Praise for
Novel & Short Story
Writer's Market

"After ten years writing and publishing fiction, *Novel & Short Story Writer's Market* remains my most important reference tool."

—I.J. Schecter, author, The Bottom of the Mug

". . . an excellent resource where writers can find market information quickly and easily. An annual must-buy for serious fiction writers."

—Writers Write, The Internet Writing Journal

". . .'there's something for everyone' in this volume offering a wide range of inside information on making a mark in the world of fiction."

—Quill & Scroll

2 0 0 1
NOVEL &
SHORT STORY
WRITER'S
MARKET

2,000 PLACES TO SELL YOUR FICTION

EDITED BY

ANNE BOWLING

ASSISTED BY

NANCY BREEN

WRITER'S DIGEST BOOKS
CINCINNATI, OHIO

If you are a publisher of fiction and would like to be considered for a listing in the next edition of *Novel & Short Story Writer's Market*, send a SASE (or SAE and IRC) with your request for a questionnaire to *Novel & Short Story Writer's Market*—QR, 1507 Dana Ave., Cincinnati OH 45207. Questionnaires received after July 15, 2001, will be held for the 2002 edition.

Editorial Director, Annuals Department: Barbara Kuroff
Managing Editor, Annuals Department: Doug Hubbuch
Production Editor: Nancy Breen

Writer's Digest Books website: www.writersdigest.com
Writer's Market website: www.writersmarket.com.

International Standard Serial Number 0897-9812
International Standard Book Number 1-58297-009-2

Cover illustration by Jim Starr

Attention Booksellers: This is an annual directory of F&W Publications.
Return deadline for this edition is April 30, 2002.

contents at a glance

Writing Fiction:

Craft & Technique 6

Personal Views 22

Electronic Publishing 39

For Mystery Writers 57

For Romance Writers 68

For Science Fiction/Fantasy & Horror Writers 78

Getting Published 95

The Markets:

Literary Agents 115

Literary Magazines 138

Small Circulation Magazines 286

Zines 320

Consumer Magazines 344

Book Publishers 386

Contests & Awards 495

Resources 545

Category Index 613

General Index 655

Contents

1 **From the Editor**

2 **The "Quick-Start" Guide to Publishing Your Fiction**

CRAFT & TECHNIQUE

6 **In Defense of the Short Story; or, Why Less is More, by Lee K. Abbott**
Award-winning short story writer Lee K. Abbott muses on the merits of the short form.

10 **Enemies of Creativity, by Jack Heffron**
How to spot them, and block them from getting between you and your writing.

17 **Smackdown! Writers Ring In on Literary vs. Genre Fiction, by Sandra Gurvis**
A spirited discussion among writers of both, on the differences and the—surprising! —similarities.

PERSONAL VIEWS

22 **John Jakes: Mastering Historical Fiction in a Fifty-Year Career, by Kelly Milner Halls**
"The Godfather" explains how to handle history in fiction.

24 **Margaret Atwood: "As a Writer, You Must Do What Beckons to You," by Katie Struckel**
The author of *Cat's Eye* and the latest *The Blind Assassin* shares her views on the role of activism, feminism and humanity in fiction.

27 **"Whatever Works, Works": Kurt Vonnegut on Flouting the Rules of Fiction, by Kelly Nickell**
Thirty years after *Slaughterhouse Five*, Vonnegut shoots straight with advice for fiction writers.

30 **Editor Robley Wilson Weighs in on Slush Pile Politics and the Value of Truth in Fiction, by Will Allison**
Outgoing editor of the venerable *North American Review* on the health of the short story.

34 **First Bylines, by Terri See and Kelly Milner Halls**
A behind-the-scenes look at first publication—novels and short story collections—with Tim Parrish, Elissa Schappell and Christopher Rice.

ELECTRONIC PUBLISHING

39 **Exploring E-Zines: A Literary Revolution Online, by Kelly Milner Halls**
A roundtable interview with the fiction editors at online lit mags *Zuzu's Petals Quarterly*, *Blue Moon Review*, *12-Gauge.com* and *Dead Mule* on getting your short fiction published electronically.

44 A Mixed Review of E-Publishing: An Interview with *PW's* John Baker, by Paula Deimling

Publishers Weekly's editorial director considers the impact of e-publishing on the book industry.

49 The Myths (and Facts) About Electronic Publishing, by Karen S. Wiesner

In defense of the e-book, an excerpt from Wiesner's *Electronic Publishing: The Definitive Guide.*

54 "Rethinking the Book:" The Electronic Literature Organization Tests Fiction's Boundaries, by Brad Vice

A group of visionaries bands together to promote experimental electronic fiction.

FOR MYSTERY WRITERS

57 Otto Penzler: Mystery Goes Mainstream, by Nicole Klungle

The founder of the Mysterious Press discusses the broadening mystery market, and what it means for writers.

60 From Editor to Writer: Martha C. Lawrence Writes What She Knows, by W.E. Reinka

The author of *Murder in Scorpio* on bringing her skills as an editor to her work as a writer.

63 Literary Mystery Appeals to Both Genre and Mainstream Readers, by Brad Vice

How Tom Franklin's mystery novella *Poachers* found crossover success.

65 Mystery Markets Appearing in this Book

67 Resources for Mystery Writers

FOR ROMANCE WRITERS

68 The Accidental Romance Novelist: A Profile of Diana Gabaldon, by Julia Cross

How the author of the bestselling *Outlander* series followed her character to success.

71 Not Just Happily-Ever-After: How to Write Real Romance, by Jennifer Crusie

The bestselling author shares nine steps to writing successful romance.

75 Romance Markets Appearing in this Book

77 Resources for Romance Writers

FOR SCIENCE FICTION/FANTASY & HORROR WRITERS

78 An Experimental Take on Horror: Mark Danielewski's *House of Leaves*, by Joshua Easton

A look behind the scenes at the creation of the novel that challenged the limits of the form.

82 *House of Leaves:* **"What a Novel Can Do That a Download Can't," by Cynthia Laufenberg**
Editor Edward Kastenmeier on acquiring Danielewski's "postmodern funhouse."

84 **Creating Believable Fantasy Worlds, by David Gerrold**
The bestselling author shares advice for maintaining realism in a fantastic setting.

90 **Science Fiction/Fantasy & Horror Markets Appearing in this Book**

94 **Resources for Science Fiction/Fantasy & Horror Writers**

GETTING PUBLISHED

95 **Ten Secrets of Successful Readings, by I.J. Schecter**
Think you're ready to promote your book? Not if you haven't read these tips first.

99 **Writing on Writing: Boost Your Income With Book Reviews, by Brad Vice**
Author Claire Messud shares tips on breaking into the book reviewing market.

101 **The Scams Are Out There!, by Nancy Breen**
Writer Beware: Read this before you seek out a publisher, and protect yourself against fraud.

105 **The Business of Fiction Writing**
Everything you need to know, from professional manuscript preparation to rights information.

THE MARKETS

115 **Literary Agents**

133 **Literary Agents Category Index**

138 **Literary Magazines**
   insider reports
   215 *McSweeney's:* **Creating a literary sensation**—An interview with Dave Eggers and the editors at this acclaimed new print and online journal.

   227 *The North American Review:* **back to the basics of storytelling**—A conversation with NAR's incoming editor Grant Tracey.

286 **Small Circulation Magazines**

320 **Zines**

344 **Consumer Magazines**
   insider reports
   361 **Changing hats: novelist's editing fuels his fiction writing**—An interview with *Harper's* acquisition editor Colin Harrison on how writing and editing work together.

   366 **The sky's the limit for fiction in *Hemispheres* magazine**—An interview with Lisa Fann, fiction editor for United Air Lines' inflight magazine, on what occasional and frequent flyers are reading.

379 *Seventeen* **magazine: looking for fiction to inspire**—Fiction editors Darcy Jacobs and Patrice Adcroft on what they want in short stories—"not just for the lip gloss set."

386 **Book Publishers**

⌐ *insider* **reports**

406 **Robert McBrearty: succeeding in the short story form**—*A Night at the Y* author on bringing a gentle humanity to short stories.

426 **Published author goes it alone for second novel**—*Angry Young Spacemen* author Jim Munroe champions self-publishing.

437 **Philip Gulley: Finding his niche in the Christian fiction market**—*Home to Harmony* author offers a homespun spin on the fast-growing genre.

461 **Jennifer Egan: Painstaking revisions, attention to detail pay off**—Author of *The Invisible Circus* advises: revise, revise, revise.

495 **Contests & Awards**

RESOURCES

545 **Conferences & Workshops**

⌐ *insider* **reports**

548 **Michael Collier: "Word has gotten out, Bread Loaf has a new vitality"**—An interview with the director of the oldest writer's conference in the U.S.

571 **Elizabeth Graver on building community among writers**—Author of *The Honey Thief* and *Unravelling* shares good reasons for writers to attend conferences, workshops and retreats.

591 **Organizations**

599 **Publications of Interest**

603 **Websites of Interest**

607 **Canadian Writers Take Note**

608 **Printing and Production Terms Defined**

610 **Glossary**

INDEXES

613 **Category Index**

655 **General Index**

From the Editor

At a used book sale recently, I found a little treasure. A skinny, first-edition hard back, copyright 1952, with a yellowed dustjacket, titled *Plots That Sell to Top-Pay Magazines*. At 50 cents—a significant savings over its original $2.95 price—who could resist? In it, author Charles Simmons details "30 basic fiction plots acceptable to leading magazines." I found use of the word "acceptable" curious—fiction must be more than "acceptable" to find publication these days. And the table of contents was so refreshingly straightforward it made me smile: Chapter 18: Girl Gets Boy. Chapter 19: Boy Gets Girl. Chapter 20: Boy and Girl Get Each Other. Chapter 21: Boy Loses Girl, and so on.

In the nearly 50 years since that book was published, those plots may endure, but Simmons might be surprised by the changes sweeping the business of fiction writing. Electronic publishing is transforming the way books are produced, short stories are distributed and, yes, even the way plot lines work. As Douglas Thornsjo, editor of the e-zine *Millennium*, puts it: "The Good: Never before has it been so cheap and so easy for publishers and writers to put material before the world. The Bad: Proliferation of electronic content on the web and elsewhere poses a serious threat to professionalism in the writing trade."

In some ways this electronic revolution is as chaotic as any political movement—change is rapid and unpredictable, opinions proliferate, and at the moment we seem to have more questions than answers as to what the field will look like once the dust has settled. To help you, the writer, navigate this brave new world, we've included a section on electronic publishing this year. In it you'll find answers to some of your technical questions on publishing your novels and short stories electronically, as in our excerpt from Karen Wiesner's *Electronic Publishing: The Definitive Guide*. You'll find forecasts from industry insiders such as *Publishers Weekly*'s John Baker and the editors of four leading electronic literary magazines. We also explore how this technology has given birth to a wholly new form, with a profile of the Electronic Literature Organization and its biennial award for hypertext fiction.

For writers who prefer their print on paper, we've included a strong line-up of inspiration, instruction and advice from some of the best in the business. You'll find profiles of veteran writers Margaret Atwood, John Jakes, and Kurt Vonnegut, in addition to young mavericks like Jim Munroe (*Angry Young Spaceman*) and Mark Danielewski (*House of Leaves*). You'll also find advice from Dave Eggers and the editors at the print and online journal *McSweeney's*. For mystery, romance and science fiction/fantasy/horror writers, we've compiled all new sections of interviews and resources to help you get your fiction in print. With these and the more than 2,000 new and updated markets for fiction, we hope you have everything you need for a productive year of writing and publishing. Good luck!

Anne Patterson Bowling.

Editor
nsswm@fwpubs.com

With many, many thanks to outgoing editor Will Allison, who set this edition on the starting block, and to former editor Barbara Kuroff, who helped it over the finish line. Thanks also to our readers who keep in touch with market information from the field, and stories of their successes.

The "Quick-Start" Guide to Publishing Your Fiction

To make the most of *Novel & Short Story Writer's Market* you need to know how to use it. And with more than 600 pages of fiction publishing markets and resources, a writer could easily get lost amidst the plethora of information. But, fear not. This "quick-start" guide will help you wind your way through the pages of *Novel & Short Story Writer's Market*, as well as the fiction publishing process, and emerge with your dream accomplished—to see your fiction in print.

1. Read, read, read.

Read numerous magazines, fiction collections and novels to determine if your fiction compares favorably with work currently being published. If your fiction is at least the same caliber as that you're reading, then move on to step two. If not, postpone submitting your work and spend your time polishing your fiction. Writing and reading the work of others are the best ways to improve craft.

For help with craft and critique of your work:

- You'll find articles on the craft and business aspects of writing fiction in the Craft & Technique section, beginning on page 6 and in the Getting Published section, beginning on page 95.
- If you're thinking about publishing your work online, see the Electronic Publishing section on page 39.
- If you're a genre writer, you will find information in For Mystery Writers, beginning on page 57, For Romance Writers, beginning on page 68 and For Science Fiction/Fantasy & Horror Writers, beginning on page 78.
- You'll find Conference & Workshop listings beginning on page 545.
- You'll find Organizations for fiction writers on page 591.

2. Analyze your fiction.

Determine the type of fiction you write to best target your submissions to markets most suitable to your work. Do you write literary, genre, mainstream or one of many other categories of fiction? There are magazines and presses seeking specialized work in each of these areas as well as numerous others.

For editors and publishers with specialized interests, see the Category Index beginning on page 613.

3. Learn about the market.

Read *Writer's Digest* magazine (F&W Publications, Inc.), *Poet's & Writers* and *Byline*. Also read *Publishers Weekly*, the trade magazine of the publishing industry, and *Independent Publisher* containing information about small- to medium-sized independent presses. And don't forget to utilize the Internet. The number of sites for writers seems to grow daily, and among them you'll find www.writersmarket.com and www.writersdigest.com (see page 603 for Websites of Interest).

4. Find markets for your work.

There are a variety of ways to locate markets for fiction. The periodicals sections of bookstores and libraries are great places to discover new journals and magazines that might be open to your type of short stories. Read writing-related magazines and newsletters for information about new markets and publications seeking fiction submissions. Also, frequently browse bookstore shelves to see what novels and short story collections are being published and by whom. Check acknowledgment pages for names of editors and agents, too. Online journals often have links to the websites of other journals that may publish fiction. And last but certainly not least, read the listings found here in *Novel & Short Story Writer's Market*.

Also, don't forget to utilize the Category Indexes at the back of this book to help you target your fiction to the right market.

5. Send for guidelines.

In the listings in this book, we try to include as much submission information as we can glean from editors and publishers. Over the course of the year, however, editors' expectations and needs may change. Therefore, it is best to request submission guidelines by sending a self-addressed stamped envelope (SASE). You can also check the websites of magazines and presses which usually contain a page with guideline information. You can find updated guidelines of many of the markets listed here at www.writersdigest.com. And for an even more comprehensive and continually updated online markets list, you can obtain a subscription to www.writersmarket.com by calling 1-800-289-0963.

6. Begin your publishing efforts with journals and contests open to beginners.

If this is your first attempt at publishing your work, your best bet is to begin with local publications or those you know are open to beginning writers. Then, after you have built a publication history, you can try the more prestigious and nationally distributed magazines. For publications and contests most open to beginners, look for the ◻ symbol preceding listing titles. Also, look for the ◪ symbol that identifies markets open to exceptional work from beginners as well as work from experienced, previously published writers.

7. Submit your fiction in a professional manner.

Take the time to show editors that you care about your work and are serious about publishing. By following a publication's or book publisher's submission guidelines and practicing standard submission etiquette, you can better ensure your chances that an editor will want to take the time to read your work and consider it for publication. Remember, first impressions last, and a carelessly assembled submission packet can jeopardize your chances before your story or novel manuscript has had a chance to speak for itself. For help with preparing submissions read The Business of Fiction Writing, beginning on page 105.

8. Keep track of your submissions.

Know when and where you have sent fiction and how long you need to wait before expecting a reply. If an editor does not respond by the time indicated in his market listing or guidelines, wait a few more weeks and then follow up with a letter (and SASE) asking when the editor anticipates making a decision. If you still do not receive a reply from the editor within a reasonable amount of time, send a letter withdrawing your work from consideration and move on to the next market on your list.

9. Learn from rejection.

Rejection is the hardest part of the publication process. Unfortunately, rejection happens to every writer, and every writer needs to learn to deal with the negativity involved. On the other hand, rejection can be valuable when used as a teaching tool rather than a reason to doubt yourself and your work. If an editor offers suggestions with his or her rejection slip, take those comments into consideration. You don't have to automatically agree with an editor's opinion of your work. It may be that the editor has a different perspective on the piece than you do. Or, you may find that the editor's suggestions give you new insight into your work and help you improve your craft.

10. Don't give up.

The best advice for you as you try to get published is be persistent, and always believe in yourself and your work. By continually reading other writers' work, constantly working on the craft of fiction writing and relentlessly submitting your work, you will eventually find that magazine or book publisher that's the perfect match for your fiction. And, *Novel & Short Story Writer's Market* will be here to help you every step of the way.

GUIDE TO LISTING FEATURES

Below you will find an example of the market listings contained in *Novel & Short Story Writer's Market*. Also included are callouts identifying the various format features of the listings. (For an explanation of the symbols used, see the front and back covers of this book.)

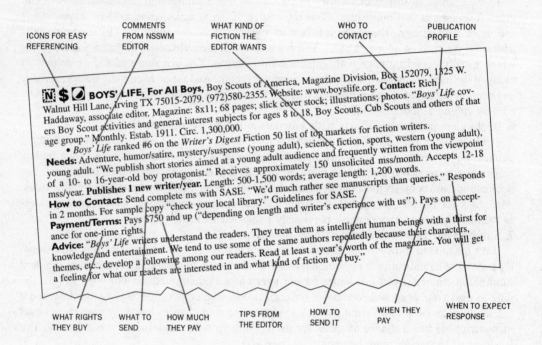

ICONS FOR EASY REFERENCING

COMMENTS FROM NSSWM EDITOR

WHAT KIND OF FICTION THE EDITOR WANTS

WHO TO CONTACT

PUBLICATION PROFILE

BOYS' LIFE, For All Boys, Boy Scouts of America, Magazine Division, Box 152079, 1325 W. Walnut Hill Lane, Irving TX 75015-2079. (972)580-2355. Website: www.boyslife.org. **Contact:** Rich Haddaway, associate editor. Magazine: 8x11; 68 pages; slick cover stock; illustrations; photos. "*Boys' Life* covers Boy Scout activities and general interest subjects for ages 8 to 18, Boy Scouts, Cub Scouts and others of that age group." Monthly. Estab. 1911. Circ. 1,300,000.
  • *Boys' Life* ranked #6 on the *Writer's Digest* Fiction 50 list of top markets for fiction writers.
Needs: Adventure, humor/satire, mystery/suspense (young adult), science fiction, sports, western (young adult), young adult. "We publish short stories aimed at a young adult audience and frequently written from the viewpoint of a 10- to 16-year-old boy protagonist." Receives approximately 150 unsolicited mss/month. Accepts 12-18 mss/year. **Publishes 1 new writer/year.** Length: 500-1,500 words; average length: 1,200 words.
How to Contact: Send complete ms with SASE. "We'd much rather see manuscripts than queries." Responds in 2 months. For sample copy "check your local library." Guidelines for SASE.
Payment/Terms: Pays $750 and up ("depending on length and writer's experience with us"). Pays on acceptance for one-time rights.
Advice: "*Boys' Life* writers understand the readers. They treat them as intelligent human beings with a thirst for knowledge and entertainment. We tend to use some of the same authors repeatedly because their characters, themes, etc., develop a following among our readers. Read at least a year's worth of the magazine. You will get a feeling for what our readers are interested in and what kind of fiction we buy."

WHAT RIGHTS THEY BUY

WHAT TO SEND

HOW MUCH THEY PAY

TIPS FROM THE EDITOR

HOW TO SEND IT

WHEN THEY PAY

WHEN TO EXPECT RESPONSE

Writing Fiction

Craft & Technique 6

Personal Views 22

Electronic Publishing 39

For Mystery Writers 57

For Romance Writers 68

For Science Fiction/Fantasy & Horror Writers 78

Getting Published 95

In Defense of the Short Story; or, Why Less Is More

BY LEE K. ABBOTT

This time she was in the third row, toward the center, hers a face even Warren Beatty might not tire to gaze upon. This time she was young, though on other occasions she had been younger or older or, not infrequently, not a "she" at all. This time she got her question in early, well before I'd had the chance to charm her and the rest of the audience with a joke or yet another display of shallow wit. This time she actually smiled when she asked—semi-chagrined, I'm hoping, to have to ask it in the first place.

"Why don't you write a novel?"

I don't think she meant to insult me. But only quick thinking and a knowing chuckle from my host, not to mention the memory of my mother wagging her finger at my nose to emphasize yet another lesson regarding good manners I'd failed to learn, kept me from saying the obvious: Why, sweet cheeks, isn't a bear a horse? Which is to say, without a lot of the hooey that nowadays attends far too many things, that she, like so many theretofore, seemed to think that in the scheme of matters literary, writing stories was decidedly minor league; that grown-ups, those with more on their minds than what *USA Today* needs only a hundred words to say, wrote novels; that a real artist(e), a typist with monstrously BIG ideas between his ears, needed at least a three-inch pile of paper to get the talk walked—all assertions as full of dangerous nonsense as any issuing from the National Rifle Association and the Republican party.

I do not think of stories, even the most traditional of them, as practice for the supposedly harder and putatively more sophisticated work that we're told the novel is. I do not think of stories as inherently an easier form to fail in. Nor do I think of stories, no matter the age or ilk, as insufficient to the task of detailing, as Updike once noted, how it is to live in the here and now. I do not think of stories as child's play, less demanding because they are less long. I do not consider stories, in fine, as efforts silly or ephemeral or provisional. Nah, I write stories, too many of them not short enough, because I can. Which is to say, with nary a twinkle in the eye, that the form suits my temperament, never mind my understanding of our goofy and condemned kind.

In the first place, as a scribbler who came of age in the 60s, I am impatient, eager to grab the next goody in the refrigerator, anxious to go on the next adventure. World peace? Yeah, today that, and tomorrow the end of hunger in Africa. What do you mean, as my father used to say, Rome wasn't built in a day? For me, you're beginning to gather, speed is of no little premium. Hence, if two or three or God help me!—four stories go bust before Independence Day, no big deal, because I know that, come Thanksgiving, I'll have at least one to be reasonably proud of, one to show to a stranger with a checkbook and a publication that reaches Americans at bulk rate.

I am also eager to horse around with the fundamentals of my faith. Second person? Why the dickens not? Ditto with the present tense. How about a story in the subjunctive mood? Can do

LEE K. ABBOTT *is the author of* Living After Midnight: A Novella and Stories. *He is the author of several other books, and has received many writing awards, including the O. Henry Award for Fiction in 1997. He is currently director of the creative writing department at Ohio State University.*

(and, golly, was once done by yours truly, an undertaking, owing to related sleights of hand with time, that nearly broke my head in half). What about multiple thirds? Or telling a story backwards. Maybe a story of one sentence (another chance, by the way, to practice one's grammar and gifts at subordination). You say you want to tell a story in 1,500 words exactly. Go to it. Not use quotation marks for dialogue? That, too. For it's a form that invites heedless experimentation—a form, in fact, whose principle virtue is its possibility, its fluidity. (You want proof? Okay, smarty-pants, define the form, beginning with the easiest of questions: how long is the story? Or this: when does a story become a novella, a novelette, or a, uh, long story? Geez, at least we know, with all due respect to the differences among, to name only a few, Spenser and Shakespeare and Petrarch, that a sonnet is 14 lines long. With a story, the "rules" are less fixed and more ambiguous. Length? Mr. E.A. Poe said it should be read at one sitting. This, of course, was before the red-eye to London, the bus ride to Katmandu—all sittings almost impossible to sit through.)

Another reason to write short is that you don't have to know very much. More proof? Try this: think of your favorite novel. Now think what X had to know to write that book—the facts, if you will. *Moby Dick*? The minutiae about knots alone were worth one darned chapter. *The Great Gatsby*? Man, how much time do you have for a lesson or two about shirts? Go ahead, try it yourself. *Cold Mountain*, by Charles Frazier. *Libra*, by Don DeLillo. And Lord help you if you should undertake to create your own world. Does the name William Faulkner mean anything to you? Or what about Ray Bradbury? The Denis Johnson who wrote *Fiskadoro*? Lordy, you might even have to invent a language a la *A Clockwork Orange*. With a story, even one about places long ago or never were, you can, well, fake it. I once, for example, wrote a story about a father who was obsessed with his brother's death on the Bataan Death March at the beginning of World War II. To do right by the material, I read one book—and, no pun intended, a short one at that—to learn the history, to find the names, to get the anecdotes. To write a story on UFOs, I read another book. To concoct some artful lies about Pancho Villa and Black Jack Pershing, maybe three books.

Washington Irving, he of the Headless Horseman and the minor role in *Catch 22*, used to say that writing at novel length inevitably lead to "dull patches." Not surprisingly, I, in the words of the miracle that is Smokey Robinson, second that emotion, especially because I agree with the aforementioned Mr. Poe that we writers ought not to write even one word that does not, as he puts it, contribute to the "unity of effect." This, folks, is hard to do. Harder than getting into heaven, methinks. The storywriter cannot be self-indulgent or indifferent to the need to hurry along to the next dramatic moment. We have to make our mark, often not subtly at all, and press on. 'His skin looked like week-old pork,' we type and are thus finished describing the software tycoon with the tongs and the barbecue mitt and a mistress with a charge card to Frederick's of Hollywood. 'Her voice made my hair melt,' we type and dare not go into any more detail about, say, her full-sprung thighs or her peculiarly fetching way of getting from hither to yon. No, the emphasis for the storywriter is brevity, an aesthetic economy where less is more.

Similarly significant to understand is that, metaphorically speaking, you don't often turn corners in stories nowadays where what you've discovered about Debbie-do or old Phinizy Spalding is grave enough to scare the pants off you, or have you wondering why that bit of "news" was yours to behold. Novelists, I think, run the risk of learning stuff about themselves through their characters that might well give the lie to the easy convictions they cleave to as citizens. What, you wonder, did it cost John O'Hara to write *Butterfield 8*? Or what horrible truth was John Cheever coming to in *Oh, What a Paradise It Seems*? And how long did it take William Styron to start breathing again when he finished the last chapter in *Lie Down in Darkness*? To be sure, such remarkable looks into the dark well of us can, and do, happen with story. In fact, I have argued elsewhere that we ought not ever to write a story that will only cost us time to get between margins. Still, with the novel—unique to its form, dear readers—much is demanded, not least a broader, more comprehensive sense of character, which is to say, finally, a more straightforward and more honest view of ourselves, the analogues for the selves we breathe into life with language. You can't, I fear, spend years with Dr. Jeykll without having more than one heart-to-heart with Señor Hyde.

I am here to say that a story is nicely accommodating to material, the "stuff" you're alive to fictionalize. In the twenty-seven years since I published my first "histoire" (the only word in French worth repeating in polite company), I've written about, oh, a duke's mixture of men and women bedeviled by the roil and rue of lived life. I've a hapless hero who killed two dogs, another who believed his mutt could speak enough English to pass the SATs. In an attempt to learn what structure alone can "say," I've told two different stories precisely the same way. I've given myself over to a guy, shaped like the Pillsbury Doughboy, who aims to get out of his draft physical by wearing India silk panties (crotchless, of course) and smooching a general or two. At various times in my career into my head, always unbidden, have sprung, in addition to the usual rakes and flounders, a football coach with a fondness for high heels, a professional "voice" breaking into his own house, a teenager watching his father destroy a brand new set of Wilson golf clubs, two former college buddies who like to hold up Stop 'n' Gos, a being from "outer-goddam-space," a mother who makes no apology for being a drunk, a twice-divorced scoundrel who likes to box waltz with women in the aisles of his local food mart, a banker who watches his wife—evidently naked, at least from the waist up—drive by in the Volvo sedan of his bridge partner, a woman in love with an ex-GI who hears voices and owns a Russian handgun to do battle with them, a smart-mouth delinquent whose directions to his place in the desert take six pages, and a session drummer with astonishingly bad taste in sweethearts. Why, I've even presumed to take up residence in the interior life of a thug named Fork—a sad sack, really, who offered to be to us what pestilence had been to our forebears. In short, whatever has interested me, and a lot certainly has, I've had a form accommodating enough to do the heavy lifting that art is.

Novel writing, so E.L. Doctorow is said to have once remarked, is like driving at night on an unfamiliar road. For the storywriter I am, that trip to the end of Lonely Street is neither less daunting nor less spooky; it's just shorter. Like our brothers and sisters who go long, we at the *to* end of narrative's *fro* must be equally watchful, equally vigilant, equally attentive to what surprises will spring out at us from the dark. I likewise believe that story writing fits well with these parlous and busy times. In my own case, I went short in part because, with a wife and two children and no little desire to be an acceptable husband and father, I had no time to go long, especially with the tenure clock ticking in the background. We had soccer practice to go to, trombone lessons to take, school plays, trips to the orthodontist—the alpha and omega, in short, of all that's involved in rearing youngsters you mean to keep clear of woe and despair and ignorance. Hence, I wrote at night, after storytime. I wrote when I didn't have class to teach (or, sigh, prepare for). I wrote when there was no department meeting, no advisee rapping at my chamber door, no sleep to have, no administrator to knock some sense into. I wrote when I didn't have papers to grade, softball to play, flesh to press, or shilly to shally. Mainly, however, I wrote short because, well, after 30 pages I began to lie.

I have, I should finally confess, tried to go long. Three times, in fact. The painful autobiographical novel (featuring a young man far too sensitive for the crudities of the modern world). The pornographic novel (yes, literally). The historical novel (see that mouth-breathing son-of-a-gun Pancho Villa from above). With each, fortunately, I learned yet more about being brief, about what to leave out, about how to cut, about why, among other things, all the little birdies go tweet-tweet-tweet. I learned the felicity of the right word at the right time. I learned, very quickly, to get to the dadgum point. I learned not to overstay my welcome, to leave the party well before the fistfights start and the drunks get to singing college fraternity songs. I learned to fish, not cut bait. I learned that a good title is worth a chapter all by its lonesome; that a name—Tump, for example, or Mr. Pitiful—is worth, at the very least, a page of vital statistics. I learned that writing is not necessarily prose. I learned, to coin a phrase, to make time fly, days and even years disappearing in a sentence. I made pals with the angel that is white space. I became explicit, maddeningly so. I learned to kill two, sometimes three, narrative birds with one stone. And, yes, I've learned what I can't do. I've learned what I have not the stamina, the time, the imagination or the courage to type—not the least valuable lesson, importantly, one can learn about one's singular, miserable self. And, best of all, I am not through learning.

I don't expect that I'll change—too little time left to become passingly good at the high and low of another genre. Besides, I've more, albeit short, to say. And short, as the poet reminds us, is sweet, right? In any event, I've nothing rousing to finish with, no rhetorical flourish of the sort you might think to underline or commit to memory. Rather, I hope my words have become a comfort to those similarly afflicted with the need to be brief. Had I been a more proficient writer, this, too, would have been shorter.

Enemies of Creativity

BY JACK HEFFRON

Jack Heffron

> "What is needed is, in the end, simply this: solitude, great inner solitude."
>
> —Rainer Maria Rilke

Getting ideas is largely a matter of showing up. As writer Ron Carlson says, it's the butt-in-the-chair approach. Waiting for inspiration is a loser's game, because without a work in progress, even if you're only doing some personal journaling and the work in progress is you, ideas that arise will have no context. They won't be recognizable as ideas. Or, they'll be great ideas for a novel or article that will never be written. And so at writers conferences and workshops, teachers will say the key is "Just do it."

And they're right. But "Just do it" is a slogan for shoes. And slogans work because they make things seem easier than they, in fact, are. If just doing it were simply a matter of deciding, anyone *could* do it. But sticking to a schedule goes beyond will. It's a matter of consciously developing a writing habit.

But there are enemies to that habit, dark forces that keep us from writing creatively. Each has its strengths and weaknesses and all can be beaten. The key is awareness. Recognize the force at work against you. Recognition is a large part of the battle against these nefarious foes.

The Procrastinator

What a great word: *procrastinator*. All of those crashing consonants, the *c*, *s* and *t*s. The Procrastinator sounds like the name of a comic book supervillain. This guy should be kicking Spiderman's butt all over New York.

Instead, he's at my house. And your house. He's convincing us we will write, yes we will, and we'll get started next week. Absolutely. No exceptions this time, no way. Well. Next week may not be ideal because there's a big meeting at work on Tuesday, which means all of those reports have to be finished, and Wednesday is parent-teacher night, and then there's soccer practice and the appointment with the eye doctor and something has to be done before the first freeze with that tree branch hanging over the garage. But the week after, no problem. We're all over it.

This is the voice of The Procrastinator. He's merciless. Very tough to beat. He can hit you with excuses so good your priest, minister, mother and therapist would absolve you of your

JACK HEFFRON *is the editorial director for Writer's Digest Books, Story Press, Walking Stick Press and Betterway Books. He was the series editor for* Best Writing on Writing *and associate editor of* Story *magazine. His short stories have appeared in numerous literary magazines, including* The North American Review *and* TriQuarterly, *and have twice been nominated for the Pushcart Prize.*

This article was excerpted from The Writer's Idea Book © 2000 *by Jack Heffron. Used with permission of Writer's Digest Books, a division of F&W Publications, Inc.*

decision not to write. They'd even write a note for you. If you want, write your own, just like you used to do in grade school in your best Mom handwriting.

How does your excuse sound? Does it ring false in your ears? Will the muse believe this excuse? Like a clever truant, make a dozen of these notes, and when you miss a day or a week or whatever your schedule calls for, write a note to the muse explaining why. Look at your excuse on the cold white paper. Does it justify not writing? This strategy can keep The Procrastinator at bay.

But maybe your excuse really is valid. Stuff comes up. It really does. We all have worthwhile reasons not to write, and if we're not writing, we're not creating new ideas. If you made a list right now for why you can't write, or couldn't write the last time your schedule said you should, I'll bet you can come up with at least five reasons, three of them excellent.

The next time you skip a writing session, write five reasons, three of them excellent, for why you must skip. These reasons are The Procrastinator's power. Now, one by one, take back the power by writing a sentence or two explaining why each excuse is not good enough or how schedules could be shifted, arrangements made, to allow you to write some other time.

By using these strategies, you can defeat The Procrastinator. Today. That's the key. Don't delay. Have you ever had a friend tell you that she's starting a diet "on Monday"? Usually she's crunching through a mouthful of Doritos at the time. Yep. Monday. That's when she's starting. Meanwhile, you couldn't be more sure that the diet will fail. You just know it. Why? Because the postponement shows the lack of commitment and desire necessary to make a diet work.

The Procrastinator feeds on delay. To vanquish him, start now. If only for five minutes. Then do five minutes tomorrow, until you're churning out ideas and writing pages. Go ahead, start now. Write a scene from your current story. Pull an unfinished poem from your files and tinker with it. Write anything. Make a list of your favorite foods or a list of your favorite friends, then explain why you like them. List ten things you hate about the holidays and explain why. Describe in detail the most romantic evening of your life. Do it now.

Really. Right now. What are you still doing here?

The Victim

All of us are, at times in our lives, victims. Life can be cruel. And we use the role of victim to stop being creative. We give up control of our creative selves because

- our families don't understand or appreciate us.
- our bosses are demanding and fill our lives with stress.
- our children are demanding and fill our lives with stress.
- our finances are a mess.
- our mates are insensitive to our needs for space to create.
- our cars refuse to run properly.
- our neighborhoods are noisy and overrun with children.

As with The Procrastinator and his excuses, The Victim makes some valid points. The key is taking back the power. In her book *Awakening the Warrior Within*, Dawn Callan speaks of "owning your victim self " as a way of finding one's inner warrior. How? Stop complaining about the forces victimizing you. Just stop. Stop making your lack of a creative life the fault of someone or something other than yourself. Any or all of the reasons on the list above might be true for you. But when you hear yourself complaining about them, hear the voice of The Victim. And, as with The Procrastinator, know that The Victim is inside you, under your control.

List the most common and frequent reasons you give for not spending enough time being creative. Next to each entry on the list, write who is in control of that situation. Now write a short plan for taking back control. It may require some tough admissions and a little creativity, but you're taking the first step toward opening your creative side.

Recognize victim talk when you hear it. Don't condemn yourself for it, just recognize what it is. Then stop. Take control. Give yourself a place to be creative again.

Taking back control is a wonderfully empowering experience. When you beat your victim self, you feel a sense of victory and you know that anything is possible. You *can* finish that novel. You *can* finish that screenplay. It really *is* within your power.

The Talker

Speaking of talk, this enemy just can't shut up. You've cooked up a great idea for a screenplay or an essay or you've made a revelation about your protagonist that will give your novel a much-needed new dimension . . . then The Talker takes over. She has to tell everyone in your writing group. She tells your mate. Or your mother. Or anyone at work who will listen. The Talker is an expert at squandering the creative nest egg. By the time you sit down to put this idea into action, it's dead, or at least not as zesty as it seemed to be a few days ago.

The Talker needs attention. The Talker needs validation. The Talker would rather talk about an idea than confront its complexities, its obstacles. The Talker wants the glory but none of the hard work that really lies at the heart of all creative efforts. The Talker is a bit of a coward, a narcissist, a layabout. If you want to develop your ideas to their full potential and to see a work through to completion, take control of The Talker. When writers tell me they can't help it, or that they *need* to talk it all out first, my advice is simple: Whenever you're talking about a work in progress, don't. Just shut up. Really. The story you're writing is a secret. Anne Tyler takes a somewhat gentler approach:

> It makes me so uncomfortable for them. If they're talking about a plot idea, I feel the idea is probably going to evaporate. I want to almost physically reach over and cover their mouths and say, "You'll lose it if you're not careful."

Writing is a private act. It is a way of communing with our imaginations, our subconscious minds, our secret lives. Bringing in a third party is almost always a bad idea. The sense of intimacy and revelation are lost, and you end up making small talk. By preserving the privacy of the creative process, you preserve the excitement of that intimacy. Getting back to that intimacy becomes a guilty pleasure, and it keeps the tension high. Ideas will spawn more ideas and you'll find yourself, and your project, rolling right along. Novelist Jay McInerney describes it this way:

> I find it helps to remove myself, as much as possible, from the world of daily life. Living in New York, it's tough to block out the din of the city. So I go away. I try to find a treehouse somewhere and pull the ladder up behind me. Once I have begun to believe in my alternate fictional universe, I can come and go from the treehouse. But it's a fragile state in the beginning.

Some writers simply think it's a jinx to talk about a work in progress. One writer I know was working on a novel for months and yet refused to even refer to the project as "a novel." She called it "this thing I'm working on" until, after more than a year, she finished it. She took care to avoid letting The Talker get so much as a toe in the door.

The best illustration of this process is also an admittedly silly one that I've used in classes and workshops for a number of years. It involves a TV commercial for grape juice. (Stick with me on this.) The commercial opened by demonstrating the way the competition made its grape juice—a rather primitive and cartoonish illustration of a big boiling vat of purple liquid. Above the boiling vat, smoke wafted into the air, and within the smoke sparkled little purple gems of flavor. Lost flavor. Flavor gone forever. Next, the illustration changed to show the sponsor's process. The vat of burbling purple stuff looked the same, but there was a cap on top of the vat, an inverted funnel with a pipe on the end that channeled the smoke (complete with sparkling purple gems of flavor) back into the vat, thus giving more flavor to the juice.

I can't believe this is how it's really done. But the ingenious ad person had created a good illustration of how The Talker can hinder the creative process. The Talker lets the steam out of your work, making it less rich and interesting. Your glistening purple gems of ideas are lost forever. Don't let that happen.

Remember some writing projects that were great at the start but stalled or remain unfinished. Write down why they weren't completed. Did you talk away any of them? Remind yourself when you're discussing a story in progress or an idea for a piece you've yet to begin that it's best to keep quiet. Tell yourself you'll talk about it after the next scene is written, then try to wait for the scene after that one.

The Critic

The biggest surprise I've found about The Critic is that he strikes every writer. As a young apprentice, I always thought that publishing a few stories would calm the critic, that I'd gain the confidence to know that I was good and wouldn't be plagued by doubt and frustration. Since then I've learned that's not the way it works. I've met esteemed writers, award winners, authors of best-selling books who still hear the voice of The Critic. As you get your chops and collect publications, your confidence grows but never to the point that The Critic is silenced. And maybe that's good, unless it's keeping you from writing, unless behind your chair The Critic is wailing an off-key version of Linda Ronstadt's classic "You're No Good."

In his book *Darkness Visible*, esteemed author William Styron discusses his nearly over-whelming feelings of self-doubt as he flies to Paris to accept an award. Despite tremendous reviews for her first novel, *A Bigamist's Daughter*, National Book Award—winner Alice McDermott still had such doubts about her ability that she considered quitting writing to attend law school.

The Critic is sometimes personified as a wicked English teacher from high school—Mrs. Crabass, she of the narrowed eyes and prodigious behind, she whose autocratic and hard-hearted insistence on rules of grammar and composition stripped us of our ability to let go, have fun and be creative. Alas, she ruined us, or nearly so, and we must fight her at every turn.

Maybe. For some reason I often hear a false note in this characterization. The majority of English teachers I've known and know would weep ecstatic tears if a student showed so much as a hint of an original thought. The Critic is, in fact, within us. We have, perhaps, absorbed the voice, from a teacher or a parent, or created the voice from our mythic personification of The Editor, who mocks with relish our feeble attempts at meaningful narrative. Once again, the voice of The Critic is our own voice. In fact, if we'd absorbed the lessons of composition from our English teachers, we may have fewer doubts about our ability.

The point here is not to "stop your whining." The Critic is a fearsome adversary, no question. And even after your flight to Stockholm to accept the Nobel prize in literature, after you win the favor and admiration of readers everywhere, that voice still will be there. Publication and praise help, no doubt. As you practice, you will gain confidence, allow yourself to experiment, even risk looking—gasp—stupid. But the real growth comes from inside, where The Critic resides. In an interview I conducted with David Guterson a couple of years ago, he spoke of this process:

> The actual act of writing is no easier than it was. You can have all the awards and sales and reviews you want, it doesn't get any easier the next day. On the other hand, I feel a deeper confidence in myself. It doesn't come from *Snow Falling on Cedars*. It comes from the years going by. I feel more confident because I've practiced more.

When you hear the voice of The Critic telling you your idea is stupid, your writing dull and pedestrian, tell the voice to wait. He may, indeed, be right. And he will have his turn, you promise, but it's not his turn now. The early draft is not the place for The Critic. If he insists on interfering, try not to fight him directly. Instead, observe the voice, name it The Critic, and let it go. You will go on writing anyway, just as you've learned to write when your kids have the TV cranked and are fighting brutally over the remote control.

Listening and letting go is the process used in meditation to let go of your Thinking Mind. The meditator knows that thoughts will intrude. When they do, she simply tells herself, "Thinking," and lets the thoughts go, without labeling them good or bad, without labeling herself weak or scattered. Don't turn The Critic into that bifocaled, bun-haired termagant with a red pen; don't turn The Critic into that bald-headed editor with a blue pen. The Critic is a necessary voice, at times. As you grow as a writer, you cultivate an aesthetic, a criteria for recognizing strong writing and weak. With this growth you become a more useful reader, of your own work and the work of others. So resist labeling The Critic.

But in the early stages of a piece, send him to a movie or on a nature hike or into the other room where he might at least fold laundry. He'll probably pop his head in from time to time, asking, "Ready for me yet?" In as kind a voice as you can muster, simply say, "Not yet."

The Judge

This guy is your conscience. I see him as Judge Kennesaw Mountain Landis, the first commissioner of baseball. You've probably seen a picture of Landis in history books—a grim-faced, fierce-eyed gent, an old-time moralist, a hard-line arbiter of right and wrong. He appears when we feel guilty about spending time writing. Would our families be better served if we were with them instead of shut behind doors with "Do not disturb" signs warning intruders to stay away? Would our spouses be grateful if we didn't head off to bed early to get up and write in the morning? Shouldn't we, for heaven's sake, be

- raking the yard?
- playing with the kids?
- cleaning the furnace filters?
- making money?
- paying bills?

How selfish of us to demand this time to indulge pointless fantasies of publication. How silly to be working through yet another draft of the memoir, dredging through events that took place twenty years go. This is the voice of The Judge. His weapon: Writer's Guilt.

Women, especially, seem to have a wrangle on their hands with this guy. In our society, women, more so than men, have been raised to ignore their needs, to put themselves at the service of their families. And families, therefore, expect this behavior. Ask your family for an hour alone in the evenings, then watch their need to bond erupt. You'll field more questions and solve more dilemmas than if you'd plopped down in front of the television with them. Or, if you do get the quiet you ask for, the voice of The Judge might start speaking in your head.

In an interview with *Publishers Weekly*, fiction writer Gish Jen spoke of fighting The Judge, even after publishing three successful books:

> Even today, I think my family would be more relieved than dismayed if I were to stop writing. I still struggle with the question, Is it selfish? It's hard on the people around me, it's hard on the children. Is it worth it? I was programmed to be selfless, and I go through periods where I wonder.

Men, too, suffer from Writer's Guilt. We feel we should be out there winning some bread, bringing home some bacon or, at the least, spending time with mate and kids. Our own fathers, by God, wouldn't be nursing along some narcissistic novel project when the grass could be cut or the garage painted. What a damp-souled, ineffectual man to have this need to create art at the expense of our dearest loved ones.

Of course, times have changed, and, I hope, things are not quite so regimented and old-fashioned in your world, but there's no denying that Writer's Guilt strikes often, and is an insidious enemy that is tough to beat. The Judge would seem to have bivouacked himself on the moral high ground with a phalanx of rocket launchers and barbed wire. To take back that ground, ask yourself why you're spending time writing rather than with family and friends and your ever-beckoning "To do" list. Is it because of your undying hope of fame and fortune? Are you seeking revenge on callous high school teachers who said you'd never be a writer? Are you intentionally hiding from responsibilities by using writing as a convenient shield?

Probably not.

If you're writing out of a need to communicate, to hear your own voice on the page, then you owe it to yourself—and to your family—to write. You have a moral imperative to do it. Try to ignore this imperative and you will unleash The Victim, the woeful sod who would write if only the world were a more understanding place. To be the best mother/father, husband/wife, son/daughter, brother/sister, friend or lover you can be, you need to have an outlet for your creativity. Even if those around you don't understand what you're doing, they should be able to understand that.

Of course, stealing creative time may require some sacrifices—getting up earlier, scheduling your time more tightly, delegating some responsibilities to family members. Can you do this and keep writing with a clear conscience? For most people, it's possible. But those blessed or cursed with an especially guilty conscience may have some trouble with The Judge. I may be one of that group. I've always admired people who put their writing first and live their lives accordingly. I remember reading John Gardner's *On Becoming a Novelist*, in which he says, in effect, use the people around you. Live off a spouse. Accept money from parents. Don't get a job. Write, write, write.

For some, this works. Books do get written that way. Take Gardner's advice at face value and make your own choices. My advice leans more to striking a balance between the needs of others and the needs of your creative life. As much as possible, meld them. Work to see them not as warring factions but as two key elements that make you a unique individual. If The Judge rears his tyrannical head, don't trust what he says. Insist upon your need for writing time. In fact, write about it.

Write about your need for a creative life or simply your need to write. Why do you do it? What needs are fulfilled through it? Call your essay "Why I Write." For examples, you can find an anthology of such essays—titled *Why I Write*, edited by Will Blythe—in which big-name authors explore their needs to write. In your essay, be honest, and be thorough. Try to achieve a better understanding of your impulse to write. Use this understanding to explain to The Judge, and to all the enemies, why you must write, despite blocks or guilt or a hundred really cool other things to do.

The following excerpt is taken from Lee Smith's essay, titled "Everything Else Falls Away," which appeared in *Why I Write*. Throughout the essay, she gives a number of reasons for writing, but this reason stands at the core:

> For me, writing is a physical joy. It is almost sexual—not the moment of fulfillment, but the moment when you open the door to the room where your lover is waiting, and everything else falls away.
>
> It *does* fall away, too. For the time of the writing, I am nobody. Nobody at all. I am a conduit, nothing but a way for the story to come to the page. Oh, but I am terribly alive then, too, though I say I am no one at all; my every sense is keen and quivering.

The Author

Last year, in one of my idea workshops at a writers conference, I guided the conferees through a few prompts to help them generate ideas for essays and articles. When the session was nearly over, a woman in the back shot a vehement arm into the air and asked with barely contained frustration, "So now what do I do with it?" Of course, I hated her on the spot.

But that's beside the point. The true point is that she missed the purpose of the workshop. We were gathered to tap into our creative selves, to generate ideas for pieces that could be developed and completed later. Instead, she was under the spell of The Author, that part of ourselves that sees every moment of writing as important and valid only if it leads to publication. That goal can impede creativity. Instead of following our own desires to write, we write with the marketplace in mind. We write about what's hot. At nearly every writers conference I attend, I sit on an editor-agent panel, fielding questions about publication. Inevitably, many people want to know what's selling. It's good for any serious writer to understand the marketplace, but writing for the marketplace is usually a bad idea. If you don't feel passionately about a subject, you won't write well about it. If you're writing for a byline or simply to see your name in print, you're probably going to find yourself blocked on a regular basis. Again, the curse of The Author.

We all like to be published. It's fun to see our words in print; it's satisfying to reach an audience of readers; it's nice to make a little money for our literary efforts. We feel validated in some way. Publication makes us feel not simply like someone who writes but like A Real Writer. All of these desires are fine. They can help keep us motivated and focused. But in the early stages of a work, you'll be more creative and successful if you send The Author away. Allow her to return at the end of the session to embrace your great work and indulge you in daydreams of glory. When you've finished a project, put The Author to work zipping off your stories to magazines everywhere.

But when you're writing, write. Enjoy the work for its own sake. Relish the process itself. If you don't, The Author will become a voracious, nagging mate who is never satisfied. Publishing is a tough business, full of frustrations for even the most successful writers. If you write primarily to be published and to be An Author, you will never be a happy writer. I swear it. Nothing will be good enough. Publications will take far too long to respond; agents and editors will be hated enemies, fickle in their tastes, cryptic in their responses; less talented writers will get ahead because of their despicably sycophantic sucking up to every well-known writer who comes to town; your work won't receive the praise it deserves; your books will have terrible covers and the publishers will be out to cheat you on your royalty statements; and no one, no one, no one will ever have the human decency to call you back. In short, no matter how much success you achieve, everything will suck.

As Pema Chódrón says throughout her book *When Things Fall Apart*, give yourself a break. Be kind and compassionate to yourself. Give your creative side the love and respect it deserves. There will be time, if you want, to confront the business of publication. Publication can be a great motivator and is not a bad ambition. But when you're trying to get words on paper, to generate ideas that interest you and fill you with that feeling of elation that making art can inspire, push The Author away.

The Capricious Guest

The composer Peter Ilyich Tchaikovsky called inspiration The Capricious Guest. Wait for him to arrive and you may be waiting for a long time. Write regularly and you will find ideas flowing through you. In his book *The Craft of Fiction*, William Knott makes the point that The Capricious Guest usually arrives when you no longer need him, when you're doing just fine on your own. He makes the point, too, that when you compare pages you've written in moments of inspiration to those you've written when simply doing your daily work, you won't notice much difference.

The key to beating all of the enemies of creativity is to do your daily work. The experience of writing, as you already know, varies greatly, from times of exquisite, nearly sybaritic delight to spirit-pummeling slogs not unlike the Bataan Death March. Realize that both are part of the process. Some days the ideas will pour forth. Other days they won't. Enemies like those we've discussed will appear. Know who they are, know where they come from and keep going.

Smackdown! Writers Ring In on Literary vs. Genre Fiction

BY SANDRA GURVIS

My sister and I both write novels. Mine tend to be tumultuous, vivid and crammed with explosive words and scenes, while hers are quiet, erudite and full of subtle, defining moments. Somewhat like our personalities, I guess, and undoubtedly the reason why they appeal to vastly different markets.

The situation is similar with genre and literary fiction. Although they are related, they seem at odds with each other at times. Like siblings, comparisons between the two can evoke strong emotions and an intense sense of rivalry. So although it's not exactly the WWF, authors in each arena have definite opinions about their chosen path and how it relates to other types of fiction writing. And even among the categories, there can be a wide divergence of views. So lace up the boxing gloves and let the match begin.

In this corner, the literary writers

Although she waited until age 38 to put her fingers to the keyboard, **Ann Arensburg** served as a literary editor for Viking and Dutton before turning to writing full-time. Her first novel, *Sister Wolf* (Knopf), won an American Book Award in 1981; her third, the Gothic-themed *Incubus* (Knopf), was published in 1999. Her short stories have been included in the O. Henry Awards anthologies.

An associate professor of English at the University of Arizona, **Elizabeth Evans** is the author of the highly acclaimed novels *The Blue Hour* (Algonquin Books) and *Carter Clay* (HarperCollins). Her newest, *Rowing in Eden*, was published in 2000 and a collection of stories, *Suicide's Girlfriend*, both from HarperCollins, is due in 2001.

The author of five novels, a memoir, and numerous short stories, **Wayne Karlin** received four Individual Artists Awards from his home state of Maryland and a fellowship from the National Endowment of the Arts. His work with both Vietnam veterans and editors and writers from both sides of that war has resulted in several anthologies and honors. He teaches language and literature at Charles County Community College.

And in this corner, the genre writers

A practicing surgical pathologist and researcher and professor at the University of Colorado Health Sciences Center, **Robert Greer** has created the CJ Floyd mystery series. Titles from Warner/Mysterious Press include *The Devil's Hatband*, *The Devil's Red Nickel*, *The Devil's Backbone* as well as *Limited Time*, a medical thriller, and *Choosing Sides*, a short story collection. He is working on a fifth novel.

Published since 1982, **Karen Harper** has written historical novels and, more recently, contemporary suspense and historical mystery. The latter, set in the Elizabethan era, include *The*

SANDRA GURVIS *is the author of eight nonfiction books, including* Careers for Nonconformists *(Marlowe, 2000), which was a selection of the Quality Paperback Book Club and the upcoming* Where Have All the Flower Children Gone? *(University Press of Mississippi) and* Day Trips from Columbus *(Globe Pequot). Her novel* The Pipe Dreamers *(www.thepipedreamers.com) will be published by Olmstead Press in 2001.*

Poysen Garden, *The Tidal Poole*, and in 2001, *The Twylight Tower*, all from Delacorte. She has tackled contemporary subjects in Amish country in *Down to the Bone* (Mira) and *Dark Road Home* (Signet) and in Appalachia (*The Baby Farm*, Mira).

Fern Michaels is a pseudonym for Mary Kuczkir, although success by any other name would smell as sweet. With seventy contemporary, romance and other novels to her credit, half of which have been *New York Times* bestsellers, she estimates that she has about 63 million books in print. Her latest hits include *Guest List* and *What You Wish For*, both from Kensington.

Round One: What is the difference between literary and genre fiction? Who are the readers?

Karen Harper: Genre fiction is aimed toward a broader group of people than literary work, which by its very nature is smaller and more defined. Also genre fiction is more uplifting; it uses heroes, rather than the anti-heroes sometimes found in literary books. With the latter, you can take more of a risk, the characters can be quirky and unlikeable.

Elizabeth Evans: Readers of literary fiction want to be engaged. They turn to stories with the expectation of finding original ideas expressed in original ways. They take delight in language and imagery and in seeing the way the author has structured the story. It's often said that readers of the pop or genre fictions tend to look for a familiar product. Maybe so, but I suspect many genre readers have missed out on a good introduction to better writing. Genres expect to produce a certain type of story; in literary fiction, the outcome can be totally surprising, yet make complete sense. I think it's a shame so many readers get stuck in the genres.

Fern Michaels: Genre or commercial fiction is for everyone, from 70-year-olds to teenagers. It's also much more action-oriented and generally provides information about a place or facet of life; the antique business, for example, or Las Vegas. Literary fiction is more serious-minded and intended to be enlightening. Personally, I think much of it is stuffy and boring. If I'm going to plunk out money for something, I want to be entertained.

Wayne Karlin: Frankly, I'm uneasy with the terms. Some fiction is written by formula—it's trying to meet or soothe, rather than challenge, preconceptions. You're giving the readers what they think they want, satisfying the customer's perceived needs. It's more plot than character-driven, providing an escape or sense of satisfaction or completion not found in real life. Literary work is written for seekers and explores the complexity of the human heart. It leaves questions, rather than providing easy answers and relies much more upon the character's internal life.

Ann Arensburg: To writers of either, there is no difference. A writer is just as serious about one as the other. People are drawn to a category, and it's a misconception that commercial writers are operating on calculation and opportunism to make money. Judith Krantz and Margaret Atwood, Harold Robbins and Norman Mailer all work under the same principles. It's the motivation and interest that makes the difference as well as the subject matter itself.

Robert Greer: The discrepancies have largely been created by the publishing industry and critics. Readers don't know or care about what kind of book XYZ is supposed to be or who published it as long as it's what they're looking for. Only writers and publishers do.

Round Two: What does your area require in terms of writing skills and techniques? What do you as an author think you bring to the table?

Karlin: My writing has been that of a witness. I've experienced and seen certain things, such as the Vietnam War, and feel a compulsion and responsibility to tell readers about it. My perceptions were so different after I came back that I felt compelled to a create new language for them, because the old way of saying things failed to adequately describe the truth of the experience. My function as a storyteller is to re-create the past and help people understand what happened and why.

Michaels: My goal is to provide entertainment, timely topics, escapism. I try to imbue a sense of family and place and always put animals in my books because I love them . . .that's my brand of storytelling. With contemporary books, you can let your imagination run wild. Historical romance readers want accuracy and adherence to the time period and will get upset if you make a mistake.

Harper: When writing for a genre, there's a particular form or expectation. You need to follow certain guidelines. If it's a mystery, there must be a crime. If it's a suspense novel, a murder can take place but the focus is more on the person's emotions, rather than the action itself. Because Americans lead faster-paced lives, it seems as if their attention spans are shorter. They want to get to the heart of things more quickly. As a result, word counts are down. That presents a challenge to me, because as a former teacher, I want to pull the reader into a culture or closed society and have him or her feel like he's come away having learned something.

Evans: It's important for me not to lie, either in the direction of the sentimental or the cynical. I try to understand what motivates my characters. What will X do to get what he or she wants? What will happen if she doesn't? What does this character say about who we are as human beings? A literary writer's goal is to make the sentences and revelations of such interest that the reader can savor the language while gaining insight.

Round Three: Do most writers have natural leanings for one or the other? Or can they develop their craft to meet the demands of their selected medium?

Arensburg: The answer to both questions is "yes." Anyone can learn to write in a certain way, but first you must be an avid reader. The best educator of writing is reading. You also need to believe in and be drawn to whatever it is your pursuing. I write to please myself and eleven other like-minded souls. And if you do have a mentor, sometimes you develop in a certain area and must overthrow him, particularly if it comes into conflict with what you want to do.

Greer: You can write in more than one genre or category. It's like being a good medical practitioner—some conditions are just inherently obvious and you can address them. I like novels heavily laden with suspense, so that's what I write. Sometimes the results are what some might call literary—and they may end up in those kinds of outlets. But I'm not thinking about that when it comes into my head and I put it down on paper.

Harper: I think that people do have innate tendencies, but that they can also re-educate themselves. When I made the switch to contemporary books and mysteries, I went on a big reading binge. I studied what was out there and looked for a twist that would help me stand out. For example, until mine came along, no mysteries had Queen Elizabeth as the central character.

Michaels: A professional writer could create anything on any subject. But most people are inclined to go with their comfort zone, with what feels most natural. For example, I could never write literature because it bores me. Why struggle if you don't have to?

Karlin: No matter what I write, the literary compulsion takes over. It's part of my personality. I could not sit down coldly and say, 'I'm going to create something that a great number of people are going to buy.'

Round Four: Are their certain routes to take for success in one or the other?

Karlin: A lot of people, particularly those just starting out, come into writing workshops and see themselves as creating a bestseller. That is wrongheaded. Most successful writers begin with small literary magazines and work their way up. Of course publishing today is totally different from the early 80s. Back then you still had a chance in the slush pile with large trade houses. Today the only way to get recognized would be to have an agent who is blown away by your work or go with a small press and hope your book gains momentum. You can also try to sell it yourself online, but that's too much like vanity publishing and you won't likely get reviews.

Arensburg: Publishing has gotten so marketing-driven that many people think there's a formula to follow to become successful. Even academic programs aren't as effective; they mostly grind out teachers of creative writing. The best writers come from seemingly nowhere; look at Raymond Carver, for example. Be the best you can be and keep submitting your work to a wide variety of publications. You also need an agent, no matter what kind of fiction you write.

Evans: Study their requirements and be selective about the outlets you write for. Avoid markets that are poorly edited; you should be proud of where your work appears. And don't pay people to publish your work.

Michaels: Decide who you want to write for and what kind of story you want to tell. Follow your publisher's guidelines; for instance, with Harlequin romances there is no explicit sex. Networking is also important. Find the organizations and clubs that cater to writers in your specialty; many offer online chat rooms and message boards, so you can live anywhere and still make valuable contacts.

Harper: Write what you really want to, whether it be full novels or short stories. Many successful genre writers started with formula publishers and expanded from there. Finish a whole manuscript; few, if any, publishers are going to buy something from an unknown that isn't complete. Especially with genres, it's a good idea to have synopses of several books mapped out, particularly if you want to write in a series.

Greer: Promotion has become increasingly important, so make sure your publisher is behind you. Some authors can do publicity themselves, but it becomes expensive and time-consuming. You also need to look professional and be well-spoken. If marketing yourself and your book is offensive to your inner being, then you might do well to stay in another line of work because these days, your book won't sell by itself.

Round Five: Is there true antagonism or conflict here? Can a novel be both genre *and* literary?

Evans: There is no conflict of interest between the books, no. There are problems within the publishing industry, which has been taken over by megacorporations which will not be satisfied by the sorts of profits traditional to the industry. This results in a marketplace where publishers put almost all of their efforts and advertising dollars behind a handful of titles by, say, a Tom Clancy or a John Grisham. Because of this, many fine works fall into obscurity.

Michaels: The friction is mostly caused by reviewers who pooh-pooh the romance industry and give us negative write-ups. Yet we make up 51 percent of the publishers' revenue! I'm proud of what I do and find it frustrating to get blistering reviews from people who haven't really read my work but would rather slice and dice it as a testament to their own superiority.

Harper: When I meet a person, I can usually tell if he or she is a "literary" reader. This is especially true with reviewers—they tend to be black-and-white about the genres, although things are slowly changing. *Publishers Weekly* now has a separate mass market section and newspapers are replacing traditional book reviewers with entertainment reporters who are more amenable to the genres.

Arensburg: Of course a novel can be both. Look at P.D. James, and the early work of Anne Rice. The categories overlap all the time. However, reviews are more important to literary books, because the publishers have ways of selling genre novels that have no relation to how they've been reviewed. Literary books have a tougher time, particularly if a reviewer doesn't quite get your subject matter. The trend towards printing them as trade paperbacks has helped somewhat, making books more affordable to readers.

Greer: Good fiction is just that, regardless of classification. The definitions are arbitrary. Consider *Huckleberry Finn* and *The Old Man and the Sea*. Both started out as so-called genre works and ended up being classics.

Winning advice

Greer: Define what you write and bring your unique experience to your books. For example, my background in health care and medicine has helped a lot in delineating my plots and characters. Do the best work you can and forget about things like figuring out your audience and finding a publisher.

Karlin: Writing workshops and communities may be a dead-end. You may end up relying too much on others' feedback rather than your own internal editor. Writing is a solitary activity. Write for the writing and let everything else take care of itself.

Evans: Read and re-read the best of contemporary authors and the classics. I write and read every day and imagine I'll be doing the same until I die. You want to keep learning new things about yourself and others and the world, and bringing these lessons to your books.

Arensburg: Make sure your interest comes from the gut and that you are writing about something you care about and are fascinated with what is real to you. Most writers could not imagine doing anything else. They put one foot in front of the other and keep at it.

Michaels: Have a distinctive voice; don't try to copy anyone. Know your subject inside out. Most importantly, be disciplined. I try to write 5000 words a day no matter what and keep a piece of paper with pencil handy so I can scribble down ideas at odd times. To paraphrase Garson Kanin, apply the seat of your pants to the seat of your chair and don't get up until you're done.

Where to Bulk Up

Literary:
Associated Writing Programs
Tallwood House MSN 1E3
George Mason University
Fairfax VA 22030
(703)993-4301 Fax: (703)993-4302
www.awpwriter.org

PEN
568 Broadway, 4th Floor
New York NY 10012
(212)334-1600
www.pen.org

PEN Center West
672 Lafayette Park Place, Suite 41
Los Angeles CA 90057
(213)365-8500
www.pen-usa-west.org

Poets and Writers
27 Spring St.
New York NY 10012
(212)226-3586
www.pw.org

Genre:
Malice Domestic
P.O. Box 31137
Bethesda MD 20824-1137
http://users.erols.com/malice

Mystery Writers of America
17 E. 47th St., 6th Floor
New York NY 10017
(212)888-8171 Fax: 212/888-8107
www.mysterywriters.net

Romance Writers of America
3707 FM 1960 West, Suite 555
Houston TX 77068
(281)440-6885 Fax: (281)440-7510
www.rwanational.com

Science Fiction Writers of America
℅ Sharon Lee, Exec. Director
P.O. Box 171
Unity ME 04988-0171

532 La Guardia Place #632
New York NY 10012-1428
www.sfwa.org

Sisters in Crime
P.O. Box 442124
Lawrence KS 66044-8933
www.sinc-ic.org

Western Writers of America
℅ Larry K. Brown
209 E. Iowa
Cheyenne WY 82009
www.westernwriters.org

John Jakes: Mastering Historical Fiction in a Fifty-Year Career

BY KELLY MILNER HALLS

When the *Los Angeles Times* called author John Jakes "the godfather of the historical novel," not an eyebrow was raised in question or challenge. Jakes has earned that kind of undisputed respect. Library and home book shelves worldwide are filled with millions of copies of his novels, including 50 million copies of his Kent Family Chronicles series alone.

Jakes celebrated half a century as a working, selling writer with an April 12, 2000 ad in the pages of *Publishers Weekly*. Although he's dedicated the vast majority of his 68 years to the craft of writing and has succeeded beyond most writers' dreams, Jakes remains soft spoken, humble and grace-filled. His *Publishers Weekly* ad was an expression of gratitude.

How has this bestselling author maintained his humility? "Simple," Jakes says. "I've tried *not* to let success affect my life and that of my family—children and grandchildren. I'm able to travel more than I once did. I drive a better car than I once did. But I wear shorts and a T-shirt on a workday, and I hope if you met me, you wouldn't guess I am what I am."

He also remembers his humble beginnings: Jakes sold his first short story for $25 as a freshman theater student at Northwestern University in Chicago, the city where he was born. "That check changed the whole direction of my life," Jakes says on his website (www.johnjakes-.com). He enrolled in the creative writing program at DePauw University, graduated in 1953 and earned an M.A. degree in American literature from Ohio State University in 1954.

Even with such impressive academic credentials, Jakes made his living by writing advertising copy for a string of corporations and agencies by day, while fine-tuning his fictional prowess at night. He sold more than 200 short stories to *Ellery Queen*, *Amazing Stories*, *Galaxy* and other well-known publications. He also sold 60 mystery, western and fantasy genre books during those early years, although he admits those niches never served him well.

"I quit writing fantasy largely because I never made a whole lot of money at it," he says. "I felt I was banging my head against a wall and making not the slightest dent. But many people still remember the cycle of Brak the Barbarian sword-and-sorcery pieces that I did and ask for a return of the character. Maybe one of these days!"

It wasn't until the early 1970's that Jakes met *The Bastard* and began to hit his historical stride. Jakes brought his hero, Phillipe Charboneau, to colonial Boston from Europe. Through Charboneau's eyes, millions of readers saw not only the power and passion of the Revolutionary War, but the evolution of a country, a family and a man. Thanks to better than 60 individual print runs, readers are still sharing Jakes's vision of *The Bastard* today.

How did he master historical authenticity? "Back when I was researching the first of the *Kent* novels, I didn't have much money," Jakes says, "but I decided I had to go to Boston anyway to see all the great Revolutionary War sites. I found many of them were gone. The site of the Boston Tea Party turned out to be an office building with a plaque on it. So I work judiciously from written sources, photos, old engravings and visits to the places if I think it

KELLY MILNER HALLS *has been a professional freelance writer for more than a decade. Her work has been featured in the* Chicago Tribune, Guideposts for Kids, FamilyFun, Highlights for Children, U*S*Kids, *and* Writer's Digest. *She is a frequent contributor to* Writer's Digest Books.

might help fill in details. I warn myself ahead of time that it might not."

When Jakes finds his historical benchmarks have been swallowed up by progress, he turns to the written word. "I tell new writers to read all you can about the period you're writing about. Absorb details large and small. Let it seep through until it's really a part of you. Then forget it—and write the story. Keep the story in the foreground. A great deal of what you've learned will come through without your forcing it. At least it does for me."

Even so, he avoids taking creative liberties with history. "I have a rule," Jakes says. "I never distort history to satisfy the story. If I make any changes at all in the historical record, they are tiny, minor, and they are always noted in the afterward of the book. I approach each novel as though it might be the *only* book about a given historical period a person reads. Hence the history must be as correct as conscientious research can make it, without spending a lifetime on one novel. I fit my characters into history and don't alter the record to suit the narrative."

Has half a century of practice made writing good historical fiction easy—or formulaic—for Jakes? "Not at all," he says. "With fiction, there are dozens of considerations, especially in a novel. Does it have the right structure? Is there a theme? If not, why not? If there is, are you beating it to death by being too obvious? Does the story move chapter-to-chapter on a rising line of suspense (what the late, great agent, Scott Meredith, called 'worry')? And on and on. I worry about dozens of elements all the time, even after the book's written. But once it's in the publication pipeline, the worry stops. By then I'm worrying about the next one."

Jakes's most recent release is *On Secret Service: A Novel* (E.P. Dutton, June 2000). Set largely in Civil War Washington DC, the novel explores political debate and intrigue during the 19th century through the eyes of four key protagonists–a spy, an actress, a Confederate belle and a Union officer.

"The story deals primarily with the development of organized wartime intelligence and counter-intelligence, which really got its start in a formal way—funded by governments for the first time on a big-time basis—during the Civil War," Jakes says. "Certainly there was spying in wartime since the earliest eras, but the Civil War brought it in as 'big business' in our country for the first time."

If Jakes seems consumed by the Civil War, he admits it's not surprising. "Of course it fascinates me, or I wouldn't return to it. It's also one of the two periods of American history that seem to exert the greatest fascination around the world." But the Civil War is not Jakes's only historic passion. "Many other periods and countries fascinate me—the Napoleonic era, the Restoration in England, the Roman Empire. My interests are wide."

So wide, in fact, that they include the dramatic arts. "I admit it, I have a writing 'sideline,' " Jakes says, "one that I have pursued since 1970. I write for the theater." Several of Jakes's plays and musicals have been published and produced. "[In 1999] we premiered a musical adaptation of *Great Expectations* I wrote with a close friend and Tony-nominated composer."

Does a musician's heart beat within Jakes's chest? "No," he says, "just a lyricist's heart. If I hadn't taken up writing novels, I probably would have tried to carve a niche as a musical book and lyric writer in New York. I think I'm pretty good at it. But if not, I have a good time at it anyway."

Historical fiction will remain Jakes's bread and butter for now. "There must be a dozen novels out there that I want to write." And if he has his way, Jakes's dedication to history in literature will stand as his professional legacy.

"I hope to be remembered first as a teller of good stories. Second, as a faithful portrayer of the colorful drama of history. And finally, as someone who has changed lives. I receive remarkable letters from men and women whose careers have been shaped by my books—most often as teachers, many of them history teachers. I'm very proud of that."

Margaret Atwood: "As a Writer, You Must Do What Beckons to You"

BY KATIE STRUCKEL

Who would have thought that when Margaret Atwood published seven of her poems on a small-bed letterpress at the age of 21, she'd emerge as one of the most respected artists of this century? Canadian-based Atwood is the author of over 50 titles, including *The Hand-maid's Tale*, *Alias Grace* and her most recent novel, *The Blind Assas-sin*. Named by *Writer's Digest* as one of the 100 Best Writers of the Century, Atwood has made a place for herself in all walks of literature.

Photo by Thies Bognar

Margaret Atwood

Being proficient at writing in a variety of forms is one of Atwood's strengths. She has written everything from fiction to poetry and most recently opera, simply because no one told her not to. "I think if I had gone to creative writing school, they probably would have said, 'Pick one or the other,' " she says. "But since there were hardly any creative writing schools at that time, I didn't see any reason why I shouldn't do what struck me."

Atwood began her writing career while still in high school, where she wrote for the school newspaper and contributed pieces to the yearbook literary section. In college she wrote for both school literary magazines and non-school publications. It was at this time that she published her poems.

"I published seven poems and made them into a little book, which cost 50 cents," she says. "I wish I had kept a lot of them." Atwood took the 200 books to local bookstores and "low and behold, some of them agreed to take those little things." Most likely those same bookstores stock Atwood's titles today.

Here Atwood takes time to share her views on the novel form, the fundamentals of writing, and the socio-political impact the writer has on society.

You've said that novels aren't sociological texts or political tracts. How would you characterize novels?

Well, novels are stories; they don't purport to be factual relations of events that have actually happened. In other words, they're not like stories in a newspaper in that you kind of hope they might be true. The idea with a novel is that it's true in a different way. It's true about human nature, but it's not true about somebody called "John Smith," whose name is also John Smith in the novel. You're telling stories about the kinds of things that happen and you're telling "what if" stories, but you're not telling, "On June the 5th, year 2000, Katie phoned Margaret and had the following conversation."

However, that's not to say that the novel has nothing to do with society. Of course it does, because you're telling "what if" stories and "this is the kind of thing that happens" stories

---

KATIE STRUCKEL *is an associate editor for* Writer's Digest *magazine, where this interview originally appeared.*

about us, who we are, where we are, where we've been and all of those kinds of things. Sometimes you're telling them about Mary Queen of Scots, but they're still about human nature.

So then, overall, you're saying a novel is about human nature and that's really the role it plays in society—to reflect our humanity.

Well, you can't help that, because human beings write them. And they write them either well or badly. But with the good ones, the reaction the reader has is "that's right," or "that's the way it is," or "that's what would have happened," or "I'm surprised to hear that, but now that you tell me, it all fits." And sometimes you say, "I don't believe that in a minute." In that case, the novel's gone off the track.

How important are the fundamentals of writing?

When I was about 17, I announced to my parents, who were quite horrified, that I was going to be a writer. My mother said, "Well, in that case, you better learn to spell." And I said, "Other people will do that for me." And you know, they do. I'm not that bad, but I would never win a spelling bee. I'm like a lot of writers in that respect—we tend to spell a little bit by ear.

As for punctuation, it's the single big argument issue when we're editing a book. The editor always wants to stick to a house style. I feel that punctuation is simply like the flats and sharps on a musical score, that punctuation has to do with the ear. The editors feel that it has to do with the rule book. So we always fight over that. I win. The buck stops with the author. The author is the one who is accountable, not the editor. So I don't want to be accountable for punctuation I don't like. My second novel, *Surfacing*, has a lot of run-on sentences in it because it's stream of consciousness in places. The galleys were edited by someone who had never edited a book of fiction before, and he took out all my punctuation and put in proper punctuation. I had to go through it with a magnifying glass and put it all back in.

How much do you allow your political activism to manifest itself in your writing?

I gave a whole lecture on this subject at Cambridge quite recently. I think that people have duties as citizens and those have nothing to do with writing. Everyone should be taking those kinds of interests in the place where they live. And, if everybody did, it would be quite a different sort of place. But writers often get shoved into the forefront, partly because they're articulate, partly because they often do have opinions. Also partly because they don't have jobs—nobody can fire them. Therefore, they find themselves being spokespersons for people who might think the same thing but would be afraid to say it. That's just a kind of job hazard.

When you look at writing in general there have been many writers, such as Charles Dickens, who have done what we might call political or social things in their novels, and there have been lots who haven't. It doesn't necessarily go with the territory. As a writer, you have to do what beckons to you as a writer. In other words, falsely straining yourself to put something like that into a book where it doesn't really belong is not doing anybody any favors. And the reader can tell. You can tell when you're being preached to and you can tell when you're being told a story—there is a difference.

I asked about your activism and its role because most of your novels tend to have a very feminist feel to them.

That's because they have women in them. Just because something has a woman in it doesn't mean it's feminist. You can call James Joyce's *Ulysses* a feminist novel and it would be. But what kind of world are we living in where half the human race is women, and if you put some of them in your book, you're a feminist? It's weird.

You put a strong woman in there and all of a sudden . . .

Then you put a weak woman in it, what is it then? You have to be either anti-feminist or a feminist, you can't just be talking about human nature. Well, too bad, I don't agree with that.

You always have highly-developed, multi-faceted, strong female characters in your fiction. Have you, or will you, ever create a strong male role?

I already have. It's just that people tend not to notice them because I'm a woman writer, so they're biased to begin with. Similarly with men who write strong women—they're often either not noticed or they're taken as some kind of criticism. You know, we could discuss Jane Austen and say, "What kind of a person is Mr. Darcy?" Where does that leave us with Jane Austen as a feminist or not a feminist? She probably wasn't even thinking about it. She had opinions about women and men, there's no doubt about that, but she was of her time and her place.

A lot of writers tend to project themselves through their characters. How do you view yourself in relation to your work?

My characters can express themselves, mostly. As for the rest of it, I don't really consider that I am putting myself into it. I mean, I don't consider it. If I wanted to write something called *This is the Story of My Life*, that's what I'd do.

In many of your novels the endings are very open and ambiguous so people can form their own opinions. Is there any particular reason why you don't provide absolute, concrete endings?

Partly because I live in the 21st century and we don't have total faith anymore in, "This is the happy ending, this is the only happy ending, and this is the only way the story can possibly end." We tend to consider alternatives. We also know that when the bride and groom walk down the aisle, that's not an ending, it's a beginning. It may not even be the first time they've done it, and it may not be the last time they're going to do it. We don't get closure in our society as much as we used to. Things are just more open-ended.

And the other reason is that I like the reader to feel that *the reader* can participate in the active imagination that is the novel.

"Whatever Works, Works": Kurt Vonnegut on Flouting the Rules of Fiction

BY KELLY NICKELL

Kurt Vonnegut has witnessed the evolution of fiction—and in some ways propelled it, perhaps. From the decreasing popularity of literary magazines and the increasing price of books, to his own evolving status as a "cult figure" and "popular author," Vonnegut has been a constant observer of—and a steady contributor to—the literary world for nearly half a century. And the oft-quoted literary giant remains a vocal commentator on the changing publishing industry.

Kurt Vonnegut

A published author of everything from novels and short stories to essays and plays, Vonnegut says fiction is an art form unto its own. "All of fiction is a practical joke—making people care, laugh, cry or be nauseated or whatever by something which absolutely is not going on at all. It's like saying, 'Hey, your pants are on fire.' "

And with his characteristic biting wit and humor, Vonnegut often combines social satire, autobiographical experiences and bits of historical fact to create a new form of literary fiction, as in *Slaughterhouse Five*, which became a No. 1 *New York Times* bestseller when it was published in 1969.

Alternating between linear and circular structures and differing points of view, Vonnegut has spent much of his life testing literary boundaries. And it's become a Vonnegut axiom that writing rules apply only to the extent that they strengthen the effect of the final piece. "You want to involve the reader," he says. "For example, *Mother Night* was a first-person confessional—the narrator ruined his life and he needn't have. But there's no way you can put together a manual about when to use first person and when to use third person.

"James Joyce broke all the rules. He's a writer like no other, and he got away with it. You have to get away with it. When I was teaching, if I gave a basic rule, it was 'whatever works, works.' I experiment, and my waste baskets are always very full of failed experiments," he says. "Can I get away with this? No. The trick is getting the reader to buy it."

It's fairly safe to assume that readers do indeed "buy it." Among his numerous honors and awards, Vonnegut has received a Guggenheim Fellowship and a National Institute of Arts and Letters grant, served as the vice president for the PEN American Center and lectured in creative writing at Harvard University and the University of Iowa.

Remember your reader

"When I teach, what I'm teaching is sociability more than anything else because that's what most beginning writers, being young, aren't doing," Vonnegut says. "I try to teach how to be a good date on a blind date and to keep the reader in mind all the time. Young writers will dump

---

KELLY NICKELL *is assistant editor of* Writer's Digest *magazine, where this interview originally appeared.*

everything they want to say on some poor reader not caring whether the reader has a good time or not."

Vonnegut's early experience in journalism—he was editor of the college newspaper in 1941 while studying biochemistry at Cornell University, and later a police reporter with the Chicago City News Bureau in 1947—clearly has influenced his style. Staying true to the basic elements of journalism, Vonnegut says he tries to give readers as much information as he can, as soon as he can—a writing trait he's also tried to teach others.

"I hate a story where on page 17 you find out, 'My God, this person is blind.' Or that this happened 100 years ago or 100 years in the future. I tell students, 'Don't withhold information from your readers, for God's sake. Tell 'em everything that's going on, so in case you die, the reader can finish the story.' "

Another Vonnegut specialty is weaving bits of factual information into his fiction's lining, to draw in readers on an emotional level. "The facts are often useful to the reader, if they're historical events. You can expect the reader to be emotionally involved. And to make the reader believe and say, 'Oh Jesus, I guess that's right.' "

Vonnegut used both historical facts and his personal experience as a World War II prisoner of war in Dresden to create *Slaughterhouse Five*. He says the latitude used when combining fact with fiction depends on how much the writer is willing to claim as fact: "The viewpoint character in *Slaughterhouse Five* was Bill Pilgrim, and he was actually a real guy from Rochester," Vonnegut says. "He never should have been in the army, and he died in Dresden and was buried over there. He just simply allowed himself to starve to death. You can do that if you're a prisoner, you can just decide not eat. He decided he didn't understand any of it, and he was right, 'cause there was nothing to understand, so he died.

"I didn't have him die in the book, but had him come home and go to optometry school. So, I didn't tell the truth about his life, but I never said it was his life in the first place."

"Write what you write"

What's the best piece of advice Vonnegut's ever received? "Quit," he says. "It's such a relief." But he didn't. "No, I didn't quit—I'm still pooping along."

Yet there were times early in his career—when he was working as a freelancer, receiving little pay and trying to raise a family—that the notion of quitting wasn't unthinkable. Fortunately, the author chose to follow the advice of agent Kenneth Littauer.

"I was working as a freelancer—it's a harrowing way to make a living-and I would talk to Ken about how to make more money and he said, 'Don't trim your sails to every wind, just go ahead and write and see what happens. Don't look at the market. Don't look at the bestseller list to see what's selling.' That wouldn't help anyway. You have to write what you write, or get out of the business."

Vonnegut's battle with depression following publication of *Slaughterhouse Five* almost did get him out of the business. He even vowed never to write again. And not until 1973 did he publish another book, *Breakfast of Champions*. Subtitled *Goodbye Blue Monday*, the book certainly didn't skirt the issue of depression, but Vonnegut says he's still not sure how the whole experience influenced his work: "There used to be a theory that tuberculosis helped to make someone a genius because they ran higher temperatures. It's now believed, and I guess it's a clinical fact, that most writers are troubled by depression. And I don't know whether it helps or not, but it sure doesn't feel good."

Whether it's his seemingly natural ability to create strong characters, or his remarkable modesty ("I certainly didn't expect to succeed to the extent I have. I didn't expect to amount to much."), generations of writers continue to attempt to follow in Vonnegut's legendary footsteps. And to these many aspiring writers, Vonnegut offers some simple advice: "Don't worry about getting into the profession—write anyway to make your soul grow. That's what the practice of any art is. It isn't to make a living, it's to make your soul grow."

On the changing fiction market

"Books don't matter as much as they used to, and they cost too much," Vonnegut says of the current state of publishing. "But publishers have to sell books to stay in business. Before television, publishers would admit that what paid the freight for everything else they published, all the serious fiction, poetry and so forth, were cook books, garden books and sex books. They had to publish those or they'd go out of business."

While many of his recent books, including *Bagombo Snuff Box*, *Fates Worse than Death: An Autobiographical Collage of the '80s* and *God Bless You, Dr. Kevorkian* showcase the shorter form—most have been collections of essays, interviews and speeches-Vonnegut says short stories seem to be losing their allure as fewer and fewer prominent magazines publish high-quality pieces.

"This country used to be crazy about short stories," he says. "New short stories would appear every week in the *Saturday Evening Post* or in *The New Yorker*, and every middle-class literate person would be talking about it: 'Hey, did you read that story by Salinger?' or 'Hey, did you read that story by Ray Bradbury?'

"But that no longer happens. No short story can cause a sensation anymore because there are too many other forms of entertainment. People can still go through old collections of short stories on their own and be absolutely wowed. But it's a private experience now."

Vonnegut in the 21st century

At what readers may hope is only a short break during a very prolific writing period, what is Vonnegut planning next? "Well, as I'm sitting around right now, I'm trying to think of what would be a neat idea. Most people do other things with their time. But writers, we'll sit around and think up neat stuff. Not something just anybody could do."

Editor Robley Wilson Weighs in on Slush Pile Politics and the Value of Truth in Fiction

BY WILL ALLISON

"The Story's death caught us all off guard. We'd been watching Poetry so closely that we failed to heed the warning signs. One day the Story was here, watching football, going to singles bars, making quiche. The next day—POOF!—we were reading about his demise in the Times, *our bagels forgotten, our untouched latté forming white rings on the dark wood of our kitchen tables."*

—From "The Death of the Short Story," by J. David Stevens
A *short-short published in* The North American Review
(November/December 1998).

Robley Wilson

Despite rumors to the contrary, the short story isn't really dead. Just ask Robley Wilson, former editor of *The North American Review*, the nation's oldest literary magazine.

"It seems to me remarkably healthy," he says. "It's only the New York publishers who pretend to think otherwise—though they continue to produce story collections. The genuine good health of the story is on display in the literary magazines."

Wilson should know. He served as editor of *The North American Review* for thirty-one years, and when he retired last spring, it marked the end of an era in the world of literary magazines.

During Wilson's tenure, *The North American Review* was a two-time winner and five-time finalist for the National Magazine Award for Fiction, the magazine equivalent of an Oscar. It's a remarkable achievement for a bimonthly with a circulation of only 4,000. It's even more remarkable when you consider the competition—big-time fiction powerhouses such as *The New Yorker*, *The Atlantic*, *Esquire* and *Harper's*. Only three other so-called "little magazines"—*Antaeus*, *The Georgia Review* and *Story*—have ever won the award. Of those other three, only *Story* equaled *The North American Review*'s feat of winning twice, and only *The Georgia Review* is still being published today.

The major annual short-story anthologies provide another yardstick of Wilson's editorial success. Work from *The North American Review* has been selected for *Best American Short Stories* eight times, the Pushcart Prize nine times, and O. Henry four times.

But there's more to Robley Wilson's literary legacy than a list of awards and honors. During his tenure, the *North American Review* nurtured some of the most important voices in contemporary American fiction, publishing early work by Raymond Carver, Gail Godwin, Joyce Carol

WILL ALLISON *is an Indianapolis-based freelance writer, former executive editor of* STORY *literary journal and former editor of* Novel & Short Story Writer's Market.

Oates and Barry Lopez. And Wilson was the first to publish T.C. Boyle and George V. Higgins, among others. (Wilson, not one to trumpet his "discoveries," is quick to point out that Higgins debuted simultaneously in *The Massachusetts Review.*)

Wilson took the helm of *The North American Review* in 1969, six years after he began teaching at Northern Iowa University, where the magazine is still published today. In addition to his teaching and editing duties, Wilson also managed to squeeze in a little writing time for himself: He is the author of three poetry collections, one chapbook, one novel, and five short-story collections, including *Dancing for Men* (University of Pittsburgh Press), winner of the 1982 Drue Heinz Literature Prize, and *Living Alone*, whose title story was selected for *The Best American Short Stories*, 1979. His fifth collection, *The Books of Lost Fathers*, is due out this spring (Johns Hopkins University Press). He was the recipient of 1983-84 Guggenheim Fellow in fiction, and he held a 1995-96 Nicholl Fellowship in Screenwriting.

Retirement has done little to slow Wilson, who now lives in Florida. His latest projects include a second novel and *100% Pure Florida Fiction* (University Press of Florida), an anthology he edited with his wife, Susan Hubbard, an associate professor of English at the University of Central Florida in Orlando and the author of two story collections.

This interview was conducted in July 2000, two months after Wilson's retirement from *The North American Review* and one week after he finished a draft of his new novel during a residency at Yaddo.

In the November/December 1998 issue, you published J. David Stevens' "The Death of the Short Story," a humorous piece in which the world mourns the passing of the short story. Every couple of years, it seems, someone steps up to the plate and announces that the form is dead—or very much alive (see Vince Passaro, *Harper's*, August 1999). What's your take on the state of the contemporary short story?

It seems to me remarkably healthy. It's only the New York publishers who pretend to think otherwise—though they continue to produce story collections. I think a lot of critics have relatively low expectations for the short story, partly because their taste has been conditioned by the myth that *The New Yorker* publishes great fiction. It doesn't; the Tina Brown ascendancy pretty thoroughly destroyed *New Yorker* fiction by bringing in sensationalism, dirty words, celebrity authors, etc. Her legacy endures, I think, so that a really fine *New Yorker* story is a kind of happy aberration.

The genuine good health of the story is on display in the literary magazines. Partly that's because lit mags are not concerned with demographics or celebrity, and partly it's because there are so few markets for fiction in large magazines.

Do you think your experience as a writer and poet influenced your approach to editing? If so, how?

Probably. It surely influenced the *NAR*'s emphasis on fiction and, more subtly, influenced my attitude toward writers. It made me less patient with them.

The North American Review's submission guidelines state, "We like stories that start quickly and have a strong narrative arc." In terms of structure, are these the main traits you looked for when you were reading manuscripts?

In general, editors have to read too many manuscripts, many of them incompetent, so they tend (I think) to look for work that will arrest them. I think it has little to do with structure, but a great deal to do with voice—by which I mean the authority that persuades a reader the author knows and believes what he's talking about. The new editors of *The North American Review* can use a phrase like "a strong narrative arc" because they haven't edited fiction before. Ultimately, they will print stories they like, and they won't defend those stories on the basis of arcs or tangents.

The guidelines also state, "We are especially interested in work that addresses contemporary North American concerns and issues, particularly with the environment, gender, race, ethnicity, and class." And on the *NAR* website, the magazine is described as taking "a broad view of current North American preoccupations—especially the problems of the environment." Would it be fair to say you had a preference for politically charged subject matter? And if so, how did this influence your selection of stories?

I remember being asked, rather nastily, at an AWP convention nearly twenty years ago if *The North American Review* sought out work that dealt with such concerns. My answer was that we did not "seek" such work—that we took it as it came. If an editor looks for excellent fiction, poetry, and essays, these concerns will appear. We published plenty of the "concerns" the new editors list in their guidelines, stories by and about gays and blacks and hispanics and the disenfranchised—but without making a special search or plea for such matters. If you advertise for politically correct material, you're going to get a lot of crap, a lot of ax-grinding, a lot of embarrassing special pleading. Truth will out; you don't have to subsidize it.

In the slush pile at *Story*, we used to see certain themes and topics again and again—coming-of-age stories, college stories, stories about sick or dying parents, stories about homeless people, etc. Were there themes or topics you saw too often at *The North American Review*? What advice would you give a young writer trying to decide what to write about, and can a writer increase her chances of publication by steering clear of certain topics?

Like *Story*, the *NAR* always had its share of such fiction. But you can't tailor your work to the magazines, can you? You don't say, "I have studied the whims of magazine X, and I am now going to write a story for magazine X." At least I hope you don't. And I guess I don't think writers—at least poets and fiction writers—"decide" what to write about. If you're a serious writer, your subject will find you—though it may not find you until you've reached middle age. Anyway, there's nothing that prevents a master storyteller from making a great story out of any of the topics you mention.

During a workshop he taught at Ohio State a few years ago, C. Michael Curtis, fiction editor of *The Atlantic*, said he could tell whether a story was a candidate for publication after reading only one paragraph. Other editors I've met say they'll read anywhere from one to five pages before they pass judgment. Can you give us some insight into your approach to reading manuscripts? How much time did you give a story to catch your interest before you moved on to the next one?

John Ciardi used to say that he could tell whether a poem was worthy of the *Saturday Review* after reading only the first line, and I think that generally editors have to be able to spot a failed story early in the read. I'd like to think that when Michael [Curtis] rejects one of my stories, he's read more than the opening paragraph—but, alas, I would echo his statement. Younger writers may resent the practice, but they should remember that all editorial judgments are subjective and/or (in the case of major magazines) conditioned by the magazine's demographics. And time is always a factor; if you read every word of every manuscript, you'd never have a life.

What were some of the most common problems you saw in manuscripts submitted to *The North American Review*?

Skipping the obvious—incompetence, banality, unearned obscenity—I'd say that a lot of promising stories fail because the author got the ending in sight and lost concentration by charging toward that ending. That, I guess, is another way of saying that the story gives itself away too soon. I'm fond of telling students that "the story knows what it wants to be," and it will fail if its writer refuses to heed that knowledge.

What's the single most valuable piece of advice you'd give a young writer interested in submitting her work to literary magazines—advice she's unlikely to hear in a creative-writing workshop?

Be patient. Tell the truth. Read. But of course any workshop would say such things. The point is, early success is neither likely nor necessarily desirable—though if it happens, it should be enjoyed to the max. Generally, writing improves with the age of the writer.

In praising *The Sun*, you once wrote, "It is livelier than most literary magazines, not ashamed to be sometimes sentimental, sometimes erotic, sometimes proletarian, sometimes downright funky." Does this statement represent a fair assessment of what you think a literary magazine should be?

Yes, I guess it does—though not in the same way Sy [Safransky, *The Sun*'s editor] perceives those adjectives. Each editor decides on his/her own mix. I'd have a fairly low "funky" threshold.

I've noticed that *The North American Review* publishes a fair number of short shorts. Does this reflect a fondness for the form, a way of dealing with space limitations, or both? And do you think a beginning writer has a better shot at publication by "going short"?

Certainly a fondness for the "form"—if done well. I'd put "form" in quotation marks because I'm not sure it's an appropriate word. The so-called short-short can assume so many shapes, it really defies definition. If you expect it to be the conventional short story writ small, then you're pretty much doomed to disappointment. If you look at most short-short anthologies, especially if they contain work by well-known writers, you find a lot of disappointing stuff. As for space limitations—the *NAR* didn't really have that as a problem.

Can you offer some recommended reading for a young writer?

Read anything and read a lot. One of the real pleasures of retirement—aside from the time freed for my own writing—is the time actually to read books!

First Bylines

BY TERRI SEE and KELLY MILNER HALLS

No writer will deny that connections are helpful—sometimes critical—in getting published. They frequently mean the difference between catching an editor's eye or sitting in the slush pile. Here three writers share their stories of first publication: a decidedly Southern short story collection; a gritty and realistic coming-of-age novel; and a short story collection (linked like a novel) about a young woman whose father is terminally ill. These writers also share how they made their very different connections work for them.

TIM PARRISH
Red Stick Men, *University Press of Mississippi*

Through a "gris-gris of gator teeth and toulene gas," the stories in Tim Parrish's first book, *Red Stick Men*, paint a rough and exotic combination of old and new South, a blend of perspective he came to from personal experience. Though Parrish now lives and teaches in Connecticut, his twenty-seven years in Baton Rouge-Red Stick, as it is known by locals, provided him with a deep range of voices and varied character types not often seen sharing the pages of Southern fiction. "I grew up on the industrial north side of town, went to college on the other side of town, played in a band all over the place, and taught at a mostly African-American high school even further north. So I feel like I know the people and the place really well," he says. This depth of connection colors the stories of *Red Stick Men*.

Dedication to revision, making time to write when it's easier not to, and "a pit-bull virus called can't-stop-writing-if-I-wanted-to" are what Parrish calls his writing fundamentals. Another essential, he says, is his ability to believe in what he's doing, even when the world doesn't provide much support for those beliefs. But Parrish readily credits a passel of folks for his success in writing. "My dad gave me the love of story-telling with his yarns from hometown Soso, Mississippi. My late high school English teacher, Fred Shirley, planted the writing bug in me by challenging me to write well and by opening up the world of literary fiction. The three books by living Southern writers that really lit up the sky for me were *Airships* by Barry Hannah, *The Watch* by Rick Bass, and *The Ice at the Bottom of the World*, by Mark Richard. When I was searching for voice and story, all three of those writers spoke to my experiences in the South by staying true to the region, but also by pushing the subject matter and language toward a New South complexity and intensity."

These attachments and his connection to community led Parrish to the work of writing and fortified him along the way. It was only fitting and comfortable, then, when the opportunity arose, to have his book considered by a Southern press. And it all happened quite "accidentally." A couple of years ago, Parrish was an invited reader at a short story conference in New Orleans. Also attending was fiction writer and University Press of Mississippi fiction editor Moira Crone.

TERRI SEE *is editor and publisher of* Greeting Card Writer *magazine, www.GreetingCardWriter.com, Director of The CardReps Agency, www.cardreps.com, and a former production editor for* Writer's Market. *She interviewed Tim Parrish and Elissa Schappell for this article.*
KELLY MILNER HALLS, *is a fulltime freelance writer, and a frequent contributor to* Writer's Digest Books. *She interviewed Christopher Rice for this article.*

Parrish sought her out to tell her how much he had liked her short story collection and a mutual admiration was born. Crone asked whether Parrish was working on anything she might be interested in. At the time, his agent was shopping a political novel of his around New York, so he told Crone no. But a few months later, Parrish pulled his novel out of circulation and contacted Crone to see if she was still interested.

"I really liked the idea of working with a Louisiana writer as my editor, and of having the book come out from the state where my parents were born," Parrish says. "Even though my agent showed little enthusiasm for my considering UPM without first shopping the book around, I submitted the book and UPM took it. I'm pretty confident (or deluded) that I could have sold the collection to a commercial press with greater circulation and more money, but I'm extremely happy that I didn't. My work with Moira Crone made all the stories better, and the folks at UPM have been wonderful, even down to letting Moira and me choose the cover art by a New Orleans artist."

Even with the support of family and friends behind him, Parrish has been visited by the same self-doubt as most writers. "I was forty when I first got published, so there was a nagging part of my brain saying it would never happen, even though I knew I had good stories to tell." One story in *Red Stick Men*, "Hardware Man," was rejected over twenty times before *Shenandoah* published it, and many of the others got roughed up too. "Rejection is a fact of life for writers, like toothaches and head colds," Parrish believes, "and you just have to find a way to handle it to survive. Every writer I know has been demoralized at some point, but the ones who end up getting published scrabble through the disappointment to get back to what's important, which is the work itself." His advice? "If you're a literary writer, love of the work—not publishing, fame, or a penchant for solitary confinement—has to be the primary motivation, or you'll go crazy. Also, try and find a community of writers who provide both support and useful feedback. And don't drink too much coffee."

ELISSA SCHAPPELL
Use Me, *William Morrow & Company*

For Elissa Schappell, writing out the complexities of people and relationships is a way of life. "I've always felt like it was my job, in my family, to see everything." Keeping diaries from an early age, Schappell believed at some point it would be important to have them. In her first book, *Use Me* (William Morrow and Co., 2000), Schappell constructs a coming-of-age novel through a series of ten short stories.

Rife with trauma and tempered with sardonic humor, the book explores topics like death, grief and abortion through the eyes of main character Evie, whose father is stricken with cancer. Critics have been kind to the title, calling it "a wonderfully satisfying book . . . that somehow fulfills the expectations of the genre in unexpected ways" (*The New York Times Book Review*). Of Schappell, author Rick Moody says "she's a challenge and a star." While *Use Me* marked Schappell's debut as a novelist, she is well-connected in publishing: she is a regular columnist for *Vanity Fair*, and a founding editor of the Portland-based literary journal *Tin House*. She also served as an editorial staffer for *The Paris Review*, and a freelance writer for magazines such as *Bomb*, *GQ*, *Spin*, *Vogue* and *Bookforum*. But with an MFA in creative writing from New York University, Schappell's first love is fiction.

Schappell started out young, writing adventure stories of "girls in go-go boots trying to conquer the world." But as Schappell developed as a writer, she came to realize she wanted to write about more personal truths and her perceptions of human experience. "I'd always written stories that were fantastic and sort of spun out of the air, and I decided to write more personal things and to take more chances," she says. But writing what is true is not often the same as writing what is pretty; and for women, Schappell believes, this presents special problems. "As women, we're supposed to 'make nice,' " she says. "But I'm very interested in going into those places where people behave in the ways that human beings really behave in the best of times and the worst of times, and writing the truth about it."

Schappell's decision to tackle tougher issues was not made overnight. "I'm as much a writer as I am a woman, but I did not have the confidence to say 'I'm going to do this. I'm going to write what I know and what I feel.' Then I was at New York University, and I saw Toni Morrison speak, and she said, 'If any of you out there need permission to write stories, I give it to you.' It stuck with me." Another turning point for Schappell was attending the Saratoga Writer's Conference and taking a class with Amy Hemphill, who encouraged her in the direction of her subject matter and style—to write from the truth and a truthful place within herself. "It was amazing to me that this was okay." The words of two writers she admired were an important reassurance, Schappell says. "Sounds kind of corny, but that's exactly what happened. Then, when my dad got sick, I thought 'he's fifty-seven years old and he's going to die.' I was then thirty-two, and I realized that if I were my father, my life would already be half-over. Was I going to pussyfoot around and not say what I felt was important?"

As fortuitously as she encountered Morrison and Hemphill, Schappell met her agent. At the time, she was an editor at *The Paris Review* and had been invited to participate in a reading by writers who worked at literary magazines. An editor at William Morrow and Company came to the reading and afterward asked to see her manuscript. Schappell sold *Use Me* on the basis of four short stories and was offered a two-book deal. Previously, all she had published were three or four short stories. "I would never have known that day would change my life. At the time I was much more focused on other things," Schappell remembers. "I did not go to that reading thinking I was going to catch someone's eye."

In addition to making the right connections at the right time, Schappell attributes her success to a love of and commitment to the craft. "You have to write every single day. I get up every morning and work. I can't wait for my brain to wake up fully because then my ego kicks in and it berates me and says things like, 'The world doesn't need more books.' The only time I feel good is when I'm writing, and it's the only thing I have ever been good at," she says. "When I'm not writing, I'm a horrible bitch and dreadful to be around. I'm happy and sane and have a clear mind when I write—and people like me much better."

CHRISTOPHER RICE
A Density of Souls, *Talk Miramax Books/Hyperion*

As you pick up *A Density of Souls*, the first novel from 22-year-old author Christopher Rice, you may be tempted to assume he's little more than a novelty—the youthful "son of Anne." Resist that temptation. Rice may be crown prince of horror's dark mistress, but he's got a writer's voice all his own.

"There is no point in being dishonest about the fact that my mother was able to get me a very powerful agent—her agent," Rice admits. "I did leap that hurdle, and that's probably not fair. But there is a common belief out there that every time one writer gets accepted, ten other 'qualified' writers are knocked out of their spot. That mindset makes it easier to say, 'Being named Rice is the only reason the books are selling,' and that's just not realistic."

Also unrealistic, according to Rice, are the reviews that suggest he should mirror his mother's gothic leaning. "That's frustrating," he admits. "Those reviews are all-out attacks. In the beginning, I was determined to adopt this very gracious attitude, but one reviewer faulted my book for *not* being supernatural? Where's the reviewer's decorum?"

Rice does admit to a certain distinctive legacy, beyond great industry contacts. "Obviously, I grew up in an atmosphere of story," he says, "with two parents [father Stan Rice is a noted poet] who were great storytellers. So I learned how to draft narrative from them. But the stories I want to tell are unique."

Indeed, *A Density of Souls* is neither gothic horror nor poetry. It is, instead, the coming-of-age account of four childhood friends from New Orleans' affluent Garden District. As Stephen, Meredith, Greg and Brandon outgrow hide-and-seek in Big Easy graveyards, differences begin to outweigh the bonds of their common past.

To magnify the shift, Rice sets his tale of teenage murder and betrayal in Cannon School—a fictitious high school dripping with money and excess. "The façade of the school's main buildings faced the wealthier Creole cottages of uptown," he writes. "The entrance doors led to the administrative hallway where the business of New Orleans's finest private school was conducted in gentle whispers punctuated by gracious laughs."

"Gracious" does not describe the growing chasms between cheerleader Meredith, football stars Greg and Brandon and their one-time playmate Stephen, a tender young theater buff who is unquestionably gay. A snickering three-against-one homophobic fire, sparked by disclosed childhood secrets, soon blazes school-wide. And Stephen's life becomes a living hell.

Is the novel autobiographical? "No," Rice says. "Most of the things that happened to Stephen never happened to me. But I was always afraid they would. I thought those fears were unrealistic, until Matthew Sheppard's death. Then I saw what hatred could really do."

Though inspired, in part, by Wyoming student Matthew Sheppard's well-documented torture and murder, Rice explored more than Stephen's outsider perspectives. He was as attentive to the self-loathing of the abusers as he was of the abused. "If I had to say the book had a message," Rice says, "it would be centered around the fact that revelation can heal the pain it causes"—a message broader than sexual orientation.

"But it certainly pleases me that the book might appeal to gay young people," Rice admits. "Growing up, I noticed a glaring lack of fiction with gay characters beyond stories of the urban gay ghettos. But I find stories of younger people living outside that reality much more fascinating. Their sex lives have not yet fully developed, and they have not yet been touched by HIV."

Though Rice writes with ease about homosexual issues, including a sprinkling of honest, occasionally graphic sexual detail, *A Density of Souls* should not be pigeon-holed as a "gay" novel. Intimidation and expectations of every adolescent kind are at the heart of the plots and subplots. How those expectations sometimes grind, one against another, is what drives the often-gripping tale.

Careful and attentive editorial direction guaranteed that balance, according to Rice. "It was a tremendously educational experience," he says. "It took me about a year-and-a-half to finish the rewrites with a very intense editor, Jonathan Burnham at Talk Miramax/Hyperion, who really loved the book. He even came down to New Orleans and met with me for a weekend to be sure we were staying on track." Though Burnham's edits were intensive, they were not entirely hands-on. "That's part of why it was so educational," Rice says. "None of the rewriting was done for me. Jonathan would nudge me, but he'd let me follow the path on my own. If I had simply gotten his written revisions, how much would I have learned?"

Growing up in a house of writers, the discipline for rewrites was not something Rice needed to learn. But he shies away from the term. "I don't use the word discipline in relation to writing," he says. "I write because I cannot *not* write. But my parents are especially respectful of the physical and mental space you need to write a novel. They don't take it personally when I slip into that world."

Does Rice have any advice for other writers facing their first novel attempt? "Again, I have to be blunt up-front and admit my mother's connections did help me get an agent. But they did not help me get an editor. So any advice I give should be taken with that in mind," he says.

"But I will tell them to strive, constantly, to put themselves in a position where they can be critiqued. Try to publish anywhere and everywhere—from the Penny Press to *The New Yorker*. Expose yourself and make yourself vulnerable. You can disregard criticism only after you learn how to listen to it."

Specialized Markets

Electronic Publishing...................................... 39

For Mystery Writers.................................... 57

For Romance Writers.................................. 68

For Science Fiction/Fantasy & Horror Writers 78

Exploring E-zines: A Literary Revolution Online

BY KELLY MILNER HALLS

For decades, publications like *Ploughshares*, *Prairie Schooner* and *The Paris Review* set the standard for literary fiction. The stories they published dazzled the well-read of an academic, paper press world, even if their reach was sometimes narrow.

But with the growth of the Internet, literary fiction has taken a brave and independent new turn. Development of the e-zine has ushered in this bold, electronic revolution. Tradition and innovation have eagerly joined hands as these venerable institutions of literary publishing have pitched camp in cyberspace, creating Web presentations of the same fine fiction formerly available only in print.

Who are these cyber-pioneers? Why have they come to the Web and where do they see this new medium going? And what do short story writers need to know before submitting their work to electronic markets? Here we talk with four of literature's electronic visionaries to find out.

The Blue Moon Review, at www.thebluemoon.com, is published by literary mainstay **Doug Lawson**, from Richmond, Virginia. Online since 1994. Lawson estimates *Blue Moon Review* has 15,000 readers per month.

Doug DuCap is the fiction editor at *Zuzu's Petals Quarterly* and *The Zuzu's Petals Literary Resource*, at www.zuzu.com, and physically based in Ithaca, New York. Online since 1995. DuCap estimates the site gets 500,000 hits per month.

Garrett Mok is the founder and publisher of the edgy *12-Gauge Review*, at www.12gauge.com, which is based in Brooklyn, New York. Online since 1995. Mok estimates 12gauge.com gets some 750 hits per day.

Valerie MacEwan spreads the infectious tone of southern literary fiction via *The Dead Mule*, at www.deadmule.com, based in Winterville, North Carolina. Online since 1996. MacEwan estimates *The Dead Mule* receives about 500 visitors per day.

What inspired you to create this publication online?

Doug Lawson: At the time, there were no online literary publications, and very few online magazines. I was facilitating writing workshops on America Online at the time, and it just seemed like a good idea; I knew enough great writers to put together a great publication, and distributing it via the Internet seemed smart—low cost, great potential audience. Fortunately, we were early enough to gain (and retain) that audience that many Websites struggle for now.

Doug DuCap: Technology is a tool like any other. When we first created *Zuzu's Petals Quarterly* in 1991, it was a traditional print magazine which featured poetry, fiction, commentary, and original art. It was a very labor-intensive process that took weeks and weeks from editing to design and from production to fulfillment. In 1995 we discovered the Internet, and it was impossible to ignore the potential productive impact this medium could have on literature and education. Moving *Zuzu's*

KELLY MILNER HALLS *is a full-time freelance writer and frequent contributor to* Writer's Digest Books. *She also interviewed John Jakes for this edition of* Novel & Short Story Writer's Market. *See the listings for* Blue Moon Review *on page 157;* Zuzu's Petal's Quarterly *on page 284;* 12-Gauge Review *on page 274; and* The Dead Mule *on page 175.*

Petals Quarterly online would enable us to cut costs and eliminate the financial barriers that kept us from distributing the magazine free of charge to a wider audience as we'd always wished, so we made the leap online.

Garrett Mok: During the pre-inception period of the grass roots magazine (1993-94), I was listening to a lot of Nirvana. I thought, and still think, that Kurt Cobain is a poet, a balls-out singer-songwriter who wore his heart on his sleeve. On April 8, 1994, Cobain took his own life with a shotgun blast to the head. And no matter what I think of weapons in general now, and also suicide, the shotgun symbolized for me, at the time, a brutally effective way out for an artist in irreversible pain. A kind of deliverance. It's a tool for the ultimate act. And the Internet presented an emerging venue alive with possibility. It was a way of creating a community out of otherwise marginalized people.

Val MacEwan: In the beginning, inspiration came from a grant from the NC Arts Council. The grant's initial purpose, highlighting writers east of I-95 in NC in a small journal, expanded to an online publication. I wanted to give writers a safe place to send their work. Few emotions can match those which accompany acceptance for print in a publication, especially the first time. It's hell to put your words out there for strangers to judge. Letting those words leave the safety of the writer's space takes tremendous courage. I wanted writers to check their e-mail, see *The Dead Mule* sender address and get a jolt of self-confidence when they read the acceptance message. And, if they are not accepted, the message is an explanation we hope leaves writers encouraged to keep trying.

How long was it before you felt your efforts were being taken seriously?

Lawson: Writers have always taken us seriously due to the careful quality evident in the work that we publish. We're read regularly now by agents and many writers have kick-started their careers via BMR publication; I'd say it depends on who you ask. *Writer's Digest* has named us among their 'Top 50 Markets for Fiction' for the last two years running, of both print and online journals. Clearly someone thinks good things about us.

DuCap: After looking at the source code of a few Websites, my co-editor and I bought a book on Web design and spent a few days learning. Then we started to organize and code Webpages to showcase the resources we already had, found some literary links on the Web, and placed our first Web issue of *Zuzu's Petals Quarterly* online as an important part of what was to be called *The Zuzu's Petals Literary Resource*. The Website was launched with 10,000 helpful addresses for writers and artists, 300 arts links organized by topic. A few days later, the Website was lucky enough to get named the NCSA/ Mosaic Pick of the Week (back when the NCSA was one of the most popular sites on the Internet) so things really got rolling.

Mok: Within just a few months. To our knowledge, we were the first-ever literary magazine online. And people noticed.

MacEwan: In 1996, many of the writers who agreed to help with the original "print" *Dead Mule* left the project when suggestions about going online began. The impression of the Internet seemed to be that of a fad or a place where copyrighted material would be stolen. A frivolous place, at best, and not taken seriously at all. The Internet had to gain legitimacy before an e-zine or a Website could. When I first spoke to anyone about an e-zine, at the Ploughshares International Writing Seminar in 1996, *Ploughshares* and *Agni* were barely online. My idea of putting the entire zine in html didn't foster much discussion. To give a true accounting, chronologically, it would be in early 1997, after being online about a year.

Have you helped launch any promising new careers?

Lawson: Sure—we published Michael Knight (*Dogfight*, Dutton), as well as Avery Chenoweth (*Wingtips*, Johns Hopkins). Aaron Even's novel *Bloodroot* is forthcoming this fall, and we were the first to excerpt that. P.J. Rondinone went on to publish *The Digital Hood* (Picador) after publishing with us. Aldo Alvarez has been a regular contributor, and his truly great collection is forthcoming from Graywolf Press.

DuCap: Author Vincent Zandri signed a six-figure, two novel deal with Dell Publishing in 1998. His story, "Simple Pleasures," appeared in the second issue of *Zuzu's Petals Quarterly*. *Our Sometime Sister*, the debut novel of Zuzu author Norah Labiner, was published by Coffee House Press and was named a Reader's Catalog Selection by *The New York Review of Books*.

Mok: We have a lot of promising talent and we continue to promote their efforts. That's our goal. Scores of our contributors later went on to win literary awards, publish novels and books of poetry, and start film and theater projects. Writers such as Doug Tanoury, Debora Lidov, Elena Georgiou, Alex Ecchevarria and numerous others.

MacEwan: I hope so. You'll have to go to www.deadmule.com for that answer. And if you were published on the *Mule*, write us and tell us how you're doing. (NewMule@DeadMule.com.)

What is the biggest challenge you face as an Internet editor that you may not have faced as an editor in traditional print?

Lawson: Our submission volumes are significant, since anyone with e-mail can send anything they want to, as often as they want to, at no expense.

DuCap: Keeping up with the mound of e-mail submissions we get in addition to the ones sent via postal mail.

Mok: This medium demands immediacy; it is a struggle to update in a timely fashion and to meet the demands of the Internet attention span.

MacEwan: Legitimacy. Making traditional print media people understand how difficult it is to format a Web page and keep a site fresh. People who are not Internet savvy buy into the "your kids can build a Web page" television hype. Also, if I don't answer a submission e-mail within 24 hours, some folks can get downright nasty.

Are you able to pay for editorial submissions? Why or why not? Are advertising clients getting any closer to funding e-zines?

Lawson: We compensate with exposure; writers gain greater mindshare among our constantly growing audience, increased sales of existing work, attention among agents and editors elsewhere. I'd like to think that's of more value than a simple $25 or $50 or $100 compensation. But that may change in the future. We've chosen not to accept advertising at present.

DuCap: *Zuzu's Petals Quarterly* is a labor of love, available free of charge on the Internet, so we're (unfortunately!) unable to pay our writers at this time. However, we plan to add more (carefully selected, tasteful) advertising to the site, so this hopefully may change.

Mok: Not at the present. We are working on it. And yes, advertising is close to funding. And as you might imagine, this is our goal.

MacEwan: We gave away *Dead Mule* t-shirts for the first two years we were online. So, I suppose you could say, yes, we paid. The shirts cost us $10. But I fund this e-zine personally, so I'm not inclined to give much away out of the goodness of my heart. Not that I don't strive to become independently wealthy someday . . . and then give away huge prizes like boat cruises through the Dismal Swamp or an all-expense-paid trip to the Pantego Mud Run or a pound of Martell's Barbecue from over in Hyde County.

What is a writer's biggest or most common mistake when it comes to submitting to your site?

Lawson: Many writers submit far before they're ready, looking for instant gratification. Though the computer may encourage rapid interactivity, real art takes time.

DuCap: Most e-zines have the same problem as print magazines; too many writers submit work without having read the magazine itself to get a sense of our editorial focus and sensibilities. Since most Web literary magazines are free of charge and consider e-mail submissions, the Internet is a convenient way for writers to familiarize themselves with publications before submitting, thus saving time, postage, and effort.

Mok: Not reading and following the guidelines. Specifically, not including full contact information in their attachments.

MacEwan: Lack of Internet savvy. Everyone should learn to copy and paste into the body of an e-mail message. And identify what you're sending in the subject line of the e-mail. A simple "Submission-short story" will do. I am willing to work with writers when they incorrectly submit, though. Most common mistake: Sending an attachment. Second most common: Sending a huge .bmp file and not knowing how to create a .jpg. Folks out there just don't seem to know how to scan at less than 600 dpi. Advice to anyone submitting to an e-zine: Every e-zine has rules. If they're not stated on a submission guideline page, e-mail and ask for them.

What's on your wish list, as far as editorial submissions are concerned?

Lawson: More brilliant writing!

DuCap: We'd like to see more hypertext fiction, strong work with a love of language and a freshness of imagery, as well as literary fiction translations.

Mok: We'd like more relevant local nonfiction-current events, restaurant reviews, cultural event coverage, etc. But of course, we are always searching for quality fiction from everywhere.

MacEwan: Abolishing passive voice from the English language. And, short pieces commenting upon Southern culture and tradition in a refreshing way. *The Dead Mule* wants writers to attempt to explain the American South, past and present. And always, stories about mules. To misquote Jerry Leath Mills, "No good Southern fiction is complete without a dead mule."

How can online publishing help a writer's career? Or more specifically, how can publishing on your site help a writer's career?

Lawson: It's a great myth that many people "surf"; most look at a set number of sites each week. Few sites have consistently provided a great literary experience over time, one good enough to keep people coming back; *BMR* is one of those. New online magazines have a difficult task in gaining eyeballs.

Writers should place their work at good, trafficked places, avoid self-publishing too much, and certainly avoid paying to have their work "showcased" online in "galleries" or "malls" where no one visits. Home pages are fine—just don't expect too many visitors until you're already famous (though it does help true fans learn more about you).

I'll note, too, that I published my own first collection as a result of an editor noticing my work in the online *Mississippi Review.*

Mok: Getting your work published at *12-Gauge.com* is not easy. And, as you know, exposure is crucial for any new writer.

MacEwan: It helps by offering a multitude of avenues for publishing. I see literary e-zines as launching pads for other forms of publication. Internet publication exposes a writer to a vast audience. As long as integrity and a common respect for copyrighted material exists (and I'm not naive; plagiarism is an age-old custom) writers can use Web publication to tweak the interest of publishers. *The Dead Mule* can facilitate a writer's career by continuing to offer quality writing and not throwing just anything on its pages.

How do you see the future of the Internet when it comes to literary fiction?

Lawson: More work will appear first online and build a following there. Print will continue to carry work that's relatively conservative or marketably literary; i.e.; proven commercially viable to a given target audience.

I'd venture to say that the vast majority of new and innovative work will be published first online in within the next five years. Many university journals will experiment with the medium first as a showcase for new writers, but will soon migrate some of the existing, established quarterlies online given the cost savings involved.

DuCap: I think that in addition to the constant need for quality fiction, e-zines will publish more and more hypertext, experimental, and interactive fiction. Also, more fiction will have an audio component (in addition to traditional text) in an effort to involve new readers as well as the vision impaired. Also, due to the global nature of the Web, literary translations should be in increased demand.

Mok: *12-Gauge.com* was one of the first literary voices on the Web, and we have watched the growth of many other sites. We know that there is an increasing cacophony of voices competing for readers' attention. Our goal is to consistently provide something smart, edgy and unique. As we noted before, the way the Internet impacts culture now is that it gives exposure to voices that otherwise would be unheard. This pattern will only increase.

MacEwan: What a difficult question! To narrow it down to a comment or two is almost impossible. A dark side exists for every comment set in a positive light. It's an endless cycle of debate which began with the invention of the printing press and will continue into cyberspace. The growth of the Internet is a double-edged sword. On one side, because of the sheer volume of Websites, you've got unlimited potential for new writers to be published, exposed. But the flip side is, by virtue of being content driven, the need for more and more fiction may cause standards to slip. With the Internet, as with anything else, the cream will rise to the top.

What has been your proudest moment as an online editor?

Lawson: Whenever I mention the journal to someone in the business and get that blink of recognition. So many people have heard of *BMR*; it's great to know that we've made an impact and brought great writers some deserved attention.

DuCap: Since our goal is to expand the reach of literary fiction and poetry beyond its traditionally academic audience, we were extremely pleased to have Zuzu.Com named one of the 30 best Websites by *Entertainment Weekly* in 1997. This was a tremendous opportunity for our writers to reach new readers, and for these new readers to make use of our ever-expanding resources.

Mok: Reader feedback has been phenomenal, and it means a great deal that what we do impacts so many people. It is our raison d'être.

MacEwan: Some of my best moments: When I saw a jogger in Central Park wearing a *Dead Mule* t-shirt. Being asked for permission for the use of *The Dead Mule* logo in *Southern Cultures*, a quarterly published by the UNC Press and Center for the Study of the American South, to illustrate an article about mules—because, as we all know, Chapel Hill is a holy place, even to this Arkansas girl.

A Mixed Review of E-Publishing: An Interview with *PW*'s John Baker

BY PAULA DEIMLING

When *Publishers Weekly*, the news magazine of book publishing and bookselling, ran its first reviews of electronic books in the summer of 1999, there was only a handful of responses from readers. "A few hailed the fact that we'd moved into the 21st century at last, and a few others deplored this thin edge of the wedge to the end of the book as we know it," observed John F. Baker, the magazine's editorial director.

Whether you agree with the former or latter take on e-publishing, or something in between, one thing is certain: E-publishing is something to be aware of in the months and years ahead. It's certainly a dynamically changing front *Publishers Weekly* editors are closely watching. The magazine recently added an e-publishing department to its pages. What started as a monthly department now appears regularly in addition to the latest news on e-publishing and e-book reviews. "That will grow slowly as I expect electronic publishing to grow slowly," Baker says.

A "PW Spotlight" in late 1999 said in part: "Loosely grouped under the rubric 'electronic publishers,' these companies have as their collective mission a better way of distributing books. Some fancy themselves software companies, others prefer to be called content-managers, still others like to be known as digital distributors.

"If their means are different, their ends are, at heart, unified: to disrupt fundamentally the business of book publishing and bookselling—not the writing or editing of books, but everything that happens afterward, or, in New Media speak, the way it is distributed to, and consumed by, the end-user."

We asked Baker for his thoughts on electronic publishing: What impact will e-publishing have on the book publishing industry? How might today's fiction writers be affected? Baker is one of the book industry's most astute observers. The former Reuters News Agency journalist started at *PW* 27 years ago as its managing editor, worked as its editor-in-chief for ten years, and for the past ten years has been the magazine's editorial director.

Want to know what agent just sold which author's book, and to what publisher, for what terms? Baker's "Hot Deals" column in *PW* is the place. In October 1999, Baker added another facet to his reporting—a twice-weekly e-mail-subscription newsletter, "Rights Alert," on book, script and licensing deals. His insight on the publishing world also extends into projects beyond his New York office, such as his 1999 book, *Literary Agents: A Writer's Introduction* (Macmillan).

Here Baker shares his views on the impact so far of e-publishing on traditional book publishing, where he sees the medium going, and what writers should consider before submitting their work to an electronic outlet.

PAULA DEIMLING *is a full-time writer and former editor of* Writer's Market. *She is one of the authors of* The Writer's Essential Desk Reference *(Writer's Digest Books). Past interviews have included Russell Banks, Jane Smiley and Isaac Asimov.*

Define e-publishing as you see it.

Any book published in a way other than the traditional printed form. Something that could be read online or played on an e-book reader or could be encrypted in such a way that it could be printed on demand. Those are the three principle approaches to electronic publishing.

Is e-publishing a disruption, or is it the cutting edge of what you're going to see in the book publishing industry?

It's a bit of both, actually. It's certainly the cutting edge in certain ways. I think obviously books that are searchable online are much more easily perused for key passages and words. In other words, for scholars looking for references, instead of searching endlessly through indexes and so forth, they can search masses of material in seconds, and obviously that's an enormous advance.

In terms of actually getting material from authors to readers, it's a rather mixed bag. There's this machinery that's evolved over the years, in effect screening out the publishable and the worthwhile from the enormous amount of material that is simply repetitive, imitative, inade-quately expressed, badly written, badly thought out, banal, etc. It seems to me if widespread electronic publishing is going to take off, and authors can simply put anything they like up and hope that somebody will pick it up and read it, all those careful safeguards and screenings are going to go out the window. It would be as if you turned over publishers' slush piles to readers anxious to see what they were missing. Publishers, in effect, have taken years trying to dissuade authors from sending unsolicited material to them so that it wouldn't hang around in the slush piles.

The agent community has been enormously built up and grown in power simply because they act as an early line of approval, a screen if you like, through which the better writers' properties and ideas are passed. It's almost as if they're throwing all this away by saying anybody can publish anything anywhere. So from that point of view, it's a pretty chaotic prospect.

The other point of course is: How does anybody get paid? It's all very well to say that authors who publish online can get royalties of 40, 50 or even 60%, but of what? How are people paying for this? Are they paying at all? Most of what is read on the Internet these days is not paid for at all. Why are they going to read novels and nonfiction works by authors they've never heard of, who haven't been promoted, edited or marketed, and pay for the privilege? I don't see it.

In your opinion, what impact will e-publishing have on the world of novels and short story collections?

I can't really foresee it having any enormous impact on fiction at all, to tell you the truth. I could be entirely out of step here. It seems to me that reading fiction in any of the currently available electronic forms is simply inferior to the experience of reading it in the printed form. As I said, the chief virtue of electronic publishing is its extreme searchability, and that doesn't really apply to fiction reading. People don't need to search fiction; they just want to keep turning the pages. For nonfiction, for biography, for historical works, for important studies of this and that and the other, for reference works, of course, it can certainly revolutionize that, and already has to a large extent.

Would there be certain types of novels that might eventually be better suited to e-publishing?

Some children's works, particularly if they could be made interactive and if the children could interact with the text and make things move in different directions by pressing certain buttons at certain points in the story. The other kind would be, and for the same reasons, science fiction where obviously you can play with the notions of reality, what's actually in print and what can be imagined on the page. You could play cyber-games with science fiction concepts that I think would be interesting. There was an avant-garde novel published by Pantheon a few months ago,

House of Leaves. It lends itself to people who like playing fancifully with the medium, but there aren't a large number of books like that. [See the interview with *House of Leaves* author Mark Danielewski on page 78.]

Will Stephen King's foray into e-publishing lend support and encouragement to other authors who might want to follow this approach?

King is such a unique case. King has an enormous body of fans, not just readers—he's collectable as well as readable. They'll pick up anything he has written. Very few authors have that kind of following. Because of his subject matter—often with teenage or young heroes becoming involved in horrific situations—he has a much younger and more technologically hip readership than most authors do. Whereas he can do almost anything, the number of popular authors who could command that kind of loyalty isn't very great. I don't think the readers, of say, Mary Higgins Clark or John Grisham are going to dart automatically to read anything they write on the Internet.

Do you think e-publishing will in any way affect the way novelists write their books?

Only in the ways I've suggested. They may seek to make it interactive in various playful and not-so-playful ways, offering people in mysteries, for instance, ways of following up on certain clues or at certain points in the action, choosing ways in which it might go in different directions. I think that could be extended to certain kinds of fiction or narrative—science fiction, fantasy and, in certain cases, mysteries.

I don't see how it would change things in other respects. Basically it's still a matter of putting one word after another; however, the words are read. Another aspect, of course, is that, at the moment, the quality of the images isn't terrific. I think it will be quite a while before anything other than utilitarian illustrations will be an important part of an e-book.

What other developments will authors be seeing on the business side of publishing?

The electronics rights auction, conducted online; and several bodies, such as rightscenter.com and rightsworld.com, that exist for the exchange of rights information and rights dealings around the world with thousands of subscribers—that will certainly continue and persist, I would think. And with the new development that electronic signatures are now acceptable, I can visualize the time when book contracts will be sent and signed over the Internet as well. At the moment, people still require paper documents, but I doubt that they will for very much longer. That's an entirely new development.

There hasn't really been enough time to know if most books, published initially as e-books, eventually will be published in printed form. Oddly enough, even people wedded to the medium still prefer to see things in print. For instance, I put out a twice-weekly e-mail newsletter called "Rights Alert" describing those rights deals. And although I can get much more into the newsletter because there are no page restrictions, everybody who gets mentioned in the newsletter says 'will I get in the print version too?' I point out to them that there is a lot of wasted readership in the print version whereas the e-mail readership is extremely focused and only people who really need the information are getting it. There's a sense of validation in seeing something in print, I think. That is still lacking in terms of the weight of the authority that it carries. I think things on the net are rightly or wrongly seen as evanescent. You can erase them at the press of a button (and you may well by accident) and they're gone. You can't do that with anything actually printed. These are people, many of them engaged in forms of electronic publishing anyway, who still want their doings described in print.

You mentioned James Ellroy, author of *L.A. Confidential* (Mysterious Press, 1990), and how his agent conducted an online auction among e-book publishers for the electronic rights to one of Ellroy's projects, while reserving the print rights for a later time. To your knowledge, how would Ellroy or other authors be compensated for their work?

There are various ways in which authors are compensated for electronic publishing. In this case, he got an advance and was to get royalties on the use of the material, and since it was going out on Contentville, which is fairly new, I don't know how or how much Contentville charges for its material. In any case, he was going to get paid a royalty on the basis of how many people hit upon his work when it appears.

But many electronic publishers don't pay anything. They say "we'll run your stuff for free and will pay you on the basis of hits" if it's a subscription thing, or some sites are supported by advertising. I think that's probably the most reliable source of support at the moment, and publishers are paid royalties on the basis of the advertising revenue that's generated by the site on which their work appears.

Then, of course, there is still a handful of electronic publishers who work on the old vanity principle, and actually charge authors to put their work online. They don't charge nearly as much as the old vanity print publishers did, who charged up to $5,000 or even $10,000 to do a very limited run of a small book. I've heard of fees of $250 or even $500 to put something online for an author. At first authors paid, and then they became aware there were a number of sites which weren't charging them anything at all, and even a handful that were paying them small advances. Most of the vanity ones have probably disappeared by now. There's an enormous rate of flux and change among these start-ups. There are a half-dozen start-ups every week and some of them last a few months and most of them have been around 18 months or, at the most, two years. For an electronic publisher, two years is really old and well-established—something to bear in mind.

The other thing authors should bear in mind is that e-publishers can be quite evanescent. They have been mostly funded by start-up capital from an IPO [Initial Public Offering of stock] or by some backer. That kind of support is extremely volatile, especially these days. It can disappear and the stock can shoot down very rapidly, or the backer can run out of money quite quickly. And off goes your publisher. It's not quite the same as a publisher that has a backlist of thousands of books and a warehouse and premises and a large staff to pay. They're not about to disappear overnight. They may be swallowed up by another publisher, but they won't actually go out of existence, whereas electronic publishers go out of existence all the time. Of the electronic publishers that have more than, say, 200 or 300 titles in their repertoire or inventory, there are very few that would have four figures worth of titles available. They're still building, growing.

For e-publishers who have been in business for two years, are you seeing any patterns in terms of what they're doing right?

One of the problems they all have is how to promote the work, how to let people know it's there. The very well-endowed electronic operations, we've all seen their extensive advertising, they spend literally millions on it. The big ones can afford to do that. The little ones can't, and how they make themselves known and make their authors known other than to a very, very limited readership of faithful cruisers of the net it's very difficult to see. How are they are going to make known the availability of the various books they're publishing? I think the whole electronic publishing business is going to rise and fall on the basis of how thoroughly the marketing and promotion of the material available is. I think that's probably its weakest link at the moment for most of them anyway, the ones without deep pockets.

For years we've heard how the lack of marketing and promotion can affect a print book, but it's ironic that electronic publishers face this same dilemma.

The machinery in place for the promotion of the print book is still infinitely more effective and efficient than anything that has so far come along for the electronic book—to say nothing of the fact that print books depend very heavily on major TV appearances by a handful of important and significant shows, and also some radio, and so electronically published authors have almost no clout at all in those areas. Bookseller coop advertising; print advertising in newspapers and magazines; television advertising when you can afford it; all of those things electronic publishing lacks at the moment.

Do you have any long-term predictions for e-publishing for, say, the next five or ten years?

Probably the area to have the most impact on authors will be the existing links between book publishers and e-publishing allies, such as book store links. E-publishers who don't have such alliances will have a harder time of it.

Is there anything you'd like to say further about e-publishing?

It seems like a very exciting possibility for writers, the way of communicating directly with the author without all the intervening screens of agent, editor, publisher, printer, reviewer, etc., but somebody has to pay the bills in order for the author to get anything at all out of the experience other than the thrill of seeing their work only rather transitorily in print and not really in a portable way. It's not quite the same thing, pressing a few buttons and seeing your words come up on a screen, as it is having a book you can carry around and show people. And therefore I think if they're aiming to make money on their writing, and get anything out of it other than the thought that a handful of readers may be looking at what they've written on their screens, they ought to look at all the alternatives very carefully. They should find out how and how much they're going to be paid, and what the outermost extremities of their likely revenues will be, and then make their decisions accordingly.

The Myths (and Facts) About Electronic Publishing

BY KAREN S. WIESNER

Electronic authors and publishers hear so many arguments against the medium. The best defense to arm yourself with, if you're an electronic author, is knowledge. Educate yourself and maybe you can win over one hard and biased heart—maybe even dozens of them!

MYTH: Electronic publishing is "buddy publishing."

FACT: I'm sure it's happened more than once—an e-publisher sets up shop and, somewhere down the line, publishes the novel of a good friend. If this publisher is putting out otherwise quality novels and gains the reputation of a top-of-the-line book publisher, wouldn't you have to assume this publisher bought the work of a friend because the work was good? And if this same work gets rave reviews, award nominations and/or award wins, wouldn't you also have to assume this publisher is accepting novels by this person on the basis of quality, not friendship? If the author sells elsewhere, you would have to conclude they're indeed talented.

Let's do a "for instance" here: say you're a modeling agent. Would you represent your ugly cousin Gertrude simply because she's family? Would you put everything you've worked for—money, reputation, present and future customers—on the line for a family member? You might . . .if you don't care anything about money, reputation or present and future customers.

A good electronic publisher only accepts quality novels. They have to because they're putting everything they have behind each novel they release. They have too much to lose to conduct business unwisely.

MYTH: Electronic publishing is vanity publishing.

FACT: A vanity publisher, or subsidy publisher, produces a book for authors willing to pay some, most, or even all of the (inflated) costs associated with production, marketing and distribution. Subsidy publishers often offer royalty contracts, but bookstores are wary of stocking books of this type. So, not only will an author pay for book production and distribution, but will most likely do the majority of the marketing themselves. Subsidy publishers have nothing to lose; the authors take all the risks.

A reputable e-publisher requires absolutely no fees—up-front or ever—from its authors. They pay generous royalty rates, as well as doing aggressive marketing. Authors and e-publishers share the risks, but the publisher almost always takes the brunt of it.

MYTH: E-publishers can't possibly justify taking X% of royalties when it doesn't cost them a dime to produce an e-book.

FACT: The scourge of the doesn't-cost-a-dime-to-produce misconception falls on both the authors and the e-publishers. Authors who sell to electronic publishers must be selling out, must be awful writers if New York won't take them on, must be adding to "the crap littering the Web left and right."Bonnee Pierson, co-publisher at Dreams Unlimited, says, "the misconception

KAREN S. WIESNER *is the author of three ongoing series published electronically by Hard Shell Word Factory. Her novel* Falling Star *was nominated for the* Romantic Times' *1999 E-Book of the Year, and was a finalist for the EPPIE.*

This article was excerpted from Electronic Publishing: The Definitive Guide *(Second Edition) © 2000 by Karen S. Wiesner, and appears here with permission of Avid Press.*

that setting up an Internet business is free only compounds the myth that e-books are of poor quality. After all, if you can set the business up for nothing, then everything is profit and who cares if you're selling quality books, right? But if people realize that it does take an investment to set up a business (and lots of time), they just might realize that a large number of us aren't going to toss away our time and money on poor quality."

"Unknown to most people, we also have investments. Yes, it may not be in an individual book, but I buy disks and packaging materials by the hundreds—an investment that's flexible and can be used on any book, but an investment nonetheless. We have to pay for Web space and we've invested literally thousands in programs. Some work and some don't, but we invest that money in the hopes to make a return and, somehow, streamline the process not just for you, but also for ourselves. We rent Web space. We pay for our Internet time . . . and we invest copious amounts of time into each manuscript. It's not just the reading and the editing. It's the formatting and coding, translating and graphics, time spent in advertising, money spent in print copies for reviews and the shipping costs to get them to the reviewers. And, eventually, ads in magazines like *Romantic Times*."

I did a chapter for an upcoming book about electronic publishing titled "Does it really cost nothing to be an e-publisher?" I interviewed thirty-one e-publishers for this chapter. More than 40% of the publishers spent between $5,000-10,000 to set up their businesses; 23% spent more than $50,000. Of these publishers, 53% said their annual investments in their e-publishing companies ranged between $5,000-10,000; 20% said it was more than $50,000 and that the majority of their profits go right back into the business. More than 60% of the e-publishers said they would remain in business indefinitely, even if they never make a profit. If you ask me, that is the supreme sacrifice of someone with a dream they intend on fulfilling, no matter what it takes. So it's definitely not "free" to be an e-publisher.

MYTH: E-publishers set up websites to sell their own books.

FACT: It's true that a lot of e-publishers are themselves authors. And yes, some electronic publishers do publish their own books and sell them on their websites.

Does that mean they receive special privileges their other authors don't? No. Their books go through an editor, they pass the same scrutiny as all other novels at that site. And does self-publishing wipe out a publisher's other credits? Not really. Does it besmirch their reputation for quality? Maybe—if both of these questions can't be answered in the affirmative: 1) Is the book selling well? 2) Has the book received good reviews?

MYTH: Electronic books are New York rejects, as in "I've read one or two e-books. They were poorly written, and not edited."

FACT: Okay, maybe it's true that many e-books are New York rejects. But, despite opinions to the contrary, New York is not the God State of all quality publishing. New York makes many, many mistakes when choosing which books to publish. (They also choose a lot of winners.) How many New York publishers have rejected books that even they loved and believed were well-written? *Countless.* New York publishers reject wonderful books for so many reasons: taboo character types/plotlines; they don't feel it will sell/don't feel it's what readers want; too realistic/gritty/controversial; not sure how to market/straddles genres/doesn't fit with the other types of books published; too category/too mainstream; not enough introspection/too much introspection/not enough action/too much action.

E-books *are* edited! E-authors do revisions just like traditional authors do. They may or may not have to do extensive revisions—because e-publishers accept only quality, nearly flawless manuscripts, and believe in retaining an author's vision.

I have no doubt the first e-books made available may well have been klunkers. Were they released by a reputable, legitimate, royalty-paying, non-subsidy publisher? That could make all the difference. The e-books nowadays are garnering rave reviews, pulling more and more readers in and receiving prestigious awards (see EPIC's Authors in the News page http://www.eclectics.com/epic/news.html for some of these).

MYTH: Electronic publishing is a flash-in-the-pan trend.

FACT: Is it? How many flash-in-the-pan trends do you know of that continue to grow by leaps and bounds in public awareness, acceptance, and technology? How many trends do you know of that have writers in all genres, traditional publishers, writing organizations all scrambling to catch up and get in on the excitement and potential profits? How many trends have e-publishers and their authors putting all their energy and their own money in, hoping to see that this venture continues to expand? Bill Gates has predicted there will be 50,000 e-books in existence by the year 2001. I think he was being extremely conservative. Hand-held readers are selling faster than companies can manufacture them. Some other amazing statistics:

- 100 million people in the U.S. have Internet access (one-half of the adult population), up from 65 million at mid-1998. That number is expected to grow to 177 million by the end of 2003.
- 221 million people world-wide have Internet access.
- Books are the most common on-line purchase.
- Of the top five most-visited retail websites ranked in the 1999 holiday season, two of them were on-line booksellers: Amazon.com—5.69 million; Barnes & Noble—1.52 million.
- 50% of merchandise purchased during the holidays were books.
- Five years after the Internet began evolving into a viable commercial enterprise, the 50 millionth American surfed online. It took radio 38 years, TV 13 years, cable TV 10 years to reach the coveted 50-million mark. It's estimated that the Internet grows by one new user every 1.67 seconds.

These are all signs of a medium here to stay.

MYTH: No one would ever want to read a book at a computer; or I'd have to print out an e-book; or I'd have to read it on a computer screen.

FACT: I can see many viable reasons for certain individuals to dislike the idea of reading at a computer—some people work all day at one, some get headaches, backaches, eye strain. Some simply don't like the idea.

However, the fact is, a lot of people do read books at the computer. A lot of people actually find it more comfortable than reading a paperback elsewhere. Some people could spend conceivably all day and night in front of a computer screen. That's where they're most happy. (Have you seen "The Net," starring Sandra Bullock? That fanatical need to be at the computer isn't mere fiction for many, many people these days!) With e-books, readers have a whole range of options on how and where to read them. You can read straight from the computer or laptop. Depending on the format you choose, you can change the font, size, as well as adjust the margins and layout. You can print a book out, again—depending on the format—in whatever layout you prefer, and read the pages in bed or in a comfy chair. You can download a book into a hand-held device and read it anywhere you want. With the hand-helds, you also have many perks—the ability to change the font size, margins, switch from landscape to portrait, turn pages. You can also "bookmark" your place. Some models even have a backlight for your convenience.

MYTH: If my book is electronically published, I won't feel like I'm really published.

FACT: Ask yourself why you would feel this way.

Is it because you've always dreamed of a book with a beautiful cover, your title, your words and your name on and in it? You'll still have that; it'll just be in a different format than you're accustomed to.

Is it because you're still a little wary of e-publishing, that you feel your friends and family won't believe you're really published? Educate yourself and then educate them.

Is it because you feel e-publishers and traditional publishers are so different? The only difference is format—in some cases—and distribution methods. The process for the author is exactly the same (try it if you don't believe me!) and just as thrilling.

MYTH: I can't get e-books at my local bookstore.

FACT: All books, including most electronic books, have an ISBN (International Standard

Book Number). The place to find an ISBN is R.R. Bowker's directory series *Books In Print*. R.R. Bowker is the leading provider of bibliographic information, supplying librarians, booksellers, and publishers.

Every book with an ISBN is registered in *Books In Print*. Most, if not all, bookstores have access to the *Books In Print* database. Since most e-books also have ISBNs registered with *Books In Print*, bookstores most certainly have the capability of ordering any book registered. Bookstores themselves may not realize this. So it's really not a question of whether or not bookstores can order e-books, but whether or not they will order them. If enough people barrage their local bookstores, the stores should not only become willing to order electronic books more readily, but may also start stocking them on their shelves.

In 1999, New Concepts Publishing announced a distribution deal with Baker & Taylor, one of the premier distributors/wholesalers in the nation. Baker & Taylor offers access to 17,000 libraries, 6,500 bookstores, and 4,000 universities. Other e-publishers will most likely follow with similar deals.

MYTH: A novel is a series of words on physical pages, between a front cover and a back cover. I could never get into the story with the glare of the computer screen.

FACT: *Webster's* definition of a book is "a long written or printed work, usually on sheets of paper fastened or bound together with covers." The definition of a novel is "a fictitious prose narrative of considerable length and complexity, portraying characters and usually presenting a sequential organization of action and scenes." By this token, a novel is a story, be it wonderful or awful; a book is simply the physical form in which a novel is read. Therefore a novel is any series of words immortalized on paper, disk, computer screen, cassette, CD and a multitude of ways not yet invented.

True story: someone I know never read an e-book in her life. She took my novel *Falling Star* to work with her. She figured she could read it on the computer there and everyone would think she was working. She ended up crying her eyes out, gave herself away and completely forgot about the glare of the computer monitor.

Don't reduce the adventure of reading to its form. Christopher Morley said, "When you sell a man a book, you don't sell him 12 ounces of paper and ink and glue—you sell him a whole new life." Every quality story will sweep you way past where you are in the physical world. It doesn't matter if you're sitting in front of a computer screen, curled up on a couch or in a basement huddled under the workbench with a flashlight.

MYTH: I believe that electronic publishing will be the wave of the future. I'll wait to hop on the wagon when it gets there.

FACT: I wouldn't count on the wagon stopping specifically by your door in the future. While electronic publishing has seemingly unlimited slots to fill and less rules for them than traditional publishers, e-publishers are just as selective . . .and they're having to turn away some authors even now—yes, even some big name, paper-published authors.

Electronic publishers have no wish to book themselves out to the year 2010 any more than traditional publishers do. It won't happen overnight, but the circle of opportunity will close a little more each year in e-publishing, making it harder for authors to break in. Finding a niche now, while the circle is wide open, could secure you a place in the future.

MYTH: If you sell to an electronic publisher, you're selling out.

FACT: Define "selling out." If you feel electronic publishing is "buddy" or vanity publishing, a flash-in-the-pan trend, e-books are New York rejects and poorly written, that you won't feel published, or your definition of a book is physical pages between two covers, see the facts above.

If you feel you're selling out because it's easier to get published electronically, think again. Books OnScreen accepts about 40% of the 80-100 monthly submissions they receive. Dead End Street accepts one to four of the 150-200 submissions they receive each month. Eastgate Systems accepts only four or five books per year of the ten to twenty they get a month. Online Originals gets 300-500 submissions per month and accepts only three per month. Crossroads gets 100-150 submissions a month and accepts only 5%. DiskUs receives 200-300 submission per month and accepts less than 5%. Nitelinks get 450 submissions a month and only accepts three per month. Electronic publishers accept only a very small percentage of their submissions. Authors won't get away with second rate or sloppy writing, blatant disregard for submission instructions or no revisions.

If your work is accepted, it's because your writing is high quality, your story is good. You've accomplished what few other authors have. You're not selling out—you're succeeding. And you're on your way!

"Rethinking the Book:" The Electronic Literature Organization Tests Fiction's Boundaries

BY BRAD VICE

When novelist Robert Coover selected the hypertext fiction novel *The Unknown* as the first-ever winner of the trAce/Alt-x award, co-author Scott Rettberg seized on the opportunity not only to transform his life, but to help transform the boundaries of literature. In 1998, Rettberg was just another starving graduate student who, with friends Dirk Stratton and William Gillespie, had spent the better part of the year dodging homework in order to complete their experimental collaborative book project *The Unknown*.

The Unknown is a book with no beginning, no end. It is a road novel of sorts, an epic adventure that tells the story of three rich and famous collaborative writers on a book tour across America. But the sequence of the journey isn't determined by page numbers; through the magic of hypertext, readers of *The Unknown* are free to wander through the narrative in any fashion they see fit.

Rettberg describes the writing of his unbounded text as "a sleep-deprived, bourbon-fueled lark. As it evolved, it became more interesting than the other writing projects I was working on. And I think also for William and Dirk. So we kept working on it over long distances." Eventually Rettberg and his friends were able to build a hypertext that was as substantial as anything else in the field up to that point. "There are a few canonical pieces out there—Michael Joyce's *afternoon, a story*; Shelly Jackson's *Patchwork Girl*; Mark Amerika's *Grammatron*—but it's very much a canon being born. It's pretty wide open right now, which is exciting, especially compared to the sort of conventional literary atmosphere that is far from wide open."

It was this sense of unbounded freedom that prompted Rettberg's next contribution to literature. At first, when the writing of *The Unknown* was complete, Rettberg thought his life would return to normal, but as it turns out publication of the novel presented opportunities that a visionary like Rettberg couldn't pass up. "We were the first, and so far the last, winners of the trAce/Alt-x Award, a prize sponsored by the trAce Online Writing Community and the Alt-x Online Publishing Network. Robert Coover was the judge, because he is a big cheerleader for literary innovation. Coover is also a professor at Brown University, and after he selected the authors of *The Unknown* for the prize, he asked if we would give a hypertext demonstration at Brown's upcoming conference on technology and literature."

It was during this conference that Rettberg wrote a proposal to found a non-profit organization dedicated to the discovery, publication and promotion of electronic literature. The proposal was met with great excitement by several writers, editors and even a few Internet start-up CEOs. Within weeks, the Electronic Literature Organization was born.

BRAD VICE *is a graduate student at the University of Cincinnati and a frequent contributor to Writer's Digest Books.*

What is the ELO, and what is its purpose?

The ELO's mission is to promote and facilitate the writing and reading of electronic literature. Ultimately, our goal is to expand the readership of literature written for electronic media. We want to support new forms of literature, which use the capabilities of emerging technologies to advance and extend literature. We hope to expand the readership and publication possibilities for these kinds of literature, both now and in the future.

You said before that the field of e-literature is wide open. What's your vision for e-literature and e-publishing? How do you see the future unfolding?

There is reason to be both optimistic and troubled about the future. New technologies have given writers the tools to work with multiple forms of media to create new kinds of literature native to the electronic media, and recently there have been advances in electronic distribution that may soon enable publishing models that remove barriers between authors and audiences. But there is a problem already in Internet culture. In accordance with the logic of a market economy, the Internet evolved first as an economic entity. Hey, what happened to the original vision of the global village that represented not only the market place, but also a gathering place where people share their culture, art and literature with an international audience? It will take a lot of effort to develop the Web as a mature cultural medium as well as a commercial one. Austria, Australia, and the United Kingdom are making cultural investments in electronic literature by sponsoring governmental and nonprofit organizations with programs that help to enable the development of new electronic art forms. We haven't seen that level of commitment in the United States, the center of the Internet economy. The Electronic Literature Organization is committed to filling that gap in our culture.

How will the ELO fill that gap? What kinds of resources do you offer visitors to your site?

ELO has grassroots membership that is steadily growing. Whether you're a member or not, you can use our website to research what's happening in the field of e-literature. We have an events bulletin that catalogs all notable events occurring in the field, and we have links to many fine publishers, and actual pieces of literature. We are all about connecting writers with publishers and readers with writers. But really we are still operating out of our seed money, and all the things we really want to do won't get going until 2001. By then, we hope to have raised enough money to have our writing prizes going. These kinds of prizes are few and far between. *The Unknown* and the e-poem "Rice," by Jenny Weight, were the first and so far the last winners of the trAce/Alt-x award. We split a thousand pounds among us—that's about $750 for each work. This was great, but ELO hopes to award prizes in fiction, poetry, drama and creative nonfiction that are worth at least $10,000. Hopefully that kind of money will keep serious artists writing for three or four months. We have an outstanding board of advisors comprised of people like Robert Coover, John Barth, T.C. Boyle, and Ursula K. LeGuin. And these are the people who will be our judges. Also, we are hoping to promote not only the prize winners, but all the truly significant entries, so even if a writer doesn't win, she may get connected with a publisher who really likes her work.

What else does 2001 hold for the ELO? In particular, how do you hope to support collaborative projects like *The Unknown* to find an audience?

ELO is dedicated to building audience awareness, so much of the year will be spent giving lectures and multimedia demonstrations at schools, colleges and libraries. In an effort to foster collaboration, we are planning to hold an international day of readings where writers from California, New York, England, Germany, all over, give readings of their works to one another over the Internet. We are also planning on having a symposium on new publishing models in

2001. We are very excited by Time Warner's recent statement that they want to "rethink the book." Rethinking the book, that's what we're all about. I think 2001, appropriately enough, will be a good year for us.

Visit the Electronic Literature Organization at www.eliterature.org. Visit The Unknown *at www.soa.uc.edu/user/unknown/trip.htm.*

Otto Penzler: Mystery Goes Mainstream

BY NICOLE R. KLUNGLE

Otto Penzler knows mysteries. You may recognize him as the founder of the Mysterious Press, or as the man who for seventeen years has published *The Armchair Detective*, an Edgar-winning quarterly devoted to the study of mystery and suspense fiction. Penzler is also the founder of the Mysterious Bookshop in Manhattan (online at www.mysteriousbookshop.com), and the man who brings you recommendations and reviews for eight mysteries every month in his "Penzler's Picks" feature on Amazon.com. The trends he has noticed in mystery publishing are perfectly clear: Mystery is more popular than ever, but changes in the way books are marketed are making it more difficult to get your mystery published.

Otto Penzler

If you want proof that mysteries have gone mainstream, Penzler says, "check the *New York Times* bestseller list. Most weeks, anywhere from five to eight are mystery/crime/suspense novels, which proves mysteries are not only being published in large numbers, but sold in large numbers." The number of mysteries among bestselling novels has increased in the last few years, and Penzler sees no reason for this to change ("unless every spot on the list is taken up by a Harry Potter book," he says grudgingly).

Mystery novels—Penzler defines a mystery as "any story in which a crime or the threat of a crime is central to the plot or theme"—are appealing to an ever-widening audience, as are mystery short stories. According to Penzler, about 1,400 new mystery novels were published in 1999. "That's a lot of books in a relatively modest-sized genre," he observes. A mystery bestseller used to sell around 100,000 copies in hardcover. Now the initial print runs of new mysteries by well-known authors, such as John Grisham and Tom Clancy, can reach three million copies. The popularity of mysteries means that readers and reviewers are now less likely to pigeonhole mysteries as category fiction. "For years, *Publishers Weekly* reviewed Dick Francis and Robert B. Parker in their mystery section. Once they made the bestseller list, they were reviewed in the fiction section. They were writing the same books; *they* didn't change. It was the public's perception that changed."

Between 800 and 1,000 original short mysteries are published every year, a number which has increased each year since the mid-1990s. Mystery short story writers can seek publication in markets as various as literary magazines, original mystery anthologies, mystery magazines (notably the long-published *Ellery Queen Mystery Magazine* and *Alfred Hitchcock Mystery Magazine*) and in mainstream magazines such as *GQ*, *Esquire* and *The New Yorker*. Literary magazines pay a nominal amount, and moderately successful mystery magazines pay more. The best-paying market for mystery short stories is large-circulation, mainstream magazines, which may pay between $5,000 and $10,000 for an original story. This is also the market getting the most exposure. Penzler notes, "If you are good enough to be published regularly anywhere with a

NICOLE R. KLUNGLE *is a freelance writer living in Cincinnati, Ohio.*

large circulation, you will become known." However, "One story won't do it," he warns.

As mysteries become more popular among readers, they are also appealing to a greater variety of authors. "Mystery fiction in general has moved very much into the mainstream, just as mainstream writers have moved toward mystery fiction." Many authors incorporate all the elements of a mystery into the novels they are writing for a general audience. "Joyce Carol Oates frequently writes suspense and psychological terror," Penzler observes. "She would never describe herself as a mystery writer, and most people wouldn't think of her as one. But there are all the elements of a mystery novel." Other nonmystery authors, including Mario Vargas Llosa, Martin Amis and Norman Mailer, have written novels that also qualify as mysteries.

The broadening base of readers for mystery stories means that what has always been true for the mystery writer is now more so: In order to succeed in the current mystery market, you can't just write a good mystery—you must write a good story.

As editor of *The Best American Mystery Stories* (Houghton Mifflin), a yearly anthology, Penzler reads every short mystery he can get his hands on. "Some are detective stories, some are crime stories, and some are pure suspense," he says, but the one thing common to all the mysteries he selects for his anthologies is that they are well written. "They have a depth of insight and originality of style that separates them from the ordinary." The best mysteries are more than mysteries: "Mystery used to be regarded as category fiction," Penzler elaborates. *The Best American Mystery Stories* anthologies, and particularly *The Best American Mystery Stories of the Century,* "have shown that they are literature."

Penzler notes that some of the biggest blockbuster successes have been in the mystery sub-genres of legal thrillers (John Grisham, Lisa Scottoline, Phillip Margolin), romantic suspense (Mary Higgins Clark, Nora Roberts, Sandra Brown) and historical mysteries (Steven Saylor, Ellis Peters, Elizabeth Peters). Series writers like Sue Grafton (*O Is for Outlaw*) and Janet Evanovich (*Hot Six*) are also succeeding with what Penzler calls a "partly gimmicky, but also very effective" approach to titling their works. "They still have to be good books, though," he points out. And while Penzler is loath to predict which subgenres will be most popular in the next five years, he does offer a warning: "The worst thing you can do is write to a perceived market. The only way a writer can succeed is to write what he or she wants to write and feels passionately about. This results in a more emotional and passionate finished work." Penzler adds, "By the time you jump onto a bandwagon, the wagon's off the trail. Create your own bandwagon."

While the Mysterious Bookshop continues to categorize mysteries into several subgenres, including suspense, espionage, cozy, hardboiled and police procedurals (just to name a few), it also maintains a large "unclassified" section for all the mysteries that do not fit neatly into one of their other categories. In the mystery market, "novelty is always desired. Many of the great writers working today are not easily classifiable. They're creating their own kind of literature. A lot of them will say, 'But I'm not a mystery writer.' They think they're writing a general category or a general novel, and indeed they are. But there are enough elements of crime, mystery and suspense that they are happily absorbed into the genre."

There is, however, a down side to the success of blockbuster mysteries. The market domination of the runaway bestseller means that midlist authors (those who don't get huge advances and are not household names, but have a steady audience and market) are getting a smaller share of the overall book market. More books are being sold now than ever, but the increase in sales can be attributed almost exclusively to bestsellers, Penzler says, and as the sales of blockbusters increase, midlist sales can only tread water. There has been a growing perception that midlist authors are being abandoned by publishing houses while bestselling authors, new or established, receive huge advances and disproportionate shares of the marketing budget. A decline in the midlist could spell trouble for the novelist trying to break into the market and for the strong, but not bestselling, mystery writer. Although a recent report to the Authors Guild reassures us that, overall, the number of midlist titles published every year has not dropped, it admits that midlist books are losing market share, and bestsellers are threatening to crowd midlist titles from the shelf and siphon away their marketing dollars.

Penzler observes that big discount warehouses, such as Sam's Club, have contributed to this trend by buying and selling a handful of titles at a huge discount. Selling a blockbuster at a substantial discount does increase the readership for that particular author, but sales of midlist titles, which are rarely discounted, cannot keep pace.

Despite industry assurances that publication of midlist titles has not decreased, some large publishers have indeed dropped some of their midlist mystery authors. Now, smaller mystery publishing houses are successfully wooing those authors and gaining market share. Unlike the large publishing houses, which have a huge overhead, small presses can make more money selling fewer books. "Smaller houses don't have the same massive overhead expenses that Random House and Simon & Schuster have, so they can make money selling 4,000 copies of a book, whereas Simon & Schuster can't turn on their lights for that amount," says Penzler. The success of small presses means that the mystery midlist will not be completely eclipsed by blockbuster novels.

But if this encouraging news leads you to think it will now be easier to publish your first mystery with a small press, think again: It is as hard as ever to break in to the mystery novel market. While large publishing houses are granting huge advances and a greater share of their marketing dollars to a few new and continuing blockbuster authors, smaller houses prefer to stick with established midlist authors. Many writers who have been rejected by big publishing houses turn to smaller houses, only to find that small houses don't have the staff necessary to read through stacks of manuscripts. "Right now, there are one million people writing books," notes Penzler. "In my small press, Mysterious Press, I received between forty and fifty manuscripts in a week. A larger publisher may receive one hundred times that amount. Who's going to read them all?"

Penzler's advice for the new mystery writer: "Get an agent." In his twenty-five years in publishing, Penzler has never accepted an unagented submission, although he knows others who will accept query letters (one page only!). "I'm not saying it's impossible to get published without an agent; you can. But it's a lot harder."

An agent is more likely to know who will look at your manuscript and whether it will sell. "If it comes through an agent, some professional has thought enough of this to take it on and send it to you." Agents get paid for what they sell; they won't represent a manuscript they think won't make it in today's market. But this doesn't mean that if one agent says no, all of them will. "Be persistent in your pursuit of an agent," says Penzler. "If one says no, don't quit."

"The market for new authors is pretty tough," he admits, so "keep your day job. There are a lot of well-established and very talented professionals who are having trouble selling books. Publishers, booksellers and authors are like farmers—there's no such thing as a really good time. 'There's too much rain,' 'there's not enough rain,' 'we have no crop this year,' 'we have so much crop that the price has been driven down.' There's always a complaint. You just have to overcome it."

With this in mind, Penzler says an author must just write a good book. Writing about your area of expertise can help, but don't try to write to a niche market. "Very talented authors always find a home, though it may take awhile."

From Editor to Writer: Martha C. Lawrence Writes What She Knows

Martha C. Lawrence

"The door crashed open with a bang. Terror propelled her to her feet. As she whirled to run, the intruder caught her and threw her to the floor. Immediately he was on top of her, his hands gripping her throat. As she stared into the livid face of her ex-boyfriend turned stalker, she had just one thought."

This isn't the opening to a Martha C. Lawrence mystery, though it could be. Lawrence encourages writers to incorporate real-life experiences into their fiction. Among her most terrifying experiences was being stalked by an ex-boyfriend who broke into her house and choked her.

And her one thought?

"If I'm ever going to write my own book, I'd better get around to it because I might not be here forever."

You'd think that if anyone would know that books don't write themselves, it would be a former editor. Why did Lawrence wait to face her insecurities and begin her own writing career until that epiphanic incident with the choking stalker, which she now refers to as "that moment of clarity?"

"People jump to the conclusion that if you have all this publishing experience, how great for you as a writer," Lawrence says. "It wasn't. It utterly shut me down because I saw how many good manuscripts were turned down every day. It was terrifying and tremendously intimidating. As a new writer, you're thinking 'who am I to think that I can prevail in this incredibly competitive market?' "

Lawrence started her publishing career in New York with Simon & Schuster in the early 1980s as an assistant to the managing editor of trade publishing. "I got to see every manuscript, fiction and non-fiction, which went into production," she recalls. "I saw every contract. I got a really good overview of what the publishing process entails."

She later returned to her native California, where she became an acquisitions editor with Harcourt Brace. There she had her own list, both fiction and non-fiction. "That's where I fell in love with mysteries—when I worked on a project called *New Black Mask Quarterly*. In the '20s, *The Black Mask* had been a magazine which ran original pulp fiction. In our quarterly anthology, we published writers like Elmore Leonard, Ed McBain, Sara Peretsky, Robert Parker, James Ellroy—it was pretty much 'you-name-it in mystery and we had it.' When I worked on that, I was having so much fun, I didn't feel like I was working."

When that "moment of clarity" prompted her to begin her first novel, Lawrence was working as a technical writer for a financial services company. In order to make time for her novel, she had to redefine her priorities. It wasn't easy.

W.E. REINKA *is a fulltime freelance writer of fiction and nonfiction. He is former books editor of the* Berkeley Insider *and the* Berkeley Voice. *He has published reviews, personal essays, profiles, business articles and travel pieces in publications nationwide.*

"I would write during my lunch hour and then come home, pick up the house and make dinner. Then I'd go back to my writing at night. I'd work until one or two in the morning. Weekends were writing weekends. There's a definite sacrifice when you're writing a book and it isn't just about time but about focus. How many things can you focus on and do well at one time? For me, three things were about it. I was a single mom, I had a job and I was a writer. Anything beyond that just fell off. I remember how difficult it was to say 'no' to my friends. A lot of wannabe writers don't understand that you have to tell the PTA 'no,' just like you have to tell your friends you can't go to the movies—unless you want to take five years to write the book."

As an editor, Lawrence saw strengths and weaknesses in other manuscripts she could draw upon when she ventured into writing fiction herself.

Simple as it sounds, the first thing Lawrence cites is the importance of a good presentation. "Typos and sloppy presentation provide the editor with a good excuse to thin the stack of prospective manuscripts."

Recalling those days when she faced stacks of unread manuscripts, she says "it's really evident when you're looking at dozens of manuscripts a day who's faking it and who's real. Write what you know and know what you write. If it's not in the author, it's not going to be in the book."

Lawrence faithfully follows that advice. During childhood, she discovered that she had psychic abilities not everyone else had when she began seeing auras and ghosts. She even dreamed in precise details events that later came to pass. So she draws on her own experience, "writing what she knows," in her mystery series revolving around licensed private investigator and parapsychologist Dr. Elizabeth Chase.

A psychic detective? Doesn't that make for short mysteries? "Psychic ability, second sight, whatever you want to call it, is not something that can be turned on and off," says Lawrence, who rolls her eyes at psychic hot lines and fortune-telling scams. "I can see auras, but not on command."

Once a professional astrologer, she expands her "write what you know" template by gathering titles from the Zodiac the way her friend and mentor, Sue Grafton, relies on the alphabet. Her first mystery, *Murder in Scorpio*, received Edgar, Anthony and Agatha awards nominations. She followed with *The Cold Heart of Capricorn*, *Aquarius Descending* and *Pisces Rising*. The Aries installment is scheduled for publication in fall, 2001.

In Lawrence's series, private eye Elizabeth Chase uses parapsychology to provide clues and hints the way other fictional gumshoes rely on sidekicks. But, just as the main detective, not the sidekick, always solves the crime, Elizabeth must still sort through evidence and hard facts to get to whodunnit. The series provides plenty of action when Chase walks into traps, ambushes and other messes her psychic ability doesn't keep her out of.

Because of her own psychic experiences, Lawrence felt called upon to establish a detective who used the right side, or intuitive, side of her brain as surely as literary predecessors used the rationally-geared left side of the brain.

"However, I knew that there was a rule in the mystery world that you can't have a psychic detective. The stereotype was that if you have a psychic detective, it's cheating. I also knew, as an editor, how critical it was to have an agent. Many houses these days won't take unagented manuscripts. So before I spent six months or a year writing a book nobody might want, I wrote three chapters and sent them to three different agents." Fortunately, she sparked interest with all three before settling on Gina Maccoby who has remained her agent throughout her career.

With more than a little irony, Lawrence claims to have lived a "charmed life." The stalking ex-boyfriend is not the only experiential grist for her writing mill. She was the victim of a serial rapist, an ordeal she calls upon in *The Cold Heart of Capricorn*. Writing that book proved valuable therapy in her recovery. Likewise, readers of *Aquarius Descending* may shiver at the authenticity of Lawrence's depiction of a religious cult. Another ordeal in her "charmed life" came at age 20, when she ran into a couple of kids who invited her to visit their "alternative community" on an isolated farm in Northern California. The alternative community turned out to be a cult. After ten days of "what amounted to imprisonment," she escaped.

Though Lawrence hit paydirt with her first manuscript, she draws on her own experience as an editor to encourage beginning writers to try try again. "Sometimes a manuscript is turned down simply because the editor has filled his or her list for the season and doesn't have any money left to buy books."

Of course, some beginning writers are turned down over craft issues. In that sense, Lawrence distinguishes fiction from non-fiction. "If you're writing fiction, you had best know how to write, and that's something for which there are no shortcuts. You must write, write and write again. You must know what prose style is. There are whole tomes available on the subject; about avoiding unnecessary adverbs and adjectives, for example."

She reminds fiction writers that awkward prose pulls down a manuscript as surely as grammatical errors. "Something as simple as inserting too many 'he saids/she saids' can slow down a manuscript and make it clunky. A beginning writer needs to weed out those obstructions. One writer I spent too much time with as an editor had an incredible story. But his skill level was not up to the story. I'd read it and write suggestions and send it back and he'd work on it some more, but we could never publish his manuscript because he was just tone deaf."

Even after years of reading manuscripts as an editor, Lawrence still defines relaxation as reading a good book. It's hard to find a crime fiction writer she hasn't read and she still enjoys reading classic literary fiction and poets such as Walt Whitman and Emily Dickinson. Now that she gets to write books for a living as well as read them, she says, without irony this time, "I lead a charmed life."

Literary Mystery Appeals to Both Genre and Mainstream Readers

BY BRAD VICE

Tom Franklin's novella "Poachers" just may be the last great mystery story of the century. 1999 was a life-changing year for the small-town Alabama native, a year in which "Poachers"—first published in a relatively small literary journal—burst into the big time. Published by William Morrow & Co. as an eponymously titled short story collection anchored by the novella, *Poachers* became a hit in both literary and mystery reading circles across the country.

Photo by Dan H. Fuller

Tom Franklin

"My agent, Nat Sobel, gets all the credit," Franklin says, in a soft, self-deprecating voice. It is hard to imagine the man with this voice writing so forcefully about greed, murder and dismemberment. "My agent subscribes to over a hundred literary journals, and he found the novella in *The Texas Review*. I think they have a novella contest now, but they didn't at the time. 'Poachers' was eighty-two pages in manuscript, so it was a kind of minor miracle it was ever published at all. Most people just don't want to give up that much space in their magazine, so I am really grateful to Paul Ruffin and George Garrett of *The Texas Review*, as well."

Just as the novella is something of a hybrid form, with the intensity of a short story and the depth of a novel, "Poachers" was also something of a hybrid in terms of its content and style. The novella's cool, polished prose attracted the attention of readers of literary fiction usually more inclined to read quiet, meditative narrative. But the plot of the novella—concerning the murder of a young game warden by three half-crazed backwoodsmen—drew the attention of readers more accustomed to selecting books from the mystery shelf at the library. Even though "Poachers" first caught the imagination of Franklin's future agent, it would soon draw praise from the editors of both *New Stories from the South* and *Best American Mystery Stories* anthologies. When Franklin's collection of short fiction, also entitled *Poachers*, hit the shelves later that year, it was awarded an Edgar, and his novella was selected by Tony Hillerman for inclusion in *The Best Mystery Stories of the Century*, an anthology that also included writers like Joyce Carol Oates, Dashiell Hammett and Ernest Hemingway.

Here Franklin discusses crossover mystery audiences, his distinctive writing style, and his upcoming novel, which he predicts will be a historical mystery.

When the book Poachers was first published, did you expect it to be a crossover success with the mystery market?

No, I didn't expect any of the success I had with "Poachers." I still can't come to think of myself as a mystery writer. Actually, I came to find out that "Poachers" technically isn't a mystery. It's a crime story, because the tension of the plot is sustained by the violence. A true

---

BRAD VICE *is a graduate student at the University of Cincinnati. His articles have also appeared in the* Guide to Literary Agents *(Writer's Digest Books). His fiction has appeared in* The Southern Review, Hayden's Ferry Review, *and* New Stories from the South.

mystery is a whodunit where the reader doesn't know the identity of the killer. Suspense novels rely on "what's going to happen next" for tension. For instance, I was told that *Crime and Punishment* would be considered a crime novel too. But the people who buy these kinds of books are fanatics, and I am very glad some of them wanted to buy my book. I would say one-third of the readers who bought my book were introduced to me through *Best American Mystery Stories*.

But if you're going to classify me as any kind of writer, I guess I am a Southern writer. I am interested in writing mostly about Clarke, Alabama, the place where I grew up. I live in Illinois now, and if I ever write anything about Illinois, at least one of the characters will be from Alabama. But having said that, I'll bet my future work will have many of the same elements as "Poachers."

Do you see yourself continuing to write mystery books, or did that just happen to be the subject of the one novella? I know there is a novel in the works, so is there any pressure for that book to be a mystery as well?

There is no pressure for the new book to be anything in particular, but there is a good deal of pressure just to get it written. The public has a short memory, and everyone wants me to be able to capitalize on the success of *Poachers*. The new novel is sort of a mystery; it's also a historical novel with a kind of western quality, too. It's called *Hell at the Breach*, and it's about a massacre that took place in southern Alabama in 1894, although I'm setting it in 1899 because that's the date on the Sears & Roebuck catalogue I'm using for research. The 'Hell at the Breach' gang was a secret society of outlaws, kind of like the Ku Klux Klan, only their crimes were politically rather than racially motivated. A mob of angry people from a northern town, tired of the gang's activities, rode into Clarke, Alabama where it was rumored the outlaws were living. Because the mob didn't know the identity of the gang members, they killed everybody—the guilty and the innocent alike. It's a complicated book about a complicated historical event. I don't want to make this a one-sided book, but to me the act of writing is the act of simplification.

The prose in *Poachers* has a very simple style—that is, it's direct and forceful. Do you see that kind of style as your trademark?

Well, many of the book's reviewers called the writing 'spare.' I never thought of my writing as spare before. But after awhile I began to take it as a compliment, because they also compared it to Raymond Carver's, whose work I love. But I don't really think about it in terms of my career. One difference between a pulp mystery and literary fiction is the time spent on the language. I agonize over every word. Sometimes publishers don't understand that, and honestly, it sounds conceited if you use that as an excuse for not getting your work in on time.

Do you have any models for your crossover career? Right now you might be compared to other hybrid writers like James Ellroy. Or maybe Joyce Carol Oates, James Lee Burke, or Walter Mosely. If *Hell at the Breach* is a success, where do you see yourself going from there?

Well, every one of those writers kind of has their own thing going. Ellroy's stuff is great because it has that historical sweep to it. Oates seems to vary between mystery novels and other kinds of books. I love James Lee Burke, but I'm never going to have a character like Dave Robicheaux. I just don't have the kind of mind to construct different plots around a single character. I'd also hate to get where my publisher or the readers were expecting a particular thing from me. Most of my heroes are Rick Bass, Barry Hannah, Larry Brown, guys like that. Currently I have been in close contact with writers like Michael Knight, Brad Watson and William Gay, other writers from the South who also seem fascinated with crime. I am very happy that many of those people seem to have liked my first book, and those are the readers I most want to impress with my next.

Mystery Markets
Appearing in This Book

Below is a list of mystery markets appearing in this edition of *Novel & Short Story Writer's Market*. To find page numbers of particular markets, go first to the General Index. Then turn to the pages those listings appear on for complete information, including who to contact and how to submit your mystery short story or novel manuscript.

Magazines

Advocate, PKA's Publication
Aguilar Expression, The
Alembic
Amelia
Analecta
Anthology
Archaeology
Armchair Aesthete, The
Art:Mag
Beginners
Beneath the Surface
Bibliophilos
Blue Murder Magazine
Blue Skunk Companion, The
Boys' Life
Capers Aweigh
Cenotaph
Chat
Children, Churches and Daddies Magazine
Chrysalis Reader
Circle Magazine, The
City Primeval
Climbing Art, The
Cochran's Corner
Cosmopolitan Magazine
Cotworld Creative Magazine
Cozy Detective, The
Crimewave
CZ's Magazine
Dagger of the Mind
Dialogue
Discovery Trails
Downstate Story
Edge, Tales of Suspense, The
Eureka Literary Magazine
Evansville Review
Free Focus/Ostentatious Mind
Fugue
Fullosia Press
Futures Magazine
Green's Magazine
Griffin, The
Grit
Hardboiled
Hemispheres
Hitchcock's Mystery Magazine, Alfred
Horsethief's Journal, The

In Posse Review
Interbang
Irreantum
Japanophile
Kids' Highway
Lamplight, The
Leapings Literary Magazine
Lite
Literary Moments
Lynx Eye
Merlyn's Pen
Missing Fez, The
MJ's Walkabout
Monkeyplanet
Murderous Intent
Musing Place, The
Mystery Time
New England Writers' Network
New Mystery
Nightfire
Northeast Arts Magazine
Northwoods Journal
Outer Darkness
Palo Alto Review
Paumanok Review, The
Peralta Press, The
Plot Line Foyer
Poetry Forum Short Stories
Portland Review
Post, The
Prisoners of the Night
PSI
Pulp Eternity Online
Queen's Mystery Magazine, Ellery
Rejected Quarterly, The
Seeking the Muse
Short Stuff Magazine for Grown-ups
Shyflower's Garden
Skylark
Snake Nation Review
SPSM&H
Storyteller, The
Strand Magazine, The
Studentswrite.com
"Teak" Roundup
Thema
3 A.M. Magazine
Threshold, The

Tucumcari Literary Review
12-Gauge.com
Urban Spaghetti
Vincent Brothers Review, The
Virginia Adversaria
Weber Studies
Woman's World Magazine
Yarns and Such
Yellow Sticky Notes

Book Publishers
Adventure Book Publishers
Ageless Press
Arcade Publishing
Authors Online Ltd.
Avalon Books
Avon Books
Bancroft Press
Bantam Books
Bantam Dell Publishing Group, The
Beggar's Press
Berkley Publishing Group, The
Carroll & Graf Publishers, Inc.
Centennial Publications
Christchurch Publishers Ltd.
Compass Point Mysteries™/Tory Corner Editions™
Cumberland House Publishing
Dan River Press
Delacorte Press
Dell
Dial Press, The
DiskUs Publishing
Duckworth Press
Dunne Books, Thomas
Fawcett
First Amendment Press International Company
Forge Books
Fort Ross Inc.
Fountainhead Productions, Inc.
Gaslight Publications
Glencannon Press, The
Gryphon Books
Harcourt Inc
Harlequin Enterprises, Ltd.

HarperTorch
Hawk Publishing Group
Hodder & Stoughton/Headline
Holt & Company, Henry
Houghton Mifflin Books for Children
Huntington Press
Insomniac Press
Island
Ivy League Press, Inc.
Kensington Publishing Corp.
LTD Books
Majestic Books
Morrow, William
Multnomah Publishers, Inc.
Mysterious Press, The
New American Library
New Hope Books, Inc.
New Victoria Publishers
Palari Publishing
Philomel Books
Pocket Books
Presidio Press
Publishers Syndication, International
Putnam's Sons, G.P.
Rainbow Books, Inc.
Random House, Inc.
RavenHaus Publishing
Regency Press
Salvo Press
Scherf Books
Scrivenery Press
Silver Dagger Mysteries
Soho Press
St. Martin's Press
Stonewall Inn
Tropical Press, Inc.
Turnstone Press
University of Nevada Press
Van Neste Books
Viking
Vista Publishing, Inc.
Walker and Company
Warner Books
Write Way Publishing
Zondervan

MYSTERY MARKETS INDEX

Resources for Mystery Writers

Below is a list of invaluable resources specifically for mystery writers. For more information on the magazines and organizations listed below, check the General Index and the Publications of Interest and Organizations sections of this book. To order any of the Writer's Digest Books titles or to get a consumer book catalog, call 1-800-289-0963. You may also order Writer's Digest Books selections through www.writersdigest.com, Amazon.com or www.barnesandnoble.com.

MAGAZINES:
- *The Armchair Detective*, P.O. Box 929, Bound Brook NJ 08805-0929
- *Mystery Readers Journal*, Mystery Readers International, P.O. Box 8116, Berkeley CA 94707
- *Writer's Digest*, 1507 Dana Ave., Cincinnati OH 45207

BOOKS:
Howdunit series (Writer's Digest Books):
- *Missing Persons: A Writer's Guide to Finding the Lost, the Abducted and the Escaped*
- *Murder One: A Writer's Guide to Homicide*
- *Armed and Dangerous: A Writer's Guide to Weapons*
- *Deadly Doses: A Writer's Guide to Poisons*
- *Cause of Death: A Writer's Guide to Death, Murder & Forensic Medicine*
- *Scene of the Crime: A Writer's Guide to Crime Scene Investigation*
- *Private Eyes: A Writer's Guide to Private Investigators*
- *Police Procedural: A Writer's Guide to the Police and How They Work*
- *Modus Operandi: A Writer's Guide to How Criminals Work*
- *Malicious Intent: A Writer's Guide to How Criminals Think*
- *Body Trauma: A Writer's Guide to Wounds and Injuries*
- *Amateur Detectives: A Writer's Guide to How Private Citizens Solve Criminal Cases*
- *Just the Facts, Ma'am: A Writer's Guide to Investigators and Investigation Techniques*
- *Rip-off: A Writer's Guide to Crimes of Deception*

Other Writer's Digest books for mystery writers:
- *How to Write Mysteries*
- *The Writer's Complete Crime Reference Book*
- *Writing the Modern Mystery*
- *Writing Mysteries: A Handbook by the Mystery Writers of America*
- *Writing the Private Eye Novel: A Handbook by the Private Eye Writers of America*
- *You Can Write a Mystery*

ORGANIZATIONS & ONLINE:
- The Mystery Writers' Forum: www.zott.com/mysforum/default.html (See complete listing in the Websites of Interest section of this book.)
- Mystery Writers of America, 17 E. 47th St., 6th Floor, New York NY 10017
- The Private Eye Writers of America, 407 W. Third St., Moorestown NJ 08057
- Sisters in Crime, P.O. Box 442124, Lawrence KS 66044-8933

The Accidental Romance Novelist: A Profile of Diana Gabaldon

BY JULIA CROSS

She says it was an accident. She didn't plan to write an award-winning romance novel that would break all the rules of the genre and evolve into a popular double trilogy. Diana Gabaldon, a former research professor with a doctorate in ecology, insists she was simply writing a novel for practice.

"I never meant to show it to anyone," she says, "let alone publish it." A natural storyteller who had sold scripts for Disney comic books in the past, Gabaldon thought the best way to learn how to write a novel would be to sit down and do it. So that's what she did.

The inspiration for the story that would become *Outlander* arrived in the form of a "rather fetching" Scottish character in a kilt on the science-fiction serial "Doctor Who." Gabaldon had never been to Scotland, and she knew no more about 18th century life in the Highlands than the average person, but she had access to a good library at Arizona State University and knew how to use it. With the time and place fixed as a starting point for her story, she got to work.

The historical novel Gabaldon intended to write might have proceeded normally from there if her heroine Claire hadn't refused to cooperate with the premise. It soon became obvious that this character preferred to speak and act like a modern Englishwoman, even in the midst of the 1745 Jacobite Rising. To accommodate her, Gabaldon found a way for Claire to travel 200 years back in time through a magical ring of stones. And that was only the beginning.

"I included any element that took my fancy," she says, "which is why I now find it on every shelf in the bookstore!"

It became so difficult to categorize the story that Gabaldon didn't know what to call it then and finds it no easier a decade later, after publishing *Outlander* and the three novels that followed: *Dragonfly in Amber*, *Voyager* and *Drums of Autumn* (the final two books in the second trilogy are still in the works). Categorizing it didn't matter much at the time, however, because she still planned to keep the novel to herself. So what happened?

Gabaldon began spending time in CompuServe's Literary Forum, where members post messages back and forth. In *The Outlandish Companion*, the book Gabaldon wrote about her popular series, she says that the forum was "the ideal social life for a busy person with small children—something like a twenty-four-hour electronic cocktail party."

She didn't tell any of her online acquaintances about the novel she was writing until she got into an argument with someone in the forum, who thought that as a father he knew what it was like to be pregnant. As a mother of three herself, Gabaldon disagreed. To make her point, she posted a fragment of her novel-in-progress, in which the character Jenny Murray describes the experience of becoming a mother to her brother Jamie.

The positive response from people in the forum, who not only praised the piece but wanted to read more of her work, encouraged Gabaldon to continue posting scenes from her growing novel. Several authors who had established an online relationship with Gabaldon insisted her work was publishable, and one recommended her to his literary agent, Perry Knowlton, who agreed to take a look at her work.

JULIA CROSS *is the founder and director of the Circle of Arts in Cincinnati, Ohio, which offers creative workshops and a website for writers at www.CircleofArts.com.*

"I sent him a rough synopsis of the book and a number of chunks, with marks on the synopsis to indicate where in the story these chunks fell," Gabaldon says, "and he took me on, on the basis of an unfinished first novel." She acknowledges that this is unusual, but believes that her track record as a freelance writer, selling Disney comics and technical articles, helped convince the agent that she was a professional who "could indeed finish the manuscript."

Six months later when the book was complete, Knowlton sent it to five editors for consideration, and three of them immediately called back with offers. The book was sold to Delacorte Press, which gave Gabaldon a three-book contract to create an *Outlander* trilogy. After that, it was up to the marketing department to decide how to present her cross-genre novel to the world.

What stopped them from selling it as an historical novel, Gabaldon says, "was the niggling difficulty that my main character was a time traveler. It didn't matter how meticulous the research, or how detailed the historical background; readers of historical fiction simply wouldn't—they thought—accept a book whose central premise included time travel."

An audience for any genre market has certain expectations, and it was difficult to know which audience would be best served. *Outlander* would come out as hardcover fiction first, as stated in the contract. But Gabaldon was surprised when, "after months of agonizing," they decided to release *Outlander* as a romance in paperback.

"What it finally came down to was that of all the categories in which this book didn't fit, romance was the largest," Gabaldon says. Her two objections to this categorization were that her book would never be reviewed by *The New York Times*, and that as a romance it wouldn't appeal to a male audience. "Well," Gabaldon recalls her agent telling her, "we could insist that they market the books as fantasy or science fiction, because of the time travel and other strange elements. But bear in mind that a bestseller in science fiction is 50,000 copies in paperback; a bestseller in romance is 500,000." Gabaldon agreed that it made sense to make *Outlander* available to as wide a readership as possible, even if it wasn't the one she had envisioned. An agreement was reached in which the books would be sold as romance but, as Gabaldon specified, "with dignified covers: no mad bosoms, no swooning clinches, no Fabio." It was also agreed that if the books became visible on *The New York Times* list, they would be repositioned as mainstream fiction, "making them safe for men to read."

Outlander sold well, and despite Gabaldon's belief that it wasn't a true romance novel, Romance Writers of America named it Best Book of the Year in 1991. The second novel in the series, *Dragonfly in Amber*, was given the same 25,000-copy print run as *Outlander*, but it sold out and went back to press twice more within the month. "That sort of thing," Gabaldon laughs, "gets a publisher's attention." When the third book, *Voyager*, came out, they printed 60,000 copies, which sold out and went back to press three times within the first week.

When *Voyager* landed on *The New York Times* list, Delacorte reissued Gabaldon's books with fresh covers as promised and began marketing them to a more mainstream audience. "They kept the original art, which I liked very much," the author says. "It's done by Kinuko Craft, who actually reads the book before doing the painting. But they replaced the style of the title and author lines, adding foil bands that covered most of the scattered flowers, which had been the only nod toward a classic romance look."

As a result, the series now claims a loyal male readership and has sold through a range of book catalogs, including those for science fiction readers and military buffs. In a review of her books for *Salon* magazine, writer Gavin McNett acknowledges their cross-genre appeal when he describes them as "the smartest historical sci-fi adventure-romance series ever written by a science Ph.D. with a background in scripting Scrooge McDuck comics."

How has Gabaldon's life changed now that she's a successful novelist? After her second book came out, she was able to retire from the university and focus on her writing full-time. She receives up to 90 e-mails a day from her fans and is in constant demand as a speaker. "Everyone wants me to stay home and write the next novel," she says, "but only after I've come to their town!"

She's hard at work on the fifth book of the *Outlander* series, tentatively titled *The Fiery Cross*, as well as a contemporary mystery set in her home state of Arizona. Gabaldon generally spends a couple of hours working on them during the day, but admits, "I'm a night person and have no functioning brain cells before 10 a.m. My prime time for writing is late at night—usually about midnight to three a.m. During those hours, 'kids are not an issue.'"

When asked how she juggles her writing projects with book tours, motherhood, and everything else, Gabaldon quips, "I don't sleep, and I don't do housework."

Gabaldon's advice to someone writing a first novel, even if it's just for practice? "There is no magic secret. You just sit still and write. That's it," she says. "The most important thing is to start. The next most important thing is to not stop. When you begin to work whole-heartedly on something, things happen."

Not Just Happily-Ever-After: How to Write Real Romance

BY JENNIFER CRUSIE

So you want to write a romance? Congratulations! You've chosen an exciting genre with a noble past, although you may find yourself arguing that with the Vast Uninformed. When I was working on my MFA in fiction, having already published three romance novels, a professor said to me, "Jenny, you write so well. Have you ever thought about writing literature?"

Heads up: *Romance fiction is literature*, the finest kind of literature, the kind that explores the most powerful emotion known to humanity, a force that has driven people to great deeds and horrible acts, that has elevated and destroyed, that can create life or inspire death. Love is not just a subject for silly love songs, and romance novels are not silly chick books with embarrassing covers. Love is a maelstrom that attacks our bodies, our minds, our hearts, and our souls, transforming us forever. And romance novels tell the stories of what happens when we get caught in that maelstrom.

A less dramatic definition: A romance is the story of two people who meet, struggle to build a relationship, and commit to spending the rest of their lives together, facing the future with optimism. Convincing an increasingly jaded readership that "this one is forever" is no easy task but it's an important one: a good romance novel does nothing less than restore a reader's faith in the power of true love, even if it's only for four hundred pages. Half the mass market fiction sold in this country is romance novels—almost 2000 romance titles were published in 1999 alone—so clearly, romance novelists are doing something right.

That also means that if you've decided you want to write a romance, there's never been a better time to write one. Unfortunately, there have also never been so many dumb assumptions about them. So first, here are some myths to wipe from your mind (or from the minds of others, by force if necessary):

Myth #1: All romances are alike.

Not even close.

Historical romances are love stories that take place before the 20th century. As we move into the 21st century, the line blurs a little more and the earlier decades of the 20th century will become more popular as settings. The key is that the story is removed from the present to a time beyond memory. Popular settings are the American west, the revolutionary period, and the Civil War; medieval and 19th century England, Scotland, and Ireland; and anything with Vikings, but just about every time period and country has been written about by now. A subset of the historical is the Regency novel; set in the early 19th century, the Regency has a set of conventions as rigid as the sonnet and should be studied apart from historical romances set in the Regency period—an entirely different kind of romance.

Contemporary romances are love stories set in the present time. This genre also has several popular subgenres, for example, the romantic comedy, a genre with its roots in the screwball

JENNIFER CRUSIE *is currently in the Ph.D. program at Ohio State University. Since her novella,* Sizzle, *was published by Silhouette in 1992, Crusie has gone on to publish several more romances, including* Anyone But You *(Harlequin) and* Welcome to Temptation *(St. Martin's Press). She currently lives near Columbus, Ohio.*

comedies of the 30s and 40s and before that in the comedies of manners by Jane Austen; and the sweet romance, generally defined as a traditional love story with no explicit sex scenes. Other subgenres combine romance with other kinds of fiction—romantic suspense, for example, combines mystery with the love story; the tradition goes back to the 19th century Gothic novel, and its 20th century roots include DuMaurier's *Rebecca*. Paranormal romances blend horror or fantasy with the love story, drawing on classics legends such as the ghost story and the vampire tale. The inspirational romance blends the story of faith with the love story. Finally, there is a growing market for erotic romance, not just love stories with explicit sex, but stories with a dual purpose to both tell the love story and to arouse.

A third kind of romance, called the series romance, encompasses both contemporary and historical elements. These books are published in a numbered series by Harlequin/Silhouette, and are divided into categories which is why they're also called category novels. Harlequin Intrigue, for example, is a category romantic suspense line, while Harlequin Romance is a traditional or sweet line.

Deciding you want to "write a romance" is like telling a waiter you'd like some food. If you aren't reading romance already, you're going to have to study the genre to find the kind of stories that you want to write, and also to understand the genre as a whole. Romance readers are extremely discerning and they can spot a faker by the end of the first chapter. Non-believers need not apply.

Myth #2: Romance novels must have a happy ending.

Nope. Romance novels must have an optimistic ending, but many romances deal with catastrophe and deep trauma. To slap a "and they all lived happily ever after without the benefit of therapy" ending on such a book would be a betrayal of the characters, and a good romance novel is first and foremost about character. The romance novel heroine is not Cinderella or Pollyanna; she knows there will be tough times ahead, but she faces them with optimism, as does the hero. No last pages with cockroaches scuttling across cracked linoleum floors while the protagonists stare sullenly at each other. "Tomorrow is another day" is writ large upon the romance protagonists' hearts.

Myth #3: Romance novels have no conflict.

Oh, please. Show me a romance in real life that has no conflict and I'll show you two first graders whose desks are not next to each other. One of the many reasons romance novels are so popular is that everybody's had at least one bad romance and would like to believe a good one is possible, even if only in the pages of a book.

However, there is a problem inherent in the romance conflict. A great fictional conflict is a fight to the end between the protagonist and the antagonist, resolved when one destroys the other completely. This is a bad beginning to a long-term relationship, so most romances that use the heroine and the hero as protagonist and antagonist end in compromise. That's good for relationships, bad for fiction climaxes. My suggestion: pit the heroine and hero against an outside antagonist and have them work together to thwart him or her, cementing their relationship during the struggle. Studies have shown that pain and stress actually make it easier for people to fall in love—think star-crossed lovers, office romances, and all those war babies—so a conflict external to the romance can actually deepen it.

Myth #4: Romance novels are soft porn for women.

First, not all romances have sex scenes.

Second, not all sex scenes are porn. (Who raised you, Kenneth Starr?)

Third, what's wrong with explicit fiction for women? We're not supposed to smudge our shiny little brains with thoughts of great sex? Romance novels encourage women to go after what they want and need, and a multiple orgasm never hurt anybody.

Romance novels are not about sex, any more than dinner is about dessert. However, sometimes dessert is a good thing. It just depends on your appetite.

Myth #5: If a romance novel is really good, a publisher will call it women's fiction and make it a hardcover.

Never confuse quality with marketing. The category printed on the spine of the book ("general fiction," "women's fiction," "romance") and the kind of cover protecting the book (hard or soft) are marketing decisions, based on getting the book to the right reader. Many terrific books are published as paperback originals; many real stinkers have hard covers.

So what exactly does determine category and cover?

The line between romance and women's fiction can be a blurry one. A romance is always a love story. Women's fiction is always about women's lives and women's relationships, although not necessarily romantic relationships, and is usually about a personal journey; that is, the woman grows and learns during the course of the novel. If a story is about a woman's journey as demonstrated in her romantic relationship, you have a novel that fits both categories. This is when the marketing department steps in because the label on the spine is about selling the book to the largest number of readers who will be satisfied by it. There are many women—poor, misguided souls—who will not read romance novels because they think they're tacky, but who will devour the same story if it's sold as women's fiction. So why not categorize all romance fiction as women's fiction? Because the most passionate book buyers shop in the romance section. It's a conundrum, so marketing makes the call.

As for packaging, books are published in both softcover and hardback because the markets for the two forms are different.

People who buy paperbacks often buy by genre; that is, they want something good to read on the plane or the beach, so they go to the mystery section or the romance section because that's what they like. They buy by author name and word of mouth, too, but they're willing to take a chance on an unknown author because the cover price is relatively cheap. The average romance reader goes through five books a week, so cover price is important to her. She'll look at a hardcover by her favorite romance author and think long and hard before plunking down the cover price. Therefore introducing a new romance author in hardcover can be very tricky. Many romance novelists who are in hardcover established their readership in paperback first; their hardcover sales come from the readers who love their work so much that they can't wait a year to read the paperback.

People who buy hardcovers buy, on the average, one book a month, and they buy because they want to read that book: they like the author, or the book has good word of mouth or it has information in it they want. They do not buy by genre, and this, coupled with the widespread misconception that romance is poor quality fiction, means that they often will not buy a romance author. This is why so many of the new romance authors that begin in hardcover are issued as General Fiction, and why so many of those romances have what has come to be known as "mainstream elements" including intricate plots and subplots apart from the romance.

Nowhere in any of this discussion has quality come up. That's because it's irrelevant. Publishers package and label books to best target the books to buyers, not to alert the readership that some aren't as good as others.

So now that you're up on romance basics and you're ready to join the party, what should you do?

1. Write the love story you want to write, the one that fills your mind waking and sleeping, the book you must write. You have to really need to write that book because if you don't, you won't.

2. As you write, study the craft of writing. Read books on it, take classes in it, go to conferences and talk to other writers, and rewrite and polish your work until it gleams. Understand point of view, plot and character arc, conflict, motif and metaphor and all the other tools that good writers understand and use. Writing stories is a very old and very honored calling and demands nothing less from you than the very best you can give. Many writers have written several books before they got one published, and many of those have been

grateful because it gave them the chance to make their mistakes in private. Nothing you write is ever wasted; it's all part of your growth as a writer.

3. Give the finished book to somebody who likes the same kind of romances you do. Ask her to be honest. When she's honest, don't argue with her or defend the book. Listen to the things she had trouble with or didn't like and try to figure out why she didn't like them. Explaining things to her is not an option; you're not going to be able to explain things to every reader when the book is published, so you have to put everything on the page so it doesn't need to be explained.

4. Study the genre. When you find romances that you like, or that are similar to the stories that you want to write or already have written, you've identified your market. You do not study the market to find out what to write, you study the market to find out which section of it will buy what you already want to write. (The best answer to the "what should I write?" question is an old one: "Write the book you want to read but can't find.")

5. Find out who edited the book that is most like yours that you liked the most (call the publishing house and ask). Write a query letter to that editor that (1) explains why you liked the book she edited, (2) tells her that you've written a book you hope she'll like as well (but not one that's better than the other book or as good as the other book), (3) describes the book's characters, conflict, and interesting plot points in a few, short, punchy sentences that are so fascinating that she must read the manuscript (think of it as a movie pitch), (4) and then give her every possible way of reaching you short of carrier pigeon (phone, fax, e-mail, snail mail, and the always popular SASE or self-addressed stamped envelope).

6. If she writes back and says, "Yes, please send the proposal," send her the first thirty to fifty pages of the book plus a synopsis of the plot, usually about one paragraph per chapter, ten to twelve double-spaced pages in length. In the cover letter, thank her for asking to see the manuscript; this is very important because it keeps you out of the slush pile, a dark place in the corner of the editor's office where manuscripts can rot for months and, in some cases, years. Include another SASE.

7. If she calls and asks to see the manuscript, congratulate yourself and send it. If you get the proposal back with a letter explaining why she isn't interested in publishing it, feel good: if she took the time to write you a letter, she's interested in you as a writer. If she sends it back with a form letter, assume she's just made a terrible mistake that she'll someday regret, and send a query letter to the next editor who edited a book you liked.

8. If she calls later and says she wants to buy it, say, "Thank you very much, I'll get back to you." There's a tendency to want to give away the farm with your first novel because you're so grateful somebody wants to publish it. This is when an agent comes in handy; agents are never grateful.

9. At some point in all of this, probably shortly after you decide you want to write a romance novel, join Romance Writers of America. RWA is one of the smartest writers' organizations around, and not the least of its benefits are its online bulletin boards where members discuss craft and industry issues and where you can get information on everything from agents to zoology (as in "never kill an animal in a romance novel"). RWA also has guidelines for recognized publishers and agents, position papers on contracts and the various rights negotiated therein, and a monthly journal that addresses the issues romance novelists are currently facing. For more information try the website at www.rwanational. com or call the office at (281)440-6885.

That's a lot to remember, but the most important part of all of this is simple: romance fiction is a vitally important form of fiction that places women at the centers of their stories and celebrates the liberating and redemptive power of love. As a romance novelist, you're part of a long tradition of life-affirming, feminist story-telling, and that tradition grows stronger every year. So welcome to the genre; we can't wait to hear what you have to say.

Romance Markets Appearing in This Book

Below is a list of romance markets appearing in this edition of *Novel & Short Story Writer's Market*. To find page numbers of particular markets, go first to the General Index. Then turn to the pages those listings appear on for complete information, including who to contact and how to submit your romance short story or novel manuscript.

Magazines
About Such Things
Advocate, PKA's Publication
Affable Neighbor
Aguilar Expression, The
Analecta
Beginners
Bibliophilos
Blue Skunk Companion, The
Bridal Guides
Brilliant Corners
Brobdingnagian Times, The
Carpe Noctem
Chat
Circle Magazine, The
Cochran's Corner
Cosmopolitan Magazine
Cotworld Creative Magazine
CZ's Magazine
Dialogue
Downstate Story
Eidolon
Eureka Literary Magazine
Evansville Review
Fugue
Futures Magazine
Gay Chicago Magazine
Gotta Write Network Litmag
Griffin, The
Grit
Home Times
Irreantum
Jive, Black Confessions, Black Romance, Bronze
    Thrills, Black Secrets
Lamplight, The
Literary Moments
Louisiana Review, The
Lynx Eye
Matriarch's Way: Journal of Female Supremacy
Merlyn's Pen
Moxie
Musing Place, The
New England Writers' Network
New Writing
Nightfire
Nite-Writer's International Literary Arts Journal
Northwoods Journal
Outer Darkness

Palo Alto Review
PeopleNet DisAbility DateNet Home Page
Plot Line Foyer
Poetry Forum Short Stories
Poskisnolt Press
Post, The
PSI
Pulp Eternity Online
Rabbit Hole Press, The
Rejected Quarterly, The
Rosebud™
Seeking the Muse
Shades of December
Short Story Writers Showcase
Short Stuff Magazine for Grown-ups
Shyflower's Garden
Skylark
SPSM&H
St. Anthony Messenger
Storyteller, The
Studentswrite.com
"Teak" Roundup
Threshold, The
Virginia Adversaria
Virginia Quarterly Review
Visions & Voices
Woman's World Magazine
Yellow Sticky Notes

Book Publishers
Adventure Book Publishers
Artemis Press
Authors Online Ltd.
Avalon Books
Avid Press, LLC
Avon Books
Bantam Books
Bantam Dell Publishing Group, The
Berkley Publishing Group, The
Dan River Press
Delacorte Press
Dell
Dial Press, The
DiskUs Publishing
Duckworth Press
First Amendment Press International Company
Fort Ross Inc.
Fountainhead Productions, Inc.
GoldenIsle Publishers Inc.

Harlequin Enterprises, Ltd.
HarperTorch
Hodder & Stoughton/Headline
ImaJinn Books
Island
Kensington Publishing Corp.
Leisure Books
LionHearted Publishing, Inc.
Love Spell
LTD Books
Majestic Books
New American Library

Pipers' Ash Ltd.
Pocket Books
Ponder Publishing Inc.
Power of Love Publishing
RavenHaus Publishing
Red Sage Publishing, Inc.
Regency Press
Russell Publishing, James
Silhouette Books
Steeple Hill
Stones Point Press
Vista Publishing, Inc.
Warner Books

Resources for Romance Writers

Below is a list of invaluable resources specifically for romance writers. For more information on the magazines and organizations listed below, check the General Index and the Publications of Interest and Organizations sections of this book. To order any of the Writer's Digest Books titles or to get a consumer book catalog, call 1-800-289-0963. You may also order Writer's Digest Books selections through www.writersdigest.com, Amazon.com or www.barnesandnoble.com.

MAGAZINES:
- *Romance Writers Report*, Romance Writers of America, 3707 FM 1960 West, Suite 555, Houston TX 77014. (281)440-6885. Fax: (281)440-7510. E-mail: infobox@rwanational. com
- *Romantic Times Magazine*, 55 Bergen St., Brooklyn NY 11201. (718)237-1097. Website: www.romantictimes.com
- *Writer's Digest*, 1507 Dana Ave., Cincinnati OH 45207

BOOKS:
- *How To Write Romances (Revised and Updated)*, Writer's Digest Books
- *Keys to Success: A Professional Writer's Career Handbook*, Attention: Handbook, Romance Writers of America, 13700 Veterans Memorial, Suite 315, Houston TX 77014-1023. (281)440-6885, ext. 21. Fax: (281)440-7510. E-mail: infobox@rwanational.com
- *Romance Writer's Sourcebook: Where to Sell Your Manuscripts*, Writer's Digest Books
- *The Writer's Guide to Everyday Life in Regency and Victorian England*, Writer's Digest Books
- *Writing Romances: A Handbook by the Romance Writers of America*, Writer's Digest Books
- *You Can Write a Romance*, Writer's Digest Books

ORGANIZATIONS & ONLINE
- Romance Writers of America, Inc. (RWA), 3703 FM 1960 West, Suite 555, Houston TX 77068. (281)440-6885, ext. 21. Fax: (281)440-7510. E-mail: infobox@rwanational.com
- Romance Writers of America regional chapters. Contact National Office (address above) for information on the chapter nearest you.
- Romance Central website: romance-central.com. Offers workshops and forum where romance writers share ideas and exchange advice about romance writing. (See complete listing in the Websites of Interest section of this book.)
- www.writersmarket.com
- www.writersdigest.com

An Experimental Take on Horror: Mark Danielewski's *House of Leaves*

BY JOSHUA EASTON

"This is not for you." With this eerie admonition on the dedication page, the reader is led into Mark Danielewski's frightening debut novel *House of Leaves* (Pantheon, 2000). But from the first page it becomes apparent that this book may not belong on the horror shelves. A substantial part of the literary landscape has been woven into this expansive work that includes Norwegian myth, a healthy dose of classical Greek subjects, existential philosophy and film theory. These themes are integrated into a layered story that is told through multiple narrators, numerous typefaces, a host of footnotes and commentators, and what is at times an overwhelming textual layout. But the 34-year-old author doesn't mind if the book is characterized as a horror novel. "It doesn't bother me that it might be put in science fiction, or horror, or literature. The fact that it is a little tricky to define is an interesting point," he says.

Identifying the story's core is difficult, but the book begins with an introduction by Johnny Truant, a 20-something tattoo assistant who has stumbled on a manuscript by a recently-deceased, blind recluse named Zampano. Truant admonishes us in the introduction that Zampano's text is a fiction. Yet the lines of reality/fiction blur in Zampano's heavily footnoted academic narrative of "The Navidson Record," purportedly a documentary of a filmmaker moving his family into a house and recording it all. Something is very wrong with the house, however, as the family soon discovers it is bigger on the inside than the outside. This foreboding premise has a profound effect on Johnny Truant, which we learn about solely through his footnotes to Zampano's text.

The story of how *House of Leaves* was published is nearly as fascinating as the complex narrative it tells. It took Danielewski over 10 years to write while working various odd jobs. "When I finished it, there were a bunch of friends that wanted to read it, and I simply didn't have the funds to copy it and send it off," he says. "So I converted it to a PDF file and posted it to an awful URL with lots of backslashes and tildes. Then I had some business cards printed up that said 'House of Leaves,' with 'House' in blue type, and just the URL address. I handed these out to friends, who would stick extras in books in bookstores, and eventually there were some strangers reading the book."

Danielewski went through the traditional channels, however, to get the book in print. "I didn't get an agent from the book being on the Internet," he cautions. "I went to a bookstore, got a book on literary agents and made a list. I sent the first 50 pages along with a letter, got a response from a few agents, flew to New York and chose one. The agent, Warren Frazier, then took the book to publishers."

Since publication, *House of Leaves* has received wide acclaim, including an extraordinary back cover blurb from *American Psycho* author Bret Easton Ellis: "A great novel, it renders most other fiction meaningless. One can imagine Thomas Pynchon, J.G. Ballard, Stephen King and David Foster Wallace bowing at Danielewski's feet, choking with astonishment, surprise, laughter and awe." With such praise, it is difficult to imagine a more intriguing debut.

Here Danielewski shares his views on what's terrifying in literature, his own highly experi-

---

JOSHUA EASTON, *a native of Kentucky, is a law student at Tulane University in New Orleans. See the interview with* House of Leaves *editor Edward Kastenmeier on page 82.*

mental approach to writing fiction, and the influence of his family on his writing process.

House of Leaves might be found someplace other than the horror shelves of bookstores. You've said that when writers really approach the deeper questions they are ultimately going to unveil something that's terrifying. Is that a good thing for a writer to pursue?

Great American literature has always been built on that. The "pilgrimage" was always in relation to some sort of fear. It was an unknown territory where there were all sorts of dangers one would have to face, whether it was crossing the Atlantic, dealing with plague or famine, the threat of already existing inhabitants, the ghosts there, etc. When you look at the literature of the past, whether it's Emily Dickinson, Melville, Hawthorne, Poe, there is always a great deal of terror in all of those adventures and ruminations. Of course with Melville, the whale is unknown and terrifying. But perhaps Emily Dickinson is one of the more extreme examples when we think about how she was writing about death and God and meaning on this earth. Frightening stuff.

Do you think that is what attracts people to the horror genre, the general fear of the unknown, or is it something that reflects other things in their lives?

Both. It also is ultimately something that steers our lives. It constantly has some bearing on the decisions we are going to make and the outcome of those decisions, or how we handle what we're afraid of. Some people deny it; they say they're not afraid, but the really successful ones tend to recognize where their fear is and learn how to handle it. They learn that some fears have to be listened to and other fears can't be listened to. I think it makes for better choices in the long run.

You mentioned Edgar Allan Poe and that brought to mind the work of your sister, the musician who goes by the name of "Poe."

Yes. We are very close, and she has been my only reader. I think that's an important thing for any writer. All you need is one reader you trust; and not even a reader to tell what's wrong with it, either, but to tell you what parts they really like. This came up very recently when someone asked if we are critical of each other's work, and when we thought about it the answer was no. In general, we're critical simply because we concentrate on what we like. Sometimes she'll write a line about some scene that I've sketched out and then she'll sing it in a way that takes it into a different emotional territory. That will actually influence me because I'll listen to it and I'll say, "Wow, I never thought something that was horrifying could actually have that element of melancholy to it." That had a very powerful effect on how I turned and shaped and directed my work. There was influence back and forth. So it really is a question of following through on those parts that really communicate and not focusing on the things that don't really work, because in the long run other people are going to tell you what doesn't work. To start a project and finish it you really need someone who's there just to encourage and tell you what they like.

The book was originally serialized on the Internet. Also some of the commentary on House of Leaves implies that the layout, the index, the blue typeface, all suggest some hypertext reference. Was this an intentional effect?

Right before the book was going to be published, based on my earlier experience I said, "Let's serialize this thing for free." We did, and a lot of people came in and read it and discussed the differences between a book that's on paper versus this sort of e-book experience. As for how the Internet might pertain to the book's design, I don't really know yet. I do caution people. I think the blue word and its relation to hyperlinks is exciting, but for the most part that element is coincidence.

Do you think you might post anything on the Internet in the future in similar fashion?

I think the Internet technology is new, but the process is not that new. What we have is the ability to look up words more quickly, and we have the ability to move around a certain space more quickly, but really books have always done that. That's why they have an appendix or an index, so you can shuttle back and forth or go to an encyclopedia or a dictionary. Now the Internet is much more vast; it provides music and pictures. So I am not really sure I would become involved in a project specifically designed for the Internet, but I certainly can't imagine not using it. It has become part of my life. It definitely is a valuable tool as a great way to conduct cursory research, to maintain contact with people, and to obtain bits of information that used to be impossible to get—like a video clip of the news when you missed it.

There had to have been a lot of research that went into this book. How did you approach it?

Writing is a process of discovery. I didn't start out researching the book and then writing the book. I began by working on a bunch of themes, and once I was deep into the book I might pursue a topic and then realize that I knew a little bit about that topic but not enough. That would force me to go to the library, or look for bibliographies on the Internet, and then I would be able to glean certain details that were pertinent. Or I would discover the theme was leading nowhere, and I had wandered too far afield. It was very organic in that sense. One of the characters would take me into a certain area; for example, the history of the Minotaur. Then suddenly I would find myself surrounded by books on that particular myth and about Knossos, and about representation of the relationship between the Minotaur and Menos throughout the ages. That would feed back into who the character of Johnny was, and how that related to the whole generational theme working in *House of Leaves*.

This book took you ten years to write. Did you know at the beginning the story was going to be about a house, or did you have different themes in mind and the house just gave you the place to talk about it?

I knew I wanted to write something big, but had no idea what it was going to be. I just felt it. So I plunged into that structure with a flashlight. I started sketching characters and then going through the characters' relationships and sketching particular themes. In 1988 or '89 I wrote the whole thing about the teacher discovering the children's drawings and how they were exactly the same. I didn't really know how that was all fitting in.

Then in 1993 I had this idea, possibly in a dream, of a house that was a quarter-inch bigger on the inside than the outside. I didn't know what the hell it was; perhaps it was a short story, a poem, or a footnote, and so I just shoved it aside. Then a few months later I realized that was what I had been looking for all along. That was the very structure that these characters inhabited, that these themes that I had been wrestling with could be construed in a physical way. From then on it was reassembling. In 1995 or '96 I tore the whole thing apart and sketched out longhand a 70-page treatment of the whole book and then I reintegrated those pieces one more time.

This being a first novel, and very unconventional at that, did you have any concerns that a publisher might not pick this up?

No, I was an absolute idiot. If I had been living in New York and knew more about the publishing world, I would not have written this book. But I was writing in a sort of bubble, while working as a plumber and at other jobs. I wanted to be true to the characters and true to my idea of how words could work on the page and my application of cinematic theory. Once it was finished, it became a lot more difficult to change, or it became difficult for a publisher to say, "Well, let's take all these one-sentence-per-page pages and combine them into ten pages," and I could say, "No, there's a reason that is the way it is." It is so much easier to change a concept or pitch, but when it was finished I could actually show how it worked. Once, I was thinking about writing a screenplay and what actors might be available or special effects to use. And my father said, "No, don't worry about the special effects. You imagine as much as you can what your story is about and the special effects people will figure out how to do it. And they will love you for raising the bar." Writers shouldn't worry about how their book might be accomplished with special effects; they should just imagine it fully, and the special effects people will figure out how to do it.

You actually spent three weeks doing the layout yourself at Pantheon's offices?

Yes. We were headed for a real train wreck. This book is very unusual in that it was purchased two years before it was published, so there were all sorts of issues to be contended with and leapt over. One of them was doing the layout for chapter nine. I had naively indicated in penciled notes how the various footnotes should be arranged on the page. I thought they would just take all of my notes and create that chapter, but my editor said, "I don't think we can do this." It might have gotten ugly. I knew this chapter wasn't finished and the pages weren't going to work as they were. So I grabbed my credit card, flew to New York and did it myself. And all the people at Pantheon were absolutely great; they found a computer and gave me the space. It was very much like a movie. I had spent nine months on all of the storyboarding and laying it out and then I had a three-week shooting schedule. I sat there 24-7 and got the thing done.

Do you have a daily writing schedule or regimen that you stick to?

I get up very early and I start writing. Initially I write four to five hours per day when I am just starting. Then once I am into the swing of things, it's anywhere from nine to twelve hours per day. The four- to five-hour schedule can last a month. I've only worked on a long project, so it's a little different. There will be breaks when I'll spend a few weeks researching, but when I get back to it I don't start with ten hours. It's like running—you have to work yourself into shape.

Johnny Truant says in the introduction, "No matter where you are, in a crowded restaurant or on some desolate street or even in the comforts of your own home, you'll watch yourself dismantle every assurance you ever lived by." Did writing the book have any effect on you in a way that he says it will?

Probably in a different way than you would expect. The story of Johnny is very complicated because he doesn't have footnotes, so in a weird way what initially seems to be the most puerile, sophomoric aspect of the book actually becomes far more complicated. Zampano actually indicates to you areas that are difficult, as well as possible ways of evaluating those areas, whereas Johnny is without footnote. There is a level of self-esteem that ironically is rising in Johnny the more he is willing to face the interior of himself, his own house. And not only is he looking at that closet but he is going into it. He is remembering it and what his past is about. He is moving away from the amazements of alcohol and drugs and starting to focus more and more on who he is and where his future lies. For me, I can't help but be a participant in that journey and feel that there is some kind of rebirth or regeneration taking place.

Any advice that you might offer to writers who are considering an unconventional or experimental form?

Pursue it only if you care little for rewards. The tricky thing is that we often imagine that if we do something unconventional, we will be rewarded for it. That is very dangerous because more than likely we will be punished for it. You can't do something unconventional for the sake of doing something unconventional. I don't really see *House of Leaves* as unconventional, but rather a book about how I read, the kind of dialogue that's in my head. You should be writing an honest reflection on how you perceive the world and how the world talks to you, and then I don't think you can go wrong.

For more information on electronic publishing, see the interview with Electronic Literature Organization founder Scott Rettberg on page 54, and the interview with Publishers Weekly *executive editor John Baker on page 44, both in the Electronic Publishing section.*

House of Leaves: "What a Novel Can Do that a Download Can't"

BY CYNTHIA LAUFENBERG

As editor for the Knopf Publishing Group, Edward Kastenmeier has worked on a diverse list of books, including *Orchid Fever* by Eric Hansen; the National Book Critics Circle Award-winning *Savage Art: A Biography of Jim Thompson*, by Robert Polito; and reprints of Bret Easton Ellis and Jonathan Lethem titles. But when friend and literary agent Warren Frazier asked him to take a look at a manuscript called *House of Leaves*, a first novel by writer Mark Danielewski, Kastenmeier discovered a book that was unlike anything he had ever worked on.

"Editors are always looking for something that's refreshing, something that doesn't appear to be like the other books they're reading," he says. *House of Leaves* captivated Kastenmeier as soon as he turned the first page. "The first thing you come across in the manuscript is the dedication, which says, 'This is not for you.' Which I thought was wonderful! I thought it was such an intriguing idea that it spurred me on to read the book. I sat down the first night and read half of it and finished it up the second night, and went to my boss and said, 'I think we really have to buy this book.' "

Danielewski's nontraditional twist on the classic horror story intrigued Kastenmeier with its unconventional approach and unique writing style. "I can't think of anybody in particular that Mark is like," Kastenmeier says. "People will say Nabokov because Nabokov wrote a lot of fiction that pushed the bounds of the genre in many different ways, so that's a very obvious parallel. It has some of the horror story elements that fans of Stephen King would like. Certainly I would imagine fans of Pynchon and DeLillo coming to a book like this and seeing something they like. But in terms of his writing style, I never really thought that Mark reminded me of anyone in particular."

Finding enthusiasm for *House of Leaves* among his coworkers wasn't a problem for Kastenmeier, as his fellow editors were captivated by the book as well. "Everybody read it, fell in love with it, and really got behind it," he says. "I was very impressed with how open everyone was to such a different and sort of challenging project." Categorizing *House of Leaves* was a little more difficult. "I think a book like this creates its own genre," Kastenmeier says. "It's as much experimental fiction as it is literary horror. It crosses so many genres. That's why I think this book defines itself; even though there are horror story elements, and it can appeal to fans of horror, it can also appeal to a lot of people who wouldn't ordinarily go to that genre because there's so much else going on."

Once *House of Leaves* was completed, finding an audience for the unique novel was the next step. "We all saw that this book could do very well for us and was a book that really deserved to reach a wide audience," Kastenmeier says. He saw *House of Leaves* as appealing mostly to the under-30 crowd, but also could see it reaching an even wider audience. "Anyone who likes a book that is nuanced and layered, that has a lot going on, can come to this book and absolutely adore it, love all the different things that Mark is experimenting with and the things he is trying to accomplish. I think it has a broad appeal, but it's always been my instinct that books of that

---

CYNTHIA LAUFENBERG *is a freelance writer living in Princeton, New Jersey. For more information on* House of Leaves, *see the interview with author Mark Z. Danielewski on page 78.*

nature appeal particularly to college students and those under 30."

With its metafictional elements, and extensive use of footnotes to propel the text, *House of Leaves* has been compared stylistically to Dave Eggers' bestselling memoir *A Heartbreaking Work of Staggering Genius*. And with similar novels finding their way onto bookstore shelves in the past year or two, Kastenmeier acknowledges that this could be indicative of a publishing trend. "It does beg the question, is there a mini-trend happening?" he says. "Periodically, there comes a time when authors and readers are interested in things that push the bounds of what a novel can be. And whether that interest is always there or whether there are moments at which that sort of interest peaks, it's hard to tell.

"This was a project long in the making, and we had reached a point where people were interested in things that were challenging the bounds of different artistic forms. I was selling *House of Leaves* when the *Blair Witch Project* was out and doing well. And here was a horror story that wasn't presented as a traditional film; it was delivered in a different way. Not to compare them too much, but it gave a context to people, to understand that there really is a market for this sort of literature."

The response to *House of Leaves* has been overwhelmingly positive from both readers and critics; *Newsweek* called it "daunting and brilliant . . . a sort of postmodern funhouse," and the *New York Times Book Review* found it to be "funny, moving, sexy, beautifully told." A cult following of sorts has even built up around the book, with signed copies of the original hardcover selling for $150 on eBay. "I could not be pleased more with the success the book has had," Kastenmeier says. "Mark put so much effort and so much energy and so much intelligence into this book. In this day and age when everyone's talking about e-books, *House of Leaves* takes the novel and tweaks it a little bit and shows you what a novel can do that a download can't. I'm pleased that people are taking up the challenge of trying to figure out all the things that Mark is trying to do, to try to figure out all the allusions and all the self-referential items."

The success of *House of Leaves* is heartening to Kastenmeier, confirming that an audience exists for novels that expand the boundaries of what fiction can be. "Periodically people talk about the death of the novel," he says. "Everybody's worried about the health of the novel, and my experience is that there's a lot of really wonderful fiction out there that's finding a significant audience—that there are plenty of people who are still reading novels and reading them closely and picking up things that offer challenges to a reader. It indicates that there's active intellectual life out there, and it makes me feel good about the state of people's relationship to literature today."

Creating Believable Fantasy Worlds

BY DAVID GERROLD

Even when you think there's nothing more to discover, keep asking.

Some fantasies are gentle, others are more detailed, and some are positively baroque. Some are rooted in history, and some are firmly grounded in thin air. But no matter how fantastic the initial premise, you are obligated to develop the world as rigorously as if you were describing an actual physical location. As with science fiction, the same strict principles of logic apply.

Suppose, for example, you want to tell a rousing adventure yarn that takes place in Atlantis, the fabled lost continent that sank beneath the sea. You are obligated to be consistent with historical fact, at least to the extent that the reader is familiar with it.

One of the first things you will have to decide is where Atlantis could be found on the ancient maps. Although all we know about Atlantis is a brief description in Plato's writings, quite a few books (of varying degrees of scholarship and research) have been published on the subject. Because your audience will be those who are interested in lost continents, you can expect them to have some familiarity with the various theories, both serious and crackpot. So you'll have to be consistent with what they know . . . or you'll have to come up with a new extrapolation even more convincing.

Many scholars think Atlantis might have existed somewhere in the Mediterranean, and they point to various sunken islands that seem to match Plato's description of the lost world. Others have said that the entire Mediterranean was once a dry valley—until the ocean broke through at Gibraltar and flooded the region. Whichever theory you subscribe to, you'll need to determine a location for your story, and you'll have to keep your descriptions consistent with what we know of ancient times.

For instance, the Sahara was once a vast savanna, a land of lush grass and forest, teeming with wildlife—until the Roman Empire stripped the land of trees and exported the animals to their arenas. They didn't see the damage they were doing because it was occurring over generations. They wanted the wood for their ships and their cities, so they took it without regard for the future—and they left behind a legacy of sand. The deserts of North Africa are man-made, but they would not have existed in the time of Atlantis, at least not on the scale we now know.

This is information that some of your readers might already know—it is also information that could surprise and delight those who have not heard this before. In either case, including it enriches the depth of your story's environment. The background of your story is more than just so much painted scenery. It's a setting that people interact with.

Try another:

Suppose you're telling a story in which your hero travels to the land of Faerie to bring King Oberon the gift of a virgin's tear wrapped in a white rose petal. For the purposes of your narrative, you want Oberon's realm to be mysterious and even a bit dangerous. You need it to be recognizably magical—you need it to be specifically *different*.

So you think for a bit. It seems to you that the most magical time of day is twilight, so you decide that the kingdom of Faerie is a twilight realm—neither day nor night. The landscape is

DAVID GERROLD *is an award-winning writer of science fiction novels, short stories and screenplays. This article was excerpted from* Worlds of Wonder © 2001 *by David Gerrold. Used with permission of Writer's Digest Books, a division of F&W Publications, Inc.*

dark and shadowy, but the sky still has light seeping through it. At the edge of your vision, there are glitters in the air—not fireflies; it's the giggling of pixies, sparkling as they dance away out of sight.

Oberon's palace is a high silken tent, seemingly made of glistening spider webs. The king and queen of Faerie sit on thrones of dandelion and rose. When they speak, you hear silver bells. The scent of lilac in moonlight comes to you.

The King of Faerie looks at you with wisdom as well as amusement. And no small amount of hostility. Foolish humans are cutting down the trees, destroying the homes of the forest folk. Foolish humans are destroying the magic in the world. Why should any human ask the mercy of the old people of the world, let alone a favor?

Yes, okay—you decide that works for your story. It's a magical mood, subtle yet dangerous, and consistent with the traditional portrayal of the land of Faerie. So now you know where your hero is going—but how does he get there?

Does he just walk into the forest? That's the traditional method, and nobody would fault you for writing it that way; but let's suppose you want to go beyond the traditional. You want to show how a human travels from the bright sunlight of the mortal realm to the twilight dreamscape of Faerie.

And here is where we begin to discover the underlying logic that your story requires. If you have decided that the land of Faerie is a dreamscape, then it cannot have a specific physical location. Nevertheless, it has to be accessible to your hero, and the method of access has to be believable within the logic of the story.

So perhaps you decide to create a bit of lore: *To reach the realm of Faerie, you must travel west until twilight.* Hmm. You think about that for a bit—what happens if you're traveling west and you don't want to end up in the land of Faerie? Stop before twilight? Maybe it would be better to make the rule: *To reach the realm of Faerie, travel west at twilight.* Or maybe: *West at twilight, when the moon is full.* That might work—especially if magic is strongest under the full moon.

Or maybe: *West until you get there.* If you're a wizard, three steps west should be sufficient. And if you have little or no belief in magic at all, you can travel west forever and never get there. So perhaps the magical beliefs and abilities of the traveler are part of the equation.

Notice that this is world-building just as rigorous as you would do for a science fiction novel. Whatever rules you set, you're going to be stuck with them until the last page of the story, so you have to be careful.

So . . . your hero travels west for three days. And as twilight creeps across the world at the end of the third day, the forest changes around him. The air turns still and the color seeps from the sky, and the sounds of the birds and the insects fade away, replaced by the distant sound of silvery bells. . . .

That works. That establishes that you reach the realm of Faerie when you're ready to step into it—and that creates it in the reader's mind as a dream reality, sideways to the land of flesh and bone.

But maybe that doesn't work for your story. . . .

Suppose you've written that the Lord of Blackmark Castle has taken grievous offense at a puckish prank. Having received no apology from Oberon, he declares war on the realm of the Old Folke. If that's your story, then Faerie has to exist as a specific physical location. Otherwise, his army could travel west forever, and never arrive at Faerie. Oberon wouldn't grant them access.

So to suit the needs of your story, you have to say that Faerie is a specific land, far to the west, shrouded in perpetual twilight.

—and the minute you make that decision, you've automatically created a whole landscape, one filled with every bit as much detail as the lunar civilization you created when your science fiction hero opened a window and looked out onto a domed-over crater with a forest growing in it; because if you've postulated a realm of magic and a realm of *not*-magic, then the reader wants to know: *What lies between the two realms?*

What's the dividing line? Is it a simple low wall that the hero steps over and he's there? On one side, spells and charms work; on the other side, they don't.

Or perhaps there's a wall of forbidding mountains, high and impenetrable; you can only enter the kingdom of magic across a narrow bridge over a deep chasm where the winds howl like ghosts.

Or maybe the transition is more gradual. The farther west the hero proceeds, the more magical the world becomes. Perhaps there are borderlands where neither magic nor mortality rule—and the hero must cross through the unformed terrain to reach the realm of Faerie. Now you must consider, *what will you find in the borderlands? What will the borderlands look like? Who lives there?* Perhaps the land itself is twisted and unreal, with the scenery shifting and changing as the winds of magic blow. Perhaps the things that live there are half-breeds of mortal and magic. They cannot survive too long in either realm.

Notice again, whatever you build, there must be an underlying logic to your construction. Some of this you will invent consciously to fit the needs of your story, and some of it will fall into place because it just *feels* right. (And when things fall into place that way, pat yourself on the back—you're in the flow.)

Stories are about journeys—not always a voyage through a physical landscape, of course, but certainly a trek through the emotional realms of life. Traveling through the terrain, physical or emotional, is the best way to demonstrate how it works. The more different aspects you portray, the more interesting it becomes.

But let's continue on a bit longer. Let's step into one of the bear traps. . . .

If there is a land to the west that is always twilight, what does this suggest about the cosmology of this world? Are we on a planet? Or are we on an endless plain? If we're on a planet, then the only way to have a realm of perpetual twilight is for the planet to have one face always turned toward the sun—and that means that Blackmark Castle is probably a molten puddle anyway. And on the other side, beyond the realm of Faerie twilight, is a realm of perpetual ice. A Nordic version of Hell perhaps?

So how do you manage this? The mortal land has a normal progression of days and nights, and a normal sky of stars; but in the land of Faerie, there is no sun or moon—halfway between night and day, the horizons glow and the sky seeps with light; in the forests and meadows, shadows spread veils of mystery. Some readers are going to wonder how you arranged the physics of this. How can an earthlike world have a habitable domain of perpetual twilight?

The easy way to resolve this is to decide that the laws of reality are different in the realm of magic—the land of Faerie is turned perpendicular to the rest of the universe, and time flows sideways. And most readers will accept that bit of double-talk as a way of lubricating the friction between the mortal world and the magic one. Especially if you're telling a good story.

Fantasy is like a soufflé. It's delicate. You have to treat it with respect. Yes, you can create things that violate the known laws of physics, but when you do, you have to balance them gently atop what the reader already knows about reality *and* fantasy. Look long and hard at what you want to build. If you write what you're willing to believe, it's likely that the audience will believe as well.

Here's an example:

Erindell moaned in distress. The entire forest roiled with disturbance. The youngtrees swayed in anguish; the bigtrees sobbed, pumping the air up through their columnar throats. The notes were so deep they were felt rather than heard—a pressure in the air that gave the travelers queasy feelings in their bellies. Despite their deafness, the horses stirred uneasily, so much that finally the riders dismounted and blindfolded the steeds to walk them in safety. All around, the rustling of leaves and branches sounded like the howling of a storm, but the air beneath remained still—as if they moved within a bubble of calm.

"What does it mean?" Vellar asked the tree-girl.

She couldn't answer. She was shaking badly, as badly as the forest. She held out a hand to touch the nearest bigtree, then recoiled as if burned. Her face showed suffering, she could barely control herself. "I don't know. Something awful has happened—might still be happening." Overcome, she collapsed sobbing to the ground.

"Say it!" Vellar commanded sharply—and regretted it instantly. The tone of his voice only made the girl howl like the trees. But he was a prince, he was used to giving orders, and the strange ways of the tree people frustrated and annoyed him. An idea came to him; he pulled off his heavy cloak and wrapped it around the girl, as if it would shield her somewhat. "Does this help?" he asked.

She nodded and managed to gasp. "Thank you."

"Is it a battle?" he asked. She shook her head. Vellar tried to think what might have panicked the trees. "Is it a forest fire?" he asked. "Or swarms of locusts?"

"Worse! Much worse! I've never felt such madness. The smell of dreadful death is in the wind—somewhere trees are dying violently. And Erindell is screaming in sympathy as well as fear." She looked as if she wanted to bolt herself. "We have to get away from here—" she tried to insist.

Vellar grabbed her arm. "Stay with us," he commanded.

Something in the distance crashed. All the travelers turned as one—just in time to see one of the biggest of the bigtrees come ripping downward, branches tearing as it toppled, all the trees around it screaming. The writhing of the forest became a wild frenzy.

"They're dying!" shrieked the girl. "They're uprooting themselves in panic! It's only going to get worse—"

"We can't go on this way!" shouted the commander of the guard. He pointed. "We have to go back."

Prince Vellar shook his head. He raised his voice to be heard. "No. We will not go back to the gray lands. We lost too many men and horses getting this far. We'll push on to the high country. If we can get above the tree line, where it's calmer, the Mage can send his soul aloft and search the horizons."

"We'll never make it to the high country—" the commander said.

Vellar turned back to the girl. She was struggling in his grasp. "Where is it safe?" he demanded. "Where can we go?"

The girl sank to her knees and dug her fingers into the soft dirt, as if she were taking root—as if she were searching for something. "Deep," she gasped. "As deep as we can get—" She opened her eyes as if she were looking into the next life—a strange expression crossed her face. Her eyes widened, almost bulging out of her skull, but she didn't seem in pain. She crooned low in her throat, as if singing to a distant ear.

Abruptly, she pulled her hands free of the dirt and pointed. "This way!"

Vellar and the others followed her—the Mage, in his hooded cloak and with his mask still shielding his face, the six remaining soldiers in their leather breastplates, the two frightened servants, and the skinny page. Around them, the wailing of the trees had reached deafening proportions. Vellar realized—*too late*—that the girl was leading them straight into the screaming heart of the forest's panic.

Suddenly, ahead—a circle of dead and dying trees—and in the center, a low mound punctuated with pig-sized openings. The tree-girl flattened herself and began crawling forward. "This way, quickly—" She glanced back. "Get down! All of you, get down and crawl!"

"No!" cried Vellar.

"Would you rather die?"

"We can't leave the horses!"

"You have to! They're the price I paid for your lives! Now follow me before it's too late—" She began crawling down into the nearest hole. The Mage was close behind her, gathering his cloak as he dropped to his knees.

"Everyone follow them—" Vellar ordered.

The commander shook his head. "Not me. Not my troops—"

"I order you—"

"No longer!" the captain of the guard cried angrily. "Not one step further. No more lives lost for this madness!"

"Then to hell with you!" said Vellar. He looked to the servants and the page. "And what about you three? Where are your loyalties?" The two servants backed away, eyes wide with fear, but the boy scrambled after the Mage.

Vellar glared angrily at the disloyal soldiers, glanced upward at the reddening sky, then reluctantly dropped to the ground and scrambled into the nest after the page.

The darkness closed in around him. His eyesight disappeared, leaving him with a confusing welter of sounds and smells and uncomfortable feelings. What was that coldness he touched? What was that distant trilling? And what was that sickening odor? The nest smelled bitter and rank.

He crawled down the cramped tunnel with a deepening feeling of despair. How had he ended up here? Had his stupid royal pride finally brought him to disaster? He thrust the thought away. The girl had been right so far. If he'd listened to her sooner, the lives of twelve good men might not have been lost to the sand beasts of the gray lands.

Vellar tumbled out into a cramped chamber, barely larger than a closet. The girl, the Mage, and the boy were arrayed closely around the edges. The Mage had produced a soft light, barely enough to see by. He held a gloved finger to the carved lips of his mask. *Make no sound.*

From above, there came the noise of screams. Men and horses alike—*the price paid for their lives.*

Vellar listened in paralyzed horror. Even after the last scream had stopped, he was sure he could still hear the sounds of death. Perhaps it wasn't death he was hearing, but hideous hunger being sated.

The girl touched his arm; she pointed to a tunnel in the floor of the chamber. "We must go down," she whispered. "The queen wants to meet you. She has never met a *man* before."

Vellar hesitated.

"You will be safe," the girl said. "The queen's daughters are as afraid of us as we are of them. They will not approach. But the queen wants to meet you. It is *not* a request," she added, unsubtly.

Vellar wanted nothing more than to head back up the way he'd come, away from this cramped confining space, away from this terrible encroaching darkness and the dreadful smell of this nest—

Notice, in this fragment of an unpublished work, there's a great deal of exposition presented. It's presented while the characters are on the move, but at the end of the section, you know that the trees are sentient enough to have emotion, emotional enough to be driven mad by the smells of other trees dying. The humans are only passing through; they've never been here before—this is a strange and terrifying place to them.

From the narrative, you know that the Mage's spirit can leave his body and go out searching, but his power appears to have limits. The girl has some kind of relationship with the forest, enough so that she can be its voice for the moment. And finally, even though it's never clearly said, there's no question that the survivors of this scene are climbing into the burrow of a colony of giant insects—termites or ants—and the queen of this colony is not only sentient, but a cruel bargainer indeed. Before we've even met her, she's collected her bloody price. Also, Vellar is of royal blood, but unused to command. He doesn't seem to deal well with anyone. He doesn't even know the girl's name yet. He has not yet matured as a leader. Oh, and by the way, the girl knows more than she's saying.

None of this is explained; *it's all shown through Vellar's eyes*. The reader identifies with Vellar, because the narrative is suffused with his thoughts and feelings—no one else's.

Overall, you should get a sense that this is a consistent and believable ecology, because everything connects to everything else. Giant insects have giant appetites; they kill trees to build their burrows—ahh, they're termites. And something that the insects are doing is driving the forest mad with fear. We don't know what, but we know that the insect burrow is at the heart of the panic. Something is happening within. The same telepathy which allows the girl to understand the moaning of the trees also allows her to mind-speak with the insects. *And the queen wants to meet Vellar!*

If the author succeeds in fitting the pieces together, you won't question them. If the pieces don't fit, you won't believe them. It really is that simple.

Science Fiction/Fantasy & Horror Markets Appearing in This Book

Below is a list of science fiction/fantasy & horror markets appearing in this edition of *Novel & Short Story Writer's Market*. To find page numbers of particular markets, go first to the General Index. Then turn to the pages those listings appear on for complete information, including who to contact and how to submit your science fiction/fantasy & horror manuscript.

Magazines (Fantasy)

Aberrations
About Such Things
Advocate, PKA's Publication
Affable Neighbor
Alembic
Amazing Stories
Amelia
Analecta
Anotherealm
Anthology
Armchair Aesthete, The
Art Times
Art:Mag
Asimov's Science Fiction
Aura Literary Arts Review
Aurealis
Barbaric Yawp
Beneath the Surface
Blue Skunk Companion, The
Cafe Irreal, The
Capers Aweigh
Cenotaph
Century
Climbing Art, The
Companion in Zeor, A
Contact Advertising
Corona
Cotworld Creative Magazine
CZ's Magazine
Dagger of the Mind
Dargonzine
Dark Matter Chronicles
Deep Outside SFFH
Dialogue
Dream International/Quarterly
Dreams & Visions
Eidolon
Electric Wine
Enigma
Eureka Literary Magazine
Evansville Review
Flesh & Blood
Fugue
Gotta Write Network Litmag
Grasslands Review
Green's Magazine
Griffin, The
Happy
Hawaii Pacific Review
Heaven Bone
Iksperament

In Posse Review
Indigenous Fiction
Interbang
Irreantum
Jackhammer E-Zine
Karitos Review, The
Lady Churchill's Rosebud Wristlet
Leading Edge, The
Leapings Literary Magazine
Lite
Literal Latté
Literary Moments
Long Shot
Lynx Eye
MacGuffin, The
Magazine of Fantasy & Science Fiction
Margin
Matriarch's Way: Journal of Female Supremacy
Merlyn's Pen
Minas Tirith Evening-Star
Missing Fez, The
Mississippi Review
Mobius
Monkeyplanet
Musing Place, The
Northwoods Journal
Oak, The
Of Unicorns and Space Stations
Office Number One
On Spec
Orphic Chronicle, The
Outer Darkness
Outer Rim—The Zine, The
Palo Alto Review
Pegasus Online
Peninsular
Penny Dreadful
Playboy Magazine
Plot Line Foyer
Poetry Forum Short Stories
Portland Review
Poskisnolt Press
Primavera
Prisoners of the Night
Psychic Radio, The
Pulp Eternity Online
Queen's Quarterly
QWF (Quality Women's Fiction)
Rabbit Hole Press, The
Ralph's Review
Rejected Quarterly, The
Rockford Review, The
Samsara

Scifi.com
Seeking the Muse
Shades of December
Short Story Writers Showcase
Shyflower's Garden
Skylark
Snake Nation Review
Songs of Innocence
Southern Humanities Review
SPSM&H
Space and Time
State of Unbeing
Studentswrite.com
Talebones
Tampa Review
Threshold, The
Thresholds Quarterly
Twilight Showcase
Urban Spaghetti
Urbanite, The
Visions & Voices
Weber Studies
Weird Tales
Windhover
Yellow Silk
Yellow Sticky Notes

Magazines (Science Fiction)

Aberrations
About Such Things
Absolute Magnitude
Advocate, PKA's Publication
Affable Neighbor
Alembic
Alien Zoo
Amazing Stories
Amelia
Analecta
Anotherealm
Anthology
Armchair Aesthete, The
Art Times
Artemis Magazine
Art:Mag
Asimov's Science Fiction
Aura Literary Arts Review
Aurealis
Barbaric Yawp
BBR Magazine
BEEF
Bear Essential Deluxe, The
Beginners
Beneath The Surface
Black Petals
Blue Skunk Companion, The
Boys' Life
Brobdingnagian Times, The
Burning Sky
Cafe Irreal, The
Callaloo
Capers Aweigh
Cenotaph
Century
Chat
Chrysalis Reader
Circle Magazine, The
Climbing Art, The
Cochran's Corner
Companion in Zeor, A
Cotworld Creative Magazine

Cozy Detective, The
Dagger of the Mind
Dark Matter Chronicles
Deep Outside SFFH
Dialogue
Downstate Story
Dream International/Quarterly
Dreams & Visions
Eidolon
Electric Wine
Eureka Literary Magazine
Evansville Review
First Class
Fugue
Futures Magazine
Gotta Write Network Litmag
Grasslands Review
Green's Magazine
Griffin, The
Grit
Happy
Hawaii Pacific Review
Home Planet News
Hurricane Alice
Iconoclast, The
In Posse Review
Indigenous Fiction
Interbang
Intertext
Irreantum
Jackhammer E-Zine
Karitos Review, The
Lady Churchill's Rosebud Wristlet
LC-39
Leading Edge, The
Leapings Literary Magazine
Left Curve
Lite
Literal Latté
Literary Moments
Long Shot
Lynx Eye
MacGuffin, The
Magazine of Fantasy & Science Fiction
Margin
Matriarch's Way: Journal of Female Supremacy
Mediphors
Mediphors
Medusa's Hairdo Magazine
Merlyn's Pen
Mindsparks
Missing Fez, The
MJ's Walkabout
Mobius
Monkeyplanet
Murderous Intent
Musing Place, The
Nightfire
Nimrod
Northwoods Journal
Nova Science Fiction Magazine
Of Unicorns and Space Stations
On Spec
Orphic Chronicle, The
Outer Darkness
Outer Rim—The Zine, The
Pacific Coast Journal
Palo Alto Review
Paumanok Review, The
Pegasus Online

Peninsular
Playboy Magazine
Plot Line Foyer
Poetry Forum Short Stories
Portland Review
Primavera
Prisoners of the Night
Psychic Radio, The
Pulp Eternity Online
Queen's Quarterly
QWF (Quality Women's Fiction)
Rabbit Hole Press, The
Rain Crow
Ralph's Review
Rejected Quarterly, The
Rockford Review, The
Rosebud™
Samsara
Scifi.com
Seeking the Muse
Shades of December
Short Story Writers Showcase
Shyflower's Garden
Silver Web, The
Skidrow Penthouse
Skylark
Snake Nation Review
SPSM&H
Space and Time
Spindrift
State of Unbeing
Struggle
Studentswrite.com
Talebones
Terra Incognita
Thema
3 A.M. Magazine
Threshold, The
Thresholds Quarterly
12-Gauge.com
Urban Spaghetti
Vincent Brothers Review, The
Visions & Voices
Weber Studies
Yellow Silk
Yellow Sticky Notes
Zopilote

Magazines (Horror)

Aberrations
Affable Neighbor
Affair of the Mind
Aguilar Expression, The
Alembic
Alien Zoo
Amazing Stories
Analecta
Anotherealm
Armchair Aesthete, The
Art:Mag
Aura Literary Arts Review
Aurealis
Barbaric Yawp
Beneath The Surface
Bibliophilos
Black Petals
Blue Skunk Companion, The
Brobdingnagian Times, The
Burning Sky
Carpe Noctem

Century
Children, Churches and Daddies Magazine
Cochran's Corner
Cotworld Creative Magazine
Dagger of the Mind
Dark Matter Chronicles
Deep Outside SFFH
Downstate Story
Dream International/Quarterly
Edge, Tales of Suspense, The
Electric Wine
Enigma
Evansville Review
Eyes
Flesh & Blood
Fugue
Futures Magazine
Grasslands Review
Griffin, The
Grue Magazine
Happy
Hunted News, The
In Posse Review
Indigenous Fiction
Interbang
Irreantum
Jackhammer E-Zine
Lite
Lynx Eye
Margin
Matriarch's Way: Journal of Female Supremacy
Merlyn's Pen
Missing Fez, The
Mobius
Monkeyplanet
Musing Place, The
New Writing
Night Terrors
Office Number One
Orphic Chronicle, The
Outer Darkness
Outer Rim—The Zine, The
Paumanok Review, The
Peninsular
Penny Dreadful
Peralta Press, The
Playboy Magazine
Psychic Radio, The
Pulp Eternity Online
QWF (Quality Women's Fiction)
Ralph's Review
Raskolnikov's Cellar and The Lamplight
Samsara
Seeking the Muse
Shyflower's Garden
Silver Web, The
Snake Nation Review
SPSM&H
Space and Time
State of Unbeing
Strand Magazine, The
3 A.M. Magazine
Threshold, The
Twilight Showcase
Urban Spaghetti
Urbanite, The
Visions & Voices
Weird Tales
Yellow Sticky Notes

Book Publishers (Fantasy)

Ace Science Fiction
Adventure Book Publishers
Affable Neighbor
Ageless Press
Alexandria Digital Literature
Artemis Press
Authors Online Ltd.
Baen Books
Bantam Books
Bantam Dell Publishing Group, The
Berkley Publishing Group, The
Circlet Press
Dan River Press
Daw Books, Inc.
Del Rey Books
Delacorte Press
Dell
Dial Press, The
DiskUs Publishing
First Amendment Press International Company
Forge Books
Fort Ross Inc.
Fountainhead Productions, Inc.
Geringer Books, Laura
Hawk Publishing Group
Hollow Earth Publishing
ImaJinn Books
Island
LTD Books
Majestic Books
New American Library
Philomel Books
Pocket Books
Pride and Imprints
Random House, Inc.
RavenHaus Publishing
Regency Press
ROC
Spectra Books
St. Martin's Press
Tor Books
TSR, Inc.
Ultramarine Publishing Co., Inc.
Warner Aspect
Warner Books
Write Way Publishing
W.W. Publications

Book Publishers (Science Fiction)

Ace Science Fiction
Adventure Book Publishers
Affable Neighbor
Ageless Press
Alexandria Digital Literature
Authors Online Ltd.
Avon Books
Baen Books
Bancroft Press
Bantam Books
Bantam Dell Publishing Group, The
Berkley Publishing Group, The
Black Heron Press
Carroll & Graf Publishers, Inc.
Circlet Press
Dan River Press
Daw Books, Inc.
Del Rey Books

Delacorte Press
Dell
Dial Press, The
DiskUs Publishing
FC2
Feminist Press at the City University of New York, The
First Amendment Press International Company
Forge Books
Fort Ross Inc.
Fountainhead Productions, Inc.
Gryphon Books
Hawk Publishing Group
ImaJinn Books
Island
LTD Books
Majestic Books
Midknight Club, The
Morrow, William
New American Library
Pig Iron Press
Pipers' Ash Ltd.
Pride and Imprints
RavenHaus Publishing
ROC
Salvo Press
Signal Crest
Soft Skull Press Inc.
Spectra Books
St. Martin's Press
Tor Books
TSR, Inc.
Ultramarine Publishing Co., Inc.
Warner Aspect
Warner Books
Wesleyan University Press
Write Way Publishing
Writers Direct
W.W. Publications

Book Publishers (Horror)

Adventure Book Publishers
Alexandria Digital Literature
Authors Online Ltd.
Bancroft Press
Beggar's Press
Dan River Press
Darktales Publications
Design Image Group Inc., The
DiskUs Publishing
Enigmatic Press
First Amendment Press International Company
Forge Books
Fountainhead Productions, Inc.
Hawk Publishing Group
ImaJinn Books
Leisure Books
LTD Books
Midknight Club, The
Morrow, William
New American Library
Palari Publishing
Pocket Books
Random House, Inc.
RavenHaus Publishing
ROC
Scherf Books
St. Martin's Press
Tor Books
Write Way Publishing

Resources for Science Fiction/ Fantasy & Horror Writers

Below is a list of invaluable resources specifically for science fiction and fantasy writers. For more information on the magazines and organizations listed below, check the General Index and the Publications of Interest and Organizations sections of this book. To order any of the Writer's Digest Books titles or to get a consumer book catalog, call 1-800-289-0963. You may also order Writer's Digest Books selections through www.writersdigest.com, Amazon.com or www.barnesandnoble.com.

MAGAZINES:
- *Locus*, P.O. Box 13305, Oakland CA 94661
- *Science Fiction Chronicle*, P.O. Box 022730, Brooklyn NY 11202-0056. (718)643-9011. Fax: (718)522-3308. E-mail: sf_chronicle@compuserve.com
- *Writer's Digest*, 1507 Dana Ave., Cincinnati OH 45207

BOOKS:
Science Fiction Writing series (Writer's Digest Books)
- *Aliens and Alien Societies: A Writer's Guide to Creating Extraterrestrial Life-forms*
- *Space Travel: A Writer's Guide to the Science of Interplanetary and Interstellar Travel*
- *Time Travel: A Writer's Guide to the Real Science of Plausible Time Travel*
- *World-Building: A Writer's Guide to Constructing Star Systems and Life-supporting Planets*

Other Writer's Digest books for science fiction & fantasy writers:
- *The Craft of Writing Science Fiction That Sells*
- *How to Write Science Fiction and Fantasy*
- *How to Write Tales of Horror, Fantasy & Science Fiction*
- *Science Fiction and Fantasy Writer's Sourcebook, 2nd Edition*
- *The Writer's Complete Fantasy Reference*
- *The Writer's Guide to Creating a Science Fiction Universe*

ORGANIZATIONS & ONLINE:
- Science Fiction & Fantasy Writers of America, Inc., P.O. Box 171, Unity ME 04988-0171. E-mail: execdir@sfwa.org. Website: www.sfwa.org/
- Con-Tour: www.con-tour.com (See complete listing in the Websites of Interest section of this book.)
- Books and Writing Online: www.interzone.com/Books/books.html

Ten Secrets of Successful Readings

BY I.J. SCHECTER

I.J. Schecter

"Truman Capote gave the best reading I ever attended. You could only see the upper half of this little old man's head as he read strictly from his very early stuff, the nice lyrical things about being reared by crazy old ladies in the Deep South. At the end of every piece, he would stride out from behind the podium, raise his book over his head, and give it one good shake, as if to say, 'This is the only thing that matters.'"

—Tom Bradley
Author of Killing Bryce

After numerous drafts and endless revisions, you complete a great manuscript. You compose an intriguing cover letter and practice your signature five times before signing it. You find the right publisher to approach. You hold your manuscript at the mouth of the mailbox for a full minute while offering a prayer to the Gods of Good Timing and Favorable Editors. Two months later you receive a letter that makes your heart stop. Someone wants to publish your book!

That blissful moment is now past and it's time to focus on a new challenge—delivering your work powerfully in a live setting. Here are ten tips to help you read your work effectively and leave your readers wanting more.

1. Determine what to read and how to read it

Recognize that your favorite story or excerpt may not lend itself to being read aloud. It may be too long or too short. It may be dialogue-heavy and difficult to follow. Its structure may be too complex.

Choose stories or excerpts with simple language, minimal dialogue (or dialogue representing few characters), clear narrative arcs (avoid tense-shifting and flashbacks) and humor.

Having chosen the story/excerpt you think is most effective, rehearse it as exhaustively as you would revise one of your manuscripts. Know where you want to pause, which words you want to emphasize. Note potential tongue-tiers, especially those that might cause embarrassment. (My agent, while promoting me at a literary festival, told a customer that my book had brought me a lot of sex. She had meant to say success. I don't believe the customer heard the corrections, as he'd rushed off—to start writing a book, no doubt).

Another way to determine how your piece will sound to an audience is to have someone else read it aloud to you. When my wife reads me a story I'm considering, it invariably teaches me new things about the way the story moves and where its strengths lie. Most material, by the time we get to reading it aloud to ourselves, has become too familiar for us to be objective about it.

2. Don't worry about "looking" like a writer

I am constantly surprised at how many writers spend their time and energy trying to achieve a look that suggests "authorness." Preparing for a reading is like preparing for a date. In wanting

I.J. SCHECTER *is a freelance writer of fiction and essays. His latest book is titled* The Bottom of the Mug, *a collection of short stories.*

to look just right, you'll be tempted to consider several different outfits, none of which will be satisfactory. This one is too stuffy. The next too casual. This one sends the wrong message.

Like a date, in coming to see you read, the audience already has declared its interest in you and probably cares little what you wear, provided you're tidy.

People have recommended I wear a smoking jacket and keep a pipe between my lips. I've been told to grow my hair long to look older. Someone even suggested I obtain spectacles with fake lenses so audiences would buy me. You don't have to create a persona to give an effective reading. Though audiences may hold you in esteem because you are published, they are under no illusions that you are something other than a real person. You needn't waste your energy worrying about looking the part. By virtue of the book with your name on it, you *are* the part.

3. Learn to conquer nerves

Okay, you've made all the right preparations and rehearsed the chosen story or section a dozen times. You're wearing your lucky underwear and carrying a picture of Ernest Hemingway in your wallet for support. Your script is marked with points of intonation. The audience shifts anxiously as a voice announces your name. It's showtime.

Public speaking comfortably outranks death as people's number one fear. You're not in the minority if you suffer sweaty palms, churning stomach, brain-lock and a host of other symptoms before mounting the platform. (In the hours leading up to a reading, I have the strange habit of yawning compulsively.) Here are some techniques to keep palms dry and stomachs calm (or, in my case, yawning, to a minimum):

• Try not to think about the size of the crowd. Many readers keep a running mental count of the number of people in the audience until it comes time to take the stage. Since no writer is ever satisfied with the size of a crowd, this can only disappoint you.

• Ignore self-doubt. Before taking the stage, you might hear a voice inside your head telling you your work isn't interesting, you've got nothing new to say, your style is overwrought, your sentences are runaway trains or your characters don't even have two dimensions. Since the voice is your own, you have every right to ignore it. And ignore it you must. You've worked hard to get to this point, and you're going to make the most of it.

• Distract yourself until it's time to read. I always try to engage people in conversation until I'm ready to go on. All I need to do with one particular friend is declare someone other than Willie Mays the greatest centerfielder of all time, and I've got an argument on my hands that can last all evening. Also, using this time to get to know your audience is a great way to show them the "real" you before the "celebrity" you takes the stage.

• Rehearse, rehearse, rehearse. Nothing helps conquer nerves like the feeling of being prepared.

4. The Sammy Davis, Jr. principle

Take the advice of Sammy Davis, Jr., who had only one rule to guide every performance he gave: No matter how many people are in the audience, give them the show of their lives. Consecutive audiences of three, two and 50 people should be viewed simply as three separate audiences who collectively total 55 potential readers. Understand that almost every author, no matter how renowned, has had to deal with tiny crowds and paper-thin publicity campaigns. Understand also that most of those enjoying success today have moved beyond their early frustrations by reaching readers a handful at a time, a couple at a time or one at a time.

One of my favorite anecdotes comes from author Rodger Kamenetz: "A well-known writer, a novelist friend of mine, was on tour with his book, and when he came to one city, only three people showed up at the bookstore. He nonetheless put his heart into the reading and tried to make everyone comfortable. After the reading, a member of the audience introduced himself. He turned out to be a local reporter; more importantly, he turned out to be a member of that year's Pulitzer Prize committee in fiction. And that year, my friend won the Pulitzer Prize in fiction. So we should never judge an audience by its size."

5. Introductions—theirs and yours

Find out who will be introducing you, then give that person a sheet with three or four points you'd like them to include—possibly a specific line from a review, an emphasis on your affiliation with the city or a distinguishing feature of your book. Politely remind the person to inform the audience whether there will be a question-and-answer period following the reading, as well as where you'll be signing copies and for how long.

Tell the audience when and how the story came to you, without sounding impressed by yourself. Use this time to be candid, genuine and funny. If your story about a teenage misfit has autobiographical roots, remark about your keen familiarity with the subject. In introducing your book about a baseball team, you might tell the crowd that writing it was the best alternative to never being able to hit a curveball.

One note of caution: Starting with a good joke can work wonders, but remember, you're not a stand-up comedian. Don't start asking if there are birthdays or out-of-towners in the crowd.

6. Be *DYNAMIC*

This doesn't mean you should do your best Jack Nicholson impression or holler, "Is everyone feeling good out there? I said, is everyone feeling GOOD?" You're an author, not a rock star. It is important, however, in the space you're given to convey energy and enthusiasm.

During the reading itself, modulate your voice more than you think you need to. Use the story as your guideline; employ dramatic pauses where appropriate and don't leave space where the story doesn't.

In order to envision the manner in which you are likely to read, think about how you conduct yourself normally. If you are a person whose natural speech is highly dynamic, your delivery might not need much fine-tuning. However, if you are soft-spoken and mild, you may require a bigger self-charge in order to read with impact.

Practice dynamic speech in the car, in the shower and in other private moments. You don't have to practice during normal conversation (you might scare off your friends), but do practice this rather than just imagining it. Then when it comes time for you to turn it on in front of an audience, it will feel natural.

Have one of your readings videotaped. Ask if you can set up a camera behind the audience. By viewing a tape of yourself, you'll be able to detect distracting or nervous movements—things like rocking back and forth or constantly moving the fingers of your free hand. Using this method, I found that when I read directly from my book without a microphone, I have a habit of alternately sliding my free hand in and out of my pocket.

7. Make eye contact

First, it is most important to make direct, rather than diffuse eye contact. Concentrating on your own effectiveness can cause you to forget about your audience and turn your gaze generally outward and "over" them, instead of meeting the eyes of individual audience members. Smiles, coupled with direct gazes, are infinitely more engaging to an audience than an exceedingly serious, remote manner. People will feel a deeper connection to you if you share the writing experience with them as much as possible, which means reading not to the general space in front of you but to the individuals within that space.

Second, be aware of the opposite behavior. The pressure to make direct eye contact can result in unintentionally "locking in" on only two or three people-those who happen to fall naturally within your line of sight or people you know and feel comfortable with. Focusing on a few audience members has the effect of alienating the rest. Try to distribute direct gazes evenly across your audience from the moment you begin speaking until the last word.

8. Avoid the panic button

Once you take your place in front of the audience, don't change your game plan. Don't switch stories as you're being announced because you think a certain line of dialogue suddenly doesn't ring true.

Even more important, don't start to fret if the audience doesn't laugh uproariously where you first think they should. It doesn't mean they don't like the story. After all, those in the crowd are as nervous to "get" the story as you are for them to like it. There will always be laughs at unexpected moments and silence where you expect laughter. Also, don't worry if the seats aren't filled; remember that people often will listen from a safe distance rather than committing themselves to a highly visible spot.

9. Answering questions

Develop interesting answers to the most common questions asked of writers so that you're not caught giving dull or predictable responses. When a customer asks how long you've been writing, say something more original than "as long as I can remember" (as if the doctor dropped his pen during your delivery, then you picked it up and wouldn't give it back). Following are five of the questions most frequently asked of writers. Take some time to think about how you might answer each one in an interesting, honest way.

What's this book about?
Where did you get the idea for this book?
What are you working on now?
How long have you been writing?
Where do you get your ideas?

The first question, "What's this book about?", is the most deceptively challenging. Pretend you are a student assigned to write a report on your own book, then study it until you can describe it in one sentence. Just as Hollywood pitchmen have only 30 seconds to sell a screenplay, you have only one chance to engage a potential reader. Don't quit until your description is concise and compelling. Practice with other books. What is *Catcher in the Rye* about, in two sentences or less? *Sons and Lovers? The Shining?*

Practice using concrete, active descriptions rather than loose, bland ones. Though you may see your book as "a study of man's eternal struggle against his own contradictions," such a description doesn't provide much information to a customer. Explaining it in simpler, livelier terms is much more effective: "It's about a Los Angeles policeman who also happens to be a cocaine trafficker."

One other note about answering questions: Don't try to be something you're not. Authors often delude themselves into thinking every answer they give must be a combination of brilliant rhetoric, profound insight, zinging wit and unfathomable depth. All that this delusion is good for is to cause perplexing answers in response to simple questions. Your wit will emerge in the course of natural dialogue. Don't force it.

10. Personalize your inscriptions

When signing copies of your books, try to individualize every inscription you can. Talk to the customer for a few moments before signing the book in order to gain information you can refer to in the inscription. If you are faced with a long line of customers, coming up with clever inscriptions will prove a greater challenge. At a minimum, make every inscription distinct by asking customers' names and addressing the book personally to them.

Always have three to five generic inscriptions prepared in case you are at a complete loss. Examples of generic inscriptions include "With best wishes," "With appreciation" and "Enjoy!", any of which are still better than your name on its own. Be conscious never to use the same generic inscription consecutively, especially with those in groups. Two different generic inscriptions are still two different inscriptions, and even the smallest effort to individualize copies will strengthen your connection to readers.

Many writers employ the five-second rule when signing. That is, if you can't think of something personal, witty or both in five seconds, write something generic. It's better than trying to buy time with idle chatter or by simply writing something non-generic which, nonetheless, is neither personal nor witty. Most important, always confirm the spelling of customers' names if they aren't obvious.

Now you're armed and ready. Knock 'em dead!

Writing On Writing: Boost Your Income with Book Reviews

BY BRAD VICE

Part French, part English, part Canadian; educated at Yale, then Cambridge, Claire Messud is a true American success story with an international flair. Messud's first novel, *When the World Was Steady*, was nominated for the PEN/Faulkner award, and her new novel *The Last Life* has met with equally good reviews. But long before Messud could make a living with her fiction, the author made ends meet as a freelance book reviewer, a habit she can't quite give up even though the dual role of author and critic is complicated at best.

Photo by Miriam Berkley

Claire Messud

Messud's reviews have frequently appeared in *The New York Times Book Review*, *The Washington Post*, *Newsday*, and *The Times of London*. Here she discusses how combining fiction writing with reviewing can pay off in more ways than one.

You started your career as a reviewer in England. How did you break into the business?

I worked in London as a journalist for *The Guardian* for two and a half years, and then I worked freelance for two and a half more. I wanted to be a novelist, and writing reviews allowed me to stay in touch with contemporary American fiction. I also liked reviewing because you know what you are getting into. Once I wrote an article on Irish immigrants in England, and I spent a month hanging out in youth hostels and the bingo parlors where the old Irish ladies spend time. I was paid two hundred pounds, about $300. In terms of time, book reviewing is comparatively manageable. But I stayed away from authors who already had seven or eight books published, because of the background research. Mostly I would sit down with a Knopf or Random House catalog and pick out new writers with a book on the way and then beg an editor to let me write about it.

Can you make a living as a book reviewer?

It's hard. *Slate* pays $1,000 for a review; *The New Yorker* pays more. But if you write for a newspaper it's only $200-400 per review. You get better rates if you are known, but it's still not very much. I continue to do it because it's engaging, not for the money. The only way to really make a living is to have a contract with a magazine to write twelve or more reviews a year for X amount of money, but that can only happen for a few people.

What's your philosophy of reviewing? Do you have any ethical concerns? Do you review your friends' books?

No. I don't even review friends of friends' books. I did it once and I didn't feel very good about it. I end up reviewing a lot of foreigners and a lot of dead people.

BRAD VICE *is a graduate student at the University of Cincinnati, and a frequent contributor to* Writer's Digest Books. *This article originally appeared in* Writer's Digest *magazine, and appears here with permission of the author.*

I try to read a book on its own terms; I try to define authorial intention. Sometimes that's clear with a successful book. Sometimes you know that you are supposed to be moved by something you've read, but it's not happening. Then you have to ask yourself why. Some reviewers seem to have a gold standard—if John Updike is our best writer, then this book falls short by so much. I don't think there is much point comparing apples to oranges, nor do I get the sense that there is a particular school to measure up to, like minimalism in the 80's. There is no longer that sort of groove. I also try not to criticize on the basis of what I want to accomplish myself. There isn't much point in saying "this book isn't serious." I mean, why review a book that isn't serious?

What kind of deadlines do you usually get?

It varies, but I guess a month or so on average. Once I had to read a book and write the review in three days. Actually I find most editors pretty far-sighted, but that doesn't mean I am on time.

Do you find that foreign newspapers have an interest in your reviews because your books have international themes and international readerships?

Well, I have contacts in Britain because I lived there. It only takes one or two editorial changes to make that not true. I was recently asked to write a review for a Canadian newspaper, but that was because I met the editor at a festival in Toronto and he wanted to commission a Canadian writer. I am a dual citizen, so that worked in my favor. I've also written for *The Irish Times*, but as far as my books having "an international readership," I don't know—it's nice to think that anybody reads them at all.

The Scams Are Out There!

BY NANCY BREEN

Woodside Literary Agency. Northwest Publishing. Deering Literary Agency/Sovereign Publications. Edit Ink. Commonwealth Publications and The Write Image (Canada). These names are now associated with some of the most notorious scams in the publishing world. Their disreputable activities have resulted in criminal investigations, class action lawsuits—and millions of dollars bilked from unsuspecting writers who believed they were entering into legitimate business arrangements with the publishers, literary agents and book doctors who preyed upon them.

How do these things happen? Could they happen to *you*? With basic knowledge of how scams operate and the obvious warning signs (not to mention a well-developed sense of skepticism), you'll be better equipped to detect a scam *before* you get taken.

HOW SCAMS WORK

Publishers: They're called subsidy, or "vanity" publishers. They recruit authors through display ads in writer's magazines, spam sent to online newsgroups or even through unsolicited letters and brochures sent by regular mail. "ATTENTION: WRITERS WANTED" they trumpet. When you respond with a query or manuscript, you receive a letter awash with praise for your writing and chock full of promises of success and exaggerated claims of all the wonderful things the publisher will do for your manuscript, from printing to promotion. Then when the contract comes, you notice the clause that states how much YOU are expected to contribute, usually a significant sum of money. For this you will receive X number of books out of X number printed, your book will be widely distributed and promoted and you will all live happily ever after.

Don't bet on it. These kinds of publishers make profits from the fees they charge writers, not from sales of the books they produce. The finished books are often of dubious quality, there's actually little or no promotional effort expended by the publisher at all and you'll be hard pressed to find your book in major bookstores (or even small ones). The publisher may not even print as many total books as promised. Without sales there are no royalties, and the hoodwinked writer ends up with little to show for a considerable investment except stacks of unsold books.

Literary agents and book doctors: Shady agents recruit writers much as subsidy publishers do—through ads, online spam and direct mail. When you submit a manuscript, the agent responds that the work isn't quite up to standard and could use some editing. And, see, publishers no longer take the time and trouble to edit manuscripts but expect polished, ready-to-print work. But don't despair! The agent gives you the name of an excellent book doctor who understands just what that agent, and today's publisher, are looking for.

For an inflated fee, the book doctor works his "magic" on your manuscript. You resubmit the work to the agent, but wouldn't you know it? In the meantime the market for your book has changed, or the agent represents an entirely different genre of writing, or . . . Well, the end of the story is you wind up with an unpublished manuscript that wasn't even particularly well "doctored," you have no representation in the marketplace and you're out a big chunk of change.

Anthologies: You see an ad calling for poets or announcing a competition that offers thousands of dollars in cash prizes. You submit a poem and, lo and behold, you receive a heartening letter:

NANCY BREEN *is the production editor for* Novel & Short Story Writer's Market *and* Poet's Market, *as well as a published poet and former senior writer at Gibson Greetings.*

Your poem didn't win but it's so good it's been chosen for inclusion in a special anthology of only the *best* poems submitted. What a feather in your cap! Now, you don't *have* to purchase an anthology if you don't want to; but should you wish to see your poem among this treasure trove of literary gems, it will cost you only $25 (or whatever—could be more). Deluxe hardbound edition, mind you. Won't you be proud to show it to your family and friends? Why, they'll probably want to buy copies for themselves.

When you receive this grand volume you may be disappointed in the quality of the other poems "chosen" to appear in this exclusive publication. Actually, everyone who entered was invited to be published, and you basically paid cash to see your poem appear in a book of no literary merit whatsoever.

These are the most common scams out there, although enterprising con artists are devising new ones all the time (modern technology, from "display" sites on the Internet to print-on-demand schemes, have opened up lots of fresh possibilities for being ripped off).

How do you protect yourself? It's important to learn the warning signs common to most publishing scams. Spotting even one of these danger signals should be enough to make you pause and ask some appropriate questions.

Here's what to watch out for:

A request for money. Here's how the legitimate system works: An agent sells your work to a publisher and takes a percentage of the sale amount as commission. A publisher agrees to publish your work and makes money off the sales of your book. At no point in this process should you be paying anyone for anything. That goes for "reading fees," "marketing fees," "contract fees" and so on.

What about contest fees? True, many literary magazines, small presses and literary organizations (such as state poetry societies) conduct contests that require entry fees (also sometimes called "reading fees"), and most of these are legitimate. The fees they charge go toward the expenses of conducting the contest, paying judges and putting up prize money, not lining someone's pocket. Also, entrants often receive a subscription to the magazine or a copy of the prize issue in exchange for the entry fee (or a copy of the winning book or chapbook in the case of small presses).

When in doubt, consider the reputation of the press, magazine or organization, how long it's been in existence and/or sponsoring the competition, how dependably winners and entrants are rewarded and the quality of the winning entries. If a competition asks for money but does not pay in cash, contributor's copies or some other tangible prize, enter your work elsewhere.

One more note about money: Do expect to pay for professional services, such as personal editing of your manuscript. However, be sure what you're being charged doesn't exceed the going rate, and have a clear understanding of the work you're paying for (simple copyediting vs. deep revision, for example). If there's a contract, read it carefully and take pains to make sure that all points are understood by both parties. And never pay the full cost of the service up front!

Referral to a specific agent, publisher or book doctor. Unscrupulous agents, publishers and book doctors could be in cahoots. For instance, an agent or publisher might suggest they'll look at your manuscript *if* it's worked on by a certain book doctor. An agent might suggest that a certain subsidy publisher is your best bet to see your work in print. And so on. If you're referred to just one individual or company, beware!

Phrases like "joint venture agreement," "author's contribution" and "co-partnership." It's that money thing again. Beware of any wording that even remotely suggests your financial participation. Your "contribution" will be bigger than you ever imagined and bring you far less than you ever wanted to believe.

Extravagant praise or unrealistic promises. Does the publisher or agent just rave about your work? Does he/she go on and on about the incredible success and financial rewards you can expect upon publication? Are you fed glorious visions of promotional campaigns and massive distribution? Don't be a chump. They're setting you up for the kill. Legitimate publishers and agents aren't going to gush all over you; and those spiels about promotional campaigns and widespread distribution are blue-sky come-ons that never materialize into anything. Great stuff for feeding your ego in the beginning, but later you'll wonder how you ever could have been so gullible.

Vagueness about details. If a publisher, agent or book doctor seems reluctant to provide basic information about his/her business activities or suggests that sharing such "confidential" information could compromise the business's operation, be on guard. It's not crossing the line to ask about sales figures, how royalties are calculated and how often they're paid, a client list (i.e., references), a complete breakdown of costs to you and whatever else you'll need to help you make a sensible, well-informed decision.

Broad, inaccurate statements about the publishing industry. This is especially true of negative statements that make it seem as if you have no hope of ever selling your manuscript; at least, not without that party's assistance. If an agent, publisher or book doctor makes claims such as "publishers don't edit manuscripts any more," kick your skepticism into high gear. Do some research on your own to find out what's really going on in the publishing world. Knowledge is power, and you'll be better able to detect the distortions in a scammer's spiel.

Display ads for agents, publishers, contests and anthologies. You're better off resisting these ads entirely. Legitimate, successful agents and publishers don't need to advertise; they're deluged with more writers than they can take on. What's more, these ads are misleading. Study them carefully and you probably won't find any mention of a fee, but you can be sure that requests for money will be introduced once you respond to the ad.

As for contests and anthologies, these ads are tempting with their promises of big cash awards. Even if the awards are actually paid to the winners, what you're more likely to receive is an invitation to buy an anthology. Understand that publications such as *Poets & Writers* run display ads for contests which are entirely legitimate, but these are usually sponsored by literary magazines and small presses. It's the ads with the grandiose titles that appear in both writer and non-writer publications that you really have to watch out for ("The Best Damn Poetry in the Cosmos Competition" or "Universal Library of Literary Giants Competition" or . . . well, you get the idea).

These are just a few of the basic tip-offs to scams that prey on writers. When searching for an agent, publisher or book doctor, apply the same common sense that you would to finding a good mechanic, caterer or carpenter. Request a resume and references. Check with the Better Business Bureau. Talk to clients past and present. Search the Internet. You can even generate a professional background check (fees for this vary, so be careful here, too).

Writers serious about their craft should never be so impatient for publication that they rush into dubious business arrangements. Unscrupulous publishers, agents and book doctors understand the vulnerability of unpublished authors who feel anxious—desperate, even—about ever seeing their work in print.

If you're good enough to be published, you're good enough to be the payee rather than the payer. On the other hand, if you really are not ready for publication, paying someone to rush things along isn't going to earn you the reputation and success you desire. So put away your checkbook and credit cards and dig out your manuscript. Concentrate your energies into making your writing the best it can be. If your work deserves an audience it will find one, without the process draining your bank account.

The scams are out there—but you do *not* have to be a victim!

If You've Been Scammed . . .

. . . or if you're trying to prevent one, the following resources should be of help:

Contact The Federal Trade Commission, Bureau of Consumer Protection (CRC-240, Washington DC 20580, 1-877-FTC-HELP(382-4357)). While they won't resolve individual consumer problems, the FTC depends on your complaints to help them investigate fraud, and your speaking up may even lead to law enforcement action. Contact them by mail or phone, or visit their website at www.ftc.gov.

Volunteer Lawyers for the Arts (1 E. 53rd St., New York NY 10022) is a group of volunteers from the legal profession who assist with questions of law pertaining to the arts, all fields. You can phone their hotline at (212)319-ARTS (2787), ext. 9 and have your questions answered for the price of the phone call. For further information you can also visit their website at www.vlany.org.

Better Business Bureau (check local listings or visit www.bbb.org)—the folks to contact if you have a complaint or if you want to investigate a publisher, literary agent or other business related to writing and writers.

It's also recommended that you contact your state's attorney general with information about scamming activity. Don't know your attorney general's name? Go to www.attorneygeneral.gov/ags. Here you'll find a wealth of contact information, including a complete list of links to the attorney general's website for each state.

For Info

There are plenty of books that can help you identify reputable publishers, literary agents, and book doctors, including *Guide to Literary Agents* (Writer's Digest Books), *Literary Marketplace* (R. R. Bowker), *Writer's Market* (Writer's Digest Books), *Writer's Guide to Book Editors, Publishers, and Literary Agents* (Prima Publishing), plus many individual titles focused on specific areas of the publishing world (finding an agent, for example).

The Internet is also a rich source of information. Simply type "publishing scams" into your favorite search engine. Here are some of the valuable sites we discovered (not only for scam information, but for good writing advice as well):

National Writers Union (www.nwu.org) includes a "Writer Alert!" section that is accessible to nonmembers.

The Science Fiction & Fantasy Writers of America site offers a comprehensive "Writer Beware" department (www.sfwa.org/beware).

Check out *Wind Publication*'s scam lowdown at http://wind.wind.org/literary.scams.htm.

At Todd Jones Pierce's Guide to Literary Agents site (www.literaryagents.org) there's a bounty of tips and advice, plus you can subscribe to a free newsletter.

The Writer's Center presents their indispensable "Scam Kit" at www.writer.org/scamkit.htm.

Even if you're not a romance writer, take a look at About.com's "Agents—Romance Fiction Net Links" (http://romancefiction.about.com/arts/romancefiction/msubagents.htm). Any writer will benefit from this page's in-depth articles and links.

The Business of Fiction Writing

It's true there are no substitutes for talent and hard work. A writer's first concern must always be attention to craft. No matter how well presented, a poorly written story or novel has little chance of being published. On the other hand, a well-written piece may be equally hard to sell in today's competitive publishing market. Talent alone is just not enough.

To be successful, writers need to study the field and pay careful attention to finding the right market. While the hours spent perfecting your writing are usually hours spent alone, you're not alone when it comes to developing your marketing plan. *Novel & Short Story Writer's Market* provides you with detailed listings containing the essential information you'll need to locate and contact the markets most suitable for your work.

Once you've determined where to send your work, you must turn your attention to presentation. We can help here, too. We've included the basics of manuscript preparation, along with a compilation of information on submission procedures and approaching markets. In addition we provide information on setting up and giving readings. We also include tips on promoting your work. No matter where you're from or what level of experience you have, you'll find useful information here on everything from presentation to mailing to selling rights to promoting your work—the "business" of fiction.

APPROACHING MAGAZINE MARKETS

While it is essential for nonfiction markets, a query letter by itself is usually not needed by most magazine fiction editors. If you are approaching a magazine to find out if fiction is accepted, a query is fine, but editors looking for short fiction want to see *how* you write. A cover letter can be useful as a letter of introduction, but it must be accompanied by the actual piece. Include basic information in your cover letter—name, address, a brief list of previous publications—if you have any—and two or three sentences about the piece (why you are sending it to *this* magazine or how your experience influenced your story). Keep it to one page and remember to include a self-addressed, stamped envelope (SASE) for reply. See the Sample Short Story Cover Letter on page 107.

Agents: Agents are not usually needed for short fiction and most do not handle it unless they already have a working relationship with you. For novels, you may want to consider working with an agent, especially if marketing to publishers who do not look at unsolicited submissions. For more on approaching agents and listings of agents willing to work with beginning and established writers, see our Literary Agents section beginning on page 115. For information on over 500 agents, see *Guide to Literary Agents* (Writer's Digest Books).

APPROACHING BOOK PUBLISHERS

Some book publishers do ask for queries first, but most want a query plus sample chapters or an outline or, occasionally, the complete manuscript. Again, make your letter brief. Include the essentials about yourself—name, address, phone number and publishing experience. Include only the personal information related to your story. Show that you have researched the market with a few sentences about why you chose this publisher. See the Sample Book Query Cover Letter on page 108.

THE SAMPLE COVER LETTER

A successful cover letter is no more than one page (20 lb. bond paper), single spaced with a double space between paragraphs, proofread carefully, and neatly typed in a standard typeface (not script or italic). The writer's name, address and phone number appear at the top, and it is addressed, ideally, to a specific editor. (If the editor's name is unavailable, address to "Fiction Editor.")

The body of a successful cover letter contains the name and word count of the story, the reason you are submitting to this particular publication, a short overview of the story, and some brief biographical information, especially when relevant to your story. Mention that you have enclosed a self-addressed, stamped envelope or postcard for reply. Also let the editor know if you are sending a disposable manuscript that doesn't need to be returned. (More and more editors prefer disposable manuscripts that save them time and save you postage.) When sending a computer disk, identify the program you are using. Remember, however, that even editors who appreciate receiving your story on a disk usually also want a printed copy. Finally, don't forget to thank the editor for considering your story.

BOOK PROPOSALS

A book proposal is a package sent to a publisher that includes a cover letter and one or more of the following: sample chapters, outline, synopsis, author bio, publications list. When asked to send sample chapters, send up to three *consecutive* chapters. An **outline** covers the highlights of your book chapter by chapter. Be sure to include details on main characters, the plot and subplots. Outlines can run up to 30 pages, depending on the length of your novel. The object is to tell what happens in a concise, but clear, manner. A **synopsis** is a very brief description of what happens in the story. Keep it to two or three pages. The terms synopsis and outline are sometimes used interchangeably, so be sure to find out exactly what each publisher wants.

MANUSCRIPT MECHANICS

A professionally presented manuscript will not guarantee publication. But a sloppy, hard-to-read manuscript will not be read—publishers simply do not have the time. Here's a list of suggested submission techniques for polished manuscript presentation:

- **Use white, 8½ × 11 bond paper,** preferably 16 or 20 lb. weight. The paper should be heavy enough so it will not show pages underneath it and strong enough to take handling by several people.
- **Type your manuscript** on a computer using a laser or ink jet printer, or on a typewriter using a new ribbon.
- **Proofread carefully.** An occasional white-out is okay, but don't send a marked-up manuscript with many typos. Keep a dictionary, thesaurus and stylebook handy and use the spellcheck function of your computer.
- **Always double space and leave a 1¼ inch margin** on all sides of the page.
- **For a short story manuscript,** your first page should include your name, address and phone number (single-spaced) in the upper left corner. In the upper right, indicate an approximate word count. Center the name of your story about one-third of the way down, skip two or three lines and center your byline (byline is optional). Skip three lines and begin your story. On subsequent pages, put last name and page number in the upper right hand corner.
- **For book manuscripts,** use a separate cover sheet. Put your name, address and phone number in the upper left corner and word count in the upper right. Some writers list their agent's name and address in the upper right (word count is then placed at the bottom of the page). Center your title and byline about halfway down the page. Start your first chapter on the next page. Center the chapter number and title (if there is one) one-third of the way down the page. Include your last name and page number in the upper right of this page and each page to follow. Start each chapter with a new page.

SAMPLE SHORT STORY COVER LETTER

Jennifer Williamson
8822 Rose Petal Ct.
Norwood OH 45212

January 15, 2001

Rebecca Rossdale
Young Woman Magazine
4234 Market St.
Chicago IL 60606

Dear Ms. Rossdale,

As a teacher and former assistant camp director I have witnessed
many a summer romance between teens working at camp. One romance in particular touched me because the young people involved
helped each other through a very difficult summer. It inspired me
to write the enclosed 8,000-word short story, "Summer Love," a
love story about two teens, both from troubled families, who find
love and support while working at a camp in upstate New York.

I think the story will fit nicely into your Summer Reading issue. My
publishing credits include stories in *Youth Today* and *Sparkle* magazines as well as publications for adults. I am also working on a
historical romance.

I look forward to hearing from you.

Sincerely,

Jennifer Williamson
(513)555-5555

Encl.: Manuscript
SASE

SAMPLE BOOK QUERY COVER LETTER

Bonnie Booth
1453 Nuance Blvd.
Norwood OH 45212

April 12, 2001

Ms. Thelma Collins
Bradford House Publishing
187 72nd St., Fifth Floor
New York NY 10101

Dear Ms. Collins,

I am a published mystery writer whose short stories have appeared in *Modern Mystery* and *Doyle's Mystery Magazine*. I am also a law student and professional hair designer and have brought these interests together in *Only Skin Deep*, my 60,000-word novel set in the glamorous world of beauty care, featuring hair designer to the stars and amateur detective Norma Haines.

In *Only Skin Deep*, Haines is helping to put together the state's largest hair design show when she gets a call from a friend at the local police station. The body of famed designer Lynette LaSalle has been found in an Indianapolis motel room. She's been strangled and her legendary blonde mane has been shaved off. Later, when the bodies of two other designers are discovered also with shaven heads, it's clear their shared occupation is more than a coincidence.

Your successful series by Ann Smythe and the bestseller *The Gas Pump Murders*, by Marc Crawford, point to the continued popularity of amateur detectives. *Only Skin Deep* would make a strong addition to your line.

Sincerely,

Bonnie Booth
(513)555-5555

Encl.: three sample chapters
       synopsis
       SASE

- **Include a word count.** If you work on a computer, chances are your word processing program can give you a word count. If you are using a typewriter, there are a number of ways to count the number of words in your piece. One way is to count the words in five lines and divide that number by five to find an average. Then count the number of lines and multiply to find the total words. For long pieces, you may want to count the words in the first three pages, divide by three and multiply by the number of pages you have.
- **Always keep a copy.** Manuscripts do get lost. To avoid expensive mailing costs, send only what is required. If you are including artwork or photos, but you are not positive they will be used, send photocopies. Artwork is hard to replace.
- **Suggest art where applicable.** Most publishers do not expect you to provide artwork and some insist on selecting their own illustrators, but if you have suggestions, please let them know. Magazine publishers work in a very visual field and are usually open to ideas.
- **Enclose a self-addressed, stamped envelope (SASE)** if you want a reply or if you want your manuscript returned. For most letters, a business-size (#10) envelope will do. Avoid using any envelope too small for an 8½ × 11 sheet of paper. For manuscripts, be sure to include enough postage and an envelope large enough to contain it.
- **Consider sending a disposable manuscript** that saves editors time and saves you money. If you are requesting a sample copy of a magazine or a book publisher's catalog, send an envelope big enough to fit.
- **When sending electronic (disk or modem) submissions,** *contact the publisher first for specific information and follow the directions carefully.* Always include a printed copy with any disk submission. *Fax or e-mail your submissions only with prior approval of the publisher.*
- **Keep accurate records.** This can be done in a number of ways, but be sure to keep track of where your stories are and how long they have been "out." Write down submission dates. If you do not hear about your submission for a long time—about three weeks to one month longer than the reporting time stated in the listing—you may want to contact the publisher. When you do, you will need an accurate record for reference.

MAILING TIPS

When mailing short correspondence or short manuscripts:
- Fold manuscripts under five pages into thirds and send in a business-size (#10) envelope.
- Mail manuscripts five pages or more unfolded in a 9 × 12 or 10 × 13 envelope.
- Mark envelopes in all caps, FIRST CLASS MAIL or SPECIAL FOURTH CLASS MANU-SCRIPT RATE.
- For return envelope, fold it in half, address it to yourself and add a stamp or, if going to a foreign country, International Reply Coupons (available for $1.05 each at the main branch of your local post office).
- Don't send by certified mail. This is a sign of a paranoid amateur and publishers do not appreciate receiving unsolicited manuscripts this way.

When mailing book-length manuscripts:

FIRST CLASS MAIL over 11 ounces (@ 65 8½ × 11 20 lb.-weight pages) automatically becomes **PRIORITY MAIL.**

METERED MAIL may be dropped in any post office box, but meter strips on SASEs should not be dated.

The Postal Service provides, free of charge, tape, boxes and envelopes to hold up to two pounds for those using PRIORITY and EXPRESS MAIL.

Requirements for mailing FOURTH CLASS and PARCEL POST have not changed.

Main branches of local banks will cash foreign checks, but keep in mind payment quoted in our listings by publishers in other countries is usually payment in their currency. Also note reporting time is longer in most overseas markets. To save time and money, you may want to include a return postcard (and IRC) with your submission and forgo asking for a manuscript to be returned.

Current Mailing Costs for First Class Postage Versus Priority

FIRST CLASS MAIL:	PRIORITY MAIL:
1 ounce = 33 cents	12 oz.-2 lbs. = $3.20
2 ounces = 55 cents	2 lbs.-3 lbs. = $4.30
each additional ounce	3 lbs.-4 lbs. = $5.40
up to 16 ounces = 22 cents	4 lbs.-5 lbs. = $6.50

If you live in Canada, see Canadian Writers Take Note on page 607.

RIGHTS

Know what rights you are selling. The Copyright Law states that writers are selling one-time rights (in almost all cases) unless they and the publisher have agreed otherwise. A list of various rights follows. Be sure you know exactly what rights you are selling before you agree to the sale.

• **Copyright** is the legal right to exclusive publication, sale or distribution of a literary work. As the writer or creator of a written work, you need simply to include your name, date and the copyright symbol © on your piece in order to copyright it. Be aware, however, that most editors today consider placing the copyright symbol on your work the sign of an amateur and many are even offended by it.

To get specific answers to questions about copyright (but not legal advice), you can call the Copyright Public Information Office at (202)707-3000 weekdays between 8:30 a.m. and 5 p.m. EST. Publications listed in *Novel & Short Story Writer's Market* are copyrighted *unless* otherwise stated. In the case of magazines that are not copyrighted, be sure to keep a copy of your manuscript with your notice printed on it. For more information on copyrighting your work see *The Copyright Handbook: How to Protect and Use Written Works* by Stephen Fishman (Nolo Press, 1992).

Some people are under the mistaken impression that copyright is something they have to send away for, and that their writing is not properly protected until they have "received" their copyright from the government. The fact is, you don't have to register your work with the Copyright Office in order for your work to be copyrighted; any piece of writing is copyrighted the moment it is put to paper. Registration of your work does, however, offer some additional protection (specifically, the possibility of recovering punitive damages in an infringement suit) as well as legal proof of the date of copyright.

Registration is a matter of filling out an application form (for writers, that's generally Form TX) and sending the completed form, a nonreturnable copy of the work in question and a check for $30 to the Library of Congress, Copyright Office, Register of Copyrights, 101 Independence Ave. SE, Washington DC 20559-6000. If the thought of paying $30 each to register every piece you write does not appeal to you, you can cut costs by registering a group of your works with one form, under one title for one $30 fee.

Most magazines are registered with the Copyright Office as single collective entities themselves; that is, the individual works that make up the magazine are *not* copyrighted individually in the names of the authors. You'll need to register your article yourself if you wish to have the additional protection of copyright registration.

• **First Serial Rights**—This means the writer offers a newspaper or magazine the right to publish the article, story or poem for the first time in any periodical. All other rights to the material remain with the writer. The qualifier "North American" is often added to this phrase to specify a geographical limit to the license.

When material is excerpted from a book scheduled to be published and it appears in a magazine or newspaper prior to book publication, this is also called first serial rights.

• **One-time Rights**—A periodical that licenses one-time rights to a work (also known as simultaneous rights) buys the *nonexclusive* right to publish the work once. That is, there is nothing to stop the author from selling the work to other publications at the same time. Simultaneous sales would typically be to periodicals without overlapping audiences.

• **Second Serial (Reprint) Rights**—This gives a newspaper or magazine the opportunity to print an article, poem or story after it has already appeared in another newspaper or magazine. Second serial rights are nonexclusive—that is, they can be licensed to more than one market.

• **All Rights**—This is just what it sounds like. All Rights means a publisher may use the manuscript anywhere and in any form, including movie and book club sales, without further payment to the writer (although such a transfer, or *assignment*, of rights will terminate after 35 years). If you think you'll want to use the material later, you must avoid submitting to such markets or refuse payment and withdraw your material. Ask the editor whether he is willing to buy first rights instead of all rights before you agree to an assignment or sale. Some editors will reassign rights to a writer after a given period, such as one year. It's worth an inquiry in writing.

• **Subsidiary Rights**—These are the rights, other than book publication rights, that should be covered in a book contract. These may include various serial rights; movie, television, audiotape and other electronic rights; translation rights, etc. The book contract should specify who controls these rights (author or publisher) and what percentage of sales from the licensing of these sub rights goes to the author. For more information, see Selling Subsidiary Rights.

• **Dramatic, Television and Motion Picture Rights**—This means the writer is selling his material for use on the stage, in television or in the movies. Often a one-year option to buy such rights is offered (generally for 10% of the total price). The interested party then tries to sell the idea to other people—actors, directors, studios or television networks, etc. Some properties are optioned over and over again, but most fail to become dramatic productions. In such cases, the writer can sell his rights again and again—as long as there is interest in the material. Though dramatic, TV and motion picture rights are more important to the fiction writer than the nonfiction writer, producers today are increasingly interested in nonfiction material; many biographies, topical books and true stories are being dramatized.

• **Electronic Rights**—These rights cover usage in a broad range of electronic media, from online magazines and databases to CD-ROM magazine anthologies and interactive games. The editor should specify in writing if—and which—electronic rights are being requested. The presumption is that unspecified rights are kept by the writer.

Compensation for electronic rights is a major source of conflict between writers and publishers, as many book publishers seek control of them and many magazines routinely include electronic rights in the purchase of all rights, often with no additional payment. Alternative ways of handling this issue include an additional 15% added to the amount to purchase first rights to a royalty system based on the number of times an article is accessed from an electronic database.

PROMOTION TIPS

Everyone agrees writing is hard work whether you are published or not. Yet, once you arrive at the published side of the equation the work changes. Most published authors will tell you the work is still hard but it is different. Now, not only do you continue working on your next project, you must also concern yourself with getting your book into the hands of readers. It becomes time to switch hats from artist to salesperson.

While even bestselling authors whose publishers have committed big bucks to promotion are asked to help in promoting their books, new authors may have to take it upon themselves to plan and initiate some of their own promotion, sometimes dipping into their own pockets. While

About Our Policies

We occasionally receive letters asking why a certain magazine, publisher or contest is not in the book. Sometimes when we contact a listing, the editor does not want to be listed because they: do not use very much fiction; are overwhelmed with submissions; are having financial difficulty or have been recently sold; use only solicited material; accept work from a select group of writers only; do not have the staff or time for the many unsolicited submissions a listing may bring.

Some of the listings do not appear because we have chosen not to list them. We investigate complaints of unprofessional conduct in editors' dealings with writers and misrepresentation of information provided to us by editors and publishers. If we find these reports to be true, after a thorough investigation, we will delete the listing from future editions. See Important Listing Information on page 114 for more about our listing policies.

If a listing appeared in our book last year but is no longer listed, we list it in the General Index, beginning on page 655, with a code explaining why it is not listed. The key to those codes is given in the introduction to the General Index. Sometimes the listing does not appear because the editor did not respond in time for our press deadline, or it may not appear for any of the reasons previously mentioned above.

There is no charge to the companies that list in this book. Listings appearing in *Novel & Short Story Writer's Market* are compiled from detailed questionnaires, phone interviews and information provided by editors, publishers and awards directors. The publishing industry is volatile and changes of address, editor, policies and needs happen frequently. To keep up with the changes between editions of the book, we suggest you check the monthly Markets columns in *Writer's Digest*. Also check the market information on the *Writer's Market* website at www.writersmarket.com, or on the *Writer's Digest* website at: www.writersdigest.com.

Club newsletters and small magazines devoted to helping writers also list market information. For those writers with access to online services, several offer writers' bulletin boards, message centers and chat lines with up-to-the-minute changes and happenings in the writing community. Some of these resources are listed in our Websites of Interest (page 603). Many magazine and book publishers offer updated information for writers on their websites. Check individual listings for those website addresses.

We rely on our readers, as well, for new markets and information about market conditions. Write us if you have any new information or if you have suggestions on how to improve our listings to better suit your writing needs.

this does not mean that every author is expected to go on tour, sometimes at their own expense, it does mean authors should be prepared to offer suggestions for promoting their books.

Depending on the time, money and the personal preferences of the author and publisher, a promotional campaign could mean anything from mailing out press releases to setting up book signings to hitting the talk-show circuit. Most writers can contribute to their own promotion by providing contact names—reviewers, home-town newspapers, civic groups, organizations—that might have a special interest in the book or the writer.

Above all, when it comes to promotion, be creative. What is your book about? Try to capitalize on it. For example, if you've written a mystery whose protagonist is a wine connoisseur, you might give a reading at a local wine-tasting or try to set something up at one of the national wine events. For more suggestions on promoting your work see *The Writer's Guide to Promotion & Publicity*, by Elane Feldman (Writer's Digest Books).

The Markets

Literary Agents 115

Literary Magazines 138

Small Circulation Magazines 286

Zines 320

Consumer Magazines 344

Book Publishers 386

Contests & Awards 495

Important Listing Information

- Listings are not advertisements. Although the information here is as accurate as possible, the listings are not endorsed or guaranteed by the editor of *Novel & Short Story Writer's Market*.
- *Novel & Short Story Writer's Market* reserves the right to exclude any listing that does not meet its requirements.

Key to Symbols and Abbreviations

N New listing in all sections
�◆ Canadian listing
◉ International listing
A Agented material only
✔ Listing includes change in contact name, address or phone
▣ Online publication
▼ Award-winning publication
$ Market pays money
⊘ Accepts no submissions
◯ Actively seeking beginning writers
◑ Seeking new and established writers
◉ Prefers working with established writers, mostly referrals
◎ Only handles specific types of work
✖ Market offers greater opportunities for unpublished writers
☐ Cable TV market (in Screenwriting section)
● Comment by editor of *Novel & Short Story Writer's Market*
ms—manuscript; **mss**-manuscripts
b&w—black and white
SASE—self-addressed, stamped envelope
SAE—self-addressed envelope
IRC—International Reply Coupon, for use on reply mail from other countries

(See Glossary for definitions of words and expressions used in writing and publishing.)

Complaint Procedure

If you feel you have not been treated fairly by a listing in *Novel & Short Story Writer's Market*, we advise you to take the following steps:

- First try to contact the listing. Sometimes one phone call or a letter can quickly clear up the matter.
- Document all your correspondence with the listing. When you write to us with a complaint, provide the details of your submission, the date of your first contact with the listing and the nature of your subsequent correspondence.
- We will enter your letter into our files and attempt to contact the listing.
- The number and severity of complaints will be considered in our decision whether or not to delete the listing from the next edition.

Literary Agents

Many publishers are willing to look at unsolicited submissions but most feel having an agent is to the writer's best advantage. In this section we include 60+ agents who specialize in fiction, or publish a significant amount of fiction. These agents were also selected because of their openness to submissions from writers.

The commercial fiction field is intensely competitive. Many publishers have smaller staffs and less time. For that reason, more book publishers are relying on agents for new talent. Some publishers are even relying on agents as "first readers" who must wade through the deluge of submissions from writers to find the very best. For writers, a good agent can be a foot in the door—someone willing to do the necessary work to put your manuscript in the right editor's hands.

It would seem today that finding a good agent is as hard as finding a good publisher. Yet those writers who have agents say they are invaluable. Not only can a good agent help you make your work more marketable, an agent acts as your business manager and adviser, keeping your interests up front during and even after contract negotiations.

Still, finding an agent can be very difficult for a new writer. If you are already published in magazines, you have a better chance than someone with no publishing credits. (Many agents routinely read periodicals searching for new writers.) Although many agents do read queries and manuscripts from unpublished authors without introduction, referrals from their writer clients can be a big help. If you don't know any published authors with agents, you may want to attend a conference as a way of meeting agents. Some agents even set aside time at conferences to meet new writers.

All the agents listed here have said they are open to working with new, previously unpublished writers as well as published writers. Most do not charge a fee to cover the time and effort involved in reviewing a manuscript or a synopsis and chapters.

USING THE LISTINGS

It is especially important when contacting these busy agents that you read individual listings carefully before submitting anything. The first information after the company name includes the address and phone, fax and e-mail address (when available). **Member Agents** gives the names of individual agents working at that company (specific types of fiction an agent handles are indicated in parenthesis after that agent's name). The **Represents:** section lists the types of fiction the agency works with. **Needs** includes any specific types of fiction the agency is currently looking for, as well as what they do not want to see. Reading the **Recent Sales** gives you the names of writers an agent is currently working with and, very importantly, publishers the agent has placed manuscripts with. **Writers' Conferences** identifies conferences an agent attends (and where you might possibly meet that agent). **Tips** presents advice directly from the agent to authors.

☑ 🜂 **ALIVE COMMUNICATIONS, INC.**, 7680 Goddard St., Suite 200, Colorado Springs CO 80920. (719)260-7080. Fax: (719)260-8223. Website: www.alivecom.com. Estab. 1989. Member of AAR, CBA. Represents 175 clients. **5% of clients are new/unpublished writers.** Currently handles: 40% nonfiction books; 10% juvenile books; 4% short story collections; 40% novels; 1% syndicated material; 5% novellas.
Member Agent(s): Rick Christian (blockbusters, bestsellers); Greg Johnson (popular/commercial nonfiction and fiction); Kathy Yanni (literary nonfiction and fiction); Jerry "Chip" MacGregor (popular/commercial nonfiction and fiction, new authors with breakout potential).
Represents: Nonfiction books, juvenile books, novels, novellas, poetry, short story collections. **Considers these fiction areas:** action/adventure; contemporary issues; detective/police/crime; family saga; historical; humor/satire; juvenile; literary; mainstream; mystery/suspense; religious/inspirational; thriller/espionage; westerns/frontier; young adult.

How to Contact: Send outline and 3 sample chapters. Include bio/résumé, publishing history and SASE. Considers simultaneous submissions, "if clearly noted in cover letter." Responds in 2 weeks to queries; 1 month to mss. Returns materials only with SASE.

Needs Actively seeking inspirational/literary/mainstream fiction and work from authors with established track record and platforms. Does not want to receive poetry, young adult paperback, scripts, dark themes. Obtains new clients through recommendations from clients and publishers.

Recent Sales: Sold 300 titles in the last year. *Left Behind* series, by Tim LaHaye and Jerry B. Jenkins (Tyndale); *Jerusalem Vigil*, by Bodie and Brock Thoene (Viking).

Terms: Agent receives 15% commission on domestic sales; 15-20% on foreign sales. Offers written contract. 60 days written notice must be given to terminate contract.

Reading List: Reads literary, religious and mainstream journals to find new clients. "Our goal is always the same—to find writers whose use of language is riveting and powerful."

Tips: "Rewrite and polish until the words on the page shine. Provide us with as much personal and publishing history information as possible. Endorsements and great connections may help, provided you can write with power and passion. Alive Communications, Inc. has established itself as a premiere literary agency and speakers bureau. Based in Colorado Springs we serve an elite group of authors and speakers who are critically acclaimed and commercially successful in both Christian and general markets."

JAMES ALLEN, LITERARY AGENT, P.O. Box 278, Milford PA 18337-0278. **Contact:** James Allen. Estab. 1974. Represents 40 clients. **10% of clients are new/previously unpublished writers.** "I handle all kinds of genre fiction (except westerns) and specialize in science fiction and fantasy." Currently handles: 2% nonfiction books; 8% juvenile books; 90% novels.

Represents: Nonfiction books, novels. **Considers these fiction areas:** action/adventure; detective/police/crime; family saga; fantasy; glitz; historical; horror; mainstream; mystery/suspense; romance (contemporary, historical); science fiction; young adult.

How to Contact: Query. Responds in 1 week to queries; 2 months to mss. "I prefer first contact to be a query letter with two- to three-page plot synopsis and SASE with a response time of one week. If my interest is piqued, I then ask for the first four chapters, response time within a month. If I'm impressed by the writing, I then ask for the balance of the manuscript, response time about two months."

Needs: Actively seeking "well-written work by people who at least have their foot in the door and are looking for someone to take them to the next (and subsequent) levels." Does not want to receive "petitions for representation from people who do not yet have even one booklength credit."

Recent Sales: Sold about 35 titles in the last year. *China Sea*, by David Poyer (St. Martin's Press), *Aranur's Tale*, by Tara K. Harper (Del Rey), *The Devil in Ol' Rosie*, by Louise Moeri (Atheneum/S&S). Other clients include Doug Allyn, Judi Lind, Robert Trout, Juanita Coulson and Jan Clark.

Terms: Agent receives 10% commission on domestic print sales; 20% on film sales; 20% on foreign sales. Offers written contract, binding for 3 years "automatically renewed. No reading fees or other up-front charges. I reserve the right to charge for extraordinary expenses (in practice, only the cost of book purchases when I need copies to market a title abroad). I do not bill the author but deduct the charges from incoming earnings."

Tips: "*First time at book length need NOT apply*—only taking on authors who have the foundations of their writing careers in place and can use help in building the rest. A cogent, to-the-point query letter is necessary, laying out the author's track record and giving a brief blurb for the book. The response to a mere 'I have written a novel, will you look at it?' is universally 'NO!' "

MARCIA AMSTERDAM AGENCY, 41 W. 82nd St., New York NY 10024-5613. (212)873-4945. **Contact:** Marcia Amsterdam. Estab. 1970. Signatory of WGA. Currently handles: 15% nonfiction books; 70% novels; 10% movie scripts; 5% TV scripts.

● Prior to opening her agency, Ms. Amsterdam was an editor.

Represents: Nonfiction, novels. **Considers these fiction areas:** action/adventure; detective; horror; humor; mainstream; mystery/suspense; romance (contemporary, historical); science fiction; thriller/espionage; westerns/frontier; young adult.

Also Handles: Feature film, TV MOW, sitcom. **Considers these script subject areas:** comedy, mainstream, mystery/suspense, romance (comedy, drama).

How to Contact: Send outline plus first 3 sample chapters and SASE. Responds in 1 month to queries.

Recent Sales: *Rosey In the Present Tense*, by Louise Hawes (Walker); *Flash Factor*, by William H. Lovejoy (Kensington). *TV scripts optioned/sold: Mad About You*, by Jenna Bruce (Columbia Tristar TV).

Terms: Agent receives 15% commission on domestic sales; 20% on foreign sales, 10% on scripts. Offers written contract, binding for 1 year, "renewable." Charges for extra office expenses, foreign postage, copying, legal fees (when agreed upon).

Tips: "We are always looking for interesting literary voices."

[N] ◐ **MEREDITH BERNSTEIN LITERARY AGENCY**, 2112 Broadway, Suite 503 A, New York NY 10023. (212)799-1007. Fax: (212)799-1145. Estab. 1981. Member of AAR. Represents approximately 100 clients. **20% of clients are new/previously unpublished writers.** Currently handles: 50% nonfiction books; 50% fiction.
  • Prior to opening her agency, Ms. Bernstein served in another agency for 5 years.
Member Agents: Meredith Bernstein; Elizabeth Cavanaugh.
Represents: Fiction and nonfiction books. **Considers these fiction areas:** romance, mystery, literary, women's fiction.
How to Contact: Query first with SASE.
Needs: Does not specialize, "very eclectic." Obtains most new clients through recommendations from others, queries and at conferences; also develops and packages own ideas.
Recent Sales: *Interview with An Angel*, by Linda Nathanson and Stephen Thayer (Dell).
Terms: Agent receives 15% commission on domestic sales; 20% on foreign sales. Charges clients $75 disbursement fee per year.
Writers' Conferences: Southwest Writers Conference (Albuquerque, August); Rocky Mountain Writers Conference (Denver, September); Beaumont (TX, October); Pacific Northwest Writers Conference; Austin League Writers Conference; Willamette Writers Conference (Portland, OR); Lafayette Writers Conference (Lafayette, LA); Surrey Writers Conference (Surrey, BC.); San Diego State University Writers Conference (San Diego, CA).

✓ ◐ **MARIA CARVAINIS AGENCY, INC.**, 1350 Avenue of the Americas, Suite 2905, New York NY 10019. (212)245-6365. Fax: (212)245-7196. E-mail: mca@mariacarvainisagency.com. **Contact:** Maria Carvainis. Estab. 1977. Member of AAR, Authors Guild, ABA, MWA, RWA, signatory of WGA. Represents 35 clients. **10% of clients are new/previously unpublished writers.** Currently handles: 34% nonfiction books; 65% novels; 1% poetry books.
  • Prior to opening her agency, Ms. Carvainis spent more than 10 years in the publishing industry as a senior editor with Macmillan Publishing, Basic Books and Avon Books, where she worked closely with Peter Mayer and Crown Publishers. Ms. Carvainis has served as a member of the AAR Board of Directors and AAR Treasurer, as well as serving as chair of the AAR Contracts Committee. She presently serves on the AAR Royalty Committee.
Represents: Nonfiction books, novels. **Considers these fiction areas:** fantasy; historical; literary; mainstream; mystery/suspense; romance; thriller; young adult.
How to Contact: Query first with SASE. Responds within 3 weeks to queries; 3 months to solicited mss.
Needs: Does not want to receive science fiction or children's. "60% of new clients derived from recommendations or conferences. 40% of new clients derived from letters of query."
Recent Sales: *The Alibi* and *Standoff*, by Sandra Brown (Warner Books); *Bearing Witness*, by Michael Kahn (TOR/Forge); *Dead of Winter*, by P.J. Parrish (Kensington); *Heroin*, by Charlie Smith (W.W. Norton). Other clients include Mary Balogh, David Bottoms, Pam Conrad, Cindy Gerard, Sarah Zsidore, Samantha James, Kristine Rolofson, William Sessions and Jose Yglesias.
Terms: Agent receives 15% commission on domestic sales; 20% on foreign sales. Offers written contract, binding for 2 years "on a book-by-book basis." Charges for foreign postage and bulk copying.
Writers' Conferences: BEA; Frankfurt Book Fair.

✓ ◐ **DON CONGDON ASSOCIATES INC.**, 156 Fifth Ave., Suite 625, New York NY 10010-7002. (212)645-1229. Fax: (212)727-2688. E-mail: congdon@veriomail.com. **Contact:** Don Congdon, Michael Congdon, Susan Ramer, Cristina Concepcion. Estab. 1983. Member of AAR. Represents approximately 100 clients. Currently handles: 50% fiction; 50% nonfiction books.
Represents: Nonfiction books, novels. **Considers all fiction areas, especially literary fiction.**
How to Contact: Query with SASE. "If interested, we ask for sample chapters and outline." Responds in 1 week to queries; 1 month to mss.
Needs: Obtains most new clients through referrals from other authors.
Recent Sales: *The Gravity of Sunlight*, by Rosa Shand (Soho); *You Only Die Twice*, by Edna Buchanan (HarperCollins).
Terms: Agent receives 15% commission on domestic sales. Charges for postage, photocopying, copyright fees and book purchases.
Tips: "Writing a query letter with a self-addressed stamped envelope is a must."

STILL LOOKING FOR AN AGENT? Pick up the 2001 edition of *Guide to Literary Agents* (Writer's Digest Books) at your local bookstore, or by calling 1-800-289-0963.

✓ ☻ **CONNOR LITERARY AGENCY**, 2911 West 71st St., Richfield MN 55423. (612)866-1426. Fax: (612)869-4074. E-mail: coolmkc@aol.com. **Contact:** Marlene Connor Lynch. Estab. 1985. Represents 50 clients. **30% of clients are new/previously unpublished writers.** Specializes in popular fiction and nonfiction. Currently handles: 50% nonfiction books; 50% novels.

  • Prior to opening her agency, Ms. Connor served at the Literary Guild of America, Simon and Schuster and Random House. She is the author of *What is Cool: Understanding Black Manhood in America* (Crown).

Member Agents: Deborah Coker (children's books); John Lynch (assistant).

Represents: Nonfiction books, novels, children's books (especially with a minority slant). **Considers these fiction areas:** contemporary issues; detective/police/crime; ethnic; experimental; family saga; horror; literary; mystery/suspense.

How to Contact: Query with outline/proposal and SASE. Considers simultaneous queries. Responds in 1 month to queries; 6 weeks to mss.

Needs: Obtains new clients through "queries, recommendations, conferences, grapevine, etc."

Recent Sales: *Essence: 25 Years of Celebrating the Black Woman* (Abrams); *Grandmother's Gift of Memories*, by Danita Green (Broadway Books).

Terms: Agent receives 15% commission on domestic sales; 25% on foreign sales. Offers a written contract, binding for 1 year.

Writers' Conferences: Howard University Publishing Institute; BEA; Detroit Writer's Conference; Mid-West Romance Writer's Conference.

Tips: "Seeking previously published writers with good sales records and new writers with real talent."

☻ **CRAWFORD LITERARY AGENCY**, 94 Evans Rd., Barnstead NH 03218. (603)269-5851. Fax: (603)269-2533. **Contact:** Susan Crawford. Estab. 1988. Represents 40 clients. **10% of clients are new/previously unpublished writers.** Specializes in celebrity and/or media-based books and authors. Currently handles: 50% nonfiction books; 50% novels.

Member Agents: Susan Crawford, Lorne Crawford (commercial fiction); Scott Neister (scientific/techno thrillers); Kristen Hales (parenting, psychology, New Age, self-help).

Represents: Commercial fiction.

How to Contact: Query with SASE. Doesn't accept queries by e-mail or fax. Considers simultaneous queries; no simultaneous ms submissions. Responds in 3 weeks to queries. Returns materials only with SASE.

Needs: Actively seeking action/adventure stories, medical thrillers, suspense thrillers, celebrity projects, self-help, inspirational, how-to and women's issues. Does not want to receive short stories or poetry. Obtains most new clients through recommendations, conferences, and queries.

Recent Sales: *Housebroken*, by Richard Karn and George Mair (HarperCollins); *Psi/Net*, by Billy Dee Williams and Rob MacGregor (TOR/Forge). Other clients include John Travolta, Ruby Dee and Ossie Davis.

Terms: Agent receives 15% commission on domestic sales; 20% on foreign sales. Offers written contract, binding for 90 days. 100% of business is derived from commissions on sales.

Writers' Conferences: International Film & Writers Workshop (Rockport ME); Maui Writers Conference.

✓ ☻ **RICHARD CURTIS ASSOCIATES, INC.**, 171 E. 74th St., Suite 2, New York NY 10021. (212)772-7363. Fax: (212)772-7393. E-mail: jhackworth@curtisagency.com. Website: www.curtisagency.com. **Contact:** Pam Valvera. Estab. 1969. Member of AAR, RWA, MWA, WWA, SFWA, signatory of WGA. Represents 100 clients. **5% of clients are new/previously unpublished writers.** Specializes in general and literary fiction and nonfiction, as well as genre fiction such as science fiction, women's romance, horror, fantasy, action-adventure. Currently handles: 50% nonfiction books; 50% novels.

  • Prior to opening his agency, Mr. Curtis was an agent with the Scott Meredith Literary Agency for 7 years and has authored over 50 published books.

Member Agents: Amy Victoria Meo, Jennifer Hackworth, Richard Curtis.

Represents: Nonfiction books, scholarly books, novels. **Considers all fiction areas.**

How to Contact: No fax or e-mail queries. Conventional queries (outline and 3 sample chapters) must be accompanied by SASE. Responds in 1 month to queries; 1 month to mss.

Needs: Obtains most new clients through recommendations from others, solicitations and conferences.

Recent Sales: Sold 100 titles in the last year. *Darwin's Radio*, by Greg Bear (Del Rey/Random House); *Ascending*, by James Gardner (Avon). Other clients include Dan Simmons, Jennifer Blake, Leonard Maltin, Earl Mindell and Barbara Parker.

Terms: Agent receives 15% commission on domestic sales; 20% on foreign sales. Offers written contract, binding on a "book by book basis." Charges for photocopying, express, fax, international postage, book orders.

Writers' Conferences: Romance Writers of America; Nebula Science Fiction Conference.

⬤**JOAN DAVES AGENCY**, 21 W. 26th St., New York NY 10010. (212)685-2663. Fax: (212)685-1781. **Contact:** Jennifer Lyons, director; Heather Currier, assistant. Estab. 1960. Member of AAR. Represents 100 clients. **10% of clients are new/previously unpublished writers.** Specializes in literary fiction and nonfiction, also commercial fiction.

Represents: Nonfiction books, novels. **Considers these fiction areas:** ethnic, family saga; gay; literary; mainstream.

How to Contact: Query with SASE. Considers simultaneous submissions. Responds in 3 weeks to queries; 6 weeks to mss. Returns materials only with SASE.

Needs: Obtains most new clients through editors' and author clients' recommendations. "A few queries translate into representation."

Recent Sales: Sold 70 titles in the last year. *Strange Fire*, by Melvin Jules Bukiet (W.W. Norton); *SLUT! Growing Up Female with a Bad Reputation*, by Leora Tannenbaum; *Candor and Perversion*, by Roger Shattuck (W.W. Norton).

Terms: Agent receives 15% commission on domestic sales; 20% on foreign sales. Offers written contract, binding on a per book basis. Charges for office expenses. 100% of business is derived from commissions on sales.

Reading List: Reads *The Paris Review*, *Missouri Review*, and *Voice Literary Supplement* to find new clients.

✔️⬤◎ **DHS LITERARY, INC.**, 6060 N. Central Expwy., Suite 624, Dallas TX 75206-5209. (214)363-4422. E-mail: submissions@dhsliterary.com. Website: www.dhsliterary.com. **Contact:** David Hale Smith, president. Estab. 1994. Represents 40 clients. **25% of clients are new/previously unpublished writers.** Specializes in commercial fiction and nonfiction for adult trade market. Currently handles: 60% nonfiction books; 40% novels.

• Prior to opening his agency, Mr. Smith was an editor at a newswire service.

Represents: Nonfiction books, novels. **Considers these fiction areas:** detective/police/crime; erotica; ethnic; feminist; gay; historical; literary; mainstream; mystery/suspense; sports; thriller/espionage; westerns/frontier.

How to Contact: One-page query via e-mail only. No paper queries accepted unless requested by agency. Will request more material if appropriate. Considers simultaneous queries. Responds in 1 month to queries.

Needs: Actively seeking thrillers, mysteries, suspense, etc., and narrative nonfiction. Does not want to receive poetry, short fiction, children's books. Obtains most new clients through referrals from other clients, editors and agents.

Recent Sales: Sold 35 titles in the last year. *Critical Space*, by Greg Rucka (Bantam).

Terms: Agent receives 15% commission on domestic sales; 25% on foreign sales. Offers written contract, with 10-day cancellation clause or upon mutual consent. Charges clients for expenses, i.e., postage, photocopying. 100% of business is derived from commissions on sales.

Reading List: Reads *Outside Magazine*, *Texas Monthly*, *Kenyon Review*, *Missouri Review* and *Mississippi Mud* to find new clients. "I like to see good writing in many formats. I'll often call a writer who has written a good short story, for example, to see if she has a novel."

Tips: "Remember to be courteous and professional, and to treat marketing your work and approaching an agent as you would any formal business matter. When in doubt, always query first via e-mail. Visit our website for more information."

✔️⬤ **ETHAN ELLENBERG LITERARY AGENCY**, 548 Broadway, #5-E, New York NY 10012. (212)431-4554. Fax: (212)941-4652. E-mail: ellenbergagent@aol.com. Website: www.ethanellenberg.org. **Contact:** Ethan Ellenberg, Michael Psaltis. Estab. 1983. Represents 70 clients. 10% of clients are new/previously unpublished writers. Currently handles: 25% nonfiction books; 75% novels.

• Prior to opening his agency, Mr. Ellenberg was contracts manager of Berkley/Jove and associate contracts manager for Bantam.

Member Agents: Michael Psaltis (commercial fiction, literary fiction, mysteries, women's fiction); Ethan Ellenberg.

Represents: Nonfiction books, novels. **Considers these fiction areas:** detective/police/crime; family saga; fantasy; historical; juvenile; literary; mainstream; mystery/suspense; picture book; romance; science fiction; thriller/espionage; young adult.

How to Contact: For fiction: Send introductory letter (with credits, if any), outline, first 3 chapters, SASE. For children's books: Send introductory letter (with credits, if any), up to 3 picture book mss, outline and first 3 chapters for longer projects, SASE. Accepts queries by e-mail but no attachments; does not accept fax queries. Considers simultaneous queries and submissions. Responds in 10 days to queries; 1 month to mss. Returns materials only with SASE.

Recent Sales: Sold over 100 titles in the last year. *Legacy Trilogy*, by Bill Keith (Avon); two contemporary romances, by Kathleen Kane (St. Martin's Press); two historical romances, by Beatrice Small (Kensington Books); *The Prairie Train*, illustrated by Eric Rohmann (Crown); *The Hero of the Herd*, by John M. Cormack.

Terms: Agent receives 15% on domestic sales; 10% on foreign sales. Offers written contract, "flexible." Charges clients for "direct expenses only: photocopying, postage." Writers reimbursed for office fees after the sale of ms.

Writers' Conferences: Attends RWA National and Novelists, Inc.

Tips: "We do consider new material from unsolicited authors. Write a good clear letter with a succinct description of your book. We prefer the first three chapters when we consider fiction. For all submissions you must include SASE for return or the material is discarded. It's always hard to break in, but talent will find a home. We continue to see natural storytellers and nonfiction writers with important books."

☑ ◐ **NICHOLAS ELLISON, INC.**, 55 Fifth Ave., 15th Floor, New York NY 10003. (212)206-6050. Fax: (212)463-8718. Affiliated with Sanford J. Greenburger Associates. **Contact:** Alička Pistek. Estab. 1983. Represents 70 clients. Currently handles: 25% nonfiction books; 75% novels.
   • Prior to becoming an agent, Mr. Ellison was an editor at Minerva Editions, Harper & Row and editor-in-chief at Delacorte.
Member Agents: Alička Pistek.
Represents: Nonfiction, novels. **Considers literary and mainstream fiction.**
How to Contact: Query with SASE. Responds in 6 weeks.
Needs: Usually obtains most new clients from word-of-mouth referrals.
Recent Sales: *The Lion's Game*, by Nelson DeMille (Warner); *Equivocal Death*, by Amy Gutman (Little, Brown). Other clients include Olivia Goldsmith, P.T. Deutermann, James Webb, Nancy Geary.
Terms: Agent receives 15% commission on domestic sales; 20% commission on foreign sales.

☑ ◖ **MARY EVANS INC.**, 242 E. Fifth St., New York NY 10003. (212)979-0880. Fax: (212)979-5344. E-mail: merrylit@aol.com. **Contact:** Carlotta Vance. Member of AAR. Represents 45 clients. Currently handles: 45% nonfiction books; 5% story collections; 50% novels.
Member Agents: Mary Evans, Tanya McKinnon.
Represents: Nonfiction books, novels. **Considers these fiction areas:** contemporary issues; ethnic; literary; upmarket.
How to Contact: Query with SASE. Responds in 1 month to queries; 2 months to mss.
Needs: Actively seeking "professional well-researched nonfiction proposals; literary novels." No children's books. Obtains most new clients through recommendations from others.
Recent Sales: Sold 15 titles in the last year. *The Amazing Adventures of Kavalier & Clay*, by Michael Chalon (Random House); *Mitten Strings for God*, by Katrina Kenison (Warner Books).
Terms: Agent receives 15% commission on domestic sales; 20% on foreign sales.

◖ **JUSTIN E. FERNANDEZ, AGENT/ATTORNEY**, (formerly Justin E. Fernandez Attorney/Agent—Agency for the Digital & Literary Arts, Inc.), P.O. Box 20038, Cincinnati OH 45220. E-mail: lit4@aol.com. **Contact:** Justin E. Fernandez. Estab. 1996. Represents 10-15 clients. **50% of clients are new/previously unpublished writers.** Currently handles: 25% nonfiction; 65% fiction; 5% digital/multimedia, 5% other. "We are presently an affiliate agency of AEI, Inc. AEI has offices in Beverly Hills and New York. AEI's web address is www.aeionline.com."
   • Prior to opening his agency, Mr. Fernandez, a 1992 graduate of the University of Cincinnati College of Law, served as a law clerk with the Ohio Court of Appeals, Second Appellate District (1992-94), and as a literary agent for Paraview, Inc., New York (1995-96).
Member Agents: Paul A. Franc (associate agent).
Represents: Nonfiction, fiction, screen/teleplays and digital art (virtual reality, music, software, multimedia/Internet-related products). **Considers most fiction genres.**
How to Contact: Query first with SASE (e-mail encouraged). Considers simultaneous queries and submissions. When hard copy is requested, be sure to include a container for the manuscript, with return address and sufficient postage affixed unless recycling is an option.
Needs: Mainstream fiction; pop culture; women's fiction; thrillers; histories; biographies; literary fiction and nonfiction; children's books; computer and Internet-related books; romance novels; African-American and Hispanic fiction; science fiction; gift and humor books; photography, art and design books; popular/mainstream science and philosophy, political science, Eastern religion, gay/lesbian fiction and nonfiction; and material for syndication (columns, cartoon strips, etc.). Usually obtains new clients through referrals or queries from listings.
Recent Sales: Sold 4 titles last year. *By Way of a Wager* and *Seeking Celeste*, by Hayley Ann Solomon (Kensington/Zebra).
Terms: Agent receives 10% commission on domestic sales; 15% on foreign sales; 25% with foreign co-agent. Offers written contract. No fees. Expenses deducted from monies received per contract terms.
Tips: "Proofread, proofread, proofread—50% of submissions have typos, usage errors, or clichés in the first several pages. Manuscripts should be double spaced, with 1-inch margins, 12 point font, and be accompanied by a return package, with sufficient postage attached (not loose) to the package. When sending e-mail follow-up messages, don't assume your name is enough information—identify the submission by title and date and method submitted."

Ⓝ Ⓞ JOYCE A. FLAHERTY, LITERARY AGENT, 816 Lynda Court, St. Louis MO 63122-5531. (314)966-3057. **Contact:** Joyce Flaherty. Estab. 1980. Member of AAR, RWA, MWA, Authors Guild. Represents 40 clients. Currently handles: 15% nonfiction books; 85% novels.
• Prior to opening her agency, Ms. Flaherty was a journalist, public relations consultant, and executive director of a large suburban Chamber of Commerce.
Member Agents: Joyce A. Flaherty.
Represents: Nonfiction books, novels. **Considers these fiction areas:** contemporary issues; family saga; feminist; historical; mainstream; military; mystery/suspense; thrillers; women's genre fiction.
How to Contact: Send outline plus 1 sample chapter and SASE. *No unsolicited mss.* Does not accept queries by e-mail or fax. Prefers to read materials exclusively. Responds in 1 month to queries; 2 months to mss unless otherwise agreed on. Returns materials only with SASE. "At this time we are adding only currently published authors." Preference given to published book authors.
Needs: Actively seeking "high concept fiction, very commercial; quality works of both fiction and nonfiction; gripping nonfiction adventure." Does not want to receive "poetry, novellas, short stories, juvenile, syndicated material, film scripts, essay collections, science fiction, traditional westerns." Obtains most new clients through recommendations from editors and clients, writers' conferences, and from queries.
Recent Sales: Sold 51 titles in the last year. *Murder of a Small Town Honey*, by Denise Swanwon (Signet/NAL); *The Irish Rogue*, by Judith E. French (Ballantine); *Primary Target*, by Joe Weber (Putnam-Berkley); *Princess*, by Gaelen Foley (Ballantine).
Terms: Agent receives 15% commission on domestic sales.
Writers' Conferences: Often attends Romance Writers of America.
Tips: "Be concise and well focused in a letter or by phone. Always include a SASE as well as your phone number. Know something about the agent beforehand so you're not wasting each other's time. Be specific about word length of project and when it will be completed if not completed at the time of contact. Be brief!"

✓ Ⓞ REECE HALSEY NORTH, 98 Main St., PMB 704, Tiburon CA 94920. (415)789-9191. Fax: (415)789-9177. E-mail: bookgirl@worldnet.att.net. Website: www.reecehalseynorth.com or www.kimberlycameron.com. **Contact:** Kimberley Cameron. Estab. 1957. Member of AAR, signatory of WGA. Represents 40 clients. **30% of clients are new/previously unpublished writers.** Specializes in mystery, literary and mainstream fiction, excellent writing. Currently handles: 30% nonfiction books; 70% fiction.
• The Reese Halsey Agency has an illustrious client list largely of established writers, including the estate of Aldous Huxley and has represented Upton Sinclair, William Faulkner and Henry Miller. Ms. Cameron has recently opened a Northern California office and all queries should be addressed to her at the Tiburon office.
Member Agents: Doris Halsey (by referral only, LA office); Kimberley Cameron (Reese Halsey North).
Represents: Fiction and nonfiction. **Considers these fiction areas:** action/adventure; contemporary issues; detective/police/crime; ethnic; family saga; historical; literary; mainstream; mystery/suspense; science fiction; thriller/espionage; women's fiction.
How to Contact: Query with SASE. Does not accept queries by e-mail or fax. Considers simultaneous queries and submissions. Responds in 3 weeks to queries; 3 months to mss.
Recent Sales: Prefers not to share information on specific sales.
Terms: Agent receives 15% commission on domestic sales of books. Offers written contract, binding for 1 year. Requests 6 copies of ms if representing an author.
Writers' Conferences: BEA, Maui Writers Conference and various writer conferences.
Reading List: Reads *Glimmer Train*, *The Sun* and *The New Yorker* to find new clients. Looks for "writing that touches the heart."
Tips: Obtains most new clients through recommendations from others and solicitation. "Please send a polite, well-written query and include a SASE with it!"

Ⓞ HARRIS LITERARY AGENCY, P.O. Box 6023, San Diego CA 92166. (619)697-0600. Fax: (619)697-0610. E-mail: hlit@adnc.com. Website: www.HarrisLiterary.com. **Contact:** Barbara J. Harris. Estab. 1998. Represents 60 clients. **65% of clients are new/previously unpublished writers.** Specializes in mainstream fiction. Currently handles: 40% nonfiction books; 60% novels.
Member Agents: Barbara J. Harris (nonfiction, fiction); Norman J. Rudenberg (fiction, science fiction, thrillers).
Represents: Nonfiction books, novels. **Considers these fiction areas:** action/adventure; contemporary young adult; detective/police/crime; humor/satire; juvenile; mainstream; mystery/suspense; science fiction; techno thriller; thriller/espionage.
How to Contact: Query with SASE. "The initial query should contain a one- to two-page description plus the author's pertinent biography, neatly typed in 12 point font with accurate spelling and proper punctuation. Make sure it is clear and succinct. Tell what the work is about and do not add hype. Include the ending and tell us how many words and pages are in your work." Accepts queries by e-mail. "Do not query by sending long e-mail messages. Tell about your work in 200-300 words." Responds in 2 weeks to queries; 1 month to mss. Returns materials only with SASE.

Needs: Obtains most new clients through directories, recommendations and internet listing.

Recent Sales: Sold 8 titles in the last year. *The Sweep of the Second Hand*, by Dean Monti (Academy Chicago Publishers); *Caught in the Web*, by Ron Joseph (Beijia Publishing House); *Meltdown*, by Rick Slater (Beijia Publishing House).

Terms: Agent receives 15% commission on domestic sales; 20% on foreign sales. Offers written contract. 30 days notice must be given to terminate contract. Charges for photocopying, postage. No reading or agency fees.

Writers' Conferences: BEA.

Tips: "Professional guidance is imperative in bringing along new writers. In the highly competitive publishing arena, strict guidelines must be adhered to." See website for agency guidelines.

☑ ◑ ◎ **THE JOY HARRIS LITERARY AGENCY, INC.**, 156 Fifth Ave., Suite 617, New York NY 10010. (212)924-6269. Fax: (212)924-6609. E-mail: gen.office@jhlitagent.com. **Contact:** Joy Harris. Member of AAR. Represents 150 clients. Currently handles: 50% nonfiction books; 50% novels.

Member Agents: Leslie Daniels.

Represents: Nonfiction, novels. **Considers "adult-type books, not juvenile." Considers all fiction areas** except fantasy; juvenile; science fiction; westerns/frontier.

How to Contact: Query with outline/proposal and SASE. Responds in 2 months to queries. *No unsolicited mss*; queries only.

Needs: Obtains new clients through recommendations from clients and editors.

Recent Sales: Sold 15 titles in the last year. Prefers not to share information on specific sales.

Terms: Agent receives 15% commission on domestic sales; 20% on foreign sales. Charges for some office expenses.

☑ ◐ **RICHARD HENSHAW GROUP**, 132 W. 22nd St., 4th Floor, New York NY 10011. (212)414-1172. Fax: (212)727-3279. E-mail: rhgagents@aol.com. Website: www.rich.henshaw.com. **Contact:** Rich Henshaw. Estab. 1995. Member of AAR, SinC, MWA, HWA, SFWA. Represents 35 clients. **20% of clients are new/ previously unpublished writers.** Specializes in thrillers, mysteries, science fiction, fantasy and horror. Currently handles: 30% nonfiction books; 70% novels.

 • Prior to opening his agency, Mr. Henshaw served as an agent with Richard Curtis Associates, Inc.

Represents: Nonfiction books, juvenile books, novels. **Considers these fiction areas:** action/adventure; detective/police/crime; ethnic; family saga; fantasy; glitz; historical; horror; humor/satire; juvenile; literary; mainstream; psychic/supernatural; romance; science fiction; sports; thriller/espionage; young adult.

How to Contact: Query with SASE. Responds in 3 weeks to queries; 6 weeks to mss.

Needs: Obtains most new clients through recommendations from others, solicitation, at conferences and query letters.

Recent Sales: Sold 17 titles in the last year. *Midnight Comes Again*, by Dana Stabenow (St. Martin's Press); *Deadstick*, by Megan Mallory Rust (Berkley); *Bad Lawyer*, by Stephen Solomita (Carroll & Graf).

Terms: Agent receives 15% commission on domestic sales; 20% on foreign sales. No written contract. Charges for photocopying manuscripts and book orders. 100% of business is derived from commission on sales.

Tips: "Always include SASE with correct return postage. Please visit our website for more information and current interests."

◐ ◎ **HOPKINS LITERARY ASSOCIATES**, PMB 327, 2117, Buffalo Rd., Rochester NY 14624-1507. (716)429-6559. E-mail: pamhopkins@aol.com. **Contact:** Pam Hopkins. Estab. 1996. Member of AAR, RWA. Represents 30 clients. **5% of clients are new/unpublished writers.** Specializes in women's fiction, particularly historical, contemporary and category romance as well as mainstream work. Currently handles: 100% novels.

Represents: Novels. **Considers these fiction areas:** historical; mainstream; romance.

How to Contact: Send outline and 3 sample chapters. No queries by e-mail or fax. Considers simultaneous queries and submissions. Responds in 2 weeks to queries; 1 month to mss. Returns material only with SASE.

Needs: Obtains most new clients through recommendations from others, solicitations and conferences.

Recent Sales: Sold 50 titles in the last year. *The Horse Soldier*, by Merline Lovelace (MIRA); *The Doctor's Wife*, by Cheryl St. John (Harlequin); *By Possession*, by Madeline Hunter (Bantam); *Fortunes Bride*, by Victoria Malvey (Pocket).

Terms: Agent receives 15% commission on domestic sales; 20% on foreign sales. No written contract. 30 day written notice must be given to terminate verbal contract.

Writer's Conferences: Romance Writers of America.

◐ **J DE S ASSOCIATES INC.**, 9 Shagbark Rd., Wilson Point, South Norwalk CT 06854. (203)838-7571. **Contact:** Jacques de Spoelberch. Estab. 1975. Represents 50 clients. Currently handles: 50% nonfiction books; 50% novels.

 • Prior to opening his agency, Mr. de Spoelberch was an editor at Houghton Mifflin.

Represents: Nonfiction books, novels. **Considers these fiction areas:** detective/police/crime; historical; juvenile; literary; mainstream; mystery/suspense; New Age; westerns/frontier; young adult.

How to Contact: Query with SASE. Responds in 2 months to queries.

Needs: Obtains most new clients through recommendations from authors and other clients.

Recent Sales: Prefers not to share information on specific sales.

Terms: Agent receives 15% commission on domestic sales; 20% on foreign sales. Charges for foreign postage and photocopying.

JABBERWOCKY LITERARY AGENCY, P.O. Box 4558, Sunnyside NY 11104-0558. (718)392-5985. **Contact:** Joshua Bilmes. Estab. 1994. Member of SFWA. Represents 40 clients. **25% of clients are new/ previously unpublished writers.** "Agency represents quite a lot of genre fiction and is actively seeking to increase amount of nonfiction projects." Currently handles: 25% nonfiction books; 5% scholarly books; 65% novel; 5% other.

Represents: Nonfiction books, scholarly books, novels. **Considers these fiction areas:** action/adventure; cartoon/comic; contemporary issues; detective/police/crime; ethnic; family saga; fantasy; gay; glitz; historical; horror; humor/satire; lesbian; literary; mainstream; psychic/supernatural; regional; science fiction; sports; thriller/espionage.

How to Contact: Query letters only with SASE; *no ms material unless requested*. Does not accept queries by e-mail or fax. Considers simultaneous queries and submissions. Responds in 2 weeks to queries. Returns materials only with SASE.

Needs: Obtains most new clients through recommendation by current clients, solicitation, "and through intriguing queries by new authors."

Recent Sales: Sold 20 titles in the last year. *Shakespeare's Trollop*, by Charlaine Harris (Dell); *Beyond the Blue Moon*, by Simon Green (Roc); *Against the Odds*, by Elizabeth Moon (Baen). Other clients include Tanya Hutt, Kristine Smith, Edo van Belkom.

Terms: Agent receives 12.5% commission on domestic sales; 20% on foreign sales. Offers written contract, binding for 1 year. Charges for book purchases, photocopying, international book/ms mailing, international long distance.

Writers' Conferences: Malice Domestic (Washington DC, May); World SF Convention (Philadelphia, August); Icon (Stony Brook NY, April).

Reading list: Reads *New Republic*, *Analog* and various newspapers to find new clients.

Tips: "In approaching with a query, the most important things to me are your credits and your biographical background to the extent it's relevant to your work. I (and most agents, I believe) will ignore the adjectives you may choose to describe your own work."

JCA LITERARY AGENCY, 27 W. 20th St., Suite 1103, New York NY 10011. (212)807-0888. Fax: (212)807-0461. **Contact:** Jeff Gerecke, Tony Outhwaite. Estab. 1978. Member of AAR. Represents 100 clients. **20% of clients are new/unpublished writers.** Currently handles: 20% nonfiction books; 5% scholarly books; 25% novels.

Member Agents: Jeff Gerecke; Tony Outhwaite.

Represents: Nonfiction books, scholarly books, novels. **Considers these fiction areas:** action/adventure; contemporary issues; detective/police/crime; family saga; historical; literary; mainstream; mystery; sports; thriller/espionage.

How to Contact: Query with SASE. Does not accept queries by fax or e-mail. Considers simultaneous queries and submissions. "We occasionally may ask for an exclusive look." Responds in 2 weeks to queries; 10 weeks to mss. Returns materials only with SASE.

Needs: Does not want to receive screenplays, poetry, children's books, science fiction/fantasy, genre romance. Obtains most new clients through recommendations, solicitations, conferences.

Recent Sales: *The Lost Glass Plates of Wilfred Eng*, by Thomas Orton (Counterpoint); *Sharp Shooter*, by David Healey (The Berkley Publishing Group/Jove); *A Healthy Place to Die*, by Peter King (St. Martin's Press). Other clients include Ernest J. Gaines, W.E.B. Griffin, Polly Whitney, David J. Garrow.

Terms: Agent receives 15% commission on domestic sales; 20% on foreign sales. No written contract. "We work with our clients on a handshake basis." Charges for postage on overseas submissions, photocopying mss for submission, books purchased for subrights submission, and bank charges, where applicable. "We deduct the cost from payments received from publishers."

Tips: "We do not ourselves provide legal, accounting, or public relations services for our clients, although some of the advice we give falls somewhat into these realms. In cases where it seems necessary we will recommend obtaining outside advice or assistance in these areas from professionals who are not in any way connected to the agency."

VIRGINIA KIDD AGENCY, INC., 538 E. Harford St., P.O. Box 278, Milford PA 18337-0728. (717)296-6205. Fax: (717)296-7266. **Contact:** James Allen. Estab. 1965. Member of SFWA, SFRA, SFTA. Represents 80 clients. Specializes in "science fiction but we do not limit ourselves to it."

● Prior to opening her agency, Ms. Kidd was a ghost writer, pulp writer and poet.

Member Agents: Virginia Kidd; James Allen; Christine Cohen (historical fiction); Nanci McCloskey (women's fiction).

Represents: Fiction. **Considers these fiction areas:** speculative fiction, science fiction, fantasy (special interest in nontraditional fantasy), mystery, literary, mainstream, feminist, glitz, suspense, historical, young adult. **Specializes in science fiction "but we do not limit ourselves to it."**

How to Contact: Query with SASE. Does not accept queries by e-mail or fax. Prefers to read materials exclusively. Responds in 1 week to queries; 6 weeks to mss.

Needs: Obtains most new clients through recommendations from others.

Recent Sales: Sold about 60 titles in the last year. *Tales from Earthsea*, by Ursula K. Le Guin (Harcourt Brace); *Pern*, by Anne McCaffrey (Del Rey); *Kingdoms of Light*, by Alan Dean Foster (Penguin Putnam). Other clients include Gene Wolfe, R.A. Lafferty, Joe L. Hensley, William Tenn and Al Coppel.

Terms: Agent receives 10% commission on domestic sales; 20% on foreign sales. Offers written contract, binding until canceled by either party. 30 days notice must be given to terminate contract. Charges for photocopying and copies of books used to market susidiary rights.

Tips: "If you have a novel of speculative fiction, romance, or mainstream that is *really extraordinary*, please query me, including a synopsis, a cv and a SASE."

KIDDE, HOYT & PICARD, 335 E. 51st St., New York NY 10022. (212)755-9461. Fax: (212)223-2501. **Contact:** Katharine Kidde, Laura Langlie. Estab. 1980. Member of AAR. Represents 80 clients. Specializes in mainstream fiction and nonfiction. Currently handles: 15% nonfiction books; 5% juvenile books; 80% novels.

• Prior to becoming agents, Ms. Kidde was an editor/senior editor at Harcourt Brace, New American Library and Putnam; Ms. Langlie worked in production and editorial at Kensington and Carroll & Graf.

Member Agents: Kay Kidde (mainstream fiction, general nonfiction, romances, literary fiction); Laura Langlie (romances, mysteries, literary fiction, general nonfiction).

Represents: Nonfiction books, novels. **Considers these fiction areas:** contemporary; detective/police/crime; feminist; gay; glitz; historical; humor; lesbian; literary; mainstream; mystery/suspense; romance (contemporary, historical, regency); thriller.

How to Contact: Query with SASE. Considers simultaneous queries and submissions. Responds in a few weeks to queries; 1 month to mss. Returns materials only with SASE.

Needs: Actively seeking "strong mainstream fiction." Does not want to receive "male adventure, science fiction, juvenile, porn, plays or poetry." Obtains most new clients through query letters, recommendations from others, "former authors from when I was an editor at NAL, Harcourt, etc.; listings in *LMP*, writers' guides."

Recent Sales: *Night Bus*, by Janice Law (Forge/TOR); *False Witness*, by Lelia Kelly (Kensington). Other clients include Michael Cadmum, Jim Oliver, Bethany Campbell and Mark Miano.

Reading List: Reads literary journals and magazines, *Harper's*, *DoubleTake*, etc. to find new clients.

Terms: Agent receives 15% commission on domestic sales; 20% on foreign sales. Charges for photocopying.

Tips: "We look for beautiful stylistic writing, and that elusive treasure, a good book (mostly fiction). As former editors, we can help launch authors."

THE KNIGHT AGENCY, P.O. Box 550648, Atlanta GA 30355. Or: 2407 Matthews St., Atlanta GA 30319. (404)816-9620. Fax: (404)237-3439. E-mail: deidremk@aol.com. Website: www.knightagency.net. **Contact:** Deidre Knight. Estab. 1996. Member of RWA, AAR, Author's Guild. Represents 30 clients. **40% of clients are new/previously unpublished writers.** Currently handles: 50% nonfiction books; 50% novels.

Represents: Nonfiction books, novels. **Considers these fiction areas:** ethnic; literary; mainstream; romance (contemporary, historical, inspirational); women's fiction; commercial fiction.

How to Contact: Query with SASE. Considers simultaneous queries and submissions. Reports in 2 weeks on queries; 6 weeks on mss.

Needs: "We are looking for a wide variety of fiction and nonfiction. In fiction, we're always looking for romance, women's fiction, ethnic and commercial fiction."

Recent Sales: Sold 40 titles in the last year. *The Highlander's Touch*, by Karen Marie Moning (Bantam Dell).

Terms: Agent receives 15% commission on domestic sales; 20-25% on foreign sales. Offers written contract, terminates upon 30-days notice. "Charge clients for photocopying, postage, overnight courier expenses. These are deducted from the sale of the book, not billed up front."

Tips: "At the Knight Agency, a client usually ends up becoming a friend."

ELAINE KOSTER LITERARY AGENCY, LLC, 55 Central Park West, Suite 6, New York NY 10023. (212)362-9488. Fax: (212)712-0164. **Contact:** Elaine Koster. Member of AAR, MWA. Represents 30 clients. **25% of clients are new/unpublished writers.** Specializes in quality fiction and nonfiction. Currently handles: 30% nonfiction books; 70% novels.

• Prior to opening her agency, Ms. Koster was president and publisher of Dutton/NAL.

Represents: Nonfiction books, novels. **Considers these fiction areas:** action/adventure; confessional; contemporary issues; detective/police/crime; ethnic; family saga; feminist; gay/lesbian; glitz; historical; literary; mainstream; mystery (amateur sleuth, cozy, culinary, malice domestic); regional; suspense; thriller/espionage.

How to Contact: Query with outline, 3 sample chapters and SASE. Does not accept queries by e-mail or fax. Prefers to read materials exclusively. Responds in 3 weeks to queries; 1 month to mss. Returns materials only with SASE.
Needs: No juvenile, screenplays. Obtains most new clients through recommendations from others.
Recent Sales: Sold 23 titles in the last year. *Special Agent*, by Candice DeLong (Hyperion); *Sounds of the River*, by Da Chen (HarperCollins); *Tilting at Windmills*, by Joseph Pittman (Pocket Books).
Terms: Agent receives 15% commission on domestic sales; 20% on foreign sales. Offers written contract, 60 days notice must be given to terminate contract. Charges for photocopying, messengers, express mail, books and book galley ordered from publisher to exploit other rights, overseas shipment of mss and books.
Tips: "We prefer exclusive submissions."

IRENE KRAAS AGENCY, 220 Copper Trail, Santa Fe NM 87505. (505)474-6212. Fax: (505)474-6216. Estab. 1990. Represents 30 clients. **75% of clients are new/unpublished writers.** Specializes in fiction only, middle grade through adult. Does not want to receive romance, short stories, plays or poetry. Currently handles: 30% juvenile books; 70% novels.
Represents: Adult fiction. **Considers these fiction areas:** action/adventure; detective/police/crime; mystery/suspense; science fiction.
How to Contact: Send cover letter and first 30 pages. Must include return postage and/or SASE. Does not accept e-mail queries. Considers simultaneous submissions. Returns materials only with SASE.
Needs: Actively seeking "books that are well written with commercial potential."
Recent Sales: *A Matter of Profit*, by Hilari Bell (Harper/Avon); *Cold Heart*, by Chandler McGraw (Bantam); *The Bean King's Daughter*, by Jennifer Stewart (Holiday House). Other clients include Denise Vitola, Shirley-Raye Redmond, Terry England and Duncan Long.
Terms: Agent receives 15% commission on domestic sales. Offers written contract, binding for 1 year "but can be terminated at any time for any reason with written notice." Charges for photocopying and postage.
Writers' Conferences: Southwest Writers Conference (Albuquerque); Pacific Northwest Conference (Seattle); Vancouver Writers Conference (Vancouver BC); Austin Writers Workshop; Wilamette Writers' Group.

PETER LAMPACK AGENCY, INC., 551 Fifth Ave., Suite 1613, New York NY 10176-0187. (212)687-9106. Fax: (212)687-9109. E-mail: renbopla@aol.com. **Contact:** Loren G. Soeiro. Estab. 1977. Represents 50 clients. **10% of clients are new/previously unpublished writers.** Specializes in commercial fiction, male-oriented action/adventure, thrillers/suspense, contemporary relationships, distinguished literary fiction, nonfiction by a recognized expert in a given field. Currently handles: 20% nonfiction books; 80% novels.
Member Agents: Peter Lampack (psychological suspense, action/adventure, literary fiction, nonfiction, contemporary relationships); Sandra Blanton (foreign rights); Loren G. Soeiro (literary and commercial fiction, mystery, suspense, nonfiction, narrative nonfiction, high-concept thrillers).
Represents: Nonfiction books, novels. **Considers these fiction areas:** action/adventure; contemporary relationships; detective/police/crime; family saga; historical; literary; mainstream; mystery/suspense; thriller/espionage.
How to Contact: Query with SASE. *No unsolicited mss.* Does not accept queries by fax. Accepts queries by e-mail. Responds in 3 weeks to queries; 2 months to mss.
Needs: Actively seeking literary and commercial fiction, thrillers, mysteries, suspense, psychological thrillers, high-concept. Does not want to receive romance, science fiction, western, academic material. Obtains most new clients from referrals made by clients.
Recent Sales: *Atlantis Found*, by Clive Cussler (Putnam); *In Her Defense*, by Stephen Horn (HarperCollins); *Summer of Storms* by Judith Kelman (Berkley).
Terms: Agent receives 15% commission on domestic sales; 20% on foreign sales.
Writers' Conferences: BEA (Chicago, June).
Tips: "Submit only your best work for consideration. Have a very specific agenda of goals you wish your prospective agent to accomplish for you. Provide the agent with a comprehensive statement of your credentials: educational and professional."

RAY LINCOLN LITERARY AGENCY, Elkins Park House, Suite 107-B, 7900 Old York Rd., Elkins Park PA 19027. (215)635-0827. **Contact:** Mrs. Ray Lincoln. Estab. 1974. Represents 30 clients. **35% of clients are new/previously unpublished writers.** Specializes in biography, nature, the sciences, fiction in both adult and children's categories. Currently handles: 30% nonfiction books; 20% juvenile books; 50% novels.
Member Agents: Jerome A. Lincoln; Mrs. Ray Lincoln.
Represents: Nonfiction books, scholarly books, juvenile books, novels. **Considers these fiction areas:** action/adventure; contemporary issues; detective/police/crime; ethnic; family saga; fantasy; feminist; gay; historical; humor/satire; juvenile; lesbian; literary; mainstream; mystery/suspense; psychic/supernatural; regional; romance (contemporary, gothic, historical); sports; thriller/espionage; young adult.
How to Contact: Query first with SASE, then on request send outline, 2 sample chapters and SASE. "I send for balance of manuscript if it is a likely project." Responds in 2 weeks to queries; 1 month to mss.
Needs: Obtains most new clients from recommendations.

Recent Sales: *The Blanders*, by Barbara Robinson (HarperCollins); *Stargirl*, by Jerry Spinelli (Knopf); *To Wanda and Me*, by Susan Katz (Simon & Schuster).

Terms: Agent receives 15% commission on domestic sales; 20% on foreign sales. Offers written contract, binding "but with notice, may be cancelled." Charges for overseas telephone calls; upfront postage fee for unpublished authors only. "I request authors to do manuscript photocopying themselves."

Tips: "I always look for polished writing style, fresh points of view and professional attitudes."

STERLING LORD LITERISTIC, INC., 65 Bleecker St., New York NY 10012. (212)780-6050. Fax: (212)780-6095. **Contact:** Peter Matson. Estab. 1952. Signatory of WGA. Represents over 600 clients. Currently handles: 50% nonfiction books, 50% novels.

Member Agents: Peter Matson; Sterling Lord; Jody Hotchkiss (film scripts); Philippa Brophy; Chris Calhoun; Jennifer Hengen; Charlotte Sheedy; George Nicholson; Neeti Madan.

Represents: Nonfiction books, novels. "Literary value considered first."

How to Contact: Query. Responds in 1 month to mss.

Needs: Obtains new clients through recommendations from others.

Recent Sales: Prefers not to share information on specific sales.

Terms: Agent receives 15% commission on domestic sales; 20% on foreign sales. Offers written contract. Charges for photocopying.

DONALD MAASS LITERARY AGENCY, 157 W. 57th St., Suite 703, New York NY 10019. (212)757-7755. **Contact:** Donald Maass, Jennifer Jackson or Michelle Brummer. Estab. 1980. Member of AAR, SFWA, MWA, RWA. Represents over 100 clients. **5% of clients are new/previously unpublished writers.** Specializes in commercial fiction, especially science fiction, fantasy, mystery, romance, suspense. Currently handles: 100% novels.

● Prior to opening his agency, Mr. Maass served as an editor at Dell Publishing (NY) and as a reader at Gollancz (London).

Member Agents: Donald Maass (mainstream, literary, mystery/suspense, science fiction); Jennifer Jackson (commercial fiction: especially romance, science fiction, fantasy, mystery/suspense); Michelle Brummer (fiction: literary, contemporary, feminist, science fiction, fantasy).

Represents: Novels. **Considers these fiction areas:** detective/police/crime; fantasy; historical; horror; literary; mainstream; mystery/suspense; psychic/supernatural; romance (historical, paranormal, time travel); science fiction; thriller/espionage.

How to Contact: Query with SASE. Considers simultaneous queries and submissions. Returns materials only with SASE. Responds in 2 weeks to queries, 3 months to mss (if requested following query).

Needs: Actively seeking "to expand the literary portion of our list and expand in romance and women's fiction." Does not want to receive nonfiction, children's or poetry.

Recent Sales: Sold over 100 titles in the last year. *Slaves of Obsession*, by Anne Perry (Ballantine); *Midnight Robber*, by Nalo Hopkinson (Warner Aspect); *The Avalanche Soldier*, by Susan Matthews (Avon Eos); *Confluence II: Ancient of Days*, by Paul McAuley (Avon Eos).

Terms: Agent receives 15% commission on domestic sales; 20% on foreign sales. Charges for large photocopying orders and book samples, "after consultation with author."

Writers' Conferences: Donald Maass: World Science Fiction Convention, Frankfurt Book Fair, Pacific Northwest Writers Conference, Bouchercon, and others. Jennifer Jackson: World Science Fiction and Fantasy Convention, RWA National, and others. Michelle Brummer: ReaderCon, World Science Fiction Convention and Luna Con.

Tips: "We are fiction specialists, also noted for our innovative approach to career planning. Few new clients are accepted, but interested authors should query with SASE. Subagents in all principle foreign countries and Hollywood. No nonfiction or juvenile works considered."

ELAINE MARKSON LITERARY AGENCY, 44 Greenwich Ave., New York NY 10011. (212)243-8480. Fax: (212)691-9014. Estab. 1972. Member of AAR and WGA. Represents 200 clients. **10% of clients are new/ unpublished writers.** Specializes in literary fiction, commercial fiction, trade nonfiction. Currently handles: 35% nonfiction books; 55% novels; 10% juvenile books.

Member Agents: Geri Thoma, Sally Wofford-Girand, Elizabeth Sheinkman, Elaine Markson.

Represents: Quality fiction and nonfiction.

How to Contact: Obtains new clients by recommendation only.

Recent Sales: *The River King*, by Alice Hoffman (Putnam); *Where the Heart Is*, by Billie Letts (Warner); *The Heartsong of Charging Elk*, by James Welch (Doubleday); *Goldman Sachs: The Culture of Success*, by Lisa Endlich (Knopf).

Terms: Agent receives 15% commission on domestic sales; 20% on foreign sales. Charges for postage, photocopying, foreign mailing, faxing, and other special expenses.

☑ Ⓜ **DORIS S. MICHAELS LITERARY AGENCY, INC.**, 1841 Broadway, Suite #903, New York NY 10023. (212)265-9474. E-mail: mail@dsmagency.com. Website: www.dsmagency.com. **Contact:** Doris S. Michaels. Estab. 1994. Member of WNBA, AAR. Represents 30 clients. **50% of clients are new/previously unpublished writers.** Currently handles: 40% nonfiction books; 60% novels.
- Prior to opening her agency, Ms. Michaels was an editor for Prentice-Hall, consultant for Prudential-Bache, and an international consultant for the Union Bank of Switzerland.

Member Agents: Faye Bender.
Represents: Nonfiction books, novels. **Considers these fiction areas:** action/adventure; contemporary issues; family saga; feminist; historical; literary; mainstream.
How to Contact: Query by e-mail. Considers simultaneous queries. *No phone calls or unsolicited mss.* Returns requested materials only with SASE,
Needs: Obtains most new clients through recommendations from others and at conferences.
Recent Sales: Sold over 30 titles in the last year. *All Roads to October*, by Maury Allen (St. Martin's Press). Other clients include Jeffrey J. Fox, Jason Kelly.
Terms: Agent receives 15% commission on domestic sales; 20% on foreign sales. Offers written contract, binding for 1 year, with 30-day cancellation clause. Charges for office expenses including deliveries, postage, photocopying and fax, not to exceed $150 for postage, photocopying, etc. without written permission. 100% of business is derived from commissions on sales.
Writers' Conferences: BEA (Chicago, June); Frankfurt Book Fair (Germany, October); London Book Fair; Society of Southwestern Authors; San Diego State University Writers' Conference; Willamette Writers' Conference; International Women's Writing Guild; American Society of Journalists and Authors; Maui Writers Conference.

Ⓜ **WILLIAM MORRIS AGENCY, INC.**, 1325 Ave. of the Americas, New York NY 10019. (212)586-5100. West Coast Office: 151 El Camino Dr., Beverly Hills CA 90212. **Contact:** Mel Berger, vice president. Member of AAR.
Member Agents: Owen Laster; Robert Gottlieb; Mel Berger; Matt Bialer; Claudia Cross; Joni Evans; Tracy Fisher; Marcy Posner; Dan Strone; Bill Contardi; Peter Franklin; Samuel Liff; Gilbert Parker; George Lane.
Represents: Nonfiction books, novels.
How to Contact: Query with SASE. Does not accept queries by fax or e-mail.
Recent Sales: Prefers not to share information on specific sales.
Terms: Agent receives 10% commission on domestic sales; 20% on foreign sales.

Ⓜ **HENRY MORRISON, INC.**, 105 S. Bedford Rd., Suite 306A, Mt. Kisco NY 10549. (914)666-3500. Fax: (914)241-7846. **Contact:** Henry Morrison. Estab. 1965. Signatory of WGA. Represents 48 clients. **5% of clients are new/previously unpublished writers.** Currently handles: 5% nonfiction books; 5% juvenile books; 85% novels; 5% movie scripts.
Represents: Nonfiction books, novels. **Considers these fiction areas:** action/adventure; detective/police/crime; family saga.
How to Contact: Query with SASE. Responds in 2 weeks to queries; 3 months to mss.
Needs: Obtains most new clients through recommendations from others.
Recent Sales: Sold 16 titles in the last year. *The Hades Factor*, by Robert Ludlum and Gayle Lynds (St. Martin's); *Burnt Sienna*, by David Morrell (Warner Books); *Driftglass*, by Samuel R. Delany (Vintage Books). Other clients include Joe Gores, Eric Lusbader, Steve Samuel, Beverly Byrnne, Patricia Keneally-Morrison and Molly Katz.
Terms: Agent receives 15% commission on domestic sales; 25% on foreign sales. Charges for ms copies, bound galleys and finished books for submission to publishers, movie producers, foreign publishers.

Ⓜ **HAROLD OBER ASSOCIATES**, 425 Madison Ave., New York NY 10017. (212)759-8600. Fax: (212)759-9428. Estab. 1929. Member of AAR. Represents 250 clients. **10% of clients are new/previously unpublished writers.** Currently handles: 35% nonfiction books; 15% juvenile books; 50% novels.
Member Agents: Phyllis Westberg, Wendy Schmalz, Emma Sweeney, Craig Tenney (not accepting new clients).
Represents: Nonfiction books, juvenile books, novels. **Considers all fiction areas.**
How to Contact: Query letter *only* with SASE. "Faxed queries not read." Responds in 1 week to queries; 3 weeks to mss.
Needs: Obtains new clients through recommendations from others.
Recent Sales: Prefers not to share information on specific sales.
Terms: Agent receives 15% commission on domestic sales; 20% on foreign sales. Charges for photocopying and express mail or package services.

☑ Ⓜ **PINDER LANE & GARON-BROOKE ASSOCIATES, LTD.**, 159 W. 53rd St., Suite 14E, New York NY 10019-6005. (212)489-0880. E-mail: pinderl@interport.net. **Contact:** Robert Thixton. Member of AAR, signatory of WGA. Represents 80 clients. **20% of clients are new/previously unpublished writers.** Specializes in mainstream fiction and nonfiction. Currently handles: 25% nonfiction books; 75% novels.

Member Agents: Nancy Coffey (contributing agent), Dick Duane, Robert Thixton.
Represents: Nonfiction books, novels. **Considers these fiction areas:** contemporary issues; detective/police/crime; family saga; fantasy; gay; literary; mainstream; mystery/suspense; romance; science fiction.
How to Contact: Query with SASE. Accepts queries by e-mail. Prefers to read materials exclusively. Responds in 3 weeks to queries; 2 months to mss.
Needs: Does not want to receive screenplays, TV series teleplays or dramatic plays. Obtains most new clients through referrals and from queries.
Recent Sales: Sold 20 titles in the last year. *Nobody's Safe* and *The 4 Phaseman*, by Richard Steinberg (Doubleday); *The Kill Box* and *The Third Consequence*, by Chris Stewart (M. Evans); *Return to Christmas*, by Chris Heimerdinger (Ballantine).
Terms: Agent receives 15% on domestic sales; 30% on foreign sales. Offers written contract, binding for 3-5 years.
Tips: "With our literary and media experience, our agency is uniquely positioned for the current and future direction publishing is taking. Send query letter first giving the essence of the manuscript and a personal or career bio with SASE."

◘ AARON M. PRIEST LITERARY AGENCY, 708 Third Ave., 23rd Floor, New York NY 10017. (212)818-0344. Fax: (212)573-9417. **Contact:** Aaron Priest or Molly Friedrich. Estab. 1974. Member of AAR. Currently handles: 25% nonfiction books; 75% fiction.
Member Agents: Lisa Erbach Vance, Paul Cirone, Aaron Priest, Molly Friedrich.
Represents: Nonfiction books, fiction.
How to Contact: Query only. SASE not required. If interested, will respond within 2 weeks of receipt of query. Will not respond if not interested. Does not accept queries by e-mail or fax. Unsolicited mss will be returned unread.
Recent Sales: *Aaron Priest: Saving Faith*, by David Baldacci (Warner); *Demolition Angel*, by Robert Crais (Doubleday). *Molly Friedrich*: *O is for Outlaw*, by Sue Grafton (Holt); *Horse Heaven*, by Jane Smiley (Knopf). *Lisa Erbach Vance: Darkest Fear*, by Harlan Coben (Delacorte); *Acid Test*, by Ross La Manina (Ballantine).
Terms: Agent receives 15% commission on domestic sales. Charges for photocopying, foreign postage expenses.

◘ ANGELA RINALDI LITERARY AGENCY, P.O. Box 7877, Beverly Hills CA 90212-7877. (310)842-7665. Fax: (310)837-8143. E-mail: e2arinaldi@aol.com. **Contact:** Angela Rinaldi. Estab. 1994. Member of AAR. Represents 50 clients. Currently handles: 50% nonfiction books; 50% novels.
  ● Prior to opening her agency, Ms. Rinaldi was an editor at NAL/Signet, Pocket Books and Bantam, and the manager of book development for *The Los Angeles Times*.
Represents: Nonfiction books, novels, TV and motion picture rights. **Considers literary and commercial fiction.**
How to Contact: For fiction, send the first 100 pages and brief synopsis with SASE. Responds in 6 weeks. Accepts queries by e-mail. Considers simultaneous queries and submissions. "Please advise if this is a multiple submission to another agent." Returns materials only with SASE.
Needs: Actively seeking commercial and literary fiction. Does not want to receive scripts, category romances, children's books, westerns, science fiction/fantasy and cookbooks.
Recent Sales: *The Starlite Drive-In*, by Marjorie Reynolds (William Morrow & Co.); *BlindSpot*, by Stephanie Kane (Bantam).
Terms: Agent receives 15% commission on domestic sales; 20% on foreign sales. Offers written contract. Charges for photocopying ("if client doesn't supply copies for submissions"). 100% of business is derived from commissions on sales. Foreign, TV and motion picture rights for clients only.

N ◘ BJ ROBBINS LITERARY AGENCY, 5130 Bellaire Ave., North Hollywood CA 91607-2908. (818)760-6602. Fax: (818)760-6616. E-mail: robbinsliterary@aol.com. **Contact:** (Ms.) B.J. Robbins. Estab. 1992. Member of Board of Directors, PEN American Center West. Represents 40 clients. **50% of clients are new/previously unpublished writers.** Currently handles: 50% nonfiction books; 50% novels.
Member Agents: Rob McAndrews (commercial fiction).
Represents: Nonfiction books, novels. **Considers these fiction areas:** contemporary issues; detective/police/crime; ethnic; family saga; literary; mainstream; mystery/suspense; sports; thriller/espionage.
How to Contact: Send outline/proposal and 3 sample chapters with SASE. Considers simultaneous queries and submissions. Responds in 2 weeks to queries; 6 weeks to mss. Returns materials only with SASE.
Recent Sales: Sold 10 titles in the last year. *Please, Please, Please*, by Renée Swindle (Dial Press); *Katie.com*, by Katherine Tarbox (Dutton); *Quickening*, by Laura Catherine Brown (Random House); *Snow Mountain Passage*, by James D. Houston (Knopf); *Stone People Medicine*, by Manny Two Feathers (New World Library).
Needs: Obtains most new clients mostly through referrals, also at conferences.
Terms: Agent receives 15% commission on domestic sales; 20% on foreign sales. Offers written contract, with 3 months notice to terminate if project is out on submission. Charges clients for postage and photocopying only. Writers charged for office fees only after the sale of ms. 100% of business is derived from commissions on sales.

Writers' Conferences: Squaw Valley Fiction Writers Workshop (Squaw Valley CA, August); Maui Writers Conference; SDSU Writers Conference.

◐ JANE ROTROSEN AGENCY LLC, 318 E. 51st St., New York NY 10022. (212)593-4330. Fax: (212)935-6985. E-mail: jrotrosen@aol.com. **Contact:** Jane Rotrosen. Estab. 1974. Member of AAR and Authors Guild. Represents over 100 clients. Currently handles: 30% nonfiction books; 70% novels.
Member Agents: Andrea Cirillo; Ruth Kagle; Annelise Robey; Margaret Ruley; Stephanie Tade.
Represents: Nonfiction books, novels. **Considers these fiction areas:** action/adventure; detective/police/crime; family saga; historical; horror; mainstream; mystery; romance; thriller/espionage; women's fiction.
How to Contact: Query with SASE. No queries by fax or e-mail. Considers simultaneous queries and submissions. Responds in 2 weeks to queries; 7 weeks to mss. Returns materials only with SASE.
Recent Sales: Sold 120 titles in the last year. Prefers not to share information on specific sales.
Terms: Agent receives 15% commission on domestic sales; 20% on foreign sales. Offers written contract, binding for 3 years. 60-days notice must be given to terminate contract. Charges for photocopying, express mail, overseas postage and book purchases.

[N] ◐ RUSSELL & VOLKENING, 50 W. 29th St., #7E, New York NY 10001. (212)684-6050. Fax: (212)889-3026. **Contact:** Joseph Regal or Jennie Dunham. Estab. 1940. Member of AAR. Represents 140 clients. **10% of clients are new/previously unpublished writers.** Currently handles: 40% nonfiction books; 5% juvenile books; 3% short story collections; 50% novels; 2% novellas.
Member Agents: Timothy Seldes (nonfiction, literary fiction); Joseph Regal (literary fiction, thrillers, nonfiction); Jennie Dunham (literary fiction, nonfiction, children's books).
Represents: Nonfiction books, novels, novellas, short story collections. **Considers these fiction areas:** action/adventure; detective/police/crime; ethnic; literary; mainstream; mystery/suspense; picture book; sports; thriller/espionage.
How to Contact: Query with SASE. Responds in 1 week to queries; 2 months to mss.
Recent Sales: *The Many Aspects of Mobile Home Living*, by Martin Clark (Knopf); *The Special Prisoner*, by Jim Lehrer (Random); *The Visitor*, by Maeve Brennan (Counterpoint); *The Beatles in Rishikesh*, by Paul Saltzman (Viking Studio); *Lanterns*, by Marian Wright Edelman (Beacon); *Places in the Dark*, by Thomas H. Cook (Bantam); *Warriors of God*, by James Reston, Jr. (Doubleday); *The Obituary Writer*, by Porter Shreve (Houghton Mifflin).
Needs: Specializes in literary fiction and narrative nonfiction. Obtains most new clients by recommendation or occasionally through query letters.
Terms: Agent receives 15% commission on domestic sales; 20% on foreign sales. Charges clients for "standard office expenses relating to the submission of materials of an author we represent, e.g., photocopying, postage."
Tips: "If the query is cogent, well written, well presented and is the type of book we'd represent, we'll ask to see the manuscript. From there, it depends purely on the quality of the work."

✓ ◐ VICTORIA SANDERS & ASSOCIATES, (formerly Victoria Sanders Literary Agency), 241 Avenue of the Americas, New York NY 10014-4822. (212)633-8811. Fax: (212)633-0525. **Contact:** Victoria Sanders and/or Diane Dickensheid. Estab. 1993. Member of AAR, signatory of WGA. Represents 75 clients. **25% of clients are new/previously unpublished writers.** Currently handles: 50% nonfiction books; 50% novels.
Member Agents: David Mayhew (lecture agent); Selena James (assistant literary agent).
Represents: Nonfiction, novels. **Considers these fiction areas:** action/adventure; contemporary issues; ethnic; family saga; feminist; gay; lesbian; literary; thriller/espionage.
How to Contact: Query with SASE. Considers simultaneous queries. Responds in 1 week to queries; 1 month to mss. Returns materials only with SASE.
Needs: Obtains most new clients through recommendations, "or I find them through my reading and pursue."
Recent Sales: Sold 20 titles in the last year. *Blindsighted*, by Karin Slaughter (Morrow); *Redemption Song*, by Dr. Bertice Berry (Doubleday); *Daughter*, by Asha Bangle (Scribner).
Terms: Agent receives 15% commission on domestic sales; 20% on foreign sales. Offers written contract, binding at will. Charges for photocopying, ms, messenger, express mail and extraordinary fees. If in excess of $100, client approval is required.
Tips: "Limit query to letter, no calls, and give it your best shot. A good query is going to get a good response."

♡ ROSALIE SIEGEL, INTERNATIONAL LITERARY AGENCY, INC., 1 Abey Dr., Pennington NJ 08534. (609)737-1007. Fax: (609)737-3708. **Contact:** Rosalie Siegel. Estab. 1977. Member of AAR. Represents 35 clients. **10% of clients are new/previously unpublished writers.** Specializes in foreign authors, especially French, though diminishing. Currently handles: 45% nonfiction books; 45% novels; 10% young adult books and short story collections for current clients.
Needs: Obtains new clients through referrals from writers and friends.
Recent Sales: Prefers not to share information on specific sales.

Terms: Agent receives 15% commission on domestic sales; 20% on foreign sales. Offers written contract, with 60-day cancellation clause. Charges for photocopying.
Tips: "I'm not looking for new authors in an active way."

◙ SPECTRUM LITERARY AGENCY, 111 Eighth Ave., Suite 1501, New York NY 10011. (212)691-7556.
Contact: Eleanor Wood, president. Represents 75 clients. Currently handles: 90% fiction; 10% nonfiction books.
Member Agents: Lucienne Diver.
Represents: Nonfiction, novels. **Considers these fiction areas:** contemporary issues; fantasy; historical; romance; mainstream; mystery/suspense; science fiction.
How to Contact: Query with SASE. Responds in 2 months to queries.
Needs: Obtains most new clients through recommendations from authors and others.
Recent Sales: Prefers not to share information on specific sales.
Terms: Agent receives 10% commission on domestic sales.

N ◙ STEELE-PERKINS LITERARY AGENCY, 26 Island Lane, Canandaigua NY 14424. (716)396-9290.
Fax: (716)396-3579. E-mail: pattiesp@aol.com. **Contact:** Pattie Steele-Perkins. Member of AAR, RWA. The Steele-Perkins Literary Agency takes an active role in marketing their clients work including preparation for media appearances. They also develop with the author individual career plans. Currently handles 100% novels.
● Prior to becoming an agent, Ms. Steele-Perkins was a TV producer/writer for 15 years.
Represents: Novels. **Considers these fiction areas:** mainstream; multicultural; romance.
How to Contact: Send outline and 3 sample chapters, include SASE. Accepts queries by e-mail. Considers simultaneous queries. Reponds in 6 weeks. Returns materials only with SASE.
Recent Sales: This agency prefers not to share information on specific sales.
Needs: Actively seeking romance, women's fiction and multicultural works. Obtains most new clients through recommendations from others, queries/solicitations.
Terms: Agent receives 15% commission on domestic sales. Offers written contract, binding for 1 year. 30-day notice must be given to terminate contract.
Writers' Conferences: National Conference of Romance Writer's of America; Book Expo America Writers' Conferences.
Tips: "Be patient. E-mail rather than call. Make sure what you are sending is the best it can be."

◙ STERNIG & BYRNE LITERARY AGENCY, 3209 S. 55, Milwaukee WI 53219-4433. (414)328-8034.
Fax: (414)328-8034. E-mail: jackbyrne@aol.com. **Contact:** Jack Byrne. Estab. 1950s. Member of SFWA and MWA. Represents 30 clients. **20% of clients are new/unpublished writers.** "We have a small, friendly, personal, hands-on teamwork approach to marketing." Currently handles: 5% nonfiction books; 40% juvenile books; 55% novels.
Member Agents: Jack Byrne.
Represents: Nonfiction books, juvenile books, novels. **Considers these fiction areas:** action/adventure; fantasy; glitz; horror; juvenile; mystery/suspense; psychic/supernatural; science fiction; thriller/espionage; young adult.
How to Contact: Query with SASE. Accepts queries by e-mail. Considers simultaneous queries; no simultaneous submissions. Responds in 3 weeks to queries; 3 months to mss. Returns materials only with SASE. "No SASE equals no return."
Needs: Actively seeking science fiction/fantasy. Does not want to receive romance, poetry, textbooks, highly specialized nonfiction.
Recent Sales: Sold 17 titles in the last year. *The Beast That Was Max*, by Gerard Daniel Houarner (Leisure); *Mark of the Cat*, by Andre Norton (Meisha Merlin). Clients include Betty Ren Wright, Lyn McComchie.
Terms: Agent receives 15% commission on domestic sales; 20% on foreign sales. Offers written contract, open/nonbinding. 60 days notice must be given to terminate contract.
Reading List: Reads *Publishers Weekly, Locus, Science Fiction Chronicles*, etc. to find new clients. Looks for "whatever catches my eye."
Tips: "Don't send first drafts; have a professional presentation . . . including cover letter; know your field (read what's been done . . . good and bad)."

◙ THE JOHN TALBOT AGENCY, 540 W. Boston Post Rd., PMB 266, Mamaroneck NY 10543-3437.
(914)381-9463. **Contact:** John Talbot. Estab. 1998. Member of the Authors Guild. Represents 50 clients. **15% of clients are new/unpublished writers.** Specializes in literary and commercial suspense fiction. Currently handles: 35% nonfiction books; 65% novels.

STILL LOOKING FOR AN AGENT? Pick up the 2001 edition of *Guide to Literary Agents* (Writer's Digest Books) at your local bookstore, or by calling 1-800-289-0963.

• Prior to becoming an agent, Mr. Talbot was a book editor at Simon & Schuster and Putnam Berkley.
Represents: Nonfiction books, novels. **Considers these fiction areas:** literary; suspense.
How to Contact: Query with SASE. Does not accept queries by fax or e-mail. Considers simultaneous queries. Responds in 1 month to queries; 2 months to mss.
Needs: Actively seeking suspense and literary fiction, "particularly by writers who are beginning to publish in magazines and literary journals." Does not want to receive children's books, science fiction, fantasy, westerns, poetry or screenplays. Obtains most new clients usually through referrals.
Recent Sales: Sold 30 titles in the last year. *Deep Sound Channel*, by Joe Buff (Bantam); *Lily of the Valley*, by Suzanne Strempek Shea (Pocket Books); *The Fuck-Up*, by Arthur Nersesian (Pocket Books/MTV). Other clients include Clarence Major, Doris Meredith, Peter Telep.
Terms: Agent receives 15% commission on domestic sales; 20% on foreign sales. Offers written contract. 2-week notice must be given to terminate contract. Charges for photocopying, overnight delivery, additional copies of books needed for use in sale of subsidiary rights, and fees incurred for submitting mss or books overseas.

PATRICIA TEAL LITERARY AGENCY, 2036 Vista Del Rosa, Fullerton CA 92831-1336. (714)738-8333. **Contact:** Patricia Teal. Estab. 1978. Member of AAR, RWA, Authors Guild. Represents 60 clients. Specializes in women's fiction and commercial how-to and self-help nonfiction. Currently handles: 10% nonfiction books; 90% novels.
Represents: Nonfiction books, novels. **Considers these fiction areas:** glitz, mainstream, mystery/suspense, romance (contemporary, historical).
How to Contact: *Published authors only.* Query with SASE. Does not accept queries by e-mail or fax. Considers simultaneous queries. Responds in 10 days to queries; 6 weeks to requested mss. Returns materials only with SASE.
Needs: Does not want to receive poetry, short stories, articles, science fiction, fantasy, Regency romance. Obtains most new clients through recommendations from authors and editors or at conferences.
Recent Sales: Sold 45 titles in the last year. *Second to None*, by Muriel Jensen (Harlequin); *Found: His Perfect Wife*, by Marie Ferrarella (Silhouette).
Terms: Agent receives 10-15% commission on domestic sales; 20% on foreign sales. Offers written contract, binding for 1 year. Charges clients for photocopying.
Writers' Conferences: Romance Writers of America conferences; Asilomar (California Writers Club); Bouchercon; BEA (Chicago, June); California State University San Diego (January); Hawaii Writers Conference (Maui).
Reading List: Reads *Publishers Weekly, Romance Report* and *Romantic Times* to find new clients. "I read the reviews of books and excerpts from authors' books."
Tips: "Include SASE with all correspondence."

THE VINES AGENCY, INC., 648 Broadway, Suite 901, New York NY 10012. (212)777-5522. Fax: (212)777-5978. E-mail: JV@Vinesagency.com. **Contact:** James C. Vines or Gary Neuwirth. Estab. 1995. Member of AAR, signatory of WGA. Represents 52 clients. **20% of clients are new/previously unpublished writers.** Specializes in mystery, suspense, science fiction, mainstream novels, screenplays, teleplays. Currently handles: 50% nonfiction books; 50% novels.
• Prior to opening his agency, Mr. Vines served as an agent with the Virginia Literary Agency.
Member Agents: James C. Vines (quality and commercial fiction); Gary Neuwirth; Ali Ryan (women's fiction and nonfiction, mainstream).
Represents: Nonfiction books, novels. **Considers these fiction areas:** action/adventure; contemporary issues; detective/police/crime; ethnic; feminist; horror; humor/satire; experimental; family saga; gay; lesbian; historical; literary; mainstream; mystery/suspense; psychic/supernatural; regional; romance (contemporary, historical); science fiction; sports; thriller/espionage; westerns/frontier; women's fiction.
Also Handles: Feature film, TV scripts, stage plays. **Considers these script subject areas:** action/adventure; comedy; detective/police/crime; ethnic; experimental; feminist; gay; historical; horror; lesbian; mainstream; mystery/suspense; romance (comedy, drama); science fiction; teen; thriller; westerns/frontier.
How to Contact: Send outline and first 3 chapters with SASE. Accepts queries by fax and e-mail. "Maximum of one page by fax or e-mail." Considers simultaneous queries and submissions. Responds in 2 weeks to queries; 1 month to mss. Returns materials only with SASE.
Needs: Obtains most new clients through query letters, recommendations from others, reading short stories in magazines, soliciting conferences.
Recent Sales: Sold 46 book titles and 5 script projects in the last year. *California Fire and Life*, by Don Winslow (Random House); *Sugar*, by Bernice McFadden (Doubleday). *Script(s) optioned/sold: Ninth Life*, by Jay Colvin (Miramax); *The Bottoms*, by Joe R. Lansdale (Mysterious Press).
Terms: Agent receives 15% commission on domestic sales; 25% on foreign sales. Offers written contract, binding for 1 year, with 30-day cancellation clause. Charges for foreign postage, messenger services and photocopying. 100% of business is derived from commissions on sales.
Writers' Conferences: Maui Writer's Conference.

Tips: "Do not follow up on submissions with phone calls to the agency. The agency will read and respond by mail only. Do not pack your manuscript in plastic 'peanuts' that will make us have to vacuum the office after opening the package containing your manuscript. Always enclose return postage."

WATKINS LOOMIS AGENCY, INC., 133 E. 35th St., Suite 1, New York NY 10016. (212)532-0080. Fax: (212)889-0506. **Contact:** Katherine Fausset. Estab. 1908. Represents 150 clients. Specializes in literary fiction, nonfiction.
Member Agents: Nicole Aragi (associate); Gloria Loomis (president); Katherine Fausset (assistant agent).
Represents: Nonfiction books, short story collections, novels. **Considers these fiction areas:** literary.
How to Contact: Query with SASE by mail only. Responds within 1 month to queries.
Recent Sales: Prefers not to share information on specific sales. Clients include Walter Mosley, Edwidge Danticat, Junot Díaz and Cornel West.
Terms: Agent receives 15% commission on domestic sales; 20% on foreign sales.

WIESER & WIESER, INC., 25 E. 21 St., 6th Floor, New York NY 10010. (212)260-0860. **Contact:** Olga Wieser. Estab. 1975. **30% of clients are new/previously unpublished writers.** Specializes in mainstream fiction and nonfiction. Currently handles: 50% nonfiction books; 50% novels.
Member Agents: Jake Elwell (history, military, mysteries, romance, sports, thrillers); Olga Wieser (psychology, fiction, pop medical, literary fiction).
Represents: Nonfiction books, novels. **Considers these fiction areas:** contemporary issues; detective/police/crime; historical; literary; mainstream; mystery/suspense; romance; thriller/espionage.
How to Contact: Query with outline/proposal and SASE. Responds in 2 weeks to queries.
Needs: Obtains most new clients through queries, authors' recommendations and industry professionals.
Recent Sales: *Cutting*, by Steven Levenkron (Norton); *Hocus Corpus*, by James N. Tucker, M.D. (Dutton/Signet); *A Little Traveling Music Please*, by Margaret Moseley (Berkley); *The Kamikazes*, by Edwin P. Hoyt (Burford Books); *Angels & Demons*, by Dan Brown (Pocket); *Headwind*, by John Nance (Putnam).
Terms: Agent receives 15% commission on domestic sales; 20% on foreign sales. Offers written contract. Charges for photocopying and overseas mailing.
Writers' Conferences: BEA; Frankfurt Book Fair.

WRITERS HOUSE, 21 W. 26th St., New York NY 10010. (212)685-2400. Fax: (212)685-1781. Estab. 1974. Member of AAR. Represents 440 clients. **50% of clients were new/unpublished writers.** Specializes in all types of popular fiction and nonfiction. No scholarly, professional, poetry or screenplays. Currently handles: 25% nonfiction books; 35% juvenile books; 40% novels.
Member Agents: Albert Zuckerman (major novels, thrillers, women's fiction, important nonfiction); Amy Berkower (major juvenile authors, women's fiction, popular and literary fiction); Merrilee Heifetz (quality children's fiction, major science fiction and fantasy authors, popular culture, literary fiction); Susan Cohen (juvenile and young adult fiction and nonfiction, Judaism, women's issues); Susan Ginsburg (serious and popular fiction, narrative nonfiction); Fran Lebowitz (juvenile and young adult, popular culture); Michele Rubin (literary fiction, mysteries); Karen Solem (contemporary and historical romance, women's fiction, narrative nonfiction, horse and animal books); Robin Rue (commercial fiction and nonfiction, YA fiction); Jennifer Lyons (literary, commercial fiction, international fiction, nonfiction and illustrated); Simon Lipskar (literary and commercial fiction, creative and narrative nonfiction, young writers).
Represents: Nonfiction books, juvenile books, novels. **Considers any fiction area.** "Quality is everything."
How to Contact: Query with SASE. Responds in 1 month to queries.
Needs: Obtains most new clients through recommendations from others.
Recent Sales: *The New New Thing*, by Michael Lewis (Norton); *Middle of Nowhere*, by Ridley Pearson (Hyperion); *Into the Garden*, by V.C. Andrews (Pocket); *Carolina Moon*, by Nora Roberts (Putnam).
Terms: Agent receives 15% commission on domestic sales; 20% on foreign sales. Offers written contract, binding for 1 year.
Tips: "Do not send manuscripts. Write a compelling letter. If you do, we'll ask to see your work."

THE WRITERS SHOP, 101 Fifth Ave., 11th Floor, New York NY 10003. (212)255-6515. Fax: (212)691-9418. Website: www.thewritersshop.com. **Contact:** Kristin Lewandowski. Member of AAR, signatory of WGA. Represents 100 clients. Currently handles 25% nonfiction books; 50% novels; 25% story collections.
Member Agents: Virginia Barber; Jennifer Rudolph Walsh; Jay Mandel.
Represents: Nonfiction books, novels, short story collections, scholarly books.
How to Contact: Query with SASE. Prefers to read materials exclusively. Reponds in 6 weeks. Returns materials only with SASE.
Recent Sales: This agency prefers not to share information on specific sales.
Needs: Obtains most new clients through recommendations from others.
Terms: Agent receives 15% commission on domestic sales.
Writers' Conferences: Bread Loaf; Squaw Valley.

Literary Agents Category Index

Agents listed in the preceeding section are indexed below according to the categories of fiction they represent. Use it to find agents who handle the specific kind of fiction you write. Then turn to those listings in the alphabetical Literary Agents section for complete contact and submission information.

Action/Adventure
Allen, Literary Agent, James
Amsterdam Agency, Marcia
Crawford Literary Agency
Halsey North, Reece
Harris Literary Agency
Harris Literary Agency, Inc., The Joy
Henshaw Group, Richard
Jabberwocky Literary Agency
JCA Literary Agency, Inc.
Koster Literary Agency, Elaine, LLC
Kraas Agency, Irene
Lampack Agency, Inc., Peter
Lincoln Literary Agency, Ray
Michaels Literary Agency, Inc., Doris S.
Morrison, Inc., Henry
Rotrosen Agency LLC, Jane
Russell & Volkening
Sanders & Associates, Victoria
Sternig & Byrne Literary Agency
Vines Agency, Inc., The

Cartoon/Comic
Harris Literary Agency, Inc., The Joy
Jabberwocky Literary Agency
Vines Agency, Inc., The

Confessional
Harris Literary Agency, Inc., The Joy
JCA Literary Agency, Inc.
Koster Literary Agency, Elaine, LLC

Contemporary Issues
Alive Communications, Inc.
Connor Literary Agency
Flaherty, Literary Agent, Joyce A.
Halsey North, Reece
Harris Literary Agency, Inc., The Joy
Jabberwocky Literary Agency
JCA Literary Agency, Inc.
Kidde, Kidde, Hoyt & Picard
Koster Literary Agency, Elaine, LLC

Lampack Agency, Inc., Peter
Lincoln Literary Agency, Ray
Michaels Literary Agency, Inc., Doris S.
Pinder Lane & Garon-Brooke Associates, Ltd.
Robbins Literary Agency, BJ
Sanders & Associates, Victoria
Spectrum Literary Agency
Vines Agency, Inc., The
Watkins Loomis Agency, Inc.
Wieser & Wieser, Inc.

Detective/Police/Crime
Alive Communications, Inc.
Allen, Literary Agent, James
Amsterdam Agency, Marcia
Connor Literary Agency
DHS Literary, Inc.
Ellenberg Literary Agency, Ethan
Halsey North, Reece
Harris Literary Agency
Harris Literary Agency, Inc., The Joy
Henshaw Group, Richard
J de S Associates Inc.
Jabberwocky Literary Agency
JCA Literary Agency, Inc.
Kidde, Kidde, Hoyt & Picard
Koster Literary Agency, Elaine, LLC
Kraas Agency, Irene
Lampack Agency, Inc., Peter
Lincoln Literary Agency, Ray
Maass Literary Agency, Donald
Morrison, Inc., Henry
Pinder Lane & Garon-Brooke Associates, Ltd.
Robbins Literary Agency, BJ
Rotrosen Agency LLC, Jane
Russell & Volkening
Vines Agency, Inc., The
Wieser & Wieser, Inc.

Erotica
DHS Literary, Inc.
Harris Literary Agency, Inc., The Joy

Ethnic
Connor Literary Agency
Daves Agency, Joan
DHS Literary, Inc.
Evans Inc., Mary
Halsey North, Reece
Harris Literary Agency, Inc., The Joy
Henshaw Group, Richard
Jabberwocky Literary Agency
JCA Literary Agency, Inc.
Knight Agency, The
Koster Literary Agency, Elaine, LLC
Kraas Agency, Irene
Lincoln Literary Agency, Ray
Robbins Literary Agency, BJ
Russell & Volkening
Sanders & Associates, Victoria
Vines Agency, Inc., The
Watkins Loomis Agency, Inc.

Experimental
Connor Literary Agency
Harris Literary Agency, Inc., The Joy
JCA Literary Agency, Inc.
Kidd Agency, Inc., Virginia
Vines Agency, Inc., The

Family Saga
Alive Communications, Inc.
Allen, Literary Agent, James
Connor Literary Agency
Daves Agency, Joan
Ellenberg Literary Agency, Ethan
Flaherty, Literary Agent, Joyce A.
Halsey North, Reece
Harris Literary Agency, Inc., The Joy
Henshaw Group, Richard
Jabberwocky Literary Agency
JCA Literary Agency, Inc.
Koster Literary Agency, Elaine, LLC
Kraas Agency, Irene
Lampack Agency, Inc., Peter
Lincoln Literary Agency, Ray
Michaels Literary Agency, Inc., Doris S.
Morrison, Inc., Henry
Pinder Lane & Garon-Brooke Associates, Ltd.
Robbins Literary Agency, BJ
Rotrosen Agency LLC, Jane
Sanders & Associates, Victoria
Vines Agency, Inc., The

Fantasy
Allen, Literary Agent, James
Carvainis Agency, Inc., Maria

Ellenberg Literary Agency, Ethan
Henshaw Group, Richard
Jabberwocky Literary Agency
Kidd Agency, Inc., Virginia
Lincoln Literary Agency, Ray
Maass Literary Agency, Donald
Pinder Lane & Garon-Brooke Associates, Ltd.
Spectrum Literary Agency
Sternig & Byrne Literary Agency

Feminist
DHS Literary, Inc.
Flaherty, Literary Agent, Joyce A.
Harris Literary Agency, Inc., The Joy
JCA Literary Agency, Inc.
Kidd Agency, Inc., Virginia
Kidde, Hoyt & Picard
Koster Literary Agency, Elaine, LLC
Lincoln Literary Agency, Ray
Michaels Literary Agency, Inc., Doris S.
Sanders & Associates, Victoria
Vines Agency, Inc., The

Gay/Lesbian
Daves Agency, Joan
DHS Literary, Inc.
Harris Literary Agency, Inc., The Joy
Jabberwocky Literary Agency
JCA Literary Agency, Inc.
Kidde, Hoyt & Picard
Koster Literary Agency, Elaine, LLC
Lincoln Literary Agency, Ray
Pinder Lane & Garon-Brooke Associates, Ltd.
Sanders & Associates, Victoria
Vines Agency, Inc., The
Watkins Loomis Agency, Inc.

Glitz
Allen, Literary Agent, James
Harris Literary Agency, Inc., The Joy
Henshaw Group, Richard
Jabberwocky Literary Agency
JCA Literary Agency, Inc.
Kidd Agency, Inc., Virginia
Kidde, Hoyt & Picard
Koster Literary Agency, Elaine, LLC
Sternig & Byrne Literary Agency
Teal Literary Agency, Patricia

Historical
Alive Communications, Inc.
Allen, Literary Agent, James
Carvainis Agency, Inc., Maria

DHS Literary, Inc.
Ellenberg Literary Agency, Ethan
Flaherty, Literary Agent, Joyce A.
Halsey North, Reece
Harris Literary Agency, Inc., The Joy
Henshaw Group, Richard
Hopkins Literary Associates
J de S Associates Inc.
Jabberwocky Literary Agency
JCA Literary Agency, Inc.
Kidd Agency, Inc., Virginia
Kidde, Hoyt & Picard
Koster Literary Agency, Elaine, LLC
Lampack Agency, Inc., Peter
Lincoln Literary Agency, Ray
Maass Literary Agency, Donald
Michaels Literary Agency, Inc., Doris S.
Rotrosen Agency LLC, Jane
Spectrum Literary Agency
Vines Agency, Inc., The
Wieser & Wieser, Inc.

Horror

Allen, Literary Agent, James
Amsterdam Agency, Marcia
Connor Literary Agency
DHS Literary, Inc.
Henshaw Group, Richard
Jabberwocky Literary Agency
JCA Literary Agency, Inc.
Maass Literary Agency, Donald
Rotrosen Agency LLC, Jane
Sternig & Byrne Literary Agency
Vines Agency, Inc., The

Humor/Satire

Alive Communications, Inc.
Amsterdam Agency, Marcia
Harris Literary Agency
Henshaw Group, Richard
Jabberwocky Literary Agency
JCA Literary Agency, Inc.
Kidde, Hoyt & Picard
Lincoln Literary Agency, Ray
Vines Agency, Inc., The

Juvenile

Alive Communications, Inc.
Ellenberg Literary Agency, Ethan
Harris Literary Agency
Henshaw Group, Richard
J de S Associates Inc.
Kraas Agency, Irene

Lincoln Literary Agency, Ray
Russell & Volkening
Sternig & Byrne Literary Agency
Vines Agency, Inc., The

Literary

Alive Communications, Inc.
Carvainis Agency, Inc., Maria
Congdon Associates, Inc., Don
Connor Literary Agency
Daves Agency, Joan
DHS Literary, Inc.
Ellenberg Literary Agency, Ethan
Ellison Inc., Nicholas
Evans Inc., Mary
Halsey North, Reece
Harris Literary Agency, Inc., The Joy
Henshaw Group, Richard
J de S Associates Inc.
Jabberwocky Literary Agency
JCA Literary Agency, Inc.
Kidd Agency, Inc., Virginia
Kidde, Hoyt & Picard
Knight Agency, The
Koster Literary Agency, Elaine, LLC
Kraas Agency, Irene
Lampack Agency, Inc., Peter
Lincoln Literary Agency, Ray
Maass Literary Agency, Donald
Markson Literary Agency, Elaine
Michaels Literary Agency, Inc., Doris S.
Pinder Lane & Garon-Brooke Associates, Ltd.
Robbins Literary Agency, BJ
Russell & Volkening
Sanders & Associates, Victoria
Talbot Agency, The John
Vines Agency, Inc., The
Watkins Loomis Agency, Inc.
Wieser & Wieser, Inc.

Mainstream

Alive Communications, Inc.
Allen, Literary Agent, James
Amsterdam Agency, Marcia
Carvainis Agency, Inc., Maria
Crawford Literary Agency
Daves Agency, Joan
DHS Literary, Inc.
Ellenberg Literary Agency, Ethan
Ellison Inc., Nicholas
Flaherty, Literary Agent, Joyce A.
Halsey North, Reece
Harris Literary Agency
Harris Literary Agency, Inc., The Joy

Henshaw Group, Richard
Hopkins Literary Associates
J de S Associates Inc.
Jabberwocky Literary Agency
JCA Literary Agency, Inc.
Kidd Agency, Inc., Virginia
Kidde, Hoyt & Picard
Knight Agency, The
Koster Literary Agency, Elaine, LLC
Kraas Agency, Irene
Lampack Agency, Inc., Peter
Lincoln Literary Agency, Ray
Maass Literary Agency, Donald
Markson Literary Agency, Elaine
Michaels Literary Agency, Inc., Doris S.
Pinder Lane & Garon-Brooke Associates, Ltd.
Robbins Literary Agency, BJ
Rotrosen Agency LLC, Jane
Russell & Volkening
Spectrum Literary Agency
Steele-Perkins Literary Agency
Teal Literary Agency, Patricia
Vines Agency, Inc., The
Watkins Loomis Agency, Inc.
Wieser & Wieser, Inc.

Multicultural
Steele-Perkins Literary Agency

Mystery/Suspense
Alive Communications, Inc.
Allen, Literary Agent, James
Amsterdam Agency, Marcia
Carvainis Agency, Inc., Maria
Connor Literary Agency
DHS Literary, Inc.
Ellenberg Literary Agency, Ethan
Flaherty, Literary Agent, Joyce A.
Halsey North, Reece
Harris Literary Agency
Harris Literary Agency, Inc., The Joy
J de S Associates Inc.
JCA Literary Agency, Inc.
Kidd Agency, Inc., Virginia
Kidde, Hoyt & Picard
Knight Agency, The
Koster Literary Agency, Elaine, LLC
Kraas Agency, Irene
Lampack Agency, Inc., Peter
Lincoln Literary Agency, Ray
Maass Literary Agency, Donald
Pinder Lane & Garon-Brooke Associates, Ltd.
Robbins Literary Agency, BJ
Rotrosen Agency LLC, Jane

Russell & Volkening
Spectrum Literary Agency
Sternig & Byrne Literary Agency
Talbot Agency, The John
Teal Literary Agency, Patricia
Vines Agency, Inc., The
Watkins Loomis Agency, Inc.
Wieser & Wieser, Inc.

Open to All Fiction Categories
Bernstein Literary Agency, Meredith
Congdon Associates, Inc., Don
Curtis Associates, Inc., Richard
Fernandez Agent/Attorney, Justin E.
Ober Associates, Harold
Writers House

Picture Book
Ellenberg Literary Agency, Ethan
Harris Literary Agency, Inc., The Joy
Russell & Volkening

Psychic/Supernatural
Harris Literary Agency, Inc., The Joy
Henshaw Group, Richard
J de S Associates Inc.
Jabberwocky Literary Agency
Lincoln Literary Agency, Ray
Maass Literary Agency, Donald
Sternig & Byrne Literary Agency
Vines Agency, Inc., The

Regional
Harris Literary Agency, Inc., The Joy
Jabberwocky Literary Agency
Knight Agency, The
Koster Literary Agency, Elaine, LLC
Lincoln Literary Agency, Ray
Vines Agency, Inc., The

Religious/Inspirational
Alive Communications, Inc.
Crawford Literary Agency
Harris Literary Agency, Inc., The Joy
J de S Associates Inc.
Knight Agency, The
Sternig & Byrne Literary Agency

Romance
Allen, Literary Agent, James
Amsterdam Agency, Marcia

Carvainis Agency, Inc., Maria
Ellenberg Literary Agency, Ethan
Flaherty, Literary Agent, Joyce A.
Harris Literary Agency, Inc., The Joy
Hopkins Literary Associates
Kidde, Hoyt & Picard
Knight Agency, The
Lincoln Literary Agency, Ray
Maass Literary Agency, Donald
Pinder Lane & Garon Brooke Associates, Ltd.
Rotrosen Agency LLC, Jane
Steele-Perkins Literary Agency
Teal Literary Agency, Patricia
Vines Agency, Inc., The
Wieser & Wieser, Inc.

Sports
DHS Literary, Inc.
Harris Literary Agency, Inc., The Joy
Henshaw Group, Richard
Jabberwocky Literary Agency
JCA Literary Agency, Inc.
Lincoln Literary Agency, Ray
Robbins Literary Agency, BJ
Russell & Volkening
Vines Agency, Inc., The

Science Fiction
Allen, Literary Agent, James
Amsterdam Agency, Marcia
Ellenberg Literary Agency, Ethan
Halsey North, Reece
Harris Literary Agency
Henshaw Group, Richard
Jabberwocky Literary Agency
Kidd Agency, Inc., Virginia
Kraas Agency, Irene
Maass Literary Agency, Donald
Pinder Lane & Garon-Brooke Associates, Ltd.
Spectrum Literary Agency
Sternig & Byrne Literary Agency
Vines Agency, Inc., The

Thriller/Espionage
Alive Communications, Inc.
Amsterdam Agency, Marcia

Carvainis Agency, Inc., Maria
Connor Literary Agency
Crawford Literary Agency
DHS Literary, Inc.
Ellenberg Literary Agency, Ethan
Flaherty, Literary Agent, Joyce A.
Halsey North, Reece
Harris Literary Agency
Harris Literary Agency, Inc., The Joy
Henshaw Group, Richard
Jabberwocky Literary Agency
JCA Literary Agency, Inc.
Kidde, Hoyt & Picard
Koster Literary Agency, Elaine, LLC
Kraas Agency, Irene
Lampack Agency, Inc., Peter
Lincoln Literary Agency, Ray
Maass Literary Agency, Donald
Robbins Literary Agency, BJ
Rotrosen Agency LLC, Jane
Russell & Volkening
Sanders & Associates, Victoria
Sternig & Byrne Literary Agency
Vines Agency, Inc., The
Wieser & Wieser, Inc.

Westerns/Frontier
Alive Communications, Inc.
Amsterdam Agency, Marcia
DHS Literary, Inc.
J de S Associates Inc.
JCA Literary Agency, Inc.
Vines Agency, Inc., The

Young Adult
Alive Communications, Inc.
Allen, Literary Agent, James
Amsterdam Agency, Marcia
Carvainis Agency, Inc., Maria
Ellenberg Literary Agency, Ethan
Harris Literary Agency, Inc., The Joy
Henshaw Group, Richard
J de S Associates Inc.
Kidd Agency, Inc., Virginia
Kraas Agency, Irene
Lincoln Literary Agency, Ray
Russell & Volkening
Sternig & Byrne Literary Agency

Literary Magazines

This section contains markets for your literary short fiction. Although definitions of what constitutes "literary" writing vary, editors of literary journals agree they want to publish the "best" fiction they can acquire. Qualities they look for in fiction include creativity, style, flawless mechanics, and careful attention to detail in content and manuscript preparation. Most of the authors writing such fiction are well-read and well-educated, and many are students and graduates of university creative writing programs.

STEPPING STONES TO RECOGNITION

Some well-established literary journals pay several hundred or even several thousand dollars for a short story. Most, though, can only pay with contributor's copies or a subscription to their publication. However, being published in literary journals offers the important benefits of experience, exposure and prestige. Agents and major book publishers regularly read literary magazines in search of new writers. Work from among these journals is also selected for inclusion in annual prize anthologies such as *The Best American Short Stories*, *Prize Stories: The O. Henry Awards*, *Pushcart Prize: Best of the Small Presses*, and *New Stories from the South: The Year's Best*.

You'll find most of the well-known prestigious literary journals listed here. Many, including *Carolina Quarterly* and *Ploughshares*, are associated with universities, while others such as *The Paris Review* are independently published.

Please pay particular attention to listings for electronic literary magazines. At a time when paper and publishing costs rise while funding to university presses continues to be cut or eliminated, electronic literary magazines are helping generate a publishing renaissance for experimental as well as more traditional literary fiction. (See the roundtable interview with editors from four such magazines on page 35.) These electronic outlets for literary fiction also benefit writers by eliminating copying and postage costs and providing the opportunity for much quicker responses to submissions. Also notice that some magazines with websites give specific information about what they offer on their websites, including updated writers guidelines and sample fiction from their publications.

SELECTING THE RIGHT LITERARY JOURNAL

Once you have browsed through this section and have a list of journals you might like to submit to, read those listings again, carefully. Remember that this is information editors present to help you in submitting work that fits their needs. The "Quick Start" Guide to Publishing Your Fiction, starting on page 2, will guide you through the process of finding markets for your fiction.

This is the only section in which you will find magazines that do not read submissions all year long. Whether limited reading periods are tied to a university schedule or meant to accommodate the capabilities of a very small staff, those periods are noted within listings. The staffs of university journals are usually made up of student editors and a managing editor who is also a faculty member. These staffs often change every year. Whenever possible, we indicate this in listings and give the name of the current editor and the length of that editor's term. Also be aware that the schedule of a university journal usually coincides with that university's academic year, meaning that the editors of most university publications are difficult or impossible to reach during the summer.

FURTHERING YOUR SEARCH

It cannot be stressed enough that reading the listings for literary journals is only the first part of developing your marketing plan. The second part, equally important, is to obtain fiction guidelines and read the actual journal you'd like to submit to with great care. Reading copies of these journals helps you determine the fine points of each magazine's publishing style and philosophy. There is no substitute for this type of hands-on research.

Unlike commercial periodicals available at most newsstands and bookstores, it requires a little more effort to obtain some of the magazines listed here. The new super chain bookstores are doing a better job these days of stocking literaries and you can find some in independent and college bookstores, especially those published in your area. You may, however, need to send for a sample copy. We include sample copy prices in the listings whenever possible. In addition to reading your sample copies, pay close attention to the **Advice** section of each listing. There you'll often find a very specific description of the style of fiction editors at that publication prefer.

Another way to find out more about literary magazines is to check out the various prize anthologies and take note of journals whose fiction is being selected for publication there. Studying prize anthologies not only lets you know which magazines are publishing award-winning work, but it also provides a valuable overview of what is considered to be the best fiction published today. Those anthologies include:

• *Best American Short Stories*, published by Houghton Mifflin, 222 Berkeley St., Boston MA 02116.

• *New Stories from the South: The Year's Best*, published by Algonquin Books of Chapel Hill, P.O. Box 2225, Chapel Hill NC 27515.

• *Prize Stories: The O. Henry Awards*, published by Doubleday/Anchor, 1540 Broadway, New York NY 10036.

• *Pushcart Prize: Best of the Small Presses*, published by Pushcart Press, Box 380, Wainscott NY 11975.

At the beginnings of listings, we include symbols to help you in narrowing your search. Keys to those symbols can be found on the inside front and back covers of this book.

For More Information

If you're interested in learning more about literary and small magazines, you may want to look at *The International Directory of Little Magazines and Small Presses* (Dustbooks, Box 100, Paradise CA 95967); the *Directory of Literary Magazines*, published by the Council of Literary Magazines and Presses (3-C, 154 Christopher St., New York NY 10014-2839); or *The Association of American University Presses Directory* (584 Broadway, New York NY 10012).

ABOUT SUCH THINGS, Literary Magazine, 1701 Delancey St., Philadelphia PA 19103. (215)849-1583. Fax: (215)735-3960. E-mail: aboutsuch@yahoo.com. Website: http://aboutsuch.homepage.com (includes writing samples, submission guidelines, ordering information, bookstore with editors' picks and writing tips, plan to add links in 2001). Editor: Laurel Webster Garver. **Contact:** E. Louise Lindinger, fiction editor. Magazine: 8½×11; perfect bound; 28-32 pages; 24 lb. paper; 80 lb. cover stock; illustrations. "Seeking stories that show contemporary people changing and growing, especially people of faith. Interested in seeing hope of healing in the midst of brokenness portrayed in fiction. Spiritual content not necessary, but gets some preference." Semiannually. Estab. 1996. Circ. 400.

Needs: Ethnic/multicultural, fantasy, historical, humor/satire (particularly with religious/inspirational elements), literary, regional, religious/inspirational, romance, science fiction (soft/sociological), allegory. No erotica, horror, occult, feminist, gay, apocalyptic fiction (end-times stories). Receives 15 unsolicited mss/month. Accepts 1-3 mss/issue; 2-6 mss/year. Does not read mss February-April and August-October. Publishes ms 3 months after acceptance. Recently published work by Eva Doyle, Deanne Devine, Shuara Wilson Shands, Bodham Hamulak and Diane C. Prochownik. Length: 300-3,000 words; average length: 2,000 words. Publishes short shorts. Also publishes cultural essays, book and film reviews and poetry. Always comments on rejected mss.

How to Contact: Send complete ms with a cover letter. Include estimated word count, address, phone number, e-mail and submission on diskette in ASCII text. Responds in up to 8 months to mss. Send SASE. Accepts simultaneous submissions and previously published submissions. Sample copy for $3 and 9 × 12 SAE with 99¢ postage. Guidelines for #10 SASE.

Payment/Terms: Pays 2 contributor's copies; additional copies $3. Acquires one-time rights. Sends galleys to author. Not copyrighted.

Advice: "We look for high quality in content, clarity, tone and characterization; also for impact, snappy dialogue, many-faceted and growing characters. Let any moral or spiritual lesson be an outgrowth of a solid plot and real characters. Be willing to let the story have resonance and tension by not tying up every loose end too tightly. Avoid making 'good' characters stereotypically 'churchy.' "

THE ABSINTHE LITERARY REVIEW, P.O. Box 328, Spring Green WI 53588. E-mail: staff@ absinthe-literary-review.com. Website: www.absinthe-literary-review.com. **Editor:** Charles Allen Wyman. Electronic literary magazine. "We publish short stories, novel excerpts, poems and occasionally essays. Our target audience is the literate individual who enjoys creative language use, character-driven fiction and the clashing of worlds-real and imagined, poetic and prosaic, archaic and modern."

Needs: "*ALR* has a special affection for the blending of archaic materials with modern subjects. Elements of myth, archetype and symbolism should figure heavily in most submissions. We favor the surrealist, the poet and the philosopher over the storyteller even in our fiction choices. We also desire submissions from highly educated writers whose work is too dense, florid or leaned for other markets. At the very least, your work should show an odd turn or a disaffected viewpoint. We abhor minimalist fiction simply because of its abundance in the present marketplace, but we can still appreciate a spare, well-done piece. Any genre work must substantially transcend traditional limitations of the form to be considered; and plot based fiction should be significantly odd." **Publishes 30-50 new writers/year.**

How to Contact: "Send fiction submissions to fiction@absinthe-literary-review.com. Though we now accept snail mail submissions, we prefer e-mail."

Payment/Terms: "We believe that writers should be paid for their work and will attempt to remit a small gratuity upon publication (usually in the $5-10 range) when funds are available. There is, however, no guarantee of payment. We are a nonprofit organization."

Advice: "Be erudite but daring in your writing. Draw from the past to drag meaning from the present. Kill cliché. Invest your work with layers of meaning that subtly reveal multiple realities. Do not submit pieces that are riddled with spelling errors and grammatical snafus."

ACM, (ANOTHER CHICAGO MAGAZINE), Left Field Press, 3709 N. Kenmore, Chicago IL 60613-5301. E-mail: solwitz@anotherchicagomag.com. Website: www.anotherchicagomag.com (includes guidelines, contest information, subscription information and samples). **Editor:** Barry Silesky. **Contact:** Sharon Solwitz, fiction editor. Magazine: 5½ × 8½; 200-220 pages; "art folio each issue." Estab. 1977.

● *ACM* is best known for experimental work and work with clear narrative voices. The editor looks for "engaged and unusual writing." The magazine receives grants from the Illinois Arts Council, the City of Chicago and the NEA.

Needs: Contemporary, ethnic, experimental, feminist, gay, lesbian, literary, prose poem and translations. No religious, strictly genre or editorial. Receives 300 unsolicited fiction mss each month. **Published several new writers in the last year.** Recently published work by Robin Hemley, Maxine Chernoff, Alyce Miller, Carol Ascher and Maureen Seaton. Also publishes creative nonfiction.

How to Contact: Unsolicited mss acceptable with SASE. "Send only one story (unless you work short, less than five pgs.) then we'll read two. We encourage cover letters." Publishes ms 6-12 months after acceptance. Sample copies are available for $8 ppd. Responds in 5 months. Receives small press collections.

Payment/Terms: Pays small honorarium when possible plus contributor's copy and 1 year subscription. Acquires first North American serial rights.

Advice: "Support literary publishing by subscribing to at least one literary journal—if not ours another. Get used to rejection slips, and don't get discouraged. Keep introductory letters short. Make sure manuscript has name and address on every page, and that it is clean, neat and proofread. We are looking for stories with freshness and originality in subject angle and style, and work that encounters the world and is not stuck in its own navel."

☑ ◎ ⚐ **THE ACORN, a Journal of the Western Sierra**, Hot Pepper Press, P.O. Box 1266, El Dorado CA 95623-1266. Phone/fax: (530)642-9265. E-mail: theacorn@visto.com or kirkcolvin@visto.com. Editor: Kirk Colvin. **Contact:** Fiction Editor. Magazine: 8½×5½; 44 pages. *The Acorn* primarily publishes work about the "western slope of Sierra Nevada and rural lifestyle, but encourages the submission of any and all good writing." Quarterly. Estab. 1993. Circ. 200.

• A work from *The Acorn* received first place for Best Western Short Fiction from the Western Writers of America.

Needs: Adventure, historical, humor/satire, literary, mainstream/contemporary, regional, senior citizen/retirement. "No porn or erotica." "We usually try to choose subjects or topics that fit the season. Historical fiction is attractive to us, but we like to see all forms of fiction." Receives 75-100 unsolicited mss/month. Accepts 5-6 mss/issue; 24 mss/year. Publishes ms 1 month after acceptance. **Publishes 5 new writers/year.** Recently published work by Taylor Graham, Kirk Colvin, Margaret S. Burns and Virgil Suarez. Length: 4,000 words maximum. Publishes short shorts. Also publishes literary essays and poetry. Often comments on rejected mss. Sponsors contest; send SASE for information.

How to Contact: Send complete ms with a cover letter. Include 1-paragraph bio and list of publications. Accepts queries/mss by e-mail. Responds in 4 months to mss. Send SASE for reply, return of ms or send a disposable copy of ms. No simultaneous submissions; accepts reprints. Electronic submissions encouraged. Sample copy for $4. Guidelines for #10 SASE.

Payment/Terms: Pays 2 contributor's copy on publication; additional copies for $3.75. Acquires one-time rights.

Advice: Looks for "memorable work that captures the flavor of our region—its history, landforms and wildlife and rural lifestyle. Good writing helps too. If we remember a story the next day, if we find ourselves thinking about the story or a character while driving around in our car, you've struck a nerve and taken a huge first step. Proper formatting will at least get your story read—fancy fonts, italics and clip art are distracting and a short cut to rejection. We encourage electronic submissions of manuscripts. Since we use an editorial board approach and have 5-6 editors reviewing each submission, electronic submissions allow us to save time and money, as well as accelerating the review process."

🄽 $◐ **ADRIFT, Writing: Irish, Irish American and . . .**, 46 E. First St. #3D, New York NY 10003. **Contact:** Thomas McGonigle, editor. Magazine: 8×11; 32 pages; 60 lb. paper stock; 65 lb. cover stock; illustrations; photos. "Irish-Irish American as a basis—though we are interested in advanced writing from anywhere." Semiannually. Estab. 1983. Circ. 1,000.

Needs: Contemporary, erotica, ethnic, experimental, feminist, gay, lesbian, literary, translations. Receives 40 unsolicited mss/month. Accepts 3 mss/issue. **published new writers within the last year.** Published work by Francis Stuart. Length: open. Also publishes literary criticism. Sometimes critiques rejected mss.

How to Contact: Send complete ms. Responds as soon as possible. SASE for return of ms. Sample copy for $5. Reviews novels or short story collections.

Payment/Terms: Pays $7.50-300 on publication for first rights.

Advice: "The writing should argue with, among others, James Joyce, Flann O'Brien, Juan Goytisolo, Ingeborg Bachmann, E.M. Cioran, Max Stirner and Patrick Kavanagh."

◖ **ADVOCATE, PKA'S PUBLICATION**, PKA Publications, 301A Rolling Hills Park, Prattsville NY 12468. (518)299-3103. Tabloid: 9⅜×12¼; 32 pages; newsprint paper; line drawings; b&w photographs. "Eclectic for a general audience." Bimonthly. Estab. 1987. Publishes 12,000 copies.

• *PKA's Advocate* editors tend to like positive, upbeat, entertaining material.

Needs: Adventure, contemporary, ethnic, experimental, fantasy, feminist, historical, humor/satire, juvenile (5-9 years), literary, mainstream, mystery/suspense, prose poem, regional, romance, science fiction, senior citizen/retirement, sports, western, young adult/teen (10-18 years). "Currently looking for equine (horses) stories, poetry, art, photos and cartoons. The *Gaited Horse Newsletter* is currently published within the pages of *PKA's Advocate*." Nothing religious, pornographic, violent, erotic, pro-drug or anti-environment. Receives 60 unsolicited mss/month. Accepts 6-8 mss/issue; 36-48 mss/year. Publishes ms 4 months to 1 year after acceptance. Length: 1,000 words preferred; 1,500 words maximum. Sometimes critiques rejected mss.

How to Contact: Send complete ms with cover letter. Responds in 2 weeks to queries; 2 months to mss. SASE. No simultaneous submissions. Sample copy for $4 (US currency for inside US; $5.25 US currency for Canada). Writers guidelines for SASE.

Payment/Terms: Pays contributor's copies. Acquires first rights.

Advice: "The highest criterion in selecting a work is its entertainment value. It must first be enjoyable reading. It must, of course, be original. To stand out, it must be thought provoking or strongly emotive, or very cleverly plotted. Will consider only previously unpublished works by writers who do not earn their living principally through writing."

◖ ◎ **AETHLON**, East Tennessee State University, Box 70, 683, Johnson City TN 37614-0683. (423)439-5994. E-mail: morefiel@etsu.edu. **Contact:** John Morefield, fiction editor. Magazine: 6×9; 180-240 pages;

illustrations; photos. "Theme: Literary treatment of sport. We publish articles on that theme, critical studies of author's treatment of sport and original fiction and poetry with sport themes. Most of our readers are academics." Semiannually. Estab. 1983. Circ. 800.

Needs: Sport. No fantasy, science fiction, mystery, nostalgia, "trick endings" or horror. "Stories must have a sport-related theme and subject; otherwise, we're wide open. No personal memoirs, mystery, sci-fi, horror, 'trick ending,' etc." Receives 15-20 fiction mss/month. Accepts 6-10 fiction mss/issue; 12-20 fiction mss/year. Publishes ms "about 1 year" after acceptance. **Publishes 2-3 new writers/year.** Recently published work by Pat Reid, Ray Gamache, Jim Denison, Tom LeClair and Peter Martinez. Length: 500-7,500; average length: 2,500-5,000 words. Also publishes literary essays, literary criticism, poetry. Sometimes critiques rejected mss.

How to Contact: Send complete ms and brief cover letter with 1-2 lines for a contributor's note. Responds in 6 months. SASE in size to fit ms. No simultaneous submissions. Final copy must be submitted on disk (WordPerfect). Sample copy for $12.50. Reviews novels and short story collections. Send books to Prof. Joe Dewey, Dept. of English, University of Pittsburgh-Johnstown, Johnstown PA 15601.

Payment/Terms: Pays 1 contributor's copy and 5 offprints.

Advice: "We are looking for well-written, insightful stories. The only criterion is literary excellence. A story should begin immediately to develop tension or conflict. It should have strong characters and a well-drawn setting. Don't be afraid to be experimental. Take more care with your manuscript. Please send a legible manuscript free of grammatical errors. Be willing to revise."

N $ ◫ AFFAIR OF THE MIND, A Literary Quarterly, Rottkamp Publishing, 8 Mare Lane, Commack NY 11725. **Contact:** Tracy Lyn Rottkamp, editor. Magazine: 9×12; 350-700 pages; glossy cover; illustrations; photos. "We use the most expensive, high-quality paper, including Ivory Linen, Gold Parchment, Antique Laid Paper, Grey Granite, etc. We are an extremely high-quality, literary, intelligent publication. We publish over 75 subject themes from world history, plays, medical theses, vignettes, philosophy, satire, memoirs, the era of French Impressionism, the Russian Revolution, the Holocaust, gay/lesbian fiction and nonfiction. We urge writers to SASE for over 8 page subject themes lists. We have been hailed in over 79 countries world-wide as being a publication of the highest caliber. We publish frequently and sporadically. In 1997, we published 32 issues; in 1998 we published 40; in 1999 we published 39." Estab. 1997. Circ. 80,000.

Needs: Erotica, ethnic/multicultural, experimental, family saga, feminist, gay, historical, horror (psychological), humor satire, lesbian, literary, military/war, New Age, psychic/supernatural/occult, thriller/espionage, translations. "No material that is immature or poorly written, inappropriate, crude, pornographic and/or raw language." SASE with 2 stamps for upcoming themes and deadlines. Receives 10,000 unsolicited mss/month. Agented fiction 50%. Recently published work by B.Z. Niditch, Ruth Wildes Schuler and Leslie Schenk. Length: maximum 500 pages; average length: 20,000 words. Publishes short shorts. Average length: 8-10 pages. Also publishes literary essays, literary criticism and poetry. We also publish novels and excerpts from novels. Please query. Always comments on rejected mss.

How to Contact: Send complete ms with a cover letter or submit through agent. Include estimated word count, brief bio, Social Security number and list of publications. Responds in 1 week to queries; 2 weeks to mss. Send SASE (or IRC) for return of ms. Accepts multiple submissions. Sample copy for $9 for regular issues; $12 for limited editions. Please affix 2 33¢ stamps on SASE when writing for guidelines. Reviews novels, short story collections and nonfiction books of interest to writers. Send review copies to Catherine Kenney, Book Review Assistant. In lower hand corner of envelope, write: Dept. BR 30G9LC.

Payment/Terms: Pays $1,000-10,000 or $700/printed page and 2-7 contributor's copies and lifetime subscription to the magazine. Pays $500/printed page for short shorts. Pays on publication for first rights. Sponsors contest: SASE for information. "Please affix two 33¢ stamps to SASE."

Advice: "Despite receiving over 20,000 manuscripts, we always read and occasionally reread every entire submission. We prefer writing with unused surprise endings, such as in the works of Guy de Maupassant, O. Henry. We also particularly like the style of Colette."

☑ $ ◫ ▽ AGNI, Creative Writing Program, Boston University, 236 Bay State Rd., Boston MA 02215. (617)353-7135. Fax: (617)353-7134. E-mail: agni@bu.edu. Website: www.bu.edu/Agni (includes names of editors, short fiction, poetry and interviews with authors). **Contact:** Askold Melnyczuk, editor. Magazine: 5½×8½; 250 pages; 55 lb. booktext paper; recycled cover stock; occasional art portfolios. "Eclectic literary magazine publishing first-rate poems and stories." Biannually. Estab. 1972.

• Work from *Agni* has been selected regularly for inclusion in both *Pushcart Prize* and *Best American Short Stories* anthologies. Jhumpa Lahiri, published in Agni 47, won Pulitzer; Ha Jin runnerup. *Agni* ranked #45 on the *Writer's Digest* "Fiction 50" list of top markets.

Needs: Stories, excerpted novels, prose poems and translations. No science fiction or romance. Receives more than 250 unsolicited fiction mss/month. Accepts 4-7 mss/issue, 8-12 mss/year. Reading period October 1 through February 15 only. **Publishes 30 new writers/year.** Recently published work by Jhumpa Lihiri, Ha Jin, Han Stavane, Frederick Basch and Thom Kennedy.

How to Contact: Send complete ms with SASE and cover letter listing previous publications. Accepts simultaneous and electronic (disk) submissions. Responds in 5 months. Sample copy for $9.

Payment/Terms: Pays $10/page up to $150; 2 contributor's copies; one-year subscription. Pays on publication for first North American serial rights. Sends galleys to author.

Advice: "Read *Agni* carefully to understand the kinds of stories we publish. Read—everything, classics, literary journals, bestsellers. People need to read and subscribe to the magazines before sending their work. It's important for artists to support the arts."

$⊘ THE AGUILAR EXPRESSION, 1329 Gilmore Ave., Donora PA 15033. (724)379-8019. **Contact:** Xavier F. Aguilar, editor. Magazine: 8½×11; 10-16 pages; 20 lb. bond paper; illustrations. "We are open to all writers of a general theme—something that may appeal to everyone." Semiannually. Estab. 1989. Circ. 150.

• The editor is particularly interested in stories about social problems (teen pregnancy, corrupt cops, political abuse, etc.) in the U.S. but publishes fiction on other topics as well.

Needs: Adventure, ethnic/multicultural, experimental, horror, mainstream/contemporary, mystery/suspense (romantic suspense), romance (contemporary). No religious, erotic or first-person stories. Want more current social issues. Receives 15 unsolicited mss/month. Accepts 1-2 mss/issue; 2-4 mss/year. Publishes ms 1 month to 1 year after acceptance. **Publishes 4-10 new writers/year (90% of works published are by new writers).** Published work by Michael D. Cohen, R.G. Cantalupo and Kent Braithwaite. Length: 750-1,500 words; average length: 1,000 words. Also publishes poetry.

How to Contact: Send complete ms with cover letter. Responds to queries in 1 week; mss in 1 month. Send SASE for reply to a query or send a disposable copy of ms. No simultaneous submissions. Sample copy for $6. Guidelines for first class stamp.

Payment/Terms: Pays $10 and 1 contributor's copy for lead story; additional copies at a reduced rate of $3. Acquires one-time rights. Not copyrighted. Write to publication for details on contests, awards or grants.

Advice: "Clean, clear copy makes a manuscript stand out."

$⊘ ⌕ ALASKA QUARTERLY REVIEW, University of Alaska—Anchorage, 3211 Providence Dr., Anchorage AK 99508. (907)786-6916. E-mail: ayaqr@uaa.alaska.edu. Website: www.uaa.alaska.edu/aqr. **Contact:** Ronald Spatz, fiction editor. Magazine: 6×9; 260 pages; 60 lb. Glatfelter paper; 10 pt. C15 black ink varnish cover stock; photos on cover only. *AQR* "publishes fiction, poetry, literary nonfiction and short plays in traditional and experimental styles." Semiannually. Estab. 1982. Circ. 2,200.

• Work appearing in the *Alaska Quarterly Review* has been selected for the *Prize Stories: The O. Henry Awards*, *Best American Essays*, *Best American Poetry*, *Beacon Best* and *Pushcart Prize* anthologies. *The Washington Post* calls the *Alaska Quarterly Review*, "one of the nation's best literary magazines."

Needs: Contemporary, experimental, literary, prose poem, translations. Receives 200 unsolicited fiction mss/month. Accepts 7-13 mss/issue, 15-24 mss/year. Does not read mss May 15 through August 15. Length: not exceeding 90 pages. **Published 4 new writers within the last year.** Published work by Richard Ford, William H. Gass, Patricia Hampl, Stuart Dybek, Alan Lightman and Hayden Carruth. Publishes short shorts.

How to Contact: Send complete mss with SASE. Accepts queries by e-mail. Simultaneous submissions "undesirable, but will accept if indicated." Responds in 2-3 months "but during peak periods a reply may take up to 6 months." Publishes ms 6 months to 1 year after acceptance. Sample copy for $6.

Payment/Terms: Pays 1 contributor's copy and a year's subscription. Pays $50-200 honorarium when grant funding permits. Acquires first rights.

Advice: "We have made a significant investment in fiction. The reason is quality; serious fiction *needs* a market. Try to have everything build to a singleness of effect."

Ⓝ ❧ ⊘ ALGONQUIN ROUNDTABLE REVIEW, Algonquin College, B122d-1385 Woodroffe Ave., Nepean, Ontario K2Y 1V8 Canada. (613)727-4723, ext. 7028. Fax: (613)727-7601. E-mail: roundtable_review@ algonquincollege.com. Website: www.algonquincollege.com/roundtable_review (includes mandate, call for submissions, submission guidelines). **Contact:** Dan Doyle and Nicholas Strachan, editors. Magazine: 8½×11; 82 pages; Plainfield Plus (120M) paper; Cornwall cover coated one side (eight point); illustrations; photos. "We are based on the idea of inclusion: a group with equal status, equal voices, sitting around a table, telling stories, reciting poetry, arguing a point, telling jokes, reading from a script, showing off photographs or graphics." Semiannual. Estab. 1999. Circ. 1,000.

Needs: Ethnic/multicultural, experimental, feminist, humor satire, literary, translations. "No clichéd stories, undue violence, or sexual/racial stereotypes. No moralizing or sentimentality either." See website for upcoming themes. Receives 15-20 unsolicited mss/month. Accepts 8-10 mss/issue; 16-20 mss/year. Publishes ms 4-6 months

---

READ 'THE BUSINESS OF FICTION WRITING' section for information on manuscript preparation, mailing tips, rights and more.

after acceptance. **Publishes 20-25 new writers/year.** Recently published work by Mairuth Sarsfield, George Elliott Clarke and Dennis York. Length: 1,000-4,000 words; average length: 2,500 words. Publishes short shorts. Average length: 600 words. Also publishes literary essays, literary criticism and poetry.

How to Contact: Send complete ms with a cover letter. Accepts submissions by e-mail and fax. Include estimated word count, brief bio and list of publications. Responds in 2 weeks to queries; 6 months to mss. Online queries preferred. Send a disposable copy of ms and #10 SASE for reply only. Accepts multiple submissions. Sample copy for $8 (Canadian). Guidelines by e-mail or visit website.

Payment/Terms: Pays 1 contributor's copy; additional copies $8. Acquires first rights.

Advice: "We prefer electronic submissions in ASCII, Rich Text format or Word Perfect (avoid macros, headers, footers and page numbers)."

N $ALLIGATOR JUNIPER, Prescott College, 301 Grove Ave., Prescott AZ 86301. (520)778-2090, ext. 2012. **Contact:** Melanie Bishop, editor. Literary magazine: 150 pages; some photos. Annual. Estab. 1995. Circ. 2,000.

Needs: Accepts 5 mss/issue; 5 mss/year. Publishes ms 3 months after acceptance. **Publishes 2 new writers/ year.** Recently published work by Melissa Pritchard, Christopher Melka, Elton Glaser and Chris Fink. Length: 30 pages. Publishes short shorts. Always comments on rejected mss.

How to Contact: Submit complete ms. Cover letter required. Include brief bio and list of publications. Responds in 2 weeks to queries; 5 months to mss. Send disposable copy of ms with #10 SASE for reply only. Accepts simultaneous and multiple submissions. Sample copy for $5. Guidelines for SASE.

Payment/Terms: Pays $500 and 4 contributor's copies; additional copies $5. Pays on acceptance for first North American serial rights.

✓ ☺ THE ALSOP REVIEW. E-mail: jw@alsopreview.com. Website: www.alsopreview.com. Managing Editor: Jaimes Alsop. **Contact:** Jamie Wasserman, editor. "*The Alsop Review* publishes only the best poetry and fiction. We are not a zine since we do not publish regular issues. Rather we are a permanent showcase."

Needs: Literary, experimental. "No genre work or humor for its own sake. No pornography." Would like to see more "experimental and unconventional works. Surprise me." Recently published work by Kyle Jarrard, Dennis Must, Kristy Nielsen, Bob Riche and Linda Sue Park. Length: no restriction.

How to Contact: By invitation only. See website for full details. Accepts submissions by e-mail only. Submit via e-mail only.

Payment/Terms: "None. We offer a permanent 'home' on the Web for writers and will pull and add material to their pages upon request. We accept previously published work."

Advice: "Read, read, read. Treat submissions to Web zines as carefully as you would to a print magazine. Research the market first. For every great Web zine, there are a hundred mediocre ones. Remember that once your work is on the Web, chances are it will be there for a very long time. Put your best stuff out there and take advantage of opportunities to re-publish work from print magazines."

$ ☺ ☑ AMELIA, 329 E St., Bakersfield CA 93304. (805)323-4064. Editor-in-Chief: Frederick A. Raborg, Jr.. **Contact:** Fiction Editor. Magazine: 5½×8½; 124-136 pages; perfect-bound; 60 lb. high-quality moistrite matte paper; kromekote cover; four-color covers; original illustrations; b&w photos. "A general review using fine fiction, poetry, criticism, belles lettres, one-act plays, fine pen-and-ink sketches and line drawings, sophisticated cartoons, book reviews and translations of both fiction and poetry for general readers with eclectic tastes for quality writing." Quarterly. Plans special fiction issue each July. Estab. 1984. Circ. 1,826.

● *Amelia* sponsors a long list of fiction awards. It ranked #23 on *Writer's Digest*'s Fiction 50 list of top markets for fiction writers.

Needs: Adventure, contemporary, erotica, ethnic, experimental, fantasy, feminist, gay, historical, humor/satire, lesbian, literary, mainstream, mystery/suspense, prose poem, regional, science fiction, senior citizen/retirement, sports, translations, western. Nothing "obviously pornographic or patently religious." Receives 160-180 unsolicited mss/month. Accepts up to 9 mss/issue; 25-36 mss/year. **Published new writers within the last year.** Published work by Michael Bugeja, Jack Curtis, Thomas F. Wilson, Maxine Kumin, Eugene Dubnov, Matt Mulhern and Merrill Joan Gerber. Length: 1,000-5,000 words; average length: 3,000 words. Usually critiques rejected mss.

How to Contact: Send complete ms with cover letter with previous credits if applicable to *Amelia* and perhaps a brief personal comment to show personality and experience. Responds in 1 week to queries; 2 weeks to 3 months to mss. SASE. Sample copy for $10.95. Guidelines for #10 SASE. Sends galleys to author "when deadline permits."

Payment/Terms: Pays $35-50 on acceptance for first North American serial rights plus 2 contributor's copies; extras with 20% discount.

Advice: "Write carefully and well, but have a strong story to relate. I look for depth of plot and uniqueness, and strong characterization. Study manuscript mechanics and submission procedures. Neatness does count. There is a sameness—a cloning process—among most magazines today that tends to dull the senses. Magazines like *Amelia* will awaken those senses while offering stories and poems of lasting value."

☑ Ⓞ **AMERICAN LITERARY REVIEW**, University of North Texas, P.O. Box 311307, Denton TX 76203-1307. (940)565-2755. Fax: (940)565-4355. Website: www.engl.unt.edu/alr/ (includes excerpts, subscription information, writer's guidelines, contest details). Editor: Lee Martin. **Contact:** Barb Rodman, fiction editor. Magazine: 7×10; 128 pages; 70 lb. Mohawk paper; 67 lb. Wausau Vellum cover. "Publishes quality, contemporary poems and stories." Semiannual. Estab. 1990. Circ. 900.

Needs: Mainstream and literary only. No genre works. Receives 50-75 unsolicited fiction mss/month. Accepts 4-8 mss/issue; 8-16 mss/year. Reading period: September 1-May 1. Publishes ms within 2 years after acceptance. Recently published work by Marianna Wright, Mark Jacobs, Tenaya Darlington and John Fulton. Length: less than 7,500 words. Critiques or comments on rejected mss when possible. Also accepts poetry and essays.

How to Contact: Send complete ms with cover letter. Responds in 2-3 months. SASE. Accepts simultaneous submissions. Sample copy for $8. Guidelines free.

Payment/Terms: Pays in contributor's copies. Acquires one-time rights.

Advice: "We like to see stories that illuminate the various layers of characters and their situations with great artistry. Give us distinctive character-driven stories that explore the complexities of human existance." Looks for "the small moments that contain more than at first appears possible, that surprise us with more truth than we thought we had a right to expect."

Ⓞ **AMERICAN WRITING; A Magazine**, Nierika Editions, 4343 Manayunk Ave., Philadelphia PA 19128. **Contact:** Alexandra Grilikhes, editor. Magazine: 8½×5½; 96 pages; matte paper and cover stock; photos. "We publish new writing that takes risks with form, point of view, language, ways of perceiving. We are interested in the voice of the loner, the artist as shaman, the powers of intuition, exceptional work of all kinds." Semiannually. Estab. 1990. Circ. 2,500.

Needs: Contemporary, excerpted novel, ethnic/multicultural, experimental, feminist, gay, lesbian, literary, translations. "We're looking for more literary, experimental, contemporary writing—writing that drives you to write it." No mainstream, romance, genre fiction, stories about sports. Receives 350 unsolicited mss/month. Accepts 4-5 mss/issue; 25 mss/year. Does not read mss June, December, January. Publishes ms 6-12 months after acceptance. Agented fiction less than 1%. **Publishes 4-6 new writers/year.** Recently published work by Cris Mazza, Pam Ryder, Saikat Mazumdor, Anne Spollen. Length: 5,000 words maximum; average length: 3,500 words. Publishes short shorts. Also publishes literary essays, personal essays, literary criticism, poetry. Critiques or comments on rejected mss "when there is time."

How to Contact: Send complete ms with a brief cover letter. Include brief bio and list of publications if applicable. "No full-length books. Send one ms at a time." Responds in 4 months. Send SASE for reply, return of ms or send a disposable copy of ms. Accepts simultaneous submissions. Sample copy for $6; guidelines for #10 SASE.

Payment/Terms: Pays 2 contributor's copies; additional copies at half price. Acquires first rights or one-time rights.

Advice: "We look for intensity, vision, voice, imaginative use of language, freshness, craft, sophistication; stories that delve. Read not just current stuff, but the old masters—Dostoyevsky, Chekhov and Hesse. Learn about subtlety and depth. Reading helps you to know who you are as a writer, writing makes you more that person, if you're lucky. Read one or two issues of the magazine *carefully*."

❧ Ⓞ **THE AMETHYST REVIEW**, Marcasite Press, 23 Riverside Ave., Truro, Nova Scotia B2N 4G2 Canada. (902)895-1345. E-mail: amethyst@col.auracom.com. Website: www.col.auracom.com/~amethyst (includes guidelines, samples of poetry and fiction, names of editors, links, etc.). **Contact:** Penny Ferguson, editor. Magazine: 8¼×6¾; 84 pages; book weight paper; card stock cover; illustrations. "We publish quality contemporary fiction and poetry of interest to the literary reader." Semiannually. Estab. 1993. Circ. 150-200.

• *The Amethyst Review* has received grants from the Nova Scotia Department of Education and Culture.

Needs: Literary. No erotica. Receives 25 unsolicited mss/month. Accepts 2-3 mss/issue; 4-6 mss/year. Publishes ms maximum 6 months after acceptance, "usually much sooner." **Publishes 8 new writers/year.** Recently published work by Hope Morritt, Sylvia Adams, Sheila MacDougall, Louisa Howerow, Susan Ioannou, Barbara Guenevere Tanner. Length: 5,000 words maximum. Publishes short shorts. Also publishes poetry.

How to Contact: Send complete ms with cover letter. Include estimated word count, a 50-word bio and list of publications. Responds in up to 7 months to mss. Send SASE or SAE and IRCs for reply, return of mss or send a disposable copy of ms. Sample copy for $6 (current) or $4 (back issues). Guidelines for SASE or SAE and IRCs. "Please do not send American stamps! We are no longer replying to submissions without adequate return postage." Reviews novels and short story collections "only by people we have published."

Payment/Terms: Pays 1 contributor's copy; additional copies $6. Pays on publication for first North American serial rights. Sponsors contest; send SASE for information.

Advice: "For us, a story must be memorable because it touches the reader's heart or imagination. Quality is our criterion. Try to delight us with originality and craft. Send for guidelines and sample. We don't look for a specific type of story. We publish the *best* of what we receive. We are seeking literary quality and accessibility. A story that stands out gives the reader a 'tingle' and stays in your mind for days to come. Pay attention to detail, don't be sloppy. Care about your subjects because if you don't neither will the reader. Dazzle us with quality instead of trying to shock us!"

N ◻ **$ ANALECTA, The Official Literary and Art Journal for the University of Texas at Austin**, Liberal Arts Council, FAC17, University of Texas, Austin TX 78712. (512)471-6563. **Contact:** Alice Wang, editor-in-chief (revolving editorship). Magazine: size varies; 200 pages; paper and cover varies; illustrations; photos. "*Analecta* is one of the largest student-run literary journals in the nation. We publish previously unpublished poems, short stories, nonfiction and drama written by college and graduate students." Annual. Estab. 1974. Circ. 1,500.

Needs: Adventure, erotica, ethnic/multicultural, experimental, family saga, fantasy, feminist, gay, glitz, historical, horror, humor satire, lesbian, literary, mainstream, military/war, mystery/suspense, New Age, psychic/supernatural/occult, regional, religious, romance, science fiction, short story collections, thriller/espionage, western. Receives 150 unsolicited mss/year. Accepts fewer than 20 mss/issue. Manuscripts are not accepted after contest deadline, usually in late October. Submission deadline in October; publication in October of next year. **Publishes 25 new writers/year.** Length: 7,000 words maximum; average length: 2,500 words. Publishes short shorts. Also publishes literary essays, literary criticism and poetry.

How to Contact: Query first. Write for cover sheet. Include SASE. Responds in 2 weeks to queries. Send a disposable copy of ms and #10 SASE for reply only. Accepts simultaneous submissions and multiple submissions. Sample copy for $8. Guidelines for SASE.

Payment/Terms: Pays $100 maximum, free subscription to the magazine and 2 contributor's copies; additional copies $8. Pays on publication for first and electronic rights. Not copyrighted. Featured writer of each issue wins $100.

$ ◻ 回 **Y** **ANTIETAM REVIEW**, Washington County Arts Council, 41 S. Potomac St., Hagerstown MD 21740-5512. Phone/fax: (301)791-3132. Executive Editor: Ethan Fischer. **Contact:** Susanne Kass and Ann Knox, fiction editors. Magazine: 8½×11; 54-68 pages; glossy paper; light card cover; photos. A literary journal of short fiction, poetry and black-and-white photographs. "Our audience is primarily in the six state region. Urban, suburban and rural writers and readers, but copies are purchased nationwide, both by libraries as well as individuals. Sales and submissions increase yearly." Annually. Estab. 1982. Circ. 1,800.

● *Antietam Review* has received several awards including First-Runner Up (1993-94) for Editorial Content from the American Literary Magazine Awards. Work published in the magazine has been included in the *Pushcart Prize* anthology and *Best American Short Stories*. The magazine also received a grant from the Maryland State Arts Council and Washington County Arts Council.

Needs: Condensed/excerpted novel, contemporary, ethnic, experimental, feminist, literary and prose poem. Wants more contemporary, ethnic, experimental. "We read manuscripts from our region only—Delaware, Maryland, Pennsylvania, Virginia, West Virginia and Washington D.C. only. We read from September 1 through February 1." No horror, romance, inspirational, pornography. Receives about 100 unsolicited mss/month. Buys 8-10 stories/year. Publishes ms 2-3 months after acceptance. **Publishes 2-3 new writers/year.** Recently published work by Marc Bookman, Tom Glenn, Richard Plant, Shirley G. Cochran, Kevin Stewart, Judy Wilson and Jamie Holland. Length: 3,000 words average. Also publishes poetry.

How to Contact: "Send ms and SASE with a cover letter. Let us know if you have published before and where." Accepts queries by e-mail. Include estimated word count, 1-paragraph bio and list of publications. Responds in 2-4 months. "If we hold a story, we let the writer know. Occasionally we critique returned ms or ask for rewrites." Sample copy for $6.50. Back issue $4.50. Guidelines for legal SAE.

Payment/Terms: "We believe it is a matter of dignity that writers and poets be paid. We have been able to give $50-100 a story and $25 a poem, but this depends on funding. Also 2 copies." Buys first North American serial rights. Sends galleys to author if requested.

Advice: "We seek high quality, well-crafted work with significant character development and shift. We seek no specific theme. We look for work that is interesting involves the reader, and teaches us a new way to view the world. A manuscript stands out because of its energy and flow. Most of our submissions reflect the times (i.e. the news, current events) more than industry trends. We also seek a compelling voice, originality, magic. We now require *accepted* stories to be put on disk by the author to cut down on printing costs. We are seeing an increase of first person narrative stories."

M **$** ◻ **THE ANTIGONISH REVIEW**, St. Francis Xavier University, P.O. Box 5000, Antigonish, Nova Scotia B2G 2W5 Canada. (902)867-3962. Fax: (902)867-5563. E-mail: tar@stfx.ca. Website: www.antigonish. com/review/. **Contact:** George Sanderson, editor. Literary magazine for educated and creative readers. Quarterly. Estab. 1970. Circ. 800.

Needs: Literary, contemporary, prose poem, translations. No erotic or political material. Accepts 6 mss/issue. Receives 50 unsolicited fiction mss each month. **Published new writers within the last year.** Published work by Arnold Bloch, Richard Butts and Helen Barolini. Length: 1,000-6,000 words. Sometimes comments briefly on rejected mss.

How to Contact: Send complete ms with cover letter. SASE ("U.S. postage not acceptable"). No simultaneous submissions. Accepts electronic (disk compatible with WordPerfect/IBM and Windows or e-mail) submissions. Prefers hard copy with disk submission. Responds in 6 months. Publishes ms 3-8 months after acceptance. Sample copy for $4. Guidelines free.

Payment/Terms: Pays $50 for stories. Authors retain copyright. Acquires first serial rights.

Advice: "Learn the fundamentals and do not deluge an editor."

$ ☑ ANTIOCH REVIEW, Box 148, Yellow Springs OH 45387-0148. (937)767-6389. Website: www.antioc h.edu/review (includes guidelines, awards, authors, titles and excerpts of current and upcoming issue, history of the Review, subscription info). Editor: Robert S. Fogarty. Associate Editor: Nolan Miller. **Contact:** Fiction Editor. Magazine: 6×9; 128 pages; 50 lb. book offset paper; coated cover stock; illustrations "seldom." "Literary and cultural review of contemporary issues in politics, American and international studies, and literature for general readership." Quarterly. Published special fiction issue last year; plans another. Estab. 1941. Circ. 5,100.

Needs: Literary, contemporary, experimental, translations. No children's, science fiction or popular market. Accepts 5-6 mss/issue, 20-24 mss/year. Receives approximately 275 unsolicited fiction mss each month. Approximately 1-2% of fiction agented. **Published 1-2 new writers/year.** Recently published work by Gordon Lish, Jean Ross Justice, Peter LaSalle, Sylvia Foley, Josie Milliken, Teresa Svoboda, Joseph Caldwell, Richard Stern, Emily Cerf and Carolyn Osborn. Length: generally under 8,000 words.

How to Contact: Send complete ms with SASE, preferably mailed flat. Responds in 2 months. Publishes ms 6-9 months after acceptance. Sample copy for $6. Guidelines for SASE.

Payment/Terms: Pays $10/page; 2 contributor's copies. $3.90 for extras. Pays on publication for first and one-time rights (rights returned to author on request).

Advice: "Our best advice, always, is to *read* the *Antioch Review* to see what type of material we publish. Quality fiction requires an engagement of the reader's intellectual interest supported by mature emotional relevance, written in a style that is rich and rewarding without being freaky. The great number of stories submitted to us indicates that fiction still has great appeal. We assume that if so many are writing fiction, many must be reading it."

☑ ◎ APOSTROPHE: University of South Carolina Beaufort Journal of the Arts, 801 Carteret St., Beaufort SC 29902. (843)521-4100. Fax: (843)522-9733. E-mail: sjtombe@gwm.sc.edu. Editor: Sheila Tombe. **Contact:** Ellen Malphrus, fiction editor. Magazine: 8×5; 70 pages. Annually. Estab. 1996. Circ. 250-300.

Needs: Literary. Does not want anything "poorly written" or "in bad taste." Receives 3 unsolicited mss/month. Accepts 3-4 mss/issue; 3-4 mss/year. Does not read mss "during semester." Publishes ms 1-2 months after acceptance. **Publishes 3 new writers/year.** Recently published work by Ian Johnson and Brewster M. Robertson. Publishes short shorts. Also publishes literary essays, literary criticism, poetry. Sometimes comments on rejected mss.

How to Contact: Send complete ms with a cover letter. Include short bio. Responds in 2 weeks to queries; 10 months to mss. Send SASE for reply, return of ms or send a disposable copy of ms. Accepts simultaneous submissions and reprints. Sample copy for $3, 8×5 SAE and 2 first-class stamps. Guidelines free for letter-size SASE.

Payment/Terms: Pays 2 contributor's copies; additional copies $5. Pays on publication for one-time rights. Not copyrighted.

Advice: Looks for "excellent prose style; nothing trite or clichéd; nothing 'crafted' à la college fiction writing course. Don't be afraid to ignore your writing instructors, when appropriate."

◎ ◎ APPALACHIAN HERITAGE, Hutchins Library, Berea College, Berea KY 40404. (606)986-9341. Fax: (606)986-9494. E-mail: sidney-farr@berea.edu. **Contact:** James E. Gage, editor. Magazine: 6×9; 80 pages; 60 lb. stock; 10 pt. Warrenflo cover; drawings; b&w photos. "*Appalachian Heritage* is a southern Appalachian literary magazine. We try to keep a balance of fiction, poetry, essays, scholarly works, etc., for a general audience and/or those interested in the Appalachian mountains." Quarterly. Estab. 1973. Circ. approximately 600.

Needs: Regional, literary, historical. "We do not want to see fiction that has no ties to Southern Appalachia." Receives 6-8 unsolicited mss/month. Accepts 2-3 mss/issue; 12-15 mss/year. Publishes ms 1-2 years after acceptance. **Published new writers within the last year.** Published work by Bettie Sellers, Robert Morgan, James Still and Wilma Dykeman. Length: 3,000 words maximum. Publishes short shorts. Length: 500 words. Occasionally critiques rejected mss.

How to Contact: Send complete ms with cover letter. Include estimated word count, 2-3-sentence bio and list of publications. Responds in 1 month to queries; 6 weeks to mss. Send SASE for reply, return of ms or send a disposable copy of ms. Accepts simultaneous and electronic submissions. Sample copy for $6. Guidelines free.

Payment/Terms: Pays 3 contributor's copies; $6 charge for extras. Acquires first North American serial rights.

Advice: "Get acquainted with *Appalachian Heritage*, as you should with any publication before submitting your work."

N ○ ◎ **ARACHNE, INC., In Praise of America's Grassroots Writers**, 2363 Page Rd., Kennedy NY 14747-9717. Editor: Susan L. Leach. **Contact:** Fiction Editor. Magazine: 8½×5½; 30 pages; 20 lb. cover stock; illustrations; photos. "Rural theme. Sedate, conservative tone." Semiannually. Estab. 1981. Circ. 500.
Needs: Literary, regional, religious/inspirational. No erotica. Publishes special fiction issues or anthologies. Receives 20 unsolicited mss/month. Accepts 1-2 mss/issue; 4-5 mss/year. "Does not read after January and July publications." Publishes ms 3 weeks after acceptance. Recently published work by Anne Thore Beecham. Length: 1,500 words. Publishes short shorts. Also publishes literary essays, literary criticism and poetry. Often comments on rejected mss.
How to Contact: Query or send complete ms with a cover letter. Include estimated word count and 250 word bio. Responds in 2 weeks to queries. Send SASE for reply, return of ms or send disposable copy of ms. No simultaneous submissions. Sample copy for $5 and 8½×5½ SAE with 3 first-class stamps. Guidelines for #10 SASE.
Payment/Terms: Pays 2 contributor's copies for first rights; additional copies $2.50. Sends galleys to author. Not copyrighted.
Advice: "Be willing to work with us to perfect your material. Don't try to do it all in one poem or short story."

N $ ◎ **ARARAT QUARTERLY**, Ararat Press, AGBU., 55 E. 59th St., New York NY 10022. (212)319-6383. **Contact:** Dr. Leo Hamalian, editor. Magazine: 8½×11; 72 pages; illustrations; b&w photos. "*Ararat* is a forum for the literary and historical works of Armenian intellectuals or non-Armenian writers writing about Armenian subjects."
Needs: Condensed/excerpted novel, contemporary, historical, humor/satire, literary, religious/inspirational, translations. Publishes special fiction issue. Receives 25 unsolicited mss/month. Accepts 5 mss/issue; 20 mss/year. Length: 1,000 words average. Publishes short shorts. Length: 500 words. Also publishes literary essays, literary criticism, poetry. Sometimes critiques rejected mss and recommends other markets.
How to Contact: Send complete ms with cover letter. Responds in 1 month to queries; 3 weeks to mss. SASE. Accepts simultaneous and reprint submissions. Sample copy for $7 and $1 postage. Free guidelines. Reviews novels and short story collections.
Payment/Terms: Pays $40-75 plus 2 contributor's copies on publication for one-time rights. Sends galleys to author.

● ▣ **ARCHIPELAGO, An International Journal On-Line of Literature, Art and Opinion**, Box 2485, Charlottesville VA 22902-2485. (804)979-5292. E-mail: editor@archipelago.org. Website: www.archipelag o.org. **Contact:** Katherine McNamara, editor. Electronic magazine: 90-100 pages in download (print) edition, available from website. "Literary (print-based, in spirit) work, meaning well-formed, fine writing, on diverse subjects and in various genres with an international tone. Readership is educated, well-read, international." Quarterly. Estab. 1997. Circ. 23 countries, 6,000 hits/month.
Needs: Literary. "No academic, self-involved, 'hip' fiction." Receives several unsolicited mss/month. Accepts 1 ms/issue. Does not read mss in the month before publication. Usually publishes ms in next issue after acceptance. Recently published work by Benjamin Cheever and Anna Maria Ortese. Publishes short shorts. Also publishes literary essays, literary criticism, poetry. Sometimes comments on rejected ms if requested.
How to Contact: Query first. Accepts queries by e-mail. Include brief bio. Responds in 2 months to queries; 4 months to mss. Send SASE for reply, return of ms. Accepts simultaneous and reprint submissions. Reviews novels, short story collections and nonfiction books of interest to writers.
Payment/Terms: No payment. Acquires first rights and first electronic rights. Sends galleys to author. Copyright reverts to author on publication.
Advice: "We look for superb writing; engaged, adult imagination. As big publishing becomes more and more part of the entertainment industry, I look for writers deeply read, thoughtful, uncontaminated by pop culture and commercial plot-lines."

✓ ◑ **ARKANSAS REVIEW, A Journal of Delta Studies**, Department of English and Philosophy, P.O. Box 1890, Arkansas State University, State University AR 72467-1890. (501)972-3043. Fax: (501)972-3045. E-mail: delta@toltec.astate.com. Website: www.clt.astate.edu/arkreview (includes guidelines, names of editors, ordering information, tables of contents). Editor: William C. Clements. **Contact:** Norman Stafford, fiction editor. Magazine: 8¼×11; 64-100 pages; coated, matte paper; matte, 4-color cover stock; illustrations; photos. Publishes articles, fiction, poetry, essays, interviews, reviews, visual art evocative of or responsive to the Mississippi River Delta. Triannually. Estab. 1996. Circ. 700.
Needs: Regional short stories, literary essays, literary criticism. "No genre fiction. Must have a Delta focus." Receives 30-50 unsolicited mss/month. Accepts 2-3 mss/issue; 5-7 mss/year. Publishes ms 6-12 months after acceptance. Agented fiction 1%. **Publishes 3-4 new writers/year.** Recently published work by Chalana Oueles, Deborah Elliott Deutschmann, Mark Sindecuse and Craig Black. Also publishes literary essays and poetry. Always comments on rejected mss.

How to Contact: Send complete ms with cover letter. Accepts queries/mss by e-mail and fax. Include bio. Responds in 1 week to queries; 4 months to mss. Send SASE for reply, return of ms or send a disposable copy of ms. Sample copy for $7.50. Guidelines free for #10 SASE.

Payment/Terms: Pays 5 contributor's copies; additional copies for $5. Acquires first North American serial rights.

Advice: "We publish new writers in every issue. We look for distinguished, mature writing, surprises, a perfect ending and a story that means more than merely what went on in it. We don't like recognizable imitations of currently fashionable writers."

✓ Ø **THE ARMCHAIR AESTHETE**, Pickle Gas Press, 31 Rolling Meadows Way, Penfield NY 14526. (716)388-6968. E-mail: bypaul@netacc.net. **Contact:** Paul Agosto, editor. Magazine: 5½ × 8½; 40-65 pages; 20 lb. paper; 110 lb. card stock color cover. *The Armchair Aesthete* seeks quality writing that enlightens and entertains a thoughtful audience (ages 9-90) with a "good read." Quarterly. Estab. 1996. Circ. 100.

Needs: Adventure, fantasy (science fantasy, sword and sorcery), historical (general), horror, humor/satire, mainstream/contemporary, mystery/suspense (amateur sleuth, cozy, police procedural, private eye/hardboiled, romantic suspense), science fiction (soft/sociological), westerns (frontier, traditional). No racist, pornographic, advert gore or material intended for children. Plans to publish special fiction issue. Receives 50 unsolicited mss/month. Accepts 8-15 mss/issue; 32-60 mss/year. Publishes ms 3-9 months after acceptance. Agented fiction less than 5%. **Publishes 10-15 new writers/year.** Recently published work by Dina Rabadi, Doug Holder, Frank Andreotti and Craig Butler. Length: 3,000 words maximum; average length: 2,000 words. Publishes short shorts. Also publishes poetry. Sometimes comments on rejected mss.

How to Contact: Send complete ms with a cover letter. Include estimated word count, 50-100 word bio and list of publications. Responds in 2-3 weeks to queries; 1-3 months to mss. Send SASE for reply, return of ms or send a disposable copy of ms. Accepts simultaneous submissions, reprints and electronic submissions. Sample copy for $3 and 2 first-class stamps. Guidelines free for #10 SASE. Reviews novels and short story collections.

Payment/Terms: Pays 1 contributor's copy on publication; additional copies for $3 (pay to P. Agosto, editor). Acquires one-time rights. Accepted works are automatically eligible for an annual contest.

Advice: "Clever, compelling storytelling has a good chance here. We look for a clever plot, thought-out characters, something that surprises or catches us off guard. Write on innovative subjects and situations. Submissions should be professionally presented and technically sound."

✓ $Ø **ARTFUL DODGE**, Dept. of English, College of Wooster, Wooster OH 44691. (330)263-2332. Website: www.wooster.edu/artfuldodge (includes writer's guidelines, editor's bios, interviews with authors, subscription information, history of the magazine). Editor-in-Chief: Daniel Bourne. **Contact:** Fiction Editor. Magazine: 100 pages; illustrations; photos. "There is no theme in this magazine, except literary power. We also have an ongoing interest in translations from Central/Eastern Europe and elsewhere." Biannual. Estab. 1979. Circ. 1,000.

Needs: Experimental, literary, prose poem, translations. "We judge by literary quality, not by genre. We are especially interested in fine English translations of significant contemporary prose writers. Translations should be submitted with original texts." Receives 40 unsolicited fiction mss/month. Accepts 5 mss/year. Published fiction by Edward Kleinschmidt, Terese Svoboda, David Surface, Leslie Pietrzyk and Zbigniew Herbert; and interviews with Tim O'Brien, Lee Smith, Michael Dorris and Stuart Dybek. **Published 1 new writer within the last year.** Length: 10,000 words maximum; 2,500 words average. Also publishes literary essays, literary criticism, poetry. Occasionally critiques rejected mss.

How to Contact: Send complete ms with SASE. Do not send more than 30 pages at a time. Responds in 1 week to 8 months. No simultaneous or reprint submissions. Sample copies are $5 for older issues; $7 for current issues. Guidelines for #10 SASE.

Payment/Terms: Pays 2 contributor's copies and honorarium of $5/page. Acquires first North American serial rights.

Advice: "If we take time to offer criticism, do not subsequently flood us with other stories no better than the first. If starting out, get as many *good* readers as possible. Above all, read contemporary fiction and the magazine you are trying to publish in."

N $ **ARTS & LETTERS**, Journal of Contemporary Culture, Georgia College & State University, Milledgeville GA 31061. Email: al@mail.gcsu.edu. Website: www.gcsu.edu (includes cover art, guidelines, editorial staff, contents of previous issues, brief introduction to Arts & Letters, competition guidelines and more). **Contact:** Kellie Wells, co-editor. Literary magazine: 7 × 10; 200 pages; 60 lb. joy white; some photos. "*Arts & Letters* publishes poetry, fiction, creative nonfiction and commentary on contemporary culture. The journal features the mentors interview series, the world of poetry translation series, and color reproductions of original artistic prints. Also is the only journal nationwide to feature authors and artists that represent such an eclectic range of creative work. Our audience is those people who make a reasoned distinction between contemporary culture and popular culture." Semiannual. Estab. 1999. Circ. 1,000.

Needs: Literary. No genre fiction. Receives 50 unsolicited mss/month. Accepts 3 mss/issue; 6 mss/year. Publishes 6-12 months after acceptance. Recently published work by Thomas E. Kennedy, Annie David, Caroline Langston and more. Length: 3,000-7,500 words; average length: 6,000 words. Sometimes comments on rejected mss.

How to Contact: Send complete ms with cover letter. Include estimated word count; brief bio and list of publications. Responds in 2 weeks to queries; 4 months to mss. Send disposable copy of ms and #10 SASE for reply only. Sample copy for $8. Guidelines for SASE, email or website.

Payment/Terms: Pays $50 or $10 per printed page and 1 contributor's copy; additional copies $5. Pays on publication for first North American serial rights. Sends galleys to author.

Advice: "An obvious, but not gimmicky, attention to and fresh usage of language. A solid grasp of the craft of story writing. Fully realized work."

☑ ◑ ◎ **ASIAN PACIFIC AMERICAN JOURNAL**, The Asian American Writers' Workshop, 16 W. 32nd St., Suite 10A, New York NY 10001. (212)494-0061. Fax: (212)494-0062. E-mail: aaww@panix.com. Website: www.aaww.org. **Contact:** Hanya Yanagihara and Jerome Chou, editors. Magazine: 5½×8½; 250 pages; illustrations. "We are interested in publishing works by writers from all segments of the Asian Pacific American community. The journal appeals to all interested in Asian-American literature and culture." Semiannually. Estab. 1992. Circ. 1,500.

Needs: Condensed/excerpted novel, erotica, ethnic/multicultural, experimental, feminist, gay, graphic novels, historical (general), humor/satire, lesbian, literary, mainstream/contemporary, regional, serialized novel, translations, Asian-American themes. "We are interested in anything related to the Asian American community." Receives 120 unsolicited mss/month. Accepts 15 mss/issue; 30 mss/year. Publishes ms 4-6 months after acceptance. Agented fiction 5%. Recently published work by David Henry Hwang, Chitra Banerjee Divakarvni, Kimiko Hahn, Bino A. Realuyo and Renna Rizzuto. Length: 3,000 words average. Publishes short shorts. Also publishes literary essays, poetry.

How to Contact: Send SASE for guidelines. Should include estimated word count, 3-5 sentence bio, list of publications. Responds in 1 month to queries; 4 months to mss. SASE for reply or send 4 disposable copies of ms. Accepts simultaneous, reprint, electronic (disk, Macintosh or IBM, preferably Microsoft Word 5 for Mac) submissions. Sample copy for $10. Guidelines for SASE.

Payment/Terms: Pays 2 contributor's copies; additional copies at 40% discount. Acquires one-time rights. Sponsors contests, awards or grants for fiction writers. "Send query with SASE."

Ⓝ **AURA LITERARY ARTS REVIEW**, University of Alabama at Brimingham, 135 HUC, 1530 3rd Ave. S, Birmingham AL 35294-1150. (205)934-3216. **Contact:** Daniel Williams, fiction editor. Literary magazine: 6×9; 110 pages; some illustrations; photos. Semiannual. Estab. 1975. Circ. 500.

Needs: Adventure, experimental, fantasy, feminist, gay, glitz, historical, horror, humor/satire, lesbian, literary, mystery, regional, science fiction, thriller/espionage. No mss longer than 5,000 words. Publishes 40 unsolicited mss/month. Accepts 8 mss/issue; 16 mss/year. Publishes 3-4 months after acceptance. **Published 2-3 new writers/ year.** Recently published work by Fred Bonnie. Length: 100-5,000 words; average length: 1,500 words. Publishes short shorts.

How to Contact: Send complete ms with cover letter. Include brief bio. Responds in 2 weeks to queries; 1 month to mss. Send SASE for return of ms or send disposable copy of ms and #10 SASE for reply only. Accepts simultaneous and multiple submissions. Sample copy for $6. Guidelines for SASE.

Payment/Terms: Pays 2 contributor's copies; additional copies $6. Acquires one-time rights.

◖ ◎ **THE AZOREAN EXPRESS**, Seven Buffaloes Press, Box 249, Big Timber MT 59011. **Contact:** Art Cuelho, editor. Magazine: 6¾×8¼; 32 pages; 60 lb. book paper; 3-6 illustrations/issue; photos rarely. "My overall theme is rural; I also focus on working people (the sweating professions); the American Indian and Hobo; the Dustbowl era; and I am also trying to expand with non-rural material. For rural and library and professor/ student, blue collar workers, etc." Semiannually. Estab. 1985. Circ. 600.

Needs: Contemporary, ethnic, experimental, humor/satire, literary, regional, western, rural, working people. Receives 10-20 unsolicited mss/month. Accepts 2-3 mss/issue; 4-6 mss/year. Publishes ms 1-6 months after acceptance. Length: 1,000-3,000 words. Also publishes short shorts, 500-1,000 words. "I take what I like; length sometimes does not matter, even when longer than usual. I'm flexible."

How to Contact: "Send cover letter with ms; general information, but it can be personal, more in line with the submitted story. Not long rambling letters." Responds in 1-4 weeks. SASE. Sample copy for $7.75 postpaid. Guidelines for SASE.

Payment/Terms: Pays in contributor's copies. "Depends on the amount of support author gives my press." Acquires first North American serial rights. "If I decide to use material in anthology form later, I have that right." Sends galleys to the author upon request.

Advice: "There would not be magazines like mine if I was not optimistic. But literary optimism is a two-way street. Without young fiction writers supporting fiction magazines the future is bleak because the commercial magazines allow only formula or name writers within their pages. My own publications receive no grants. Sole support is from writers, libraries and individuals."

■ **BABEL, the Multilingual, Multicultural Online Journal of Arts and Ideas**, E-mail: malcolm@towero fbabel.com. Website: www.towerofbabel.com. **Contact:** Malcolm Lawrence, editor-in-chief. Electronic zine. Publishes "regional reports from international stringers all over the planet, as well as features round table discussions, fiction, columns, poetry, erotica, travelogues, reviews of all the arts and editorials. We are an online community involving an extensive group of over 50 artists, writers and programmers, and over 150 translators representing (so far) 35 of the world's languages."
Needs: "There are no specific categories of fiction that we are not interested in. Possible exceptions: lawyers/ vampires, different genders hailing from different planets, cold war military scenarios and things that go bump in the suburban night." Recently published work by Nicholas P. Snoek, Yves Jaques, Doug Williamson, A.L. Fern, Laura Feister, Denzel J. Hankinson, Pete Hanson and Malcolm Lawrence.
How to Contact: Send queries/mss by e-mail. "Please send submissions with a résumé/cv or biography, as Microsoft Word attached to e-mail." Reviews novels and short story collections.
Advice: "We would like to see more fiction with first-person male characters written by female authors as well as more fiction with first-person female characters written by male authors. The best advice we could give to writers wanting to be published in our publication is simply to know what you're writing about and to write passionately about it. We should also mention that the phrase 'dead white men' will only hurt your chances. The Internet is the most important invention since the printing press and will change the world in the same way. One look at *Babel* and you'll see our predictions for the future of electronic publishing."

✔ ⦿ **THE BALTIMORE REVIEW**, Baltimore Writers' Alliance, P.O. Box 410, Riderwood MD 21139. (410)377-5265. Fax: (410)377-4325. E-mail: hdiehl@bcpl.net. Website: www.baltimorewriters.org (includes guidelines, info about Baltimore Writers' Alliance and Writer's Forum). Editor: Barbara Diehl. **Contact:** Fiction Editor. Magazine: 6×9; 136 pages; 60 lb. paper; 10 pt. CS1 gloss film cover. Showcase for the best short stories and poetry by writers in the Baltimore area and beyond. Semiannually. Estab. 1996.
Needs: Ethnic/multicultural, experimental, literary, mainstream/contemporary. "Would like to see more well-written literary and somewhat traditional stories." No science fiction, westerns, children's, romance, etc. Accepts 8-12 mss/issue; 16-24 mss/year. Publishes ms 1-9 months after acceptance. **Publishes "at least a few" new writers/year.** Recently published work by Michael Larkin, M.E. Grow and Molly Bruce Jacobs. Length: short shorts to 6,000 words maximum; average length: 3,000 words. Also publishes poetry.
How to Contact: Send complete ms with a cover letter. Include estimated word count, brief bio and list of publications. Responds in 1-3 months. Send SASE for reply, return of ms or send a disposable copy of ms. Accepts simultaneous submissions. Sample copy for $8. Guidelines free for #10 SASE. No e-mail or fax submissions.
Payment/Terms: Pays 2 contributor's copies on publication. Acquires first North American serial rights.
Advice: "We look for compelling stories and a masterful use of the English language. We want to feel that we have never heard this story, or this voice, before. Read the kinds of publications you want your work to appear in. Make your reader believe, and care."

Ⓝ ⚘ ✔ $⦿ **B&A: NEW FICTION**, P.O. Box 702, Station P, Toronto, Ontario M5S 2Y4 Canada. Fax: (416)696-5075. E-mail: bloodaphorisms@hotmail.com. Website: www.gutterpress.com. Publisher: Sam Hiyate. Managing Editor: Kristi-ly Green. **Contact:** Elaine O'Connor and Rick Kang, editors. Magazine: 8½×11; 48 pages; bond paper; illustrations. "We publish new and emerging writers whose work is fresh and revealing, and impacts on a literary readership." Quarterly. Estab. 1990. Circ. 2,500.
Needs: Experimental, literary. No gratuitous violence, pornography or exploitive fiction. Publishes anthology periodically. Receives 100 unsolicited mss/month. Accepts 10 mss/issue; 24-40 mss/year. Publishes ms 3-6 months after acceptance. Length: 150-7,000 words; average length: 2,500 words. Often critiques rejected mss. Sponsors fiction contest: $2,000 (Canadian) in prizes; up to 2,500 words; $18 entry fee includes subscription. SASE for information.
How to Contact: Send complete ms with a cover letter. Should include estimated word count, short bio, list of publications with submission. SASE for reply to a query or return of ms. Accepts simultaneous (please advise) and electronic (e-mail and disk with hard copy) submissions. Sample copy for $6. Guidelines for SASE.
Payment/Terms: Pays subscription to the magazine plus $35/printed page. Additional copies $6. Acquires first North American serial rights, electronic distribution for current issue sampling on Home Page, and the right to use work in anthology.
Advice: "Read *B&A* first. Know what kind of literary magazine you are submitting to. If it is consistent with your work, send us your best."

⦿ **BARBARIC YAWP**, Bone World Publishing, 3700 County Rt. 24, Russell NY 13684-3198. (315)347-2609. Editor: John Berbrich. **Contact:** Nancy Berbrich, fiction editor. Magazine: digest-size; 60 pages; 24 lb. paper; matte cover stock. "We are not preachers of any particular poetic or literary school. We publish any type of quality material appropriate for our intelligent and wide-awake audience." Quarterly. Estab. 1997. Circ. 100.
Needs: Adventure, experimental, fantasy (science, sword and sorcery), historical, horror, humor/satire, literary, mainstream/contemporary, psychic/supernatural/occult, regional, religious/inspirational, science fiction (hard, soft/sociological). Wants more humor, satire and adventure. "We don't want any pornography, gratuitous violence

or whining." Receives 30-40 unsolicited mss/month. Accepts 10-12 mss/issue; 40-48 mss/year. Publishes ms within 6 months after acceptance. **Publishes 3-5 new writers/year.** Recently published work by Mark Spitzer, Errol Miller and Jeff Grimshaw. Length: 1,000 words maximum; average length: 600 words. Publishes short shorts. Also publishes literary essays, literary criticism, poetry. Often comments on rejected mss.

How to Contact: Send complete ms with a cover letter. Include estimated word count, brief bio and list of publications. Responds in 2 weeks to queries; 4 months to mss. Send SASE for reply, return of ms or send a disposable copy of ms. Accepts simultaneous submissions and reprints. Sample copy for $3. Guidelines for #10 SASE.

Payment and Terms: Pays 1 contributor's copy; additional copies $3. Acquires one-time rights.

Advice: "We are primarily concerned with work that means something to the author, but which is able to transcend the personal into the larger world. Send whatever is important to you. We will use Yin and Yang. Work must hold my interest and be well-crafted. Read, read, read; write, write, write—then send us your best. Don't get discouraged. Believe in yourself. Take risks. Do not fear rejection."

THE BARCELONA REVIEW, Correu Vell 12 - 2, 08002 Barcelona, Spain. Phone/fax: (00) 34 93 319 15 96. E-mail: editor@barcelonareview.com. Website: www.barcelonareview.com. **Contact:** Jill Adams, editor. "*TBR* is an international review of contemporary, cutting-edge fiction published in English, Spanish and Catalan. Our aim is to bring both new and established writers to the attention of a larger audience."

● *The Barcelona Review* ranked #10 on *Writer's Digest*'s Fiction 50 list of top markets for fiction writers. *TBR* has also been named "Best Online Only Literary Review" by Nan A. Talese/Doubleday.

Needs: Short fiction. Length: 4,000 words maximum. Also publishes articles and essays, book and film reviews and author interviews. "Most, but not all of our fiction lies somewhere out of the mainstream. Our bias is towards potent and powerful cutting-edge material; given that general criteria we are open to all styles and techniques and all genres. No slice-of-life stories, vignettes or sentimental writing, and nothing that does not measure up in your opinion, to the quality of work in our review, which we expect submitters to be familiar with." **Published 20 new writers in 1999.** "That number will increase as the quality of writing presents itself." Published work by Irvine Welsh, Pagan Kennedy, Pinckney Benedict and A.M. Home.

How to Contact: Send submissions by e-mail as an attached file. Hard copies accepted but cannot be returned. No simultaneous submissions.

Payment/Terms: "In lieu of pay we offer a highly professional Spanish translation to English-language writers and vice versa to Spanish writers."

Advice: "We're after original, potent and powerful writing with a contemporary feel that is literarily sound. We'd like to see more risks being taken, more writing with imaginative distinction."

BATHTUB GIN, Pathwise Press, P.O. Box 2392, Bloomington IN 47402. (812)323-2985. E-mail: charter@ bluemarble.net. Website: www.bluemarble.net/~charter/btgin.htm (includes guidelines, news, links and catalogue). Editors: Chris Harter and Tom Maxedon. **Contact:** Fiction Editor. Magazine: 8½×5½; 48-52 pages; recycled 20-lb. paper; 60-lb. card cover; illustrations; photos. "*Bathtub Gin* is looking for work that has some kick to it. We are very eclectic and publish a wide range of styles. Audience is anyone interested in new writing and art that is not being presented in larger magazines." Semiannually. Estab. 1997. Circ. 150.

Needs: Condensed/excerpted novel, experimental, gay, humor/satire, lesbian, literary. "No horror, science fiction, historical unless they go beyond the usual formula." Want more experimental fiction. Receives 20 unsolicited mss/month. Accepts 2-3 mss/issue. Does not read mss September 15-December 1 and March 15-July 1; "we publish in mid-October and mid-April." **50% of works published are by new writers.** Recently published work by Laura J. Cutler, Phillip Good, Greggory Moore and Allen Purdy. Length: 10 double-spaced pages maximum. Publishes short shorts. Also publishes literary essays, literary criticism, poetry. Often comments on rejected ms.

How to Contact: Send complete ms with a cover letter. Include estimated word count, 3-5 line bio. Accepts queries by e-mail. Responds in 1-2 months. Send SASE for reply, return of ms or send a disposable copy of ms. Accepts simultaneous, reprint and electronic submissions (modem). Sample copy for $5 with 6×9 SAE and 4 first-class stamps. Guidelines for #10 SASE. Reviews novels and short story collections.

Payment/Terms: Pays 1 contributor's copy; discount on additional copies. Rights revert to author upon publication.

Advice: "We are looking for writing that contains strong imagery, is complex, and is willing to take a chance with form and structure. Query first and obtain a sample of a magazine to see what it is looking for and if you really want to be published there."

BAYBURY REVIEW, 40 High St., Highwood IL 60040. E-mail: baybury@flash.net. Website: www.ba yburyreview.com (includes writers' guidelines, names of editors, excerpts from old and new issues, subscription information and links to related sites). Editor: Janet St. John. **Contact:** Pamela Sourelis, fiction editor. Magazine: 5½×8½; 80-120 pages; card cover, perfect-bound; b&w line art. "*Baybury Review* publishes quality fiction, poetry and nonfiction by emerging and established writers." Annually. Estab. 1997. Circ. 400.

Needs: Literary fiction. No erotica, horror, or children's fiction. Wants more short shorts and non-linear narratives. Receives 800 mss/year. Accepts 3-4 mss/year. **Publishes 2-6 new writers/year.** Recently published work by Curtis Smith, Greg Melaik, Linda Lewis, Danny Sklar and Michael Cook. Length: 5,000 words maximum. Publishes short shorts. Also publishes prose poetry and book reviews.

How to Contact: Open to unsolicited mss from August 1 through December 31 only. Send complete ms with SASE and optional cover letter. Responds in 3 months. Accepts simultaneous submissions (please notify of acceptance elsewhere). Publishes ms up to 1 year after acceptance. Sample copy for $6.

Payment/Terms: Pays 2 contributor's copies. Acquires first North American serial rights.

Advice: "We are particularly interested in writers who explore the boundaries of conventional form. Read and look through many different literary journals. Find the best 'home' for your work—where it seems to fit best. We are somewhat discouraged by the fact that many money-making, established, and grant-supported literary journals keep repeat publishing well-known writers when they could be supporting more unrecognized and talented writers. We are dedicated to publishing these lesser known writers."

BBR MAGAZINE, P.O. Box 625, Sheffield, S1 3GY, United Kingdom. E-mail: magazine@bbr-online.com. Website: www.bbr-online.com/magazine (includes names of editors, writer's guidelines and more). **Contact:** Chris Reed, editor. Annually. Circ. 3,000. Publishes 20,000-30,000 words/issue.

Needs: Science fiction, literary. "*Back Brain Recluse*, the award-winning British fiction magazine, actively seeks new fiction that ignores genre pigeonholes. We tread the thin line between experimental speculative fiction and avant-garde literary fiction." No genre fiction, or science fiction, fantasy or horror.

How to Contact: Enclose a SASE for the return of your ms. Accepts queries by e-mail. "We are unable to reply to writers who do not send return postage. We recommend two IRCs plus disposable ms for non-UK submissions. One US$ is an acceptable (and cheaper!) alternative to IRCs. Please send all submissions to Chris Reed, BBR, P.O. Box 625, Sheffield S1 3GY, UK. We aim to reply to all submissions within 2 months, but sometimes circumstances beyond our control may cause us to take longer. Please enclose SAE if enquiring about a manuscript's status. No responsibility can be accepted for loss or damage to unsolicited material, howsoever caused."

Payment/Terms: Sample copy available in US for $10 from BBR, % Anne Marsden, 31192 Paseo Amapola, San Juan Capistrano CA 92675-2227. (Checks payable to Anne Marsden).

Tips: "Guidelines are not there for the editor's amusement. If you're serious about being published, pay attention to what the guidelines say. Familiarity with the magazine is *strongly* advised."

BEACON STREET REVIEW, 100 Beacon St., Emerson College, Boston MA 02116. (617)824-8750. E-mail: beaconstreetreview@hotmail.com. Editor: Siobhan McFarland. **Contact:** Genevieve Hamilton, fiction editor. Editors change each year. Magazine: 5½×8½; 100 pages; 60 lb. paper. The *Beacon Street Review*, a journal of new prose and poetry, is published twice a year by students in the graduate writing, literature and publishing department of Emerson College. Semiannual. Estab. 1986. Circ. 800.

Needs: Literary. Receives 120 mss/year. Accepts 5-10 mss/issue; 10-20 mss/year. Does not read mss in the summer. Publishes ms 1-2 months after acceptance. **Publishes 8 new writers/year.** Recently published work by Matthew Goodman, Keith Regan and D.M. Gordon. Length: 20 pages maximum. Publishes short shorts. Also publishes literary essays and poetry. Sometimes comments on rejected mss.

How to Contact: Send complete ms with a cover letter. Accepts submissions by e-mail. Include estimated word count and bio. Responds in 2 weeks to queries; 2 months to mss. Send disposable copy of ms. Accepts simultaneous submissions. Sample copy for $3 with 6×9 SAE. Guidelines free. Reviews novels, short story collections and nonfiction books of interest to writers.

Payment/Terms: Pays 3 contributor's copies; additional copies $1.50. Pays on publication for one-time rights. Sponsors Editor's Choice Award. One piece is selected from every two issues for a $75 award judged by an established local author.

$ THE BELLINGHAM REVIEW, Western Washington University, MS9053, Bellingham WA 98225. Website: www.wwu.edu/~bhreview (includes guidelines, poetry, fiction, nonfiction). Editor: Robin Hemley. **Contact:** Fiction Editor. Magazine: 5½×8; 120 pages; 60 lb. white paper; varied cover stock. "A literary magazine featuring original short stories, novel excerpts, essays, short plays and poetry of palpable quality." Semiannually. Estab. 1977. Circ. 1,500.

• The editors would like to see more humor and literary fiction.

Needs: All genres/subjects considered. Accepts 1-2 mss/issue. Does not read between May 2 and September 30. Publishes short shorts. **Publishes 8-10 new writers/year.** Published work by Sharon Solwitz, Michael Martone, Lee Upton and Bret Lott. Length: 10,000 words or less. Also publishes poetry.

How to Contact: Send complete ms. Responds in 3-6 months. Publishes ms an average of 6 months after acceptance. Sample copy for $5. Reviews novels and short story collections.

Payment/Terms: Pays 1 contributor's copy plus 2-issue subscription and $250. Charges $2.50 for extra copy. Acquires first North American serial and one-time rights.

Advice: "We look for work that is ambitious, vital, and challenging both to the spirit and the intellect. We hope to publish important works from around the world, works by older, neglected writers, and works by unheralded but talented new writers."

☑ ◑ **BELLOWING ARK, A Literary Tabloid**, P.O. Box 5564, Shoreline WA 98155. (206)440-0791. Editor: R.R. Ward. **Contact:** Fiction Editor. Tabloid: 11½×17½; 28 pages; electro-brite paper and cover stock; illustrations; photos. "We publish material which we feel addresses the human situation in an affirmative way. We do not publish academic fiction." Bimonthly. Estab. 1984. Circ. 650.

• Work from *Bellowing Ark* appeared in the *Pushcart Prize* anthology. The editor says he's using much more short fiction and prefers positive, life-affirming work. Remember, he likes a traditional, narrative approach and "abhors" minimalist and post-modern work.

Needs: Contemporary, literary, mainstream, serialized/excerpted novel. No science fiction or fantasy. Receives 600-800 unsolicited fiction mss/year. Accepts 2-5 mss/issue; 10-20 mss/year. Time varies, but publishes ms not longer than 6 months after acceptance. **Published 10-50 new writers/year.** Recently published work by Robin Sterns, Shelley Uva, Tanyo Ravicz, Susan Montag and E.R. Romaine. Length: 3,000-5,000 words average ("but no length restriction"). Publishes short shorts. Also publishes literary essays, literary criticism, poetry. Sometimes critiques rejected mss.

How to Contact: No queries. Send complete ms with cover letter and short bio. "Prefer cover letters that tell something about the writer. Listing credits doesn't help." No simultaneous submissions. Responds in 6 weeks to mss. SASE. Sample copy for $3, 9×12 SAE and $1.21 postage.

Payment/Terms: Pays in contributor's copies. Acquires all rights, reverts on request.

Advice: "*Bellowing Ark* began as (and remains) an alternative to the despair and negativity of the Workshop/ Academic literary scene; we believe that life has meaning and is worth living—the work we publish reflects that belief. Learn how to tell a story before submitting. Avoid 'trick' endings—they have all been done before and better. *Bellowing Ark* is interested in publishing writers who will develop with the magazine, as in an extended community. We find *good* writers and stick with them. This is why the magazine has grown from 12 to 28 pages."

☑ ◑ 🐱 **BELOIT FICTION JOURNAL**, Box 11, 700 College St., Beloit College WI 53511. (608)363-2577. E-mail: darlingr@beloit.edu. **Editor:** Clint McCown. Magazine: 6×9; 250 pages; 60 lb. paper; 10 pt. C1S cover stock; illustrations; photos on cover. "We are interested in publishing the best contemporary fiction and are open to all themes except those involving pornographic, religiously dogmatic or politically propagandistic representations. Our magazine is for general readership, though most of our readers will probably have a specific interest in literary magazines." Annual. Estab. 1985.

• Work first appearing in *Beloit Fiction Journal* has been reprinted in award-winning collections, including the *Flannery O'Connor* and the *Milkweed Fiction Prize* collections and has won the Iowa Short Fiction award.

Needs: Contemporary, literary, mainstream, prose poem, spiritual and sports. Wants more experimental and short shorts. No pornography, religious dogma, science fiction, horror, political propaganda. Receives 400 unsolicited fiction mss/month. Accepts 20 mss/year. Replies take longer in summer. Reads mss August 1-December 1. Publishes ms within 9 months after acceptance. **Publishes 3 new writers/year.** Recently published work by Rick Bass, Mariette Ansay and David Milofsky. Length: 250 words-10,000 words; average length: 5,000 words. Sometimes critiques rejected mss and recommends other markets.

How to Contact: Send complete ms with cover letter. Responds in 1 week to queries; 2 months to mss. SASE for ms. Accepts simultaneous submissions if identified as such. Sample copy for $14; back issues $7. Guidelines for #10 SASE.

Advice: "We're looking for a strong opening paragraph, interesting narrative line, compelling voice and unusual subject matter. Many of our contributors are writers whose work we have previously rejected. Don't let one rejection slip turn you away from our—or any—magazine."

▧ 🐱 ◑ **BENEATH THE SURFACE**, McMaster University Society of English, Dept. of English, Chester New Hall, McMaster University, Hamilton, Ontario L8S 4S8 Canada. **Contact:** E.M. Frail, co-editor. Editors change every April. Magazine: 21cm × 13.5cm; 25-55 pages; illustrations; photos. "Primarily, university audience intended. Also targets general reading public." Annually. Estab. 1984. Circ. varies.

Needs: Drama, ethnic/multicultural, experimental, fantasy (non-formula), feminist, gay, historical (general), horror, humor/satire, lesbian, literary, mystery/suspense (non-formula), psychic/supernatural/occult, science fiction (non-formula). Accepts 6 mss/issue. Does not read mss during summer months. Publishes ms 1-6 months after acceptance. **Publishes 6-10 new writers/year.** Recently published work by J.P. Lamarche, Sean L. Erdy and Delia DeSantis. Length: 3,000 words maximum. Publishes short stories. Also publishes literary essays, poetry.

How to Contact: Send complete ms with a cover letter. Should include short bio and list of publications. Responds in 6 months to mss. Send a disposable copy of ms. Accepts electronic submissions (disk or modem). Sample copy for $4.

Payment/Terms: Pays contributor's copies. Not copyrighted; copyrights belong to authors.
Advice: "Avoid formula fiction. For experimental writers: we are looking for *your* experimentation, not someone else's."

BIBLIOPHILOS, A Journal for Literati, Savants, Bibliophiles, Amantes Artium, and Those Who Love Animals, 200 Security Building, Fairmont WV 26554-2834. (304)366-8107. Fax: (304)366-8461. Editor: Gerald J. Bobango, Ph.D. **Contact:** Fiction Editor. Literary magazine: 5½ × 8; 64-72 pages; white glossy paper; illustrations; photos. Magazine "for literate persons who are academically and scholastically oriented, focused on the liberal arts, ⅓ fiction. Nonfiction includes criticism, history, art, music, theology, philosophy, educational theory, economics. In fiction we look for that which shows the absurdity of our slavish devotion to technology and all-encompassing big government; that which is not politically correct; that which exposes the egregious dumbing down of education; traditional pre-1960 American values." Estab. 1981. Circ. 200.
Needs: Adventure, ethnic/multicultural, family saga, historical (general, US, Eastern Europe), horror (psychological, supernatural), humor, satire, literary, mainstream/contemporary, military/war, mystery/suspense (police procedural, private eye/hardboiled, courtroom), regional (New England, Middle Atlantic), romance (gothic, historical, regency period), short story collections, thriller/espionage, translations, western (frontier saga, traditional), Civil War, US ethnic history, immigration, 19th century politics. "No science fiction, high tech, Erma Bombeck material, 'how I found Jesus and it changed my life.'" Receives 15 unsolicited mss/month. Accepts 2 mss/issue; 6-7 mss/year. Publishes ms 5-8 months after acceptance. **Publishes 2-3 new writers/year.** Recently published work by Johnnie Mae Hawkins, Lenore McComas Caberly, George R. Higinbotham and Robert Walter. Length: 1,500-3,000 words. Publishes short shorts. Length: 1,000 words. Also publishes literary essays, literary criticism and poetry. Often comments on rejected ms.
How to Contact: Query with clips of published work. Include bio, SASE and $5 for sample issue. Responds in 2 weeks to queries. Accepts simultaneous and reprint submissions. Sample copy for $5. Guidelines for SASE. Reviews novels, short story collections and nonfiction books of interest to writers. Send books to editor.
Payment/Terms: Pays subscription to magazine and 3 contributor's copies; additional copies $5. Acquires first North American serial rights.
Advice: "Use correct English, correctly written and punctuated. No jargon, cant, or short-cut language. Type the manuscript on a typewriter, not on a word-processor or computer and you'll have an advantage over other contributors from the start. Scholarly magazines and journals are becoming a rarity. If you use 'feel' rather than 'think' as your verb of choice, better look elsewhere."

BLACK JACK, Seven Buffaloes Press, Box 249, Big Timber MT 59011. **Contact:** Art Cuelho, editor. "Main theme: Rural. Publishes material on the American Indian, farm and ranch, American hobo, the common working man, folklore, the Southwest, Okies, Montana, humor, Central California, etc. for people who make their living off the land. The writers write about their roots, experiences and values they receive from the American soil." Annually. Estab. 1973. Circ. 750.
Needs: Literary, contemporary, western, adventure, humor, American Indian, American hobo, and parts of novels and long short stories. "Anything that strikes me as being amateurish, without depth, without craft, I refuse. Actually, I'm not opposed to any kind of writing if the author is genuine and has spent his lifetime dedicated to the written word." Receives approximately 10-15 unsolicited fiction mss/month. Accepts 5-10 mss/year. Length: 3,500-5,000 words (there can be exceptions).
How to Contact: Query for current theme with SASE. Responds in 1 month to queries and mss. Sample copy for $7.75 postpaid.
Payment/Terms: Pays 1-2 contributor's copies. Acquires first North American serial rights and reserves the right to reprint material in an anthology or future *Black Jack* publications. Rights revert to author after publication.
Advice: "Enthusiasm should be matched with skill as a craftsman. That's not saying that we don't continue to learn, but every writer must have enough command of the language to compete with other proven writers. Save postage by writing first to find out the editor's needs. A small press magazine always has specific needs at any given time. I sometimes accept material from writers that aren't that good at punctuation and grammar but make up for it with life's experience. This is not a highbrow publication; it belongs to the salt-of-the-earth people."

BLACK LACE, BLK Publishing Co., P.O. Box 83912, Los Angeles CA 90083-0912. (310)410-0808. Fax: (310)410-9250. E-mail: newsroom@blk.com. Website: www.blk.com. Editor: Alycee Lane. **Contact:** Fiction Editor. Magazine: 8⅛ × 10⅞; 48 pages; book stock; color glossy cover; illustrations; photos. "*Black Lace* is a lifestyle magazine for African-American lesbians. Published quarterly, its content ranges from erotic imagery to political commentary." Estab. 1991.
   ● Member: COSMEP. The editor would like to see more full-length erotic fiction, politically-focused articles on lesbians and the African-American community as a whole, and nostalgia and humor pieces.
Needs: Ethnic/multicultural, lesbian. "Avoid interracial stories or idealized pornography." Accepts 4 mss/year. Published work by Nicole King, Wanda Thompson, Lynn K. Pannell, Sheree Ann Slaughter, Lyn Lifshin, JoJo and Drew Alise Timmens. Publishes short shorts. Also publishes literary essays, literary criticism, poetry.

How to Contact: Query first with clips of published work or send complete ms with a cover letter. Should include bio (3 sentences). Send a disposable copy of ms. No simultaneous submissions. Accepts electronic submissions. Sample copy for $7. Guidelines free.
Payment/Terms: Pays 2 contributor's copies. Acquires first North American serial rights and right to anthologize.
Advice: *Black Lace* seeks erotic material of the highest quality. The most important thing is that the work be erotic and that it feature black lesbians or themes. Study the magazine to see what we do and how we do it. Some fiction is very romantic, other is highly sexual. Most articles in *Black Lace* cater to black lesbians between these two extremes."

☑ $◫ ☒ BLACK WARRIOR REVIEW, Box 862936, Tuscaloosa AL 35486-0027. (205)348-4518. Website: www.sa.ua.edu/osm/bwr (includes writer's guidelines, names of editors, short fiction). Editor-in-Chief: T.J. Beitelman. **Contact:** Jennifer Davis, fiction editor. Magazine: 6×9; 200 pages; illustrations; photos. "We publish contemporary fiction, poetry, reviews, essays, photography and interviews for a literary audience. We strive to publish the most compelling, best written work that we can find regardless of genre or type, for a literate audience." Semiannually. Estab. 1974. Circ. 2,000.
   • Work that appeared in the *Black Warrior Review* has been included in the *Pushcart Prize* anthology, *The Year's Best Fantasy & Horror*, *Harper's Magazine*, *Best American Short Stories*, *Best American Poetry* and in *New Short Stories from the South*.
Needs: Contemporary, literary, short and short-short fiction. Want "work that is conscious of form, good experimental writing, short-short fiction, writing that is more than competent—that sings." No genre fiction please. Receives 200 unsolicited fiction mss/month. Accepts 5 mss/issue, 10 mss/year. Approximately 5% of fiction is agented. **Publishes 5 new writers/year.** Recently published work by Ingrid Hill, Jane Buchbinder, Mark Wisniewski and Linnea Johnson. Length: 7,500 words maximum; average length: 2,000-5,000 words. Also publishes essays, poetry. Occasionally critiques rejected mss. Unsolicited novel excerpts are not considered unless the novel is already contracted for publication.
How to Contact: Send complete ms with SASE (1 story per submission). Accepts simultaneous submissions. Responds in 4 months. Publishes ms 2-5 months after acceptance. Sample copy for $8. Guidelines for SASE. Reviews novels and short story collections.
Payment/Terms: Pays up to $100 per story and 2 contributor's copies. Pays on publication.
Advice: "We look for attention to the language, freshness, honesty. Also, send us a clean, well-printed, typo-free manuscript. Become familiar with the magazine prior to submission. We're increasingly interested in considering good experimental writing and in reading short-short fiction. We read year round. We get a good number of stories, many of them competent but lacking a truly new vision or aesthetic. The stories we publish pay particular attention to language. They're fresh and honest. Read. Read. Read. Sometimes people forget the symbiotic relationship between reading good stories and writing good stories. Also, become familiar with the magazine prior to submission. The traditional 20-page short story is on the verge of becoming a dinosaur. Very short fiction (1-7 pages or so) and creative nonfiction seem to be asserting themselves as viable forms. We'd like to see more quality work in these new 'genres.' "

☑ ○ ◎ BLUE MESA REVIEW, University of New Mexico, Dept. of English, Humanities Bldg., Room 217, Albuquerque NM 87131. (505)277-6155. Fax: (505)277-5573. E-mail: bluemesa@unm.edu. Website: www. unm.edu/~bluemesa (includes writer's guidelines, names of editors, short fiction). **Contact:** Julie Shigekuni. Magazine: 6×9; 300 pages; 55 lb. paper; 10 pt CS1; photos. "*Blue Mesa Review* publishes the best/most current creative writing on the market." Annually. Estab. 1989. Circ. 1,200.
Needs: Adventure, ethnic/multicultural, experimental, feminist, gay, historical, humor/satire, lesbian, literary, mainstream/contemporary, regional, westerns. Contact for list of upcoming themes. Receives 300 unsolicited mss/year. Accepts 100 mss/year. Accepts mss July 1-October 1; all submissions must be postmarked by October 1; reads mss November-December; responds in January. Publishes ms 5-6 months after acceptance. Published work by Kathleen Spivack, Roberta Swann and Tony Mares. Publishes short shorts. Also publishes literary essays, poetry.
How to Contact: Send 2 copies of complete ms with a cover letter. Send SASE for reply. Sample copy for $12. Reviews novels, short story collections, poetry and nonfiction.
Payment/Terms: Pays 1 contributor copy for First North American serial rights.
Advice: "Contact us for complete guidelines. All submissions must follow our guidelines."

MARKET CONDITIONS are constantly changing! If you're still using this book and it is 2002 or later, buy the newest edition of *Novel & Short Story Writer's Market* at your favorite bookstore or order from Writer's Digest Books by calling 1-800-289-0963.

⚫ ▣ **THE BLUE MOON REVIEW**, P.O. Box 48, Ivy VA 22945-0045. E-mail: editor@thebluemoon.com; fiction@thebluemoon.com. Website: www.TheBlueMoon.com. **Contact:** Doug Lawson, editor. Electronic magazine: Illustrations and photos. Quarterly. Estab. 1994. Circ. 16,000.

• See the interview with *Blue Moon Review* editor Doug Lawson on page 39 in the Electronic Publishing section.

Needs: Experimental, feminist, gay, lesbian, literary, mainstream/contemporary, regional, translations. No genre fiction or condensed novels. Receives 40-70 unsolicited mss/month. Accepts 7-10 mss/issue; 51-60 mss/year. Publishes ms up to 9 months after acceptance. Published work by Edward Falco, Deborah Eisenberg, Robert Sward and Eva Shaderowfsky. Length: 3,000 words maximum. Publishes short shorts. Also publishes literary essays, literary criticism, poetry. Sometimes comments on rejected mss.

How to Contact: Electronic submissions only. Send ASCII file attachment, or include ms in body of e-mail. "Please direct your query/submission to the appropriate editor." Send complete ms with a cover letter. Include a brief bio, list of publications and e-mail address if available. Responds in 2 months to mss. Sample copy and guidelines available at above website. Reviews novels and short story collections.

Payment/Terms: Offers prizes for fiction and poetry. Acquires first North American serial rights and non-exclusive use of electronic rights. Rights revert to author upon request.

Advice: "We look for strong use of language or strong characterization. Manuscripts stand out by their ability to engage a reader on an intellectual or emotional level. Present characters with depth regardless of age and introduce intelligent concepts that have resonance and relevance."

✅ ⚪ ◎ **THE BLUE SKUNK COMPANION**, The Blue Skunk Society Inc., P.O. Box 8400, MSU 59, Mankato MN 56002-8400. (507)388-8519. Editor: Connie Colwell. **Contact:** Blake Hoena, fiction editor. Magazine: 8×11; 35-45 pages; illustrations; photos. "We publish fiction, poetry, nonfiction and essays that are inspired by life, not by classic literature, periods or styles. We intend to reach readers that wish to be entertained and moved no matter their age, race or culture." Semiannual. Estab. 1997. Circ. 100-500.

Needs: Adventure, condensed/excerpted novel, ethnic/multicultural, experimental, fantasy (contemporary), historical (general), horror, humor/satire, literary, mainstream/contemporary, mystery/suspense (contemporary), psychic/supernatural/occult, regional, romance (contemporary), science fiction (contemporary), translations. "We do not want fiction/prose that falls into clichés." Receives 10-20 unsolicited mss/month. Accepts 5-7 mss/issue; 10-14 mss/year. Publishes ms 4-6 months after acceptance. Published work by Roger Sheffer, Brian Batt, Samuel Dollar and Kevin Langton. Length: 1,000-7,000 words; average length: 1,000-4,000 words. Also publishes literary essays, literary criticism, poetry. Often comments on rejected mss.

How to Contact: Send complete ms with a cover letter. Include estimated word count, ½-1-page bio and list of publications. Responds in 1 month to queries; 2-3 months to mss. SASE. Accepts simultaneous submissions. Sample copy for $5 and 9×12 SAE with 6 first-class stamps. Guidelines for 4×12 SASE. Reviews novels and short story collections.

Payment/Terms: Pays free subscription to the magazine; additional copies for $5. Pays on publication for first rights. Not copyrighted.

Advice: "We look for a voice that sounds like a 'person' and not like a 'writer.' Good use of language as function, taste and art; not a boastful vocabulary. Try to avoid genre until you have a good grasp of mainstream and contemporary prose. Once that has been achieved, then your genre fiction will be much better. Always be fresh with ideas and themes. We feel that good fiction/prose can be found on the back shelves of bookstores and not on the bestsellers list."

⚫ ◎ **BLUELINE**, English Dept., SUNY, Potsdam NY 13676. (315)267-2043. E-mail: blueline@potsdam.edu. Website: www.potsdam.edu/engl/blueline.html. Editor: Rick Henry. **Contact:** Fiction Editor. Magazine: 6×9; 180 pages; 70 lb. white stock paper; 65 lb. smooth cover stock; illustrations; photos. "*Blueline* is interested in quality writing about the Adirondacks or other places similar in geography and spirit. We publish fiction, poetry, personal essays, book reviews and oral history for those interested in the Adirondacks, nature in general, and well-crafted writing." Annually. Estab. 1979. Circ. 400.

Needs: Adventure, contemporary, humor/satire, literary, prose poem, regional, reminiscences, oral history, nature/outdoors. Receives 8-10 unsolicited fiction mss/month. Accepts 6-8 mss/issue. Does not read January through August. Publishes ms 3-6 months after acceptance. **Published new writers within the last year.** Published fiction by Jeffrey Clapp. Length: 500-3,000 words; average length: 2,500 words. Also publishes literary essays, poetry. Occasionally critiques rejected mss.

How to Contact: Send complete ms with SASE, word count and brief bio. Submit mss September through November 30. Responds in 2-10 weeks. Sample copy for $6. Guidelines for 5×10 SASE.

Payment/Terms: Pays 1 contributor's copy for first rights. Charges $7 each for 3 or more extra copies.

Advice: "We look for concise, clear, concrete prose that tells a story and touches upon a universal theme or situation. We prefer realism to romanticism but will consider nostalgia if well done. Pay attention to grammar and syntax. Avoid murky language, sentimentality, cuteness or folksiness. We would like to see more good fiction related to the Adirondacks. If manuscript has potential, we work with author to improve and reconsider for publication. Our readers prefer fiction to poetry (in general) or reviews. Write from your own experience, be specific and factual (within the bounds of your story) and if you write about universal features such as love, death, change, etc., write about them in a fresh way. Triteness and mediocrity are the hallmarks of the majority of stories seen today."

✓ ⬭ **BOGG, A Magazine of British & North American Writing**, Bogg Publications, 422 N. Cleveland St., Arlington VA 22201. (703)243-6019. **Contact:** John Elsberg, US editor. Magazine: 6×9; 68-72 pages; 70 lb. white paper; 70 lb. cover stock; line illustrations. "American and British poetry, prose poems, experimental short 'fictions,' reviews, and essays on small press." Published "two or three times a year." Estab. 1968. Circ. 850.
   ● The editors at *Bogg* are most interested in short, wry or semi-surreal fiction.
Needs: Very short experimental fiction and prose poems. "We are always looking for work with British/Commonwealth themes and/or references." Receives 25 unsolicited fiction mss/month. Accepts 1-2 mss/issue; 3-6 mss/year. Publishes ms 3-18 months after acceptance. **Published 25% new writers within the last year.** Recently published work by Dan Lenihan, Harriet Zinnes, Laurel Speer and Brian Johnson. Length: 300 words maximum. Also publishes literary essays, literary criticism, poetry. Occasionally critiques rejected mss.
How to Contact: Query first or send ms (2-6 pieces) with SASE. Responds in 1 week to queries; 2 weeks to mss. Sample copy for $3.50 or $4.50 (current issue). Reviews novels and short story collections.
Payment/Terms: Pays 2 contributor's copies; reduced charge for extras. Acquires one-time rights.
Advice: "We look for voice and originality. Don't follow the MFA hard. Read magazine first. We are most interested in prose work of experimental or wry nature to supplement poetry, and are always looking for innovative/imaginative uses of British themes and references."

Ⓝ ⬭ **BOOKPRESS, The Newspaper of the Literary Arts**, The Bookery, 215 N. Cayuga St., Ithaca NY 14850. (607)277-2254. Fax: (607)275-9221. E-mail: bookpress@thebookery.com. Website: www.thebookery. com/bookpress (includes current issue, credits and archives). **Contact:** Jack Goldman, editor-in-chief. Newspaper: 16 pages; newsprint; Illustrations and photos. Contains book reviews, analysis, fiction and excerpts from published work. Monthly. Estab. 1991. Circ. 20,000.
Needs: Condensed/excerpted novel, feminist, gay, historical, lesbian, literary, regional. No new age. Publishes special fiction issues or anthologies. Receives 10-12 unsolicited mss/month. Accepts 0-2 mss/issue. Does not read during the summer. Publishes ms 1-3 months after acceptance. **Publishes 5-10 new writers/year.** Recently published work by J. Robert Lennon, Brian Hall and Robert Sward. Length: 4,000 words maximum; average length: 2,000 words. Also publishes literary essays, literary criticism and poetry.
How to Contact: Send complete ms with a cover letter. Also include on disk in Microsoft Word or .rif format. Submissions accepted via e-mail. Include 3-sentence bio. Responds in 1 month to mss. Send SASE for return of ms. Accepts simultaneous submissions. Sample copy and guidelines free. Reviews novels or short story collections. Send books to editor.
Payment/Terms: Pays free subscription to newspaper.
Advice: "Send a brief, concise cover letter. No overwriting or overly cerebral academic work. The author's genuine interest and passion for the topic makes for good work."

$⬭ **BOULEVARD**, Opojaz Inc., PMB 332, 4579 Laclede Ave., St. Louis MO 63108-2103. (314)361-2986. Editor: Richard Burgin. **Contact:** Fiction Editor. Magazine: 5½×8½; 150-225 pages; excellent paper; high-quality cover stock; illustrations; photos. "*Boulevard* aspires to publish the best contemporary fiction, poetry and essays we can print. While we frequently publish writers with previous credits, we are very interested in publishing less experienced or unpublished writers with exceptional promise." Published 3 times/year. Estab. 1986. Circ. about 3,500.
   ● *Boulevard* ranked #32 on the *Writer's Digest* "Fiction 50" list of top markets.
Needs: Contemporary, experimental, literary. Does not want to see "anything whose first purpose is not literary." No science fiction, erotica, westerns, horror, romance. Receives over 600 mss/month. Accepts about 10 mss/issue. Does not accept manuscripts between April 1 and October 1. Publishes ms less than 1 year after acceptance. Agented fiction ⅓-¼. Length: 8,000 words maximum; average length: 5,000 words. Publishes short shorts. **Publishes 10 new writers/year.** Recently published work by Melissa Pritchard, Peter LaSalle and Robert Phillips. Also publishes literary essays, literary criticism, poetry. Sometimes critiques rejected mss and recommends other markets.
How to Contact: Send complete ms with cover letter. Responds in 2 weeks to queries; 3 months to mss. SASE for reply. Accepts simultaneous submissions. Sample copy for $8 and SAE with 5 first-class stamps.
Payment/Terms: Pays $50-300; contributor's copies; charges for extras. Acquires first North American serial rights. Does not send galleys to author unless requested.
Advice: "Surprising, intelligent, eloquent work always makes an impression." We are open to different styles of imaginative and critical work and are mindful of Nabokov's dictum 'There is only one school, the school of talent.' Above all, when we consider the very diverse manuscripts submitted to us for publication, we value original sensibility, writing that causes the reader to experience a part of life in a new way. Originality, to us, has

little to do with a writer intently trying to make each line or sentence odd, bizarre, or eccentric, merely for the sake of being 'different.' Rather, originality is the result of the character or vision of the writer; the writer's singular outlook and voice as it shines through in the totality of his or her work."

[N] ⊘ BRAIN, CHILD, The Magazine for Thinking Mothers, March Press, P.O. Box 1161, Harrisonburg VA 22803. (540)574-2379. E-mail: editor@brainchildmag.com. Website: www.brainchildmag.com (includes excerpts, guidelines, mission statement, editorial staff info, subscription info). **Contact:** Jennifer Niesslein and Stephanie Wilkinson, co-editors. Magazine: 7¾×10; 60-100 pages; 80 lb matte cover; illustrations; photos. "*Brain, Child* is a new quarterly magazine spotlighting women's own experience of motherhood. Instead of focusing on childbearing tips and techniques, like most parenting publications, our writers explore the more personal transformations that motherhood brings. Each issue is packed with essays, in-depth features, humor, reviews, news and fiction, plus superb art, photography, cartoons and more." Quarterly. Estab. 2000. Circ. 8,000. Member: IPA.
Needs: Literary, mainstream. Receives less than 20 unsolicited mss/month. Accepts 1 ms/issue; 4 mss/year. Publishes ms 6 months after acceptance. Recently published work by Susan Cheever and Barbara Kingsolver. Length: 1,000-5,000 words; average length: 2,500 words. Will consider short shorts but prefer longer pieces. Also publishes literary essays. Sometimes comments on rejected mss.
How to Contact: Send complete ms with a cover letter. Accepts submissions by e-mail (be sure to copy and paste the ms into the body of the e-mail). Include estimated word count, brief bio and list of publications. Responds in 6 weeks to queries; 10 weeks to mss. Send SASE (or IRC) for return of ms or send a disposable copy of ms and #10 SASE for reply only. Occasionally accepts previously published work and multiple submissions (no more than 2 at once). Sample copy for $5. Guidelines for SASE or on website. Reviews novels, short story collections and nonfiction books of interest to women.
Payment/Terms: "Our fees vary, depending on a number of considerations. In general, though, payment is modest for now." Pays on publication for electronic rights and the right to include the piece in a *Brain, Child*/March Press anthology, should one ever happen. Sends galleys to author.
Advice: "Since much of *Brain, Child* is made of personal essays, we have to walk a strict line between fiction and fact (i.e., stories should read like stories, not essays). We look for strongly developed characters in fiction. We're open to myriad subjects, but are most interested in literary stories that resonate with women as mothers and individuals."

☑ ⊘ ⍦ THE BRIAR CLIFF REVIEW, Briar Cliff College, 3303 Rebecca St., Sioux City IA 51104-0100. (712)279-1651 or 279-5321. Fax: (712) 279-5410. E-mail: currans@briar-cliff.edu. Website: www.briar-cliff.edu/bcreview (includes writer's guidelines, contest guidelines, previous contest winners and their winning poems/short stories and cover artwork). Managing Editor: Tricia Currans-Sheehan. **Contact:** Phil Hey, fiction editor. Magazine: 8½×11; 80 pages; 70 lb. Finch Opaque cover stock; illustrations; photos. "*The Briar Cliff Review* is an eclectic literary and cultural magazine focusing on (but not limited to) Siouxland writers and subjects. We are happy to proclaim ourselves a regional publication. It doesn't diminish us; it enhances us." Annually. Estab. 1989. Circ. 750.
● *The Briar Cliff Review* has received The Gold Crown and Silver Crown awards from the Columbia Scholastic Press Association and the National Pacemaker Award from the Associated Collegiate Press.
Needs: Ethnic/multicultural, feminist, historical, humor/satire, literary, mainstream/contemporary, regional. No romance, horror or alien stories. Accepts 5 mss/year. Reads mss only between August 1 and November 1. Publishes ms 3-4 months after acceptance. **Published 10-14 new writers/year.** Recently published work by Jacob Appel, Laura Wilson, Cynthia Gregory, Robley Wilson and Bill Franzen. Length: 2,500-4,000 words; average length: 3,000 words. Also publishes literary essays, literary criticism and poetry. Sometimes comments on rejected mss.
How to Contact: Send complete ms with a cover letter. Include estimated word count, bio and list of publications. Responds in 4-5 months to mss. Send a SASE for return of ms. Accepts electronic submissions (disk). Accepts simultaneous submissions. Sample copy for $10 and 9×12 SAE. Guidelines free for #10 SASE. Reviews novels and short story collections.
Payment/Terms: Pays 2 contributor's copies for first rights; additional copies available for $5.
Advice: "So many stories are just telling. We want some action. It has to move. We prefer stories in which there is no gimmick, no mechanical turn of events, no moral except the one we would draw privately."

⊘ BRILLIANT CORNERS, A Journal of Jazz & Literature, Lycoming College, Williamsport PA 17701. (570)321-4279. Fax: (570)321-4090. E-mail: feinstei@lycoming.edu. **Contact:** Sascha Feinstein, editor. Journal: 6×9; 100 pages; 70 lb. Cougar opaque, vellum, natural paper; photographs. "We publish jazz-related literature—fiction, poetry and nonfiction." Semiannually. Estab. 1996. Circ. 1,200.
Needs: Condensed/excerpted novel, ethnic/multicultural, experimental, literary, mainstream/contemporary, romance (contemporary). Receives 10-15 unsolicited mss/month. Accepts 1-2 mss/issue; 2-3 mss/year. Does not read mss May 15-September 1. Publishes ms 4-12 months after acceptance. Very little agented fiction. Publishes short shorts. Also publishes literary essays, literary criticism and poetry. Often comments on rejected mss.

How to Contact: Send complete ms with a cover letter. Include 1-paragraph bio and list of publications. Responds in 2 weeks to queries; 1-2 months to mss. SASE for return of ms or send a disposable copy of ms. Accepts unpublished work only. Sample copy for $7. Reviews novels and short story collections. Send books to editor.

Payment/Terms: Pays 2 contributor's copies. Acquires first North American serial rights. Sends galleys to author when possible.

Advice: "We look for clear, moving prose that demonstrates a love of both writing and jazz. We primarily publish established writers, but we read all submissions carefully and welcome work by outstanding young writers."

[N] [⊕] THE BROWN CRITIQUE, 98 Park St., 2nd Floor, Calcutta, West Bengal India 700-017. Phone: (91) 033-280-1386. E-mail: gayatrimajumdar@usul.edu. Website: www.browncritique.com. **Contact:** Gayatri Majumdar, editor. Literary magazine: 60-100 pages; rice and art; some illustrations; photos. Quarterly. Estab. 1995.

Needs: Ethnic/multicutural, humor/satire, literary, religion/insperational, translations. Receives 5-10 unsolicited mss/month. Accepts 2 mss/issue; 10 mss/year. Publishes 6 months after acceptance. **Publishes 5 new writers/ year.** Recently published work by Siddhartha Choudbury, Ronita Torcato, and Abbas Zaidi. Length: 1,000-5,000 words; average length: 3,000 words. Publishes short shorts; average length: 1,000 words. Sometimes comments on rejected mss.

How to Contact: Send complete ms with cover letter. Include brief bio. Responds in 2 months to queries and mss. Send disposable copy of ms and #10 SASE for reply only.

Payments/Terms: Pays in 1 contributor's copy; additional copies $2.50. Acquires all rights.

Advice: "Originality and unpretention-ness. Do not let trends and fashions overwhelm you. Just write. Then re-write."

[◐] BUTTON, New England's Tiniest Magazine of Poetry, Fiction & Gracious Living, 4222 Flora Place, St. Louis MO 63110. E-mail: buttonx26@aol.com. Editor: S. Cragin. **Contact:** W.M. Davies, fiction editor. Magazine: 4×5; 34 pages; bond paper; color cardstock cover; illustrations; photos. Semiannually. Estab. 1993. Circ. 1,500.

Needs: Literary. No genre fiction, science fiction, techno-thriller. Wants more of "anything Herman Melville, Henry James or Betty MacDonald would like to read." Receives 20-40 unsolicited mss/month. Accepts 1-2 mss/ issue; 3-5 mss/year. Publishes ms 3-9 months after acceptance. Published work by Sven Birkerts, Stephen Mc-Cauley, Wayne Wilson, Romayne Dawney, Brendan Galvin, They Might Be Giants and Lawrence Millman. Length: 500-2,500 words. Also publishes literary essays, poetry. Sometimes comments on rejected mss "if it shows promise."

How to Contact: Request guidelines. Send ms with bio, list of publications and advise how you found magazine. Responds in 1 month to queries; 2-4 months to mss. SASE. Sample copy for $2. Guidelines for SASE. Reviews novels and short story collections. Send book to editor. Sponsors poetry contest, for more info send SASE.

Payment/Terms: Pays honorarium and multiple free subscriptions to the magazine on publication. Acquires first North American serial rights. Sends galleys to author if there are editorial changes.

Advice: "What makes a manuscript stand out? Flannery O'Connor once said, 'Don't get subtle till the fourth page,' and I agree. We publish fiction in the 1,000-3,000 word category, and look for interesting, sympathetic, believable characters and careful setting. I'm really tired of stories that start strong and then devolve into dialogue uninterupted by further exposition. Also, no stories from a mad person's POV unless it's really tricky and skillful. Advice to prospective writers: continue to read at least ten times as much as you write. Read the best, and read intelligent criticism if you can find it. *No beginners please.* Please don't submit more than once a year—it's more important that you work on your craft rather than machine-gunning publications with samples, and don't submit more than 3 poems in a batch (this advice goes for other places, you'll find . . .)."

[✔] [$◐] BYLINE, Box 130596, Edmond OK 73013-0001. (405)348-5591. E-mail: cwall@bylinemag.com. Website: www.bylinemag.com (includes writer's guidelines, names of editors, contest list and rules, ad rates and sample article from magazine). Editor-in-Chief: Marcia Preston. **Contact:** Carolyn Wall, fiction editor. Monthly magazine "aimed at encouraging and motivating all writers toward success, with special information to help new writers. Articles center on how to write better, market smarter, sell your work." Estab. 1981.

● Byline ranked #21 on *Writer's Digest's* Fiction 50 list of top markets for fiction writers.

Needs: Literary, genre, general fiction. Receives 100-200 unsolicited fiction mss/month. Does not want to see erotica or explicit graphic content. No science fiction or fantasy. Accepts 1 ms/issue; 11 mss/year. **Published many new writers within the last year.** Recently published work by Lucrecia Guerrero, Jim Finley and O'Neil De Noux. Length: 2,000-4,000 words. Also publishes poetry and articles.

How to Contact: Send complete ms with SASE. Accepts simultaneous submissions, "if notified. For us, no cover letter is needed." Responds in 6-12 weeks. Publishes ms an average of 3 months after acceptance. Sample copy for $4. Guidelines for #10 SASE.

Payment/Terms: Pays $100 on acceptance and 3 contributor's copies for first North American rights.

Advice: "We look for good writing that draws the reader in; conflict and character movement by story's end. We're very open to new writers. Submit a well-written, professionally prepared ms with SASE. No erotica or senseless violence; otherwise, we'll consider most any theme. We also sponsor short story and poetry contests. Read what's being published. Find a good story, not just a narrative reflection. Keep submitting."

$ 🖊 🏆 💻 THE CAFE IRREAL, International Imagination. E-mail: cafeirreal@iname.com. Website: home.sprynet.com/~awhit. **Contact:** Alice Whittenburg, G.S. Evans, editors. E-zine; illustrations. *"The Cafe Irreal* is a webzine focusing on short stories and short shorts of an irreal nature." Semiannually.
• *The Cafe Irreal* has been named an "Editor's Pick" at aol.com.
Needs: Experimental, fantasy (literary), science fiction (literary), translations. "No horror or 'slice-of-life' stories; no genre or mainstream science fiction or fantasy." Accepts 10-15 mss/issue; 20-30 mss/year. Publishes mss 6 months after acceptance. Recently published translations of works by Cristovan Buarque and Vit Erban. Length: no minimum; 2,000 words maximum (excerpts from longer works accepted). Publishes short shorts. Also publishes literary essays, literary criticism. Often comments on rejected ms.
How to Contact: "We only accept electronic submissions. E-mail us with complete manuscript as enclosed text, HTML or ASCII file." Include estimated word count. Responds in 2 months to mss. Accepts reprint submissions if indicated as such. See website for sample copy and guidelines.
Payment/Terms: Pays 1¢/word, $2 minimum on publication for first rights, one-time rights. Sends galleys (the html document via e-mail) to author.
Advice: "Forget formulas. Write about what you *don't* know, take me places I couldn't *possibly* go, don't try to make me care about the characters. Read short fiction by writers such as Kafka, Kobo Abe, Julio Cortazar, Leonara Carrington and Stanislaw Lem. Also read our website and guidelines."

✔ 🖊 ◎ CALLALOO, A Journal of African-American and African Diaspora Arts and Letters, Dept. of English, 322 Bryan Hall, University of Virginia, Charlottesville VA 22904. (804)924-6637. Fax: (804)924-6472. E-mail: callaloo@virginia.edu. Website: www.people.virginia.edu/~callaloo (includes sample issues, copyright information, editorial information, submission guidelines). **Editor:** Charles H. Rowell. Magazine: 7×10; 250 pages. Scholarly magazine. Quarterly. "Devoted to publishing fiction, poetry, drama of the African diaspora, including North, Central and South America, the Caribbean, Europe and Africa. Visually beautiful and well-edited, the journal publishes 3-5 short stories in all forms and styles in each issue." Estab. 1976. Circ. 2,000.
• One of the leading voices in African-American literature, *Callaloo* has received NEA literature grants. Work published in *Callaloo* received a 1994 *Pushcart Prize* anthology nomination and inclusion in *Best American Short Stories*.
Needs: Contemporary, ethnic (black culture), feminist, historical, humor/satire, literary, prose poem, regional, science fiction, serialized/excerpted novel, translations. Also publishes poetry and drama. "Would like to see more well-crafted, literary fiction particularly dealing with the black middle class, immigrant communities and/ or the black South." No romance, confessional. Themes for 2001: Confederate Flag; 2 retrospective issues; Best of Diaspora issue. Accepts 3-5 mss/issue; 10-20 mss/year. Length: 50 pages maximum. **Publishes 5-10 new writers/year.** Published work by Chinua Achebe, Rita Dove, Reginald McKnight, Caryl Philips, Jewell Parker Rhodes and John Edgar Wideman.
How to Contact: Submit complete ms in triplicate and cover letter with name, mailing address, e-mail address, if possible and loose stamps. Accepts queries by e-mail and fax. Responds to queries in 2 weeks; 6 months to mss. Previously published work accepted "only as part of a special issue or if solicited." Sample copy for $10.
Payment/Terms: Pays in contributor's copies. Acquires all rights. Sends galleys to author.
Advice: "We strongly recommend looking at the journal before submitting."

◐ CALYX, A Journal of Art & Literature by Women, Calyx, Inc., P.O. Box B, Corvallis OR 97339. (541)753-9384. Fax: (541)753-0515. E-mail: calyx@proaxis.com. Director: Margarita Donnelly. **Contact:** Beverly McFarland, senior editor. Magazine: 6×8; 128 pages per single issue; 60 lb. coated matte stock paper; 10 pt. chrome coat cover; original art. Publishes prose, poetry, art, essays, interviews and critical and review articles. *"Calyx* exists to publish women's literary and artistic work and is committed to publishing the work of all women, including women of color, older women, working class women, and other voices that need to be heard. We are committed to nurturing beginning writers." Biannually. Estab. 1976. Circ. 6,000.
Needs: Receives approximately 1,000 unsolicited prose and poetry mss when open. Accepts 4-8 prose mss/ issue; 9-15 mss/year. Reads mss October 1-December 15; submit only during this period. Mss received when not reading will be returned. **Publishes 10-20 new writers/year.** Published work by Margaret Willey, Chitrita Banerji, Torie Olsen, Catherine Brady, Deidre Duffy and Andrea Silva. Length: 5,000 words maximum. Also publishes literary essays, literary criticism, poetry.
How to Contact: Send ms with SASE and bio. Accepts requests for guidelines by e-mail. Accepts simultaneous submissions. Responds in 8 months to mss. Publishes ms an average of 8 months after acceptance. Sample copy for $9.50 plus $2 postage. Guidelines available for SASE. Reviews novels, short story collections, poetry and essays.
Payment/Terms: "Combination of payment, free issues and 1 volume subscription."

Advice: Most mss are rejected because "the writers are not familiar with *Calyx*—writers should read *Calyx* and be familiar with the publication."

⊕ ◎ **CAMBRENSIS**, 41 Heol Fach, Cornelly, Bridgend, Mid-Glamorgan, CF33 4LN Wales. Editor: Arthur Smith. **Contact:** Fiction Editor. Quarterly. Circ. 500.
Needs: "Devoted solely to the short story form, featuring short stories by writers born or resident in Wales or with some Welsh connection; receives grants from the Welsh Arts' Council and the Welsh Writers' Trust; uses artwork—cartoons, line-drawings, sketches etc." Length: 2,500 words maximum.
How to Contact: Writer has to have some connection with Wales. SAE and IRCs or similar should be enclosed with "air mail" postage to avoid long delay.
Payment/Terms: Writers receive 3 copies of magazine. Send IRCs for a sample copy. Subscriptions via Blackwell's Periodicals, P.O. Box 40, Hythe Bridge Street, Oxford, OX1 2EU, UK or Swets & Zeitlinger B V, P.O. Box 800, 2160 S Z Lisse, Holland.

⊠ ◑ ◎ **CAPERS AWEIGH, Cape Breton Poetry & Fiction**, Capers Aweigh Press, 39 Water St., Glace Bay, Sydney, Nova Scotia B1A 1R6 Canada. (902)849-0822. E-mail: capersaweigh@hotmail.com. Editor: John MacNeil. **Contact:** Fiction Editor. Magazine: 5×8; 80 pages; bond paper; Cornwall-coated cover. "*Capers Aweigh* publishes poetry and fiction of, by and for Cape Bretoners." Publication frequency varies. Estab. 1992. Circ. 500.
Needs: Adventure, ethnic/multicultural, fantasy, feminist, historical, humor/satire, literary, mainstream, contemporary, mystery/suspense, psychic/supernatural/occult, regional, science fiction. List of upcoming themes available for SASE. Receives 2 unsolicited mss/month. Accepts 30 mss/issue. Publishes ms 9 months after acceptance. Published work by C. Fairn Kennedy and Shirley Kiju Kawi. Length: 2,500 words. Publishes short shorts. Also publishes literary criticism, poetry. Sponsors contests only to Cape Bretoners fiction writers.
How to Contact: Query first. Send SASE for reply or send a disposable copy of ms. Accepts electronic submissions (IBM). Sample copy for $4.95 and 6×10 SAE.
Payment/Terms: Pays free subscription to the magazine and 1 contributor's copy; additional copies for $4.95. Acquires first North American serial rights. Sends galleys to author.

⊠ $◑ **THE CAPILANO REVIEW**, 2055 Purcell Way, North Vancouver, British Columbia V7J 3H5 Canada. (604)984-1712. Fax: (604)983-7520. E-mail: erains@capcollege.bc.ca. Website: www.capcollege.bc.ca/dept/TCR/tcr.html (includes guidelines, excerpts and complete bibliography of 25 years worth of contributors). Editor: Ryan Knighton. **Contact:** Fiction Editor. Magazine: 6×9; 90-120 pages; book paper; glossy cover; perfect-bound; illustrations; photos. Magazine of "fresh, innovative art and literature for literary/artistic audience." Triannually. Estab. 1972. Circ. 900.
Needs: Experimental, literary and drama. Receives 80 unsolicited mss/month. Accepts 3-4 mss/issue; 10 mss/year. **Published new writers within the last year.** Published work by Keith Harrison, Kim Echlin and Jack Hodgins. Length: 4,000 words average. Also publishes literary essays, poetry.
How to Contact: Send complete ms with cover letter and SASE or IRC. Include 2- to 3-sentence bio and brief list of publications. Responds to mss in 2-4 months. Send SAE with IRCs for return of ms. Sample copy for $9 (Canadian). "No U.S. postage please—we cannot use it."
Payment/Terms: Pays $50-200, 2 contributor's copies and one year subscription. Pays on publication for first North American serial rights.
Advice: "We are looking for exceptional, original style; strong thematic content; innovation and quality writing. Read several issues before submitting and make sure your work is technically perfect."

⊕ ✓ ◎ **THE CARIBBEAN WRITER**, The University of the Virgin Islands, RR 02, Box 10,000—Kingshill, St. Croix, Virgin Islands 00850. (340)692-4152. Fax: (340)692-4026. E-mail: qmars@uvi.edu. Website: http://rps.uvi.edu/CaribbeanWriter (includes writer's guidelines and excerpts from past publications). **Contact:** Erika J. Waters, editor. Magazine: 6×9; 304 pages; 60 lb. paper; glossy cover stock; illustrations; photos. "*The Caribbean Writer* is an international magazine with a Caribbean focus. The Caribbean should be central to the work, or the work should reflect a Caribbean heritage, experience or perspective." Annually. Estab. 1987. Circ. 1,500.
Needs: Contemporary, historical (general), humor/satire, literary, mainstream and prose poem. Receives 800 unsolicited mss/year. Accepts 60 mss/issue. Also accepts poetry, essays, translations, plays. **Publishes approximately 20% new writers/year.** Recently published work by Kamau Brathwaite, Geoffrey Philp, Opal Palmer Adisa, Fred D'Aguiar and Marvin E. Williams.
How to Contact: Send complete ms with cover letter. Accepts queries/mss by e-mail and disk. "Blind submissions only. Send name, address and title of manuscript on separate sheet. Title only on manuscript. Manuscripts will not be considered unless this procedure is followed." Responds "once a year." SASE (or IRC). Accepts simultaneous submissions and multiple submissions. Sample copy for $7 and $2 postage.
Payment/Terms: Pays 2 contributor's copies. Annual prizes for best story ($400); for best poem ($300); $200 for first publication; best work by Caribbean author ($500); best work by Virgin Islands author ($100).

Terms: Acquires one-time rights.

Advice: Looks for "work which reflects a Caribbean heritage, experience or perspective."

☑ ◐ ♈ CAROLINA QUARTERLY, Greenlaw Hall CB #3520, University of North Carolina, Chapel Hill NC 27599-3520. (919)962-0244. Fax: (919)962-3520. E-mail: cquarter@unc.edu. Website: www.unc.edu/depts/cqonline (includes writer's guidelines, current contents, index to past contributors). **Contact:** Chad Trevitte, editor-in-chief. Literary journal: 70-90 pages; illustrations. Publishes fiction for a "general literary audience." Triannually. Estab. 1948. Circ. 1,400.

● Work published in *Carolina Quarterly* has been selected for inclusion in *Best American Short Stories*, in *New Stories from the South: The Year's Best*, and *Best of the South. Carolina Quarterly* received a special mention in 1999 *Pushcart Prize* stories.

Needs: Literary. "We would like to see more short/micro-fiction and more stories by minority/ethnic writers." Receives 150-200 unsolicited fiction mss/month. Accepts 4-5 mss/issue; 14-16 mss/year. Does not read mss June-August. Publishes ms an average of 4 months after acceptance. **Publishes 1-2 new writers/year.** Published work by Clyde Edgerton, Barry Hannah and Doris Betts. Length: 7,000 words maximum; no minimum. Also publishes short shorts, literary essays, poetry. Occasionally critiques rejected mss.

How to Contact: Send complete ms with cover letter and SASE to fiction editor. Accepts queries by phone, fax and e-mail. No simultaneous submissions. Responds in 2-4 months. Sample copy for $5; writer's guidelines for SASE.

Payment/Terms: Pays in contributor's copies for first rights.

Ⓝ CARVE MAGAZINE, SAO Box 187, University of Washington, Box 352238, Seattle WA 98195. (206)706-8611. E-mail: melvino@u.washington.edu. Website: www.carvezine.com (includes entire content—stories, art gallery, submission guidelines and more). **Contact:** Melvin Sterne, managing editor. Literary magazine, online magazine and e-zine specializing in short stories/literary fiction. Some photos. "*Carve Magazine* seeks fine literary fiction of any length. We are loosely dedicated to fiction in the Ray Carver Tradition, with precise writing free of gimmicks. We will, however, consider any work if it 'knocks our socks off.' We publish for a worldwide audience and would like to preserve the art of the short story. We accept submissions worldwide and guidelines are available worldwide online." Bimonthly. Estab. 2000. Circ. 6,000.

Needs: Literary. Receives 20 unsolicited mss/month. Accepts 6-10 mss/issue; 36-60 mss/year. Publishes ms immediately after acceptance. **Publishes 6-15 new writers/year.** Recently published work by Daniel Greenstone, Alexandra Thompson, Pieter Hudsen and more. Average length: 3,500 words. Publishes short shorts. Sometimes comments on rejected mss.

How to Contact: Electronically through our website. Responds in 1 month to mss. Guidelines on website.

Payment/Terms: Acquires one time rights for annual print anthology. Sends galleys to author.

Advice: "We only accept electronic submissions. One, respect your work, clean it up. Don't send sloppy work. Two, follow the guidelines. Page numbers makes our job easier. Three, Send us your best work. We want to make you famous! Four, we like thoughtful fiction that asks deep questions. Our goals are to use web technology to preserve the art of the short story. Our costs are minimal—subscriptions are free—and as more magazines succumb to financial pressures, we want to see web technology fully utilized to preserve costs."

◐ ◎ CAYO, A Chronicle of Life in the Keys, P.O. Box 4516, Key West FL 33041. (305)296-4286. **Contact:** Alyson Matley, editor. Magazine: 8½ × 11; 40-48 pages; glossy paper; 70 lb. cover stock; illustrations; photos. Magazine on Keys-related topics or by Keys authors. Quarterly. Estab. 1993. Circ. 1,000.

Needs: Condensed/excerpted novel, experimental, literary, regional. Receives 4-5 unsolicited mss/month. Accepts 2-3 mss/issue; 8-12 mss/year. Published work by Alma Bond, Robin Shanley and Lawrence Ferlinghetti. Length: 800 words-3,000 words; average length: 3,000 words. Publishes short shorts. Also publishes literary essays, poetry. Often comments on rejected mss.

How to Contact: Send complete ms with a cover letter. Include bio and list of publications with submission. Responds in 6 weeks to queries; 3 months to mss. Send SASE for reply, return of ms or send a disposable copy of ms. Accepts simultaneous, reprint and electronic (ASCII text on disk) submissions. Sample copy for $4. Guidelines for #10 SASE.

Payment/Terms: Pays in contributor's copies. Acquires one-time rights.

Advice: "The story has to stand on its own and move the reader."

Ⓝ ■ CENOTAPH, Fiction for the New Millennium, Cayuse Press, P.O. Box 66003, Burien WA 98166-0003. E-mail: editor@cenotaph.net. Website: www.cenotaph.net (includes submission guidelines, features, writer's resources and two writers forums). **Contact:** Barbara Benepe, editor-in-chief. Electronic literary journal. "Published quarterly, *Cenotaph* is fiction for the new millennium, and seeks innovative fiction, shimmering with vision and originality for a literate audience." Estab. 1999.

Needs: Adventure, ethnic/multicultural (general), fantasy, historical, literary, mainstream, mystery/suspense, thriller/espionage, translations, cross-genre, science fiction, surrealism, magic realism, speculative. Romance (of any orientation) is acceptable if not sexually graphic. No children's, young adult or erotica. Receives 15 unsolicited mss/month. Publishes 10-12 mss/issue; 40-48 mss/year. Publishes ms 2-6 months after acceptance. **Willing to publish new writers.** Recently published work by Don Taylor, Kimberly Townsend Palmer, Janet Buck, J. Michael Yates, Jo Nelson and Mary Chandler. Length: 800-2,500 words; average length: 1,500 words; prefers 1,000 words. Sometimes comments on rejected mss.

How to Contact: Send complete ms with a cover letter by e-mail only. No attachments will be accepted. Include estimated word count, 100-200 word bio and list of publications. Responds in 2 months after deadline to mss. Accepts multiple submissions. Prefers unpublished work, but will consider previously published, with proper documentation. Writer retains copyright. Guidelines and deadlines available on website or by return e-mail to guidelines@cenotaph.net.

Payment/Terms: Acquires one-time rights.

Advice: "Read and study the guidelines, then follow them when submitting. We are always looking for new voices and original stories. Short works best on the Internet. We're more attracted to stories under 1,000 words. We look forward to working with you."

N $ CENTURY, Century Publishing, P.O. Box 150510, Brooklyn NY 11215-0510. E-mail: editor@centurymag.com. Website: www.centurymag.com (includes excerpts, writer's guidelines, online order form). **Contact:** Robert Killheffer, editor. Literary Magazine: 6×9; 96-112 pages; acid free. "We seek to publish the broadest rang of imaginative or speculative fiction, ranging from science fiction, fantasy, magic realism, surrealism, and even mainstream fiction that has a quirky, offbeat sensibility." Quarterly. Estab. 1995. Circ. 2,000.

Needs: Experimental, fantasy, feminist, historical, horror, literary, science fiction. Receives 200 unsolicited mss/months. Accepts 6-7 mss/issue; 24-28 mss/year. Publishes 6-9 months after acceptance. Agented fiction 7%. **Publishes 1-2 new writers/year.** Recently published work by F. Brett Cox, Greer Gilman, and Ben Miller. Length: 250-20,000 words; average length: 6,000. Publishes short shorts. Sometimes comments on rejected mss.

How to Contact: Send complete ms with cover letter. Include estimated word count and list of publications. Responds in 2 weeks to queries; 2 months to mss. Send SASE for return of ms or send disposable copy of ms and #10 SASE for reply only. Accepts multiple submissions. Sample copy for $7. Guidelines for SASE.

Payment/Terms: Pays 4¢/word and 5 contributor's copies; additional copies $3.60. Pays on acceptance for First World English and non-exclusive reprint. Sends galleys to author.

Advice: "Read lots of every kind of work, but most importantly, take a look at at least one issue of our magazine to get a sense of our tastes."

CHANTEH, The Iranian Cross-Cultural Quarterly, P.O. Box 703, Falls Church VA 22046. (703)533-1727. Fax: (703)536-7853. **Contact:** Saïdeh Pakravan, editor. Magazine: 8½×11; 80 pages; illustrations; photos. "A multicultural magazine for second-generation immigrants and exiles adapting to new environments." Quarterly. Estab. 1992. Circ. 1,200.

Needs: Ethnic/multicultural (general), historical (Middle East), humor/satire, literary, mainstream/contemporary. No romance, erotic, science fiction. Receives 100 unsolicited mss/month. Accepts 1-2 mss/issue; 10 mss/year. Publishes ms 6 months after acceptance. **Publishes 50% new writers.** Length: 7,500 maximum; average length: 3,000 words. Publishes short shorts. Also publishes literary essays, literary criticism, poetry.

How to Contact: Send complete ms with a cover letter. Include 25-word bio. Responds in 6 weeks. Send disposable copy of ms. Accepts simultaneous submissions. Reviews novels, short story collections and nonfiction books of interest to writers.

Payment/Terms: Pays 2 contributor's copies. Acquires first North American serial rights.

Advice: "The material should preferably, though not exclusively, relate to the cross-cultural experience. This is more a trend than a fast rule. An exceptional submission will always be considered on its own merit."

$ CHAPMAN, 4 Broughton Place, Edinburgh EH1 3RX Scotland. **Contact:** Joy Hendry, fiction editor. Phone: (+44)131 557 2207. Fax: (+44)131 556 9565. E-mail: editor@chapman-pub.co.uk.pub.uk. Website: www.chapman.pub.uk (includes samples from current issues, guidelines, catalog). "*Chapman*, Scotland's quality literary magazine, is a dynamic force in Scotland, publishing poetry, fiction, criticism, reviews; articles on theatre, politics, language and the arts. Our philosophy is to publish new work, from known and unknown writers, mainly Scottish, but also worldwide." Quarterly. Circ. 2,000. Publishes 4-6 stories/issue. Estab. 1970.

Needs: No horror, science fiction. **Publishes 25 new writers/year.** Recently published work by Quim Monzo, Dilys Rose, Leslie Schenck. Length: 1,000-6,000 words.

How to Contact: Include SAE and return postage (or IRC) with submissions.

Payment/Terms: Pays £7/page. Sample copy available for £5 (includes postage).

Tips: "We seek challenging work which attempts to explore difficult/new territory in content and form, but lighter work, if original enough, is welcome."

$ THE CHARITON REVIEW, Truman State University, Kirksville MO 63552. (816)785-4499. Fax: (816)785-7486. Editor: Jim Barnes. **Contact:** Fiction Editor. Magazine: 6×9; approximately 100 pages; 60 lb. paper; 65 lb. cover stock; photographs on cover. "We demand only excellence in fiction and fiction translation for a general and college readership." Semiannually. Estab. 1975. Circ. 700.

Needs: Literary, contemporary, experimental, translations. Accepts 3-5 mss/issue; 6-10 mss/year. **Published new writers within the last year.** Published work by Ann Townsend, Glenn DelGrosso, Paul Ruffin and X.J. Kennedy. Length: 3,000-6,000 words. Also publishes literary essays, poetry. Critiques rejected mss when there is time.

How to Contact: Send complete ms with SASE. No book-length mss. No simultaneous submissions. Responds in less than 1 month to mss. Publishes ms an average of 6 months after acceptance. Sample copy for $5 with SASE. Reviews novels and short story collections.

Payment/Terms: Pays $5/page up to $50 maximum and contributor's copy on publication; additional copies for $5.50. Buys first North American serial rights; rights returned on request.

Advice: "Do not ask us for guidelines: the only guidelines are excellence in all matters. Write well and study the publication you are submitting to. We are interested only in the very best fiction and fiction translation. We are not interested in slick material. We do not read photocopies, dot-matrix, or carbon copies. Know the simple mechanics of submission—SASE, no paper clips, no odd-sized SASE, etc. Know the genre (short story, novella, etc.). Know the unwritten laws. There is too much manufactured fiction; assembly-lined, ego-centered personal essays offered as fiction."

✓ $ ☑ ⚑ THE CHATTAHOOCHEE REVIEW, Georgia Perimeter College, 2101 Womack Rd., Dunwoody GA 30338. (770)551-3019. Managing Editor: Jo Ann Yeager Adkins. **Contact:** Fiction Editor. Magazine: 6×9; 150 pages; 70 lb. paper; 80 lb. cover stock; illustrations; photos. Quarterly. Estab. 1980. Circ. 1,250.
● Fiction from *The Chattahoochee Review* has been included in *Best New Stories of the South.*

Needs: Literary, mainstream. No juvenile, romance, science fiction. Receives 900 unsolicited mss/year. Accepts 5 mss/issue. **Published new writers within the last year.** Recently published work by Merrill Joan Gerber, Mary Ann Taylor-Hall, Anthony Grooms and Greg Johnson. Length: 2,500 words average. Also publishes creative nonfiction, interviews with writers, poetry reviews, poetry. Sometimes critiques rejected mss.

How to Contact: Send complete ms with cover letter, which should include sufficient bio for notes on contributors' page. Responds in 2-4 months. SASE. May consider simultaneous submission "reluctantly." Sample copy for $6. Fiction and poetry guidelines available on request. Reviews novels and short story collections.

Payment/Terms: Pays $20/page fiction; $15/page nonfiction; $50/poem. Acquires first rights.

Advice: "Arrange to read magazine before you submit to it." Known for publishing Southern regional fiction.

$ ☑ ⚑ CHELSEA, Chelsea Associates, Inc., Box 773, Cooper Station, New York NY 10276-0773. E-mail: rafoerster@aol.com. Editor: Richard Foerster. **Contact:** Fiction Editor. Magazine: 6×9; 185-235 pages; 60 lb. white paper; glossy, full-color cover; artwork; occasional photos. "We have no consistent theme except for single special issues. Otherwise, we use general material of an eclectic nature: poetry, prose, artwork, etc., for a sophisticated, literate audience interested in avant-garde literature and current writing, both national and international." Annually. Estab. 1958. Circ. 1,800.
● *Chelsea* sponsors the Chelsea Awards. Entries to that contest will also be considered for the magazine, but writers may submit directly to the magazine as well.

Needs: Literary, contemporary short fiction, poetry and translations. "No science fiction, romance, divorce, racist, sexist material or I-hate-my-mother stories. We look for serious, sophisticated literature from writers willing to take risks with language and narrative structure." Receives approximately 200 unsolicited fiction mss each month. Approximately 1% of fiction is agented. **Publishes 1-2 new writers/year.** Length: not over 25 printed pages. Publishes short shorts of 6 pages or less. Sponsors annual Chelsea Award, $1,000 (send SASE for guidelines).

How to Contact: Send complete ms with SASE and succinct cover letter with previous credits. No inquiries by e-mail. No simultaneous submissions. Responds in 5 months to mss. Publishes ms within a year after acceptance. Sample copy for $7.

Payment/Terms: Pays contributor's copies and $15 per printed page for first North American serial rights plus one-time non-exclusive reprint rights.

Advice: "Familiarize yourself with issues of the magazine for character of contributions. Manuscripts should be legible, clearly typed, with minimal number of typographical errors and cross-outs, sufficient return postage. Most manuscripts are rejected because they are conventional in theme and/or style, uninspired, contrived, etc. We see far too much of the amateurish love story or romance. We would like to see more fiction that is sophisticated, with attention paid to theme, setting, language as well as plot. Writers should say something that has never been said before or at least say something in a unique way. There is too much focus on instant fame and not enough attention to craft. Our audience is sophisticated, international, and expects freshness and originality."

$ ☑ ⚑ CHICAGO REVIEW, 5801 S. Kenwood Ave., Chicago IL 60637. (773)702-0887. E-mail: chicago-review@uchicago.edu. Website: humanities.uchicago.edu (includes guidelines, editors' names, subscription information). **Contact:** William Martin, fiction editor. Magazine for a highly literate general audience: 6×9; 128 pages; offset white 60 lb. paper; illustrations; photos. Quarterly. Estab. 1946. Circ. 3,500.
● The *Chicago Review* has won two *Pushcart* prizes and an Illinois Arts Council Award.

Needs: Literary, contemporary and experimental. Accepts up to 5 mss/issue; 20 mss/year. Receives 80-100 unsolicited fiction mss each week. **Publishes 2 new writers/year.** Published work by Hollis Seamon, Tom House, Rachel Klein and Doris Dörrie. No preferred length, except will not accept book-length mss. Also publishes literary essays, literary criticism, poetry. Sometimes recommends other markets.

How to Contact: Send complete ms with cover letter. Accepts queries/mss by e-mail. SASE. No simultaneous submissions. Responds in 4-5 months to mss. Sample copy for $8. Guidelines via website or with SASE. Reviews novels and short story collections. Send books to Book Review Editor.

Payment/Terms: Pays 3 contributor's copies and subscription.

Advice: "We look with interest at fiction that addresses subjects inventively, work that steers clear of clichéd treatments of themes. We're always eager to read writing that experiments with language, whether it be with characters' viewpoints, tone or style. We like a strong voice capable of rejecting gimmicks in favor of subtleties. We are most impressed by writers who have read both deeply and broadly, but display their own inventiveness. However, we have been receiving more submissions and are becoming more selective."

N **CHILDREN, CHURCHES AND DADDIES MAGAZINE, the unreligious, non-family oriented literary & art publication**, Scars Publications and Design, P.O. Box 150, Intercourse PA 17534. E-mail: ccandd96@pa.freei.net or ccandd96@aol.com. Website: www.yotko.com/scars. **Contact:** Janet Kuypers, publisher. E-zine: illustrations; photos. "We prefer anything off the beaten track. We shy away from romantic or science fiction writing—we like writing that seems very real and gripping." Monthly. Estab. 1993.

Needs: Adventure, experimental, feminist, gay, horror (psychological, supernatural), lesbian, literary, mainstream, mystery/suspense, psychic/supernatural/occult. "No religious or gushy family material." Accepts 1 ms/issue; 10 mss/year. **Publishes 7 new writers/year.** Recently published work by Cheryl Townsend, Lisa Newkirk and Kirt Nimmo. Publishes short shorts. Also publishes literary essays, literary criticism and poetry. Comments on rejected mss if requested.

How to Contact: Query first. Accepts submissions by e-mail and disk. Responds in 2 weeks to queries and mss. Send SASE (or IRC) for return of ms or send a disposable copy of ms and #10 SASE for reply only. Accepts simultaneous submissions, previously published work and multiple submissions. Sample copy "as book collection" for $12.

Payment/Terms: No payment. Acquires one-time rights. Sponsors contest. $11 entry fee. "Winners are included in the book and receive a copy of that book." Keep it under 10 pages, if you can.

Advice: "If it relates to how the world fits into a person's life (political story, a day in the life, coping with issues that people face), it will probably win us over faster. Please tell the story like it actually happened—what makes a story believable is the detail given in it that pulls the reader in. Make our reader see the scene, smell the food, feel the wind on their face. They'll remember the story more when they put an issue down if they feel like they lived the story instead of merely reading it. They can take something from it, and when they do you know you've done something right."

CHIRON REVIEW, 702 N. Prairie, St. John KS 67576-1516. (316)549-6156. E-mail: chironreview@hotmail.com. Website: www.geocities.com/SoHo/Nook/1748 (includes writer's guidelines, names of editors, chat line, sample poems and contest info). Editor: Michael Hathaway. **Contact:** Fiction Editor. Tabloid: 10×13; minimum 24 pages; newsprint; illustrations; photos. Publishes "all types of material, no particular theme; traditional and off-beat, no taboos." Quarterly. Estab. 1982. Circ. 1,200.

• *Chiron Review* is known for publishing experimental and "sudden" fiction.

Needs: Contemporary, experimental, humor/satire, literary. No didactic, religious or overtly political writing. Receives 100 mss/month. Accepts 1-3 ms/issue; 4-12 mss/year. Publishes ms within 6-18 months of acceptance. **Publishes 100 new writers and poets/year.** Published work by Janice Eidus, David Newman, Craig Curtis, Jay Marvin and Ad Hudler. Length: 3,500 maximum. Publishes short shorts. Sometimes recommends other markets to writers of rejected mss.

How to Contact: Responds in 6-8 weeks. SASE. No simultaneous or reprint submissions. Deadlines: November 1 (Winter), February 1 (Spring), May 1 (Summer), August 1 (Autumn). Sample copy for $4 ($8 overseas). Guidelines for #10 SASE.

Payment/Terms: Pays 1 contributor's copy; extra copies at 50% discount. Acquires first rights.

Advice: "Research markets thoroughly."

CHRISTIANITY AND THE ARTS, P.O. Box 118088, Chicago IL 60611. (312)642-8606. Fax: (312)266-7719. E-mail: chrnarts@aol.com. Website: www.christianarts.com. Editor: Marci Whitney-Schenck. **Contact:** Terrence Neal Brown, P.O. Box 381528, Germantown TN 38183. Magazine: 8½×11; 52 pages; 60 lb. gloss paper; illustrations; photos. Publishes work on "Christian expression—visual arts, dance, music, literature, film. We reach Protestant, Catholic, and Orthodox readers throughout the United States and Canada. Our readers tend to be upscale and well-educated, with an interest in several disciplines, such as music and the visual arts." Quarterly. Estab. 1994. Circ. 5,000.

• *Christianity and the Arts* received an award for Best Special Interest Magazine from Associated Church Press in 1999.

Needs: Mainstream/contemporary, religious/inspirational. No erotica. "We generally treat two themes in each issue." Receives 3-4 unsolicited mss/month. "We hope to publish one fiction manuscript per issue." Publishes ms 6 months after acceptance. Length: 3,000 words maximum. Publishes short shorts. Also publishes literary essays. Sometimes comments on rejected mss.
How to Contact: Send complete ms with a cover letter. Include bio, estimated word count and list of publications. SASE for reply. Accepts simultaneous submissions. Sample copy for $6. Reviews novels and short story collections.
Payment/Terms: No payment. Sends galleys to author.
Advice: "Fiction is difficult for us to publish in our print edition at this time. But try us and be patient. We do publish fiction on our website."

✅ 💲🖋 **CHRYSALIS READER, Journal of the Swedenborg Foundation**, The Swedenborg Foundation, 320 N. Church St., West Chester PA 19380-3213. (610)430-3222. Send mss to: Rt. 1, Box 4510, Dillwyn VA 23936. (804)983-3021. **Editor:** Carol S. Lawson. Book series: 7½×10; 192 pages; archival paper; coated cover stock; illustrations; photos. "A literary magazine centered around one theme per issue. Publishes fiction, essays and poetry for intellectually curious readers interested in spiritual topics." Biannually. Estab. 1985. Circ. 3,000.
Needs: Fiction (leading to insight), contemporary, experimental, historical, literary, mainstream, mystery/suspense, science fiction, spiritual, sports. No religious, juvenile, preschool. Upcoming themes: "Serendipity" (September 2000). Receives 50 mss/month. Accepts 15-20 mss/issue; 20-40 mss/year. Publishes ms within 2 years of acceptance. Published work by Robert Bly, Larry Dossey, John Hitchcock, Barbara Marx Hubbard and Linda Pastan. Length: 2,000-3,500 words. Also publishes literary essays, literary criticism, chapters of novels, poetry. Sometimes critiques rejected mss and recommends other markets.
How to Contact: Query first and send SASE for guidelines. Responds in 2 months. SASE. No simultaneous, reprinted or in-press material. Sample copy for $10. Guidelines for #10 SASE.
Payment/Terms: Pays $75-250 and 5 contributor's copies on publication for one-time rights. Sends galleys to author.
Advice: Looking for "1. *Quality*; 2. appeal for our audience; 3. relevance to/illumination of an issue's theme."

💲🖋📷 **CICADA**, 329 "E" St., Bakersfield CA 93304. (805)323-4064. **Contact:** Frederick A. Raborg, Jr., editor. Magazine: 5½×8¼; 24 pages; matte cover stock; illustrations; photos. "Oriental poetry and fiction related to the Orient for general readership and haiku enthusiasts." Quarterly. Estab. 1985. Circ. 810.
Needs: *All with Oriental slant:* Adventure, contemporary, erotica, ethnic, experimental, fantasy, feminist, historical (general), horror, humor/satire, lesbian, literary, mainstream, mystery/suspense, psychic/supernatural/occult, regional, contemporary romance, historical romance, young adult romance, science fiction, senior citizen/retirement and translations. "We look for strong fiction with Oriental (especially Japanese) content or flavor. Stories need not have 'happy' endings, and we are open to the experimental and/or avant-garde. Erotica is fine; pornography, no." Receives 30 unsolicited mss/month. Accepts 1 ms/issue; 4 mss/year. Publishes ms 6 months to 1 year after acceptance. Agented fiction 5%. Published work by Gilbert Garand, Frank Holland and Jim Mastro. Length: 500-3,000 words; average length: 2,000 words. Critiques rejected ms when appropriate. Also publishes poetry.
How to Contact: Send complete ms with cover letter. Include Social Security number and appropriate information about the writer in relationship to the Orient. Responds in 2 weeks to queries; 3 months to mss (if seriously considered). SASE. Sample copy for $6. Guidelines for #10 SASE.
Payment/Terms: Pays $10-25 and contributor's copies on publication for first North American serial rights; charges for additional copies. $5 kill fee.
Advice: Looks for "excellence and appropriate storyline. Strong characterization and knowledge of the Orient are musts. Neatness counts high on my list for first impressions. A writer should demonstrate a high degree of professionalism."

Ⓝ **CICADA**, Carus Publishing Company, 315 Fifth St., Peru IL 61354. (815)224-6656. Fax: (815)224-6615. E-mail: mmiklavcic@caruspub.com. Website: www.cricketmag.com or www.cicadamag.com. **Contact:** Deborah Vetter, executive editor. Senior Editor: John D. Allen. Literary magazine: 128 pages; some illustrations. Bimonthly. Estab. 1998. Circ. 12,500.
Needs: Young adult/teen (adventure, fantasy/science fiction, historical, mystery/suspense, romance, sports, western, humor). "Our readership is age 14-21. Submissions should be tailored for high-school and college-age audience, not junior high or younger." Accepts 10 mss/issue; 60 mss/year. Publishes 1 year after acceptance. Length: 3,000-15,000 words; average length: 5,000 words. Also publishes poetry. Sometimes comments on rejected mss.
How to Contact: Send complete ms with cover letter. Include estimated word count and brief bio. Responds in 3 months to mss. Send SASE for return of ms or send disposable copy of ms and #10 SASE for reply only. Accepts simultaneous and multiple submissions. (Prefers original mss if ms is tagged as simultaneous submission.) Sample copy for $8.50. Guidelines for SASE or on website. Reviews novels "geared toward our teen readership."

Payment/Terms: Fiction and articles pay 25¢/word and 2 contributor's copies. Poems: up to $3/line and 2 contributor's copies; additional copies $4. Pays on publication. Sends edited ms for author approval. "For stories and poems previously unpublished, CICADA purchases first publication rights in the English language as well as additional rights options. *CICADA* also requests the rights to reprint the work in any volume or anthology published by Carus Publishing Company upon payment of half the original fee. For stories and poems previously published, *CICADA* purchases second North American publication rights. Fees vary, but are generally less than fees for first publication rights. For recurring features, *CICADA* purchases the material outright. The work becomes the property of *CICADA,* and is copyrighted in the name of Carus Publishing Company. A flat fee per feature is usually negotiated. For commissioned artwork, first publication rights plus promotional rights (promotions, advertising, or any other form not offered for sale), subject to the terms outlined: Physical art remains the property of the illustrator; payment is made within 45 days of acceptance; *CICADA* retains the additional, nonexclusive right to reprint the work in any volume or anthology published by *CICADA* subject to pro-rata share of 7% royalty of net sales."

Advice: "Quality writing, good literary style, genuine teen sensibility, depth, humor, good character development, avoidance of stereotypes. Read several issues to familiarize yourself with our style."

✓ $ ◧ CIMARRON REVIEW, Oklahoma State University, 205 Morrill, Stillwater OK 74074-0135. (405)744-9476. E-mail: cimarronreview@hotmail.com. Website: cimarronreview.okstate.edu. **Associate Editors:** Todd Peterson and Jennifer Schell. Magazine: 6×9; 150 pages. "Poetry and fiction on contemporary themes; personal essay on contemporary issues that cope with life in the 20th century, for educated literary readers. We work hard to reflect quality. We are eager to receive manuscripts from both established and less experienced writers that intrigue us by their unusual perspective, language, imagery and character." Quarterly. Estab. 1967. Circ. 500.

Needs: Literary and contemporary. "Would like to see more language-aware writing that gets away from the crutch of first person." No collegiate reminiscences, science fiction or juvenilia. Accepts 6-7 mss/issue, 24-28 mss/year. **Published 8 new writers/year.** Published work by Jose Saramago, Adam Braver, Jonathan Ames and Ryan Williams. Also publishes literary essays, literary criticism, poetry.

How to Contact: Send complete ms with SASE. "Short cover letters are appropriate but not essential, except for providing *CR* with the most recent mailing address available." No simultaneous submissions. Responds in 3 months to mss. Publishes ms within 1 year after acceptance. Sample copy with SASE and $5. Reviews novels, short story collections, and poetry collections.

Payment/Terms: Pays one-year subscription to author, plus $50 for each prose piece. Acquires all rights on publication. "Permission to reprint granted freely."

Advice: "Don't try to pass personal essays off as fiction. Short fiction is a genre uniquely suited to the modern world. *CR* seeks an individual, innovative style that focuses on contemporary themes."

○ CITY PRIMEVAL: Narratives of Urban Reality, P.O. Box 30064, Seattle WA 98103. (206)440-0791. Editor: David Ross. **Contact:** Fiction Editor. Magazine: 6×9; 72 pages; 60 lb. paper; card cover stock; illustrations; photos. *City Primeval* "features work in the new genre: urban narrative." Quarterly. Estab. 1995. Circ. 200.

Needs: Adventure, literary, military/war, mystery/suspense, thriller/espionage. Receives 75-150 unsolicited mss/month. Accepts 6-10 mss/issue; 36-60 mss/year. Publishes ms 3-6 months after acceptance. **Publishes 6-10 new writers/year.** Recently published work by Robin Sterns, Robert R. Ward, P.F. Allen, Susan Montag and Diane Trzcinski. Word length: 5,000 words average; 10,000 words maximum. Publishes short shorts. Also publishes literary essays and poetry. Sometimes comments on or critiques rejected ms.

How to Contact: Send complete ms with a cover letter. Include 6-12 line bio. Responds to mss in 6 weeks. Send SASE for return of ms. No simultaneous submissions. Sample copy for $5. Guidelines for SASE.

Payment/Terms: Pays 1 contributor's copy. Payment on publication. Acquires first North American serial rights.

Advice: "Must meet editorial requirements—request guidelines before submitting. Know the market."

⬡ ✓ ○ ◎ THE CLAREMONT REVIEW, The Contemporary Magazine of Young Adult Writers, The Claremont Review Publishers, 4980 Wesley Rd., Victoria, British Columbia V8Y 1Y9 Canada. (604)658-5221. Fax: (604)658-5387. E-mail: aurora@home.com. Website: www.claremont.sd63.bc.ca. **Contact:** Kim Andeil, Bill Stenson, Susan Stenson, Rob Filgate, Janice McCachen, Kim LeMieux and Susan Field, editors. Magazine: 6×9; 110-120 pages; book paper; soft gloss cover; b&w illustrations. "We are dedicated to publishing emerging young writers aged 13-19 from anywhere in the English-speaking world, but primarily Canada and the U.S." Biannually. Estab. 1992. Circ. 700.

Needs: Young adult/teen ("their writing, not writing for them"). Plans special fiction issue or anthology. Receives 10-12 unsolicited mss/month. Accepts 10-12 mss/issue; 20-24 mss/year. Publishes ms 3 months after acceptance. **Publishes 200 new writers/year.** Recently published work by Alan Herring, Phoebe Prileaux, Michael Mulley and Elissa Hintz. Length: 5,000 words maximum; 1,500-3,000 words preferred. Publishes short shorts, prose and poetry. Always comments on rejected mss.

How to Contact: Send complete ms with cover letter. Include 2-line bio, list of publications and SASE. Responds in 6 weeks-3 months. Accepts simultaneous and electronic (disk or modem) submissions. Sample copy for $6 with 6×9 SASE and $2 Canadian postage. Guidelines free with SASE.
Payment/Terms: Pays 1 contributor's copy on publication for first North American and one-time rights. Additional copies for $5.
Advice: Looking for "good concrete narratives with credible dialogue and solid use of original detail. It must be unique, honest and a glimpse of some truth. Send an error-free final draft with a short covering letter and bio; please, read us first to see what we publish."

THE CLIMBING ART, 6390 E. Floyd Dr., Denver CO 80222-7638. Phone/fax: (303)757-0541. E-mail: rmorrow@dnvr.uswest.net. Editor: Ron Morrow. **Contact:** Fiction Editor. Magazine: 5½×8½; 150 pages; illustrations; photos. "*The Climbing Art* publishes literature, poetry and art for and about the spirit of climbing." Semiannually. Estab. 1986. Circ. 1,200.
Needs: Adventure, condensed/excerpted novel, ethnic/multicultural, experimental, fantasy, historical, literary, mainstream/contemporary, mystery/suspense, regional, science fiction, sports, translations. "No religious, rhyming, or non-climbing related." Receives 50 unsolicited mss/month. Accepts 4-6 mss/issue; 10-15 mss/year. Publishes ms up to 1 year after acceptance. Agented fiction 10%. **Publishes 25-30 new writers/year.** Recently published work by Reg Saner, Robert Walton and Gary Every. Length: 500-10,000 words. Publishes short shorts. Also publishes literary essays, literary criticism, poetry. Sometimes comments on rejected mss. Sometimes sponsors contests.
How to Contact: Send complete ms with a cover letter. Include estimated word count, 1-paragraph bio and list of publications. Accepts queries/mss by fax or e-mail. Responds in 1 month to queries; 2-8 weeks to mss. SASE. Accepts simultaneous and electronic submissions. Sample copy $7. Reviews novels and short story collections.
Payment/Terms: Pays free subscription and 2 contributor's copies; additional copies for $4. Acquires one-time rights.
Advice: Looks for knowledge of subject matter and love of the sport of climbing. "Read several issues first and make certain the material is related to climbing and the spirit of climbing. We have not seen enough literary excellence."

THE COE REVIEW, Coe College, 1220 First Ave. NE, Cedar Rapids IA 52402. (319)399-8000. E-mail: caukema@coe.edu. **Contact:** Nate Ochs, editor. Editors change each year. Magazine: 150 pages; illustrations; photos. "We are a college literary magazine specializing in experimental poetry and fiction." Annual. Estab. 1971. Circ. 500.
Needs: Experimental. Next year's theme: "The Swimsuit Issue." Receives 50-75 unsolicited mss/month. Accepts 10 mss/year. Does not read mss June-August. Publishes ms 2 months after acceptance. **"Most of our authors are previously unpublished."** Recently published work by Marge Piercy, Shana Fried and Alan Webber. Length: 1,200-2,500 words. Publishes short shorts. Also publishes poetry.
How to Contact: Send complete ms with a cover letter. Include brief bio. Send SASE (or IRC) for return of ms. Accepts previously published work and multiple submissions. Sample copy for $4. Guidelines for SASE.
Payment/Terms: Pays 2 contributor's copies; additional copies $4. Acquires first North American serial rights.
Advice: "We appreciate quality experimental fiction: texts that push boundaries in genre but are comprehensible. Try to get a copy and look at it prior to submitting. It is obvious when someone who has never seen a copy of our magazine submits."

COLLAGES AND BRICOLAGES, The Journal of International Writing, P.O. Box 360, Shippenville PA 16254. E-mail: cb@penn.com. **Contact:** Marie-José Fortis, editor. Magazine: 8½×11; 100-150 pages; illustrations. "The magazine includes essays, short stories, occasional interviews, short plays, poems that show innovative promise. It is often focus- or issue-oriented—themes can be either literary or socio-political." Annually. Estab. 1987.
Needs: Contemporary, ethnic, experimental, feminist, humor/satire, literary, philosophical works. "Also symbolist, surrealist b&w designs/illustrations are welcome." Receives about 60 unsolicited fiction mss/month. Publishes ms 6-9 months after acceptance. **Published new writers within the last year.** Recently published work by Mark Antony Rossi, Crystal E. Wilkinson, Anne Blonstein and Pedro Shimose. Publishes short shorts. Also publishes literary essays, literary criticism, poetry. Critiques rejected ms "when great potential is manifest."
How to Contact: Send complete ms with cover letter that includes a short bio. Responds in 1-3 months. SASE. Sample copy for $10; older back issues $5. Reviews novels and short story collections. "How often and how many per issue depends on reviewers available. Only send material between August 15 and December 15."
Payment/Terms: Pays 2 contributor's copies. Acquires first rights. Rights revert to author after publication.
Advice: "Avoid following 'industry trends.' Do what you must do. Write what you must write. Write as if words were your bread, your water, a great vintage wine, salt, oxygen. Also, very few of us have a cornucopia budget, but it is a good idea to look at a publication before submitting."

☑ **$ ⊘ COLORADO REVIEW**, English Department, Colorado State University, Fort Collins CO 80523. (970)491-5449. E-mail: coloradoreview@lamar.colostate.edu. Editor: David Milofsky. **Contact:** Fiction Editor. Literary journal: 200 pages; 70 lb. book weight paper. Triquarterly. Estab. 1966. Circ. 1,300.

• *Colorado Review*'s circulation has increased from 500 to 1,300.

Needs: Contemporary, ethnic, experimental, literary, mainstream, translations. No genre fiction. Receives 600 unsolicited fiction mss/month. Accepts 3-4 mss/issue. **Published new writers within the last year.** Published work by T. Alan Broughton, Elizabeth Gaffney, Ann Hood and Robert Boswell. Length: under 6,000 words. Does not read mss May through August. Also publishes literary essays, book reviews, poetry. Occasionally critiques rejected mss.

How to Contact: Send complete ms with SASE (or IRC) and brief bio with previous publications. Responds in 3 months. Publishes ms 6-12 months after acceptance. Sample copy for $10. Reviews novels or short story collections.

Payment/Terms: Pays $5/printed page for fiction; 2 contributor's copies; extras for $5. Pays on publication for first North American serial rights. "We assign copyright to author on request." Sends galleys to author.

Advice: "We are interested in manuscripts that show craft, imagination, and a convincing voice. If a story has reached a level of technical competence, we are receptive to the fiction working on its own terms. The oldest advice is still the best: persistence. Approach every aspect of the writing process with pride, conscientiousness—from word choice to manuscript appearance."

☑ **⊘ COLUMBIA: A JOURNAL OF LITERATURE & ART**, 415 Dodge Hall, Columbia University, New York NY 10027. (212)854-4216. E-mail: arts-litjournal@columbia.edu. Prose Editor: Scott Snyder. **Contact:** Rargi McNeil, editor-in-chief. Editors change each year. Magazine: 5¼×8¼; approximately 200 pages; coated cover stock; illustrations; photos. "We accept short stories, novel excerpts, translations, interviews, nonfiction, artwork and poetry." Biannually.

Needs: Literary and translations. "No genre unless it transcends the genre." Upcoming theme: "Vice." Accepts 5-15 mss/issue. Receives approximately 125 unsolicited fiction mss each month. Does not read mss May 1 to August 31. Recently published work by Donald Anderson, Gabriel Neruda and Andy Gersick. Published 5-8 unpublished writers within the year. Length: 25 pages maximum. Publishes short shorts.

How to Contact: Send complete ms with SASE. Accepts computer printout submissions. Responds in 2-3 months. Sample copy for $8.

Payment/Terms: Offers yearly contest with guest editors and cash awards. Offers one editor's award at $250/issue. Send SASE for guidelines.

Advice: "Because our staff changes each year, our specific tastes also change, so our best advice is to write what you want to write."

N COMPOST, a journal of art, literature, and idea, P.O. Box 226, Jamaica Plain MA 02130. (617)524-1456. E-mail: kgallagh@tufts.edu. **Contact:** Kevin Gallagher, editor. Literary magazine: 9½×11; 87 pages; some illustrations; photos. "*Compost* was founded in 1992 to help foster a better understanding among the world's people through art, literature and ideas. Each issue features the literature of another country, Boston area literature, and submissions from the U.S., in addition to art and photography." Annual. Estab. 1992. Circ. 1,000.

Needs: Experimental, literary, translation. Accepts 1-3 mss/year. Agented fiction 5%. Publishes 30% of issues total. Recently published work by Colum Mcann, Andre Carpenter, Ed Bullins, Robert Pinsky. Length: 1,000-7,000. Publishes short shorts. Also publishes literary essays, literary criticism, and poetry. Rarely comments on rejected mss.

How to Contact: Send complete ms with cover letter. Include brief bio. Responds in 8 months to queries and mss. Send SASE for return of ms. Sample copy free with SASE.

Payment/Terms: Acquires first rights.

Advice: "Truth and originality."

N CONCHO RIVER REVIEW, Fort Concho Museum Press, 630 S. Oakes, San Angelo TX 76903. Fax: (915)942-2269. E-mail: me.hartje@mailserv.angelo.edu. **Contact:** Mary Ellen Hartje, fiction editor. Magazine: 6½×9; 100-125 pages; 60 lb. Ardor offset paper; Classic Laid Color cover stock; b&w drawings. "We publish any fiction of high quality—no thematic specialties—*contributors must be residents of Texas or the Southwest generally.*" Semiannually. Estab. 1987. Circ. 300.

• The magazine is considering featuring "guest editors" with each issue, but manuscripts should still be sent to the editor, Mary Ellen Hartje.

Needs: Contemporary, ethnic, historical, humor/satire, literary, regional and western. No erotica; no science fiction. Receives 10-15 unsolicited mss/month. Accepts 3-6 mss/issue; 8-10 mss/year. Publishes ms 4 months after acceptance. **Publishes 4 new writers/year.** Recently published work by Gordon Alexander, Riley Froh, Gretchen Geralds and Kimberly Willis Holt. Length: 1,500-5,000 words; average length: 3,500 words. Also publishes literary essays, poetry.

How to Contact: *Send submissions to Mary Ellen Hartje, English Dept., Angelo State University, San Angelo, TX 76909.* Send complete ms with SASE; cover letter optional. Responds in 3 weeks to queries; 3-6 months to mss. SASE for ms. Accepts simultaneous submissions (if noted). Sample copy for $4. Guidelines for #10 SASE. Reviews novels and short story collections. Books to be reviewed should be sent to Dr. James Moore.
Payment/Terms: Pays in contributor's copies; $4 charge for extras. Acquires first rights.
Advice: "We prefer a clear sense of conflict, strong characterization and effective dialogue."

[N] [symbol] CONDUIT, Conduit, Inc., 510 Eighth Ave. NE, Minneapolis MN 55413. (612)362-0995. E-mail: conduit@bitstream.net. Editor: William Waltz. **Contact:** Brett Astor, fiction editor. Magazine: 5×10; 64 pages; letterpress cover; illustrations; photos. "*Conduit* is primarily a poetry magazine, but we're eager to include lively fiction. *Conduit* publishes work that is intelligent, serious, irreverent and daring." Biannual. Estab. 1993. Circ. 1,000.
Needs: Experimental, literary, translations. Receives 100 unsolicited mss/month. Accepts 4 mss/issue; 12 mss/year. Publishes ms 3-6 months after acceptance. Length: 1,500-3,000 words maximum. Publishes short shorts. Also publishes poetry.
How to Contact: Send complete ms with a cover letter. Responds in 6-24 weeks. Send SASE for reply, return of ms or send a disposable copy of ms. Sample copy for $6, postage/envelope included. Guidelines free for SASE.
Payment/Terms: Pays 3 contributor's copies. Acquires first North American serial rights.
Advice: "Write and send work that feels like it is absolutely essential, but avoid the leg-hold traps of self-importance and affectation."

[check] $[symbol] [Y] CONFRONTATION, English Dept., C.W. Post of Long Island University, Brookville NY 11548. (516)299-2720. Fax: (516)299-2735. Editor: Martin Tucker. Associate Editor: Jonna Semeiks. **Contact:** Fiction Editor. Magazine: 6×9; 250-350 pages; 70 lb. paper; 80 lb. cover; illustrations; photos. "We like to have a 'range' of subjects, form and style in each issue and are open to all forms. Quality is our major concern. Our audience is made up of literate, thinking people; formally or self-educated." Semiannually. Estab. 1968. Circ. 2,000.
 • *Confrontation* has garnered a long list of awards and honors, including the Editor's Award for Distinguished Achievement from CCLM (now the Council of Literary Magazines and Presses) and NEA grants. Work from the magazine has appeared in numerous anthologies including the *Pushcart Prize, Best Short Stories* and *O. Henry Prize Stories*.
Needs: Literary, contemporary, prose poem, regional and translations. No "proseletyzing" literature. Accepts 30 mss/issue; 60 mss/year. Receives 400 unsolicited fiction mss each month. Does not read June through September. Approximately 10-15% of fiction is agented. **Publishes 20-25 new writers/year.** Published work by Arthur Miller, Cynthia Ozick, Irving Fieldman, Nadine Gordimer and Stephen Dixon. Length: 500-4,000 words. Publishes short shorts. Also publishes literary essays, poetry. Critiques rejected mss when there is time. Sometimes recommends other markets.
How to Contact: Send complete ms with SASE. "Cover letters acceptable, not necessary. We accept simultaneous submissions but do not prefer them." Accepts diskettes if accompanied by computer printout submissions. Responds in up to 2 months to mss. Publishes ms 6-12 months after acceptance. Sample copy for $3. Reviews novels, short story collections, poetry and literary criticism.
Payment/Terms: Pays $20-250 on publication for all rights "with transfer on request to author"; 1 contributor's copy; half price for extras.
Advice: "Keep trying."

[N] $ CONVERSELY, Conversely, Inc., PMB #121, 3053 Fillmore St., San Francisco CA 94123-4009. E-mail: writers@conversely.com. Website: www.conversely.com. "We are a webszine, all our content is online."
Contact: Alejandro Gutierrez, editor. Online magazine. Illustrations; photos. "*Conversely* is dedicated to exploring relationships between women and men, every stage, every aspect, through different forms of writing, essays, memoirs, and fiction. Our audience is both female and male, mostly between 18-35 age range. We look for writing that is intelligent, provocative, and witty; we prefer topics that are original and appealing to our readers." Monthly, some sections are published weekly. Estab. 2000.
Needs: Literary, "must be about relationships between women and men." No erotica, gothic, science fiction, romance. Receives 300 unsolicited mss/month. Accepts 1-2 mss/issue; 12-18 mss/year. Publishes ms 3 months after acceptance. Length: 500-3,000 words; average length: 2,500 words. Publishes short shorts.
How to Contact: Send complete ms with cover letter. Accepts submissions by e-mail. "We much prefer e-mail over regular mail." Include estimated work count, brief bio, list of publications and if ms is simultaneous or previously published. Responds in 2 weeks to queries; 2 months to mss. Send disposable copy of ms and #10 SASE for reply only (include e-mail and phone number if sending by regular mail). Accepts simultaneous submissions and previously published submissions. Guidelines for e-mail on website.
Payment/Terms: Pays $50-100. Pays on publication for electronic rights (60 days exclusive, non-exclusive there after). Sends galleys to author.

Advice: "We look for stories that hold attention from start to finish, that cover original topics or use a fresh approach, that have a compelling narrative voice. We prefer stories that deal with relationships in a manner that is complex and insightful, honest, and that surprise by revealing more about a character than was expected. Keep in mind our target audience. Know when to start and know where to end, what to leave out and what to keep in."

N: ☑ CORONA, Marking the Edges of Many Circles, Dept. of History and Philosophy, Montana State University, Bozeman MT 59717. (406)994-5200. Co-Editors: Lynda Sexson, Michael Sexson. Managing Editor: Sarah Merrill. **Contact:** Fiction Editor. Magazine: 7×10; 130 pages; 60 lb. "mountre matte" paper; 65 lb. Hammermill cover stock; illustrations; photos. "Interdisciplinary magazine—essays, poetry, fiction, imagery, science, history, recipes, humor, etc., for those educated, curious, with a profound interest in the arts and contemporary thought." Published occasionally. Estab. 1980. Circ. 1,000.
Needs: Comics, contemporary, experimental, fantasy, feminist, humor/satire, literary, prose poem. "Our fiction ranges from the traditional Talmudic tale to fiction engendered by speculative science, from the extended joke to regional reflection—if it isn't accessible and original, please don't send it." Receives varying number of unsolicited fiction mss/month. Accepts 6 mss/issue. **Published new writers within the last year.** Published work by Rhoda Lerman and Stephen Dixon. Publishes short shorts. Also publishes literary essays, poetry. Occasionally critiques rejected mss.
How to Contact: Query. Responds in 6 months to mss. Sample copy for $7.
Payment/Terms: Pays 2 free contributor's copies; discounted charge for extras. Acquires first rights. Sends galleys to author upon request.
Advice: "Be knowledgeable of contents other than fiction in *Corona*; one must know the journal."

☑ ☑ COTTONWOOD, Box J, 400 Kansas Union, University of Kansas, Lawrence KS 66045-2115. (785)864-2528. Fax: (785)864-4298. E-mail: tlorenz@eagle.cc.ukans. **Contact:** Tom Lorenz, fiction editor. Magazine: 6×9; 100 pages; illustrations; photos. "*Cottonwood* publishes high quality prose, poetry and artwork and is aimed at an audience that appreciates the same. We have a national scope and reputation while maintaining a strong regional flavor." Semiannually. Estab. 1965. Circ. 500.
  • *Cottonwood* is a member of Council of Literary Magazines and Presses.
Needs: "We publish only literary prose and poetry." Receives 25-50 unsolicited mss/month. Accepts 5-6 mss/issue; 10-12 mss/year. Publishes ms 6-18 months after acceptance. Agented fiction 10%. **Publishes 1-3 new writers/year.** Recently published work by Connie May Fowler, Oakley Hall and Cris Mazza. Length: 1,000-10,000 words; average length: 2,000-5,000 words. Publishes short shorts. Length: 1,000 words. Rarely publishes literary essays; publishes literary criticism, poetry. Sometimes comments on rejected mss.
How to Contact: Send complete ms with a cover letter or submit through agent. Include 4-5 line bio and brief list of publications. Responds in up to 4 months. SASE for return of ms. Accepts simultaneous submissions. Sample copy for $8.50, 9×12 SAE and $1.90. Reviews novels and short story collections. Send books to review editor at our Cottonwood address.
Payment/Terms: Pays 1 contributor's copy; additional copies $5. Pays on publication for one-time rights.
Advice: "We're looking for depth and/or originality of subject matter, engaging voice and style, emotional honesty, command of the material and the structure. *Cottonwood* publishes high quality literary fiction, but we are very open to the work of talented new writers. Write something honest and that you care about and write it as well as you can. Don't hesitate to keep trying us. We sometimes take a piece from a writer we've rejected a number of times. We generally don't like clever, gimmicky writing. The style should be engaging but not claim all the attention for itself."

☑ ☑ CRAB CREEK REVIEW, P.O. Box 840, Vasmon WA 98070. (206)772-8489. Website: www.crabcreek review.org. **Contact:** Kimberly Allison, Harris Levinson, Laura Sinai and Terri Stone, editors. Magazine: 6×9 paperbound; 80-112 pgs., line drawings. "Magazine publishing poetry, short stories, and cover art for an audience interested in literary, visual and dramatic arts and in politics." Published twice yearly. Estab. 1983. Circ. 450.
Needs: Contemporary, humor/satire, literary and translations. No confession, erotica, horror, juvenile, preschool, religious/inspirational, romance or young adult. Receives 100 unsolicited mss/month. **Published new writers within the last year.** Recently published work by David Lee, Andrena Zawinski, Deborah Byrne and Judith Skillman. Length: 1,200-6,000 words; average length: 3,000 words. Publishes short shorts.
How to Contact: Send complete ms with short list of credits. Responds in 2-4 months. SASE. No simultaneous submissions. Sample copy for $5. *Anniversary Anthology* $3.
Payment/Terms: Pays 2 contributor's copies; $4 charge for extras. Acquires first rights. Rarely buys reprints.
Advice: "We appreciate 'sudden fictions.' Type name and address on each piece. Enclose SASE. Send no more than one story in a packet (except for short shorts—no more than three, ten pages total). Know what you want to say and say it in an honest, clear, confident voice."

☑ $☑ CRAB ORCHARD REVIEW, A Journal of Creative Works, Southern Illinois University at Carbondale, English Department, Faner Hall, Carbondale IL 62901-4503. (618)453-6833. Fax: (618)453-8224.

Website: www.siu.edu/~crborchd (includes contest information and guidelines). Editor: Richard Peterson. Prose Editor: Carolyn Alessio. Managing Editor: Jon Tribble. **Contact:** Fiction Editor. Magazine: 5½×8½; 250 pages; 55 lb. recycled paper, card cover; photo on cover. "This twice-yearly journal will feature the best in contemporary fiction, poetry, creative nonfiction, reviews and interviews." Estab. 1995. Circ. 1,500.

Needs: Condensed/excerpted novel, ethnic/multicultural, literary, translations. No science fiction, romance, western, horror, gothic or children's. Wants more novel excerpts that also work as stand alone pieces. List of upcoming themes available on website. Receives 75 unsolicited mss/month. Accepts 5-10 mss/issue, 10-18 mss/year. Does not read during the summer. Publishes ms 9-12 months after acceptance. Agented fiction 5%. Recently published work by Gordon Weaver, Ellen Slezak, Tim Parrish and Gina Ochsner. **Publishes 1 new writer/year.** Length: 1,000-6,500 words; average length: 2,500 words. Also publishes literary essays and poetry. Rarely comments on rejected mss.

How to Contact: Send complete ms with a cover letter. Include brief bio and list of publications. Responds in 3 weeks to queries; up to 9 months to mss. Send SASE for reply, return of ms. Accepts simultaneous submissions. Sample copy for $6. Guidelines for #10 SASE. Reviews books, small press and university press novels and story collections only. Reviews done in house by staff. Send review copies to Managing Editor Jon Tribble.

Payment/Terms: Pays $100 minimum; $5/page maximum plus 2 contributor's copies for first North American serial rights, plus a year's subscription.

Advice: "We look for well-written, provocative, fully realized fiction that seeks to engage both the reader's senses and intellect. Don't submit too often to the same market, and don't send manuscripts that you haven't read over carefully. Writers can't rely on spell checkers to catch all errors. Always include a SASE. Read and support the journals you admire so they can continue to survive."

◙ CRANIA, A Literary/Arts Magazine, 1072 Palms Blvd., Venice CA 90291. E-mail: editor@crania.com. Website: www.crania.com. **Contact:** Dennis Hathaway, editor. "To bring literary and visual works of art of the highest quality to an audience potentially much larger than the audience reached by print media."

Needs: Fiction, poetry, essays, reviews. No genre fiction. Recently published work by Alyson Hagy, Alvin Greenberg, Amy Gerstler and Alex Keegan.

How to Contact: Electronic submissions only. Send ms by e-mail.

Advice: "*Crania* welcomes submissions from new writers, but the magazine is not a bulletin board site where anyone can post their work. We urge potential contributors to read the magazine carefully, and to submit work that shows a facility with craft and a commitment to the idea of writing as an art."

☑ ◙ THE CREAM CITY REVIEW, University of Wisconsin-Milwaukee, Box 413, Milwaukee WI 53201. (414)229-4708. E-mail: creamcity@csd.uwm.edu. Website: www.uwm.edu:80/Dept/English/CCR (includes writer's guidelines, names of editors, table of contents from past issues, cover art scanned and magazine's history). Editors-in-Chief: Kyoko Yoshida and Peter Whalen. **Contact:** Steve Nelson, fiction editor. Editors rotate. Magazine: 5½×8½; 200-300 pages; 70 lb. offset/perfect-bound paper; 80 lb. cover stock; illustrations; photos. "General literary publication—an eclectic and electric selection of the best we receive." Semiannually. Estab. 1975. Circ. 2,000.

Needs: Ethnic, experimental, literary, prose poem, regional, translations. "Would like to see more international writings, intranational writing." Does not want to see horror, formulaic, racist, sexist, pornographic, homophobic, science fiction, romance. Receives approximately 300 unsolicited fiction mss each month. Accepts 6-10 mss/issue. Does not read fiction or poetry May 1 through August 31. **Publishes 10 new writers/year.** Recently published work by Pete Fromm. Length: 1,000-10,000 words. Publishes short shorts. Also publishes literary essays, literary criticism, poetry.

How to Contact: Send complete ms with SASE. Accepts simultaneous and multiple submissions if notified. Submissions on disk. Responds in 6 months. Sample copy for $5 (back issue), $7 (current issue). Reviews novels and short story collections.

Payment/Terms: Pays 1 year subscription or in copies. Acquires first rights. Sends galleys to author. Rights revert to author after publication.

Advice: "Read as much as you write so that you can examine your own work in relation to where fiction has been and where fiction is going. We are looking for strong, consistent, fresh voices."

☑ ◙ ☯ THE CRESCENT REVIEW, The Crescent Review, Inc., P.O. Box 7959, S. Brunswick NC 28470-7959. E-mail: crescent@nccoast.net. Website: www.crescentreview.org (includes essays, interviews, guidelines, and more). Editor: J.T. Holland. **Contact:** Fiction Editor. Magazine: 6×9; 160 pages. Triannually. Estab. 1982.

CHECK THE CATEGORY INDEXES, located at the back of the book, for publishers interested in specific fiction subjects.

• Work appearing in *The Crescent Review* has been included in *O. Henry Prize Stories*, *Best American Short Stories*, *Pushcart Prize* and *Black Southern Writers* anthologies and in the *New Stories from the South*. *The Crescent Review* ranked #41 on the *Writer's Digest* "Fiction 50" list of top markets.

Needs: "Well-crafted stories." Wants shorter-length pieces (though will publish stories in the 6,000-9,000 word range). Wants stories where choice has consequences. Conducts two annual writers contests: The Renwick-Sumerwell Award (exclusively for new unpublished writers) and the Chekhov Award for Fine Storytelling. Does not read submissions May-June and November-December.

How to Contact: Responds in up to 6 months. SASE. Sample issue for $10.

Payment/Terms: Pays 2 contributor's copies; discount for contributors. Acquires first North American serial rights.

CRIMEWAVE, TTA Press, 5 Martins Lane, Witcham, Ely, Cambs CB6 2LB England. E-mail: ttapress@aol.com. Website: www.tta-press.freewire.co.uk (includes news, biographies, secure credit card transaction facility). **Contact:** Andy Cox, fiction editor. Magazine: 128 pages; lithographed, color; perfect bound. Magazine publishes "modern crime fiction from across the waterfront, from the misnamed cozy to the deceptively subtle hardboiled." Biannual, published in April and October.

Needs: Mystery (amateur sleuth, cozy, police procedural, private eye/hardboiled), suspense, thriller, etc. Accepts 15 mss/issue. Recently published work by Chaz Brenchley, James Lovegrove, Tom Piccirilli and Lev Raphael.

How to Contact: Send complete ms with a cover letter. "Send one story at a time plus adequate return postage, or disposable ms plus 2 IRC's or e-mail address—but no e-mail submissions. No reprints." Query by e-mail. Sample copy: $12 US, £7 Europe or for 2 issues: $22, £15.

Payment/Terms: "Relatively modest flat fee, but constantly increasing." Contract on acceptance, payment on publication.

CRUCIBLE, English Dept., Barton College, College Station, Wilson NC 27893. (252)399-6456. Editor: Terrence L. Grimes. **Contact:** Fiction Editor. Magazine of fiction and poetry for a general, literary audience. Annually. Estab. 1964. Circ. 500.

Needs: Contemporary, ethnic, experimental, feminist, literary, regional. Receives 20 unsolicited mss/month. Accepts 5-6 mss/year. Publishes ms 4-5 months after acceptance. Does not normally read mss from April 30 to December 1. Published work by Mark Jacobs, William Hutchins and Guy Nancekeville. Length: 8,000 words maximum.

How to Contact: Send 3 complete copies of ms unsigned with cover letter which should include a brief biography, "in case we publish." Responds in 6 weeks to queries; 4 months to mss (by July 1). SASE. Sample copy for $6. Guidelines free.

Payment/Terms: Pays contributor's copies. Acquires first rights.

Advice: "Write about what you know. Experimentation is fine as long as the experiences portrayed come across as authentic, that is to say, plausible."

CUTBANK, English Dept., University of Montana, Missoula MT 59812. (406)243-6156. E-mail: cutbank@selway.umt.edu. Website: www.umt.edu/cutbank (includes writer's guidelines, names of editors, interviews with authors and excerpts). **Contact:** Fiction Editor. Editors change each year. Magazine: 5½×8½; 115-130 pages. "Publishes serious-minded and innovative fiction and poetry from both well known and up-and-coming authors." Semiannually. Estab. 1973. Circ. 600.

Needs: "Innovative, challenging, experimental material." No "science fiction, fantasy or unproofed manuscripts." Receives 200 unsolicited mss/month. Accepts 6-12 mss/year. Does not read mss from April 1-August 15. Publishes ms up to 6 months after acceptance. **Publishes 4 new writers/year.** Recently published work by Dan Barden and Todd Pierce. Length: 40 pages maximum. Also publishes literary essays, literary criticism, poetry. Occasionally critiques rejected mss.

How to Contact: Send complete ms with cover letter, which should include "name, address, publications." Responds in 4 months to mss. SASE. Accepts simultaneous submissions. Sample copy for $4 (current issue $6.95). Guidelines for SASE. Reviews novels and short story collections. Send books to fiction editor.

Payment/Terms: Pays 2 contributor's copies. Rights revert to author upon publication, with provision that *Cutbank* receives publication credit.

Advice: "Strongly suggest contributors read an issue. We have published stories by Kevin Canty, Chris Offutt and Pam Houston in recent issues, and like to feature new writers alongside more well-known names. Send only your best work."

THE DALHOUSIE REVIEW, Room 114, 1456 Henry St., Halifax, Nova Scotia B3H 3J5 Canada. (900)494-2541. Fax: (902)494-3561. E-mail: dalhousie.review@dal.ca. Website: www.dal.ca/~dalrev. Editor: Dr. Ronald Huebert. Magazine: 15cm×23cm; approximately 140 pages; photographs sometimes. Publishes articles, book reviews, short stories and poetry. Published 3 times a year. Circ. 650.

Needs: Literary. Length: 5,000 words maximum. Also publishes essays on history, philosophy, etc., and poetry. Recently published work by Mark Blagrave, Joy Hewitt Mann and Gideon Forman.

How to Contact: Send complete ms with cover letter. SASE (Canadian stamps). Sample copy for $10 (Canadian) including postage. Occasionally reviews novels and short story collections.

N THE DEAD MULE. E-mail: editor@deadmule.com. Website: www.deadmule.com. **Contact:** Valerie Mac-Ewan, editor. *"The Dead Mule* is an online literary magazine featuring Southern fiction, articles, poetry and essays, and is proud to claim a long heritage of Southern literary excellence. We've been online since early 1996. In Internet years, that's a century." Estab. 1996.
  • See the interview with *Dead Mule* editor Valerie MacEwan on page 39 in the Electronic Publishing
  Section.
Needs: Literary.
How to Contact: Send complete ms by e-mail. Do not send attachments—copy and paste your submission into the body of the e-mail. Length: 2,500 words maximum.
Advice: "You've worked hard on whatever it is you wrote. Don't blow it all by not submitting correctly."

$ ◙ ☑ DENVER QUARTERLY, University of Denver, Denver CO 80208. (303)871-2892. **Contact:** Bin Ramke, editor. Magazine: 6×9; 144-160 pages; occasional illustrations. "We publish fiction, articles and poetry for a generally well-educated audience, primarily interested in literature and the literary experience. They read *DQ* to find something a little different from a strictly academic quarterly or a creative writing outlet." Quarterly. Estab. 1966. Circ. 2,000.
  • *Denver Quarterly* received an Honorable Mention for Content from the American Literary Magazine
  Awards and selections have been anthologized in the *Pushcart Prize* anthologies.
Needs: "We are interested in experimental fiction (minimalism, magic realism, etc.) as well as in realistic fiction and in writing about fiction. No sentimental, science fiction, romance or spy thrillers. No stories longer than 15 pages!" **Published 5 new writers within the last year.** Recently published work by Frederick Busch, Judith E. Johnson, Stephen Alter and Harriet Zinnes. Also publishes poetry.
How to Contact: Send complete ms and brief cover letter with SASE. Does not read mss May-September 15. Do not query. Responds in 3 months to mss. Publishes ms within a year after acceptance. Accepts simultaneous submissions. Sample copy $6.
Payment/Terms: Pays $5/page for fiction and poetry and 2 contributor's copies for first North American serial rights.
Advice: "We look for serious, realistic and experimental fiction; stories which appeal to intelligent, demanding readers who are not themselves fiction writers. Nothing so quickly disqualifies a manuscript as sloppy proofreading and mechanics. Read the magazine before submitting to it. We try to remain eclectic, but the odds for beginners are bound to be small considering the fact that we receive nearly 10,000 mss per year and publish only about ten short stories."

🔳 ☑ $ DESCANT, Descant Arts & Letters Foundation, P.O. Box 314, Station P, Toronto, Ontario M5T 1L4. (416)593-2557. Fax: (416)593-9362. E-mail: descant@web.net. Website: www.descant.on.ca (includes guidelines, editors' names, excerpts and subscription information.) Editor: Karen Mulhallen. **Contact:** Nathan Whitlock, managing editor. Quarterly literary journal. Estab. 1970. Circ. 1,200.
Needs: Literary. No gothic, religious, beat. **Publishes 20 new writers/year.** Recently published work by Andrew Pyper, Douglas Gloner and Judith McCormack. Also publishes poetry and literary essays. Submit seasonal material 4 months in advance.
How to Contact: Send complete ms. Sample copy for $8.50. Guidelines for SASE.
Payment/Terms: Pays $100 (Canadian). Pays on publication.
Advice: "Familiarize yourself with our magazine before submitting."

N DESPERATE ACT, Box 1081, Pittsford NY 14534. E-mail: des@aol.com. **Contact:** Gary Wiener, Steve Engle, editors. Magazine: 5½×8½; 76-100 pages; 20 lb. paper; 80 lb. cover stock; illustrations; photos. Annually. Estab. 1995. Circ. 200.
Needs: Humor/satire, literary, mainstream/contemporary. List of upcoming themes available for SASE. Receives 5-10 unsolicited mss/month. Accepts 2-3 mss/issue. Publishes ms 6-12 months after acceptance. **Publishes several new writers/year.** Recently published work by Wendy Low, William Heyer, Martin Prieto and Ruth Lunt. Length: 2,500 words maximum. Publishes short shorts. Also publishes literary essays, literary criticism, poetry. Sometimes comments on rejected ms.
How to Contact: Send complete ms with a cover letter. Accepts queries/mss by e-mail. Include estimated word count, short bio. Responds in 2-3 weeks to queries; 3-6 months to mss. SASE for return of ms or send a disposable copy of ms. Accepts simultaneous submissions. Sample copy for $5. Guidelines free. Reviews novels, short story collections and nonfiction books of interest to writers.
Payment/Terms: Pays 1 contributor's copy; additional copies $5. Acquires first North American serial rights. Not copyrighted.
Advice: "We favor regional writers but will consider good work from anywhere."

THE DISTILLERY: ARTISTIC SPIRITS OF THE SOUTH, Motlow St. Community College, P.O. Box 88100, Tullahoma TN 37388-8100. (931)393-1500. Fax: (931)393-1681. Website: mscc.cc.tn.us/www/distill ery (includes guidelines, contributor list and staff info). **Contact:** Inman Majors, editor. Magazine: 88 pages; color cover; color/b&w art and photos. "The editors seek well-crafted, character-driven fiction." Semiannually. Estab. 1994. Circ. 750.

• Work from *The Distillery* has been anthologized in *Best New Stories from the South*.

Needs: Literary. Receives 50-60 unsolicited mss/month. Accepts 3-4 mss/issue; 6-8 mss/year. Does not read mss June 1-August 1. Publishes ms 6-12 months after acceptance. **Publishes 3-4 new writers/year.** Recently published work by Janice Daugharty, Elaine Palencia and Virgil Suarez. Length: 4,000 words maximum; average length: 2,000-4,000 words. Also publishes literary essays, literary criticism, poetry and book reviews.

How to Contact: Send complete ms with a cover letter. Include estimated word count, brief bio, list of publications. Responds in 2 weeks to queries; 3 months to mss. SASE for reply. Send a disposable copy of ms. Sample copy for $7.50. Guidelines for SASE. Occasionally reviews novels, short story collections and poetry collections. Send books to editor.

Payment/Terms: Pays 2 contributor's copies on publication; additional copies for $7.50. Acquires first North American serial rights.

Advice: "Send us your best work. We would rather publish the best story by an unknown writer than a throwaway from a 'name' author. We are southern by region and sensibility but like good writing set in all manner of locale. We have a sense of humor, but please don't send the exercises in 'local color' that play to every conceivable stereotype of the region; we are fervently praying that the 'Aunt Momma at the Dairy Queen' brand of fiction will die a quick and painful death. Otherwise, we're wide open for submissions."

$ DOUBLETAKE, 55 Davis Square, Somerville MA 02144-2908. **Contact:** Fiction Editor.

Needs: "Realistic fiction in all of its variety; it's very unlikely we'd ever publish science fiction or gothic horror, for example." Buys 12 mss/year. Length: 3,000-8,000 words.

How to Contact: Send complete ms with cover letter. Accepts simultaneous submissions. Responds in 3 months to mss. Sample copy for $12. Guidelines for #10 SASE.

Payment/Terms: Pays "competitively." Pays on acceptance for first North American serial rights.

Advice: "Use a strong, developed narrative voice. Don't attempt too much or be overly melodramatic, lacking in subtlety, nuance and insight."

$ DOWNSTATE STORY, 1825 Maple Ridge, Peoria IL 61614. (309)688-1409. E-mail: ehopkins@ prairienet.org. Website: www.wiu.edu/users/mfgeh/dss (includes guidelines, names of editors, short fiction and reviews). **Contact:** Elaine Hopkins, editor. Magazine: illustrations. "Short fiction—some connection with Illinois or the Midwest." Annually. Estab. 1992. Circ. 500.

Needs: Adventure, ethnic/multicultural, experimental, historical, horror, humor/satire, literary, mainstream/contemporary, mystery/suspense, psychic/supernatural/occult, regional, romance, science fiction, westerns. No porn. Wants more political fiction. Accepts 10 mss/issue. Publishes ms up to 1 year after acceptance. Length: 300-2,000 words. Publishes short shorts. Also publishes literary essays.

How to Contact: Send complete ms with a cover letter. Responds "ASAP." SASE for return of ms. Accepts simultaneous submissions. Sample copy for $8. Guidelines for SASE.

Payment/Terms: Pays $50 maximum on acceptance for first rights.

1812, A Literary Arts Magazine, P.O. Box 1812, Amherst NY 14226-7812. E-mail: info@newwriting.c om. Website: www.newwriting.com. **Contact:** Richard Lynch, fiction editor. Magazine: Illustrations and photographs. "We want to publish work that has some *bang*." Annually. Estab. 1994.

• Work published in *1812* has been described as "experimental, surreal, bizarre."

Needs: Experimental, humor/satire, literary, mainstream/contemporary, translations. Does not want to see "stories about writers, stories about cancer, stories containing hospitals or stories that sound like they've been told before." Also publishes literary essays, literary criticism, poetry. Often comments on rejected mss.

How to Contact: Send complete ms with a cover letter. Include brief list of publications. Responds in 2 months. SASE for return of ms. Accepts simultaneous, reprint and electronic submissions. Reviews novels and short story collections.

Payment/Terms: Payment is "arranged." Acquires one-time rights.

Advice: "Our philosophy can be summed up in the following quote from Beckett: 'I speak of an art turning from it in disgust, weary of its puny exploits, weary of pretending to be able, of being able, of doing a little better the same old thing, of going a little further along a dreary road.' Too many writers copy. We want to see writing by those who aren't on the 'dreary road.' "

$ ELECTRIC WINE, A Magazine of Science Fiction, Fantasy and Horror, PMB #182, 2500 Dallas Hwy., Suite 202, Marietta GA 30064. (770)425-3006. E-mail: electricwine@netscape.net. Website: www.electricwine.com (includes science fiction, fantasy and horror, both short stories and poetry. The website also features editorials and book reviews, artwork, guidelines, special articles.) **Contact:** Diana Sharples and

James Rasmussen, co-editors. Online magazine: illustrations; photos. "We publish pro-quality science fiction, fantasy and horror-fiction and poetry—and articles such as book reviews, convention reports, historical or science essays and editorials. Readers from teen to adult. With illustrations to go along with stories, we are unique among online science fiction magazines and offer a variety of writing styles in our fiction." Bimonthly. Estab. 1999.

Needs: Fantasy (all subgenres), historical (of interest to genre readers), horror (dark fantasy, futuristic, psychological, supernatural), psychic/supernatural/occult, science fiction (all subgenres). "No media-related stories (i.e., Star Trek, Xena, etc.) and role-playing adventures." Receives 100 unsolicited mss/month. Accepts 6 mss/issue; 36 mss/year. Pays within 30 days of receipt of signed contract. Agented fiction 1%. **Publishes 50% new writers/ year.** Recently published work by Sherwood Smith, Gerald W. Page and Wendy Webb. Length: 1,000-5,000 words; average length: 4,000 words. "We publish one novella-length story (5,000-15,000 words) per issue." Publishes short shorts. Average length: 1,200 words. Also publishes literary essays, literary criticism and poetry. Often comments on rejected mss.

How to Contact: Send complete ms with a cover letter. Prefer submissions by e-mail and disk. Include estimated word count, brief bio and list of publications. Responds in 1 week to queries; 3 weeks to mss. Send a disposable copy of ms and #10 SASE for reply only. Accepts previously published work. Guidelines for SASE or by e-mail. Reviews novels, short story collections and nonfiction books of interest to writers.

Payment/Terms: Pays 1¢/word with $5 minimum. Pays on acceptance for worldwide electronic rights, first or reprint.

Advice: "We are looking for worlds, characters and creatures that carry us away into wondrous realms of fantasy, horror and science fiction. We want to be lured into new places, explore unique experiences, and be inspired by new ideas. Your job as a writer is to fulfill this task, by bringing worlds, people and plots to life. We love finding new talent and are willing to help a new author along . . . if the story has real potential. The best way to tell what kind of writing we're looking for is to read the 'zine. (What kind of research could be more fun?)"

☑ ◎ **ELYSIAN FIELDS QUARTERLY: The Baseball Review**, P.O. Box 14385, St. Paul MN 55114-0385. (651)644-8558. Fax: (651)644-8086. E-mail: info@efqreview.com. Website: www.efqreview.com (includes ordering capabilities, back issues, affiliated products, sample stories, distribution information, e-mail addresses of staff and links). **Editor:** Stephen Lehman. Magazine: 6×9; 96 pages; 60 lb. paper; gloss/varnish cover; illustrations; and photos. *Elysian Fields Quarterly* is "unique because nobody covers baseball the way that we do, with such an offbeat, irreverent manner and yet with full appreciation for the game." Quarterly. Estab. 1992. Circ. 1,035.

Needs: "Any fiction piece about baseball will be considered. We do not want to see general fiction that tries to be a baseball story by making tangential connections to baseball, but in reality is not a fiction piece about baseball." Receives 3-5 unsolicited mss/month. Accepts 2-3 mss/issue; 10-15/year. Publishes ms 3-9 months after acceptance. **Publishes 10-12 new writers/year.** Recently published work by W.P. Kinsella, Donald Dewey, Rick Wilber, Lynn Rigney Schott, William McGill and George Bowering. Word length: 2,000-3,000 words average; 1,000 words minimum; 4,000 words maximum. Does not generally publish short shorts "but we don't rule out any good writing." Length: 750. Also publishes literary essays, literary criticism and poetry. Very rarely comments on or critiques rejected ms.

How to Contact: Send complete ms with a cover letter. Accepts inquiries by e-mail. "E-mail submissions should be properly formatted or in readable attachments." Include 50 word bio. Responds in 2-3 months. Send SASE for reply, return of ms or send a disposable copy of ms. "Will occasionally consider" simultaneous and reprint submissions. Sample copy for $7.50. Guidelines free. "We review baseball books and novels of interest to our readership."

Payment/Terms: Pays 4 contributor's copies; additional copies $5.95. Acquires one-time rights and the right to reprint in any anthologies. Sponsors contest: Dave Moore Award for the "most important baseball book."

Advice: "Originality, creativity, believability—is it truly a baseball story? We do not pay attention to industry trends; we just try to publish good writing, not what is trendy."

Ⓝ ❧ ◎ **EMPLOI PLUS**, DGR Publication, 1256 Principale North St., #203, L'Annonciation, Quebec J0T 1T0 Canada. Phone/fax: (819)275-3293. **Contact:** Daniel G. Reid, fiction editor. Magazine: 7×8½; 12 pages; illustrations; photos. Bilingual (French/English) magazine publishing Canadian and American authors. Every 2 or 3 years. Estab. 1990. Circ. 500.

Needs: Serialized novel. Recently published work by Robert Biro and D.G. Reid. Also publishes poetry.

How to Contact: *Closed to unsolicited submissions.* Sample copy free.

◎ **EMRYS JOURNAL**, The Emrys Foundation, P.O. Box 8813, Greenville SC 29604. E-mail: jhn@ghs.org. **Editor:** Jeanine Halva-Neubauer. Catalog: 9×9¾; 120 pages; 80 lb. paper. "We publish short fiction, poetry, and essays. We are particularly interested in hearing from women and other minorities. We are mindful of the southeast but not limited to it." Annually. Estab. 1984. Circ. 400.

Needs: Contemporary, feminist, literary, mainstream and regional. Reading period: August 1-December 1, 2000. Accepts 18 mss/issue. Publishes mss in April. Length: 6,000 words maximum; average length: 3,500 words. Publishes short shorts. Recently published work by Colby Willis and Mary Sharratt.
How To Contact: Send complete ms with cover letter. Responds in 6 weeks. SASE. Sample copy for $15 and 7×10 SAE with 4 first-class stamps. Guidelines for #10 SASE.
Payment/Terms: Pays in contributor's copies. Acquires first rights.
Advice: Looks for "fiction by women and minorities, especially but not exclusively southeastern."

$ **EPOCH MAGAZINE**, 251 Goldwin Smith Hall, Cornell University, Ithaca NY 14853-3201. (607)255-3385. Fax: (607)255-6661. **Contact:** Michael Koch, editor. (Submissions should be sent to Michael Koch). Magazine: 6×9; 128 pages; good quality paper; good cover stock. "Top level fiction and poetry for people who are interested in good literature." Published 3 times a year. Estab. 1947. Circ. 1,000.

- Work originally appearing in this quality literary journal has appeared in numerous anthologies including *Best American Short Stories, Best American Poetry, Pushcart Prize, The O. Henry Prize Stories, Best of the West* and *New Stories from the South.*

Needs: Literary, contemporary and ethnic. No science fiction. Accepts 15-20 mss/issue. Receives 500 unsolicited fiction mss each month. Does not read in summer (April 15-September 15). **Published new writers in the last year.** Published work by Ron Hansen, Susan Choi, Robert Coover, Lily Tuck and Jhumpa Lahiri. Length: no limit. Also publishes personal essays, poetry. Critiques rejected mss when there is time. Sometimes recommends other markets.
How to Contact: Send complete ms with SASE. No simultaneous submissions. Responds in 1 month to mss. Publishes ms an average of 6 months after acceptance. Sample copy for $5.
Payment/Terms: Pays $5-10/printed page and contributor copies on publication for first North American serial rights.
Advice: "Read the journals you're sending work to."

EUREKA LITERARY MAGAZINE, 300 E. College Ave., Eureka College, Eureka IL 61530-1500. (309)467-6336. E-mail: llogsdon@eureka.edu. **Contact:** Loren Logsdon, editor. Magazine: 6×9; 100 pages; 70 lb. white offset paper; 80 lb. gloss cover; photographs (occasionally). "We seek to be open to the best stories that are submitted to us. We do not want to be narrow in a political sense of the word. Our audience is a combination of professors/writers and general readers." Semiannually. Estab. 1992. Circ. 500.
Needs: Adventure, ethnic/multicultural, experimental, fantasy (science), feminist, historical, humor/satire, literary, mainstream/contemporary, mystery/suspense (private eye/hardboiled, romantic), psychic/supernatural/occult, regional, romance (historical), science fiction (soft/sociological), translations. "We try to achieve a balance between the traditional and the experimental. We do favor the traditional, though. We look for the well-crafted story, but essentially any type of story that has depth and substance to it—any story that expands us as human beings and celebrates the mystery and miracle of the creation. Make sure you have a good beginning and ending, a strong voice, excellent use of language, good insight into the human condition, narrative skill, humor—if it is appropriate to the subject. No drug stories of any kind, stories with gratuitous violence or stories with heavy propaganda." Receives 30 unsolicited mss/month. Accepts 4 mss/issue; 8-9 mss/year. Does not read mss mainly in late summer (August). **Publishes 3-4 new writers/year.** Recently published work by Charles Edward Brooks, Frank Scozzari, Michael Smith, Ashley Thomas Memory, Regina Villiers, Dale Cramer and David Michael Slater. **Publishes 5-8 new writers/year.** Length: 7,000-8,000 words; average length: 4,500 words. Publishes short shorts. Also publishes poetry.
How to Contact: Send complete ms with a cover letter. Should include estimated word count and bio (short paragraph). Responds in 1 week to queries; 4 months to mss. Send SASE for reply, return of ms or send a disposable copy of ms. Accepts simultaneous submissions and multiple submissions. Sample copy for $7.50.
Payment/Terms: Pays free subscription to the magazine and 2 contributor's copies. Acquires first rights or one-time rights.
Advice: "Does the writer tell a good story—one that would interest a general reader? Is the story provocative? Is its subject important? Does the story contain good insight into life or the human condition? We don't want anything so abstract that it seems unrelated to anything human. We appreciate humor and effective use of language, stories that have powerful, effective endings. Take pains with the beginning and ending of the story; both must work. Be sure the voice is genuine. Be sure the manuscript is free from serious surface errors and is easy to read. We would suggest that writers should avoid sending a manuscript that appears to have made the rounds. Always send an SASE. Send one story at a time unless the stories are very short."

EVANSVILLE REVIEW, University of Evansville, 1800 Lincoln Ave., Evansville IN 47722. (812)488-1114. E-mail: evansvillereview@yahoo.com. **Contact:** Erica Schmidt, editor. Editors change every 1-2 years. Magazine: 6×9; 180 pages; 70 lb. white paper; glossy full color cover; perfect bound. Annually. Estab. 1990. Circ. 2,500.
Needs: "We're open to all creativity. No discrimination. All fiction, screenplays, nonfiction, poetry, interviews, photo essays and anything in between." No children or young adult. List of upcoming themes available for

SASE. Receives over 1,000 unsolicited mss/year. Does not read mss February-August. Agented fiction 2%. **Publishes 15 new writers/year.** Recently published work by Arthur Miller, Christopher Bigsby, Julia Kasdorf, Vivian Shipley, Dale Ray Phillips and Reginald Gibbons. Also publishes literary essays, poetry.

How to Contact: Send complete ms with a cover letter, e-mail or fax. Include 150 word or less bio and list of publications. Responds in 2 weeks to queries; 3 months to mss. Send SASE for reply, return of ms or send a disposable copy of ms. Accepts simultaneous and reprint submissions. Sample copy for $5. Guidelines free.

Payment/Terms: Pays 2 contributor's copies on publication. Acquires one-time rights. Sends galleys to author if requested. Not copyrighted.

Advice: "Because editorial staffs roll over every 1-2 years, the journal always has a new flavor."

EVENT, Douglas College, Box 2503, New Westminster, British Columbia V3L 5B2 Canada. Fax: (604)527-5095. E-mail: event@douglas.bc.ca. Website: www.douglas.bc.ca/event (includes guidelines, contest information, contents and author information, names of editors). Editor: Calvin Wharton. **Contact:** Christine Dewar, fiction editor. Assistant Editor: Bonnie Bauder. Magazine: 6×9; 144 pages; quality paper and cover stock. "Primarily a literary magazine, publishing poetry, fiction, reviews; for creative writers, artists, anyone interested in contemporary literature." Triannually. Estab. 1971. Circ. 1,000.

● Fiction originally published in *Event* has been included in *Best Canadian Stories*, and the publication was nominated for a Western Magazine Award in 2000.

Needs: Literary, contemporary, feminist, humor, regional. "No technically poor or unoriginal pieces." Receives approximately 100 unsolicited fiction mss/month. Accepts 6-8 mss/issue. **Published new writers within the last year.** Recently published work by Julie Keith, Andrew Pyper and Kenneth Harvey. Length: 5,000 words maximum. Also publishes poetry.

How to Contact: Send complete ms, bio and SAE with Canadian postage or IRC. Responds in 1-4 months to mss. Publishes ms 6-12 months after acceptance. Sample copy for $5.

Payment/Terms: Pays $22/page and 2 contributor's copies on publication for first North American serial rights.

Advice: "A good narrative arc is hard to find."

EWGPRESENTS, 406 Shady Lane, Cayce SC 29033. (803)794-8869. E-mail: EWGBet@aol.com. Website: www.webpanache.com/EWGPresents/. **Contact:** EWGBet@aol.com, fiction editor. Electronic zine. "A contemporary journal of literary quality by new and established writers. *EWGPresents* continues to provide an online forum for writers to present their works internationally, and to usher literature into the digital age."

Needs: Literary. "No pornography or excessive violence and gore beyond the legitimate needs of a story. When in doubt, leave it out." **Publishes 50-60 new writers/year.** Recently published work by Tessa Nardi, L.C. Mohr, Mary Gordon, Jeffrey L. Jackson and Vasilis Afxentiou.

How to Contact: Send queries/mss by e-mail. No attachments. Submissions should be directed to specific departments with work on the body of the e-mail. Read and adhere to guidelines provided at the zine.

Advice: "We seek well-written, professionally executed fiction, with attention to basics—grammar, punctuation, usage. Be professional. Be creative. And above all, be yourself. A writer must speak with their own voice. Let us hear your voice. We have the means to reach a universal audience by the click of a mouse. Writers are gifted with a new medium of exposure and the future demands taking advantage of this format. Without a doubt, electronic publishing will be a major factor in gaining new audiences and recognition for today's writer."

EXPLORATIONS, UAS Explorations, University of Alaska Southeast, 11120 Glacier Highway, Juneau AK 99801. Fax: (907)465-6406. E-mail: fnamp@uas.alaska.edu. **Contact:** Art Petersen, editor. Magazine: 5½×8¼; 60 pages; heavy cover stock; b&w illustrations; photos. "Poetry, prose and art—we strive for artistic excellence." Annually. Estab. 1981. Circ. 750.

Needs: Experimental, humor/satire, traditional quality fiction, poetry, and art. Receives about 1,200 mss/year. **75% of work is by new writers.** Recently published work by Charles Bukowski, William Everson, David Ray, Ania Savage and Nicchia P. Leamer.

How to Contact: *Reading/entry fee $6/story required.* Send name, address and short bio on *back* of first page of each submission. All submissions entered in contest. Submission postmark deadline is May 15. Responds in July. Mss cannot be returned. Accepts simultaneous and reprint submissions. Sample copy for $5.

Payment/Terms: Pays 2 contributor's copies. Acquires one-time rights (rights remain with the author). Also awards 7 annual prizes of $1,000 for best story or poem, $500 for best story or poem in genre other than 1st Place, and more.

Advice: "It is best to send for full guidelines with a SASE or via e-mail. Concerning poetry and prose, standard form as well as innovation are encouraged; appropriate and fresh *imagery* (allusions, metaphors, similes, symbols . . .) as well as standard or experimental form draw editorial attention. 'Language really spoken by men' and women and authentically rendered experience are encouraged. Unfortunately, requests for criticism usually cannot be met. The prizes for 2000 were awarded by Art Petersen, *Explorations* editor."

☑ ◑ ▣ **THE FAIRFIELD REVIEW**, 1 Kings Highway N., Westport CT 06880. (203)255-1199. Fax: (203)256-1970. E-mail: FairfieldReview@hpmd.com. Website: www.fairfieldreview.org. **Editors:** Edward and Janet Granger-Happ. Electronic magazine. "Our mission is to provide an outlet for poetry, short stories and essays, from both new and established writers and students, which are accessible to the general public."
Needs: Short stories, poetry, essays. Would like to see more stories "rich in lyrical imagery and those that are more humorous." **Publishes over 20 new writers/year.** Recently published work by Rowan Wolf and Kristen Huston. "We encourage students and first-time writers to submit their work."
How to Contact: Electronic submissions preferred. Fax submissions accepted.
Advice: "In addition to the submission guidelines found in each issue on our website, we recommend reading the essay *Writing Qualities to Keep in Mind* from our Editors and Authors page on the website. Keep to small, directly experienced themes; write crisply using creative, poetic images; avoid the trite expression."

◑ ◎ **FEMINIST STUDIES**, Department of Women's Studies, University of Maryland, College Park MD 20742. (301)405-7415. Fax: (301)314-9190. E-mail: femstud@umail.umd.edu. Website: www.inform.umd.edu/femstud. Editor: Claire G. Moses. **Contact:** Shirley Lim, fiction editor. Magazine: journal-sized; about 200 pages; photographs. "Scholarly manuscripts, fiction, book review essays for professors, graduate/doctoral students; scholarly interdisciplinary feminist journal." Triannually. Estab. 1974. Circ. 7,500.
Needs: Contemporary, ethnic, feminist, gay, lesbian. Receives about 15 poetry and short story mss/month. Accepts 2-3 mss/issue. "We review fiction twice a year. Deadline dates are May 1 and December 1. Authors will receive notice of the board's decision by June 30 and January 30, respectively." Published work by Bell Chevigny, Betsy Gould Gibson and Joan Jacobson. Sometimes comments on rejected mss.
How to Contact: Send complete ms with cover letter. No simultaneous submissions. Sample copy for $15. Guidelines free.
Payment/Terms: Pays 2 contributor's copies and 10 tearsheets. Sends galleys to authors.

▼ ◑ **FICTION**, % Dept. of English, City College, 138th St. & Convent Ave., New York NY 10031. (212)650-6319/650-6317. Managing Editor: Michael W. Pollock. **Contact:** Mark J. Mirsky, editor. Magazine: 6×9; 150-250 pages; illustrations; occasionally photos. "As the name implies, we publish *only* fiction; we are looking for the best new writing available, leaning toward the unconventional. *Fiction* has traditionally attempted to make accessible the unaccessible, to bring the experimental to a broader audience." Biannually. Estab. 1972. Circ. 4,500.
   ● *Fiction* ranked #48 on *Writer's Digest*'s "Fiction 50" list of top markets. Stories first published in *Fiction* have been selected for inclusion in the *Pushcart Prize* and *Best of the Small Presses* anthologies.
Needs: Contemporary, experimental, humor/satire, literary and translations. No romance, science-fiction, etc. Receives 200 unsolicited mss/month. Accepts 12-20 mss/issue; 24-40 mss/year. Does not read mss May-October. Publishes ms 1-12 months after acceptance. Agented fiction 10-20%. Published work by Harold Brodkey, Joyce Carol Oates, Peter Handke, Max Frisch, Susan Minot and Adolfo Bioy-Casares. Length: 5,000 words maximum. Publishes short shorts. Sometimes critiques rejected mss and recommends other markets.
How to Contact: Send complete ms with cover letter. Responds in approximately 3 months to mss. SASE. Accepts simultaneous submissions, but please advise. Sample copy for $5. Guidelines for SASE.
Payment/Terms: Pays in contributor's copies. Acquires first rights.
Advice: "The guiding principle of *Fiction* has always been to go to terra incognita in the writing of the imagination and to ask that modern fiction set itself serious questions, if often in absurd and comic voices, interrogating the nature of the real and the fantastic. It represents no particular school of fiction, except the innovative. Its pages have often been a harbor for writers at odds with each other. As a result of its willingness to publish the difficult, experimental, unusual, while not excluding the well known, *Fiction* has a unique reputation in the U.S. and abroad as a journal of future directions."

▼ $◑ **THE FIDDLEHEAD**, University of New Brunswick, Campus House, Box 4400, Fredericton, New Brunswick E3B 5A3 Canada. (506)453-3501. Fax: (506)453-5069. E-mail: fid@nbnet.nb.ca. Editor: Ross Leckie. **Contact:** Mark A. Jarman, fiction editor. Magazine: 6×9; 104-128 pages; ink illustrations; photos. "No criteria for publication except quality. For a general audience, including many poets and writers." Quarterly. Estab. 1945. Circ. 1,000.
Needs: Literary. No non-literary fiction. Receives 100-150 unsolicited mss/month. Buys 4-5 mss/issue; 20-40 mss/year. Publishes ms up to 1 year after acceptance. Small percent agented fiction. **Publishes 30 new writers/year.** Published work by J.A. McCormack, Madeleine Thien, Susan Fettell and Tamas Dobozy. Length: 50-3,000 words average. Publishes short shorts. Occasionally critiques rejected mss.
How to Contact: Send complete ms with cover letter. Send SASE and *Canadian* stamps or IRCs for return of mss. Accepts reprint submissions. No simultaneous submissions. Responds in 6 months. Sample copy for $7 (US). Reviews novels and short story collections—*Canadian only.*
Payment/Terms: Pays $10-12 (Canadian)/published page and 1 contributor's copy on publication for first or one-time rights.
Advice: "Write well. Less than 5% of the material received is published."

FIRST CLASS, Four-Sep Publications, P.O. Box 12434, Milwaukee WI 53212. E-mail: chriftor@execpc .com. Website: www.execpc.com/~chriftor (includes all information regarding Four-Sep Publications). **Contact:** Christopher M, editor. Magazine: 8½×11; 48-56 pages; 24 lb./60 lb. offset paper; craft cover; illustrations; photos. "*First Class* features short fiction and poetics from the cream of the small press and killer unknowns— mingling before your very hungry eyes. I publish plays, too." Triannually. Estab. 1995. Circ. 200-400.
Needs: Erotica, literary, mainstream, science fiction (soft/sociological), short story collections, post-modern. "No religious or traditional poetry, or 'boomer angst'—therapy-driven self loathing." Receives 20-30 unsolicited mss/month. Accepts 3-4 mss/issue; 10-12 mss/year. Publishes ms 2-3 months after acceptance. **Publishes 5-6 new writers/year.** Recently published work by Gerald Locklin, John Bennett and B.Z. Niditch. Length: 5,000-8,000 words; average length: 2,000-3,000 words. Publishes short shorts. Length: 500 words. Also publishes poetry. Sometimes comments on rejected mss.
How to Contact: Send complete ms with a cover letter. Accepts queries by e-mail. Include 1 page bio and SASE. Responds in 1 week to queries; 2 weeks to mss. Send SASE for reply, return of ms or send a disposable copy of ms. Accepts simultaneous submissions and reprints. Sample copy for $5. Guidelines free for #10 SASE. Reviews novels and short story collections. Send books to Christopher M.
Payment/Terms: Pays 1 contributor's copy; additional copies $4. Pays on publication for one-time rights.
Advice: "Don't bore me with puppy dogs and the morose/sappy feelings you have about death. Belt out a good, short, thought-provoking, graphic, uncommon piece."

$ ☑ ▼ FIVE POINTS: A Journal of Literature and Art, Georgia State University, University Plaza, Atlanta GA 30303-3083. (404)651-0071. Fax: (404)651-3167. E-mail: msexton@gsu.edu. Website: www.webdels ol.com/fivepoints (includes excerpts from issue, guidelines, announcements and links). Editors: Pam Durban and David Bottoms. **Contact:** Pam Durban, fiction editor. Magazine: 6×9; 200 pages; cotton paper; glossy cover; and photos. *Five Points* is "committed to publishing work that compels the imagination through the use of fresh and convincing language." Triannually. Estab. 1996. Circ. 2,000.
• *Five Points* won the CELJ award for Best New Journal.
Needs: List of upcoming themes available for SASE. Receives more than 250 unsolicited mss/month. Accepts 4 mss/issue; 15-20 mss/year. Does not read mss April 30-September 1. Publishes ms up to 6 months after acceptance. Publishes 1 new writer/year. Recently published work by Frederick Busch, Ursula Hegi and Melanie Rae Thon. Word length: 7,500 words average. Publishes short shorts. Also publishes literary essays and poetry. Sometimes comments on or critiques rejected ms.
How to Contact: Send complete ms with a cover letter. Include 3-4 line bio and list of publications. Send SASE for reply to query. No simultaneous submissions. Sample copy $5. Guidelines free.
Payment/Terms: Pays $15/page minimum; $250 maximum, free subscription to magazine and 2 contributor's copies; additional copies $3. Acquires first North American serial rights. Sends galleys to author. Sponsors contest: Paul Bowles Prize, annual award for fiction published in *Five Points*.
Advice: "We place no limitations on style or content. Our only criterion is excellence. If your writing has an original voice, substance, and significance, send it to us. We will publish distinctive, intelligent writing that has something to say and says it in a way that captures and maintains our attention."

THE FLORIDA REVIEW, Dept. of English, University of Central Florida, Orlando FL 32816. (407)823-2038. Fax: (407)823-6582. Website: pegasus.cc.ucf.edu/~english/floridareview/home.htm (includes writer's guidelines, contest information and covers and table of contents of the six most recent issues. **Contact:** Pat Rushin. Magazine: 7×10; 120 pages; semigloss full-color cover; perfect-bound. "We publish fiction of high 'literary' quality—stories that delight, instruct and aren't afraid to take risks. Our audience consists of avid readers of contemporary fiction, poetry and personal essay." Semiannually. Estab. 1972. Circ. 1,000.
Needs: Contemporary, experimental and literary. "We welcome experimental fiction, so long as it doesn't make us feel lost or stupid. We aren't especially interested in genre fiction (science fiction, romance, adventure, etc.), though a good story can transcend any genre." Receives 200 mss/month. Accepts 4-6 mss/issue; 8-12 mss/year. Publishes ms within 3-6 months of acceptance. **Publishes 2-4 new writers/year.** Recently published work by Richard Wirick, Daniel Ort and Debbie Lee Wesselmann. Also publishes literary criticism, poetry and essays.
How to Contact: Send complete ms with cover letter. Responds in 4 months. SASE required. Accepts simultaneous submissions. Sample copy for $6. Guidelines for SASE. Reviews novels and short story collections.
Payment/Terms: Pays in contributor's copies. Small honorarium occasionally available. "Copyright held by U.C.F.; reverts to author after publication. (In cases of reprints, we ask that a credit line indicate that the work first appeared in the *F.R.*)"
Tips: "We're looking for writers with a fresh voice, engaging situations and are not afraid to take risks. Read contemporary writers/literary magazines."

N: FLYWAY, A Literary Review, Iowa State University, 206 Ross Hall, Ames IA 50011. (515)294-8273. Fax: (515)294-6814. E-mail: flyway@iastate.edu. Website: www.engl.istate.edu/main/flyway/flyway.html. **Contact:**

Stephen Pett, editor. Literary magazine: 8½×11; 64 pages; quality paper; cover stock; some illustrations; photos. "We publish quality fiction. Our stories are accompanied by brief commentaries by their authors. The sort of thing a writer might say introducing a piece at a reading." Triannual. Estab. 1995. Circ. 500.

Needs: Literary. Receives 50 unsolicited mss/month. Accepts 2-5 mss/issue; 10-12 mss/year. Published 5 months after acceptance. **Publishes 7-10 new writers/year.** Recently published work by Duane Miatum, Christina D. Allen-Yazzie, Jacob Appel. Length: 5,000 words; average length: 3,500 words. Publishes short shorts; average length: 500 words. Often comments on rejected mss.

How to Contact: Send complete ms with cover letter. Send SASE. Sample copy for $8. Guidelines for SASE.

Payment/Terms: Pays 1 contributor's copy; additional copies $6. Pays on publication for one-time rights.

Advice: "Quality, originality, voice, drama tension. Make it as strong as you can."

⬛ **FOLIO: A LITERARY JOURNAL**, Department of Literature, Washington DC 20016. (202)885-2990. Editor changes yearly. **Contact:** Editor. Magazine: 6×9; 64 pages. "Fiction is published if it is well written. We look for fresh language, engaging plot and character development." Semiannually. Estab. 1984.

Needs: Contemporary, literary, mainstream, prose poem, translations, essay, b&w art or photography. No pornography. Occasional theme-based issues. See guidelines for info. Receives 150 unsolicited mss/month. Accepts 3-5 mss/issue; 6-40 mss/year. Does not read mss during April-August. **Publishes new writers.** Published work by Henry Taylor, Kermit Moyer, Linda Pastan. Length: 4,500 words maximum; average length: 2,500 words. Publishes short shorts. Occasionally critiques rejected mss.

How to Contact: Send complete ms with cover letter. Include a brief bio. Responds in 2 months. SASE. Accepts simultaneous and reprint submissions (if noted). Sample copy for $5. Guidelines for #10 SASE.

Payment/Terms: Pays in contributor's copies. Acquires first North American rights. "$100 award for best fiction, poetry and art. Query for guidelines."

N: ⊕ $ FRANK, An International Journal of Contemporary Writing and Art, 32 rue Edouard Vaillant, 93100 Montreuil, France. **Editor:** David Applefield. "Semiannual journal edited and published in Paris in English." Circ. 3,000. Publishes 20 stories/issue. "At *Frank*, we publish fiction, poetry, literary and art interviews, and translations. We like work that falls between existing genres and has social or political consciousness." Send IRC or $5 cash. Must be previously unpublished in English (world). Pays 2 copies and $10 (US)/printed page. "Send your most daring and original work. At *Frank*, we like work that is not too parochial or insular, however, don't try to write for a 'French' market." Sample copy $10 (US/air mail included), $38 for 4 issues; guidelines available upon request. Subscriptions, inquiries, and an online edition of *Frank* available at www.paris-anglo.com/frank.

⬛ **FRONTIERS: A Journal of Women Studies**, Washington State University, Frontiers, Women's Studies, Box 644007, Pullman WA 99164-4007. E-mail: frontier@wsu.edu. **Contact:** Fiction Editor. Magazine: 6×9; 200 pages; photos. "Women studies; academic articles in all disciplines; criticism; exceptional creative work (art, short fiction, photography, poetry)."

Needs: Feminist, multicultural, lesbian. "We want to see fiction that deals with women's lives and experience from a feminist perspective." Receives 15 unsolicited mss/month. Accepts 7-12 mss/issue. Publishes ms 6-12 months after acceptance. **Publishes 2 new writers/year.** Recently published work by Elizabeth Bell, Nadine Chapman, Tricia Currans-Sheehan and Alethea Eason.

How to Contact: Send 3 copies of complete ms with cover letter. Responds in 1 month to queries; up to 6 months to mss. SASE. Writer's guidelines for #10 SASE. Sample copy for $15.

Payment/Terms: Pays 2 contributor's copies. Acquires first North American serial rights.

Advice: "We are a *feminist* journal. *Frontiers* aims to make scholarship in women studies, and *exceptional* creative work, accessible to a cross-disciplinary audience inside and outside academia. Read short fiction in *Frontiers* before submitting."

$⬜ **FUGUE, Literary Digest of the University of Idaho**, English Dept., Rm. 200, Brink Hall, University of Idaho, Moscow ID 83844-1102. (208)885-6156. Fax: (208)885-5944. E-mail: witt931@novell.uidaho.edu. Website: www.uidaho.edu/LS/Eng/Fugue (includes writer's guidelines, names of editors, short fiction). **Contact:** Ryan Witt, managing editor. Editors change frequently. Send to Executive Editor. Magazine: 6×9; 60-100 pages; 20 lb. stock paper. "We are interested in all classifications of fiction—we are not interested in pretentious 'literary' stylizations. We expect stories to be written in a manner engaging for anyone, not just academics and literati. If we could put together an 'ideal' issue, we would probably have 6 or 7 pieces of fiction, each of which would run no more than 10 pages (printed—probably 15 or 16 manuscript pages), a modest essay, and maybe 10 or a dozen poems. The fiction would include a couple of solid 'mainstream/literary' stories, at least one 'regional/local' story (preferably by a writer from the inland Northwest), at least one story by an ethnic writer (Chicano, Native American, Asian-American, African-American), at least one story that had some sort of international or cosmopolitan angle (set, perhaps, in Hong Kong or Quito and written by someone who really knew what he or she was doing), and at least one story that would be 'experimental' (including postmodernism, fantasy, surrealism . . .). Wit and humor are always welcome." Semiannually. Estab. 1990. Circ. 300.

Needs: Adventure, ethnic/multicultural, experimental, fantasy, historical, humor/satire, literary, mainstream/contemporary, regional. "We're looking for good ethnic fiction by ethnic writers; work with a cosmopolitan/international flavor from writers who know what they're doing; and intelligent and sophisticated mainstream and postmodern work." Does not want to see Dungeons & Dragons, Sword & Sorcery, Harlequin, "Cowboy Adventure Stories," True Confessions, etc. No genre fiction. Receives 80 unsolicited mss/month. Accepts 4-8 mss/issue; 8-16 mss/year. Publishes ms 1 year after acceptance. **Publishes 6-7 new writers/year.** Recently published work by Ed McClanahan, Sophia Dembling, Jacob M. Appel and Denise Haver. Length: 50-6,000 words; average length: 3,000 words. Publishes short shorts. Also publishes literary essays and poetry. Sometimes comments on rejected mss.

How to Contact: Send complete ms with cover letter. "Obtain guidelines first." Include estimated word count and list of publications. Report in 2 weeks to queries; 2-3 months to mss. SASE for a reply to a query or return of ms. No simultaneous submissions. Sample copy for $5. Guidelines for #10 SASE.

Payment/Terms: Pays $10-20 on publication for first North American serial rights. All contributors receive a copy; extra copies available at a discount.

Advice: Looks for "competent writing, clarity and consideration for the reader; also stylistic flair/energy. Here are what we consider the characteristics of a 'good' story: distinct voice; the quality of strangeness; engaging, dynamic characters; engaging language, style, craftsmanship; emotional resonance ('snap'); and an un-put-down-ability. Be original and inventive. Take chances, but present your work as a professional. Proper manuscript format is essential."

N **$** **FUTURES MAGAZINE, for Writers and Artists**, 3039 38th Ave. S, Minneapolis MN 55406-2140. (612)724-4023. E-mail: barbl@tela.com. Website: www.firetowrite.com (includes excerpts, writer's guidelines, names of editors, interviews with authors, fiction, contests, cover art, color posters and greeting cards for writers for sale). **Contact:** Brian Lawrence or Babs Lackey. Magazine: 8½×11; 75 pages; illustrations; photos. "We are multi-genre as well as literary—we offer inspiration and guidance and we're fun! We help writers—entering and nominating for Edgars, Derringer Award, Pushcart Prize, New Century Award and more." Bimonthly. Estab. 1998. Circ. 2,000.

Needs: Comics/graphic novels, ethnic/multicultural, experimental, feminist, gay, glitz, horror, humor satire, lesbian, literary, mainstream, mystery/suspense (amateur sleuth, cozy, police procedural, private eye/hardboiled), psychic/supernatural/occult, romance, science fiction, thriller/espionage, western, young adult/teen. No erotica. List of upcoming themes available for SASE. Receives 80 unsolicited mss/month. Accepts 20-25 mss/issue; 150 mss/year. Publishes ms 6-12 months after acceptance. **Publishes at least 30% new writers/year.** Recently published work by Earl Staggs, Kris Neri, Michael Mallory and RC Hildebrandt (Pushcart winner). Length: 6,000 words maximum; average length: 2,500 words. Publishes short shorts. Average length: 300-1,000 words. Also publishes literary essays, literary criticism and poetry. Sometimes comments on rejected mss.

How to Contact: Send complete ms with a cover letter. Accepts submissions by e-mail. Include estimated word count and brief bio. Responds in 1 week to queries; 2 weeks to mss. Send SASE (or IRC) for return of ms or send a disposable copy of ms and #10 SASE for reply only. Accepts simultaneous submissions. Sample copy for $3.95. Guidelines for SASE or by e-mail.

Payment/Terms: Pays $10-25 plus many awards (2 publishers choices in each issue receive additional fee and award); additional copies $4. Acquires first rights. Sponsors contests. Visit website for details.

Advice: "Never give up! Don't let rejections get you down. Keep writing and vow to improve your craft daily!"

✓ **GARGOYLE**, % Atticus Books, 2308 Mt. Vernon Ave., Alexandria VA 22301. (703)548-7580. Website: www.atticusbooks.com. **Contact:** Richard Peabody and Lucinda Ebersole, editors. Literary magazine: 6×9; 350 pages; illustrations; photos. "*Gargoyle* is a literary magazine for poets and writers who actually read and care about what their peers are writing." Annually. Estab. 1976. Circ. 3,000.

Needs: Erotica, ethnic/multicultural, experimental, gay, lesbian, literary, mainstream/contemporary, translations, "good short stories with sports and music backgrounds." No romance, horror, science fiction. Receives 50-200 unsolicited mss/month. Accepts 15 mss/issue. Reads in summer (June, July, August). Publishes ms 6-12 months after acceptance. Agented fiction 5%. **Publishes 5-6 new writers/year.** Recently published work by Kim Addonizio, Mary Caponegro, Billy Childish, Helen Schulman and Curtis White. Length: 30 pages maximum; average length: 5-10 pages. Publishes short shorts. Length: 2-3 pages. Also publishes literary essays, criticism and poetry. Sometimes comments on rejected ms.

How to Contact: Send complete ms. Responds in 2 weeks to queries; 3 months to mss. Send SASE for reply, return of ms or send a disposable copy of ms. Accepts simultaneous submissions. Sample copy for $12.

Payment/Terms: Pays 1 contributor's copy; additional copies for ½ price. Acquires first rights, first North American rights or first British rights. Sends prepublication galleys to author.

Advice: "Read a copy. Our favorite living writers are Paul Bowles and Jeanette Winterson. That should give you a clue. We are, as far as I can tell, one of the few magazines that likes both realism and experimental work. Both poles are welcome."

$ **GEIST, The Canadian Magazine of Ideas and Culture**, The Geist Foundation, 103-1014 Homer St., Vancouver, British Columbia V6B 2W9 Canada. (604)681-9161. Fax: (604)669-8250. E-mail: geist@ geist.com. Website: www.geist.com (includes guidelines, names of editors, short fiction, issue previews). Editor: Barbara Zatyko. **Contact:** Fiction Editor. Magazine: 8 × 10½; illustrations; photos. "*Geist Magazine* is particularly interested in writing that blurs the boundary between fiction and nonfiction. Each issue and most of the writing in *Geist* explores the physical and mental landscape of Canada." Quarterly. Estab. 1990. Circ. 5,000.
- *Geist* was nominated for best regular column and best magazine of the year at the Western Magazine Awards.

Needs: Condensed/excerpted novel, literary. "Rarely publish works in passive voice." Receives 25 unsolicited mss/month. Accepts 10 mss/issue; 40 mss/year. Publishes ms 2-12 weeks after acceptance. **Publishes 20 new writers/year.** Recently published work by Myrna Kostash, Alberto Manguel and Ann Diamond. Length: 200-5,000 words. Publishes short shorts.

How to Contact: Send complete ms with a cover letter. Accepts queries by e-mail. Prefer snail mail. Include estimated word count and 1-2 line bio. Responds in 1 week to queries; 2 months to mss. Send SASE for reply, return of ms or send a disposable copy of ms. Accepts reprint submissions. Guidelines for SASE. Reviews novels and short story collections. Send books to Shannon Emmerson.

Payment/Terms: Pays $50-250 on publication and 8 contributor's copies; additional copies for $2. Acquires first rights. Send a SASE requesting contest guidelines.

Advice: "Each issue of Geist is a meditation on the imaginary country that we inhabit. Often that imaginary country has something to do with some part of Canada. A sense of Canadian place is central to the work we publish. Recommended reading: George Orwell's essay "Politics and the English Language"; back issues of *Geist*; and *Granta*."

$ **GEORGE & MERTIE'S PLACE: ROOMS WITH A VIEW**, P.O. Box 10335, Spokane WA 99209-1335. (509)325-3738. E-mail: geomert@icehouse.net. **Contact:** George Thomas and Mertie Duncan, editors. Microzine: 8½ × 11; 4-8 pages; heavy stock, colored paper; illustrations. "We want well-written fiction and poetry, political and philosophical debate, humor, satire and jeremiad. Our audience is literate Americans who like to read and to think. They enjoy the use of language." Monthly. Estab. 1995. Circ. 60.

Needs: Anything well written. Receives 20-30 unsolicited mss/month. Accepts 1-2 mss/issue; 10-15 mss/year. "We work 3 months ahead." Published work by Sybil Smith, Jeff Grimshaw and Robert Walter. Length: 1-2,500 words; average length: 1,000 words. Publishes short shorts. Also publishes humor and poetry. Comments on rejected mss.

How to Contact: Send complete ms with a cover letter. Include word count and a very brief bio. Responds in 2 months. Send SASE for reply, return of ms or send a disposable copy of ms. No simultaneous submissions. Sample copy for $2 and SASE. Also may purchase samples through infopost.com. Guidelines for SASE.

Payment/Terms: Pays 1¢/word, at publication and 1 contributor's copy; additional copies for $1.50. Acquires first North American serial rights and republication in GMP anthology. Not copyrighted. Each issue has a $25 "favorite of issue" prize and GMP awards a $100 prize for favorite of the year (at end of each publication year) which will be decided by someone other than the editors.

Advice: "We look for style in the work and an interesting narrative persona. *GMP*'s editors enjoy Kerouac, Kafka, Carver, Austen, Yeats, Genet, Miller, Frost, Carlyle, Stafford, Nin, Steinbeck, Fellini, Chaucer, Mishima, Hanshan, Kubric, Lapham, all those Russians, and many more (even Pope and Swift)! Old dogs with new tricks, our goal is to create a short, scruffy, entertaining, sometimes querulous monthly bark with a bite that does tricks but won't roll over."

$ **THE GEORGIA REVIEW**, The University of Georgia, Athens GA 30602-9009. (706)542-3481. Fax: (706)542-0047. E-mail: bkeen@arches.uga.edu. Website: www.uga.edu/~garev (includes writer's guidelines, names of editors, order/subscription info, guestbook, current issue contents and more). Acting Editor: Stephen Corey. **Contact:** William Trowbridge and Jonathan David Ingle, assistant editors. Journal: 7 × 10; 208 pages (average); 50 lb. woven old-style paper; 80 lb. cover stock; illustrations; photos. "*The Georgia Review* is a journal of arts and letters, featuring a blend of the best in contemporary thought and literature—essays, fiction, poetry, visual art and book reviews for the intelligent nonspecialist as well as the specialist reader. We seek material that appeals across disciplinary lines by drawing from a wide range of interests." Quarterly. Estab. 1947. Circ. 6,000.
- *The Georgia Review* was a finalist for the National Magazine Award in Fiction in 2000.

Needs: Experimental and literary. "We're looking for the highest quality fiction—work that is capable of sustaining subsequent readings, not throw-away pulp magazine entertainment. Nothing that fits too easily into a 'category.' " Receives about 300 unsolicited fiction mss/month. Accepts 3-4 mss/issue; 12-15 mss/year. Does not read unsolicited mss May 15-August 15. Would prefer *not* to see novel excerpts. **Published new writers within the last year.** Published work by Eudora Welthy, Barry Lopez, Kevin Brockmeier and Teresa S. Mathes. Length: Open. Also publishes literary essays, literary criticism, poetry. Occasionally critiques rejected mss.

How to Contact: Send complete ms (one story) with SASE. No multiple submissions. Usually responds in 3 months. Sample copy for $6; guidelines for #10 SASE. Reviews short story collections.

Payment/Terms: Pays minimum $40/printed page on publication for first North American serial rights, 1 year complimentary subscription and 1 contributor's copy; reduced charge for additional copies. Sends galleys to author.

GERTRUDE: A Journal of Voice & Vision, P.O. Box 270814, Ft. Collins CO 80527-0814. (970)491-5957. E-mail: ErickD@FRII.com. **Editor:** Eric Delehoy. Magazine: 5×8½, 36-48 pages; 60 lb. paper; glossy card cover; illustrations; photos. *Gertrude* is a "biannual publication featuring the voices and visions of the gay, lesbian, bisexual, transgender and supportive community." Estab. 1999. Circ. 550.

Needs: Ethnic/multicultural, feminist, gay, humor satire, lesbian, literary, mainstream. No erotica, pornography or science fiction. Wants more humorous and multicultural fiction. Receives 3-5 unsolicited mss/month. Accepts 2-3 mss/issue; 4-6 mss/year. Publishes ms 1-2 months after acceptance. **Publishes 4-5 new writers/year.** Recently published work by Christopher Thomas, Demrie Alonzo, Noah Tysick and Christine McGuire. Word length: 1,500 words average; 200 words minimum; 2,500 words maximum. Publishes short shorts. Length: 250 words. Also publishes poetry. Often comments on or critiques rejected ms.

How to Contact: Send complete ms with a cover letter. Include estimated word count, 1 paragraph bio and list of publications. Responds in 4 months to mss. Send SASE for reply to query and a disposable copy of ms. No simultaneous submissions. Accepts multiple submissions (no more than three) and reprint submissions. Sample copy for $4.95, 6×9 SAE and 3 1st class stamps. Guidelines for #10 SASE.

Payment/Terms: Pays 1-2 contributor's copies; additional copies $3.95. Payment on publication. Author retains rights upon publication. Not copyrighted. Sponsors contest: "The Gerty," editors choice award. All accepted work is automatically considered.

Advice: "We look for strong characters, vivid detail and believable dialogue. Show us through words—don't tell us. We look for work that conveys the strength of the human spirit whether seriously or comically. Spell check and have someone else read your work. Just because we might not accept your work doesn't mean it is poorly written. Much has to do with editorial tastes. We tend to be eclectic. We are concerned with the quality of work and what it has to say to our readers."

THE GETTYSBURG REVIEW, Gettysburg College, Gettysburg PA 17325. (717)337-6770. Fax: (717)337-6775. Website: www.gettysburgreview.com (includes writer's guidelines, staff biographies and excerpts from the most recent issues). Editor: Peter Stitt. **Contact:** Mark Drew, assistant editor. Magazine: 6¾×10; 170 pages; acid free paper; full color illustrations. "Quality of writing is our only criterion; we publish fiction, poetry, and essays." Quarterly. Estab. 1988. Circ. 4,500.

• Work appearing in *The Gettysburg Review* has also been included in *Prize Stories: The O. Henry Awards*, the *Pushcart Prize* anthology, *Best American Fiction, Best American Poetry, New Stories from the South*, *Harper's* and elsewhere. It is also the recipient of a Lila Wallace-Reader's Digest grant and NEA grants.

Needs: Contemporary, experimental, historical, humor/satire, literary, mainstream, regional and serialized novel. No fantasy, horror or romance. "We require that fiction be intelligent, and aesthetically written." Receives 350 mss/month. Accepts 4-6 mss/issue; 16-24 mss/year. Publishes ms within 1 year of acceptance. **Publishes 1-5 new writers/year.** Published work by Robert Olen Butler, Joyce Carol Oates, Naeem Murr, Tom Perrotta, Alison Baker and Peter Baida. Length: 1,000-20,000 words; average length: 3,000 words. Occasionally publishes short shorts. Also publishes literary essays, some literary criticism, poetry. Sometimes critiques rejected mss.

How to Contact: Send complete ms with cover letter September through May. Responds in up to 6 months. SASE. No simultaneous submissions. Sample copy for $7 (postage paid). Does not review books per se. "We do essay-reviews, treating several books around a central theme." Send review copies to editor.

Payment/Terms: Pays $25/printed page, subscription to magazine and contributor's copy on publication for first North American serial rights. Charge for extra copies.

Advice: "Reporting time can take more than three months. It is helpful to look at a sample copy of *The Gettysburg Review* to see what kinds of fiction we publish before submitting."

GINOSKO, between literary vision and spiritual realities, P.O. Box 246, Fairfax CA 94978. (415)460-8436. E-mail: RobertPaulCesaretti@hotmail.com. **Contact:** Robert Cesaretti, editor. Magazine: 4×6; 50-60 pages; standard paper; card cover; illustrations; photos. Published "when material permits."

Needs: Experimental, literary, stylized; "consider 'Pagan Night' by Kate Braverman, 'Driving the Heart' by Jason Brown, 'Customs of the Country' by Madison Smartt Bell." Does not want conventional work. Wants more work like Kate Braverman. Receives 15-20 unsolicited mss/month. Length: 500-15,000.

How to Contact: Send complete ms with a cover letter. Responds in 3 months to mss. SASE for return of ms. Accepts simultaneous and reprint submissions.

Payment/Terms: Pays 1 contributor's copy. Acquires one-time rights.

Advice: "I am looking for a style that conveys spiritual hunger and depth yet avoids religiosity and convention— *Between literary vision and spiritual realities.*"

$ ☑ ⊻ GLIMMER TRAIN STORIES, Glimmer Train Press, 710 SW Madison St., Suite 504, Portland OR 97205. (503)221-0836. E-mail: linda@glimmertrain.com. Website: www.glimmertrain.com (includes writer's guidelines, story excerpts and a Q&A section for writers). **Editors:** Susan Burmeister-Brown and Linda Burmeister Davies. Magazine: 6¾×9¼; 160 pages; recycled, acid-free paper; 20 illustrations; 12 photographs. Quarterly. Estab. 1991. Circ. 21,000.
  ● *Glimmer Train* was ranked #4 on *Writer's Digest's* "Fiction 50" list of top markets for fiction writers. The magazine also sponsors an annual short story contest for new writers and a very short fiction contest.
Needs: Literary. Receives 3,000 unsolicited mss/month. Accepts 10 mss/issue; 40 mss/year. Reads in January, April, July, October. Publishes ms 6-12 months after acceptance. Agented fiction 20%. **Publishes "about 8" new writers/year.** Recently published work by Judy Budnitz, Brian Champeau, Ellen Cooney, Andre Dubus III, Thomas Kennedy, Chris Offutt, Alberto Rios and Monica Wood. Length: 1,200-12,000 words.
How to Contact: Send complete ms with a cover letter. Include estimated word count. Responds in 3 months. Send SASE for return or send a disposable copy of ms (with stamped postcard or envelope for notification). Accepts simultaneous submissions. Sample copy for $10. Guidelines for #10 SASE.
Payment/Terms: Pays $500 and 10 contributor's copies on acceptance for first rights.
Advice: "If you're excited about a story you've written, send it to us! If you're not very excited about it, wait and send one that you are excited about. When a story stays with us after the first reading, it gets another reading. Those stories that simply don't let us set them aside, get published. Read good fiction. It will often improve the quality of your own writing."

⊠ $ ☑ ⊻ GRAIN, Saskatchewan Writers' Guild, Box 1154, Regina, Saskatchewan S4P 3B4 Canada. (306)244-2828. Fax: (306)244-0255. E-mail: grain.mag@sk.sympatico.ca. Website: www.skwriter.com (includes history, news, subscription and contest information). Editor: Elizabeth Philips. **Contact:** Dianne Warren, fiction editor. Literary magazine: 6×9; 128 pages; Chinook offset printing; chrome-coated stock; some photos. "Fiction and poetry for people who enjoy high quality writing." Quarterly. Estab. 1973. Circ. 1,300.
  ● *Grain* won magazine of the year-Saskatchewan at the Western Magazine awards and was ranked #42 on *Writer's Digest*'s Fiction 50 list of top markets for fiction writers.
Needs: Contemporary, experimental, literary, mainstream and prose poem. Want to see more magic realism. "No propaganda—only artistic/literary writing." No genre fiction. No mss "that stay *within* the limits of conventions such as women's magazine type stories, science fiction; none that push a message." Receives 80 unsolicited fiction mss/month. Accepts 8-12 mss/issue; 32-48 mss/year. Recently published work by Douglas Glover, Cyril Dabydeen, Lewis Horne and Anita Shir-Jacob. Length: "No more than 30 pages." Also publishes poetry and creative nonfiction. Occasionally critiques rejected mss.
How to Contact: Send complete ms with SASE (or IRC) and brief letter. Accepts queries by e-mail or fax. No simultaneous submissions. Responds within 4 months to mss. Publishes ms an average of 4 months after acceptance. Sample copy for $7.95 plus postage.
Payment/Terms: Pays $40/page up to $175 and 2 contributor's copies on publication for first Canadian serial rights. "We expect acknowledgment if the piece is republished elsewhere."
Advice: "Submit a story to us that will deepen the imaginative experience of our readers. *Grain* has established itself as a first-class magazine of serious fiction. We receive submissions from around the world. If Canada is a foreign country to you, we ask that you *do not* use U.S. postage stamps on your return envelope. If you live outside Canada and neglect the International Reply Coupons, we *will not* read or reply to your submission. We look for attention to detail, credibility, lucid use of language and metaphor and a confident, convincing voice. Sweat the small stuff. Make sure you have researched your piece, that the literal and metaphorical support one another."

Ⓝ $ ☑ ⊻ ▢ GRAND STREET, 214 Sullivan St., Suite 6C, New York NY 10012. (212)533-2944. Fax (212)533-2737. Website: www.grandstreet.com. Editor: Jean Stein. **Contact:** Benjamin Anastas, associate editor. Magazine: 7¾×9½; 240-270 pages; illustrations; art portfolios. "We publish new fiction and nonfiction of all types." Quarterly. Estab. 1981. Circ. 7,000.
  ● Work published in *Grand Street* has been included in the *Best American Short Stories*.
Needs: Poetry, essays, translations. Agented fiction 90%. Published work by Durs Grunbëin, José Saramago, Ozren Kebo, Jorge Luis Borgers and Mike Davis. Length: 9,000 words maximum; average length: 4,000 words.
How to Contact: *Not accepting unsolicited fiction mss.* Sample copy for $15; $18 overseas and Canada.
Payment/Terms: Pays $250-1,000 and 2 contributor's copies on publication for first North American serial rights. Sends galleys to author.

⊕ $ ☑ GRANTA, The Magazine of New Writing, 2-3 Hanover Yard, Noel Rd., London N1 8BE England. Phone: 0701 704 9776. Fax: 0701 704 0474. E-mail: editorial@grantamag.co.uk. **Contact:** Ian Jack, editor. Magazine: paperback, 270 pages approx.; photos. "*Granta* magazine publishes fiction, reportage, biography and autobiography, history, travel and documentary photography. It rarely publishes 'writing about writing.' The realistic narrative—the story—is its primary form." *Granta* has been called "the most impressive literary magazine of its time" by *The London Daily Telegraph*, and has published Salman Rushdie, Martin Amis, Saul Bellow and Paul Theroux, among others. Quarterly. Estab. 1979. Circ. 90,000.

Needs: Literary. "No fantasy, science fiction, romance, historical, occult or other 'genre' fiction." Themes decided as deadline approaches. Receives 100 unsolicited mss/month. Accepts 0-1 ms/issue; 1-2 mss/year. Percentage of agented fiction varies. **Publishes 1-2 new writers/year.** Length: open.

How to Contact: Query first. *No e-mail submissions.* Responds in 1 month to queries; 3 months to mss. Send SAE and IRCs for reply, return of ms or send a disposable copy of ms. Accepts simultaneous submissions. Sample copy £7.99.

Payment/Terms: Pays £75-5,000 and 3 contributor's copies. Acquires variable rights. Pays on publication. Sends galleys to author.

Advice: "We are looking for the best in realistic stories; originality of voice; without jargon, connivance or self-conscious 'performance'—writing that endures."

GRASSLANDS REVIEW, P.O. Box 626, Berea OH 44017. (440)243-4842. E-mail: glreview@aol.com. Website: hometown.aol.com/glreview/prof/index.htm (includes guidelines, contest information, sample text, table of contents for latest issue). Editor: Laura B. Kennelly. **Contact:** Fiction Editor. Magazine: 6×9; 80 pages. *Grasslands Review* prints creative writing of all types; poetry, fiction, essays for a general audience. "Designed as a place for new writers to publish." Semiannually. Estab. 1989. Circ. 300.

Needs: Contemporary, ethnic, experimental, fantasy, horror, humor/satire, literary, prose poem, regional, science fiction and western. Nothing pornographic or overtly political or religious. Accepts 1-3 mss/issue. Reads only in October and March. Publishes ms 6 months after acceptance. **Publishes 15 new writers/year.** Recently published work by Matthew Pitt and Edward Brooks. Length: 100-3,500 words; average length: 1,500 words. Publishes short shorts (100-150 words). Also publishes poetry. Sometimes critiques rejected mss and recommends other markets.

How to Contact: Send complete ms in October or March *only* with cover letter. No simultaneous submissions. Responds in 3 months to mss. SASE. Sample copy for $4.

Payment/Terms: Pays in contributor's copies. Acquires one-time rights. Publication not copyrighted.

Advice: "A fresh approach, imagined by a reader for other readers, pleases our audience. We are looking for fiction which leaves a strong feeling or impression—or a new perspective on life. The *Review* began as an in-class exercise to allow experienced creative writing students to learn how a little magazine is produced. It now serves as an independent publication, attracting authors from as far away as the Ivory Coast, but its primary mission is to give unknown writers a start."

THE GREEN HILLS LITERARY LANTERN, Published by North Central Missouri College and co-published by The North Central Missouri Writer's Guild, P.O. Box 375, Trenton MO 64683. (660)359-3948, ext. 324. Fax: (660)359-3202. E-mail: jsmith@mail.ncmc.cc.mo.us. Website: www.ncmc.cc.mo.us. (includes writer's guidelines, excerpts from current issue, subscription information). Editor: Jack Smith. **Contact:** Sara King, fiction editor. Magazine: 6×9; 200 pages; good quality paper with glossy 4-color cover. "The mission of *GHLL* is to provide a literary market for quality fiction writers, both established and beginners, and to provide quality literature for readers from diverse backgrounds. We also see ourselves as a cultural resource for North Central Missouri. Our publication works to publish the highest quality fiction—dense, layered, subtle, and, at the same time, fiction which grabs the ordinary reader. We tend to publish traditional short stories, but we are open to experimental forms." Annually. Estab. 1990. Circ. 500.

• *The Green Hills Literary Lantern* received a Missouri Arts Council grant in 2000.

Needs: Ethnic/multicultural, experimental, feminist, humor/satire, literary, mainstream/contemporary and regional. "Fairly traditional short stories but we are open to experimental. Our main requirement is literary merit. Wants more quality fiction about rural culture." No adventure, crime, erotica, horror, inspirational, mystery/suspense, romance. Receives 30 unsolicited mss/month. Accepts 7-10 mss/issue. Publishes ms 6-12 months after acceptance. Recently published work by J. Morris, Dennis Vannatta, Karl Harshbarger, and Robert Garner McBrearty. Publishes 0-1 new writer/year. Length: 7,000 words maximum; average length: 3,000 words. Publishes short shorts. Also publishes poetry. Sometimes comments on rejected mss.

How to Contact: Send complete ms with a cover letter. Include bio (50-100 words) with list of publications. Accepts queries (only) by e-mail. Responds in 4 months to mss. SASE for return of ms. Accepts simultaneous submissions and multiple submissions (2-3). Sample copy for $7 (includes envelope and postage).

Payment/Terms: Pays two contributor's copies. Acquires one-time rights. Sends galleys to author.

Advice: "We look for strong character development, substantive plot and theme, visual and forceful language within a multilayered story. Make sure your work has the flavor of life—a sense of reality. A good story, well-crafted, will eventually get published. Find the right market for it, and above all, don't give up."

$ ⊘ GREEN MOUNTAINS REVIEW, Johnson State College, Box A-58, Johnson VT 05656. (802)635-1350. Editor-in-Chief: Neil Shepard. **Contact:** Tony Whedon, fiction editor. Magazine: digest-sized; 160-200 pages. Semiannual. Estab. 1975 (new series, 1987). Circ. 1,700.

• *Green Mountains Review* has received a Pushcart Prize and Editors Choice Award.

Needs: Adventure, contemporary, experimental, humor/satire, literary, mainstream, serialized/excerpted novel, translations. Receives 80 unsolicited mss/month. Accepts 6 mss/issue; 12 mss/year. Publishes ms 6-12 months after acceptance. Reads mss September 1 through March 1. **Publishes 0-4 new writers/year.** Recently published work by Howard Norman, Debra Spark, Valerie Miner and Peter LaSalle. Length: 25 pages maximum. Publishes short shorts. Also publishes literary criticism, poetry. Sometimes critiques rejected mss.

How to Contact: Send complete ms with cover letter. "Manuscripts will not be read and will be returned between March 1 and September 1." Responds in 1 month to queries; 6 months to mss. SASE. Accepts simultaneous submissions (if advised). Sample copy for $5.

Payment/Terms: Pays contributor's copies, 1-year subscription and small honorarium, depending on grants. Acquires first North American serial rights. Rights revert to author upon request. Sends galleys to author upon request.

Advice: "We're looking for more rich, textured, original fiction with cross-cultural themes. The editors are open to a wide spectrum of styles and subject matter as is apparent from a look at the list of fiction writers who have published in its pages. One issue was devoted to Vermont fiction, and another issue filled with new writing from the People's Republic of China, and a recent issue devoted to literary ethnography."

⊘ ◎ ▣ THE GREEN TRICYCLE: "The fun-to-read lit mag!" Cayuse Press, P.O. Box 66003, Burien WA 98166-0003. E-mail: editor@greentricycle.com. Website: http://greentricycle.com ("The website offers everything writers need for publication in the *Green Tricycle*. You'll find guidelines, themes, deadlines, current and archived issues, tools and tips for writers, freebies, and access to the five forums open to all writers.") **Contact:** B. Benepe, editor. "*The Green Tricycle* is an online thematic literary journal, with three themes per issue. Each piece is limited to 200 words. We accept poetry, micro-fiction, mini-essays, letters, and drama, as long as it addresses the theme in an original manner." Quarterly. Estab. 1999.

Needs: Literary. Wants more mystery, literary and cross-genre. "No erotica, horror, or occult—too much of that is on the Internet already." List of upcoming themes available on website. Receives 40-100 unsolicited mss/month. Accepts 2-5 mss/issue; 8-10 mss/year. Publishes ms 1-3 months after acceptance. Agented fiction 10%. **Publishes 10 new writers/year.** Recently published work by J. Michael Yates, Suzanne Ruth Thurman, Deena L. Trouten and Jo Nelson. Word length: 175 words average; 100 words minimum; 200 words maximum. Also publishes literary essays and poetry. Sometimes comments on or critiques rejected ms.

How to Contact: Send complete ms with a cover letter. "Online submissions only. No attachments." Include estimated word count, 25-30 word bio and list of publications. Responds in 2 months. Sample copy and guidelines free online. Reviews novels, short story collections and nonfiction books of interest to writers. Contact the publisher.

Payment/Terms: Acquires one-time rights. Sponsors contest: information on website.

Advice: "I look for originality. A creative approach to the theme catches my attention. Be original. Read the magazine. Sloppy mechanics are sickening. Write the best you can without using four-letter words."

▨ ⊘ GREEN'S MAGAZINE, Fiction for the Family, Green's Educational Publications, Box 3236, Regina, Saskatchewan S4P 3H1 Canada. **Contact:** David Green, editor. Magazine: 5¼×8½; 96 pages; 20 lb. bond paper; matte cover stock; line illustrations. Publishes "solid short fiction suitable for family reading." Quarterly. Estab. 1972.

Needs: Adventure, fantasy, humor/satire, literary, mainstream, mystery/suspense and science fiction. No erotic or sexually explicit fiction. Receives 20-30 mss/month. Accepts 10-12 mss/issue; 40-50 mss/year. Publishes ms within 3-6 months of acceptance. Agented fiction 2%. **Publishes 6 new writers/year.** Recently published work by Robert Redding, Gordon C. Wilson and Mary Wallace. Length: 1,500-4,000 words; 2,500 words preferred. Also publishes poetry. Sometimes critiques rejected mss.

How to Contact: Send complete ms. "Cover letters welcome but not necessary." Responds in 2 months. SASE (or IRC). No simultaneous submissions. Sample copy for $5. Guidelines for #10 SASE (IRC). Reviews novels and short story collections.

Payment/Terms: Pays in contributor's copies. Acquires first North American serial rights.

Advice: "No topic is taboo, but we avoid sexuality for its own sake, and dislike material that is needlessly explicit or obscene. We look for strongly written stories that explore their characters through a subtle blending of conflicts. Plots should be appropriate, rather than overly ingenious or reliant on some *deus ex machina*. It must be a compression of experience or thoughts, in a form that is both challenging and rewarding to the reader. We have no form rejection slip. If we cannot use a submission, we try to offer constructive criticism in our personal reply. Often, such effort is rewarded with reports from our writers that following our suggestions has led to placement of the story or poem elsewhere."

◐ 🏆 **THE GREENSBORO REVIEW**, English Dept., 134 McIver Bldg., UNC Greensboro, P.O. Box 26170, Greensboro NC 27402-6170. (336)334-5459. E-mail: jlclark@uncg.edu. Website: www.uncg.edu/eng/mfa (includes writer's guidelines, literary awards guidelines, address, deadlines, subscription information). **Contact:** Jim Clark, editor. Fiction editor changes each year. Send mss to the editor. Magazine: 6×9; approximately 128 pages; 60 lb. paper; 65 lb. cover. Literary magazine featuring fiction and poetry for readers interested in contemporary literature. Semiannually. Circ. 800.

Needs: Contemporary and experimental. Accepts 6-8 mss/issue, 12-16 mss/year. 10% of all work published is by previously unpublished autors. Recently published work by Robert Morgan, George Singleton, Robert Olmstead, Jean Ross Justice, Dale Ray Phillips and Kelly Cherry. Length: 7,500 words maximum.

How to Contact: Send complete ms with SASE. No simultaneous submissions or previously published works. Unsolicited manuscripts must arrive by September 15 to be considered for the spring issue and by February 15 to be considered for the fall issue. Manuscripts arriving after those dates may be held for the next consideration. Responds in 4 months. Sample copy for $5.

Payment/Terms: Pays in contributor's copies. Acquires first North American serial rights.

Advice: "We want to see the best being written regardless of theme, subject or style. Recent stories from *The Greensboro Review* have been included in *The Best American Short Stories*, *Prize Stories: The O. Henry Awards*, *New Stories from the South*, and *Pushcart Prize*, anthologies recognizing the finest short stories being published."

⦙Ⓝ⦙ ◐ **THE GRIFFIN**, Gwynedd-Mercy College, P.O. Box 901, 1325 Sumneytown Pike, Gwynedd Valley PA 19437-0901. (215)646-7300. Fax: (215)923-3060. E-mail: z31w@aol.com. **Contact:** Anne K. Kaler, Ph.D., editor. Editor: Susan E. Wagner. Literary magazine: 8½×5½; 112 pages. "*The Griffin* is a literary journal sponsored by Gwynedd-Mercy College. It's mission is to enrich society by nurturing and promoting creative writing that demonstrates a unique and intelligent voice. We seek writing which accurately reflects the human condition with all its intellectual, emotional, and ethical challenges." Semiannual. Estab. 1999. Circ. 500.

Needs: Adventure, ethnic/multicultural (general), family saga, fantasy, feminist, historical, horror, humor/satire, literary, mainstream, mystery/suspense, religious (general), romance, science fiction, thriller/espionage, western. "No slasher, graphic violence or sex." Receives 2-3 unsolicited mss/month. Accepts mss depending on the quality of work submitted. Published 3-6 months after acceptance. **Publishes 15 new writers/year.** Recently published work by Pat Carr, Donna Dvorak-Knieriem, Ryan G. Van Cleave. Length: 2,500 words; average length: 2,000. Publishes short shorts; average length: 1,000. Also publishes literary essays and poetry.

How to Contact: Send complete ms with cover letter. Accepts submissions by e-mail, fax and disk. Include estimated word count and brief bio. Responds in 1 month to queries; 6 months to mss. Send SASE for return of ms or send disposable copy of ms and #10 SASE for reply only. Sample copy for $6. Guidelines for SASE or e-mail.

Payment/Terms: Pays in 2 contributor's copies; additional copies for $6. Pays on publication for one-time rights.

Advice: "Looking for well constructed works that explore universal qualities, respect for the individual and community, justice and integrity. Check our description and criteria. Rewrite until you're sure every word counts. We publish the best work we find regardless of industry trends."

✓ $◐ **GULF COAST, A Journal of Literature & Fine Arts**, Dept. of English, University of Houston, Houston TX 77204-3012. (713)743-3223. Fax: (713)743-3215. Website: www.gulfcoast.uh.edu. **Contact:** Miah Arnold, fiction editor. Editors change each year. Magazine: 6×9; 144 pages; stock paper, gloss cover; illustrations; photos. "Innovative fiction for the literary-minded." Estab. 1984. Circ. 1,500.

• Work published in *Gulf Coast* has been selected for inclusion in the *Pushcart Prize* anthology and *Best American Short Stories*.

Needs: Contemporary, ethnic, experimental, literary, regional, translations. Wants more "cutting-edge, experimental" fiction. No children's, genre, religious/inspirational. Receives 150 unsolicited mss/month. Accepts 8-10 mss/issue; 16-20 mss/year. Publishes ms 6 months-1 year after acceptance. Agented fiction 5%. Published work by Amy Storrow, Beverly Lowry, Diana Joseph, Karen Mary Penn and J. David Stevens. Length: no limit. Publishes short shorts. Sometimes critiques rejected mss.

How to Contact: Send complete ms with brief cover letter. "List previous publications; please notify us if the submission is being considered elsewhere." Responds in 6 months. Accepts simultaneous submissions. Back issue for $6, 7×10 SAE and 4 first-class stamps. Guidelines on website or for #10 SASE.

Payment/Terms: Pays contributor's copies and *small* honorariam for one-time rights.

Advice: "Rotating editorship, so please be patient with replies. As always, please send one story at a time."

◐ **GULF STREAM MAGAZINE**, Florida International University, English Dept., North Miami Campus, N. Miami FL 33181. (305)919-5599. Editor: Lynne Barrett. **Contact:** Fiction Editor. Editors change every 1-2 years. Magazine: 5½×8½; 96 pages; recycled paper; 80 lb. glossy cover; cover illustrations. "We publish *good quality*—fiction, nonfiction and poetry for a predominately literary market." Semiannually. Estab. 1989. Circ. 500.

Needs: Contemporary, literary, mainstream. Plans special issues. Receives 100 unsolicited mss/month. Accepts 5 mss/issue; 10 mss/year. Does not read mss during the summer. Publishes ms 3-6 months after acceptance. **Publishes 2-5 new writers/year.** Published work by Christine Liotta, Jane McCafferty, Steven Almond and

Charles Radke. Length: 7,500 words maximum; average length: 5,000 words. "Usually longer stories do not get accepted. There are exceptions, however." Publishes short shorts. Also publishes poetry. Sometimes critiques rejected mss.

How to Contact: Send complete manuscript with cover letter including list of previous publications and a short bio. Responds in 3 months. SASE. Accepts simultaneous submissions "if noted." Sample copy for $4. Guidelines free.

Payment/Terms: Pays in gift subscriptions and contributor's copies. Acquires first North American serial rights.

Advice: "Looks for good concise writing—well plotted with interesting characters."

HALF TONES TO JUBILEE, English Dept., Pensacola Junior College, 1000 College Blvd., Pensacola FL 32504-8910. (850)484-1450. Editor: Walter Spara. **Contact:** Fiction Editor. Magazine: 6×9; approx. 100 pages. "No theme, all types published." Annually. Estab. 1985. Circ. 500.

● "We run a national poetry contest every spring. Deadline: May 15. Prizes: $300, $200 and $100."

Needs: Open. Accepts approx. 6 mss/issue. "We publish in September." Published work by Mark Spencer (fiction), Larry Rubin and B.Z. Niditch (poetry). Length: 1,500 words average. Publishes short shorts. Also publishes poetry.

How to Contact: Send complete ms with cover letter. SASE. Sample copy for $4. Guidelines free.

Payment/Terms: Pays 1 contributor's copy. Acquires one-time rights.

Advice: "We are moving away from linear development; we are noted for innovation in style."

✓ $ HAPPY, The Happy Organization, 240 E. 35th St., 11A, New York NY 10016. (212)689-3142. Fax: (212)683-1669. E-mail: bayardx@aol.com. Editor: Bayard. **Contact:** Fiction Editor. Magazine: 5½×8; 100 pages; 60 lb. text paper; 150 lb. cover; perfect-bound; illustrations; photos. Quarterly. Estab. 1995. Circ. 500.

● *Happy* was ranked #20 on *Writer's Digest*'s "Fiction 50" list of top markets for fiction writers.

Needs: Erotica, ethnic/multicultural, experimental, fantasy, feminist, gay, horror, humor/satire, lesbian, literary, psychic/supernatural/occult, science fiction. No "television rehash or religious nonsense." Want more work that is "strong, angry, empowering." Receives 300-500 unsolicited mss/month. Accepts 30-40 mss/issue; 100-150 mss/year. **30-50% of work published is by new writers.** Publishes ms 6-12 months after acceptance. Length: 6,000 words maximum; average length: 1,000-3,500 words. Publishes short shorts. Often comments on rejected mss.

How to Contact: Send complete ms with a cover letter. Include estimated word count. Accepts queries by e-mail. Responds in 1 week to mss. Send SASE for reply, return of ms or send a disposable copy of ms. Accepts simultaneous submissions. Sample copy for $15.

Payment/Terms: Pays 1¢/word, minimum $5 on publication and 1 contributor's copy for one-time rights.

Advice: "No more grumbling about what you should be—become what you intended!"

Ⓝ $ THE HARPWEAVER, Harpweaver, Brock University, St. Catherines, Ontario L2S 3A1 Canada. Phone/fax: (905)688-5550. E-mail: harpweav@spartan.or.brocku.ca. **Contact:** Co-editor. Magazine: 5½×8½; 100-128 pages; illustrations; photos. Publishes short fiction, reviews, poetry and visual arts for a general, literate audience. Semiannual. Estab. 1996. Circ. 500.

Needs: Welcomes all categories and styles of fiction. Receives 10-15 mss/month. Accepts 2-3 mss/issue; 4-6 mss/year. Publishes ms 3 months after acceptance. **Publishes 1-2 new writers/year.** Length: 5,000 words maximum. Publishes short shorts. Also publishes poetry.

How to Contact: Send complete ms with a cover letter. Accepts submissions by e-mail. Include estimated word count, brief bio and list of publications. Responds in 2 months to mss. Send SASE. Accepts multiple submissions. Sample copy for $4. Guidelines by e-mail. Reviews novels, short story collections and nonfiction books of interest to writers.

Payment/Terms: Pays $10 minimum. Pays on publication for one-time rights. Not copyrighted.

✓ $ HAYDEN'S FERRY REVIEW, NSSWM Box 871502, Arizona State University, Tempe AZ 85287-1502. (480)965-1243. Fax: (480)965-2229. E-mail: hfr@asu.edu. Website: www.statepress.com/hfr. **Contact:** Fiction Editor. Editors change every 1-2 years. Magazine: 6×9; 128 pages; fine paper; illustrations; photos. "Contemporary material by new and established writers for a varied audience." Semiannually. Estab. 1986. Circ. 1,300.

● Work from *Hayden's Ferry Review* has been selected for inclusion in *Pushcart Prize* anthologies.

Needs: Contemporary, experimental, literary, prose poem, regional. Possible special fiction issue. Receives 250 unsolicited mss/month. Accepts 5 mss/issue; 10 mss/year. Publishes mss 3-4 months after acceptance. Published work by T.C. Boyle, Raymond Carver, Ken Kesey, Rita Dove, Chuck Rosenthal and Rick Bass. Length: No preference. Publishes short shorts. Also publishes literary essays.

How to Contact: Send complete ms with cover letter. Responds in up to 5 months from deadline to mss. SASE. Sample copy for $6. Guidelines for SAE.

Payment/Terms: Pays 2 contributor's copies; $25/page with a maximum of $100. Acquires first North American serial rights. Sends page proofs to author.

N **$** **THE HEARTLANDS TODAY**, The Firelands Writing Center, Firelands College of BGSU, Huron OH 44839. (419)433-5560. Editors: Larry Smith, Nancy Dunham, Connie W. Everett, David Shevin and Zita Sodeika. **Contact:** Fiction Editor. Magazine: 6×9; 160 pages; b&w illustrations; 15 photos. *Material must be set in the Midwest.* "We prefer material that reveals life in the Midwest today for a general, literate audience." Annually. Estab. 1991.
Needs: Ethnic, humor, literary, mainstream, regional (Midwest). Receives 15 unsolicited mss/month. Accepts 6 mss/issue. Does not read mss August-December. "We edit between January 1 and June 5. Submit then." 2000 theme was "The Midwest: Crossings and Turnings." Publishes ms 6 months after acceptance. Published work of Wendell Mayo, Tony Tomassi, Gloria Bowman. Length: 4,500 words maximum. Also publishes literary essays, poetry. Sometimes critiques rejected mss.
How to Contact: Send complete ms with cover letter. Responds in 2 months to mss. Send SASE for ms, not needed for query. Accepts simultaneous submissions, if noted. Sample copy for $5. "We edit January to June. June 5th deadline."
Payment/Terms: Pays $10-25 on publication and 1 contributor's copy for first rights.
Advice: "We look for writing that connects on a human level, that moves us with its truth and opens our vision of the world. If writing is a great escape for you, don't bother with us. We're in it for the joy, beauty or truth of the art. We look for a straight, honest voice dealing with human experiences. We do not define the Midwest, we hope to be a document of the Midwest. If you feel you are writing from the Midwest, send your work to us. We look first at the quality of the writing."

N **HEAVEN BONE**, Heaven Bone Press, Box 486, Chester NY 10918. (914)469-9018. E-mail: heavenbone@aol.com. **Contact:** Steven Hirsch and Kirpal Gordon, editors. Magazine: 8½×11; 96-116 pages; 60 lb. recycled offset paper; full color cover; computer clip art, graphics, line art, cartoons, halftones and photos scanned in tiff format. "Expansive, fine surrealist and experimental literary, earth and nature, spiritual path. We use current reviews, essays on spiritual and esoteric topics, creative stories. Also: reviews of current poetry releases and expansive literature." Readers are "scholars, surrealists, poets, artists, musicians, students." Annually. Estab. 1987. Circ. 2,500.
Needs: Esoteric/scholarly, experimental, fantasy, psychic/supernatural/occult, regional, spiritual. "No violent, thoughtless, exploitive or religious fiction." Receives 45-110 unsolicited mss/month. Accepts 5-15 mss/issue; 12-30 mss/year. Publishes ms 2 weeks-10 months after acceptance. **Publishes 3-4 new writers/year.** Published work by Keith Abbott and Stephen-Paul Martin. Length: 1,200-5,000 words; average length: 3,500 words. Publishes short shorts. Also publishes literary essays, literary criticism, poetry. Sometimes critiques rejected mss.
How to Contact: Query first; send complete ms with cover letter. Include short bio of recent activities. Responds in 3 weeks to queries; up to 10 months to mss. Send SASE for reply or return of ms. Accepts reprint submissions. Accepts electronic submissions via "Apple Mac versions of Macwrite, Microsoft Word or Writenow 3.0." Sample copy for $7. Guidelines free. Reviews novels and short story collections.
Payment/Terms: Pays in contributor's copies; charges for extras. Acquires first North American serial rights. Sends galleys to author, if requested.
Advice: "Read a sample issue first. Our fiction needs are temperamental, so please query first before submitting. We prefer shorter fiction. Do not send first drafts to test them on us. Please refine and polish your work before sending. Always include SASE. We are looking for the unique, unusual and excellent."

N **HIDDEN MANNA, Faith and Story**, 17914 Valley Knoll, Houston TX 77084-5904. E-mail: hiddenmanna@triquetra.org. Website: www.triquetra.org (includes writer's guidelines, vision statement). **Contact:** Daniel C. Massey, editor. Magazine: 8½×5½; 32 pages; Cougar Opaque 60 lb. paper; Wausau Royal Fiber Spice 80 lb. cover; illustrations. "HM is dedicated to the belief that a faith fed by stories endures. HM publishes Christian and Jewish fiction that raises more questions than answers, that is artistic not didactic. Narrative poetry also considered." Quarterly. Estab. 1999. Circ. 500.
Needs: Literary, religious (general religious). No romance, science fiction. Receives 60 unsolicited mss/month. Accepts 20 mss/year. Publishes ms up to 6 months after acceptance. Length: 500-4,000 words. Publishes short shorts. Also publishes literary essays, literary criticism and poetry.
How to Contact: Send complete ms with a cover letter. Include estimated word count, bio and list of publications. Responds in 6 months to queries and mss. Send SASE or disposable copy of ms. Accepts simultaneous submissions and reprints. Sample copy for $4 with 6×9 SAE and 3 first-class stamps. Guidelines free for letter size SAE and 1 first-class stamp or on website.
Payment/Terms: Pays free subscription to the magazine, 5 contributor's copies; additional copies $4. Pays on publication for one-time rights.
Advice: "Fiction should be surprising, with a keen attention to language. The best fiction makes riddles out of answers. Hidden Manna is not a traditional evangelistic magazine. It is a literary journal tackling difficult questions of faith for an audience that is adult, ecumenical and intelligent. Most 'Christian fiction' is either romance

fiction or apocalyptic fantasies. The rest is typically evangelical drama. A new form of Christian fiction needs to emerge. The rapid change in society has led us into fantasy and escape. Our hope is that a new form of fiction can also lead to renewal."

THE HIGGINSVILLE READER, The Higginsville Writers, P.O. Box 141, Three Bridges NJ 08887. (908)788-0514. E-mail: hgvreader@yahoo.com. **Contact:** Frank Magalhaes, Amy Finkenaur and Kathe Palka, editors. Magazine: 7×7½; 16 pages; 20 lb. white paper; illustrations; photos. "*HR* is a small literary quarterly geared to a general adult audience. Though small, our distribution is national as are our contributors. We print the best short fiction, essays and poetry culled from the submissions received. We have eclectic tastes and print a broad range of styles." Quarterly. Estab. 1991. Circ. 200.

Needs: Humor satire, literary, mainstream, translations. "No young adult/teen, children's/juvenile, senior citizen/retirement." Receives 3-10 unsolicited mss/month. Accepts 2 mss/issue; 6-8 mss/year. Publishes ms 1 year after acceptance. **Publishes 1 new writer/year.** Recently published work by Jim Meirose, R.C. Ringer, Glen Retiet and Patricia Bindert. Length: 3,500 maximum; average length: 1,500-2,500 words. Publishes short shorts. Also publishes literary essays, literary criticism and poetry. Sometimes comments on rejected mss.

How to Contact: Send complete ms with a cover letter. Accepts submissions by e-mail. Include estimated word count and brief bio. Responds in 2 weeks to queries; 3 weeks to mss. Send SASE (or IRC) for return of ms or send a disposable copy of ms and #10 SASE for reply only. Accepts simultaneous submissions and previously published work. "Accepts multiple submissions but no more than 3 works at a time. Require notification on simultaneous submissions." Sample copy for $1.50 plus 75¢ foreign postage. Guidelines for SASE or by e-mail.

Payment/Terms: Pays 1 contributor's copy; additional copies $1.50 or 8 copies for $10, 20 copies for $20. Pays on publication for one-time rights. Not copyrighted.

Advice: "We look for work that engages the reader's interest. Vivid imagery/language and consistency in the story are important."

$ **HIGH PLAINS LITERARY REVIEW**, 180 Adams St., Suite 250, Denver CO 80206. Phone/fax: (303)320-6828. Editor-in-Chief: Robert O. Greer, Jr. **Contact:** Fiction Editor. Magazine: 6×9; 135 pages; 70 lb. paper; heavy cover stock. "The *High Plains Literary Review* publishes poetry, fiction, essays, book reviews and interviews. The publication is designed to bridge the gap between high-caliber academic quarterlies and successful commercial reviews." Triannually. Estab. 1986. Circ. 2,200.

Needs: Most pressing need: outstanding essays, serious fiction, contemporary, humor/satire, literary, mainstream, regional. No true confessions, romance, pornographic, excessive violence. Receives approximately 400 unsolicited mss/month. Accepts 4-6 mss/issue; 12-18 mss/year. Publishes ms usually 6 months after acceptance. **Published new writers within the last year.** Recently published work by Naton Leslie, Tony Ardizzone, Cris Mazza and Gordon Weaver. Length: 1,500-8,000 words; average length: 4,200 words; prefers 3,000-6,000 words. Also publishes literary essays, literary criticism, poetry. Occasionally critiques rejected mss.

How to Contact: Send complete ms with cover letter. Include brief publishing history. Responds in 4 months. Send SASE for reply or return of ms. Accepts simultaneous submissions. Sample copy for $4.

Payment/Terms: Pays $5/page for prose and 2 contributor's copies on publication for first North American serial rights. "Copyright reverts to author upon publication." Sends copy-edited proofs to the author.

Advice: "*HPLR* publishes *quality* writing. Send us your very best material. We will read it carefully and either accept it promptly, recommend changes or return it promptly. Do not start submitting your work until you learn the basic tenets of the game including some general knowledge about how to develop characters and plot and how to submit a manuscript. I think the most important thing for any new writer interested in the short story form is to have a voracious appetite for short fiction, to see who and what is being published, and to develop a personal style."

HILL AND HOLLER: Southern Appalachian Mountains, Seven Buffaloes Press, P.O. Box 249, Big Timber MT 59011. **Editor:** Art Cuelho. Magazine: 5½×8½; 80 pages; 70 lb. offset paper; 80 lb. cover stock; illustrations; photos rarely. "I use mostly rural Appalachian material: poems and stories, and some folklore and humor. I am interested in heritage, especially in connection with the farm." Annually. Published special fiction issue. Estab. 1983. Circ. 750.

Needs: Contemporary, ethnic, humor/satire, literary, regional, rural America farm. "I don't have any prejudices in style, but I don't like sentimental slant. Deep feelings in literature are fine, but they should be portrayed with tact and skill." Receives 10 unsolicited mss/month. Accepts 4-6 mss/issue. Publishes ms 6 months-1 year after acceptance. Length: 2,000-3,000 words average. Also publishes short shorts of 500-1,000 words.

A BULLET INTRODUCES COMMENTS by the editor of *Novel & Short Story Writer's Market* indicating special information about the listing.

How to Contact: Query first. Responds in 1 month to queries. SASE. Sample copy for $7.75 postpaid.
Payment/Terms: Pays in contributor's copies. Acquires first North American serial rights "and permission to reprint if my press publishes a special anthology." Sometimes sends galleys to author.
Advice: "In this Southern Appalachian rural series I can be optimistic about fiction. Appalachians are very responsive to their region's literature. I have taken work by beginners that had not been previously published. Be sure to send a double-spaced clean manuscript and SASE. I have the only rural press in North America; maybe even in the world. So perhaps we have a bond in common if your roots are rural."

N ◐ **Y HOME PLANET NEWS**, Home Planet Publications, P.O. Box 415, New York NY 10009. (718)769-2854. **Contact:** Enid Dame and Donald Lev, co-editors. Tabloid: 11½ × 16; 24 pages; newsprint; illustrations, photos. "*Home Planet News* publishes mainly poetry along with some fiction, as well as reviews (books, theater and art), and articles of literary interest. We see *HPN* as a quality literary journal in an eminently readable format and with content that is urban, urbane and politically aware." Triannually. Estab. 1979. Circ. 1,000.
● *HPN* has received a small grant from the Puffin Foundation for its focus on AIDS issues.
Needs: Ethnic/multicultural, experimental, feminist, gay, historical, lesbian, literary, mainstream/contemporary, science fiction (soft/sociological). No "children's or genre stories (except rarely some science fiction)." Upcoming themes: "Midrash." Publishes special fiction issue or anthology. Receives 12 mss/month. Accepts 1 ms/ issue; 3 mss/year. Reads fiction mss only from February to May. Publishes 1 year after acceptance. Published work by Maureen McNeil, Eugene Stein, B.Z. Niditch, Walter Jackman and Layle Silbert. Length: 500-2,500 words; average length: 2,000 words. Publishes short shorts. Also publishes literary criticism, poetry.
How to Contact: Send complete ms with a cover letter. Responds in 6 months to mss. Send SASE for reply, return of ms or send a disposable copy of the ms. Sample copy for $3. Guidelines for SASE.
Payment/Terms: Pays 3 contributor's copies; additional copies $1. Acquires one-time rights.
Advice: "We use very little fiction, and a story we accept just has to grab us. We need short pieces of some complexity, stories about complex people facing situations which resist simple resolutions."

◐ ▤ **THE HORSETHIEF'S JOURNAL, Celebrating the Literature of the New West**, Cayuse Press, P.O. Box 66003, Burien WA 98166-0003. E-mail: cayuse-press@usa.com. Website: www.cayuse-press.com (includes submission guidelines, deadlines, current and archived issues, tools and tips for writers and a poetry forum). **Contact:** Barbara Benepe, editor-in-chief. Electronic literary journal. "*The Horsethief's Journal* is a triannual online literary journal showcasing the best in contemporary poetry, short fiction and memoir for the general reader." Estab. 1998.
Needs: Adventure, ethnic/multicultural (general), historical, literary, mainstream, mystery/suspense, regional (western US), thriller/espionage, translations, cross-genre fiction. No erotica, horror, occult, children's, young adult. Receives 30 unsolicited mss/month. Accepts 2-5 mss/issue; 6-15/year. Publishes ms 1-3 months after acceptance. **Publishes 25 new writers/year.** Recently published work by J. Michael Yates, Robert J. Kelley and Cris Bisch. Length: 200-3,000 words; average length: 1,500 words. Publishes short shorts. Length: 300 words. Also publishes literary essays and poetry. Sometimes comments on rejected ms.
How to Contact: Send complete ms with a cover letter by e-mail only; no attachments. Include estimated word count, 100-200 word bio and list of publications. Responds in 2 months to mss. Inquire about simultaneous and reprint submissions. Guidelines available on website. Reviews novels, short story collections and nonfiction books of interest to writers. Send books to editor.
Payment/Terms: Acquires one-time rights.
Advice: "We're looking for stories with an original slant. No cliched plots, characters or themes. Polish. Polish. Polish. Poor diction, grammar errors—bad mechanics in general—will get you a rejection. Read the magazine. Be original."

▨ ◐ **THE HUDSON REVIEW**, 684 Park Ave., New York NY 10021. Fax: (212)774-1911. Website: www.litline.org/hudson (includes partial text, table of contents and subscription information). **Contact:** Paula Deitz, fiction editor. Magazine: 4½ × 7½; 176 pages; 50 Basis Miami book vellum paper; 65 Basis Torchglow cover. "*The Hudson Review* is a sourcebook of American culture that explores the current trends in literature and the arts. Each issue features poetry and fiction, essays on literary and cultural topics, book reviews, reports from abroad, and chronicles covering recent developments in film, theater, dance, music and art. We encourage and publish new writing in order to bring the creative imagination of today to a varied, responsive audience." Quarterly. Estab. 1948. Circ. 4,500. "Writers who wish to send unsolicited mss outside the normal reading period (June 1 to November 30) must have a subscription."
Needs: Literary. Receives 375 unsolicited mss/month. Accepts 1-2 mss/issue; 4-8 mss/year. Does not read from December 1 through May 31 (except for subscribers). **Publishes 75% new writers/year.** Recently published work by Gary Krist, William Trevor and Henry Shukman. Length: 10,000 words maximum; average length: 8,000 words. Also publishes literary essays, literary criticism and poetry.

How to Contact: Send complete ms with a cover letter. Include estimated word count. Responds in 6 weeks to queries; 3 months to mss. Send SASE for reply, return of ms or send disposable copy of ms. No simultaneous submissions. Sample copy for $9. Guidelines free. Reviews novels and short story collections. Send book to editor.

Payment/Terms: Pays 2 contributor's copies; additional copies $4. Sends galleys to author.

Advice: "We do not specialize in publishing any particular 'type' of writing; our sole criterion for accepting unsolicited work is literary quality. The best way for you to get an idea of the range of work we publish is to read a current issue."

THE HUNTED NEWS, The Subourban Press, P.O. Box 9101, Warwick RI 02889-9101. (401)826-7307. **Contact:** Mike Wood, editor. Magazine: 8½×11; 30-35 pages; photocopied paper. "I am looking for good writers in the hope that I can help their voices be heard. Like most in the small press scene, I just wanted to create another option for writers who otherwise might not be heard." Annually. Estab. 1991. Circ. 200.

Needs: Experimental, historical, horror, literary, mainstream/contemporary, regional, religious/inspirational, translations. "No self-impressed work, shock or experimentation for its own sake." Would like to see more religious/spiritual fiction. Receives 50-60 unsolicited mss/month. Acquires 3 mss/issue. Publishes ms within 3-4 months after acceptance. **Publishes 5 new writers/year.** Published work by Alfred Schwaid, Steve Richmond, Darryl Smyers and Charles Bukowski. Length: 700 words maximum. Publishes short shorts. Also publishes literary essays, literary criticism and poetry. Often comments on rejected mss.

How to Contact: Send complete ms with cover letter. Responds in 1 month. Send SASE for return of ms. Accepts simultaneous and reprint submissions. Sample copy for 8½×11 SAE and 3 first-class stamps. Guidelines free. Reviews novels or short story collections.

Payment/Terms: Pays 3-5 contributor's copies. Acquires one-time rights.

Advice: "I look for an obvious love of language and a sense that there is something at stake in the story, a story that somehow needs to be told. Write what you need to write, say what you think you need to say, no matter the subject, and take a chance and send it to me. A writer will always find an audience if the work is true."

$ **THE ICONOCLAST**, 1675 Amazon Rd., Mohegan Lake NY 10547-1804. **Contact:** Phil Wagner, editor. Journal. 8½×5½; 32-40 pages; 20 lb. white paper; 50 lb. cover stock; illustrations. "*The Iconoclast* is a self-supporting, independent, unaffiliated general interest magazine with an appreciation of the profound, absurd and joyful in life. Material is limited only by *its* quality and *our* space. We want readers and writers who are open-minded, unafraid to think, and actively engaged with the world." Published 8 times/year. Estab. 1992. Circ. 700-3,000 (special issues).

• *The Iconoclast* has grown from a 16-page newsletter to a 32-40-page journal and is, subsequently, buying more fiction.

Needs: Adventure, ethnic/multicultural, humor/satire, literary, mainstream/contemporary, science fiction. Wants to see more "literary fiction with plots." "Nothing militant, solipsistic, or silly." Receives 100 unsolicited mss/month. Accepts 3-6 mss/issue; 25-30 mss/year. Publishes ms 6-9 months after acceptance. **Publishes 8-10 new writers/year.** Recently published work by W.P. Kinsella, Lilia Levin and E.G. Silverman. Length: 100 words minimum; occasionally longer; 2,000-2,500 words preferred. Publishes short shorts. Also publishes essays, poetry. Sometimes comments on rejected mss.

How to Contact: Send complete ms. Responds in 1 month. Send SASE for reply, return of ms or send a disposable copy of the ms labeled as such. Sample copy for $2. Reviews novels and short story collections.

Payment/Terms: Pays 1¢/word on acceptance for subscribers and 2-5 contributor's copies; additional copies $1.20 (40% discount). Acquires one-time rights.

Advice: "We like fiction that has something to say (and not about its author). We hope for work that is observant, intense and multi-leveled. Follow Pound's advice—'make it new.' Write what you want in whatever style you want without being gross, sensational, or needlessly explicit—then pray there's someone who can appreciate your sensibility. Read good fiction. It's as fundamental as learning how to hit, throw and catch is to baseball. With the increasing American disinclination towards literature, stories must insist on being heard. Read what is being published—then write something better—and different. Do all rewrites before sending a story out. Few editors have time to work with writers on promising stories; only polished."

THE IDAHO REVIEW, Boise State University, English Dept., 1910 University Dr., Boise ID 83725. (208)426-1002. Fax: (208)426-5426. **Contact:** Mitch Wieland, editor. Magazine: 6×9; 180-200 pages; acid-free accent opaque paper; coated cover stock; photos. "A literary journal for anyone who enjoys good fiction." Annual. Estab. 1998. Circ. 1,000. Member: C.L.M.P.

• Three stories from *The Idaho Review* were listed in "100 Other Distinguished Short Stories" in *The Best American Short Stories, 1999.*

Needs: Experimental, literary. No genre fiction of any type. Receives 150 unsolicited mss/month. Accepts 5-7 mss/issue; 5-7 mss/year. "We do not read from December 16-August 31." Publishes ms 1 year after acceptance.

Agented fiction 5%. **Publishes 1 new writer/year.** Recently published work by Stephen Dixon, Stephen Minot and Alan Cheuse. Length: open; average length: 7,000 words. Publishes short shorts. Average length: 750 words. Also publishes literary essays. Sometimes comments on rejected mss.
How to Contact: Send complete ms with a cover letter. Include estimated word count, brief bio and list of publications. Responds in 5 months to mss. Send SASE (or IRC) for return of ms or send a disposable copy of ms and #10 SASE for reply only. Accepts simultaneous submissions. Sample copy for $8.95. Guidelines for SASE. Reviews novels, short story collections and nonfiction books of interest to writers.
Payment/Terms: Pays free subscription to the magazine and 5 contributor's copies; additional copies $5. Pays on publication for first North American serial rights. Sends galleys to author.
Advice: "We look for strongly crafted work that tells a story that needs to be told. We demand vision and intelligence and mystery in the fiction we publish."

⬤ THE IDIOT, Anarchaos Press, 1706 S. Bedford St., Los Angeles CA 90035. E-mail: purple-hayes@juno.com. President for Life: Sam Hayes. **Contact:** Sam Hoel, emperor of ice cream. Magazine: 5½×8½; 48 pages; 20 lb. white paper; cardboard cover; illustrations. "For people who enjoy Dennis Miller, Woody Allen, S.J. Perelman, James Thurber, and Camus. We're looking for black comedy. Death, disease, and Dr. Seuss are all subjects of comedy. Nothing is sacred, but it needs to be funny. I don't want whimsical, I don't want amusing, I don't want some fanciful anecdote about a trip you took with your uncle when you were eight, I want laugh-out-loud-fall-on-the-floor-funny. If it's cute, give it to your mom, your sweetheart, or your puppy dog. Length doesn't matter, but most comedy is like soup. It's an appetizer, not a meal. Short is often better. Bizarre, obscure, referential, and literary are all appreciated. My audience is mostly comprised of bitter misanthropes who play Russian Roulette between airings of 'The Simpsons' each day. I want dark." Annually. Estab. 1993. Circ. 250-300.
Needs: Humor/satire. Wants more short, dark humor. Publishes ms 6-12 months after acceptance. **Publishes 1-3 new writers/year.** Recently published work by Joe Deasy, Dan Medeiros, Brian Campbell and Mark Romyn. Length: 2,000 words maximum; average length: 500 words. Mostly looking for short shorts. Also publishes poetry. Sometimes comments on rejected mss.
How to Contact: Send complete ms with a cover letter. Include estimated word count and bio (30-50 words). Accepts queries/mss by e-mail. Responds in 1 month to queries; 3 months to mss. Send SASE for reply, return of ms or send a disposable copy of ms. Accepts simultaneous, reprint and electronic submissions. Sample copy for $5.
Payment/Terms: Pays 1 contributor copy. Acquires one-time rights. Sends galleys to author if time permits.
Advice: "Nothing over 2,000 words unless it's the funniest damned thing on the face of this or any other Earth."

Ⓝ ⬤ ILLYA'S HONEY, The Dallas Poets Community, P.O. Box 225435, Dallas TX 75222. E-mail: illyashoney@hotmail.com. Website: www.dallaspoets.org. **Contact:** Ann Howells or Meghan Ehrlich, fiction editors. Magazine: 5½×8½; 24 pages; 24 lb. paper; glossy cover; photos. Quarterly. Estab. 1994. Circ. 125.
Needs: Ethnic/multicultural, experimental, feminist, gay, historical, humor satire, lesbian, literary, mainstream, regional, flash fiction. Receives 10 unsolicited mss/month. Accepts 2-8 mss/year. Publishes ms 1-3 months after acceptance. **Publishes 1-2 new writers/year.** Recently published work by Christopher Soden, Brandon Brown and Nancy McGovern. Publishes short shorts. Average length: 200 words. Also publishes poetry. Sometimes comments on rejected mss.
How to Contact: Send complete ms with a cover letter. Include estimated word count and brief bio. Responds in 6 months. Send SASE (or IRC) for return of ms or send a disposable copy of ms and #10 SASE for reply only. Accepts multiple submissions. Sample copy for $6. Guidelines for SASE or by e-mail.
Payment/Terms: Pays 1 contributor's copy; additional copies $6. Pays on publication for first North American serial rights.

✔ $⬤ 🗹 INDIANA REVIEW, Ballantine Hall, 465, 1020 E. Kirkwood Ave., Bloomington IN 47405. (812)855-3439. Website: www.indiana.edu/~inreview/ir.html. **Contact:** Shannon Gibmey, fiction editor. Editors change every 2 years. Magazine: 6×9; 160 pages; 50 lb. paper; Glatfelter cover stock. *Indiana Review* looks for stories which integrate theme, language, character and form. We like mature, sophisticated fiction which has consequence beyond the world of its narrator. Semiannually. Estab. 1976. Circ. 2,000.
  ● *Indiana Review* won the 1996 American Literary Magazine Award. Work published in *Indiana Review* was selected for inclusion in the *O. Henry Prize Stories* anthology. This publication ranked #30 on *Writer's Digest*'s Fiction 50 list of top markets for fiction writers.
Needs: Ethnic, literary, regional, translations. Also considers novel excerpts. No genre fiction. Receives 200 unsolicited mss each month. Accepts 7-9 prose mss/issue. Published work by Jason Brown, Dan Chaon, Stuart Dubek, Kathy Acker and Antonya Nebon. Length: 1-35 magazine pages. Also publishes literary essays, poetry and reviews.
How to Contact: Send complete ms with cover letter. Cover letters should be *brief* and demonstrate specific familiarity with the content of a recent issue of *Indiana Review*. SASE. Accepts simultaneous submissions (if

notified *immediately* of other publication). Responds in 3 months. Publishes ms an average of 3-6 months after acceptance. Does not read mid-December through mid-January. Sample copy for $8. Sponsors annual $1,000 fiction contest. SASE for guidelines.

Payment/Terms: Pays $5/page and 2 contributor's copies for first North American serial rights.

Advice: "Because our editors change each year, so do our literary preferences. It's important that potential contributors are familiar with the most recent issue of *Indiana Review* via library, sample copy or subscription. Beyond that, we look for prose that is well crafted and socially relevant. Dig deep. Don't accept you first choice descriptions when you are revising. Cliché and easy images sink 90% of the stories we reject. Understand the magazines you send to—investigate! As people write more and more short-shorts, the beauty of longer pieces becomes even more apparent and attractive to us."

$ 🖉 🝐 INDIGENOUS FICTION, Wondrously Weird & Offbeat, I.F. Publishing, P.O. Box 2078, Redmond WA 98073-2078. E-mail: deckr@earthlink.net. Publisher/Managing Editor: Sherry Decker. Associate Editors: Evelyn Gratrix and Becky Warden. **Contact:** Fiction Editor. Magazine: 5½×8½; 60-70 pages; 20 lb. white paper; 4-color glossy cover; illustrations. "*I.F.* wants literary stories from all areas: fantasy, dark fantasy, science fiction, horror, mystery and mainstream." Triannual. Estab. 1998. Circ. 250 estimated.

● Awarded Honorable Mention by Datlow and Windling for *Year's Best Fantasy & Horror Collection* (St. Martin's Press).

Needs: Adventure, ethnic/multicultural, experimental, fantasy (science fantasy, sword and sorcery, contemporary), feminist, horror, humor/satire, literary, mainstream/contemporary, suspense, psychic/supernatural/occult, science fiction (soft/sociological, cross-genre). "No porn; children-physical/sexual abuse; hard-tech science fiction; gore; vignettes; it-was-all-a-dream; evil cats, unicorns; sweet nostalgia." Receives 200 unsolicited mss/month. Accepts 6-8 mss/issue; 16-24 mss/year. Publishes ms 1 year maximum after acceptance. **Publishes 1-2 new writers/year.** Recently published work by Stepan Chapman, Kathryn Kulpa, Patricia Russo, Jeffrey Thomas and Rhonda Eikamp. Length: 500-8,000 words; average length: 4,500 words. Sometimes comments on rejected ms.

How to Contact: Send complete ms with a cover letter. Include estimated word count, brief bio and list of publications. Responds in 1 week to queries; 2 weeks to mss. Send SASE for reply, return of ms or send a disposable copy of ms. Accepts only queries by e-mail. Accepts simultaneous submissions. Guidelines for #10 SASE. Sample copy $6, $7 Canada, $8 overseas.

Payment/Terms: Pays $5-20 for work between 500-8,000 words. Accepted works of at least 1,500 words also receives contributor's copy. Additional copies $4.75. Sends galleys to authors in US.

Advice: "We want wonderful writing—unusual stories of the supernatural or the unexplained, dark moody stories, bizarre, odd occurrences mixed with stark reality." Looks for "distinctive writing, lack of adverbs, a sense of wonder and professional manuscript. There is not such thing as a 'born writer.' Take classes. Keep taking classes."

☑ 🖉 INTERBANG: Dedicated to perfection in the art of writing, P.O. Box 1574, Venice CA 90294. (310)450-6372. E-mail: heather@interbang.net. Website: www.interbang.net (includes back issues and writer's guide). **Contact:** Heather Hoffman, editor. Magazine: 8½×7, 30 pages; 60 lb. paper; card cover stock; illustrations; photos. "We publish well-crafted writing on a variety of topics." Quarterly. Estab. 1995. Circ. 2,000.

Needs: Adventure, ethnic/multicultural, experimental, family saga, fantasy (space fantasy, sword and sorcery), feminist, gay, glitz, historical (general), horror (dark fantasy, futuristic, psychological, supernatural), humor satire, lesbian, literary, mainstream, military/war, mystery/suspense (amateur sleuth, cozy, police procedural, private eye/hardboiled), New Age, psychic/supernatural/occult, regional, science fiction (hard science/technological, soft/sociological), short story collections, thriller/espionage, translations. No travel or children's. Receives 50 unsolicited mss/month. Accepts 5 mss/issue; 25 mss/year. Publishes ms 1 month after acceptance. Agented fiction 5%. **Publishes 50 new writers/year.** Recently published work by John Thomas, Coral Suter and Carol Lewis. Word length: 2,500 word average. Publishes short shorts. Also publishes literary essays. Sometimes comments on or critiques rejected ms.

How to Contact: Send complete ms with a cover letter. Accepts inquiries by e-mail. Include estimated word count and bio. Responds in 2 weeks to queries; 3 months to mss. Send SASE for reply, return of ms or send a disposable copy of ms. Accepts simultaneous submissions. Sample copy free. Reviews novels, short story collections and nonfiction books. Send books to editor.

Payment/Terms: Pays free subscription to the magazine, an *Interbang* T-shirt and 5 contributor's copies. Payment on publication. Acquires one-times rights.

Advice: "We're looking for well-written stories with strong, vivid descriptions, well-developed characters and complex themes. Focus on a consistent narrative style. We do not publish stories that read like a TV show. We want stories with style and depth."

☑ 🖉 INTERNATIONAL QUARTERLY, Essays, Fiction, Drama, Poetry, Art, Reviews, P.O. Box 10521, Tallahassee FL 32302-0521. Fax: (850)224-5127. Website: www.internationalquarterly.org. **Contact:** Van K. Brock, editor. Magazine: 7½×10; 176 pages; 50 lb. text paper; 60 lb. gloss cover; fine art illustrations.

"*International Quarterly* seeks to bridge boundaries between national, ethnic and cultural identities, and among creative disciplines, by providing a venue for dialogue between exceptional writers and artists and discriminating readers. We look for work that reveals character and place from within." Quarterly. Estab. 1993.

Needs: Ethnic/multicultural, experimental, humor/satire, literary, mainstream/contemporary, regional, translations. "We would consider work in any of the genres that transcends the genre through quality of language, characterization and development. Our sympathies are strongly feminist. Many of the genre categories imply simplistic and limited literary purposes. Any genre can transcend its limits. No issue is limited to work on its regional or thematic focus." Accepts 5 mss/issue; 20 mss/year. "We read all year, but fewer readers are active in July and August." Publishes ms 3-9 months after acceptance. Recently published work by Mark Apelman and Alyson Shaw. Publishes short shorts. Also publishes literary essays, literary criticism (for general readers), poetry. Sometimes comments on rejected mss.

How to Contact: Query first or send complete ms with a cover letter. Include estimated word count, bio, list of publications. Include rights available. "We prefer first rights for all original English texts." Responds in 2 weeks to queries; 4 months to mss. Send SASE for reply, return of ms or send a disposable copy of ms. Accepts simultaneous, reprint (please specify) and electronic submissions. Sample copy for $6 (a reduced rate) and 4 first-class stamps. Guidelines for #10 SASE. Reviews novels and short story collections. Send books to Book Review Editor.

Payment/Terms: Pays free subscription to magazine and 2 contributor's copies. Acquires first North American serial rights. Sends galleys to author.

Advice: "We would like to see more fiction break out of conventional thinking and set fictional modes without straining or trying to shock and fiction that presents the world of its characters from inside the skin of the culture, rather than those outside of the culture, tourists or short-termers, as it were, commenting on the world of a story's subjects from outside, lamenting that it has fallen into our consumerist ways, etc., lamentable as that may be. Works we publish do not have to be foreign, they may arise out of a profound understanding of any culture or locale, as long as they provide the reader with an authentic experience of that locale, whatever the origin of the author. We have no taboos, but we want writing that understands and creates understanding, writers who want to go beyond cultural givens."

$ ☐ ▼ THE IOWA REVIEW, University of Iowa, 308 EPB, Iowa City IA 52242. (319)335-0462. E-mail: iowa-review@uiowa.edu. Website: www.uiowa.edu/~iareview. Editor: David Hamilton. **Contact:** Fiction Editor. Magazine: 6×9; 200 pages; first-grade offset paper; Carolina CS1 10-pt. cover stock. "Stories, essays, poems for a general readership interested in contemporary literature." Triannual. Estab. 1970. Circ. 2,000.

• *The Iowa Review* ranked #49 in *Writer's Digest*'s "Fiction 50" list of top markets. Work published in *Iowa Review* regularly has been selected for inclusion in the *Pushcart Prize* and *Best American Short Stories* anthologies.

Needs: "We feel we are open to a range of styles and voices and always hope to be surprised by work we then feel we need." Receives 600 unsolicited fiction mss/month. Agented fiction less than 2%. Accepts 4-6 mss/issue, 12-18 mss/year. Does not read mss April-August. "We discourage simultaneous submissions, and although we will try, we can no longer promise to read manuscripts not entrusted to us alone for a three-month period, not including a month around Christmas." **Published new writers within the last year.** Recently published work by Joshua Harmon, Katherine Vaz, Mary Helen Stefaniak and Robert Anderson. Also publishes literary essays, literary criticism, poetry.

How to Contact: Send complete ms with cover letter. "Don't bother with queries." SASE for return of ms. Responds in 4 months to mss. Publishes ms an average of 6-12 months after acceptance. Sample copy for $6. Guidelines for SASE. Reviews novels and short story collections (3-6 books/year).

Payment/Terms: Pays $10/page on publication and 2 contributor's copies; additional copies 30% off cover price. Acquires first North American serial rights.

Advice: "We have no set guidelines as to content or length; we look for what we consider to be the best writing available to us and are pleased when writers we believe we have discovered catch on with a wider range of readers. It is never a bad idea to look through an issue or two of the magazine prior to a submission."

✓ ◐ ◎ IRIS: A Journal About Women, Box 323 HSC, University of Virginia, Charlottesville VA 22908. (804)924-4500. E-mail: iris@virginia.edu. Website: www.virginia.edu/%Ewomenctr/pubs/iris/irishome.html (includes last issue cover and table of contents). Coordinating Editor: Eileen Boris. **Contact:** Fiction Editor. Magazine: 8½×11; 80 pages; glossy paper; heavy cover; illustrations; artwork; photos. "Material of particular interest to women. For a feminist audience, college educated and above." Semiannually. Estab. 1980. Circ. 3,500.

Needs: Experimental, feminist, lesbian, literary, mainstream. "I don't think what we're looking for particularly falls into the 'mainstream' category—we're just looking for well-written stories of interest to women (particularly feminist women)." Receives 300 unsolicited mss/year. Accepts 5 mss/year. Publishes ms within 1 year after acceptance. **Publishes 1-2 new writers/year.** Recently published work by Sibyl Johnston and Barbara Drake. Length: 2,500-4,000 words average. Sometimes critiques rejected mss.

How to Contact: Send complete ms with cover letter. Include "previous publications, vocation, other points that pertain. Make it brief!" Accepts queries by e-mail. Responds in 3 months to mss. SASE. Accepts simultaneous submissions. Accepts electronic submissions via disk or modem. Sample copy for $5. Guidelines with SASE. Label: Fiction Editor.

Payment/Terms: Pays in contributor's copies and 1 year subscription. Acquires one-time rights.

Advice: "I select mss which are lively imagistically as well as in the here-and-now; I select for writing which challenges the reader. My major complaint is with stories that don't elevate the language above the bland sameness we hear on the television and everyday. Read the work of the outstanding women writers, such as Alice Munroe and Louise Erdrich."

N $ ☉ ☺ IRREANTUM, Exploring Mormon Literature, The Association for Mormon Letters, 1925 Terrace Dr., Orem UT 84097-8060. (801)226-5585. E-mail: irreant@cs.com. Website: http://cc.weber.edu/~bypar kinson/irreantum.html (includes purpose and philosophy, submission guidelines, archives of past issues and order forms). **Contact:** Tory Anderson. Magazine or Zine: 8½×5½; 68-100 pages; 20 lb. paper; 20 lb. color cover; illustrations; photos. "While focused on Mormonism, *Irreantum* is a cultural, humanities-oriented magazine, not a religious magazine. Our guiding principle is that Mormonism is grounded in a sufficiently unusual, cohesive and extended historical and cultural experience that it has become like a nation, an ethnic culture. We can speak of a Mormon literature at least as surely as we can of a Jewish or Southern literature. *Irreantum* publishes stories, one-act dramas, stand-alone novel and drama excerpts, and poetry by, for or about Mormons (as well as author interviews, essays and reviews). The magazine's audience includes readers of any or no religious faith who are interested in literary exploration of the Mormon culture, mindset and worldview through Mormon themes and characters. *Irreantum* is currently the only magazine devoted to Mormon literature." Quarterly. Estab. 1999. Circ. 400.

Needs: Adventure, ethnic/multicultural (Mormon), experimental, family saga, fantasy, feminist, historical, horror, humor/satire, literary, mainstream, mystery/suspense, New Age, psychic/supernatural/occult, regional (Western USA/Mormon), religious, romance, science fiction, thriller/espionage, translations, young adult/teen. Receives 5 unsolicited mss/month. Accepts 3 mss/issue; 12 mss/year. "We are looking to increase fiction." Publishes ms 3-12 months after acceptance. **Publishes 6 new writers/year.** Recently published work by Ed Snow, Benson Parkinson, John Bennion and Marilyn Brown. Length: 1,000-7,000 words; average length: 5,000 words. Publishes short shorts. Also publishes literary essays, literary criticism and poetry. Sometimes comments on rejected mss.

How to Contact: Send complete ms with a cover letter. Accepts submissions by e-mail and disk. "Note: Submissions by other than e-mail or floppy are discouraged." Include brief bio and list of publications. Responds in 2 weeks to queries; 2 months to mss. Send a disposable copy of ms and #10 SASE for reply only. Accepts simultaneous submissions, previously published work and multiple submissions. Sample copy for $4. Guidelines available via e-mail. Reviews novels, short story collections and nonfiction books of interest to writers. Send review copies to Irreantum, c/o AML, 1925 Terrace Dr., Orem UT 84097.

Payment/Terms: Pays $0-100 and 2 contributor's copies; additional copies $3. Pays on publication for one-time and electronic rights.

Advice: "*Irreantum* is not interested in didactic or polemnical fiction that primarily attempts to prove or disprove Mormon doctrine, history or corporate policy. We encourage beginning writers to focus on human elements first, with Mormon elements introduced only as natural and organic to the story. Readers can tell if you are honestly trying to explore the human experience or if you are writing with a propagandistic agenda either for or against Mormonism."

N ☉ THE JABBERWOCK REVIEW, Mississippi State University, P.O. Box 6025, Dept. of English, Mississippi State MS 39762. (662)325-0992. Website: www.msstate.edu/org/jabberwock/ (includes writer's guidelines, interviews with authors, community-related events). **Contact:** Fiction Editor (revolving editorship). Magazine: 8½×5½; 120 pages; glossy cover; illustrations; photos. "We are located in the South—love the South—but we publish good writing from anywhere and everywhere. And from anyone. We respect writers of reputation—and print their work—but we take great delight in publishing new and emerging writers as well." Semiannual. Estab. 1979. Circ. 500.

Needs: Ethnic/multicultural, experimental, feminist, gay, lesbian, literary, mainstream, regional, translations. Editorial calendar available for SASE or on website. Receives 150 unsolicited mss/month. Accepts 7-8 mss/issue; 15 mss/year. "We do not read during the summer (May 1 to September 1). Manuscripts send during that time will be held until fall, when we start reading again." Publishes ms 4-6 months after acceptance. Agented fiction 5%. **Publishes 1-5 new writers/year.** Recently published work by James Wilcox and R.M. Kinder. Length: 250-5,000 words; average length: 4,000 words. Publishes short shorts. Average length: 1,000 words. Also publishes literary essays and poetry. Sometimes comments on rejected mss.

How to Contact: Send complete ms with a cover letter. Include estimated word count, brief bio, Social Security number and list of publications. Responds in 5 months to mss. Send SASE (or IRC) for return of ms. Accepts simultaneous submissions. Sample copy for $4. Guidelines for SASE or by e-mail.

Payment/Terms: Pays 2 contributor's copies. Pays on publication for first rights. Sends galleys to author. Sponsors contests. Visit website or write for guidelines.

Advice: "It might take a few months to get a response from us, but your manuscript will be read with care. Our editors enjoy reading submissions (really!) and will remember writers who are persistent and commited to getting a story 'right' through revision."

✅ $ ◱ ◎ **JAPANOPHILE**, Box 7977, Ann Arbor MI 48107. (734)930-1553. Fax: (734)930-9968. E-mail: japanophile@aol.com. Website: www.japanophile.com (includes writer's guidelines, sample fiction). **Contact:** Susan Lapp and Ashby Kinch, editors. Magazine: 5¼×8½; 58 pages; illustrations; photos. Magazine of "articles, photos, poetry, humor, short stories about Japanese culture, not necessarily set in Japan, for an adult audience, most with a college background and who like to travel." Quarterly. Estab. 1974. Circ. 800.

● Most of the work included in *Japanophile* is set in recent times, but the magazine will accept material set back as far as pre-WWII.

Needs: Adventure, historical, humor/satire, literary, mainstream, and mystery/suspense. No erotica, science fiction or horror. Published special fiction issue last year; plans another. Receives 40-100 unsolicited fiction mss/month. Accepts 12 mss/issue, 15-20 mss/year. Recently published work by Suzanne Kamata, Amy Chavez and Matt Malcomson. Publishes 12 previously unpublished writers/year. Length: 2,000-6,000 words; average length: 3,200 words. Also publishes essays, book reviews, literary criticism and poetry.

How to Contact: Send complete ms with SASE, cover letter, bio and information about story. Accepts queries/mss by e-mail and fax. Accepts simultaneous and reprint submissions. Responds in 2 months to mss. Sample copy for $4; guidelines for #10 SASE.

Payment/Terms: Pays $20 on publication for all rights, first North American serial rights or one-time rights (depends on situation). Stories submitted to the magazine may be entered in the annual contest. *A $5 entry fee must accompany each submission* to enter contest. Prizes include $100 plus publication for the best short story. Deadline: December 31.

Advice: "We look for originality and sensitivity to cultural detail. Clarity and directness of expression make manuscripts stand out. Short stories usually involve Japanese and 'foreign' (non-Japanese) characters in a way that contributes to understanding of Japanese culture and the Japanese people. However, a *good* story dealing with Japan or Japanese cultural aspects anywhere in the world will be considered, even if it does not involve this encounter or meeting of Japanese and foreign characters. Some stories may also be published in an anthology with approval of the author and additional payment."

◱ **THE JOURNAL**, Dept of English, Ohio State University, 164 W. 17th St., Columbus OH 43210. (614)292-4076. Website: www.cohums.ohio-state.adu/english/journals/the-journal. **Contact:** Kathy Fagan (poetry); Michelle Herman (fiction), editors. Magazine: 6×9; 150 pages. "We are open to all forms of quality fiction." For an educated, general adult audience. Semiannually. Estab. 1973. Circ. 1,500.

Needs: No romance, science fiction or religious/devotional. Accepts 2 mss/issue. Receives approximately 100 unsolicited fiction mss/month. "Usually" publishes ms within 1 year of acceptance. Agented fiction 10%. **Published new writers within the last year.** Recently published work by Stephen Dixon, Norma Rosen, Mark Jacobs and Liza Wieland. Length: Open. Also accepts poetry. Critiques rejected mss when there is time.

How to Contact: Send complete ms with cover letter. Responds "as soon as possible," usually 3 months. SASE. Sample copy for $7; guidelines for SASE.

Payment/Terms: Pays $25 stipend when funds are available; contributor's copies; $7 charge for extras.

Terms: Acquires First North American serial rights. Sends galleys to author.

Advice: Mss are rejected because of "lack of understanding of the short story form, shallow plots, undeveloped characters. Cure: read as much well-written fiction as possible. Our readers prefer 'psychological' fiction rather than stories with intricate plots. Take care to present a clean, well-typed submission."

◱ **THE JOURNAL**, Poetry Forum, 5713 Larchmont Dr., Erie PA 16509. Phone/fax: (814)866-2543. (Faxing hours: 8-10 a.m. and 5-8 p.m.) E-mail: 75562.670@compuserve.com. **Contact:** Gunvor Skogsholm, editor. Journal: 5½×8½; 18-20 pages; light card cover. Looks for "good writing—for late teens to full adulthood." Quarterly. Estab. 1989. Circ. 200.

● *The Journal* is edited by Gunvor Skogsholm, the editor of *Poetry Forum Short Stories* and *Short Stories Bimonthly*. This magazine is not strictly a pay-for-publication, "subscribers come first.'

Needs: Mainstream. Plans annual special fiction issue. Want more "work born from the human condition rather than from so called trends." No extreme horror. Receives 25-30 unsolicited mss/month. Accepts 1 ms/issue; 7-10 mss/year. Publishes mss 2-28 weeks after acceptance. Agented fiction 1%. **Publishes 50 new writers/year.** Recently published work by C.S. Craggs and Jan Haight. Length: 150 words minimum; average length: 300 words; 500 words preferred. Publishes short shorts. Length: 400 words. Sponsors contest. Send SASE for details.

How to Contact: Send complete ms. Accepts queries/mss by e-mail, fax, disk. Responds in 7 months to mss. SASE. Accepts simultaneous submissions. Accepts electronic disk submissions. Sample copy for $3. Guidelines for SASE.

Payment/Terms: No payment. Acquires one-time rights. Not copyrighted.

Advice: "Subscribers come first!" Looks for "a good lead stating a theme, support of the theme throughout and an ending that rounds out the story or article. Make it believable, please don't preach, avoid propaganda, and don't say, 'This is a story about a retarded person'; instead, prove it by your writing. Show, don't tell. Avoid using 'slang expressions' and 'street' language (except for in a dialogue)."

THE JOURNAL OF AFRICAN TRAVEL-WRITING, P.O. Box 346, Chapel Hill NC 27514-0346. (919)929-0419. E-mail: ottotwo@email.unc.edu. Website: www.unc.edu/~ottotwo/ (includes guidelines, selected texts, table of contents). **Contact:** Amber Vogel, editor. Magazine: 7×10; 96 pages; 50 lb. paper; illustrations. "*The Journal of African Travel-Writing* presents materials in a variety of genres that explore Africa as a site of narrative." Semiannually. Estab. 1996. Circ. 600.
• Sponsors annual award for best piece published in the journal.
Needs: Adventure, condensed/excerpted novel, ethnic/multicultural, historical, literary, translations. Accepts 1-4 mss/issue. Publishes ms 4-6 months after acceptance. Recently published work by Eileen Drew, Lisa Fugard and Sandra Jackson-Opoku. Also publishes literary essays, literary criticism and poetry. Sometimes comments on rejected mss.
How to Contact: Send complete ms with a cover letter. Sample copy for $6. Reviews novels and short story collections. Send books to editor.
Payment/Terms: Pays 5 contributor's copies for first rights. Sends galleys to author.

KALEIDOSCOPE: International Magazine of Literature, Fine Arts, and Disability, 701 S. Main St., Akron OH 44311-1019. (330)762-9755. Fax: (330)762-0912. E-mail: mshiplett@udsakron.org. Website: www.udsakron.org (includes guidelines, upcoming issue themes and information on the editors). Editor-in-Chief: Darshan Perusek, Ph.D. Senior Editor: Gail Willmott. **Contact:** Fiction Editor. Magazine: 8½×11; 56-64 pages; non-coated paper; coated cover stock; illustrations (all media); photos. "*Kaleidoscope* Magazine explores the experiences of disability through literature and the fine arts. Unique in the field of disability studies, it is not an advocacy, rehabilitation, or independent living journal but expresses the experiences of disability from the perspective of individuals, families, healthcare professionals, and society as a whole. Each issue explores a specific theme which deals with disability. Readers include people with and without disabilities." Semiannually. Estab. 1979. Circ. 1,000.
• *Kaleidoscope* has received awards from the American Heart Association, the Great Lakes Awards Competition and Ohio Public Images. The editors are looking for more fiction .
Needs: Personal experience, drama, fiction, essay, artwork. "Would like to see more fiction with emphasis on character study instead of action." Upcoming theme: "Deaf Culture & Art (deadline March 2001) and "International Fiction/Art" (deadline August 2001). No fiction that is stereotypical, patronizing, sentimental, erotic, romantic or maudlin. Receives 20-25 unsolicited fiction mss/month. Accepts 10 mss/year. Approximately 1% of fiction is agented. **Published new writers within the last year.** Recently published work by John Bayley and Rick Moody. Length: 5,000 words maximum. Also publishes poetry.
How to Contact: Query first or send complete ms and cover letter. Accepts queries by fax. Include author's educational and writing background and if author has a disability, how it has influenced the writing. Accepts simultaneous submissions. Responds in 1 month to queries; 6 months to mss. Sample copy for $4. Guidelines for #10 SASE.
Payment/Terms: Pays $10-125 and 2 contributor's copies on publication; additional copies $5. Acquires first rights. Reprints permitted with credit given to original publication.
Advice: "Read the magazine and get submission guidelines. We prefer that writers with a disability offer original perspectives about their experiences; writers without disabilities should limit themselves to our focus in order to solidify a connection to our magazine's purpose. Do not use stereotypical, patronizing and sentimental attitudes about disability."

KALLIOPE, A Journal of Women's Art, Florida Community College at Jacksonville, 3939 Roosevelt Blvd., Jacksonville FL 32205. (904)381-3511. Website: www.fccj.org/kalliope (includes guidelines, subscription information, contents of current issue, contests, cassette information, back issues, events, history and post address). Editor: Mary Sue Koeppel. **Contact:** Fiction Editor. Magazine: 7¼×8¼; 76-88 pages; 70 lb. coated matte paper; Bristol cover; 16-18 halftones per issue. "A literary and visual arts journal for women, *Kalliope* celebrates women in the arts by publishing their work and by providing a forum for their ideas and opinions." Short stories, poems, plays, essays, reviews and visual art. Triannually. Estab. 1978. Circ. 1,550.
• *Kalliope* ranked #46 on *Writer's Digest's* Fiction 50 of top markets for fiction writers. *Kalliope* has received the Frances Buck Sherman Award from the local branch of the National League of Pen Women. The magazine has also received awards and grants for its poetry, grants from the Florida Department of Cultural Affairs and the Jacksonville Club Gallery of Superb Printing Award.
Needs: "Quality short fiction by women writers." No science fiction. Accepts 2-4 mss/issue. Receives approximately 100 unsolicited fiction mss each month. **Publishes 3 new writers/year.** Recently published work by

Edith Pearlman, Janice Daugharety, Susan Hubbard and Marey Gardner. Preferred length: 750-2,000 words, but occasionally publishes longer (and shorter) pieces. Also publishes poetry. Critiques rejected mss "when there is time and if requested."

How to Contact: Send complete ms with SASE and short contributor's note. No simultaneous submissions. Responds in 3 months on ms. Publishes ms an average of 1-3 months after acceptance. Sample copy: $7 for current issue; $4 for issues from '78-'88. Reviews short story collections.

Payment/Terms: Pays 2 contributor's copies or 1-years subscription for first rights. Discount for extras. "We accept only unpublished work. Copyright returned to author upon request."

Advice: "Read our magazine. The work we consider for publication will be well written and the characters and dialogue will be convincing. We like a fresh approach and are interested in new or unusual forms. Make us believe your characters; give readers an insight which they might not have had if they had not read you. We would like to publish more work by minority writers." Manuscripts are rejected because "1) nothing *happens*!, 2) it is thinly disguised autobiography (richly disguised autobiography is OK), 3) ending is either too pat or else just trails off, 4) characterization is not developed, and 5) point of view falters."

KARAMU, English Department, Eastern Illinois University, 600 Lincoln Ave., Charleston IL 61920. (217)581-6297. Editors: Olga Abella and Lauren Smith. **Contact:** Fiction Editor. Literary magazine: 5×8; 132-136 pages; illustrations; photos. "*Karamu* is a literary magazine of ideas and artistic expression independently produced by the faculty members and associates of Eastern Illinois University. Contributions of essays, fiction, poetry and artwork of interest to a broadly educated audience are welcome." Annually. Estab. 1969. Circ. 400.

Needs: Adventure, ethnic/multicultural, experimental, feminist, gay, historical, humor satire, lesbian, literary, mainstream/contemporary, regional. No pornographic, religious, or moralistic work. List of upcoming editorial themes available for SASE. Receives 50-60 unsolicited mss/month. Accepts 7-10 fiction mss/issue. Does not read mss April 2-September 1. Publishes ms 1 year after acceptance. **Publishes 3-6 new writers/year.** Recently published work by Mary-Lou Brockett-Devine, Virgil Suarez, Diane Farrington and Meg Mocer. Length: 3,500 words maximum. Publishes short shorts, poetry and essays. Sometimes comments on rejected ms.

How to Contact: Query first. Includes estimated word count, 1-paragraph bio and list of publications. Responds in 1 week to queries. Send SASE for reply. Accepts simultaneous submissions. Sample copy for $7.50 or $6 for back issues. Guidelines for SASE.

Payment/Terms: Pays 1 contributor's copy; additional copies for $5. Acquires one-time rights.

Advice: Looks for "development of characters, strong voice and original story line."

THE KARITOS REVIEW, Karitos Christian Arts Festival, 35689 N. Helendale Rd., Ingleside IL 60041. (847)587-9111. E-mail: robuserid@prodigy.net or bob@intersurfer.com. Website: www.karitos.com (includes writer's guidelines and information about our writer's conference). **Contact:** Gina Merritt, fiction editor. Magazine: 8½×5½; 48 pages; illustrations. "The *Karitos Review* publishes poetry, fiction and essays. Our audience is multicultural, mostly evangelical Christians involved in the arts. Though we are evangelical, not everything we publish is religious. We are especially interested in receiving material from writers whose work falls between the Christian and secular markets." Annual. Estab. 1999. Circ. 150.

Needs: Ethnic/multicultural, experimental, fantasy, historical, humor/satire, literary, mainstream, psychic/supernatural/occult, religious (general, inspirational, fantasy, mystery/suspense, thriller), science fiction, translations, western. The editor reports a need for more fiction submissions. No romance, graphic sex and nothing with anti-Christian bias. No religious stereotypes. No formulaic Christian fiction. List of upcoming themes available online. Accepts 4-5 mss/issue; 4-5 mss/year. Does not read mss over the summer. **Publishes 2 new writers/year.** Recently published work by Dennis Van Wey, John Desjarlais and Melissa Merritt. Length: 2,500 words maximum; average length: 1,000-1,500 words. Publishes short shorts. Also publishes literary essays and poetry. Sometimes comments on rejected mss.

How to Contact: Send complete ms with a cover letter. Accepts submissions by e-mail. Include estimated word count, brief bio, list of publications, phone number and/or e-mail address. Responds in 2 weeks to queries; 4 months to mss. Send SASE (or IRC) for return of ms or send a disposable copy of ms and #10 SASE for reply only. Accepts simultaneous submissions and previously published work. Sample copy for $2 plus 6×9 SASE with 77¢ postage. Guidelines on website.

Payment/Terms: Pays 2-3 contributor's copies; additional copies $2. Pays on publication for one-time and first rights.

Advice: "We want quality material written from a Christian worldview. Read a sample copy. Much material that is appropriate for other Christian publications does not fit our style."

KELSEY REVIEW, Mercer County College, P.O. Box B, Trenton NJ 08690. (609)586-4800, ext. 3326. E-mail: kelsey.review@mccc.edu. Website: www.mccc.edu (includes deadlines and writer's guidelines). **Contact:** Robin Schore, editor-in-chief. Magazine: 7×14; 80 pages; glossy paper; soft cover. "Must live or work in Mercer County, NJ." Annually. Estab. 1988. Circ. 1,750.

Needs: Open. Regional (Mercer County only). Receives 120 unsolicited mss/year. Accepts 24 mss/issue. Reads mss only in May. Publishes ms 1-2 months after acceptance. **Publishes 6 new writers/year.** Recently published work by Janet Kirk, Noreen Duncan and Bruce Petronio. Length: 2,000 words maximum. Publishes short shorts. Also publishes literary essays, literary criticism and poetry. Always comments on rejected mss.
How to Contact: Send complete ms with cover letter. SASE for return of ms. Accepts queries/mss by e-mail. Accepts multiple submissions. Responds in 2 months. Sample copy free.
Payment/Terms: Pays 5 contributor's copies. Rights revert to author on publication.
Advice: Looks for "quality, intellect, grace and guts. Avoid sentimentality, overwriting and self-indulgence. Work on clarity, depth and originality."

☑ $⊘ ☷ **THE KENYON REVIEW**, Kenyon College, Gambier OH 43022. (740)427-5208. Fax: (740)427-5417. E-mail: kenyonreview@kenyon.edu. Website: www.kenyonreview.org (includes excerpts, advertising information, issue highlights, writer's guidelines, summer programs and author bios and photos). Editor: David H. Lynn. **Contact:** Fiction Editor. "Fiction, poetry, essays, book reviews." Triannually. Estab. 1939. Circ. 5,000.
• Work published in the *Kenyon Review* has been selected for inclusion in *Pushcart Prize* anthologies.
Needs: Condensed/excerpted novel, contemporary, ethnic, experimental, feminist, gay, historical, humor/satire, lesbian, literary, mainstream, translations. Receives 400 unsolicited mss/month. Unsolicited mss typically read only from September 1 through March 31. Publishes ms 12-18 months after acceptance. Recently published work by David Baker, Rick Bass, Rachel Hadas and Cathy Song. Length: 3-15 typeset pages preferred.
How to Contact: Send complete ms with cover letter. Responds to mss in 4 months. SASE. No simultaneous submissions. Sample copy for $9.
Payment/Terms: Pays $10-15/page on publication for first-time rights. Sends copyedited version to author for approval.
Advice: "Read several issues of our publication. We remain invested in encouraging/reading/publishing work by writers of color, writers expanding the boundaries of their genre, and writers with unpredictable voices and points of view."

◎ **KEREM, Creative Explorations in Judaism**, Jewish Study Center Press, Inc., 3035 Porter St. NW, Washington DC 20008. (202)364-3006. Fax: (202)364-3806. Website: www.kerem.com. **Contact:** Sara R. Horowitz and Gilah Langner, editors. Magazine: 6×9; 128 pages; 60 lb. offset paper; glossy cover; illustrations; photos. "*Kerem* publishes Jewish religious, creative, literary material—short stories, poetry, personal reflections, text study, prayers, rituals, etc." Annually. Estab. 1992. Circ. 2,000
Needs: Jewish: feminist, humor/satire, literary, religious/inspirational. Receives 10-12 unsolicited mss/month. Accepts 1-2 mss/issue. Publishes ms 2-10 months after acceptance. Recently published work by Marge Piercy, William Novak and Anita Diamant. Length: 6,000 words maximum. Also publishes literary essays, poetry.
How to Contact: Send complete ms with a cover letter. Should include 1-2 line bio. Responds in 2 months to queries; 5 months to mss. Send SASE for reply, return of ms or send a disposable copy of ms. Accepts simultaneous submissions. Sample copy for $8.50.
Payment/Terms: Pays free subscription and 2-10 contributor's copies. Acquires one-time rights.
Advice: "Should have a strong Jewish content. We want to be moved by reading the manuscript!"

[N] **KESTREL, A Journal of Literature and Art**, Division of Language and Literature, Fairmont State College, 1201 Locust Ave., Fairmont WV 26554-2470. (304)367-4815. Fax: (304)367-4896. E-mail: kestrel@mail.fscwv.edu. Website: www.fscwv.edu/pubs/kestrel/kestrel.html (includes issue contents, contests, guidelines, subscription forms, festival itinerary). Editors: Mary Stewart and John Hoppenthaler. **Contact:** Fiction Editor. Magazine: 6×9; 100 pages; 60 lb. paper; glossy cover; photographs. "An eclectic journal publishing the best fiction, poetry, creative nonfiction and artwork for a literate audience. We strive to present contributors' work in depth." Semiannually. Estab. 1993. Circ. 500.
• *Kestrel* has received funding grants from the NEA and the West Virginia Commission of the Arts.
Needs: Condensed/excerpted novel, literary, translations. "No pornography, children's literature, romance fiction, pulp science fiction—formula fiction in general." Upcoming theme: West Coast Authors/Spring 2001. Receives 100-150 unsolicited mss/month. Acquires 10-20 mss/issue; 20-40 mss/year. Publishes ms 3-12 months after acceptance. Recently published work by Cáit R. Coogan, Sharon Dilworth, Peter Paul Sweeney and John Maher. Length: 1,500-6,000 words. Publishes short shorts. Also publishes literary essays and poetry. Sometimes comments on rejected mss.
How To Contact: Send complete ms with "short but specific" cover letter. Include list of publications. Responds in 3-6 months to mss. SASE for return of ms or disposable copy of ms. No simultaneous submissions. Accepts electronic (disk) submissions. Sample copy for $6.
Payment/Terms: Pays 5 contributor's copies. Rights revert to contributor on publication.
Advice: Looks for "maturity, grace and verve . . . whether you're 21 or 81 years old. Live with a story for a year or more before you send it anywhere, not just *Kestrel.*"

☑ $ 🔲 **KIDS' HIGHWAY, Oo! What a Ride!**, P.O. Box 6275, Bryan TX 77805-6275. (979)778-5894. E-mail: kidshighway@att.net. Website: http://home.att.net/~kidshighway (includes mission statement, updated table of contents, contest winners, contest information, writer's guidelines, short fiction, e-mail address and subscription information). Editor: Miranda Garza. **Contact:** Hector Cole Garza, fiction editor. Magazine: 8½×11; 22 pages; illustrations. *"Kids' Highway* is a literary magazine that has something for everyone. It has fiction for kids and a tear-out section for adults. We do publish nonfiction." Published 5 times/year. Estab. 1999.

Needs: Adventure, children's/juvenile (adventure, animal, fantasy, mystery, series), mystery/suspense (amateur sleuth, cozy), young adult/teen (adventure, fantasy/science fiction, mystery/suspense, series, western). "We are looking for young writers as well as new ones. No ghosts, magic, occult, horror, religious, political, experimental, problem novels, gay or lesbian." Accepts 5-6 mss/issue; 25-30 mss/year. Publishes ms up to 6 months after acceptance. **Publishes 50% new writers.** Recently published work by David Labounty, Guy Belleranti and Lily Erlic. Length: childrens stories, 1,200 words maximum; adult stories, 900-2,200 words. Publishes short shorts. Length: 50-400 words. Also publishes poetry. Poetry length: 20 lines maximum. Often comments on rejected mss.

How to Contact: Send complete ms with a cover letter. "Send SASE for reply. Send disposable copy of manuscript or send adequate postage for return of manuscript." Accepts queries/mss by e-mail. Include estimated word count, 100 word maximum bio. "If student, include age in cover letter or on manuscript." Responds in 2 months. Send SASE for reply, return of ms or send a disposable copy of ms. Accepts simultaneous submissions and reprints. Sample copy for $3, 9×12 SAE and 3 first-class stamps. Guidelines free for #10 SASE. Reviews novels and short story collections. Send books to Miranda Garza (children's novels and juvenile fiction).

Payment/Terms: Fiction and nonfiction over 400 words: $5 and copy. Poetry: $2 plus copy. Work under 400 words and fillers: pays in copies only. Pays on publication for one-time, reprint rights and selective nonexclusive electronic rights. Sends galleys to author "upon request and with SASE."

Advice: "We look for stories that are unique and entertaining. It has to be original and fun with a surprising and/or satisfying ending. Neatness counts as well as good grammar. Be different but not gross. Have fun with your story. Think 'entertaining' when writing it."

🔲 **KIOSK**, English Department, S.U.N.Y. at Buffalo, 306 Clemens Hall, Buffalo NY 14260. (716)645-2575. E-mail: ed-kiosk@acsu.buffalo.edu. Website: wings.buffalo.edu/kiosk (includes writer's guidelines, names of editors, representative fiction and poetry from issues). **Contact:** Kevin Grauke, editor-in-chief. Magazine: 5½×8½; 150 pages; 80 lb. cover; illustrations. "We seek innovative, non-formula fiction and poetry." Annually. Estab. 1986. Circ. 500.

Needs: Literary. "While we subscribe to no particular orthodoxy, we are most hospitable to stories with a strong sense of voice, narrative direction and craftsmanship." No genre fiction. Wants more experimental fiction. Receives 50 mss/month. Accepts 10-20 mss/issue. Publishes ms within 6 months of acceptance. **Published new writers within the last year.** Recently published work by Mark Jacobs, Jay Atkinson and Richard Russo. Length: 7,500 words maximum; 3,000 words preferred. Publishes short shorts, "the shorter the better." Also publishes poetry. Sometimes critiques rejected mss.

How to Contact: Send complete mss with cover letter. Accepts queries/mss by e-mail. Does not read from June through August. Responds in 4 months to mss. SASE. Accepts simultaneous and reprint submissions. Sample copy for $5. Guidelines for SASE.

Payment/Terms: Pays in contributor's copies. Acquires one-time rights.

Advice: "First and foremost, *Kiosk* is interested in sharp writing. Make it new, but also make it worth the reader's effort. Demand our attention with the first paragraph and maintain it to the end. Read as many different journals as possible. See what people are writing and publishing."

🔲 **KOJA**, 7314 21 Avenue #6E, Brooklyn NY 11204-5906. Website: www.monkeyfish.com/koja (includes sample writing from the premier issue). **Contact:** Mike Magazinnik, editor. Magazine: 8½×11; 64 pages; color cover; illustrations. "The magazine is dedicated to experimental prose/poetry from American authors, and Russian authors living in the US and writing in English. We publish only experimental works." Biennial. Estab. 1996. Circ. 300. "Authors need to buy a sample issue before submitting their works. The cost of the sample issue is $7."

Needs: "We do not publish anything except for experimental literary fiction." Receives 20-30 unsolicited mss/month. Accepts 5-10 mss/issue. Publishes ms up to 2 years after acceptance. **Publishes 20 new writers/year.** Recently published work by Raymond Federman, Richard Vostelanetz, Doug Rice and Lance Olsen. Word length: no minimum; 3,000 words maximum. Publishes short shorts: "any length." Also publishes poetry. Sometimes comments on or critiques rejected ms.

How to Contact: Send complete ms with a cover letter. Include 1-2 paragraph bio. Responds to queries in 1 week; 4 months to mss. "All submissions must be accompanied by $7 to cover the cost of a sample issue. All submissions without $7 will be returned unread." Send SASE for reply, return of ms or send a disposable copy of ms. No simultaneous submissions. Sample copy for $7. Reviews novels, short story collections and poetry of interest to writers. Send book to editor. "Please send only experimental works. We do not guarantee the review of your work will appear in the magazine."

Payment/Terms: Pays 1 contributor's copy; additional copies $7. Acquires first North American serial rights.
Advice: "We look for a fresh approach to writing prose; challenging the boundaries of prose, as well as narrative structure. Please send only experimental work, and only after having seen a sample copy. We receive a lot of works unrelated to the mission of the magazine."

N ★ $ ⃠ KRATER QUARTERLY, P.O. Box 1371, Lincoln Park MI 48146. E-mail: kraterquarterly@aol.com. Website: www.kraterquarterly.com (includes text only for contact info, writer's guidelines and contest info). **Contact:** Leonard D. Fritz, editor. Magazine: standard size; 52 pages; white wove paper; 80 lb. glossy cover; illustrations; photos. A literary magazine of outstanding short fiction and poetry. Quarterly. Estab. 1998. Circ. 4,000.
Needs: Literary, mainstream. No genre fiction. Receives 200 unsolicited mss/month. Accepts 4-6 mss/issue; 16-24 mss/year. Publishes ms 6 months after acceptance. Agented fiction 10%. **Publishes 10-12 new writers/year.** Length: 750-5,000 words; average length: 3,000 words. Sometimes comments on rejected mss.
How to Contact: Send complete ms with a cover letter. Include estimated word count, brief bio and list of publications. Responds in 1 month to queries; 3 months to mss. Send SASE (or IRC) for reply or send a disposable copy of ms. Accepts simultaneous submissions. Sample copy for $5. Guidelines for SASE.
Payment/Terms: Pays $50 minimum and 3 contributor's copies; additional copies $3.50. Acquires first North American serial rights. Rights revert back to author. Sponsors the Erskine Caldwell Award for Short Fiction (see listing in Contests & Awards).
Advice: "Obviously, read us before submitting. Submit one stylish, high-quality story (in a professional format) per mailing, please. New writers—we like you!"

🌐 ◎ LA KANCERKLINIKO, 162 rue Paradis, 13006 Marseille France. Phone/fax: 2-48-61-81-98. E-mail: a.lazarus-1.septier@wanadoo.fr. **Contact:** Laurent Septier, fiction editor. Circ. 300. Quarterly. Publishes 40 pages of fiction annually. "An esperanto magazine which appears 4 times annually. Each issue contains 32 pages. *La Kancerkliniko* is a political and cultural magazine."
Needs: Science fiction. Short stories or very short novels. "The short story (or the very short novel) must be written only in esperanto, either original or translation from any other language." Wants more science fiction. **Publishes 2-3 new writers/year.** Recently published work by Mao Zifu, Manvelde Sabrea, Stefan Maul and Aldo déGiorgi. Length: 15,000 words maximum.
How to Contact: Accepts queries/mss by e-mail and fax.
Payment/Terms: Pays in contributor's copies. Sample copy on request with 3 IRCs from Universal Postal Union.

✓ ◎ THE LAMPLIGHT, Beggar's Press, 8110 N. 38 St., Omaha NE 68112. (402)455-2615. E-mail: beggpress124@aol.com. Editor: Richard R. Carey. **Contact:** Fiction Editor. Magazine: 8½ × 11; 60 pages; 20 lb. bond paper; 65 lb. stock cover; some illustrations; a few photos. "Our purpose is to establish a new literature drawn from the past. We relish foreign settings in the 19th century when human passions transcended computers and fax machines. We are literary but appeal to the common intellect and the mass soul of humanity." Semiannually.
Needs: Historical (general), humor/satire, literary, mystery/suspense (literary). "Settings in the past. Psychological stories. Would like to see more historical humor." Plans special fiction issue or anthology in the future. Receives 120-140 unsolicited mss/month. Accepts 6 mss/issue; 12 mss/year. Publishes ms 4-12 months after acceptance. **Publishes 4-5 new writers/year.** Published work by James Scoffield and Fred Zydek. Length: 500-3,500 words; 2,000 words preferred. Publishes short shorts. Length: 300 words. Also publishes literary criticism and poetry. Critiques or comments on rejected mss.
How to Contact: Send complete ms with cover letter. Include estimated word count, bio (a paragraph or two) and list of publications. Responds in 1 month to queries; 2½ months to mss. SASE. Accepts simultaneous and reprint submission. Sample copy for $10.95, 9 × 12 SAE. Guidelines for #10 SASE. Reviews novels and short story collections.
Payment/Terms: Pays 1 contributor's copy. Acquires first North American serial rights.
Advice: "We deal in classical masterpieces. Every piece must be timeless. It must live for five centuries or more. We judge on this basis. These are not easy to come by. But we want to stretch authors to their fullest capacity. They will have to dig deeper for us, and develop a style that is different from what is commonly read in today's market. We promote our writers after publication."

N 🌐 LANDFALL/UNIVERSITY OF OTAGO PRESS, University of Otago Press, P.O. Box 56, Dunedin, New Zealand. Fax: (64)3 479-8385. E-mail: university.press@stonebow.otago.ac.nz. Editor: Justin Paton. **Contact:** Fiction Editor.
Needs: Publishes fiction, poetry, commentary and reviews of New Zealand books. Length: maximum 10,000 words but shorter work is preferred. "We concentrate on publishing work by New Zealand writers, but occasionally accept work from elsewhere."

N **$** **⊘** **◎** **THE LARCOM REVIEW, The Arts and Literature of New England**, The Larcom Press, P.O. Box 161, Prides Crossing MA 01965. (978)927-8707. Fax: (978)927-8904. E-mail: amp@larcompress.com. Website: www.larcompress.com. **Contact:** Susan Oleksiw, editor. Magazine: 8½×5½; 200-250 pages; acid free paper; 10 pt. CIS cover; illustrations; photos. "We showcase contemporary work by writers and artists of New England as well as exploring work of earlier times. We are interested in all aspects of the six states of this region. Our work is targeted towards New Englanders but not limited to them." Semiannual. Estab. 1999. Circ. 800. Member: American Booksellers Association.

Needs: Family saga, literary, mainstream, personal essays. "No violence, sexual themes." Receives 200-300 unsolicited mss/month. Accepts 6-10 mss/issue; 15-30 mss/year. Publishes ms 2-3 months after acceptance. **Publishes 1-2 new writers/year.** Recently published work by Susan Barrie, Kelly Brennan, Rose Moss, Edith Pearlman, Herb Kenny and Dorothy Stephens. Length: 3,000 words maximum; average length: 1,500-2,500 words. Publishes short shorts. Also publishes literary essays, literary criticism and poetry. Often comments on rejected mss.

How to Contact: Send complete ms with a cover letter or query first with article or book review. Accepts submissions by mail. Include an estimated word count, brief bio and telephone number. Send SASE (or IRC) for return of ms. Accepts simultaneous submissions and no more than 2 multiple submissions. Sample copy for $7. Guidelines for SASE. Reviews nonfiction books of interest to New England.

Payment/Terms: Pays $25-300 and 1 contributor's copy; additional copies discounted 50%. Pays on publication for first North American serial rights. Sends galleys to author.

N **$** **◻** **LC-39, A Magazine of Science Fiction Literature**, Launch Publications, P.O. Box 9307, Baltimore MD 21228-9307. E-mail: editor.lc-39@home.com. Website: http://members.home.net/editor.lc-39 (includes writer's guidelines, story synopsis, subscription information, author biographies). **Contact:** Matthew Walls, editor. Magazine: 7×8½; 128 pages; 70 lb. Patina Matte paper; 80 lb. Lustro Enamel cover. "*LC-39* publishes character-driven science fiction: stories that use the fantastical qualities of this genre to explore some aspect of what it means to be human in this vast and seemingly uncaring universe." Semiannual. Estab. 1999. Circ. 500.

Needs: Science fiction. Receives 30 unsolicited mss/month. Accepts 20 mss/year. Publishes ms 3-6 months after acceptance. **Publishes 3 new writers/year.** Recently published work by Bruce Boston, John B. Rosenman and Stephanie Bedwell-Grime. Length: 20,000 words maximum; average length: 6,300 words. Publishes short shorts. Average length: 500 words. Also publishes poetry. Sometimes comments on rejected mss.

How to Contact: Send complete ms with a cover letter. Include estimated word count and brief bio. Responds in 1 week to queries; 2 months to mss. Send SASE (or IRC) for return of ms or send a disposable copy of ms and #10 SASE for reply only. Accepts previously published work and multiple submissions. Sample copy for $6. Guidelines for SASE.

Payment/Terms: Pays $250 and 2 contributor's copies; additional copies $3.60. Pays on publication for first North American serial rights. Acquires first rights. Sends galleys to author.

Advice: "*LC-39* was built on the idea that quality science fiction should be treated no differently from 'literary' fiction and that is deserves a quality home. *LC-39* departs from the tradition of the science fiction 'pulp,' providing an eloquent presentation where an author's words are allowed room to flow across a page, not be forced into it."

☑ **◯** **LEAPINGS LITERARY MAGAZINE**, 2455 Pinercrest Dr., Santa Rosa CA 95403-8946. (707)544-4861. Fax: (707)568-7531. E-mail: editserv@compuserve.com. Website: home.inreach.com/editserv/leapings.h tml (includes writer's guidelines). Editor: S.A. Warner. **Contact:** Fiction Editor. Magazine: 5×8; 40 pages; 20 lb. paper; glossy cover; illustrations; photos. "Eclectic magazine emphasizing diversity." Semiannually. Estab. 1998. Circ. 200.

Needs: Adventure, ethnic/multicultural, experimental, fantasy, feminist, humor satire, literary, mainstream, mystery/suspense, science fiction. No romance. Receives 30 unsolicited mss/month. Accepts 2 mss/issue; 4 mss/year. Publishes ms 6 months after acceptance. Less than 10% of fiction accepted is agented. **Publishes 5 new writers/year.** Publishes short shorts. Also publishes literary essays, literary criticism, poetry. Sometimes comments on rejected mss.

How to Contact: Send complete ms with a cover letter. Include estimated word count. Responds in 6 weeks. Send SASE for reply, return of ms or send a disposable copy of ms. No simultaneous submissions. Sample copy for $5. Guidelines free for #10 SASE. Reviews novels and short story collections. Send books to S.A. Warner.

Payment/Terms: Pays 2 contributor's copies; additional copies $5. Pays on publication for first rights.

Advice: Looks for "good presentation and sound writing showing the writer has worked at his/her craft. Write and rewrite and only submit it when you've made the work as crisp and clear as possible."

SENDING TO A COUNTRY other than your own? Be sure to send International Reply Coupons (IRC) instead of stamps for replies or return of your manuscript.

☑ ⬓ **THE LICKING RIVER REVIEW**, University Center, Northern Kentucky University, Highland Heights KY 41076. (859)572-5416. E-mail: lrr@nku.edu. **Contact:** Andrew Miller, faculty advisor. Magazine: 7×11; 104 pages; photos. Annually. Estab. 1991. Circ. 1,500.

Needs: Experimental, literary, mainstream/contemporary. No erotica. Wants more experimental. Receives 40 unsolicited mss/month. Accepts 7-9 mss/year. Does not read mss January through July. Publishes ms 6 months after acceptance. Recently published work by Dallas Wiebe, George Malko, Laurie Jones Neighbor, Brett Weaver, Pax Riddle and dayna marie. Length: 5,000 words maximum. Publishes short shorts. Also publishes poetry.

How to Contact: Send complete ms with a cover letter. Accepts queries by e-mail. Include list of publications. Responds in 6 months to mss. SASE for return of manuscript or send disposable copy of ms. No simultaneous submissions. Sample copy for $5.

Payment/Terms: Pays 2 contributor's copies on publication.

Advice: Looks for "good writing and an interesting and well-told story. Read a sample copy first. Don't do what everybody else is doing. Be fresh, original. Write what you like—it will show."

☑ ⬓ **LIGHT QUARTERLY**, P.O. Box 7500, Chicago IL 60680. Editor: John Mella. **Contact:** Fiction Editor. Magazine: 6×9; 64 pages; Finch opaque (60 lb.) paper; 65 lb. color cover; illustrations. "Light and satiric verse and prose, witty but not sentimental. Audience: intelligent, educated, usually 'professional.' " Quarterly. Estab. 1992. Circ. 1,000.

Needs: Humor/satire, literary. Receives 10-40 unsolicited fiction mss/month. Accepts 2-4 mss/issue. Publishes ms 6-24 months after acceptance. Published work by X.J. Kennedy, J.F. Nims and John Updike. Length: 600-2,000 words; 1,200 words preferred. Publishes short shorts. Also publishes literary essays, literary criticism and poetry. Sometimes comments on rejected mss.

How to Contact: Query first. Include estimated word count and list of publications. Responds in 1 month to queries; 4 months to mss. Send SASE for reply, return of ms or send a disposable copy of ms. No simultaneous submissions. Accepts electronic submissions (disk only). Sample copy for $6 (plus $2 for 1st class). Guidelines for #10 SASE. Reviews novels and short story collections. Send review copies to review editor.

Payment/Terms: Pays contributor's copies (2 for domestic; 1 for foreign). Acquires first North American serial rights. Sends galleys to author.

Advice: Looks for "high literary quality; wit, allusiveness, a distinct (and distinctive) style. Read guidelines or issue first."

Ⓝ $⬓ **LIGHTHOUSE STORY COLLECTIONS, Timeless Stories for Family Reading**, Lighthouse Story Collections, P.O. Box 48114, Watauga TX 76148. (817)581-8868. E-mail: lighthouse48114@aol.com. **Contact:** Joyce Parchman or Doris Best, editors. Literary magazine: 8×5½; 52-56 pages; 60 lb. white paper; bristol cover stock. "All material is G-rated, no violence, bad language." Quarterly. Estab. 1999. Circ. 200.

Needs: Children's/juvenile (adventure, animal, easy-to-read, fantasy, historical, mystery, preschool, sports, ages 3-10), historical, mainstream, religious. Receives 25-30 unsolicited mss/month. Accepts 8 mss/issue; 24 mss/year. Publishes ms 6-12 months after acceptance. **Publishes 10-12 new writers/year.** Length: 500-3,000 words; average length: 1,800 words. Publishes short shorts; average length: 1,000 words. Also publishes poetry.

How to Contact: Request writer's guidelines. Accepts submissions by e-mail and on disk. Include estimated word count, brief bio, social security number and age group mss is for. Responds in 1 month to queries; 3 months to mss. Send SASE or IRC for return of ms or send disposable copy of ms and #10 for reply only. Sample copy for $3.50 with 6×9 SAE and $1 US postage. Guidelines free by SASE, e-mail or fax.

Payment/Terms: Pays $50 and 1 contributor's copy; additional copies $3. Pays on publication for first North American serial rights.

Advice: "Well written, strong main characters, good grammar, and can be read by the whole family."

☑ ⬓ **LITE, Baltimore's Literary Newspaper**, P.O. Box 26162, Baltimore MD 21210. E-mail: lite@toadmail.com. Website: LiteCircle.dragonfire.net (includes guidelines, current and back issues, literary news, staff contact information). **Editor:** David W. Kriebel. Tabloid: 11×14; 16 pages; 30 lb. newsprint paper; 2-4 illustrations; some photos. "Poetry, short fiction, occasional nonfiction pieces, satire. Our audience is intelligent, literate, and imaginative. They have the ability to step back and look at the world from a different perspective." Bimonthly. Estab. 1989. Circ. 10,000.

Needs: Experimental, fantasy, historical (general), horror, humor/satire, literary, mystery/suspense (private eye), psychic/supernatural/occult, science fiction (hard science, soft/sociological). "No erotica, gay, lesbian. Nothing demeaning to any ethnic or religious group. No stories with an obvious or trite 'message.' No violence for its own sake." Receives 20-30 unsolicited mss/month. Accepts 1-2 mss/issue; 12-18 mss/year. Publishes mss 1-3 months after acceptance. **Publishes more than 30 new writers/year.** Recently published work by Elizabeth Stevens, Elisa Vietta Ritchie and Catharine Asaro. Length: 3,000 words maximum (however, will consider serializing longer pieces); 1,500 words preferred. Publishes short shorts. Also publishes poetry. Comments on or critiques rejected mss if requested with SASE.

How to Contact: Request guidelines, then send ms and cover letter. Encourages electronic submissions. Include "information on the writer, focusing on what led him to write or create visual art. We want to know the person, both for our contributors guide 'Names in Lite' and to help build a network of creative people." Responds in up to 1 year. SASE. Accepts simultaneous submissions, but prefer them not to be sent to other Baltimore publications. Sample copy for 9×12 SAE and 3 first-class stamps. Guidelines for #10 SASE.

Payment/Terms: Pays 5 contributor's copies; 5 extras for 9×12 SASE with 4 first-class stamps. Acquires one-time rights.

Advice: "We first look for quality writing, then we look at content and theme. It's not hard to tell a dedicated writer from someone who only works for money or recognition. Fiction that resonates in the heart makes us take notice. It's a joy to read such a story." Known for "offbeat, creative, but not overtly sexual or violent. We like characterization and the play of ideas. We don't like contrived plots or political propaganda masquerading as literature."

N $ ○ ▣ LITERAL LATTÉ, Mind Stimulating Stories, Poems & Essays, Word Sci, Inc., 61 E. Eighth St., Suite 240, New York NY 10003. (212)260-5532. E-mail: litlatte@aol.com. Website: www.literal-latte.com (includes excerpts, writer's guidelines, names of editors, interviews with authors, fiction not included in print version). **Contact:** Jenine & Jeff Bockman, editors. Magazine: 11×17; 24 pages; newsprint paper; 50 lb. cover; illustrations; photos. Publishes great writing in many flavors and styles. Bimonthly. Estab. 1994. Circ. 25,000. Member: CLMP.

Needs: Experimental, fantasy, literary, science fiction. Receives 4,000 mss/month. Accepts 4-6 mss/issue; 30 mss/year. Publishes ms 6 months after acceptance. Agented fiction 5%. **Publishes 6 new writers/year.** Length: 500-6,000 words; average length: 4,000 words. Publishes short shorts. Often comments on rejected mss.

How to Contact: Send complete ms with a cover letter. Include estimated word count and brief bio. Responds in 6 months to mss. Send SASE for return of mss or send a disposable copy of ms and #10 SASE for reply only or e-mail for reply only. Accepts simultaneous and multiple submissions. Sample copy for $3. Guidelines for SASE, e-mail of check website. Reviews novels, short story collections and nonfiction books of interest to writers.

Payment/Terms: Pays 10 contributor's copies, a free subscription to the magazine and 2 gift certificates; additional copies $1. Pays on publication for first and one-time rights. Sponsors contest; guidelines for SASE, e-mail or on website.

Advice: "Words make a manuscript stand out, words beautifully woven together in striking and memorable patterns."

N ○ LITERARY MOMENTS, Larnette Phillips and Company, P.O. Box 30534, Pensacola FL 32503-1534. **Contact:** Larnette Phillips, publisher/editor. Magazine: 8½×11; 32-50 pages; 24 lb. gray/white (not recycled) paper; 67 lb. gray/granite cover; illustrations. "*Literary Moments* is a quarterly literary journal that focuses on publishing only those writers who are unpublished or minimally published in fiction." Quarterly. Estab. 1999. Circ. 2,000.

Needs: Adventure, children's/juvenile, family saga, fantasy, historical, humor satire, literary, mainstream, mystery/suspense, religious, romance, science fiction, western, young adult/teen. "I will not print anything containing graphic sex, graphic violence or profanity." Accepts 3-10 mss/issue; 40 mss/year. Publishes ms 3-6 months after acceptance. Recently published work by Ed Sullivan, Linda Olson and Paula Patrick. Length: 1,200-1,500 words; average length: 1,500 words. Publishes short shorts. Average length: 1,200 words. Also publishes literary essays and poetry. Always comments on rejected mss.

How to Contact: Include estimated word count, brief bio and Social Security number with submissions. Send SASE (or IRC) for return of ms. Sample copy for $12.50. Guidelines for SASE.

Payment/Terms: "Submissions are only accepted through my writing competitions which are held three times annually (writing competition deadlines are February 25, May 31 and September 21 of each year). Maximum word length is 1,500. Cash prizes are $500 (1st Prize); $250 (2nd Prize); $100 (3rd Prize) as long as subscription base continues at a level to warrant pay out since I do not solicit advertising revenue and support this publication solely by its subscription base. Winners also receive publication in the magazine plus two contributor copies." Pays on publication for one-time rights.

◲ ▣ THE LITERARY REVIEW, An International Journal of Contemporary Writing, Fairleigh Dickinson University, 285 Madison Ave., Madison NJ 07940. (973)443-8564. Fax: (973)443-8364. E-mail: tlr@fdu.edu. Website: www.webdelsol.com/tlr/ (includes subscription information, writer's guidelines, names of editors, chapbooks and selections from printed issues). **Contact:** Walter Cummins, editor-in-chief. Magazine: 6×9; 140 pages; professionally printed on textpaper; semigloss card cover; perfect-bound. "Literary magazine specializing in fiction, poetry, and essays with an international focus." Quarterly. Estab. 1957. Circ. 2,300.

● This magazine has received grants from a wide variety of international sources including the Spanish Consulate General in New York, the Program for Cultural Cooperation between Spain's Ministry of Culture and U.S. Universities, Pro Helvetia, the Swiss Center Foundation, The Luso-American Foundation, Japan-U.S. Friendship Commission. Work published in *The Literary Review* has been included in *Editor's Choice*, *Best American Short Stories* and *Pushcart Prize* anthologies. The editor would like to see more fiction with an international theme.

Needs: Works of high literary quality only. Receives 50-60 unsolicited fiction mss/month. Approximately 1-2% of fiction is agented. **Published 5-6 new writers/year.** Recently published work by Dale Kushner, Allen Learst and Susan Schwartz Sensted. Length: 5,000 words maximum. Acquires 10-12 mss/year. Does not read submissions during June, July and August. Also publishes literary essays, literary criticism, poetry. Occasionally critiques rejected mss.
How to Contact: Send 1 complete ms with SASE. "Cover letter should include publication credits." Responds in 3 months to mss. Publishes ms an average of 1½-2 years after acceptance. Considers multiple submissions. Sample copy for $5; guidelines for SASE. Reviews novels and short story collections.
Payment/Terms: Pays 2 contributor's copies; 25% discount for extras. Acquires first rights.
Advice: "We want original dramatic situations with complex moral and intellectual resonance and vivid prose. We don't want versions of familiar plots and relationships. Too much of what we are seeing today is openly derivative in subject, plot and prose style. We pride ourselves on spotting new writers with fresh insight and approach."

THE LITTLE MAGAZINE, State University of New York at Albany, English Department, Albany NY 12222. E-mail: litmag@csc.albany.edu. Website: www.albany.edu/~litmag. **Contact:** Dimitri Anastasopoulos, Christina Milletti, Manny Savopoulos, editors. "Web-based journal; publishes CD-ROM issue every 2 years. Includes fiction and poetry for a literary audience; also illustrations; photos; artwork. Fiction and poetry for a literary audience." Annually. Estab. 1965.
● *The Little Magazine* has published entirely on the Web since 1995.
Needs: Literary, multi-media, hypertext, experimental. No genre fiction or long pieces not suitable for web publication. Receives "roughly" 600 mss/issue over a 3-month reading period. Accepts 20 mss/issue. Does not read June through August. Submissions accepted on a rolling basis September through May. Publishes ms 6 months after acceptance. **Publishes 10 new writers/year.** Recently published work by Stuart Moulthrop and Mark Amerika. Length: no limit. Publishes short shorts.
How to Contact: Send complete ms with SASE (or IRC) *on disk* (IBM or Mac) or by e-mail. Hard copy submissions also accepted. Responds in 2 months to queries; in 4 months to mss. Accepts simultaneous and reprint submissions. Sample copy for $15.
Payment/Terms: Pays 2 contributor's copies (when published on CD-ROM).
Terms: Acquires first North American serial rights.
Advice: "We're looking for high-quality fiction and poetry that has been conceived as, or lends itself to, multi-media or hypertext production."

THE LONG STORY, 18 Eaton St., Lawrence MA 01843. (978)686-7638. E-mail: rpbtls@aol.com. Website: www.litline.org/ls/longstory.html (includes writer's guidelines, cumulative index, editorials and a description of the magazine). **Contact:** R.P. Burnham, editor. Magazine: 5½×8½; 150-200 pages; 60 lb. paper; 65 lb. cover stock; illustrations (b&w graphics). For serious, educated, literary people. No science fiction, adventure, romance, etc. "We publish high literary quality of any kind, but especially look for stories that have difficulty getting published elsewhere—committed fiction, working class settings, left-wing themes, etc." Annually. Estab. 1983. Circ. 1,200.
Needs: Contemporary, ethnic, feminist and literary. Receives 30-40 unsolicited mss/month. Accepts 6-7 mss/issue. **50% of writers published are new.** Length: 8,000-20,000 words. Best length: 8,000-12,000 words.
How to Contact: Send complete ms with a brief cover letter. Responds in 2 months. Publishes ms an average of 3 months to 1 year after acceptance. SASE. May accept simultaneous submissions ("but not wild about it"). Sample copy for $6.
Payment/Terms: Pays 2 contributor's copies; $5 charge for extras. Acquires first rights.
Advice: "Read us first and make sure submitted material is the kind we're interested in. Send clear, legible manuscripts. We're not interested in commercial success; rather we want to provide a place for long stories, the most difficult literary form to publish in our country."

LONZIE'S FRIED CHICKEN®, A journal of accessible southern fiction & poetry, Southern Escarpment Company, P.O. Box 189, Lynn NC 28750. E-mail: lonziesfriedchic@hotmail.com. Website: www.lonziesfried chicken.com (includes thumbnail photos of each issue, editors notes and list of contributor's from each issue, bookstore list & writers' guidelines, subscription and ordering info, story behind the name). **Contact:** E.H. Goree, editor/publisher. Literary magazine: 5½×8½; about 100 pages; 65 lb. paper; cardstock cover stock; photos for cover only. "*Lonzie's Fried Chicken* publishes the best work by regional writers and poets. Our focus is to promote both new and established writers. Our growing subscribers' list contains readers from all parts of the US, from all walks of life. We have published 117 writers and poets, many of them never published, as of our fourth issue. *Lonzie's* is an independent publication, funded by subscriptions and bookstore sales." Semiannual. Estab. 1998. Circ. 1,000.
Needs: Historical (general), humor/satire, literary, mainstream, regional (southern US themes). "No gore, hate, erotica, fantasy, science fiction, no essays about your great aunt's funeral." Receives 50 unsolicited mss/month. Accepts 8-12 mss/issue; 16-24 mss/year. Publishes ms 1-6 months after acceptance. **Publishes 10-15 new writers/**

year. Recently published work by Mark Creech, Betty Wilson Beamguard, Melissa A. Hinnant. Length: 1,000-4,000 words; average length: 2,500 words. Publishes short shorts; average length: 200 words. Also publishes poetry. Only comments on rejected ms upon requests and if time permits.

How to Contact: Send complete ms with cover letter. Submit by regular mail only. Responds in 4 months to mss. Send SASE for return of ms or send disposable copy of ms and #10 SASE for reply only. Accepts simultaneous submissions if notified and multiple submissions. Sample copy for $6. Guidelines for SASE.

Payment/Terms: Pays 3 contributor's copies; additional copies $5. Pays on publication for first rights and anthology.

Advice: "We look for subtlety & humor, rejecting the quaint & too-cute. We want your well-written short & short-short stories & novel excerpts with a feel for the region. Writers don't have to live in or be from the south; some of our favorite pieces were written by transplants, some by folks who merely drove through the south! We are interested in work by all writers who write southern-style pieces. Send only your best work."

LOST AND FOUND TIMES, Luna Bisonte Prods, 137 Leland Ave., Columbus OH 43214. (614)846-4126. **Editor:** John M. Bennett. Magazine: 5½ × 8½; 56 pages; good quality paper; good cover stock; illustrations; photos. Theme: experimental, avant-garde and folk literature, art. Published irregularly (twice yearly). Estab. 1975. Circ. 375.

Needs: Contemporary, experimental, literary, prose poem. Prefers short pieces. The editor would like to see more short, extremely experimental pieces. "No 'creative writing' workshop stories." Also publishes poetry. Accepts approximately 2 mss/issue. **Published new writers within the last year.** Published work by Spryszak, Steve McComas, Willie Smith, Rupert Wondolowski, Al Ackerman.

How to Contact: Query with clips of published work. SASE. No simultaneous submissions. Responds in 1 week to queries, 2 weeks to mss. Sample copy for $6.

Payment/Terms: Pays 1 contributor's copy. Rights revert to authors.

LOUISIANA LITERATURE, A Review of Literature and Humanities, Southeastern Louisiana University, SLU 792, Hammond LA 70402. (504)549-5783. Fax: (504)549-5021. E-mail: ngerman@selu.edu. Website: www.selu.edu. Editor: Jack Bedell. **Contact:** Norman German, fiction editor. Magazine: 6¾ × 9¾; 150 pages; 70 lb. paper; card cover; illustrations. "Essays should be about Louisiana material; preference is given to fiction and poetry with Louisiana and Southern themes, but creative work can be set anywhere." Semiannually. Estab. 1984. Circ. 400 paid; 500-700 printed.

• The editor would like to see more stories with firm closure.

Needs: Literary, mainstream, regional. "No sloppy, ungrammatical manuscripts." Receives 100 unsolicited fiction mss/month. Accepts mss related to special topics issues. May not read mss June through July. Publishes ms 6-12 months maximum after acceptance. **Publishes 4 new writers/year.** Recently published work by Anthony Bukowski, Tim Parrish, Robert Phillips and Andrew Otis Haschemeyer. Length: 1,000-6,000 words; 3,500 words preferred. Also publishes literary essays (Louisiana themes), literary criticism, poetry. Sometimes comments on rejected mss.

How to Contact: Send complete ms. Responds in 3 months to mss. SASE. Sample copy for $8. Reviews novels and short story collections (mainly those by Louisiana authors).

Payment/Terms: Pays usually in contributor's copies. Acquires one-time rights.

Advice: "Cut out everything that is not a functioning part of the story. Make sure your manuscript is professionally presented. Use relevant specific detail in every scene. We love detail, local color, voice and craft. Any professional manuscript stands out."

THE LOUISIANA REVIEW, % Division of Liberal Arts, Louisiana State University at Eunice, P.O. Box 1129, Eunice LA 70535. (337)550-1328. E-mail: mgage@lsue.edu. **Contact:** Dr. Maura Gage, editor. Magazine: 7½ × 11; 124 pages; glossy cover; illustrations; photos. "While we will accept some of the better works submitted by our own students, we prefer excellent work by Louisiana writers as well as those outside the state who tell us their connection to it." Annual. Estab. 1999. Circ. 500-700.

Needs: Ethnic/multicultural (Cajun or Louisiana culture), historical (Louisiana-related or setting), regional (Louisiana), romance (gothic). Receives 25 unsolicited mss/month. Accepts 5-7 mss/issue. Does not read mss April-December. Publishes ms up to 11 months after acceptance. Recently published work by R.C. Ferrari, David Pulling and Susan LeJeune. Length: 2,000-10,000 words; average length: 5,000 words. Publishes short shorts. Also publishes poetry. Sometimes comments on rejected mss.

How to Contact: Send complete ms with a cover letter. Accepts submissions by disk (with a hard copy attached, Microsoft Word only). Include letter stating connection to Louisiana. Responds in 5 weeks to queries; 10 weeks to mss. Send SASE (or IRC) for return of ms. Accepts simultaneous submissions, previously published work and multiple submissions. "Please identify these works as such." Sample copy for $3. Reviews novels, short story collections and nonfiction books of interest to writers.

Payment/Terms: Pays 1-2 contributor's copies; additional copies $5. Pays on publication for one-time rights. Not copyrighted (but has an ISSN #).

Advice: "We do like to have fiction play out visually as a film would rather than remain static and lack drama."

THE LOUISVILLE REVIEW, College of Arts and Sciences, Spalding University, 851 S. Fourth St., Louisville KY 40203. (502)585-9911, ext. 223. E-mail: louisvillereview@spalding.edu. Website: www.louisviller eview.org. **Contact:** Sera Jeter Naslund, editor. Literary magazine. Semiannual. Estab. 1976.

Needs: Literary. Receives 25-30 unsolicited mss/month. Accepts 4-6 mss/issue; 8-12 mss/year. Published ms 6 months after acceptance. **Publishes 2-4 new writers/year.** Recently published work by Maura Stanton, David Kaplan, David Ray. Publishes short shorts. Also publishes literary essays and poetry. Sometimes comments on rejected mss.

How to Contact: Send complete ms with cover letter. Include estimated word count, brief bio and list of publications. Responds in 6 months to queries and mss. Send SASE for return of ms or send disposable copy of ms and #10 SASE for reply only.

Payment/Terms: Pays 2 contributor's copies.

LULLWATER REVIEW, Emory University, P.O. Box 22036, Atlanta GA 30322. E-mail: leahwolfson @hotmail.com. Editor-in-Chief: Leah Wolfson. Associate Editor: Alicia Galindo. **Contact:** Robyn Turner, fiction editor. Magazine: 6×9; 100 pages; 60 lb. paper; photos. "We look for fiction that reflects the issues and lifestyles of today, in whatever form it might arrive, whether as a story, short story or a novel excerpt. We hope to reach the average person, someone who might not ordinarily read a publication like ours, but might be attracted by our philosophy." Semiannually. Circ. 2,000. Member: Council of Literary Magazines and Presses.

Needs: Condensed/excerpted novel, ethnic/multicultural, experimental, feminist, gay, humor/satire, lesbian, literary, mainstream/contemporary, regional. "No romance or science fiction, please." Receives 75-115 unsolicited mss/month. Accepts 3-7 mss/issue; 6-14 mss/year. Does not read mss in June, July, August. Publishes ms within 2 months after acceptance. **25% of work published is by new writers.** Recently published work by Greg Jenkins, Thomas Juvik, Jimmy Gleacher, Carla Vissers and Judith Sudnolt. Length: 30 pages maximum; average length: 10 pages. Publishes short shorts. Length: 300-500 words. Also publishes poetry. Sponsors contest; send SASE for information in early Fall.

How to Contact: Send complete ms with cover letter. Include bio and list of publications. Responds in 2 weeks to queries; 4 months to mss. Send SASE for reply, return of ms or send a disposable copy of ms. Accepts simultaneous submissions. Sample copy for $5. Back copy $4. Guidelines for SASE.

Payment/Terms: Pays 3 contributor's copies; additional copies for $5. Acquires first North American serial rights.

Advice: "We at the *Lullwater Review* look for clear cogent writing, strong character development and an engaging approach to the story in our fiction submissions. Stories with particularly strong voices and well-developed central themes are especially encouraged. Be sure that your manuscript is ready before mailing it off to us. Revise, revise, revise!"

LUMMOX JOURNAL, Lummox Press, P.O. Box 5301, San Pedro CA 90733-5301. (562)439-9858. E-mail: lumoxraindog@earthlink.net. **Contact:** Raindog, editor. Magazine: digest size; 24-36 pages; photocopy paper; illustrations; photos. "*The Lummox Journal* focuses on the process of creativity using interviews, reviews, articles and essays as exploratory tools. Lummox Press also publishes a series of poetry books entitled The Little Red Books. Audience: the curious literary bohemian." Estab. 1996. Circ. 200.

● *Lummox Journal* charges an annual reading fee of $5.

Needs: "Stories that highlight the creative process. Longer works may be serialized. Publishes prose and special poetry issues. Publishes special fiction and poetry anthology. Receives 30-40 unsolicited mss/month. **Publishes 10-15 new writers/year.** Recently published work by Clive Matson, Todd Moore and A.D. Winans. Length: 900 words maximum; average length: 750 words. Publishes short shorts. Also publishes literary essays, literary criticism and poetry.

How to Contact: Query first. E-mail preferred. Include cover letter and brief bio and estimated word count. Responds in 2 months to queries. Send SASE for reply, return of ms or send disposable copy of ms. Accepts simultaneous and electronic (disk only) submissions. Sample copy for $2 and a 6×9 SAE with 2 first-class stamps. Guidelines for #10 SASE. Reviews books, CDs, chapbooks. Send in care of Raindog.

Payment/Terms: Pays 1 contributor's copy for one-time rights; additional copies $1. Not copyrighted.

Advice: Looks for "well-crafted, focused work (not buzzword rants), strength and genuine believability. Make sure it's the draft you want to see in print—editor seldom cuts work down."

LYNX EYE, ScribbleFest Literary Group, 1880 Hill Dr., Los Angeles CA 90041-1244. (323)550-8522. Fax: (323)550-8243. E-mail: pamccully@aol.com. **Contact:** Pam McCully, co-editor. Magazine: 5½×8½; 120 pages; 60 lb. book paper; varied cover stock. "*Lynx Eye* is dedicated to showcasing visionary writers and artists, particularly new voices." Quarterly. Estab. 1994. Circ. 500.

● A story from *Lynx Eye* has been chosen for reprint in the *Best Mystery Stories* anthology.

Needs: Adventure, condensed/excerpted novel, erotica, ethnic/multicultural, experimental, fantasy (science), feminist, gay, historical, horror, humor/satire, lesbian, literary, mainstream/contemporary, mystery/suspense, romance, science fiction, serialized novel, translations, westerns. No horror with gratuitous violence or YA stories. Receives 500 unsolicited mss/month. Accepts 30 mss/issue; 120 mss/year. Publishes ms approximately 3 months after acceptance (contract guarantees publication within 12 months or rights revert and payment is kept by author). **Publishes 30 new writers/year.** Recently published work by Anjali Banerjee, Jean Ryan, Karen Wendy Gilbert, Jack Random and Robert R. Gass. Length: 500-5,000 words; average length: 2,500 words. Also publishes artwork, literary essays, poetry. Often comments on rejected mss.

How to Contact: Send complete ms with a cover letter. Include name and address on page one; name on *all* other pages. Responds in 3 months. Send SASE for reply, return of ms or send a disposable copy of ms. Accepts simultaneous submissions. Sample copy for $7.95. Guidelines for #10 SASE.

Payment/Terms: Pays $10 on acceptance and 3 contributor's copies for first North American serial rights; additional copies $3.95.

Advice: "We consider any well-written manuscript. Characters who speak naturally and who act or are acted upon are greatly appreciated. Your high school English teacher was correct. Basics matter. Imaginative, interesting ideas are sabotaged by lack of good grammar, spelling and punctuation skills. Most submissions are contemporary/mainstream. We could use some variety. Please do not confuse confessional autobiographies with fiction."

✔ ◑ **THE MACGUFFIN**, Schoolcraft College, Department of English, 18600 Haggerty Rd., Livonia MI 48152-2696. (734)462-4400, ext. 5292 or 5327. Fax: (734)462-4679. E-mail: macguffin@schoolcraft.cc.mi.us. Website: www.macguffin.org (includes excerpts, guidelines, contests and special issues). Editor: Arthur J. Lindenberg. **Contact:** Elizabeth Kircos, fiction editor. Magazine: 6×9; 164 pages; 60 lb. paper; 110 lb. cover; b&w illustrations; photos. "*The MacGuffin* is a literary magazine which publishes a range of material including poetry, nonfiction and fiction. Material ranges from traditional to experimental. We hope our periodical attracts a variety of people with many different interests." Triannual. Quality fiction a special need. Estab. 1984. Circ. 600.

Needs: Adventure, contemporary, ethnic, experimental, fantasy, historical (general), humor/satire, literary, mainstream, prose poem, psychic/supernatural/occult, science fiction, translations. No religious, inspirational, juvenile, romance, horror, pornography. Upcoming themes: "Dreams of Travel; Thoughts of Home." The issue focuses on place. This will be published in June, 2001. We will consider works until March 15, 2001. Receives 25-40 unsolicited mss/month. Accepts 5-10 mss/issue; 10-30 mss/year. Does not read mss between July 1 and August 15. Publishes ms 6 months to 2 years after acceptance. Agented fiction: 10-15%. **Published 30 new writers within the last year.** Recently published work by Brian Bedard, Sharon Dilworth and Rustin Larson. Length: 100-5,000 words; average length: 2,000-2,500 words. Publishes short shorts. Also publishes literary essays. Occasionally critiques rejected mss and recommends other markets.

How to Contact: Send complete ms with cover letter, which should include: "1. *brief* biographical information; 2. note that this *is not* a simultaneous submission." Responds in 3 months. SASE. Accepts reprint and electronic (disk) submissions. Sample copy for $7; current issue for $8. Guidelines free.

Payment/Terms: Pays 2 contributor's copies. Acquires one-time rights.

Advice: "We want to give promising new fiction writers the opportunity to publish alongside recognized writers. Be persistent. If a story is rejected, try to send it somewhere else. When we reject a story, we may accept the next one you send us. When we make suggestions for a rewrite, we may accept the revision. There seems to be a great number of good authors of fiction, but there are far too few places for publication. However, I think this is changing. Make your characters come to life. Even the most ordinary people become fascinating if they live for your readers."

✔ ◐ **THE MADISON REVIEW**, Department of English, Helen C. White Hall, 600 N. Park St., University of Wisconsin, Madison WI 53706. (608)263-0566. **Contact:** Jessica Agneessens, fiction editor. Magazine: 6×9; 180 pages. "Magazine of fiction and poetry with special emphasis on literary stories and some emphasis on Midwestern writers." Semiannually. Estab. 1978. Circ. 1,000.

Needs: Experimental and literary stories, prose poems, novel excerpts and stories in translation. No historical fiction. Receives 10-50 unsolicited fiction mss/month. Acquires approximately 6 mss/issue. Does not read mss May through September. **Published new writers within the last year.** Published work by Leslie Pietrzyk, Stephen Shugart and Ira Gold. Length: 4,000 words average. Also publishes poetry.

How to Contact: Send complete ms with cover letter and SASE. Include estimated word count, 1-page bio and list of publications. "The letters should give one or two sentences of relevant information about the writer—just enough to provide a context for the work." Responds in 6 months to mss. Publishes ms an average of 4 months after acceptance. Sample copy for $3.

Payment/Terms: Pays 2 contributor's copies; $2.50 charge for extras.

Terms: Acquires first North American serial rights.

🍁 ✔ $ 🖊 **MALAHAT REVIEW**, University of Victoria, P.O. Box 1700, STN CSC, Victoria, British Columbia V8W 2Y2 Canada. (250)721-8524. E-mail: malahat@uvic.ca (for queries only). Website: web.uvic.ca/malahat (includes guidelines, contest info, names of editors and recent contributors). **Contact:** Marlene Cookshaw, editor. Quarterly. Circ. 1,200.

• *The Malahat Review* has received the National Magazine Award for poetry and fiction.

Needs: "General fiction and poetry." Responds in 3 months. Publishes 3-4 stories/issue. **Publishes 4-5 new writers/year.** Recently published work by Niki Singh, Mark Anthony Jarman, Elizabeth Moret Ross, Andrew Pyper and Chris Fink. Length: 10,000 words maximum.

How to Contact: "Enclose proper postage on the SASE." Sample copy: $10 available through the mail; guidelines available upon request. No simultaneous submissions.

Payment/Terms: Pays $30/printed page and contributor's copies.

Advice: "We do encourage new writers to submit. Read the magazines you want to be published in, ask for their guidelines and follow them. Write for information on *Malahat*'s novella competitions."

$ ☑ ☒ MANOA, A Pacific Journal of International Writing, English Dept., University of Hawaii, Honolulu HI 96822. (808)956-3070. Fax: (808)956-7808. E-mail: mjournal-1@hawaii.edu. Website: www.hawaii.edu/mjournal (includes writer's guidelines, names of editors, short fiction and poetry). Editor: Frank Stewart. **Contact:** Ian MacMillan, fiction editor. Magazine: 7 × 10; 240 pages. "An American literary magazine, emphasis on top US fiction and poetry, but each issue has a major guest-edited translated feature of recent writings from an Asian/Pacific country." Semiannually. Estab. 1989.

• *Manoa* has received numerous awards, and work published in the magazine has been selected for prize anthologies.

Needs: Contemporary, excerpted novel, literary, mainstream and translation (from US and nations in or bordering on the Pacific). "Part of our purpose is to present top U.S. fiction from throughout the U.S., not only to U.S. readers, but to readers in Asian and Pacific countries. Thus we are not limited to stories related to or set in the Pacific—in fact, we do not want exotic or adventure stories set in the Pacific, but good US literary fiction of any locale." Accepts 8-10 mss/issue; 16-20/year. Publishes ms 6-24 months after acceptance. Agented fiction 10%. **Publishes 1-2 new writers/year.** Recently published work by Robert Olen Butler, Monica Wood and Barry Lopez. Publishes short fiction. Also publishes essays, book reviews, poetry.

How to Contact: Send complete ms with cover letter or through agent. Responds in 6 months. SASE. Accepts simultaneous submissions; query before sending e-mail. Sample copy for $10. Reviews novels and short story collections. Send books or reviews to Reviews Editor.

Payment/Terms: Pays "highly competitive rates so far," plus contributor's copies for first North American serial rights and one-time reprint rights. Sends galleys to author.

Advice: "*Manoa*'s readership is (and is intended to be) mostly national, not local. It also wants to represent top US writing to a new international market, in Asia and the Pacific. Altogether we hope our view is a fresh one; that is, not facing east toward Europe but west toward 'the other half of the world.' "

☑ ☑ MANY MOUNTAINS MOVING, a literary journal of diverse contemporary voices, 420 22nd St., Boulder CO 80302-7909. (303)545-9942. Fax: (303)444-6510. E-mail: mmm@mmminc.org. **Contact:** Naomi Horii, editor. Magazine: 6 × 8¾; 250 pages; recycled paper; color/heavy cover; illustrations; photos. "We publish fiction, poetry, general-interest essays and art. We try to seek contributors from all cultures." Triannually. Estab. 1994. Circ. 2,500.

Needs: Ethnic/multicultural, experimental, feminist, gay, historical, humor/satire, lesbian, literary, mainstream/contemporary, translations. No genre fiction. Plans special fiction issue or anthology. Receives 300 unsolicited mss/month. Accepts 4-6 mss/issue; 12-18 mss/year. Publishes ms 2-8 months after acceptance. Agented fiction 1%. Recently published work by Tony Ardizzone, Michael Dorsey, Daniela Kuper and Michael Ramos. "We try to publish at least one new writer per issue; more when possible." Length: 3,000-10,000 words average. Publishes short shorts. Also publishes literary essays, poetry. Sometimes comments on rejected mss.

How to Contact: Send complete ms with a cover letter. Include estimated word count, list of publications. Responds in 2 weeks to queries; 3 months to mss. Send SASE for reply, return of ms or send a disposable copy of ms. Accepts simultaneous submissions. Sample copy for $6.50 and enough IRCs for 1 pound of airmail/printed matter. Guidelines for #10 SASE.

Payment/Terms: Pays 3 contributor's copies; additional copies for $3. Acquires first North American serial rights. Sends galleys to author "if requested." Sponsors a contest, $200 prize. Send SASE for guidelines. Deadline: December 31.

Advice: "We look for top-quality fiction with fresh voices and verve. Read at least one issue of our journal to get a feel for what kind of fiction we generally publish."

Ⓝ ☑ ☒ THE MARLBORO REVIEW, The Marlboro Review Inc., P.O. Box 243, Marlboro VT 05344-0243. (802)254-4938. E-mail: marlboro@marlbororeview.com. Website: www.marlbororeview.com (includes excerpts, guidelines, subscription forms, short reviews, more). **Contact:** Helen Fremont, fiction editor. Magazine: 6 × 9; 80-120 pages; 60 lb. paper; photos. "We are interested in cultural, philosophical, scientific and literary issues. Approached from a writer's sensibility. Our only criterion for publication is strength of work." Semiannual. Estab. 1996. Circ. 300. Member: CLMP, AWP

• Works published in *The Marlboro Review* received Pushcart Prizes in 1997, 1998, 1999.

Needs: Literary, translations. Receives 60 unsolicited mss/month. Accepts 2-3 mss/issue; 4-6 mss/year. Publishes ms 1 year after acceptance. Recently published work by Jenny Browne, Kathleen Lester, Nancy Eimers and Alberto Rios. Length: 500-12,000 words; average length: 7,000 words. Publishes short shorts. Average length: 1,000 words. Also publishes literary essays, literary criticism and poetry.

How to Contact: Send complete ms with a cover letter. Include a brief cover letter (short bio, publication history if appropriate). Responds in 3 months to queries; 4 months to mss. Send SASE (or IRC) for return of ms or send a disposable copy of ms and #10 SASE for reply only. Accepts simultaneous submissions and multiple submissions. Sample copy for $8.75. Guidelines for SASE or on website. Reviews novels, short story collections and nonfiction books of interest to writers. Send review copies to Ellen Dudley, editor.

Payment/Terms: Pays 2 contributor's copies; additional copies $5. Pays on publication. All rights revert to author on publication. Sometimes sends galleys to author.

Advice: "We're looking for work with a strong voice and sense of control. Do your apprenticeship first. The minimalist impulse seems to be passing and for that we are grateful. We love to see great, sprawling, musical, chance-taking fiction. *The God of Small Things* is the favorite of more than one editor here."

$ 🖊 🎭 THE MASSACHUSETTS REVIEW, South College, University of Massachusetts, Amherst MA 01003. (413)545-2689. Fax: (413)577-0740. E-mail: massrev@external.umass.edu. Website: www.litline.org/html/massreview.html (includes general overview, information on editors, excerpts, guidelines). Editors: Mary Heath, Jules Chametzky, Paul Jenkins. **Contact:** Fiction Editor. Magazine: 6×9; 172 pages; 52 lb. paper; 65 lb. vellum cover; illustrations; photos. Quarterly. Estab. 1959. Circ. 1,200.

• Stories from the *Massachusetts Review* have been anthologized in the *100 Best American Short Stories of the Century* and the *Pushcart Prize* anthology. This magazine ranked #26 on *Writer's Digest's* Fiction 50 list of top markets for fiction writers.

Needs: Short stories. Wants more prose less than 30 pages. No mystery or science fiction. Does not read fiction mss June 1-October 1. **Publishes 3-5 new writers/year.** Recently published work by Vern Rutsala, Peter Love and Neal Durando. Approximately 5% of fiction is agented. Also accepts poetry. Critiques rejected mss when time permits.

How to Contact: Send complete ms. No ms returned without SASE. Accepts simultaneous submissions, if noted. Responds in 2 months. Publishes ms an average of 9-12 months after acceptance. Sample copy for $8. Guidelines available for SASE.

Payment/Terms: Pays $50 maximum on publication for first North American serial rights.

Advice: "Shorter rather than longer stories preferred (up to 28-30 pages)." Looks for works that "stop us in our tracks." Manuscripts that stand out use "unexpected language, idiosyncrasy of outlook and are the opposite or ordinary."

✓ 🖊 MATRIARCH'S WAY; JOURNAL OF FEMALE SUPREMACY, Artemis Creations, 3395 Nostrand Ave., 2J, Brooklyn NY 11229-4053. Phone/fax: (718)648-8215. E-mail: artemispub@aol.com. Website: http://members.aol.com/femdombook (includes contest news, subscription info, purpose). Editor: Shirley Oliveira. **Contact:** Fiction Editor. Magazine: 5½×8½; illustrations; photos. *Matriarch's Way* is a "matriarchal feminist" publication. Biannual. Estab. 1996.

Needs: Condensed/excerpted novel, erotica (quality), ethnic/multicultural, experimental, fantasy (science, sword and sorcery), feminist (radical), horror, humor/satire, literary, psychic/supernatural/occult, religious/inspirational, romance (futuristic/time travel, gothic, historical), science fiction (soft/sociological), serialized novel. "No Christian anything." Want more "femme dominant erotica and sci-fi." Upcoming themes: "Science of Matriarchy" and "What it Means to be a Female 'Other.' " Receives 10 unsolicited mss/week. Often comments on rejected mss. **50% of work published is by new writers.**

How to Contact: Query first, query with clips of published work or query with synopsis plus 1-3 chapters of novel. Accepts queries/mss by e-mail and disk. Include estimated word count, bio and list of publications with submission. Responds in 1 week to queries; 6 weeks to mss. SASE for reply or send a disposable copy of ms. Sample copy for $10. Reviews novels and short story collections and excerpts "We need book reviewers, original or reprints. We supply books."

Payment/Terms: Pays 1 copy of published issue. Acquires one-time rights.

Advice: Looks for "a knowledge of subject, originality and good writing style. If you can best Camille Paglia, you're on your way!" Looks for "professional writing—equates with our purpose/vision—brave and outspoken."

📰 McSWEENEY'S, 394A Ninth St., Brooklyn NY 11215. E-mail: printsubmissions@mcsweeneys.net or websubmissions@mcsweeneys.net. Website: www.mcsweeneys.net. **Contact:** Dave Eggers, Sean Wilsey, Todd Pruzen, Lawrence Weschler, Diane Vadino and Kevin Shay, editors. "*Timothy McSweeney's Internet Tendency* is an offshoot of *Timothy McSweeney's Quarterly Concern*, a journal created by nervous people in relative obscurity, and published four times a year."

• See the interview with the editor of McSweeney's on page 215.

Needs: Literary.

How to Contact: Submit the first 300 words of ms via e-mail, to the "print submissions" or "web submissions" address. Include a "brief and sober" bio and cover letter. Attach the entire ms to the e-mail submission, if possible as an Microsoft Word file. Attachments in BinHex form cannot be read. If your piece is under 1,000 words, paste the entire submission into the e-mail. "Stories submitted without the author's phone number cannot be considered." Responds in up to 4 months to mss. "Please be patient." Sometimes comments on rejected ms. SASE for editor comments.

Payment/Terms: Pays contributor copies for stories published in the print edition.

Advice: "Do not submit your written work to both the print submissions address and the web submissions address, as seemingly hundreds of writers have been doing lately. If you submit a piece of writing intended for the magazine to the web submissions address, you will confuse us, and if you confuse us, we will accidently delete your work without reading it, and then we will laugh and never give it another moment's thought, and sleep the carefree sleep of young children. This is very, very serious."

N **◑** **◎** **MEDIPHORS, A Literary Journal of the Health Professions**, Mediphors, Inc., P.O. Box 327, Bloomsburg PA 17815. E-mail: mediphor@ptd.net. Website: www.mediphors.org (includes guidelines, staff listing, poems, short stories, essays, art and photographs from recent/past issues). **Contact:** Eugene Radice, editor. Magazine: 8½×11; 80 pages; glossy white paper; 70 lb. color cover; illustrations; photos. "We publish short stories and short-shorts broadly related to medicine and health." Semiannual. Estab. 1993. Circ. 1,000.

Needs: Experimental, historical (medicine), humor satire, literary, mainstream, science fiction (hard science/technological, soft/sociological). "No fantasy, romance, religious." Receives 80 unsolicited mss/month. Accepts 14 mss/issue; 28 mss/year. Publishes ms 10 months after acceptance. Agented fiction 5%. **Publishes 8 new writers/year.** Recently published work by Richard Selzer and Abraham Verghese. Length: 4,500 maximum words; average length: 3,500 words. Publishes short shorts. Average length: 500 words. Also publishes literary essays and poetry. Sometimes comments on rejected mss.

How to Contact: Send complete ms with a cover letter. Include brief bio and list of publications. Responds in 3 weeks to queries; 4 months to mss. Send SASE (or IRC) for return of ms or send a disposable copy of ms and #10 SASE for reply only. Accepts simultaneous submissions and multiple submissions. Sample copy for $6. Guidelines for SASE or on website.

Payment/Terms: Pays 2 contributor's copies; additional copies $5. Pays on publication for first North American serial rights.

Advice: Looks for "high quality writing that shows fresh perspective in the medical and health fields. Accurate knowledge of subject material. Situations that explore human understanding in adversity. Order a sample copy for examples of work. Start with basic quality writing in short story and create believable, engaging stories concerning medicine and health. Knowledge of the field is important since the audience includes professionals within the medical field. Don't be discouraged. We enjoy receiving work from beginning writers. Avoid superficial violence, sex and clichés with nothing more than shock effect."

N **MERIDIAN, The Semiannual from the University of Virginia**, University of Virginia, P.O. Box 400121, Charlottesville VA 22904-4121. (804)924-3354. Fax: (804)924-1478. E-mail: meridian@virginia.edu. Website: www.engl.virginia.edu/meridian (includes excerpts, cover, guidelines, contact info). **Contact:** Fiction Editor. Literary magazine: 6×9; 160 pages; some illustrations. "Produced in affiliation with the University of Virginia's M.F.A. Program in Creative Writing, *Meridian* seeks to publish the best fiction, poetry, and other writing from established and emerging writers." Semiannual. Estab. 1998. Circ. 500.

Needs: "We are open to a variety, but don't want erotica, romance, young adult, children/juvenile." Receives 20-30 unsolicited mss/month. Accepts 3 mss/issue; 6 mss/year. Publishes ms 3-6 months after acceptance. Agented fiction 5%. **Publishes 3 new writers/year.** Recently published work by Jeannie Rothrock, Elizabeth Oness, George Garrett. Length: 1,000-5,000 words; average length: 4,000. Publishes short shorts. Also publishes literary essays, literary criticism and poetry. Rarely comments on rejected mss.

How to Contact: Send complete ms with cover letter. Include estimated word count, brief bio, list of publications and e-mail address. Responds in 1 month to queries; 4 months to mss. Send SASE for return of ms or send disposable copy of ms and #10 SASE for reply only. Accepts simultaneous and multiple submissions. Sample copy for $7. Guidelines for SASE or on website.

Payment/Terms: Pays in 2 contributor's copies; additional copies $3.50. Acquires first North American serial rights. Sends galleys to author.

Advice: "Strong action, vivid characters, dynamic languages. Keep cover letters brief and factual."

✓ **$◯** **◎** **☑** **MERLYN'S PEN: Fiction, Essays and Poems by America's Teens, Grades 6-12**, Box 1058, East Greenwich RI 02818. (401)885-5775. Fax: (401)885-5222. E-mail: merlynspen@aol.com. Website: www.merlynspen.com (includes writer's guidelines, the first page of most stories that appear in our anthology collection: *The American Teen Writer Series*). **Contact:** R. Jim Stahl, publisher. Magazine: 8⅜×10⅞; 100 pages; 70 lb. paper; 12 pt. gloss cover; illustrations; photos. Student writing only (grades 6 through 12) for libraries, homes and English classrooms. Annual (each November). Estab. 1985. Circ. 6,000.

insider report

McSweeney's: creating a literary sensation

When a new literary journal opens its doors, there is usually a buzz among writers' circles: people are excited about having a new venue for their stories and a place to read the work of fresh or even favorite voices. But for a literary journal to cause the national stir that *McSweeney's* has in the last year, well, fiction writers everywhere have cause to rejoice. Not only has *McSweeney's* and its website, www.mcsweeneys.net, provided new opportunities for writers, but it's gotten the attention of people outside the literary world—a rare and wonderful occurrence for a literary journal.

Articles featuring *McSweeney's* have appeared in magazines ranging from *Poets & Writers* to *The New Yorker* and *The Village Voice* to *Salon.com*. And people are also taking note of the stories published in *McSweeney's*. Judy Budnitz's story, "Flush," was selected for inclusion in *Prize Stories: The O. Henry Awards* and Paul Maliszewski's "Two Prayers" was selected for the Pushcart Prize collection. And in spite of today's somewhat inhospitable climate for short stories, a number of writers who started at *McSweeney's* have since signed book deals for collections of their work.

Part of what makes *McSweeney's* so attractive to readers is its sense of play, quirky sense of humor, and willingness to experiment with form, as in the staff's own description of the quarterly found on their website: "McSweeney's is a quarterly publication. Its issues are on average 280 pages, and are perfect-bound. The contents of McSweeney's include fiction, nonfiction, drawings of hairy people, and very little poetry."

McSweeney's strives to mirror the sense of play found in the text by breaking away from the traditional form of the literary journal. The journal is longer than most. The third issue had color foldouts and an actual story by David Foster Wallace printed on the spine. And Issue Four, according to the website, "starts with a box, within which are fourteen separate booklets, most of the stories having been granted their own binding and color covers." The *McSweeney's* website continues this experimentation with hypertext links that give articles a sense of fluidity.

Part of the media excitement surrounding *McSweeney's* is because of Dave Eggers, one of the magazine's founding editors. Eggers's memoir, the bestselling *A Heartbreaking Work of Staggering Genius* (Simon & Schuster, 2000) has made quite a splash of its own in the publishing world, using metafictional techniques in a memoir format, punctuated liberally with outright silliness. Readers familiar with Eggers's earlier publishing effort, the (now folded) San Francisco-based magazine *Might*, may recognize the zany Eggers's sensibility echoed in *McSweeney's*, and the standards of literary quality Eggers helped maintain as an editor with *Esquire*.

Some readers may have been drawn originally to *McSweeney's* and its website because of Eggers's success, but the reason people keep coming back may be its infectious energy. That energy stems from not only the talented writers in the journal but also from the many editors who work to make the journal a success. Here, these editors—Dave Eggers, Sean Wilsey,

Todd Pruzen, Lawrence Weschler, Diane Vadino and Kevin Shay—share a behind-the-scenes glimpse of *McSweeney's*, including how they select fiction for the journal. Their wittiness comes through in their answers, but also apparent is their genuine care about the fiction and nonfiction in *McSweeney's*.

Describe your personal motivation behind working on *McSweeney's*.
We all help out because we like publishing things. That's the beginning and end of it.

In an interview with *Poets & Writers*, Dave Eggers said that the goal of *McSweeney's* is to get stories out "now." What type of fiction are you looking for? For example, do you want current events worked into the stories that would give them this sense of "now"? What other qualities make a *McSweeneys* story?
We really don't publish anything with any sort of timely element. That's just not a factor. What we mean by "now" is just trying to speed up the process of publishing in general, especially with regard to books. By keeping our operation small and streamlined, we're able to cut out many of the more superfluous steps, and thus shrink the time between when something is written and when it's given to readers.

Why do you place such importance on speed?
We feel a certain amount of the fun is lost when one waits a year to publish a story, or eighteen months to publish a book. All authors express frustration at having to wait so long to see their work in print. By the time it appears, you've moved on, improved, your work having taken a new direction. But this issue of speed, we should say, really applies more to our book publishing than the journal. Our books will be published within a few months of the manuscript being finished, for the same reason that, say, fruit is delivered fresh. Freshness is good. Books are good when fresh.

The first book you're publishing through your McSweeney's book label is *The Neal Pollack Anthology of American Literature* which according to your website "features the best of Neal's work for *McSweeney's*, and a number of new pieces, interviews, segues and paraphernalia." What types of work are you interested in for your book label?
It's impossible to say. Late 19th century French imperialism. Cookbooks for Andorrans. Gardening guides for the ambidextrous. Our next book, *Lemon*, by Lawrence Krauser, is about love between man and fruit. But it's a very serious book.

How do your goals for the Internet version differ from the print version?
The web version is much more ephemeral, of course. It's lighter in tone and more accessible. Sometimes it's even timely. And it's been a very good—and cheap!—tool in getting the word out about the journal, about book tours, news, all that. And we'll be using the website more and more, to promote and sell the books we'll be publishing.

How should writers approach *McSweeneys*?
First of all, we would like to say that nothing brings us more joy than to publish unpublished or underpublished writers. Just under half of each print version of *McSweeney's* consists of work we've received, unsolicited, through the mail. But it's hard to read all the submissions.

So we, like most magazines, find ourselves sorting through the submissions, and piling them in order of apparent possibility.

What are common mistakes writers make when submitting to McSweeney's?
The first red flag is a lack of a cover letter. Such submissions are usually photocopies of stories written years ago, and are sent out, blindly, to dozens of magazines. These we read with the least sense of urgency, because we figure that if the writer can't find time to glance at the magazine to which they're submitting, why should that magazine find the time to read their work? The relationship should be one of mutual respect. Thus, we would much rather publish a writer who knows what we're doing, who likes what we do, who buys *McSweeney's* or borrows it and has read it.

Do you think this advice carries over to writers who are submitting work to any magazine or journal?
Many on our staff have read submissions for other, more venerable magazines and report the same problems. Too many writers are greatly reducing their chances of getting published by simply picking up a writer's guide, entering three dozen magazines' addresses into their databases, and throwing their work to the wind. A more personal, attentive approach provides greater benefits to everyone involved. If you look at the journals to which you submit—thus better discerning which outlets would be appropriate for your work—then chances are you'll save yourself a lot of time and stamps, and increase your rate of success. And you'll save the magazines time, too. We just hate reading the words: "To Whom It May Concern." Our staff has been the same since our inception; it makes our day when people use our names.

What is the goal of McSweeney's?
We really consider this a community endeavor, and prefer working with people who treat us like a friendly neighbor, as opposed to some faceless Publishing Outlet. A primary goal of *McSweeney's* is to make the relationship between writer, publisher and reader a tighter and more immediate one, and a more personal one. Make our day by confirming that there are actual people out there enjoying what we're doing, and who want to be a part of it. That keeps us happy and keeps us working.
    —Donya Dickerson

● Winner of the Paul A. Witty Short Story Award and Selection on the New York Public Library's Book List of Recommended Reading. Merlyn's Pen has also received a Parent's Choice Gold Award.
Needs: Adventure, fantasy, historical, horror, humor/satire, literary, mainstream, mystery/suspense, romance, science fiction, western, young adult/teen. "Would like to see more humor." Also publishes editorial reviews, poetry. Must be written by students in grades 6-12. Receives 1,200 unsolicited fiction mss/month. Accepts 50 mss/issue; 50 mss/year. Publishes ms 3 months to 1 year after acceptance. **Publishes 50 new writers/year.** Length: 25 words minimum; no maximum; average length: 1,500 words. Publishes short shorts. Responds to rejected mss.
How to Contact: Send for cover-sheet template. Accepts queries/mss by fax. Accepts multiple submissions. *Charges submission fee: $1/title. For an additional $4, authors receive an extended editorial critique (100 or more words) of their submission in addition to the standard yes/no response.* Responds in 10 weeks.
Payment/Terms: Three copies of *Merlyn's Pen* plus up to 1,000 words $10; over 1,000 words $75; over 3,000 words $175; over 5,000 words $200. Published works become the property of Merlyn's Pen, Inc.
Advice: "Write what you *know*; write where you are. We look for the authentic voice and experience of young adults."

$ ⊠ MICHIGAN QUARTERLY REVIEW, University of Michigan, 3032 Rackham, Ann Arbor MI 48109-1070. (734)764-9265. E-mail: mqr@umich.edu. Website: www.umich.edu/~mqr (includes history and description of magazine; of current and forthcoming issues, subscription information). Editor: Laurence Goldstein. **Contact:** Fiction Editor. "An interdisciplinary journal which publishes mainly essays and reviews, with some high-quality fiction and poetry, for an intellectual, widely read audience." Quarterly. Estab. 1962. Circ. 1,800.

● Stories from *Michigan Quarterly Review* have been selected for inclusion in *The Best American Short Stories* O. Henry and Pushcart Prize volumes.

Needs: Literary. No "genre" fiction written for a "market." "Would like to see more fiction about social, political, cultural matters, not just centered on a love relationship or dysfunctional family." Receives 200 unsolicited fiction mss/month. Accepts 2 mss/issue; 8 mss/year. **Publishes 1-2 new writers/year.** Published work by Nicholas Delbanco, Elizabeth Searle, Marian Thurm and Tennessee Williams. Length: 1,500-7,000 words; average length: 5,000 words. Also publishes poetry, literary essays.

How to Contact: Send complete ms with cover letter. "I like to know if a writer is at the beginning, or further along, in his or her career. Don't offer plot summaries of the story, though a background comment is welcome." Responds in 2 months. SASE. No simultaneous submissions. Sample copy for $2.50 and 2 first-class stamps.

Payment/Terms: Pays $8-10/printed page on publication for first rights. Awards the Lawrence Foundation Prize of $1,000 for best story in *MQR* previous year.

Advice: "There's no beating a good plot and interesting characters, and a fresh use of the English language. (Most stories fail because they're written in such a bland manner, or in TV-speak.) Be ambitious, try to involve the social world in the personal one, be aware of what the best writing of today is doing, don't be satisfied with a small slice of life narrative but think how to go beyond the ordinary."

$ ⊘ ⊠ MID-AMERICAN REVIEW, Department of English, Bowling Green State University, Bowling Green OH 43403. (419)372-2725. Website: www.bgsu.edu/midamericanreview (includes submission guidelines, sample work and contest info). **Fiction Editor:** Michael Czyzniejewski. Magazine: 6×9; 100-150 pages; 60 lb. bond paper; coated cover stock. "We publish serious fiction and poetry, as well as critical studies in contemporary literature, translations and book reviews." Biannually. Estab. 1981.

Needs: Experimental, literary, memoir, prose poem, traditional and translations. Receives about 150 unsolicited fiction mss/month. Accepts 6-8 mss/issue. Approximately 5% of fiction is agented. **Published 5-10 new writers within the last year.** Recently published work by Dan Chaon, Bernard Cooper, Michael Knight and Pamela Painter. Length: 25 pages maximum. Also publishes literary essays and poetry. Occasionally critiques rejected mss. Sponsors the Sherwood Anderson Short Fiction Award.

How to Contact: Send complete ms with SASE. No simultaneous submissions. Responds in about 6 months. Publishes ms an average of 6 months after acceptance. Sample copy for $5. Reviews novels and short story collections. Send books to editor-in-chief.

Payment/Terms: Payment offered pending funding; pays 2 contributor's copies; charges for additional copies. Acquires first North American serial rights.

Advice: "We look for well-written stories that make the reader want to read on past the first line and page. Clichéd themes and sloppy writing turn us off immediately. Read literary journals to see what's being published in today's market. We tend to publish work that is more non-traditional in style and form, but are open to all literary non-genre submissions."

Ⓝ ⊘ THE MIDDAY MOON, Essays, Fiction, Poetry, Other Things of That Sort, Montag Publishing, P.O. Box 368, Waite Park MN 56387. (320)656-5473. E-mail: smontag@montagpublishing.com. Website: www. montagpublishing.com. **Contact:** Susan Montag, editor. Magazine: 8½×11; 32-48 pages; 80 lb. Number 3 Gloss enamel text paper; self cover; illustrations; photos. "*The Midday Moon* is a literary magazine for those not interested in gloom and depression. We want to appeal to open-minded people who want to 'think smart, feel good and laugh at humor their coworkers don't get.' We have a unique section called 'What the Writers Read', a book review section." Estab. 2000. Circ. 300.

Needs: Literary, mainstream. "No romance, erotica, western, horror." Receives about 20 unsolicited mss/month. Accepts 2-3 mss/issue; 8-12 mss/year. Publishes ms 2 months after acceptance. **Publishes 10 new writers/ year.** Recently published Christopher Meeks, Athena Stevens and Karen Patterson-Nourie. Length: 6,000 words maximum; average length: 3-5,000 words. Publishes short shorts. Also publishes literary essays, literary criticism and poetry. Sometimes comments on rejected mss.

How to Contact: Send complete ms with a cover letter. Include estimated word count, brief bio and list of publications. Responds in 1 month to queries and mss. Send SASE (or IRC) for return of ms or send a disposable copy of ms and #10 SASE for reply only. Accepts simultaneous submissions, previously published work and multiple submissions. Sample copy for $4.50. Guidelines for SASE.

Payment/Terms: Pays 2 contributor's copies; additional copies $3.50. Pays on publication.

Advice: "We look for fiction that is concise and thought provoking. The story should begin with the first sentence. Research the market and send for sample copies."

⊚ **MINAS TIRITH EVENING-STAR**, W.W. Publications, Box 7871, Flint MI 48507. Editor: Philip Helms. **Contact:** Fiction Editor. Magazine: 5½×8½; 24 pages; typewriter paper; black ink illustrations; photos. Magazine of J.R.R. Tolkien and fantasy—fiction, poetry, reviews, etc. for general audience. Quarterly. Published special fiction issue; plans another. Estab. 1967. Circ. 500.
Needs: "Fantasy and Tolkien." Receives 5 unsolicited mss/month. Accepts 1 ms/issue; 5 mss/year. **Published new writers within the last year.** Length: 5,000 words maximum; 1,000-1,200 words preferred. Publishes short shorts. Also publishes literary essays, literary criticism, poetry. Occasionally critiques rejected mss.
How to Contact: Send complete ms and bio. Responds in 2 months. SASE. No simultaneous submissions. Accepts reprint submissions. Sample copy for $2. Reviews novels and short story collections.
Terms: Acquires first rights.
Advice: Goal is "to expand knowledge and enjoyment of J.R.R. Tolkien's and his son Christopher Tolkien's works and their worlds."

📰 ⃝ **MINDPRINTS, A Literary Journal**, Allan Hancock College, Disabled Student Programs and Services, 800 S. College Dr., Santa Maria CA 93454-6399. (805)922-6966, ext. 3274. Fax: (805)922-3556. E-mail: htcdsps@sbceo.org. **Contact:** Paul Fahey, editor. 1 year term. Next year's editor is Margaret Tillery. Magazine: 6×9; 100 pages; 70 lb. perfect bound paper; glossy cover; illustrations; photos. "*Mindprints* is a quality college publication of short fiction, memoir, poetry and art for writers with disabilities and writers with an interest in the field." Annual. Estab. 2000. Circ. 500.
Needs: Literary, short shorts, flash fiction, memoir. Accepts 50 mss/issue. Does not read mss June-August. Publishes ms 6 months after acceptance. Length: 250-750 words; average length: 500-600 words. Publishes short shorts. Average length: 600-750 words. Also publishes poetry. Sometimes comments on rejected mss.
How to Contact: Send complete ms with a cover letter. Submission deadline: March 1. Include estimated word count, brief bio and list of publications. Responds in 3 months to mss. Send a disposable copy of ms and #10 SASE for reply only. Accepts simultaneous submissions, previously published work and multiple submissions (2 short shorts or 5 poems). Sample copy for $5. Guidelines for SASE.
Payment/Terms: Pays 1 contributor's copy; additional copies $5. Acquires one-time rights. Not copyrighted.

✅ ⃝ **THE MINNESOTA REVIEW, A Journal of Committed Writing**, Dept. of English, University of Missouri, Columbia MO 65211. (573)882-3059. Fax: (573)882-5785. **Contact:** Jeffrey Williams, editor. Magazine: 5¼×7½; approximately 200 pages; some illustrations; occasional photos. "We emphasize socially and politically engaged work." Semiannually. Estab. 1960. Circ. 1,500.
Needs: Experimental, feminist, gay, historical, lesbian, literary. Receives 50-75 mss/month. Accepts 3-4 mss/issue; 6-8 mss/year. Publishes ms within 6-12 months after acceptance. Published work by Laura Nixon Dawson, Jameson Currier, Jiqi Kajane and Stephen Guiterrez. Length: 1,500-6,000 words preferred. Publishes short shorts. Also publishes literary essays, literary criticism, poetry. Occasionally critiques rejected mss and recommends other markets.
How to Contact: Send complete ms with optional cover letter. Responds in 3 weeks to queries; 3 months to mss. SASE. Accepts simultaneous submissions. Reviews novels and short story collections. Send books to book review editor.
Payment/Terms: Pays in contributor's copies. Charge for additional copies. Acquires first rights.
Advice: "We look for socially and politically engaged work, particularly short, striking work that stretches boundaries."

📰 $⃝ **THE MISSING FEZ, A Quarterly Publication of Unconventional and Otherwise Abnormal Literature**, Red Felt Publishing, 1720 N. Dodge Blvd., Tucson AZ 85716. (520)323-1486. E-mail: missingfez@hotmail.com. **Contact:** Eleanor Horner, fiction editor. Magazine: 8½×7; 36-40 pages; semigloss paper; glossy cover. "We strive to publish fiction of high quality which for some reason falls outside the traditional literary spectrum." Quarterly. Estab. 2000. Circ. 1,000.
Needs: Erotica, experimental, fantasy (space fantasy), feminist, gay, horror, humor satire, literary, mainstream, mystery/suspense (private eye/hardboiled), psychic/supernatural/occult, science fiction, thriller/espionage. "Please do not send anecdotes or lessons of morality." Receives 30 unsolicited mss/month. Accepts 4-5 mss/issue; 16-20 mss/year. Publishes ms 6 months after acceptance. Agented fiction 20%. **Publishes 10 new writers/year.** Recently published work by Jonathon Earney and Michael Blackwell. Length: 10-8,000 words; average length: 5,000 words. Publishes short shorts. Average length: 1,000 words. Also publishes poetry. Always comments on rejected mss.
How to Contact: Send complete ms with a cover letter and $3 reading fee payable to: Red Felt Publishing. Include estimated word count and list of publications. Responds in 6 weeks to mss. Send a disposable copy of ms and #10 SASE for reply only. Accepts simultaneous submissions. Sample copy for $2. Guidelines for SASE or by e-mail.
Payment/Terms: Pays $25 and 2 contributor's copies; additional copies $2. Pays on acceptance for first rights. Sponsors contest. Send SASE for guidelines.
Advice: "We get a lot of stories about morality and doing the right thing—we would like to see less of this."

⬤ **MISSISSIPPI REVIEW**, University of Southern Mississippi, Box 5144, Hattiesburg MS 39406-5144. (601)266-4321. E-mail: fb@netdoor.com. Website: www.sushi.st.usm.edu/mrw/. **Contact:** Rie Fortenberry, managing editor. "Literary publication for those interested in contemporary literature—writers, editors who read to be in touch with current modes." Semiannually. Estab. 1972. Circ. 1,500.

- The *Mississippi Review* ranked #5 on *Writer's Digest*'s "Fiction 50" list of top markets for fiction writers.

Needs: Literary, contemporary, fantasy, humor, translations, experimental, avant-garde and "art" fiction. Quality writing. No juvenile or genre fiction. Buys varied amount of mss/issue. Does not read mss in summer. Published work by Jason Brown, Terese Svoboda and Barry Hannah. Length: 30 pages maximum.

How to Contact: Not currently reading unsolicited work. Sample copy for $8.

Payment/Terms: Pays in contributor's copies. Acquires first North American serial rights.

Advice: "May I suggest that you enter our annual *Mississippi Review* Prize competition (see Contests section in this book) or submit the work via e-mail to our World Wide Web publication, which is a monthly (except August) and publishes more new work than we are able to in the print version. Send submissions to fb@netdoor. com as ASCII files in the text of your e-mail message, or as Microsoft Word of WordPerfect attachments to your message."

$ ⬤ 🔲 **THE MISSOURI REVIEW**, 1507 Hillcrest Hall, University of Missouri—Columbia, Columbia MO 65211. (573)882-4474. Fax: (573)884-4671. Website: www.missourireview.org (includes guidelines, contest information, staff photos, editorial column, short fiction, poetry, essays, interviews, features and book reviews). **Contact:** Speer Morgan, editor. Magazine: 6×9; 212 pages. Theme: fiction, poetry, essays, reviews, interviews, cartoons, "all with a distinctly contemporary orientation. For writers, and the general reader with broad literary interests. We present nonestablished as well as established writers of excellence. The *Review* frequently runs feature sections or special issues dedicated to particular topics frequently related to fiction." Published 3 times/academic year. Estab. 1977. Circ. 6,800.

- *The Missouri Review* ranked #38 on *Writer's Digest*'s "Fiction 50" list of top markets for fiction writers. This magazine had stories anthologized in the *Pushcart Prize Anthology*, *Best American Short Stories*, *Best American Erotica* and *New Stories From the South*.

Needs: Condensed/excerpted novel, ethnic/multicultural, humor/satire, literary, contemporary. "No genre or flash fictions; no children's." Receives approximately 400 unsolicited fiction mss each month. Accepts 5-6 mss/issue; 15-20 mss/year. **Publishes 6-10 new writers/year.** Recently published work by William Gay, Frederick Busch and Nicola Mason. No preferred length. Also publishes personal essays, poetry. Often critiques rejected mss.

How to Contact: Send complete ms with SASE. Include brief bio and list of publications. Responds in 10 weeks. Send SASE for reply, return of ms or send disposable copy of ms. Sample copy for $8.

Payment/Terms: Pays $20/page minimum on signed contract for all rights.

Advice: Awards William Peden Prize in fiction; $1,000 to best story published in *Missouri Review* in a given year. Also sponsors Editors' Prize Contest with a prize of $1,500 for fiction, $1,000 for essays and the Larry Levis Editors' Prize for poetry, with a prize of $1,500; and the Tom McAfee Discovery Prize in poetry for poets who have not yet published a book.

⬤ **MOBIUS, The Journal of Social Change**, 1250 E. Dayton #3, Madison WI 53703. (608)255-4224. E-mail: smfred@aol.com. **Contact:** Fred Schepartz, editor. Magazine: 8½×11; 32-64 pages; 60 lb. paper; 60 lb. cover. "Looking for fiction which uses social change as either a primary or secondary theme. This is broader than most people think. Need social relevance in one way or another. For an artistically and politically aware and curious audience." Quarterly. Estab. 1989. Circ. 1,500.

Needs: Contemporary, ethnic, experimental, fantasy, feminist, gay, historical, horror, humor/satire, lesbian, literary, mainstream, prose poem, science fiction. "No porn, no racist, sexist or any other kind of ist. No Christian or spiritually proselytizing fiction." Receives 15 unsolicited mss/month. Accepts 3-5 mss/issue. Publishes ms 3-9 months after acceptance. Published work by JoAnn Yolanda Hernández, Patricia Stevens and Rochelle Schwab. Length: 500-5,000 words; 3,500 words preferred. Publishes short shorts. Length: 500 words. Always critiques rejected mss.

How to Contact: Send complete ms with cover letter. Responds in 4 months. SASE. Accepts simultaneous and reprint submissions. Sample copy for $2, 9×12 SAE and 3 first-class stamps. Guidelines for SASE. "Please include return postage, not IRCs, in overseas submissions."

Payment/Terms: Pays contributor's copies. Acquires one-time rights and electronic rights for www version.

Advice: "We like high impact, we like plot and character-driven stories that function like theater of the mind." Looks for "first and foremost, good writing. Prose must be crisp and polished; the story must pique my interest and make me care due to a certain intellectual, emotional aspect. Second, *Mobius* is about social change. We want stories that make some statement about the society we live in, either on a macro or micro level. Not that your story needs to preach from a soapbox (actually, we prefer that it doesn't), but your story needs to have *something* to say."

N ☑ ▣ MONKEYPLANET, Monkeyplanet.com, 20 Highland Ave., Suite 3A, Metuchen NJ 08840. (732)548-8700. Fax: (732)548-7888. E-mail: editor@monkeyplanet.com. Website: www.monkeyplanet.com (includes stories, editors, authors, guidelines and art gallery). **Contact:** Perry Waddell, editor-in-chief. Magazine: 100 pages. "*Monkeyplanet* is an online magazine for those too young to be Baby Boomers and too old for Gen X. *Monkeyplanet* has fiction, travel, poetry, reviews and short stories." Quarterly. Estab. 1998. Circ. "thousands of website hits."

Needs: Adventure, ethnic/multicultural, experimental, fantasy, feminist, gay, glitz, historical, horror, hummor/satire, lesbian, literary, mainstream, mystery/suspense, regional, science fiction, thriller/espionage. List of upcoming themes available online. Receives 5 unsolicited mss/month. Accepts 12 mss/issue; 48 mss/year. Publishes ms 1-2 weeks after acceptance. Agented fiction 1%. **Publishes 10 new writers/year.** Recently published work by Rick Overton, Mark Salon and Anya Krugoudy Silver. Length: 300-1,500 words; average length: 300 words. Publishes short shorts. Average length: 300 words. Also publishes literary essays, literary criticism and poetry.

How to Contact: Query with clips of published work. Accepts submissions by e-mail and disk. Include estimated word count, brief bio and list of publications. Responds in 2 months to queries. Send SASE (or IRC) for return of ms or send a disposable copy of ms and #10 SASE for reply only. Accepts simultaneous submissions, previously published work and multiple submissions. Guidelines on website. Reviews novels, short story collections and nonfiction books of interest to writers. Send review copies to editor.

Payment/Terms: Acquires one-time electronic rights.

☑ ◎ THE MUSING PLACE, The Literary & Arts Magazine of Chicago's Mental Health Community, The Thresholds, 2700 N. Lakeview, Chicago IL 60614. (773)281-3800, ext. 2491. Fax: (773)281-8790. E-mail: jscudder@thn.thresholds.org. **Contact:** Jennifer Scudder, editor. Magazine: 8½ × 11; 36 pages; 60 lb. paper; glossy cover; illustrations. "We are mostly a poetry magazine by and for mental health consumers. We want to give a voice to those who are often not heard. All material is composed by mental health consumers. The only requirement for consideration of publication is having a history of mental illness." Semiannually. Estab. 1986. Circ. 1,000.

Needs: Adventure, condensed/excerpted novel, ethnic/multicultural, experimental, fantasy (science fantasy, sword and sorcery), feminist, gay, historical (general), horror, humor/satire, lesbian, literary, mainstream/contemporary, mystery/suspense, regional, romance, science fiction and serialized novel. Publishes ms up to 6 months after acceptance. Published work by Allen McNair, Donna Willey and Mark Gonciarz. Length: 700 words maximum; average length: 500 words. Length: 500 words. Also publishes poetry.

How to Contact: Send complete ms with a cover letter. Include bio (paragraph) and statement of having a history of mental illness. Responds in 6 months. Send a disposable copy of ms. Accepts simultaneous and reprint submissions. Sample copy free.

Payment/Terms: Pays contributor's copies. Acquires one-time rights.

☑ NEBO, A Literary Journal, Arkansas Tech University, Dept. of English, Russellville AR 72801. (501)968-0256. Editors change each year. **Contact:** Dr. Michael Karl Ritchie, editor. Literary, fiction and poetry magazine: 5×8; 50-60 pages. For a general, academic audience. Annually. Estab. 1983. Circ. 500.

Needs: Literary, mainstream, reviews. Upcoming theme: pop icon fiction and poetry (fiction and poetry that plays with the roles of pop icons). Receives 20-30 unsolicited fiction mss/month. Accepts 2 mss/issue; 6-10 mss/year. Does not read mss May 1-September 1. **Published new writers within the last year.** Published work by Steven Sherrill, J.B. Bernstein, Jameson Currier, Tricia Lande and Joseph Nicholson. Length: 3,000 words maximum. Also publishes literary essays, literary criticism, poetry. Occasionally critiques rejected mss.

How to Contact: Send complete ms with SASE and cover letter with bio. No simultaneous submissions. Responds in 3 months to mss. Publishes ms an average of 6 months after acceptance. Sample copy for $6. "Submission deadlines for all work are November 15 and January 15 of each year." Reviews novels and short story collections.

Payment/Terms: Pays 1 contributor's copy. Acquires one-time rights.

Advice: "A writer should carefully edit his short story before submitting it. Write from the heart and put everything on the line. Don't write from a phony or fake perspective. Frankly, many of the manuscripts we receive should be publishable with a little polishing. Manuscripts should *never* be submitted with misspelled words or on 'onion skin' or colored paper."

☑ THE NEBRASKA REVIEW, University of Nebraska at Omaha, Omaha NE 68182-0324. (402)554-3159. E-mail: jreed@unomaha.edu. **Contact:** James Reed, fiction editor. Magazine: 5½ × 8½; 108 pages; 60 lb. text paper; chrome coat cover stock. "*TNR* attempts to publish the finest available contemporary fiction and poetry for college and literary audiences." Publishes 2 issues/year. Estab. 1973. Circ. 1,000.

● *TNR* received a special mention for the Pushcart Prize and had work published in *Best New Stories of the South.*

Needs: Contemporary, humor/satire, literary and mainstream. No genre fiction. Receives 40 unsolicited fiction mss/month. Accepts 4-5 mss/issue, 8-10 mss/year. Reads for the *Nebraska Review* Awards in Fiction and Poetry and Creative Nonfiction September 1 through November 30. Open to submissions January 1-April 30; does not read May 1-August 31. **Publishes 2/3 new writers/year.** Published work by Cris Mazza, Mark Wisniewski, Stewart O'Nan, Elaine Ford and Tom Franklin. Length: 5,000-6,000 words average. Also publishes poetry.

How to Contact: Send complete ms with SASE. Responds in 6 months. Publishes ms an average of 6-12 months after acceptance. Sample copy for $4.50.

Payment/Terms: Pays 2 contributor's copies plus 1 year subscription; additional copies $4. Acquires first North American serial rights.

Advice: "Write stories in which the lives of your characters are the primary reason for writing and techniques of craft serve to illuminate, not overshadow, the textures of those lives. Sponsors a $500 award/year—write for rules."

☑ ⊘ ◎ **NEOTROPE**, Broken Boulder Press, P.O. Box 172, Lawrence KS 66044-0172. (785)331-0270. E-mail: apowell10@hotmail.com. Website: www.brokenboulder.com (includes submission guidelines, ordering information and addresses, samples of published work, and general information about our press). Editors: Adam Powell, Paul Silvia. **Contact:** Fiction Editor. Magazine: 5½ × 8½; 90 pages; perfect-bound; illustrations; photos. "We view *Neotrope* as a deprogramming tool for refugees from MPW programs and fiction workshops. We are seeking highly original and aggressively experimental fiction. We publish new and progressive forms of fiction writing, stories that are experimental in structure, style, subject matter and execution. We don't target any specific groups, but trust our audience to define itself." Published annually in August. Estab. 1998. Circ. 1,000.

Needs: Experimental fiction and drama. "No genre fiction, nothing traditional." Receives 30-50 unsolicited mss/month. Accepts 12-16 mss/issue. Publishes ms up to 1 year after acceptance. **Publishes 1-16 new writers/ year.** Recently published works by Joy Kaplan, Davis Schneiderman, Tom Whalen and Bill D. Michele. Length: open. Publishes short shorts. Always comments on rejected ms.

How to Contact: Send complete ms with a cover letter and SASE. Responds in 2 weeks. Accepts simultaneous submissions, "but if we accept it we will use it, regardless of any other magazine's decision." Sample copy for $5 postpaid. Guidelines free.

Payment/Terms: Pays 2 contributor's copies; additional copies at cost. Acquires one-time rights. Sometimes sends galleys to author.

Advice: "If it reminds me of something I've seen before, it's not ready for *Neotrope*. You can never take too much time to develop your art. I despise this unwritten code of honor among editors which prohibits all but the most general and impersonal replies with returned manuscripts. Most editors don't even bother to sign their names to a xeroxed rejection slip. Those people who are confident enough to set themselves up as the caretakers of contemporary literature have an obligation to prove their worth by helping other writers along."

Ⓜ **NERVE COWBOY**, Liquid Paper Press, P.O. Box 4973, Austin TX 78765. Editors: Joseph Shields and Jerry Hagins. **Contact:** Fiction Editor. Magazine: 7 × 8½; 60-64 pages; 20 lb. paper; card stock cover; illustrations. "*Nerve Cowboy* publishes adventurous, comical, disturbing, thought-provoking, accessible poetry and fiction. We like to see work sensitive enough to make the hardest hard-ass cry, funny enough to make the most hopeless brooder laugh and disturbing enough to make us all glad we're not the author of the piece." Semiannually. Estab. 1996. Circ. 250.

• Sponsors an annual chapbook contest for fiction or poetry. Deadline January 15. Send SASE for details.

Needs: Literary. No "racist, sexist or overly offensive" work. Wants more "unusual stories with rich description and enough twists and turns that leaves the reader thinking." Receives 40 unsolicited mss/month. Accepts 2-3 mss/issue; 4-6 mss/year. Publishes ms 6-12 months after acceptance. **Publishes 5-10 new writers/year.** Published work by Albert Huffstickler, Mark Smith, Catfish McDaris, Laurel Speer, Brian Prioleau, Marcy Shapiro, Susanne R. Bowers and Adam Gurvitch. Length: 1,500 words maximum; average length: 750-1,000 words. Publishes short shorts. Also publishes poetry.

How to Contact: Send complete ms with a cover letter. Include bio and list of publications. Responds in 2 weeks to queries; 2 months to mss. Send SASE for reply, return of ms or send disposable copy of ms. No simultaneous submissions. Accepts reprints. Sample copy for $4. Guidelines for #10 SASE.

Payment/Terms: Pays 1 contributor's copy for one-time rights.

Advice: "We look for writing which is very direct and elicits a visceral reaction in the reader. Read magazines you submit to in order to get a feel for what the editors are looking for. Write simply and from the gut."

☑ ⊘ ♈ **NEW DELTA REVIEW**, Creative Writing Programs, English Dept./Louisiana State University, Baton Rouge LA 70803-5001. (504)388-4079. E-mail: wwwndr@unix1.snce.lsu.edu. Editor-in-Chief: Andrew Spear. **Contact:** Sean Cavenaugh, fiction editor. Editors change every year. Magazine: 6 × 9; 75-125 pages; high quality paper; glossy card cover; b&w illustrations and artwork. "No theme or style biases. Poetry, fiction primarily; also literary interviews and reviews." Semi-annual. Estab. 1984. Circ. 500.

• *New Delta Review* also sponsors the Eyster Prizes for fiction and poetry. See the listing in the Contest and Awards Section of this book. Work from the magazine has been included in the *Pushcart Prize* anthology. This publication ranked #43 on *Writer's Digest*'s Fiction 50 list of top markets for fiction writers.

Needs: Contemporary, humor/satire, literary, mainstream, prose poem, translations. No novel excerpts, adventure, sci-fi, juvenile. Receives 200 unsolicited mss/ month. Accepts 3-4 mss/issue, 6-8 mss/year. **Published new writers within the last year.** Recently published work by George Berridge, Jr., Ted Graf, Hayley R. Mitchell and Rebecah Edwards. Length: 250 words minimum; average length: 20 ms pages. Publishes short shorts. Also publishes poetry. Rarely critiques rejected mss.
How to Contact: Send complete ms with cover letter. Cover letter should include estimated word count, bio, Social Security number and "credits, if any; no synopses, please." Accepts queries/mss by fax. No simultaneous submissions. Responds to queries in 3 weeks; 3 months to mss. SASE (or IRC). Mss deadlines September 1 for fall; February 15 for spring. Sample copy for $6. Reviews novels and short story collections.
Payment/Terms: Pays in contributor's copies. Charge for extras.
Terms: Acquires first North American serial rights. Sponsors award for fiction writers in each issue. Eyster Prize-$50 plus notice in magazine. Mss selected for publication are automatically considered.
Advice: "We want fiction that compels the reader to continue reading until the end. Keep reading what is being published in the small journals and 'Best of' anthologies, and write, and then rewrite."

$ ◯ NEW ENGLAND REVIEW, Middlebury College, Middlebury VT 05753. (802)443-5075. E-mail: nereview@mail.middlebury.edu. Website: www.middlebury.edu/~nereview (includes guidelines, staff, ordering information, sample works from current and back issues). **Contact:** Stephen Donadio, editor. Magazine: 7 × 10; 180 pages; 50 lb paper; coated cover stock. A literary quarterly publishing fiction, poetry and essays with special emphasis on contemporary cultural issues, both in the US and abroad. For general readers and professional writers. Quarterly. Estab. 1977. Circ. 2,000.
Needs: Literary. Receives 250 unsolicited fiction mss/month. Accepts 5 mss/issue; 20 mss/year. Does not read ms June-August. **Publishes 1-2 new writers/year.** Recently published work by Tom Paine, Madison Smart Bell, Robert Cohen, Debrah Spark. Publishes ms 3-9 months after acceptance. Agented fiction: less than 5%. Prose length: 10,000 words maximum, double spaced. Novellas: 30,000 words maximum. Publishes short shorts occasionally. Sometimes critiques rejected mss.
How to Contact: Send complete ms with cover letter. "Cover letters that demonstrate that the writer knows the magazine are the ones we want to read. We don't want hype, or hard-sell, or summaries of the author's intentions. Will consider simultaneous submissions, but must be stated as such." Responds in 15 weeks to mss. SASE.
Payment/Terms: Pays $10/page, $20 minimum and 2 contributor's copies on publication; charge for extras. Acquires first rights and reprint rights. Sends galleys to author.
Advice: "It's best to send one story at a time, and wait until you hear back from us to try again."

$ ◯ NEW LETTERS MAGAZINE, University of Missouri-Kansas City, University House, 5101 Rockhill Rd., Kansas City MO 64110. (816)235-1168. Fax: (816)235-2611. Website: www.umkc.edu/newletters. **Contact:** James McKinley, editor. Magazine: 14 lb. cream paper; illustrations. Quarterly. Estab. 1971 (continuation of *University Review,* founded 1935). Circ. 2,500.
Needs: Contemporary, ethnic, experimental, humor/satire, literary, mainstream, translations. No "bad fiction in any genre." **published work by new writers within the last year.** Published work by Tess Gallagher, Jimmy Carter and Amiri Baraka. Agented fiction: 10%. Also publishes short shorts. Rarely critiques rejected mss.
How to Contact: Send complete ms with cover letter. Does not read mss May 15-October 15. Responds in 3 weeks to queries; 3 months to mss. SASE for ms. No simultaneous or multiple submissions. Sample copy $5.50 or on website.
Payment/Terms: Pays honorarium—depends on grant/award money; 2 contributor's copies. Sends galleys to author.
Advice: "Seek publication of representative chapters in high-quality magazines as a way to the book contract. Try literary magazines first."

◯ ▼ NEW ORLEANS REVIEW, Box 195, Loyola University, New Orleans LA 70118. (504)865-2295. Fax: (504)865-2294. E-mail: noreview@loyno.edu. **Contact:** Sophia Stone, editor. Magazine: 8½ × 11; 160 pages; 60 lb. Scott offset paper; 12 + King James C1S cover stock; photos. "Publishes poetry, fiction, translations, photographs, nonfiction on literature and film. Readership: those interested in current culture, literature." Quarterly. Estab. 1968. Circ. 1,300.
• Work from the *New Orleans Review* has been anthologized in *Best American Short Stories.*
Needs: "Storytelling between traditional and experimental." No romance. Want more experimental fiction. **Publishes 6-8 new writers/year.** Recently published work by Laurie Blauner, Valerie Martin, John Keegan, Sheila Mulligan Webb, R.M. Berry, Moira Crone and Charlotte Forbes.
How to Contact: Send complete ms with SASE. Accepts queries/mss by fax. Does not accept simultaneous submissions. Accepts disk submissions; inquire about system compatibility. Prefers hard copy with disk submission. Responds in 3 months. Sample copy for $9.
Payment/Terms: "Inquire." Most payment in copies. Pays on publication for first North American serial rights.

N ⊕ ◑ NEW SHETLANDER, Shetland Council of Social Service, 11 Mounthodly St., Lerwick, Shetland Scotland 2E1 0BJ United Kingdom. Phone: 01595 693816. Fax: 01595 696787. E-mail: shetlandcss@zetnet.co. uk. **Contact:** John Hunter or Alex Cluness. Magazine: A4/A5; 34 pages; glossy paper; illustrations; photos. Quarterly. Estab. 1947. Circ. 2,000.
Needs: Literary. Receives 20 unsolicited mss/month. Accepts 2 mss/issue; 8 mss/year. Publishes ms 2-3 months after acceptance. **Publishes 10-20 new writers/year.** Length: 1,700 words maximum; average length: 1,000 words. Publishes short shorts. Average length: 700-1,000 words. Also publishes literary essays, literary criticism and poetry. Sometimes comments on rejected mss.
How to Contact: Send complete ms with a cover letter. Accepts submissions by e-mail, fax and disk. Include estimated word count and brief bio. Responds in 4 months to queries. Send SASE (or IRC) for return of ms or send a disposable copy of ms and #10 SASE for reply only. Accepts previously published work and multiple submissions. Sample copy free. Reviews novels, short story collections and nonfiction books of interest to writers.
Payment/Terms: Pays contributor's copies; additional copies £1-80. Not copyrighted.
Advice: "Editorial committee select manuscripts."

N ◑ NEW STONE CIRCLE, New Stone Circle, 1185 E. 1900 North Rd., White Heath IL 61884. (217)762-5801. **Contact:** Mary Hays, fiction editor. Magazine: 8½ × 5½; 40-58 pages; illustrations; photos. Annual. Estab. 1994. Circ. 100.
Needs: "No racist or misogynist work." Receives 30 unsolicited mss/month. Accepts 4-5 mss/issue; 4-10 mss/year. Publishes ms 1 year after acceptance. Agented fiction 1%. **Publishes 1-2 new writers/year.** Recently published work by Joan Joffe Hall, Joy Clumsky and Susan Sonde. Publishes short shorts.
How to Contact: Send complete ms with a cover letter. Accepts submissions by disk. Include brief bio and list of publications. Responds in 2 months to queries; 6 months to mss. Send SASE (or IRC) for return of ms or send a disposable copy of ms and #10 SASE for reply only. Accepts simultaneous submissions, previously published work and multiple submissions. Sample copy for $4.50. Guidelines for SASE. Reviews novels and short story collections.
Payment/Terms: Pays 1 contributor's copy; additional copies $3.50. Pays on publication for one-time rights. Sends galleys to author. Sponsors contest. Send SASE for guidelines.

⊕ $ NEW WELSH REVIEW, Chapter Arts Centre, Market Rd., Cardiff Wales CF5 1QE United Kingdom. Phone: 01222 665529. Fax: 01222 665529. E-mail: robin@nwrc.demon.co.uk. Editor: Robin Reeves. **Contact:** Fiction Editor. "*NWR*, a literary quarterly ranked in the top five of British Literary magazines, publishes stories, poems and critical essays. The best of Welsh writing in English, past and present, is celebrated, discussed and debated. We seek poems, short stories, reviews, special features/articles and commentary." Accepts 16-20 mss/year.
Needs: Short fiction. "No extremes, such as extreme thriller, erotica etc. where emphasis is placed on sensational-izing." Length: 2,000-3,000 words. **Approximately 20% of fiction published each year from new writers.** Recently published work by Sian James, Ron Berry, Alun Richards, Lloyd Rees, Roger Granelli and Herbert Williams.
How to Contact: Accepts queries by e-mail. Do not send mss by e-mail.
Terms: Pays "cheque on publication and one free copy."

N ⊕ ◑ Ⓐ THE NEW WRITER, P.O. Box 60, Cranbrook Kent TN17 2ZR United Kingdom. 01580 212626. Fax: 01580 212041. E-mail: thenewwriter@hotmail.com. Website: www.tnwriter.free-online.co.uk (in-cludes editorials, guidelines, extracts, links, etc.) **Contact:** Suzanne Ruthven, editor. Magazine: A4; 48 pages; illustrations; photos. Contemporary writing magazine which publishes "the best in fact, fiction and poetry." Publishes 10 issues per annum. Estab. 1996. Circ. 1,500. "We consider short stories from subscribers only but we may also commission guest writers."
Needs: "We will consider all categories apart from stories written for children." Accepts 4 mss/issue; 40 mss/year. Publishes ms up to 1 year after acceptance. Agented fiction 5%. **Majority of work is by previously unpublished writers.** Recently published work by Tom McConville, Theodore Hannon and Kerrie Maxwell. Length: 2,000-5,000 words; average length: 3,500 words. Publishes short shorts. Average length: 1,500 words. Also publishes literary essays, literary criticism and poetry. Often comments on rejected mss.
How to Contact: Query with clips of published work. Accepts queries but not mss by e-mail and fax. Include estimated word count, brief bio and list of publications. Responds in 4 weeks to queries; 8 weeks to mss. Send SASE (or IRC) for return of ms or send a disposable copy of ms and #10 SASE for reply only. Accepts simultaneous submissions. Sample copy for SASE and A4 SAE with IRCs only. Guidelines for SASE. Reviews novels, short story collections and nonfiction books of interest to writers.
Payment/Terms: Pays £10 per story by credit voucher; additional copies £1.50. Pays on publication for first rights. Sponsors contest.
Advice: "Hone it—always be prepared to improve the story. It's a competitive market."

○ ■ **NEW WRITING, A Literary Magazine for New Writers**, P.O. Box 1812, Amherst NY 14226-7812. (716)834-1067. E-mail: 1812@newwriting.com. Website: www.newwriting.com. **Contact:** Sam Meade, editor. Electronic magazine; illustrations; photos. "We publish work that is deserving." Annually. Estab. 1994.
Needs: Work by new writers: action, experimental, horror, humor/satire, literary, mainstream/contemporary, romance, translations, westerns. **Publishes 20 new writers/year.** Recently published work by Rob Roberge and Dom Leone. Length: open. Publishes short shorts. Often comments on rejected mss. Sponsors an annual award.
How to Contact: Send complete ms with a cover letter. "When sending e-mail do not send attached files." Include *brief* list of publications and *short* cover letter. Responds in 2 months. Send SASE for return of ms. Accepts simultaneous submissions. Reviews novels and short story collections.
Payment/Terms: Acquires one-time rights.
Advice: "Don't send first copies of *any* story. Always read over, and rewrite!" Avoid "stories with characters who are writers, stories that start with the character waking, and death and dying stories—we get too many of them."

N $ ○ **NEW YORK STORIES**, English Dept., LaGuardia Community College, E-103, 31-10 Thomson Ave., Long Island City NY 11101. (718)482-5673. **Contact:** Daniel Caplice Lynch, editor. Magazine: 9×11; 64-96 pages; photos. Quarterly. Estab. 1998.
Needs: Condensed/excerpted novel, ethnic/multicultural, experimental, feminist, gay, humor/satire, lesbian, literary, mainstream/contemporary, regional. Receives 300 unsolicited mss/month. Accepts 5-10 mss/issue; 20-40 mss/year. Does not read June through August. Publishes ms 6 months after acceptance. Agented fiction 5%. **Publishes 2 new writers/year.** Length: 100 words minimum; average length: 2,500-3,000 words. Publishes short shorts. Also publishes literary essays, especially about New York. Sometimes comments on rejected mss.
How to Contact: Send complete ms with a cover letter. Include 1-paragraph bio and Social Security number. Responds in 2 months to queries; 3 months to mss. Send SASE for return of ms or send disposable copy of ms. Accepts simultaneous submissions and reprints. Guidelines for #10 SASE or by e-mail.
Payment/Terms: Pays $100 minimum; $1,000 maximum on publication.
Advice: "Fresh angles of vision, dark humor and psychological complexity are hallmarks of our short stories. Present characters who are 'alive.' Let them breathe. To achieve this, revise, revise, revise. Lately, the industry of publishing fiction seems to be playing it safe. We want your best—no matter what."

N ○ ◎ **NIGHTFIRE**, Camel's Back Books, P.O. Box 181126, Boston MA 02118. (617)825-5866. Fax: (617)282-5749. E-mail: nightfir10@aol.com. **Contact:** Michael Dubson, editor. Magazine: 6×9; 60-80 pages; 50 lb. uncoated book stock; colored cover stock/tape binding. "The theme of *Nightfire* is that there is much to celebrate in the lives of gay men, our primary target audience, and to survive in this culture is a triumph. To thrive and excel is a miracle. *Nightfire* will honor and exhault this phenomena in our work, and give gay authors a chance to express ideas not likely to be found in commercial, mainstream gay magazines." Quarterly. Estab. 2000. Small Publishers of North America, Publishers Marketing Association.
Needs: Adventure, erotica, experimental, family saga, gay, humor satire, literary, mainstream, mystery/suspense, New Age, psychic/supernatural/occult, romance, science fiction. "Must be for and about gay men." "Nothing that promotes or glorifies violence, particularly male-to-male violence. Homophobia must be portrayed as bad/harmful. Nothing dry or academic. Let passion—in all its forms—drive your prose." Accepts 5-7 mss/issue; 20-28 mss/year. Publishes ms 3 months after acceptance. Length: 1,000-5,000 words; average length: 2,500 words. Publishes short shorts. Average length: 1,250 words. Also publishes literary essays and poetry. Sometimes comments on rejected mss.
How to Contact: Send complete ms with a cover letter. Accepts submissions by e-mail, fax. Include estimated word count and brief bio. Responds in 1 week to queries; 3 months to mss. Send SASE (or IRC) for return of ms or send a disposable copy of ms and #10 SASE for reply only. Accepts simultaneous submissions and multiple submissions. Sample copy for $8. Guidelines for SASE, by e-mail or fax.
Payment/Terms: Pays 2 contributor's copies; additional copies $4. Pays on publication for first rights.
Advice: "We're looking for strong characters who are survivors—able to stand up against all adversaries—internal, external, societal, etc. Stories may end sadly or badly; but the power and strength of the character must always be clear. Write from the heart—what are the things, the people, the experiences you really care about? Make these the material of your stories. Make your goal as a writer to make your reader and editor feel. Gay publications are growing in both number and in size and we want *Nightfire* to be a part of that trend, but we also want it to challenge and counter some of the main streaming that goes on. We also want to find and give voice to new writers."

✓ $ ○ **NIMROD, International Journal of Prose and Poetry**, University of Tulsa, 600 S. College Ave., Tulsa OK 74104-3126. (918)631-3080. Fax: (918)631-3033. E-mail: nimrod@utulsa.edu. Website: www.utulsa.edu/nimrod/ (includes writer's guidelines, excerpts from published work, contest rules, theme issue announcements, ed-in-chief name and subscription/sample issue order form). **Contact:** Gerry McLoud, fiction editor. Magazine: 6×9; 192 pages; 60 lb. white paper; illustrations; photos. "We publish one thematic issue and one awards issue each year. A recent theme was "Islands in the Sea and of the Mind," a compilation of poetry and prose from all over the world. We seek vigorous, imaginative, quality writing. Our mission is to discover new writers and publish experimental writers who have not yet found a 'home' for their work." Semiannually. Estab. 1956. Circ. 3,000.

Needs: "We accept contemporary poetry and/or prose. May submit adventure, ethnic, experimental, prose poem or translations." No science fiction or romance. Upcoming theme: "The Celtic Fringe (2001). Receives 120 unsolicited fiction mss/month. **Published 5-10 new writers within the last year.** Published work by Sarah Flygare, Jennifer Ward, Ruth Schwartz and Lucia Cordell Getsi. Length: 7,500 words maximum. Also publishes poetry.

How to Contact: SASE for return of ms. Accepts queries by e-mail. Accepts simultaneous submissions. Responds in 5 months. Sample copy: "to see what *Nimrod* is all about, send $10 for a back issue. To receive a recent awards issue, send $10 (includes postage)."

Payment/Terms: Pays 2 contributor's copies.

Advice: "We have not changed our fiction needs: quality, vigor, distinctive voice. We have, however, increased the number of stories we print. See current issues. We look for fiction that is fresh, vigorous, distinctive, serious and humorous, seriously-humorous, unflinchingly serious, ironic—whatever. Just so it is quality. Strongly encourage writers to send #10 SASE for brochure for annual literary contest with prizes of $1,000 and $2,000."

96 Inc., P.O. Box 15559, Boston MA 02215-0011. (617)267-0543. Fax: (617)262-3568. **Contact:** Julie Anderson and Vera Gold, fiction editors. Magazine: 8½×11; 50 pages; 20 lb. paper; matte cover; illustrations; photos. "*96 Inc.* promotes the process; integrates beginning/young with established writers; reaches out to audiences of all ages and backgrounds." Annual. Estab. 1992. Circ. 3,000.

Needs: All types, styles and subjects. Receives 200 unsolicited mss/month. Accepts 12-15 mss/issue; 30 mss/ year. Agented fiction 10%. **Publishes 4-5 new writers/year.** Recently published work by Judith Stitzel, Aaron Alexander, Susan Green and Linda Goldberg. Length: 1,000-7,000 words. Publishes short shorts. Also publishes literary essays, literary criticism and poetry. Sometimes comments on rejected mss.

How to Contact: Query first. Include estimated word count, bio (100 words) and list of publications. Responds in 3 weeks to queries; up to 1 year to mss. Send SASE for reply, return of ms or send a disposable copy of ms. Accepts simultaneous and electronic submissions. Sample copy for $7.50. Guidelines for #10 SASE. Reviews novels and short story collections on occasion.

Payment/Terms: Pays modest sum if funds are available, not depending on length or merit, free subscription and 4 contributor's copies on publication for one-time rights.

Advice: Looks for "good writing in any style. Pays attention to the process. Read at least one issue. Be patient— it takes a very long time for readers to go through the thousands of manuscripts."

NITE-WRITER'S INTERNATIONAL LITERARY ARTS JOURNAL, Nite Owl Press, 137 Pointview Rd., Suite 300, Pittsburgh PA 15227. (412)885-3798. E-mail: nitewriterarts@aol.com. Website: http://pages. about.com/nitewriter/index/html. Editor: John A. Thompson, Sr. Associate Editor: Bree A. Orner. **Contact:** Fiction Editor. Magazine: 8½×11; 30-50 pages; bond paper; illustrations. "*Nite-Writer's International Literary Arts Journal* is dedicated to the emotional intellectual with a creative perception of life." Quarterly. Estab. 1993. Circ. 250.

Needs: Adventure, erotica, historical, humor/satire, literary, mainstream/contemporary, religious/inspirational, romance, senior citizen/retirement, sports, young adult/teen (adventure). Plans special fiction issue or anthology. Receives 3-5 unsolicited mss/month. Accepts 1-2 mss/issue; 5-8 mss/year. Publishes ms within 1 year after acceptance. Published work by Julia Klatt Singer, Jean Oscarson Schoell, Lawrence Keough and S. Anthony Smith. Length: 1,500 words average. Publishes flash fiction of 1,000 words. Also publishes literary essays, literary criticism, poetry. Often comments on rejected mss.

How to Contact: Send complete ms with a cover letter. Include estimated word count, 1-page bio, list of publications. Responds in 6 months. SASE for return of ms. Accepts simultaneous submissions. Sample copy for $6, 9×13 SAE and 6 first-class stamps. Guidelines for legal size SASE.

Payment/Terms: Does not pay. Copyright reverts to author upon publication.

Advice: "Read a lot of what you write, study the market; don't fear rejection, but use it as a learning tool to strengthen your work before resubmitting. Express what the heart feels."

$ THE NORTH AMERICAN REVIEW, University of Northern Iowa, Cedar Falls IA 50614. (319)273-6455. Fax: (319)273-4326. E-mail: nar@edu. Website: http://webdelsol.com/NorthAmRev/NAR. Editor: Vince Gotera. **Contact:** Grant Tracey, fiction editor. "The NAR is the oldest literary magazine in America and one of the most respected; though we have no prejudices about the subject matter of material sent to us, our first concern is quality." Bimonthly. Estab. 1815. Circ. 4,000.

● See the interview with *North American Review* fiction editor Grant Tracey on page 227.

Needs: Open (literary). Reads mss from January 1 to April 1 only.

How to Contact: Send complete ms with SASE. No simultaneous submissions. Sample copy for $5.

Payment/Terms: Pays $5 per 350 words of prose, $20 minimum and 2 contributor's copies; additional copies $4.50. Pays on publication for first North American serial rights.

insider report

North American Review: back to the basics of storytelling

Grant Tracey

Grant Tracey has big boots to fill. He has taken over as fiction editor of the celebrated *The North American Review*, following the retirement of Robley Wilson, a well-regarded figure who played a major role in rebuilding the magazine since 1968. Despite obvious respect for his esteemed predecessor, Tracey is more than ready to saddle up and steer the magazine's fiction into new frontiers—entirely clear when you consider he started reading submissions and working on his editorial agenda six months before his "official" starting date, in June 2000. "I'm excited to be part of the adventure," he says.

Since its inception in 1815, *The North American Review* has a proven track record of showcasing fresh talents with literary staying power, publishing such giants as Walt Whitman, Henry James, Joseph Conrad, John Steinbeck and Maxine Hong Kingston. Tracey hopes to discover more writers who will have wide appeal long after they land a byline in *The North American Review*. "Of course I don't want to take the magazine too far afield from where it's been recently, but I do want to open up what *The North American Review* publishes, and find writers whose voices haven't been heard. And I want to reach readers who haven't been reading us."

How does one "open up" *The North American Review*? For Tracey, it's pretty simple: Make the publication more accessible to readers at large, not just workshop graduates and scholars. "Too many literary magazines are for writers only," he says. "I want people who aren't writers to read our stories and enjoy them. I don't want somebody to pick up our magazine and think, 'Man, what are these guys writing about?' *The North American Review* has had a sort of cerebral aesthetic, and I want to move away from that a bit and give it more heart."

Tracey hopes to help usher in new publishing trends and doesn't hold back his disappointment with the literary angst (what he calls "art brut") that's permeated the short story the past few decades. "The time of cynicism and angst in fiction has passed," he says. "I've grown tired of the notion that a story has to be dark and cynical to make great writing. The negativity coming from writers and journals over the years has gotten really old for me. There's a lot more to explore."

It's not that Tracey longs for feel-good stories with a guaranteed psychological boost; he merely wants writers to open something other than a cynical vein. "I say let's let *The North American Review* become a place where writers don't have to take themselves so seriously. Of course I'll still publish the darker stuff if it's written well, but so many other venues publish that material. And too often writers shy away from more positive stories, thinking they aren't cool or publishable. I disagree. I know it might sound cliché, but I do want stories with heart in which the writer treats characters with respect." That doesn't mean Tracey wants fluff; it just means he wishes to publish something other than a bimonthly roster of downbeat stories.

Tracey also isn't too keen on minimalism ("A little Raymond Carver goes a long way for me," he admits) or interior stories with a grand epiphany. "I don't need too much of either of those," he says. "There's too much minimalist stuff out there, and I honestly get bored by stories in which everything is in a character's head, and the story goes nowhere until suddenly there's some great revelation at the end. I like a story to be going somewhere at all times. I want a narrative payoff."

So what, specifically, is Tracey looking for at *The North American Review?* "I would like to see an honest story about the working class, or women's narrative, or a multicultural/ethnic piece, and I could definitely go for some humor, magical realism, or something entirely absurd. I'll go for anything as long as it's done well."

Satirical stories also appeal to Tracey. "We definitely want more humorous writing," he says. "I just published a story in which a guy dresses up like Shane, but the catch is that he wields a cell phone. So the cell phone replaces the pistol. I think the story is an insightful comment on our time—and it's fun to read. I'd love to have more of that kind of material."

Tracey also desires less defeatist love stories, those that go right up to the edge of emotion without lapsing into effusive sentimentality. "Can't we have a tender story with a couple changing in the bathroom and talking?" he asks. "That way we can pick up from the nuances of the conversation the love and tenderness between them. I see nothing wrong with stories that have charm and beauty."

One other area in fiction Tracey would like to explore is publishing sports literature. "I'd love a story that takes little moments in sports and familiarizes them. If, for example, I got a story with momentum about what goes on in a goalie's head during a penalty shot, that would interest me. What's the player's experience of the event? How does he see it from an angle that's completely different from how the crowd sees it? I'd like to see a sports story that lets me see something in a way I can't see it on TV."

No matter what you write, Tracey has his storytelling criteria. "A story should have a solid plot and an equally strong narrative arc. It needs to go in an interesting direction, offer some surprises and have character development," he says. "I don't have to like a character to appreciate him. And that's what I want to see that I don't see that often—a character I can sympathize with and understand, even if the character is a complete jerk. I want to feel what the character feels and grasp why the character acts how he does. A good story will provide that."

If it sounds as though Tracey wants to move back a step to the basics of storytelling, that's because he does. It's no coincidence his favorite writers came from the '30s and '40s, when telling a solid, clear story mattered. "Those writers connected with their readers, which is the key," Tracey says. "So, yes, there might be a bit of a 'retro element' to what I like, but for me it all comes down to good storytelling." And that, ultimately, is what *The North American Review* is about.

(See the interview with retired *North American Review* editor Robley Wilson on page 30.)
—*Don Prues*

Advice: "We are interested in high-quality fiction on any subject, but we are especially interested in work that addresses contemporary North American concerns and issues, particularly the environment, gender, race, ethnicity and class. We like stories that start quickly and have a strong narrative arc. We'd also like to see more stories engaged with wonder and humor."

N **NORTH ATLANTIC REVIEW,** North Eagle Corp. of NY, 15 Arbutus Lane, Stony Brook NY 11790. (631)689-8266. E-mail: 75467.112@compuserve.com. Website: www2.sunysuffolk.edu/gillj. **Contact:** John Gill, editor. Magazine: 7×9; 320 pages; glossy cover. "General interest." Estab. 1989. Circ. 1,000.

• *North Atlantic Review* tends to accept traditional fiction.

Needs: General fiction. Has published special fiction issue. Accepts 40 mss/year. Publishes ms 6-10 months after acceptance. Length: 3,000-7,000 words average. Publishes short shorts. Sometimes critiques rejected mss.

How to Contact: Send complete ms with cover letter. Responds in 6 months to queries. SASE. Accepts simultaneous and photocopied submissions. Sample copy for $10.

✔ ⊘ **NORTHEAST ARTS MAGAZINE**, P.O. Box 4363, Portland ME 04101. **Contact:** Mr. Leigh Donaldson, publisher. Magazine: 6½×9½; 32-40 pages; matte finish paper; card stock cover; illustrations; photos. Bimonthly. Estab. 1990. Circ. 750.

Needs: Ethnic, gay, historical, literary, mystery/suspense (private eye), prose poem (under 2,000 words). No obscenity, racism, sexism, etc. Receives 50 unsolicited mss/month. Accepts 1-2 mss/issue; 5-7 mss/year. Publishes ms 2-4 months after acceptance. Agented fiction 20%. Length: 750 words preferred. Publishes short shorts. Sometimes critiques rejected mss.

How to Contact: Send complete ms with cover letter. Include short bio. Responds in 1 month to queries; 4 months to mss. SASE. Accepts simultaneous submissions. Sample copy for $4.50, SAE and 75¢ postage. Guidelines free.

Payment/Terms: Pays 2 contributor's copies. Acquires first North American serial rights. Sometimes sends galleys to author.

Advice: Looks for "creative/innovative use of language and style. Unusual themes and topics."

⊘ ▼ **NORTHWEST REVIEW**, 369 PLC, University of Oregon, Eugene OR 97403. (503)346-3957. Website: darkwing.uoregon.edu/~engl/deptinfo/NWR.html. Editor: John Witte. **Contact:** Janice MacCrae, fiction editor. Magazine: 6×9; 140-160 pages; high quality cover stock; illustrations; photos. "A general literary review featuring poems, stories, essays and reviews, circulated nationally and internationally. For a literate audience in avant-garde as well as traditional literary forms; interested in the important writers who have not yet achieved their readership." Triannual. Estab. 1957. Circ. 1,200.

• *Northwest Review* ranked #30 on *Writer's Digest*'s "Fiction 50" list of top markets for fiction writers. Also received the Oregon Governor's Award for the Arts. Work published here tends to be heavy on character and theme.

Needs: Contemporary, experimental, feminist, literary and translations. Accepts 4-5 mss/issue, 12-15 mss/year. Receives approximately 100 unsolicited fiction mss each month. **Published new writers within the last year.** Published work by Diana Abu-Jaber, Madison Smartt Bell, Maria Flook and Charles Marvin. Length: "Mss longer than 40 pages are at a disadvantage." Also publishes literary essays, literary criticism, poetry. Critiques rejected mss when there is time. Sometimes recommends other markets.

How to Contact: Send complete ms with SASE. "No simultaneous submissions are considered." Responds in 4 months. Sample copy for $4. Reviews novels and short story collections. Send books to John Witte.

Payment/Terms: Pays 3 contributor's copies and one-year subscription; 40% discount on extras. Acquires first rights.

$ ⊘ **NORTHWOODS JOURNAL, A Magazine for Writers**, Conservatory of American Letters, P.O. Box 298, Thomaston ME 04861. (207)354-0998. Fax: (207)354-8953. E-mail: cal@americanletters.org. Website: www.americanletters.org (includes guidelines and catalogue). Editor: R.W. Olmsted. **Contact:** Ken Sieben, fiction editor (submit fiction to Ken Sieben, 253 Ocean Ave., Sea Bright NJ 07760). Magazine: 5½×8½; 32-64 pages; white paper; 70 lb. text cover; offset printing; some illustrations; photos. "No theme, no philosophy—for people who read for entertainment." Quarterly. Estab. 1993. Circ. 500.

Needs: Adventure, experimental, fantasy (science fantasy, sword and sorcery), literary, mainstream/contemporary, mystery/suspense (amateur sleuth, police procedural, private eye/hard-boiled, romantic suspense), psychic/supernatural/occult, regional, romance (gothic, historical), science fiction (hard science, soft/sociological), sports, westerns (frontier, traditional). Publishes special fiction issue or anthology. "Would like to see more first-person adventure." No porn or evangelical. Receives 20 unsolicited mss/month. Accepts 12-15 mss/year. **Publishes 15 new writers/years.** Recently published work by Paul A. Jurvie, Richard Vaughn, Bryn C. Gray and Sandra Thompson. Length: 2,500 words maximum. Also publishes literary essays, literary criticism and poetry.

How to Contact: *Charges $3 reading fee per 2,500 words.* Read guidelines *before* submitting. Send complete ms with a cover letter. Include word count and list of publications. There is a $3 fee per story (make checks payable to Ken Sieben. The magazine gets none of the reading fee). Responds in 2 days to queries; by next deadline plus 5 days to mss. Send SASE for reply, return of ms or send a disposable copy of ms. No simultaneous submissions. No electronic submissions. Sample copies: $5.50 next issue, $8.45 current issue, $12.50 back issue (if available), all postage paid. Guidelines for #10 SASE. Reviews novels, short story collections and poetry.

Payment/Terms: Varies, "minimum $3/published page on acceptance for first North American serial rights."

Advice: "Read guidelines, read the things we've published. Know your market."

$ ⊘ **NOTRE DAME REVIEW**, University of Notre Dame, English Department, Creative Writing, Notre Dame IN 46556. (219)631-6952. Fax: (219)631-8209. E-mail: english.ndreview.1@nd.edu. Website: www.nd.

edu/~ndr/review.htm (includes guidelines, editors, additional poetry, fiction, book reviews, art, audio clips of authors and photos). Senior Editor: Steve Tomasula. Editor: John Matthias. **Contact:** William O'Rourke, fiction editor. Literary magazine: 6×9; 115 pages; 50 lb. smooth paper; illustrations; photos. "The *Notre Dame Review* is an independent, non-commercial magazine of contemporary American and international fiction, poetry, criticism and art. We are especially interested in work that takes on big issues by making the invisible seen, that gives voice to the voiceless. In addition to showcasing celebrated authors like Seamus Heaney and Czelaw Milosz, the *Notre Dame Review* introduces readers to authors they may have never encountered before, but who are doing innovative and important work. In conjunction with the *Notre Dame Review*, the on-line companion to the printed magazine, the *Notre Dame Re-view* engages readers as a community centered in literary rather than commercial concerns, a community we reach out to through critique and commentary as well as aesthetic experience." Semiannually. Estab. 1995. Circ. 2,000.

• Short story originally published in the *Notre Dame Review* was published in *Best American Short Stories*.

Needs: "We're eclectic." No genre fiction. Upcoming theme issues planned. List of upcoming themes or editorial calendar available for SASE. Receives 75 unsolicited fiction mss/month. Accepts 4-5 mss/issue; 10 mss/year. Does not read mss May through August. Publishes ms 6 months after acceptance. **Publishes 2 new writers/year.** Recently published work by Ed Falco, Jarda Cerverka and David Green. Length: 3,000 words maximum. Publishes short shorts. Also publishes literary criticism and poetry. Sometimes comments on rejected ms.

How to Contact: Send complete ms with cover letter. Include 4-sentence bio. Responds in 4 months. Send SASE for response, return of ms, or send a disposable copy of ms. Accepts simultaneous submissions. Sample copy for $6.

Payment/Terms: Pays $5-25 and contributor's copies. Pays on publication for first North American serial rights.

Advice: "We're looking for high quality work that takes on big issues in a literary way. Please read our back issues before submitting."

☑ $ ◎ **NOW & THEN,** Center for Appalachian Studies and Services, East Tennessee State University, Box 70556, Johnson City TN 37614-0577. (423)439-6173. E-mail: cass@etsu.tn.net. Website: www.cass.etsu.edu/net. **Contact:** Editor. Magazine: 8½×11; 36-52 pages; coated paper and cover stock; illustrations; photos. Publication focuses on Appalachian culture, present and past. Readers are mostly people in the region involved with Appalachian issues, literature, education." Triannually. Estab. 1984. Circ. 1,250.

Needs: Ethnic, literary, regional, serialized/excerpted novel, prose poem. "Absolutely has to relate to Appalachian theme. Can be about adjustment to new environment, themes of leaving and returning, for instance. Nothing unrelated to region." Upcoming themes: Rivers & Valleys; Writing Revisited. Buys 2-3 mss/issue. Publishes ms 3-4 months after acceptance. **Published new writers within the last year.** Published work by Lee Smith, Pinckney Benedict, Gurney Norman, George Ella Lyon. Length: 3,000 words maximum. Publishes short shorts. Also publishes literary essays, poetry.

How to Contact: Send complete ms with cover letter. Responds in 3 months. Include "information we can use for contributor's note." SASE (or IRC). Accepts simultaneous submissions, "but let us know when it has been accepted elsewhere right away." Sample copy for $5. Reviews novels and short story collections. Send books to: Marianne Worthington, Dept. of Communications & Theatre Arts, Cumberland College, 6000 College Station Dr., Williamsburg KY 40769.

Payment/Terms: Pays up to $75 per story, contributor's copies.

Terms: Holds copyright.

Advice: "Keep in mind that *Now & Then* only publishes fiction related to the Appalachian region (all of West Virginia and parts of 12 other states from southern New York to northern Mississippi, Alabama and Georgia). Plus we only publish fiction that has some plausible connection to a specific issues themes. Get the guidelines. We like to offer first-time publication to promising writers."

☑ $ ◎ **OASIS, A Literary Magazine,** P.O. Box 626, Largo FL 33779-0626. (727)449-2186. E-mail: oasislit@aol.com. Website: www.litline.org/oasis/oasis.html (includes writer's guidelines, names of editors, short fiction, poetry). Editor: Neal Storrs. **Contact:** Fiction Editor. Magazine: 70 pages. "Literary magazine first, last and always—looking for styles that delight and amaze, that are polished and poised. Next to that, content considerations relatively unimportant—open to all." Quarterly. Estab. 1992. Circ. 500.

Needs: High-quality writing. Also publishes translations. Receives 150 unsolicited mss/month. Accepts 6 mss/issue; 24 mss/year. Publishes ms 4-6 months after acceptance. **Publishes 2 new writers/year.** Recently published work by Wendell Mayo, Al Masarik and Mark Wisniewski. Length: no minimum or maximum. Also publishes literary essays and poetry. Occasionally comments on rejected mss.

How to Contact: Send complete ms with or without a cover letter. Accepts queries/mss by e-mail. Usually reports same day. Send SASE for reply, return of ms or send a disposable copy of ms. Accepts simultaneous, reprint and electronic (e-mail) submissions. Sample copy for $7.50. Guidelines for #10 SASE.

Payment/Terms: Pays $15-30 and 1 contributor's copy on publication for first rights.

Advice: "If you want to write good stories, read good stories. Cultivate the critical ability to recognize what makes a story original and true to itself."

$⊘ ◖ THE OHIO REVIEW, 344 Scott Quad, Ohio University, Athens OH 45701-2979. (740)593-1900. Fax: (740)597-2967. **Contact:** Wayne Dodd, editor. Magazine: 6×9; 200 pages; illustrations on cover. "We attempt to publish the best poetry and fiction written today. For a mainly literary audience." Semiannually. Estab. 1971. Circ. 3,000.

• *The Ohio Review* will not accept unsolicited ms until September 2001.

Needs: Contemporary, experimental, literary. "We lean toward contemporary on all subjects." Receives 150-200 unsolicited fiction mss/month. Accepts 5 mss/issue. Does not read mss June 1-September 15. Publishes ms 6 months after acceptance. Also publishes poetry. Sometimes critiques rejected mss and/or recommends other markets.

How to Contact: Send complete ms with cover letter. Responds in 3 weeks. SASE. Sample copy for $6. Guidelines for #10 SASE.

Payment/Terms: Pays $5/page, free subscription to magazine and 2 contributor's copies on publication for first North American serial rights. Sends galleys to author.

Advice: "We feel the short story is an important part of the contemporary writing field and value it highly. Read a copy of our publication to see if your fiction is of the same quality. So often people send us work that simply doesn't fit our needs."

✓ ◖ ♈ OLD CROW REVIEW, FKB Press, P.O.Box 403, Easthampton MA 01027-0403. E-mail: oldcrow @yahoo.com. Editor: John Gibney. **Contact:** Karen Malley, fiction editor. "*Old Crow Review* publishes the finest short and serialized fiction from new and established writers." Magazine: 5½×8½; 100 pages; 20 lb. paper; 90 lb. cover stock; illustrations; photos. Semiannually. Estab. 1991. Circ. 500.

• William Monahan's "Experiments in Vacuo" received a *Pushcart* Prize.

Needs: Erotica, literary, mainstream/contemporary, psychic/supernatural/occult, regional, translations. Receives 400-500 unsolicited mss/month. Accepts 3-5 mss/issue; 6-10 mss/year. Publishes ms 1-3 months after acceptance. Agented fiction 20%. Recently published work by Robert L. Mayne, Stephen Jones and Katherine Toy Miller. Length: 6,000 words maximum; average length: 3,000 words. Publishes short shorts. Also publishes literary essays, literary criticism and poetry.

How to Contact: Send complete ms with a cover letter. Should include estimated word count, bio (2-5 sentences) and list of publications. Responds in 3 months to queries and mss. Send SASE for reply, return of ms or send a disposable copy of ms. Accepts simultaneous and reprint submissions. Sample copy for $5; make check payable to Tawnya Kelley Tiskus. Guidelines for #10 SASE.

Payment/Terms: Pays 1 contributor's copy; additional copies for $5.

Advice: "A piece must seem true to us. If it strikes us as a truth we never even suspected, we build an issue around it. We haven't seen enough writers taking risks with their stories. Avoid sending pieces which sound just like somebody else's. Take the time to make a story tight and complete."

◖ OPEN SPACES QUARTERLY, PMB 134, 6327 C SW Capitol Hwy., Portland OR 97201-1937. (503)227-5764. Fax: (503)227-3401. E-mail: info@open-spaces.com. Website: www.open-spaces.com (includes overview, contents of current and back issues, sample articles and creative writing, submission guidelines, contact information). Editor: Penny Harrison. **Contact:** A. Bradley, fiction editor. Magazine: 64 pages; illustrations; photos. "We are a high-quality, general-interest publication with an intelligent, well-educated readership appreciative of well-written, insightful work." Quarterly. Estab. 1997.

Needs: "Excellence is the issue—not subject matter." Accepts 2 mss/issue; 8 mss/year. Recently published work by William Kittredge, Terence O'Donnell, Pattiann Rogers and David James Duncan. Publishes short shorts. Also publishes literary essays and poetry. Sometimes comments on rejected mss.

How to Contact: Send complete ms with a cover letter. Accepts queries/mss by fax. Include short bio, social security number and list of publications. SASE for return of ms or send a disposable copy of ms. Sample copy for $10. Guidelines free for SASE.

Payment/Terms: Pays on publication.

Advice: "The surest way for a writer to determine whether his or her material is right for us is to read the magazine."

🅽 ▦ $◖ OTHER VOICES, Other Voices Publishing Society, Garneau, P.O. Box 52059, 8210-109 St., Edmonton, Alberta T6G 2T5 Canada. (780)497-5356. E-mail: editor@othervoices.ab.ca. Website: www.othervoic es.ab.ca (includes excerpts, upcoming issues, names of editors, newsletter). **Contact:** Jannie Edwards, fiction editor. Magazine: 4¼×5½; 150 pages; illustrations; photos. "While our magazine is not limited to the publication of women artists, we encourage, in particular, work by women speaking from diverse cultural, sexual and regional perspectives. *Other Voices* is committed to helping underrepresented voices find the space to be heard." Biannual. Estab. 1987. Circ. 400. Member: Alberta Magazine Publisher's Association.

• From 1997-1999, fiction writers published in *Other Voices* were nominated for the Journey Prize.

Needs: Erotica, ethnic/multicultural, experimental, family saga, feminist, gay, historical, humor satire, lesbian, literary, New Age. Receives 30 unsolicited mss/month. Accepts 6 mss/issue; 12 mss/year. Publishes ms 3 weeks after acceptance. **Publishes 2 new writers/year.** Recently published work by Karen Solie, Mark Storey and Gideon Forman. Length: 2,500-5,000 words; average length: 3,000 words. Publishes short shorts. Average length: 500 words. Also publishes literary essays and poetry. Sometimes comments on rejected mss.

How to Contact: Send complete ms with a cover letter. Accepts submissions by e-mail and disk. Include estimated word count, brief bio and list of publications. Responds in 3 weeks to queries; 4 months to mss. Send SASE (or IRC) for return of ms or send a disposable copy of ms and #10 SASE for reply only. Accepts multiple submissions. Sample copy for $12 (US); $10 (Canadian). Guidelines for SASE or by e-mail. Reviews novels, short story collections and nonfiction books of interest to writers.

Payment/Terms: Pays $30; additional copies $8 (Canadian). Pays on publication for electronic rights (we will ask individual authors if we wish to publish on our website). Not copyrighted. Sponsors annual contest with prizes of $500 (poetry, fiction).

Advice: "Our magazine has expanded from publishing exclusively women's writing to publishing other voices more generally. We provide a space for both emerging and established writers who might otherwise not have the space to be heard."

N ◯ **OTHER VOICES**, The University of Illinois at Chicago, Dept. of English (M/C 162), 601 S. Morgan St., Chicago IL 60607. (312)413-2209. Website: www.othervoicesmagazine.org (includes writer's guidelines, names of editors, e-mail address and subscription information). Editors: Lois Hauselman and Gina Frangello. **Contact:** Fiction Editor. Magazine: 5⅞×9; 168-205 pages; 60 lb. paper; coated cover stock; occasional photos. "Original, fresh, diverse stories and novel excerpts" for literate adults. Semiannually. Estab. 1985. Circ. 1,500.

● *Other Voices* ranked #25 on *Writer's Digest's* "Fiction 50" list of top markets for fiction writers. Work from *OV* was included in *Best American Short Stories of the Century* and *Pushcart Best of the Small Presses 2000. Other Voices* has received 17 Illinois Arts Council Awards since it began.

Needs: Contemporary, excerpted novel, experimental, humor/satire and literary. No taboos, except ineptitude and murkiness. No science fiction, romance, horror. Would like to see more one-act plays and experimental literary stories. Receives 300 unsolicited fiction mss/month. Accepts 20-23 mss/issue. **Publishes 6 new writers/year. Publishes new writers.** Recently published work by Aimee Bender, Wanda Coleman, Kate Small and Dan Chaon. Length: 5,000 words maximum; average length: 4,000 words.

How to Contact: Send ms with SASE October 1 to April 1 only. No e-mail submissions. No multiple submissions. Mss received during non-reading period are returned unread. Cover letters "should be brief and list previous publications. Also, list title of submission. Most beginners' letters try to 'explain' the story—a big mistake." Accepts simultaneous submissions. Responds in 3 months to mss. Sample copy for $7 (includes postage). Guidelines for #10 SASE.

Payment/Terms: Pays in contributor's copies and modest cash gratuity. Acquires one-time rights.

Advice: "There are so *few* markets for *quality* fiction! By publishing 40-45 stories a year, we provide new and established writers a forum for their work. Send us your best voice, your best work, your best best. The market has been saturated with certain themes. We get too many stories derivative of *Bastard Out of Carolina* and second person stories that sound dated."

✓ $ ◯ ◎ THE OXFORD AMERICAN, The Southern Magazine of Good Writing, P.O. Box 1156, Oxford MS 38655. (662)236-1836. Website: www.oxfordamericanmag.com. **Contact:** Marc Smirnoff, editor. Magazine: 8½×11; 100 pages; glossy paper; glossy cover; illustrations; photos. Bimonthly. Estab. 1992. Circ. 40,000.

Needs: Regional (Southern); stories set in the South. Published work by Lewis Nordan, Donna Tartt, Florence King and Tony Earley. Also publishes literary essays. Sometimes comments on rejected mss.

How to Contact: Send complete ms. Send SASE for reply, return of ms or send a disposable copy of ms. No simultaneous submissions without indicating as such. No e-mail or faxed submissions. "No further guidelines available than those stated here." Sample copy for $4.50. "We review Southern novels or short story collections only."

Payment/Terms: Pays $100 minimum on publication for first rights; prices vary.

Advice: "I know you've heard it before—but we appreciate those writers who try to get into the spirit of the magazine which they can best accomplish by being familiar with it."

✓ ◯ ⚲ OXFORD MAGAZINE, Bachelor Hall, Miami University, Oxford OH 45056. (513)529-5253. Editor: Deborah Kennedy. Editors change every year. **Send submissions to:** "Fiction Editor." Magazine: 6×9; 120 pages; illustrations. Annually. Estab. 1985. Circ. 1,000.

● *Oxford* has been awarded two Pushcart Prizes.

Needs: Literary, ethnic, experimental, humor/satire, feminist, gay/lesbian, translations. Receives 150 unsolicited mss/month. Reads mss September through January. **Published new writers within the last year.** Published work by Stephen Dixon, Andre Dubus and Stuart Dybek. Length: 2,000-4,000 words average. "We will accept long fiction (over 6,000 words) only in cases of exceptional quality." Publishes short shorts. Also publishes poetry.

How to Contact: Send complete ms with cover letter, which should include a short bio or interesting information. Accepts simultaneous submissions, if notified. Responds in 2 months, depending upon time of submissions; mss received after January 31 will be returned. SASE. Sample copy for $5.
Payment/Terms: Pays in contributor's copies. Acquires one-time rights.
Advice: "*Oxford Magazine* is looking for humbly vivid fiction; that is to say, fiction that illuminates, which creates and inhabits an honest, carefully rendered reality populated by believable, three-dimensional characters. We want more stories—from undiscovered writers—that melt hair and offer the heat of a character at an emotional crossroads. Send us stories that are unique; we want fiction no one else but you could possibly have written."

◐ ⬛ ▣ **OYSTER BOY REVIEW OF FICTION AND POETRY**, P.O. Box 77842, San Francisco CA 94107-0842. E-mail: obr@levee67.com. Website: www.levee67.com (includes full contents of all issues; also related links). **Contact:** Damon Sauve, editor. Electronic and print magazine. "An independent literary magazine of poetry and fiction published in North Carolina in print and electronic form. We're interested in the underrated, the ignored, the misunderstood, and the varietal. We'll make some mistakes. The editors tend to select experimental and traditional narrative fiction. Our audience tends to be young, unpublished writers or writers of considerable talent who have published in the bigger little magazines but like the harder literary edge *Oyster Boy* promotes. We publish kick-ass, teeth-cracking stories."
● Work from *Oyster Boy* was selected for the *Pushcart Prize 1999* anthology.
Needs: "Fiction that revolves around characters in conflict with themselves or each other; a plot that has a beginning, a middle, and an end; a narrative with a strong moral center (not necessarily 'moralistic'); a story with a satisfying resolution to the conflict; and an ethereal something that contributes to the mystery of a question, but does not necessarily seek or contrive to answer it." No genre fiction. **Publishes 20 new writers/year.** Recently published work by Michael Rumaker, Charlotte Morgan, Paul Dilsaver.
How to Contact: Electronic and traditional submissions accepted. "E-mail submissions should be sent as the body-text of the e-mail message, or as an attached ASCII-text file.
Advice: "Keep writing, keep submitting, keep revising."

◐ **PACIFIC COAST JOURNAL**, French Bread Publications, P.O. Box 23868, San Jose CA 95153-3868. E-mail: paccoastj@bjt.net. Website: www.bjt.net/~stgraham/pcj (includes guidelines, contest information, past published work). Editor: Stillson Graham. **Contact:** Stephanie Kylkis, fiction editor. Magazine: 5½×8½; 40 pages; 20 lb. paper; 67 lb. cover; illustrations; b&w photos. "Slight focus toward Western North America/Pacific Rim." Quarterly (or "whenever we have enough money"). Estab. 1992. Circ. 200.
Needs: Ethnic/multicultural, experimental, feminist, historical, humor/satire, literary, science fiction (soft/sociological, magical realism). No children. Receives 30-40 unsolicited mss/month. Accepts 3-4 mss/issue; 10-12 mss/year. Publishes ms 6-18 months after acceptance. **Publishes 3-5 new writers/year.** Recently published work by Tamara Jane, Lisa Garrigues and Charles Ordine. Length: 4,000 words maximum; 2,500 words preferred. Publishes short shorts. Also publishes literary essays and poetry. Sometimes comments on rejected mss. Sponsors contest. Send SASE for details.
How to Contact: Send complete ms with a cover letter. Include 3 other publication titles that are recommended as good for writers. Responds in 6 months. Send SASE for reply, return of ms or send a disposable copy of ms. Accepts simultaneous, reprint and electronic submissions (Mac or IBM disks). Sample copy for $2.50, 6×9 SASE. Reviews novels and short story collections.
Payment/Terms: Pays 1 contributor's copy. Acquires one-time rights.
Advice: "We tend to comment more on a story not accepted for publication when an e-mail address is provided as the SASE. There are very few quality literary magazines that are not backed by big institutions. We don't have those kinds of resources so publishing anything is a struggle. We have to make each issue count."

◐ **PACIFIC ENTERPRISE, A Magazine for Enterprising Filipinos and Friends**, P.O. Box 1907, Fond du Lac WI 54936-1907. (920)922-9218. E-mail: rudyled@vbe.com. **Contact:** Rudy Ledesma, editor. Magazine: 8½×11; 36-44 pages; 35 lb. stock newsprint paper; coated enamel cover; illustrations; photos. "*Pacific Enterprise* welcomes submissions of unpublished works from emerging and established writers. Although our primary audience is Filipino Americans, we welcome submissions from everyone. Our aim is to publish the best work we can find regardless of the author's country of origin." Published "once or twice a year." Estab. 1998. Circ. 3,000.
Needs: Literary. "No fantasy, juvenile, western, romance, horror, science fiction." Receives about 3 unsolicited mss/month. Accepts 0-3 mss/issue; 2-3 mss/year. Publishes ms 6-12 months after acceptance. Recently published work by Val Vallejo and Holly Lalena Day. Length: 700-5,000 words. Publishes short shorts. Length: 500 words. Also publishes literary essays, literary criticism, poetry. Sometimes comments on rejected mss.
How to Contact: Send complete ms with short bio. Accepts queries/mss by e-mail. Include estimated word count, 4-5 sentence bio and list of publications. Responds in 6 months "or longer." Send a disposable copy of ms. Accepts simultaneous submissions. Sample copy for $4, 9×12 SAE and 3 first-class stamps. Guidelines free. Reviews novels and short story collections. Send books to the editor at above address.

Payment/Terms: Pays 2 contributor's copies; additional copies $2.95 plus postage. Pays on publication for first North American serial rights. Sends galleys to author.

Advice: "We're looking for a strong command of language; something happening in the story; a story that surprises us. Request a sample copy and send in your work."

☑ $◐ ▣ **PAINTED BRIDE QUARTERLY**, Painted Bride Art Center, 230 Vine St., Philadelphia PA 19106. (215)925-9914. Website: www.webdelsol/pbq. **Contact:** Kathy Volk-Miller, fiction editor. Literary magazine: 6×9; 96-100 pages; illustrations; photos. Quarterly. Estab. 1973. Circ. 1,000.

● *Painted Bride Quarterly* is now a quarterly online magazine with an annual anthology.

Needs: Contemporary, ethnic, experimental, feminist, gay, lesbian, literary, prose poem and translations. **Published new writers within the last year.** Recently published work by Lisa Borders, Jeannie Tietja, Kevin Miller, Mark LaMonda and Jennifer Moses. Length: 5,000 words maximum; average length: 3,000 words. Publishes short shorts. Also publishes literary essays, literary criticism, poetry. Occasionally critiques rejected mss.

How to Contact: Send complete ms. Responds in 6 months. SASE. Sample copy for $6. Reviews novels and short story collections. Send books to editor.

Payment/Terms: Pays $5/accepted piece and 1 contributor's copy, 1 year free subscription, 50% off additional copies. Acquires first North American serial rights.

Advice: Looks for "freshness of idea incorporated with high-quality writing. We receive an awful lot of nicely written work with worn-out plots. We want quality in whatever—we hold experimental work to as strict standards as anything else. Many of our readers write fiction; most of them enjoy a good reading. We hope to be an outlet for quality. A good story gives, first, enjoyment to the reader. We've seen a good many of them lately, and we've published the best of them."

◐ **PALO ALTO REVIEW, A Journal of Ideas**, Palo Alto College, 1400 W. Villaret, San Antonio TX 78224. (210)921-5021. Fax: (210)921-5008. E-mail: eshull@accd.edu. **Contact:** Bob Richmond and Ellen Shull, editors. Magazine: 8½×11; 60 pages; 60 lb. natural white paper (50% recycled); illustrations; photos. "Not too experimental nor excessively avant-garde, just good stories (for fiction). Ideas are what we are after. We are interested in connecting the college and the community. We would hope that those who attempt these connections will choose startling topics and interesting angles with which to investigate the length and breadth of the teaching/learning spectrum, life itself." Semiannually (spring and fall). Estab. 1992. Circ. 500-600.

Needs: Adventure, ethnic/multicultural, experimental, fantasy, feminist, historical, humor/satire, literary, mainstream/contemporary, mystery/suspense, regional, romance, science fiction, translations, westerns. Upcoming themes: "Beginnings" (spring 2001). Upcoming themes available for SASE. Receives 100-150 unsolicited mss/month. Accepts 2-4 mss/issue; 4-8 mss/year. Does not read mss March-April and October-November when putting out each issue. Publishes ms 2-15 months after acceptance. **Publishes 30 new writers/year.** Published work by Layle Silbert, Naomi Chase, Kenneth Emberly, C.J. Hannah, Tom Juvik, Kassie Fleisher and Paul Perry. Length: 5,000 words maximum. Publishes short shorts. Also publishes articles, interviews, literary essays, literary criticism, poetry. Always comments on rejected mss.

How to Contact: Send complete ms with a cover letter. "Request sample copy and guidelines." Accepts queries by e-mail. Include brief bio and brief list of publications. Responds in 4 months. Send SASE for reply, return of ms or send a disposable copy of ms. Accepts simultaneous and electronic (Macintosh disk) submissions. Sample copy for $5. Guidelines for #10 SASE.

Payment/Terms: Pays 2 contributor's copies; additional copies for $5. Acquires first North American serial rights.

Advice: "Good short stories have interesting characters confronted by a dilemma working toward a solution. So often what we get is 'a moment in time,' not a story. Generally, characters are interesting because readers can identify with them. Edit judiciously. Cut out extraneous verbiage. Set up a choice that has to be made. Then create tension—who wants what and why they can't have it."

◐ **PANGOLIN PAPERS**, Turtle Press, P.O. Box 241, Nordland WA 98358. (360)385-3626. **Contact:** Pat Britt, editor. Magazine: 5½×8½; 120 pages; 24 lb. paper; 80 lb. cover. "Best quality literary fiction for an informed audience." Triannually. Estab. 1994. Circ. 500.

Needs: Condensed/excerpted novel, experimental, humor/satire, literary, translations. No "genre such as romance or science fiction." Plans to publish special fiction issues or anthologies in the future. Receives 20 unsolicited mss/month. Accepts 7-10 mss/issue; 20-30 mss/year. Publishes ms 4-12 months after acceptance. Agented fiction 10%. **Publishes 3-4 new writers/year.** Published work by Jack Nisbet and Barry Gifford. Length: 100-7,000 words; average length: 3,500 words. Publishes short shorts. Length: 400 words. Also publishes literary essays. Sometimes comments on rejected mss.

How to Contact: Send complete ms with a cover letter. Include estimated word count and short bio. Responds in 2 weeks to queries; 2 months to mss. Send SASE for reply, return of ms or send a disposable copy of ms. No simultaneous submissions. Sample copy for $5 and $1.50 postage. Guidelines for #10 SAE.

Payment/Terms: Pays 2 contributor's copies. Offers annual $200 prize for best story. Acquires first North American serial rights. Sends galleys to author.

Advice: "We are looking for original voices. Follow the rules and be honest in your work."

⬛ ◩ ▣ **PAPERPLATES, a magazine for fifty readers**, Perkolator Kommunikation, 19 Kenwood Ave., Toronto, Ontario M6C 2R8 Canada. (416)651-2551. Fax: (416)651-2910. E-mail: paper@perkolator.com. Website: www.perkolater.com. **Contact:** Bernard Kelly, editor. Electronic magazine. Published 2-3 times/year. Estab. 1990.

• *Paperplates* is now published entirely online.

Needs: Condensed/excerpted novel, ethnic/multicultural, feminist, gay, lesbian, literary, mainstream/contemporary, translations. "No science fiction, fantasy or horror." Receives 2-3 unsolicited mss/week. Accepts 2-3 mss/issue; 6-9 mss/year. Publishes ms 6-8 months after acceptance. Published work by Celia Lottridge, C.J. Lockett, Deirdre Kessler and Marvyne Jenoff. Length: 1,500-7,500 words; average length: 5,000 words. Publishes short shorts. Also publishes literary essays, literary criticism and poetry.

How to Contact: Send complete ms with a cover letter. Responds in 6 weeks to queries; 3 months to mss. Send SASE for reply, return of ms or send a disposable copy of ms. Accepts simultaneous submissions and electronic submissions. Guidelines for #10 SASE.

Payment/Terms: Pays 2 contributor's copies on publication; additional copies for $5. Acquires first North American serial rights.

✔ $ ◩ ▼ **THE PARIS REVIEW**, 45-39 171 Place, Flushing NY 11358 (*business office only, send mss to address below*). (212)861-0016. Fax: (212)861-4504. Website: www.parisreview.com. **Contact:** George A. Plimpton, editor. Magazine: 5¼×8½; about 260 pages; illustrations; photos (unsolicited artwork not accepted). "Fiction and poetry of superlative quality, whatever the genre, style or mode. Our contributors include prominent, as well as less well-known and previously unpublished writers. Writers at Work interview series includes important contemporary writers discussing their own work and the craft of writing." Quarterly.

Needs: Literary. Receives about 1,000 unsolicited fiction mss each month. **Published new writers within the last year.** Published work by Raymond Carver, Elizabeth Tallent, Rick Bass, John Koethe, Sharon Olds, Derek Walcott, Carolyn Kizer, Tess Gallagher, Peter Handke, Denis Johnson, Bobbie Ann Mason, Harold Brodkey, Joseph Brodsky, John Updike, Andre Dubus, Galway Kinnell, E.L. Doctorow and Philip Levine. No preferred length. Also publishes literary essays, poetry.

How to Contact: *Send complete ms with SASE to Fiction Editor, 541 E. 72nd St., New York NY 10021.* Responds in 8 months. Accepts simultaneous submissions. Sample copy for $12. Writer's guidelines for #10 SASE (from Flushing office). Sponsors annual Aga Khan Fiction Contest award of $1,000.

Payment/Terms: Pays up to $1,000. Pays on publication for all rights. Sends galleys to author.

◩ **PARTING GIFTS**, 3413 Wilshire, Greensboro NC 27408-2923. E-mail: rbixby@aol.com. Website: users.aol.com/marchst (includes guidelines, samples, free websites and newsletter). **Contact:** Robert Bixby, editor. Magazine: 5×7; 60 pages. "High-quality insightful fiction, very brief and on any theme." Semiannually. Estab. 1988.

Needs: "Brevity is the second most important criterion behind literary quality." Publishes ms within one year of acceptance. Published work by Russ Thorburn, Curt Smith, Rosaleen Bertolino and David Schuman. Length: 250-1,000 words. Also publishes poetry. Sometimes critiques rejected mss.

How to Contact: Send complete ms with cover letter. Accepts simultaneous submissions. Responds in 1 day to queries; 1 week to mss. SASE.

Payment/Terms: Pays in contributor's copies. Acquires one-time rights.

Advice: "Read the works of Amy Hempel, Jim Harrison, Kelly Cherry, C.K. Williams and Janet Kauffman, all excellent writers who epitomize the writing *Parting Gifts* strives to promote. I need more than ever for my authors to be better read. I sense that many unaccepted writers have not put in the hours reading."

✔ $ ◩ **PARTISAN REVIEW**, 236 Bay State Rd., Boston MA 02215. (617)353-4260. Fax: (617)353-7444. E-mail: partisan@bu.edu. Website: www.partisanreview.com (includes excerpts, writer's guidelines and subscription information). Editor-in-Chief: William Phillips. Editor: Edith Kurzweil. **Contact:** Fiction Editor. Magazine: 6×9; 160 pages; 40 lb. paper; 60 lb. cover stock. "Theme is of world literature and contemporary culture: fiction, essays and poetry with emphasis on the arts and political and social commentary, for the general intellectual public and scholars." Quarterly. Estab. 1934. Circ. 8,000.

Needs: Contemporary, experimental, literary, prose poem, regional and translations. Receives 100 unsolicited fiction mss/month. Buys 1-2 mss/issue; 4-8 mss/year. **Published new writers within the last year.** Recently published work by Leonard Michaels, Muriel Spark and Doris Lessing. Length: open.

How to Contact: Send complete ms with SASE and cover letter listing past credits. No simultaneous submissions. Responds in 4 months to mss. Sample copy for $6 and $1.50 postage.

Payment/Terms: Pays $25-200 and 2 contributor's copies. Pays on publication for first rights.

Advice: "Please research the type of fiction we publish. Often we receive manuscripts which are entirely inappropriate for our journal. Sample copies are available for sale and this is a good way to determine audience."

Ⓝ ◩ **PASSAGES NORTH**, Northern Michigan University, Department of English, 1401 Presque Isle Ave., Marquette MI 49855-5363. (906)227-1795. Fax: (906)227-1096. E-mail: khanson@nmu.edu. Editor: Kate Myers

Hanson. **Contact:** Candice Rowe and John Smolens, fiction editors. Magazine: 8×5½; 110-130 pages; 80 lb. paper. "*Passages North* publishes quality fiction, poetry and creative nonfiction by emerging and established writers." Readership: General and literary. Semiannual. Estab. 1979. Circ. 1,000.

Needs: Ethnic/multicultural, literary, mainstream/contemporary, regional. "Seeking more multicultural work." No genre fiction, science fiction, "typical commercial press work." Receives 100-200 mss/month. Accepts 8-12 fiction mss/year. Does not read May through August. **25% of mss published are from new writers.** Recently published works by W.P. Kinsella, Jack Gantos, Bonnie Campbell, Anthony Bukoski and Peter Orner. Length: 5,000 words maximum. Critiques returned mss when there is time. Also publishes interviews with authors.

How to Contact: Send complete ms with SASE and estimated word count. No electronic or fax submissions. Responds in 2 months. Accepts simultaneous submissions. Sample copy for $7. Guidelines free.

Payment/Terms: Pays 2 contributor's copies. Rights revert to author on request.

Tips: "We look for voice, energetic prose, writers who take risks. Revise, revise. Read what we publish."

THE PAUMANOK REVIEW. E-mail: paumanok @etext.org. Website: www.etext.org/Fiction/Paumanok (includes full text of magazine, guidelines, archives and publishing information). **Contact:** Katherine Arline, editor. Online magazine. "TPR is dedicated to publishing and promoting the best in world art and literature. The audience is 25-50, well-educated and looking for insight and entertainment from talented new and established voices." Quarterly. Estab. 2000.

Needs: Experimental, historical, horror (psychological), humor satire, literary, mainstream, mystery/syspense, science fiction (hard science/technological, soft/sociological), western. List of upcoming themes available online. Receives 30 unsolicited mss/month. Accepts 4-6 mss/issue; 16-24 mss/year. Publishes ms 6 weeks after acceptance. **Publishes 4 new writers/year.** Recently published work by Ace Boggess, Tim Rees and Renee Carter Hall. Length: 1,500-6,000 words; average length: 3,000 words. Publishes short shorts. Average length: 800 words. Also publishes literary essays and poetry. Always comments on rejected mss.

How to Contact: Send complete ms with a cover letter. Accepts submissions by e-mail. Include estimated word count, brief bio, list of publications and where you discovered TPR. Responds in 1 week to queries; 1 month to mss. Accepts simultaneous submissions and previously published work. Sample copy and guidelines online.

Payment/Terms: Free classified ads for the life of the magazine. Acquires one-time and anthology rights. Rights revert at publication. Sends galleys to author.

Advice: "TPR was created to bridge the gap between highly specialized e-zines and affluent mega-zines closed to new writers. TPR is the ideal place for a writer's first electronic submission since the process closely follows print publishing's methods."

PEARL, A Literary Magazine, Pearl, 3030 E. Second St., Long Beach CA 90803-5163. Phone/Fax: (562)434-4523. E-mail: mjohn5150@aol.com. Website: www.pearlmag.com (includes writer's guidelines, contest guidelines, subscription information, books, current issue, about the editors.) **Contact:** Joan Jobe Smith, Marilyn Johnson and Barbara Hauk, editors. Magazine: 5½×8½; 96 pages; 60 lb. recycled, acid-free paper; perfect-bound; coated cover; b&w drawings and graphics. "We are primarily a poetry magazine, but we do publish some *very short* fiction and nonfiction. We are interested in lively, readable prose that speaks to *real* people in direct, living language; for a general literary audience." Biannually. Estab. 1974. Circ. 600.

Needs: Contemporary, humor/satire, literary, mainstream, prose poem. "We will only consider short-short stories up to 1,200 words. Longer stories (up to 4,000 words) may only be submitted to our short story contest. All contest entries are considered for publication. Although we have no taboos stylistically or subject-wise, obscure, predictable, sentimental, or cliché-ridden stories are a turn-off." Publishes an all fiction issue each year. Receives 10-20 unsolicited mss/month. Accepts 1-10 mss/issue; 12-15 mss/year. Submissions accepted September-May *only.* Publishes ms 6 months to 1 year after acceptance. **Publishes 1-5 new writers/year.** Recently published work by Gina Ochsner, Helena Maria Viramontes, Stephanie Dickinson, Lisa Glatt, Gerald Locklin and Dave Newman. Length: 500-1,200 words; average length: 1,000 words. Also publishes poetry. Sponsors an annual short story contest. Send SASE for complete guidelines.

How to Contact: Send complete ms with cover letter including publishing credits and brief bio. Accepts simultaneous submissions. Responds in 2 months to mss. SASE. Sample copy for $7 (postpaid). Guidelines for #10 SASE.

Payment/Terms: Pays 2 contributor's copies. Acquires first North American serial rights. Sends galleys to author.

Advice: "We look for vivid, *dramatized* situations and characters, stories written in an original 'voice,' that make sense and follow a clear narrative line. What makes a manuscript stand out is more elusive, though—more to do with feeling and imagination than anything else . . .'"

THE PEGASUS REVIEW, P.O. Box 88, Henderson MD 21640-0088. (410)482-6736. **Contact:** Art Bounds, editor. Magazine: 5½×8½; 6-8 pages; illustrations. "*The Pegasus Review* is a bimonthly, done in a calligraphic format and occasionally illustrated. Each issue is based on a specific theme." Estab. 1980. Circ. 120.

● Because *The Pegasus Review* is done in calligraphy, fiction submissions must be very short. Two pages, says the editor, are the ideal length.

Needs: Humor/satire, literary, prose poem and religious/inspirational. Wants more short-shorts and theme-related fiction. Upcoming themes: "Teacher Teaching" (March/April); "Leadership" (May/June); "Imagination" (July/August); "Ages Youth" (September/October); "Forgiveness" (November/December). Receives 35 unsolicited mss/month. Accepts "about" 50 mss/year. "Try to approach themes in various ways, rather than the traditional manner. Themes may be approached by means of poetry, short short fiction or essays . . . even an appropriate cartoon." **Publishes 10 new writers/year.** Recently published work by Frederick Foote, Mildred Kadison, Judi Rypma and Patrick Flavin. Publishes short shorts of 2-3 pages; 500 words. Themes are subject to change, so query if in doubt. "Occasional critiques."

How to Contact: Send complete ms. SASE "a must." Brief cover letter with author's background, name and prior credits, if any. Simultaneous submissions acceptable, if so advised. Responds in 2 months. Sample copy for $2.50. Guidelines for SAE. Subscription: $12/year.

Payment/Terms: Pays 2 contributor's copies. Occasional book awards. Acquires one-time rights.

Advice: "Study various writing publications. Pay strict attention to indicated guidelines. They serve a definite purpose. Join a local writers' group, especially one that does critiquing. Above all, don't be afraid of rewriting: it comes with the craft. Circulate your work and keep it circulating. Our publication is open to novice and professional writers alike."

PEMBROKE MAGAZINE, Box 1510, University of North Carolina at Pembroke, Pembroke NC 28372. (910)521-6358. Editor: Shelby Stephenson. **Contact:** Fran Oxendine, managing editor. Magazine: 6×9; approximately 200 pages; illustrations; photos. Magazine of poems and stories plus literary essays. Annually. Estab. 1969. Circ. 500.

Needs: Open. Receives 120 unsolicited mss/month. Publishes short shorts. **Published new writers within the last year.** Published work by Fred Chappell, Robert Morgan. Length: open. Occasionally critiques rejected mss and recommends other markets.

How to Contact: Send complete ms. No simultaneous submissions. Responds in up to 3 months. SASE. Sample copy for $8 and 9×10 SAE.

Payment/Terms: Pays 1 contributor's copy.

Advice: "Write with an end for *writing*, not publication."

N ⊕ $ PENINSULAR, Literary Magazine, Cherrybite Publications, Linden Cottage, 45 Burton Rd., Little Neston, Cheshire CH64 4AE England. Phone: 0151 353 0967. Fax: 0870 165 6282. E-mail: helicon @globalnet.co.uk. **Contact:** Shelagh Nugent, editor. Magazine: 80 pages; card cover. "We're looking for brilliant short fiction to make the reader think/laugh/cry. A lively, up and coming quality magazine." Quarterly. Estab. 1985. Circ. 400. "We ask only that a potential writer buy at least one copy. Subscribing is not essential."

Needs: Adventure, ethnic/multicultural (general), fantasy (space fantasy), gay, historical (general), horror (futuristic, psychological, supernatural), humor/satire, lesbian, literary, New Age, psychic/supernatural/occult, science fiction (soft/sociological). "I'll read anything but avoid animals telling the story and clichés. Also avoid purple prose." Receives 50 unsolicited mss/month. Accepts 10 mss/issue; 40 mss/year. Publishes ms 3-6 months after acceptance. Recently published work by Sally Zigmond, Alex Keegan, Jo Good and Lesley Gleeson. Length: 1,000-4,000 words; average length: 3,000 words. Publishes short shorts. Average length: 1,000 words. Also publishes literary criticism. Often comments on rejected mss.

How to Contact: Send for guidelines. Prefers hard copy for submissions. Include estimated word count. Responds in 1 week to queries; 2 weeks to mss. "I often write comments on the manuscript." Accepts simultaneous submissions and previously published work. Sample copy for $5. Guidelines for SASE with 2 IRCs or by e-mail. Reviews novels, short story collections and nonfiction books of interest to writers. Send review copies to the editor.

Payment/Terms: Pays £5 sterling per 1,000 words or can pay in copies and subscriptions; additional copies £5 sterling or equivalent in dollars cash. Pays on publication for one-time rights. Sponsors contest. "Send IRCs for current competition details."

Advice: "We look for impeccable presentation and grammar, outstanding prose, original story line and the element of difference that forbids me to put the story down. A good opening paragraph usually grabs me. Read one or two copies and study the guidelines. A beginning writer should read as much as possible. The trend seems to be for stories written in first person/present tense and for stories without end leaving the reader thinking 'so what?' Stories not following this trend stand more chance of being published by me!"

PENNSYLVANIA ENGLISH, Penn State DuBois, College Place, DuBois PA 15801. (814)375-4814. Fax: (814)375-4784. E-mail: ajv2@psu.edu. **Contact:** Antonio Vallone, editor. Magazine: 5½×8½; up to 180 pages; perfect bound; full color cover featuring the artwork of a Pennsylvania artist. "Our philosophy is quality. We publish literary fiction (and poetry and nonfiction). Our intended audience is literate, college-educated people." Annually. Estab. 1985. Circ. 300.

Needs: Short shorts, literary, contemporary mainstream. No genre fiction or romance. Publishes ms within 12 months after acceptance. **Publishes 2-3 new writers/year.** Recently published work by Dave Kress, Dan Leone and Paul West. Length: "no maximum or minimum." Publishes short shorts. Also publishes literary essays, literary criticism, poetry. Sometimes critiques rejected mss.

How to Contact: Send complete ms with cover letter. Responds in 2 months. SASE. Accepts simultaneous submissions.

Payment/Terms: Pays in 3 contributor's copies. Acquires first North American serial rights.

Advice: "Quality of the writing is our only measure. We're not impressed by long-winded cover letters or résumés detailing awards and publications we've never heard of. Beginners and professionals have the same chance with us. We receive stacks of competently written but boring fiction. For a story to rise out of the rejection pile, it takes more than basic competence."

THE PERALTA PRESS, The Peralta Community College District, 333 E. Eighth St., Oakland CA 94606. (510)466-7200. **Contact:** Jay Rubin, editor. Literary magazine: 6×9; 150 pages; some illustrations; photos. "*The Peralta Press* publishes short fiction, short creative non-fiction and poetry without any pre-determined editorial themes. Goal is to include approximately 20 prose pieces and 50 poems." Annual. Estab. 2000. Circ. 1,000.

Needs: Adventure, erotica, ethnic/multicultural, feminist, gay, glitz, historical, horror, humor/satire, lesbian, mainstream, military/war, mystery/suspense, psychic/supernatural/occult. Receives 12 unsolicited mss/month. Accepts 10-15 mss/issue; 10-15 mss/year. Publishes ms 5-6 months after acceptance. **Publishes 50% new writers/year.** Length: 1,000-2,000 words; average length: 1,800. Publishes short shorts; average length: 1,100 words. Also publishes literary essays, literary criticism and poetry. Sometimes comments on rejected mss.

How to Contact: Send complete ms with cover letter. Include estimated word count and brief bio in 50 words. Send SASE for return of ms or send disposable copy of ms and #10 SASE for reply only. Accepts simultaneous submissions and previously published submissions. Sample copy for $10. Guidelines for SASE.

Payment/Terms: Pays 1 contributor's copy; additional copies $10. Acquires one-time rights and electronic rights.

Advice: "A clean, well-formatted copy with a strong intro and compelling characters. Please edit, revise, edit, revise, edit . . ."

PEREGRINE, The Journal of Amherst Writers & Artists Press, AWA Press, P.O. Box 1076, Amherst MA 01004-1076. (413)253-3307. Fax: (413)253-7764. Website: www.amherstwriters.com (includes writer's guidelines, names of editors, excerpts from publication and interviews with authors). **Contact:** Nancy Rose, managing editor. Magazine: 6×9; 120 pages; 60 lb. white offset paper; glossy cover. "*Peregrine* has provided a forum for national and international writers for 20 years, and is committed to finding excellent work by new writers as well as established authors. We publish what we love, knowing that all editorial decisions are subjective, and that all work has a home somewhere." Annually.

Needs: Poetry and prose—short stories, short short stories, personal essays. No previously published work. No children's stories. Publishes 2 pages in each issue of work in translation. "We welcome work reflecting diversity of voice." Accepts 6-12 fiction mss/issue. Publishes ms an average of 4 months after acceptance. **Published 3-5 new writers/year.** Recently published work by Cynthia Coffin, Andrew Lopenzina, Jim Goodspeed, Jr. and Dianna Hunter. "We like to be surprised. We look for writing that is honest, unpretentious, and memorable." Length: 3,000 words maximum. Short pieces have a better chance of publication. *Peregrine* sponsors an annual contest (The *Peregrine* Prize) and awards $500 each for fiction and poetry, and $100 "Best of the Nest" awarded to a local author.

How to Contact: Send #10 SASE to "Peregrine Guidelines" or visit website for writer's guidelines. Send ms with cover letter; include 40-word biographical note, prior publications and word count. Accepts simultaneous submissions. Enclose sufficiently stamped SASE for return of ms; if disposable copy, enclose #10 SASE for response. Deadline for submission: April 1, 2001. Read October-April. Sample copy $10.

Payment/Terms: Pays contributor's copies. All rights return to writer upon publication.

Advice: "We look for heart and soul as well as technical expertise. Trust your own voice. Familiarize yourself with *Peregrine*." Every ms is read by three or more readers.

PIF. (360)493-0596. E-mail: editor@pifmagazine.com. Website: http://pifmagazine.com. **Contact:** Camille Renshaw, senior editor. Fiction Editor: Jen Bergmark (fiction@pifmagazine.com). Literary magazine: 5½×8½; 150 pages; perfect bound. Biannual. Electronic magazine (pifmagazine.com): circ. 100,000. Monthly. Estab. 1995.

● *Pif* ranked #16 on *Writer's Digest*'s "Fiction 50" list of top markets for fiction writers.

Needs: Literary, experimental, very short ("micro") fiction. Receives 200-300 mss/month. Accepts 2-3 mss/electronic issue; more mss per print issue. Publishes 1-4 months after acceptance. Reads year round. Length: 4,000 words maximum. Recently published work by Marcy Dermansky, Michael Largo, Deena Larson and Kathryn Kulpa. **Publishes several new writers/year.** Also publishes poetry, book reviews, essays and interviews.

How to Contact: Electronic submissions only. Online submissions form and guidelines at http://pifmagazine. com/submit/. Submissions will be considered for both the print journal and electronic magazine. Responds in 6 weeks. Accepts simultaneous submissions. Sometimes comments on rejected mss.
Payment/Terms: Pays $50-200 on publication.
Advice: "We're open to all forms of fiction, as long as the writing is compelling. It's always exciting when a writer has been paying attention and every sentence in a story feels absolutely essential."

☑ $ ◙ **PIG IRON PRESS**, Box 237, 27 N. Phelps, Youngstown OH 44501. (330)747-6932. Fax: (330)747-0599. **Editor:** Jim Villani. Annual series: 8½ × 11; 144 pages; 60 lb. offset paper; 85 pt. coated cover stock; b&w illustrations; b&w 120 line photos. "Contemporary literature by new and experimental writers." Annually. Estab. 1975. Circ. 1,000.
● At press time, Pig Iron Press was not accepting unsolicited submissions.
Needs: Literary and thematic. No mainstream. Accepts 60-70 mss/issue. Receives approximately 75-100 unsolicited mss/month. Recently published work by Charles Darling, Jim Sanderson and J.D. Winans. Length: 8,000 words maximum. Also publishes literary nonfiction, poetry. Sponsors contest. Send SASE for details.
How to Contact: Send complete ms with SASE. No simultaneous submissions. Responds in 4 months. Sample copy for $5.
Payment/Terms: Pays $5/printed page and 2 contributor's copies on publication for first North American serial rights; $5 charge for extras.
Advice: "Looking for work that is polished, compelling and magical."

Ⓝ ◯ **PIKEVILLE REVIEW**, Pikeville College, Sycamore St., Pikeville KY 41501. (606)432-9612. Fax: (606)432-9238. E-mail: eward@pc.edu. Website: www.pc.edu (includes writer's guidelines, names of editors, short fiction). Editor: Elgin M. Ward. **Contact:** Fiction Editor. Magazine: 8½ × 6; 120 pages; illustrations; photos. "Literate audience interested in well-crafted poetry, fiction, essays and reviews." Annually. Estab. 1987. Circ. 500.
Needs: Ethnic/multicultural, experimental, feminist, humor/satire, literary, mainstream/contemporary, regional, translations. Receives 25 unsolicited mss/month. Accepts 3-4 mss/issue. Does not read mss in the summer. Publishes ms 6-8 months after acceptance. **Publishes 20 new writers/year.** Recently published work by Jim Wayne Miller and Robert Morgan. Length: 15,000 words maximum; average length: 5,000 words. Publishes short shorts. Also publishes literary essays and poetry. Often critiques rejected mss. Sponsors occasional fiction award: $50.
How to Contact: Send complete ms with cover letter. Include estimated word count. Send SASE for reply, return of ms or send a disposable copy of ms. Accepts simultaneous submissions. Sample copy for $4. Reviews novels and short story collections.
Payment/Terms: Pays 5 contributor's copies; additional copies for $4. Acquires first rights.
Advice: "Send a clean manuscript with well-developed characters."

🌐 $ **PLANET-THE WELSH INTERNATIONALIST**, P.O. Box 44, Aberystwyth, Ceredigion, SY23 3ZZ Cymru/ Wales UK. Phone: 01970-611255. Fax: 01970-611197. **Contact:** John Barnie, fiction editor. Bimonthly. Circ. 1,400. Publishes 1-2 stories/issue.
Needs: "A literary/cultural/political journal centered on Welsh affairs but with a strong interest in minority cultures in Europe and elsewhere." Recently published work by Arthur Winfield Knight, Roger Granelli, Sian James, Jan Morris and Guy Vanderhaeghe. Length: 1,500-4,000 words maximum.
How to Contact: No submissions returned unless accompanied by an SAE. Writers submitting from abroad should send at least 3 IRCs for return of typescript; 1 IRC for reply only.
Payment/Terms: Writers receive 1 contributor's copy. Payment is at the rate of £40 per 1,000 words for prose; a minimum of £25 per poem (in the currency of the relevant country if the author lives outside the UK). Sample copy: cost (to USA & Canada) £2.87. Writers' guidelines for SAE.
Advice: "We do not look for fiction which necessarily has a 'Welsh' connection, which some writers assume from our title. We try to publish a broad range of fiction and our main criterion is quality. Try to read copies of any magazine you submit to. Don't write out of the blue to a magazine which might be completely inappropriate to your work. Recognize that you are likely to have a high rejection rate, as magazines tend to favor writers from their own countries."

🌐 ☑ ▢ **THE PLAZA, A Space for Global Human Relations**, U-Kan Inc., Yoyogi 2-32-1, Shibuya-ku, Tokyo 151-0053, Japan. Tel: +81-(3)-3379-3881. Fax: +81-(3)-3379-3882. E-mail: plaza@u-kan.co.jp. Website: u-kan.co.jp (includes contribution guide, contents of the current and back issues, representative works by *The Plaza* writers). **Contact:** Leo Shunji Nishida, publisher/fiction editor. "*The Plaza* is an intercultural and bilingual magazine (English and Japanese). Our focus is the 'essence of being human.' Some works are published in both Japanese and English (translations by our staff if necessary). The most important criteria is artistic level. We look for works that reflect simply 'being human.' Stories on intercultural (not international) relations are desired. *The Plaza* is devoted to offering a spiritual *Plaza* where people around the world can share their creative work. We introduce contemporary writers and artists as our generation's contribution to the continuing human heritage." Quarterly. Online publication which is freely available to all readers on the Internet.

Needs: Length: less than 2,500 words (longer stories may be recommended for serial publication). Wants to see more fiction "of not human beings, but being human. Of not international, but intercultural. Of not social, but human relationships." No political themes: religious evangelism; social commentary. Publishes about 2 stories/issue. **Publishes 3 new writers/year.** Recently published work by Michael Hoffman, Bun'ichirou Chino and Isabel Wendell.

How to Contact: Send complete ms with cover letter. Accepts queries/mss by e-mail and fax. "The most important consideration is that which makes the writer motivated to write. If it is not moral but human, or if it is neither a wide knowledge nor a large computer-like memory, but rather a deep thinking like the quietness in the forest, it is acceptable. While the traditional culture of reading of some thousands of years may be destined to be extinct under the marvellous progress of civilization, *The Plaza* intends to present contemporary works as our global human heritage to readers of forthcoming generations."

☑ $☑ **PLEIADES**, Department of English & Philosophy, Central Missouri State University, Martin 336, Warrensburg MO 64093-5046. (660)543-4425. Fax: (660)543-8544. E-mail: rmk8708@cmsu2.cmsu.edu. Website: www.cmsu.edu/englphil/pleiades.htm (includes guidelines, editors, sample poetry or prose). **Contact:** R.M. Kinder, fiction editor. Poetry: Kevin Prufer. Magazine: $5\frac{1}{2} \times 8\frac{1}{2}$; 150 pages; 60 lb. paper; perfect-bound; 8 pt. color cover. Sponsored in part by Missouri Arts Council. "*Pleiades* emphasizes cultural diversity, publishes poetry, fiction, essays, occasional drama, interviews and reviews for a general educated audience." Semiannually. Estab. 1939. Circ. 2,000.

● A story first published by Pleiades was awarded a Pushcart Prize and was selected for Norton Anthology of Best Fantasy and Horror.

Needs: Ethnic/multicultural, experimental, especially cross-genre, feminist, gay, humor/satire, literary, mainstream/contemporary, regional, translations. "No westerns, romance, mystery, etc. Nothing pretentious, didactic or overly sentimental." Receives 100 unsolicited mss/month. Accepts 8 mss/issue; 16 mss/year. "We're slower at reading manuscripts in the summer." Publishes ms 6-12 months after acceptance. **Publishes 1-2 new writers/year.** Recently published work by Edith Pearlman, Alan Cheuse, Alexandra Grilikes and Richard Burgin. Length: 800-8,000 words; average length: 3,000-6,000 words. Also publishes literary essays, literary criticism and poetry. Sometimes comments on rejected mss.

How to Contact: Send complete ms with a cover letter. Accepts queries by e-mail but not submissions. Include 75-100 bio, Social Security number and list of publications. Responds in 3 weeks to queries; 4 months to mss. Send SASE for reply, return of ms or send a disposable copy of ms. Accepts simultaneous submissions. Sample copy (including guidelines) for $6.

Payment/Terms: Pays $10 or subscription and 1 contributor's copy on publication. Acquires first North American serial rights.

Advice: Looks for "a blend of language and subject matter that entices from beginning to end. Send us your best work. Don't send us formula stories. While we appreciate and publish well-crafted traditional pieces, we constantly seek the story that risks, that breaks form and expectations and wins us over anyhow."

Ⓝ $☑ ▣ **PLOT LINE FOYER**, G.S. & S., 3601 Owens St., Bryan TX 77808-0969. (979)778-0248. E-mail: PlotLineFoyer@att.net. Website: http://home.att.net/~plotlinefoyer (includes contest news/rules, fiction, poetry, articles on herbs and essential oils, as well as guidelines and contact information). **Contact:** Hector Garza III, executive editor. Online magazine: illustrations; photos. "Plot Line Foyer is a place where you have choices, where you have simplicity with no excuses, where you can come and enjoy a cup of virtual coffee or tea. Sit back and take a moment from surfing to enjoy good fiction or nonfiction. Research herbs, ask or answer a question concerning usage. Use one of our plotlines as a springboard to a new story or as a safety net for an old one. Enter a mind warp with a poem as your star or not." Bimonthly. Estab. 2000.

Needs: Adventure, comics/graphic novels, ethnic/multicultural (general: Asian/Mexican), family saga, fantasy (space fantasy), humor satire, mainstream, mystery/suspense (amateur sleuth, cozy, police procedural, private eye/hardboiled, futuristic), romance (futuristic/time travel, romantic suspense), science fiction, thriller/espionage, western, young adult/teen (mystery/suspense). "Anything that has to do with the use of herbs as they relate to health." No alternative lifestyles, child/spousal abuse, New Age, spiritual, religious, political, occult, erotica, experimental, horror. Receives 160 unsolicited mss/month. Accepts 2 mss/issue; 30 mss/year. Publishes ms 1-3 months after acceptance. **Publishes 4 new writers/year.** Recently published work by Pamela Garza, H. Turnip Smith and Jill Williams. Length: 200-3,000 words; average length: 2,000 words. Publishes short shorts. Average length: 500 words. Also publishes literary essays and poetry.

How to Contact: Send complete ms with a cover letter. Accepts submissions by e-mail and snail mail. Include estimated word count and brief bio. Responds in 2 weeks to queries; 2 months to mss. Send SASE (or IRC) for return of ms or send a disposable copy of ms and #10 SASE for reply only. Accepts simultaneous submissions, previously published work and multiple submissions. Sample copy on website. Guidelines on website or by e-mail.

Payment/Terms: Pays $2-5. Pays on acceptance for electronic rights. Sponsors contests. Information online at website.
Advice: "We love it when a writer can go beyond the meaning of a word and show us a new one by exploiting the language, not being a slave to it. Coin new phrases, make up new words and show us they belong. Reading 'was' in every sentence is distracting."

✔ $ ◢ ♀ **PLOUGHSHARES,** Emerson College, 120 Boylston St., Boston MA 02116. (617)824-8753. Website: www.emerson.edu/ploughshares. Editor: Don Lee. **Contact:** Fiction Editor. "Our mission is to present dynamic, contrasting views on what is valid and important in contemporary literature, and to discover and advance significant literary talent. Each issue is guest-edited by a different writer. We no longer structure issues around preconceived themes." Triquarterly. Estab. 1971. Circ. 6,000.
- Work published in *Ploughshares* has been selected regularly for inclusion in the *Best American Short Stories* and *O. Henry Prize* anthologies. In fact the magazine has the honor of having the most stories selected from a single issue (three) to be included in *B.A.S.S.* Guest editors have included Richard Ford, Tim O'Brien and Ann Beattie. *Ploughshares* ranked #22 on *Writer's Digest*'s "Fiction 50" list of top markets for fiction writers.

Needs: Literary. "No genre (science fiction, detective, gothic, adventure, etc.), popular formula or commercial fiction whose purpose is to entertain rather than to illuminate." Buys 30 mss/year. Receives 1,000 unsolicited fiction mss each month. **Published new writers within the last year.** Published work by Rick Bass, Joy Williams and Andre Dubus. Length: 300-6,000 words.
How to Contact: Reading period: postmarked August 1 to March 31. Cover letter should include "previous pubs." SASE. Responds in 5 months to mss. Sample copy for $8. (Please specify fiction issue sample.) Current issue for $9.95. Guidelines for #10 SASE.
Payment/Terms: Pays $25/page, $50 minimum per title; $250 maximum, plus copies and a subscription on publication for first North American serial rights. Offers 50% kill fee for assigned ms not published.
Advice: "Be familiar with our fiction issues, fiction by our writers and by our various editors (e.g., Sue Miller, Tobias Wolff, Rosellen Brown, Richard Ford, Jayne Anne Phillips, James Alan McPherson) and more generally acquaint yourself with the best short fiction currently appearing in the literary quarterlies, and the annual prize anthologies (*Pushcart Prize, O. Henry Awards, Best American Short Stories*). Also realistically consider whether the work you are submitting is as good as or better than—in your own opinion—the work appearing in the magazine you're sending to. What is the level of competition? And what is its volume? Never send 'blindly' to a magazine, or without carefully weighing your prospect there against those elsewhere. Always keep a log and a copy of the work you submit."

✿ ✔ ◢ **THE PLOWMAN,** Box 414, Whitby, Ontario L1N 5S4 Canada. (905)668-7803. **Contact:** Tony Scavetta, editor. Tabloid: 20 pages; illustrations; photos. "An international journal publishing all holocaust, religion, didactic, ethnic, eclectic, love and other stories." Quarterly. Estab. 1988. Circ. 10,000.
Needs: No science fiction. **Publishes 50 new writers/year.** Published work by B. Fleming, P. Larty, B. Lilley, B. McCann Jr., Y. Nair and D. Garza. Length: 7,000 words maximum, poetry: 38 lines or less. "All manuscripts are appraised and a written report given to author for a minimal cost."
How to Contact: Send complete ms with cover letter. Responds in 2 months. Accepts simultaneous and reprint submissions. Sample copy and guidelines for SAE.
Payment/Terms: Pays in contributor's copies; charges for extras. Acquires one-time rights. Sends galleys to author. 20% royalties paid.
Advice: "No satanic or rude language." Looks for "detail, excellent English and language as well as quality. Be patient and submit to different publishers."

◢ **POETRY FORUM SHORT STORIES,** Poetry Forum, 5713 Larchmont Dr., Erie PA 16509. Phone/fax: (814)866-2543 (fax hours 8-10 a.m., 5-8 p.m.). E-mail: 75562.670@compuserve.com. **Contact:** Gunvor Skogsholm, editor. Newspaper: 7×8½; 34 pages; card cover; illustrations. "Human interest themes (no sexually explicit or racially biased or blasphemous material) for the general public—from the grassroot to the intellectual." Quarterly. Estab. 1989. Circ. 400.
Needs: Confession, contemporary, ethnic, experimental, fantasy, feminist, historical, literary, mainstream, mystery/suspense, prose poem, religious/inspirational, romance, science fiction, senior citizen/retirement, young adult/teen. "No blasphemous, sexually explicit material." Publishes annual special fiction issue. Receives 50 unsolicited mss/month. Accepts 12 mss/issue; 40 mss/year. Publishes ms 6 months after acceptance. Agented fiction less than 1%. **80% of work published is by new writers.** Recently published work by Scott Fields and Frank Bland. Length: 500-5,000 words; average length: 2,000 words. Also publishes literary essays, literary criticism, poetry.
How to Contact: *This magazine charges a "professional members" fee of $36 and prefers to work with subscribers.* The fee entitles you to publication of a maximum of 3,000 words. Send complete ms with cover

letter. Accepts queries/mss by e-mail and fax. Responds in up to 2 months to mss. SASE. Accepts simultaneous and reprint submissions. "Accepts electronic submissions via disk gladly." Sample copy for $3. Guidelines for SASE. Reviews novels and short story collections.

Payment/Terms: Preference given to submissions by subscribers. Acquires one-time rights.

Advice: "Tell your story with no padding as if telling it to a person standing with one hand on the door ready to run out to a meeting. Have a good lead. This is the 'alpha & omega' of all good story writing. Don't start with 'This is a story about a boy and a girl. Avoid writing how life 'ought to be,' rather write how life is."

☑ ◐ ☼ PORCUPINE LITERARY ARTS MAGAZINE, P.O. Box 259, Cedarburg WI 53012-0259. (262)375-3128. E-mail: ppine259@aol.com. Website: members.aol.com/ppine259 (includes writer's guidelines, cover art, subscription information, table of contents). Editor: W.A. Reed. **Contact:** Chris Skoczynski, fiction editor. Magazine: 5×8½; 100 pages; glossy color cover stock; illustrations and photos. Publishes "primarily poetry and short fiction. Novel excerpts are acceptable if self-contained. No restrictions as to theme or style." Semiannually. Estab. 1996. Circ. 1,500.

● *Porcupine Literary Arts Magazine* was named Best Literary/Arts Magazine by *Milwaukee Magazine* (1997).

Needs: Condensed/excerpted novel, ethnic/multicultural, literary, mainstream/contemporary. No pornographic or religious. Receives 20 unsolicited mss/month. Accepts 3 mss/issue; 6 mss/year. Publishes ms within 6 months of acceptance. **Publishes 4-6 new writers/year.** Published work by Terri Brown-Davidson, Mary Ann Cain and Karl Voskuil. Length: 2,000-7,500 words; average length: 3,500 words. Publishes literary essays and poetry. Sometimes comments on rejected mss.

How to Contact: Send complete ms with a cover letter. Accepts queries/mss by e-mail. Include estimated word count, 5-line bio and list of publications. Responds in 2 weeks to queries; 2 months to mss. Send SASE for reply, return of ms or send a disposable copy of ms. No simultaneous submissions. Sample copy for $5. Guidelines for #10 SASE.

Payment/Terms: Pays 1 contributor's copy on publication; additional copies for $8.95. Acquires one-time rights.

Advice: Looks for "believable dialogue and a narrator I can see and hear and smell. Form or join a writers' group. Read aloud. Rewrite extensively."

☑ ◐ PORTLAND REVIEW, Portland State University, Box 347, Portland OR 97207-0347. (503)725-4533. Fax: (503)725-4534. E-mail: review@vanguard.vg.pdx.edu. Website: www.angelfire.com/in/portlandreview.com (includes writer's guidelines, e-mail and links to other journals). Editor: Ryan Spear. **Contact:** Haley Hach, assistant editor. Magazine: 9×6; 100 pages; b&w art and photos. "We seek to publish fiction in which content takes precedence over style." Quarterly. Estab. 1954. Circ. 300.

● The editors say they are looking for experimental work "dealing with the human condition."

Needs: Adventure, ethnic/multicultural, experimental, fantasy (science), feminist, gay, historical, humor/satire, lesbian, literary, mainstream/contemporary, mystery/suspense, regional, science fiction. Wants more humor. Receives about 100 mss each month. Accepts 4-6 mss/issue; 10-12 mss/year. Also publishes critical essays, poetry, drama, interviews and reviews. Published work by Ian McMillan, Heather King and Benjamin Chambers.

How to Contact: Submit complete ms with short bio. Accepts queries/mss by e-mail and fax. Manuscripts returned only if SASE is supplied. Accepts simultaneous and electronic submissions (if noted). Responds in "several" months. Sample copy for $6 plus $1 postage.

Payment/Terms: Pays contributor's copies. Acquires one-time rights.

Advice: "Our editors, and thus our tastes/biases change annually, so keep trying us."

☑ ◐ POTOMAC REVIEW, The Quarterly with a Conscience—and a Lurking Sense of Humor, Potomac Review, Inc., P.O. Box 354, Port Tobacco MD 20677. (301)934-1412. Fax: (301)753-1648. E-mail: elilu@juno.com. Website: www.meral.com/potomac (includes editor's note, contents page, contact information, submission guidelines, some sampling of stories, poems). Editor: Eli Flam. **Contact:** Fiction Editor. Magazine: 5½×8½; 128 pages; 50 lb. paper; 65 lb. cover; illustrations. *Potomac Review* "explores the topography and inner terrain of the Mid-Atlantic and beyond via a challenging diversity of prose, poetry and b&w artwork." Estab. 1994. Circ. 2,000.

**FOR EXPLANATIONS OF THESE SYMBOLS,
SEE THE INSIDE FRONT AND BACK COVERS OF THIS BOOK.**

Needs: Excerpted novel—"stories with a vivid, individual quality that get at 'the concealed side' of life. Regionally rooted, with a cross-cutting theme each issue (e.g., 'On the Trails,' summer 2000); we also keep an eye on the wider world." No "overly experimental" fiction. Wants more "fiction that gets inside its characters." Upcoming themes (subject to change): "Along the Potomac" and "Homing in on Native Americans." Receives 100 unsolicited mss/month, assigns some nonfiction pieces. Accepts 20-30 mss/issue of all sorts; 80-120 mss/year. Publishes ms within a year after acceptance as a rule. Agented fiction 5%. **Publishes up to 24 new writers/year.** Recently published work by Breena Clarke, G.C. Waldrep, Ben Passikov, David B. Bowes, E. Ethelbert Miller and Saïdeh Pakravan. Length: 100-3,000 words; average length: 2,000 words. Publishes short shorts. Length: 250 words. Also publishes poetry, essays and cogent, issue-oriented nonfiction. Humor is welcome.
How to Contact: Send complete ms with a cover letter. Include estimated word count, 2-3 sentence bio, list of publications and SASE. Responds in 2 weeks to queries; 3 months to mss. Send SASE for reply, return of ms or send a disposable copy of ms. Accepts simultaneous and reprint submissions. Sample copy for $5. Submission guidelines for #10 SASE. Reviews novels, short story collections, other books.
Payment/Terms: Pays 1 or more contributor's copy; $75 for assigned nonfiction; additional copies for $3.
Advice: "Some kind of vision should be inherent in your writing, something to say *inter alia* about life in these or other times. Read all possible magazines that might take your work; work at your last, first and last, like an old-fashioned shoemaker, daily and with dedication. Learn, above all, to rewrite; and when to stop." Fiction selected must "educate, challenge and divert in fresh ways; have something to say, in an original voice; and convey ethical depth, and a corresponding vision."

$ POTTERSFIELD PORTFOLIO, P.O. Box 40, Station A, Sydney, Nova Scotia B1P 6G9 Canada. Website: www.chebucto.ns.ca/culture/WFNS/Pottersfield/potters.html. **Contact:** Douglas Arthur Brown, editor. Magazine: 8×11; 60 pages; illustrations. "Literary magazine interested in well-written fiction and poetry. No specific thematic interests or biases." Triannually. Estab. 1979. Circ. 1,000.
Needs: Receives 40-50 fiction mss/month. Buys 4-5 fiction mss/issue. Recently published work by David Adams Richards, Vivette Kady and M.J. Hull. Length: 4,000 words maximum. Sometimes comments on rejected mss.
How to Contact: Send complete ms with SASE and cover letter. Include estimated word count and 50-word bio. No simultaneous submissions. No fax or e-mail submissions. Responds in 3 months. SASE. Sample copy for $7 (US).
Payment/Terms: Pays contributor's copy plus $5 Canadian per printed page to a maximum of $25 on publication for first Canadian serial rights.
Advice: "Provide us with a clean, proofread copy of your story. Include a brief cover letter with biographical note, but don't try to sell the story to us. *Always* include a SASE with sufficient *Canadian* postage, or IRCs, for return of the manuscript or a reply from the editors."

$ PRAIRIE FIRE, Prairie Fire Press Inc., 100 Arthur St., Room 423, Winnipeg, Manitoba R3B 1H3 Canada. (204)943-9066. Fax: (204)942-1555. Managing Editor: Andris Taskans. Magazine: 6×9; 160 pages; offset bond paper; sturdy cover stock; illustrations; photos. "Essays, critical reviews, short fiction and poetry. For writers and readers interested in Canadian literature." Published 4 times/year. Estab. 1978. Circ. 1,500.
• *Prairie Fire* authors recently received the National Magazine Silver Award for Fiction, the Western Magazine Gold Award for Fiction and the Journey Prize (fiction).
Needs: Literary, contemporary, experimental, prose poem, reviews. "We will consider work on any topic of artistic merit, including short chapters from novels-in-progress. We wish to avoid gothic, confession, religious, romance and pornography." Buys 3-6 mss/issue, 12-24 mss/year. Does not read mss in summer. **Published new writers within the last year.** Recently published work by Carol Shields, Timothy Findley, George Bowering and David Bergen. Receives 100-120 unsolicited fiction mss each quarter. Publishes short shorts. Length: 5,000 words maximum; average length: 2,500 words. Also publishes literary essays, literary criticism, poetry.
How to Contact: Send complete ms with IRC w/envelope and short bio. No simultaneous submissions. Responds in 6 months. Sample copy for $10 (Canadian). Reviews novels and short story collections. Send books to Andris Taskans.
Payment/Terms: Pays $40 for the first page, $35 for each additional page; 1 contributor copy; 60% of cover price for extras. Pays on publication for first North American serial rights. Rights revert to author on publication.
Advice: "We are publishing more fiction. Read our publication before submitting. We prefer Canadian material. Most mss are not ready for publication. Be neat, double space, and put your name and address on everything! Be the best writer you can be."

THE PRAIRIE JOURNAL OF CANADIAN LITERATURE, Prairie Journal Press, Box 61203, Brentwood Postal Services, Calgary, Alberta T2L 2K6 Canada. Website: www.geocities.com/Athens/Ithaca/4436. **Contact:** A.E. Burke, editor. Journal: 7×8½; 50-60 pages; white bond paper; Cadillac cover stock; cover illustrations. Journal of creative writing and scholarly essays, reviews for literary audience. Semiannually. Published special fiction issue last year. Estab. 1983.
Needs: Contemporary, literary, prose poem, regional, excerpted novel, novella, double-spaced. Canadian authors given preference. Publishes "a variety of types of fiction—fantasy, psychological, character-driven, feminist, etc.

We publish authors at all stages of their careers from well-known to first publication." No romance, erotica, pulp, westerns. Publishes anthology series open to submissions: *Prairie Journal Poetry II* and *Prairie Journal Fiction III*. Receives 50 unsolicited mss each month. Accepts 10-15 mss/issue; 20-30 mss/year. Suggests sample issue before submitting ms. **Publishes 20 new writers/year.** Published work by Magie Dominic, Allison Kydd, Nancy Ellen Russell, Carla Mobley, Patrick Quinn. Length: 100-3,000 words; average length: 2,500 words. Suggested deadlines: April 1 for spring/summer issue; October 1 for fall/winter. Also publishes literary essays, literary criticism, poetry. Sometimes critiques rejected mss and recommends other markets.

How to Contact: Send complete ms. Responds in 1 month. SASE. Sample copy for $8 (Canadian) and SAE with $1.10 for postage or IRC. Include cover letter of past credits, if any. Reply to queries for SAE with 55¢ for postage or IRC. No American stamps. Reviews excerpts from novels and short story collections. Send only 1 story.

Payment/Terms: Pays contributor's copies and modest honoraria. Acquires first North American serial rights. In Canada author retains copyright with acknowledgement appreciated.

Advice: "We like character-driven rather than plot-centered fiction." Interested in "innovational work of quality. Beginning writers welcome! There is no point in simply republishing known authors or conventional, predictable plots. Of the genres we receive fiction is most often of the highest calibre. It is a very competitive field. Be proud of what you send. You're worth it."

PRAIRIE SCHOONER, University of Nebraska, English Department, 201 Andrews Hall, Lincoln NE 68588-0334. (402)472-0911. Fax: (402)472-9771. E-mail: eflanaga@unlnotes.unl.edu. Website: www.unl.edu/schooner/psmain.htm (includes guidelines, editors, table of contents and excerpts of current issue). **Contact:** Hilda Raz, editor. Magazine: 6×9; 200 pages; good stock paper; heavy cover stock. "A fine literary quarterly of stories, poems, essays and reviews for a general audience that reads for pleasure." Quarterly. Estab. 1926. Circ. 3,200.

● *Prairie Schooner*, one of the oldest publications in this book, has garnered several awards and honors over the years. Work appearing in the magazine has been selected for anthologies including *Pushcart Prizes* and *Best American Short Stories*.

Needs: Good fiction (literary). Accepts 4-5 mss/issue. Receives approximately 500 unsolicited fiction and poetry mss each month. Mss are read September through May only. **Published new writers within the last year.** Recently published work by Maxine Kumin, Janet Burroway, Marilyn Hacker and Denise Duhamel. Length: varies. Also publishes poetry. Offers annual prize of $1,000 for best fiction, $1,000 for excellence in writing, $500 for best new writer (poetry or fiction), two $500 awards for best poetry (for work published in the magazine in the previous year).

How to Contact: Send complete mss with SASE and cover letter listing previous publications—where, when. Accepts queries/mss by e-mail or fax. Responds in 4 months. Sample copy for $5. Reviews novels, poetry and short story collections.

Payment/Terms: Pays in contributor's copies and prize money awarded. Acquires all rights. Will reassign rights upon request after publication.

Advice: "*Prairie Schooner* is eager to see fiction from beginning and established writers. Be tenacious. Accept rejection as a temporary setback and send out rejected stories to other magazines. *Prairie Schooner* is not a magazine with a program. We look for good fiction in traditional narrative modes as well as experimental, meta-fiction or any other form or fashion a writer might try. Create striking detail, well-developed characters, fresh dialogue; let the images and the situations evoke the stories themes. Too much explication kills a lot of otherwise good stories. Be persistent. Keep writing and sending out new work. Be familiar with the tastes of the magazines where you're sending. We are receiving record numbers of submissions. Prospective contributors must sometimes wait longer to receive our reply."

PRIMAVERA, Box 37-7547, Chicago IL 60637-7547. (312)324-5920. Editorial Board. Magazine: 5½×8½; 128 pages; 60 lb. paper; glossy cover; illustrations; photos. Literature and graphics reflecting the experiences of women: poetry, short stories, photos, drawings. "We publish original fiction that reflects the experiences of women. We select works that encompass the lives of women of different ages, races, sexual orientations and social classes." Annually. Estab. 1975. Circ. 1,000.

● *Primavera* has won grants from the Illinois Arts Council, the Puffin Foundation and from Chicago Women in Publishing.

Needs: Literary, contemporary, fantasy, feminist, gay/lesbian, humor and science fiction. "We dislike slick stories packaged for more traditional women's magazines. We publish only work reflecting the experiences of women, but also publish manuscripts by men." Accepts 6-10 mss/issue. Receives approximately 40 unsolicited fiction mss each month. **Published new writers within the last year.** Published work by Sheila Thorne, Nicole L. Reid, Stacy Lynn Smith and Marianna Wright. Length: 25 pages maximum. Also publishes poetry. Critiques rejected mss when there is time. Often gives suggestions for revisions and invites re-submission of revised ms. Occasionally recommends other markets.

How to Contact: Send complete ms with SASE. No post cards. Cover letter not necessary. No simultaneous submissions. Responds in 6 months to mss. Publishes ms up to 1 year after acceptance. Sample copy for $5; $10 for recent issues. Guidelines for SASE.

Payment/Terms: Pays 2 contributor's copies. Acquires first rights.

Advice: "We're looking for artistry and deftness of untrendy, unhackneyed themes; an original slant on a well-known theme, an original use of language, and the highest literary quality we can find."

PRISM INTERNATIONAL, Buch E462-1866 Main Mall, University of British Columbia, Vancouver, British Columbia V6T 1Z1 Canada. (604)822-2514. Fax: (604)822-3616. E-mail: prism@intercha nge.ubc.ca. Website: www.arts.ubc.ca/prism/ (includes entire year of issues, writer's guidelines, contest informa-tion, PRISM news and e-mail address). Executive Editor: Belinda Bruce. **Contact:** Andrea MacPherson and Chris Labonté, editors. Magazine: 6×9; 72-80 pages; Zephyr book paper; Cornwall, coated one side cover; artwork on cover. "An international journal of contemporary writing—fiction, poetry, drama, creative nonfiction and translation." Readership: "public and university libraries, individual subscriptions, bookstores—a world-wide audience concerned with the contemporary in literature." Quarterly. Estab. 1959. Circ. 1,200.

• PRISM *international* has won numerous magazine awards and stories first published in PRISM have been included in the *Journey Prize Anthology* every year since 1991.

Needs: New writing that is contemporary and literary. Short stories and self-contained novel excerpts. Works of translation are eagerly sought and should be accompanied by a copy of the original. No gothic, confession, religious, romance, pornography, or sci-fi. Also looking for creative nonfiction that is literary, not journalistic, in scope and tone. Buys approximately 70 mss/year. Receives over 100 fiction unsolicted mss each month. "PRISM publishes both new and established writers; our contributors have included Franz Kafka, Gabriel Garcia Marquez, Michael Ondaatje, Margaret Laurence, Mark Anthony Jarman, Gail Anderson-Dargatz and Eden Robin-son." **Publishes 7 new writers/year.** Recently published works by Billie Livingston, Rob McLennan, Jean McNeil and Kate Small. Submissions should not exceed 5,000 words "though flexible for outstanding work" (only one long story per submission, please). Publishes short shorts. Also publishes poetry and drama. Sponsors annual short fiction contest with $2,000 (Canadian) grand prize: send SASE for details.

How to Contact: Send complete ms with SASE or SAE, IRC and cover letter with bio, information and publications list. Accepts multiple submissions. "Keep it simple. U.S. contributors take note: Do note send U.S. stamps, they are not valid in Canada. Send International Reply Coupons instead." Responds in 6 months. Sample copy for $5 (U.S./Canadian).

Payment/Terms: Pays $20 (Canadian)/printed page, 1 year's subscription on publication for first North Ameri-can serial rights. Selected authors are paid an additional $10/page for digital rights.

Advice: "Read several issues of our magazine before submitting. We are committed to publishing outstanding literary work in all genres. We look for strong, believeable characters; real voices; attention to language; interest-ing ideas and plots. Send us fresh, innovative work which also shows a mastery of the basics of good prose writing. Poorly constructed or sloppy pieces will not receive serious consideration. We welcome e-mail submissions and are proud to be one of few print literary journals who offer additional payment to select writers for digital publication. Too many e-mail submissions, however, come to us unpolished and unprepared to be published. Writers should craft their work for e-mail submission as carefully as they would for submissions through tradi-tional methods. They should send one piece at a time and wait for our reply before they send another."

THE PROSE MENAGERIE. E-mail: caras@reporters.net. Website: www.geocities.com/Sotto/Studios/ 5116/index.html. **Contact:** Cara Swann, editor. E-zine. "*The Prose Menagerie* is a mixture of interesting prose, essays, articles as well as fiction (short stories/novellas/poetry)."

Needs: Literary. No erotica. Wants more "meaningful themes." **Publishes 1-2 new writers/weekly.** Recently published work by Allen Woodman, John K. Trammell and Zalman Velvel.

How to Contact: Send queries/mss by e-mail. Send in body of e-mail and/or attached as plain ASCII text file only. No MS Word files accepted.

Payment/Terms: "Since *The Prose Menagerie* is only available online, the writer maintains copyright; and while there is no payment, there is wide exposure for new and unknown writers, eagerly promoted along with those who do have name recognition."

Advice: "Submit a piece of writing that has meaning, whether it is poetry, fiction or articles. Also open to those who wish to present ideas for regular columns and book reviews."

PROVINCETOWN ARTS, Provincetown Arts, Inc., 650 Commercial St., P.O. Box 35, Province-town MA 02657. (508)487-3167. Fax: (508)487-8634. **Contact:** Christopher Busa, editor. Magazine: 9×12; 184 pages; 60 lb. coated paper; 12 pcs. cover; illustrations; photos. "*PA* focuses broadly on the artists, writers and theater of America's oldest continuous art colony." Annually. Estab. 1985. Circ. 8,000.

• *Provincetown Arts* is a recipient of a CLMP seed grant. Provincetown Arts Press has an award-winning poetry series.

Needs: Plans special fiction issue. Receives 300 unsolicited mss/year. Buys 5 mss/issue. Publishes ms 3 months after acceptance. Published work by Carole Maso and Hilary Masters. Length: 1,500-8,000 words; average length: 3,000 words. Publishes short shorts. Also publishes literary essays, literary criticism, poetry. Sometimes critiques rejected mss and recommends other markets.

How to Contact: Send complete ms with cover letter including previous publications. No simultaneous submissions. Responds in 2 weeks to queries; 3 months to mss. SASE. Sample copy for $7.50. Reviews novels and short story collections.

Payment/Terms: Pays $75-300 on publication for first rights. Sends galleys to author.

PUCKERBRUSH REVIEW, Puckerbrush Press, 76 Main St., Orono ME 04473. (207)866-4868/581-3832. Editor: Constance Hunting. **Contact:** Fiction Editor. Magazine: 9×12; 80-100 pages; illustrations. "We publish mostly new Maine writers; interviews, fiction, reviews, poetry for a literary audience." Semiannually. Estab. 1979. Circ. approx. 500.

Needs: Belles-lettres, experimental, gay (occasionally), literary. "Wants to see more original, quirky and well-written fiction." No genre fiction. "Nothing cliché." Receives 30 unsolicited mss/month. Accepts 6 mss/issue; 12 mss/year. Publishes ms 1 year after acceptance. **Publishes 10 new writers/year.** Recently published work by Beth Lurie, Beth Round, Miriam Colwell, Christopher Fahy and Farnham Blair. Sometimes publishes short shorts. Also publishes literary essays, literary criticism, poetry. Sometimes critiques rejected mss.

How to Contact: Send complete ms with cover letter. "No disks please!" Responds in 2 months. SASE. Accepts simultaneous submissions. Sample copy for $2. Guidelines for SASE. Sometimes reviews novels and short story collections.

Payment/Terms: Pays in contributor's copies.

Advice: "I don't want to see tired plots or treatments. I want to see respect for language—the right words. Be true to yourself, don't follow fashion."

PUERTO DEL SOL, New Mexico State University, Box 3E, Las Cruces NM 88003-0001. (505)646-3931. Fax: (505)646-2345. E-mail: kwest@nmsu.edu. Editors: Kay West, Antonya Nelson and Kevin McIlvoy. Magazine: 6×9; 200 pages; 60 lb. paper; 70 lb. cover stock; photos sometimes. "We publish quality material from anyone. Poetry, fiction, art, photos, interviews, reviews, parts-of-novels, long poems." Semiannually. Estab. 1961. Circ. 1,500.

● *Puerto Del Sol* ranked #46 on *Writer's Digest*'s "Fiction 50" list of top markets.

Needs: Contemporary, ethnic, experimental, literary, mainstream, prose poem, excerpted novel and translations. Receives varied number of unsolicited fiction mss/month. Acquires 8-10 mss/issue; 12-15 mss/year. Does not read mss March through August. **Published 8-10 new writers/year.** Published work by Dagobeuto Gilb, Wendell Mayo and William H. Cobb. Also publishes poetry. Occasionally critiques rejected mss.

How to Contact: Send complete ms with SASE. Accepts simultaneous submissions. Responds in 3 months. Sample copy for $7.

Payment/Terms: Pays 2 contributor's copies. Acquires one-time rights (rights revert to author).

Advice: "We are open to all forms of fiction, from the conventional to the wildly experimental, as long as they have integrity and are well written. Too often we receive very impressively 'polished' mss that will dazzle readers with their sheen but offer no character/reader experience of lasting value."

QUARTER AFTER EIGHT, A Journal of Prose and Commentary, QAE, Ellis Hall, Ohio University, Athens OH 45701. (740)593-2827. **Contact:** Thom Conroy and Christina Veladota, editors-in-chief. Magazine: 6×9; 310 pages; 20 lb. glossy cover stock; photos. "We look to publish work which somehow addresses, in its form and/or content, the boundaries between poetry and prose." Annually.

Needs: Condensed/excerpted novel, erotica, ethnic/multicultural, experimental, gay, humor/satire, lesbian, literary, mainstream/contemporary, translations. Send SASE for list of upcoming themes. Receives 75-100 unsolicited mss/month. Accepts 40-50 mss/issue. Does not read mss mid-March to mid-September. Publishes ms 6-12 months after acceptance. Agented fiction 15%. **Publishes 10-15 new writers/year.** Recently published work by Sandra Alcosser, David Baratier, Joan Connor, Colette Inez, Jane Miller and Denise Duhomel. Length: 10,000 words maximum; average length: 3,000 words. Publishes short shorts. Also publishes literary essays, literary criticism, prose poetry. Also sponsors an annual prose contest: $300 award. Sometimes comments on rejected ms.

How to Contact: Send complete ms with a cover letter. Include short bio and list of publications. Responds in 3 months. Send SASE for return of ms or send a disposable copy of ms. Accepts simultaneous submissions and miltiple submissions (up to 5 short works and 2 longer works). Sample copy for $10, 8×11 SAE and $1.60 postage. Guidelines for #10 SASE. Reviews novels and short story collections. Send books to Book Review Editor, Patrick Madden.

Payment/Terms: Pays 2 contributor's copies; additional copies $10. Acquires first North American serial rights. Rights revert to author upon publication. Sponsors contest. Send SASE for guidelines.

Advice: "We're interested in seeing more stories that push language and the traditional form to their limits."

☑ $◻☑ **QUARTERLY WEST**, University of Utah, 200 S. Central Campus Dr., Room 317, Salt Lake City UT 84112-9109. (801)581-3938. Fax: (801)581-3299. Website: chronicle.utah.edu/QW/QW.html (includes novella guidelines, submission guidelines, recent issues with samples of contributors' work). Editors: Margot Schilpp and Lynn Kilpatrick. **Contact:** Aaron Sanders, fiction editor. Magazine: 6×9; 224 pages; 60 lb. paper; 5-color cover stock; illustrations; photos rarely. "We try to publish a variety of fiction and poetry from all over the country based not so much on the submitting author's reputation but on the merit of each piece. Our publication is aimed primarily at an educated audience interested in contemporary literature and criticism." Semiannually. "We sponsor a biennial novella competition." (Next competition held in 2000). Estab. 1976. Circ. 1,800.
  • *Quarterly West* ranked #50 on *Writer's Digest*'s "Fiction 50" list of top markets. *Quarterly West* is a past recipient of grants from the NEA and was awarded First Place for Editorial Content from the American Literary Magazine Awards. Work published in the magazine has been selected for inclusion in the *Pushcart Prize* anthology and *The Best American Short Stories* anthology.
Needs: Literary, contemporary, experimental, translations. No detective, science fiction or romance. Accepts 6-10 mss/issue, 12-20 mss/year. Receives 300 unsolicited fiction mss each month. **Publishes 3 new writers/year.** Published work by Laurie Foos, Catherine Ryan Hyde, Drew Dunphy and Susan Steinberg. No preferred length; interested in longer, "fuller" short stories, as well as short shorts. Critiques rejected mss when there is time.
How to Contact: Send complete ms. Brief cover letters welcome. Send SASE for reply or return of ms. Accepts simultaneous submissions with notification. Responds in 3 months; "sooner, if possible." Sample copy for $7.50.
Payment/Terms: Pays $15-500 and 2 contributor's copies on publication for all rights (negotiable).
Advice: "We publish a special section of short shorts every issue, and we also sponsor a biennial novella contest. We are open to experimental work—potential contributors should read the magazine! We solicit occasionally, but tend more toward the surprises—unsolicited. Don't send more than one story per submission, but submit as often as you like."

◻ ⊕ $◻ **QWF (QUALITY WOMEN'S FICTION), Breaking the Boundaries of Women's Fiction**, P.O. Box 1768, Rugby, Warks CVZ1 4ZA United Kingdom. 01788 334302. Fax: 01788 334702. E-mail: qwfeditor@aol.com. **Contact:** Jo Good, editor. Magazine: A5; 80-90 pages; glossy paper. "*QWF* gets under the skin of the female experience and exposes emotional truth." Bimonthly. Estab. 1994. Circ. 2,000.
Needs: Erotica, ethnic/multicultural, experimental, fantasy, feminist, gay, horror (psychological, supernatural), humor satire, lesbian, literary, New Age, psychic/supernatural/occult, science fiction (soft/sociological), translations. Receives 30-50 unsolicited mss/month. Accepts 12 mss/issue; 72 mss/year. Does not read mss June-August. Publishes ms up to 18 months after acceptance. **Publishes 20 new writers/year.** Recently published work by Julia Darling, Sally Zigmond and Diana Forrester. Length: 1,000-4,500 words; average length: 2,500 words. Publishes short shorts. Average length: 900 words. Also publishes literary criticism. Always comments on rejected mss.
How to Contact: Send complete ms, cover letter and 3 IRCs. Accepts submissions by disk. Include estimated word count, brief bio, list of publications and IRCs or stamps. Responds in 2 weeks to queries; 3 months to mss. Send SASE (or IRC) for return of ms or send a disposable copy of ms and #10 SASE for reply only. Accepts previously published work. Guidelines for SASE, by e-mail or fax. Reviews novels, short story collections and nonfiction books of interest to writers.
Payment/Terms: Pays £10 sterling maximum. Pays on publication for first British serial rights. Sponsors contest. SASE or IRC for details.
Advice: "Take risks with subject matter. Study at least one copy of *QWF*. Ensure story is technically sound."

◻ ◻ **THE RABBIT HOLE PRESS**, 2 Huntingwood Crescent, Brampton, Ontario L6S 1S6 Canada. E-mail: rabbit.hole@3web.net. **Contact:** Alice Cobham, editor. Magazine: digest sized; saddle stitched; desktop published; illustrations; photos. "Rabbit Hole Press is a one-person operation on a part-time basis. We publish original poetry, short fiction, essays, art and photography by new and unpublished writers/artists. We seek to provide a forum for beginning writers." Quarterly. Estab. 1999. Circ. 500.
Needs: Adventure, erotica, ethnic/multicultural, experimental, fantasy (space fantasy, sword and sorcery), feminist, gay, historical, horror (dark fantasy, futuristic, psychological, supernatural), humor satire, lesbian, literary, mainstream, military/war, mystery/suspense, New Age, psychic/supernatural/occult, regional, romance, science fiction, thriller/espionage. "We want eclectic, provocative, culturally diverse, metaphysical, philosophical, imaginative, radical, 'how deep is the rabbit hole?' submissions." Publishes ms 3-4 months after acceptance.
How to Contact: Send complete ms with a cover letter. Accepts submissions by e-mail. Include estimated word count and brief bio. Responds in 1 month to queries; 3 months to mss. Send SASE (or IRC) for return of ms or send a disposable copy of ms and #10 SASE for reply only. Accepts simultaneous submissions. Sample copy for $5 (US).
Payment/Terms: Pays contributor's copy.
Advice: "Read, read and write, write. Learn your craft at the feet of the masters, but develop your own voice. Be original, honest and true to yourself. Believe in your potential and don't be discouraged by rejection. You are unique; never give up."

$ ⬛ RAIN CROW, (formerly 32 Pages), 2127 W. Pierce Ave. Apt. 2B, Chicago IL 60622-1824. (773)562-5786. Fax: (503)214-6615. E-mail: submissions@rain-crow.com. Website: http://rain-crow.com/ (includes writer's guidelines, sample issue, back issue sales, advertising rates). **Contact:** Michael S. Manley, editor. Magazine/journal: 8½×11; 96-128 pages; white bond paper; glossy cover; illustrations; photos. "*32 Pages* publishes new and experienced writers in many styles and genres. I look for eclectic, well-crafted, entertaining fiction aimed at those who enjoy literature for its pleasures." Triannually. Estab. 1997. Circ. 1,000. Member: CLMP.

Needs: Erotica, experimental, literary, mainstream, science fiction, short story collections, translations. "No propaganda, juvenile, formulaic fiction. No poetry." Receives 20-30 unsolicited mss/month. Accepts 6-10 mss/issue; 18-30 mss/year. Publishes ms within 6 months after acceptance. **Publishes several new writers/year.** Published work by Susan Neville, Peter Johnson, William Stuckey, Carolyn Allesio and James Clarage. Length: 250-8,000 words; average length: 3,500 words. Publishes short shorts. Also publishes literary essays, poetry. Sometimes comments on rejected mss.

How to Contact: Send complete ms with a cover letter. May also e-mail submissions. Include list of publications. Responds in 3 months. Send SASE for reply, return of ms or send a disposable copy of ms. Accepts simultaneous submissions, reprints and electronic submissions. Sample copy for $2.50. Guidelines for #10 SASE (1 IRC). Reviews novels, short story collections and nonfiction books. Send review copies to Michael Manley, editor.

Payment/Terms: Pays $5-190 per page on publication, free subscription to magazine and 2 contributor's copies; additional copies for $2.75. Acquires one-time rights and one-time electronic rights. Sends galleys to author. Watch for announcements in writer's publications and on our website for contests."

Advice: "We look for attention to craft: voice, language, character and plot working together to maximum effect. We look for stories that deserve rereading. We look for stories we would gladly recommend others read. Send your best work. Present your work professionally. Unique, credible settings and situations that entertain get the most attention. Get used to rejections."

⬛ RAMBUNCTIOUS REVIEW, Rambunctious Press, Inc., 1221 W. Pratt Blvd., Chicago IL 60626-4329. **Contact:** Nancy Lennon, Richard Goldeman and Elizabeth Hausler, editors. Magazine: 10×7; 48 pages; illustrations; photos. Annually. Estab. 1983. Circ. 300.

Needs: Experimental, feminist, humor/satire, literary, mainstream/contemporary. No mystery or drama. Upcoming themes: Courage (Fall 2001), deadline "early to middle 2001." List of upcoming themes available for SASE. Receives 30 unsolicited mss/month. Accepts 4-5 mss/issue. Does not read mss May through August. Publishes ms 5-6 months after acceptance. **Publishes 6 new writers/year.** Published work by Ben Satterfield and Brian Skinner. Length: 12 double-spaced pages. Publishes short shorts. Also publishes poetry. Sometimes comments on rejected ms. Sponsors contest. Send SASE for details.

How to Contact: Send complete ms with a cover letter. Include estimated word count. Responds in 9 months. Send SASE for reply, return of ms or send a disposable copy of ms. Accepts simultaneous submissions. Sample copy for $4.

Payment/Terms: Pays 2 contributor's copies. Acquires one-time rights.

⬛ RASKOLNIKOV'S CELLAR and THE LAMPLIGHT, The Beggars's Press, 8110 N. 38th St., Omaha NE 68112-2018. (402)455-2615. Editor: Richard Carey. **Contact:** Danielle Staton, fiction editor. Magazine: 8½×12; 60-150 pages; 20 lb. bond paper; 12pt soft cover. "Our purpose is to encourage writing in the style of the past masters and to hold back illiteracy in our generation." Semiannually. Estab. 1952. Circ. 1,200.

● Member: International Association of Independent Publishers and the Federation of Literary Publishers.

Needs: Historical, horror, humor/satire, literary, serialized novels, translations. No "religious, sentimental, folksy, science fiction or ultra modern." Publishes special fiction issue or anthologies. Receives 135 unsolicited mss/month. Accepts 15 mss/issue; 30-45 mss/year. Publishes ms 2-6 months after acceptance. Agented fiction 5%. Published work by James Scoffield, Richard Davignon and Philip Sparacino. Length: 50-3,000 words; average length: 1,500-2,000 words. Publishes short shorts. Also publishes literary essays, literary criticism and poetry.

How to Contact: Send complete ms with a cover letter. Include estimated word count and 1 page bio. Responds in 2 months to queries; 4 months to mss. Accepts simultaneous submissions. Sample copy for $10 plus 9×12 SAE with 2 first-class stamps. Guidelines for #10 SAE with 2 first-class stamps. Reviews novels or short story collections. Send books to Danielle Staton.

Payment/Terms: Pays 1 contributor's copy for first North American serial rights.

Advice: "We judge on writing style as well as content. If your style of writing and your word usage do not attract us at once, there is faint hope of the content and the plot saving the story. Read and learn from the great writers of the past. Set your stories in the un-computer age, so your characters have time to think, to feel, to react. Use your glorious language to the fullest. Our subscribers can read quite well. The strongest way to say anything is to never quite say it."

Ⓝ RATTAPALLAX, Rattapallax Press, 532 La Guardia Place, Suite 353, New York NY 10012. (212)560-7459. E-mail: rattapallax@hotmail.com. Website: www.rattapallax.com. **Contact:** George Dickerson, editor-in-chief. Literary magazine: 6×9; 128 pages; bound; some illustrations; photos. "General readership. Our stories must be character driven with strong conflict. All accepted stories are edited by our staff and the writer before publication to ensure a well-crafted and written work." Semiannual. Estab. 1999. Circ. 2,000.

Needs: Literary. Receives 15 unsolicited mss/month. Accepts 3 mss/issue; 6 mss/year. Publishes 3-6 months after acceptance. Agented fiction 15%. **Publishes 5-10 new writers/year.** Recently published work by W.R. Marcy, Karen Swanson, James Ragan. Length: 1,000-10,000 words; average length: 5,000. Publishes short shorts; average length: 1,000 words. Also publishes poetry. Often comments on rejected mss.

How to Contact: Send complete ms with cover letter. Reports in 3 months to queries and mss. Send SASE for return of ms. Sample copy for $7.95. Guidelines for SASE or e-mail.

Payment/Terms: Pays 2 contributor's copies; additional copies $7.95. Pays on publication for first North American serial rights. Sends galleys to author.

Advice: "Character driven, well-crafted, strong conflict."

THE RAVEN CHRONICLES, A Magazine of Transcultural Art, Literature and the Spoken Word, The Raven Chronicles, 1634 11th Ave., Seattle WA 98122-2419. (206)323-4316. Fax: (206)323-4316. E-mail: ravenchron@speakeasy.org. Website: www.speakeasy.org/ravenchronicles (includes guidelines, editors, short fiction, prose, poetry, separate monthly topics for online publication). Managing Editor: Phoebe Bosché. **Contact:** Kathleen Alcala, fiction editors. Poetry Editors: Tiffany Midge and Jody Aliesan. Webmaster: Scott Martin. Magazine: 8½×11; 48-64 pages; 50 lb. book paper; glossy cover; b&w illustrations; photos. "*The Raven Chronicles* is designed to promote transcultural art, literature and the spoken word." Triannually. Estab. 1991. Circ. 2,500-5,000.

● This magazine is a frequent winner of Bumbershoot Bookfair awards. The magazine also received grants from the Washington State Arts Commission, the Seattle Arts Commission, the King County Arts Commission and ATR, a foundation for social justice projects.

Needs: Political, cultural essays, ethnic/multicultural, literary, regional. No romance, fantasy, mystery or detective. Receives 300-400 mss/month. Buys 20-40 mss/issue; 60-120 mss/year. Publishes 3-6 months after acceptance. **Publishes 50-100 new writers/year.** Published work by David Romtvedt, Sherman Alexie, D.L. Birchfield, Nancy Redwine, Diane Glancy, Greg Hischak and Sharon Hashimoto. Length: 2,500 words maximum; average length: 2,000 words. Publishes short shorts. Length: 300-500 words. Also publishes literary essays, reviews, literary criticism, poetry. Sometimes critiques rejected mss.

How to Contact: Send complete ms with a cover letter. Include estimated word count. Accepts queries/mss by e-mail. Responds in 8 months on manuscripts. Send SASE for return of ms. Accepts simultaneous submissions. Sample copy for $4. Guidelines for #10 SASE.

Payment/Terms: Pays $10-40 plus 2 contributor's copies; additional copies at half cover cost. Pays on publication for first North American serial rights. Sends galleys to author.

Advice: Looks for "clean, direct language, written from the heart and experimental writing. Read sample copy, or look at *Before Columbus* anthologies and *Greywolf Annual* anthologies."

REALPOETIK: A Little Magazine of the Internet, 840 W. Nickerson St. #11, Seattle WA 98119. (206)282-3776. E-mail: salasin@scn.org. Website: www.scn.org/arts/realpoetik. "This is an archive/website for the mailing list/e-mail aspect of *RealPoetik*." Editor: Sal Salasin. **Contact:** Fiction Editor. E-zine. "We publish the new, lively, exciting and unexpected in vernacular English. Any vernacular will do." Weekly. Estab. 1993.

Needs: "We do not want to see anything that fits neatly into categories. We subvert categories." Publishes ms 2-4 months after acceptance. **Publishes 20-30 new writers/year.** Word length: 250-500 average. Publishes short shorts. Also publishes literary essays, literary criticism and poetry. Sometimes comments on or critiques rejected ms.

How to Contact: "E-mail to salsanis@scn.org." Responds to queries in 1 month. Send SASE for reply, return of ms or send a disposable copy of ms. No simultaneous submissions. Reviews novels, short story collections and poetry.

Payment/Terms: Acquires one-time rights. Sponsors contest.

Advice: "Be different, but interesting. Humor and consciousness are always helpful. Write short. We're a postmodern e-zine."

RECURSIVE ANGEL. (914)765-1156. Fax: (914)765-1157. E-mail: recangel@calldei.com. Website: www.recursiveangel.com. Managing Editor: David Sutherland. **Contact:** Paul Kloppenborg, fiction editor. E-zine. "*Recursive Angel* looks for and pays a fee for high quality, cutting edge fiction, poetry and art. We prefer the serious writer with a preference to the philosophical/experimental in works accepted."

Needs: Literary. "Wants experimental, no standard storyline or topic. Would like to see more of those stories that take risks with ones imagination as well as reach for broader world views." **Publishes 50-60 new writers/year.** Recently published work by Beth Spencer, Mark Budman and Coral Hull.

How to Contact: Send queries/mss by e-mail. "Our guidelines with the appropriate editorial contacts are listed on our web pages."

Payment/Terms: Pays $15/short story; $10/poem.

Advice: "Take a chance with your writing, push the envelope. Electronic publishing is alive and healthy! We see thousands of readers per month and have received positive write-ups/reviews from the *New York Times Online*, *Poets & Writers* and *The Boston Review*."

RED CEDAR REVIEW, Dept. of English, 17C Morrill Hall, Michigan State University, East Lansing MI 48824. (517)655-6307. E-mail: rcreview@msu.edu. Website: www.msu.edu/~rcreview (includes writer's guidelines, editors' names, subscription information). Editors change yearly. **Contact:** Jim Oliver, fiction editor. Magazine: 5½×8½; 100 pages. Theme: "literary—poetry and short fiction." Biannual. Estab. 1963. Circ. 400.

Needs: Literary. "Good stories with character, plot and style, any genre, but with a real tilt toward literary fiction." Accepts 3-4 mss/issue, 6-10 mss/year. **Publishes 4 new writers/year.** Recently published work by Marc Bookman and Catherine Ryan Hyde. Length: 5,000 words maximum.

How to Contact: Query with unpublished ms with SASE. No simultaneous submissions. Responds in 3 months to mss. Publishes ms up to 4 months after acceptance. Sample copy for $4.

Payment/Terms: Pays 2 contributor's copies. $6 charge for extras. Acquires first rights.

Advice: "It would be nice to see more stories that self-confidently further our literary tradition in some way, stories that 'marry artistic vision with moral insight.' What does your story discover about the human condition? What have you done with words and sentences that's new? Hundreds of journals get hundreds of manuscripts in the mail each month. Why does yours need to get printed? I don't want to learn yet again that innocent people suffer, that life is hollow, that the universe is meaningless. Nor do I want to be told that a warm kitten can save one from the abyss. I want an honest, well crafted exploration of where and what we are. Something after which I can no longer see the world in the same way."

RED ROCK REVIEW, Community College of Southern Nevada, 3200 E. Cheyenne Ave., N. Las Vegas NV 89030. (702)651-4094. **Contact:** Dr. Richard Logsdon, senior editor. Magazine: 5×8; 125 pages. "We're looking for the very best literature. Stories need to be tightly crafted, strong in character development, built around conflict. Poems need to be tightly crafted, characterized by expert use of language." Semiannual. Estab. 1995. Circ. 250. Member: CLMP.

Needs: Experimental, literary, mainstream. Receives 125 unsolicited mss/month. Accepts 5-7 mss/issue; 10-14 mss/year. Does not read mss during summer. Publishes ms 3-5 months after acceptance. **Publishes 5-10 new writers/year.** Recently published work by Kari Brooks, Robert Thomas, Shaun Griffin and David Lee. Length: 1,500-5,000 words; average length: 3,500 words. Publishes short shorts. Average length: 3,500 words. Also publishes literary essays, literary criticism and poetry. Sometimes comments on rejected mss.

How to Contact: Send complete ms with a cover letter. Accepts submissions by e-mail and disk. Include brief bio and list of publications. Responds in 2 weeks to queries; 2 months to mss. Send SASE (or IRC) for return of ms. Accepts simultaneous submissions and multiple submissions. Sample copy for $5.50. Guidelines for SASE, by e-mail or on website.

Payment/Terms: Pays 2 contributor's copies. Pays on acceptance for first rights.

RED WHEELBARROW, (formerly Bottomfish Magazine). De Anza College, 21250 Stevens Creek Blvd., Cupertino CA 95014. (408)864-8600. E-mail: splitter@cruzio.com. Website: www.deanza.fhda.edu/bottomfish/bottomfish.html (includes guidelines, names of editors, short fiction, authors, links). **Contact:** Randolph Splitter, editor-in-chief. Magazine: 6×9; 80-100 pages; White Bristol vellum cover; b&w high contrast illustrations; photos. "Contemporary poetry, fiction, creative nonfiction, b&w graphics, comics and photos." Annual. Estab. 1976. Circ. 500.

Needs: "Careful, thoughtful, personal writing. Diverse styles and voices." Receives 50-100 unsolicited fiction mss/month. Accepts 5-6 mss/issue. **Publishes 1-3 new writers/year.** Recently published work by Michelle Cacho-Negrete, Chitra Banerjee Divakaruni and Eleanor Swanson. Length: 4,000 words maximum; average length: 2,500 words.

How to Contact: Reads mss September through February. Submission deadline: December 31; publication date: April. Accepts queries by e-mail (no mss). Submit 1 short story or up to 3 short shorts with cover letter, brief bio and SASE. "Sorry, we cannot return manuscripts." No reprints. Responds in 6 months. Publishes mss an average of 3 months after acceptance. Sample copy for $5.

Payment/Terms: Pays 2 contributor's copies. Acquires one-time rights.

Advice: "Write freely, rewrite carefully. Move beyond clichés and stereotypes."

REFLECT, 1317-D Eagles Trace Path, Chesapeake VA 23320. (757)547-4464. **Contact:** W.S. Kennedy, editor. Magazine: 5½×8½; 48 pages; pen & ink illustrations. "Spiral Mode fiction and poetry for writers and poets—professional and amateur." Quarterly. Estab. 1979.

Needs: Spiral fiction. "The four rules to the Spiral Mode fiction form are: (1) The story a situation or condition. (2) The outlining of the situation in the opening paragraphs. The story being told at once, the author is not overly-involved with dialogue and plot development, may concentrate on *sound, style, color*—the superior elements in art. (3) The use of a concise style with euphonic wording. Good poets may have the advantage here. (4) The

involvement of Spiral Fiction themes—as opposed to Spiral Poetry themes—with love, and presented with the mystical overtones of the Mode." No "smut, bad taste, socialist." Accepts 2-6 mss/issue; 8-24 mss/year. Publishes ms 3 months after acceptance. **Publishes 6 new writers/year.** Recently published work by Dr. Elaine Hatfield, Ruth Schuler, Joan P. Kincaid and Susan Tanaka. Length: 2,500 words maximum; average length: 1,500 words average. Publishes short shorts. Sometimes critiques rejected mss.
How to Contact: Send complete ms with cover letter. Responds in 2 months to mss. SASE. No simultaneous submissions. Sample copy for $2. (Make checks payable to W.S. Kennedy.) Guidelines in each issue of *Reflect*.
Payment/Terms: Pays contributor's copies. Acquires one-time rights. Publication not copyrighted.
Advice: "Subject matter usually is not relevant to the successful writing of Spiral Fiction, as long as there is some element or type of *love* in the story, and provided that there are mystical references. (Though a dream-like style may qualify as 'mystical.')"

$☑ ◖ THE REJECTED QUARTERLY, A Journal of Quality Literature Rejected at Least Five Times, Black Plankton Press, P.O. Box 1351, Cobb CA 95426. E-mail: bplankton@juno.com. Editor: Daniel Weiss. **Contact:** Daniel Weiss, Jeff Ludecke, fiction editors. Magazine: 8½×11; 40 pages; 60 lb. paper; 8 pt. coated cover stock; illustrations. "We want the best literature possible, regardless of genre. We do, however, have a bias toward the unusual and toward speculative fiction. We aim for a literate, educated audience. *The Rejected Quarterly* believes in publishing the highest quality rejected fiction and other writing that doesn't fit anywhere else. We strive to be different, but will go for quality every time, whether conventional or not." Quarterly. Estab. 1998.
Needs: Experimental, fantasy, historical, humor/satire, literary, mainstream/contemporary, mystery/suspense, romance (futuristic/time travel only), science fiction (soft/sociological), sports. "No vampire fiction." Receives 30 unsolicited mss/month. Accepts 4-6 mss/issue; 16-24 mss/year. Publishes ms 1-12 months after acceptance. **Publishes 1-2 new writers/year.** Recently published work by Vera Searles, Lance Carrey, Arthur Winefeld Knight, Kay Haugaard, Jessiyka Anya Blau and Thomas E. Kennedy. Length: no mimimum; 8,000 words maximum; average length: 5,000 words. Publishes short shorts. Also publishes literary essays, literary criticism, poetry. Often comments on rejected ms.
How to Contact: Send complete ms with a cover letter and 5 rejection slips. Include estimated word count, 1-paragraph bio and list of publications. Accepts queries by e-mail. Responds in 2 weeks to queries; 3 months to mss. Send SASE for reply, return of ms or send a disposable copy of ms. Accepts reprint submissions. Sample copy $6 (IRCs for foreign requests). Reviews novels, short story collections and nonfiction.
Payment/Terms: Pays $5 on acceptance and 1 contributor's copy for first rights; additional copies, one at cost, others $5. Sends galleys to author if possible.
Advice: "We are looking for high-quality writing that tells a story or expresses a coherent idea. We want unique stories, original viewpoints and unusual slants. We are getting far too many inappropriate submissions. Please be familiar with the magazine. Be sure to include your rejection slips! Send out quality rather than quantity. Work on one piece until it is as close to a masterpiece in your own eyes as you can get it. Find the right place for it. Be selective in ordering samples, but do be familiar with where you're sending your work."

◖ RHINO, The Poetry Forum, P.O. Box 554, Winnetka IL 60093. Website: www.rhinopoetry.com (includes guidelines, events, and excerpts). **Contact:** Alice George, Deborah Nodler Rosen, Helen Degen Cohen, Kathleen Kirk, editors. Magazine: 5½×7½; 90-120 pages; glossy cover stock; illustrations; photos. "An eclectic magazine looking for strong voices and risk-taking." Annually. Estab. 1976.
Needs: Erotica, ethnic/multicultural, experimental, feminist, humor/satire, literary, mainstream/contemporary, regional. "No long stories—we only print short-shorts/flash fiction." Receives 60 unsolicited mss/month. Accepts 1-2 mss/issue. Publishes ms up to 9 months after acceptance. Publishes 4 new writers/year. Recently published work by Barry Siles Ky and S.I. Weisenberg.. Length: flash fiction/short shorts (under 500 words) only. Also publishes literary essays. Sometimes comments on rejected ms.
How to Contact: Send complete ms with a cover letter. Include bio. Responds in 1 month to queries; 3 months to mss. Send SASE for reply, return of ms or send a disposable copy of ms. Accepts simultaneous submissions. Sample copy $5. Guidelines free.
Payment/Terms: Pays 2 contributor's copies; additional copies $3.50. Acquires one-time rights. Sends galleys to author.

☑ ◖ RIO GRANDE REVIEW, UT El Paso's literary magazine, Student publications, 105 E. Union, University of Texas at El Paso, El Paso TX 79968-0062. (915)747-5161. Fax: (915)747-8031. E-mail: rgr@mail.ut ep.edu. Website: www.utep.edu/proscmine/rgr/. Editor: Adriana Chavez. Editors change each year. **Contact:** Fiction Editor. Magazine: 6×9; approximately 200 pages; 70 lb. paper; 85 lb. cover stock; illustrations; photos. "We publish any work that challenges writing and reading audiences alike. The intended audience isn't any one sect in particular; rather, the work forcing readers to think as opposed to couch reading is encouraged." Semiannually. Estab. 1984. Circ. 1,000.
Needs: Experimental, feminist, gay, humor/satire, lesbian, mainstream/contemporary, flash fiction, short drama, short fiction. No regional, "anything exclusionarily academic." Receives 40-45 unsolicited mss/month. Accepts

3-4 mss/issue; 6-8 mss/year. Publishes ms approximately 2 months after acceptance. **Publishes 5 new writers/ year.** Published work by Lawrence Dunning, James J. O'Keeffe and Carole Bubash. Length: 1,100-2,000 words; average length: 1,750 words. Publishes short shorts. Also publishes poetry. Sometimes comments on rejected mss.

How to Contact: Send complete ms with a cover letter. Include estimated word count, 40-word bio and list of publications. Responds in 3 months to queries; 4 months to mss. Send SASE for reply and disposable copy of ms. Accepts electronic submissions. Sample copy for $5.

Payment/Terms: Pays 2 contributor's copies on publication; additional copies for $5. Acquires "one-time rights that revert back to the author but the *Rio Grande Review* must be mentioned."

Advice: "Be patient. If the beginning fiction writer doesn't make it into the edition the first time, re-submit. Be persistent. One huge category that the *RGR* is branching into is flash fiction. Because the attention span of the nation is dwindling, thereby turning to such no-brain activities as television and movies, literature must change to accommodate as well."

☑ $◙ **RIVER STYX**, Big River Association, 634 N. Grand Blvd., 12th Floor, St. Louis MO 63103-1218. Website: www.riverstyx.org (includes writer's guidelines, names of editors, contest and theme issue information, excerpts and art from publication). **Contact:** Richard Newman, editor. Magazine: 6×9; 100 pages; color card cover; perfect-bound; b&w visual art. "No theme restrictions; only high quality, intelligent work." Triannual. Estab. 1975.

Needs: Excerpted novel chapter, contemporary, ethnic, experimental, feminist, gay, satire, lesbian, literary, mainstream, prose poem, translations. No genre fiction, "less thinly veiled autobiography, or science fiction." Receives 150-200 unsolicited mss/month. Accepts 1-3 mss/issue; 3-8 mss/year. Reads only May through November. Published work by Richard Burgin, Lucia Perillo, Linda Wendling and Ken Harvey. Length: no more than 20-30 manuscript pages. Publishes short shorts. Also publishes poetry. Sometimes critiques rejected mss and recommends other markets.

How to Contact: Send complete ms with name and address on every page. SASE required. Responds in 5 months to mss. Accepts simultaneous submissions, "if a note is enclosed with your work and if we are notified immediately upon acceptance elsewhere." Sample copy for $7.

Payment/Terms: Pays 2 contributor's copies, 1-year subscription and $8/page "if funds available." Acquires first North American serial rights.

Advice: "We want high-powered stories with well-developed characters. We like strong plots, usually with at least three memorable scenes, and a subplot often helps. No thin, flimsy fiction with merely serviceable language. Short stories shouldn't be any different than poetry–every single word should count. One could argue every word counts more since we're being asked to read 10 to 30 pages."

◙ **ROANOKE REVIEW**, English Department, Roanoke College, Salem VA 24153. (703)375-2500. Editor: Robert R. Walter. **Contact:** Fiction Editor. Magazine: 6×9; 40-60 pages. Semiannually. Estab. 1967. Circ. 300.

Needs: Receives 50-60 unsolicited mss/month. Accepts 2-3 mss/issue; 4-6 mss/year. Publishes ms 6 months after acceptance. Length: 2,500-7,500 words. Publishes short shorts. Occasionally critiques rejected mss.

How to Contact: Send complete ms with a cover letter. Responds in 2 weeks to queries; 3 months to mss. SASE for query. Sample copy for $3.

Payment/Terms: Pays in contributor's copies.

☑ $◙ **ROCKET PRESS**, P.O. Box 672, Water Mill NY 11976-0672. E-mail: RocketUSA@delphi.com. Website: www.people.delphi.com/rocketusa. **Contact:** Darren Johnson, editor. 16-page newspaper. "A Rocket is a transcendental, celestial traveler—innovative and intelligent fiction and poetry aimed at opening minds—even into the next century." Biannually. Estab. 1993. Circ. 500-2,000.

Needs: Erotica, experimental, humor/satire, literary, special interests (prose poetry). "No historical, romance, academic." Publishes annual special fiction issue or anthology. Receives 20 unsolicited mss/month. Accepts 2-4 mss/issue; 8-16 mss/year. Recently published work by Chris Woods, Roger Lee Kenvin and Ben Ohmart. Publishes 1 new writer/year. Length: 500-2,000 words; average length: 1,000 words. Publishes short shorts. Length: 400 words. Also publishes poetry. Sometimes comments on rejected mss.

How to Contact: "E-mail submissions preferred," or send SASE for reply, return of ms or send a disposable copy of ms. Accepts simultaneous submissions. Responds in 3 months. Current issue $2, past issue $1.

Payment/Terms: Pays 1¢/word. Acquires one-time rights.

Advice: "Your first paragraph is crucial. Editors are swamped with submissions, so a plain or clumsy lead will send your manuscript to the recycling bin. Also, too many writers come off as self-important. When writing a cover letter really try to talk to the editor—don't just rattle off a list of publications you've been in."

◙ **THE ROCKFORD REVIEW**, The Rockford Writers Guild, Box 858, Rockford IL 61105. **Contact:** David Ross, editor-in-chief. Magazine: 5⅜×8½; 50 pages; b&w illustrations; b&w photos. "We look for prose and poetry with a fresh approach to old themes or new insights into the human condition." Triquarterly. Estab. 1971. Circ. 750.

Needs: Ethnic, experimental, fantasy, humor/satire, literary, regional, science fiction (hard science, soft/sociological). Published work by Kevin Mims, Bill Embly, William Gorman and Melanie Coronetz. Length: Up to 1,300 words. Also publishes one-acts and essays.

How to Contact: Send complete ms. "Include a short biographical note—no more than four sentences." Accepts simultaneous submissions. Responds in 2 months to mss. SASE. Sample copy for $5. Guidelines for SASE.

Payment/Terms: Pays contributor's copies. "Two $25 editor's choice cash prizes per issue." Acquires first North American serial rights.

Advice: "Any subject or theme goes as long as it enhances our understanding of our humanity." Wants more "satire and humor, good dialogue."

N ⊛ $ 🗹 ⊚ ROOM OF ONE'S OWN, P.O. Box 46160, Suite D, Vancouver, British Columbia V6J 5G5 Canada. Website: www.islandnet.com/Room/enter (includes selected works from current issue). **Contact:** Growing Room Collective. Magazine: 96 pages; illustrations; photos. Quarterly. Estab. 1975.

Needs: Feminist, literary. "No humor, science fiction, romance." Receives 60-100 unsolicited mss/month. Accepts 18-20 mss/issue; 75-80 mss/year. Publishes ms 1 year after acceptance. **Publishes 15-20 new writers/ year.** Length: 5,000 maximum. Publishes short shorts. Also publishes poetry. Sometimes comments on rejected mss.

How to Contact: Send complete ms with a cover letter. Accepts submissions by disk. Include estimated word count and brief bio. Send a disposable copy of ms and #10 SASE for reply only. Accepts multiple submissions. Reviews novels, short story collections and nonfiction books of interest to writers. Send review copies to Virginia Aulen.

Payment/Terms: Pays $35, free subscription to the magazine and 2 contributor's copies. Pays on publication for first North American serial rights.

🗹 SALT HILL, Salt Hill, English Dept., Syracuse University, Syracuse NY 13244-1170. (315)425-9371. Fax: (315)443-3660. E-mail: cbkoplik@syr.edu. Website: www.hypertext.com/sh (includes writer's guidelines, short fiction, links, audio). **Contact:** Caryn Koplik, editor. Magazine: 5½ × 8½; 120 pages. 4-color cover; illustrations; photos. Publishes fiction with "fresh imagery, original language and tonal and structural experimentation." Semiannual. Estab. 1994. Circ. 1,000.

● Member: CLMP. Sponsors short short fiction contest. Deadline September 15. Send SASE for details.

Needs: Erotica, ethnic/multicultural, experimental, gay, humor/satire, lesbian, literary, translations. No genre fiction. Receives 40-50 unsolicited mss/month. Accepts 3-5 mss/issue; 6-10 mss/year. Publishes ms 2-8 months after acceptance. **Publishes 2 new writers/year.** Recently published work by Christine Schutt, Edra Ziesk and Mark Kipniss. Length: 4,500 words maximum. Publishes short shorts. Also publishes literary essays, literary criticism and poetry.

How to Contact: Send complete ms with a cover letter. Include 3-5 sentence bio and estimated word count. Accepts fiction queries/mss by e-mail. Responds in 6 months to mss. Send SASE for reply, return of ms or send disposable copy of ms. Accepts simultaneous submissions. Sample copy for $8. Guidelines for #10 SASE. Reviews novels or short story collections. Send books to "Book Review Editor."

Payment/Terms: Pays 1 contributor's copy; additional copies $7. Acquires first North American serial rights and web rights.

Tips: "Read everything you can, think about what you read, understand the structures, characters, etc.—then write, and write, and write again."

⊚ SAMSARA, The Magazine of Suffering, P.O. Box 367, College Park MD 20741-0367. Website: members .aol.com/rdfgoalie/ (includes writer's guidelines and tips for writers). **Contact:** R. David Fulcher, editor. Magazine: 8½ × 11; 50-80 pages; Xerox paper; poster stock cover; illustrations. "*Samsara* publishes only stories or poems relating to suffering." Semiannual. Estab. 1994. Circ. 250.

Needs: Condensed/excerpted novel, erotica, experimental, fantasy (science fantasy, sword and sorcery), horror, literary, mainstream/contemporary, science fiction (hard science, soft/sociological). Receives 80 unsolicited mss/ month. Accepts 17-20 mss/issue; 40 mss/year. "*Samsara* closes to submission after the publication of each issue. However, this schedule is not fixed." Publishes ms 4 months after acceptance. Recently published work by D.F. Lewis, D. Ceder and Christopher Hivner. Average length: 2,000 words. Publishes short shorts. Also publishes poetry. Sometimes comments on rejected ms.

How to Contact: Send complete ms with a cover letter. Include estimated word count, 1-page bio and list of publications. Responds in 6 months to queries. Send SASE for reply, return of ms or send a disposable copy of ms. Accepts simultaneous and reprint submissions. Sample copy for $5.50. Guidelines for #10 SASE.

Payment/Terms: Pays 1 contributor's copy. Acquires first North American serial rights and reprint rights.

Advice: "We seek out writers who make use of imagery and avoid over-writing. Symbolism and myth really make a manuscript stand out. Read a sample copy. Too many writers send work which does not pertain to the guidelines. Writers should avoid sending us splatter-punk or gore stories."

SANSKRIT, Literary Arts Magazine of UNC Charlotte, University of North Carolina at Charlotte, Highway 49, Charlotte NC 28223-0001. (704)547-2326. Fax: (704)547-3394. E-mail: sanskrit@email.uncc.edu. Website: www.uncc.edu/life/sanskrit (includes 1999, 2000 editions). **Contact:** Tamara Titus, literary editor. Magazine: 9×12, 64 pages. "*Sanskrit* is an award-winning magazine produced with two goals in mind: service to the student staff and student body, and the promotion of unpublished and beginning artists. Our intended audience is the literary/arts community of UNCC, Charlotte, other schools and contributors and specifically individuals who might never have read a litarary magazine before." Annually. Estab. 1968.

• *Sanskrit* has received the Pacemaker Award, Associated College Press, Gold Crown Award and Columbia Scholastic Press Award.

Needs: "Not looking for any specific category—just good writing." Receives 50 unsolicited mss/month. Acquires 2-3 mss/issue. Publishes in late March. Deadline: first Friday in November. Published work by Bayard. Length: 250-3,500 words. Publishes short shorts. Also publishes poetry. Seldom critiques rejected mss.

How to Contact: Send complete manuscript with cover letter. Accepts queries/mss by e-mail. SASE. Accepts simultaneous submissions. Sample copy for $10; additional copies $7. Guidelines for #10 SAE.

Payment/Terms: Pays contributor's copy. Acquires one-time rights. Publication not previously copyrighted.

Advice: "Remember that you are entering a market often saturated with mediocrity—an abundance of cute words and phrases held together by cliques simply will not do."

SANTA MONICA REVIEW, Santa Monica College, 1900 Pico Blvd., Santa Monica CA 90405. (310)434-4242. **Contact:** Andrew Tonkovich, editor. Magazine: 250 pages. "The editors are committed to fostering new talent as well as presenting new work by established writers. There is also a special emphasis on presenting and promoting writers who make their home in Southern California." Estab. 1989. Circ. 1,500.

Needs: Literary, experimental. No "genre writing, no TV, no clichés, no gimmicks." Want more "self conscious, smart, political, humorous, digressive, meta-fiction." Publishes special fiction issues or anthologies. Receives 250 unsolicited mss/month. Accepts 10 mss/issue; 20 mss/year. Agented fiction 10%. **Publishes 3-4 new writers/ year.** Recently published work by Jim Krusoe, Aimee Bender, Gregg Bills, Judith Grossman and Amy Gerstler. Also publishes literary essays, memoirs and novel chapters.

How to Contact: Send complete ms with a cover letter. Responds in 3 months. Send a disposable copy of ms. Accepts simultaneous submissions. Sample copy for $7.

Payment/Terms: Pays 2 contributor's copies. Acquires first North American serial rights. Sends galleys to author.

SEEKING THE MUSE: Inspired Works of Creativity, D&K Publications, P.O. Box 650, Cerro Gordo IL 61818-0650. (217)763-3311. E-mail: jagusch@one-eleven.net. Website: http://sites.netscape.net/jagusch/homepage (includes writer's guidelines). **Contact:** Kris Jagusch, editor/publisher. Magazine: 8½×5½; 60 pages; 20 lb. bond paper; cardstock cover; illustrations. Semiannual. Estab. 1999. Circ. 100.

Needs: Adventure, children's/juvenile (adventure, animal, fantasy, historical, mystery, sports), experimental, family saga, fantasy (space fantasy, sword and sorcery), feminist, historical, horror (dark fantasy, futuristic, psychological, supernatural), humor/satire, literary, mainstream, mystery/suspense (amateur sleuth, cozy, police procedural, private eye/hardboiled), romance (contemporary, futuristic/time travel, gothic, historical, regency period, romantic suspense), science fiction (hard science/technological, soft/sociological), thriller/espionage, young adult/teen (adventure, fantasy/science fiction, historical, horror, mystery/suspense, romance, sports, western). Receives 10 unsolicited mss/month. Accepts 5 mss/issue; 10 mss/year. Does not read mss December 1-31. Publishes ms 6 months after acceptance. **Publishes 2-3 new writers/year.** Recently published work by Nancy Furstinger, Kristin Nymoen and Anne Christiansen-Bullers. Length: 1,500 words maximum; average length: 1,000 words. Publishes short shorts. Average length: 750 words. Also publishes literary essays and poetry. Often comments on rejected mss.

How to Contact: Send complete ms with a cover letter. Accepts submissions by e-mail. "But only if contained within the body of the e-mail, not as an attachment." Include estimated word count, brief bio and list of publications. Responds in 3 months to queries and mss. Send SASE (or IRC) for return of ms or send a disposable copy of ms and #10 SASE for reply only. Accepts simultaneous submissions, previously published work and up to 5 multiple submissions. Sample copy for $5 (US); $6.50 (Canadian and UK). Guidelines for SASE or e-mail. Reviews nonfiction "only if they are geared toward kick-starting or maintaining the writer's creativity."

Payment/Terms: Pays 1 contributor's copy; additional copies $5 (US) or $6.50 (Canadian and UK). Pays on publication for one-time rights.

SEEMS, Lakeland College, Box 359, Sheboygan WI 53082-0359. (920)565-1276. Fax: (920)565-1206. E-mail: kelder@excel.net. **Contact:** Karl Elder, editor. Magazine: 7×8½; 40 pages. "We publish fiction and poetry for an audience which tends to be highly literate. People read the publication, I suspect, for the sake of reading it." Published irregularly. Estab. 1971. Circ. 300.

Needs: Literary. Accepts 4 mss/issue. Receives 12 unsolicited fiction mss each month. **Publishes 1-2 new writers/year.** Published work by Sapphire and other emerging writers. Length: 5,000 words maximum. Publishes short shorts. Also publishes poetry. Critiques rejected mss when there is time.

How to Contact: Send complete ms with SASE. Responds in 2 months to mss. Publishes ms an average of 1-2 years after acceptance. Sample copy for $4.
Payment/Terms: Pays 1 contributor's copy; $4 charge for extras. Rights revert to author.
Advice: "Send clear, clean copies. Read the magazine in order to help determine the taste of the editor." Mss are rejected because of "lack of economical expression, or saying with many words what could be said in only a few. Good fiction contains all of the essential elements of poetry; study poetry and apply those elements to fiction. Our interest is shifting to story poems, the grey area between genres."

$⊘ SENSATIONS MAGAZINE, 2 Radio Ave., A5, Secaucus NJ 07094-3843. Founder: David Messineo. **Contact:** Fiction Editor. Magazine: 8½×11; 200 pages; 20 lb. paper; full color cover; color photography. "We publish short stories and poetry, no specific theme." Magazine also includes the Rediscovering America in Poetry research series. Semiannually. Estab. 1987.
• *Sensations Magazine* is one of the few markets accepting longer work and is a 3-time winner in the American Literary Magazine Awards.
Needs: "*Sensations Magazine* celebrates its 15th anniversary in 2002 with a two-part issue. Starting January 1, 2001, fiction writers should request submission guidelines for the '15th Anniversary Fiction Contest.' There will be an entry fee, which will cover your receiving the Part 2 issue, containing 10-15 stories. Issue will be released December 15, 2002." Accepts 2-4 mss/issue. Publishes ms 2 months after acceptance. **Publishes 2-4 new writers/year.** Recently published work by Ken Sieben.
How to Contact: Send SASE for guidelines. Accepts simultaneous submissions. Accepts e-mail queries. *"Do not submit material before reading submission guidelines."*
Payment/Terms: Pays $100 for the story judged by one of our fiction editors.
Advice: "Each story must have a strong beginning that grabs the reader's attention in the first two sentences. Characters have to be realistic and well-described. Readers must like, hate, or have some emotional response to your characters. Setting, plot, construction, attention to detail—all are important. Purchase a sample copy first and read the stories. Develop long-term relationships with five magazines whose editorial opinions you respect. Naturally, we'd like to be one of the five."

⊕✓ SEPIA, Poetry & Prose Magazine, Kawabata Press, Knill Cross House, Knill Cross, Millbrook, Nr Torpoint, Cornwall PL10 1DX England. **Contact:** Colin David Webb, editor-in-chief. Published 3 times/year.
Needs: "Magazine for those interested in modern un-clichéd work." No science fiction, detective "or any typical genre." Contains 32 pages/issue. **Publishes 5-6 new writers/year.** Length: 200-4,000 words (for short stories).
How to Contact: Always include SAE with IRCs. Send $1 for sample copy and guidelines. Subscription $5; "no cheques!"
Payment/Terms: Pays 1 contributor's copy.

$⊙ THE SEWANEE REVIEW, University of the South, 735 University Ave., Sewanee TN 37383-1000. (931)598-1246. E-mail: rjones@sewanee.edu. Website: www.sewanee.edu/sreview/home.html (includes extracts from recent and back issues, magazine's history, writers' guidelines, links to other literary sites). Editor: George Core. **Contact:** Fiction Editor. Magazine: 6×9; 192 pages. "A literary quarterly, publishing original fiction, poetry, essays on literary and related subjects, book reviews and book notices for well-educated readers who appreciate good American and English literature." Quarterly. Estab. 1892. Circ. 3,500.
• *The Sewanee Review* won *The Year's Best Fantasy and Horror, Twelfth Annual Collection.*
Needs: Literary, contemporary. No erotica, science fiction, fantasy or excessively violent or profane material. Buys 10-15 mss/year. Receives 100 unsolicited fiction mss each month. Does not read mss June 1-August 31. **Publishes 2-3 new writers/year.** Recently published work by Richard Rees, William Hoffman, Gladys Swan and Mark Saunders. Length: 6,000-7,500 words. Critiques rejected mss "when there is time." Sometimes recommends other markets.
How to Contact: Send complete ms with SASE and cover letter stating previous publications, if any. Responds in 6 weeks to mss. Sample copy for $7.25.
Payment/Terms: Pays $10-12/printed page; 2 contributor's copies; $4.25 charge for extras. Pays on publication for first North American serial rights and second serial rights by agreement. Writer's guidelines for SASE.
Advice: "Send only one story at a time, with a serious and sensible cover letter. We think fiction is of greater general interest than any other literary mode."

✓⊘ SHADES OF DECEMBER, Box 244, Selden NY 11784. (631)736-4155. E-mail: eilonwy@innocent. com. Website: www2.fastdial.net/~fc2983 (includes guidelines, reviews, sample work, upcoming themes). **Contact:** Alexander Danner, editor. Magazine: 8½×5½; 60 pages. "Good writing comes in all forms and should not be limited to overly specific or standard genres. Our intended audience is one that is varied in taste and open to the unorthodox." Quarterly. Estab. 1998. Circ. 200-300. Reading fee of $1 for non-electronic submissions.
Needs: Experimental, fantasy, humor/satire, literary, mainstream/contemporary, psychic/supernatural/occult, romance, science fiction. "We are not limited in the categories of writing that we will consider for publication."

Accepts 1-3 mss/issue; 4-12 mss/year. Publishes ms 1-4 months after acceptance. 50% new writers/issue. **Publishes 2-6 new writers/year.** Recently published work by Joe Lucia, Julie Meslin, Hank Ballenger and Tom Bierowski. Length: 2,500 words maximum. Publishes short shorts. Also publishes literary essays, scripts, poetry. Sometimes comments on rejected ms.
How to Contact: Send complete ms with a cover letter. Include bio (50 words or less) and list of publications. Responds in up to 10 weeks. Send SASE for reply, return of ms or send a disposable copy of ms. Accepts simultaneous and reprint submissions. Electronic submissions preferred; $1 reading fee for nonelectronic submissions. Make checks payable to Alexander Danner. Sample copy $3. Guidelines for #10 SASE.
Payment/Terms: Pays 2 contributor's copies. Acquires one-time rights.
Advice: "We like to see work that strays from the conventional. While we print good writing in any form, we prefer to see work that takes risks."

● SHATTERED WIG REVIEW, Shattered Wig Productions, 425 E. 31st, Baltimore MD 21218. (410)243-6888. **Contact:** Collective, editor. Attn: Sonny Bodkin. Magazine: 8½×8½; 70 pages; "average" paper; cardstock cover; illustrations; photos. "Open forum for the discussion of the absurdo-miserablist aspects of everyday life. Fiction, poetry, graphics, essays, photos." Semiannually. Estab. 1988. Circ. 500.
Needs: Confession, contemporary, erotica, ethnic, experimental, feminist, gay, humor/satire, lesbian, literary, prose poem, psychic/supernatural/occult, regional. Does not want "anything by Ann Beattie or John Irving." Receives 15-20 unsolicited mss/month. Publishes ms 2-4 months after acceptance. **Published new writers within the last year.** Published work by Al Ackerman, Kim Harrison and Mok Hossfeld. Publishes short shorts. Also publishes literary criticism, poetry. Sometimes critiques rejected mss and recommends other markets.
How to Contact: Send complete ms with cover letter. Responds in 2 months. Send SASE for return of ms. Accepts simultaneous and reprint submissions. Sample copy for $4.
Payment/Terms: Pays in contributor's copies. Acquires one-time rights.
Advice: "The arts have been reduced to imploding pus with the only material rewards reserved for vapid stylists and collegiate pod suckers. The only writing that counts has no barriers between imagination and reality, thought and action. Send us at least three pieces so we have a choice."

$● SHENANDOAH, The Washington and Lee Review, 2nd Floor, Troubadour Theater, Lexington VA 24450-0303. (540)463-8765. Fax: (540)463-8461. Website: www.wlu.edu/~shenando (includes samples, guidelines and contents). Editor: R.T. Smith. **Contact:** Fiction Editor. Magazine: 6×9; 124 pages. "We are a literary journal devoted to excellence." Quarterly. Estab. 1950. Circ. 2,000.
Needs: Literary. Receives 400-500 unsolicited fiction mss/month. Accepts 5 mss/issue; 20 mss/year. Does not read mss during summer. Publishes ms 6-12 months after acceptance. **Publishes 2 new writers/year.** Published work by Kent Nelson, Barry Gifford, Nicholas Delbanco and Reynolds Price. Publishes short shorts. Also publishes literary essays, literary criticism and poetry.
How to Contact: Send complete ms with cover letter. Include a 3-sentence bio and list of publications ("just the highlights"). Responds in 10 weeks to mss. Send a disposable copy of ms. Sample copy for $5. Guidelines for #10 SASE. Reviews novels and short story collections.
Payment/Terms: Pays $25/page, $2.50/line (poetry) and free subscription to the magazine on publication. Acquires first North American serial rights. Sends galleys to author. Sponsors contest.
Advice: Looks for "thrift, precision, originality. As Frank O'Connor said, 'Get black on white.' "

□ SHORT STORIES BIMONTHLY, Poetry Forum, 5713 Larchmont Dr., Erie PA 16509. Phone/fax: (814)866-2543. E-mail: 75562.670@compuserve.com. **Contact:** Gunvor Skogsholm, editor. Newsletter: 11×17; 14 pages; 20 lb. paper; illustrations. Magazine "provides an outlet for the beginner writer, as well as the advanced to express their ideas to a greater audience." Estab. 1992. Circ. 400.
Needs: Literary, mainstream. No extreme horror or pornography. Wants more "deeply felt works, dealing with some aspect of the human condition." Receives 30 unsolicited mss/month. Accepts 8-10 mss/issue; 48-60 mss/year. Publishes ms 1-9 months after acceptance. **Publishes 33-42 new writers/year.** Published work by James Hinton, Sara Stevenson and Christopher Binkhouse. Length: 600-4,000 words; average length: 1,800 words. Publishes short shorts. Length: 600 words. Also publishes literary essays and literary criticism.
How to Contact: Send complete ms with a cover letter. Accepts queries/mss by e-mail and fax. Include estimated word count. Responds in up to 6 months to mss. Send SASE for reply, return of ms or send a disposable copy of ms. Accepts simultaneous and electronic submissions. Sample copy for $3. Guidelines free. Favors submissions from subscribers. "We exist by subscriptions and advertising." Reviews novels and short story collections.
Payment/Terms: Acquires one-time rights. Sponsors contests, awards or grants for fiction writers. Send SASE.
Advice: "Be original, be honest. Write from your deepest sincerity—don't play games with the readers. Meaning: we don't want the last paragraph to tell us we have been fooled."

$● SHORT STUFF MAGAZINE FOR GROWN-UPS, Bowman Publications, P.O. Box 7057, Loveland CO 80537. (970)669-9139. **Contact:** Donna Bowman, editor. Magazine: 8½×11; 40 pages; bond paper; enamel cover; b&w illustrations; photos. "Nonfiction is regional—Colorado and adjacent states. Fiction and humor must be tasteful, but can be any genre, any subject. We are designed to be a 'Reader's Digest' of fiction. We are found in professional waiting rooms, etc." Publishes 6 issues/year.

Needs: Adventure, contemporary, historical, humor/satire, mainstream, mystery/suspense (amateur sleuth, English cozy, police procedural, private eye, romantic suspense), regional, romance (contemporary, gothic, historical), western (frontier). No erotica. Wants to see more humor or cozy mystery. "We use holiday themes. Need 3 month lead time. Issues are Valentine (February/March); Easter and St. Patrick's Day (April/May); Mom's and Dad's (June/July); Americana (August/September); Halloween (October/November); and Holiday (December/January). Receives 500 unsolicited mss/month. Accepts 9-12 mss/issue; 76 mss/year. **90% of stories published are written by new writers.** Recently published work by Bill Hallstead, Eleanor Sherman, Guy Belleranti, Judith Grams, Gloria Amoury, Charles Langley, Erika Leck, Diane Sawyer and Jacque Hall. Length: 1,500 words maximum; average length: 1,000 words.

How to Contact: Send complete ms with cover letter. SASE. Responds in 6 months. Sample copies for $1.50 and 9×12 SAE with $1.50 postage. Guidelines for SASE.

Payment/Terms: Pays $10-50 "at our discretion" and subscription to magazine. $1-5 for fillers (less than 500 words). "We do not pay for single jokes or poetry, but do give free subscription if published." Pays on publication for first North American serial rights.

Advice: "We seek a potpourri of subjects each issue. A new slant, a different approach, fresh viewpoints—all of these excite us. We don't like gore, salacious humor or perverted tales. Prefer third person, past tense. Be sure it is a story with a beginning, middle and end. It must have dialogue. Many beginners do not know an essay from a short story. Essays frequently used if *humorous*. We'd like to see more young (25 and over) humor; 'clean' humor is hard to come by. Length is a big factor. Writers who can tell a good story in a thousand words are true artists and their work is highly prized by our readers. Stick to the guidelines. We get manuscripts of up to 10,000 words because the story is 'unique and deserving.' We don't even read these."

✔ $ 🖉 ▣ **SIDE SHOW, Short Story Anthology**, Somersault Press, P.O. Box 1428, El Cerrito CA 94530-1428. (510)965-1250. E-mail: jisom@atdial.net. **Contact:** Shelley Anderson and Marjorie K. Jacobs, editors. Book (paperback): 5½×8½; 300 pages; 50 lb. paper; semigloss card cover with color illustration; perfect-bound. "Quality short stories for a general, literary audience." Estab. 1991. Circ. 3,000.

● Previously published as an annual anthology, from now on *Side Show* will publish a book once they have the requisite number of publishable stories (approximately 20-25). There is no longer a yearly deadline. Stories are accepted year round. Work published in *Side Show* has been selected for inclusion in the *Pushcart Prize* anthology.

Needs: Contemporary, ethnic, feminist, gay, humor/satire, literary, mainstream. Nothing genre, religious, pornographic, essays, novels, memoirs. Receives 50-60 unsolicited mss/month. Accepts 25-30 mss/issue. Publishes ms up to 9 months after acceptance. **Publishes 5-10 new writers/per book.** Recently published work by George Harrar, Elisa Jenkins and Miguel Rios. 25% of fiction by previously unpublished writers. Length: Open. Critiques rejected mss, if requested.

How to Contact: Accepts queries by e-mail. All submissions entered in contest. *$10 entry fee* (includes subscription to *Side Show*). No guidelines. Send complete ms with cover letter and entry fee. Responds in 1 month to mss. SASE. Accepts simultaneous submissions. Multiple submissions encouraged (entry fee covers all submissions mailed in same envelope). Sample copy for $10 and $2 postage and handling ($.83 sales tax CA residents).

Payment/Terms: Pays $5/printed page. Pays on publication for first North American serial rights. Sends galleys to author. All submissions entered in our contest for cash prizes of $200 (1st), $100 (2nd) and $75 (3rd).

Advice: Looks for "readability, vividness of characterization, coherence, inspiration, interesting subject matter, imagination, point of view, originality, plausibility. If your fiction isn't inspired, you probably won't be published by us (i.e., style and craft alone won't do it)."

$ 🖉 **THE SILVER WEB, A Magazine of the Surreal**, Buzzcity Press, Box 38190, Tallahassee FL 32315. (850)385-8948. Fax: (850)385-4063. E-mail: annkl9@mail.idt.net. **Contact:** Ann Kennedy, editor. Magazine: 8½×11; 80 pages; 20 lb. paper; full color; perfect bound; glossy cover; b&w illustrations; photos. "Looking for unique character-based stories that are off-beat, off-center and strange, but not inaccessible." Semiannually. Estab. 1989. Circ. 2,000.

● Work published in *The Silver Web* has appeared in *The Year's Best Fantasy and Horror* (DAW Books) and *The Year's Best Fantastic Fiction*.

Needs: Experimental, horror, science fiction (soft/sociological). No "traditional storylines, monsters, vampires, werewolves, etc." *The Silver Web* publishes surrealistic fiction and poetry. Work too bizarre for mainstream, but perhaps too literary for genre. This is not a straight horror/sci-fi magazine. No typical storylines." Receives 500 unsolicited mss/month. Accepts 8-10 mss/issue; 16-20 mss/year. Does not read mss October through December. Publishes ms 6-12 months after acceptance. Recently published work by Brian Evenson, Jack Ketchum and Joel Lane. Length: 100-8,000 words; average length: 6,000 words. Publishes short shorts. Also publishes poetry. Sometimes critiques rejected ms.

How to Contact: Send complete ms with a cover letter. Include estimated word count. Responds in 1 week to queries; 2 months to mss. Send SASE for reply, return of ms or send a disposable copy of ms plus SASE for reply. Accepts simultaneous and reprint submissions. Sample copy for $7.20. Guidelines for #10 SASE. Reviews novels and short story collections.

Payment/Terms: Pays 2-3¢/word and 2 contributor's copies; additional copies for $4. Acquires first North American serial rights, reprint rights or one-time rights.

Advice: "I have a reputation for publishing excellent fiction from newcomers next to talented, established writers, and for publishing cross-genre fiction. No traditional, standard storylines. I'm looking for beautiful writing with plots that are character-based. Tell a good story; tell it with beautiful words. I see too many writers writing for the marketplace and this fiction just doesn't ring true. I'd rather read fiction that comes straight from the heart of the writer." Read a copy of the magazine, at least get the writer's guidelines.

SINISTER WISDOM, A Journal for the Lesbian Imagination in the Arts and Politics, Sinister Widsom, Inc., Box 3252, Berkeley CA 94703. Magazine: 5½ × 8½; 128-144 pages; 55 lb. stock; 10 pt C1S cover; illustrations; photos. Lesbian-feminist journal, providing fiction, poetry, drama, essays, journals and artwork. Triannually. Past issues included "Lesbians of Color," "Old Lesbians/Dykes" and "Lesbians and Religion." Estab. 1976. Circ. 2,000.

Needs: Lesbian: erotica, ethnic, experimental. No heterosexual or male-oriented fiction; no 70s amazon adventures; nothing that stereotypes or degrades women. List of upcoming themes available for SASE and on website. Receives 30 unsolicited mss/month. Accepts 6 mss/issue; 24 mss/year. Publishes ms 3 months to 1 year after acceptance. **published new writers within the last year.** Published work by Jacqueline Miranda, Amanda Esteva and Sharon Bridgeforth; Length: 500-4,000 words; average length: 2,000 words. Publishes short shorts. Also publishes literary essays, literary criticism, poetry. Sometimes critiques rejected mss.

How to Contact: Send 1 copy of complete ms with cover letter, which should include a brief author's bio to be published when the work is published. Accepts simultaneous submissions, if noted. Responds in 6 months. SASE. Sample copy for $7.50. Guidelines for #10 SASE. Reviews novels and short story collections. Send books to "Attn: Book Review."

Payment/Terms: Pays 2 contributor's copies. Acquires one-time rights.

Advice: *Sinister Wisdom* is "a multicultural lesbian journal reflecting the art, writing and politics of our communities."

SKIDROW PENTHOUSE, Skidrow Penthouse Press, 44 Four Corners Rd., Blairstown NJ 07825. **Contact:** Rob Cook and Stephanie Dickinson, editors. Magazine: 8½ × 5½; 160 pages; illustrations; photos. "We're interested in publishing anything from micro-fiction to connected short stories to serializations of novels." Semiannual. Estab. 1998. Circ. 500.

Needs: Experimental, literary, mainstream, psychic/supernatural/occult, science fiction (soft/sociological), translations. Publishes ms 1 year after acceptance. Recently published work by Chris Belden, Gil Fagiani and Frances Broderick. Publishes short shorts. Also publishes literary essays, literary criticism and poetry. Sometimes comments on rejected mss.

How to Contact: Send complete ms with a cover letter. Include estimated word count and brief bio. Responds in 6 weeks to mss. Send SASE (or IRC) for return of ms or send a disposable copy of ms and #10 SASE for reply only. Accepts simultaneous submissions, previously published work and multiple submissions. Sample copy for $8. Guidelines for SASE. Reviews novels, short story collections and nonfiction books of interest to writers.

Payment/Terms: Pays 1 contributor's copy. Pays on publication for one-time rights.

Advice: "We like experimental, traditional, humor, erotica, etc. But we don't care for poorly crafted stories or stories that feel as if they were written in one short sitting. Too much is haphazard and without emotional content. We're looking for heart and craft."

SKIPTRACER, (formerly Brunswick Pop Underground), % S. Indrisek, Rutgers University, 31226 RPO Way, New Brunswick NJ 08901-8812. E-mail: bigmonkeycar@aol.com. **Contact:** Scott Indrisek, editor. Magazine: digest-sized; 20-30 pages; xerox paper; cover varies; illustrations; photos. "We look for excellent writing that doesn't suffer from typical clichés—edgy, modern, exciting prose and nonrhyming poetry." Semiannual. Estab. 1998. Circ. varies.

Needs: Experimental, literary, mainstream, short story collections. "No horror, science fiction, fantasy, *Reader's Digest* parables." Receives 30 unsolicited mss/month. Accepts 20 mss/year. Does not read mss June-August. **Publishes 10 new writers/year.** Recently published work by Michael McNeilley, Helen Hsi, Michael W. Dean and Jim Chandler. Length: 2,000-7,000 words. Also publishes poetry. Always comments on rejected mss.

How to Contact: Send complete ms with a cover letter. Accepts submissions by e-mail. Include bio and list of publications. Responds in 2 months to mss. Send SASE or disposable copy of ms. Accepts simultaneous submissions. Sample copy for $2 with 8 × 12 SASE. Guidelines free.

Payment/Terms: Pays 5 contributor's copies; additional copies $2. Pays on publication for first rights.

Advice: "We're looking for experimentation, new thoughts and ideas. Nothing overly stodgy or pseudo-intellectual. We don't follow the trends of the mainstream publishing era. Fiction is dying out in mainstream magazines and poetry even more so. Our magazine wants to bring writing out to an intelligent, modern audience."

✓ ◐ **SKYLARK**, Purdue University Calumet, 2200 169th St., Hammond IN 46323-2094. (219)989-2273. Fax: (219)989-2165. E-mail: poetpam.49@yahoo.com. Editor-in-Chief: Pamela Hunter. **Contact:** Fiction Editor. Magazine: 8½×11; 100 pages; illustrations; photos. "*Skylark* presents short stories, essays and poetry which capture a positive outlook on life through vivid imagery, well-developed characterization and unself-conscious plots. We publish adults, both beginners and professionals, and young authors side be side to complement the points of view of writers of all ages." Annually. Estab. 1971. Circ. 1,000.
Needs: Contemporary, ethnic, experimental, feminist, humor/satire, literary, mainstream, prose poem, spiritual and sports. Wants to see more experimental and avant garde fiction. No erotica, science fiction, overly-religious stories. Upcoming theme: "Education" (submit by April 2001). Receives 20 mss/month. Accepts 8 mss/issue. **Publishes 6 new writers/year.** Recently published work by Earl M. Coleman, Joanne Zimmerman and Virginia A. Deweese. Length: 4,000 words maximum. Also publishes essays and poetry.
How to Contact: Send complete ms. Send SASE for return of ms. Accepts queries/mss by fax. Responds in 4 months. No simultaneous submissions. Sample copy for $8; back issue for $6.
Payment/Terms: Pays 3 contributor's copies. Acquires first rights. Copyright reverts to author.
Advice: "We seek fiction that presents effective imagery, strong plot, and well-developed characterization. Graphic passages concerning sex or violence are unacceptable. We're looking for dramatic, closely-edited short stories. Manuscript must require little editing both for content and syntax. Author must be sincere in the treatment of plot, characters and tone. Please state in your cover letter that the story is not being considered elsewhere. We live in one of the most industrialized sections of the country. We are looking for stories set in steel mills and refractories, etc. We especially need stories set in these areas but we rarely find such stories."

✓ ◐ ◎ **SLIPSTREAM**, Box 2071, New Market Station, Niagara Falls NY 14301. (716)282-2616. E-mail: editors@slipstreampress.org. Website: www.slipstreampress.org (includes guidelines, editors, current needs, info on current and past releases, sample poems, contest info.). Editor: Dan Sicoli. **Contact:** Robert Borgatti, co-editor. Magazine: 7×8½; 80-100 pages; high quality paper; card cover; illustrations; photos. "We use poetry and short fiction with a contemporary urban feel." Estab. 1981. Circ. 500.
Needs: Contemporary, erotica, ethnic, experimental, humor/satire, literary, mainstream and prose poem. No religious, juvenile, young adult or romance. Occasionally publishes theme issues; query for information. Receives over 25 unsolicited mss/month. Accepts 2-4 mss/issue; 6 mss/year. Published work by Kirby Wright, Jessica Treat and C. Abe Gaustad. Length: under 15 pages. Publishes short shorts. Rarely critiques rejected mss. Sometimes recommends other markets.
How to Contact: "Query before submitting." Responds within 2 months. Send SASE for reply or return of ms. Sample copy for $6. Guidelines for #10 SASE.
Payment/Terms: Pays 2 contributor's copies. Acquires one-time rights.
Advice: "Writing should be honest, fresh; develop your own style. Check out a sample issue first. Don't write for the sake of writing, write from the gut as if it were a biological need. Write from experience and mean what you say, but say it in the fewest number of words."

◐ **THE SMALL POND MAGAZINE**, Box 664, Stratford CT 06615. (203)378-4066. Editor: Napoleon St. Cyr. **Contact:** Fiction Editor. Magazine: 5½×8½; 42 pages; 60 lb. offset paper; 65 lb. cover stock; illustrations (art). "Features contemporary poetry, the salt of the earth, peppered with short prose pieces of various kinds. The college educated and erudite read it for good poetry, prose and pleasure." Triannually. Estab. 1964. Circ. 300.
Needs: "Rarely use science fiction or the formula stories you'd find in *Cosmo*, *Redbook*, *Ladies Home Journal*, etc. Philosophy: Highest criteria, originality, even a bit quirky is OK. Don't mind O. Henry endings but better be exceptional. Readership: College grads, and college staff, ⅓ of subscribers are college and university libraries." No science fiction, children's. Accepts 10-12 mss/year. Longer response time in July and August. Receives approximately 40 unsolicited fiction mss each month. **Publishes 1-2 new writers/year.** Recently published work by Peter Baida, Stephen V. Smith, Stuart Mitchner, Margaret Haller and James Bellarosa. Length: 200-2,500 words. Critiques rejected mss when there is time. Sometimes recommends other markets.
How to Contact: Send complete ms with SASE and short vita. Responds in up to 3 months. Publishes ms an average of 2-18 months after acceptance. Sample copy for $4; $3 for back issues.
Payment/Terms: Pays 2 contributor's copies for all rights; $3/copy charge for extras, postage paid.
Advice: "Send for a sample copy first. All mss must be typed. Name and address and story title on front page, name of story on succeeding pages and paginated. I look for polished, smooth progression—no clumsy paragraphs or structures where you know the author didn't edit closely. Also, no poor grammar. Beginning and even established poets read and learn from reading lots of other's verse. Not a bad idea for fiction writers, in their genre, short or long fiction."

SNAKE NATION REVIEW, Snake Nation Press, Inc., #2 West Force St., 110, Valdosta GA 31601. (912)244-0752. Fax: (912)253-9125 (call first). Editor: Jean Arambula. **Contact:** Nancy Phillips, fiction editor. 6×9; 110 pages; acid free 70 lb. paper; 90 lb. cover; illustrations; photos. "We are interested in all types of stories for an educated, discerning, sophisticated audience." Quarterly. Estab. 1989. Circ. 2,000.

● *Snake Nation Review* receives funding from the Georgia Council of the Arts, the Georgia Humanities Council and the Porter/Fleming Foundation for Literature.

Needs: "Short stories of 5,000 words or less, poems (any length), art work that will be returned after use." Condensed/excerpted novel, contemporary, erotica, ethnic, experimental, fantasy, feminist, gay, horror, humor/satire, lesbian, literary, mainstream, mystery/suspense, prose poem, psychic/supernatural/occult, regional, science fiction, senior citizen/retirement. "We want our writers to have a voice, a story to tell, not a flat rendition of a slice of life." Plans annual anthology. Receives 50 unsolicited mss/month. Buys 8-10 mss/issue; 40 mss/year. Publishes ms 6 months after acceptance. Agented fiction 1%. Recently published work by Robert Earl Price and O. Victor Miller. Length: 300-5,500 words; average length: 3,500 words. Publishes short shorts. Length: 500 words. Also publishes literary essays, poetry. Reviews novels and short story collections. Sometimes critiques rejected mss and recommends other markets.

How to Contact: Send complete ms with cover letter. Responds to queries in 3 months. SASE. Sample copy for $6, 8×10 SAE and 90¢ postage. Guidelines for SASE.

Payment/Terms: Pays 2 contributor's copies for one-time rights. Sends galleys to author.

Advice: "Looks for clean, legible copy and an interesting, unique voice that pulls the reader into the work." Spring contest: short stories (5,000 words); $300 first prize, $200 second prize, $100 third prize; entry fee: $5 for stories, $1 for poems. Contest Issue with every $5 fee.

$ SNOWY EGRET, P.O. Box 9, Bowling Green IN 47833. Publisher: Karl Barnebey. Editor: Philip Repp. **Contact:** Fiction Editor. Magazine: 8½×11; 50 pages; text paper; heavier cover; illustrations. "*Snowy Egret* explores the range of human involvement, particularly psychological, with the natural world. It's fiction depicts characters who identify strongly with nature, either positively or negatively, and who grow in their understanding of themselves and the world of plants, animals and landscape." Semiannually. Estab. 1922. Circ. 500.

Needs: Nature writing, including 'true' stories, eye-witness accounts, descriptive sketches and traditional fiction. "We are interested in penetrating psychological and spiritual journeys of characters who have strong ties to or identifications with the natural world. No works written for popular genres: horror, science fiction, romance, detective, western, etc." Receives 25 unsolicited mss/month. Accepts up to 6 mss/issue; up to 12 mss/year. Publishes ms 6-12 months after acceptance. **Publishes 2 new writers/year.** Published works by James Hinton, Thomas Filer, David Abrams and Suzanne Kamata. Length: 500-10,000 words; 1,000-3,000 words preferred. Publishes short shorts. Length: 400-500 words. Sometimes critiques rejected mss.

How to Contact: Send complete ms with cover letter. "Cover letter optional: do not query." Responds in 2 months. SASE. Accepts simultaneous (if noted) and electronic (Mac, ASCII) submissions. Sample back issues for $8 and 9×12 SAE. Send #10 SASE for writer's guidelines.

Payment/Terms: Pays $2/page and 2 contributor's copies; charge for extras. Pays on publication for first North American serial rights and reprint rights. Sends galleys to author.

Advice: Looks for "honest, freshly detailed pieces with plenty of description and/or dialogue which will allow the reader to identify with the characters and step into the setting. Characters who relate strongly to nature, either positively or negatively, and who, during the course of the story, grow in their understanding of themselves and the world around them."

SNREVIEW: Starry Night Review—A Literary E-Zine, 197 Fairchild Ave, Fairfield CT 06432-4856. (203)366-5991. Fax: (203)336-4753. E-mail: SNReviewezine@aol.com. Website: members.aol. com/jconlin1221/snreview.htm. **Contact:** Joseph Conlin, editor. E-zine specializing in literary short stories, essays and poetry. "The *SNReview* searches for material that not only has strong characters and plot but also a devotion to imagery." Quarterly. Estab. 1999.

Needs: "We only want literary and mainstream." Receives 10 mss/month. Accepts 5 mss/issue; 20 mss/year. Publishes ms 6 months after acceptance. **Publishes 20 new writers/year.** Recently published work by John Jennings. Word length: 4,000 words average; 1,500 words minimum; 7,000 words maximum. Also publishes literary essays, literary criticism and poetry.

How to Contact: Send complete ms with a cover letter via e-mail only. Include 100 word bio and a list of publications. Responds in 1 month. Accepts simultaneous and reprint submissions. Sample copy and guidelines free on website.

Payment/Terms: Acquires first rights. Sends prepublication webpages to the author.

SO TO SPEAK, A Feminist Journal of Language and Art, George Mason University, 4400 University Dr., MS 2D6, Fairfax VA 22030-4444. (703)993-3625. E-mail: sts@gmu.edu. Website: www.gmu.edu/org/sts. **Contact:** Anne William Davis, fiction editor. Editors change every year. Magazine: 7×10; approximately 70 pages. "We are a feminist journal of high-quality material." Semiannual. Estab. 1988. Circ. 1,300.

Needs: Ethnic/multicultural, experimental, feminist, lesbian, literary, mainstream/contemporary, regional, translations. "No science fiction, mystery, genre romance, porn (lesbian or straight)." Receives 100 unsolicited mss/month. Accepts 2-3 mss/issue; 6 mss/year. Publishes ms 6 months after acceptance. **Publishes 2 new writers/year.** Recently published work by Deborah J.M. Owen and Sally Chandler. Length: 6,000 words maximum; average length: 4,000 words. Publishes short shorts. Also publishes literary essays, literary criticism, book reviews, poetry and artwork. Sometimes comments on rejected mss.

How to Contact: Send complete ms with a cover letter. Include bio (50 words maximum) and SASE. Responds in 6 months to mss. SASE for return of ms or send a disposable copy of ms. Accepts simultaneous submissions. Sample copy for $5. Guidelines for #10 SASE. We do not read between March 15 and August 15.

Payment/Terms: Pays contributor's copies for first North American serial rights.

Advice: "Every writer has something they do exceptionally well; do that and it will shine through in the work. We look for quality prose with a definite appeal to a feminist audience. We are trying to move away from strict genre lines."

THE SOFT DOOR, 1800 U.S. Rt. 6 East, Bradner OH 43406. E-mail: terria@bgnet.bgsu.edu. **Contact:** T. Williams, editor. Magazine: 8½×11; 100 pages; bond paper; heavy cover; illustrations; photos. "We publish works that explore human relationships and our relationship to the world." Irregularly.

Needs: Literary, mainstream/contemporary. No science fiction or romance. Receives 25 mss/month. Accepts 5 mss/year. Does not read mss November through December. Publishes ms up to 2 years after acceptance. **Publishes 3 new writers/year.** Published work by Mark Sa Franko, Simon Peter Buehrer, E.S. Griggs, Jennifer Casteen and Jim Feltz. Length: 10,000 words maximum; average length: 5,000 words. Publishes short shorts. Also publishes poetry. Sometimes comments on rejected mss.

How to Contact: Send complete ms with a cover letter. Include "short statement about who you are and why you write, along with any successes you have had. Please write to me like I am a human being." Send SASE for reply, return of ms or send a disposable copy of ms. "Please include SASE with all correspondence. Do not send postcards." Accepts simultaneous submissions. Sample copy for $12. Make checks payable to T. Williams.

Payment/Terms: Pays 1 contributor's copy. Acquires one-time rights.

Advice: "Read as much contemporary fiction and poetry as you can get your hands on. Write about your deepest concerns. What you write can, and does, change lives. Always interested in works by Native American writers. I also don't get enough work by and about women. Be patient with the small presses. We work under terrific pressure. It's not about money; it's about the literature, caring about ideas that matter."

SONGS OF INNOCENCE, Pengradonian Publications, P.O. Box 719, New York NY 10101-0719. E-mail: mmpendragon@aol.com. Website: http://hometown.aol.com/mmpinnocence/index.html (includes writer's guidelines, subscription information, and links). Editor: Michael Pendragon. **Contact:** Fiction Editor. Literary magazine/journal: 8½×5½; 120 pages; perfect bound; illustrations. "A literary publication which celebrates the nobler aspects of humankind and the human experience. Along with sister-publication, *Penny Dreadful*, *Songs* seeks to provide a forum for poetry and fiction in the 19th century/Romantic/Victorian tradition." Triannually. Circ. estimated 250.

Needs: Fantasy, historical (19th century or earlier), literary, New Age, psychic/supernatural/occult. No "children's/young adult; modern tales; Christian (or anything dogmatic)." Receives 100 unsolicited mss/month. Accepts 10 mss/issue; 30 mss/year. Publishes ms up to 2 years after acceptance. Length: 500-5,000 words. Publishes short shorts. Also publishes literary essays, literary criticism, poetry. Often comments on rejected mss. Published works by John Berbrich, John B. Ford, Ann Kucera and Jason E. Schlismann.

How to Contact: Send complete ms with a cover letter. Include estimated word count, 1 page or less bio and list of publications. Accepts mss by e-mail or disk. Responds in 3 weeks to queries; up to 3 months to mss. SASE for reply and send a disposable copy of ms. Accepts simultaneous submissions and reprints. Sample copy for $5, 9×6 SAE. Guidelines for SASE.

Payment/Terms: Pays 1 contributor's copy; additional copies $5 each. Pays on publication for one-time rights. Sends galleys to author.

Advice: "We prefer tales set in 1910 or earlier (preferably earlier). We prefer prose in the 19th century/Victorian style. We do not like the terse, modern, post-Hemingway 'see Dick run' style. Tales should transcend genres and include a spiritual supernatural element (without becoming fantasy). Avoid strong language, sex, etc. Include name and address on the title page. Include word count on title page. Double space, 12-pt. Times/Courier font, etc. (usual professional format). We select stories/poems that appeal to us and do not base selection on whether one has been published elsewhere."

SOUTH CAROLINA REVIEW, Strode Tower, Clemson University, Clemson SC 29634-1503. (864)656-5399. Fax: (864)656-1345. E-mail: cwayne@clemson.edu. Editor: Wayne Chapman. **Contact:** Fiction Editor. Magazine: 6×9; 200 pages; 60 lb. cream white vellum paper; 65 lb. cream white vellum cover stock. Semiannually. Estab. 1967. Circ. 700.

Needs: Literary and contemporary fiction, poetry, essays, reviews. Receives 50-60 unsolicited fiction mss each month. Does not read mss June through August or December. **Published new writers within the last year.** Published work by Joyce Carol Oates, Rosanne Coggeshall and Stephen Dixon. Rarely critiques rejected mss.
How to Contact: Send complete ms with SASE. Requires text on disk upon acceptance in WordPerfect or Microsoft Word format. Responds in 4 months to mss. "No unsolicited reviews." Sample copy for $5.
Payment/Terms: Pays in contributor's copies.

☑ Ⓞ **SOUTH DAKOTA REVIEW,** University of South Dakota, Box 111, University Exchange, Vermillion SD 57069. (605)677-5966. Fax: (605)677-5298. E-mail: bbedard@usd.edu. Website: www.usd.edu/engl/SDR/index.html (includes masthead page with editors' names and submission/subscription guidelines, sample covers, sample story and essay excerpts and poems). Editor: Brian Bedard. **Contact:** Fiction Editor. Magazine: 6×9; 140-170 pages; book paper; glossy cover stock; illustrations sometimes; photos on cover. "Literary magazine for university and college audiences and their equivalent. Emphasis is often on the American West and its writers, but will accept mss from anywhere. Issues are generally personal essay, fiction, and poetry with some literary essays." Quarterly. Estab. 1963. Circ. 500.
  ● The *South Dakota Review* ranked #47 on *Writer's Digest*'s "Fiction 50" list of top markets.
Needs: Literary, contemporary, ethnic, excerpted novel, regional. "We like very well-written, thematically ambitious, character-centered short fiction. Contemporary western American setting appeals, but not necessary. No formula stories, horror, or adolescent 'I' narrator." Receives 40 unsolicited fiction mss/month. Accepts about 40 mss/year. Summer editor accepts mss in April through June. Agented fiction 5%. Publishes short shorts of 5 pages double-spaced typescript. **Publishes 3-5 new writers/year.** Published work by Steve Heller, H.E. Francis, James Sallis, Ronna Wineberg, Lewis Horne and Rita Welty Bourke. Length: 1,000-6,000 words. (Has made exceptions, up to novella length.) Sometimes recommends other markets.
How to Contact: Send complete ms with SASE. Accepts queries/mss by fax. "We like cover letters that are not boastful and do not attempt to sell the stories but rather provide some personal information about the writer which can be used for a contributor's note." Responds in 10 weeks. Publishes ms an average of 1-6 months after acceptance. Sample copy for $5.
Payment/Terms: Pays 1-year subscription, plus 2-4 contributor's copies, depending on length of ms; cover price charge for extras while issue is current, $3 when issue becomes a back issue.. Acquires first and reprint rights.
Advice: Rejects mss because of "careless writing; often careless typing; stories too personal ('I' confessional); aimlessness of plot, unclear or unresolved conflicts; subject matter that editor finds clichéd, sensationalized, pretentious or trivial. We are trying to use more fiction and more variety."

☑ Ⓞ ◎ **SOUTHERN HUMANITIES REVIEW,** Auburn University, 9088 Haley Center, Auburn University AL 36849. Website: www.auburn.edu/english/shr/home.htm. Co-editors: Dan R. Latimer and Virginia M. Kouidis. **Contact:** Fiction Editor. Magazine: 6×9; 100 pages; 60 lb. neutral pH, natural paper; 65 lb. neutral pH med. coated cover stock; occasional illustrations; photos. "We publish essays, poetry, fiction and reviews. Our fiction has ranged from very traditional in form and content to very experimental. Literate, college-educated audience. We hope they read our journal for both enlightenment and pleasure." Quarterly. Estab. 1967. Circ. 800.
Needs: Serious fiction, fantasy, feminist, humor and regional. Receives approximately 25 unsolicited fiction mss each month. Accepts 1-2 mss/issue, 4-6 mss/year. Slower reading time in summer. **Published new writers within the last year.** Published work by Anne Brashler, Heimito von Doderer and Ivo Andric. Length: 3,500-15,000 words. Also publishes literary essays, literary criticism, poetry. Critiques rejected mss when there is time. Sometimes recommends other markets.
How to Contact: Send complete ms (one at a time) with SASE and cover letter with an explanation of topic chosen—"special, certain book, etc., a little about author if he/she has never submitted." Responds in 3 months. Sample copy for $5. Reviews novel and short story collections.
Payment/Terms: Pays 2 contributor's copies; $5 charge for extras. Rights revert to author upon publication. Sends galleys to author.
Advice: "Send us the ms with SASE. If we like it, we'll take it or we'll recommend changes. If we don't like it, we'll send it back as promptly as possible. Read the journal. Send typewritten, clean copy carefully proofread. We also award annually the Hoepfner Prize of $100 for the best published essay or short story of the year. Let someone whose opinion you respect read your story and give you an honest appraisal. Rewrite, if necessary, to get the most from your story."

$ Ⓞ ▨ **THE SOUTHERN REVIEW,** Louisiana State University, 43 Allen Hall, Baton Rouge LA 70803. (225)388-5108. Fax: (225)388-5098. E-mail: bmacon@lsu.edu. Website: www.lsu.edu/guests/wwwtsm (includes subscription information, staff, guidelines, table of contents, current issue). **Contact:** James Olney and Dave Smith, editors. Magazine: 6¾×10; 240 pages; 50 lb. Glatfelter paper; 65 lb. #1 grade cover stock. "A literary quarterly publishing critical essays, poetry and fiction for a highly intellectual audience." Quarterly. Estab. 1935. Circ. 3,100.

• *The Southern Review* ranked #40 on *Writer's Digest*'s "Fiction 50" list of top fiction markets. Several stories published in *The Southern Review* were Pushcart Prize selections.

Needs: Literary. "We emphasize style and substantial content. No mystery, fantasy or religious mss." Accepts 4-5 mss/issue. Receives approximately 300 unsolicited fiction mss each month. Does not read mss June through August. Publishes ms 6-9 months after acceptance. Agented fiction 1%. **Publishes 4-6 new writers/year.** Published work by Rick Bass, Andrea Barrett, Ann Beattie, Robert Olen Butler, Tracy Daugherty, Ellen Douglas, Pam Durban, Ehud Havazelet, Mark Jacobs, Bobbie Ann Mason, Joyce Carol Oates, Gerald Shapiro, June Spence and Scott Ely. Length: 2,000-10,000 words. Also publishes literary essays, literary criticism, poetry. Sponsors annual contest for best first collection of short stories published during the calendar year.

How to Contact: Send complete ms with cover letter and SASE. "Prefer brief letters giving information on author concerning where he/she has been published before, biographical info and what he/she is doing now." Responds in 2 months to mss. Sample copy for $8. Guidelines free for SAE. Reviews novels and short story collections.

Payment/Terms: Pays $12/printed page and 2 contributor's copies. Pays on publication for first North American serial rights. Sends galleys to author.

Advice: "Develop a careful, clear style. Although willing to publish experimental writing that appears to have a valid artistic purpose, *The Southern Review* avoids extremism and sensationalism."

☑ ◐ **SOUTHWEST REVIEW**, P.O. Box 750374, 307 Fondren Library West, Southern Methodist University, Dallas TX 75275-0374. (214)768-1037. Fax: (214)768-1408. E-mail: swr@mail.smu.edu. Editor: Willard Spiegelman. **Contact:** Elizabeth Mills, senior editor. Magazine: 6×9; 144 pages. "The majority of our readers are college-educated adults who wish to stay abreast of the latest and best in contemporary fiction, poetry, literary criticism and books in all but the most specialized disciplines." Quarterly. Estab. 1915. Circ. 1,600.

Needs: "High literary quality; no specific requirements as to subject matter, but cannot use sentimental, religious, western, poor science fiction, pornographic, true confession, mystery, juvenile or serialized or condensed novels." Receives approximately 200 unsolicited fiction mss each month. Published work by Bruce Berger, Thomas Larsen, Alice Hoffman, Matthew Sharpe, Floyd Skloot, Daniel Harris and Daniel Stern. Length: prefers 3,000-5,000 words. Also publishes literary essays and poetry. Occasionally critiques rejected mss.

How to Contact: Send complete ms with SASE. Responds in 6 months to mss. Publishes ms 6-12 months after acceptance. Sample copy for $6. Guidelines for SASE.

Payment/Terms: Payment varies; writers receive 3 contributor's copies. Pays on publication for first North American serial rights. Sends galleys to author.

Advice: "We have become less regional. A lot of time would be saved for us and for the writer if he or she looked at a copy of the *Southwest Review* before submitting. We like to receive a cover letter because it is some reassurance that the author has taken the time to check a current directory for the editor's name. When there isn't a cover letter, we wonder whether the same story is on 20 other desks around the country."

☑ ◐ ◎ **SOUTHWESTERN AMERICAN LITERATURE**, Center for the Study of the Southwest, Southwest Texas State University, 601 University Dr., San Marcos TX 78666. (512)245-2232. Fax: (512)245-7462. E-mail: mb13@swt.edu. Editor: D.M. Heaberlin. **Contact:** Mark Busby, fiction editor. Magazine: 6×9; 125 pages; 80 lb. cover stock. "We publish fiction, nonfiction, poetry, literary criticism and book reviews. Generally speaking, we want material concerning the Greater Southwest, or material written by southwestern writers." Semiannually. Estab. 1971. Circ. 300.

• A poem published in *Southwestern American Literature* was selected for the anthology, *Best Texas Writing 2.*

Needs: Ethnic/multicultural, literary, mainstream/contemporary, regional. No science fiction or romance. Receives 10-15 unsolicited mss/month. Accepts 1-2 mss/issue; 4-5 mss/year. Publishes ms up to 6 months after acceptance. **Publishes 1-2 new writers/year.** Published work by Jerry Craven, Paul Ruffin, Robert Flynn and Philip Heldrich. Length: 6,250 words maximum; average length: 6,000 words. Publishes short shorts. Also publishes literary essays, literary criticism, poetry. Sometimes comments on rejected ms.

How to Contact: Send complete ms with a cover letter. Include estimated word count, 200-word bio and list of publications. Accepts queries by e-mail. Responds in 2 months. SASE for return of ms. Accepts simultaneous submissions. Sample copy $7. Guidelines free. Reviews novels and short story collections. Send books to Mark Busby.

Payment/Terms: Pays 2 contributor's copies; additional copies $7. Acquires first rights.

Advice: "We look for crisp language, interesting approach to material; regional emphasis is desired but not required. Read widely, write often, revise carefully. We are looking for stories that probe the relationship between the tradition of Southwestern American literature and the writer's own imagination in creative ways. We seek stories that move beyond stereotype and approach the larger defining elements of regional literature with three qualities: originality, supple language, and humanity. We want stories with regional elements and also ones that, as William Faulkner noted in his Nobel Prize acceptance speech, treat subjects central to good literature—the old verities of the human heart such as honor and courage and pity and suffering, fear and humor, love and sorrow."

☑ ◐ **SOU'WESTER**, Box 1438, Southern Illinois University—Edwardsville, Edwardsville IL 62026-1438. (618)650-3190. Managing Editor: Fred W. Robbins. **Contact:** Fiction Editor. Magazine: 6×9; 120 pages; Warren's Olde Style paper; 60 lb. cover. General magazine of poetry and fiction. Biannually. Estab. 1960. Circ. 300.

> ● The *Sou'wester* is known for publishing traditional, well-developed and carefully crafted short stories. Work published here has received an Illinois Arts Council Literary Award for "Best Illinois Fiction" and the Daniel Curley Award.

Needs: "The best work we can find, no matter who the author is." No science fiction or fantasy. Receives 50-100 unsolicited fiction mss/month. Accepts 6 mss/issue; 12 mss/year. **Publishes 3-4 new writers/year.** Published work by Robert Wexelblatt, Julie Simon, John Pesta, Ellen Slezak and David Starkey. Length: 10,000 words maximum. Also publishes poetry. Occasionally critiques rejected mss.
How to Contact: Send complete ms with SASE. Accepts simultaneous submissions. Responds in 8 months. Publishes ms an average of 6 months after acceptance. Sample copy for $5.
Payment/Terms: Pays 2 contributor's copies; $5 charge for extras. Acquires first serial rights.
Advice: "Work on polishing your sentences."

Ⓝ ◯ **SPEAK UP**, Speak Up Press, P.O. Box 100506, Denver CO 80250. (303)715-0837. Fax: (303)715-0793. E-mail: SpeakUPres@aol.com. Website: www.speakuppress.org. **Contact:** G. Bryant, senior editor. Magazine: 5½×8½; 64 pages; 55 lb. Glat. Supple Opaque Recycled Natural paper; 12 pt. CIS cover; illustrations; photos. "*Speak Up* features the original fiction, nonfiction, poetry, plays, photography and artwork of young people 13-19 years old. *Speak Up* provides a place for teens to be creative, honest and expressive in an uncensored environment." Annual. Estab. 1999. Circ. 1,200.
Needs: Young adult/teen. Receives 20 unsolicited mss/month. Accepts 14 mss/issue; 14 mss/year. Publishes ms 3-5 months after acceptance. **Publishes 13 new writers/year.** Length: 5,000 words maximum; average length: 500 words. Publishes short shorts. Also publishes literary essays and poetry.
How to Contact: Send complete ms with a cover letter. Accepts submissions by e-mail and fax. Include cover letter. Responds in 3 months to queries. Send SASE (or IRC) for return of ms. Accepts simultaneous submissions, previously published work and multiple submissions. Sample copy free. Guidelines for SASE, by e-mail, fax or on website.
Payment/Terms: Pays 2 contributor's copies. Pays on publication for all, first North American serial or one-time rights.

◑ **SPINDRIFT**, Shoreline Community College, 16101 Greenwood Ave. North, Seattle WA 98133. (206)546-5864. **Contact:** Carol Orlock, editor. Magazine: 140 pages; quality paper; photographs; b&w artwork. "We look for fresh, original work that is not forced or 'straining' to be literary." Annually. Estab. around 1967. Circ. 500.

> ● *Spindrift* has received awards for "Best Literary Magazine" from the Community College Humanities Association both locally and nationally and awards from the Pacific Printing Industries.

Needs: Contemporary, ethnic, experimental, historical (general), prose poem, regional, science fiction, serialized/excerpted novel, translations. No romance, religious/inspirational. Receives up to 150 mss/year. Accepts up to 20 mss/issue. Does not read during spring/summer. Publishes ms 3-4 months after acceptance. **Published new writers within the last year.** Published work by David Halpern and Jana Harris. Length: 250-4,500 words maximum. Publishes short shorts.
How to Contact: Send complete ms, and "bio, name, address, phone and list of titles submitted." Responds in 2 weeks to queries; juries after February 1 and responds by March 15 with SASE. Sample copy for $6.50, 8×10 SAE and $1 postage.
Payment/Terms: Pays in contributor's copies; charge for extras. Acquires first rights. Publication not copyrighted.
Advice: "The tighter the story the better. The more lyric values in the narrative the better. Read the magazine, keep working on craft. Submit by February 1."

Ⓝ ◕ **SPINNING JENNY**, Black Dress Press, P.O. Box 213, New York NY 10014. E-mail: submissions@blackdresspress.com. Website: www.blackdresspress.com (includes guidelines, subscription information, catalog). **Contact:** C.E. Harrison. Magazine: 60 lb. paper; offset printed; perfect bound; illustrations. Literary magazine publishing short stories and novel excerpts. Estab. 1994. Member: CLMP.
Needs: Experimental, literary. Publishes ms less than 1 year after acceptance. **Publishes 3 new writers/year.**
How to Contact: Send complete ms with a cover letter. Accepts submissions by e-mail. Responds in 2 months. Send SASE (or IRC) for return of ms or send a disposable copy of ms and #10 SASE for reply only. Accepts electronic submissions. Guidelines for SASE or on website.
Payment/Terms: Pays 5 contributor's copies.

VISIT THE WRITER'S MARKET WEBSITE at www.writersmarket.com for hot new markets, daily market updates, writers' guidelines and much more.

☑ $ ⊘ ◎ **SPSM&H**, *Amelia* Magazine, 329 "E" St., Bakersfield CA 93304. (661)323-4064. Editor: Frederick A. Raborg, Jr. **Contact:** Fiction Editor. Magazine: 5½ × 8¼; 24 pages; matte cover stock; illustrations; photos. "*SPSM&H* publishes sonnets, sonnet sequences and fiction, articles and reviews related to the form (fiction may be romantic or Gothic) for a general readership and sonnet enthusiasts." Quarterly. Estab. 1985. Circ. 600.

• This magazine is edited by Frederick A. Raborg, Jr., who is also editor of *Amelia* and *Cicada*.

Needs: Adventure, confession, contemporary, erotica, ethnic, experimental, fantasy, feminist, gay, historical, horror, humor/satire, lesbian, literary, mainstream, mystery/suspense, regional, romance (contemporary, historical), science fiction, senior citizen/retirement, translations and western. All should have romantic element. "We look for strong fiction with romantic or Gothic content, or both. Stories need not have 'happy' endings, and we are open to the experimental and/or avant-garde. Erotica is fine; pornography, no." Receives 30 unsolicited mss/month. Accepts 1 ms/issue; 4 mss/year. Publishes ms 6-12 months after acceptance. Agented fiction 5%. Published work by Brad Hooper, Mary Louise R. O'Hara and Clara Castelar Bjorlie. Length: 500-3,000 words; average length: 2,000 words average. Critiques rejected ms when appropriate; recommends other markets.

How to Contact: Send complete ms with cover letter. Include Social Security number. Responds in 2 weeks. SASE. Sample copy for $6. Guidelines for #10 SASE.

Payment/Terms: Pays $10-25 and contributor's copies. Pays on publication for first North American serial rights; charge for extra copies.

Advice: "A good story line (plot) and strong characterization are vital. I want to know the writer has done his homework and is striving to become professional."

🌐 $ **STAND MAGAZINE**, School of English, University of Leeds, Leeds LS2 9JT England. Phone: (44)113 223 4794. Fax: (44)113 233 4791. E-mail: stand@english.novell.leeds.ac.uk. **Contact: Michael Hulse and John Kinsella, editors.** "*Stand* is an international quarterly publishing poetry, short stories, reviews, criticism and translations." Circ. 4,500. Quarterly.

Needs: Literary. **Publishes 10 new writers/year.** Recently published Michael Mott, Christopher Hope and Penelope. Length: 5,000 words maximum.

How to Contact: "Read copies of the magazine before submitting. Enclose sufficient IRCs for return of mss/reply. No more than 6 poems or 2 short stories at any one time. Should not be under consideration elsewhere."

Payment/Terms: £75 per 1,000 words of prose on publication (or in US dollars); contributor's copies. Sponsors biennial short competition: First prize, £1,500. Send 2 IRCs for information. Sample copy: £11.

$ ◯ ◎ ▼ **STONE SOUP, The Magazine By Young Writers and Artists**, Children's Art Foundation, Box 83, Santa Cruz CA 95063. (831)426-5557. E-mail: gmandel@stonesoup.com. Website: www.stonesoup.com (includes writer's guidelines, sample copy, links, projects, international children's art). **Contact:** Ms. Gerry Mandel, editor. Magazine: 7 × 10; 48 pages; high quality paper; photos. Stories, poems, book reviews and art by children through age 13. Readership: children, librarians, educators. Published 6 times/year. Estab. 1973. Circ. 20,000.

• This is known as "the literary journal for children." *Stone Soup* has previously won the Ed Press Golden Lamp Honor Award and the Parent's Choice Award.

Needs: Fiction by children on themes based on their own experiences, observations or special interests. Also, some fantasy, mystery, adventure. No clichés, no formulas, no writing exercises; original work only. Receives approximately 1,000 unsolicited fiction mss each month. Accepts approximately 15 mss/issue. **Published new writers within the last year.** Length: 150-2,500 words. Also publishes literary essays and poetry. Critiques rejected mss upon request.

How to Contact: Send complete ms with cover letter. "We like to learn a little about our young writers, why they like to write, and how they came to write the story they are submitting." SASE. No simultaneous submissions. Responds in 1 month to mss. Does not respond to mss that are not accompanied by an SASE. Publishes ms an average of 3-6 months after acceptance. Sample copy for $4. Guidelines for SASE. Reviews children's books.

Payment/Terms: Pays $25 plus 2 contributor's copies; $2.50 charge for extras. Buys all rights. Subscription: $33/year.

Advice: Mss are rejected because they are "derivatives of movies, TV, comic books; or classroom assignments or other formulas."

🌐 ☑ ⊘ ◎ **STORYBOARD, A Journal of Pacific Imagery**, Division of English, University of Guam, Mangilao, Guam 96923. Phone: (671)735-2749. Fax: (671)734-0010. E-mail: rburns@uoga.uog.edu. Website: www.uog2.uog.edu/strybrd/STORYBOARD. **Contact:** Robert A. Burns, general editor. Editors change each year. Magazine: 100 pages; illustrations; photos. "A multilingual journal with a focus on Pacific writing and writers. We publish short fiction, creative nonfiction and poetry." Annually. Estab. 1991. Circ. 300. Member: Council of Literary Magazines and Presses.

• Material sent to *Storyboard* must relate to the Pacific region or be written by an indigenous Pacific writer.

Needs: Ethnic/multicultural (Pacific region), experimental, family saga, regional (Pacific region). Receives 10-15 unsolicited mss/month. Accepts 30-40 mss/issue. Publishes ms 6-12 months after acceptance. Agented fiction 50-75%. Length: 1,000 words average. Publishes short shorts. Also publishes poetry.

How to Contact: Send complete ms with a cover letter. Accepts queries/mss by e-mail. Include bio. Responds in 1 month to queries; 6 months to mss. Send SASE for reply, return of ms or send a disposable copy of ms. Sample copy $6 and 7×10 SAE. Guidelines free.

Payment/Terms: Pays 2 contributor's copies; additional copies $7.50.

◙ STORYQUARTERLY, Box 1416, Northbrook IL 60065-1416. (847)564-8891. Co-editors: Anne Brashler and Marie Hayes. **Contact:** Fiction Editor. Magazine: approximately 6×9; 240 pages; good quality paper; illustrations; photos. A magazine devoted to the short story and committed to a full range of styles and forms. Annually. Estab. 1975. Circ. 3,000.

 • *StoryQuarterly* ranked #35 on *Writer's Digest*'s "Fiction 50" list of top markets. *StoryQuarterly* received honorable mention in *Best Essays* O'Henry Awards and *Best American Stories 1999*. The publication also won the First Story Award from the Illinois Arts Council, 1999.

Needs: "Great humor, serious and well-written stories about life." No sci-fi, horror, animal-oriented or sex-driven stories. Receives 200 unsolicited fiction mss/month. Accepts 20 mss/issue. **Published new writers within the last year.** Recently published work by Stephen Dixon, Pamela Painter, Alice Hoffman, Lois Hauselman, Oliver Broudy, Mark Halliday and S.L. Wisenberg.

How to Contact: Send complete ms with SASE. Accepts simultaneous submissions. Responds in 3 months to mss. Sample copy for $6.

Payment/Terms: Pays 3 contributor's copies for one-time rights. Copyright reverts to author after publication.

Advice: "Send one manuscript at a time, subscribe to the magazine, send SASE." Fiction selected based on "the voice, the story and the author's control. Read. Read. Read. Don't be self-obsessed. Enjoy and be proud of being a writer. A sense of humor helps. Literary magazines (university affiliated and/or independent) deal with reality in ways the industry trends do not. We do not deal in fairy tale endings."

☑ ◙ STOVEPIPE, A Journal of Little Literary Value, P.O. Box 1076, Georgetown KY 40324. (502)868-6573. Fax: (502)868-6566. E-mail: troyteegarden@worldradio.org. Website: www.worldradio.org/soup.html. Editor: Troy Teegarden. **Contact:** Fiction Editor. Magazine: 8½×5½; 30-60 pages; 70 lb. paper; card stock cover; illustrations. "We like to have a good time with what we read. We publish fiction, nonfiction, poetry and black and white art." Quarterly. Estab. 1995. Circ. 250.

Needs: Comics/graphic novels, experimental, humor/satire, literary, short story collections. No religious, fantasy. Want more experimental, humor and fringe. Receives 50 unsolicited mss/month. Accepts 1-2 mss/issue; 4-8 mss/year. Publishes ms 1-3 months after acceptance. **Publishes 4-8 new writers/year.** Recently published work by Mike Francis and Steven Carter. Length: 3,500 words maximum. Publishes short shorts. "We really dig short short stories." Also publishes poetry. Often comments on rejected ms.

How to Contact: Send complete ms with a cover letter. Accepts queries by e-mail. Include estimated word count, short but informative bio and list of publications. Responds in 2 weeks to queries; 1 month to mss. Send SASE for reply, return of ms. Sample copy $2 or send 5½×8½ SAE with 78¢ postage. Guidelines for #10 SASE.

Payment/Terms: Pays 1 year subscription; additional copies $2. Acquires one-time rights.

Advice: "Stories must be interesting and new and they must offer something original to the reader. We don't see much fiction but would like to publish more. We look for originality, creativity, strong characters and unique perspectives. Write for yourself. Just because we don't publish it doesn't mean it's not good. We are very particular."

◙ STRUGGLE, A Magazine of Proletarian Revolutionary Literature, Box 13261, Detroit MI 48213-0261. (213)273-9039. E-mail: timhall@megsinet.net. **Contact:** Tim Hall, editor. Magazine: 5½×8½; 36-72 pages; 20 lb. white bond paper; colored cover; illustrations; occasional photos. Publishes material related to "the struggle of the working class and all progressive people against the rule of the rich—including their war policies, racism, exploitation of the workers, oppression of women, etc." Quarterly. Estab. 1985. Subscription: $10/year in US, $12 to libraries, $15 foreign.

Needs: Contemporary, ethnic, experimental, feminist, historical (general), humor/satire, literary, prose poem, regional, science fiction, senior citizen/retirement, translations, young adult/teen (10-18). "The theme can be approached in many ways, including plenty of categories not listed here. Would like to see more fiction that depicts the life, work and struggle of the working class of every background; also the struggles of the 1930s and 60s illustrated and brought to life." No romance, psychic, mystery, western, erotica, religious. Receives 10-12 unsolicited fiction mss/month. Publishes ms 6 months or less after acceptance. **Published new writers within the last year.** Recently published work by Greg Norton, David Poyner, Billie Louise Jones and Dennis Hammond. Length: 4,000 words maximum; average length: 1,000-3,000 words. Publishes short shorts. Normally critiques rejected mss.

How to Contact: Send complete ms; cover letter optional. "Tries to" report in 3-4 months. SASE. Accepts simultaneous and reprint submissions. Sample copy for $2.50. Make checks payable to Tim Hall-Special Account.

Payment/Terms: Pays 2 contributor's copies. No rights acquired. Publication not copyrighted.
Advice: "Write about the oppression of the working people, the poor, the minorities, women, and if possible, their rebellion against it—we are not interested in anything which accepts the status quo. We are not too worried about plot and advanced technique (fine if we get them!)—we would probably accept things others would call sketches, provided they have life and struggle. For new writers: just describe for us a situation in which some real people confront some problem of oppression, however seemingly minor. Observe and put down the real facts. Experienced writers: try your 'committed'/experimental fiction on us. We get poetry all the time. We have increased our fiction portion of our content in the last few years. The quality of fiction that we have published has continued to improve. If your work raises an interesting issue of literature and politics, it may get discussed in letters and in my editorial. I suggest ordering a sample."

$ SUB-TERRAIN, P.O. Box 1575, Bentall Centre, Vancouver BC V6C 2P7 Canada. (604)876-8710. Fax: (604)879-2667. E-mail: subter@pinc.com. Fiction Editors: D.E. Bolen and Brian Kaufman. Magazine: 8½×11; 40 pages; offset printed paper; illustrations; photos. "*Sub-Terrain* provides a forum for work that pushes the boundaries in form or content." Estab. 1988.
Needs: "Primarily a literary magazine; also interested in erotica, experimental, humor/satire." Receives 100 unsolicited mss/month. No horror, romance, science fiction. Accepts 15-20 mss/issue. Publishes ms 1-4 months after acceptance. **Publishes 6-10 new writers/year.** Recently published work by Tammy Armstrong and Carrie MacDonald. Length: 200-3,000 words. Publishes short shorts. Length: 200 words. Also publishes literary essays, literary criticism, poetry. Sometimes critiques rejected mss and "at times" recommends other markets.
How to Contact: Send complete ms with cover letter. Accepts multiple submissions. Responds in 1 month to queries; 3 months to mss. SASE. Sample copy for $5. Also features book review section. Send books marked "Review Copy, Managing Editor."
Payment/Terms: Pays (for solicited work) $25/page; $20/poem. Acquires one-time rights.
Advice: "We look for contemporary, modern fiction with something special in the voice or style, not simply something that is a well-written story—a new twist, a unique sense or vision of the world, the stuff that every mag is hoping to find. Read a sample copy before submitting."

SULPHUR RIVER LITERARY REVIEW, P.O. Box 19228, Austin TX 78760-9228. (512)292-9456. **Contact:** James Michael Robbins, editor. Magazine: 5½×8½; 145 pages; illustrations; photos. "*SRLR* publishes literature of quality—poetry and short fiction with appeal that transcends time. Audience includes a broad spectrum of readers, mostly educated, many of whom are writers, artists and educators." Semiannually. Estab. 1978. Circ. 400.
Needs: Ethnic/multicultural, experimental, feminist, humor/satire, literary, mainstream/contemporary and translations. No "religious, juvenile, teen, sports, romance or mystery." Receives 20-30 unsolicited mss/month. Accepts 4-5 mss/issue; 8-10 mss/year. Publishes ms 1-2 years after acceptance. **Publishes few new writers/year.** Published work by Hugh Fox, Angela Hall, Rafael Courtoisie, Warren Carrier and Emilia Pardo Bazán. Publishes short shorts. Also publishes literary essays, literary criticism and poetry. Critiques or comments on rejected mss when requested.
How to Contact: Send complete ms with a cover letter. Include short bio and list of publications. Responds in 1 week to queries; 1 month to mss. Send SASE for reply, return of ms or send a disposable copy of ms. No simultaneous submissions. Sample copy for $7.
Payment/Terms: Pays 2 contributor's copies; additional copies for $7. Acquires first North American serial rights.
Advice: Looks for "Quality. Imagination served perfectly by masterful control of language."

SUNDOG: THE SOUTHEAST REVIEW, English Department, Florida State University, Tallahassee FL 32306-1036. (850)644-2640. E-mail: sundog@english.fsu.edu. Website: www.english.fsu.edu/sundog/ (includes names of editors and writer's guidelines). **Contact:** Jarret Keene, fiction editor. Magazine: 6×9; 60-100 pages; 70 lb. paper; 10 pt. Krome Kote cover; illustrations; photos. Biannually. Estab. 1979. Circ. 2,000.
Needs: "We want stories (under 3,000 words) with striking images, fresh language, and a consistent voice." Would like to see more literary fiction. No genre or formula fiction. **Publishes 4-6 new writers/year.** "We receive approximately 180 submissions per month; we accept less than 5%. We will comment briefly on rejected mss when time permits." Upcoming themes: Southern Gothic, deadline March 15, 2001; Giant Robots, deadline August 15, 2001. Recently published work by G. Travis Regier, Rita Ciresi, Stephen Dixon, Susan Hubbard, Pat Rushin and Tracy Daugherty.
How to Contact: Send complete ms with SASE and a brief cover letter. Responds in 2 months. Publishes ms an average of 2-6 months after acceptance. Sample copy for $5. Subscriptions for $9.
Payment/Terms: Pays 2 contributor's copies. Acquires first North American serial rights which then revert to author.

Advice: "Avoid trendy experimentation for its own sake (present-tense narration, observation that isn't also revelation). Fresh stories, moving, interesting characters and a sensitivity to language are still fiction mainstays. Also publishes winner and runners-up of the World's Best Short Short Story Contest sponsored by the Florida State University English Department."

SYCAMORE REVIEW, Department of English, Purdue University, West Lafayette IN 47907. (765)494-3783. Fax: (765)494-3780. E-mail: sycamore@expert.cc.purdue.edu. Website: www.sla.purdue.edu/academic/engl/sycamore (includes back and current issues, index, submission guidelines, subscription information, journal library). Editor-in-Chief: Numsiric Kunakemakorn. Editors change every two years. **Contact:** Rebecca Rauve, fiction editor. Magazine: 5½×8½; 150-200 pages; heavy, textured, uncoated paper; heavy laminated cover. "Journal devoted to contemporary literature. We publish both traditional and experimental fiction, personal essay, poetry, interviews, drama and graphic art. Novel excerpts welcome if they stand alone as a story." Semiannually. Estab. 1989. Circ. 1,000.

• Work published in *Sycamore Review* has been selected for inclusion in the *Pushcart Prize* anthology. The magazine was also named "The Best Magazine from Indiana" by the *Clockwatch Review*.

Needs: Contemporary, experimental, humor/satire, literary, mainstream, regional, translations. "We generally avoid genre literature, but maintain no formal restrictions on style or subject matter. No science fiction, romance, children's." Would like to see more experimental fiction. Publishes ms 3 months to 1 year after acceptance. **10% of material published is by new writers.** Recently published work by Lucia Perillo, June Armstrong, W.P. Osborn and William Giraldi. Length: 250 words minimum; 3,750 words preferred. Also publishes poetry, "this most recently included Billy Collins, Thomas Lux, Kathleen Peirce and Vandana Khanna." Sometimes critiques rejected mss and recommends other markets.

How to Contact: Send complete ms with cover letter. Cover letter should include previous publications and address changes. Only reads mss September through March 31. Responds in 4 months. SASE. Accepts simultaneous submissions. Sample copy for $7. Guidelines for #10 SASE.

Payment/Terms: Pays in contributor's copies; charge for extras. Acquires one-time rights.

Advice: "We publish both new and experienced authors but we're always looking for stories with strong emotional appeal, vivid characterization and a distinctive narrative voice; fiction that breaks new ground while still telling an interesting and significant story. Avoid gimmicks and trite, predictable outcomes. Write stories that have a ring of truth, the impact of felt emotion. Don't be afraid to submit, send your best."

$ TAKAHE, P.O. Box 13-335, Christchurch, 8001, New Zealand. (03)382-1813. E-mail: isamoyn@ihug.co.nz. Website: www.nzwriters.co.nz (includes writer's guidelines and the names of editors). **Contact:** Bernadette Hall, fiction editor. "A literary magazine which appears three or four times a year, and publishes short stories and poetry by both established and emerging writers. The publisher is the Takahe Collective Trust, a charitable trust formed by established writers to help new writers and get them into print."

Needs: Publishes 25 new writers/year. Recently published work by Sarah Quigley, Michael Harlow, Kapka Kassabora, Fiona Farrell, David Hill and Mark Pirie.

How to Contact: Send complete ms with bio. SASE with IRCs for overseas submissions.

Payment/Terms: "There is a small payment for work published. $NZ30 ($US20) to each writer/poet appearing in a particular issue regardless of number/length of itmes, but the amount is subject to change according to circumstaces. Editorials and literary commentaries are by invitation only and not being covered by our grant, are not paid for. All contributors receive two copies of the issue in which theirwork appears. Copyright reverts to the author on publication."

Advice: "While insisting on correct British spelling (or recognised spellings in foreign languages), smart quotes, and at least internally-consistent punctuation, we, nonetheless, try to allow some latitude in presentation. Any use of foreign languages must be accompanied by an English translation."

TALKING RIVER REVIEW, Lewis-Clark State College, Division of Literature and Languages, 500 8th Ave., Lewiston ID 83501. (208)799-2307. Fax: (208)799-2324. E-mail: triver@lcsc.edu. Editor: Dr. Carmen Burton. **Contact:** Claire Davis, fiction editor. Magazine: 6×9; 150 pages; 60 lb. paper; coated, color cover; illustrations; photos. "We publish the best work by well-known and unknown authors; our audience is literary but unpretentious." Semiannually. Estab. 1994. Circ. 750.

Needs: Condensed/excerpted novel, ethnic/multicultural, feminist, historical, humor/satire, literary, mainstream/contemporary, regional. "Wants more well-written, character-driven stories that surprise and delight the reader with fresh, arresting yet unself-conscious language, imagery, metaphor, revelation." No surprise endings; plot-driven stories; or stories that are sexist, racist, homophobic, erotic for shock value, romance. Receives 200 unsolicited mss/month. Accepts 5-8 mss/issue; 10-15 mss/year. Does not read March to September. Publishes ms up to 1 year after acceptance. Agented fiction 10%. **Publishes 10 new writers/year.** Recently published work by Gary Gildner, William Kittredge, David Long and Mary Clearman Blew. Length: 7,500 words maximum; average length: 3,000 words. Also publishes literary essays and poetry. Sometimes comments on rejected mss.

How to Contact: Send complete manuscript with a cover letter. Include estimated word count, 2-sentence bio, Social Security number and list of publications. Responds in 3 months to mss. Send SASE for reply, return of ms or send disposable copy of ms. Accepts simultaneous submissions if indicated. Sample copy for $5. Guidelines for #10 SASE. Subscription: $14/year.
Payment/Terms: Pays 2 contributor's copies and a year's subscription for one-time rights; additional copies $4.
Advice: "Revise, revise, revise. Read more widely, including poetry."

$◻ TAMEME, New Writing from North America/Nueva Literatura de Norteamérica, Tameme, Inc., 199 First St., Los Altos CA 94022. (650)941-2037. Fax: (650)941-5338. E-mail: editor@tameme.org. Website: www.tameme.org (includes editor, contributors, writer's guidelines, staff, index of magazine). Editor: C.M. Mayo. **Contact:** Fiction Editor. Magazine: 6×9; 220 pages; good quality paper; heavy cover stock; illustrations; photos. "*Tameme* is an annual fully bilingual magazine dedicated to publishing new writing from North America in side-by-side English-Spanish format. *Tameme*'s goals are to play an instrumental role in introducing important new writing from Canada and the United States to Mexico, and vice versa, and to provide a forum for the art of literary translation." Estab. 1996. Circ. 1,000. Member: Council of Literary Magazines and Presses (CLMP).
Needs: Ethnic/multicultural, literary, translations. No genre fiction. Plans special fiction issue or anthology. Receives 10-15 unsolicited mss/month. No romance, mystery or western. Accepts 3-4 mss/issue; 6-8 mss/year, "but we are a new magazine so these numbers may not be indicative of a year from now." Publishes ms 1 year after acceptance. Agented fiction 5%. **Publishes 1-3 new writers/year.** Published work by Fabio Morábito, Margaret Atwood, Juan Villoro, Jaime Sabines, Edwidge Danticat, A. Manette Ansay, Douglas Glover and Marianne Toussaint. Publishes short shorts. Also publishes literary essays and poetry.
How to Contact: Send complete ms with a cover letter. Translators query or submit mss with cover letter, curriculum vita and samples of previous work. Include 1-paragraph bio and list of publications. Responds in 6 weeks to queries; 3 months to mss. Send SASE for reply, return of ms or send a disposable copy of ms. Accepts simultaneous submissions. Sample copy for $14.95. Guidelines for SASE.
Payment/Terms: Pays 3 contributor's copies to writers; $20 per double-spaced WordPerfect page to translators. Pays on publication for one-time rights. Sends galleys to author.
Advice: "We're looking for whatever makes us want to stand up and shout YES! Read the magazine, send for guidelines (with SASE), then send only your best, with SASE. No electronic submissions please."

☑ $◻ TAMPA REVIEW, 401 W. Kennedy Blvd., Box 19F, University of Tampa, Tampa FL 33606-1490. (813)253-6266. Fax: (813)258-7593. E-mail: utpress@alpha.utampa.edu. Website: www.tampareview.utampa. edu. Editor: Richard Mathews. **Contact:** Lisa Birnbaum, Kathleen Ochshorn, fiction editors. Magazine: 7½×10½; hardback; approximately 100 pages; acid-free paper; visual art; photos. "Interested in fiction of distinctive literary quality." Semiannually. Estab. 1988.
Needs: Contemporary, ethnic, experimental, fantasy, historical, literary, mainstream, prose poem, translations. "We are far more interested in quality than in genre. Nothing sentimental as opposed to genuinely moving, nor self-conscious style at the expense of human truth." Buys 4-5 mss/issue. Publishes ms within 7 months-1 year of acceptance. Agented fiction 60%. Published work by Elizabeth Spencer, Lee K. Abbott, Lorrie Moore, Gordon Weaver and Tim O'Brien. Length: 250-10,000 words. Publishes short shorts "if the story is good enough." Also publishes literary essays (must be labeled nonfiction), poetry.
How to Contact: Send complete ms with cover letter. Include brief bio. No simultaneous submissions. SASE. Reads September through December; reports January through March. Sample copy for $5 (includes postage) and 9×12 SAE. Guidelines on website or for #10 SASE.
Payment/Terms: Pays $10/printed page on publication for first North American serial rights. Sends galleys to author upon request.
Advice: "There are more good writers publishing in magazines today than there have been in many decades. Unfortunately, there are even more bad ones. In T. Gertler's *Elbowing the Seducer*, an editor advises a young writer that he wants to hear her voice completely, to tell (he means 'show') him in a story the truest thing she knows. We concur. Rather than a trendy workshop story or a minimalism that actually stems from not having much to say, we would like to see stories that make us believe they mattered to the writer and, more importantly, will matter to a reader. Trim until only the essential is left, and don't give up belief in yourself. And it might help to attend a good writers' conference, e.g. Wesleyan or Bennington."

◆ ☑ ◻ "TEAK" ROUNDUP, The International Quarterly, West Coast Paradise Publishing, P.O. Box 2093, Sardis, British Columbia U2R 1A7 Canada. (604)824-9528. Fax: (604)824-9541. E-mail: wcpp@telus.net. **Contact:** Yvonne and Robert Anstey, editors. Magazine: 5½×8½; 60 pages; 20 lb. copy paper; card stock cover; illustrations; photos. " *'Teak' Roundup* is a general interest showcase for prose and poetry. No uncouth material." Quarterly. Estab. 1994. Circ. 200.
Needs: Adventure, children's/juvenile, condensed/excerpted novel, ethnic/multicultural, historical, humor/satire, literary, mainstream/contemporary, mystery/suspense (police procedural), regional, religious/inspirational, romance (contemporary, historical), sports, westerns, young adult/teen (adventure). "No uncouth or porn. No war

or violence." List of upcoming themes available for SASE. Receives 25 unsolicited mss/month. Accepts 20 mss/issue. Publishes ms 3-6 weeks after acceptance. **Publishes 20 new writers/year.** Recently published work by Ann Carson, Philip Fletcher and Rita Campbell. Length: 1,000 words maximum. Also publishes literary essays, literary criticism and poetry. Often comments on rejected ms.

How to Contact: *Accepts work from subscribers only.* Subscription for $17 (Canadian); $13 (US). Query first or send complete ms with a cover letter. Include estimated word count and brief bio. Responds in 1 week. Send SASE for reply, return of ms or send a disposable copy of ms. Accepts simultaneous, reprint and electronic submissions. Sample copy for $5 (Canadian); $3 (US). Guidelines for #10 SASE. Reviews novels and short story collections.

Payment/Terms: Acquires one-time rights (unreserved reprint if "Best of" edition done later.)

Advice: "Subscribe and see popular work which is enjoyed by our growing audience. Many good writers favor us with participation in subscribers-only showcase for prose and poetry. No criticism of generous contributors."

TEARS IN THE FENCE, 38 Hod View, Stourpaine, Nr. Blandford Forum, Dorset DT11 8TN England. Phone: 01258-456803. Fax: 01258-454026. E-mail: poets@wanderingdog.co.uk. Editor: David Caddy. **Contact:** Fiction Editor. Three issues per annum. The editor looks for "the unusual, perceptive and risk-taking as well as the imaginistic and visionary."

• *Tears in the Fence* has expanded to 112 pages and is accepting more prose and prose poems.

Needs: A magazine of poetry, fiction, criticism and reviews, open to a variety of contemporary voices from around the world. Upcoming themes: "Difference and the Other" (June 2001). **Publishes 1-2 new writers/year.** Recently published work by Gerald Locklin, Martin Hubbard, Norman Lock, Nigel Jarrett, Brian George and Sarah Connor. Publishes short and long fiction. Publishes 4-5 stories/issue.

Payment/Terms: Pays £7.50 per story plus complimentary copy of the magazine. Sample copy for $5 (US).

Advice: "Look for firm narrative control with an economical style that takes the reader far beyond the obvious and inconsequential. Explore the market by buying sample copies."

THE TEXAS REVIEW, Texas Review Press at Sam Houston State University, Huntsville TX 77341-2146. (936)294-1992. Fax: (936)294-1414 (inquiries only). Website: www.shsu.edu/~eng_www/trp.html. **Contact:** Paul Ruffin, editor. Magazine: 6×9; 148-190 pages; best quality paper; 70 lb. cover stock; illustrations; photos. "We publish top quality poetry, fiction, articles, interviews and reviews for a general audience." A member of the Texas A&M University Press consortium. Semiannually. Estab. 1976. Circ. 1,200.

Needs: Literary and contemporary fiction. "We are eager enough to consider fiction of quality, no matter what its theme or subject matter. No juvenile fiction." Accepts 4 mss/issue. Receives approximately 40-60 unsolicited fiction mss each month. Does not read June-August. **Published new writers within the last year.** Published work by George Garrett, Ellen Gilchrist and Fred Chappell. Length: 500-10,000 words. Critiques rejected mss "when there is time." Recommends other markets.

How to Contact: Send complete ms, cover letter optional. SASE. No mss accepted via fax. Responds in 3 months to mss. Sample copy for $5.

Payment/Terms: Pays contributor's copies plus one year subscription. Acquires first North American serial rights. Sends galleys to author.

THEMA, Box 8747, Metairie LA 70011-8747. (504)887-1263. E-mail: thema@home.com. Website: www.litline.org (includes guidelines, list of upcoming themes and back issues). **Editor:** Virginia Howard. Magazine: 5½×8½; 200 pages; Grandee Strathmore cover stock; b&w illustrations. "Different specified theme for each issue—short stories, poems, b&w artwork must relate to that theme." Triannually. Estab. 1988.

• Ranked #33 on *Writer's Digest*'s "Fiction 50" list of top markets for fiction writers. *Thema* received a Certificate for Excellence in the Arts from the Arts Council of New Orleans.

Needs: Adventure, contemporary, experimental, humor/satire, literary, mainstream, mystery/suspense, prose poem, psychic/supernatural/occult, regional, science fiction, sports, western. "Each issue is based on a specified premise—a different unique theme for each issue. Many types of fiction acceptable, but must fit the premise. No pornographic, scatologic, erotic fiction." Upcoming themes (deadlines for submission in 2001): "What Sarah (or Edward) Remembered" (March 1); "The Third One" (July 1); and "The Power of Whim" (November 1). Publishes ms within 6 months of acceptance. **Publishes 10-15 new writers/year.** Recently published work by Nancy Gronbach, C.M. Mayo and Muriel Moulton. Length: fewer than 6,000 words preferred. Also publishes poetry. Sometimes critiques rejected mss and recommends other markets.

How to Contact: Send complete ms with cover letter, include "name and address, brief introduction, specifying the intended target issue for the mss." Accepts queries by e-mail. Accepts simultaneous submissions. Responds in 1 week to queries; 5 months after deadline for specified issue. SASE. Sample copy for $8. Guidelines available on website or for SASE.

Payment/Terms: Pays $25; $10 for short shorts on acceptance for one-time rights.

Advice: "Do not submit a manuscript unless you have written it for a specified premise. If you don't know the upcoming themes, send for guidelines first, before sending a story. We need more stories told in the Mark Twain/ O. Henry tradition in magazine fiction."

THIN AIR, Graduate Creative Writing Association of Northern Arizona University, P.O. Box 23549, Flagstaff AZ 86002. Website: www.nau.edu/~english/thinair. **Contact:** Fiction Editor. Editors change each year. Magazine: 8½×11; 50-60 pages; illustrations; photos. Publishes "contemporary voices for a literary-minded audience." Semiannually. Estab. 1995. Circ. 500.

Needs: Condensed/excerpted novel, ethnic/multicultural, experimental, literary, mainstream/contemporary. "No children's/juvenile." Editorial calendar available for SASE. Receives 75 unsolicited mss/month. Accepts 5-8 mss/issue; 10-15 mss/year. Does not read mss May-September. Publishes ms 6-9 months after acceptance. Solicited fiction 35%. **Publishes 3-8 new writers/year.** Recently published work by Stephen Dixon, Henry H. Roth, Brian Evenson, Charles Bowden, Sean Caughlin, Patricia Lawrence and Craig Rullman. Length: 6,000 words maximum. Publishes short shorts. Also publishes literary essays, literary criticism, creative nonfiction, poetry and interviews. Recent interviews include Thom Jones, Alan Lightman and Rick Bass

How to Contact: Send complete ms with a cover letter. Include estimated word count and list of publications. Responds in 1 month to queries; 5 months to mss. Send SASE for reply, return of ms or send a disposable copy of ms. Accepts simultaneous submissions. Sample copy for $5. Guidelines free. Reviews novels and short story collections.

Payment/Terms: Pays 2 contributor's copies; additional copies for $4. Pays on publication for first North American serial rights. Sponsors contest; send SASE for guidelines.

Advice: Looks for "writers who know how to create tension and successfully resolve it."

THE THIRD ALTERNATIVE, TTA Press, 5 Martins Lane, Witcham, Ely, Cambs CB6 2LB England. E-mail: ttapress@aol.com. Website: www.tta.press.freewiz.co.uk (includes news, art, interviews, stories, links, contributor's guidelines). **Contact:** Andy Cox, fiction editor. Quarterly. Publishes 8 stories/issue. A4, 68 pages, lithographed, color, laminated.

Needs: "Modern fiction: no mainstream or genre clichés. Innovative, quality science fiction/fantasy/horror and slipstream material (cross-genre)." Recently published M. John Harrison, Christopher Priest and Ran Watson. Length: No minimum; no maximum (no serials).

How to Contact: Only send one story at a time, mailed flat or folded no more than once. USA stamps are not acceptable as return postage (UK stamps, 2 IRCs or an e-mail address—but no submissions via e-mail). "A covering letter is appreciated." Standard ms format and SAE (overseas: disposable ms and 2 IRCs). No simultaneous submissions. Reprints only in exceptional circumstances.

Payment/Terms: Payment is £20 per 1,000 words. $7 sample copy, $36 6-issue subscription. US checks acceptable, payable to TTA Press.

THIRD COAST, Dept. of English, Western Michigan University, Kalamazoo MI 49008-5092. (616)387-2675. Fax: (616)387-2562. Website: www.wmich.edu/thirdcoast (includes guidelines, editors names and samples of past fiction we have published are all available on the website). Managing Editor: Shanda Blue. **Contact:** Lisa Lishman and Chris Torockio, fiction editors. Magazine: 6×9; 150 pages. "We will consider many different types of fiction and favor that exhibiting a freshness of vision and approach." Semiannually. Estab. 1995. Circ. 600.

● *Third Coast* has received *Pushcart Prize* nominations. The editors of this publication change with the university year.

Needs: Literary. "While we don't want to see formulaic genre fiction, we will consider material that plays with or challenges generic forms." Receives approximately 100 unsolicited mss/month. Accepts 6-8 mss/issue; 15 mss/year. Publishes ms 3-6 months after acceptance. Recently published work by Peter Ho Davies, Sharon Dilworth, Trudy Lewis and Mark Winegardner. Length: no preference. Publishes short shorts. Also publishes literary essays, poetry and interviews. Sometimes comments on rejected mss.

How to Contact: Send complete ms with a cover letter. Include list of publications. Responds in 2 months to queries; 5 months to mss. Send SASE for reply or return of ms. No simultaneous submissions. Sample copy for $6. Guidelines for #10 SASE.

Payment/Terms: Pays 2 contributor's copies as well as 1 year subscription to the publication; additional copies for $4. Acquires first North American serial rights.

Advice: "Of course, the writing itself must be of the highest quality. We love to see work that explores non-western contexts, as well as fiction from all walks of American (and other) experience."

THE THIRD HALF MAGAZINE, "Amikeco," 16, Fane Close, Stamford, Lincolnshire PE9 1HG England. Phone: (01780)754193. **Contact:** Kevin Troop, fiction editor. Published irregularly (when enough work is ready).

Needs: "*The Third Half* literary magazine publishes mostly poetry, but editorial policy is to publish as much *short* short story writing as possible in separate books." Recently published work by Steve Sneyd and Michael Newman. Length: 2,000 words maximum.

Payment/Terms: Pays in contributor's copies. Sample copy £4.95; £5.50 by post in England; £7 overseas.

13TH MOON, A Feminist Magazine, Dept. of English, University at Albany, Albany NY 12222. (518)442-4181. Editor: Judith Johnson. **Contact:** Judith Fetterly and Hollis Seamon, fiction editors. Magazine: 6×9; 300 pages; 50 lb. paper; heavy cover stock; illustrations; photos. "Feminist literary magazine for feminist women and men." Annually. Estab. 1973. Circ. 2,000.
Needs: Ethnic/multicultural, experimental, feminist, lesbian, literary, romance, science fiction, translations. No fiction by men. List of upcoming themes available for SASE. Receives 20 or more unsolicited mss/month. Accepts 30 mss/year. Does not read mss June-August. Time varies between acceptance and publication. Published work by F.R. Lewis, Jan Ramjerdi and Wilma Kahn. Length: Open. Publishes short shorts. Also publishes poetry. Sometimes critiques rejected mss.
How to Contact: Query first; send complete ms with cover letter and SASE (or IRC). Include bio and list of publications. Responds in 2 months to queries; 1 year to mss. SASE. Sample copy for $10. Guidelines for SASE.
Payment/Terms: Pays 2 contributor's copies.
Terms: Acquires first North American serial rights.
Advice: Looks for "*unusual* fiction with feminist appeal."

$ THIS MAGAZINE, Red Maple Foundation, 401 Richmond St. W., Suite 396, Toronto, Ontario M5V 3A8 Canada. (416)979-8400. E-mail: thismag@web.net. Website: www.thismag.org (includes writer's guidelines). **Contact:** Chris Chambers, literary editor. Magazine: 8½×11; 48 pages; bond paper; non-coated cover; illustrations; photos. "Alternative general interest magazine." Bimonthly. Estab. 1966. Circ. 7,000.
 • *This Magazine* has won national Canadian Magazine awards, and *Utne Reader's* alternative press awards for cultural coverage. *This Magazine* is not currently accepting unsolicited manuscripts.

3 A.M. MAGAZINE, The Hour of the Wolf, 3 A.M. Publishing, 218 Main St., #118, Kirkland WA 98033. (206)610-7341. E-mail: editor@3ampublishing.com. Website: www.3ampublishing.com. **Contact:** Kenneth Wilson. Online magazine. "3 A.M. Publishing's website specializes in no-holds-barred popular literature and on-edge journalism. Featuring an exciting suspenseful collection of e-books and short stories, we are a highly visited site in the online literary world." Monthly. Estab. 1998. Circ. more than 32,000 users a month.
Needs: Adventure, comics/graphic novels, experimental, historical (general), horror (psychological, supernatural, original), humor/satire, military/war, mystery/suspense (surreal), psychic/supernatural/occult, science fiction (soft/sociological), thriller/espionage. "No fantasy, romance, erotica.:" Accepts 15 (online) mss/issue. Publishes mss 30 days after acceptance. Recently pubished work by Tom Waltz, Kaley Noonan, Klaus D. Yurk. Length: 3,000-10,000 words; average length: 5,000. Accepts short shorts; average length: 500 words. Also publishes literary essays and literary criticism. Sometimes comments on rejected mss.
How to Contact: Query first or query via website. Accepts submissions by e-mail. Include estimated word count, brief bio and list of publications. Responds in 1 month to queries; 2 months to mss. Accepts simultaneous submissions. Sample copy and guidelines on website.
Payment/Terms: Pays a percentage of ebook sales online for electronic rights. No payment for short stories.
Advice: "Sharp writing style, intrigue and entertainment level. Read through our online publication, get a grasp for our different themes, these attempt something that we haven't seen before."

$ THE THREEPENNY REVIEW, P.O. Box 9131, Berkeley CA 94709. (510)849-4545. **Contact:** Wendy Lesser, editor. Tabloid: 10×17; 40 pages; Electrobrite paper; white book cover; illustrations. "Serious fiction." Quarterly. Estab. 1980. Circ. 9,000.
 • *The Threepenny Review* ranked #26 on *Writer's Digest's* "Fiction 50" list of top markets for fiction writers, and has received GE Writers Awards, CLMP Editor's Awards, NEA grants, Lila Wallace grants and inclusion of work in the *Pushcart Prize Anthology*.
Needs: Literary. "Nothing 'experimental' (ungrammatical)." Receives 300-400 mss/month. Accepts 3 mss/ issue; 12 mss/year. Does *not* read mss June through August. Publishes 6-12 months after acceptance. Agented fiction 5%. Published Sigrid Nunez, Dagoberto Gilb, Gina Berriault and Leonard Michaels. Length: 5,000 words maximum. Publishes short shorts. Also publishes literary essays, literary criticism, poetry.
How to Contact: Send complete ms with a cover letter. Responds in 1 month to queries; 2 months to mss. Send SASE for reply, return of ms or send a disposable copy of the ms. No simultaneous submissions. Sample copy for $7. Guidelines for #10 SASE. Reviews novels and short story collections.
Payment/Terms: Pays $200 plus free subscription to the magazine; additional copies at half price. Pays on acceptance for first North American serial rights. Sends galleys to author.

$ TIN HOUSE, 2601 NW Thurman St., Portland OR 97210. (503)274-4393. Fax: (503)222-1154. E-mail: tinhouse@europa.com. Editor: Win McCormack. **Contact:** Rob Spillman and Elissa Schappell, fiction editors. Literary magazine: 5¾×8¼; 200 pages, 50 lb. paper; glossy cover stock; illustrations and photos. Quarterly.
 • See the interview with *Tin House* fiction co-editor Elissa Schappell on publication of her first novel, *Use Me* (William Morrow & Company, 2000), on page 35.

Needs: Experimental, literary. Accepts 3-4 mss/issue. Publishes ms up to one year after acceptance. Length: 2,000-5,000 words; average length: 3,500 words. Publishes short shorts. Also publishes literary essays, literary criticism and poetry.

How to Contact: Send complete ms with a cover letter or submit through an agent. Include estimated word count. Responds in 6 weeks to mss. Send SASE for return of ms. Accepts simultaneous submissions. Sample copy for $9.95. Guidelines for $2.

Payment/Terms: Pays $100-1,000 plus 2 contributor's copies; additional copies $9.95. Acquires first North American serial and Anthology rights.

Advice: "Our criteria are boldness of concept, intense level of emotion and energy, precision of observation, deployment of imagination, grace of style. Any sentence read at random is impeccable and as good as any other in the work. Do not send anything that does not make you feel like laughing or crying, or both, when you read it yourself."

N ◐ ◎ TRANSITION, An International Review, Duke University Press, 69 Dunster St., Cambridge MA 02138. (617)496-2845. Fax: (617)496-2877. E-mail: transition@fas.harvard.edu. Website: www.transitionmagazine.com. (includes contents of all issues, abstracts, editorial history and current info, purchasing and subscription info). **Contact:** Michael Vazquez, executive editor. Magazine: 9½ × 6½; 150-175 pages; 70 lb. Finch Opaque paper; 100 lb. white Warren Lustro dull cover; illustrations; photos. "*Transition* magazine is a quarterly, international review known for compelling and controversial writing on race, ethnicity, culture and politics. This prestigious magazine is edited at Harvard University, and editorial board members include heavy-hitters such as Toni Morrison, Jamaica Kincaid and bell hooks. The magazine also attracts famous contributors such as Spike Lee, Philip Gourevitch and Carlos Fuentes." Quarterly. Estab. 1961. Circ. 3,500.

● Winner of Alternative Press Award for international reporting 1999, 1995; American Association of University Publishers Outstanding Design 1997.

Needs: Ethnic/multicultural (general), historical, humor satire, literary, regional (Africa diaspora, India, Third World, etc.) Receives 10 unsolicited mss/month. Accepts 4-6 mss/year. Publishes ms 6-12 months after acceptance. Agented fiction 30-40%. **Publishes 2-5 new writers/year.** Recently published work by George Makana Clark, Paul Beatty and Victor D. LaValle. Length: 4,000-8,000 words; average length: 6,000 words. Also publishes literary essays and literary criticism. Sometimes comments on rejected mss.

How to Contact: Send complete ms with a cover letter or query with clips of published work. Include brief bio and list of publications. Responds in 2 months to queries; 4 months to mss. Send disposable copy of ms and #10 SASE for reply only. Accepts simultaneous submissions. Sample copy for $8.99 through website. Guidelines for SASE. Reviews novels, short story collections and nonfiction books of interest to writers.

Payment/Terms: Pays 3 contributor's copies. Rights negotiable. Sends galleys to author.

Advice: "*Transition* is always looking for remarkable writing from Africa and beyond. Please read the magazine before submitting."

◐ ▼ TRIQUARTERLY, Northwestern University, 2020 Ridge Ave., Evanston IL 60208-4302. (847)491-7614. **Contact:** Susan Hahn, editor. Magazine: 6 × 9¼; 240-272 pages; 60 lb. paper; heavy cover stock; illustration; photos. "A general literary quarterly. We publish short stories, novellas or excerpts from novels, by American and foreign writers. Genre or style is not a primary consideration. We aim for the general but serious and sophisticated reader. Many of our readers are also writers." Triannual. Estab. 1964. Circ. 5,000.

● Stories from *Triquarterly* have been reprinted in *The Best American Short Stories*, *Pushcart Prizes* and *O'Henry Prize* Anthologies.

Needs: Literary, contemporary and translations. "No prejudices or preconceptions against anything *except* genre fiction (romance, science fiction, etc.)." Accepts 10 mss/issue, 30 mss/year. Receives approximately 500 unsolicited fiction mss each month. Will begin reading October 1, 2001. Agented fiction 10%. **Publishes 1-5 new writers/year.** Recently published work by John Barth, Chaim Potok, Joyce Carol Oates, Hélène Cixous, Charles Baxter, Margot Livesey and Robert Girardi. Length: no requirement. Publishes short shorts.

How to Contact: Send complete ms with SASE. No simultaneous submissions. Responds in 4 months to mss. Publishes ms an average of 6-12 months after acceptance. Sample copy for $5.

Payment/Terms: Pays 2 contributor's copies on publication for first North American serial rights. Cover price less 40% discount for extras. Sends galleys to author. Honoraria vary, depending on grant support.

◐ TUCUMCARI LITERARY REVIEW, 3108 W. Bellevue Ave., Los Angeles CA 90026. **Contact:** Troxey Kemper, editor. Magazine: 5½ × 8½; about 40 pages; 20 lb. bond paper; 67 lb. cover stock; few illustrations; photocopied photos. "Old-fashioned fiction that can be read and reread for pleasure; no weird, strange pipe dreams and no it-was-all-a-dream endings." Bimonthly. Estab. 1988. Circ. small.

Needs: Adventure, contemporary, ethnic, historical, humor/satire, literary, mainstream, mystery/suspense, regional (southwest USA), senior citizen/retirement, western (frontier stories). No "sci-fi, occult, violence, liquor, tobacco, sex sex sex, dirty language for no reason or romance. Would like to see more Western, mystery and O. Henry endings." No drugs/acid rock, occult, pornography, horror, martial arts or children's stories. Accepts 6 or

8 mss/issue; 35-40 mss/year. Publishes ms 2-6 months after acceptance. **Publishes 12 new writers/year.** Published work by Wilma Elizabeth McDaniel, Ruth Daniels, Andy Peterson, Jim Boone and Bobby Rivera. Length: 400-1,200 words preferred. Also publishes rhyming poetry.

How to Contact: Send complete ms with or without cover letter. Responds in 2 weeks. SASE. Accepts simultaneous and reprint submissions. Sample copy for $2. Guidelines for #10 SASE.

Payment/Terms: Pays in contributor's copies. Acquires one-time rights. Publication not copyrighted.

Advice: "Computers/printers are 'nice' but sometimes handwritten work on 3-hole lined notebook paper is interesting, too. Think of some stories you read in English class when you were in grade school/high school. Try something, *but not the same story*, along those lines. Not a rehash of Hollywood 'plots' done over and over and over."

N 12-GAUGE.COM, (formerly *12-Gauge Review*), InGauge Media LLC, 192 Washington Park, 3rd Floor, Brooklyn NY 11205. (718)852-4816. Fax: (718)222-3737. E-mail: info@12-gauge.com. Website: www.12gauge.com. **Contact:** Eric Seadale, managing editor. Online magazine. Monthly. Estab. 1995.

• See the interview with *12-Gauge.com* editor Garrett Mok on page 39 in the Electronic Publishing section.

Needs: Comics/graphic novels, erotica, ethnic/multicultural, experimental, gay, glitz, humor/satire, lesbian, literary, mainstream, military/war, regional, science fiction (hard science, soft/sociological). Receives 100 unsolicited mss/month. Accepts 2 mss/issue; 24/year. Publishes ms 3-4 weeks after acceptance. Agented fiction: 5%. Publishes 10-12 previously unpublished writers/year. Length: 5,000 words maximum; average length: 3,000. Publishes short shorts. Also publishes essays, criticism, poetry. Sometimes comments on rejected mss.

How to Contact: Send complete ms with cover letter. Accepts submissions by e-mail or on disk. Include estimated word count, brief bio, list of publications and contact information. Simultaneous and previously published submissions okay. Guidelines available via e-mail or on website.

Payment/Terms: Negotiable. Acquires one-time rights.

Advice: "Work must be original but shouldn't try too hard."

⚫ UNMUZZLED OX, Unmuzzled Ox Foundation Ltd., 105 Hudson St., New York NY 10013. (212)226-7170. E-mail: mandreox@aol.com. **Contact:** Michael Andre, editor. Magazine: 5½×8½. "Magazine about life for an intelligent audience." Published irregularly. Estab. 1971. Circ. 7,000.

• Recent issues of this magazine have included poetry, essays and art only. You may want to check before sending submissions or expect a long response time.

Needs: Contemporary, literary, prose poem and translations. No commercial material. Receives 20-25 unsolicited mss/month. Also publishes poetry. Occasionally critiques rejected mss.

How to Contact: "Please no phone calls and no e-mail submissions. Correspondence by mail *only*. Cover letter is significant." Responds in 1 month. SASE. Sample copy for $10.

Payment/Terms: Contributor's copies.

◩ URBAN SPAGHETTI, Literary Arts Journal, P.O. Box 5186, Mansfield OH 44901-5186. E-mail: editor@urban-spaghetti.com. Website: www.urban-spaghetti.com. Editor: Cheryl Dodds. **Contact:** Fiction Editor. Literary magazine: 8½×7; 50-90 pages; 60-80 lb. bond paper; illustrations; photos. "Our focus extends a hand to new writers and poets who share a sense of social responsibility in their writing and offer a fresh presentation and language which challenges us." Semiannually. Estab. 1998.

Needs: Adventure, ethnic/multicultural, experimental, fantasy, feminist, historical, horror, humor satire, literary, mainstream/contemporary, military/war, mystery/suspense, science fiction, western. Receives 200 unsolicited mss/month. Accepts 2-5 mss/issue; 4-10 mss/year. Does not read December-June. Publishes ms 2-5 months after acceptance. Length: 3,500 words maximum. Publishes short shorts. Also publishes literary essays, criticism and poetry. Often comments on rejected ms.

How to Contact: Send complete ms with a cover letter. Include estimated word count and 1-paragraph bio. Responds in 1 week to queries; 2 months to mss. Send SASE for reply or return of ms. Accepts simultaneous submissions with notification. Reviews short story collections and nonfiction books of interest to writers. Send books to editor.

Payment/Terms: Pays 2 contributor's copies; additional copies $7. Acquires first rights. See website for details.

Advice: Looks for "excellent writing, strong voice, good characterization and craft. Proof read, use fresh language, do not use 'shock factor' without well-crafted purpose, make us believe. *Urban Spaghetti* wants to promote new writers. We want to be a resource for innovative new voices."

$ ◩ ◎ THE URBANITE, Surreal & Lively & Bizarre, Urban Legend Press, P.O. Box 4737, Davenport IA 52808. Website: members.tripod.com/theurbanite/ (includes information on current and upcoming issues and also features a fiction showcase). **Editor:** Mark McLaughlin. Magazine: 8½×11; 52-80 pages; bond paper; coated cover; saddle-stitched; illustrations. "We look for quality fiction with a surrealistic tone. We publish character-oriented, sophisticated fiction that expands the boundaries of the speculative genres. Our readers appreciate the best in imaginative fiction." Each issue includes a featured writer, a featured poet and a featured artist. Published three times a year. Estab. 1991. Circ. 500-1,000.

● *The Urbanite* ranked as #19 on the *Writer's Digest* "Fiction 50" list of top markets.

Needs: Experimental, fantasy (dark fantasy), horror, humor/satire, literary, psychic/supernatural/occult, science fiction (soft/sociological). "We love horror, but please, no tired, gore-ridden horror plots. Horror submissions must be subtle and sly. Want more unusual, stylish stories with a sense of 'voice.' Also, more bizarre humor." Upcoming themes: "The Zodiac" and "All Horror" issue. List of upcoming themes available for SASE. Receives over 800 unsolicited mss/month. Accepts 15 mss/issue; 45 mss/year. Publishes ms 6 months after acceptance. **Publishes at least 2-3 new writers/year.** Published work by Basil Copper, Wilum Pugmire, Hertzan Chimera, Marni Scofidio Griffin, Alexa de Monterice and Thomas Ligotti. Length: 500-3,000 words; 2,000 words preferred. Publishes short shorts. Length: 350 words preferred. Also publishes poetry. Sometimes comments on rejected mss.

How to Contact: Include estimated word count, 4 to 5-sentence bio, Social Security number and list of publications. Responds in 1 month to queries; 4 months to mss. Send large SASE for reply and return of ms, or send a stamped, self-addressed business-size envelope and a disposable copy of ms. Sample copy for $5. Guidelines for #10 SASE.

Payment/Terms: Pays 2-3¢/word and 2 contributor's copies. Featured authors receive 3¢/word, 6 contributor's copies and a lifetime subscription to the magazine. Authors of stories in our website's fiction showcase receive $25. Acquires first North American serial rights and nonexclusive rights for public readings.

Advice: "The tone of our magazine is unique, and we strongly encourage writers to read an issue to ascertain the sort of material we accept. The number one reason we reject many stories is because they are inappropriate for our publication: in these cases, it is obvious that the writer is not familiar with *The Urbanite*. We are known for publishing quality horror—work from *The Urbanite* has been reprinted in *Year's Best Fantasy & Horror, The Year's Best Fantastic Fiction*, England's *Best New Horror*, volumes 7 and 8, and on the *Masters of Terror Website*. We want to see more bizarre (yet urbane and thought-provoking) humor. Excellence is priority number one. We simply want stories that are well-written, compelling and unique. Find your own 'voice.' Put your own style and personality into your work!"

[N] ◖ US1 WORKSHEETS, % US1 Poet's Cooperative, P.O. Box 127, Kingston NJ 08528-0127. Editor: Rotating board. **Contact:** Fiction Editor. Magazine: 5½×8½; 72 pages. Publishes poetry and fiction. Annually. Estab. 1973.

Needs: "No restrictions on subject matter or style. Good storytelling or character delineation appreciated. Audience does not include children." **Publishes 1-2 new writers/year.** Recently published work by Alicia Ostriker, Joan Baranow, Lois Marie Harrod, Frederick Tibbetts and Rod Tulloss. Publishes short shorts. Word limit for prose: 2,000 words.

How to Contact: Query first "or send a SAE postcard for reading dates. We read only once a year." Responds to queries "as soon as possible." SASE. Sample copy for $4.

Payment/Terms: Pays in contributor's copies. Acquires one-time rights. Copyright "reverts to author."

[N] ○ ◎ VALLEY GRAPEVINE, Seven Buffaloes Press, Box 249, Big Timber MT 59011. Editor/Publisher: Art Cuelho. Theme: "poems, stories, history, folklore, photographs, ink drawings or anything native to the Great Central Valley of California, which includes the San Joaquin and Sacramento valleys. Focus is on land and people and the oil fields, farms, orchards, Okies, small town life, hobos." Readership: "rural and small town audience, the common man with a rural background, salt-of-the-earth. The working man reads *Valley Grapevine* because it's his personal history recorded." Annually. Estab. 1978. Circ. 500.

Needs: Literary, contemporary, ethnic (Arkie, Okie), regional and western. No academic, religious (unless natural to theme), or supernatural material. Receives approximately 4-5 unsolicited fiction mss each month. Length: 2,500-10,000 (prefers 5,000) words.

How to Contact: Query. SASE for query, ms. Responds in 1 week. Sample copy available to writers for $7.75.

Payment/Terms: Pays 1-2 contributor's copies. Acquires first North American serial rights. Returns rights to author after publication, but reserves the right to reprint in an anthology or any future special collection of Seven Buffaloes Press.

Advice: "Buy a copy to get a feel of the professional quality of the writing. Know the theme of a particular issue. Some contributors have 30 years experience as writers, most 15 years. Age does not matter; quality does."

[N] ○ VICTORY PARK, The Journal of the New Hampshire Institute of Art, 148 Concorde St., Manchester NH 03104. **Contact:** Joe Monninger, fiction editor. Magazine: 6×9; 96-112 pages; 60 lb. bond paper; semi-gloss cover; illustrations; photos. "*Victory Park* is an art-based literary journal covering broad themes each issue for a primarily New England audience." Semiannual. Estab. 1997. Circ. 550. Member: CLMP, AAWP.

Needs: Ethnic/multicultural, experimental, family saga, historical (general), humor satire, literary, mainstream, regional (New England). "No writing for children; translations; pornography, science fiction." Upcoming themes: Fall/Winter issue, deadline September 15; Spring/Summer issue, deadline March 15. Receives 400 unsolicited mss/month. Accepts 1-3 mss/issue; 2-6 mss/year. **Publishes 8-10 new writers/year.** Length: 5,000 words maximum; average length: 3,000 words. Publishes short shorts. Also publishes literary criticism and poetry.

How to Contact: Send complete ms with a cover letter. Accepts submissions by disk. Include estimated word count and brief bio. Accepts simultaneous submissions and multiple submissions. Sample copy for $5. Guidelines for SASE.

Payment/Terms: Pays 2 contributor's copies; additional copies $10. Pays on publication for first North American serial or one-time rights.

Advice: "We're looking for well-written, organic stories that explore the human relationship to art, place, emotion. Avoid the maudlin, the shock/schlock, the coming-of-age story; science fiction, childrens (fables, etc.), pornography."

N ⊘ $ **THE VINCENT BROTHERS REVIEW**, The Vincent Brothers Company, 4566 Northern Circle, Riverside OH 45424-5733. **Editor:** Kimberly Willardson. Magazine: 5½ × 8¼; 88-100 perfect-bound pages; 60 lb. white coated paper; 60 lb. Oxford (matte) cover; b&w illustrations; photos. "We publish at least two theme issues per year. Writers must send SASE for information about upcoming theme issues. Each issue of *TVBR* contains poetry, b&w art, at least six short stories and usually one nonfiction piece. For a mainstream audience looking for an alternative to the slicks." Triannually. Estab. 1988. Circ. 400.

● *TVBR* was ranked #12 in the *Writer's Digest's* "Fiction 50." It has received grants from the Ohio Arts Council for the last six years. The magazine sponsors a fall fiction contest; deadline in October. Contact them for details.

Needs: Adventure, condensed/excerpted novel, contemporary, ethnic, experimental, feminist, historical, humor/satire, literary, mainstream, mystery/suspense (amateur sleuth, cozy, private eye), prose poem, regional, science fiction (soft/sociological), senior citizen/retirement, serialized novel, translations, western (adult, frontier, traditional). "We focus on the way the story is presented rather than the genre of the story. No racist, sexist, fascist, etc. work." Receives 200-250 unsolicited mss/month. Buys 6-10 mss/issue; 30 mss/year. Publishes ms 2-4 months after acceptance. **Publishes 8-12 new writers/year.** Published work by Gordon C. Wilson, Tom D. Ellison, Nikolaus Maack, Laurel Jenkins-Crowe and Ariel Smart. Length: 250-7,000 words; average length: 2,500 words. Maximum 10,000 words for novel condensations. Publishes short shorts. Length: 250-1,000 words. Also publishes literary essays, literary criticism, poetry. Often critiques rejected mss and sometimes recommends other markets.

How to Contact: "Send query letter *before* sending novel excerpts or condensations! *Send only one short story at a time*—unless sending short shorts." Send complete ms. Accepts simultaneous submissions, but not preferred. Responds in 1 month to queries; 3 months to mss with SASE. Sample copy for $6.50; back issues for $4.50. Guidelines for #10 SASE. Reviews novels and short story collections.

Payment/Terms: Pays $15-250 on acceptance for first North American serial rights. $200 first place; $100 second; $50 third for annual short story contest. Charge (discounted) for extras.

Advice: "The best way to discover what *TVBR* editors are seeking in fiction is to read at least a couple issues of the magazine. We are typical readers—we want to be grabbed by the first words of a story and rendered unable to put it down until we've read the last word of it. We want stories that we'll want to read again. This doesn't necessarily mean we seek stories that grab the reader via shock tactics; gross-out factors; surface titillation; or emotional manipulation. Good writers know the difference. Research the markets. Read good writing. Dig deep to find original and compelling narrative voices. It's amazing how many dozens and dozens of stories we receive sound/read so very much alike. We've noticed a marked increase in violent and/or socially ill/deviant-themed stories. Hmm. Is this art imitating life or life imitating art or is it just writers desperate to shock the reader into believing this now passes for originality? Incest stories have been done and done well, but that doesn't mean everyone should write one. Same goes for divorce, death-watch, I-killed-my-boss (spouse, etc.) and got-away-with-it stories."

N $ **VIRGINIA ADVERSARIA**, Empire Publishing Inc., P.O. Box 2349, Poquoson VA 23662. E-mail: empirepub@hotmail.com. **Contact:** Bill Glose, editor. Literary magazine: 7 × 10; 56 pages; some illustrations; photos. Quarterly. Estab. 2000. Circ. 2,500.

Needs: Adventure, ethnic/multicultural, family saga, historical, humor/satire, literary, mainstream, mystery/suspense, regional, romance, thriller/espionage. No erotica or horror. Receives 25 unsolicited mss/month. Accepts 4-8 mss/issue; 20-30 mss/year. Publishes ms 4-7 months after acceptance. Length: 6,000 words; average length: 3,000 words. Publishes short shorts. Also publishes literary essays and poetry. Often comments on rejected mss.

How to Contact: Send complete ms with cover letter. Accepts submissions on disk. Include estimated word count, brief bio and social security number. Responds in 1 month to queries and mss. Send SASE for return of ms. Accepts simultaneous, previously published and multiple submissions. Sample copy for $4.95. Guidelines for SASE.

Payment/Terms: Pays 1¢/word and 1 contributor's copies; additional copies for $3. Pays on publication for one-time rights. Sends galleys to author.

Advice: "Ask yourself if you are excited about the piece you're sending. If you aren't, chances are we won't be either. We want pieces with energy and emotion, something that will leave us saying, Wow! Beginning writers are more successful sending short personal vignettes to the Reflections column."

N ◯ WAR, LITERATURE & THE ARTS: An International Journal of the Humanities, Dept. of English & Fine Arts, United States Air Force Academy, 2354 Fairchild Dr., Suite 6D45, USAF Academy CO 80840-6242. (719)333-3930. Fax: (719)333-3932. E-mail: donald.anderson@usafa.af.mil. Website: www.usafa. edu/dfeng/wla. **Contact:** Donald Anderson, editor. Magazine: 6×9; 200 pages; illustrations; photos. "*WLA* seeks artistic depictions of war from all periods and cultures. From time immemorial, war and art have reflected one another. It is the intersection of war and art that *WLA* seeks to illuminate." Semiannual. Estab. 1989. Circ. 500. Member: Council of Editors of Learned Journals, CLMP.

Needs: No fantasy, science fiction. Accepts 2 mss/issue; 4 mss/year. Publishes ms 1 year after acceptance. Agented fiction 50%. **Publishes 2 new writers/year.** Recently published work by Paul West, Philip Caputo, Robert Morgan and Philip Appleman. Publishes short shorts. Also publishes literary essays, literary criticism and poetry. Sometimes comments on rejected mss.

How to Contact: Send complete ms with a cover letter. Include brief bio and list of publications. Responds in 6 weeks to queries; 6 months to mss. Send a disposable copy of ms and #10 SASE for reply only. Accepts simultaneous submissions "if told." Sample copy for $5. Guidelines on website. Reviews novels, short story collections and nonfiction books of interest to writers. Send review copies to the editor.

Payment/Terms: Pays 2 contributor's copies; additional copies $5. Pays on publication for first North American serial and electronic rights. Sends galleys to author.

Advice: "Our only criterion is literary excellence and fresh language. Our current writer's guidelines are 'Make the world new.' "

⊕ ✓ WASAFIRI, Dept. of English, Queen Mary & Westfield College, University of London, Mile End Road, London EI4NS UK. E-mail: wasafiri@qmw.ac.uk. Website: www.qmw.ac.uk/wasafiri (includes writer's guidelines, editors, content/backlist). **Contact:** Ms. Susheila Nasta, editor. Bi-annual. Circ. 5,000. Publishes 2-3 short stories/issue. "Publishes critical articles, interviews, fiction and poetry by and about African, Asian, Caribbean, Pacific and Black British writers." Length: 500-2,000 words. Pays contributor's copies. "We welcome any writing for consideration which falls into our areas of interest. Work from writers outside Britain is a major part of our interest. Articles should be double-spaced and follow MLA guidelines."

Needs: Literary. No romance, science fiction, fantasy. Would like to see more contemporary, adventurous fiction. Recently published work by Jamal Mahoub, Leila Aboulela and Meera V. Pilay. **Publishes 20% new writers/ year.** Upcoming themes: "Focus on Africa" (spring); "Travel" (autumn).

Advice: "We're looking for clarity of style and nonflowery language. Read extensively, and read and reread your own writing."

❀ ✓ $◯ WASCANA REVIEW OF CONTEMPORARY POETRY AND SHORT FICTION, University of Regina, Regina, Saskatchewan S4S 0A2 Canada. (306)585-4299. E-mail: kathleen.wall@uregina. ca. Website: www.uregina.ca/english/wrhome.htm. Editor: Dr. Kathleen Wall. **Contact:** Dr. Jeanne Shami, fiction editor. "Literary criticism, fiction and poetry for readers of serious fiction." Semiannually. Estab. 1966. Circ. 500.

Needs: Literary and humor. Upcoming themes: "Revisiting the Past: Sources, Inspirations, Intertexts." Buys 8-10 mss/year. Receives approximately 20 unsolicited fiction mss/month. Agented fiction 5%. **Publishes 1-2 new writers/year.** Length: 2,000-6,000 words. Occasionally recommends other markets.

How to Contact: Accepts queries by e-mail. Send complete ms with SASE. Responds in 2 months to mss. Publishes ms an average of 6 months after acceptance. Sample copy for $5. Guidelines with SASE.

Payment/Terms: Pays $3/page for prose; $10/page for poetry; 2 contributor's copies. Pays on publication for first North American rights.

Advice: "Stories are often technically incompetent or deal with trite subjects. Usually stories are longer than necessary by about one-third. Be more ruthless in cutting back on unnecessary verbiage. All approaches to fiction are welcomed by the *Review* editors—but we continue to seek the best in terms of style and technical expertise. As our calls for submission state, the *Wascana Review* continues to seek "short fiction that combines craft with risk, pressure with grace."

◯ WASHINGTON SQUARE, Literary Review of New York University's Creative Writing Program, (formerly Ark/Angel Review), NYU Creative Writing Program, 19 University Place, 3rd Floor, Room 310, New York NY 10003-4556. (212)998-8816. Fax: (212)995-4017. Editor: Jennifer Keller. **Contact:** David Pucell, fiction editor. Editors change each year. Magazine: 5½×8½; 144 pages; photographs. "*Washington Square* is the literary review produced by New York University's Graduate Creative Writing Program. We publish outstanding works of fiction and poetry by the students and faculty of NYU as well as the work of writers across the country." Semiannually. Estab. 1996 (we were previously called Ark/Angel Review, estab. 1987). Circ. 1,000.

Needs: Condensed/excerpted novel, ethnic/multicultural, experimental, literary, mainstream/contemporary. No adventure, children's, erotica. Receives 75 unsolicited mss/month. Accepts 5 mss/issue; 10 mss/year. Publishes ms 3-5 months after acceptance. Agented fiction 20%. Published work by Dika Lam, Sarah Inman, Jessica Anya Blau, Irene Korenfield. Length: 7,000 words maximum; average length: 5,000 words. Publishes short shorts. Also publishes poetry. Sometimes comments on rejected mss.

How to Contact: Send complete ms with a cover letter. Include estimated word count (only put name on first page). Responds in 2 weeks to queries; 6 weeks to mss. Send SASE for reply, return of ms or send a disposable copy of ms. Accepts simultaneous submissions. Sample copy for $6.

Payment/Terms: Pays 3 contributor's copies; additional copies for $6. Acquires first North American serial rights. "Each fall we sponsor a short story contest. Send SASE for more info."

Advice: "We look for compelling, original, outstanding fiction. Please send polished, proofread manuscripts only."

⬤ ▣ WEB DEL SOL, E-mail: editor@webdelsol.com. Website: www.webdelsol.com. **Contact:** Michael Neff, editor. Electronic magazine. "The goal of *Web Del Sol* is to use the medium of the Internet to bring the finest in contemporary literary arts to a larger audience. To that end, *WDS* not only publishes collections of work by accomplished writers and poets, but hosts other literary arts publications on the WWW such as *Ploughshares*, *AGNI, North American Review, Zyzzyva, Flashpoint, 5-Trope, Global City Review, The Literary Review* and *The Prose Poem*.

• *Web Del Sol* ranked #24 on *Writer's Digest*'s "Fiction 50" list of top markets for fiction writers.

Needs: "*WDS* publishes work considered to be literary in nature, i.e., non-genre fiction. *WDS* also publishes poetry, prose poetry, essays and experimental types of writing." Publishes short shorts. **Publishes 30-40 new writers/year.** Recently published work by Robert Olen Butler, Forrest Gander, Xue Di, Michael Buceja, Martine Billen and Roldey Wilson. "Currently, *WDS* published Featured Writer/Poet websites, approximately 15 per year at this time; but hopes to increase that number substantially in the coming year. *WDS* also occasionally publishes individual works and plans to do more of these also."

How to Contact: "Submissions by e-mail from September through November and from January through March only. Submissions must contain some brief bio, list of prior publications (if any), and a short work or prortion of that work, neither to exceed 1,000 words. Editors will contact if the balance of work is required."

Advice: "*WDS* wants fiction that is absolutely cutting edge, unique and/or at a minimum, accomplished with a crisp style and concerning subjects not usually considered the objects of literary scrutiny. Read works in such publications as *Conjunctions* (www.conjunctions.com) and *North American Review* (webdelsol.com/NorthAmRe view/NAR) to get an idea what we are looking for."

Ⓝ 🌐 WESPENNEST, Zeitschrift Fur Brauchbare Texte Und Bilder, Wespennest Zeitschrift und Edition, Rembrandtstrasse 31/4, Vienna 1020 Austria. Phone: +43-1-332-6697. Fax: +43-1-333-2970. E-mail: office@w espennest.at. Website: www.wespennest.at. **Contact:** Andrea Zederbauer. Literary magazine: 230×300mm; 120 pages; some photos. Quarterly. Estab. 1969. Circ. 5,000.

Needs: Experimental, literary, translations. Receives 50 unsolicited mss/year. Recently published work by Friedrich Achleitner, Erwin Riess, and Peter Gorsen. Publishes short shorts. Also publishes literary essays, literary criticism, and poetry.

How to Contact: Query first. Accepts submissions by e-mail, fax or on disk. Include brief bio and list of publications. Responds in 2 months to queries. Reviews novels, short story and nonfiction books. Contact: Thomas Eder.

Payment/Terms: Pays 2 contributor's copies. Acquires one-time rights.

🌿 $ ◨ WEST COAST LINE, A Journal of Contemporary Writing & Criticism, 2027 E. Academic Annex, Simon Fraser University, Burnaby, British Columbia V5A 1S6 Canada. (604)291-4287. Fax: (604)291-4622. E-mail: wcl@sfu.ca. Website: www.sfu.ca/west-coast-line. **Contact:** Roger Farr, managing editor. Magazine: 6×9; 128-144 pages. "Poetry, fiction, criticism—modern and contemporary, North American, experimental, avant-garde, cross-cultural. Readers include academics, writers, students." Triannual. Estab. 1990. Circ. 600.

Needs: Experimental, ethnic/multicultural, feminist, gay, literary. "We do not publish journalistic writing or strictly representational narrative." Receives 30-40 unsolicited mss/month. Accepts 2-3 mss/issue; 3-6 mss/year. Publishes ms 2-10 months after acceptance. **Publishes 3 new writers/year.** Recently published work by Rita Wong, Bruce Andrews, Lisa Roberts, Dodie Bellem and Dan Ferrell. Length: 3,000-4,000 words. Publishes short shorts. Length: 250-400 words. Also publishes literary essays and literary criticism.

How to Contact: Send complete ms with a cover letter. "We supply an information form for contributors." Responds in 3 months. Send SAE with IRCs, not US postage, for return of ms. No simultaneous submissions. Sample copy for $10. Guidelines free.

Payment/Terms: Pays $3-8/page (Canadian); subscription; 2 contributor copies; additional copies for $6-8/copy, depending on quantity ordered. Pays on publication for one-time rights.

MARKET CONDITIONS are constantly changing! If you're still using this book and it is 2002 or later, buy the newest edition of *Novel & Short Story Writer's Market* at your favorite bookstore or order from Writer's Digest Books by calling 1-800-289-0963.

Advice: "Special concern for contemporary writers who are experimenting with, or expanding the boundaries of conventional forms of poetry, fiction and criticism; also interested in criticism and scholarship on Canadian and American modernist writers who are important sources for current writing. We recommend that potential contributors send a letter of enquiry or read back issues before submitting a manuscript."

○ WESTERN HUMANITIES REVIEW, % University of Utah English Dept., 255 S. Central Campus Dr., Room 3500, Salt Lake City UT 84112-0494. (801)581-6070. Fax: (801)581-3392. Editor: Barry Weller. **Contact:** Karen Brennan, fiction editor. Magazine: 95-120 pages. Biannually. Estab. 1947. Circ. 1,200.
Needs: Experimental, literary. Receives 100 unsolicited mss/month. Accepts 3-5 mss/issue; 6-10 mss/year. Does not read mss July-September. Publishes ms within 1-4 issues after acceptance. Published work by Stephen Dixon, Benjamin Wessman, Jeanne Schinto and Wendy Rawlings. Length: open. Publishes short shorts. Also publishes literary essays, literary criticism and poetry. Sometimes comments on rejected mss.
How to Contact: Send complete ms with a cover letter. Include list of publications. Responds in 3 weeks to queries; 6 months to mss. Send SASE for reply, return of ms or send a disposable copy of ms. Accepts simultaneous submissions. Sample copy for $8.
Payment/Terms: Pays 2 contributor's copies; additional copies for $3.50. Acquires first North American serial rights. Sends galleys to author.

○ WESTVIEW, A Journal of Western Oklahoma, Southwestern Oklahoma State University, 100 Campus Dr., Weatherford OK 73096-3098. (580)774-3168. Editor: Fred Alsberg. **Contact:** Fiction Editor. Magazine: 8½×11; 44 pages; 24 lb. paper; slick color cover; illustrations; photos. Biannual. Estab. 1981. Circ. 400.
Needs: Contemporary, ethnic (especially Native American), humor, literary, prose poem. No pornography, violence, or gore. No overly sentimental. "We are particularly interested in writers of the Southwest; however, we accept work of quality from elsewhere." Receives 20 unsolicited mss/month. Accepts 5 mss/issue; 10 mss/year. Publishes ms 3-12 months after acceptance. Published work by Diane Glancy, Wendell Mayo, Jack Matthews, Mark Spencer and Pamela Rodgers. Length: 2,000 words average. Also publishes literary essays, literary criticism, poetry. Occasionally critiques rejected mss.
How to Contact: Accepts simultaneous submissions. Send complete ms with SASE. Responds in 2 months. "We welcome submissions on a 3.5 disk formatted for WordPerfect 5.0, IBM or Macintosh. Please include a hard copy printout of your submission."
Payment/Terms: Pays contributor's copy for first rights.

○ WHETSTONE, Barrington Area Arts Council, P.O. Box 1266, Barrington IL 60011. (847)382-5626. **Contact:** Sandra Berris, Marsha Portnoy and Jean Tolle, co-editors. Magazine: 9×6; 130 pages; heavy cover stock. "We try to publish the best quality nonfiction, fiction and poetry for the educated reader." Annually. Estab. 1984. Circ. 700. Member: CLMP.
● *Whetstone* has received numerous Illinois Arts Council Awards.
Needs: Humor/satire, literary, mainstream/contemporary. "No genre, formula or plot driven fiction." Receives 100 unsolicited mss/month. Accepts 8-10 mss/year. Publishes ms by December 1 of year accepted. Recently published work by Barbara Croft, Ann Joslin Will, James Reed, Leslie Pietzyk and Scott Blackwood. **Publishes 1-2 new writers/year.** Length: 3,000 words average; 6,000 words maximum. Also publishes poetry. Sometimes comments on rejected mss "depending on the work. We often write out the readers' responses if they are helpful. A work gets a minimum of two readers and up to four or five."
How to Contact Send complete ms with a cover letter. Include a 50-word bio. Reports in 3-6 months on mss "or sooner depending on the time of the year." Send SASE for return of ms or reply only. Simultaneous submissions OK. Sample copy (including guidelines) for $5.
Payment/Terms: Pays a variable amount and 2 contributor's copies. Pays on publication for first North American serial rights. Sends galleys to author. "We frequently work with writers on their pieces. All works selected for publication are considered for the $500 Whetstone Prize and the $250 McGrath Award."
Advice: "We like strong characterization and, of course, a coherent plot. We like texture and a story which resonates. Read the journal and other small literary journals. Study good writing wherever you find it. Learn from editorial comments. Read. Read. Read, but do it as a writer reads. We're seeing too many childhood trauma stories. There are only so many of these we can accept."

☑ ○ WHISKEY ISLAND MAGAZINE, Dept. of English, Cleveland State University, Cleveland OH 44115-2440. (216)687-2056. Fax: (216)687-6943. E-mail: whiskeyisland@csuohio.edu. Website: www.csuohio.edu/whiskey_island (includes writer's guidelines, contest guidelines, staff information, history, short fiction, poetry, subscription information). Editors change each year. Magazine of fiction and poetry, including experimental works, with no specific theme. "We provide a forum for new writers and new work, for themes and points of view that are both meaningful and experimental, accessible and extreme." Biannually. Estab. 1978. Circ. 2,500.

Needs: "Would like to see more short shorts, flash fiction." Receives 100 unsolicited fiction mss/month. Accepts 46 mss/issue. Reads submissions September through April only. **Publishes 5-10 new writers/year.** Published Vickie A. Carr and John Fulmer. Length: 5,000 words maximum. Also publishes poetry (poetry submissions should contain no more than 10 pages).

How to Contact: Send complete ms with SASE. Accepts queries/mss by fax. No simultaneous or previously published submissions. Responds in 4 months to mss. Sample copy for $5.

Payment/Terms: Pays 2 contributor's copies. Acquires one-time rights.

Advice: "We seek a different voice, controlled language and strong opening. Childhood memoirs are discouraged."

$ ◻ 🛡 WILLOW SPRINGS, Eastern Washington University, 526 Fifth St., MS-1, Cheney WA 99201. (509)458-6429. **Contact:** Christopher Howell, editor. Magazine: 9×6; 128 pages; 80 lb. glossy cover. "*Willow Springs* publishes literary poetry and fiction of high quality, a mix of new and established writers." Semiannually. Estab. 1977. Circ. 1,200.

● *Willow Springs* is a member of the Council of Literary Magazines and Presses and AWP. The magazine has received grants from the NEA and a CLMP excellence award.

Needs: Parts of novels, short stories, literary, prose poems, poems and translations. "No genre fiction please." Receives 150 unsolicited mss/month. Accepts 2-4 mss/issue; 4-8 mss/year. Does not read mss May 15-September 15. Publishes ms 6-12 months after acceptance. **Published new writers within the last year.** Recently published work by James Grabill, Amy Newman and Jonathan Penne. Length: 5,000-11,000 words. Also publishes literary essays, literary criticism and poetry. Rarely critiques rejected mss.

How to Contact: Send complete ms with cover letter. Include short bio. No simultaneous submissions. Responds in 2 weeks to queries. Sample copy for $5.50.

Payment/Terms: Pays $20-50 and 2 contributor's copies for first North American rights.

Advice: "We hope to attract good fiction writers to our magazine, and we've made a commitment to publish three-four stories per issue. We like fiction that exhibits a fresh approach to language. Our most recent issues, we feel, indicate the quality and level of our commitment."

Ⓝ ◯ WINDHOVER: A Journal of Christian Literature, University of Mary Hardin-Baylor, P.O. Box 8008, Belton TX 76513. (254)295-4564. E-mail: dwnixon@umhb.edu. Website: www.uclj.com (includes excerpts, writer's guidelines, names of editors). **Contact:** Donna Walker-Nixon, editor. Magazine: 6×9; white bond paper. "We want to publish literary fiction by writers of faith." Annual. Estab. 1997. Circ. 500.

Needs: Ethnic/multicultural (general), experimental, family saga, fantasy, historical (general), humor/satire, literary. "No erotica." Receives 30 unsolicited mss/month. Accepts 5 mss/issue; 5 mss/year. Publishes ms 1 year after acceptance. **Publishes 5 new writers/year.** Recently published work by Walt McDonald, James Schaap, Jeanne Murray Walker and David Hopes. Length: 1,500-4,000 words; average length: 3,000 words. Publishes short shorts. Average length: 150 words. Also publishes literary essays and poetry. Sometimes comments on rejected mss.

How to Contact: Send complete ms with a cover letter. Accepts submissions by e-mail. Include estimated word count, brief bio and list of publications. Responds in 3 weeks to queries; 4 months to mss. Send SASE (or IRC) for return of ms or send a disposable copy of ms and #10 SASE for reply only. Accepts simultaneous submissions. Sample copy for $6. Guidelines by e-mail.

Payment/Terms: Pays 2 contributor's copies; additional copies $6. Pays on publication for first rights.

Advice: "Be patient. We have an editorial board and sometimes replies take longer than I like. We particularly look for convincing plot and character development."

◯ WISCONSIN REVIEW, University of Wisconsin, Box 158, Radford Hall, Oshkosh WI 54901. (920)424-2267. **Contact:** Debbie Martin, editor. Editors change every year. Send submissions to "Fiction Editor." Magazine: 6×9; 60-100 pages; illustrations. Literary prose and poetry. Triannual. Estab. 1966. Circ. 2,000.

Needs: Literary and experimental. Receives 30 unsolicited fiction mss each month. **Publishes 3 new writers/year.** Length: up to 5,000 words. Publishes short shorts.

How to Contact: Send complete ms with SASE and cover letter with bio notes. Accepts simultaneous submissions. Responds in 6 months. Publishes ms an average of 1-3 months after acceptance. Sample copy for $4.

Payment/Terms: Pays 2 contributor's copies. Acquires first rights.

Advice: "We look for well-crafted work with carefully developed characters, plots and meaningful situations. The editors prefer work of original and fresh thought when considering a piece of experimental fiction."

✓ $◻ WITNESS, OCC, 27055 Orchard Lake Rd., Farmington Hills MI 48334. (734)996-5732. E-mail: stinepj@umick.edu. **Contact:** Peter Stine, editor. Magazine: 6×9; 192 pages; photos. "*Witness* highlights role of modern writer as witness to his/her times." Semiannually. Estab. 1987. Circ. 3,000.

Needs: Ethnic/multicultural, experimental, literary. Upcoming theme: "Animals in America" (deadline July 15, 2001). List of upcoming themes available for SASE. Receives 250 unsolicited mss/month. Accepts 12 mss/issue; 24 mss/year. Publishes ms 1-2 years after acceptance. Agented fiction 10%. **Publishes 4 new writers/year.**

Recently published works by Thomas Lynch, Joyce Carol Oates and Maxine Kumin. Length: 1,000-7,000 words; average length: 4,000 words. Publishes short shorts. Also publishes literary essays, poetry. Sometimes comments on rejected mss.
How to Contact: Send complete ms with a cover letter. Include estimated word count, list of publications. Responds in 1 month to queries; 3 month to mss. SASE for reply or send disposable copy of ms. Accepts simultaneous submissions. Sample copy for $9. Guidelines free.
Payment/Terms: Pays $6/page for prose; $10/page for poetry and 2 contributor's copies; additional copies $7. Payment on publication. Acquires one-time rights. Sponsors contest: send SASE for information.

THE WORCESTER REVIEW, Worcester Country Poetry Association, Inc., 6 Chatham St., Worcester MA 01609. (508)797-4770. Website: www.geocities.com/Paris/LeftBank/6433. Editor: Rodger Martin. **Contact:** Fiction Editor. Magazine: 6×9; 100 pages; 60 lb. white offset paper; 10 pt. CS1 cover stock; illustrations; photos. "We like high quality, creative poetry, artwork and fiction. Critical articles should be connected to New England." Annually. Estab. 1972. Circ. 1,000.
Needs: Literary, prose poem. "We encourage New England writers in the hopes we will publish at least 30% New England but want the other 70% to show the best of writing from across the US." Receives 20-30 unsolicited fiction mss/month. Accepts 2-4 mss/issue. Publishes ms an average of 6 months to 1 year after acceptance. Agented fiction less than 10%. Published work by Robert Pinsky, Marge Piercy, Wes McNoir and Deborah Diggeso. Length: 1,000-4,000 words; average length: 2,000 words. Publishes short shorts. Also publishes literary essays, literary criticism, poetry. Sometimes critiques rejected mss and recommends other markets.
How to Contact: Send complete ms with cover letter. Responds in 9 months to mss. SASE. Accepts simultaneous submissions if other markets are clearly identified. Sample copy for $6; guidelines free.
Payment/Terms: Pays 2 contributor's copies and honorarium if possible for one-time rights.
Advice: "Send only one short story—reading editors do not like to read two by the same author at the same time. We will use only one. We generally look for creative work with a blend of craftsmanship, insight and empathy. This does not exclude humor. We won't print work that is shoddy in any of these areas."

WRITER TO WRITER, P.O. Box 2336, Oak Park IL 60303. Phone/Fax: (708)763-0193. E-mail: blcroft@aol.com. **Contact:** Barbara Croft, fiction editor. Magazine: 8½×11; 32 pages; illustrations. "*Writer to Writer* is primarily oriented toward essays on writing for published sophisticated writers, but uses one story per issue. *Writer to Writer* exists to provide a forum in which working writers can discuss issues of interest with colleagues." Semiannual. Estab. 1997. Circ. 100.
Needs: Literary. "No genre fiction; and we use almost no humor." Receives 10-12 unsolicited mss/month. Accepts 1 ms/issue; 2 mss/year. Publishes ms 2-3 months after acceptance. **Publishes 1 new writer/year.** Recently published work by Rick Christman and Doris Vidivar. Length: 1,000-3,500 words; average length: 2,000 words. Publishes short shorts. Also publishes literary essays and poetry. Often comments on rejected mss.
How to Contact: Send complete ms with a cover letter. Include brief bio and list of publications. Responds in 3 weeks. Send SASE (or IRC) for return of ms or send a disposable copy of ms. Accepts simultaneous submissions. Sample copy for $5. Guidelines for SASE. Reviews novels, short story collections and nonfiction books of interest to writers. Send review copies to fiction or poetry editor.
Payment/Terms: Pays 2 contributor's copies and free subscription to the magazine; additional copies $5. Pays on publication for one-time rights. Sends galleys to author.
Advice: "Present your work professionally. We like the skillful use of language, fresh approach to themes and characters."

WRITERS' FORUM, University of Colorado at Colorado Springs, Colorado Springs CO 80933-7150. Fax: (719)262-4557. E-mail: kpellow@brain.uccs.edu. **Contact:** C. Kenneth Pellow, editor. "Ten to fifteen short stories or self-contained novel excerpts published once a year along with 25-35 poems. Highest literary quality only: mainstream, avant-garde, with preference to western themes. For small press enthusiasts, teachers and students of creative writing, commercial agents/publishers, university libraries and departments interested in contemporary American literature." Estab. 1974.
Needs: Contemporary, ethnic (Chicano, Native American, not excluding others), literary and regional (West). Want more fiction "with pressing, relevant social/domestic issues and those with fully realized characters." Receives approximately 50 unsolicited fiction mss each month and will publish new as well as experienced authors. **Publishes 1-3 new writers/year.** Recently published work by Toni Graham, Mark Lewandowski, Ben Brooks and Mary Clyde. Length: 1,500-8,500 words. Also publishes literary essays, literary criticism, poetry. Critiques rejected mss "when there is time and perceived merit."
How to Contact: Send complete ms and letter with relevant career information with SASE. Accepts queries by e-mail. Submissions read year-round. Accepts simultaneous submissions. Responds in 2 months to mss. Publishes ms an average of 6 months after acceptance. Sample back copy $8 to *NSSWM* readers. Current copy $10. Make checks payable to "Writers' Forum."
Payment/Terms: Pays 2 contributor's copies. Cover price less 50% discount for extras. Acquires one-time rights.

Advice: "Read our publication. Be prepared for constructive criticism. We especially seek submissions with a strong voice that show immersion in place (trans-Mississippi West) and development of credible characters. Probably the TV-influenced fiction with trivial dialogue and set-up plot is the most quickly rejected. Our format—a 5½×8½ professionally edited and printed paperback book—lends credibility to authors published in our imprint. Never consider a piece 'finished'; keep it in revision; keep it in circulation. Do not get discouraged!"

WRITING FOR OUR LIVES, Running Deer Press, 647 N. Santa Cruz Ave., Annex, Los Gatos CA 95030-4350. (408)354-8604. **Contact:** Janet M. McEwan, editor. Magazine: 5¼×8¼; 80 pages; 70 lb. recycled white paper; 80 lb. recycled cover. "*Writing For Our Lives* is a periodical which serves as a vessel for poems, short fiction, stories, letters, autobiographies, and journal excerpts from the life stories, experiences and spiritual journeys of women. Audience is women and friends of women." Annually. Estab. 1992. Circ. 600.
Needs: Ethnic/multicultural, experimental, feminist, humor/satire, lesbian, literary, translations, "autobiographical, breaking personal or historical silence on any concerns of women's lives. *Women writers only, please.* We have no preannounced themes." Receives 15-20 unsolicited mss/month. Accepts 10 mss/issue; 20 mss/year. Publishes ms 2-24 months after acceptance. **Publishes 3-5 new writers/year.** Recently published work by Sabah Akbur, Anjali Banerjee, Debra Kay Viest, Eison M. Ortiz and Luci Yammamoto. Length: 2,100 words maximum. Publishes short shorts. Also publishes poetry. Rarely comments on rejected mss.
How to Contact: Send complete ms and bio with a cover letter. "Publication date is October. Closing dates for mss are 2/15 and 8/15. Initial report immediate; next report, if any, in 1-18 months." Send 2 SASE's for reply, and one of them must be sufficient for return of ms if desired. Accepts simultaneous and reprint submissions. Sample copy for $6-8 (in California add 8.25% sales tax), $9-11 overseas. Guidelines for #10 SASE.
Payment/Terms: Pays 2 contributor's copies; additional copies for 50% discount and 1 year subscription at 50% discount. Acquires one-time rights in case of reprints and first worldwide English language serial rights.
Advice: "It is in our own personal stories that the real herstory of our time is told. This periodical is a place for exploring the boundaries of our empowerment to break long historical and personal silences. While honoring the writing which still needs to be held close to our hearts, we can begin to send some of our heartfelt words out into a wider circle."

WV, The magazine of Emerging Writers, The Writers Voice of the West Side YMCA, 5 W. 63rd St., New York NY 10023. (212)875-4124. E-mail: wswritersvoice@ymcanyc.org. Website: www.ymcanyc.org (includes full information about our workshops, readings, contests, magazine). **Contact:** David Andrews, managing editor. Magazine: 8½×11; 64 pages; coated paper; glossy cover; illustrations. "*WV* is for writers who are coming into their own. We specifically look for writers who are on the cusp of publishing and also look for non-mainstream writers doing outstanding work." Semiannual. Estab. 1998. Circ. 1,000. Member: CLMP.
Needs: Comics/graphic novels, erotica, experimental, feminist, gay, lesbian, literary. Receives 30 unsolicited mss/month. Accepts 10-12 mss/issue; 20-25 mss/year. Publishes ms 2-6 months after acceptance. **Publishes 15-20 new writers/year.** Recently published work by Gerry Gomez Pearlberg, Caroline Koeppel and Essence Mason. Length: 5,000 words maximum; average length: 3,000-5,000 words. Publishes short shorts. Average length: 500-1,000 words. Also publishes poetry. Sometimes comments on rejected mss.
How to Contact: Send complete ms with a cover letter. Include estimated word count and brief bio. Responds in 6 months to mss. Send a disposable copy of ms and #10 SASE for reply only. Accepts simultaneous submissions and multiple submissions. Sample copy for $5. Guidelines for SASE, by e-mail or on website.
Payment/Terms: Pays 5 contributor's copies and free subscription to the magazine. Pays on publication for one-time rights. Not copyrighted. Sponsors contest. "The Writer's Voice awards are part of our literary arts center. Award winners may be considered for *WV*."
Advice: "We are seeing pieces that straddle the line between fiction and memoir—usually not successfully. Please seriously consider what genre a piece is, and work to the requirements of that form."

XAVIER REVIEW, Xavier University, 1 Drexel Dr., New Orleans LA 70125-1098. (504)485-7944. Fax: (504)485-7197. E-mail: rnlcoll@bellsouth.net (correspondence only—no mss). Managing Editor: Robert E. Skinner. Associate Editor: Richard Collins. Assistant Editor: Patrice Melnick. Production Consultant: Mark Whitaker. **Contact:** Thomas Bonner, Jr., editor. Magazine: 6×9; 75 pages; 50 lb. paper; 12 pt. CS1 cover; photographs. Magazine of "poetry/fiction/nonfiction/reviews (contemporary literature) for professional writers/libraries/colleges/universities." Semiannual. Estab. 1980. Circ. 500.
Needs: Contemporary, ethnic, experimental, historical (general), literary, Latin American, prose poem, Southern, religious, serialized/excerpted novel, translations. Receives 100 unsolicited fiction mss/month. Accepts 2 mss/issue; 4 mss/year. Does not read mss during the summer months. **Publishes 2-3 new writers/year.** Published work by Randall Ivey, Rita Porteau, John Goldfine and Christine Wiltz. Length: 10-15 pages. Publishes literary criticism, literary essays, books of creative writing and poetry. Occasionally critiques rejected mss.
How to Contact: Send complete ms. Include 2-3 sentence bio. SASE. Responds in 10 weeks. Sample copy for $5.
Payment/Terms: Pays 2 contributor's copies.

$ ⊘ THE YALE REVIEW, Yale University/Blackwell Publishers Inc., P.O. Box 208243, New Haven CT 06520-8243. (203)432-0499. Fax: (203)432-0510. Editor: J.D. McClatchy. **Contact:** Susan Bianconi, fiction editor. Magazine: 9¼×6; 180-190 pages; book stock paper; glossy cover; illustrations; photos. "*The Yale Review* is meant for the well-read general reader interested in a variety of topics in the arts and letters, in history, and in current affairs." Quarterly. Estab. 1911. Circ. 7,000.
Needs: Mainstream/contemporary. Receives 80-100 unsolicited mss/month. Accepts 1-3 mss/issue; 7-12 mss/year. Publishes ms 3 months after acceptance. Agented fiction 25%. Published work by Steven Millhauser, Deborah Eisenberg, Jeffrey Eugenides, Sheila Kohler, Joe Ashby Porter, Julie Orringer, John Barth and James McCourt. Publishes short shorts (but not frequently). Also publishes literary essays, poetry.
How to Contact: Send complete ms with a cover letter. Include estimated word count and list of publications. Responds in 1 month to queries; 2 months to mss. Send SASE for reply, return of ms or send a disposable copy of ms. Always include SASE. No simultaneous submissions. Reviews novels and short story collections. Send books to the editors.
Payment/Terms: Pays $300-400 on publication and 2 contributor's copies; additional copies for $8.50. Sends galleys to author. "Awards by the editors; cannot be applied for."
Advice: "We find that the most accomplished young writers seem to be people who keep their ears open to other voices; who read widely."

THE YALOBUSHA REVIEW, The Literary Journal of the University of Mississippi, University of Mississippi, P.O. Box 186, University MS 38677-0186. (601)232-7439. E-mail: yalobush@olemiss.edu. Editors change each year. Magazine: 5½×8½; 130 pages; 60 lb. off-white; card cover stock. "We look for high-quality fiction, poetry, and creative essays; and we seek a balance of regional and national writers." Annually. Estab. 1995. Circ. 500.
Needs: Literary. "No genre or formula fiction." List of upcoming themes available for SASE. Receives 30 unsolicited mss/month. Accepts 3-6 mss/issue. Does not read mss April through August. Published work by Larry Brown, Cynthia Shearer and Eric Miles Williamson. Length: 35 pages maximum; average length: 15 pages average. Publishes short shorts. Also publishes literary essays and poetry. Sometimes comments on rejected mss.
How to Contact: Send complete ms with a cover letter. Responds in 1 month to queries; reporting time to mss varies. Send SASE for reply, return of ms or send a disposable copy of ms. Accepts electronic submissions.
Payment/Terms: Pays 2 contributor's copies. Pays on publication for first North American serial rights.
Advice: "We look for writers with a strong, distinct voice and good stories to tell."

$ ⊘ YELLOW SILK: Journal of Erotic Arts, Verygraphics, Box 6374, Albany CA 94706. (510)644-4188. **Contact:** Lily Pond, editor. "We are interested in nonpornographic erotic literature: joyous, mad, musical, elegant, passionate, real and profound. 'All persuasions; no brutality' is our editorial policy. Literary excellence is a priority; innovative forms are welcomed, as well as traditional ones." Annual. Estab. 1981.
Needs: Erotica, ethnic, experimental, fantasy, feminist/lesbian, gay, humor/satire, literary, prose poem, science fiction and translations. No "blow-by-blow" descriptions. "We're looking for excellent work dealing with human relationships in their erotic, spiritual, emotional and behavioral manifestations." Nothing containing brutality. Accepts 16-20 mss/year. **Publishes 20 new writers/year.** Recently published work by Mary Gordon, Tobias Wolff, Richard Zimler and Jane Smiley. Length: no preference. Rarely critiques rejected mss.
How to Contact: Send complete ms with SASE and include short, *personal* bio notes. No queries. No pre-published material. No simultaneous submissions. Name, address and phone number on each page. Accepts submissions on disk *with* hard copy only. Responds in 6 months to mss. Publishes ms up to 3 years after acceptance.
Payment/Terms: Competitive payment on publication for all periodical and anthology rights for one year following publication, at which time rights revert back to author; and nonexclusive reprint, electronic and anthology rights for the duration of the copyright are held.
Advice: "Read, read, read! Including our magazine—plus Nabokov, Ntozaké Shangé, Rimbaud, Virginia Woolf, William Kotzwinkle, James Joyce. Then send in your story! Trust that the magazine/editor will not rip you off—they don't. As they say, 'find your own voice,' then trust it. Most manuscripts I reject appear to be written by people without great amounts of writing experience. It takes years (frequently) to develop your work to publishable quality; it can take many rewrites on each individual piece. Don't give up! I also see many approaches to sexuality (for my magazine) that are trite and not fresh. The use of language is not original, and the people do not seem real. However, the gems come too, and what a wonderful moment that is. Please don't send me anything with blue eye shadow."

⊘ YEMASSEE, The literary journal of the University of South Carolina, Department of English, University of South Carolina, Columbia SC 29208. (803)777-2085. Fax: (803)777-9064. E-mail: Liskerr@vmisc. edu. Website: www.cla.sc.edu/ENGL/yemassee/index.htm (includes cover of latest issue, origin of name and subscription info). **Contact:** Lisa Kerr, editor. Magazine: 5½×8½; 60-80 pages; 60 lb. natural paper; 65 lb. cover; cover illustration. "We are open to a variety of subjects and writing styles. *Yemassee* publishes primarily fiction and poetry, but we are also interested in one-act plays, brief excerpts of novels, essays, reviews and interviews with literary figures. Our essential consideration for acceptance is the quality of the work." Semiannually. Estab. 1993. Circ. 375.

- Stories from *Yemassee* have been selected for publication in *Best New Stories of the South.*

Needs: Condensed/excerpted novel, ethnic/multicultural, experimental, feminist, gay, historical, humor/satire, lesbian, literary, regional. No romance, religious/inspirational, young adult/teen, children's/juvenile, erotica. Wants more experimental. Receives 10 unsolicited mss/month. Accepts 1-3 mss/issue; 2-6 mss/year. "We hold manuscripts until our reading periods—October 1 to November 15 and March 15 to April 30." Publishes ms 2-4 months after acceptance. **Publishes 6 new writers/year.** Published work by Robert Coover, Chris Railey, Virgil Suarez, and Susan Ludvigson. Length: 4,000 words or less. Publishes short shorts. Also publishes literary essays and poetry.

How to Contact: Send complete ms with a cover letter. Include estimated word count, brief bio, Social Security number and list of publications. Responds in 2 weeks to queries, 4 months after deadlines to mss. Send SASE for reply, return of ms or send disposable copy of ms. Accepts simultaneous submissions. Sample copy for $5. Guidelines for #10 SASE.

Payment/Terms: Pays 2 contributor's copies; additional copies $2.75. All submissions are considered for the *Yemassee* awards—$200 each for the best poetry and fiction in each issue when funding permits. Acquires first rights

Advice: "Our criteria are based on what we perceive as quality. Generally that is work that is literary. We are interested in subtlety and originality, interesting or beautiful language; craft and precision. Read more, write more and revise more. Read our journal and any other journal before you submit to see if your work seems appropriate. Send for guidelines and make sure you follow them."

N ◎ ZAUM, the literary review of Sonoma State University, Sonoma State University/English Department, 1801 E. Cotati Ave., Rohnert Park CA 94928. Website: www.sonoma.edu/English/Zaum. Editor: Leah Greenstein. **Contact:** Scott Green, prose editor. Magazine: perfect bound. "Our journal concentrates on undergraduate and graduate writing that pushes traditional boundaries, is well-crafted, leaning towards avant-garde. All writers must be enrolled as a graduate or undergraduate student at the time of submission." Annual. Estab. 1996. Circ. 500.

Needs: Erotica, experimental, slice-of-life vignettes. No religious work. Accepts 5-7 mss/issue. Publishes ms 6-8 months after acceptance. Length: 2,500 words maximum.

How to Contact: Send complete ms with a cover letter. Accepts submissions by e-mail. Include brief bio. Responds in 2 weeks to queries; 3 months to mss. Guidelines for #10 SASE.

Payment/Terms: Pays 1 contributor's copy. Pays on publication for first North American serial rights.

Advice: "All writers must be enrolled as a graduate or undergraduate student at the time of submission."

☑ $ ◎ ▣ ZOETROPE: All-Story, AZX Publications, 1350 Avenue of the Americas, 24th Floor, New York NY 10019. (212)708-0400. Fax: (212)708-0475. E-mail: info@allstory.com. Website: www.zoetrope-stories .com (includes information on short story contests, online writer's workshop, monthly magazine that publishes the top two submissions each month and chats with writers, editors, etc.) **Contact:** Adrienne Brodeur, editor. Magazine: 10½×14; 60 pages; illustrations; photos. Quarterly. "*Zoetrope: All-Story* bridges the worlds of fiction and film by publishing stories that have been or may be adapted for film." Estab. 1997. Circ. 40,000.

- Library Journal named *Zoetrope: All-Story* one of the ten best new magazines. Stories from *Zoetrope* have received the O. Henry Prize, the Pushcart Prize and have been reprinted in *New Stories from the South* and received honorable mentions in *Best American Short Stories. Zoetrope: All-Story* was ranked #2 on the *Writer's Digest*'s "Fiction 50" list of top markets for fiction writers.

Needs: Literary, mainstream/contemporary, one act plays. No genre fiction or excerpts from larger works. Receives 500 unsolicited mss/month. Accepts 7-8 mss/issue; 28-32 mss/year. Publishes ms 2-6 months after acceptance. Agented fiction 15%. **Publishes 4-6 new writers/year.** Recently published work by Melissa Bank, Heidi Julavits, Ana Menendez, Robert Olen Butler and Francine Prose. Length: 7,000 words maximum.

How to Contact: Send complete manuscript (no more than 2) with a cover letter. Include estimated word count and list of publications. Accepts simultaneous submissions. Sample copy for $5.95 and 9×12 SAE and $1.70 postage. Guidelines for #10 SASE. *No unsolicited submissions from June 1-August 31.*

Payment/Terms: Pays $1,400 for first serial rights and 2 year option on movie rights for unsolicited submissions; $5,000 for commissioned works.

Advice: "We like fiction that really tells a full story. Voices that we haven't heard before and solid prose help a story stand out."

◎ ▣ ZUZU'S PETALS QUARTERLY, P.O. Box 4853, Ithica NY 14852. (607)844-9009. E-mail: info@zu zu.com. Website: www.zuzu.com. **Contact:** Doug DuCap, fiction editor. Internet magazine. "Arouse the senses; stimulate the mind." Estab. 1992.

- See the interview with *Zuzu's Petals Quarterly* fiction editor Doug DuCap on page 39.

Needs: Ethnic/multicultural, feminist, gay, humor/satire, lesbian, literary, regional. No "romance, sci-fi, the banal, TV style plotting." Receives 110 unsolicited mss/month. Accepts 1-3 mss/issue; 4-12 mss/year. Publishes ms 4-6 months after acceptance. Agented fiction 10%. Published work by Norah Labiner, Jean Erhardt and LuAnn Jacobs. Length: 1,000-6,000 words. Publishes short shorts. Length: 350 words. Also publishes literary essays, literary criticism and poetry. Sometimes comments on rejected mss.

How to Contact: Send complete ms with a cover letter. Include estimated word count and list of publications. Responds in 2 weeks to queries; 2 weeks to 2 months to mss. Send SASE (or IRC) for reply, return of ms or send a disposable copy of ms. Accepts simultaneous and electronic submissions. Back issue for $5. Guidelines free. Reviews novels and short story collections. Send to Doug DuCap.

Advice: Looks for "strong plotting and a sense of vision. Original situations and true to life reactions."

☑ $ ▨ ◎ **ZYZZYVA, the last word: west coast writers & artists**, POB 590069, San Francisco CA 94159-0069. (415)752-4393. Fax: (415)752-4391. E-mail: editor@zyzzyva.org. Website: www.zyzzyva.org (includes guidelines, names of editors, selections from current issues, editor's note). Editor: Howard Junker. **Contact:** Fiction Editor. Magazine: 6×9; 208 pages; graphics; photos. "Literate" magazine featuring West Coast writers and artists. Triquarterly. Estab. 1985. Circ. 4,000.

● *Zyzzyva* ranked #18 on *Writer's Digest*'s "Fiction 50" list of top markets for fiction writers, and was recently profiled in *Poet's & Writer's* magazine.

Needs: Contemporary, experimental, literary, prose poem. West Coast US writers only. Receives 400 unsolicited mss/month. Accepts 5 fiction mss/issue; 20 mss/year. Agented fiction: 10%. **Publishes 20 new writers/year.** Recently published work by Robert Glück, Joy Harjo and Dorianne Laux. Length: varies. Also publishes literary essays.

How to Contact: Send complete ms. "Cover letters are of minimal importance." Responds in 2 weeks to mss. SASE. No simultaneous or reprint submissions. Sample copy for $5. Guidelines on masthead page.

Payment/Terms: Pays $50 on acceptance for first North American serial rights.

Advice: "Keep the faith."

Small Circulation Magazines

This section of *Novel & Short Story Writer's Market* contains general interest, special interest, regional and genre magazines with circulations of under 10,000. Although these magazines vary greatly in size, theme, format and management, the editors are all looking for short stories for their respective publications. Their specific fiction needs present writers of all degrees of expertise and interests with an abundance of publishing opportunities.

Although not as high-paying as the large-circulation consumer magazines, you'll find some of the publications listed here do pay writers 1-5¢/word or more. Also unlike the big consumer magazines, these markets are very open to new writers and relatively easy to break into. Their only criteria is that your story be well written, well presented, and suitable for their particular readership.

DIVERSITY IN OPPORTUNITY

Among the diverse publications in this section are magazines devoted to almost every topic, every level of writing and every type of writer. Some of the markets listed here publish fiction about a particular geographic area or by authors who live in that locale. Even more specialized editorial needs than genre and regional fiction include *The Pipe Smoker's Ephemeris* and *Rosebud, For People Who Enjoy Writing*.

SELECTING THE RIGHT MARKET

Your chance for publication begins as you zero in on those markets most likely to be interested in your work. If you write genre fiction, check out specific sections for lists of magazines publishing in that genre (mystery, page 57; romance, page 68; science fiction/fantasy & horror, page 78). For other types of fiction, begin by looking at the Category Index starting on page 613. If your work is more general, or, in fact, very specialized, you may wish to browse through the listings, perhaps looking up those magazines published in your state or region. Also check the Zine section for other specialized and genre publications.

In addition to browsing through the listings and using the Category Index, check the ranking codes at the beginning of listings to find those most likely to be receptive to your work. This is especially true for beginning writers, who should look for magazines that say they are especially open to new writers (□) and for those giving equal weight to both new and established writers (◐). The ★ symbol indicates markets that offer writers greater opportunities by buying a large amount of freelance/unagented manuscripts, or by otherwise being very open to new writers. For more explanation about these codes, see the inside front and back covers of this book.

Once you have a list of magazines you might like to try, read their listings carefully. Much of the material within each listing carries clues that tell you more about the magazine. The "Quick Start" Guide to Publishing Your Fiction starting on page 2 describes in detail the listing information common to all the markets in our book.

The physical description appearing near the beginning of the listings can give you clues about the size and financial commitment to the publication. This is not always an indication of quality, but chances are a publication with expensive paper and four-color artwork on the cover has more prestige than a photocopied publication featuring a clip art self-cover. For more information on some of the paper, binding and printing terms used in these descriptions, see Printing and Production Terms Defined on page 608.

FURTHERING YOUR SEARCH

It cannot be stressed enough that reading the listing is only the first part of developing your marketing plan. The second part, equally important, is to obtain fiction guidelines and read the actual magazine. Reading copies of a magazine helps you determine the fine points of the magazine's publishing style and philosophy. There is no substitute for this type of hands-on research.

Unlike commercial magazines available at most newsstands and bookstores, it requires a little more effort to obtain some of the magazines listed here. You may need to send for a sample copy. We include sample copy prices in the listings whenever possible. See The Business of Fiction Writing for the specific mechanics of manuscript submission. Above all, editors appreciate a professional presentation. Include a brief cover letter and send a self-addressed envelope for a reply or a self-addressed envelope in a size large enough to accommodate your manuscript, if you would like it returned. Be sure to include enough stamps or International Reply Coupons (for replies from countries other than your own) to cover your manuscript's return. Many publishers today appreciate receiving a disposable manuscript, eliminating the cost to writers of return postage and saving editors the effort of repackaging manuscripts for return.

Most of the magazines listed here are published in the US. You will also find some English-speaking markets from around the world. These foreign publications are denoted with a 🌐 symbol at the beginning of listings. To make it easier to find Canadian markets, we include a 🍁 symbol at the start of those listings.

ABERRATIONS, Science Fiction, Fantasy and Horror, Sirius Fiction, P.O. Box 460430, San Francisco CA 94146-0430. Editor: Richard Blair. Magazine: digest size; 64 pages; 80 lb. pulp paper; 40 lb. enamel cover; illustrations; photos. "A magazine of speculative stories running the gamut from pulp-era science fiction/fantasy/horror of the 30s and 40s to the experimental and literary work of today." Monthly. Estab. 1992. Circ. 1,500.
Needs: Experimental, fantasy (science fantasy, sword and sorcery), horror, science fiction (hard science, soft/sociological). No true-crime stories. Receives 250-300 unsolicited mss/month. Accepts 10 mss/issue; 120 mss/year. Publishes ms 1 year after acceptance. Agented fiction 1-2%. Recently published work by Paul Di Filippo, Don Webb, Carrie Martin, T. Jackson King, Lois Tilton, Gerard Daniel Houarner, Kent Brewster, Uncle River and Brian Plante. Length: 1-8,000 words. Publishes short shorts. Also publishes literary essays and literary criticism. Sometimes comments on rejected mss.
How to Contact: Send complete ms with a cover letter. Include estimated word count. Responds in 2 weeks to queries; 4 months to mss. Send SASE for reply, return of ms or send disposable copy of ms. No simultaneous submissions. Sample copy for $4.50. Guidelines for #10 SASE. Reviews novels and short story collections. Send books to "John F.D. Taff, Reviews Editor."
Payment/Terms: Pays ½ cent/word plus two contributor's copies for first English language serial rights.
Advice: "We like stories that take chances (whether this be through characterization, plotting or structuring) as well as those that take a more traditional approach to sf/f/h."

🔳 🚫 ◎ THE ABIKO QUARTERLY WITH JAMES, Finnegan's Wake Studies, ALP Ltd., 8-1-7 Namiki, Abiko, Chiba Japan 270-1165. (011)81-471-69-7319. E-mail: alp@mil.net.ne.jp. Website: www.user3.all net.ne.jp/hce/. **Contact:** Annie Bilton, senior reader. Magazine: B5; 350 pages; illustrations; photos. "We primarily publish James Joyce *Finnegan's Wake* essays, The James Joyce Fiction Contest Award winners, The Thelma & Charlie Willis Memorial Poetry Prize winners and Japanese writers and expatriates here in Japan and abroad." Annual. Estab. 1989. Circ. 500. "Due to the economy in Japan, we request that a writer pay $15 postage and handling fees to receive 1 complimentary copy."
Needs: Experimental (in the vein of James Joyce), literary, inspirational. Also essays on James Joyce's *Finnegan's Wake* from around the world. Receives very few unsolicited mss/month. Accepts 12 mss/issue. Recently published work by Annie Bilton, John Cross, L. Friedman and M. Garrison. Length: 5,000 words maximum; average length: 15 pages. Publishes short shorts. Average length: 3-4 pages. Also publishes literary essays (James Joyce *Finnegan's Wake* essays), literary criticism and poetry. Always comments on rejected mss.
How to Contact: Send complete ms with a cover letter. Include brief bio and artwork. Responds in 1 week to queries; 3 months to mss. Send a disposable copy of ms and #10 SASE for reply only. Accepts multiple submissions. Sample copy for $20. Guidelines for SASE. "Do not send American postage. It won't fly in Japan." Reviews novels, short story collections and nonfiction books of interest to writers. Send review copies to Brian Daldorph % of ALP Ltd.
Payment/Terms: Pays 1 contributor's copy; additional copies $25. Copyright reverts to author upon publication. "We require camera-ready copy. The writer is welcome to accompany it with appropriate artwork."

N 🌐 $ 💿 🖥 **ADHOCITY.COM, 500 Words**, Adhoc Publishing Limited, 35 Parkside, Cambridge CB1 1JE United Kingdom. 01223 568960. Fax: 01223 509963. E-mail: 500w@adhoc-guides.com. Website: www.adhocity.com. **Contact:** Colin Greenland, fiction editor. Online magazine with quarterly paper magazine which includes highlights from the website: 72 pages; illustrations; photos. "We only publish 500-word stories in the fiction section of our site." Estab. 1999.

• Finalist for 1998 Financial Times Business Website of the Year.

Needs: "We will consider any subject if well written—*500 words only.*" Receives 50-100 unsolicited mss/ month. Accepts 1 ms/month; 12 mss/year. Publishes ms 1 month after acceptance. **Publishes 3 new writers/ year.** Recently published work by Stephen D. Rogers, Colin Greenland and Ceri Jordan. Length: 480-520 words; average length: 500 words. Publishes short shorts. Average length: 500 words.

How to Contact: "E-mail and ask for guidelines or visit section of website 'short story.' " Include estimated word count and brief bio. Accepts simultaneous submissions, previously published work and multiple submissions. Sample copy and guidelines on website.

Payment/Terms: Pays £200 (UK sterling). Pays on publication for first British serial rights.

Advice: "Read the guidelines on www.adhocity.com (click on short story button)."

N ⚪ **ALEMBIC**, Singularity Rising Press, P.O. Box 28416, Philadelphia PA 19149. (610)460-0588. E-mail: alembic33@yahoo.com. **Contact:** Larry Farrell, editor. Magazine: 8½×11; 64 pages; bond paper; illustrations. "*Alembic* is a literary endeavor magically bordering intersecting continua." The magazine publishes poems, stories and art. Quarterly. Estab. 1999. Circ. 100.

Needs: Fantasy (space fantasy, sword and sorcery), horror (dark fantasy, futuristic, psychological, supernatural), literary, mystery/suspense (amateur sleuth, cozy, police procedural, private eye/hardboiled), science fiction (hard science/technological, soft/sociological), thriller/espionage. No children's, religious, romance. Receives 15 unsolicited mss/month. Accepts 6 mss/issue; 24 mss/year. Publishes ms 6 months after acceptance. **Publishes 15 new writers/year.** Recently published work by Jebediah E. Cornblack III and F. Colin Spross. Length: 1,000-5,000 words; average length: 3,000 words. Publishes short shorts. Average length: 1,000 words. Also publishes poetry. Often comments on rejected mss.

How to Contact: Send complete ms with a cover letter. Include estimated word count, brief bio and list of publications. Responds in 3 weeks to queries; 3 months to mss. Accepts multiple submissions. Sample copy for $3.50. Guidelines for SASE or by e-mail. Reviews novels, short story collections and nonfiction books of interest to writers.

Payment/Terms: Pays 1 contributor's copy; additional copies $2. Pays on publication for first North American serial rights. Sends galleys to author. Not copyrighted. Sponsors contest. Send for guidelines.

Advice: "Write, rewrite and rewrite again. After all that, keep on submitting. A rejection never killed anyone."

✅ ⚪ **ANTHOLOGY**, Inkwell Press, P.O. Box 4411, Mesa AZ 85211-4411. (480)461-8200. E-mail: lisa@ink wellpress.com. Website: www.anthologymagazine.com (includes guidelines and links to literary sites). **Contact:** Elissa Harris, prose editor. Magazine: 8½×11; 20-28 pages; 20 lb. paper; 60-100 lb. cover stock; illustrations; photos. "Our intended audience is anyone who likes to read." Bimonthly. Estab. 1994. Circ. 500-1,000.

Needs: Adventure, children's/juvenile (5-9 and 10-12 years); fantasy (science fantasy, sword and sorcery), humor/satire, literary, mystery/suspense (amateur sleuth, police procedural, private eye/hardboiled), science fiction (hard science, soft/sociological). *Anthology* maintains an ongoing series of short stories based in the Mythical City of Haven. Receives 10-20 unsolicited mss/month. Accepts 2 mss/issue; 12 mss/ year. Publishes ms 6-12 months after acceptance. **Publishes 8-10 new writers/year.** Recently published work by Claudine R. Moreau and Claire Mulligan. Length: 3,000-6,000 words average; Haven stories 3,000-5,000 words. Publishes short shorts. Also publishes poetry.

How to Contact: Send complete ms with a cover letter. Include estimated word count. Responds in 1 month to queries; 2 months to mss. Send SASE for reply, return of ms or send disposable copy of ms. Accepts simultaneous, reprint and electronic (disk or modem) submissions. Sample copy for $3.95. Guidelines for 4½×9½ SASE. Reviews chapbooks and audio books.

Payment/Terms: Pays 1 contributor's copy; additional copies $2. Haven stories pay $5. Acquires one-time rights. *Anthology* retains rights to reprint any Haven story; however, author may submit the story elsewhere for simultaneous publication.

Advice: "Is there passion in the writing? Is there forethought? Will the story make an emotional connection to the reader? Send for guidelines and a sample issue. If you see that your work would not only fit into, but add something to *Anthology*, then send it."

$ ⚪ **ARCHAEOLOGY**, P.O. Box 1264, Huntington WV 25714. Magazine: 8½×11; 24 pages; illustrations; photos. Authors are "archaeology writers who have a message for children and young adults." Quarterly. Estab. 1993. Circ. 9,000.

Needs: Children's/juvenile (adventure, historical, mystery, preschool, series), historical, mystery/suspense (procedural), young adult/teen (adventure, historical, mystery/suspense, series, western), archaeology. Receives 25 unsolicited mss/month. Accepts 1-2 mss/issue; 12-16 mss/year. Publishes ms 1-3 months after acceptance. Published work by Linda Lyons and Rocky Nivison. Length: 500 words minimum. Also publishes literary essays, criticism and poetry. Always comments on rejected ms.

How to Contact: Send complete ms with a cover letter. Include estimated word count, bio and list of publications. Responds in 1 month to queries; 2 months to mss. Send SASE for reply, return of ms or send disposable copy of ms. Accepts simultaneous and reprint submissions. Sample copy for $3.50. Guidelines free.

Payment/Terms: Pays 1¢/word maximum and 2 contributor's copies. Pays on acceptance for first rights. Sends prepublication galleys to author.

Advice: "Guidelines are the best reference to knowing if a manuscript or filler is acceptable for a magazine. Writers' time and resources can be saved by submitting their work to publications that need their style of writing. Guidelines for *Archaeology* are sent for a SASE."

$ ☑ **ARTEMIS MAGAZINE, Science and Fiction for a Space-Faring Age**, 1380 East 17th St., Suite 201, Brooklyn NY 11230-6011. E-mail: magazine@lrcpubs.com. Website: www.lrcpublications.com (includes writer's guidelines, names of editors, reviews, author information, letters, news, etc.). **Contact**: Ian Randal Strock, editor. Magazine: 8½×11; 64 pages; glossy cover; illustrations. "The magazine is an even mix of science and fiction. We are a proud sponsor of the Artemis Project, which is constructing a commercial, manned moon base." Quarterly. Estab. 1999.

Needs: Adventure, science fiction, thriller/espionage. Receives 200 unsolicited mss/month. Accepts 4-7 mss/issue. Publishes ms 3-12 months after acceptance. Recently published work by Joseph J. Lazzaro, Fred Lerner, Ron Collins, Linda Dunn, Stanley Schmidt and Jack Williamson. Length: 1-15,000 words; average length: 2,000-8,000 words. Publishes short shorts. Also publishes poetry. Often comments on rejected ms.

How to Contact: Send complete ms with a cover letter. Include estimated word count, 1-3-paragraph bio, Social Security number, list of publications. Responds in 1 month to mss. Send SASE for reply, return of ms or send a disposable copy of ms. Sample copy for $5 and a 9×12 SAE with 4 first-class stamps. Guidelines for SASE. Reviews novels, short story collections and nonfiction books of interest to writers and readers. Send books to editor.

Payment/Terms: Pays 3-5¢/word and 3 contributor's copies on acceptance for first rights. Sends prepublication galleys to author.

Advice: "*Artemis Magazine* publishes the best science and science fiction based, in some way, on lunar development. The more closely related to the Project the better, but do not sacrifice a good story or informative article simply to get in a reference to the Project. Present lunar development in a positive, entertaining manner. The moon is an attractive goal, to which people want to go. Please remember that we are part of the Artemis Project, so stories about colonists bashing the company that got them there probably won't make the cut."

N 🌐 **$ AUREALIS**, Australian Fantasy and Science Fiction, P.O. Box 2164, Mt. Waverley, Victoria 3149 Australia. Website: aurealis.hl.net (includes writer's guidelines, names of editors, interviews with authors, chat line, competitions, market news, online ordering, online bookshop). **Contact:** Dirk Strasser and Stephen Higgins, fiction editors. Zine specializing in science fiction, fantasy and horror. Semiannually. Circ. 2,500.

Needs: Publishes 7 stories/issue: science fiction, fantasy and horror short stories. **Publishes 4 new writers/year.** Published work by Terry Dowling and Sean McMullen. Length: 2,000-8,000 words.

How to Contact: "No reprints; no stories accepted elsewhere. Send one story at a time." Guidelines for SAE with IRC. Sample copy for $10 (Aus).

Payment/Terms: Pays 2-6¢ (Aus)/word and contributor's copy.

Advice: "Read the magazine. It is available in the UK and North America."

N $ ☑ ◎ **THE BARK, The Modern Dog Culture Magazine**, The Bark, Inc., 2810 Eighth, Berkeley CA 94710. (510)704-0827. Fax: (510)704-0933. E-mail: editor@thebark.com. Website: www.thebark.com. **Contact:** Claudia Kawczynska, editor-in-chief. Magazine: 8×10; 80 pages; matte gloss paper; illustrations; photos. "We are the only cultural/literary arts publication for the modern dog lover. We explore the unique bond between ourselves and our dogs." Quarterly. Estab. 1997. Circ. 60,000. Member: IPA.

Needs: Adventure, children's/juvenile (adventure, animal), comics/graphic novels, feminist, gay, humor/satire, literary, short story collections. Receives 15 unsolicited mss/month. Publishes ms 6 months after acceptance. **Publishes 12 new writers/year.** Recently published work by Cynthia Heimel, Caroline Knapp and Paul Auster. Length: 500-2,000 words; average length: 1,200 words. Publishes short shorts. Also publishes literary essays and poetry.

READ 'THE BUSINESS OF FICTION WRITING' section for information on manuscript preparation, mailing tips, rights and more.

How to Contact: Query with clips of published work. Accepts submissions by e-mail and disk. Include estimated word count, brief bio, Social Security number and list of publications. Responds in 1 month to queries; 4 months to mss. Send a disposable copy of ms and #10 SASE for reply only. Accepts simultaneous submissions, previously published work and multiple submissions. Sample copy for $5. Guidelines for SASE or by e-mail. Reviews novels, short story collections and nonfiction books of interest to writers.
Payment/Terms: Pays $100, free subscription to the magazine and contributor's copies. Pays on publication for first rights. Sends galleys to author.

$ ⬛ **BASEBALL**, P.O. Box 1264, Huntington WV 25714. Magazine: 8½×11; illustrations; photos. Quarterly. Estab. 1998. Circ. 9,000.
Needs: Children's/juvenile (sports), young adult/teen (sports), baseball. Length: 500 words minimum. Also publishes literary essays, criticism and poetry. Often comments on rejected ms.
How to Contact: Send complete ms with a cover letter. Include estimated word count, bio and list of publications. Responds in 1 month to queries; 2 months to mss. Send SASE for reply, return of ms or send disposable copy of ms. Accepts simultaneous and reprint submissions. Sample copy for $3.50. Guidelines free.
Payment/Terms: Pays 1¢/word maximum and contributor's copies. Pays on acceptance for first rights. Sends prepublication galleys to author.

N BEGINNERS, A Magazine for the Novice Writer, Beginnings Publishing, P.O. Box 92-N, Shirley NY 11967. (631)924-7824. E-mail: scbeginnings@juno.com. Website: www.scbeginnings.com (includes guidelines, subscriptions, reader's reviews, bulletin board for posting work for critiquing). **Contact:** Jenine Boisits, editor. Magazine: 8½×11; 54 pages; matte; glossy cover; some photos. "We are a magazine dedicated to the novice writer. We only publish work by beginners. We do accept articles by professionals pertaining to the craft of writing. We have had many new writers go on to be published elsewhere after being featured in our magazine." Semiannual. Estab. 1998. Circ. 1,000.
Needs: Adventure, family saga, mystery/suspense (amateur sleuth), romance (contemporary), science fiction (soft/sociological). No erotica or horror. Receives 125 unsolicited mss/month. Accepts 9 mss/issue; 18-20 mss/year. Publishes ms 3-4 months after acceptance. **Publishes 100% new writers/year.** Recently published work by Ann F. Shalaski, Patricia Woo, Lois Peterson. Length: 3,000 words; average length: 2,500. Publishes short shorts. Average length: 900 words. Also publishes poetry. Often comments on rejected mss.
How to Contact: Send complete ms with cover letter. Accepts submissions by e-mail. Include estimated word count and brief bio. Responds in 6 weeks to mss. Send disposable copy of ms and #10 SASE for reply only; however, will accept SASE for return of ms. Accepts simultaneous submissions and previously published submissions. Sample copy for $4. Guidelines for SASE, e-mail or on website.
Payment/Terms: Pays 1 contributor's copy; additional copies $3. Pays on publication for first North American serial rights.
Advice: "Originality, presentation, proper grammar and spelling a must. Non-predictable endings. Many new writers confuse showing vs. telling. Writers who have that mastered stand out. Study the magazine. Check and double check your work. Original storylines, well thought-out, keep up a good pace. Presentation is important, too! Rewrite, rewrite!"

⬜ ◎ **BLACKFIRE**, BLK Publishing Co., P.O. Box 83912, Los Angeles CA 90083-0912. (310)410-0808. Fax: (310)410-9250. E-mail: newsroom@blk.com. Website: www.blk.com. **Contact:** Alan Bell, editor. Magazine: 8⅛×10⅞; 68 pages; color glossy throughout; illustrations; photos. Bimonthly magazine featuring the erotic images, experiences and fantasies of black gay and bisexual men. Estab. 1992.
Needs: Ethnic/multicultural, gay. No interracial stories or idealized pornography. Accepts 4 mss/issue. Published work by Terrance 'Kenji' Evans, Geoff Adams, Shawn Hinds, Stefan Collins and Robert Wesley. Publishes short shorts. Also publishes poetry.
How to Contact: Query first, query with clips of published work or send complete ms with a cover letter. Should include bio (3 sentences). Send a disposable copy of ms. Accepts simultaneous and electronic submissions. Sample copy for $7. Guidelines free.
Payment/Terms: Pays $50-100, 5 contributor's copies. Acquires first North American serial rights and right to anthologize.
Advice: "*Blackfire* seeks erotic material of the highest quality. The most important thing is that the work be erotic and that it features black gay men or themes. Study the magazine to see what we do and how we do it. Some fiction is very romantic, other is highly sexual. Most articles in *Blackfire* cater to black gay/bisexual men between these two extremes."

✅ **$** ⬛ 🔲 **BOY'S QUEST**, The Bluffton News Publishing & Printing Co., P.O. Box 227, Bluffton OH 45817-0227. (419)358-4610. Fax: (419)358-5027. Website: www.boysquest.com (includes samples of magazine content, order form). **Contact:** Marilyn Edwards, editor. Magazine: 7×9; 50 pages; enamel paper; illustrations; photos. "Magazine for boys 5-13, wholesome, encouraging kindness, helping others, etc." Bimonthly. Estab. 1994.

• *Boy's Quest* received an EDPRESS Distinguished Achievement Award for Excellence in Educational Journalism, and a Silver Award-Gallery of Superb Printing.

Needs: Children's/juvenile (5-9 years, 10-13 years) adventure, ethnic/multicultural, historical, sports. No violence, romance, fads. "We would like to see more wholesome adventure and humorous stories." Upcoming themes: disasters, achievers, racing, water, inventions, bugs, horses, space, flying, boats, forest animals, and frogs, turtles, snakes. List of upcoming themes available for SASE. Receives 300-400 unsolicited mss/month. Accepts 20-40 mss/year. Agented fiction 2%. **Publishes 40 new writers/year.** Recently published work by Eve Marar, John Hillman, Marcie Tichenor, John Thomas Waite, Carolyn Mott Ford and Robert Redding. Length: 500 words maximum; average length: 300-500 words. Publishes short shorts. Length: 250-400 words. Also publishes poetry. Always comments on rejected mss.

How to Contact: Send complete ms with a cover letter. Include estimated word count, 1 page bio, Social Security number, list of publications. Responds in 2-4 weeks to queries; 6-10 weeks to mss. Accepts simultaneous, multiple and reprint submissions. Sample copy for $4. Guidelines for #10 SASE. Reviews novels and short story collections.

Payment/Terms: Pays 5¢/word and 1 contributor's copy; additional copies $4, $2.50 for 10 or more. Pays on publication for first North American serial rights.

$◐ BRIDAL GUIDES, P.O. Box 1264, Huntington WV 25714. Magazine: 8½×11; illustrations; photos. Quarterly. Estab. 1993. Circ. 9,000.

Needs: Children's/juvenile, romance, young adult/teen (romance); the emphasis is on weddings. Receives 25 unsolicited mss/month. Accepts 1-4 mss/issue; 24-30 mss/year. Publishes ms 1-3 months after acceptance. Length: 500 words minimum. Also publishes literary essays, criticism and poetry. Always comments on rejected ms.

How to Contact: Send complete ms with a cover letter. Include estimated word count, bio and list of publications. Responds in 1 month to queries; 2 months to mss. Send SASE for reply, return of ms or send disposable copy of ms. Accepts simultaneous and reprint submissions. Sample copy for $3.50. Guidelines free.

Payment/Terms: Pays 1¢/word and 2 contributor's copies. Pays on acceptance for first rights. Sends prepublication galleys to author.

◪ ✓ $◐ ◎ CHRISTIAN COURIER, Reformed Faith Witness, Unit 4, 261 Martindale Rd., St. Catharines, Ontario L2W 1A1 Canada. (905)682-8311. Fax: (905)682-8313. E-mail: cceditor@aol.com. **Contact:** Harryder Nederlander, editor. Tabloid; 11½×14; 20 pages; newsprint; illustrations; photos. Bi-weekly. Estab. 1945. Circ. 4,000.

Needs: Historical, religious/inspirational, senior citizen/retirement, sports. No "sentimental 'religious' stuff; superficial moralizing." Receives 5-10 unsolicited mss/month. Accepts 12 mss/year. Does not read mss from the end of July through early August. Publishes ms within a month after acceptance. Length: no minimum; 1,400 words maximum; average length: 1,200 words. Publishes short shorts. Length 500 words. Also publishes literary essays (if not too technical), literary criticism and poetry.

How to Contact: Send complete ms with a cover letter. Include word count and bio (100 words maximum). Responds in 6 weeks to mss. Send a disposable copy of ms. Accepts simultaneous, reprint and electronic submissions. Sample copy free. Guidelines for SASE.

Payment/Terms: Pays $25-60 on publication and 1 contributor's copy (on request). Acquires one-time rights.

Advice: Looks for work "geared to a Christian audience but reflecting the real world, real dilemmas, without pat resolutions—written in an engaging, clear manner."

ℕ ○ THE CIRCLE MAGAZINE, Circle Publications, 1325 S. Cocalico Rd., Denver PA 17517. Phone/fax: (610)670-7017. E-mail: circlemag@aol.com. Website: www.circlemagazine.com (includes guidelines, poetry and fiction not in print issue, links, etc.) **Contact:** Penny Talbert, editor. Magazine: 8½×5½; 40-48 pages; white offset paper; illustrations; photos. *"The Circle* is an eclectic mix of culture and subculture. Our goal is to provide the reader with thought-provoking reading that they remember." Quarterly.

Needs: Adventure, experimental, humor/satire, literary, mainstream, mystery/suspense, New Age, psychic/supernatural/occult, romance, science fiction, thriller/espionage. No religious fiction. Receives 50 unsolicited mss/month. Accepts 3-5 mss/issue; 12-20 mss/year. Publishes ms 1-4 months after acceptance. Recently published work by David McDaniel, Bart Stewart, Ace Boggess and Stephen Forney. Length: 2,000-6,000 words; average length: 3,500 words. Publishes short shorts. Average length: 1,200 words. Also publishes literary essays, literary criticism and poetry. Sometimes comments on rejected mss.

How to Contact: Send complete ms with a cover letter. Accepts submissions by e-mail, fax and disk. Include estimated word count, brief bio and list of publications. Responds in 1 month to queries; 4 months to mss. Send SASE (or IRC) for return of ms or send a disposable copy of ms and #10 SASE for reply only. Accepts simultaneous submissions, previously published work and multiple submissions. Sample copy for $4. Guidelines on website.

Payment/Terms: Pays 1 contributor's copy; additional copies $4. Pays on publication for one-time and electronic rights.

Advice: "The most important thing is that submitted fiction keeps our attention and interest. The most typical reason for rejection: bad endings! Proofread your work and send it in compliance with our guidelines."

$ ◎ ⚑ CLUBHOUSE MAGAZINE, Focus on the Family, 8605 Explorer Dr., Colorado Springs CO 80920. (719)531-3400, ext. 1860. Fax: (719)531-3499. **Contact:** Jesse Florea, editor. Associate Editor: Annette Brashler Bourland. Magazine: 24 pages; illustrations; photos. Christian children's magazine. Monthly. Estab. 1987. Circ. 126,000.

• *Clubhouse Magazine* has received Evangelical Press Association awards for fiction and art.

Needs: Adventure, children's/juvenile (8-12 years), religious/inspirational, sports. No animal fiction or where the main character is not between the ages of 8-12 and dealing with issues appropriate to the age level. Would like to see more historical fiction with Bible-believing/Christian protagonist. Receives 100 unsolicited mss/month. Accepts 1 ms/issue; 12 mss/year. **Publishes 8 new writers/year.** Recently published work by Nancy N. Rue, Sigmund Brouwer and Katherine Bond. Length: 500-1,200 words average. Publishes short shorts.

How to Contact: Send complete ms with a cover letter. Include estimated word count, Social Security number and list of publications. Responds in 6 weeks to queries and mss. Send SASE for reply, return of ms or send disposable copy of ms. Accepts simultaneous submissions. Sample copy for $1.50. Writer's guidelines free.

Payment/Terms: Pays $25-250 and 5 contributor's copies. Pays on acceptance for first rights.

Advice: "*Clubhouse* readers are 8- to 12-year-old boys and girls who desire to know more about God and the Bible. Their parents (who typically pay for the membership) want wholesome, educational material with scriptural or moral insight. The kids want excitement, adventure, action, humor or mystery. Your job as a writer is to please both the parent and child with each article."

◘ COCHRAN'S CORNER, 1003 Tyler Court, Waldorf MD 20602-2964. Phone/fax: (301)870-1664. President: Ada Cochran. **Contact:** Jeanie Saunders, editor. Magazine: 5½×8; 52 pages. "We publish fiction, nonfiction and poetry. Our only requirement is no strong language." For a "family" audience. Quarterly magazine. Estab. 1986. Circ. 500.

Needs: Adventure, children's/juvenile, historical, horror, humor/satire, mystery/suspense, religious/inspirational, romance, science fiction, young adult/teen (10-18 years). Would like to see more mystery and romance fiction. "Mss must be free from language you wouldn't want your/our children to read." Plans a special fiction issue. Receives 50 mss/month. Accepts 4 mss/issue; 8 mss/year. Publishes ms by the next issue after acceptance. **Publishes approximately 30 new writers/year.** Published work by James Hughes, Ellen Sandry, James Bennet, Susan Lee and Judy Demers. Length: 300-1,000 words; 500 words preferred. Also publishes literary essays, literary criticism, poetry.

How to Contact: "Right now we are forced to limit acceptance to *subscribers only.*" Send complete ms with cover letter. Responds in 3 weeks to queries; 6-8 weeks to mss. SASE for manuscript. Accepts simultaneous and reprint submissions. Sample copy for $5, 9×12 SAE and 90¢ postage. Guidelines for #10 SASE.

Payment/Terms: Pays in contributor's copies. Acquires one-time rights.

Advice: "I feel the quality of fiction is getting better. The public is demanding a good read, instead of having sex or violence carry the story. I predict that fiction has a good future. We like to print the story as the writer submits it if possible. This way writers can compare their work with their peers and take the necessary steps to improve and go on to sell to bigger magazines. Stories from the heart desire a place to be published. We try to fill that need. Be willing to edit yourself. Polish your manuscript before submitting to editors."

◘ THE COZY DETECTIVE, Mystery Magazine, Meager Ink Publishing, 686 Jakes Ct., McMinnville OR 97128. Phone/fax: (503)472-4896. E-mail: papercapers@yahoo.com. Editor: David Workman. **Contact:** Charlie Bradley, fiction editor. Magazine: 8½×5½; 80 pages; illustrations; photos. Publishes mystery/suspense fiction and true crime stories for mystery buffs. Quarterly. Estab. 1994. Circ. 2,000.

Needs: Condensed/excerpted novel, mystery/suspense (amateur sleuth, cozy, police procedural, private eye/hardboiled), science fiction (mystery), serialized novel, young adult (mystery). No "sex, violence or vulgarity." Publishes special fiction issues or anthologies. Receives 15-25 unsolicited mss/month. Accepts 5 mss/issue; 20 mss/year. Does not read mss June-August. Recently published work by Kris Neri, Wendy Dager, Ruth Latta, James Geisert, C. Lester Bradley and Robert W. Kreps. Length: 6,000 words maximum; will consider longer stories for two-part series. Publishes short shorts. Also publishes poetry. Sometimes comments on rejected ms.

How to Contact: Send complete ms with a cover letter. Include 1-paragraph bio and estimated word count. Responds in 2 months to queries; 6 months to mss. Send SASE for reply, return of ms or send disposable copy of ms. Accepts simultaneous, reprint and electronic submissions. Sample copy for $2.95. Guidelines for #10 SASE. Reviews novels and short story collections. Send books to "Review Editor."

Payment/Terms: Pays 2 contributor's copies; additional copies $1.50. Acquires first North American serial rights.

Advice: "Do your best work—don't rush. Try to make your plot secondary to characters in the story. We look for action, crisp dialogue and original use of old ideas. We love a good mystery."

✓ ◘ **CZ'S MAGAZINE**, CZA, 3300 St. Joachim, St. Ann MO 63074. (314)890-2060. E-mail: submissions @cza.com. Website: www.cza.com/ (includes guidelines, reader participation in giving comments on stories and poems). **Contact:** Loretta Nichols, editor. Electronic magazine. "This publication is produced for writers who want to be published in a general subject magazine. We publish general topics and wholesome plots. Family reading. Inspirational type stories and poems." Triquarterly. Estab. 1997. Circ. 200.

Needs: Adventure, children's/juvenile (10-12 years), experimental, fantasy (science fantasy, sword and sorcery), feminist, humor/satire, literary, mainstream/contemporary, mystery/suspense (amateur sleuth, police procedural, romantic suspense), psychic/supernatural/occult, religious/inspirational, romance (contemporary, futuristic/time travel, gothic), young adult/teen (adventure, mystery, romance, science fiction), interviews. Would like to see more inspirational and romance fiction. "No porn." Receives 20 unsolicited mss/month. Accepts 3 mss/issue; 12 mss/year. **Publishes 10 new writers/year.** Recently published work by Kenneth Goldman and Jack Fisher. Length: 500-3,000 words; average length: 1,500 words. Publishes short shorts. Also publishes literary essays, literary criticism and poetry. Sometimes comments on rejected mss.

How to Contact: Send complete ms with a cover letter only. Accepts queries/mss by e-mail only. Include estimated word count, bio and list of publications. Responds in 6 months. Send SASE for reply, return of ms or send a disposable copy of ms. Accepts simultaneous submissions and reprints. Sample copy for $2. Guidelines free. Reviews novels and short story collections. Send books to editor.

Payment/Terms: Varies.

Advice: "Send your work with SASE. I always publish unpublished authors first (unless their work is not fitting)."

$ ◘ **DAGGER OF THE MIND, Beyond The Realms Of Imagination**, K'yi-Lih Productions (a division of Breach Enterprises), 1317 Hookridge Dr., El Paso TX 79925-7808. (915)591-0541. **Contact:** Arthur William Lloyd Breach, executive editor. Magazine. 8½×11; 62-86 pages; hibright paper; high glossy cover; from 5-12 illustrations. "Our aim is to provide the reading, educated public with thought-provoking, intelligent fiction without graphic sex, violence and gore. We publish science fiction, fantasy, horror, mystery and parapsychological/fortean nonfiction material." Quarterly. Estab. 1990. Circ. 5,000.

• Do not send this publication "slasher" horror. The editor's preferences lean toward *Twilight Zone* and similar material. He says he added mystery to his needs but has received very little quality material in this genre.

Needs: Lovecraftian, *Twilight Zone* fiction. Intelligent, well-crafted and thought provoking, exactly like the television series. Adventure, experimental, fantasy, horror, mystery/suspense (private eye, police procedural), science fiction (hard science, soft/sociological). Nothing sick and blasphemous, vulgar, obscene, racist, sexist, profane, humorous, weak, exploited women stories and those with idiotic puns. No westerns or slasher. Plans special paperback anthologies. Receives 500 unsolicited mss/month. Accepts 8-15 mss/issue; 90-100 mss/year depending upon length. Publishes ms 2 years after acceptance. Agented fiction 30%. **Publishes 1-2 new writers/ year.** Published work by Sidney Williams, Jessica Amanda Salmonson and Donald R. Burleson. All lengths are acceptable; from short shorts to novelette lengths. Also publishes literary essays, literary criticism, poetry. Sometimes comments on rejected mss.

How to Contact: All mail should be addressed to Arthur Breach. Send complete manuscript with cover letter. "Include a bio and list of previously published credits with tearsheets. I also expect a brief synopsis of the story." Responds in 6 months to mss. SASE. Accepts simultaneous submissions "as long as I am informed that they are such." Accepts electronic submissions. Sample copy for $3.50, 9×12 SAE and 5 first-class stamps. Guidelines for #10 SASE.

Payment/Terms: Pays ½-1¢/word and 1 contributor's copy. Pays on publication for first rights (possibly anthology rights as well).

Advice: "Do not send *revised* stories unless requested. I'm a big fan of the late H.P. Lovecraft. I love reading through Dunsanian and Cthulhu Mythos tales. I'm constantly on the lookout for this special brand of fiction. If you want to grab my attention immediately, write on the outside of the envelope 'Lovecraftian submission enclosed.' There are a number of things which make submissions stand out for me. Is there any sensitivity to the tale? I like sensitive material, so long as it doesn't become mushy. Another thing that grabs my attention are characters which leap out of the pages at you. Move me, bring a tear to my eye; make me stop and think about the world and people around me. Frighten me with little spoken truths about the human condition. In short, show me that you can move me in such a way as I have never been moved before."

$ ◘ **DANCE**, P.O. Box 1264, Huntington WV 25714. Magazine: 8½×11; illustrations; photos. Quarterly. Estab. 1993. Circ. 9,000.

Needs: Children's/juvenile, young adult/teen, dance. Receives 25 unsolicited mss/month. Accepts 1-2 mss/issue; 12-16 mss/year. Publishes ms 1-3 months after acceptance. Length: 500 words minimum. Also publishes literary essays, criticism and poetry. Always comments on rejected ms.

How to Contact: Send complete ms with a cover letter. Include estimated word count, bio and list of publications. Responds in 1 month to queries; 2 months to mss. Send SASE for reply, return of ms or send disposable copy of ms. Accepts simultaneous and reprint submissions. Sample copy for $3.50. Guidelines free.

Payment/Terms: Pays 1¢/word and contributor's copies. Pays on acceptance for first rights. Sends prepublication galleys to author.

N $ ☐ ▣ DARK MATTER CHRONICLES, Eggplant Productions, P.O. Box 2248, Schiller Park IL 60176. (847)928-9925. Fax: (801)720-0706. E-mail: darkmatter@eggplant-productions.com. Website: www.eggp lant-productions.com/darkmatter (includes sign up form, writer's guidelines, links, news). **Contact:** Raechel Henderson, editor. E-zine specializing in fiction and reviews. "*Dark Matter Chronicles* is a PDF publication which is e-mailed to subscribers twice a month. This publication reviews fantasy, science fiction and horror websites and other electronic media (including e-books) and features one piece of short fiction in each issue. Our goal is to guide readers to quality speculative fiction sites and offer webmasters/editors a place for feedback on their work." Biweekly. Estab. 1999. Circ. 270. Member: Zine Guild.
Needs: Fantasy (space fantasy, sword and sorcery), horror (dark fantasy, futuristic, psychological, supernatural), science fiction (hard science/technological, soft/sociological). Speculative fiction only. Receives 15 unsolicited mss/month. Accepts 1 ms/issue; 24 mss/year. Publishes ms 2-4 months after acceptance. **Publishes 12 new writers/year.** Recently published work by Andrew L. Burt, Steve Lazarowitz and Maren Henry. Length: 500-3,000 words; average length: 1,800 words. Publishes short shorts. Average length: 1,000 words. Always comments on rejected mss.
How to Contact: Send complete ms with a cover letter. Only accepts submissions by e-mail. "Submissions sent to the P.O. Box will be returned unread." Include estimated word count and contact info. Responds in 1 month to queries and ms. Accepts simultaneous submissions, previously published work and multiple submissions. Sample copy free. Guidelines on website. Reviews websites and e-books.
Payment/Terms: Pays ¼¢/word. Pays on publication for one-time rights. Sends galleys to author. Not copyrighted.
Advice: "As always, I look for a story that moves me. I want to care about the characters and their situations. If I feel something during and after I read the story I will publish it."

✓ $ ☑ ▣ DEEP OUTSIDE SFFH, 6549 Mission Gorge Rd., PMB 260, San Diego CA 92120. Website: www.clocktowerfiction.com/Outside. **Contact:** John Cullen and Brian Callahan, editors. Web-only magazine. "*Outside* is a paying professional magazine of SF and dark imaginative fiction, aimed at people who love to read well-plotted, character-driven genre fiction. We are interested in fiction that transcends the limitations and ventures outside the stereotypes of genre fiction." Monthly. Estab. 1998. Circ. 3,000+
Needs: Fantasy (dark), horror (dark fantasy, futuristic, psychological), science fiction (hard science/technological, soft/sociological). No pornography, excessive gore, "or vulgarity unless it directly furthers the story (sparingly, at that)." No sword and sorcery, elves, high fantasy, cookie-cutter space opera. Receives 100-150 unsolicited mss/month. Accepts 1 ms/issue; 12 mss/year. Publishes ms 1-3 months after acceptance. **Publishes 10% new writers/year.** Recently published work by Andrew Vachss, Melanie Tem, and Joe Murphy. Length: 2,000-4,000 words. Often comments on rejected ms.
How to Contact: Send complete ms with a cover letter. "Manuscripts must be sent by postal mail only." Include estimated word count; list of publications. Responds in 3 months. Send disposable copy of ms and SASE for reply.
Payment/Terms: Pays 3¢/word on acceptance for first rights. Sends prepublication galleys to author.
Advice: "We look for the best quality story. Genre comes second. We look for polished, first-rate, professional fiction. It is most important to grab us from the first three paragraphs-not only as a common standard but because that's how we lead with both the monthly newsletter and the main page of the magazine. Please read the tips and guidelines at the magazine's website for up-to-the-moment details. Do not send envelopes asking for guidelines, please—all the info is online at our website."

N ⊕ ◨ ◎ DIALOGOS, Hellenic Studies Review, Frank Cass Publishers, Newbury House, 890-900 Eastern Ave., Ilford, Essex 192 7HH United Kingdom. Website: www.frankcass.com. **Contact:** Dr. David Ricks, fiction editor. Learned journal with literary element: 150 pages; glossy cover. "*Dialogos* encompasses Greek language, literature, history, culture and thought from ancient times and the present; it encourages the submission of translations and original literary work. It is directed to an informed but open-minded scholarly audience." Estab. 1994. Circ. 300.
Needs: Ethnic/multicultural (Greek), translations. Accepts 1 ms/year. Publishes ms 1 year after acceptance. **Publishes 1-2 new writers/year.** Length: 8,000 words maximum; average length: 7,000 words. Publishes short shorts. Also publishes literary essays, literary criticism and poetry. Sometimes comments on rejected mss.
How to Contact: Query first. Responds in 2 weeks to queries; 3 months to mss. Send a disposable copy of ms and #10 SASE for reply only. Guidelines by e-mail. Reviews novels, short story collections and nonfiction books of interest to writers. Send review copies to David Ricks.
Payment/Terms: Pays 1 contributor's copy plus 25 off prints; additional copies $29.50. Pays on publication. Rights revert to author. Sends galleys to author.
Advice: "Must have a strong Greek relevance."

☑ ⊘ ◎ **DREAM INTERNATIONAL/QUARTERLY,** U.S. Address: Charles I. Jones, #H-1, 411 14th St., Ramona CA 92065-2769. (760)789-1020. **Contact:** Charles I. Jones, editor-in-chief. Magazine: 8½×11; 143 pages; Xerox paper; parchment cover stock; some illustrations; photos. "Publishes fiction and nonfiction that is dream-related or clearly inspired by a dream. Also dream-related fantasy and poetry." Quarterly. Estab. 1981. Circ. 65-100.

Needs: Confession, erotica (soft), fantasy (dream), historical, horror, humor/satire, literary, prose poem, psychic/supernatural/occult, science fiction, young adult/teen (10-18). "We would like to see submissions that deal with dreams that have an influence on the person's daily waking life. Suggestions for making dreams beneficial to the dreamer in his/her waking life. We would also like to see more submissions dealing with lucid dreaming." Receives 35-40 unsolicited mss/month. Accepts 20 mss/issue; 50-55 mss/year. Publishes ms 8 months to 3 years after acceptance. Agented fiction 1%. **Publishes 40-50 new writers/year.** Recently published work by Tim Scott, Carmen M. Pursifull and Allen Underwood. Length: 1,000-1,500 words. Publishes short shorts. Also publishes literary essays, poetry (poetry submissions to Carmen M. Pursifull, 809 W. Maple St., Champaign IL 61820-2810. Hard copy only for poetry. No electronic submissions please! Send SASE for poetry guidelines).

How to Contact: Submit ms. Responds in 6 weeks to queries; 3 months to mss. SASE. Accepts simultaneous and reprint submissions. Sample copy for $13. Guidelines $2 with SAE and 2 first-class stamps. Subscription: $50 (1-year); $100 (2-year). "Accepted mss will not be returned unless requested at time of submission."

Payment/Terms: Pays in contributor's copy (contributors must pay $3 for postage and handling). Acquires first North American serial and electronic rights. Sends prepublication galleys to author on request.

Advice: "Write about what you know. Make the reader 'stand up and take notice.' Avoid rambling and stay away from chichés in your writing unless, of course, it is of a humorous nature and is purposefully done to make a point."

☒ $ ⊘ **DREAMS & VISIONS, New Frontiers in Christian Fiction,** Skysong Press, 35 Peter St. S., Orillia, Ontario L3V 5AB Canada. Website: www.bconnex.net/~skysong. **Contact:** Steve Stanton, editor. Magazine: 5½×8½; 56 pages; 20 lb. bond paper; glossy cover. "Contemporary Christian fiction in a variety of styles for adult Christians." Triannual. Estab. 1989. Circ. 200.

Needs: Contemporary, experimental, fantasy, humor/satire, literary, religious/inspirational, science fiction (soft/sociological). "All stories should portray a Christian world view or expand upon Biblical themes or ethics in an entertaining or enlightening manner." Receives 20 unsolicited mss/month. Accepts 7 mss/issue; 21 mss/year. Publishes ms 2-6 months after acceptance. Length: 2,000-6,000 words; average length: 2,500 words.

How to Contact: Send complete ms with cover letter. "Bio is optional: degrees held and in what specialties, publishing credits, service in the church, etc." Responds in 1 month to queries; 4 months to mss. SASE. Accepts simultaneous submissions. Sample copy for $4.95. Guidelines for SASE or on website.

Payment/Terms: Pays ½¢/word and contributor's copy. Acquires first North American serial rights and one-time, non-exclusive reprint rights.

Advice: "In general we look for work that has some literary value, that is in some way unique and relevant to Christian readers today. Our first priority is technical adequacy, though we will occasionally work with a beginning writer to polish a manuscript. Ultimately, we look for stories that glorify the Lord Jesus Christ, stories that build up rather than tear down, that exalt the sanctity of life, the holiness of God, and the value of the family."

Ⓝ ⊕ $ ◎ **EIDOLON, The Journal of Australian Science Fiction and Fantasy,** P.O. Box 225, North Perth, Western Australia 6906. E-mail: eidolon@eidolon.net. **Contact:** Jeremy Byrne, editor. Magazine: A5 size; 124 pages; gloss cover; illustrations; photos. "Primarily Australian science fiction, fantasy and horror magazine." Quarterly. Estab. 1990. Circ. 350.

Needs: Fantasy, psychic/supernatural/occult, romance (futuristic/time travel), science fiction, young adult/teen (horror, science fiction). Receives 25 unsolicited mss/month. Accepts 6 mss/issue; 25 mss/year. Publishes ms up to 1 year after acceptance. Agented fiction less than 1%. Recently published work by Terry Dowling, Sean Williams, Simon Brown, Jack Dann, Damien Broderick, Stephen Bedman. Length: 10,000 words maximum; average length: 4,000 words. Publishes short shorts.

How to Contact: Send complete ms with a cover letter. Include estimated word count, 100-word bio, list of publications and e-mail address. Send SASE for reply and a disposable copy of ms. No simultaneous submissions. Publishes fiction by Australians only. Sample copy for $8 Aus. Guidelines for #10 SASE or SAE with 1 IRC.

Payment/Terms: Pays $20 and 1 contributor's copy. Acquires first Australian rights and optional electronic reproduction rights. Sends galleys to author.

INTERESTED IN A PARTICULAR GENRE? Check our sections for: **Mystery,** page 57; **Romance,** page 68; **Science Fiction/Fantasy & Horror,** page 78.

Advice: Looks for "sophisticated, original explorations of fantastic themes, surprising plots and intelligent characterization. Proof carefully, work hard on dialogue. Make sure you know the field you're writing in well to avoid rehashing old themes. We expect writers to avoid stereotypical, sexist, racist or otherwise socially unacceptable themes and styles."

N **O ENIGMA,** Audrecieus/Bettle Press, 402 South 25 St., Philadelphia PA 19146. (215)545-8694. E-mail: sydx@att.net. **Contact:** Syd Bradford, publisher. Magazine: 8½×11; 100 pages; 24 lb. white paper; illustrations; photos. "Everything is done—except printing—by me, the publisher. No editors, etc. Eclectic—I publish articles, fiction, poetry." Quarterly. Estab. 1989. Circ. 60.
Needs: Adventure, experimental, fantasy, gay, historical, horror, humor/satire. Accepts 70 mss/issue. Publishes ms 2 months after acceptance. **Publishes 20 new writers/year.** Length: 1,000-3,000 words; average length: 1,500 words. Publishes short shorts. Also publishes literary essays, literary criticism and poetry.
How to Contact: Send complete ms with a cover letter. Accepts submissions by e-mail. Include brief bio. Send SASE (or IRC) for return of ms. Sample copy for $5. Guidelines for SASE. Reviews novels, short story collections and nonfiction books of interest to writers.
Payment/Terms: Pays 1 contributor's copy; additional copies $5. Sends galleys to author.
Advice: "I look for imaginative writing, excellent movement, fine imagery, stunning characters."

✓ **O EYES,** 3610 North Doncaster Ct., Apt. X7, Saginaw MI 48603-1862. (517)498-4112. E-mail: fjm3eyes @aol.com. Website: http://members.aol.com/eyeonweb/index.html (includes guidelines, contact information, stories and reviews). **Contact:** Frank J. Mueller, III, editor. Magazine: 8½×11; 40+ pages; 20 lb. paper; Antiqua parchment, blue 65 lb. cover. "No specific theme. Speculative fiction and surrealism most welcome. For a general, educated, not necessarily literary audience." Estab. 1991.
Needs: Contemporary, horror (psychological), mainstream, ghost story. "Especially looking for speculative fiction and surrealism. Would like to see more ghost stories, student writing. Dark fantasy OK, but not preferred." No sword/sorcery, overt science fiction, pornography, preachiness or children's fiction. Accepts 5-9 mss/issue. Publishes ms up to 1 year or longer after acceptance. **Publishes 15-20 writers/year.** Length: 6,000 words maximum. Sometimes comments on rejected mss.
How to Contact: Query first or send complete ms. A short bio is optional. Responds in 1 month to queries; 3 months or longer to mss. SASE. No simultaneous submissions. Sample copy for $4; extras $4. Subscriptions $14. (Checks to Frank J. Mueller III.) Guidelines for #10 SASE.
Payment/Terms: Pays one contributor's copy. Acquires one-time rights.
Advice: "Pay attention to character. A strong plot, while important, may not be enough alone to get you in *Eyes*. Atmosphere and mood are also important. Please proofread. If you have a manuscript you like enough to see it in *Eyes*, send it to me. Above all, don't let rejections discourage you. I would encourage the purchase of a sample to get an idea of what I'm looking for. Read stories by authors such as Algernon Blackwood, Nathaniel Hawthorne, Shirley Jackson, Henry James and Poe. Also, please write for information concerning chapbooks."

N **$ O O FLESH & BLOOD, Quiet Tales of Horror & Dark Fantasy,** Flesh & Blood Press, 121 Joseph St., Bayville NJ 08721. E-mail: HorrorJack@aol.com. Website: www.geocities.com/soho/lofts/3459/fnb.h tml (includes news, updates, guidelines, sales, releases). **Contact:** Jack Fisher, senior editor/publisher. Magazine: digest sized; 44-52 pages; 60 lb. paper; thick/glossy cover; illustrations. "We publish fiction with heavy emphasis on the supernatural, fantastic and bizarre." Triannual. Estab. 1997. Circ. 500.
Needs: Fantasy (light), horror (dark fantasy, supernatural). "We love unique ghost stories. Also, retakes on old stories like *Peter Pan* accepted." "No psychological, revenge, old-storyline stories." Receives 250 unsolicited mss/month. Accepts 4-6 mss/issue; 20-25 mss/year. Publishes ms 6-10 months after acceptance. Agented fiction 1%. **Publishes 2-6 new writers/year.** Recently published work by Mark McLaughlin, Charlee Jacob and DF Lewis. Length: 500-4,000 words; average length: 2,000 words. Publishes short shorts. Average length: 100-500 words. Also publishes poetry. Often comments on rejected mss.
How to Contact: Send complete ms with a cover letter. Accepts submissions by e-mail. Include brief bio and list of publications. Responds in 2 weeks to queries; 3 months to mss. Send SASE (or IRC) for return of ms. Accepts previously published work and multiple submissions. Sample copy for $4. Guidelines free for SASE or by e-mail.
Payment/Terms: Pays $5-80 plus 1 contributor's copy. Pays within 3 months after acceptance for first North American serial rights.
Advice: "Too many fiction submissions today are cliché, rushed and sloppy. Offer new, original ideas and present them properly and professionally."

🌐 **O FORESIGHT,** 44 Brockhurst Rd., Hodge Hill, Birmingham B36 8JB England. 0121.783.0587. **Contact:** John Barklam, editor. Fiction Editor: Judy Barklam. Quarterly.
Needs: Magazine including "new age material, world peace, psychic phenomena, research, occultism, spiritualism, mysticism, UFOs, philosophy, etc. Shorter articles required on a specific theme related to the subject matter of *Foresight* magazine." Length: 300-1,000 words.

How to Contact: Send SAE with IRC for return of ms.
Payment/Terms: Pays in contributor's copies. Sample copy for 75p and 50p postage.

$ ⬛ FREE FOCUS/OSTENTATIOUS MIND, Wagner Press, Bowbridge Press, P.O. Box 7415, JAF Station, New York NY 10116-7415. **Contact:** Patricia Denise Coscia, editor. Editors change each year. Magazine: 8 × 14; 10 pages; recycled paper; illustrations; photos. "*Free Focus* is a small-press magazine which focuses on the educated women of today, and *Ostentatious Mind* is designed to encourage the intense writer, the cutting reality." Bimonthly. Estab. 1985 and 1987. Circ. 100 each.
Needs: Experimental, feminist, humor/satire, literary, mainstream/contemporary, mystery/suspense (romantic), psychic/supernatural/occult, westerns (traditional), young adult/teen (adventure). "X-rated fiction is not accepted." List of upcoming themes available for SASE. Plans future special fiction issue or anthology. Receives 1,000 unsolicited mss/month. Does not read mss February to August. Publishes ms 3-6 months after acceptance. **Publishes 200 new writers/year.** Published work by Edward Janz. Length: 1,000 words maximum; average length: 500 words. Publishes short shorts. Also publishes literary essays, literary criticism and poetry. Always comments on rejected mss. Sponsors contest for work submitted to *Free Focus*.
How to Contact: Query with clips of published work or send complete ms with a cover letter. Should include 100-word bio and list of publications. Responds in 3 months. Send SASE for reply. Accepts simultaneous submissions. Sample copy for $3, #10 SAE and $1 postage. Guidelines for #10 SAE and $1 postage. Reviews novels and short story collections.
Payment/Terms: Pays $2.50-5 and 2 contributor's copies; additional copies $2. Pays on publication for all rights. Sends galleys to author.
Advice: "This publication is for beginning writers. Do not get discouraged; submit your writing. We look for imagination and creativity; no x-rated writing."

ℕ GAY CHICAGO MAGAZINE, Gernhardt Publications, Inc., 3115 N. Broadway, Chicago IL 60657-4522. (773)327-7271. Publisher: Ralph Paul Gernhardt. Associate Publisher: Jerry Williams. **Contact:** Jeff Rossen, entertainment editor. Magazine: 8½ × 11; 80-144 pages; newsprint paper and cover stock; illustrations; photos. Entertainment guide, information for the gay community.
Needs: Erotica (but no explicit hard core), lesbian, gay and romance. Receives "a few" unsolicited mss/month. Acquires 10-15 mss/year. **Published new writers within the last year.** Length: 1,000-3,000 words.
How to Contact: Send all submissions Attn: Jeff Rossen. Send complete ms with SASE. Accepts 3.5 disk submissions and Macintosh or ASCII Format, "also accepts floppies and zips." Responds in 6 weeks to mss. Free sample copy for 9 × 12 SAE and $1.45 postage.
Payment/Terms: Minimal. 5-10 free contributor's copies; no charge for extras "if within reason." Acquires one-time rights.

$ ⬛ GHOST TOWN, P.O. Box 1264, Huntington WV 25714. Magazine: 8½ × 11; illustrations; photos. Quarterly. Estab. 1999.
Needs: Children's/juvenile (historical), historical (ghost towns), western, young adult/teen (historical). Receives 50 unsolicited mss/month. Accepts 1-2 mss/issue; 12-16 mss/year. Publishes ms 1-3 months after acceptance. Length: 500 words minimum. Also publishes literary essays, criticism and poetry. Always comments on rejected ms.
How to Contact: Send complete ms with a cover letter. Include estimated word count, bio and list of publications. Responds in 1 month to queries; 2 months to mss. Send SASE for reply, return of ms or send disposable copy of ms. Accepts simultaneous and reprint submissions. Sample copy for $3.50. Guidelines free.
Payment/Terms: Pays 1¢/word and contributor's copies. Pays on acceptance for first rights. Sends prepublication galleys to author.

$ ⬛ ◎ GRUE MAGAZINE, Hell's Kitchen Productions, P.O. Box 370, New York NY 10108-0370. Phone/fax: (212)245-2329. E-mail: nadramia@panix.com. **Contact:** Peggy Nadramia, editor. Magazine: 5½ × 8½; 96 pages; 60 lb. paper; 10 pt. C1S film laminate cover; illustrations; photos. "We look for quality short fiction centered on horror and dark fantasy—new traditions in the realms of the gothic and the macabre for horror fans well read in the genre, looking for something new and different, as well as horror novices looking for a good scare." Triannually. Estab. 1985.
Needs: Horror, psychic/supernatural/occult. No fantasy or science fiction. Receives 250 unsolicited fiction mss/month. Accepts 10 mss/issue; 25-30 mss/year. Publishes ms 1-2 years after acceptance. **Publishes 10-15 new writers/year.** Recently published work by Wayne Allen Sallee, Kevin Filan, A.R. Morlan and Denise Dumars. Length: 6,500 words maximum; average length: 4,000 words. Sometimes critiques rejected ms.
How to Contact: Send complete ms with cover letter. "I like to hear where the writer heard about *Grue*, his most recent or prestigious sales, and maybe a word or two about himself." Responds in 3 weeks to queries; 6 months to mss. Send SASE for return of ms. Sample copy for $5. Guidelines for #10 SASE.
Payment/Terms: Pays ½¢/word and 2 contributor's copies. Pays on publication for first North American serial rights.

Advice: "Remember that readers of *Grue* are mainly seasoned horror fans, and *not* interested or excited by a straight vampire, werewolf or ghost story—they'll see all the signs, and guess where you're going long before you get there. Throw a new angle on what you're doing; put it in a new light. How? Well, what scares *you*? What's *your* personal phobia or anxiety? When the writer is genuinely, emotionally involved with his subject matter, and is totally honest with himself and his reader, then we can't help being involved, too, and that's where good writing begins and ends."

✔ ◐ **HARD ROW TO HOE DIVISION**, Potato Eyes Foundation, P.O. Box 541-I, Healdsburg CA 95448. (707)433-9786. **Contact:** Joe Armstrong, editor. Newsletter: 8½×11; 12 pages; 60 lb. white paper; illustrations; photos. "Book reviews, short story and poetry of rural USA including environmental and nature subjects." Triannually. Estab. 1982. Circ. 150.
• *Hard Row to Hoe* was called "one of ten best literary newsletters in the U.S." by *Small Press* magazine.
Needs: Rural America. "No urban material or stories of pets. Would like to see stories that depict organic farming." Receives 8-10 unsolicited mss/month. Acquires 1 ms/issue; 3-4 mss/year. Publishes ms 6-9 months after acceptance. **Publishes 1-2 new writers/year.** Recently published work by Deborah Rowland Stambul and Karen Richardson Kettner. Length: 2,000-2,200 words; average length: 1,500 words. Publishes short shorts. Sometimes comments on rejected mss.
How to Contact: Send complete ms with cover letter. Responds in 1 month to mss. SASE. Accepts multiple submissions. Sample copy for $2. Guidelines for legal-size SASE.
Payment/Terms: Pays 2 contributor's copies. Acquires one-time rights.
Advice: "Be certain the subject fits the special need."

$ ◐ **HARDBOILED**, Gryphon Books, P.O. Box 209, Brooklyn NY 11228-0209. **Contact:** Gary Lovisi, editor. Magazine: Digest-sized; 100 pages; offset paper; color cover; illustrations. Publishes "cutting edge, hard, noir fiction with impact! Query on nonfiction and reviews." Quarterly. Estab. 1988.
• By "hardboiled" the editor does not mean rehashing of pulp detective fiction from the 1940s and 1950s but, rather, realistic, gritty material. Lovisi could be called a pulp fiction "afficionado," however. He also publishes *Paperback Parade* and holds an annual vintage paperback fiction convention each year.
Needs: Mystery/suspense (private eye, police procedural, noir). Receives 40-60 mss/month. Accepts 10-20 mss/year. Publishes ms within 6 months-2 years of acceptance. **Published many new writers within the last year.** Published work by Andrew Vachss, Joe Lansdale, Bill Nolan, Richard Lupoff, Bill Pronzini and Eugene Izzi. Length: 2,000-3,000 words. Sometimes comments on rejected mss and recommends other markets.
How to Contact: Query first or send complete ms with cover letter. Query with SASE only on anything over 3,000 words. No full-length novels. Responds in 1 month to queries; 2 months to mss. SASE. Accepts simultaneous submissions, but query first. Sample copy for $8. Subscriptions are 5 issues $35.
Payment/Terms: Pays $5-50 and 2 contributor's copies. Pays on publication for first North American serial rights. Copyright reverts to author.

◐ **HAWAII PACIFIC REVIEW** Hawaii Pacific University, 1060 Bishop St., Honolulu HI 96813. (808)544-1107. **Contact:** Catherine Sustana, fiction editor. Magazine: 6×9; 100-150 pages; quality paper; glossy cover; illustrations; original artwork. "The *Review* seeks to reflect the cultural diversity that is the hallmark of Hawaii Pacific University. Consequently, we welcome material on a wide variety of themes and we encourage experimental styles and narrative techniques. Categories: fiction, poetry, personal essays." Annual. Estab. "nationwide in 1988."
Needs: Adventure, contemporary, ethnic, experimental, fantasy, humor/satire, literary, mainstream, regional, science fiction, translations. No romance, confessions, religious or juvenile. Receives approx. 50 unsolicited fiction mss/month. Accepts 4-8 mss/issue. Reading period is September 1 through December 31. Publishes ms 3-12 months after acceptance. **Published new writers within the last year.** Length: 5,000 words maximum. Publishes short shorts. Also publishes literary essays, poetry. Sometimes critiques rejected mss or recommends other markets.
How to Contact: Send complete ms with cover letter, which should include a brief bio. Responds in 4 months. SASE. Accepts simultaneous submissions. Guidelines for #10 SASE.
Payment/Terms: Pays in contributor's copies. Acquires first North American serial rights. Rights revert to author upon publication.

✔ $ ◐ ▼ **HOPSCOTCH: THE MAGAZINE FOR GIRLS**, The Bluffton News Publishing & Printing Co., P.O. Box 164, Bluffton OH 45817-0164. (419)358-4610. Fax: (419)358-5027. Website: hopscotchmagazine. com (includes samples of articles and order info). **Contact:** Marilyn Edwards, editor. Magazine: 7×9; 50 pages; enamel paper; pen & ink illustrations; photos. Publishes stories for and about girls ages 5-13. "We are trying to produce a wholesome magazine for girls 5-13, encouraging childhood. There is nothing on makeup, boyfriends, fads, clothing, etc." Bimonthly. Estab. 1989. Circ. 9,000.
• *Hopscotch* is indexed in the *Children's Magazine Guide* and *EdPress* and has received a Parents' Choice Gold Medal Award and EdPress Awards.

Needs: Children's/juvenile (5-9, 10-13 years): adventure, ethnic/multicultural, historical (general), sports. No fantasy, science fiction, romance. "We would like to see more stories that rhyme and stories that have a moral." Upcoming themes: Hamsters; Names; The Circus; Zoo Animals; Hats; Women of Courage; Ballet; That's Entertainment; Weather; Astronomy; Water Creatures; It's a Mystery. "All writers should consult the theme list before sending in articles." Current theme list available for SASE. Receives 300-400 unsolicited mss/month. Accepts 20-40 mss/year. Agented fiction 2%. Published work by Lois Grambling, Betty Killion, John Thomas Waite, Kelly Musselman, Marilyn Helmer and Joyce Styron Madsen. Length: 300-750 words; 500-750 words preferred. Publishes short shorts. Length: 250-400 words. Also publishes poetry, puzzles, hidden pictures and crafts. Always comments on rejected mss.
How to Contact: Send complete ms with cover letter. Include estimated word count, 1-page bio, Social Security number and list of publications. Responds in 1 month to queries; 10 weeks to mss. Send SASE for reply, return of ms or send disposable copy of the ms. Accepts simultaneous, multiple and reprint submissions. Sample copy for $4. Guidelines for #10 SASE. Reviews novels and short story collections.
Payment/Terms: Pays 5¢/word (extra for usable photos or illustrations) and 1 contributor's copy; additional copies $4; $2.50 for 10 or more. Pays before publication for first North American serial rights
Advice: "Make sure you have studied copies of our magazine to see what we like. Follow our theme list. We are looking for wholesome stories. This is what our publication is all about."

◙ HURRICANE ALICE, A Feminist Quarterly, Hurricane Alice Fn., Inc., Dept. of English, Rhode Island College, Providence RI 02908. (401)456-8377. E-mail: mreddy@grog.ric.edu. **Contact:** Maureen Reddy, executive editor. Fiction is collectively edited. Tabloid: 11 × 17; 12-16 pages; newsprint stock; illustrations; photos. "We look for feminist fictions with a certain analytic snap, for serious readers, seriously interested in emerging forms of feminist art/artists." Quarterly. Estab. 1983. Circ. 600-700.
Needs: Experimental, feminist, gay, humor/satire, lesbian, science fiction, translations, work by young women. "No coming-out stories, defloration stories, abortion stories, dreary realism. Would like to see more speculative and experimental fiction." Receives 30 unsolicited mss/month. Publishes 8-10 stories annually. Publishes mss up to 1 year after acceptance. **Publishes 4-5 new writers/year.** Published work by Vickie Nelson, Mary Sharratt and Kathryn Duhamel. Length: up to 3,500 words maximum. Publishes short shorts. Occasionally comments on rejected mss.
How to Contact: Send complete ms with cover letter. "A brief biographical statement is never amiss. Writers should be sure to tell us if a piece was commissioned by one of the editors." Responds in 9 months. SASE for response. Accepts simultaneous submissions, but must be identified as such. Sample copy for $2.50, 11 × 14 SAE and 2 first-class stamps.
Payment/Terms: Pays 6 contributor's copies. Acquires one-time rights.
Advice: "Fiction is a craft. Just because something happened, it isn't a story; it becomes a story when you transform it through your art, your craft."

Ⓝ ◙ HYBOLICS, Da Literature and Culture of Hawaii, Hybolics, Inc., P.O. Box 3016, Aiea HI 96701. (808)366-1272. E-mail: hybolics@lava.net. Website: www.hybolics.com (includes writer's guidelines and back issue ordering information). **Contact:** Fiction Editor. Magazine: 8½ × 11; 80 pages; 80 lb. coated paper; cardstock cover; illustrations; photos. "We publish da kine creative and critical work dat get some kine connection to Hawaii." Semiannual. Estab. 1999. Circ. 1,000.
Needs: Comics/graphic novels, ethnic/multicultural, experimental, humor/satire, literary. "No genre fiction." Receives 5 unsolicited mss/month. Accepts 5 mss/issue; 10 mss/year. Publishes ms 1 year after acceptance. **Publishes 2 new writers/year.** Recently published work by Darrell Lum, Rodney Morales, Lee Cataluna and Lisa Kanae. Length: 1,000-8,000 words; average length: 4,000 words. Publishes short shorts. Also publishes literary essays, literary criticism and poetry.
How to Contact: Send complete ms with a cover letter. Include estimated word count, brief bio and list of publications. Responds in 5 weeks to queries; 5 months to mss. Send SASE (or IRC) for return of ms or send a disposable copy of ms and #10 SASE for reply only. Sample copy for $13.35. Guidelines for SASE.
Payment/Terms: Pays 2 contributor's copies; additional copies $7.25. Pays on publication for first rights. Sends galleys to author.

$ ◙ ◎ Ⓥ IN THE FAMILY, The Magazine for Lesbians, Gays, Bisexuals and their Relations P.O. Box 5387, Takoma Park MD 20913. (301)270-4771. Fax: (301)270-4660. E-mail: helenalips@aol.com. Website: www.inthefamily.com (includes writer's guidelines, bulletin board, overview of magazine content and back issue themes). Editor: Laura Markowitz. **Contact:** Helena Lipstadt, fiction editor. Magazine: 8½ × 11, 32 pages; coated paper; coated cover; illustrations; photos. "We use a therapy lens to explore the diverse relationships and families of lesbians, gays, bisexuals and their straight relations." Quarterly. Estab. 1995. Circ. 2,000.
  • Received 1997 Excellence in Media Award from the American Association for Marriage and Family Therapy. Member of IPA.
Needs: Ethnic/multicultural, feminist, gay, humor/satire, lesbian. No erotica. Would like to see more short stories. List of upcoming themes available for SASE. Receives 25 unsolicited mss/month. Accepts 1 ms/issue; 4 mss/

year. Publishes ms 3-6 months after acceptance. **Publishes 3 new writers/year.** Published work by James Young, Ellen Hawley, Daniel Cox, Shoshana Daniel and Martha Davis. Length: 2,500 words maximum; average length: 2,000 words. Publishes short shorts. Also publishes literary essays and poetry. Sometimes comments on rejected mss.

How to Contact: Send complete ms with a cover letter. Include estimated word count and 40-word bio. Responds in 6 weeks to queries and mss. Send SASE for reply, return of ms or send disposable copy of ms. Accepts multiple submissions. Sample copy for $5.50. Guidelines free. Reviews novels and short story collections. Send books to Book Review Editor.

Payment/Terms: Pays $25-50, free subscription to magazine and 5 contributor's copies. Acquires first rights.

Advice: "Story must relate to our theme of gay/lesbian/bi relationships and family in some way. Read a few issues and get a sense for what we publish. Shorter is better. Go deep, write from the gut, but not just your pain; also your joy and insight."

N ⬇ $⊘ ⊻ INDIAN LIFE, Intertribal Christian Communications, P.O. Box 3765, RPO Redwood Centre, Winnepeg, Manitoba R2W 3R6 Canada. (204)661-9333. Fax: (204)661-3982. E-mail: jim.editor@indianl ife.org. Website: www.indianlife.org. **Contact:** Jim Uttley, editor. Religious tabloid: 11 × 17; 16 pages; newsprint paper; illustrations; photos. "*Indian Life* is an Aboriginal newspaper which seeks to present positive news stories of Native Americans and deals with social issues facing Aboriginal people. It is our mission to bring hope, healing and honor to Native Americans." Bimonthly. Estab. 1968. Circ. 32,000. Member: Evangelical Press Association, Native American Journalists Association.

• *Indian Life* won the Award of Excellence from EPA (1997, 1998).

Needs: Adventure, children's/juvenile (adventure, animal, easy-to-read, historical), comics/graphic novels, ethnic/multicultural (Native American), historical, religious (children's religious, general religious, inspirational), western (frontier saga, traditional). "No writing which berates or puts down Native Americans. Writers must write from Native perspective." Please contact editor by phone for upcoming themes. Receives 4 unsolicited mss/month. Accepts 1 ms/issue; 6 mss/year. Publishes ms 2 months after acceptance. Agented fiction 1%. **Publishes 3 new writers/year.** Length: 500-2,000 words; average length: 800-1,500 words. Publishes short shorts. Average length: 800 words. Also publishes literary essays, literary criticism and poetry. Often comments on rejected mss.

How to Contact: Query first. Accepts submissions by e-mail, fax and disk. Include estimated word count and brief bio. Responds in 1 month to queries; 2 months to mss. Send a disposable copy of ms and #10 SASE for reply only. Accepts simultaneous submissions, previously published work and multiple submissions. Sample copy for SASE with $2 postage. Guidelines for SASE, by e-mail, fax or on website. Reviews novels, short story collections and nonfiction books of interest to writers.

Payment/Terms: Pays $50-100 (Canadian) and 3 contributor's copies; additional copies 25¢. Pays on publication for first rights. Plans to sponsor contest.

Advice: "Research, research, research. Do everything you can to get heart for Native Americans."

N INKY TRAIL NEWS, Inky Trail News, 70 Macomb Place, #226, Mt. Clemens MI 48043. E-mail: inkytrails @prodigy.net. Website: www.inkytrails.com. **Contact:** Wendy Fisher, editor. Tabloid newspaper: 24-28 pages; newsprint; some illustrations; photos. "Friendship newsletter for women/seniors, penpals, journaling, memories, crafts and more." Bimonthly. Estab. 1993. Circ. 500.

Needs: Historical (general memories), mainstream, women penpals, new writers, homelife, personal journals, gardening, seniors, crafts. Receives 2-3 unsolicited mss/month. Accepts 2-3 mss/issue. Publishes 3-4 months after acceptance. **Publishes 60-100 new writers/year.** Length: 600 words; average length: 600-800 words. Publishes short shorts.

How to Contact: Send complete ms with cover letter. Accepts submissions by e-mail or on disk. Responds to queries and ms within days (if submitted by e-mail). Send SASE for return of ms or send a disposable copy of ms and #10 SASE for reply only. Accepts simultaneous submissions, previously published work and multiple submissions. Sample copy for $3. Guidelines for SASE, e-mail or on website.

Payment/Terms: Pays 6 contributor's copies or free subscription to magazine; additional copies $1. Pays on publication for one-time and electronic rights.

Advice: "Use our topics."

◐ ◎ ITALIAN AMERICANA, URI/CCE 80 Washington St., Providence RI 02903-1803. (401)277-5306. Fax: (401)277-5100. Website: www.uri.edu/prov/italian/italian.html (includes writer's guidelines, names of editors). **Contact:** Carol Bonomo Albright and John Paul Russo, editors. Poetry Editor: Dana Gioia. Magazine: 6 × 9; 200 pages; varnished cover; perfect-bound; photos. "*Italian Americana* contains historical articles, fiction, poetry and memoirs, all concerning the Italian experience in the Americas." Semiannual. Estab. 1974. Circ. 1,200.

Needs: Italian American: literary. No nostalgia. Receives 10 mss/month. Accepts 3 mss/issue; 6-7 mss/year. Publishes up to 1 year after acceptance. Agented fiction 5%. **Publishes 1-2 new writers/year.** Recently published work by Mary Caponegro and Tony Ardizzone. Length: 20 double-spaced pages. Publishes short stories. Also publishes literary essays, literary criticism, poetry. Sometimes comments on rejected mss. Sponsors $500-1,000 literature prize annually.

How to Contact: Send complete ms (in triplicate) with a cover letter. Accepts queries/mss by fax. Include 3-5 line bio, list of publications. Responds in 1 month to queries; 2 months to mss. Send SASE for reply, return of ms or send a disposable copy of ms. No simultaneous submissions. Sample copy for $7. Guidelines for SASE. Reviews novels and short story collections. Send books to Professor John Paul Russo, English Dept., Univ. of Miami, Coral Gables, FL 33124.

Payment/Terms: Awards two $250 prizes to best fiction of year and 1 contributor's copy; additional copies $7. Acquires first North American serial rights.

Advice: "Please individualize characters, instead of presenting types (i.e., lovable uncle, etc.). No nostalgia."

☑ ◎ JEWISH CURRENTS MAGAZINE, 22 E. 17th St., New York NY 10003-1919. (212)924-5740. Fax: (212)414-2227. **Contact:** Morris U. Schappes, editor-in-chief. Magazine: 5½ × 8½; 48 pages. "We are a secular, progressive, independent Jewish monthly, pro-Israel though not Zionist, printing fiction, poetry, articles and reviews on Jewish politics and history, Holocaust/Resistance; mideast peace process, Black-Jewish relations, labor struggles, women's issues. Audience is secular, left/progressive, Jewish, mostly urban." Monthly. Estab. 1946. Circ. 2,000.

● This magazine may be slow to respond. They continue to be backlogged.

Needs: Contemporary, ethnic, feminist, historical, humor/satire, literary, senior citizen/retirement, translations. "We are interested in *authentic* experience and readable prose; humanistic orientation. Must have Jewish theme. Could use more humor; short, smart, emotional and intellectual impact. No religious, sectarian; no porn or hard sex, no escapist stuff. Go easy on experimentation, but we're interested." Upcoming themes (submit at least 3 months in advance): "Black-Jewish Relations" (February); "Holocaust/Resistance" (April); "Israel" (May); "Jews in the USSR & Ex-USSR" (July-August). Receives 6-10 unsolicited fiction mss/month. Accepts 0-1 ms/issue; 8-10 mss/year. **Publishes 4 new writers/year.** Published work by Stephanie Savage, Judy Cohen and Janusz Korczak. Length: 1,000-3,000 words; average length: 1,800 words. Also publishes literary essays, literary criticism, poetry.

How to Contact: Send complete ms with cover letter. "Writers should include brief biographical information, especially their publishing histories." SASE. Responds in 2 months to mss. Publishes ms 2-24 months after acceptance. Accepts mss by fax. Sample copy for $3 with SAE and 3 first-class stamps. Reviews novels and short story collections.

Payment/Terms: Pays complimentary one-year subscription and 6 contributor's copies. "We readily give reprint permission at no charge." Sends galleys to author.

Advice: Noted for "stories with Jewish content and personal Jewish experience—e.g., immigrant or Holocaust memories, assimilation dilemmas, dealing with Jewish conflicts OK. Space is increasingly a problem. Be intelligent, imaginative, intuitive and absolutely honest. Have a musical ear, and an ear for people: how they sound when they talk, and also hear what they don't say."

⊕ ☑ $ ◎ JEWISH QUARTERLY, P.O. Box 2078, London W1A1JR England. E-mail: editor@jewquart. freeserve.co.uk. Website: www.jq.ort.org/ (includes magazine info, covers, excerpts from articles). **Contact:** Matthew Reisz, editor. Quarterly.

Needs: "It deals in the broadest sense with all issues of Jewish interest." Accepts 1-3 mss/issue. Length: 1,500-7,000 words.

Payment/Terms: Pays £50.

Advice: "Work should have either a Jewish theme in the widest interpretation of that phrase or a theme which would interest our readership. The question which contributors should ask is 'Why should it appear in the *Jewish Quarterly* and not in another periodical?' "

☑ ◯ JOURNAL OF POLYMORPHOUS PERVERSITY Wry-Bred Press, Inc., 10 Waterside Plaza, Suite 20-B, New York NY 10010. (212)689-5473. Fax: (212)689-6859. E-mail: info@psychhumor.com. Website: www. psychhumor.com (includes excerpts). **Contact:** Glenn Ellenbogen, editor. Magazine: 6¾ × 10; 24 pages; 60 lb.

FOR EXPLANATIONS OF THESE SYMBOLS,
SEE THE INSIDE FRONT AND BACK COVERS OF THIS BOOK.

paper; antique india cover stock; illustrations with some articles. "*JPP* is a humorous and satirical journal of psychology, psychiatry, and the closely allied mental health disciplines." For "psychologists, psychiatrists, social workers, psychiatric nurses, *and* the psychologically sophisticated layman." Semiannual. Estab. 1984.

Needs: Humor/satire. "We only consider materials that are funny or that relate to psychology *or* behavior." Receives 50 unsolicited mss/month. Accepts 8 mss/issue; 16 mss/year. Most writers published last year were previously unpublished writers. Length: 4,000 words maximum; average length: 1,500 words. Comments on rejected mss.

How to Contact: Send complete ms *in triplicate*. Include cover letter and SASE. Responds in 3 months to mss. SASE. Accepts multiple submissions. Sample copy for $7. Guidelines for #10 SASE.

Payment/Terms: Pays 2 contributor's copies; additional copies $7.

Advice: "We will *not* look at poetry. We only want to see intelligent spoofs of scholarly psychology and psychiatry articles written in scholarly scientific language. Take a look at *real* journals of psychology and try to lampoon their *style* as much as their content. There are few places to showcase satire of the social sciences, thus we provide one vehicle for injecting a dose of humor into this often too serious area. Occasionally, we will accept a piece of creative writing written in the first person, e.g. 'A Subjective Assessment of the Oral Doctoral Defense Process: I Don't Want to Talk About It, If You Want to Know the Truth' (the latter being a piece in which Holden Caulfield shares his experiences relating to obtaining his Ph.D. in Psychology). Other creative pieces have involved a psychodiagnostic evaluation of The Little Prince (as a psychiatric patient) and God being refused tenure (after having created the world) because of insufficient publications and teaching experience."

KRAX MAGAZINE, 63 Dixon Lane, Leeds LS12 4RR, Yorkshire, Britain, U.K. **Contact:** Andy Robson, fiction editor. "*Krax* publishes lighthearted, humorous and whimsical writing. It is for anyone seeking light relief at a gentle pace." Appears 1-2 times/year.

Needs: "We publish mostly poetry of a lighthearted nature but use comic or spoof fiction, witty and humorous essays." Accepts 1 ms/issue. **Publishes 6-7 new writers/year (poetry).** Recently published work by Jim Sullivan. Length: 2,000 words maximum.

How to Contact: No specific guidelines.

Payment/Terms: Pays contributor's copies. Sample copy for $1 direct from editor.

Advice: "Don't spend too long on scene-setting or character construction as this inevitably produces an anti-climax in a short piece. Send IRCs or currency notes for return postal costs."

LEFT CURVE, P.O. Box 472, Oakland CA 94604. (510)763-7193. E-mail: leftcurv@wco.com. Website: www.ncal.verio.com/~leftcurv. **Contact:** Csaba Polony, editor. Magazine: 8½ × 11; 130 pages; 60 lb. paper; 100 pt. C1S Durosheen cover; illustrations; photos. "*Left Curve* is an artist-produced journal addressing the problem(s) of cultural forms emerging from the crises of modernity that strive to be independent from the control of dominant institutions, based on the recognition of the destructiveness of commodity (capitalist) systems to all life." Published irregularly. Estab. 1974. Circ. 2,000.

Needs: Contemporary, ethnic, experimental, historical, literary, prose poem, regional, science fiction, translations, political. "We publish critical, open, social/political-conscious writing." Upcoming theme: "Cyber-space and Nature." Receives approximately 12 unsolicited fiction mss/month. Accepts approximately 1 ms/issue. Publishes ms a maximum of 12 months after acceptance. Published work by Péter Lengyel and Michael Filas. Length: 500-2,500 words; average length: 1,200 words. Publishes short shorts. Sometimes comments on rejected mss.

How to Contact: Send complete ms with cover letter. Include "statement of writer's intent, brief bio and reason for submitting to *Left Curve*." Accepts electronic submissions; "prefer 3½ disk and hard copy, though we do accept e-mail submissions." Responds in 6 months. SASE. Sample copy for $10, 9 × 12 SAE and $1.24 postage. Guidelines for 1 first-class stamp.

Payment/Terms: Pays in contributor's copies. Rights revert to author.

Advice: "Dig deep; no superficial personalisms, no corny satire. Be honest, realistic and gorge out the truth you wish to say. Understand yourself and the world. Have writing be a means to achieve or realize what is real."

LONG SHOT, Long Shot Productions, P.O. Box 6238, Hoboken NJ 07030. Website: www.longshot.org (includes excerpts, writer's guidelines, names of editors, interview w/ authors, poetry, fiction, books to order). **Contact:** Nancy Mercado. Literary magazine: 5 × 8; 160 pages; white paper; 10pt C1S cover stock; some illustrations; photos. "Writing for the real world. Dark, gritty, humorous, light, fantastic, surreal, imaginative." Semiannual. Estab. 1982.

Needs: Comics/graphic novels, erotica, ethnic (general and specific culture), fantasy, feminist, gay, humor/satire, lesbian, literary, science fiction. "No grad school writing program processed fiction." Receives 50 unsolicited mss/month. Accepts 2-3 mss/issue; 4-6 mss/year. Publishes ms 4-6 months after acceptance. Recently published work by Robert Press, John Richey, Nicholasa Mohr. Length: 1-12 pages; average length: 5 pages. Publishes short shorts. Also publishes poetry. Rarely comments on rejected mss.

How to Contact: Send complete ms with cover letter or submit through an agent. Accepts submissions on disk, definitely no e-mail submissions. Responds in 4 months to queries; 2 months to mss. Accepts simultaneous submissions. Sample copy for $8. Guidelines by e-mail or on website.

Payment/Terms: Pays 3 contributor's copies; additional copies 60% of the cover price. Pays on publication for first North American serial and electronic rights.
Advice: "We like work that captures our attention immediately and impresses us with its passion, style and point of view. Read our magazine."

MAIL CALL JOURNAL, Keeping the Spirit of the Civil War Soldier Alive!, Distant Frontier Press, P.O. Box 5031, Dept. N, South Hackensack NJ 07606. (201)296-0419. E-mail: mcj@historyonline.net. Website: www.historyonline.net. **Contact:** Anna Pansini, managing editor. Newsletter: 8½×11; 8 pages; 20 lb. paper; illustrations. *Mail Call Journal* focuses on the soldiers' lives during the Civil War and publishes Civil War soldiers' letters, diaries, memoirs and stories of the individual soldiers as well as poems. Bimonthly. Estab. 1990. Circ. 500.
Needs: Historical (American Civil War). Receives 20 unsolicited mss/month. Accepts 2 mss/issue; 10 mss/year. Publishes ms up to 2 years after acceptance. **Publishes 10 new writers/year.** Length: 500-1,500 words. Also publishes literary essays, literary criticism and poetry. Sometimes comments on rejected ms.
How to Contact: Send complete ms with a cover letter mentioning "any relations from the Civil War period for reference only, not a determining factor." Accepts queries/mss by e-mail. Responds in 1 year. SASE for return of ms. Accepts simultaneous, reprint and electronic (disk) submissions. Sample copy and guidelines are included in a writer's packet for $5.
Payment/Terms: Pays in contributor's copies. Acquires one-time rights for print and Internet publication.
Advice: Wants more "personal accounts" and no "overused themes. Write from your heart but use your head. Our readers are knowledgeable about the basics of the Civil War, so go beyond that."

MAJESTIC BOOKS P.O. Box 19097A, Johnston RI 02919-0097. (401)421-5311. E-mail: majesticbk@aol.com. **Contact:** Cindy MacDonald, fiction editor. Bound softcover short story anthologies; 5½×8½; 192 pages; 60 lb. paper; C1S cover stock. "Majestic Books is a small press which was formed to give children an outlet for their work. We publish softcover bound anthologies of fictional stories by children, for children and adults who enjoy the work of children." Triannual. Estab. 1993. Circ. 250.
Needs: Stories written on any subject by children (under 18) only. Children's/juvenile (10-12 years), young adult (13-18 years). Receives 50 unsolicited mss/month. Accepts 100 mss/year. Publishes ms 1 year maximum after acceptance. **Publishes 100 new writers/year.** Published work by Michelle Foley, Beth Woodward, Emily Breyfogle and Susan Chaves. Length: 2,000 words maximum. Publishes short shorts. Also publishes literary essays.
How to Contact: Send complete ms with a cover letter. Include estimated word count and author's age. Accepts submissions by e-mail. Responds in 3 weeks. Send SASE for reply. Accepts simultaneous submissions. Sample copy for $5. Guidelines for #10 SASE.
Payment/Terms: Pays 10% royalty for all books sold due to the author's inclusion.
Advice: "We love stories that will keep a reader thinking long after they have read the last word. Be original. We have received some manuscripts of shows we have seen on television or books we have read. Write from inside you, and you'll be surprised at how much better your writing will be. Use *your* imagination."

MEDIPHORS, A Literary Journal of the Health Professions, P.O. Box 327, Bloomsburg PA 17815. E-mail: mediphor@ptd.net. Website: www.mediphors.org (includes writer's guidelines, names of editors, samples of short stories, essays, poetry, photography, covers and current contents, art and more). **Contact:** Eugene D. Radice, MD, editor. Magazine: 8½×11; 73 pages; 20 lb. white paper; 70 lb. cover; illustrations; photos. "We publish broad work related to medicine and health including essay, short story, commentary, fiction, poetry. Our audience: general readers and health care professionals." Semiannual. Estab. 1993. Circ. 900.
Needs: "Short stories related to health." Adventure, experimental, historical, humor/satire, literary, mainstream/contemporary, science fiction (hard science, soft/sociological), medicine. "No religious, romance, suspense, erotica, fantasy." Receives 50 unsolicited mss/month. Accepts 14 mss/issue; 28 mss/year. Publishes ms 10 months after acceptance. Agented fiction 2%. **Publishes 20 new writers/year.** Length: 4,500 words maximum; average length: 2,500 words. Publishes short shorts. Also publishes literary essays and poetry. Sometimes comments on rejected mss.
How to Contact: Send complete ms with a cover letter. Include estimated word count, bio (paragraph) and any experience/employment in the health professions. Responds in 4 months to mss. Send SASE for reply, return of ms or send a disposable copy of ms. No simultaneous submissions. Sample copy for $6. Guidelines for #10 SASE.
Payment/Terms: Pays 2 contributor's copies; additional copies for $5.50 Acquires first North American serial rights.
Advice: Looks for "high quality writing that shows fresh perspective in the medical and health fields. Accurate knowledge of subject material. Situations that explore human understanding in adversity. Order a sample copy for examples of work. Start with basic quality writing in short story and create believable, engaging stories concerning medicine and health. Knowledge of the field is important since the audience includes professionals within the medical field. Don't be discouraged. We enjoy receiving work from beginning writers."

N ◑ MEDUSA'S HAIRDO MAGAZINE, Byrd White Press, 2631 Seminole Ave., Ashland KY 41102. E-mail: medusashairdo@yahoo.com. Website: http://victorian.fortunecity.com/brambles/4/mh/ (includes guidelines, news, cover art). **Contact:** Beverly Moore, editor. Magazine: 8½×11; 24 pages; glossy cover; illustrations. "We are the magazine of modern mythology—not a rehash of classical myth, but the stories that define or describe our times." Semiannual. Estab. 1995. Circ. 50.

Needs: Humor/satire, literary, mainstream, science fiction (soft/sociological). "No erotica or extreme violence. I'm also not likely to accept politically slanted stories in categories like ethnic, feminist, religious, etc." Receives 30 unsolicited mss/month. Accepts 4-6 mss/issue; 8-12 mss/year. Publishes ms 1 year after acceptance. Length: 4,000 words maximum; average length: 2,000 words. Publishes short shorts. Average length: 1,000 words. Also publishes poetry. Often comments on rejected mss.

How to Contact: Send complete ms with a cover letter. Accepts submissions by e-mail as text only. Include estimated word count and cover letter with name, address, e-mail, subtitles. Responds in 2 weeks to queries; 2 months to mss. Send a disposable copy of ms and #10 SASE for reply only. Accepts simultaneous submissions, previously published work and multiple submissions (3 stories maximum). Sample copy for $4.50. Guidelines for SASE or by e-mail.

Payment/Terms: Pays 1 contributor's copy; additional copies $4.50. Acquires first North American serial rights.

Advice: "Let me know in your cover letter that your are a beginner. I'll try to help."

N $ MINDSPARKS, The Magazine of Science and Science Fiction, (I, II, IV), Molecudyne Research, P.O. Box 1302, Laurel MD 20725-1302. (410)715-1703. E-mail: asaro@sff.net. Website: www.sff.net/people/asaro/ (includes interviews, reviews, information on the Skolian Empire/Ruby Dynasty books, science articles). **Contact:** Catherine Asaro, editor. Magazine: 8½×11; 44 pages; 20 lb. white paper; 60 lb. cover; illustrations; photos. "We publish science fiction and science articles." Published on a varied schedule. Estab. 1993. Circ. 1,000.

● *Mindsparks* is in the process of changing from a paper magazine to an electronic publication. For more information, either write the above editorial address or check the website.

Needs: Science fiction (hard science, soft/sociological), young adult (science fiction). "No pornography." Receives 50 unsolicited submissions/month. Accepts 2-4 mss/issue; 12-14 mss/year. Publishes ms 1-24 months after acceptance. **Publishes an average of 10 new writers/year.** Published work by Hal Clement, G. David Nordley, Lois Gresh and Paul Levinson. Length: 8,000 words maximum; average length: 4,000 words. Publishes short shorts. Also publishes literary essays, literary criticism and poetry. Often comments on rejected mss.

How to Contact: Send complete ms with a cover letter. Include estimated word count and list of publications. "Prefers initial contact be made by mail." Responds in 3 months. Send SASE for reply, return of ms or send a disposable copy of ms. Accepts simultaneous submissions. Sample copy for $4.50, 8½×11 SAE and $1 postage or 2 IRCs. Guidelines for #10 SASE. Reviews novels and short story collections.

Payment/Terms: Pays 2¢/word. Pays on publication for first North American serial rights. Sends galleys to author.

Advice: Looks for "well-written, well-researched, interesting science ideas with good characterization and good plot. Read a copy of the magazine. We receive many submissions that don't fit the intent of *Mindsparks*."

✓ $ ◎ THE MIRACULOUS MEDAL, The Central Association of the Miraculous Medal, 475 E. Chelten Ave., Philadelphia PA 19144-5785. (215)848-1010. Fax: (215)848-1014. Website: www.cmphila.org/camm/. Editor: Rev. William J. O'Brien, C.M. **Contact:** Charles Kelly, general manager. Magazine. Quarterly.

Needs: Religious/inspirational. Receives 25 unsolicited fiction mss/month. Accepts 2 mss/issue; 8 mss/year. Publishes ms up to 2 years or more after acceptance.

How to Contact: Query first with SASE. Sample copy and fiction guidelines free.

Payment/Terms: Pays 2¢/word minimum. Pays on acceptance for first rights.

N $◑ ◎ MOXIE, For the Woman Who Dares, Moxie, 1230 Glen Ave., Berkeley CA 94708. (510)540-5510. Fax: (510)540-8595. E-mail: emily@moxiemag.com. Website: www.moxiemag.com (includes entirely original content, no overlap with print edition—articles, short stories, book reviews and poems). **Contact:** Emily Hancock, editor. Magazine: 8¼×10¾; 56 pages; illustrations; photos. "Our audience is smart, gutsy women who want something more than fashion, sex and beauty in a magazine." Quarterly. Estab. 1998. Circ. under 10,000. Member: IPA.

Needs: Essays, family saga, feminist, romance (contemporary). Upcoming theme: Family/Friends/Lovers. List of upcoming themes available for SASE. Receives 40-60 unsolicited mss/month. Accepts 20-30 mss/issue; 90-100 mss/year. **Publishes 80 new writers/year.** Recently published work by dgk goldberg, Danya Ruttenberg and Jessica Leigh Lebos. Length: 750-4,000 words; average length: 1,500-2,000 words. Publishes short shorts. Average length: 750 words. Also publishes literary essays, literary criticism and poetry. Often comments on rejected mss.

How to Contact: Send complete ms with a cover letter by e-mail only. Include estimated word count and e-mail address. Responds in 2 weeks to mss. Accepts simultaneous submissions and previously published work. Sample copy for $5. Guidelines free or by e-mail. Reviews novels, short story collections and nonfiction books of interest to writers.

Payment/Terms: Pays $10-25 and 3 contributor's copies; additional copies $5. Pays on publication. Sends galleys to author.

⚇ MSLEXIA, For Women Who Write, Mslexia Publications Ltd., P.O. Box 656, Newcastle Upon Tyne NE99-2RP United Kingdom. Phone: (00)44-191-2819772. Fax: (00)44-191-2819445. E-mail: lisa@mslexia.dem on.co.uk. Website: www.mslexia.co.uk. **Contact:** Debbie Taylor. Magazine: A4; 60 pages; some illustrations; photos. "*Mslexia* is for women who write, who want to write, who have a special interest in women's writing, who teach creative writing. *Mslexia* is a blend of features, articles, advice, listings, and original prose & poetry. Many parts of the magazine are open to submission from any women. Please request contributor's guidelines prior to sending in work." Quarterly. Estab. 1999. Circ. 6,000.

Needs: Each issue is dedicated to a specific theme. Themes for SASE. Some themes included erotica, death writing from a male perspective & body image. No work of men. Receives 100-200 unsolicited mss/month. Accepts 5-6 mss/issue; 20-25 mss/year. Publishes ms 3-4 months after acceptance. **Publishes 10-15 new writers/ year.** Length: 2,000 words; average length: 1,000-2,000 words. Publishes short shorts. Average length: 1,000-2,000 words. Also publishes poetry.

How to Contact: Query first. Accepts submissions by e-mail, fax, and disk. Responds in 2 weeks to queries; 3 months to mss. Send disposable copy of ms and #10 for reply only. Sample copy for £4.95 (sterling). Guidelines for SASE, e-mail, fax or on website.

Payment/Terms: Pays £25 sterling/poem or 1,000 words of prose; additional copies £4.95 sterling. Pays on publication for one-time rights.

Advice: "Prose—An unusual slant on the theme. Well structured, short pieces. Also intelligent, humorous, or with a strong sense of voice. Poetry—Innovative diction use/syntax, free verse or intelligent subversion of form, well crafted structured. Consider the theme and all obvious interpretations of it. Try to think of a new angle/ slant. Dare to be different. Make sure the piece is strong on craft as well as content."

☑ $▢ ◎ MURDEROUS INTENT, Mystery Magazine, Deadly Alibi Press. (360)695-9004. Fax: (360)693-3354. E-mail: madison@teleport.com. Website: www.murderousintent.com (includes writer's guide-lines, short fiction, articles, interviews, table of contents, minisynopsis corner, subscription and convention infor-mation). **Contact:** Margo Power, editor. Magazine: 8½×11; 64 pages; newsprint; glossy 2-color cover; illustra-tions; photos, cozy/soft boiled mystery magazine publishing fiction, nonfiction and interviews. Quarterly. Estab. 1995. Circ. 7,000.

● Several *Murderous Intent* authors have been short fiction Derringer Award recipients, Edgar nominees, and one story was purchased for a film.

Needs: Mystery/suspense (amateur sleuth, cozy, police procedural, private eye), psychic/supernatural/occult, science fiction (with mystery) "occasionally." No true crime, no cannibal stories, no stories with excessive violence, language or sex. (Nothing but mystery/suspense with a little ghostly presence now and then). Receives 200 unsolicited queries/month. Accepts 10-14 mss/issue; 40-48 mss/year. Publishes ms up to 18 months after acceptance. **Publishes 10 or more new writers/year. Publishes 30% new writers/year.** Published work by Toni L.P. Kelner, Carol Cail, Michael Mallory, Seymour Shubin and L.L. Thrasher. Length: 250-5,000 words; average length: 2,000-4,000 words. Publishes short shorts. Length: 250-400 words. Also publishes mystery-related essays and poetry. Sometimes comments on rejected mss. Annual contest, 2,000 words, mystery. Deadline: August 1. $10 entry fee. SASE. E-mail for guidelines, different theme each year.

How to Contact: Email queries only. Include a brief story synopsis, word count, telephone number, e-mail and address. "If it looks like something that fits the magazine we will send guidelines for submitting the story. All snail mail submissions will be returned unopened." Only 1 story/submission. Responds in 1 week to queries, 2 weeks to mss. Sample copy for $5.95, 9×12 SAE and 4 first-class stamps. Guidelines for #10 SASE. "Minisy-nopsis Corner" for authors to submit minisynopses of their new mystery novels (free).

Payment/Terms: Pays $10 and 1 contributor's copy; additional copies $3.50 (issue their story appears in). Pays on acceptance for first North American serial rights.

Advice: "The competition is tough so write the mystery you love—build characters people will remember—and surprise us."

$▢ MYSTERY TIME, An Anthology of Short Stories, Hutton Publications, P.O. Box 2907, Decatur IL 62524-2907. **Contact:** Linda Hutton, editor. Booklet: 5½×8½; 52 pages; bond paper. "Semiannual collection of short stories with a suspense or mystery theme for mystery buffs, with an emphasis on women writers and women protagonists. We focus on older women, both as characters and as authors. It is our goal to encourage middle-aged and older females by presenting a positive, up-beat picture of them and their lives." Estab. 1983.

Needs: Mystery/suspense only. Receives 10-15 unsolicited fiction mss/month. Accepts 20-24 mss/year. **Publishes 5-6 new writers/year.** Published work by Barbara Deming, Patricia Harrington, and Elizabeth Hawn. Length: 1,500 words maximum. Occasionally comments on rejected mss and recommends other markets.

How to Contact: Send complete ms with SASE. "No cover letters." Accepts simultaneous and previously published submissions. Responds in 1 month to mss. Publishes ms an average of 6-8 months after acceptance. Accepts previously published work. Sample copy for $4. Guidelines for #10 SASE. Reviews mysteries and women's studies books. Send galleys or book with SASE.

Payment/Terms: Pays ¼-1¢/word and 1 contributor's copy; additional copies $2.50. Pays on acceptance for one-time rights.

Advice: "Study a sample copy and the guidelines. Too many amateurs mark themselves as amateurs by submitting blindly."

✓ $ Ⓞ NEW ENGLAND WRITERS' NETWORK, P.O. Box 483, Hudson MA 01749-0483. (978)562-2946. Fax: (978)568-0497. E-mail: NEWNmag@aol.com. Editor: Glenda Baker. **Contact:** Liz Aleshire, fiction editor. Poetry Editor: Judy Adourian. Magazine: 8½×11; 24 pages; coated cover. "We are devoted to helping new writers get published and to teaching through example and content. We are looking for well-written stories that grab us from the opening paragraph." Quarterly. Estab. 1994. Circ. 200.

● *New England Writers' Network* has a new feature called First Fiction. A story by a previously unpublished fiction writer is spotlighted under the heading First Fiction.

Needs: Adventure, condensed/excerpted novel, ethnic/multicultural, humor/satire, literary, mainstream/contemporary, mystery/suspense, religious/inspirational, romance. "We will consider anything except pornography or extreme violence." Accepts 5 mss/issue; 20 mss/year. Reads mss only from June 1 through September 1. Publishes ms 4-12 months after acceptance. **Publishes 4-6 new writers/year.** Published work by Arline Chase, James Calandrillo, Pat Carr, Nick Hubacker and Steve Burt. Length: 2,000 words maximum. Publishes short shorts. Also publishes poetry and 3-4 personal essays per issue. Always comments on rejected mss.

How to Contact: Send complete ms with a cover letter. Include estimated word count. Bio on acceptance. Responds in 4 months. SASE for return of ms. No simultaneous submissions. Sample copy for $5.50. Guidelines free. "We do not review story collections or novels. We do publish 2,000-word (maximum) novel excerpts. Writer picks the excerpt—do not send novel."

Payment/Terms: Pays $10 for fiction, $5 for personal essays, $3 per poem and 1 contributor's copy. Pays on publication for first North American serial rights.

Advice: "Give us a try! Please send for guidelines and a sample."

Ⓝ Ⓞ NEW METHODS, The Journal of Animal Health Technology, P.O. Box 22605, San Francisco CA 94122-0605. **Contact:** Ronald S. Lippert, AHT, editor. Newsletter ("could become magazine again"): 8½×11; 2-4 pages; 20 lb. paper; illustrations; "rarely" photos. Network service in the animal field educating services for mostly professionals in the animal field; e.g., animal health technicians. Monthly. Estab. 1976. Circ. 5,608.

Needs: Animals: contemporary, experimental, historical, mainstream, regional. No stories unrelated to animals. Receives 12 unsolicited fiction mss/month. Accepts one ms/issue; 12 mss/year. Length: Open. "Rarely" publishes short shorts. Occasionally critiques rejected mss. Recommends other markets.

How to Contact: Query first with theme, length, expected time of completion, photos/illustrations, if any, biographical sketch of author, all necessary credits or send complete ms. Response time varies (up to 4 months). SASE for query and ms. Accepts simultaneous submissions. Sample copy and guidelines for $2.90.

Payment/Terms: No payment. Acquires one-time rights. Back issue and guidelines only with SASE for $2, must mention Writer's Digest Books.

Advice: Sponsors contests: theme changes but generally concerns the biggest topics of the year in the animal field. "Emotion, personal experience—make the person feel it. We are growing."

✓ $ Ⓞ NEWFANGLED FAIRY TALES, Meadowbrook Press, 5451 Smetana Dr., Minnetonka MN 55343. (952)930-1100. **Contact:** Bruce Lansky, editor. Assistant Editor: Megan McGinnis. Anthology series for children ages 8-12. Annual.

Needs: Children's/juvenile short stories (8-12 years). No novels or picture books. Receives 25-30 unsolicited submissions/month for each series. Accepts 8-10 mss/issue. Publishes ms 1 year after acceptance. **Publishes 10-15 new writers/year.** Length: 1,800 words maximum; average length: 1,200-1,500 words. Sometimes comments on or critiques rejected mss.

How to Contact: Query first. Include estimated word count and list of publications. Responds in 3 months. Send SASE for reply, return of ms or send disposable copy of ms. Accepts simultaneous submissions and reprints. Guidelines for #10 SASE. Address all submissions to Megan McGinnis, assistant editor.

Payment/Terms: Pays $500 on publication for nonexclusive worldwide rights.

Advice: "Read our guidelines before submitting. All our anthology series for children have very strict guidelines. Also, please read the books to get a feel for what types of stories we publish. Our series consistently feature short stories by previously unpublished writers—we consider stories on their own merits, not on the reputations of the authors."

☑ $⃠ ▣ **NIGHT TERRORS**, 1202 W. Market St., Orrville OH 44667-1710. (330)683-0338. E-mail: dedavidson@night-terrors-publications.com. Website: www.night-terrors-publications.com (includes updated guidelines, bios of the editor and writers, short fiction, order info, links to other sites of interest to writers and readers of horror). **Contact:** D.E. Davidson, editor/publisher. Magazine: 8½×11; 52 pages; 80 lb. glossy cover; illustrations; photos. *Night Terrors* publishes quality, thought-provoking horror fiction for literate adults. Quarterly. Estab. 1996. Circ. 1,000.

• *Night Terrors* has had 22 stories listed in the Honorable Mention section of *The Year's Best Fantasy and Horror, Annual Collections.* Five *Night Terror* stories were nominated for the Horror Writer's Association's Bram Stoker Award for Short Fiction 1997, 1998.

Needs: Horror, psychic/supernatural/occult. "*Night Terrors* does not accept stories involving abuse, sexual mutilation or stories with children as main characters. We publish traditional supernatural/psychological horror for a mature audience. Our emphasis is on literate work with a chill." Receives 50 unsolicited mss/month. Accepts 12 mss/issue; 46 mss/year. Does not read mss June-August. Publishes ms 2-6 months after acceptance. **Publishes 16 new writers/year.** Published work by John M. Clay, Ken Goldman, and Barbara Rosen. Length: 2,000-5,000 words; average length: 3,000 words. Often comments on rejected mss.

How to Contact: Send complete ms with a cover letter. Include estimated word count, 50-word bio and list of publications. Responds in 1 week to queries; 3 months to mss. Send SASE for reply, return of ms or send a disposable copy of ms. Accepts simultaneous submissions. Sample copy for $6 (make checks to Night Terrors Publications). Guidelines free for #10 SASE.

Payment/Terms: Pays up to $100 and 1-2 contributor's copy; additional copies for $4.50. Pays on publication for first North American serial rights. Sends galleys to author.

Advice: "I publish what I like. I like stories which involve me with the viewpoint character and leave me with the feeling that his/her fate could have or might be mine. Act professionally. Check your work for typos, spelling, grammar, punctuation, format. Send your work flat. And if you must, paper clip it, don't staple. Include a brief, to-the-point cover letter."

◪ **THE OAK**, 1530 Seventh St., Rock Island IL 61201. (309)788-3980. **Contact:** Betty Mowery, editor. Magazine: 8½×11; 8-20 pages. "To provide a showcase for new authors while showing the work of established authors as well; to publish wholesome work, something with a message." Bimonthly. Estab. 1991. Circ. 300.

• "The Gray Squirrel," a section in *Oak,* uses fiction and poetry only from authors age 60 and up.

Needs: Adventure, contemporary, experimental, fantasy, humor, mainstream, prose poem. No erotica or love poetry. Receives 25 mss/month. Accepts up to 12 mss/issue. Publishes ms within 3 months of acceptance. **Published new writers within the last year.** Length: 500 words maximum.

How to Contact: Send complete ms. Responds in 1 week. SASE. Accepts simultaneous and reprint submissions. Sample copy for $3. Subscription $10 for 4 issues.

Payment/Terms: None, but not necessary to buy a copy in order to be published. Acquires first rights.

Advice: "I do not want erotica, extreme violence or killing of humans or animals for the sake of killing. Just be yourself when you write. Please include SASE or manuscripts will be destroyed. Be sure name and address are on the manuscript. Study the markets for length of manuscript and what type of material is wanted."

🦋 ☑ $⃠ ◐ **ON SPEC**, Box 4727, Edmonton, Alberta T6E 5G6 Canada. (780)413-0215. Fax: (780)413-1538. E-mail: onspec@earthling.net. Website: www.icomm.ca/onspec (includes writer's guidelines, past editorials, excerpts from published fiction, links to writer's Internet resources). **Contact:** The Editors. Magazine: 5¼×8; 112 pages; illustrations. "Provides a venue for Canadian speculative writing—science fiction, fantasy, horror, magic realism." Quarterly. Estab. 1989. Circ. 2,000.

Needs: Fantasy and science fiction. No condensed or excerpted novels, no religious/inspirational stories. "We would like to see more horror, fantasy, science fiction—well-developed stories with complex characters and strong plots." Receives 50 mss/month. Accepts 10 mss/issue; 40 mss/year. "We read manuscripts during the month after each deadline: February 28/May 31/August 31/November 30." Publishes ms 6-18 months after acceptance. **Publishes new writers, number varies.** Length: 1,000-6,000 words; average length: 4,000 words. Also publishes poetry. Often comments on rejected mss.

How to Contact: Send complete ms with a cover letter. No submissions by e-mail or fax. Include estimated word count, 2-sentence bio and phone number. Responds in 5 months to mss. SASE for return of ms or send a disposable copy of ms plus #10 SASE for response. Include Canadian postage or IRCs. Accepts simultaneous submissions. Sample copy for $6. Guidelines for #10 SASE.

Payment/Terms: Pays $40-180 and 2 contributor's copies; additional copies for $4. Pays on acceptance for first North American serial rights.

Advice: "We're looking for original ideas with a strong SF element, excellent dialogue, and characters who are so believable, our readers will really care about them."

THE PIPE SMOKER'S EPHEMERIS, The Universal Coterie of Pipe Smokers, 20-37 120 St., College Point NY 11356-2128. **Contact:** Tom Dunn, editor. Magazine: 8½×11; 84-116 pages; offset paper and cover; illustrations; photos. Pipe smoking and tobacco theme for general and professional audience. Irregular quarterly. Estab. 1964.
Needs: Pipe smoking related: historical, humor/satire, literary. Publishes ms up to 1 year after acceptance. Length: 5,000 words maximum; average length: 2,500 words. Also publishes short shorts. Occasionally critiques rejected mss.
How to Contact: Send complete ms with cover letter. Responds in 2 weeks to mss. Accepts simultaneous submissions and reprints. Sample copy for 8½×11 SAE and 6 first-class stamps.
Payment/Terms: Acquires one-time rights.

POSKISNOLT PRESS, Yesterday's Press, Yesterday's Press, JAF Station, Box 7415, New York NY 10116-4630. **Contact:** Patricia D. Coscia, editor. Magazine: 7×8½; 20 pages; regular typing paper. Estab. 1989. Circ. 100.
Needs: Contemporary, erotica, ethnic, experimental, fantasy, feminist, gay, humor/satire, lesbian, literary, mainstream, prose poem, psychic/supernatural/occult, romance, senior citizen/retirement, western, young adult/teen (10-18 years). "X-rated material is not accepted!" Plans to publish a special fiction issue or anthology in the future. Receives 50 unsolicited mss/month. Accepts 30 mss/issue; 100 mss/year. Publishes ms 6 months after acceptance. Length: 100-500 words; average length: 200 words. Publishes short shorts. Length: 100-500 words. Sometimes comments on rejected mss and recommends other markets.
How to Contact: Query first with clips of published work or send complete ms with cover letter. Responds in 1 week to queries; 6 months to mss. SASE. Accepts simultaneous submissions. Sample copy for $5 with #10 SAE and $2 postage. Guidelines for #10 SAE and $2 postage.
Payment/Terms: Pays with subscription to magazine or contributor's copies; charges for extras. Acquires all rights, first rights or one-time rights.

$ THE POST, Publishers Syndication International, P.O. Box 6218, Charlottesville VA 22906-6218. (804)964-1194. Fax: (804)964-0096. E-mail: asam@hombuslib.com. Website: www.hombuslib.com/. **Contact:** A.P. Samuels, editor. Magazine: 8½×11; 32 pages. Monthly. Estab. 1988.
Needs: Adventure, mystery/suspense (private eye), romance (romantic suspense, historical, contemporary), western (traditional). "No explicit sex, gore, weird themes, extreme violence or bad language." Receives 35 unsolicited mss/month. Accepts 1 ms/issue; 12 mss/year. Time between acceptance and publication varies. Agented fiction 10%. **Publishes 1-3 new writers/year.** Length: 10,000 words average.
How to Contact: Send complete ms with cover letter. Responds to mss in 5 weeks. Guidelines for #10 SASE.
Payment/Terms: Pays ½-4¢/word. Pays on acceptance for all rights.
Advice: "Manuscripts must be for a general audience."

PRAYERWORKS, Encouraging, God's people to do the real work of ministry—intercessory prayer, The Master's Work, P.O. Box 301363, Portland OR 97294-9363. (503)761-2072. Fax: (503)760-1184. E-mail: jay4prayer@aol.com. Editor: V. Ann Mandeville. Newsletter: 5½×8; 4 pages; bond paper. "Our intended audience is 70% retired Christians and 30% families. We publish 350-500 word devotional material—fiction, nonfiction, biographical poetry, clean quips and quotes. Our philosophy is evangelical Christian serving the body of Christ in the area of prayer." Estab. 1988. Circ. 1,000.
Needs: Religious/inspirational. "Subject matter may include anything which will build a relationship with the Lord—prayer, ways to pray, stories of answered prayer, teaching on a Scripture portion, articles that will build faith, or poems will all work. We even use a series occasionally." Publishes 2-6 months after acceptance. Published work by Barb Marshal, Mary Hickey and Vann Mandeville. Length: 350-500 words; average length: 350-500 words. Publishes short shorts. Also publishes poetry. Often comments on rejected mss.
How to Contact: Send complete ms with a cover letter. Include estimated word count and a very short bio. Responds in 1 month. Send SASE for reply, return of ms or send a disposable copy of ms. Accepts simultaneous submissions and reprints. Sample copy and guidelines for #10 SASE.
Payment/Terms: Pays free subscription to the magazine and contributor's copies on publication. Writer retains all rights. Not copyrighted.

VISIT THE WRITER'S MARKET WEBSITE at www.writersmarket.com for hot new markets, daily market updates, writers' guidelines and much more.

Advice: Stories "must have a great take-away—no preaching; teach through action. Be thrifty with words— make them count."

☑ $ ⬛ ◎ **PRISONERS OF THE NIGHT, An Adult Anthology of Erotica, Fright, Allure and . . . Vampirism,** MKASHEF Enterprises, P.O. Box 688, Yucca Valley CA 92286-0688. E-mail: alayne@inetworld.n et. Website: www.asidozines.com (includes guidelines, excerpts, submission and subscription information). **Contact:** Alayne Gelfand, editor. Magazine: 8½×11; 50-80 pages; 20 lb. paper; slick cover; illustrations. "An adult, erotic vampire anthology of original character stories and poetry. Heterosexual and homosexual situations." Annual. Estab. 1987. Circ. 5,000.
Needs: "All stories must be erotic vampire stories, with unique characters, unusual situations." Adventure, contemporary, erotica, fantasy, feminist, gay, lesbian, literary, mystery/suspense, prose poem, psychic/supernatural/occult, science fiction (soft/sociological). No fiction that deals with anyone else's creations, i.e., no "Dracula" stories. No traditional Gothic, humor "or stereotypical vampires, please." Receives 100-150 unsolicited fiction mss/month. Accepts 5-12 mss/issue. Publishes ms 1-11 months after acceptance. **Publishes 1-5 new writers/ year.** Published work by Keil Stuart, Wendy Rathbone, James Dorr and Charlee Jacob. Length: 8,000 words maximum. Publishes short shorts. Sometimes comments on rejected mss.
How to Contact: Send complete ms with short cover letter. "A very brief introduction of author to the editor; name, address, *some* past credits if available." Responds in 3 weeks to queries; 4 months to mss. Reads *only* September through March. SASE. Accepts electronic submissions via Word, Word for Windows 98, ASCII rich text disk. Sample copy #1-4, $15; #5, $12; #6-9, $9.95; #10, $7.95; #11, $9.95. Guidelines for #10 SASE.
Payment/Terms: Pays 1¢/word for fiction. Pays on acceptance for first North American serial rights.
Advice: Looks for "clean, professional presentation. Interesting writing style that flows from word-one and sucks the reader in. An interesting idea/concept that appears at the beginning of a story. Read at least the most current issue of the publication to which you submit and read the guidelines before submitting. Know your market!"

$ ⬛ **PSI,** P.O. Box 6218, Charlottesville VA 22906-6218. (804)964-1194. Fax: (804)964-0096. E-mail: asam @esinet.net. **Contact:** A.P. Samuels, editor. Magazine: 8½×11; 32 pages; bond paper; self cover. "Mystery and romance." Bimonthly. Estab. 1987.
Needs: Adventure, romance (contemporary, historical, young adult), mystery/suspense (private eye), western (traditional). No ghoulish, sex, violence. Wants to see more believable stories. Receives 35 unsolicited mss/ month. Accepts 1-2 mss/issue. **Publishes 1-3 new writers/year.** Length: 10,000 (stories) and 30,000 (novelettes) words average. Comments on rejected mss "only on a rare occasion."
How to Contact: Send complete ms with cover letter. Responds in 2 weeks to queries; 6 weeks to mss. SASE. Accepts electronic submissions via disk.
Payment/Terms: Pays 1-4¢/word plus royalty. Pays on acceptance for all rights.
Advice: "Manuscripts must be for a general audience. Just good plain story telling (make it compelling). No explicit sex or ghoulish violence."

Ⓝ **THE PSYCHIC RADIO,** 1111 Elmwood Ave., Rochester NY 14620-3005. (716)472-3230, ext. 1288. **Contact:** Lester Billips Jr., editor. Magazine: full size; 30-50 pages; typing paper; card cover. "My magazine is to fiction, what 'alternative rock' is to music. *Psychic Radio* offers straight talk about problems long kept in the dark. My intended audience is anyone concerned with the moral fiber of our country." Quarterly. Estab. 2001.
Needs: Fantasy (sword and sorcery), horror (futuristic, psychological, supernatural), new age, psychic/supernatural/occult, religious (general, inspirational, religious fantasy), science fiction (soft/sociological). Accepts 5-10 mss/issue; 20-25 mss/year. Publishes in 3-4 months after acceptance. Publishes short shorts. Also publishes literary essays and poetry. Sometimes comments on rejected mss.
How to Contact: Send complete ms with cover letter. Include estimated word count and brief bio. Responds in 1 month to queries and mss. Send SASE for return of ms or send a disposable copy of ms and #10 SASE for reply only. Accepts simultaneous submissions, previously published work and multiple submissions. Sample copy for $2.50. Guidelines for SASE.
Payment/Terms: Pays $20-50 plus contributor's copies; additional copies $2.50. Pays on acceptance for one-time rights.
Advice: "Relevance to the growing psychic problem in America today. Be honest and be urgent."

Ⓝ $ ⬛ ▢ **PULP ETERNITY ONLINE,** Eternity Press, P.O. Box 930068, Norcross GA 30003. (770)934-6598. E-mail: pulpeternity@hotmail.com. Website: www.pulpeternity.com (includes fiction, guidelines, contests, reviews). **Contact:** Steve Algieri, editor. Online magazine. "We publish unique fiction with a leaning toward genre fiction (science fiction, fantasy, horror, mystery, romance, historical, alternative) with defined integral settings and strong ethnic/cultural/historical elements." Monthly. Estab. 1997. Circ. 10,000.
Needs: Erotica, ethnic/multicultural, experimental, fantasy (space fantasy, sword and sorcery, romance), feminist, gay, historical (general and romance), horror (dark fantasy, futuristic, psychological, supernatural), lesbian, mainstream, mystery/suspense (amateur sleuth, cozy, police procedural, private eye/hardboiled), psychic/supernatural/

occult, romance (contemporary, futuristic/time travel, gothic, historical, regency period, romantic suspense), science fiction (hard science/technological, soft/sociological), thriller/espionage. "No young adult or children's, child abuse, religious." Sponsors Best of the Web Contest and Anthology. Runs December-March each year. Published in May. List of upcoming themes available for SASE. Receives 300-500 unsolicited mss/month. Accepts 1-3 mss/issue; 15-25 mss/year. Publishes ms 6 months after acceptance. **Publishes 5 new writers/year.** Recently published work by William R. Eakin, Geoffrey Landis and Brian A. Hopkins. Length: 100-3,000 words; average length: 2,000 words. Publishes short shorts. Average length: 1,000 words. Also publishes literary criticism. Always comments on rejected mss.

How to Contact: Send complete ms with a cover letter. Accepts submissions by e-mail and disk. Include estimated word count. Responds in 1 week to queries; 1 month to mss. Send SASE (or IRC) for return of ms or send a disposable copy of ms and #10 SASE for reply only. Accepts simultaneous submissions. Sample copy free. Guidelines for SASE or by e-mail. Reviews novels, short story collections and nonfiction books of interest to writers.

Payment/Terms: Pays 5¢/word ($5-150). Pays on publication for nonexclusive, one-time print and audio rights. Sends galleys to author. Sponsors contest. Details posted online or available for SASE.

Advice: "We're different and proud of it. As other publishers further chop up fiction into tidy and smaller units, we endeavor to publish fiction that cannot be classified."

🅾 QUEEN OF ALL HEARTS, Queen Magazine, Montfort Missionaries, 26 S. Saxon Ave., Bay Shore NY 11706-8993. (516)665-0726. Fax: (516)665-4349. E-mail: pretre@worldnet.att.net. **Contact:** Roger M. Charest, S.M.M., managing editor. Magazine: 7¾×10¾; 48 pages; self cover stock; illustrations; photos. Magazine of "stories, articles and features on the Mother of God by explaining the Scriptural basis and traditional teaching of the Catholic Church concerning the Mother of Jesus, her influence in fields of history, literature, art, music, poetry, etc." Bimonthly. Estab. 1950. Circ. 2,500.
   ● *Queen of All Hearts* received a Catholic Press Award for General Excellence (third place) and a Prayer and Spirituality Journalism Award.

Needs: Religious/inspirational. "No mss not about Our Lady, the Mother of God, the Mother of Jesus." **Publishes 6 new writers/year.** Published work by Richard O'Donnell and Jackie Clements-Marenda. Length: 1,500-2,000 words. Sometimes recommends other markets.

How to Contact: Send complete ms with SASE. Accepts queries/mss by e-mail and fax (mss by permission only). Responds in 1 month to mss. Publishes ms 6-12 months after acceptance. Sample copy for $2.50 with 9×12 SAE.

Payment/Terms: Varies. Pays 6 contributor's copies.

Advice: "We are publishing stories with a Marian theme."

⬛✅ $⬜ ◎ QUEEN'S QUARTERLY, A Canadian Review, Queen's University, Kingston, Ontario K7L 3N6 Canada. Phone/fax: (613)533-2667. Fax: (613)533-6822. E-mail: qquarter@post.queensu.ca. Website: info.queensu.ca./quarterly. **Contact:** Boris Castel, editor. Magazine: 6×9; 800 pages/year; illustrations. "A general interest intellectual review, featuring articles on science, politics, humanities, arts and letters. Book reviews, poetry and fiction." Quarterly. Estab. 1893. Circ. 3,000.

Needs: Adventure, contemporary, experimental, fantasy, historical, humor/satire, literary, mainstream, science fiction and women's. "*Special emphasis on work by Canadian writers.*" Accepts 2 mss/issue; 8 mss/year. **Published new writers within the last year.** Published work by Gail Anderson-Dargatz, Mark Jarman, Rick Bowers and Dennis Bock. Length: 2,000-3,000 words. Also publishes literary essays, literary criticism, poetry.

How to Contact: "Send complete ms with SASE." Accepts submissions by e-mail. Responds within 3 months. Sample copy for $6.50. Reviews novels and short story collections.

Payment/Terms: Pays $100-300 for fiction, 2 contributor's copies and 1-year subscription; additional copies $5. Pays on publication for first North American serial rights. Sends galleys to author.

🅽 🅾 REFLECTIONS, Literary Journal, Piedmont Community College, P.O. Box 1197, Roxboro NC 27573. (336)599-1181. E-mail: furbisd@piedmont.cc.nc.us. **Contact:** Dean Furbish, founding editor. Magazine: 124 pages. "We publish work which addresses and transcends humanity and cultures." Annual. Estab. 1999. Circ. 500.

Needs: Literary, translations. Receives 3 unsolicited mss/month. Accepts 5 mss/issue. Publishes ms up to 1 year after acceptance. **Publishes 2 new writers/year.** Length: 5,000 words maximum; average length: 2,500 words. Publishes short shorts. Also publishes poetry.

How to Contact: Send complete ms with a cover letter. Include estimated word count, brief bio and SASE. Send SASE (or IRC) for return of ms or send a disposable copy of ms and #10 SASE for reply only. Accepts multiple submissions. Sample copy for $6. Guidelines for SASE or by e-mail.

Payment/Terms: Pays 1 contributor's copy; additional copies $6 pre-publication; $7 post-publication. Pays on publication for first North American serial rights. Writers are automatically considered for $50 annual Editor's Choice Award for best fiction.

Advice: "We look for good writing with a flair, which captivates an educated lay audience. Must speak to the human condition."

$ ⬤ ROSEBUD™, For People Who Enjoy Good Writing, P.O. Box 459, Cambridge WI 53523. Phone/fax: (608)423-9609. Website: www.hyperionstudio.com/rosebud (includes writer's guidelines, contests, preview, *Rosebud* bulletin board, teachers guide to current issue, outreach programs and advertising rates). **Contact:** Roderick Clark, editor. Magazine: 7×10; 136 pages; 60 lb. matte; 100 lb. cover; illustrations. Quarterly. Estab. 1993. Circ. 11,000.

Needs: Adventure, condensed/excerpted novel, ethnic/multicultural, experimental, historical (general), humor/satire, literary, mainstream/contemporary, psychic/supernatural/occult, regional, romance (contemporary), science fiction (soft/sociological), serialized novel, translations. Each submission must fit loosely into one of the following categories to qualify. City and Shadow (urban settings), Songs of Suburbia (suburban themes), These Green Hills (nature and nostalgia), En Route (any type of travel), Mothers, Daughters, Wives (relationships), Ulysses' Bow (manhood), Paper, Scissors, Rock (childhood, middle age, old age), The Jeweled Prize (concerning love), Lost and Found (loss and discovery), Voices in Other Rooms (historic or of other culture), Overtime (involving work), Anything Goes (humor), I Hear Music (music), Season to Taste (food), Word Jazz (wordplay), Apples to Oranges (miscellaneous, excerpts, profiles). Publishes annual special fiction issue or anthology. Receives 1,200 unsolicited mss/month. Accepts 16 mss/issue; 64 mss/year. Publishes ms 1-3 months after acceptance. **70% of work published is by new writers.** Published work by Seamus Heany, Louis Simpson, Allen Ginsberg and Philip Levine. Length: 1,200-1,800 words average. Occasionally uses longer pieces and novel excerpts (prepublished). Publishes short shorts. Also publishes literary essays. Often comments on rejected mss.

How to Contact: Send complete ms with a cover letter. Include estimated word count and list of publications. Responds in 3 months to mss. SASE for return of ms. Accepts simultaneous and reprints submissions. Sample copy for $6.95. Guidelines for legal SASE.

Payment/Terms: Pays $15 and 3 contributor's copies; additional copies $4.40. Pays on publication for one-time rights.

Advice: "Each issue will have six or seven flexible departments (selected from a total of sixteen departments that will rotate). We are seeking stories, articles, profiles, and poems of: love, alienation, travel, humor, nostalgia and unexpected revelation. Something has to 'happen' in the pieces we choose, but what happens inside characters is much more interesting to us than plot manipulation. We like good storytelling, real emotion and authentic voice."

N SHYFLOWER'S GARDEN, Shyflower's Enterprises Ltd., 1307 NW 1st St., Faribault MN 55021. (507)334-7469. E-mail: shyflowe@means.net. Website: www.shyflowersgarden.com. **Contact:** Linda Paquette, CFO-managing editor. Online magazine: 50 pages; some illustrations; photos. "Types of material wanted: Fiction, poetry, essays, articles, original humor, photographs, art contributed humor. Adult audience." Monthly. Estab. 2000. Circ. 84 subscribers; 1,000 visitors/month.

Needs: Adventure, erotica, ethnic/multicultural, experimental, fantasy (space, sword/sorcery), feminist, gay, historical (general), horror (dark fantasy, futuristic, psychological, supernatural), humor/satire, lesbian, literary, mainstream, military/war, mystery/suspense (amateur sleuth, private eye/hardboiled), new age, religious (general, inspirational), romance (futuristic/time travel, gothic, romantic suspense), science fiction (soft/sociological), thriller/espionage, western (traditional). Receives 55 unsolicited mss/month. Accepts 7 mss/issue; 84 mss/year. Publishes ms 1-6 months after acceptance. Recently published work by Jennifer Currington, Joe Miller, Maureen McMahon. Length: 2,500 words; average length: 1,700 words. Publishes short shorts. Also publishes literary essays and poetry. Always comments on rejected mss.

How to Contact: Send e-mail query. Include estimated word count, brief bio, social security number, website and e-mail address. Responds in 1 month to queries and mss. Accepts simultaneous submissions, previously published work and multiple submissions. Guidelines by e-mail or on website.

Payment/Terms: Pays $50 or 4¢/word plus free subscription to magazine. Acquires one-time, electronic and re-sale rights. Sometimes sends galleys to author.

Advice: "Content, readability, length, style. We prefer the type of writing that is written as if the author were telling the story to a friend. Read our mission statement, read our guidelines, familiarize yourself with the type of material we publish before submitting. Don't be afraid to query and ask any questions you may have."

✓ ⬤ ▼ SKIPPING STONES: A Multicultural Children's Magazine, P.O. Box 3939, Eugene OR 97403-0939. (541)342-4956. E-mail: skipping@efn.org. Website: www.efn.org/~skipping (includes writer's guidelines). **Contact:** Arun N. Toké, executive editor. Magazine: 8½×11; 36 pages; recycled 50 lb. halopaque paper; 100 lb. text cover; illustrations; photos. "*Skipping Stones* is a multicultural, international, nature awareness magazine for children 8-16, and their parents and teachers." Published 5 times a year. Estab. 1988. Circ. 2,500.

Needs: Children's/juvenile (8-16 years): ethnic/multicultural, feminist, religious/inspirational, young adult/teen, international, nature. No simplistic, fiction for the sake of fiction, mystery, violent/abusive language or science fiction. "We want more authentic pieces based on truly multicultural/intercultural/international living experiences of authors. We welcome works by people of color." Upcoming themes: "Living Abroad," "Crosscultural Communications," "Challenging Disabililty," "Humor Unlimited," "Folktales," "Turning Points in Life . . .," "Raising Children: Rewards, Punishments." List of upcoming themes available for SASE. Receives 50 mss/ month. Accepts 5-8 mss/issue; 20-25 mss/year. Publishes ms 3-6 months after acceptance. **Publishes up to 100 new writers/year.** Published work by Linda Grennell, Almira Gilles, Joseph Chu, Lily Hartmannn and Peter Chase. Length: 250-1,000 words; average length: 750 words. Publishes short shorts. Also publishes literary essays and poetry (by youth under 18). Often comments on rejected mss. Sponsors contests and awards for writers under 17 years of age.

How to Contact: Send complete ms with a cover letter. Accepts queries/mss by e-mail. Include 50- to 100-word bio with background, international or intercultural experiences. Responds in 1 month to queries; 4 months to mss. Send SASE for reply, return of ms or send a disposable copy of ms. Accepts simultaneous submissions. Sample copy for $5, and 4 first-class stamps. Guidelines for #10 SASE.

Payment/Terms: Pays 1-4 contributor's copies; additional copies for $3. Acquires first North American serial rights and nonexclusive reprint rights.

Advice: Looking for stories with "multicultural/multiethnic theme. Realistic and suitable for 8 to 16 year olds (with use of other languages when appropriate). Promoting social and nature awareness. In addition to encouraging children's creativity, we also invite adults to submit their own writing and artwork for publication in *Skipping Stones*. Writings and artwork by adults should challenge readers to think and learn, cooperate and create."

✓ $ ⊘ SPACE AND TIME, 138 W. 70th St. (4B), New York NY 10023-4468. Website: www.cith.org/ space&time.html (includes guidelines, staff, current and future contents, back issues/books for sale). Editor: Gordon Linzner. **Contact:** Gerard Houarner, fiction editor. Magazine: 8½×11; 48 pages; 50 lb. paper; index card cover stock; illustrations; photos. "We publish science fiction, fantasy, horror and our favorite, that-which-defies-categorization." Biannual. Estab. 1966. Circ. 2,500. Member: Small Press Center and the Small Press Genre Organization.

Needs: Fantasy (science, sword and sorcery, undefinable), horror, science fiction (hard science, soft/sociological, undefinable). Receives 100 unsolicited mss/month. Accepts 12 mss/issue; 24 mss/year. Publishes ms 6-18 months after acceptance. **Publishes 2-6 new writers/year.** Recently published work by Charlee Jacob, Patricia Russo, and Chris Huntington. Length: 10,000 words maximum; average length: 5,000 words. Publishes short shorts. Also publishes poetry. Send poems to Linda D. Addison. Often comments on rejected mss.

How to Contact: Send complete ms. Include estimated word count. Responds in 1 week to queries; 3 months to mss. Send SASE for reply, return of ms or send a disposable copy of ms. Sample copy for $6.50 and 9×12 SAE. Guidelines for #10 SASE or SAE and 1 IRC.

Payment/Terms: Pays 1¢/word, $5 minimum and 2 contributor's copies; additional copies $3. Pays on acceptance for first North American serial rights and option to reprint in context of magazine.

Advice: Looks for "good writing, strong characterization and unusual plot or premise."

Ⓝ STEPPING OUT OF THE DARKNESS, Puritan Newsletter, P.O. Box 712, Hingham MA 02043. (781)878-5531. **Contact:** Editor. Newsletter/magazine: 9-12 pages. "Our main focus is on New England in earlier centuries. We uncover lost spiritual truths in Holy living (with the help of such great figures as Richard Baxter, Gov. John Winthrop, Cotton Mather and many more.) We also print current concerns, poetry and inspirational fiction. We like to see work from children and teens as well as adults. Our publication is read by Christians and also those who are unsure about God. We also print Jewish stories." Monthly. Estab. 1998. Circ. 50.

Needs: Children's/juvenile (historical, ages: 7-10), family saga, historical (general), humor/satire, religious (children's, general, inspirational, religious thriller), thriller/espionage, young adult/teen (adventure, historical, problem novels), general family, Jewish stories. Accepts 1 mss/issue; 12 mss/year. Publishes ms 2-4 months after acceptance. Length: 500-1,400 words; average length: 900. Publishes short shorts; average length: 700 words. Also publishes poetry. Always comments on rejected mss.

How to Contact: Send complete ms with cover letter. Include estimated word count and brief bio. Responds in 2 months to queries; 4 months to mss. Send disposable copy of ms and #10 SASE for reply only. Accepts multiple submissions. Sample copy for $3. Guidelines for SASE.

Payment/Terms: Pays 1 contributor's copy and free subscription to magazine; additional copies $1.50. Acquires one-time rights.

Ⓝ STORY DIGEST, The Magazine for Writers, Shaun Lockhart Communications, P.O. Box 744, Louisville KY 40201-0744. (502)635-5453. Fax: (502)635-7072. E-mail: storydigest@aol.com. Website: www.storydigest.com (includes links, magazine description, editors' names, guidelines). **Contact:** Shaun Lockhart, editor. Estab. 1996. Bimonthly. Circ. 5,000. Magazine: 5½×8½; 72 pages; glossy cover; illustrations; photos. "*Story Digest* is a writer's guide to networking and freelancing opportunities. This magazine infuses life and imagination into news, features, reports, fiction and poetry, all dealing with writing. We aim to inspire, enlighten and entertain writers who have an interest in expanding their careers. *Story Digest* publishes a wide range of material, as long as it relates to the writer or writer's craft.

Needs: "We are looking for interesting stories in all forms that relate to writing or writers. These stories can be in the form of mystery, horror, thriller, and so on. Please do not send stories that do not adhere to our criteria."

List of themes available with SASE. Receives 30 unsolicited mss/month. Accepts 10 mss/issue; 60-70 mss/year. Publishes ms 2 months after acceptance. Agented fiction less than 5%. **Publishes 5-7 new writers/year.** Recently published work by Linda Cervantes Rose, Beverly Fratoni, Sheila Mead, Meher Baba, Thomas Abernathy. Length: 4,000 words maximum. Also publishes literary essays, poetry, criticism, nonfiction. Often comments on rejected mss; "sometimes we will comment and ask writers to resubmit."

How to Contact: Send complete ms with floppy disk, or query with ms by e-mail. Include estimated word count, brief bio, photo or art suggestions. Responds in 2 months to mss. SASE. Simultaneous submissions and reprints okay. Sample copy for $3. Also reviews novels, short story collections, and nonfiction books of interest to writers.

Payment/Terms: Pays 3 contributors copies; additional copies for $3. Acquires first or reprint rights.

Advice: "We look at fiction writing to first make sure it fits our criteria. Afterwards, we ask how the piece can inspire, enlighten or entertain our readers. Does this piece offer a glimpse into the life of a writer? How so? The best tip we can offer beginning writers is to simply write. Before submitting to our publication or any other, understand the format and structure. Editors are sometimes not sympathetic to you as a beginning writer when they have tons of work to do. Because we have limited staff, the trend we adopted recently was to only accept work submitted by disk or e-mail. It otherwise would be difficult and time consuming to reproduce into magazine format the large amount of material we receive."

✓ ○ **THE STORYTELLER, A Writers Magazine,** 2441 Washington Rd., Maynard AR 72444. (870)647-2137. Fax: (870)647-2137. E-mail: storyteller1@cox-internet.com. **Contact:** Regina Cook Williams, editor. Tabloid: 8½×11; 64 pages; typing paper; illustrations. "This magazine is open to all new writers regardless of age. I will accept short stories in any genre and poetry in any type. Please keep in mind, this is a family publication." Quarterly. Estab. 1996.

Needs: Adventure, historical, humor/satire, literary, mainstream/contemporary, mystery/suspense, regional, religious/inspirational, romance, senior citizen/retirement, sports, westerns, young adult/teen. "I will not accept pornography, erotica, science fiction, new age, foul language, horror or graphic violence." Wants more well-plotted mysteries. Publishes ms 3-9 months after acceptance. **Publishes 150 new writers/year.** Published work by Randy Offner, Frank McKinley, Dusty Richards, and Tony Killerman. Length: 200-1,500 words. Publishes short shorts. Also publishes literary essays and poetry. Sometimes comments on rejected mss.

How to Contact: Nonsubscribers must pay reading fee: $1/poem, $2/short story. Send complete ms with a cover letter. Include estimated word count and 5-line bio. Responds in 1 month to queries; 2 months to mss. Send SASE for reply, return of ms or send a disposable copy of ms. Accepts simultaneous and reprint submissions. "*Must* tell where and when it was first published." Sample copy for $6. Guidelines for #10 SASE.

Payment/Terms: Readers vote quarterly for their favorites in all categories. Winning authors receive certificate of merit and free copy of issue in which their story or poem appeared."

Advice: Looks for "professionalism, good plots and unique characters. Purchase a sample copy so you know the kind of material we look for. Even though this is for unpublished writers, don't send us something you would not send to paying markets." Would like more "well-plotted mysteries and suspense and a few traditional westerns. Avoid sending anything that children or young adults would not (or could not) read, such as really bad language."

THE STRAND MAGAZINE, Box 1418, Birmingham, MI 48012-1418. (800)300-6657. Fax: (248)874-1046. E-mail: strandmag@worldnet.att.net. **Contact:** A. F. Gullie, editor. Quarterly mystery magazine. Estab. 1998. "After an absence of nearly half a century, the magazine known to millions for bringing Sir Arthur Conan Doyle's ingenious detective, Sherlock Holmes, to the world has once again appeared on the literary scene. First launched in 1891, *The Strand* included in its pages the works of some of the greatest writers of the 20th century: Agatha Christie, Dorothy Sayers, Margery Allingham, W. Somerset Maugham, Graham Greene, P.G. Wodehouse, H.G. Wells, Aldous Huxley and many others. In 1950, economic difficulties in England caused a drop in circulation which forced the magazine to cease publication."

Needs: Mysteries, detective stories, tales of terror and the supernatural "written in the classic tradition of this century's great authors. Stories can be set in any time or place, provided they are well written and the plots interesting and well thought out. We are NOT interested in submissions with any sexual content." Length: 2,000-6,000 words, "however, we may occasionally publish short shorts of 1,000 words or sometimes go as long as a short novella."

How to Contact: Send complete ms, typed, double-spaced on one side of each page. SASE (IRCs if outside the US). Responds in 4 months.

Payment/Terms: Pays $25-$50 on acceptance for first North American serial rights.

Ⓝ **STUDENTSWRITE.COM,** (formerly Texas Young Writers' Newsletter), P.O. Box 90046, San Antonio TX 78209-9046. E-mail: editor@studentswrite.com. Website: www.studentswrite.com. **Contact:** Susan Currie, editor. Online publication. "*Studentswrite.com* teaches young writers about the art and business of writing, and also gives them a place to publish their best work. We publish articles by adults with experience in publishing, and poetry and short stories by young writers 12-19." New work posted monthly. Estab. 2000.

Needs: Open to authors ages 12-19 only. Adventure, ethnic/multicultural, fantasy (children's fantasy, science fantasy), historical, humor/satire, literary, mainstream/contemporary, mystery/suspense, romance, science fiction, young adult/teen. "Anything by young writers, 12-19. No erotica, horror, gay/lesbian or occult." Receives 10 unsolicited mss/month. Accepts 3 mss/issue; 30 mss/year. Publishes ms 3 months after acceptance. Length: 500-2,000 words; average length: 900 words. Publishes short shorts. Also publishes poetry. Always comments on rejected ms.

How to Contact: Send complete ms with a cover letter. Include estimated word count and 50-100 word bio. Responds in 1 month. Send SASE for reply, return of ms. Guidelines for #10 SASE, "please specify adult or young writer's guidelines."

Payment/Terms: Acquires first rights. Not copyrighted.

Advice: "Please read back issues and study the sort of fiction we publish, and make sure it fits our newsletter. Since *TYWN* is sent to schools and young people, we prefer upbeat, nonviolent stories. I look for work that is highly original, creative, and appropriate for our audience. Manuscripts that are professional and striking stand out. I haven't seen enough stories with strong characters and involving plots. I don't want to see dull stories with dull characters. We want to show our young writers terrific examples of stories that they can learn from."

🌐 ✔ ◑ **STUDIO: A JOURNAL OF CHRISTIANS WRITING,** 727 Peel St., Albury 2640 Australia. Phone/fax: (+61)26021-1135. E-mail: pgrover@bigpond.com. **Contact:** Paul Grover, managing editor. Quarterly. Circ. 300.

Needs: "*Studio* publishes prose and poetry of literary merit, offers a venue for new and aspiring writers, and seeks to create a sense of community among Christians writing." Accepts 20-30 mss/year. **Publishes 40 new writers/year.** Recently published work by Andrew Lenodowen and Benjamin Gilmour. Length: 500-5,000 words.

How to Contact: Send SASE. "Overseas contributors must use International postal coupons in place of stamped envelope." Responds in 1 month to ms. Sample copy for $8 (Aus).

Payment/Terms: Pays in copies; additional copies are discounted. "Copyright of individual published pieces remains with the author, while each edition as a whole is copyright to studio." Subscription $48 (Australian) for 4 issues (1 year). International draft in Australian dollars and IRC required.

✔ $ 🖊 ◑ **TALEBONES, Fiction on the Dark Edge,** Fairwood Press, 5203 Quincy Ave. SE, Auburn WA 98092-8723. (253)735-6552. E-mail: talebones@nventure.com. Website: www.fairwoodpress.com (includes guidelines, submission requirements, excerpts, news about the magazine, bios). **Contact:** Patrick and Honna Swenson, editors. Magazine: digest size; 84 pages; standard paper; glossy cover stock; illustrations; photos. "We like stories that have punch, but still entertain. We like dark science fiction and dark fantasy, humor, psychological and experimental works." Quarterly. Estab. 1995. Circ. 600.

● *Talebones* was nominated for the International Horror Guild Award for Best Publication.

Needs: Fantasy (dark), humor/satire, science fiction (hard science, soft/sociological, dark). "No straight slash and hack horror. No cat stories or stories told by young adults. Would like to see more science fiction." Receives 200 mss/month. Accepts 6-7 mss/issue; 24-28 mss/year. Publishes ms 3-4 months after acceptance. **Publishes 2-3 new writers/year.** Recently published work by Mary Soon Lee, Bruce Holland Rogers and M. Christian.. Length: 1,000-6,000 words; average length: 3,000-4,000 words. Publishes short shorts. Length: 1,000 words. Also publishes poetry.

How to Contact: Send complete ms with a cover letter. Accepts queries/submissions by e-mail and on disk. Include estimated word count and 1-paragraph bio. Responds in 1 week to queries; 1 month to mss. Send SASE for reply, return of ms or send a disposable copy of ms. Sample copy for $5. Guidelines for SASE. Reviews novels and short story collections.

Payment/Terms: Pays $10-100 and 1 contributor's copy; additional copies $3. Pays on acceptance for first North American serial rights. Sends galleys to author.

Advice: "The story must be entertaining, but should blur the boundary between science fiction and horror. Most of our stories have a dark edge to them, but often are humorous or psychological. Be polite and know how to properly present a manuscript. Include a cover letter, but keep it short and to the point."

✔ $ ◑ 🖊 **TERRA INCOGNITA, A New Generation of Science Fiction,** 52 Windermere Ave., Lansdowne PA 19050-1812. E-mail: terraincognita@writeme.com. Website: www.voicenet.com/~inognit (includes writer's guidelines, names of editors, excerpts from previous issues, advice for writers, subscription information). **Contact:** Jan Berrien Berends, editor/publisher. . Magazine: 64 pages; e-brite paper; full-color glossy cover; illustrations; photos. "*Terra Incognita* is devoted to earth-based science fiction stories and relevant nonfiction articles. Readers of quality fiction—even those who are not science fiction fans—enjoy *TI*. Audience ranges from ages 18 and upward. We encourage feminist and socially conscious submissions." Quarterly. Estab. 1996.

● A story published in *Terra Incognito* was included in the sixteenth annual collection of *The Year's Best Science Fiction*, edited by Gardner Dozois.

Needs: Science fiction (hard science, soft/sociological). "No horror, fantasy, pornography. No sexism and gratuitous sex and violence, racism or bias; avoid prose poems and vignettes. We prefer character-driven stories with protagonists and plots." Receives 200-300 unsolicited mss/month. Accepts 6-10 mss/issue; 25-35 mss/year. Publishes ms 3 months to 1 year after acceptance. Published work by L. Timmel Duchamp, Mary Soon Lee, Terry McGarry, W. Gregory Stewart, Sally Caves, Don D'Ammassa. Length: 100-15,000 words; average length: 5,000 words. Publishes short shorts. Also publishes literary essays, literary criticism and poetry.

How to Contact: Send complete ms with cover letter. Include estimated word count and anything you think might be interesting in a cover letter. Accepts multiple submissions. Responds in 2 weeks to queries; 3 months to mss. Send SASE for reply, return of ms or send a disposable copy of ms. "A cover letter is optional; a SASE is not." Sample copy for $5; $6 overseas. Fiction guidelines for #10 SASE. Reviews novels and short story collections.

Payment/Terms: Pays at least 3¢/word and 2 contributor's copies; additional copies $5. Pays on acceptance for first North American serial rights.

Advice: Looks for "good writing and literary merit; a story that grabs our interest and holds it straight through to the end. Write as well as you can (which means—don't overwrite, but do use the words themselves to advance your story), and tell us a story—preferably one we haven't heard before. Don't get your great idea rejected on account of lousy grammar or poor manuscript format. We take all submissions seriously."

☑ ◖ **THE THRESHOLD,** Crossover Press, P.O. Box 101362, Pittsburgh PA 15237. E-mail: threshmag@aol .com. Website: www.thresholdmagazine.com (includes fiction and poetry, interviews, meet the editors, tutoring services, excerpts from magazine, subscriber information, activities page and guestbook). **Contact:** Don H. Laird and Michael Carricato, editors. Magazine: 8½ × 11; 48 pages; colored bond paper; card cover; illustrations. "*The Threshold* is a journal that promotes new and established writers. Our goal is to provide a forum for all genres of fiction. Our audience is in search of the best new short fiction exhibited with the graphic flourishes that have become the trademark of our publication." Our audience is both young and old, and they are in search of one thing: imaginative short fiction and poetry." Quarterly. Estab. 1996. Circ. 1,000.

Needs: Adventure, erotica, experimental, fantasy, gay, horror, humor/satire, lesbian, literary, mainstream/contemporary, mystery/suspense, psychic/supernatural/occult, romance (contemporary, futuristic/time travel/gothic), science fiction, serialized novel. No slice of life vignettes. Publishes special fiction issues or anthologies. Receives 80 unsolicited mss/month. Accepts 6-8 mss/issue, 24-32 mss/year. Publishes ms up to 5 months after acceptance. **Publishes 8-10 new writers/year.** Recently published work by Michael Kent, Renne Carter Hall, Sherrie Brown, Edward Hunter, Steve Burt. Length: 8,000 words maximum; average length: 3,000-5,000 words. Publishes short shorts. Also publishes poetry.

How to Contact: Send complete ms with a cover letter. Include estimated word count and 2-paragraph bio. Responds in 2 weeks to queries; 4-6 months to mss. Send SASE for reply, return of ms or send disposable copy of ms. Accepts simultaneous and multiple submissions. Sample copy for $5.95. Guidelines for #10 SASE.

Payment/Terms: Pays 1 contributor's copy and up to $25 under special arrangement with publisher. Acquires one-time rights.

Advice: "Good writers are a dime a dozen. Good storytellers are priceless. Make it interesting, but above all, be imaginative! Most publications print stories, we illuminate them. To better understand this unique approach, however, we highly recommend reading an issue or two before submitting your work."

☑ ◖ ◎ **THRESHOLDS QUARTERLY, School of Metaphysics Associates Journal,** SOM Publishing, School of Metaphysics World Headquarters, HCR1, Box 15, Windyville MO 65783. (417)345-8411. Fax: (417)345-6668 (call first, computerized). Website: www.som.org. **Contact:** Dr. Barbara Condron, editor. Senior Editor: Dr. Laurel Clark. Magazine: 7 × 10; 32 pages; line drawings and b&w photos. "The School of Metaphysics is a nonprofit educational and service organization invested in education and research in the expansion of human consciousness and spiritual evolution of humanity. For all ages and backgrounds. Themes: dreams, healing, science fiction, personal insight, morality tales, fables, humor, spiritual insight, mystic experiences, religious articles, creative writing with universal themes." Quarterly. Estab. 1975. Circ. 5,000.

Needs: Adventure, fantasy, humor, psychic/supernatural, religious/inspirational, science fiction. Upcoming themes: "Dreams, Visions, and Creative Imagination" (February); "Health and Wholeness" (May); "Intuitive Arts" (August); "Man's Spiritual Consciousness" (November). Receives 5 unsolicited mss/month. Length: 4-6 double-spaced typed pages. Publishes short shorts. Also publishes literary essays and poetry. Often comments on rejected mss.

How to Contact: Query with outline; will accept unsolicited ms with cover letter; no guarantee on time length to respond. Include bio (1-2 paragraphs). Send SASE for reply, return of ms or send a disposable copy of ms. Sample copy for 9 × 12 SAE and $1.50 postage. Guidelines for #10 SASE.

Payment/Terms: Pays up to 5 contributor's copies. Acquires all rights.

Advice: "We encourage works that have one or more of the following attributes: uplifting, educational, inspirational, entertaining, informative and innovative."

☑ ◎ UP DARE?, la Pierna Tierna Press, P.O. Box 100, Shartlesville PA 19554. (610)488-6894. **Contact:** Mary M. Towne and Loring D. Emery, editors. "The only requirement is that all submitted material must pertain to folks with physical or psychological handicaps-fiction or non-fiction." Magazine: digest-sized; 48 pages; illustrations. Estab. 1997.

Needs: Fiction and poetry. Looks for "honesty, plain language and message." No smut. Published work by Dan Buck, Karen Elkins, Sylvia Mais-Harak, Betty June Silconas, Vanda One and Denise Corrigan.

How to Contact: "We will take single-spaced and even double-sided submissions so long as they are legible. We prefer to optically scan all material to avoid typos. We will not insist on an SASE if you truly have financial limitations. We're trying to make it as easy as possible. We will take short (250 words or less) pieces in Braille." Sample copy for $2.50. Guidelines for #10 SASE.

Advice: "We will not use euphemisms—a chair with a leg missing is a 'three-legged chair,' not a 'challenged seat.' We would like to hear from folks who are handicapped, but we aren't closing the door to others who understand and help or just have opinions to share. We will take reprints if the original appearance is identified."

☑ $☑ VIRGINIA QUARTERLY REVIEW, One West Range, P.O. Box 400223, Charlottesville VA 22904-4223. (804)924-3124. Fax: (804)924-1397. **Contact:** Staige Blackford, editor. "A national magazine of literature and discussion. A lay, intellectual audience; people who are not out-and-out scholars but who are interested in ideas and literature." Quarterly. Estab. 1925. Circ. 4,000.

Needs: Adventure, contemporary, ethnic, feminist, humor, literary, romance, serialized novels (excerpts) and translations. "No pornography." Buys 3 mss/issue, 20 mss/year. Length: 3,000-7,000 words.

How to Contact: Query or send complete ms. SASE. Responds in 2 weeks to queries, 2 months to mss. Sample copy for $5.

Payment/Terms: Pays $10/printed page. Pays on publication for all rights. "Will transfer upon request." Offers Emily Clark Balch Award for best published short story of the year.

Advice: Looks for "stories with a somewhat Southern dialect and/or setting. Humor is welcome; stories involving cancer and geriatrics are not."

☑ $☑ ◎ ▣ WEBER STUDIES: Vices and Viewpoints of the Contemporary West, 1214 University Circle, Ogden UT 84408-1214. (801)626-6616. E-mail: swhoward@weber.edu. Website: http://weberstudi es.weber.edu (includes full web edition of journal). **Contact:** Sherwin W. Howard, editor. Magazine: 7½×10; 120-140 pages; coated paper; 4-color cover; illustrations; photos. *Weber Studies* publishes work that "provides insight into the culture and environment (both broadly defined) of the contemporary western United States." Triannual "with occasional 4th issues." Estab. 1984. Circ. 1,000.

Needs: Adventure, comics/graphic novels, ethnic/multicultural, experimental, fantasy (space fantasy), feminist, gay, historical, humor satire, lesbian, literary, mainstream, military/war, mystery/suspense, New Age, psychic/supernatural/occult, regional (contemporary western US), science fiction, short story collections, translations, western (frontier saga, traditional, contemporary). No children's/juvenile, erotica, religious or young adult/teen. Receives 50 unsolicited mss/month. Accepts 3-6 mss/issue; 9-18 mss/year. Publishes ms up to 18 months after acceptance. **Publishes "few" new writers/year.** Recently published work by Joseph Ditta, Ron McFarland, Lawrence Dunning, M.L. Archer, and Eleanor Swanson. Length: 5,000 words maximum. Publishes short shorts. Also publishes critical essays, poetry and personal narrative. Sometimes comments on rejected ms.

How to Contact: Send complete ms with a cover letter. Include estimated word count, bio (not necessary), and list of publications (not necessary). Responds to mss in 3 months. Send SASE for return of ms or disposable copy of ms. Accepts multiple submissions. Sample copy for $7.

Payment/Terms: Pays $70-150, free subscription to the magazine and 1 contributor's copy. Pays on publication for first serial rights, electronic edition rights and requests electronic archive permission. Sends galleys to author.

Advice: "Is it true? Is it new? Is it interesting? Will the story appeal to educated readers who are concerned with the contemporary western United States? Declining public interest in reading generally is of concern. We publish both in print media and electronic media because we believe the future will expect both options."

$☑ WEIRD TALES, Terminus Publishing Co., Inc., 123 Crooked Lane, King of Prussia PA 19406-2570. (610)275-4463. E-mail: owlswick@netaxs.com. **Contact:** George H. Seithers and Darrell Schweitzer, editors. Magazine: 8½×11; 68 pages; white, non-glossy paper; glossy 4-color cover; illustrations. "We publish fantastic fiction, supernatural horror for an adult audience." Quarterly. Estab. 1923. Circ. 10,000.

Needs: Fantasy (sword and sorcery), horror, supernatural/occult, translations. "We want to see a wide range of fantasy, from sword and sorcery to supernatural horror. We can use some unclassifiables." No hard science fiction or non-fantasy. Receives 400 unsolicited mss/month. Accepts 8 mss/issue; 32 mss/year. Publishes ms 6-18 months after acceptance. Agented fiction 10%. **Publishes 6 new writers/year.** Published work by Tanith Lee, Thomas Ligotti, Ian Watson and Lord Dunsany. Length: 10,000 words maximum (very few over 8,000); average length: 4,000 words. "No effective minimum. Shortest we ever published was about 100 words." Publishes short shorts. Also publishes poetry. Always comments on rejected mss.

How to Contact: Send complete ms. Include estimated word count. Responds in 2-3 weeks to mss. Send SASE for reply, return of ms or send a disposable copy of ms with SASE. No simultaneous submissions. No reprint submissions, "but will buy first North American rights to stories published overseas." Sample copy for $4.95. Guidelines for #10 SASE. Reviews novels and short story collections relevant to the horror/fantasy field.
Payment/Terms: Pays 3¢/word minimum and 2 contributor's copies. Acquires first North American serial rights plus anthology option. Sends galleys to author.
Advice: "We look for imagination and vivid writing. Read the magazine. Get a good grounding in the contemporary horror and fantasy field through the various 'best of the year' anthologies. Avoid the obvious cliches of technicalities of the hereafter, the mechanics of vampirism, generic Tolkien-clone fantasy. In general, it is better to be honest and emotionally moving rather than clever. Avoid stories which have nothing of interest save for the allegedly 'surprise' ending."

N ✉ $ ▢ ◎ THE WESTCOAST FISHERMAN, Westcoast Publishing Ltd., 1496 W. 72nd Ave., Vancouver, British Columbia V6P 3C8 Canada. (640)266-8611. Fax: (604)266-6437. E-mail: fisherman@west-coast.com. **Contact:** David Rahn, editor. Magazine: 20cm×27cm; 56-88 pages; newsprint; glossy cover stock; illustrations; photos. "*The Westcoast Fisherman* is a nonpolitical, nonaligned trade magazine serving the commercial fishing industry of Canada's west coast. It is distributed to selected areas of the commercial fishing industry and sold at selected newsstands." Monthly. Estab. 1986. Circ. 8,000.
Needs: Condensed/excerpted novel, historical, humor/satire, regional. "Nothing on sport fishing. Submissions must be closely tied to commercial fishing, preferably in British Columbia. Seasonality is good, e.g., salmon in summer, herring in spring, etc." Receives 1 unsolicited ms/month. Accepts approximately 6 mss/year. Publishes ms 1-3 months after acceptance. Published work by Pete Fletcher. Length: 800-2,500 words; average length: 1,200 words. Also publishes poetry.
How to Contact: Query with clips of published work or send complete ms with a cover letter. Include 10-20 word bio and where piece has previously appeared, if applicable. Responds in 1 month. Send disposable copy of ms. Accepts simultaneous, reprint and electronic (disk or modem) submissions. Sample copy for $3. Guidelines free. Reviews novels or short story collections "if on topic, definitely."
Payment/Terms: Pays 10-15¢/word and 2-10 contributor's copies; additional copies $3. Pays on publication for one-time rights. Sponsors annual fiction contest. Timing and conditions change from year to year.
Advice: "We are interested in fiction produced by fishermen or coastal dwellers, or which shows familiarity with their work and world."

✓ ▢ THE WHITE CROW, Osric Publishing, P.O. Box 4501, Ann Arbor MI 48106-4501. E-mail: chris@osric.com. Website: www.osric.com/whitecrow/ (includes writer's guidelines, staff contact list, excerpts from publication). **Contact:** Christopher Herdt, editor. Zine: 5½×8; 32 pages; 20 lb. white paper; 60 lb. cover stock; illustrations; photos. "We seek solid literary works which will appeal to an intelligent but not necessarily literary audience." Quarterly. Estab. 1994. Circ. 200.
Needs: Ethnic/multicultural, experimental, humor/satire, literary, translations. Receives 6 mss/month. Accepts 1-2 mss/issue; 6 mss/year. Publishes ms up to 4 months after acceptance. **Publishes 1 new writer/year.** Recently published work by Delia DeSantis and Jas Isle. Length: 300-3,000 words; average length: 2,500 words. Publishes short shorts. Also publishes literary essays and poetry. Always comments on rejected mss.
How to Contact: Send complete ms with cover letter. Include estimated word count and a 30-word bio. Responds in 6 months. Send SASE for return of ms. Accepts simultaneous submissions and reprints. Sample copy for $2.
Payment/Terms: Pays 1 contributor's copy; additional copies for $1. Acquires one-time rights. Not copyrighted.
Advice: "Is the story focused? Is it driven by a coherent, meaningful idea that can be grasped by an intelligent (but not literary) reader? We're here to edit a publication, not your writing, so please proofread your ms. Running spell check is a fabulous idea too."

◎ WISCONSIN ACADEMY REVIEW, Wisconsin Academy of Sciences, Arts & Letters, 1922 University Ave., Madison WI 53705-4099. (608)263-1692. Fax: (608)265-3039. E-mail: joanfischer@facstaff.wisc.edu. Website: www.wisconsinacademy.org (includes writer's guidelines, names of editors, interviews with authors and excerpts from publication). **Contact:** Joan Fischer, editor. Magazine: 8½×11; 48-52 pages; 75 lb. coated paper; coated cover stock; illustrations; photos. "The *Review* reflects the focus of the sponsoring institution with its editorial emphasis on Wisconsin's intellectual, cultural, social and physical environment. It features short fiction,

MARKET CONDITIONS are constantly changing! If you're still using this book and it is 2002 or later, buy the newest edition of *Novel & Short Story Writer's Market* at your favorite bookstore or order from Writer's Digest Books by calling 1-800-289-0963.

poetry, essays, nonfiction articles and Wisconsin-related art and book reviews for people interested in furthering regional arts and literature and disseminating information about sciences." Quarterly. Estab. 1954. Circ. approximately 1,800.

Needs: Experimental, historical, humor/satire, literary, mainstream, prose poem. No genre fiction. "Author must have a Wisconsin connection or fiction must have strong Wisconsin theme or setting." Receives 5-6 unsolicited fiction mss/month. Accepts 1-2 mss/issue; 6-8 mss/year. **Published new writers within the last year.** Length: 1,000-3,500 words. Also publishes poetry; "will consider" literary essays, literary criticism.

How to Contact: Send complete ms with SAE and state author's connection to Wisconsin, the prerequisite. Accepts multiple submissions. Sample copy for $3. Guidelines for SASE. Reviews books on Wisconsin themes.

Payment/Terms: Pays 3-5 contributor's copies. Acquires first rights on publication.

Advice: "Manuscript publication is at the discretion of the editor based on space, content and balance. We accept only previously unpublished poetry and fiction. We publish emerging as well as established authors; fiction and poetry, without names attached, are sent to reviewers for evaluation."

N $ ⊘ ◎ WRITER'S GUIDELINES & NEWS, The Who, What, When and Where Magazine for Writers, P.O. Box 18566, Sarasota FL 34276. (941)924-3201. Fax: (941)925-4468. E-mail: writersgn@aol.com. **Contact:** Ned Burke, editor. Magazine: 8½×11; 52 pages; 60 lb. white paper; glossy cover; illustrations; photos. "*WG&N* is a mostly nonfiction magazine for writers. Occasionally publishes fiction 'with a writing slant.'" Quarterly. Estab. 1988. Circ. 2,500.

Needs: Fiction with a "writing slant." Humor/satire, literary, mainstream. No erotica. Receives 20-50 unsolicited mss/month. Accepts 2 mss/issue; 10 mss/year. Publishes ms 4-6 months after acceptance. Agented fiction 10%. **Publishes 2-4 new writers/year.** Length: 1,000-2,000 words; average length: 1,500 words. Publishes short shorts. Average length: 300 words. Also publishes literary essays, literary criticism and poetry.

How to Contact: Send complete ms with a cover letter. Include estimated word count, brief bio and list of publications. Responds in 4 months to queries and mss. Send SASE (or IRC) for return of ms. Sample copy for $5. Guidelines for SASE. Reviews novels, short story collections and nonfiction books of interest to writers. Send review copies to Carrillee Collins.

Payment/Terms: Pays $50 maximum, free subscription to the magazine and 1 contributor's copy; additional copies $5. Pays on publication for one-time rights.

N ◯ ◎ YARNS AND SUCH, Creative With Words Publications, Box 223226, Carmel CA 93922. Fax: (831)655-8627. E-mail: cwwpub@usa.net. Website: members.tripod.com/CreativeWithWords (includes themes, guidelines, submittal form, cost of back issues, advertising rates, editorial statement; editing tips of current issue; best of the month salute and winning writing). **Contact:** Brigitta Geltrich (General Editor) and Bert Hower (Nature Editor), editors. Booklet: 5½×8½; more than 50 pages; bond paper; illustrations. Folklore. 12-14 issues annually. Estab. 1975. Circ. varies.

Needs: Ethnic, humor/satire, mystery/suspense (amateur sleuth, private eye), regional, folklore. "Poems have a better chance to be accepted. Do not submit essays. Four times a year we publish an anthology of the writings of young writers, titled: *We are Writers Too!*" No violence or erotica, overly religious fiction or sensationalism. List of themes available for SASE. Receives 500 unsolicited fiction mss/month. Publishes ms 1-2 months after deadline. **Published new writers within the last year.** Length: 1,500 words average; limits poetry to 20 lines or less, 46 characters per line or less. Critiques rejected mss "when requested, *then we charge $20/prose, up to 1,000 words.*"

How to Contact: Query first or send complete ms with cover letter and SASE. Accepts queries/mss by e-mail with writer's e-mail address given. "Reference has to be made to which project the manuscript is being submitted. Unsolicited mss without SASE will be destroyed after holding them 1 month." Responds in 2 weeks to queries; 2 months to mss; longer on specific thematic anthologies. Accepts electronic (disk) submissions via Macintosh and IBM/PC. Sample copy for $6. Guidelines for #10 SASE.

Payment/Terms: No payment; 20% reduction on each copy ordered; 30% reduction on each copy on orders of 10 or more. Acquires one-time rights. Offers "Best of the Month" one free copy and publishing on the web.

Advice: "We have increased the number of anthologies we are publishing to 12-14 per year and offer a greater variety of themes. We look for clean family-type fiction. Also, we ask the writer to look at the world from a different perspective, research topic thoroughly, be creative, apply brevity, tell the story from a character's viewpoint, tighten dialogue, be less descriptive, proofread before submitting and be patient. We will not publish every manuscript we receive. It has to be in standard English, well-written, proofread. We do not appreciate receiving manuscripts where we have to do the proofreading and the correcting of grammar."

$ ⊘ YELLOW STICKY NOTES, P.O. Box 452, Greenfield IN 46140. (317)462-0037. E-mail: suwk@aol.com. Website: www.wordmuseum.com (includes writer's guidelines, editors, list of articles in upcoming issue). **Contact:** Su Kopil, editor. Magazine: 8×11; 60 pages; paper varies; glossy cover; illustrations; photos. "*Yellow Sticky Notes* is a multi-genre magazine for writers and readers. It includes articles, interviews, short fiction and poetry. Semiannual. Estab. 1999. Circ. 2,000.

Needs: Adventure, children's/juvenile (adventure, animal, easy-to-read, fantasy, historical, mystery, preschool, series, sports), comics, ethnic/multicultural, fantasy (space fantasy, sword and sorcery, romance), historical, horror (psychological, supernatural), literary, mainstream, military/war, mystery/suspense (amateur sleuth, cozy, police procedural, private eye/hardboiled), regional, religious (children's religious, general religious, inspirational, religious fantasy, religious mystery/suspense, religious thriller, religious romance), romance (contemporary, futuristic/time travel, gothic, historical, regency period, romantic suspense), science fiction (hard science/technological, soft/sociological), thriller/espionage, western (frontier saga, traditional), young adult/teen (adventure, easy-to-read, fantasy/science fiction, historical, horror, mystery/suspense, problem novels, romance, series, sports, western). "We are a family oriented publication. No inappropriate themes or issues. Accepts 2 mss/issue; 4 mss/year. Does not read from August-Nov. or from Feb.-April. Publishes ms 6 months after acceptance. Agented fiction 2%. **Publishes 1 new writer/year.** Published work by Vicki Nince, Lori Soard, Cathy McDavid and Hilary Anne Brown. Length: 1,000-2,500 words; average length: 2,000 words. Publishes short shorts. Average length: 500 words. Also publishes literary essays and poetry. Sometimes comments on rejected ms.

How to Contact: Query first by e-mail. "No postal submissions." Include estimated word count, 1-2 paragraph bio and list of publications. Responds in 6 weeks to queries. Accepts simultaneous and reprint submissions. Sample copy for $8.99. Guidelines free on website or for SASE.

Payment/Terms: Pays $1-10 and 1 contributor's copy. Pays on publication for first rights. Sends prepublication galleys to author.

Advice: "We like stories that are unique. Make us laugh, cry or smile. Make certain the manuscript is clean. Watch for spelling and grammatical errors. Clean up passive writing."

N **©** **ZOPILOTE**, Oldie Publications, 824 S. Mill Ave., Suite 219, Tempe AZ 85281. (480)557-7195. Fax: (480)838-7264. E-mail: zopilote@inficad.com. Website: www.zopilote.com. **Contact:** Marco Albarrán, publisher. Magazine: 8½×11; 26 pages; illustrations; photos. "*Zopilote* magazine is one of the few cultural magazines that promotes indigenous and Latino cultures in the U.S. We publish material pertinent to the history, ways of life, philosophies, traditions and changes taking place right now." Bimonthly. Estab. 1993. Circ. 5,000. Member: Council of Literary Magazines and Presses.

Needs: Comics/graphic novels, ethnic/multicultural (indigenous Latino), historical (indigenous Latino), literary, science fiction (ancient science of the Americas), western (indigenous Latino). "No religious, romance, erotica." Receives 5-10 unsolicited mss/month. Accepts 3 mss/issue; 18-20 mss/year. Publishes ms 3-5 months after acceptance. **Publishes 60-70% new writers/year.** Recently published work by Roberto Rodriquez, Cristina Gonzalez and Carmen Vaxones Martinez. Length: 150-500 words; average length: 300 words. Publishes short shorts. Also publishes literary essays, literary criticism and poetry. Sometimes comments on rejected mss.

How to Contact: Send complete ms with a cover letter. Accepts submissions by e-mail. Include estimated word count, brief bio and list of publications. Responds in 6 weeks. Send a disposable copy of ms and #10 SASE for reply only. Accepts simultaneous submissions, previously published work and multiple submissions. Sample copy free for 8½×11 SAE and $3 postage. Guidelines by e-mail. Reviews novels, short story collections and nonfiction books of interest to writers.

Payment/Terms: Pays 5 contributor's copies; additional copies $3.50.

Zines

The zine market is nearly unparalleled in dynanism and opportunity. Vastly different from one another in appearance and content, the common source of zines seems to be a need to voice opinions. Although they've always been around, it was not until the '70s, and possibly beginning with the social upheaval of the '60s, that the availability of photocopiers and computers provided an easy, cheap way to produce the self-published and usually self-written "zines." And now, with the cyberspace explosion, an overwhelming number of "e-zines" are springing up in an electronic format every day.

SELF-EXPRESSION AND ARTISTIC FREEDOM

The editorial content of zines runs the gamut from traditional and genre fiction to personal rants and highly experimental work. Artistic freedom, however, is a characteristic of all zines. Although zine editors are open to a wide range of fiction that more conventional editors might not consider, don't make the mistake of thinking they expect any less from writers than the editors of other types of publications. Zine editors look for work that is creative and well presented and that shows the writer has taken time to become familiar with the market. And since most zines are highly specialized, familiarity with the niche markets they offer is extremely important.

Some of the zines listed here have been published since the early '80s, but many are relatively new and some were just starting publication as they filled out the questionnaire to be included in this edition of *Novel & Short Story Writer's Market*. Unfortunately, due to the waning energy and shrinking funds of their publishers (and often a lack of material), few last for more than several issues. Fortunately, though, some have been around since the late '70s and early '80s, and hundreds of new ones are launched every day.

While zines represent the most volatile group of publications in *Novel & Short Story Writer's Market*, they are also the most open to submissions by beginning writers. As mentioned above, the editors of zines are often writers themselves and welcome the opportunity to give others a chance at publication.

SELECTING THE RIGHT MARKET

Your chance for publication begins as you zero in on the zines most likely to be interested in your work. Begin by browsing through the listings. This is especially important since zines are the most diverse and specialized markets listed in this book. If you write genre fiction, check out the specific sections for lists of magazines publishing in that genre (mystery, page 57; romance, page 68; science fiction/fantasy & horror, page 78). For other types of fiction, check the Category Index (starting on page 613) for the appropriate subject heading.

In addition to browsing through the listings and using the Category Index, check the ranking codes at the beginning of listings to find those most likely to be receptive to your work. Most all zines are open to new writers (❑) or to both new and established writers (◨). For more explanation about these codes, see the inside front and back covers of this book.

Once you have a list of zines you might like to try, read their listings carefully. Zines vary greatly in appearance as well as content. Some paper zines are photocopies published whenever the editor has material and money, while others feature offset printing and regular distribution schedules. And a few have evolved into four-color, commercial-looking, very slick publications. The physical description appearing near the beginning of the listings gives you clues about the size and financial commitment to the publication. This is not always an indication of quality, but chances are a publication with expensive paper and four-color artwork on the cover has more prestige than a photocopied publication featuring a clip art self-cover. If you're a new writer or your work is considered avant garde, however, you may be more interested in the photocopied zine or one of the electronic zines. For more information on some of the paper, binding and printing terms used in these descriptions, see Printing and Production Terms Defined on page 608. Also, The "Quick Start" Guide to Publishing Your Fiction, starting on page 2, describes in detail the listing information common to all markets in our book.

FURTHERING YOUR SEARCH

Reading the listings is only the first part of developing your marketing plan. The second part, equally important, is to obtain fiction guidelines and a copy of the actual zine. Reading copies of the publication helps you determine the fine points of the zine's publishing style and philosophy. Especially since zines tend to be highly specialized, there is no substitute for this hands-on, eyes-on research. With e-zines, all the information you need is available on their websites.

Unlike commercial periodicals available at most newsstands and bookstores, it requires a little more effort to obtain most of the paper zines listed here. You will probably need to send for a sample copy. We include sample copy prices in the listings whenever possible.

$ ABSOLUTE MAGNITUDE, Science Fiction Adventures, DNA Publications, P.O. Box 2988, Radford VA 24143-2988. E-mail: dnapublications@iname.com. **Editor:** Warren Lapine. Zine: 8½×11; 64 pages; newsprint; color cover; illustrations. "We publish technical science fiction that is adventurous and character driven." Quarterly. Estab. 1993. Circ. 9,000.
• *Absolute Magnitude* ranked #15 on *Writer's Digest's* Fiction 50 list of top fiction markets.
Needs: Science fiction: adventure, hard science. No fantasy, horror, funny science fiction. Receives 300-500 unsolicited mss/month. Accepts 7-10 mss/issue; 28-40 mss/year. Publishes ms 3-6 months after acceptance. Agented fiction 5%. Published work by Hal Clement, Chris Bunch, C.J. Cherryh, Barry B. Longyear and Harlan Ellison. Length: 1,000-25,000 words; average length: 5,000-12,000 words. Publishes very little poetry. Often comments on rejected ms.
How to Contact: Do NOT query. Send complete ms with a cover letter. Should include estimated word count and list of publications. Send SASE for reply or return of ms. Sample copy for $5. Reviews novels and short story collections.
Payment/Terms: Pays 1-5¢/word on publication for first North American serial rights; 1¢/word for first reprint rights. Sometimes sends galleys to author.
Advice: "We want good writing with solid characterization, also character growth, story development, and plot resolution. We would like to see more character-driven stories."

N ⊘ AFFABLE NEIGHBOR, P.O. Box 3635, Ann Arbor MI 48106-3635. E-mail: affableneighbor@yahoo o.com. **Editor:** Joel Henry-Fisher. **Contact:** Joel Henry-Fisher, Leigh Chalmers, fiction editors. Zine: size/pages vary; usually photocopy paper and cover stock; illustrations; photos. "Counter-culture zine publishing high and low art and experimentation of all forms, advocating the Affable Neighbor Worldview®." Estab. 1994. Circ. under 500.
Needs: Adventure, comics/graphic novels, erotica, ethnic/multicultural, experimental, fantasy, feminist, gay, glitz, historical, horror, humor/satire, lesbian, literary, psychic/supernatural/occult, romance ("kamp/sleaze perhaps"), science fiction, short story collections, translations, collage/text. "No pro-religious—unless, perhaps, fringe related; no tired, formulaic writings." Receives 15 unsolicited mss/month. Accepts 1-2 mss/issue. **Publishes 12 new writers/year.** Recently published work by Marshall Stanley, Scott Hoye, Cairn Smith, and Geoff Daily. Length: short. Publishes short shorts (under 500 words). Also publishes literary essays, literary criticism, poetry. Sometimes comments on rejected ms.
How to Contact: Send complete ms with a cover letter. Responds in approximately 1 week. Send SASE for reply, return of ms or send a disposable copy of ms. Accepts simultaneous and reprint submissions. Sample copy for 3 first-class stamps, if available. Reviews novels, short story collections and nonfiction books of interest. Send books to Leigh Chalmers, Assistant Editor, Affable Neighbor, 729 E. Burnside #210, Portland OR 97214. Send disposable copies or SASE.
Payment/Terms: Pays free subscription if requested and contributor's copies. Not copyrighted.
Advice: "We like interesting and exciting works—experimental, brash, and sometimes dead-serious."

✓ ◯ ▣ AKP ZINE: Powerful Imaginations, Silly and Strange, (formerly *Kasper Zine*), %AKP, P.O. Box 2474, Athens GA 30612-0474. E-mail: zine@akp.cc. Website: www.akpzine.com (includes writer's guidelines and a discussion board). **Contact:** Adrian Pritchett, editor. Electronic zine specializing in humor. Publishes "prose, photography, and artwork that is weird, silly, or wonderful." Estab. 1996.

Needs: Humor satire. Accepts 3 mss/year. Publishes ms 2 months after acceptance. Recently published works by Adrian Pritchett, Alvin Shubert, and David Lee. Length: 200-5,000 words. Publishes short shorts. Length: 200 words.
How to Contact: Query first. Send queries/mss by e-mail. Include 75-word bio; e-mail and website addresses. Responds in 1 week to queries; 2 months to mss. Accepts simultaneous submissions and reprints. Guidelines for #10 SASE.
Advice: "A manuscript stands out if it balances nonsense with enough plot to be readable and hilarious."

ALIEN ZOO, 8936 N. Central Ave., Phoenix AZ 85020. (602)850-3253. Fax: (602)850-3255. E-mail: james@alienzoo.com. Website: www.alienzoo.com. **Contact:** James McCarty, acquisitions editor. E-zine. Biweekly.
Needs: Comics/graphic novels, horror (futuristic, supernatural), psychic/supernatural/occult, science fiction (hard science/technological, soft/sociological), young adult/teen (fantasy/science fiction). No gothic or erotic. Receives 300 unsolicited mss/month. Accepts 5-10 mss/issue; 150 mss/year. Publishes ms 1-2 months after acceptance. Agented fiction 35%. **Publishes 10-20 new writers/year.** Recently published work by Jim Marrs, Paul Davids, Chris Mercer, and Wendell Davis. Average length: 3,000 words. Publishes short shorts. Sometimes comments on rejected mss.
How to Contact: Send complete ms with cover letter. Accepts submissions by e-mail, fax, disk. Include estimated word count, brief bio and Social Security number. Send SASE for return of ms or send a disposable copy of ms and #10 SASE for reply only. Accepts previously published work and multiple submissions. Sample copy free with SASE. Guidelines for SASE, e-mail or fax. Reviews novels, short story collections and nonfiction.
Payment/Terms: Pay is negotiable; percentage of banner ad revenue. Acquires first North American serial rights and electronic rights. Sends galleys to author.

$☐▣ ANOTHEREALM, 287 Gano Ave., Orange Park FL 32073-4307. (904)269-5429. E-mail: goldstrm @tu.infi.net. Website: www.anotherealm.com. **Contact:** Jean Goldstrom, editor. "We are the most read science fiction/fantasy/horror e-zine on the Internet." Weekly. Estab. 1998.
   ● *Anotherealm* is a member of the Zine Guild.
Needs: Fantasy (space fantasy, sword and sorcery), horror (dark fantasy, futuristic, psychological, supernatural), science fiction (hard science/technological, soft/sociological). No gore, porn, slasher. Receives 100 unsolicited mss/month. Accepts 104 mss/year. Publishes ms 3 months after acceptance. **Publishes 50 new writers/year.** Recently published work by d.g.k. goldberg, Justin Stanchfield and Darin Park. Word length: 5,000 words maximum. Rarely comments on rejected mss.
How to Contact: Send complete ms with a cover letter by e-mail. Include estimated word count. Responds to mss in 2 months. Accepts previously published work and multiple submissions. Sample copy and guidelines free on website.
Payment/Terms: Pays $10. Pays on acceptance for electronic rights.
Advice: "Same as everyone else—editor's prejudice view of 'the best.' Read my book *How to Write Creatively for Internet Magazines.*"

ANY DREAM WILL DO, The First Ever Manic Zine, Any Dream Will Do. E-mail: mail@anydrea mzine.com. Website: www.anydreamzine.com. **Contact:** Jean M. Bradt, Ph.D., editor. "An online fiction magazine for writers and readers who are recovering from mental illness, or who care about us. We publish, free of charge, stories from the mentally ill perspective." Estab. 2000.
Needs: Fiction only. "No porn, poems, true life stories, political material, or depressing accounts of hopeless or perverted people, please. Short stories are fine. A science fantasy is OK if it stars real characters and has a real plot, ending with a clear-cut message or twist. Science fantasy or not, we like endings that are satisfying or evoke strong positive or negative emotions." Publishes ms 1 month after acceptance. **Mostly publishes stories from new writers.** Length: 4,000 words maximum. Publishes short shorts. Often comments on rejected mss.
How to Contact: Send ms as attachment by e-mail. Include brief bio indicating your relationship to persons diagnosed with mental illness. Responds in 3 weeks to queries and mss. Accepts simultaneous submissions and previously published submissions. Sample copy on website.
Advice: "Read several stories on our website before starting to write. Proof your story many times before submitting it. Make the readers think. Above all, present people diagnosed with mental illness realistically rather than with prejudice."

ART:MAG, P.O. Box 70896, Las Vegas NV 89170-0896. (702)734-8121. **Contact:** Peter Magliocco, editor. Zine: 7×8½×8½, 8½×14, also 8½×11; 70-90 pages; 20 lb. bond paper; b&w pen and ink illustrations; photos. Publishes "irreverent, literary-minded work by committed writers," for "small press, 'quasi-art-oriented' " audience. Annual. Estab. 1984. Circ. under 500.
Needs: Condensed/excerpted novel, confession, contemporary, erotica, ethnic, experimental, fantasy, feminist, gay, historical (general), horror, humor/satire, lesbian, literary, mainstream, mystery/suspense, prose poem, psychic/supernatural/occult, regional, science fiction, translations and arts. Wants to see more "daring and thought-

provoking" fiction. No "slick-oriented stuff published by major magazines." Receives 1 plus ms/month. Accepts 1-2 mss/year. Does not read mss July-October. Publishes ms within 3-6 months of acceptance. **Publishes 1-2 new writers/year.** Recently published work by Alan Catlin, T. Kilgore Splake, Peter Magliocco and the Mag Man. Length: 250-3,000 words; 2,000 words preferred. Also publishes literary essays "if relevant to aesthetic preferences," literary criticism "occasionally," poetry. Sometimes comments on rejected mss.

How to Contact: Send complete ms with cover letter. Responds in 3 months. SASE for ms. Accepts simultaneous submissions. Sample copy for $5, 6×9 SAE and 79¢ postage. Two-year subscription for $10. Guidelines for #10 SASE.

Payment/Terms: Pays contributor's copies. Acquires one-time rights.

Advice: "Seeking more novel and quality-oriented work, usually from solicited authors. Magazine fiction today needs to be concerned with the issues of fiction writing itself—not just with a desire to publish or please the largest audience. Think about things in the fine art world as well as the literary one and keep the hard core of life in between."

babysue, P.O. Box 8989, Atlanta GA 31106-8989. (404)320-1178. Websites: www.babysue.com and www.LMNOP.com (includes comics, poetry, fiction and a wealth of music reviews). **Contact:** Don W. Seven, editor. Zine: 8½×11; 32 pages; illustrations; photos. "*babysue* is a collection of music reviews, poetry, short fiction and cartoons for anyone who can think and is not easily offended." Biannual. Estab. 1983. Circ. 5,000.

• Sometimes funny, very often perverse, this 'zine featuring mostly cartoons and "comix" definitely is not for the easily offended.

Needs: Erotica, experimental and humor/satire. Receives 5-10 mss/month. Accepts 3-4 mss/year. Publishes ms within 3 months of acceptance. Published work by Daniel Lanette, Massy Baw, Andrew Taylor and Barbara Rimshaw. Publishes short shorts. Length: 1-2 single-spaced pages.

How to Contact: Query with clips of published work. SASE. Accepts simultaneous submissions. No submissions via e-mail.

Payment/Terms: Pays 1 contributor's copy.

Advice: "Create out of the love of creating, not to see your work in print!"

BEEF: the meat. (218)838-8333. E-mail: beef@the-meat.net. Website: www.the-meat.net. **Contact:** Joy Olivia Miller, editor-in-chief. Electronic zine. *BEEF* is "high brow content hidden in fun articles, reviews, stories and poetry. The point of *BEEF* is to entertain."

Needs: "No historical melodramatic pieces or pornographic work. Would like to see more dark comedy first person or modern and sci-fi." **Publishes 10 new writers/year.** Recently published work by Michelle Trella, Brian Zomchek and Christina Walker.

How to Contact: Accepts queries/mss by e-mail.

Advice: "Entertaining commentary on pop culture issues is a major theme . . . *BEEF* is mainly reviews and essays; however, fiction that would be appropriate/interesting to an audience of those age 18-28 is printed. Tends to be a college-educated crowd. Make your work fun and true to life. Honesty pays off. Although print will never die, the electronic publishing arena IS the future."

THE BITTER OLEANDER, 4983 Tall Oaks Dr., Fayetteville NY 13066-9776. (315)637-3047. Fax: (315)637-5056. E-mail: bones44@ix.netcom.com. Website: www.bitteroleander.com. **Contact:** Paul B. Roth, editor. Zine specializing in poetry and fiction: 6×9; 128 pages; 55 lb. paper; 12 pt. CIS cover stock; photos. "We're interested in the surreal; deep image; particularization of natural experiences." Semiannual. Estab. 1974. Circ. 1,500.

• In 1998 *The Bitter Oleander* received a Hemingway grant from the French Ministry of Culture and was listed in *Best of American Poetry,* 1999.

Needs: Experimental, new age/mystic/spiritual, translations. "No pornography; no confessional; no romance." Receives 100 unsolicited mss/month. Accepts 1-2 mss/issue; 2-4 mss/year. Does not read mss in July. Publishes ms 4-6 months after acceptance. Recently published work by Robert Bly, Charles Wright, Louis Simpson, Marjorie Agosín, Duane Locke and Alan Britt. Length: 1,000-2,000 words. Publishes short shorts. Length: 1,500 words. Also publishes literary essays, poetry. Always comments on rejected ms.

How to Contact: Send complete ms with a cover letter. Include estimated word count, 50-word bio and list of publications. Responds in 1 week to queries; 1 month to mss. Send SASE for reply, return of ms. Sample copy for $8, 7×10 SAE with 4 first-class stamps. Guidelines for #10 SASE.

Payment/Terms: Pays 1 contributor's copy; additional copies $8. Acquires first rights.

Advice: "We're interested in originality."

BLACK PETALS, Fossil Publications, 11627 Taft, Wichita KS 67209-1036. E-mail: blackptls@aol.com. Website: http://hometown.aol.com/blackptls/Bptls1.html (includes writer's guidelines, subscription information, addresses, editors' names, sample story). **Contact:** Kenneth James Crist, editor. Zine specializing in horror/

science fiction: digest size; over 88 pages; photocopied; illustrations. "A little something special for those special readers of oddity and terror. *Black Petals* is about the dark side of science fiction and the bizarre and unusual in horror—mature audience *only*." Quarterly. Estab. 1997. Circ. 200.

Needs: Experimental, horror, psychic/supernatural; science fiction (soft/sociological). Wants more hard core horror. No children's or romance, "Star Trek," vampires, stories from "beyond the grave. We don't get nearly enough science fiction that is based on current scientific fact—or even scientific speculation. We look for original ideas, strong characters, emotional involvement, good, vivid background." Receives over 10-15 unsolicited mss/month. Accepts 14-20 mss/issue. **Publishes 3-5 new writers/year.** Recently published work by Lee Clark, D.F. Lewis and Scott Urban. Length: no minimum; 3,500 words maximum; average length: 1,500 words. Publishes short shorts. Also publishes poetry. Always comments on rejected mss.

How to Contact: Send complete ms. Include estimated word count and list of publications. Responds in 2-4 weeks to queries and mss. "Disposable copies please. No e-mail submissions, query first." Accepts simultaneous and multiple submissions and reprints. Sample copy for $3.50. Guidelines for #10 SASE.

Payment/Terms: Pays contributor's copies; additional copies $3.50.

Advice: "My best advice—submit! How do you know if you'll get published unless you submit! Also, obtain a sample copy, follow guidelines and don't watch the mailbox. New unpublished writers are high on my list. If I have time I'll even help edit a manuscript. If I reject a manuscript, I encourage writers to send something else. Don't ever be discouraged, and don't wallpaper your office with rejection notes—toss them!"

N: ◎ **BLUE MURDER MAGAZINE**, Blue Murder, LLC, 2340 NW Thurman St., Portland OR 97210-2579. (503)220-4041. Fax: (502)220-4077. E-mail: info@bluemurder.com. Website: www.bluemurder.com (includes the entire magazine). **Contact:** Elise Lyons. Online e-zine specializing in crime noir fiction; 75 pages. "Hard-boiled, crime noir fiction. Our magazine was the first of its kind on the web. Our audience (worldwide) enjoys reading crime/mystery fiction." Bimonthly. Estab. 1998.

Needs: Mystery/suspense (police procedural, private eye/hardboiled). No romantic mysteries, horror, gothic, cozy or cat mysteries. Receives 400-500 mss/month. Accepts 12-15 mss/issue; 70-100 mss/year. Publishes ms 1-6 months after acceptance. Agented fiction 10%. **Publishes 2-5 new writers/year.** Recently published work by Kate Thornton, Andrew Vachss, and Kris Neri. Length: 250-3,000 words. Publishes short shorts. Also publishes literary essays and literary criticism. Accepts submissions by e-mail. Include estimated word count and brief bio. Responds in 1 week to queries and mss. Online submissions only. Accepts simultaneous submissions and multiple submissions. Sample copy free upon request. Guidelines for e-mail and on website. Reviews novels, short story collections and nonfiction books of interest. Contact: David Firks.

Payment/Terms: Pays $20-100. Pays on publication for one-time rights and electronic rights.

Advice: "A manuscript should have voice, be unique. The first two paragraphs are very important. The short story should move the reader at lightening pace. Read as much as you can, everything you can. Know what crime noir fiction is about. Read our back issues."

◎ ◎ **BOTH SIDES NOW, Journal of Spiritual Alternatives**, Free People Press, 10547 State Highway 110 N., Tyler TX 75704-3731. (903)592-4263. **Contact:** Elihu Edelson, editor. Zine: 8½×11; 20 pages; bond paper and cover; b&w line illustrations. "*Both Sides Now* explores the Aquarian frontier as the world witnesses the end of an old order and enters a New Age. Its contents include opinion, commentary, philosophy and creative writing for all who are interested in New Age matters." Published irregularly. Estab. 1969. Circ. 200.

Needs: Material with New Age slant, including fables, fantasy, humor/satire, myths, parables, psychic/supernatural, spiritual/inspirational, romance (futuristic/time travel), political, science fiction (utopian, soft/sociological). Length: "about 2 magazine pages, more or less." Also publishes literary essays, book reviews and poetry. Often comments on rejected mss with "brief note."

How to Contact: Send complete ms with SASE. Include brief bio and list of publications. Accepts simultaneous submissions and previously published work. Responds in 3 months to mss. Send SASE for reply, return of ms or send a disposable copy of ms. Sample copy for $2. Reviews "New Age fiction."

Payment/Terms: Pays 5 contributor's copies plus subscription. "Authors retain rights."

Advice: Looks for "tight, lucid writing that leaves the reader with a feeling of delight and/or enlightenment. Heed our editorial interests. Short pieces preferred as space is very limited. We plan to publish more fiction; emphasis has been on nonfiction to date."

⊕ ◎ **THE BROBDINGNAGIAN TIMES**, 96 Albert Rd., Cork, Ireland. Phone: (21)311227. **Contact:** Giovanni Malito, editor. Zine specializing in short international work: 6×8½; 8 pages; 80 gramme paper; illustrations. "There are no obvious editorial slants. We are interested in any prose from anyone anywhere provided it is short (1,000 words maximum)." Quarterly. Estab. 1996. Circ. 250.

CHECK THE CATEGORY INDEXES, located at the back of the book, for publishers interested in specific fiction subjects.

Needs: Ethnic/multicultural, experimental, horror, humor/satire, literary, romance (contemporary), science fiction (hard science/technological, soft/sociological). "No ghost stories/dysfunctional family stories/first sex stories." Receives 4-6 unsolicited mss/month. Accepts 2 mss/issue; 8 mss/year. Publishes ms in next issue after acceptance. **Publishes 2-3 new writers/year.** Published work by D.F. Lewis, Christopher Woods, Michael Wynne, Laura Lush, Ruba Neda and Jon Rourke. Length: 50-1,000 words; average length: 600 words. Publishes short shorts. Average length: 500 words. Also publishes literary essays, poetry. Always comments on rejected ms.

How to Contact: Send complete ms with a cover letter. Include estimated word count. Responds in 1 week to queries; 3 weeks to mss. Send SASE (IRCs) for reply, return of ms or send a disposable copy of ms. Accepts simultaneous and reprint submissions. Sample copy for #10 SAE and 2 IRCs. Guidelines for #10 SAE and 1 IRC.

Payment/Terms: Pays 2 contributor's copies; additional copies for postage. Acquires one time rights for Ireland/U.K. Sends galleys to author if required. Copyrighted Ireland/U.K.

Advice: "Crisp language. Economy of language. These are important, otherwise almost anything goes."

✓ Ⓞ **BURNING SKY: Adventures in Science Fiction Terror**, Thievin' Kitty Publications, P.O. Box 341, Marion MA 02738. E-mail: theedge@capecod.net. Website: www.capecod.net/thievinkitty or www.angelfire .com/biz3/GFGpg/ (includes guidelines, current and back issue information, cover art, ordering information, information on editors). **Contact:** Greg F. Gifune, editor. Associate editors: Carla Gifune and Chuck Deude. Zine specializing in science fiction horror: digest; 30-40 pages; white bond; glossy card cover. *Burning Sky* publishes "sci/fi horror blends ONLY." Triannual. Estab. 1998. Circ. 250.

● "In the Ending" by James H. Bearden was recommended for the Stoker Award.

Needs: Horror and science fiction blends. Receives more than 100 unsolicited mss/month. Accepts 5-6 mss/issue; 15-18 mss/year. Does not read January, May and September. Publishes ms 1-4 months after acceptance. Agented fiction 1-2%. **Publishes 1-3 new writers/year.** Published work by D. F. Lewis, Michael Laimo, Suzanne Donahue, Christopher Stires, Denis Kirk and Stephen van Maanen. Length: 500-3,500 words; average length: 2,000-3,000 words. Also publishes literary criticism. Often comments on rejected ms.

How to Contact: Send complete ms with a cover letter. Accepts queries by e-mail, but no mss. Include estimated word count, bio, list of publications and cover letter. Responds in 1 week to queries; 2 months to mss. Send SASE for reply, return of ms or send a disposable copy of ms. Sample copy for $4 in US, $5 elsewhere. Reviews novels, short story collections and nonfiction books of interest to writers. Send books to editor.

Payment/Terms: Pays 1 contributor's copy; additional copies $3. Pays on publication. Sends galleys to author on request.

Advice: "We like strong, concise, lean writing, stories that follow our very specific guidelines of blending sci-fi and horror, stories with an 'edge of your seat' quality. Thought-provoking, tension filled and genuinely frightening stories with realistic dialogue and a gritty style. Do not send straight sci-fi or horror stories. We need elements of both. Read a copy. *Burning Sky* is a very particular market, but we are proud to have published three first stories in our first three issues, along with more established writers. Send us a well written story in proper manuscript format that fits our guidelines. We don't want highly technical or introverted ramblings—we want exciting, highly entertaining and frightening stories."

Ⓝ Ⓜ **$** Ⓞ **CHIAROSCURO: Treatments of Light and Shade in Words**. E-mail: brett.savory@hom e.com. Website: www.gothic.net/chiaroscuro/chizine. **Contact:** Brett A. Savory, editor-in-chief. E-zine specializing in dark fiction. "Just give us your best and darkest." Quarterly. Estab. 1999. Circ. 10,000.

Needs: "Anything so long as it's dark and well-written. No vampires or monsters (traditional), unless a new spin is somehow put on it." Receives 50 unsolicited mss/month. Accepts 3 mss/issue; 12 mss/year. Publishes ms 1-75 days after acceptance. Recently published work by Philip Nutman, John Shirley and Sandra Kasturi. Length: 5,000 words maximum; average length: 3,000-4,000 words. Publishes short shorts. Average length: 1,500 words. Also publishes poetry. Sometimes comments on rejected mss.

How to Contact: Send complete ms with a cover letter. Accepts only submissions by e-mail. Include estimated word count, brief bio and list of publications. Responds immediately to queries; 10 weeks to mss. Guidelines by e-mail. Reviews novels, short story collections and nonfiction books of interest to writers.

Payment/Terms: Pays $50 maximum or 1¢/word. Pays on acceptance (usually) for electronic and anthology rights under the Chiaroscuro name for "year's best." Sends galleys electronically to author. Sponsors contest. See website for details.

Advice: "Avoid pointless bloodshed. Bloodshed that is integral is fine, but hack and slash for the sake of hacking and slashing is boring. Please, for the love of all the gods that ever were, no more vampires!"

Ⓝ Ⓞ **CHILDREN, CHURCHES AND DADDIES LITERARY MAGAZINE, the un-religious, non-family oriented publication**, Scars Publications and Design, 2628 N. Troy, #2, Chicago IL 60647-1137. E-mail: ccandd96@aol.com. Website: www.yotko.com/scars (includes all issues, writings, guidelines). **Contact:** Janet Kuypers, editor-in-chief. E-zine and literary magazine: laser paper; CMYK color cover stock; some illustrations; photos. "We look for detail-oriented writing that makes you feel as you lived in the scenes. We appreciate a gripping sense of action." Annual. Estab. 1993.

Needs: Ethnic/multicutural, feminist, gay, horror (futuristic, psychological, supernatural), lesbian, literary, mainstream, mystery/suspense, psychic/supernatural/occult. No religious, romantic or children's writings. Accepts 25-45 mss/year. Publishes ms 1 year after acceptance. Agented fiction 60-80%. **Publishes 85% new writers/year.** Recently published work by Mackenzie Silver, Shannon Peppers, and Helena Wolfe. Publishes short shorts. Also publishes poetry.

How to Contact: Send complete ms with cover letter by e-mail. Include e-mail address. Responds in 1 month to queries; 2 months to mss. Send SASE for return of ms or send a disposable copy of the ms and #10 SASE for reply only. Sample copy free on website. Guidelines for SASE, e-mail, or on website.

Payment/Terms: Pays with publication of work. Acquires one-time and electronic rights.

Advice: "Use descriptive detail, gripping philosophy and logic and reason. View our issues and guidelines online and enter our contest."

[N] [logo] CLARK STREET REVIEW, P.O. Box 1377, Berthoud CO 80513-2377. (970)669-5175. E-mail: clarkreview@earthlink.net. Website: http://home.earthlink.net/~clarkreview/ (includes guidelines only). **Contact:** Ray Foreman, editor. Zine specializing in poetry and short fiction: 5½ × 8½; 20 pages; 20 lb. paper; 20 lb. cover stock. "We publish only narrative poetry and short shorts with communicable content tuned to the spoken language and distinguished by clarity and humanity. We are small enough to bore a reader and publish often enough to make him know we are alive and stamping our feet." Bimonthly. Estab. 1998. Circ. 100.

Needs: Mainstream. Receives 10 unsolicited mss/month. Accepts 20-40 mss/year. Publishes ms 6 months after acceptance. Recently published work by Tad Wojnicki, Ray Clark Dickson and Steven Levi. Length: 800 words maximum; average length: 400-700 words. Also publishes literary essays, literary criticism and poetry.

How to Contact: Send complete ms with a cover letter. Include estimated word count. Responds in 1 month. Send a disposable copy of ms and #10 SASE for reply only. Accepts simultaneous submissions, previously published work and multiple submissions. Sample copy for $2. Guidelines for SASE or by e-mail.

Payment/Terms: Pays 1 contributor's copy; additional copies $1. Pays on publication for one-time rights.

Advice: "I will look at beginning writer's work, but I won't read past five lines if he doesn't hook me before that. Writing a short short is difficult because there's no room to recover if you screw up in the beginning."

[N] [logo] [logo] COLE'S COMIC DESK, G.S.&S., 3601 Owens St., Bryan TX 77808-0969. E-mail: colescomicdesk@mailcity.com. Website: www.colescomicdesk.tripod.com. **Contact:** Cole, executive editor. E-zine specializing in comic book reviews, news and stories. Weekly reviews. Bimonthly stories. Estab. 1999.

Needs: Comic book reviews, short stories about comic book characters. Publishes ms 1-2 months after acceptance. **Publishes 50% new writers/year.** Story length: 150-500 words; review lengths: 200 words. Publishes short shorts. Average length: 75-150 words.

How to Contact: E-mail submissions only. Include estimated word count and brief bio. Responds in 2 weeks to queries; 1 month to mss. Accepts simultaneous submissions, previously published work and multiple submissions. Sample copy and guidelines available on website. Reviews novels, short story collections, or nonfiction books of interest to writers.

Payment/Terms: Pays on publication for one-time and electronic rights.

Advice: "I want to be zapped into the world you create. While I'm there, don't use any wording to remind me of where I came from. Don't use other writers' words to describe or compare. Work hard at being the first to come up with tomorrow's cliché phrase."

[check] [logo] [logo] A COMPANION IN ZEOR, 307 Ashland Ave., Egg Harbor Township NJ 08234-5568. (606)645-6938. Fax: (606)645-8084. E-mail: klitman323@aol.com or karenlitman@juno.com. Website: www.simegen.com/sgfandom/rimonslibrary/cz. (includes guidelines, back issue flyers, etc.). **Contact:** Karen Litman, editor. Fanzine: 8½ × 11; 60 pages; "letter" paper; heavy blue cover; b&w line illustrations; occasional b&w photos. Publishes science fiction based on the various Universe creations of Jacqueline Lichtenberg. Occasional features on Star Trek, and other interests, convention reports, reviews of movies and books, recordings, etc. Published irregularly. Estab. 1978. Circ. 300.

● *Companion in Zeor* is one fanzine devoted to the work and characters of Jacqueline Lichtenberg. Lichtenberg's work includes several future world, alien and group culture novels and series including the Sime/Gen Series and The Dushau trilogy. She's also penned two books on her own vampire character and she co-authored *Star Trek Lives*.

Needs: Fantasy, humor/satire, prose poem, science fiction. "No vicious satire. Nothing X-rated. Homosexuality prohibited unless *essential* in story. Occasionally receives one manuscript a month." Publication of an accepted ms "goes to website posting." Occasionally comments on rejected mss and recommends other markets.

How to Contact: Query first or send complete ms with cover letter. "Prefer cover letters about any writing experience prior, or related interests toward writing aims." Responds in 1 month. SASE. Accepts simultaneous submissions. Sample copy price depends on individual circumstances. Guidelines for #10 SASE. "I write individual letters to all queries. No form letter at present." SASE for guidelines or can be sent by e-mail. Reviews science fiction/fantasy collections or titles. "We can accept e-mail queries and manuscripts through AOL providers."

Payment/Terms: Pays in contributor's copies. Acquires first rights. Acquires website rights as well.

Advice: "Send concise cover letter asking what the author would like me to do for them if the manuscript cannot be used by my publication. They should follow guidelines of the type of material I use, which is often not done. I have had many submissions I cannot use as they are general fiction. Ask for guidelines before submitting to a publication. Write to the best of your ability and work with your editor to develop your work to a higher point than your present skill level. Take constructive criticism and learn from it. Electronic web publishing seems the way the industry is heading. I would not have thought of a website a few years ago. Receipt of manuscripts can only be through klitman323@aol.com. Juno cannot handle attachments. People can learn more through the domain—www.simegen.com/index.html."

⬛ ⬛ **DARGONZINE.** E-mail: dargon@shore.net. Website: www.dargonzine.org. **Contact**: Ornoth D.A. Liscomb, editor. Electronic zine specializing in fantasy. "*DargonZine* is a collaborative anthology, designed to give aspiring amateur writers the opportunity to interact with a live readership as well as other writers. Our goal is to write fantasy fiction that is mature, emotionally compelling and professional."
Needs: Fantasy. "We only accept fantasy fiction that is developed within our common milieu. We would like to see more fantasy stories with characters who are easy to identify with, which offer the reader an emotionally compelling experience, and restore a sense of wonder that modern fantasy has lost. Membership in the Dargon Project is a requirement for publication." **Publishes 6-10 new writers/year.** Recently published work by Bryan Read, Mark A. Murray, Dafydd Cyhoeddwr, Jim Ownes and Max Khaytsus.
How to Contact: Guidelines available on website.
Payment/Terms: "Authors retain all rights to their stories, and our only compensation is the growth and satisfaction that comes with working with other writers through peer review and close collaboration."
Advice: "Start by reading our Readers' and Writers' FAQs on our website. We have a strong idea of what makes good fantasy fiction, and we live with certain restrictions as a part of our collaborative milieu. Furthermore, writing for *DargonZine* requires a nontrivial commitment of time."

✓ ⬛ ⬛ **DIXIE PHOENIX, Marching to the beat of a different drummer since 1992**, P.O. Box 5676, Arlington VA 22205. E-mail: jsmosby@gateway.net. Website: www.dixiephoenix.com (includes writer's guidelines, zine history, selected articles, collected reviews, a few recipes and a growing number of links). **Contact:** Mike & Bjorn Munson, editors. Zine specializing in literature/essays: $5\frac{1}{2} \times 8\frac{1}{2}$; 48 pages; 60 lb. standard paper; 60-70 lb. color cover; illustrations; photos. "Our audience appears to be of all religious and political persuasions from fringe to mainstream. We try to make each issue intriguing, informative, edifying and entertaining. We're a 'Mom & Pop publication' not a corporate operation." Triannual. Estab. 1992. Circ. 500.
Needs: Historical (general), humor/satire, literary, mainstream/contemporary, regional, religious/inspirational, translations, travel essays, Celtic and Southern themes, Southern ghost stories, regional from all walks of life; folklore from around the world. Wants more "transcendental, regional" fiction. No poetry, children's/juvenile, erotica (no profanity in general), psychic/occult, romance. Receives 16-25 unsolicited mss/month. Accepts 1-2 mss/issue; 3-4 mss/year. Publishes ms 6-18 months after acceptance. **Publishes 2-3 new writers/year.** Recently published Errol Miller, Patricia G. Rourke and Gerald Wheeler. Length: 250-7,000 words; average length: 1,500 words. Publishes short shorts. Also publishes literary essays, literary criticism. "We have regular columns concerning history, culture and spirituality." Sometimes comments on rejected mss. "We are not accepting any poetry at this time."
How to Contact: Query first or e-mail. Accepts submissions by e-mail in ASCII, "(unsolicited attachments are deleted). Include SASE and a "nice friendly letter telling us about themselves and/or their writing." Responds in 1 month to queries; 4 months to mss. Accepts simultaneous submissions, reprints and electronic submissions. Sample copy for $2. Reviews novels and short story collections (also music).
Payment/Terms: Pays 3 contributor's copies; additional copies for $2. Pays on publication for one-time rights.
Advice: "We value sincerity over shock value. Fiction with a 'Phoenix Flavor' has a subject of personal exploration/discovery/epiphany/subjectivity whether spiritual, emotional, intellectual, etc. Definitely get a sample copy of our publication to get an idea of what we're about. Do many drafts and learn to critique your own work. Polish, polish, polish. No work is ever completely done."

✓ ⬛ ⬛ **DUCT TAPE PRESS**. E-mail: ducttapepress@yahoo.com. Website: www.io.com/~crberry/DuctT ape (includes all zine content). **Contact:** Josh Wardrip, editor. Electronic zine. "We seek writing that is perhaps riskier than what mainstream journals typically publish but we also demand the writing be very well crafted."
Needs: Experimental, literary. "No genre fiction that fails to challenge the conventions of the given genre." **Publishes 50-60 new writers/year.** Recently published work by Michael Largo, Jay Marvin, Michael Rothenberg, Scott Holstad and Anjana Basu. Also publishes poetry.
How to Contact: Send queries/mss by e-mail.
Advice: Looks for "daring, envelope-pushing writing that displays intelligence, attention to craft and imagination. We see a lot of writing that combines a few of these attributes, but rarely all of them. Familiarize yourself with the publication. A casual perusal should give you a general indication of the kind of material we favor. Don't assume that because we are a non-paying electronic zine we set lower standards than print publications. Please send your best work."

THE EDGE, TALES OF SUSPENSE, Thievin' Kitty Publications, P.O. Box 341, Marion MA 02738. E-mail: theedge@capecod.net. Websites: www.angelfire.com/biz3/GFGpg/ or www.capecod.net/thievinkitty/ (includes guidelines, samples, and updates. **Contact:** Greg F. Gifune, editor. Associate Editors: Carla S. Gifune, Chuck A. Deude. Zine specializing in varied genre suspense: digest-sized; 80-88 pages; heavy stock paper; heavy card cover. "We publish a broad range of genres, subjects and styles. While not an easy magazine to break into, we offer thrilling, 'edge of your seat' fiction from both seasoned and newer writers. We focus on the writing, not illustrations or distracting bells and whistles. Our goal is to present a quality, entertaining publication." Triannual. Estab. 1998. Circ. 1,000.
Needs: Adventure, erotica, gay, horror, lesbian, mystery/suspense (police procedural, private eye/hardboiled, noir), psychic/supernatural/occult, westerns with supernatural or horror element only. "Emphasis is on horror, crime and blends." No children's, young adult, romance, humor. Receives over 100 unsolicited mss/month. Accepts 10-12 mss/issue; 30-36 mss/year. Publishes ms 1-4 months after acceptance. Agented fiction 1-2%. **Publishes 1-6 new writers/year.** Published work by Ken Goldman, John Roux, Scott Urban, Stefano Donati, Suzanne Donahue, Robert Dunbar and Michael Laimo. Length: 700-8,000 words; average length: 2,500-4,500 words. Also publishes poetry. Always comments on rejected ms.
How to Contact: Send complete ms with a cover letter. Include estimated word count, brief bio and list of publications. Responds in 8 weeks. Send SASE for reply, return of ms or send a disposable copy of ms. Accepts simultaneous submissions but not preferred. Sample copy for $6 U.S., $7 elsewhere (includes postage). Guidelines for #10 SASE. No e-mail submissions.
Payment/Terms: Pays 1 contributor's copy; additional copies $5. Acquires one-time rights.
Advice: "We look for taut, tense thrillers with realistic dialogue, engaging characters, strong plots and endings that are both powerful and memorable. Graphic violence, sex and profanity all have their place but do not have to be gratuitous. We will not accept anything racist, sexist, sacrilegious, or stories that depict children or animals in violent or sexual situations!"

ENCOUNTER, meeting God Face-to-Face, (formerly *Straight*), Standard Publishing, 8121 Hamilton Ave., Cincinnati OH 45231. (513)931-4050. Fax: (513)931-0950. E-mail: kcarr@standardpub.com. Website: www.standardpub.com (includes lists of Standard Publishing's products and how to order them). **Contact:** Kelly Carr, editor. Zine specializing in Christian teens: 8½ × 11; 8 pages; glossy paper; illustrations; photos. "We seek to cause teens to look at their relationship with God in a new light and encourage them to live out their faith." Weekly. Estab. 1951. Circ. 35,000.
Needs: Religious, young adult/teen. Short stories that have Christian principles. "No non-religious fiction." Upcoming themes: media, crises, family life, Book of James, Satan-angels-demons, Book of Galatians, contentment. List of upcoming themes available for SASE. Receives 35 unsolicited mss/month. Accepts 2 mss/issue; 45 mss/year. Publishes ms 1 year after acceptance. Length: 800-1,100 words. Always comments on rejected mss.
How to Contact: Send complete ms with a cover letter. Accepts ms on disk; must call first. Include estimated word count and Social Security number. Responds in 3 months. Send SASE (or IRC) for return of ms or send a disposable copy of ms and #10 SASE for reply only. Accepts simultaneous submissions, previously published work and multiple submissions. Sample copy free for 11 × 13 SASE. Guidelines for SASE.
Payment/Terms: Pays 6-8¢/word and 5 contributor's copies. Pays on acceptance for first rights.
Advice: "We look for realistic teenagers with up-to-date dialogue who cope with modern-day problems."

THE FIREFLY, a tiny glow in a forest of darkness, 300 Broadway St., #107, St. Paul MN 55101. (651)291-5291. E-mail: spiderkirby@hotmail.com. **Contact:** Jane Kirby, editor. Zine specializing in revolutionary family life: 8½ × 11; 8-10 pages; some illustrations; photos. "Revolutionary, outside of mainstream parenting life, environmental, political, home birth, etc. . ." Quarterly. Estab. 1990. Circ. 300.
Needs: Ethnic/multicultural (Native American politics), feminist, birth, parenting, breastfeeding, homeschooling. Publishes ms 3-6 months after acceptance. Length: 1,000 words. Publishes literary essays, literary criticism and poetry. Sometimes comments on rejected mss.
How to Contact: Send complete ms with cover letter. Include brief bio. Responds in 6 weeks to queries and mss. Send SASE for reply to query, SASE for return of ms, or send a disposable copy of ms. Accepts simultaneous submissions and reprints. Sample copy for SASE. Reviews novels, short story collections, or nonfiction books of interest to writer.
Payment/Terms: Pays 5 contributor's copies. Acquires one-time rights.

FULLOSIA PRESS, Rockaway Park Philosophical Society, 299-9 Hawkins Ave., Suite 865, Ronkonkoma NY 11779. Fax: (631)588-9428. E-mail: deanofrpps@aol.com. Website: www.angelfire.com/bc2/Fullos iaPress/. **Contact:** J.D. Collins, editor. E-zine. "One-person, part-time. Publishes fiction and nonfiction. Our publication is right wing and conservative but amenable to the opposition's point of view. We promote an independent America. We are anti-global, anti-UN. Collects unusual news from former British or American provinces. Fiction interests include military, police, private detective, courthouse stories." Monthly. Estab. 1999. Circ. 100. Member: Vast Rightwing Conspiracy.

Needs: Historical (American), military/war, mystery/suspense, thriller/espionage. List of upcoming themes for SASE. Publishes ms 1 week after acceptance. Recently published work by Grant DeMan and HM Pax. Length: 500-2,000 words; average length: 750 words. Publishes short shorts. Also publishes literary essays. Always comments on rejected mss.

How to Contact: Query first. Accepts submissions by e-mail, fax and disk. Include brief bio and list of publications. Responds in 1 week to queries; 1 month to mss. Send SASE (or IRC) for return of ms. Accepts simultaneous submissions, previously published work and multiple submissions. Guidelines for SASE. Reviews novels, short story collections and nonfiction.

Payment/Terms: No payment. Acquires electronic rights.

Advice: "Make your point quickly. After five pages, everybody hates you and your characters."

$ ◐ THE FUNNY TIMES, 2176 Lee Rd., Cleveland Heights OH 44118. (216)371-8600. E-mail: ft@funnyti mes.com. Website: www.funnytimes.com (includes information about *The Funny Times*, cartoon of the week and laugh links). **Contact**: Ray Lesser and Susan Wolpert, editors. Zine specializing in humor: tabloid; 24 pages; newsprint; illustrations. *The Funny Times* is a "liberal-left monthly humor review." Estab. 1985. Circ. 55,000.

Needs: "Anything funny." Receives hundreds of unsolicited mss/month. Accepts 5 mss/issue; 60 mss/year. Publishes ms 1-6 months after acceptance. Agented fiction 10%. **Publishes 10 new writers/year.** Length: 500-700 words average. Publishes short shorts.

How to Contact: Send complete ms with a cover letter. Include list of publications. Responds in 3 months. Send SASE for return of ms or disposable copy of ms. Accepts simultaneous and reprint submissions. Sample copy for $3, 11 × 14 SAE and 77¢ 1st class postage. Guidelines for #10 SASE.

Payment/Terms: Pays $50, free subscription to the zine and 5 contributor's copies. Pays on publication for one-time rights.

Advice: "It must be funny."

$ ◻ ◐ ▣ GOTTA WRITE NETWORK LITMAG, Maren Publications, 515 E. Thacker, Hoffman Estates IL 60194-1957. E-mail: netera@aol.com or GWNLitmag@aol.com. Website: members.aol.com/gwnlit mag/. **Contact:** Denise Fleischer, editor. Magazine: 8½ × 11; 48-84 pages; saddle-stapled ordinary paper; matte card or lighter weight cover stock; illustrations. Magazine "serves as an open forum to discuss new markets, successes and difficulties. Gives beginning writers their first break into print and promotionally supports established professional novelists." Now accepting fiction for GWN's website. Distributed through the US, Canada and England. Semiannual. Estab. 1988. Circ. 200-300.

● In addition to publishing fiction, *Gotta Write Network Litmag* includes articles on writing techniques, small press market news, writers' seminar reviews, and features a "Behind the Scenes" section in which qualified writers can conduct e-mail interviews with small press editors and established writers. Those recently interviewed have included Literal Hatte's editors, romance author Jen Holing, *Writer's Digest* editor Melanie Rigney, authors Beverly Connor, R. Barri Flowers and J.G. Passarella.

Needs: Adventure, contemporary, fantasy, historical, humor/satire, literary, mainstream, prose poem, romance (gothic), science fiction (hard science, soft/sociological). "Currently seeking work with a clear-cut message or a twist at the very end. All genres accepted with the exception of excessive violence, sexual overtones or obscenity." Receives 75-150 unsolicited mss per month. Accepts 1-6 mss per issue; up to 20 mss a year. Publishes mss 6-12 months after acceptance. Length: 10 pages maximum for short stories. Also publishes poetry.

How to Contact: Send complete ms with cover letter. Include "who you are, genre, previous publications and focused area of writing." Responds in 4 months (later during publication months). SASE ("no SASE, no response"). Responds on fax submissions within days. Responds by fax. Accepts electronic (e-mail) submissions but no attached mail. Sample copy for $6. Guidelines for SASE.

Payment/Terms: Pays $10 or 2 contributor's copies for first North American serial rights.

Advice: "If I still think about the direction of the story after I've read it, I know it's good. Organize your thoughts on the plot and character development (qualities, emotions) before enduring ten drafts. Make your characters come alive by giving them a personality and a background, and then give them a little freedom. Let them take you through the story."

Ⓝ ✖ ◐ IKSPERAMENT, a literary experiment, 616 Norman Crescent, Midland, Ontario L4R 4N5 Canada. (705)526-4102. E-mail: athan55@hotmail.com. Website: www.move.to/danonline. **Contact:** Dan Johnson, editor. E-zine specializing in experimental work. Quarterly. Estab. 1999.

Needs: Experimental, gay, lesbian, literary, translation. No mainstream. Receives 2 unsolicited mss/month. Accepts 1 mss/issue. Publishes ms 1-2 months after acceptance. **Publishes 3-4 new writers/year.** Recently published work by Sean Van der Lee, Elana Wolff, and Richard M. Grove. Length: 500-3,000 words; average length: 2,000. Publishes short shorts. Average length: 1,000 words. Publishes literary essays, literary criticism and poetry. Sometimes comments on rejected mss.

How to Contact: Send complete ms with cover letter. Accepts submissions by e-mail and disk. Include estimated word count, brief bio and list of publications. Accepts previously published work and multiple submissions. Guidelines on website. Reviews novels, short story collections and nonfiction books of interest.

Payment/Terms: Acquires first rights. Copyrights remain with author. Sends galleys to author via e-mail.
Advice: Wants "new, fresh writing, especially experimental and freestyle. Send via e-mail in body of message. Makes web formatting easier and editor happier."

N ⊘ IN POSSE REVIEW, Web Del Sol, 239 Duncan St., San Francisco CA 94131. E-mail: submissions@w ebdelsol.com. Website: www.webdelsol.com. **Contact:** Rachel Callaghan, editor. Poetry Editor: Ilya Kaminsky. E-zine specializing in literary fiction, poetry, and creative nonfiction. "The best of literary fiction, creative nonfiction and poetry from, well, whoever writes it—we welcome all serious writers; especially those who can demonstrate fresh new style and a slightly skewed point of view. *IPR* is interested in looking for non-PC work concerning ethnic issues. See website for details." Quarterly or triannual.
Needs: Adventure, erotica, ethnic/multicultural, experimental, family saga, fantasy, feminist, gay, historical, horror (literary), humor/satire, lesbian, literary, mystery/suspense, science fiction, western (literary). Accepts 8 mss/issue; 25 mss/year. Publishes ms 3 months after acceptance. **Publishes 10 new writers/year.** Length: 3,500 words; average length: 1,500 words. Publishes short shorts. Average length: 500 words. Also publishes literary essays and poetry. Sometimes comments on rejected mss.
How to Contact: Cut and paste ms into e-mail. Include estimated word count, brief bio and list of publications. Responds in 3 months to mss. Accepts multiple submissions but limit is 2 short stories. Guidelines on website.
Payment/Terms: Acquires electronic rights for 120 days. Sends galleys to author by e-mail.
Advice: "We have very eclectic tastes, whatever turns us on at that moment. Different, surprising, cutting edge, intriguing, but well-written is best. A manuscript that stands out is one we would consider printing out. Make sure you have a complete story, not slice-of-life or good start. Wait after writing and re-read. Use spelling and grammar checkers."

⊘ 🏆 ▣ INTERTEXT. E-mail: editors@intertext.com. Submissions to: submissions@intertext.com. Website: www.intertext.com. **Contact:** Jason Snell, editor. Electronic zine. "Our readers are computer literate (because we're online only) and appreciate entertaining fiction. They're usually accepting of different styles and genres—from mainstream to historical to science fiction to fantasy to horror to mystery—because we don't limit ourselves to one genre. They just want to read a story that makes them think or transports them to an interesting new place."

• *InterText* author Stan Houston's *Bite Me, Deadly* was named one of the top net fiction stories of the year by *Pulp Eternity Magazine*.

Needs: "Well-written fiction from any genre or setting." Especially looking for intelligent science fiction. No "exploitative sex or violence. We will print stories with explicit sex or violence, but not if it serves no purpose other than titillation." No pornography, fan fiction, novels or by-the-book swords and sorcery. **Publishes 16 new writers/year.** Published work by E. Jay O'Connell, Richard Kadrey, Levi Asher, Marcus Eubanks and William Routhier.
How to Contact: Electronic submissions only. Stories should be in ASCII, HTML, or Microsoft Word formats. Full guidelines available on website.
Advice: "Have a clear writing style—the most clever story we've seen in months still won't make it if it's written badly. Try to make our readers think in a way they haven't before, or take them to a place they've never thought about before. And don't be afraid to mix genres—our readers have come to appreciate stories that aren't easily labeled as being part of one genre or another."

$ ⊘ 🏆 ▣ JACKHAMMER E-ZINE, 9220 Jill Lane #2E, Schiller Park IL 60176. (847)928-9925. E-mail: jackhammer@eggplant-productions.com. Website: www.eggplant-productions.com. "The entire content of *Jackhammer E-zine* (including limited archives) can be found on the website, writer's guidelines, submission information and submission addresses are also available." **Contact:** Raechel Henderson, editor. E-zine specializing in science fiction, fantasy, horror and nonfiction. "*Jackhammer E-zine* is a weekly themed e-zine. Each week we propose a 'Question of the Week' and all fiction and nonfiction published in that issue touches upon the 'Question of the Week.' We publish short fiction and short articles, preferring informative and personal essays over 'rants.' Our intended audience is anyone who likes to ask 'What if?'" Estab. 1997. Circ. 1,000.

• *Jackhammer E-zine* is a member of the Zine Association, for e-zines in the science fiction, fantasy, horror genres. *Jackhammer E-zine* has received the Page One Award for Literary Contribution in 1999, the Blue Moon Award for Website Excellence in 1999 and Eternity Online's Best of the Web: Editor of the Year award in 1999.

Needs: Fantasy (space fantasy, sword and sorcery, magic realism, modern fantasy), horror (dark fantasy, futuristic, psychological, supernatural), science fiction (soft/sociological), speculative fiction. "Other categories such as ethnic/multicultural, feminist, gay and occult would also be considered if they fall under the umbrella of speculative fiction. No splatterpunk, gore, straight erotica, anything that could be considered R-rated material." List of upcoming themes available at www.eggplant-productions.com/jackhammer/guidelines.html. Receives 80 unsolicited mss/month. Accepts 3 mss/issue; 156 mss/year. Publishes ms 1-12 months after acceptance. **Publishes 80 new writers/year.** Word length: 1,500 words average; 175 words minimum; 2,000 words maximum. Publishes short shorts. Length: 375 words. Often comments on rejected ms.

How to Contact: Send complete ms by e-mail. "We only accept e-mail submissions. Snail mail submissions are returned unread to the sender." Include estimated word count, 50 word bio, the question the story is being submitted for and a valid e-mail address. Responds in 1-2 weeks. Accepts simultaneous and reprint submissions. Sample copy and guidelines free.

Payment/Terms: Pays $5-20. Payment on publication. Acquires first Worldwide electronic rights or Worldwide Electronic rights if applicable. "Eggplant Productions holds the rights up until 90 days after publication during which the work can not appear anywhere else on the Web."

Advice: "A properly formatted manuscript is always appreciated. What I really want in a story is to feel something after reading it. If a story makes me laugh, grin, cry or shudder, I'm going to buy it. If the story doesn't affect me one way or the other I'll pass it on. Read the guidelines carefully. Read them a third time. If you still have a question then you can e-mail me. Electronic publishing is still struggling for respectability and so my goal with *Jackhammer E-zine* is to provide quality short stories to readers. By 'quality' I mean stories that elicit an emotional response in readers. Also, by 'quality' I mean polished stories. Many places on the Web post stories that are still in the rough draft stage. Make sure your work is ready to be viewed by others before you send it out."

N $ 🖫 LADY CHURCHILL'S ROSEBUD WRISTLET, An Occasional Outburst, Gleek It, Inc., 106 Warren St., Brighton MA 02115. (617)266-7746. E-mail: lcrw@hotmail.com. Website: www.netcolony.com/arts/lcrw (includes guidelines, contents and occasional extras not in the zine). **Contact:** Gavin Grant, editor. Zine: half legal size; 40 pages; 60 lb. paper; cardstock cover; illustrations; photos. Semiannual. Estab. 1996. Circ. 200.
Needs: Comics/graphic novels, experimental, fantasy, feminist, literary, science fiction, short story collections, translations. Receives 1 unsolicited ms/month. Accepts 4-6 mss/issue; 8-12 mss/year. Publishes ms 6 months after acceptance. **Publishes 2-4 new writers/year.** Recently published work by Kelly Link, Lucy Snyder, Margaret Muirhead and Stuart Davies. Length: 200-7,000 words; average length: 3,500 words. Publishes short shorts. Average length: 500 words. Also publishes literary essays and poetry. Sometimes comments on rejected mss.
How to Contact: Send complete ms with a cover letter. Accepts submissions by e-mail and disk. Include estimated word count. Responds in 2 weeks to queries; 1 month to mss. Send SASE (or IRC) for return of ms or send a disposable copy of ms and #10 SASE for reply only. Accepts simultaneous submissions, previously published work and multiple submissions. Sample copy for $3. Guidelines by e-mail. Reviews novels, short story collections and nonfiction books of interest to writers.
Payment/Terms: Pays $5-10 and 2 contributor's copies; additional copies $3. Pays on publication for first or one-time rights.
Advice: "I like fiction that tends toward the speculative."

N $ ◯ THE LEADING EDGE, Magazine of Science Fiction and Fantasy, TLE Press, 3163 JKHB, Provo UT 84602. (801)378-4455. E-mail: tle@byu.edu. Website: www.tle.clubs.byu.edu (includes excerpts; writer's, artist's, advertising guidelines; previews; subscription information). **Contact:** Douglas Summers Stay, editor. Fiction Director: Peter Ahlstrom. Zine specializing in science fiction: 5½×8½; 120 pages; card stock; some illustrations. "*The Leading Edge* is dedicated to helping new writers make their way into publishing. We send critiques back with every story. We don't print anything with heavy swearing, violence that is too graphic, or explicit sex. We have an audience that is about 50% Mormon." Semiannual. Estab. 1981. Circ. 400.
Needs: Fantasy (space fantasy, sword/sorcery), science fiction (hard science/technological, soft/sociological). Receives 60 unsolicited mss/month. Accepts 6 mss/issue; 12 mss/year. Publishes ms 1-6 months after acceptance. **Publishes 4 new writers/year.** Recently published work by Brent Chesley, Randal S. Doering, and Richard R. Harris. Length: 12,000 words maximum; average length 7,000 words. Publishes short shorts. Average length: 1,200 words. Also publishes poetry. Always comments on rejected mss.
How to Contact: Send complete ms with cover letter. Include estimated word count, brief bio and list of publications. Responds in up to 5 months on mss. Send disposable copy of ms and #10 SASE for reply only. Accepts multiple submissions. Sample copy for $4.50. Guidelines for SASE. Reviews novels, short story collections and nonfiction books of interest. Contact: Peter Ahlstrom, nonfiction editor.
Payment/Terms: Pays 1¢/word; $100 maximum and 2 contributor's copies; additional copies $3.95. Pays on publication for first North American serial rights. Sends galleys to author.
Advice: "We are looking for new ideas and strong plots in science fiction. We could use more creative high fantasy submissions. We publish at least one humorous piece in each issue. Try to base a story on the latest scientific discoveries rather than old clichés like time travel or space cowboys. Fantasy stories need good characterization and should inspire awe in the reader."

✓ ◯ LIQUID OHIO, Voice of the Unheard, Grab Odd Dreams Press, P.O. Box 60265, Bakersfield CA 93386-0265. (805)871-0586. E-mail: grab_odd_dream@hotmail.com. Website: www.chickpages.com/zinescene/notaprettygirl1914. **Contact:** Christa Hart, fiction editor. Magazine: 8×11; 13-25 pages; copy paper; illustrations; photos. Quarterly. Estab. 1995. Circ. 500.

Needs: Experimental, humor/satire, literary. Receives 15-20 unsolicited mss/month. Accepts 2 mss/issue; 24-30 mss/year. Publishes ms 1-3 months after acceptance. **Publishes 40-60 new writers/year.** Recently published work by Janet Kuypers, Peter Gorman and Christine Brandel. Length: 2,500-3,000 words; average length: 1,500-1,800 words. Publishes short shorts. Also publishes literary essays, literary criticism, poetry.

How to Contact: Send complete ms with a cover letter. Should include estimated word count. Responds in 1 month to queries; 3 months to mss. Send SASE for reply, return of ms or send a disposable copy of ms. Accepts simultaneous submissions, reprint and electronic submissions. Sample copy for $3, 11 × 14 SAE and 3 first-class stamps. Guidelines for #10 SASE.

Payment/Terms: Pays 3 contributor's copies. Acquires one-time rights.

Advice: "We like things that are different, but not too abstract or 'artsy' that one goes away saying, 'huh?' Write what you feel, not necessarily what sounds deep or meaningful—it will probably be that naturally if it's real. Send in anything you've got—live on the edge. Stories that are relatable, that deal with those of us trying to find a creative train in the world. We also love stories that are extremely unique, e.g., talking pickles, etc."

N **$** **O** **©** **LITERALLY HORSES, Poetry, Fiction, Nonfiction & Other Expressions of the Horse**, Equestrienne Ltd., 208 Cherry Hill St., Kalamazoo MI 49006. (616)345-5915. **Contact:** Laurie A. Cerny, publisher/editor. Zine specializing in horse/cowboy-related fiction/poetry: 5¼ × 8½; 20 pages; 20 lb. paper; 20 lb. cover stock; illustrations; photos. "We showcase poetry/fiction that has a horse/cowboy, western lifestyle theme. Most of the mainstream horse publications, as well as ones that publish western history, ignore these genres. I'm very interested in subject material geared toward the English riding discipline of the horse industry, as well as horse racing, driving. etc." Quarterly. Estab. 1999. Circ. 1,000. Member: Publishers Marketing Association, American Horse Publications.

Needs: Children's/juvenile (horse; ages 7-13), comics/graphic novels, western (frontier saga, traditional, cowboy/rodeo related). "No horror, gay, erotica." Receives 1-5 unsolicited mss/month. Accepts 2-3 mss/year. Publishes ms 6 months after acceptance. **Publishes 25 new writers/year.** Recently published work by Kim Marie Wood, Wally Badgett and John R. Erickson. Length: 1,500-2,500 words; average length: 1,500 words. Publishes short shorts. Average length: 500 words. Also publishes literary criticism and poetry. Sometimes comments on rejected mss.

How to Contact: Send complete ms with a cover letter. Include brief bio. Responds in 6 weeks to mss. Send a disposable copy of ms and #10 SASE for reply only. Accepts simultaneous submissions, previously published work and multiple submissions. Sample copy for $2.25. Guidelines for SASE. Reviews novels, short story collections and nonfiction books of interest to writers.

Payment/Terms: Pays $3/poem, $12/short story and 2 contributor's copies; additional copies $2. Pays on publication for one-time rights. Not copyrighted. Sponsors annual contest. Deadline is May 15 of each year. SASE for rules.

Advice: "Right now many other mainstream literary publications seem to be interested in very dark, disturbed fiction. I'm focusing on fiction that is positive (it still may deal with hard issues) and spiritual. A reader should come away feeling good and not depressed after reading the fiction in *Literally Horses*."

N **O** **©** **MARGIN: Exploring Modern Magical Realism**, 9407 Capstan Dr. NE, Bainbridge Island WA 98110-4624. E-mail: msellma@attglobal.net. Website: www.angelfire.com/wa2/index.html (includes fiction excerpts, short stories, links, reading lists, special features, reviews, essays, creative nonfiction, articles). **Contact:** Tamara Kaye Sellman, editor. E-zine specializing in magical realism. "*Margin* seeks to publish high-quality works of magical realism which might otherwise be skipped over by print publishers, who seem to be concerned only with marketability and quality in literature." Perpetual, always accessible. Estab. 2000. Circ. 1,500 visitors a month.

Needs: Ethnic/multicultural, experimental, fantasy (magic realism), feminist, gay, historical, horror (supernatural), lesbian, mainstream, psychic/supernatural/occult, regional, science fiction (only if bridges with magical realism), translations (query first). Receives 100 mss/month. Accepts 1% of mss received. Publishes ms within 6 months after acceptance. **Publishes 1% new writers/year.** Recently published work by Brandy Bauer, Anne Spollen and Katherine Voz. Length: 3,500 words maximum. Publishes short shorts. Also publishes literary essays and literary criticism. Sometimes comments on rejected mss.

How to Contact: Send complete ms with cover letter. Query first on translated work. Accepts submissions by e-mail. "We prefer e-mail but accept surface mail subs too." Include brief bio, list of publications, list of 10 recommended works of magic realism, the author's 100-word definition of magic realism. Responds in 3 months

● **A BULLET INTRODUCES COMMENTS** by the editor of *Novel & Short Story Writer's Market* indicating special information about the listing.

to queries and mss. Send SASE for return of ms or send a disposable copy of ms and #10 SASE for reply only. Accepts simultaneous submissions and previously published work. Sample copy free on website. Guidelines for SASE, e-mail or on website. Reviews novels, short story collections, and nonfiction books of interest to writers.
Payment/Terms: Funds distributed to contributors as they are acquired. Acquires first, first North American serial, one-time and electronic rights, reprint; nonexclusive reprint depends on the rights available.
Advice: Looks for "technical strength, unique, engaging style, well-developed and inventive story. Manuscript must be magic realism. Do not send more than one manuscript. Always enclose SASE. Do not inquire before 3 months. Send us your 'A' list, no works-in-progress."

N ⃞ ⃞ **MILKWOOD REVIEW, an interdisciplinary journal of literature and the other arts.** Website: www.geocities.com/milkwoodreview (includes complete publication). **Contact:** Susan Atefat Peckham, founding editor. E-zine specializing in literature and the other arts. "The *Milkwood Review* is an interdisciplinary journal specializing in short fiction, poetry, creative nonfiction, and hypertext. Because the journal is published on the Web, we seek to create an environment for the work that makes use of the Internet's multimedia capacities. All work, for example, is published with real-audio excerpts of passages read by the author. We are also very open to experimental presentation. *Milkwood* is not designed to compete with print journals but to provide an alternative avenue of publication for authors whose work may benefit from a multimedia presentation." Estab. 2000.
Needs: Ethnic/multicultural, experimental, family saga, feminist, historical, humor/satire, literary, hypertext. Accepts mss 3-5/issue. Publishes when all required materials are submitted. Publishes short shorts. Also publishes literary essays, literary criticism, and poetry. Sometimes comments on rejected mss.
How to Contact: Send complete ms with cover letter. Accepts submissions by e-mail or disk (WordPerfect only). Include brief bio and list of publications. Responds in 2 weeks to queries; 2 months to mss. Send disposable copy of ms and #10 SASE for reply only. Accepts simultaneous submissions, previously published work and multiple submissions. Reviews novels, short story collections, and nonfiction books. Contact: Joel Peckham.
Payment/Terms: Payment is publication. Acquires first North American serial rights and electronic rights. Sometimes sends galleys to authors.
Advice: "Looking for a strong narrative drive and a lyric pulse. Someone who understands the musical qualities of the language. Avoid fuzzy abstractions. Be persistant and respond to criticism if given. We wouldn't give suggestions if we weren't interested in the work."

⃞ **MILLENNIUM: A Journal for Tomorrowland.** E-mail: dsp@ctel.net. Website: www.etext.org/Zines/Millenium. **Contact:** Douglas Thornsjo, editor. Electronic zine. "Our theme, if there is one, is 'Look ahead into the past,' or 'Don't be fooled by the present,' or 'Don't let some suited corporate bastard dictate the future. If it's possible to be respectful and revolutionary at the same time, that's what *Millennium* tries for."
Needs: Literary. "No aimless (meta-fiction); religious or propagandistic; emotionally trite; graphically violent; stories that aren't about anything; stories that are about too much; stories by authors who can't be bothered to think about their readers. Interested in all genres, but the story and characters should be larger than the genre. The qualities we most value are grace, substance, character and sense of purpose that isn't overblown or sententious." Recently published works by Bruce Canwell and Richard Nostbakken.
How to Contact: Accepts queries/mss by e-mail only. "No paper submissions will be considered. Plain text preferred, but MS Word5 or earlier is OK."
Advice: "Always keep in mind Mark Twain's rules for short fiction especially including this one: 'A tale should arrive somewhere and accomplish something.' Editorial writers: our editorial bias is 'slightly left of center,' but we will not publish propaganda or religious material of any sort. Read good writers and try to be as good as what you read. Download and read the magazine (it is always free)." On electronic publishing—"The Good: never before has it been so cheap or so easy for publishers and writers to put material before the world. The Bad: promoting an electronic publication and getting people to visit the site still requires money. Until publishers and especially writers find a way to derive real income from electronic publishing, it will never be a serious alternative to print. Proliferation of electronic content on the web and elsewhere poses a serious threat to professionalism in the writing trade. Electronic publications are still not as attractive to consumers (nor as convenient) as paper publications. The Ugly: the field is crowded to such an extent that far from providing an outlet, electronic publishing may just be one more means by which writers find themselves disenfranchised and devalued."

N ⃞ ⃞ **MJ'S WALKABOUT, G.S.&S.,** 3601 Owens St., Bryan TX 77808-0969. Fax: (979)778-0248. E-mail: mjswalkabout@mailcity.com. Website: www.mjswalkabout.tripod.com (includes guidelines, poems, kids' stories and poetry, fiction, travel pieces, links, reviews [book, comic and videos]). **Contact:** Em Jay, managing editor. Online magazine. "Writers have the unique station of tour guide, using the transport of fiction, travel pieces and poetry." Bimonthly. Estab. 1999.
Needs: Adventure, children's/juvenile (adventure, animal, historical, mystery, series, age: young adult and up), ethnic/multicultural (general), humor/satire, mystery/suspense (amateur sleuth, cozy, police procedural, private eye/hardboiled), science fiction, thriller/espionage, western, young adult/teen (adventure, fantasy/science fiction, historical, mystery/suspense, series, sports, western, reviews of books, comics & videos), travelling pieces (fiction

that takes place in some exotic country or nonfiction explaining a traveling adventure). Receives 20 unsolicited mss/month. Accepts 50% mss/issue. Publishes ms 1 month after acceptance. Recently published work by Jessica Steinmets, Shayla Price, and Barry Smith. Length: 100-3,000 words. Publishes short shorts. Average length: 500 words. Also publishes literary essays and poetry. Often comments on rejected mss.

How to Contact: Send complete ms with cover letter by e-mail only. Include estimated word count, brief bio, list of publications and valid e-mail address. Responds in 2 weeks to queries; 2 months to mss. Accepts simultaneous submissions, previously published work and multiple submissions. Guidelines by e-mail or on website. Reviews novels, short story collections and nonfiction books.

Payment/Terms: Pays writers in "a beautiful page and links to sites of their choice." Pays on publication for one-time and electronic rights.

Advice: "I challenge writers to take me to a place I've never been before with words, phrases, subjects, and tidbits. I want to see, feel, smell, touch, and hear the world you create or report. Don't assume I have been there. Do it right and you'll succeed in showing me that I haven't. Clear, color photos are a plus (submitted by e-mail or link). If I have to re-read a sentence to find out what the writer means, it's on its way to the rejection route. After writing your piece, give it a cooling-off period of at least a few days (1 month is even better). Then approach it again with the intent of picking it apart word by word, searching for the one that fits better, that's more concise, more appealing, more reader friendly, more stimulating, more 'you,' in each and every case."

☑ ◑ ▣ **moonbomb press**. E-mail: paul@moonbomb.com. Website: www.moonbomb.com. **Contact:** Paul C. Choi, editor. Electronic zine. "We are contemporary, urban, irreverent, ethnic, random."

Needs: Short stories, poetry, short plays, any fictional format, autobiographical non-fiction, fictional journalism. No children's fiction. Wants more fictional realism and essays. "The main thing we seek in any piece of writing is a clear, identifiable voice. If this voice is also unique, we are even more pleased." **Publishes 2 new writers/ year.** Recently published work by Eve Pearlman and Sheryl Ridenour.

How to Contact: Electronic submissions only.

Advice: "Be bold. Do not try to be what you are not. Anything so contrived is obviously so. Content and structure are important, but the voice, the heart behind the writing is even more essential."

$◑ **MUSHROOM DREAMS**, 14537 Longworth Ave., Norwalk CA 90650-4724. **Contact:** Jim Reagan, editor. Magazine: 8½×5½; 32 pages; 20 lb. paper; heavy cover stock; illustrations. "Eclectic content with emphasis on literary quality." Semiannual. Estab. 1997. Circ. 100.

Needs: Realistic or naturalistic fiction. No gay, lesbian. Receives 10-15 unsolicited mss/month. Accepts 3 mss/ issue; 6 mss/year. Publishes ms 6-12 months after acceptance. Recently published work by William E. Meyer, Jr., John Taylor and Edward M. Turner. Length: 250-1,800 words; average length: 1,500 words. Publishes short shorts. Length: 250 words. Also publishes poetry. Often comments on rejected ms.

How to Contact: Send complete ms with a cover letter. Include estimated word count, short paragraph bio. Responds in 1 week to queries; 6 weeks to mss. Send SASE for reply or return of ms. Accepts simultaneous and reprint submissions. Sample copy $1. Guidelines free.

Payment/Terms: Pays $2-20 and 2 contributor's copies on publication for first rights; additional copies $1.

☑ ◑ ▣ **NEWS OF THE BRAVE NEW WORLD**, 114 Britt Court, Chapel Hill NC 27514. Fax: (919)962-2388. E-mail: olaf@indy95.chem.unc.edu. Website: http://indy95.chem.unc.edu. **Contact:** Olaf Kohlmann, editor. Electronic zine. "We serve as a platform for fresh, new authors in need of an outlet for their creative work without the usual rip-off practices, Therefore, this magazine is free of charge for readers and writers. It is published in two languages, i.e. English and German, with different material in each section."

Needs: Erotica, humor, short stories, poems, essays, reviews and novels (no excerpts, only complete works). Want more "dark and/or intelligent humor, erotic (not porn) and everything that offers surprises. No badly written fiction, extremely conservative writings, copycats of bestseller authors, predictable and boring stuff. We believe in a sparse layout to focus attention to the written word. There is no specific theme, because we do not want to tell the contributors what they have to write about." **Publishes 20-50 new writers/year.** Recently published work by Aloke Roy, Brian Downes, Tom Sanders, Vasilis Afxentiou, Charlie Dickinson, Martha Nemes Fried and Stephanie Savage.

How to Contact: Accepts queries/mss by e-mail. "Send as e-mail attachments, Word 6.0 documents or Text-only files. No Macintosh please. We cannot read it."

Advice: "Read your submissions at least twice. Correct spelling and grammar mistakes. We publish your work as it is submitted, and part of our philosophy is not to edit anything. It is certainly embarrassing for the author, and the publisher as well, if a work contains many mistakes."

Ⓝ $◑ ◎ **NOVA SCIENCE FICTION MAGAZINE**, Nova Publishing Company, 17983 Paseo Del Sol, Chino Hills CA 91709-3947. (909)393-0806. **Contact:** Wesley Kawato, editor. Zine specializing in evangelical Christian science fiction: 8½×5½; 64 pages; cardstock cover. "We publish science fiction short stories, no fantasy or horror. One story slot per issue will be reserved for a story written from an evangelical Christian viewpoint. We also plan to carry one article per issue dealing with science fiction wargaming." Quarterly. Estab. 1999. Circ. 25.

Needs: Science fiction (hard science/technological, soft/sociological, religious). "No stories where the villain is a religious fanatic and stories that assume the truth of evolution." Accepts 3 mss/issue; 12 mss/year. Publishes ms 3 months after acceptance. **Publishes 5 new writers/year.** Recently published work by Wesley Kawato, Tom Cron, Robert Alley, Ellen Straw, Kurt Sidaway and Dan Lea. Length: 250-8,000 words; average length: 4,000 words. Publishes short shorts. Average length: 250 words. Sometimes comments on rejected mss.

How to Contact: Query first. Include estimated word count and list of publications. Responds in 3 months to queries and mss. Send SASE (or IRC) for return of ms. Accepts previously published work and multiple submissions. Sample copy for $6. Guidelines free for SASE.

Payment/Terms: Pays $1.25-40. Pays on publication for first North American serial rights. Not copyrighted.

Advice: "Although committed to publishing a mixture of secular and Christian stories, *Nova Science Fiction* considers itself a pioneer in developing a new sub genre we call evangelical Christian science fiction."

NUTHOUSE, Essays, Stories and Other Amusements, Twin Rivers Press, P.O. Box 119, Ellenton FL 34222. Website: members.aol.com/Nuthous499/index.html (includes writer's guidelines, readers' letters, excerpts). **Contact:** Dr. Ludwig "Needles" Von Quirk, chief of staff. Zine: digest-sized; 12-16 pages; bond paper; illustrations; photos. "Humor of all genres for an adult readership that is not easily offended." Published every 6 weeks. Estab. 1993. Circ. 100.

Needs: Humor/satire: erotica, experimental, fantasy, feminist, historical (general), horror, literary, main-stream/contemporary, mystery/suspense, psychic/supernatural/occult, romance, science fiction and westerns. Plans annual "Halloween Party" issue featuring humorous verse and fiction with a horror theme. Receives 30-50 unsolicited mss/month. Accepts 5-10 mss/issue; 50-60 mss/year. Publishes ms 6-12 months after acceptance. Published work by Dale Andrew White, Mitchell Nathanson, Rob Loughran, Vanessa Dodge, Ken Rand, Don Hornbostel and Michael McWey. Length: 100-1,000 words; average length: 500 words. Publishes short shorts. Length: 100-250 words. Also publishes literary essays, literary criticism and poetry. Often comments on rejected mss.

How to Contact: Send complete ms with a cover letter. Include estimated word count, bio (paragraph) and list of publications. Responds in 1 month to mss. SASE for return of ms or send disposable copy of ms. Accepts simultaneous and reprint submissions. Sample copy for $1 (payable to Twin Rivers Press). Guidelines for #10 SASE.

Payment/Terms: Pays 1 contributor's copy. Acquires one-time rights. Not copyrighted.

Advice: Looks for "laugh-out-loud prose. Strive for original ideas; read the great humorists—Saki, Woody Allen, Robert Benchley, Garrison Keillor, John Irving—and learn from them. We are turned off by sophomoric attempts at humor built on a single, tired, overworked gag or pun; give us a story with a beginning, middle and end."

NUVEIN ONLINE, (626)401-3466. Fax: (626)401-3460. E-mail: ediaz@earthlink.net or ediaz@nuvein.com. Website: www.nuvein.com. **Editor:** Enrique Diaz. Electronic zine. "We are open to short works of fiction which explore topics divergent from the mainstream. Especially welcome are stories with a point of view opposite traditional and stereotypical views of minorities, including women and gays. Our philosophy is to provide a forum for voices rarely heard in other publications."

• *Nuvein Online* has been awarded the Visionary Media Award.

Needs: Short fiction, serials, graphic e-novels and poetry. Wants more "experimental, cyberfiction, serialized fiction, ethnic, as well as pieces dealing with the exploration of sexuality." **Publishes 4 new writers/year.** Recently published work by Ronald L. Boerem, Holly Day, Enrique Diaz, Rick Stepp-Bolling and Scott Essman.

How to Contact: Send queries/mss by e-mail.

Advice: "Read over each submission before sending it, and if you, as the writer, find the piece irresistible, e-mail it to us immediately!"

$ OF UNICORNS AND SPACE STATIONS, %Gene Davis, P.O. Box 200, Bountiful UT 84011-0200. Website: www.genedavis.com. **Contact:** Gene Davis, senior editor. Zine: $5\frac{1}{2} \times 8\frac{1}{2}$; 60 pages; 20 lb. white paper; card cover stock; illustrations. "We want science fiction and fantasy of a positive nature, that gives us ideas, that warns us about the future and gives potential answers. It should be for adults, though graphic sex, violence and offensive language are not considered." Biannual. Estab. 1994. Circ. 100.

Needs: Fantasy (science fantasy, sword and sorcery), science fiction (hard science, soft/sociological, utopian). Wants "clear writing that is easy to follow." Receives 20 unsolicited mss/month. Accepts 9-13 mss/issue; approximately 25 mss/year. Publishes ms 6-12 months after acceptance. **Publishes approximately 4 new writers/year.** Recently published work by John Light and Jackie Shank. Length: 3,000 words average. Publishes short shorts. Also publishes poetry. Sometimes comments on rejected mss.

How to Contact: Send complete ms (clean, well-written, not stapled) with a cover letter. Include estimated word count, bio (75 words or less) and writer's classification of the piece (science fiction, fantasy, poetry).

Responds in 3 months. Send SASE for reply, return of ms or send a disposable copy of ms. Accepts simultaneous, reprint and electronic (disk only) submissions. If a subscriber, e-mail submissions OK. Sample copy for $4. Guidelines for #10 SASE.

Payment/Terms: Pays 5¢/word and 1 contributor's copy for stories; $5/poem and 1 contributor's copy for poetry; additional copies for $4. Acquires one-time rights.

Advice: "Keep trying. It may take several tries to get published. Most stories I see are good. You just need to find an editor that goes ga-ga over your style."

◑ OFFICE NUMBER ONE, 2111 Quarry Rd., Austin TX 78703. E-mail: onocdingus@aol.com. **Contact:** Carlos B. Dingus, editor. Zine: 8½×11; 12 pages; 60 lb. standard paper; b&w illustrations; photos. "I look for short stories, imaginary news stories or essays (under 400 words) that can put a reader on edge—avoid profanity or obscenity, make a point that frees the reader to see several worlds." Biannual zine specializing in satire, humor and views from alternate realities. Estab. 1989. Circ. 1,000.

Needs: Fictional news articles, experimental, fantasy, horror, humor/satire, literary, psychic/supernatural/occult, also fictional reviews, limericks. Receives 16 unsolicited mss/month. Buys 1-3 mss/issue; 16 mss/year. Publishes ms 6-12 months after acceptance. **Publishes 10-15 new writers/year.** Length: 400 words maximum, 150 best. Also publishes literary essays and poetry. Sometimes comments on rejected mss if requested.

How to Contact: Send complete ms with optional cover letter. Should include estimated word count with submission. Responds in 6-8 weeks to mss. Send SASE for reply, return of ms or send disposable copy of ms. Will consider simultaneous submissions, reprints. Sample copy for $2 with SAE and 3 first-class stamps. Guidelines for SASE.

Payment/Terms: Pays 1 contributor's copy. Additional copies for $1 plus $1.50 postage and 9×12 SASE. Acquires one-time rights.

Advice: "Clean writing, no unnecessary words, clear presentation. Express *one* good idea. Write for an audience that you can identify. I'm planning to publish more *shorter* fiction. I plan to be more up-beat and to focus on a journalistic style—and broaden what can be accomplished within this style. It seems like the Internet is taking away from print media. However, I also think the Internet cannot replace print media for fiction writing."

$ ◑ ▣ THE ORPHIC CHRONICLE: The Online Magazine of SF, Fantasy and Horror, P.O. Box 171202, Arlington TX 76003-1202. (818) 457-4436. E-mail: editor@orphic-chronicle.com. Website: www.orphic-chronicle.com. "This is an online magazine. The entire issue: short fiction, poetry, reviews, features and our SF autograph section is on the WWW." **Contact:** S. Kay Elmore, editor. E-zine specializing in science fiction, fantasy and horror. Quarterly. Estab. 1996. Circ. 3,000.

● *The Orphic Chronicle* is a member of the Zine Association, for e-zines in the science fiction, fantasy and horror genres.

Needs: Fantasy (space fantasy, sword and sorcery), horror (dark fantasy, futuristic, psychological, supernatural), psychic/supernatural/occult, science fiction (hard science/technological, soft/sociological, space opera). "No vampire fiction, no fan fiction, no serial killers." Upcoming themes: "Halloween mini-issue" (October 15, 2000). Accepts 6-8 mss/issue, 24-30 ms/year. Publishes ms 2-6 month after acceptance. **Publishes 10-15 new writers/ year.** Recently published work by Dean Loftis, Michael Williams, Sephera Giron, John Shanadan, Robert J. Tiess, Tom Gerencer and Bob Barrett. Length: no minimum; 10,000 words maximum; average length: 4,000 words. Publishes short shorts. Also publishes poetry. Sometimes comments on rejected ms.

How to Contact: Send complete ms via e-mail. Include estimated word count, 1 paragraph bio, list of publications, mailing address and your website and e-mail addresses. Responds in 1-3 months. Send SASE for reply, return of ms or send a disposable copy of ms. No simultaneous submissions; accepts reprints. Sample copy free. Guidelines free for SAE. Reviews novels, short story collections and nonfiction books of interest to writers. Send books to above address.

Payment/Terms: Pays $5. Pays on publication for first rights and reprint (one-time) rights if applicable.

Advice: "A strong, believable plot and traditional story forms are preferred. Give me good characters, readable dialogue and use your best English skills. Violence and gore must be justified, and your horror had better be horrific. Back up the science in your fiction, and make your fantasy truly fantastic. Send your best work. I suggest you have a friend help you double-check it for simple errors. Online science fiction/speculative fiction genre e-zines are the future of the small press short fiction market. Where once people ran a few thousand copies and begged distributors to carry them, we now publish online and reach worldwide with our publications—for a fraction of the cost."

◑ ♟ OUTER DARKNESS, Where Nightmares Roam Unleashed, Outer Darkness Press, 1312 N. Delaware Place, Tulsa OK 74110. **Contact:** Dennis Kirk, editor. Zine: 8½×5½; 60-80 pages; 20 lb. paper; 90 lb. glossy cover; illustrations. Specializes in imaginative literature. "Variety is something I strive for in *Outer Darkness*. In each issue we present readers with great tales of science fiction and horror along with poetry, cartoons and interviews/essays. I seek to provide readers with a magazine which, overall, is fun to read. My readers range in age from 16 to 70." Quarterly. Estab. 1994. Circ. 500.

• Fiction published in *Outer Darkness* has received honorable mention in *The Year's Best Fantasy and Horror.*

Needs: Fantasy (science), horror, mystery/suspense (with horror slant), psychic/supernatural/occult, romance (gothic), science fiction (hard science, soft/sociological). No straight mystery, pure fantasy—works which do not incorporate elements of science fiction and/or horror. Wants more "character-driven tales—especially in the genre of science fiction. I do not publish works with children in sexual situations, and graphic language should be kept to a minimum." Receives 50-75 unsolicited mss/month. Accepts 7-9 mss/issue; 20-50 mss/year. **Publishes 3-5 new writers/year.** Recently published work by Charlee Jacob, Gene Kokayko, Scott Thomas and Frank Andreotti. Length: 1,000-5,000 words; average length: 3,000 words. Also publishes literary essays and poetry. Always comments on rejected mss.

How to Contact: Send complete ms with a cover letter. Include estimated word count, 50- to 75-word bio, list of publications and "any awards, honors you have received." Responds in 1 week to queries; 1-2 months to mss. Send SASE for reply, return of ms or send a disposable copy of ms. Accepts simultaneous and multiple submissions. Sample copy for $3.95. Guidelines for #10 SASE.

Payment/Terms: Pays 3 contributor's copies for fiction, 2 for poetry and art. Pays on publication for one-time rights.

Advice: "Suspense is one thing I look for in stories. I want stories which grab the reader early on . . . and don't let go. I want stories which start off on either an interesting or suspenseful note. Read the works of Alan Dean Foster, Robert Bloch, William Greenleaf and Richard Matheson. Don't be discouraged by rejections. The best writers have received their share of rejection slips. Be patient. Take time to polish your work. Produce the best work you can and continue to submit, regardless of rejections. New writers now have more markets than ever before. I believe readers are searching for more 'traditional' works and that's what I strive to feature."

✅ 🌀 **THE OUTER RIM—THE ZINE**, (formerly Jupiter's Freedom), P.O. Box 110217, Palm Bay FL 32911-0217. (321)725-6243. E-mail: contact@theouterrim.org. Website: www.theouterrim.org (includes entire magazine, writer's guidelines, subscription, news, how to contact and more). **Contact:** Christine Smalldone, editor. Zine: 8½×11; 20-30 pages; 20 lb. paper, 70 lb. cover stock; illustrations; photos. Quarterly science fiction zine "that tries to flow and grow in the sci-fi, horror, fantasy and surreal aspects of this mixed genre, trying to publish the best in these areas that have shown a new direction or approach in the realm of sci-fi, to engulf those who love sci-fi and all its elements in a visual landscape of words." Estab. 1998.

Needs: Fantasy (space fantasy), horror (dark fantasy, futuristic, psychological), science fiction (hard science/ technological, soft/sociological). Upcoming themes: "It Came From Outer Space—All About the Final Frontier and Its Family Members" and "Animal Extinct—From the Dog Pound to the Cat Lick, We Love Animals." Receives 10-20 unsolicited mss/month. Accepts 3-5 mss/issue; 12-16 mss/year. Publishes ms 2-4 months after acceptance. **Publishes 10-15 new writers/year.** Recently published work by Suzi Kosturin, Joe Wocoski, Tom Brinck. Length: 5,000-15,000 words; average length: 10,000 words. Publishes short shorts. Length: 500 words. Also publishes poetry. Often comments on rejected ms.

How to Contact: Send complete ms with a cover letter. Accepts queries/mss by e-mail. Include estimated word count, bio, list of publications. Responds in 2 weeks to queries; 1 month to mss. Send SASE for reply, return of ms or send a disposable copy of ms. Accepts simultaneous submissions. Sample copy for $5 and 9½×11 envelope with 3 first-class stamps. Guidelines for #10 SASE.

Payment/Terms: Pays 1 contributor's copy; additional copies $1. Acquires one-time rights.

Advice: "Stay true and close to yourself, your style and your goals. Even if your story is bizarre and abstract, always write from your heart and talent, but don't be afraid to be different."

🅽 🌀 🖥 **PEGASUS ONLINE, the Fantasy and Science Fiction Ezine**. E-mail: editors@pegasusonline .com or scottMarlow@pegasusonline.com. Website: www.pegasusonline.com. **Contact:** Scott F. Marlowe, editor. Electronic zine. "*Pegasus Online* focuses upon the genres of science and fantasy fiction. We look for original work which inspires and moves the reader, writing which may cause him or her to think, and maybe even allow them to pause for a moment to consider the how's and why's of those things around us."

Needs: Fantasy, science fiction. "More specifically, fantasy is to be of the pure fantastic type: dragons, goblins, magic and everything else you can expect from something not of this world. Science fiction can or cannot be of the 'hard' variety." No "excessive profanity or needless gore." **Publishes 12 new writers/year.**

How to Contact: Electronic submissions only. Send mss by e-mail.

Advice: "Tell a complete tale with strong characters and a plot which draws the reader in from the very first sentence to the very last. The key to good fiction writing is presenting readers with characters they can identify with at some level. Your characters certainly can be larger than life, but they should not be all-powerful. Also, be careful with grammar and sentence structure. We get too many submissions which have good plot lines, but are rejected because of poor English skills. The end-all is this: we as humans read because we want to escape from reality for a short time. Make us feel like we've entered your world and make us want to see your characters succeed (or not, depending on your plot's angle), and you've done your job and made us happy at the same time."

✓ ◐ ◎ ⚱ **PENNY DREADFUL, Tales & Poems of Fantastic Terror**, Pendragonian Publications, P.O. Box 719, New York NY 10101-0719. E-mail: mmpendragon@aol.com. Website: www.hometown.aol.com/mmpendragon/index.html. **Contact:** Michael Pendragon, editor. Zine specializing in horror: 8½ × 5½; 140 pages; illustrations; photos. Publication to "celebrate the darker aspects of man, the world and their creator. We seek to address a highly literate audience who appreciate horror as a literary art form." Triannual. Estab. 1996. Circ. 500.

• *Penny Dreadful* won several Honorable Mentions in St. Martin's Press's *The Year's Best Fantasy and Horror* competition.

Needs: Fantasy (dark symbolist), horror, psychic/supernatural/occult. Wants more "tales set in and in the style of the 19th century." No modern settings "constantly referring to 20th century persons, events, products, etc." List of upcoming themes available for SASE. Receives 100 unsolicited mss/month. Accepts 10 mss/issue; 30 mss/year. "*Penny Dreadful* reads all year until we have accepted enough submissions to fill more than one year's worth of issues." **Publishes 1-3 new writers/year.** Recently published work by James S. Dorr, Scott Thomas, John B. Ford, Susan E. Abramski, Paul Bradshaw and John Light. Length: 500-5,000 words. Publishes short shorts. Also publishes poetry. Always comments on rejected mss.

How to Contact: Send complete ms with a cover letter. Include estimated word count, bio and list of publications. Responds in 3 months to queries and mss. Send SASE for reply, return of ms or send disposable copy of ms. Accepts simultaneous submissions and reprints. Sample copy for $5. Subscription for $12. Guidelines for #10 SASE.

Payment/Terms: Pays 1 contributor copy. Acquires one-time rights. Sends galleys to author. Not copyrighted.

Advice: Whenever possible, try to submit to independent zines specializing in your genre. Be prepared to spend significant amounts of time and money. Expect only one copy as payment. Over time—if you're exceptionally talented and/or lucky—you may begin to build a small following."

◎ ▣ **PEOPLENET DISABILITY DATENET HOME PAGE, "Where People Meet People,"**, Box 897, Levittown NY 11756-0897. (516)579-4043. E-mail: mauro@idt.net. Website: http://idt.net/~mauro (includes writer's guidelines, articles, stories, poems). **Contact:** Robert Mauro, editor. "Romance stories featuring disabled characters." Estab. 1995.

Needs: Romance, contemporary and disabled. Main character must be disabled. Upcoming theme: "Marriage between disabled and non-disabled." Accepts 3 mss/year. Publishes immediately after acceptance. **Publishes 5-10 new writers/year.** Length: 1,500 words. Publishes short shorts. Length: 750 words. Also publishes poetry. Especially looking for book reviews on books dealing with disabled persons and sexuality.

How to Contact: Send complete ms by e-mail. Guidelines online.

Payment/Terms: Acquires first rights.

Advice: "We are looking for romance stories of under 1,000 words on romance with a disabled man or woman as the main character. No sob stories or 'super crip' stories. Just realistic romance. No porn. Erotica okay. Love, respect, trust, understanding and acceptance are what I want."

◯ **BERN PORTER COSMOGRAPHIC**, 50 Salmond St., Belfast ME 04915. (207)338-4303. E-mail: bpinternational@hotmail.com. **Contact:** Natasha Bernstein and Sheila Holtz, editors. Magazine: 8½ × 11; 8 pages; illustrations; photos. "Experimental prose and poetry at the edge of established literary forms." Monthly. Estab. 1997.

Needs: Experimental, literary, prose poem, translations, international. "No long conventional narratives. Want more short vignettes and surreal prose-poems." Receives 30-50 unsolicited mss/month. Publishes ms immediately after acceptance. **Publishes 12 new writers/year.** Published work by Stephen Jama, Natasha Bernstein, C.A. Conrad, T. Anders Carson and Anne Welsh. Length: 2 pages maximum. Publishes short shorts.

How to Contact: Query first. Accepts queries by e-mail. Responds in 1 week. Accepts simultaneous and reprint submissions. Sample copy $2. Guidelines free.

Payment/Terms: Pays in copies.

Advice: "Do not compromise your style and vision for the sake of the market. Megamarketing of authors by big mega publishers sucks. We seek to counter this trend by giving voice to authors who would not be heard in that world."

✓ ◐ ◎ **QECE, Question Everything Challenge Everything**, 406 Main St. #3C, Collegeville PA 19426. E-mail: qece@yahoo.com. **Contact:** Larry Nocella, editor. Zine: 5½ × 8½; 60 pages; copy paper; copy paper cover; illustrations; photos; color artwork centerfold. Zine "seeking to inspire free thought and action by encouraging a more questioning mentality. Intended for dreamers and quiet laid-back rebels." Biannual. Estab. 1996. Circ. 300.

• QECE was listed among *Maximumrocknroll's Zine Top Ten*.

Needs: Experimental. "Anything that inspires others to question and challenge conventions of fiction. Aggressive, compelling, short, fun is OK too. No lame stuff. Be wary of anything too foo-foo literary." No genre fiction, no formulas. Receives 15 unsolicited mss/month. Accepts 1 ms/issue; 3 mss/year. Publishes ms 6 months after acceptance. **Publishes 12 new writers/year.** Recently published work by Andy Rant, Lisa Cellini and Colin Develin. Length: 1,000 words average. Publishes short shorts. Always comments on rejected mss.

How to Contact: Send complete ms with a cover letter. Include estimated word count and 25 words or less bio. Responds in 4 months. Send SASE for reply, return of ms or send a disposable copy of ms. Accepts simultaneous and e-mail submissions. Sample copy for $3. Guidelines free for #10 SASE.

Payment/Terms: Pays 2 contributor's copies; additional copies for $3 (make checks out to Larry Nocella). Acquires one-time rights.

Advice: "Ignore 'trends'; be yourself as much as possible and you'll create something unique. Be as timeless as possible. Avoid obscure, trendy references. Tie comments about a current trend to timeless observation. If it's in the 'news' chances are it won't be in QECE, The 'news' is a joke. Tell me something I need to know. Favor anecdotes and philosophy over intense political opinions. I'd prefer to hear about personal experiences and emotions everyone can relate to. Criticism is welcome, though. QECE can be negative, but remember it is positive too. Just go for it! Send away and let me decide! Get busy!"

N ◯ RALPH'S REVIEW, RC Publications, 129A Wellington Ave., Albany NY 12203-2637. (518)459-0883. E-mail: rcpub@juno.com. **Contact:** Ralph Cornell, editor. Zine: 8½×11; 20-35 pages; 20 lb. bond paper and cover. "To let as many writers as possible get a chance to publish their works, fantasy, sci-fi, horror, poetry. We are adding home remedies and gardening tips. Audience: adult, young adult, responsible, self-contained, conscious human beings." Quarterly. Estab. 1988. Circ. 200.

Needs: Adventure, fantasy (science fantasy), horror, humor/satire, literary, psychic/supernatural/occult, science fiction, stamp and coin collecting, dinosaurs, environmental, fishing. No extreme violence, racial, gay/lesbian/x-rated. Publishes annual special fiction issue or anthology. Receives 10-15 unsolicited mss/month. Accepts 1-2 mss/issue; 12-15 mss/year. Publishes ms 2-4 months after acceptance. Published work by Ralph Cornell, Celeste Plowden, Bob Holmes and Renese Carlisle. **Publishes 10-20 new writers/year.** Length: 50-2,000 words; average length: 500-1,000 words. $2 reading fee for all stories over 500 words. Publishes short shorts. Also publishes poetry. Sometimes comments on rejected mss.

How to Contact: Send complete ms with a cover letter. Include 1-paragraph bio and list of publications. Responds in 3 weeks to queries; 3 months to mss. Send SASE for reply, return of ms or send a disposable copy of ms. Accepts simultaneous and reprint submissions. Sample copy for $2, 9×12 SAE and 5 first-class stamps. Guidelines for #10 SASE. Reviews novels or short story collections.

Payment/Terms: Pays 1 contributor's copy; additional copies for $2. Acquires first North American serial rights.

Advice: Looks for manuscripts "that start out active and continue to grow until you go 'Ahh!' at the end. Something I've never read before. Make sure spelling is correct, content is crisp and active, characters are believable. Must be horrific, your worst nightmare, makes you want to look in the corner while sitting in your own living room."

N ◯ ▢ RENAISSANCE ONLINE MAGAZINE, P.O. Box 3246, Pawtucket RI 02861-2331. E-mail: kridolfi@renaissancemag.com. Website: www.renaissancemag.com (includes archives and guidelines). **Contact:** Kevin Ridolfi, editor. Electronic zine. "*Renaissance* provides an open forum and exchange for an online community seeking for diversity on the jumbled and stagnant Internet. Works should be well-written and should deal with the effective resolution of a problem."

Needs: Short fiction, serial fiction, poetry, essays, humor, young adult. "No lewd, adult fiction." **Publishes 6 new writers/year.** Recently published work by Sharon Suendsen, Rob Kerr, and Steve Mueske. Length: 800-2,000 words.

How to Contact: Electronic and traditional submissions accepted, electronic (e-mail) submissions preferred.

Advice: "Browse through *Renaissance*'s past issues for content tendencies and submission requirements. Don't be afraid to go out on a short limb, but please limit yourself to our already existing categories."

◯ S.L.U.G. FEST, LTD., A Magazine of Free Expression, SF, Ltd., P.O. Box 1238, Simpsonville SC 29681-1238. Editor: M.T. Nowak. **Contact:** M. Tatlow, fiction editor. Zine: 8½×11; 70 pages; 20 lb. paper; 30 lb. cover stock; illustrations. "We are dedicated to publishing the best poetry and fiction we can find from writers who have yet to be discovered." Quarterly. Estab. 1991. Circ. 1,000.

Needs: Adventure, ethnic/multicultural, experimental, feminist, historical, humor/satire, literary, mainstream/contemporary, regional, "philosophies, ramblings." "No poor writing." Receives 30 unsolicited mss/month. Accepts 5-10 mss/issue; 20-40 mss/year. Publishes mss 3 months after acceptance. **Publishes 10-15 new writers/year.** Length: 1,000-5,000 words preferred. Publishes short shorts. Also publishes literary essays, literary criticism and poetry. Often comments on and comments on rejected mss.

How to Contact: Send complete ms with a cover letter. Include estimated word count. Responds in 5 weeks. Send SASE for reply, return of ms or send a disposable copy of ms. Accepts simultaneous, reprint and electronic submissions. Sample copy for $5. Guidelines free. Reviews novels and short story collections.

Payment/Terms: Pays 1 contributor's copy. Rights revert to author upon publication.

Advice: "We look for humor, quality of imagery. Get our interest. Style and content must grab our editors. Strive for a humorous or unusual slant on life."

N $ ⊘ ▣ SCIFI.COM, USA Networks, 48 Eighth Ave., PMB 405, New York NY 10014. (212)989-3742. E-mail: datlow@www.scifi.com. Website: www.scifi.com (includes all fiction, guidelines, editorial information). **Contact:** Ellen Datlow, fiction editor. E-zine specializing in science fiction. "Largest and widest-ranging science fiction site on the Web. Affiliated with the Sci Fi Channel, *Science Fiction Weekly*. News, reviews, comics, movies, and interviews." Weekly. Estab. 2000. Circ. 50,000/day.
Needs: Fantasy (urban fantasy), science fiction (hard science/technological, soft/sociological). Receives 75 unsolicited mss/month. Accepts 1 mss/issue; 35 mss/year. Publishes ms 6 months after acceptance. Agented fiction 2%. Recently published work by Chris Fowler, Kim Newman and Pat Cadigan. Length: 1,500-25,000 words; average length: 7,500 words. Publishes short shorts. Average length: 1,000 words. Sometimes comments on rejected mss.
How to Contact: Send complete ms with cover letter. Include estimated word count and list of publications. Responds in 1 week to queries; 2 months to mss. Send SASE for return of ms or send a disposable copy of ms and #10 SASE for reply only. Guidelines for SASE or on website.
Payment/Terms: Pays 20¢/word up to $4,000. Pays on acceptance for first, electronic and anthology rights (to be negotiated).
Advice: Wants "crisp, evocative writing, interesting characters, good storytelling. Check out the kinds of fiction we publish if you can. If you read one, then you know what I want."

☒ ✓ ▣ SHADOW VOICES. E-mail: vcj@interlog.com. Website: www.geocities.com/Athens/styx/1713/index.html. **Contact:** Vida Janulaitis, editor. Electronic zine. "If you speak of the unknown and reach into the darkness of your soul, share your deepest thoughts. Send me your poetry and short stories."
Needs: "Well-written fiction or poetry that reveals your inner thoughts. We want more fiction that allows the writer to reveal a different side of life and put those feelings into words. The best writing grabs your attention from the beginning and surprises you in the end." Recently published work by Will Ackerman, Rich Logsdon and Vida Janulaitis. Publishes new and established writers.
How to Contact: Accepts queries/mss by e-mail. "Each and every submission should be sent on a separate e-mail, no file attachments please. At the top of each page place 'the title of the work,' your real name, complete e-mail address and a short bio. Please indicate submission in the e-mail subject line."
Advice: "Please edit your work carefully. I will assume poetic license. Most of all, write what's inside of you and be sincere about it. Everyone has a unique style, make yours stand out."

✓ ○ ▣ SHORT STORY WRITERS SHOWCASE, E-mail: sswseditor@yahoo.com. Website: www.ssws.net. **Contact:** Melissa K. Beynon, editor. Electronic zine specializing in genre short stories. "Post stories in a variety of genres with one goal in mind: entertain an intelligent population with the written word. If readers learn, feel, and visit again, the site is a success." Estab. 1997.
Needs: Fantasy, romance, science fiction. "Want all genres of short stories that are written with intelligence, honesty and with the reader's entertainment always in mind. Visitors to *SSWS* range in age from 8 to over 100. I accept stories written by all ages. I will not accept stories with explicit sex, unnecessary violence or harsh language, prejudice without change or involving a subject that could prove dangerous to young readers (like hopelessness). I would love to see more fantasy, romance and science fiction on *SSWS* in the future." **Publishes 100 new writers/year.** Recently published work by David R. Dixon, Matt Mitchell, Bill Monks, Patrick Nilsson, Melissa Kelly, Nora M. Mulligan and Bryan Nally. Length: 10,000 words maximum. Often comments on rejected mss.
How to Contact: Accepts mss by e-mail. "I use Microsoft Word (the latest version) to read e-mailed contributions, usually as an attachment. If I can't read the format, I always reply to the contributor with suggestions on how to make it so I can read it."
Advice: "Read, read and re-read your work. Have friends, teachers and anyone who'll sit still long enough read it. Listen to their advice. If you confuse, frustrate, or bore them, you'll confuse, frustrate or bore me. And pay attention to your word processor's spelling and grammar checker please, it isn't perfect."

N $ ○ ▣ SPELLBOUND MAGAZINE, A fantasy magazine for young readers, Eggplant Productions, 9220 Jill Lane, #2E, Schiller Park IL 60176. (847)928-9925. Fax: (801)720-0706. E-mail: spellbound@eggplant-productions.com. Website: www.eggplant-productions.com/spellbound/ (includes writer's guidelines, upcoming themes and previews of issues). **Contact:** Raechel Henderson, fiction editor. E-zine and magazine: A5; 64 pages; 20 lb paper; 80 lb cover stock; some illustrations. "*Spellbound* is devoted to publishing fantasy fiction and poetry which engages young readers. We want to introduce readers to the fantasy genre in all its wonderful forms." Quarterly. Estab. 1999. Circ. Less than 100.

Needs: Children's/juvenile (fantasy). No "After School Special" types of fiction. Receives 15 unsolicited mss/month. Accepts 5 mss/issue; 20 mss/year. Publishes ms 6-12 months after acceptance. **Publishes 50% new writers/year.** Length: 500-2,500 words; average length: 1,800 words. Publishes short shorts. Average length: 1,000 words. Also publishes poetry. Always comments on rejected mss.

How to Contact: Send complete ms with cover letter. Only accepts e-mail submissions. Include estimated word count, brief bio and postal mailing address. Responds in 6 weeks to queries and mss. Accepts simultaneous and multiple submissions. Sample copy for $5. Guidelines on website.

Payment/Terms: Pays $5 and 2 contributor's copies; additional copies $2. Pays on publication for first North American serial rights.

Advice: "I am looking for fiction that makes me feel something, stories that use bold images and memorable characters. Ultimately, I choose the types of stories I would have liked to read as a child. Read the guidelines carefully. Keep in mind the age of our audience and have fun with the story."

✓ ◑ ▣ **STATE OF UNBEING,** 1700 Nueces St., #106, Austin TX 78701. (512)630-7574. E-mail: kilgore @apoculpro.org. Website: www.apoculpro.org (includes writer's guidelines, editor names, contributors, fiction, past issues, interviews with authors, history, special events, mailing list information, illumination, every answer). **Contact:** Kilgore Trout, editor. E-zine. "We thrive off the new, fresh, unique-absurdity is worshipped, everything is embraced. If you are four years old and wield a crayon, write and submit." Monthly. Estab. 1994. Circ. "several hundred."

Needs: Adventure, erotica, ethnic/multicultural, experimental, family saga, fantasy, feminist, gay, glitz, historical, horror, humor satire, lesbian, literary, New Age, psychic/supernatural/occult, regional, religious, science fiction, short story collections, thriller/espionage, translations. No children's. Receives 5-20 unsolicited mss/month. Accepts 5-20 mss/issue; 60-100 mss/year. Publishes ms 1-2 months after acceptance. **Publishes 20 new writers/year.** Recently published work by Robert James Berry, J. Lang Wood, and D.L. Brown. Length: 3 words minimum; average length: 1,200 words. Also publishes literary essays, criticism and poetry. Sometimes comments on rejected ms.

How to Contact: Query or send complete ms with a cover letter. Accepts queries and mss by e-mail. Include bio. Responds in 1 month to queries and mss. Send SASE for reply, return of ms or send disposable copy of ms. Accepts simultaneous and reprint submissions.

Payment/Terms: Acquires one-time rights.

Advice: "We look for writing that is nonstandard, unique, things I will not read about in *Reader's Digest*. Don't think, write."

◑ ▣ **STORY BYTES—Very Short Stories,** E-mail: editor@storybytes.com. Website: www.storybytes. com (includes issues, mailing lists, subscription info, submission guidelines). **Contact:** M. Stanley Bubien, editor. Electronic zine. "*Story Bytes—Very Short Stories* is strictly an electronic publication, appearing on the Internet in three forms. First, the stories are sent to an electronic mailing list of readers. They also get placed on the *Story Bytes* website, in both HTML and PDF format."

Needs: "Stories must be very short—having a length that is the power of 2 specifically: 2, 4, 8, 16, 32, 64, 128, 256, 512, 1,024 and 2,048 words long." No sexually explicit material. "Would like to see more material dealing with religion. Not necessarily 'inspirational' stories, but those that show the struggles of living a life of faith in a realistic manner." **33% of works published are by new writers.** Recently published work by Richard K. Weems, Joseph Lerner, Lisa Cote, Thomas Sennet, Mark Hansen and Wendy Williams. Preferred length: 256-512 words. Publishes short shorts.

How to Contact: Accepts queries/mss by e-mail. "I prefer plain text with story title, authorship and word count. Only accepts electronic submissions." See website for complete guidelines.

Advice: "In *Story Bytes*, the very short stories themselves range in topic. Many explore a brief event—a vignette of something unusual, unique and, at times, something even commonplace. Some stories can be bizarre, while others quite lucid. Some are based on actual events, while others are entirely fictional. Try to develop conflict early on (in the first sentence if possible!), and illustrate or resolve this conflict through action rather than description. I believe we'll find an audience for electronic published works primarily in the short story realm. Very few people want to sit in front of their computer to read *War and Peace!* But, most people gladly read e-mail, and messages in this form can easily range from 2 to 1,000 words."

◑ **TRANSCENDENT VISIONS,** Toxic Evolution Press, 251 S. Olds Blvd., 84-E, Fairless Hills PA 19030-3426. (215)547-7159. **Contact:** David Kime, editor. Zine: letter size; 24 pages; xerox paper; illustrations. "*Transcendent Visions* is a literary zine by and for people who have been labeled mentally ill. Our purpose is to illustrate how creative and articulate mental patients are." Quarterly. Estab. 1992. Circ. 200.

SENDING TO A COUNTRY other than your own? Be sure to send International Reply Coupons (IRC) instead of stamps for replies or return of your manuscript.

● *Transcendent Visions* has received excellent reviews in many underground publications.

Needs: Experimental, feminist, gay, humor/satire, lesbian. Especially interested in material dealing with mental illness. "I do not like stuff one would find in a mainstream publication. No porn." Receives 5 unsolicited mss/month. Accepts 7 mss/issue; 20 mss/year. Publishes ms 3-4 months after acceptance. Published work by Claudine R. Moreau, Roger Coleman, and Dan Buck. Length: under 10 pages typed, double-spaced. Publishes short shorts. Also publishes poetry.

How to Contact: Send complete ms with cover letter. Include half-page bio. Responds in 2 weeks to queries; 1 month to mss. Send disposable copy of ms. Accepts simultaneous submissions and reprints. Sample copy for $2.

Payment/Terms: Pays 1 contributor's copy on publication. Acquires one-time rights.

Advice: "We like unusual stories that are quirky. Please do not go on and on about what zines you have been published in or awards you have won, etc. We just want to read your material, not know your life story. Please don't swamp me with tons of submissions. Send up to five stories. Please print or type your name and address."

$ ⊘ ▣ TWILIGHT SHOWCASE, 1436 Fifth St., Waynesboro VA 22980. (540)949-4294. E-mail: gconn @rica.net. Website: home.rica.net/gconn. **Contact:** Gary W. Conner, editor. Electronic zine. "We're interested in growing various subgenres of fantasy, those mainly being horror, dark fantasy and speculative fiction. We like a nice mix of writers you've read within these genres and writers you've never heard of." Monthly.

Needs: Fantasy (dark), horror, speculative fiction. No vampire fiction. **75% of works published are by new writers.** Recently published work by Philip Nutman, David Niall Wilson, Brett A. Savory, Patricia Lee Macomber, Mehitobel Wilson, D.F. Lewis, David Whitman, Weston Ochse, Ken Goldman and Michael Laimo.

How to Contact: Prefers queries/mss by e-mail. "Submissions should be carefully edited and e-mailed to strangeconcepts@rica.net. They may be sent in the body of the e-mail, in MSWord, MS Works, .rtf, or HTML formats.

Payment/Terms: Writers receive ½¢/word. Pays on publication.

Advice: "We enjoy concise writing and original plots with well-rounded characters. We want stories that have a beginning, middle and an end. Read the magazine. Won't cost you a thing. Web fiction is flourishing, as it gives any number of new writers an opportunity to make themselves heard. I have read so many incredible stories on the Internet that I am actually a fan of people I've never seen in print. There are some great e-zines out there."

Ⓝ ⚘ ⊘ ◎ URBAN GRAFFITI, Greensleeve Editions, P.O. Box 41164, Edmonton, Alberta T6J 6M7 Canada. E-mail: cogwheels@worldgate.com. **Contact:** Mark McCawley, editor. Zine specializing in fiction: 7×11; 28 pages; Xerox paper; some illustrations; photos. "Litzine of transgressive, discursive, post-realist writing (primarily fiction) concerned with the struggles of hard-edged urban living, alternative lifestyles, deviant culture, and presented in their most raw and unpretentious form. Adult audience/adult themes. Anti-literary. No-holds-barred exploration of the underside of contemporary urban existance (using sex, violence, shock value, parody, cynicism, irony, and black humour to do so)." Semiannual. Estab. 1993. Circ. 250.

Needs: Comics/graphic novels, erotica, gay, humor/satire, lesbian. No middle class dramas, cute college tales, or glossy vignettes of modern life. Receives 200 unsolicited mss/month. Accepts 10-15 mss/issue; 20-30 mss/year. Publishes ms 3-12 months after acceptance. **Publishes 2-3 new writers/year.** Recently published work by Matthew Firth, Glenn Gustafson and Sonja Saikaley. Length: 500-7,000 words; average length: 3,000 words. Publishes short shorts. Average length: 1,000 words. Also publishes poetry.

How to Contact: Send complete ms with cover letter. Accepts submissions by e-mail or disk. Include estimated word count and creative bio. Responds in 2 weeks to queries; 3 months to mss. Send disposable copy of ms and #10 SASE for reply only. Accepts multiple submissions. Sample copy for $3. Guidelines for SASE or by e-mail. Reviews novels, short story collections and nonfiction books.

Payment/Terms: Pays in 5 contributor's copies; additional copies for $4. Pays on publication for first anthology rights.

Advice: Considers "how well manuscripts adheres to the mandate of the litzine. Be honest and trust your instincts. If it's raunchy, realistic and puts forth the author's own viewpoint (or world view), the better chance the author has of being accepted by my publication."

Ⓝ $ ⊘ ▣ VISIONS & VOICES, Mystic Visions, P.O. Box 6848, New Albany IN 47151-6848. E-mail: vandv@mysticvisions.com. Website: www.mysticvisions.com/vandv/index.htm (includes subscription info, current issue, issue archives, about V&V, writer's guidelines, publishing calendar, contact info, advertising rates). **Contact:** Dawn Seewer, editor-in-chief. E-zine specializing in speculative romance writing and reading. "*Visions & Voices* is a subscription webzine dedicated to providing a quality online publication celebrating fantasy, futuristic/science fiction, paranormal, and time travel romance. In each issue, you will find how-to articles on writing, inspirations, fiction, poetry and publisher profile along with two years of back issues online in our archives." Quarterly. Estab. 2000.

Needs: Fantasy (space fantasy, sword/sorcery, magic, romance), horror (dark fantasy, futuristic, psychological, supernatural), New Age, psychic/supernatural/occult, romance (futuristic/time travel, gothic), science fiction (soft sociological, sci-fi romance), nonfiction (how-to articles on writing). No gay, gore, straight erotica, contemporary romance, suspense romance, children or young adult. Length: 5,000 words; average length: 3,000 words. Publishes short shorts. Average length: 1,000 words. Also publishes poetry. Often comments on rejected mss.

How to Contact: Send complete ms with cover letter. Accepts submissions by e-mail. Include estimated word count and brief bio. Responds in 1 week to queries; 1 month to mss. Send SASE for return of ms or send a disposable copy of ms and #10 SASE for reply only. Accepts simultaneous submissions, previously published work and multiple submissions. Sample copy for free on website. Guidelines for SASE, e-mail or on website.

Payment/Terms: Pays $2-5 and 1 contributor's copies. Pays on publication for electronic, one-time electronic and non-exclusive rights to retain work in the archives. Would have rights for 90 days.

Advice: "We are looking for original stories with multi-dimensional characters and interesting settings. We are especially interested in those speculative works that cross genres with romance; however, we will consider works of pure fantasy, science fiction and paranormal. Also looking for poetry and true tales of personal experiences dealing with the unusual. Also looking for how-to articles about writing speculative romance and the writing life. Please read the guidelines before submitting material. Properly-submitted work is reviewed first."

☑ ◯ ▣ **VOIDING THE VOID**℠, 8 Henderson Place, New York NY 10028. (212)628-2799. E-mail: mail@vvoid.com. or EELIPP@aol.com. Website: www.voidingthevoid.com. **Contact:** E.E. Lippincott, editor-in-chief. Electronic zine and hard copy specializing in personal world views: 8½×11; 8 pages; mock newsprint hard copy. "A small reader specializing in individuals' fictional and nonfictional views of the world around them." Monthly. Estab. 1997. Circ. 500 both in US and UK.

Needs: All categories. "We will consider anything the potential contributor feels is appropriate to the theme 'tangibility.' All fiction genres OK." Publishes holiday issues; submit at least 1 month prior to holiday. Receives 100 unsolicited mss/month. Accepts 5-10 mss/issue; 120 mss/year. Publishes ms immediately to 3 months after acceptance. Recently published work by Erik Seims, Craig Coleman, R. Ambardar, T. Liam Vederman and Jenny Wu. Length: no length restrictions. Publishes short shorts. Also publishes literary essays, literary criticism, poetry. Always comments on rejected ms.

How to Contact: Send complete ms with a cover letter; send electronic submissions via website or direct e-mail. Include estimated word count. Responds in 2 weeks to queries; 3 months to mss. Send SASE for reply or return of ms. Accepts simultaneous and reprint (with date and place indicated) submissions. Guidelines for #10 SASE. Reviews novels and short story collections

Payment/Terms: Pays 4 contributor's copies. Acquires one-time rights. Individual issues not copyrighted.

Advice: "*Voiding the Void* is not about the 'writing' or the 'art' so much as it is about the human being behind it all."

◯ ▣ **WILMINGTON BLUES**. E-mail: editor@wilmingtonblues.com. Website: www.wilmingtonblues.com. **Contact:** Trace Ramsey, editor. Electronic zine.

Needs: Humor/satire, literary. Receives 60-80 unsolicited mss/month. Publishes ms 1 month after acceptance. **Publishes as many new writers as possible.** Recently published work by Alex Stolis and Steve Gibbs. Length: 250-10,000 words; average length: 2,500 words. Publishes short shorts. Length: 250 words. Also publishes essays, poetry. Often comments on rejected mss.

How to Contact: Electronic submission only. "Please submit work as a text attachment to an e-mail." Include estimated word count, bio, e-mail address. Responds in 2 weeks to queries; 1 month to mss. Accepts simultaneous submissions.

Payment/Terms: Acquires one-time rights.

Advice: "If your work has something to offer, it will be published. We offer comments on work that isn't accepted, and we encourage resubmissions!"

Consumer Magazines

In this section of *Novel & Short Story Writer's Market* are consumer magazines with circulations of more than 10,000. Many have circulations in the hundreds of thousands or millions. While much has been made over the shrinking consumer magazine market for fiction—*Ms. Magazine* and *Cosmopolitan* have stopped running it, for example—new markets are opening. Both United Air Lines inflight magazine *Hemispheres* and *Seventeen* magazine have this year placed new emphasis on publishing fiction (see the Insider Reports with *Hemispheres* and *Seventeen* editors on pages 366 and 379, respectively). And among the oldest magazines listed here are ones not only familiar to us, but also to our parents, grandparents and even great-grandparents: *The Atlantic Monthly* (1857); *The New Yorker* (1925); *Capper's* (1879); *Amazing Stories* (1926); *Esquire* (1933); and *Jack and Jill* (1938).

Consumer periodicals make excellent markets for fiction in terms of exposure, prestige and payment. Because these magazines are well-known, however, competition is great. Even the largest consumer publications buy only one or two stories an issue, yet thousands of writers submit to these popular magazines.

Despite the odds, it is possible for talented new writers to break into print in the magazines listed here. Your keys to breaking into these markets are careful research, professional presentation and, of course, top-quality fiction.

TYPES OF CONSUMER MAGAZINES

In this section you will find a number of popular publications, some for a broad-based, general-interest readership and others for large but select groups of readers—children, teenagers, women, men and seniors. There are also religious and church-affiliated magazines, publications devoted to the interests of particular cultures and outlooks, and top markets for genre fiction.

SELECTING THE RIGHT MARKET

Unlike smaller journals and publications, most of the magazines listed here are available at newsstands and bookstores. Many can also be found in the library, and guidelines and sample copies are almost always available by mail. Start your search, then, by familiarizing yourself with the fiction included in the magazines that interest you.

Don't make the mistake of thinking, just because you are familiar with a magazine, that their fiction is the same today as when you first saw it. Nothing could be further from the truth—consumer magazines, no matter how well established, are constantly revising their fiction needs as they strive to reach new readers and expand their audience base.

In a magazine that uses only one or two stories an issue, take a look at the nonfiction articles and features as well. These can give you a better idea of the audience for the publication and clues to the type of fiction that might appeal to them.

If you write genre fiction, check out the specific sections for lists of magazines publishing in that genre (mystery, page 57; romance, page 68; science fiction/fantasy & horror, page 78). For other types of fiction look in the Category Index beginning on page 613. There you will find a list of markets that say they are looking for a particular subject.

FURTHERING YOUR SEARCH

See The "Quick Start" Guide to Publishing Your Fiction (page 3) for information about the material common to all listings in this book. In this section in particular, pay close attention to the number of submissions a magazine receives in a given period and how many they publish in the same period. This will give you a clear picture of how stiff your competition can be. Also, the ⚃ symbol before a listing identifies markets that offer writers greater opportunities by buying a large amount of freelance/unagented manuscripts.

While many of the magazines listed here publish one or two pieces of fiction in each issue, some also publish special fiction issues once or twice a year. We have indicated this in the listing information. We also note if the magazine is open to novel excerpts as well as short fiction and we advise novelists to query first before submitting long work.

The Business of Fiction Writing, beginning on page 105, covers the basics of submitting your work. Professional presentation is a must for all markets listed. Editors at consumer magazines are especially busy, and anything you can do to make your manuscript easy to read and accessible will help your chances of being published. Most magazines want to see complete manuscripts, but watch for publications in this section that require a query first.

As in the previous section, we've included our own comments in many of the listings, set off by a bullet (●). Whenever possible, we list the publication's recent awards and honors. We've also included any special information we feel will help you in determining whether a particular publication interests you.

The maple leaf symbol (🍁) identifies our Canadian listings. You will also find some English-speaking markets from around the world. These foreign magazines are denoted with 🌐 at the beginning of the listings. Remember to use International Reply Coupons rather than stamps when you want a reply from a country other than your own.

For More Information

For more on consumer magazines, see issues of *Writer's Digest* (by F&W Publications) and other industry trade publications available in larger libraries.

For news about some of the genre publications listed here and information about a particular field, there are a number of magazines devoted to genre topics, including *The Mystery Review*, *Locus* (for science fiction); *Science Fiction Chronicle*; and *Romance Writers' Report* (available to members of Romance Writers of America). Addresses for these and other industry magazines can be found in the Publications of Interest section of this book.

Membership in the national groups devoted to specific genre fields is not restricted to novelists and can be valuable to writers of short fiction in these fields. Many include awards for "Best Short Story" in their annual contests. For information useful to genre writers, see For Mystery Writers, page 57; For Romance Writers, page 68; and For Science Fiction/Fantasy & Horror Writers, page 78. Also see the Organizations section of this book.

⚃ $ 🖋 **AFRICAN VOICES, A Soulful Collection of Art and Literature,** African Voices Communications, Inc., 270 W. 96th St., New York NY 10025. (212)865-2982. Fax: (212)316-3335. Website: www.africanvoices.com. Editor: Carolyn A. Butts. Managing Editor: Layding Kaliba. **Contact:** Kim Horne, fiction editor. Book Review Editor: Debbie Officer. Magazine: 32 pages; illustrations; photos. "*AV* publishes enlightening and entertaining literature on the varied lifestyles of people of color." Quarterly. Estab. 1993. Circ. 20,000.
Needs: African-American: children's/juvenile (10-12 years), condensed/excerpted novel, erotica, ethnic/multicultural, gay, historical (general), horror, humor/satire, literary, mystery/suspense, psychic/supernatural/occult, religious/inspirational, science fiction, young adult/teen (adventure, romance). List of upcoming themes available for SASE. Publishes special fiction issue. Receives 20-50 unsolicited mss/month. Accepts 20 mss/issue. Publishes ms 3-6 months after acceptance. Agented fiction 5%. Published work by Junot Díaz, Michel Marriott and Carol Dixon. Length: 500-3,000 words; average length: 2,000 words. Occasionally publishes short shorts. Also publishes literary essays and poetry.
How to Contact: Query with clips of published work. Include short bio. Responds in 3 months to queries and mss. Send SASE for return of ms. Accepts simultaneous, reprint and electronic submissions. Sample copy for $5 and 9 × 12 SASE. Guidelines free. Subscriptions are $12 for 1 year. Reviews novels and short story collections. Send books to Book Editor.

Payment/Terms: Pays $25 maximum, free subscription and 5 contributor's copies. Pays on publication for first North American serial rights.

Advice: "A manuscript stands out if it is neatly typed with a well-written and interesting story line or plot. Originality encouraged. We are interested in more horror, erotic and drama pieces. *AV* wants to highlight the diversity in our culture. Stories must touch the humanity in us all."

★ $ ◩ **AIM MAGAZINE,** P.O. Box 1174, Maywood IL 60153. (773)874-6184. Fax: (206)543-2746. Editor: Myron Apilado, EdD. **Contact:** Mark Boone, fiction editor. Magazine: 8½ × 11; 48 pages; slick paper; photos and illustrations. Publishes material "to purge racism from the human bloodstream through the written word—that is the purpose of *Aim Magazine.*" Quarterly. Estab. 1973. Circ. 10,000.

● *Aim* sponsors an annual short story contest.

Needs: Open. No "religious" mss. Published special fiction issue last year; plans another. Receives 25 unsolicited mss/month. Buys 15 mss/issue; 60 mss/year. **Publishes 40 new writers/year.** Published work by Christina Touregny, Thomas Lee Harris, Michael Williams and Jake Halpern. Length: 800-1,000 words average. Publishes short shorts. Sometimes comments on rejected mss.

How to Contact: Send complete ms. Include SASE with cover letter and author's photograph. Accepts simultaneous submissions. Responds in 1 month. Sample copy for $4 with SAE (9 × 12) and $1.80 postage. Guidelines for #10 SASE.

Payment/Terms: Pays $15-25. Pays on publication for first rights.

Advice: "Search for those who are making unselfish contributions to their community and write about them. Write about your own experiences. Be familiar with the background of your characters." Known for "stories with social significance, proving that people from different ethnic, racial backgrounds are more alike than they are different."

$ ◩ **AMAZING® STORIES,** Wizards of the Coast, P.O. Box 707, Renton WA 98057-0707. (425)204-2263. Fax: (425)204-5928. E-mail: amazing@wizards.com. Website: www.wizards.com/amazing (includes fiction guidelines, short features and teasers for coming and current issues). Editor-in-Chief: Mr. Kim Mohan. **Contact:** Pamela Mohan, associate editor. Magazine: 8⅜ × 10¾; 100 pages; saddle-stitched; color illustrations; rarely photos. Magazine of science fiction stories for adults and young adults. Quarterly. Estab. 1926. Circ. 30,000.

● *Amazing Stories* ranked #15 on *Writer's Digest*'s "Fiction 50" list of top markets.

Needs: Science fiction (hard science, soft/sociological), occasionally fantasy, rarely horror. "We prefer science fiction to dominate our content, but we will not turn away a well-written fantasy or horror piece. Low priority to heroic, pseudo-Medieval fantasy and stories derivative of folk tales; no gratuitous gore or offensive language." Receives 250-300 unsolicited fiction mss/month. Accepts 6-8 mss/issue. Publishes ms 4-8 months after acceptance. Agented fiction less than 5%. Published work by Orson Scott Card, Kristine Kathryn Rusch, Ben Bova, Ursula K. Le Guin, Neal Barrett, Jr. and Jack Williamson; published new writers within the last year. Length: 1,000-8,000 words; can go to 10,000 words for work of exceptional merit. Not actively seeking serializations or excerpts from longer works. Usually comments on rejected ms.

How to Contact: Send complete ms with a cover letter. Include list of other professional credits in the genre. Responds in 60 days. SASE. No simultaneous submissions. Sample copy for $8 (includes first-class postage and handling). Guidelines for #10 SASE or available at website.

Payment/Terms: Pays 6-10¢/word. Pays on acceptance for first worldwide rights in the English language. Sends comp copies to author.

Advice: "Read writer's guidelines. Write a good, short query letter. Your manuscript should look professional. We are not likely to publish sword and sorcery fantasy; ethnic fantasy that is a rehash or an interpretation of a myth or legend; and horror that relies on gratuitous vulgarity or excessive gore to make the story work."

$ ◡ ▼ **AMERICAN GIRL,** Pleasant Company Publications, Box 620986, Middleton WI 53562-0986. (608)836-4848. E-mail: readermail.ag.pleasantco.com. Website: www.americangirl.com. Editor: Kristi Thom. **Contact:** Magazine Department Assistant. Magazine: 8½ × 11; 52 pages; illustrations; photos. Four-color bimonthly magazine for girls age 8-12. "Our mission is to celebrate girls, yesterday and today. We publish fiction up to 2,300 words and the protagonist is a girl between 8-12. We want thoughtfully developed children's literature with good characters and plots." Estab. 1991. Circ. 700,000.

● *American Girl* won the 2000 and 1999 Parent's Choice Gold Award. Pleasant Company is known for its series of books featuring girls from different periods of American history.

Needs: Children's/juvenile (girls 8-12 years): "contemporary, realistic fiction, adventure, historical, problem stories." No romance, science fiction, fantasy. Receives 100 unsolicited mss/month. Accepts 1 ms/year. Length: 2,300 words maximum. Publishes short shorts. Also publishes literary essays and poetry (if age appropriate). **Publishes 2-3 new writers year.** Recently published work by Kay Thompson, Mavis Jukes and Susan Shreve.

How to Contact: Query with published samples. Include bio (1 paragraph). Send SASE for reply, return of ms or send a disposable copy of ms. Accepts multiple submissions. Send SASE for guidelines. Sample copy for $3.95 plus $1.93 postage.

Payment/Terms: Pays in cash; amount negotiable. Pays on acceptance for first North American serial rights. Sends galleys to author.

Advice: "We're looking for excellent character development within an interesting plot."

■ $ ▣ **THE ANNALS OF ST. ANNE DE BEAUPRÉ**, Redemptorist Fathers, P.O. Box 1000, St. Anne de Beaupré, Quebec G0A 3C0 Canada. (418)827-4538. Fax: (418)827-4530. **Contact:** Father Roch Achard, C.Ss.R., editor. Magazine: 8×11; 32 pages; glossy paper; photos. "Our aim is to promote devotion to St. Anne and Catholic family values." Monthly. Estab. 1878. Circ. 50,000.

Needs: Religious/inspirational. "We only wish to see something inspirational, educational, objective, uplifting. Reporting rather than analysis is simply not remarkable." Receives 50-60 unsolicited mss/month. Published work by Beverly Sheresh, Eugene Miller and Aubrey Haines. Publishes short stories. Length: 1,500 maximum. Always comments on rejected ms.

How to Contact: Send complete, typed, double spaced ms with a cover letter. Include estimated word count. Responds in 3 weeks. Send SASE for reply or return of ms. No simultaneous submissions. Free sample copy and guidelines.

Payment/Terms: Pays 3-4¢/word on acceptance and 3 contributor's copies on publication for first North American rights.

✓ ▣ ◉ **APPALACHIA JOURNAL**, Appalachian Mountain Club, 5 Joy St., Boston MA 02108. (617)523-0636. **Contact:** Lucille Daniel, editor. Magazine: 6×9; 160 pages; 60 lb. recycled paper; 10 pt. CS1 cover; 5-10 illustrations; 20-30 photos. "*Appalachia* is the oldest mountaineering and conservation journal in the country. It specializes in backcountry recreation and conservation topics (hiking, canoeing, cross-country skiing, etc.) for outdoor (including armchair) enthusiasts." Semiannually (June and December). Estab. 1876. Circ. 15,000.

Needs: Prose, poem, sports. Receives 5-10 unsolicited mss/month. Accepts 1-2 mss/issue; 2-4 mss/year. Publishes ms 6-12 months after acceptance. Length: 500-4,000 words average. Publishes short shorts.

How to Contact: Send complete ms with cover letter. No simultaneous submissions. Responds in 1 month to queries; 3 months to mss. SASE (or IRC) for query. Sample copy for $5. Guidelines for #10 SAE.

Payment/Terms: Pays contributor's copies. Occasionally pays $100-300 for a feature—usually assigned.

Advice: "All submissions should be related to conservation, mountaineering, and/or backcountry recreation both in the Northeast and throughout the world. Most of our journal is nonfiction. The fiction we publish is mountain-related and often off-beat. Send us material that says, I went to the wilderness and *thought* this; not I went there and did this."

$ ▣ **ART TIMES, Commentary and Resources for the Fine and Performing Arts**, P.O. Box 730, Mt. Marion NY 12456. Phone/fax: (914)246-6944. **Contact:** Raymond J. Steiner, editor. Magazine: 12×15; 24 pages; Jet paper and cover; illustrations; photos. "Arts magazine covering the disciplines for an over-40, affluent, arts-conscious and literate audience." Monthly. Estab. 1984. Circ. 20,000.

Needs: Adventure, contemporary, ethnic, fantasy, feminist, gay, historical, humor/satire, lesbian, literary, mainstream and science fiction. "We seek quality literary pieces. Nothing violent, sexist, erotic, juvenile, racist, romantic, political, etc." Receives 30-50 mss/month. Accepts 1 ms/issue; 11 mss/year. Publishes ms within 48-60 months of acceptance. Publishes 1-5 new writers/year. Length: 1,500 words maximum. Publishes short shorts.

How to Contact: Send complete ms with cover letter. Accepts simultaneous submissions. Responds in 6 months. SASE. Sample copy for $1.75, 9×12 SAE and 3 first-class stamps. Guidelines for #10 SASE.

Payment/Terms: Pays $25, free one-year subscription to magazine and 6 contributor's copies. Pays on publication for first North American serial rights.

Advice: "Competition is greater (more submissions received), but keep trying. We print new as well as published writers."

■ $ ▣ ▼ **ASIMOV'S SCIENCE FICTION**, 475 Park Ave. S., Floor 11, New York NY 10016-6901. (212)686-7188. Fax: (212)686-7414. E-mail: asimovs@dellmagazines.com. Website: www.asimovs.com (includes guidelines, names of editors, short fiction, interviews with authors, editorials, and more). **Contact:** Gardner Dozois, editor. Executive Editor: Sheila Williams. Magazine: 5¼×8¼ (trim size); 144 pages; 30 lb. newspaper; 70 lb. to 8 pt. C1S cover stock; illustrations; rarely photos. Magazine consists of science fiction and fantasy stories for adults and young adults. Publishes "the best short science fiction available." Estab. 1977. Circ. 50,000. 11 issues/year (one double issue).

● Named for a science fiction "legend," *Asimov's* regularly receives Hugo and Nebula Awards. Editor Gardner Dozois has received several awards for editing including Hugos and those from *Locus* and *Science Fiction Chronicle* magazines. This publication ranked #11 on the *Writer's Digest* Fiction 50 list of top markets for fiction writers.

Needs: Science fiction (hard science, soft sociological), fantasy. No horror or psychic/supernatural. Receives approximately 800 unsolicited fiction mss each month. Accepts 10 mss/issue. Publishes ms 6-12 months after acceptance. Agented fiction 10%. **Publishes 6 new writers/year.** Published work by Robert Silverberg, Connie Willis and Greg Egan. Length: up to 20,000 words. Publishes short shorts. Comments on rejected mss "when there is time."

How to Contact: Send complete ms with SASE. Responds in 3 months. Guidelines for #10 SASE. Sample copy for $5 and 9×12 SASE. Reviews novels and short story collections. Send books to Book Reviewer.

Payment/Terms: Pays 6-8¢/word for stories up to 7,500 words; 5¢/word for stories over 12,500; $450 for stories between those limits. Pays on acceptance for first World English serial rights plus specified foreign rights, as explained in contract. Very rarely buys reprints. Sends galleys to author.

Advice: "We are looking for character stories rather than those emphasizing technology or science. New writers will do best with a story under 10,000 words. Every new science fiction or fantasy film seems to 'inspire' writers—and this is not a desirable trend. Be sure to be familiar with our magazine and the type of story we like; workshops and lots of practice help. Try to stay away from trite, cliched themes. Start in the middle of the action, starting as close to the end of the story as you possibly can. We like stories that extrapolate from up-to-date scientific research, but don't forget that we've been publishing clone stories for decades. Ideas must be fresh."

$ ⬛ ◎ THE ASSOCIATE REFORMED PRESBYTERIAN, The Associate Reformed Presbyterian, Inc., 1 Cleveland St., Greenville SC 29601. (864)232-8297. **Contact:** Ben Johnston, editor. Magazine: 8½×11; 32-48 pages; 50 lb. offset paper; illustrations; photos. "We are the official magazine of our denomination. Articles generally relate to activities within the denomination—conferences, department work, etc., with a few special articles that would be of general interest to readers." Monthly. Estab. 1976. Circ. 6,100.

Needs: Contemporary, juvenile, religious/inspirational, spiritual, young adult/teen. "Stories should portray Christian values. No retelling of Bible stories or 'talking animal' stories. Stories for youth should deal with resolving real issues for young people." Receives 30-40 unsolicited fiction mss/month. Accepts 10-12 mss/year. Publishes ms within 1 year after acceptance. Published work by Lawrence Dorr, Jan Johnson and Deborah Christensen. Length: 300-750 words (children); 1,250 words maximum (youth). Sometimes comments on rejected mss.

How to Contact: Include cover letter. Responds in 6 weeks to queries and mss. Accepts simultaneous submissions. Sample copy for $1.50; Guidelines for #10 SASE.

Payment/Terms: Pays $20-75 for first rights and contributor's copies.

Advice: "Currently we are seeking stories aimed at the 10 to 15 age group. We have an oversupply of stories for younger children."

Ⓝ $ ⬛ Ⓨ THE ATLANTIC MONTHLY, 77 N. Washington St., Boston MA 02114. (617)854-7749. Fax: (617)854-7877. Editor: William Whitworth. **Contact:** C. Michael Curtis, senior editor. Managing Editor: Cullen Murphy. General magazine for the college educated with broad cultural interests. Monthly. Estab. 1857. Circ. 500,000.

● *The Atlantic Monthly* ranked #1 on the *Writer's Digest*'s "Fiction 50" list of top markets for fiction writers.

Needs: Literary and contemporary. "Seeks fiction that is clear, tightly written with strong sense of 'story' and well-defined characters." Accepts 15-18 stories/year. Receives 1,000 unsolicited fiction mss each month. **Publishes 3-4 new writers/year.** Recently published work by Mary Gordon, John Updike and Roxana Robinson. Preferred length: 2,000-6,000 words.

How to Contact: Send cover letter and complete ms with SASE. Responds in 2 months or less to mss.

Payment/Terms: Pays $3,000/story. Pays on acceptance for first North American serial rights.

Advice: When making first contact, "cover letters are sometimes helpful, particularly if they cite prior publications or involvement in writing programs. Common mistakes: melodrama, inconclusiveness, lack of development, unpersuasive characters and/or dialogue."

$ ⬛ ◎ BALLOON LIFE, The Magazine for Hot Air Ballooning, 2336 47th Ave., SW, Seattle WA 98116. (206)935-3649. Fax: (206)935-3326. E-mail: tom@balloonlife.com. Website: www.balloonlife.com/ (includes guidelines, sample issues). **Contact:** Tom Hamilton, editor. Magazine: 8½×11; 48 pages; color, b&w photos. Publishes material "about the sport of hot air ballooning. Readers participate in hot air ballooning as pilots, crew, official observers at events and spectators."

Needs: Humor/satire, related to hot air ballooning. "Manuscripts should involve the sport of hot air ballooning in any aspect. Prefer humor based on actual events; fiction seldom published." Accepts 4-6 mss/year. Publishes ms within 3-4 months after acceptance. Length: 800-1,500 words; average length: 1,200 words. Publishes short shorts. Length: 400-500 words. Sometimes comments on rejected mss and recommends other markets.

How to Contact: Send complete ms with cover letter that includes Social Security number. Accepts queries/mss by e-mail and fax (ms by permission only). Responds in 3 weeks to queries; 2 weeks to mss. SASE. Accepts simultaneous and reprint submissions. Sample copy for 9×12 SAE and $1.94 postage. Guidelines for #10 SASE.

Payment/Terms: Pays $25-75 and contributor's copies. Pays on publication for first North American serial, one-time or other rights.

Advice: "Generally the magazine looks for humor pieces that can provide a light-hearted change of pace from the technical and current event articles. An example of a work we used was titled 'Balloon Astrology' and dealt with the character of a hot air balloon based on what sign it was born (made) under."

☑ $⊘ **THE BEAR DELUXE MAGAZINE,** Orlo, 2516 NW 29th, P.O. Box 10342, Portland OR 97296. (503)242-1047. Fax: (503)243-2645. E-mail: bear@orlo.org. Website: www.orlo.org/beardeluxe/ (writing and contest guides). **Contact:** Thomas L. Webb, editor. Magazine: 11×14; 60 pages; newsprint paper; Kraft paper cover; illustrations; photos. "*The Bear Deluxe* has an environmental focus, combining all forms and styles. Fiction should have environmental thread to it and should be engaging to a cross-section of audiences. The more street-level, the better." Triannual. Estab. 1993. Circ. 17,000.
● *The Bear Deluxe* has received a publishing grant from the Oregon Council for the Humanities.
Needs: Environmentally focused: humor/satire, literary, science fiction. "We would like to see more nontraditional forms." No childrens or horror. List of upcoming themes available for SASE. Receives 20-30 unsolicited mss/month. Accepts 2-3 mss/issue; 8-12 mss/year. Publishes ms 6 months after acceptance. Recently published work by Robert Sullivan, Bruce Holland, Rocco Lo Bosco, Gina Ochsuer, Art Gibney, Martin John Brocon and Sara Backer. **Publishes 3-5 new writers/year.** Length: 900-4,000 words; average length: 2,500 words. Publishes short shorts. Also publishes literary essays, literary criticism, poetry, reviews, opinion, investigative journalism, interviews and creative nonfiction. Sometimes comments on rejected mss.
How to Contact: Send complete ms with a cover letter and clips. Include estimated word count, 10 to 15-word bio, list of publications, copy on disk, if possible. Accepts queries/mss by e-mail (mss by permission only). Responds in 3 months to queries; 6 months to mss. Send a disposable copy of mss. Accepts simultaneous and electronic (disk is best, then e-mail) submissions. Sample copy for $3, 7½×11 SAE and 5 first-class stamps. Guidelines for #10 SASE. Reviews novels and short story collections. Send SASE for "Edward Abbey" fiction contest and guidelines.
Payment/Terms: Pays free subscription to the magazine, contributor's copies and 5¢ per published word; additional copies for postage. Acquires first or one-time rights. Not copyrighted. Sponsors contests and awards for fiction writers.
Advice: "Keep sending work. Write actively and focus on the connections of man, nature, etc., not just flowery descriptions. Urban and suburban environments are grist for the mill as well. Have not seen enough quality humorous and ironic writing. Interview and artist profile ideas needed. Juxtaposition of place welcome. Action and hands-on great. Not all that interested in environmental ranting and simple 'walks through the park.' Make it powerful, yet accessible to a wide audience."

Ⓝ ⊕ **BEST MAGAZINE,** 197 Marsh Wall, London E14 9SG England. **Contact:** Louise Court, editor. Weekly. Circ. 570,000. Publishes 52 stories/issue; plus 15 commissioned stories in spring, summer and autumn fiction specials. Weekly mainstream women's magazine combining features and practicals. Looks for "twist in the tale, pacy, strong fiction." Length: 900-1,500 words. Pays £100 sterling plus contributor's copies. "Write for guidelines first. Type and double space your story, be sure your name is on it, and keep a copy. Send a SAE, but above all read a copy of *Best* first to get the feel of it."

☑ $⊘ **BOMB MAGAZINE,** New Art Publications, 594 Broadway, Suite 905, New York NY 10012. (212)431-3943. Fax: (212)431-5880. E-mail: suzan@bombsite.com. Editor-in-Chief: Betsy Sussler. **Contact:** Suzan Sherman, associate editor. Magazine: 11×14; 104 pages; 70 lb. glossy cover; illustrations; photos. Publishes "work which is unconventional and contains an edge, whether it be in style or subject matter." Quarterly. Estab. 1981.
Needs: Contemporary, experimental, novel excerpts. No genre: romance, science fiction, horror, western. Upcoming theme: "The Americas," featuring work by artists and writers from Central and South America. Receives 50 unsolicited mss/week. Accepts 6 mss/issue; 24 mss/year. Publishes ms 3-6 months after acceptance. Agented fiction 70%. **Publishes 4 new writers/year.** Published work by Yusef Komunyakaa, Javier Marias, and W. G. Sebald. Length: 10-12 pages average. Publishes interviews.
How to Contact: Send complete ms up to 25 pages in length with cover letter. Responds in 4 months to mss. SASE. Sample copy for $4.50 with $1.67 postage.
Payment/Terms: Pays $100 and contributor's copies. Pays on publication for first or one-time rights. Sends galleys to author.
Advice: "We are committed to publishing new work that commercial publishers often deem too dangerous or difficult. The problem is, a lot of young writers confuse difficult with dreadful. Read the magazine before you even think of submitting something."

$⊘ ⦿ **BOSTON REVIEW A political and literary forum,** 30 Wadsworth St., E53-407, MIT, Cambridge MA 02139. (617)253-3642. Fax: (617)252-1549. E-mail: bostonreview@mit.edu. Website: www-polisci.m it.edu/bostonreview/ (includes full issue 1 month after publication, poetry and fiction links page, guidelines and contests guidelines, bookstore listing and subscription info). Managing Editor: Jeff Decker. **Contact:** Jodi Daynard, fiction editor. A bimonthly magazine "providing a forum of ideas in politics, literature and culture. Essays, reviews, poetry and fiction are published in every issue. Audience is well educated and interested in under recognized writers." Magazine: 10¾ × 14¾; 56 pages; newsprint. Estab. 1975. Circ. 30,000.

● *Boston Review* is the recipient of a Pushcart Prize in poetry.

Needs: Contemporary, ethnic, experimental, literary, prose poem, regional, translations. No romance, erotica, genre fiction. Receives 150 unsolicited fiction mss/month. Buys 4-6 mss/year. Publishes ms an average of 4 months after acceptance. Recently published work by David Mamet, Rhoda Stamell, Jacob Appel, Elisha Porat and Diane Williams. Length: 4,000 words maximum; average length: 2,000 words. Occasionally comments on rejected ms.

How to Contact: Send complete ms with cover letter and SASE. "You can almost always tell professional writers by the very thought-out way they present themselves in cover letters. But even a beginning writer should find some link between the work (its style, subject, etc.) and the publication—some reason why the editor should consider publishing it." No queries or manuscripts by e-mail. Responds in 4 months. Accepts simultaneous submissions (if noted). Sample copy for $4.50. Reviews novels and short story collections. Send books to Matthew Howard, managing editor.

Payment/Terms: Pays $50-100 and 5 contributor's copies. Pays after publication for first rights.

Advice: "I'm looking for stories that are emotionally and intellectually substantive and also interesting on the level of language. Things that are shocking, dark, lewd, comic, or even insane are fine so long as the fiction is *controlled* and purposeful in a masterly way. Subtlety, delicacy and lyricism are attractive too. Work tirelessly to make the work truly polished before you send it out. Make sure you know the publication you're submitting— don't send blind."

☑ $ 🔘 **BOWHUNTER MAGAZINE, The Number One Bowhunting Magazine**, Primedia Special Interest Publications, 6405 Flank Dr., Harrisburg PA 17112. (717)657-9555. Fax: (717)657-9552. Founder/Editor-in-Chief: M.R. James. Associate Publisher/Managing Editor: Jeffrey S. Waring. **Contact:** Dwight Schuh, editor. Magazine: 8 × 10½; 150 pages; 75 lb. glossy paper; 150 lb. glossy cover stock; illustrations; photos. "We are a special interest publication for people who hunt with the bow and arrow. We publish hunting adventure and how-to stories. Our audience is predominantly male, 30-50, middle income." Bimonthly. Circ. 180,000.

● Themes included in most fiction considered for *Bowhunter* are pro-conservation as well as pro-hunting.

Needs: Bowhunting, outdoor adventure. "Writers must expect a very limited market. We buy only one or two fiction pieces a year. Writers must know the market—bowhunting—and let that be the theme of their work. No 'me and my dog' types of stories; no stories by people who have obviously never held a bow in their hands." Receives 25 unsolicited fiction mss/month. Accepts 30 mss/year. Publishes ms 3 months to 2 years after acceptance. Length: 500-2,000 words; average length: 1,500 words. Publishes short shorts. Length: 500 words. Sometimes comments on rejected mss and recommends other markets.

How to Contact: Query first or send complete ms with cover letter. Responds in 2 weeks to queries; 1 month to mss. Sample copy for $2 and 8½ × 11 SAE with appropriate postage. Guidelines for #10 SASE.

Payment/Terms: Pays $100-350. Pays on acceptance for first worldwide serial rights.

Advice: "We have a resident humorist who supplies us with most of the 'fiction' we need. But if a story comes through the door which captures the essence of bowhunting and we feel it will reach out to our readers, we will buy it. Despite our macho outdoor magazine status, we are a bunch of English majors who love to read. You can't bull your way around real outdoor people—they can spot a phony at 20 paces. If you've never camped out under the stars and listened to an elk bugle and try to relate that experience without really experiencing it, someone's going to know. We are very specialized; we don't want stories about shooting apples off people's heads or of Cupid's arrow finding its mark. James Dickey's *Deliverance* used bowhunting metaphorically, very effectively . . . while we don't expect that type of writing from everyone, that's the kind of feeling that characterizes a good piece of outdoor fiction."

🅽 $ 🔘 **BOYS' LIFE, For All Boys**, Boy Scouts of America, Magazine Division, Box 152079, 1325 W. Walnut Hill Lane, Irving TX 75015-2079. (972)580-2355. Website: www.boyslife.org. **Contact:** Rich Haddaway, associate editor. Magazine: 8 × 11; 68 pages; slick cover stock; illustrations; photos. "*Boys' Life* covers Boy Scout activities and general interest subjects for ages 8 to 18, Boy Scouts, Cub Scouts and others of that age group." Monthly. Estab. 1911. Circ. 1,300,000.

● *Boys' Life* ranked #6 on the *Writer's Digest* Fiction 50 list of top markets for fiction writers.

Needs: Adventure, humor/satire, mystery/suspense (young adult), science fiction, sports, western (young adult), young adult. "We publish short stories aimed at a young adult audience and frequently written from the viewpoint of a 10- to 16-year-old boy protagonist." Receives approximately 150 unsolicited mss/month. Accepts 12-18 mss/year. **Publishes 1 new writer/year.** Published work by Donald J. Sobol, Geoffrey Norman, G. Clifton Wisler and Marlys Stapelbroek. Length: 500-1,500 words; average length: 1,200 words. "Very rarely" comments on rejected ms.

How to Contact: Send complete ms with SASE. "We'd much rather see manuscripts than queries." Responds in 2 months. Accepts multiple submissions. For sample copy "check your local library." Guidelines for SASE.

Payment/Terms: Pays $750 and up ("depending on length and writer's experience with us"). Pays on acceptance for one-time rights.

Advice: "*Boys' Life* writers understand the readers. They treat them as intelligent human beings with a thirst for knowledge and entertainment. We tend to use some of the same authors repeatedly because their characters, themes, etc., develop a following among our readers. Read at least a year's worth of the magazine. You will get a feeling for what our readers are interested in and what kind of fiction we buy."

$ 🖉 ◎ BUGLE, Elk Country and the Hunt, Rocky Mountain Elk Foundation, P.O. Box 8249, Missoula MT 59807-8249. (406)523-4570. Fax: (406)523-4550. E-mail: bugle@rmef.org. Website: www.rmef.org. Editor: Dan Crockett. **Contact:** Lee Cromrich, assistant editor. Magazine: 8½×11; 114-172 pages; 55 lb. Escanaba paper; 80 lb. sterling cover; b&w, 4-color illustrations; photos. "The Rocky Mountain Elk Foundation is a nonprofit conservation organization established in 1984 to help conserve critical habitat for elk and other wildlife. *BUGLE* specializes in research, stories (fiction and nonfiction), art and photography pertaining to the world of elk and elk hunting." Bimonthly. Estab. 1984.

Needs: Elk-related adventure, children's/juvenile, historical, human interest, natural history, conservation. "We would like to see more humor. No formula outdoor or how-to writing." Upcoming themes; "Bowhunting" and "Women in the Outdoors." Receives 10-15 unsolicited mss/month. Accepts 5 mss/issue; 18-20 mss/year. Publishes ms 6 months after acceptance. **Publishes 10 new writers/year.** Published work by Hal Herring and Frederick Benton. Length: 1,500-5,000 words; 2,500 words preferred. Publishes short shorts. Also publishes literary essays and poetry.

How to Contact: Query first or send complete ms with a cover letter. Accepts queries/mss by e-mail and fax (ms by permission only). Include estimated word count and bio (100 words). Responds in 4 weeks on queries; 12 weeks on ms. Send SASE for reply, return of ms or send a disposable copy of ms. Sample copy for $5. Guidelines free.

Payment/Terms: Pays 20¢/word maximum. Pays on acceptance for one-time rights.

Advice: "We accept fiction and nonfiction stories about elk that show originality, and respect for the animal and its habitat."

N $ 🖉 ◎ ▼ CALLIOPE, World History for Young People, Cobblestone Publishing, Co., 30 Grove St., Suite C, Peterborough NH 02740. Fax: (603)924-7380. E-mail: cfbakeriii@meganet.net. Website: www.cobblestonepub.com. Editor: Lou Waryncia. **Contact:** Rosalie Baker, managing editor. Magazine. "*Calliope* covers world history (east/west) and lively, original approaches to the subject are the primary concerns of the editors in choosing material. For 8-14 year olds." Monthly except June, July, August. Estab. 1990. Circ. 11,000.

 • Cobblestone Publishing also publishes the children's magazines *Cobblestone* and *Faces* listed in this section. *Calliope* has received the Ed Press Golden Lamp and One-Theme Issue awards.

Needs: Material must fit upcoming theme; write for themes and deadlines. Childrens/juvenile (8-14 years). "Authentic historical and biographical fiction, adventure, retold legends, etc. relating to the theme." Send SASE for guidelines and theme list. Published after theme deadline. Recently published work by Duane Damon and Amita V. Sarin. Publishes 5-10 new writers/year. Length: 800 words maximum. Publishes short shorts. Also publishes poetry.

How to Contact: Query first or query with clips of published work (if new to *Calliope*). Include a brief cover letter stating estimated word count and 1-page outline explaining information to be presented, extensive bibliography of materials used. Responds in several months (if interested, response 5 months before publication date). Send SASE (or IRC) for reply (writers may send a stamped reply postcard to find out if query has been received). Sample copy for $4.95, 7½×10½ SAE and $2 postage. Guidelines for #10 SAE and 1 first-class stamp or on website.

Payment/Terms: Pays 20-25¢/word. Pays on publication for all rights.

Tips: "We primarily publish historical nonfiction. Fiction should be retold legends or folktales related to appropriate themes."

$ 🖉 ▼ CAMPUS LIFE MAGAZINE, Christianity Today, Inc., 465 Gundersen Dr., Carol Stream IL 60188. (630)260-6200. Fax: (630)260-0114. E-mail: cledit@aol.com. Website: www.campuslife.net. **Contact:** Christopher Lutes, managing editor. Magazine: 8¼×11¼; 100 pages; 4-color and b&w illustrations; 4-color and b&w photos. "Teen magazine with a Christian point of view." Articles "vary from serious to humorous to current trends and issues, for teen readers." Bimonthly. Estab. 1942. Circ. 100,000.

 • *Campus Life* regularly receives awards from the Evangelical Press Association.

Needs: "All fiction submissions must be contemporary, reflecting the teen experience in the '90s. We are a Christian magazine but are *not* interested in sappy, formulaic, sentimentally religious stories. We *are* interested in well-crafted stories that portray life realistically, stories high school and college youth relate to. Writing must reflect a Christian world view. If you don't understand our market and style, don't submit." Accepts 5 mss/year. Reading and response time slower in summer. **Published new writers within the last year.** Length: 1,000-2,000 words average, "possibly longer."

How to Contact: Query with short synopsis of work, published samples and SASE. Responds in 6 weeks to queries. Sample copy for $3 and 9½×11 envelope.

Payment/Terms: Pays "generally" 15-20¢/word and 2 contributor's copies. Pays on acceptance for one-time rights.

Advice: "We print finely-crafted fiction that carries a contemporary teen (older teen) theme. First person fiction often works best. Ask us for sample copy with fiction story. We want experienced fiction writers who have something to say to young people without getting propagandistic."

$☑ CAPPER'S, Ogden Publications, Inc. 1503 S.W. 42nd St., Topeka KS 66609-1265. (785)274-4346. Fax: (785)274-4305. E-mail: cappers@kspress.com. Website: www.cappers.com (includes sample items from publication and subscription information). **Contact:** Ann Crahan, editor. Magazine: 36-56 pages; newsprint paper and cover stock; photos. A "clean, uplifting and nonsensational newspaper for families, from children to grandparents." Biweekly. Estab. 1879. Circ. 250,000.

● *Capper's* is interested in longer works of fiction, 7,000 words or more. They would like to see more stories with older characters.

Needs: Serialized novels suitable for family reading. "We accept novel-length stories for serialization. No fiction containing violence, sexual references or obscenity. We would like to see more western romance, pioneer stories." Receives 2-3 unsolicited fiction mss each month. Accepts 4-6 stories/year. Recently published work by C.J. Sargent and Mona Exinger. Published new writers within the last year. Length: 7,000-40,000 words.

How to Contact: Send complete ms with SASE. Cover letter and/or synopsis helpful. Responds in 8 months on ms. Sample copy for $2.

Payment/Terms: Pays $75-300 for one-time serialization and contributor's copies (1-2 copies as needed for copyright). Pays on acceptance for second serial (reprint) rights and one-time rights.

Advice: "Since we publish in serialization, be sure your manuscript is suitable for that format. Each segment needs to be compelling enough so the reader remembers it and is anxious to read the next installment. Please proofread and edit carefully. We've seen major characters change names partway through the manuscript."

N $☑ ◎ CARPE NOCTEM, CN Publishing, 2633 Vista Way, #112, Oceanside CA 92054. (619)441-8121. Fax: (619)441-8180. E-mail: info@carpenoctem.com. Website: www.carpenoctem.com (includes past issues, excerpts, writer's guidelines, art guidelines, goth clubs and events, subscription information, music and merchandise). **Contact:** Michael T. Huyck, Jr., fiction editor. All fiction should be sent to Michael Huyck at PMB 251, 510 E. 17th St., Idaho Falls ID 83494, (619)441-8121. Magazine: 8½×11; 90 pages; 60 lb. glossy paper; 4-color, 80 lb. glossy cover; illustrations; photos. "*Carpe Noctem Magazine* is the fastest growing dark/alternative periodical for all media aspects of horror, science fiction, fantasy and alternative music. We specialize in the promotion of cutting edge artists and writers, avant garde cinema, and music for the dark at heart. *Carpe Noctem* is filled with interviews, fiction, art, photography, reviews and articles that all give its readers glimpses into the less traveled places in all media." Quarterly. Estab. 1994. Circ. 20,000.

● *Carpe Noctem* has twice been nominated for best publication by the International Horror Guild.

Needs: Comics/graphic novels, erotica, experimental, gay, horror (dark fantasy, psychological, supernatural, death-positive), lesbian, psychic/supernatural/occult, romance (gothic). "No children's fiction, religion (of any sort), high tech science fiction or high fantasy." Receives 25 unsolicited mss/month. Accepts 4 mss/issue; 16 mss/year. Publishes ms 6 months after acceptance. **Publishes 4 new writers/year.** Recently published work by Andrew Vachss, Mick Garris and Caitlin R. Kiernan. Length: 3,000 words maximum; average length: 2,500 words. Publishes short shorts. Sometimes comments on rejected mss.

How to Contact: Send complete ms with a cover letter. Accepts submissions by e-mail (preferred) and disk (must be accompanied by hard copy). Include estimated word count, brief bio and list of publications. Responds in 2 months. Send SASE (or IRC) for return of ms or send a disposable copy of ms and #10 SASE for reply only. Sample copy for $5.95. Guidelines for SASE or by e-mail. Reviews novels, short story collections and nonfiction books of interest to writers.

Payment/Terms: Pays 3¢/word. Pays on publication for first North American serial rights.

Advice: "Work should have a darkly romantic angle and present a 'death positive' perspective. Give us originality, literacy, intelligence and taste. Plot is absolutely necessary—problem presented and problem resolved. The best manuscripts provide a plot I care about, characters I can 'see' and a continuous authorial voice."

⊕ ☑ $CHAT, King's Reach Tower, Stamford St., London SE1 9LS England. 0870-444-5000. Website: www.ipc.co.uk. **Contact:** Olwen Rice, fiction editor. Weekly. Circ. 500,000.

Needs: Publishes mysteries, thrillers, science fiction and romance. Publishes 1 story/issue; 1/Christmas issue; 1/Summer special. Length: 800 words maximum.

How to Contact: "I accept and buy fiction from anyone, anywhere. Send material with reply coupons if you want your story returned."

Payment/Terms: Payment "negotiated with the fiction editor and made by cheque." Guidelines for SAE and IRCs.

◼ ✓ $ ⊘ ❑ **CHICKADEE**, Owl Communications, 179 John St., Suite 500, Toronto, Ontario M5T 3G5 Canada. (416)340-2700. Fax: (416)340-9769. E-mail: owl@owlkids.com. Website: www.owlkids.com. **Contact:** Hilary Bain, editor. Magazine: 8½×11¾; 36 pages; glossy paper and cover stock; illustrations; photos. "*Chickadee* is created to give children aged 6-9 a lively, fun-filled look at the world around them. Each issue has a mix of activities, puzzles, games and stories." Published 10 times/year. Estab. 1979. Circ. 80,000.

● *Chickadee* has won several awards including the Ed Press Golden Lamp Honor award and the Parents' Choice Golden Seal awards.

Needs: Juvenile. No religious material. Accepts 1 ms/issue; 10 mss/year. Publishes ms an average of 1 year after acceptance. Published new writers within the last year. Length: 300-900 words.

How to Contact: Send complete ms and cover letter with $1 or IRC to cover postage and handling. Accepts simultaneous submissions Responds in 2 months. Sample copy for $4.50. Guidelines for SAE and IRC.

Payment/Terms: Pays $25-250 (Canadian) and 2 contributor's copies. Pays on acceptance for all rights. Occasionally buys reprints.

Advice: "Read back issues to see what types of fiction we publish. Common mistakes include loose, rambling, and boring prose; stories that lack a clear beginning, middle and end; unbelievable characters; and overwriting."

✓ $ ⊘ **CHILDREN'S DIGEST**, Children's Better Health Institute, P.O. Box 567, 1100 Waterway Blvd., Indianapolis IN 46206. (317)634-1100. **Contact:** Lisa Hoffman, editor. Magazine: 7×10⅛; 36 pages; reflective and preseparated illustrations; color and b&w photos. Magazine with special emphasis on health, nutrition, exercise and safety for preteens.

● Other magazines published by Children's Better Health Institute and listed in this book are *Children's Playmate, Humpty Dumpty, Jack and Jill* and *Turtle*.

Needs: "Realistic stories, short plays, adventure and mysteries. Humorous stories are highly desirable. We especially need stories that *subtly* encourage readers to develop better health or safety habits. Stories should not exceed 1,500 words." Receives 40-50 unsolicited fiction mss each month. Published work by Judith Josephson, Pat McCarthy and Sharen Liddell; published new writers within the last year.

How to Contact: Currently not accepting unsolicited mss. Sample copy for $1.75. Guidelines for SASE.

Payment/Terms: Pays 12¢/word minimum with up to 10 contributor's copies on publication for all rights.

Advice: "We try to present our health-related material in a positive—not a negative—light, and we try to incorporate humor and a light approach wherever possible without minimizing the seriousness of what we are saying. Fiction stories that deal with a health theme need not have health as the primary subject but should include it in some way in the course of events. Most rejected health-related manuscripts are too preachy or they lack substance. Children's magazines are not training grounds where authors learn to write 'real' material for 'real' readers. Because our readers frequently have limited attention spans, it is very important that we offer them well-written stories."

◎ **CHILDREN'S PLAYMATE**, Children's Better Health Institute, P.O. Box 567, 1100 Waterway Blvd., Indianapolis IN 46206. (317)636-8881. **Contact:** Terry Harshman, editor. Magazine: 7½×10; 48 pages; preseparated and reflective art; b&w and color illustrations. Juvenile magazine for children ages 6-8 years. Published 8 times/year.

● *Children's Digest, Humpty Dumpty, Jack and Jill* and *Turtle* magazines are also published by Children's Better Health Institute and listed in this book.

Needs: Juvenile with special emphasis on health, nutrition, safety and exercise. "Our present needs are for short, entertaining stories with a subtle health angle. Seasonal material is also always welcome." No adult or adolescent fiction. Receives approximately 150 unsolicited fiction mss each month. Published work by Batta Killion, Ericka Northrop, Elizabeth Murphy-Melas; published new writers within the last year. Length: 300-700 words.

How to Contact: Send complete ms with SASE. Indicate word count on material and date sent. Responds in 3 months. Sample copy for $1.75. Writer's guidelines for SASE.

Payment/Terms: Pays up to 17¢/word and 10 contributor's copies. Pays on publication for *all* rights.

Advice: "Stories should be kept simple and entertaining. Study past issues of the magazine—be aware of vocabulary limitations of the readers."

✓ ◯ ◎ **CITYCYCLE MOTORCYCLE NEWS MAGAZINE**, Motormag Corp., P.O. Box 808, Nyalk NY 10960-0808. (914)353-MOTO. Fax: (914)353-5240. E-mail: bigcheese@motorcyclenews.com. Website: www.motorcyclenews.com (includes short fiction, interviews with authors). **Contact:** Mark Kalan, editor. Magazine: tabloid; 64 pages; newsprint; illustrations; photos. Monthly magazine about motorcyling. Estab. 1990. Circ. 50,000.

Needs: "Anything about motorcycles." No "sexual fantasy." Accepts 10 mss/year. Publishes ms 2-6 months after acceptance. Length: 750-2,000 words. Publishes short shorts. Also publishes literary essays, literary criticism and poetry. Sometimes comments on rejected mss.

How to Contact: Query with clips of published work. Responds in 1 month to queries. Send SASE for reply. Accepts reprints. Sample copy for $3 and 9×12 SAE. Guidelines for #10 SASE. Reviews novels and short story collections. Send books to editor.

Payment/Terms: Pays up to $150. Pays on publication for one-time rights.

Advice: "Articles, stories and poetry can be about any subject, fiction or non-fiction, as long as the subject pertains to motorcycles or the world of motorcycling. Examples would include fiction or non-fiction stories about traveling cross-country on a motorcycle, biker lifestyle or perspective, motorcycling/biker humor, etc. Stories should reflect the love of riding motorcycles and the experience of what riding is like. Romance is fine. Science fiction is fine as long as it will interest our mostly male audience."

$ ☑ CLUBHOUSE, Focus on the Family, 8605 Explorer Dr., Colorado Springs CO 80920. (719)531-3400. **Contact:** Jesse Florea, editor. Associate Editor: Annette Brashler Bourland. Magazine: 8×11; 24 pages; illustrations; photos. Publishes literature for kids aged 8-12. "Stories must have moral lesson included. *Clubhouse* readers are 8- to 12-year-old boys and girls who desire to know more about God and the Bible. Their parents (who typically pay for the membership) want wholesome, educational material with Scriptual or moral insight. The kids want excitement, adventure, action, humor or mystery. Your job as a writer is to please both the parent and child with each article." Monthly. Estab. 1987. Circ. 126,000.

Needs: Children's/juvenile (8-12 years), religious/inspirational. No science fiction. Receives 150 unsolicited ms/month. Accepts 1 ms/issue. Agented fiction 15%. **Publishes 8 new writers/year.** Published work by Sigmund Brower and Nancy Rue. Length: 500-1,600 words.

How to Contact: Send complete ms with cover letter. Include estimated word count, bio and list of publications. Responds in 6 weeks. Send SASE for reply, return of ms or send a disposable copy of ms. Sample copy for $1.50. Guidelines free.

Payment/Terms: Pays $250 maximum and 2 contributor's copies; additional copies $1.50. Pays on acceptance for first North American serial rights.

Advice: Looks for "humor with a point, historical fiction featuring great Christians or Christians who lived during great times; contemporary, exotic settings; holiday material (Christmas, Thanksgiving, Easter, President's Day); parables; fantasy (avoid graphic descriptions of evil creatures and sorcery); mystery stories; choose-your-own adventure stories and westerns. No contemporary, middle-class family settings (we already have authors who can meet these needs) or stories dealing with boy-girl relationships."

Ⓝ ◐ $ ☒ COBBLESTONE, Discover American History, 30 Grove St., Suite C, Peterborough NH 03458. (603)924-7209. Fax: (603)924-7380. Website: www.cobblestonepub.com. **Contact:** Meg Chorlian, editor. Magazine. "Historical accuracy and lively, original approaches to the subject are primary concerns of the editors in choosing material. For 8-14 year olds." Monthly (except June, July and August). Estab. 1979. Circ. 33,000.

● Cobblestone Press also publishes *Calliope* and *Faces*, listed in this section. *Cobblestone* has received Ed Press and Parent's Choice awards.

Needs: Material must fit upcoming theme; write for theme list and deadlines. Childrens/juvenile (8-14 years). "Authentic historical and biographical fiction, adventure, retold legends, etc., relating to the theme." Upcoming themes available for SASE. Published after theme deadline. Accepts 1-2 fiction mss/issue. Length: 800 words maximum. Publishes short shorts. Also publishes poetry.

How to Contact: Query first or query with clips of published work (if new to *Cobblestone*). Include estimated word count. "Include detailed outline explaining the information to be presented in the article and bibliography of material used." Responds in several months. If interested, responds to queries 5 months before publication date. Send SASE (or IRC) for reply or send self-addressed postcard to find out if query was received. Accepts electronic submissions (disk, Microsoft Word or MS-DOS). Sample copy for $4.95, 7½×10½ SAE and $2 postage. Guidelines for #10 SAE and 1 first-class stamp or on website.

Payment/Terms: Pays 20-25¢/word. Pays on publication for all rights.

Advice: Writers may send $8.95 plus $3 shipping for *Cobblestone*'s index for a listing of subjects covered in back issues.

Ⓒ CONTACT PUBLICATIONS, Box 3431, Ft. Pierce FL 34948. (561)464-5447. E-mail: nietzche@cadv.com. Website: www.cadv.com (includes short fiction club information). **Contact:** Herman Nietzche, editor. Magazines and newspapers "specializing in alternative lifestyles." Publications vary in size, 56-80 pages. "Group of 26 erotica, soft core publications for swingers, single males, married males, gay males, transgendered and bisexual persons." Bimonthly, quarterly and monthly. Estab. 1975. Circ. combined is 2,000,000.

● This is a group of regional publications with explicit sexual content, graphic personal ads, etc. Not for the easily offended.

Needs: Erotica, fantasy, swinger, fetish, gay, lesbian. Receives 8-10 unsolicited mss/month. Accepts 1-2 mss/issue; 40-50 mss/year. Publishes ms 1-3 months after acceptance. **Publishes 3-6 new writers/year.** Length: 2,000-3,500 words. Sometimes comments on rejected mss.

How to Contact: Query first, query with clips of published work or send complete ms with cover letter. SASE. Accepts submissions by e-mail and on disk. Accepts simultaneous, multiple and reprint submissions. Sample copy for $7. Guidelines with SASE.

Payment/Terms: First submission, free subscription to magazine; subsequent submissions $25 on publication for all rights or first rights; all receive 3 contributor's copies.

Advice: "Know your grammar! Content must be of an adult nature but well within guidelines of the law. Fantasy, unusual sexual encounters, swinging stories or editorials of a sexual bent are acceptable. Read Henry Miller!"

$ ⬭ ⬭ CORNERSTONE MAGAZINE, Cornerstone Communications, Inc., 939 W. Wilson Ave., Chicago IL 60640. (773)561-2450 ext. 2394. Fax (773)989-2076. Editor: Jon Trott. **Contact:** Submission Editor. Magazine: 8½×11; 64 pages; 35 lb. coated matie paper; self cover; illustrations; photos. "For adults, 18-45. We publish nonfiction (essays, personal experience, religious), music interviews, current events, film and book reviews, fiction, poetry. *Cornerstone* challenges readers to look through the window of biblical reality. Known as avant-garde, yet attempts to express orthodox belief in the language of the nineties." Approx. quarterly. Estab. 1972. Circ. 38,000.

• *Cornerstone Magazine* has won numerous awards from the Evangelical Press Association.

Needs: Ethnic/multicultural, fantasy (science fantasy), humor/satire, literary, mainstream/contemporary, religious/inspirational. Special interest in "issues pertinent to contemporary society, seen with a biblical worldview." No "pornography, cheap shots at non-Christians, unrealistic or syrupy articles." Receives 60 unsolicited mss/month. Accepts 1 mss/issue; 3-4 mss/year. Does not read mss during Christmas/New Year's week and the month of July. Published work by Dave Cheadle, C.S. Lewis and J.B. Simmonds. Length: 250-2,500 words; average length: 1,200 words. Publishes short shorts. Length: 250-450 words. Also publishes literary essays, literary criticism and poetry.

How to Contact: Send all submissions, by e-mail, to: fiction@cornerstonemag.com. Please send the submission as html or ASCII text. If e-mail if unavailable, we accept hard copies. Will consider simultaneous submissions and reprints. Reviews novel and short story collections. Reviews novels and short story collections.

Payment/Terms: Pays 8-10¢/word maximum and 6 contributor's copies. Pays on publication for first serial rights.

Advice: "Articles may express Christian world view but shouldn't be unrealistic or syrupy. We're looking for high-quality fiction with skillful characterization and plot development and imaginative symbolism." Looks for "mature Christian short stories, as opposed to those more fit for church bulletins. We want fiction with bite and an edge but with a Christian worldview."

⬭ COSMOPOLITAN MAGAZINE, The Hearst Corp., 224 W. 57th St., New York NY 10019. (212)649-2000.

• *Cosmopolitan* no longer publishes short fiction or novel excerpts.

N ⬭ ★ ⬭ ⬭ COTWORLD CREATIVE MAGAZINE, Cotworld Independent, 2008-66 Isabella St., Toronto, Ontario M4Y-1N3 Canada. (416)964-1241. E-mail: webmaster@cotworld.com. Website: www.cotworld. com. **Contact:** Mark O'Sullivan, editor-in-chief. "*Cotworld* is a purely online entity. We feature poetry and short stories by unpublished authors." Online magazine: some illustrations; photos. "*Cotworld* is about brutal honesty, and good writing. We will publish anything as long as we feel it is quality, thought-provoking writing." Monthly. Estab. 1999. Circ. approximately 14,000 hits/month.

Needs: Adventure, comics/graphic novels, erotica, ethnic/multicultural, family saga, fantasy, feminist, gay, glitz, historical, horror, humor/satire, lesbian, literary, mainstream, military/war, mystery/suspense, new age, psychic/supernatural/occult, regional, religious, romance, science fiction, thriller/espionage, translation, and western. List of upcoming themes available online. Accepts 4-5 mss/issue; 48-60 mss/year. Publishes ms 1 month after acceptance. **Publishes 90 new writers/year.** Recently published work by Tom O'Brien, Ian Wolff and Rhod Broadwater. Length: 2,000-3,500 words; average length: 2,500 words. Publishes short shorts. Average length: 2,500 words. Also publishes literary essays and poetry.

How to Contact: E-mail or mail submissions with contact information and brief personal bio to webmaster. Accepts ms by e-mail and on disk. Responds in 1 month to queries. Send SASE or IRC for return of mss or send disposable copy of ms and #10 SASE for reply only. Accepts simultaneous, previously published work or multiple submissions. Sample copy free. Guidelines on website. Reviews novels, short story collections and nonfiction books.

Payment/Terms: "The writer retains all ownership. We're just a showcase."

Advice: "We're looking for a quality writing style; well thought-out storyline; thought-provoking content and brutal honestly."

✓ $ ⬭ COUNTRY WOMAN, Reiman Publications, 5400 South 60th St., Greendale WI 53129. (414)423-0100. Editor: Ann Kaiser. **Contact:** Kathleen Pohl, executive editor. Magazine: 8½×11; 68 pages; excellent quality paper; excellent cover stock; illustrations and photographs. "Stories should have a rural theme and be of specific interest to women who live on a farm or ranch, or in a small town or country home, and/or are simply interested in country-oriented topics." Bimonthly. Estab. 1971.

Needs: Fiction must be upbeat, heartwarming and focus on a country woman as central character. "Many of our stories and articles are written by our readers!" Published work by Edna Norrell, Millie Thomas Kearney and Rita Peterson. **Published new writers within last year.** Publishes 1 fiction story/issue. Length: 1,000 words.

How to Contact: Send $2 and SASE for sample copy and writer's guidelines. All manuscripts should be sent to Kathy Pohl, Executive Editor. Responds in 3 months. Include cover letter and SASE. Accepts simultaneous and reprint submissions.

Payment/Terms: Pays $90-125 for fiction. Pays on acceptance for one-time rights.

Advice: "Read the magazine to get to know our audience. Send us country-to-the-core fiction, not yuppie-country stories—our readers know the difference! Very traditional fiction—with a definite beginning, middle and end, some kind of conflict/resolution, etc. We do not want to see contemporary avant-garde fiction—nothing dealing with divorce, drugs, etc., or general societal malaise of the '90s."

CREATIVE KIDS, Prufrock Press, P.O. Box 8813, Waco TX 76714-8813. (254)756-3337. Fax: (254)756-3339. E-mail: creative_kids@prufrock.com. Website: www.prufrock.com (includes catalog, submission guidelines and information about our staff). **Contact:** Libby Lindsey, editor. Magazine: 7×10½; 36 pages; illustrations; photos. Material by children for children. Published 4 times/year. Estab. 1980. Circ. 45,000.

• *Creative Kids* featuring work by children has won Ed Press and Parents' Choice Gold and Silver Awards.

Needs: "We publish work by children ages 8-14." Publishes short stories, essays, games, puzzles, poems, opinion pieces and letters. Accepts 3-4 mss/issue; 12-16 mss/year. Publishes ms up to 2 years after acceptance. **Published new writers within the last year.** No novels.

How to Contact: Send complete ms with cover letter; include name, age, birthday, home address, school name and address, grade, statement of originality signed by teacher or parent. Must include SASE for response. Do not query. Responds in 1 month to mss. SASE. Sample copy for $3. Guidelines for SASE.

Payment/Terms: Pays 1 contributor's copy. Acquires all rights.

Advice: "*Creative Kids* is designed to entertain, stimulate and challenge the creativity of children ages 8 to 14, encouraging their abilities and helping them to explore their ideas, opinions and world. Your work reflects you. Make it neat, have it proofread and follow ALL guidelines."

CRICKET MAGAZINE, Carus Corporation, P.O. Box 300, Peru IL 61354. (815)224-6656. **Contact:** Marianne Carus, editor-in-chief. Magazine: 8×10; 64 pages; illustrations; photos. Magazine for children, ages 9-14. Monthly. Estab. 1973. Circ. 71,000.

• *Cricket* ranked #31 on the *Writer's Digest* Fiction 50 list of top markets for fiction writers. *Cricket* has received a Parents Choice Award, and awards from Ed Press. Carus Corporation also publishes *Spider, the Magazine for Children, Ladybug, the Magazine for Young Children, Babybug,* and *Cicada.*

Needs: Adventure, contemporary, ethnic, fantasy, historic fiction, folk and fairytales, humorous, juvenile, mystery, science fiction and translations. No adult articles. All issues have different "mini-themes." Receives approximately 1,100 unsolicited fiction mss each month. Publishes ms 6-24 months or longer after acceptance. Accepts 180 mss/year. Agented fiction 1-2%. **Published new writers within the last year.** Published work by Peter Dickinson, Mary Stolz and Jane Yolen. Length: 500-2,000 words.

How to Contact: Do not query first. Send complete ms with SASE. List previous publications. Responds in 3 months to mss. Sample copy for $5. Guidelines for SASE.

Payment/Terms: Pays up to 25¢/word and 2 contributor's copies; $2 charge for extras. Pays on publication for first rights. Sends edited mss for approval. Buys reprints.

Advice: "Do not write *down* to children. Write about well-researched subjects you are familiar with and interested in, or about something that concerns you deeply. Children *need* fiction and fantasy. Carefully study several issues of *Cricket* before you submit your manuscript." Sponsors contests for readers of all ages.

CRUSADER MAGAZINE, Calvinist Cadet Corps, Box 7259, Grand Rapids MI 49510-7259. (616)241-5616. **Contact:** G. Richard Broene, editor. Magazine: 8½×11; 24 pages; illustrations; photos. Magazine "for boys (ages 9-14) who are members of the Calvinist Cadet Corps. *Crusader* publishes stories and articles that have to do with the interests and concerns of boys, teaching Christian values subtly." 7 issues/year. Estab. 1958. Circ. 12,000.

Needs: Adventure, comics, juvenile, religious/inspirational, spiritual and sports. No fantasy, science fiction, fashion, horror or erotica. List of upcoming themes available for SASE. Receives 60 unsolicited fiction mss/month. Buys 3 mss/issue; 18 mss/year. Publishes ms 4-11 months after acceptance. Published work by Sigmund Brouwer, Douglas DeVries and Betty Lou Mell. **Publishes 0-3 new writers/year.** Length: 800-1,500 words; average length: 1,200 words. Publishes short shorts.

How to Contact: Send complete ms and SASE with cover letter including theme of story. Responds in 3 months. Accepts simultaneous, multiple and previously published submissions. Sample copy with a 9×12 SAE and 4 first-class stamps. Guidelines for #10 SASE.

Payment/Terms: Pays 4-6¢/word and 1 contributor's copy. Pays on acceptance for one-time rights. Buys reprints.

Advice: "On a cover sheet, list the point your story is trying to make. Our magazine has a theme for each issue, and we try to fit the fiction to the theme. All fiction should be about a young boy's interests—sports, outdoor activities, problems—with an emphasis on a Christian perspective. No simple moralisms. Avoid simplistic answers to complicated problems."

☑ $ ◻ **DIALOGUE, A World of Ideas for Visually Impaired People of All Ages**, Blindskills Inc., P.O. Box 5181, Salem OR 97304-0181. (800)860-4224. (503)581-4224. Fax: (503)581-0178. E-mail: blindskl@te leport.com. Website: www.blindskills.com. **Contact:** Carol McCarl, editor/publisher. Magazine: 9×11; 130 pages; matte stock. Publishes information of general interest to visually impaired. Quarterly. Estab. 1961. Circ. 15,000.

Needs: Adventure, contemporary, fantasy, humor/satire, literary, mainstream, mystery/suspense, romance, science fiction, senior citizen/retirement. No erotica, religion, confessional or experimental. Receives approximately 10 unsolicited fiction mss/month. Accepts 3 mss/issue, 12 mss/year. Publishes ms an average of 1 year after acceptance. Published work by Kim Rush, Diana Braun and Eric Cameron. Published new writers within the last year. Length: 800-1,200 words; average length: 1,000 words. Publishes short shorts. Occasionally comments on rejected mss. Sometimes recommends other markets. "We primarily feature blind or visually impaired (legally blind) authors."

How to Contact: Query first or send complete ms with SASE. Also send statement of visual disability. Responds in 2 weeks to queries; 6 weeks to mss. Accepts electronic submissions on disk; IBM and compatible; Word Perfect 5.1 or 6.0 preferred. Sample copy for $6 and #10 SAE with 1 first-class stamp. Guidelines free.

Payment/Terms: Pays $15-30 and contributor's copy. Pays on acceptance for first rights.

Advice: "Authors should be blind or visually impaired. We prefer contemporary problem stories in which the protagonist solves his or her own problem. We are looking for strongly-plotted stories with definite beginnings, climaxes and endings. Characters may be blind, sighted or visually in-between. Because we want to encourage any writer who shows promise, we may return a story for revision when necessary."

$ ◻ **DISCOVERIES**, WordAction Publishing Company, 6401 The Paseo, Kansas City MO 64131. (816)333-7000 ext. 2359. Fax: (816)333-4439. **Contact:** Emily J. Freeburg, assistant editor. Story paper: 8½×11; 4 pages; illustrations. "Committed to reinforce the Bible concept taught in Sunday School curriculum, for ages 8-10 (grades 3-4)." Weekly.

Needs: Religious stories, puzzles, Bible trivia, 100-200 words. "Avoid fantasy, science fiction, personification of animals and cultural references that are distinctly American." Accepts 1 story, 1 Bible trivia, and 1 puzzle/issue. Publishes ms 1-2 years after acceptance. **Publishes 5-10 new writers/year.** Story length: 500 words.

How to Contact: Send complete ms with cover letter and SASE. Send SASE for sample copy and guidelines.

Payment/Terms: Pays 5¢/word. Pays on acceptance or on publication for multiple rights.

Advice: "Stories should vividly portray definite Christian emphasis or character building values, without being preachy."

☑ $ ◻ **DISCOVERY TRAILS**, Gospel Publishing House, 1445 N. Boonville Ave., Springfield MO 65802-1894. (417)862-2781. Fax: (417)862-6059. E-mail: discoverytrails@gph.org. Website: www.radiantlife.org. **Contact:** Sinda S. Zinn, editor. Magazine: 8×10; 4 pages; coated offset paper; art illustrations; photos. "A Sunday school take-home paper of articles and fictional stories that apply Christian principles to everyday living for 10- to 12-year-old children." Weekly. Estab. 1954. Circ. 40,000.

Needs: Contemporary, juvenile, religious/inspirational, spiritual, sports. Adventure and mystery stories and serials are welcome. No Biblical fiction, Halloween, Easter "bunny," Santa Claus or science fiction. Accepts 2 mss/issue. **Published new writers within the last year.** Published work by Lucinda J. Rollings, Karen Cogan, A.J. Sckut and Terry Miller Shannon. Length: 800-1,000 words. Publishes short shorts.

How to Contact: Send complete ms with SASE. Accepts submissions by e-mail. Responds in 6 weeks. Free sample copy and guidelines with SASE.

Payment/Terms: Pays 7-10¢/word and 3 contributor's copies. Pays on acceptance.

Advice: "Know the age level and direct stories or articles relevant to that age group. Since junior-age children (grades 5 and 6) enjoy action, fiction provides a vehicle for communicating moral/spiritual principles in a dramatic framework. Fiction, if well done, can be a powerful tool for relating Christian principles. It must, however, be realistic and believable in its development. Make your children be children, not overly mature for their age. We would like more serial stories. Write for contemporary children, using setting and background that includes various ethnic groups."

☑ $ ◻ 🔲 **ESQUIRE, The Magazine for Men**, Hearst Corp., 250 W. 55th St., New York NY 10019. (212)649-4020. Website: www.esquiremag.com. Editor: David Granger. **Contact:** Adrienne Miller, literary editor. Magazine. Monthly. Estab. 1933. Circ. 750,000. General readership is college educated and sophisticated, between ages 30 and 45.

● *Esquire* is well-respected for its fiction and has received several National Magazine Awards. Work published in *Esquire* has been selected for inclusion in the *Best American Short Stories* anthology.

Needs: No "pornography, science fiction or 'true romance' stories." Publishes special fiction issue in July. Receives "thousands" of unsolicited mss/year. Rarely accepts unsolicited fiction. Published work by T.C. Boyle and Raymond Carver.

How to Contact: Send complete ms with cover letter or submit through an agent. Accepts simultaneous submissions. Guidelines for SASE.

Payment/Terms: Pays in cash on acceptance, amount undisclosed. Publishes ms an average of 2 months after acceptance.

Advice: "Submit one story at a time. Worry a little less about publication, a little more about the work itself."

$ ☑ ◎ EVANGEL, Light & Life Communications, P.O. Box 535002, Indianapolis IN 46253-5002. (317)244-3660. **Contact:** Julie Innes, editor. Sunday school take-home paper for distribution to adults who attend church. Fiction involves people coping with everyday crises, making decisions that show spiritual growth. Magazine: 5½×8½; 8 pages; 2- and 4-color illustrations; color and b&w photos. Weekly. Estab. 1897. Circ. 22,000.

Needs: Religious/inspirational. "No fiction without any semblance of Christian message or where the message clobbers the reader." Receives approximately 300 unsolicited fiction mss/month. Accepts 3-4 mss/issue, 156-200 mss/year. **Publishes 90 new writers/year.** Published work by Karen Leet and Dennis Hensley. Length: 500-1,200 words.

How to Contact: Send complete ms with SASE. Responds in 2 months. Accepts electronic submissions (3½ inch disk-WordPerfect); send hard copy with disk. Sample copy and writer's guidelines with #10 SASE.

Payment/Terms: Pays 4¢/word and 2 contributor's copies. Pays on publication.

Advice: "Choose a contemporary situation or conflict and create a good mix for the characters (not all-good or all-bad heroes and villains). Don't spell out everything in detail; let the reader fill in some blanks in the story. Keep him guessing." Rejects mss because of "unbelievable characters and predictable events in the story."

N: $ ☑ ◎ FACES, People, Places and Cultures, A Cobblestone Publication, Cobblestone Publishing, Co., 30 Grove St., Suite C, Peterborough NH 03458. (603)924-7209. Fax: (603)924-7380. E-mail: faces@cob blestonepub.com. Website: www.cobblestonepub.com. Editor: Elizabeth Crooker. **Contact:** Lou Waryncia, managing editor. Magazine. *Faces* is a magazine about people and places in the world for 8 to 14-year-olds. Estab. 1984. Circ. 15,000. Monthly, except June, July and August.

● Cobblestone also publishes *Cobblestone* and *Calliope*, listed in this section.

Needs: All material must relate to theme; send for theme list. Children's/juvenile (8-14 years), "retold legends, folk tales, stories from around the world, etc., relating to the theme." Length: 800 words preferred. Publishes short shorts.

How to Contact: Query first or query with clips of published work (send query 6-9 months prior to theme issue publication date). Include estimated word count and bio (2-3 lines). Responds 4 months before publication date. Send SASE for reply. Sample copy for $4.95, 7½×10½ SAE and $2 postage. Guidelines for SASE.

Payment/Terms: Pays 20-25¢/word. Pays on publication for all rights.

☑ $ ☑ ◎ FIRST HAND, Experiences for Loving Men, First Hand Ltd., Box 1314, Teaneck NJ 07666. (201)836-9177. Fax: (201)836-5055. E-mail: firsthand3@aol.com. **Contact:** Don Dooley, editor. Magazine: digest size; 130 pages; illustrations. "Half of the magazine is made up of our readers' own gay sexual experiences. Rest is fiction and columns devoted to health, travel, books, etc." Publishes 16 times/year. Estab. 1980. Circ. 60,000.

Needs: Erotica, gay. "Should be written in first person." No science fiction or fantasy. Erotica should detail experiences based in reality. Receives 75-100 unsolicited mss/month. Accepts 6 mss/issue; 72 mss/year. Publishes ms 9-18 months after acceptance. Length: 2,000-3,750 words; 3,000 words preferred. Sometimes comments on rejected mss.

How to Contact: Send complete ms with cover letter. Include name, address, telephone and Social Security number and "advise on use of pseudonym if any. Also whether selling all rights or first North American rights." No simultaneous submissions. Responds in 2 months. SASE. Sample copy for $5. Guidelines for #10 SASE.

Payment/Terms: Pays $100-150 on publication for all rights or first North American serial rights.

Advice: "Avoid the hackneyed situations. Be original. We like strong plots."

☑ $ ☑ THE FRIEND MAGAZINE, The Church of Jesus Christ of Latter-day Saints, 50 E. North Temple, 24th Floor, Salt Lake City UT 84150-3226. (801)240-2210. **Contact:** Vivian Paulsen, editor. Magazine: 8½×10½; 50 pages; 40 lb. coated paper; 70 lb. coated cover stock; illustrations; photos. Publishes for 3- to 11-year-olds. Monthly. Estab. 1971. Circ. 275,000.

Needs: Children's/juvenile: adventure, ethnic, some historical, humor, mainstream, religious/inspirational, nature. Length: 1,000 words maximum. Publishes short shorts. Length: 250 words.

How to Contact: Send complete ms. "No query letters please." Responds in 2 months. SASE. Sample copy for $1.50 with 9½×11 SAE and four 33¢ stamps.

Payment/Terms: Pays 10-13¢/word. Pays on acceptance for all rights.

Advice: "The *Friend* is particularly interested in stories with substance for tiny tots. Stories should focus on character-building qualities and should be wholesome without moralizing or preaching. Boys and girls resolving conflicts is a theme of particular merit. Since the magazine is circulated worldwide, the *Friend* is interested in stories and articles with universal settings, conflicts and characters. Other suggestions include rebus, picture, holiday, sports, and photo stories, or manuscripts that portray various cultures. Very short pieces (up to 250 words) are desired for younger readers and preschool children. Appropriate humor is a constant need."

☑ $ ◑ **GOLF JOURNAL,** United States Golf Assoc., Golf House, P.O. Box 708, Far Hills NJ 07931-0708. (908)234-2300. Fax: (908)781-1112. E-mail: golfjournal@usga.org. Website: www.golfjournal.org (includes excerpts from publication). **Contact:** Brett Avery, editor. Managing Editor: Rich Skyzinski. Magazine: 48-56 pages; self cover stock; illustrations; photos. "The magazine's subject is golf—its history, lore, rules, equipment and general information. The focus is on amateur golf and those things applying to the millions of American golfers. Our audience is generally professional, highly literate and knowledgeable; they read *Golf Journal* because of an interest in the game, its traditions, and its noncommercial aspects." Published 9 times/year. Estab. 1948. Circ. 650,000.

Needs: Poignant or humorous essays and short stories. "Golf jokes will not be used." Accepts 12 mss/year. Published new writers within the last year. Length: 1,000-2,000 words.

How to Contact: Send complete ms with SASE. Responds in 2 months to mss. Sample copy for SASE.

Payment/Terms: Pays $500-1,500 and 5 contributor's copies. Pays on acceptance.

Advice: "Know your subject (golf); familiarize yourself first with the publication." Rejects mss because "fiction usually does not serve the function of *Golf Journal*, which, as the official magazine of the United States Golf Association, deals chiefly with the history, lore and rules of golf."

🅽 $ ◑ **GOOD HOUSEKEEPING,** 959 Eighth Ave., New York NY 10019. **Contact:** Fiction Editor. "It is now our policy that all submissions of unsolicited fiction received in our offices will be read and, if found to be unsuitable for us, destroyed by recycling. If you wish to introduce your work to us, you will be submitting material that will not be critiqued or returned. The odds are long that we will contact you to inquire about publishing your submission or to invite you to correspond with us directly, so please be sure before you take the time and expense to submit it that it is our type of material."

Advice: "We welcome short fiction submissions (1,000-3,000 words). We look for stories with strong emotional interest—stories revolving around, for example, courtship, romance, marriage, family, friendships, personal growth, coming of age. The best way to gauge whether your story might be appropriate for us is to read the fiction in several of our recent issues. (We are sorry but we cannot furnish sample copies of the magazine.) We prefer double-spaced, typewritten (or keyboarded) manuscripts, accompanied by a short cover letter listing any previous writing credits. (We're sorry, but no e-mailed or faxed submissions will be accepted.) Make sure that your name and address appear on the manuscript and that you retain a copy for yourself."

☑ $ ◑ **GRIT, American Life & Traditions,** Ogden Publications, Inc., 1503 S.W. 42nd St., Topeka KS 66609-1265. (785)274-4300. Fax: (785)274-4305. E-mail: grit@cjnetworks.com. Website: www.grit.com (includes cover story from current issue plus titles of other features and book and products store). **Contact:** Donna Doyle, editor-in-chief. Note on envelope: Attn: Fiction Department. Tabloid: 50 pages; 30 lb. newsprint; illustrations; photos. "*Grit* is a 'good news' publication and has been since 1882. Fiction should be 1,200 words or more and interesting, inspiring, perhaps compelling in nature. Audience is *conservative*; readers tend to be 40+ from smaller towns, rural areas who love to read." Biweekly. Estab. 1882. Circ. 200,000.

● *Grit* is considered one of the leading family-oriented publications.

Needs: Adventure, nostalgia, condensed novelette, mainstream/contemporary (conservative), mystery/suspense, light religious/inspirational, romance (contemporary, historical), science fiction, westerns (frontier, traditional). "No sex, violence, drugs, obscene words, abuse, alcohol, or negative diatribes." Upcoming themes: "Gardening" (January/February); "Love & Romance (February); "Presenting the Harvest" (June); "Back to School" (August); "Health Issue" (September); "Home for the Holidays" (November); "Christmas Theme" (December); special storytellers issue (5-6 mss needed; submit in June). Buys 1 mss/issue; 26 mss/year. **Publishes 20 new writers/year.** Recently published work by Jack Kriege, Fatima Atchley, Tim Myers and Margaret Tauber. Length: 1,200 words minimum; 4,000-6,000 words maximum for serials; average length: 1,500 words. Also publishes poetry.

How To Contact: Send complete ms with cover letter. Include estimated word count, brief bio, Social Security number, list of publications with submission. Send SASE for return of ms. No simultaneous submissions. Sample copy for $4 postage/appropriate SASE. No e-mail submissions. Accepts fax submissions.

Payment/Terms: Pays up to 22¢/word. Purchases first North American serial or one-time rights.

Advice: Looks for "well-written, fast-paced adventures, lessons of life, wholesome stories with heart. Especially need serials with cliffhangers. Prefer western, historical with romantic interest and mysteries."

$ ◑ 🏆 **GUIDEPOSTS FOR KIDS,** P.O. Box 638, Chesterton IN 46304. Website:www.gp4k.com (for children, includes sample stories, games, interactives). **Contact:** Mary Lou Carney, editor-in-chief. Magazine: 8¼×10¾; 32 pages. "Value-centered bimonthly for kids 7-12 years old. Not preachy, concerned with contemporary issues." Bimonthly. Estab. 1990. Circ. 200,000.

● The magazine publishes many new writers but is primarily a market for writers who have already been published. *Guideposts for Kids* received Awards of Excellence from the Ed Press Association and also has received from SCBWI the Angel Awards.

Needs: Children's/juvenile: fantasy, historical (general), humor, mystery/suspense, holidays. "No 'adult as hero' or 'I-prayed-I-got' stories." Receives 200 unsolicited mss/month. Accepts 1-2 mss/issue; 6-10 mss/year. Recently published work by Beverly Patt and Lisa Harkrader. Length: 600-1,400 words; 1,300 words preferred. Publishes short shorts. Also publishes small amount of poetry. Sometimes comments on rejected mss; "only what shows promise."

How to Contact: Send complete ms with cover letter. Include estimated word count, Social Security number, phone number and SASE. Responds in 2 months. Send SASE for reply, return of ms or send disposable copy of ms. Accepts simultaneous submissions. Sample copy for $3.25. Guidelines for #10 SASE.

Payment/Terms: $250-600 and 2 contributor's copies; additional copies available. Pays on acceptance for all rights.

Advice: "We're looking for the good stuff. Fast-paced, well-crafted stories aimed at kids 8-12 years of age. Stories should reflect strong traditional values. Don't preach. This is not a Sunday School handout, but a good solid piece of fiction that reflects traditional values and morality. Build your story around a solid principle and let the reader gain insight by inference. Don't let adults solve problems. While adults can appear in stories, they can't give the characters life's answers. Don't make your kid protagonist grateful and awed by sage, adult advice. Be original. We want a good mix of fiction—contemporary, historical, fantasy, sci-fi, mystery—centered around things that interest and concern kids. A kid reader should be able to identify with the characters strongly enough to think. *'I know just how he feels!'* Create a plot with believable characters. Here's how it works: the story must tell what happens when someone the reader likes (character) reaches an important goal (climax) by overcoming obstacles (conflict). Let kids be kids. Your dialogue (and use plenty of it!) should reflect how the kids sound, think and feel. Avoid slang, but listen to how real kids talk before you try and write for them. Give your characters feelings and actions suitable for the 4th to 6th grader."

$ ☺ ☑ HARPER'S MAGAZINE, 666 Broadway, 11th Floor, New York NY 10012. (212)614-6500. Website: www.harpers.org (includes submission guidelines). **Editor:** Lewis H. Lapham. Magazine: 8 × 10¾; 80 pages; illustrations. Magazine for well-educated, widely read and socially concerned readers, college-aged and older, those active in political and community affairs. Monthly. Circ. 218,000.

● See the interview with *Harper's* editor Colin Harrison on page 361.

Needs: Contemporary and humor. Stories on contemporary life and its problems. Receives 600 unsolicited fiction mss/year. Accepts 12 mss/year. Recently published work by David Guterson, David Foster Wallace, Johnathan Franzen, Steven Millhauser, Lisa Roney, Rick Moody and Steven Dixon. Published new writers within the last year. First published David Foster Wallace. Length: 1,000-5,000 words.

How to Contact: Query to managing editor, or through agent. Responds in 6 weeks to queries.

Payment/Terms: Pays $500-2,000. Pays on acceptance for rights, which vary on each author materials and length. Sends galleys to author.

[N] $ ☑ HEMISPHERES, The Magazine of United Airlines, Pace Communications, 1301 Carolina St., Greensboro NC 27401. (336)378-6065. Fax: (336)378-8265. Website: www.hemispheresmagazine.com (includes mastheads, archived travel articles, information about Faux Faulkner and Imitation Hemingway contests). **Contact:** Lisa Fann, articles editor. Magazine: 8 × 10; 190 pages; 45 lb. paper; 120 lb. West Vaco cover; illustrations; photos. "*Hemispheres* is an inflight magazine that interprets 'inflight' to be a mode of delivery rather than an editorial genre. As such, *Hemispheres*' task is to engage, intrigue and entertain its primary readers—an international, culturally diverse group of affluent, educated professionals and executives who frequently travel for business and pleasure on United Airlines. The magazine offers a global perspective and a focus on topics that cross borders as often as the people reading the magazine. That places our emphasis on ideas, concepts, and culture rather than products. We present that perspective in a fresh, artful and sophisticated graphic environment. Monthly. Estab. 1992. Circ. 500,000.

● *Hemispheres* won 15 awards in 2000 alone for design, journalism, editorials and feature profiles. See the interview with *Hemispheres* articles editor Lisa Fann on page 366.

Needs: Ethnic/multicultural, historical, humor/satire, literary, mainstream, mystery/suspense, regional. Receives 5-10 unsolicited ms/month. Publishes 1 ms/issue; 12-14 mss/year. Publishes ms 4-6 months after acceptance. **Publishes 1 new writer/year.** Recently published work by Frederick Waterman, Nero Blanc and O'Neil DeNoux. Length: 1,000-3,500 words.

How to Contact: Send complete ms with cover letter. Include estimated word count, brief bio and list of publications. Responds in 2 months to queries and mss. Send disposable copy of ms or SASE for reply. Accepts multiple submissions. Sample copy for $7.50. Guidelines for SASE.

Payment/Terms: Varies by author. Pays by the word and in contributor's copies; additional copies $7.50. Buys first world rights. Sometimes sends galleys to author. Sponsors the Faux Faulkner and Imitation Hemingway competitions. Details on website.

insider report

Changing hats: novelist's editing fuels his fiction writing

Colin Harrison, the novelist, takes his table near the back of Noho Star Restaurant in downtown Manhattan. The table is wide enough to accommodate his working manuscript pages. He will spread them out, most of them loose-leaf or legal pad pages, scattering them across the table within sight of most any patron. It's his routine during the workday week, and says it will not change any time soon. It is Harrison's "writerly conditioning" to write during a typical two-hour lunch break, which is otherwise sandwiched by the nine-to-six time-frame of his demanding *other* job.

Colin Harrison

© Joyce Ravid

He enjoys Noho's lunch fare, but the restaurant is also a convenient two-minute walk from the *Harper's* magazine offices where Harrison, the deputy editor, changes hats to solicit, acquire, and edit some of the country's most cutting-edge short fiction and journalism. In his position of making such decisions for this highly influential magazine, Harrison must work steadily, with a level of concentration that attends to *Harper's* nonfiction or short stories at hand. Any inclination to dwell on his own fictional characters or plot twists in the novel-in-progress "stays at the restaurant or at home," he says, and rarely trickles into the day job.

Harrison sees this as a benefit to both occupations. "As a novelist, I have a couple of hours at midday to let out the wild creative juices and just let go, work on pushing the novel somewhere," he says. "I push quickly because of the fast-paced nature of my editorial job. It instills pacing. I'm so used to magazine deadlines, to the inescapable task of always facing someone's piece of journalism or short story. It's a fact that pages are just going to sit and sit if they're not 'gotten to,' whether it's editing or my novel writing."

At the restaurant, there's no set work strategy. Whatever Harrison has on hand he uses: "I can work between a laptop and sheets of paper. Whatever I pick up at the office and leave with. I don't have time to fiddle. And I don't have a plan for that day. I might revise, I might invent, or I might scribble notes. I do what needs to get done on that day. I sit down, order lunch, and get on with writing. I may be a little more organized at home, but not all the time." He encourages writers to take on an approach that works best for them, regardless of the opportunity. Yet there is a bottom line, he says, and it's not to let too much time slip away before a strict, self-imposed period of writing gets done.

A typical heavy week of work for Harrison, then, is to write at lunch three or four days a week and, at home, three nights a week from 10 p.m. to 1 a.m., and occasional weekend afternoons. "There are always adjustments, and a lot of times when this routine is juggled and often not even workable. But I don't dally too long before I'm doing some writing or researching."

Integrating his writing and editing

If his personal and public writer-based demands during the day aren't complex enough, Harrison's domestic life in Brooklyn, where he lives, makes his routine even more rare yet satisfying. He's married to bestselling novelist and memoirist, Kathryn Harrison. With three children, the household duties must be shared between the writers, and both Colin and Kathryn have always understood that their arrangements factor in time when each can work on a writing project. "Kathryn can generally work during the day; that's best for her," Harrison says. "So it doesn't present a real scheduling dilemma. If there's a conflict, we can simply work it out."

Their marriage, Harrison says, affords them the chance to confer with each other about their writing, but there's never pressure to do so. Their fiction, on the whole, is so aesthetically different that they've each carved their own path. "We don't collide out of any defensiveness or any big concern for what the other's doing," he says. The couple met in their 20s at the Iowa Writer's Workshop. Both now have published several novels, and in 2000 both published a new novel only a few months apart—Colin published *Afterburn* (Farrar, Strauss & Giroux), and Kathryn published *The Binding Chair* (Random House).

There's no doubt in Harrison's mind that constantly being surrounded at *Harper's* magazine by work from some of the finest fiction writers and journalists would help inspire any serious writer to pay attention to craft. "I'm really fortunate in that capacity," he says. "This is my work, to edit, but in front of me is the best writing by some of our best writers." Some of the writers he's worked with just in the last year include Francine Prose, Robert Stone, Ha Jin, Barbara Ehrenrich, David Guterson, David Foster Wallace, Bobbie Ann Mason, Annie Proulx, Bob Shacochis and Sebastian Junger.

And he recognizes the depth in which *Harper's* expansive journalism and essays play a role in his own thinking about the art of a story. "My editing of all these narrative pieces that come in keeps me tuned in to how important revision is, how important shaping and sculpting a story is, all these tools we need as fiction writers, or writers period. I'm lucky; my editorial work puts me on top of it and keeps me there."

Keeping on top of his fiction

Harrison's success has been elevated recently by his move to Farrar, Strauss & Giroux and an accompanying two-book and low seven-figure deal, complete also with heavy marketing and critical praise for *Afterburn*. The FS&G novel garnered a 100,000-copy first printing, two book club deals, an audio deal, five foreign-rights deals, and an eight-city U.S. tour.

While Harrison considers his third novel, *Manhattan Nocturne* (Crown Publishers), a decent break-out novel and one that helped pave the way for the new, two-book contract, he realized that as a novelist he couldn't become complacent and simply "write the same novel over." Still, he says, he faced these hard facts: he again wanted to use Manhattan as both a setting and eventual metaphor because of the exotically fast-paced and chaotic place it can be. His prose is not flashy but concise and poignant—tight sentences work the plot to a frenzied pace which mimics the embattled lives of his characters. So, these were core elements in *Manhattan Nocturne* and even his second novel, *Bodies Electric*. What could he do differently?

"Since I have no problem with readers identifying my stories as thrillers, I was confident I was going to 'thrill,' as one of my heroes, Joseph Conrad, also thrilled. I wanted to get more deeply into structure, and then character, and then plot," he says. "First it was structure. Definitely. Very crucial to me. *Nocturne* is in a strict first person. I wanted to mix it up more in the next novel. So in *Afterburn*, I torqued the structure. *Afterburn* uses three third-person point-of-view narratives that interweave. I found these intersecting points-of-view really deepened the suspense. It turned out to be a leap for the better."

What effectively happened as well with this new structure, he says, is that he began to sharpen each chapter as a scene. Yet as each chapter/scene became very different, or used a different point of view, the chapters curiously began to have a collective feel about them. "There were big differences between chapters, but the interweaving and intersecting gave them a simultaneous ring. The back-and-forth points of view became layered, and the different chapters gelled. I was shooting for that."

Harrison approaches each novel "organically at first," he says. He outlines sporadically, with some gleaning of where a plot or character might go. He relies upon whatever happens next, though, to guide him through a scene or chapter. "I do pay attention to a larger outline, but I put my emphasis on just letting go, seeing where the narrative leads. Too much list-making can be destructive; you wind up not finding out surprising things that can happen if you don't leave yourself open."

If Harrison's recent success seems like a natural ascension into major publishing respectability, it has come with a price and a "fierce determination," he says. Years ago, in his 20s, he decided to work hard at writing and publishing, and to not make excuses for failing. His apprenticeship between the ages of 21-25 entailed writing a first novel that he wound up stuffing in a drawer for eternity, he says. "I thought it was okay, but once I finished I knew it was awful. It's a gift that it will never be published."

At least it was a stepping stone to crafting his first published novel, *Break and Enter*. That novel presented an even clearer picture of certain subject matter that fascinated Harrison enough to integrate into future novels. Many of his characters and storylines revolve around the calamities and explicitly brutal consequences that human deception, greed, and lovelessness foster "when let on the loose," he says. His characters are "high stakes players" and pay equally for their valor or their greed. It's Harrison's exploration of our primarily urban culture, whose core is sadly driven by money and materialism, he says, and he wants to take actions and characterizations to extremes.

The importance of being tenacious

Similarly, he suggests that writers challenge themselves and not play it safe. "I don't like easy stories with easy-going characters. Stories should be concerned with consequences; a story will deal with characters' choices. Since that's the case, I don't want my characters' choices or consequences to be predictable."

The publication of *Break and Enter* was an original move itself. After one agent failed to sell the novel, Harrison asked another agent to take it on; he was turned down. A third agent took it on and Harrison and the agent sold it to Crown Publishers immediately—in just three days. "Crown bought it that quickly. You never know what's going to happen."

As for the earlier rejections of *Break and Enter*, they didn't faze Harrison: "You have to be persistent and not afraid. Thick-skinned," he urges. "You have to go on if you encounter a 'No, we can't publish it' response. You have to have a huge desire, more than you might imagine."

Some film industry interest has been expressed in Harrison's novels, but that doesn't change his goals or dissuade him from writing literary stories. His novels *Break and Enter* and *Manhattan*

Nocturne are currently under option, while *Bodies Electric* is being shopped around Hollywood and the newest, *Afterburn*, has yet to be optioned. Yet Harrison remains clear-eyed and blunt about what it means to be a writer, and what considerations a would-be writer should have before "taking the plunge," as he says.

"I'd truthfully say this: if you don't need to write, don't do it. You won't drive yourself to do as well as you can. That's a fact. Think twice. And if you need to, do it. Don't complain about it—the other job, the time, the rejections. If you're in it, you're in it. You don't have to be."

If anything, Harrison never veers from perhaps the most practical reality of all and his most emphatic point to any writer: "The world is not waiting for your book. It's really a minefield. It's just not all tulips. You have to study the field you're working in, know it extremely well, and you have to desire it above all. Otherwise, why bother?"

—*Jeff Hillard*

Advice: "In our information-saturated, hyperlinked age, fiction is often viewed as a bit superfluous. It doesn't solve whatever problem we have this second, and so is often relegated to a position of entertainment—something enjoyable to be fit in around the more important aspects of life. But good fiction has much longer lasting value—it should entertain, certainly, but it should also cause us to reconsider, to look at things from another perspective, to mull over what's really important. It should encourage us to explore with new eyes the mysteries of life."

☑ $ ◎ **HIGHLIGHTS FOR CHILDREN**, 803 Church St., Honesdale PA 18431. (570)253-1080. Editor: Kent L. Brown, Jr. **Contact:** Marileta Robinson, senior editor. Magazine: 8½×11; 42 pages; uncoated paper; coated cover stock; illustrations; photos. Monthly. Circ. 2.8 million. Highlights publishes "general interest for children between the ages of 2 and 12. Our philosophy is 'fun with a purpose.' "
● *Highlights* is very supportive of writers. The magazine sponsors a contest and a workshop each year at Chautauqua (New York). Several authors published in *Highlights* have received SCBWI Magazine Merit Awards. *Highlights* ranked #36 on the *Writer's Digest*'s Fiction 50 list of top markets for fiction writers.
Needs: Juvenile (ages 2-12). Unusual stories appealing to both girls and boys; stories with good characterization, strong emotional appeal, vivid, full of action. "Begin with action rather than description, have strong plot, believable setting, suspense from start to finish." Length: 400-900 words. "We also need easy stories for very young readers (100-400 words)." No war, crime or violence. Receives 600-800 unsolicited fiction mss/month. Accepts 6-7 mss/issue. Also publishes rebus (picture) stories of 125 words or under for the 3- to 7-year-old child. **Publishes 30 new writers/year.** Recently published work by Susan Campbell Bartoletti, Beverly J. Letchworth, Cheryl Fusco Johnson, Rushkin Bond and James M. Janik. Comments on rejected mss occasionally, "especially when editors see possibilities in story."
How to Contact: Send complete ms with SASE and include a rough word count and cover letter "with any previous acceptances by our magazine; any other published work anywhere." Accepts multiple submissions. Responds in 2 months. Guidelines with SASE.
Payment/Terms: Pays 14¢ and up/word. Pays on acceptance for all rights. Sends galleys to author.
Advice: "We accept a story on its merit whether written by an unpublished or an experienced writer. Mss are rejected because of poor writing, lack of plot, trite or worn-out plot, or poor characterization. Children *like* stories and learn about life from stories. Children learn to become lifelong fiction readers by enjoying stories. Feel passion for your subject. Create vivid images. Write a child-centered story; leave adults in the background."

$ ◎ ▼ **ALFRED HITCHCOCK'S MYSTERY MAGAZINE**, Dell Magazines, 475 Park Ave. S., New York NY 10016. (212)686-7188. Website: www.mysterypages.com (includes guidelines, story excerpts, subscription forms and logic puzzles). **Contact:** Cathleen Jordan, editor. Mystery fiction magazine: 5¼×8⅜; 144 pages; 28 lb. newsprint paper; 60 lb. machine-/coated cover stock; illustrations; photos. Published 11 times/year, including 1 double issue. Estab. 1956. Circ. 615,000 readers.
● Stories published in *Alfred Hitchcock's Mystery Magazine* have won Edgar Awards for "Best Mystery Story of the Year," Shamus Awards for "Best Private Eye Story of the Year" and Robert L. Fish Awards for "Best First Mystery Short Story of the Year." *Alfred Hitchcock's Mystery Magazine* ranked #13 on the *Writer's Digest* Fiction 50 list of top markets for fiction writers.

Needs: Mystery and detection (amateur sleuth, private eye, police procedural, suspense, etc.). No sensationalism. Number of mss/issue varies with length of mss. Length: up to 14,000 words. Also publishes short shorts. Recently published work by Walter Satterthwait, Joseph Hansen, Rob Kantner and Ann Ripley.
How to Contact: Send complete ms and SASE. Responds in 2 months. Guidelines for SASE. Sample issue for $5.
Payment/Terms: Pays 8¢/word. Pays on acceptance.

☑ $ ▱ ◎ **HOME TIMES,** Neighbor News, Inc., 3676 Collin Dr. #16, West Palm Beach FL 33406. (561)439-3509. **Contact:** Dennis Lombard, editor. Newspaper: tabloid; 24 pages; newsprint; illustrations; photos. "Conservative news, views, fiction, poetry, sold to general public." Weekly. Estab. 1990. Circ. 5,000.
Needs: Adventure, historical (general), humor/satire, literary, mainstream, religious/inspirational, sports. No romance. "All fiction needs to be related to the publication's focus on current events and conservative perspective—we feel you must examine a sample issue because *Home Times* is *different*." Nothing "preachy or doctrinal, but Biblical worldview needed." Receives 40 unsolicited mss/month. Accepts 2-4 mss/issue. Publishes ms 1-9 months after acceptance. **Publishes 10-15 new writers/year.** Recently published work by Cal Thomas, Chuck Colson, Armstrong Williams and Bruce Bartlett. Length: 500-800 words; average length: 700 words.
How to Contact: Send complete ms with cover letter including word count. "Absolutely no queries." Include in cover letter "one to two sentences on what the piece is and who you are." Responds in 1 month to mss. SASE. Accepts simultaneous and reprint submissions. Sample current issue for $3. Guidelines for #10 SASE.
Payment/Terms: Pays $5-50 for one-time rights.
Advice: "We are particularly interested in "Guidepost"-like stories of hope and faith. We are very open to new writers, but read our newspaper—get the drift of our rather unusual conservative, pro-Christian, but non-religious content. Looks for "creative nonfiction on historical and issues subjects." Send $12 for a writer's subscription (12 current issues)."

$ ▱ **HUMPTY DUMPTY'S MAGAZINE,** Children's Better Health Institute, Box 567, 1100 Waterway Blvd., Indianapolis IN 46206. (317)636-8881. Fax: (317)684-8094. Website: www.satevepost.org/kidsonline. **Contact:** Nancy S. Axelrad, editor. Magazine: 7⅝×10⅛; 36 pages; 35 lb. paper; coated cover; illustrations; some photos. Children's magazine "seeking to encourage children, ages 4-6, in healthy lifestyle habits, especially good nutrition and fitness." Publishes 8 issues/year.
● The Children's Better Health Institute also publishes *Children's Digest, Children's Playmate, Jack and Jill* and *Turtle,* also listed in this section.
Needs: Juvenile health-related material and material of a more general nature. No inanimate talking objects, animal stories and science fiction. Wants more "health and fitness stories with a positive slant." Rhyming stories should flow easily with no contrived rhymes. Receives 100-200 unsolicited mss/month. Accepts 2-3 mss/issue. Publishes 1-2 unpublished writers/year. Length: 300 words maximum.
How to Contact: Send complete ms with SASE. No queries. Responds in 3 months. Sample copy for $1.75. Editorial guidelines for SASE.
Payment/Terms: Pays up to 22¢/word for stories plus 10 contributor's copies. Pays on publication for all rights. (One-time book rights returned when requested for specific publication.)
Advice: "In contemporary stories, characters should be up-to-date, with realistic dialogue. We're looking for health-related stories with unusual twists or surprise endings. We want to avoid stories and poems that 'preach.' We try to present the health material in a positive way, utilizing a light humorous approach wherever possible." Most rejected mss "are too wordy or not age appropriate."

🅽 $ **HUSTLER BUSTY BEAUTIES,** HG Publications, Inc., 8484 Wilshire Blvd., Suite 900, Beverly Hills CA 90211. (323)651-5400. **Contact:** N. Morgen Hagen, editor. Magazine: 8×11; 100 pages; 60 lb. paper; 80 lb. cover; illustrations; photos. "Adult entertainment and reading centered around large-breasted women for an over-18 audience, mostly male." Published 13 times/year. Estab. 1988. Circ. 150,000.
Needs: Adventure, erotica, fantasy, mystery/suspense. All must have erotic theme. Receives 25 unsolicited fiction mss/month. Accepts 1 ms/issue; 6-12 mss/year. Publishes mss 3-6 months after acceptance. Published work by Mike Dillon and H.H. Morris. Length: 1,000-2,000 words; 1,600 words preferred.
How to Contact: Query first. Then send complete ms with cover letter. Responds in 2 weeks to queries; 1 month to mss. SASE. Sample copy for $5. Guidelines free.
Payment/Terms: Pays $350-500 (fiction) and $50 (erotic letters). Pays on publication for all rights.
Advice: Looks for "1. plausible plot, well-defined characters, literary ingenuity; 2. hot sex scenes; 3. readable, coherent, grammatically sound prose."

☑ $ ▱ ◎ ▯ **IN TOUCH FOR MEN,** 13122 Saticoy St., North Hollywood CA 91605-3402. (800)637-0101. Fax: (818)764-2307. E-mail: info@intouchformen.com. Website: www.intouchformen.com (includes a retrospective of all back issues, hyperfiction, magazine and video sales sections, and other things of interest to our readers). **Contact:** Alan W. Mills, editor. Magazine: 8×10¾; 100 pages; glossy paper; coated cover; illustra-

insider report

The sky's the limit for fiction in *Hemispheres* magazine

Lisa Fann

With the number of paperback novels sold in airport gift shops, it would seem natural that a magazine published especially for airline passengers would prominently feature fiction. Passengers obviously want a diversion to take their minds off the somewhat tedious task of flying to their next destination. Yet many of the inflight magazines found in the back pocket of each airline seat either bury their fiction in a plethora of travel-related articles or don't publish fiction at all. *Hemispheres* magazine, the award-winning inflight publication for United Airlines, is looking to change all that, using fiction as a way to differentiate themselves in the market.

"'Inflight,' as we see it, is a means of distribution rather than an editorial genre," says Lisa Fann, articles editor at *Hemispheres*, who has been with the magazine since its inception in 1992. "*Hemispheres* is a magazine that just happens to be distributed on a plane. And there are advantages to this. Sitting on an airplane is a wonderful time to slow down and think about life. Because of this, *Hemispheres* has always been more about ideas than things, and fiction is an important part of our mix of articles." Due to popular demand, fiction pieces have recently been taking up more space in the magazine. "It has been exciting for me to see the large numbers of letters we receive complimenting the stories and asking for more," Fann says. "Fiction is one of the most popular sections we run. In response to this, we have recently decided to commit to one or two short stories an issue."

Fiction in *Hemispheres* typically runs from 1,500 to 4,000 words, and speaks mainly to its core audience of well-educated, affluent, well-traveled business professionals in their 40s from all parts of the world. But because of the distribution of the magazine—making it available to every passenger who flies on United Airlines—fiction published in *Hemispheres* must be suitable for a wide age-range of readers. And just because readers are sitting on a plane taking them to a new destination doesn't mean that all stories must focus on characters who are traveling.

"Since *Hemispheres* is a travel magazine, I am particularly drawn to stories with an evocative sense of place," Fann says. "Stories [should] give insight into another culture and the way human strengths and weaknesses play out in that particular context—universal themes in a specific setting. But the stories don't have to have that cultural angle. Our favorite stories are thought provoking, or offer a fresh vision of the world, or are playful and employ sophisticated word play and use of language."

Hemispheres has won a number of awards in its brief eight-year history, including the honor of being named the United States' best monthly travel magazine for two years in a row by the Society of American Travel Writers. It is the only inflight magazine to have won a James Beard

Culinary award for journalism (over magazines such as *Saveur* and *GQ*), and recently won a Best Single-Topic Column honor from the National Headliner Awards, beating out such stalwarts as *Newsweek* magazine.

The editors of *Hemispheres* want to expand their tradition of publishing high-level, award-winning writing into the fiction pages of the magazine, so run-of-the-mill stories just won't do. *Hemispheres* seeks stories that stir the soul and engage readers to think. And because *Hemispheres* is an inflight magazine, stories involving air disasters such as plane crashes or hijackings are strictly forbidden. Fann explains how a fiction piece published in *Hemispheres* needs to be more than just a nice little story to entertain weary business travelers on cross-country flights: "Novelist Alice Hoffman said, 'I have always believed that it is in fiction that the deepest, most soul-searching truths can be found.' Because fiction is not restrained by sticking to the facts, it can more easily delve into the core of truth, the reality underneath everyday reality. It is an agile tool with which to explore the human condition because it engages our hearts and creativity in a way that nonfiction can't."

While the editors at *Hemispheres* prefer to receive material from established writers, they are very open to hearing from talented, unpublished writers. But in the piles of unsolicited submissions that come across the desks of Fann and Senior Editor Selby Bateman, there are few stories that reach the sophistication and quality *Hemispheres* requires. Many stories are rejected because they contain poorly thought-out, hackneyed plots and one-dimensional characters, or because they're not appropriate for the audience that *Hemispheres* serves. Writers must familiarize themselves with *Hemispheres* before submitting their work to make sure their stories will fit the magazine's sensibility. A good way to get to know *Hemispheres*, if you're not taking a United Airlines flight anytime soon, is to visit the website at www.hemispheresmagazine .com. The website is more than just an online version of the print product. "Our theory behind the website is *Hemispheres* as a resource rather than simply a digital version," Fann says. "You can type in a location and access all the articles we've published about that place. We also run some of the fiction stories from the print magazine as well as information on and past winners of the Faux Faulkner and Imitation Hemingway contests."

Distilling the philosophy of the *Hemispheres* editorial staff, Fann says, "Most of all, we want fiction that involves our readers, immerses them emotionally and intellectually. We don't require happy endings, but neither do we seek tales of dark despair. Remember that we circulate globally, and we are looking for writers, in English, from all over the world."

—*Cynthia Laufenberg*

---

tions; photos. "*In Touch* is a gay adult publication which focuses on youth and takes a lighthearted approach to sexuality. We publish erotic fiction which portrays a positive view of homosexuality. We also publish two other magazines, *Indulge* and *Blackmale*." Monthly. Estab. 1973. Circ. 70,000.

● *In Touch for Men* has had eleven stories published in *Fiction 3: Best Gay Erotica* in 2000.

Needs: Confession, gay erotica, romance (contemporary, historical). All characters must be over 18 years old. Stories must have an explicit erotic content. No heterosexual or internalized homophobic fiction. Accepts 7 mss/month; 80 mss/year. Publishes ms 6 months after acceptance. **Publishes 20 new writers/year.** Recently published work by Barry Alexander, L.M. Ross, Roddy Martin and Derek Adams. Length: up to 3,500 words maximum; average length: 2,500 words. Sometimes comments on rejected mss and recommends other markets.

How to Contact: Send complete ms with cover letter, name, address and Social Security number. Accepts queries and mss by e-mail and fax (mss by permission only). Responds in 2 weeks to queries; 2 months to mss. SASE. Accepts simultaneous, multiple and reprint submissions, if from local publication. Accepts disk submissions (call before sending by modem). Sample copy for $6.95. Guidelines free. Reviews novels and short story collections.

Payment/Terms: Pays $25-75 (except on rare occasions for a longer piece). Pays on publication for one-time rights.

Advice: Publishes "primarily erotic material geared toward gay men. We sometimes run nonfiction or features about gay issues. I personally prefer (and accept) manuscripts that are not only erotic/hardcore, but show a developed story, plot and a concise ending (as opposed to just sexual vignettes that basically lead nowhere). If it has a little romance, too, that's even better. Emphasis still on the erotic, though. We now only use 'safe sex' depictions in fiction, hoping that it will prompt people to act responsibly. We have a new interest in experimental fiction as long as it does not violate the standards of the homoerotic genre. All fiction must conform to the basic rules of the genre. Beyond that, we look for inventive use of language, unique content, exciting themes and, on occasion, experimental structures or subversive issues. If you're writing for a genre, know that genre, but don't be afraid to twist things around just enough to stand out from the crowd. Our website is becoming increasingly important to us. We have our eyes open for interesting hyperfiction because we want people to keep returning to our site, hoping that they might subscribe to the magazine."

$ ⬛ ◎ INDIA CURRENTS, The Complete Indian American Magazine, Box 21285, San Jose CA 95151. (408)274-6966. Fax: (408)274-2733. **Contact:** Vandana Kumar, managing editor. E-mail: editor@indiacurrents.com. Magazine: 8½×11; 104 pages; newsprint paper; illustrations; photos. "The arts and culture of India as seen in America for Indians and non-Indians with a common interest in India." Monthly. Estab. 1987. Circ. 25,000.
Needs: All Indian content: contemporary, ethnic, feminist, historical (general), humor/satire, literary, mainstream, regional, religious/inspirational, romance, translations (from Indian languages). "We seek material with insight into Indian culture, American culture and the crossing from one to another." Receives 12 unsolicited mss/month. Accepts 1 ms/issue; 12 mss/year. Publishes ms 2-6 months after acceptance. **Published new writers within the last year.** Published work by Chitra Divakaruni, Jyotsna Sreenivasan and Rajini Srikanth. Length: 2,000 words.
How to Contact: Send complete ms with cover letter and clips of published work. Responds in 3 months to mss. SASE. Accepts simultaneous and reprint submissions. Accepts electronic submissions. Sample copy for $3.
Payment/Terms: Pays $50/1,000 words. Pays on publication for one-time rights (print and website).
Advice: "Story must be related to India and subcontinent in some meaningful way. The best stories are those which document some deep transformation as a result of an Indian experience, or those which show the humanity of Indians."

N ❋ ✔ ⬇ INDIAN LIFE MAGAZINE, Indian Life Ministries, P.O. Box 3765, RPO, Red Wood Center, Station B, Winnipeg, Manitoba R2W 3R6 Canada. (204)661-9333 or (800)665-9275 in Canada only. Fax: (204)661-3982. E-mail: jim.editor@indianlife.org. Website: www.indianlife.org. **Contact:** Jim Uttley, editor. Newspaper: 11×17 Tabloid; 24 pages; newsprint paper and cover stock; illustrations; full cover; photos. A nondenominational Christian newspaper written and read mostly by Native Americans. Bimonthly. Estab. 1979. Circ. 32,000.
  • *Indian Life Magazine* has won several awards for "Higher Goals in Christian Journalism" and "Excellence" from the Evangelical Press Association. The magazine also won awards from the Native American Press Association.
Needs: Contemporary stories of Native Americans in everyday life. Ethnic (Indian), historical (general), juvenile, religious/inspirational, young adult/teen, native testimonies, bible teaching articles. No erotic or stories of Native American spirituality. Upcoming themes: "TV and its effect on Native culture" and "Prisons, and prison life." **Publishes 4 new writers/year.** Recently published work by Crying Wind and Helen Lieschid. Length: 1,000-1,200 words average.
How to Contact: Query letter preferred. Accepts submissions by e-mail, fax and disk. Accepts simultaneous submissions. Responds in 1 month to queries. $2.50 or SASE ("U.S. stamps no good up here"). Sample copy and guidelines for $2.50 and 8½×11 SAE. Guidelines for $2.50 and #10 SAE.
Advice: "Keep it simple with an Indian viewpoint at about a ninth grade reading level. Read story out loud. Have someone else read it to you. If it doesn't come across smoothly and naturally, it needs work."

⊕ $◎ IRELAND'S OWN, 1 North Main St., Wexford, Ireland. **Contact:** Gerry Breen and Margaret Galvin, editors. Weekly. Circ. 50,000. Publishes 2 stories/issue. "*Ireland's Own* is a homey family-oriented weekly magazine with a story emphasis on the traditional values of Irish society. Short stories must be written in a straightforward nonexperimental manner with an Irish orientation." Length: 1,800-2,000 words. Pays £40-50 on publication. "Study and know the magazine's requirements, orientation and target market. Guidelines and copies sent out on request."

$⬛◎ JACK AND JILL, The Children's Better Health Institute, P.O. Box 567, 1100 Waterway Blvd., Indianapolis IN 46206. (317)636-8881. **Contact:** Daniel Lee, editor. Children's magazine of articles, stories and activities, many with a health, safety, exercise or nutritional-oriented theme, ages 7-10 years. Monthly except January/February, April/May, July/August, October/November. Estab. 1938. Circ. 360,000.
  • The Children's Better Health Institute also publishes *Children's Digest, Children's Playmate, Humpty Dumpty* and *Turtle*, listed in this section.

Needs: Science fiction, mystery, sports, adventure, historical fiction and humor. Health-related stories with a subtle lesson. Published new writers within the last year. Buys 30-35 mss/year. Length: 500-800 words.
How to Contact: Send complete ms with SASE. Responds in 3 months to mss. Sample copy for $1.75. Guidelines for SASE.
Payment/Terms: Pays up to 20¢/word on publication for all rights.
Advice: "Try to present health material in a positive—not a negative—light. Use humor and a light approach wherever possible without minimizing the seriousness of the subject. We need more humor and adventure stories."

N $ ⊘ JIVE, BLACK CONFESSIONS, BLACK ROMANCE, BRONZE THRILLS, BLACK SE-CRETS, TRUE BLACK EXPERIENCE, Sterling/Mcfadden, 233 Park Ave. S., Fifth Floor, New York NY 10003. (212)780-3500. **Contact:** Janet Pastaina, editor. Magazine: 8½×11; 72 pages; newsprint paper; glossy cover; 8×10 photographs. "We publish stories that are romantic and have romantic lovemaking scenes in them. Our audience is basically young. However, we have a significant audience base of housewives. The age range is from 18-49." Bimonthly (*Jive* and *Black Romance* in odd-numbered months; *Black Confessions* and *Bronze Thrills* in even-numbered months). 6 issues per year. Estab. 1962. Circ. 100,000.
Needs: Confession, romance (contemporary, young adult). No "stories that are stereotypical to black people, ones that do not follow the basic rules of writing, or ones that are too graphic in content and lack a romantic element." Receives 20 or more unsolicited fiction mss/month. Accepts 6 mss/issue (2 issues/month); 144 mss/year. Publishes ms an average of 2-3 months after acceptance. Published work by Linda Smith; published new writers within the last year. Length: 5,000-5,800 words.
How to Contact: Query with clips of published work or send complete ms with cover letter. "A cover letter should include an author's bio and what he or she proposes to do. Of course, address and phone number." Responds in 2 months. SASE. Sample copy for 9×12 SAE and 5 first-class stamps; guidelines for #10 SAE and 2 first-class stamps.
Payment/Terms: Pays $100-125. Pays on publication for all rights.
Advice: "Our five magazines are a great starting point for new writers. We accept work from beginners as well as established writers. Please study and research black culture and lifestyles if you are not a black writer. Stereotypical stories are not acceptable. Set the stories all over the world and all over the USA—not just down south. We are not looking for 'the runaway who gets turned out by a sweet-talking pimp' stories. We are looking for stories about all types of female characters. Any writer should not be afraid to communicate with us if he or she is having some difficulty with writing a story. We are available to help at any stage of the submission process. We are buying all of our work from freelance writers."

$ ⊘ KIDZ CH@T, 8121 Hamilton Ave., Cincinnati OH 45231-2396. (513)931-4050. **Editor:** Gary Thacker. Magazine (Sunday school take-home paper): 5⅜×8⅜; 8 pages; Choctaw matte 45 lb. paper; illustrations; photos. "*Kidz Ch@t* correlates with Standard Publishing's Middler Sunday school curriculum. Features tie into the theme of the Sunday school lesson each week." Weekly. Estab. 1999. Circ. 55,000.
   • *Kidz Ch@t* is not accepting unsolicited mss at this time.

N ♥ A ✿ LADIES' HOME JOURNAL, Published by Meredith Corporation, 125 Park Ave., 20th Floor, New York NY 10017. (212)557-6600. **Editor-in-Chief:** Myrna Blyth. **Contact:** Shana Aborn, books/fiction editor. Managing Editor: Carolyn Noyes. Magazine: 190 pages; 34-38 lb. coated paper; 65 lb. coated cover; illustrations; photos.
   • *Ladies' Home Journal* has won several awards for journalism.
Needs: Book mss and short stories, *accepted only through an agent*. Return of unsolicited material cannot be guaranteed. Published work by Fay Weldon, Anita Shreve, Jane Shapiro and Anne Rivers Siddons. Length: approximately 2,000-2,500 words.
How to Contact: Send complete ms with cover letter (credits). Accepts simultaneous submissions. Publishes ms 4-12 months after acceptance.
Payment/Terms: Acquires First North American rights.
Advice: "Our readers like stories, especially those that have emotional impact. Stories about relationships between people—husband/wife—mother/son—seem to be subjects that can be explored effectively in short stories. Our readers' mail and surveys attest to this fact: Readers enjoy our fiction and are most keenly tuned to stories dealing with children. Fiction today is stronger than ever. Beginners can be optimistic; if they have talent, I do believe that talent will be discovered. It is best to read the magazine before submitting."

N ⊕ $ THE LADY, 39-40 Bedford St., Strand, London WC2E 9ER England. Phone: (0207)379 4717. **Contact:** Beverly Davies. Magazine. Weekly. Estab. 1885. Circ. 42,000.
Needs: Family saga, feminist, historical, literary, mainstream, mystery/suspense (cozy), regional, romance (contemporary, gothic, historical, Regency, romantic suspense). Buys 1 ms/issue. Length: 2,000 words. Also publishes poetry.
How to Contact: Send complete ms with cover letter. Accepts submissions by fax. Include estimated word count. Responds in 1 month to queries, 3 months to mss. SASE. Accepts multiple submissions.

Payment/Terms: Pays variable rate and 1 contributor's copy. Buys first British serial rights.

$ ◑ ◎ ▼ LADYBUG, The Cricket Magazine Group, P.O. Box 300, Peru IL 61354. (815)224-6656. **Contact:** Marianne Carus, editor-in-chief. Editor: Paula Morrow. Magazine: 8 × 10; 36 pages plus 4-page pullout section; illustrations. "*Ladybug* publishes original stories and poems by the world's best children's authors. For young children, ages 2-6." Monthly. Estab. 1990. Circ. 128,000.

 • *Ladybug* was ranked #23 on the *Writer's Digest*'s Fiction 50 list of top markets for fiction writers. *Ladybug* has received the Parents Choice Award; the Golden Lamp Honor Award and the Golden Lamp Award from Ed Press; and Magazine Merit awards from the Society of Children's Book Writers and Illustrators.

Needs: Fantasy (children's), folk tales, juvenile, picture stories, preschool, read-out-loud stories and realistic fiction. Length: 300-750 words preferred.

How to Contact: Send complete ms with cover letter. Include word count on ms (do not count title). Responds in 3 months. SASE. Accepts reprints are. Guidelines for SASE. Sample copy for $5. For guidelines *and* sample send 9 × 12 SAE (no stamps required) and $5.

Payment/Terms: Pays up to 25¢/word (less for reprints). Pays on publication for first publication rights or second serial (reprint) rights. For recurring features, pays flat fee and copyright becomes property of The Cricket Magazine Group.

Advice: Looks for "well-written stories for preschoolers: age-appropriate, not condescending. We look for rich, evocative language and sense of joy or wonder."

$ ◯ ◎ ▼ LIGUORIAN, "A Leading Catholic Magazine," Liguori Publications, 1 Liguori Dr., Liguori MO 63057-9998. (800)464-2555. Fax: (800)325-9526. E-mail: aweinert@liguori.org. Website: www.liguori.org (*Liguorian* magazine is part of Liguori Publications website. It includes condensed articles from present issue, writer's guidelines and subscription information.) **Contact:** Fr. Allan Weinert, CSSR, editor-in-chief. Magazine: 5 × 8½; 64 pages; b&w illustrations; photos. "*Liguorian* is a general interest magazine firmly committed to orthodox Catholic Christianity. Our effort is to inform and inspire, making spirituality accessible to our readers and assisting them in those matters most important to them—their families, their work, their own personal growth—as they live out their life in an ever-changing world." Monthly. Estab. 1913. Circ. 330,000.

 • *Liguorian* received Catholic Press Association awards for 2000 including Second Place: General Excellence (including stories); and First Place: Best Short Story ("The Receiving Blanket," by Amy Viets).

Needs: Religious/inspirational, young adult and senior citizen/retirement (with moral Christian thrust), spiritual. "Stories submitted to *Liguorian* must have as their goal the lifting up of the reader to a higher Christian view of values and goals. We are not interested in contemporary works that lack purpose or are of questionable moral value." Receives approximately 25 unsolicited fiction mss/month. Accepts 12 mss/year. **Publishes 5-6 new writers/year.** Recently published work by Darlene Takarsh, Mary Beth Teymaster and Maeve Mullen Ellis. Length: 1,500-2,000 words preferred. Also publishes short shorts. Occasionally comments on rejected mss "if we feel the author is capable of giving us something we need even though this story did not suit us."

How to Contact: Send complete ms with SASE. Accepts disk submissions compatible with IBM, using a WordPerfect 5.1 program; prefers hard copy with disk submission. Accepts submissions by e-mail and fax. Responds in 3 months to mss. Sample copy and guidelines for #10 SASE.

Payment/Terms: Pays 10-12¢/word and 5 contributor's copies. Pays on acceptance for all rights. Offers 50% kill fee for assigned mss not published.

Advice: "First read several issues containing short stories. We look for originality and creative input in each story we read. Since most editors must wade through mounds of manuscripts each month, consideration for the editor requires that the market be studied, the manuscript be carefully presented and polished before submitting. Our publication uses only one story a month. Compare this with the 25 or more we receive over the transom each month. Also, many fiction mss are written without a specific goal or thrust, i.e., an interesting incident that goes nowhere is *not a story*. We believe fiction is a highly effective mode for transmitting the Christian message and also provides a good balance in an unusually heavy issue."

▨ LILITH MAGAZINE, The Independent Jewish Women's Magazine, 250 W. 57th St., Suite 2432, New York NY 10107. (212)757-0818. E-mail: lilithmag@aol.com. Editor: Susan Weidman Schneider. **Contact:** Yona Zeldis, fiction editor. Magazine: 48 pages; 80 lb. cover; b&w illustrations; b&w and color photos. Publishes work relating to Jewish feminism, for Jewish feminists, feminists and Jewish households. Quarterly. Estab. 1976. Circ. 25,000.

Needs: Ethnic, feminist, lesbian, literary, prose poem, religious/inspirational, spiritual, translation, young adult. "Nothing that does not in any way relate to Jews, women or Jewish women." Receives 15 unsolicited mss/month. Accepts 1 ms/issue; 4 mss/year. Publishes ms up to 1 year after acceptance. Published work by Lesléa Newman, Marge Piercy and Gloria Goldreich. Publishes short shorts.

How to Contact: Send complete ms with cover letter, which should include a 2-line bio. Responds in 2 months to queries; 6 months to mss. SASE. Accepts simultaneous and reprint submissions but must be indicated in cover letter. Sample copy for $6. Writer's guidelines for #10 SASE. Reviews novels and short story collections. Send books to Susan Weidman Schneider.
Payment/Terms: Varies. Acquires first rights.
Advice: "Read the magazine to be familiar with the kinds of material we publish."

☑ $ ◉ ◎ **LIVE,** Assemblies of God, 1445 Boonville, Springfield MO 65802-1894. (417)862-2781. Fax: (417)862-6059. E-mail: rl-live@gph.org. Website: www.radiantlife.org (includes writer's guidelines, names of editors, short fiction and non-fiction and devotionals). **Contact:** Paul W. Smith, editor. "A take-home story paper distributed weekly in young adult/adult Sunday school classes. *Live* is a story paper primarily. Stories in both fiction and narrative style are welcome. Poems, first-person anecdotes and humor are used as fillers. The purpose of *Live* is to present in short story form realistic characters who utilize biblical principles. We hope to challenge readers to take risks for God and to resolve their problems scripturally." Weekly. Circ. 115,000.
Needs: Religious/inspirational prose, poem and spiritual. "Inner city, ethnic, racial settings." No controversial stories about such subjects as feminism, war or capital punishment. Accepts 2 mss/issue. **Publishes 75-100 new writers/year.** Recently published work by Carrie Darlington, Chris Williams, Melodie Wright and Dorothy B. Kidney. Length: 500-1,700 words.
How to Contact: Send complete ms. Accepts disk submissions. Accepts queries by e-mail and fax. Social Security number and word count must be included. Accepts simultaneous submissions. Responds in 6 weeks. Sample copy and guidelines for SASE.
Payment/Terms: Pays 10¢/word (first rights); 7¢/word (second rights). Pays on acceptance.
Advice: "Study our publication and write good, inspirational true to life or fiction stories that will encourage people to become all they can be as Christians. Stories should go somewhere! Action, not just thought—life; interaction, not just insights. Heroes and heroines, suspense and conflict. Avoid simplistic, pietistic conclusions, preachy, critical or moralizing. We don't accept science or Bible fiction. Stories should be encouraging, challenging, humorous. Even problem-centered stories should be upbeat." Reserves the right to change titles, abbreviate length and clarify flashbacks for publication.

☑ $ ◉ ☿ **MAGAZINE OF FANTASY & SCIENCE FICTION,** P.O. Box 1806, New York NY 10159-1806. Phone/fax: (212)982-2676. E-mail: gordonfsf@aol.com. Website: www.fsfmag.com or www.sfsite.com/fsf (includes writer's guidelines, letter column, subscription information, nonfiction features, current issue, information on back issues and links). **Contact:** Gordon Van Gelder, editor. Magazine: illustrations on cover only. Publishes science fiction and fantasy. "We aspire to publish science fiction and fantasy of the highest entertainment quality. Our readers are age 13 and up." Monthly. Estab. 1949. Circ. 50,000.
 ● *Magazine of Fantasy and Science Fiction* has won numerous Nebula awards and ranks #3 on the *Writer's Digest* Fiction 50 list of top markets for fiction writers.
Needs: Fantasy and science fiction. "We're always looking for more science fiction." Receives 500-700 unsolicited fiction submissions/month. Buys 8 fiction mss/issue ("on average"); 100-140 mss/year. Time between acceptance and publication varies; up to 3 years. **Publishes 6-10 new writers/year.** Recently published work by Ray Bradbury, Ursula K. LeGuin, Joyce Carol Oates and Robert Sheckley. Length: 25,000 words maximum. Publishes short shorts. Comments on rejected ms, "if quality warrants it." Sometimes recommends other markets.
How to Contact: Send complete ms with cover letter. Responds in 1 month to queries; 2 months to mss. SASE (or IRC). Sample copy for $5. Guidelines for SASE.
Payment/Terms: Pays 5-8¢/word. Pays on acceptance for first North American serial rights; foreign, option on anthology if requested.
Advice: "Our only real criterion for selecting fiction is how strongly it affects us when we read it. The manuscripts that stand out most are the ones that are prepared properly. Read a copy of the magazine first."

☑ $ ◉ ◎ **MATURE YEARS,** United Methodist Publishing House, 201 Eighth Ave. S., Nashville TN 37202. (615)749-6292. Fax: (615)749-6512. E-mail: matureyears@4mpublishing.org. **Contact:** Marvin W. Cropsey, editor. Magazine: 8½×11; 112 pages; illustrations; photos. Magazine "helps persons in and nearing retirement to appropriate the resources of the Christian faith as they seek to face the problems and opportunities related to aging." Quarterly. Estab. 1953.
Needs: Humor, intergenerational relationships, nostalgia, older adult issues, religious/inspirational, spiritual (for older adults). "We don't want anything poking fun at old age, saccharine stories or anything not for older adults. Must show older adults (age 55 plus) in a positive manner." Accepts 1 ms/issue, 4 mss/year. Publishes ms 1 year after acceptance. Published work by Ann S. Gray, Betty Z. Walker and Vickie Elaine Legg. Published new writers within the last year. Length: 1,000-1,800 words.
How to Contact: Send complete ms with SASE and Social Security number. No simultaneous submissions. Responds in 2 months. Sample copy for 10½×11 SAE and $5.
Payment/Terms: Pays 6¢/word. Pays on acceptance.

Advice: "Practice writing dialogue! Listen to people talk; take notes; master dialogue writing! Not easy, but well worth it! Most inquiry letters are far too long. If you can't sell me an idea in a brief paragraph, you're not going to sell the reader on reading your finished article or story."

$ MESSENGER OF THE SACRED HEART, Apostleship of Prayer, 661 Greenwood Ave., Toronto, Ontario M4J 4B3 Canada. (416)466-1195. **Contact:** Rev. F.J. Power, S.J. and Alfred DeManche, editors. Magazine: 7×10; 32 pages; coated paper; self-cover; illustrations; photos. Magazine for "Canadian and U.S. Catholics interested in developing a life of prayer and spirituality; stresses the great value of our ordinary actions and lives." Monthly. Estab. 1891. Circ. 14,000.
Needs: Religious/inspirational. Stories about people, adventure, heroism, humor, drama. No poetry. Accepts 1 ms/issue. Length: 750-1,500 words. Recommends other markets.
How to Contact: Send complete ms with SAE. Rarely buys reprints. Responds in 1 month. Sample copy for $1.50 (Canadian).
Payment/Terms: Pays 6¢/word and 3 contributor's copies. Pays on acceptance for first North American serial rights.
Advice: "Develop a story that sustains interest to the end. Do not preach, but use plot and characters to convey the message or theme. Aim to move the heart as well as the mind. If you can, add a light touch or a sense of humor to the story. Your ending should have impact, leaving a moral or faith message for the reader."

$ MONTANA SENIOR NEWS, Barrett-Whitman Co., Box 3363, Great Falls MT 59403. (406)761-0305. Fax: (406)761-8358. E-mail: montsrnews@imt.net. **Contact:** Jack Love, editor. Tabloid: 11×17; 60-80 pages; newsprint paper and cover; illustrations; photos. Publishes "everything of interest to seniors, except most day-to-day political items like Social Security and topics covered in the daily news. Personal profiles of seniors, their lives, times and reminiscences." Bimonthly. Estab. 1984. Circ. 28,000.
Needs: Historical, senior citizen/retirement, western (historical or contemporary). No fiction "unrelated to experiences to which seniors can relate." Buys 1 or fewer mss/issue; 4-5 mss/year. Length: 500-800 words preferred. Publishes short stories. Length: under 500 words.
How to Contact: Send complete ms with cover letter and phone number. Only responds to selected mss. Accepts simultaneous and reprint submissions. Accepts queries by e-mail. Sample copy for 9×12 SAE and $2 postage and handling.
Payment/Terms: Pays 4¢/word. Pays on publication for first rights or one-time rights.

MS MAGAZINE, 20 Exchange Place, 22nd Floor, New York NY 10005.
● *Ms Magazine* is no longer publishing fiction.

$ MY FRIEND, The Catholic Magazine for Kids, Pauline Books & Media, 50 St. Paul's Ave., Boston MA 02130. (617)522-8911. E-mail: myfriend@pauline.org. **Contact:** Sister Kathryn James Hermes, editor. Magazine: 8½×11; 32 pages; smooth, glossy paper and cover stock; illustrations; photos. Magazine of "religious truths and positive values for children in a format which is enjoyable and attractive. Each issue contains lives of saints, short stories, science corner, contests, projects, etc." Monthly during school year (September-June). Estab. 1979. Circ. 11,000.
● *My Friend* received third place in the Catholic Press Association's Best Short Story competition in 1999.
Needs: Juvenile, religious/inspirational, spiritual (children), sports (children). Receives 60 unsolicited fiction mss/month. Accepts 3-4 mss/issue; 30-40 mss/year. Published work by Mary Bahr and Sandra Humphrey. Published new writers within the past year. Length: 600-1,000 words; average length: 800 words.
How to Contact: Send complete ms with SASE. Responds in 3 months to mss. Publishes ms an average of 1 year after acceptance. Sample copy for $2 and 9×12 SAE ($1.24 postage).
Payment/Terms: Pays $20-150 (stories, articles).
Advice: "We are particularly interested in fun and amusing stories with backbone. Good dialogue, realistic character development, current lingo are necessary. We have a need for each of these types at different times. We prefer child-centered stories in a real-world setting."

$ NA'AMAT WOMAN, Magazine of NA'AMAT USA, The Women's Labor Zionist Organization of America, 350 Fifth Ave., Suite 4700, New York NY 10118-3903. (212)565-5222. **Contact:** Judith A. Sokoloff, editor. "Magazine covering a wide variety of subjects of interest to the Jewish community—including political and social issues, arts, profiles; many articles about Israel; and women's issues. Fiction must have a Jewish theme. Readers are the American Jewish community." Published 4 times/year. Estab. 1926. Circ. 20,000.
Needs: Contemporary, ethnic, literary. Receives 10 unsolicited fiction mss/month. Accepts 3-5 fiction mss/year. Length: 1,500-3,000 words. Also buys nonfiction.
How to Contact: Query first or send complete ms with SASE. Responds in 3 months to mss. Free sample copy for 9×11½ SAE and $1.20 postage.

Payment/Terms: Pays 10¢/word and 2 contributor's copies. Pays on publication for first North American serial rights; assignments on work-for-hire basis.

Advice: "No maudlin nostalgia or romance; no hackneyed Jewish humor and no poetry."

N $ ⊘ ◎ ▼ NEW ERA MAGAZINE, (I, II, IV), The Church of Jesus Christ of Latter-day Saints, 50 E. North Temple St., Salt Lake City UT 84150. (801)240-2951. Fax: (801)240-2270. **Contact:** Larry A. Hiller, editor. Magazine: 8×10½; 51 pages; 40 lb. coated paper; illustrations; photos. "We will publish fiction on any theme that strengthens and builds the standards and convictions of teenage Latter-day Saints ('Mormons')." Monthly. Estab. 1971. Circ. 220,000.

● *New Era* is a recipient of the Focus on Excellence Award from Brigham Young University. The magazine also sponsors a writing contest.

Needs: Stories on family relationships, self-esteem, dealing with loneliness, resisting peer pressure and all aspects of maintaining Christian values in the modern world. "All material must be written from a Latter-day Saint ('Mormon') point of view—or at least from a generally Christian point of view, reflecting LDS life and values. Would like to see more fiction with a lighthearted approach to self-esteem or peer pressure." No science fiction or fantasy. Receives 30-35 unsolicited mss/month. Accepts 1 ms/issue; 12 mss/year. Publishes ms 3 months to 3 years after acceptance. Published work by A.E. Cannon, on Smurthwaite, Jack Weyland and Alma Yates. Publishes 2-3 new writers/year. Length: 250-2,000 words; average length: 1,500 words.

How to Contact: Send complete ms. Responds in 2 months. SASE. Accepts disk submissions (WordPerfect, MacIntosh). Sample copy for $1.50 and 9×12 SAE with 2 first-class stamps. Guidelines for #10 SASE.

Payment/Terms: Pays $50-375 and contributor's copies. Pays on acceptance for all rights (will reassign to author on request).

Advice: "Each magazine has its own personality—you wouldn't write the same style of fiction for *Seventeen* that you would write for *Omni*. Very few writers who are not of our faith have been able to write for us successfully, and the reason usually is that they don't know what it's like to be a member of our church. You must study and research and know those you are writing about. We love to work with beginning authors, and we're a great place to break in if you can understand us." Sponsors contests and awards for LDS fiction writers. "We have an annual contest; entry forms are in each October issue. Deadline is January; winners published in September."

✔ $ ◉ NEW MYSTERY, The Best New Mystery Stories, 101 W. 23rd St., PH-1#7, New York NY 10011-7703. (212)353-1582. E-mail: editorial@newmystery.com. Website: www.NewMystery.com (includes book and film reviews, short shorts and investigative journalism). **Contact:** Charles Raisch III, editor. Magazine: 8½×11; 96 pages; illustrations; photos. "Mystery, suspense and crime." Quarterly. Estab. 1990. Circ. 90,000.

● Fiction published in *New Mystery* has been nominated for Edgar, Blaggand Shamus, Macavity and Anthony awards for best short story of the year. Response time for this magazine seems to be slower in summer months. The mystery included here is varied and realistic.

Needs: Mystery/suspense (cozy to hardboiled). No horror or romance. Wants more suspense and espionage. Plans special annual anthology. Receives 350 unsolicited mss/month. Buys 6-10 ms/issue. Agented fiction 50%. **Publishes 1 new writer/issue.** Published work by Stuart Kaminsky, Andrew Greeley and Rosemary Santini. Length: 3,000-5,000 words preferred. Also buys short book reviews 500-3,000 words. Sometimes comments on rejected mss.

How to Contact: *New Mystery charges a $7 fee for purchase of a contributor's packet, which includes guidelines and 2 sample copies.* Send complete ms with cover letter. "We cannot be responsible for unsolicited manuscripts." Responds in 1 month to ms. SASE. Sample copy for $5, 9×12 SAE and 4 first-class stamps.

Payment/Terms: Pays $25-1,000. Pays on publication for negotiated rights.

Advice: Stories should have "believable characters in trouble; sympathetic lead; visual language." Sponsors "Annual First Story Contest."

$ ◉ THE NEW YORKER, The New Yorker, Inc., 4 Times Square, New York NY 10036. **Contact:** Fiction Department. A quality magazine of interesting, well-written stories, articles, essays and poems for a literate audience. Weekly. Estab. 1925. Circ. 750,000.

How to Contact: Send complete ms with SASE. Responds in 3 months to mss. Publishes 1 ms/issue.

Payment/Terms: Varies. Pays on acceptance.

Advice: "Be lively, original, not overly literary. Write what you want to write, not what you think the editor would like. Send poetry to Poetry Department."

✔ $ ⊘ NUGGET, Dugent Corp., 2201 W. Sample Rd., Building Q, Suite 4A, Pompano Beach FL 33073. (954)917-5820. **Contact:** Christopher James, editor-in-chief. A newsstand magazine designed to have erotic appeal for a fetish-oriented audience. Published 13 times a year. Estab. 1956. Circ. 100,000.

Needs: Offbeat, fetish-oriented material encompassing a variety of subjects (B&D, TV, TS, spanking, amputeeism, golden showers, infantalism, catfighting, etc.). Most of fiction includes several sex scenes. No fiction that concerns children or religious subjects. Accepts 2 mss/issue. Agented fiction 5%. Length: 2,000-3,500 words.

How to Contact: Send complete ms with SASE. Responds in 1 month. Sample copy for $5. Guidelines for legal-sized SASE.

Payment/Terms: Pays minimum $200 and 1 contributor's copy. Pays on publication for first rights.

Advice: "Keep in mind the nature of the publication, which is fetish erotica. Subject matter can vary, but we prefer fetish themes."

$ ◢ ODYSSEY, Adventures in Science, Cobblestone Publishing, Inc., 30 Grove St., Suite C, Peterborough NH 03458. (603)924-7209. **Contact:** Elizabeth E. Lindstrom, senior editor. Magazine. "Scientific accuracy, original approaches to the subject are primary concerns of the editors in choosing material. For 10-16 year olds." Monthly (except July and August). Estab. 1991. Circ. 30,000.

Needs: Material must match theme; send for theme list and deadlines. Children's/juvenile (10-16 years), "authentic historical and biographical fiction, science fiction, retold legends, etc., relating to theme." List of upcoming themes available for SASE. Length: 750-1,000 words.

How to Contact: Query first or query with clips of published work (if new to *Odyssey*). "Include estimated word count and a detailed 1-page outline explaining the information to be presented; an extensive bibliography of materials authors plan to use." Responds in several months. Send SASE for reply or send stamped postcard to find out if ms has been received. Sample copy for $4.50, 9 × 12 SAE and $1.05 postage. Guidelines for SASE.

Payment/Terms: Pays 20-25¢/word. Pays on publication for all rights.

Advice: "We also include in-depth nonfiction, plays and biographies."

N $ ◢ ◎ ON OUR BACKS, The Best of Lesbian Sex, HAF Enterprises, 3415 Cesar Chavez, #101, San Francisco CA 94110. (415)648-9464. Fax: (415)648-4705. E-mail: staff@onourbacksmag.com. Website: www.onourbacksmag.com. **Contact:** Tristan Taormino, editor. Magazine: 8½ × 11; 48 pages; uncoated paper; glossy cover; illustrations; photos. "*On Our Backs* is a lesbian sex magazine which publishes photographs, erotic fiction, features, interviews, advice, reviews and other sex nonfiction. *OOB* is the only national sex magazine produced by and for lesbians." Bimonthly. Estab. 1984. Circ. 50,000.

• *On Our Backs* was one of UTNE's "Ten Magazines to Make a Difference in the Eighties."

Needs: Erotica, lesbian. Receives 20-30 unsolicited mss/month. Accepts 2 mss/issue; 12 mss/year. Publishes ms 2-4 months after acceptance. **Publishes 2-4 new writers/year.** Recently published work by Joan Nestle, Peggy Munson, Toni Amato and Cecilia Tan. Length: 1,000-2,000 words; average length: 1,300 words. Publishes short shorts. Average length: 1,000 words.

How to Contact: Send complete ms with a cover letter. Include estimated word count and complete contact information, including phone number and/or e-mail address. Responds in 1 month to queries; 6 months to mss. Send a disposable copy of ms and #10 SASE for reply only. Accepts simultaneous submissions, previously published work and multiple submissions. Sample copy for $5.95. Guidelines for SASE or e-mail.

Payment/Terms: Pays $100, 1 contributor's copy and free subscription to the magazine; additional copies $5.95. Pays on publication for all rights.

$ ◢ ◎ OPTIONS, The *Bi*-Monthly, AJA Publishing, Box 170, Irvington NY 10533. E-mail: dianaeditr@aol.com. Website: www.youngandtight.com/men (includes short fiction). **Contact:** Diana Sheridan, associate editor. Magazine: digest-sized; 114 pages; newsprint paper; glossy cover stock; illustrations; photos. Sexually explicit magazine for and about bisexuals. "Please read our Advice subhead." 10 issues/year. Estab. 1982. Circ. 100,000.

Needs: Erotica, bisexual, gay, lesbian. "First person as-if-true experiences." Accepts 6 unsolicited fiction mss/issue. "Very little" of fiction is agented. **Published new writers within the last year.** Length: 2,000-3,000 words. Sometimes comments on rejected mss.

How to Contact: Send complete ms with or without cover letter. Responds in 3 weeks. SASE. Accepts electronic submissions (disk or e-mail as textfiles). "Submissions on disk welcome, but please include hard copy too." Sample copy for $2.95 and 6 × 9 SAE with 5 first-class stamps. Guidelines for SASE.

Payment/Terms: Pays $100. Pays on publication for all rights. Will reassign book rights on request.

Advice: "Read a copy of *Options* carefully and look at our spec sheet before writing anything for us. That's not new advice, but to judge from some of what we get in the mail, it's necessary to repeat. We only buy two bi/lesbian pieces per issue; need is greater for bi/gay male mss. Though we're a bi rather than gay magazine, the emphasis is on same-sex relationships. If the readers want to read about a male/female couple, they'll buy another magazine. Gay male stories sent to *Options* will also be considered for publication in *Beau*, or one of our other gay male magazines. Must get into the hot action by 1,000 words into the story. (Sooner is fine too!) *Most important:* We *only* publish male/male stories that feature 'safe sex' practices unless the story is clearly something that took place pre-AIDS."

⊕ ✓ $ ◢ PEOPLE'S FRIEND, D.C. Thomson & Co., Ltd., 80 Kingsway East, Dundee DD4 8SL Scotland. 01382 223131. Fax: 01382 452491. **Contact:** Fiction Editor. Weekly. Estab. 1869. Circ. 470,000.

Needs: Specializes in women's fiction. Would like to see more young romances. "British backgrounds preferred (but not essential) by our readership. Quite simply, we aim to entertain. Stories should have believable, well-developed characters in situations our readers can relate to. Our readers tend to be traditionalists." No stories of the supernatural, or extreme sex or violence. Published work by Betty McInnes, Shirley Worral and Christina Jones. "We actively encourage new authors and do our best to help and advise." Publishes 5 stories/issue. Length: 1,000-3,000 words.

How to Contact: Accepts multiple submissions. Sample copy and guidelines available on application.

Payment/Terms: Pays $75-85 and contributor's copies.

Advice: Looks for manuscript with "emotional content and characterization. It must make enjoyable reading; it mustn't shock."

$ ☑ PLAYBOY MAGAZINE, 680 N. Lake Shore Dr., Chicago IL 60611. (312)751-8000. **Contact:** Fiction Editor. Monthly magazine. "As the world's largest general-interest lifestyle magazine for men, *Playboy* spans the spectrum of contemporary men's passions. From hard-hitting investigative journalism to light-hearted humor, the latest in fashion and personal technology to the cutting edge of the popular culture, *Playboy* is and always has been both guidebook and dream book for generations of American men . . . the definitive source of information and ideas for over 10 million readers each month. In addition, *Playboy*'s 'Interview' and '20 Questions' present profiles of politicians, athletes and today's hottest personalities." Estab. 1953, Circ. 3,283,000.

How to Contact: Query first. "Fiction manuscripts must be no longer than 7,500 words for acceptance." Send SASE for guidelines.

Advice: "*Playboy* does not consider poetry, plays, story outlines or novel-length manuscripts."

☑ $ ☑ ☑ POCKETS, Devotional Magazine for Children, The Upper Room, 1908 Grand Ave., Box 340004, Nashville TN 37203-0004. (615)340-7333. E-mail: pockets@upperroom.org. Website: www.upperroom.org/pockets (includes themes, guidelines and contest guidelines). Editor: Janet R. Knight. Associate Editor: Lynn W. Gilliam. **Contact:** Patricia McIntyre, editorial assistant. Magazine: 7×9; 48 pages; 50 lb. white econowrite paper; 80 lb. white coated, heavy cover stock; color and 2-color illustrations; some photos. Magazine for children ages 6-12, with articles specifically geared for ages 8 to 11. "The magazine offers stories, activities, prayers, poems—all geared to giving children a better understanding of themselves as children of God." Published monthly except for January. Estab. 1981. Estimated circ. 99,000.

● *Pockets* has received honors from the Educational Press Association of America. The magazine's fiction tends to feature children dealing with real-life situations "from a faith perspective." *Pockets* ranked #15 on the *Writer's Digest* Fiction 50 list of top markets for fiction writers.

Needs: Adventure, contemporary, ethnic, historical (general), juvenile, religious/inspirational and suspense/mystery. No fantasy, science fiction, talking animals. "All submissions should address the broad theme of the magazine. Each issue is built around one theme with material which can be used by children in a variety of ways. Scripture stories, fiction, poetry, prayers, art, graphics, puzzles and activities are all included. Submissions do not need to be overtly religious. They should help children experience a Christian lifestyle that is not always a neatly-wrapped moral package, but is open to the continuing revelation of God's will. Seasonal material, both secular and liturgical, is desired. No violence, horror, sexual and racial stereotyping or fiction containing heavy moralizing." No talking animal stories or fantasy. Receives approximately 200 unsolicited fiction mss/month. Accepts 4-5 mss/issue; 44-60 mss/year. **Publishes 10-12 new writers/year.** Published work by Peggy King Anderson, Angela Gibson and John Steptoe. Length: 600-1,600 words; average length: 1,200 words. Publishes short shorts.

How to Contact: Send complete ms with SASE. Accepts previously published submissions. Responds in 1 month to mss. Publishes ms 1 year to 18 months after acceptance. Sample copy free with SAE and 4 first-class stamps. Guidelines and themes for SASE. "Strongly advise sending for themes or checking website before submitting."

Payment/Terms: Pays 14¢/word and 2-5 contributor's copies; $1.95 charge for extras; $1 each for 10 or more. Pays on acceptance for first North American serial rights.

Advice: "Listen to children as they talk with each other. Please send for a sample copy as well as guidelines and themes. Many manuscripts we receive are simply inappropriate. Each issue is theme-related. Please send for list of themes. New themes published in December of each year. Include SASE." Sponsors annual fiction writing contest. Deadline: Aug. 15. Send for guidelines. $1,000 award and publication.

☑ ☑ PORTLAND MAGAZINE, Maine's City Magazine,, 578 Congress St., Portland ME 04101. (207)775-4339. Fax: (207)775-2334. E-mail: staff@portlandmagazine.com. Website: www.portlandmonthly.com. **Contact:** Colin Sargent, editor. Magazine: 56 pages; 60 lb. paper; 80 lb. cover stock; illustrations; photos. "City lifestyle magazine—style, business, real estate, controversy, fashion, cuisine, interviews and art relating to the Maine area." Monthly. Estab. 1986. Circ. 100,000.

Needs: Contemporary, historical, literary. Receives 20 unsolicited fiction mss/month. Accepts 1 mss/issue; 10 mss/year. Publishes short shorts. Published work by Janwillem van de Wetering, Sanford Phippen and Mame Medwed. Length: 3 double-spaced typed pages.

How to Contact: Query first. "Fiction below 700 words, please." Send complete ms with cover letter. Responds in 6 months. SASE. Accepts electronic submissions.

Payment/Terms: Pays on publication for first North American serial rights.

Advice: "We publish ambitious short fiction featuring everyone from Frederick Barthelme to newly discovered fiction by Edna St. Vincent Millay."

N ☑ $☐ PURPOSE, Herald Press, 616 Walnut Ave., Scottdale PA 15683-1999. (412)887-8500. Fax: (412)887-3111. E-mail: horsch@mph.org. Website: www.mph.org (includes information about products, editors' names, guidelines). **Contact:** James E. Horsch, editor. Magazine: 5⅜ × 8⅜; 8 pages; illustrations; photos. "Magazine focuses on Christian discipleship—how to be a faithful Christian in the midst of everyday life situations. Uses story form to present models and examples to encourage Christians in living a life of faithful discipleship." Weekly. Estab. 1968. Circ. 12,200.

Needs: Historical, religious/inspirational. No militaristic/narrow patriotism or racism. Receives 100 unsolicited mss/month. Accepts 3 mss/issue; 140 mss/year. Length: 750 words maximum; average length: 500 words. Occasionally comments on rejected mss.

How to Contact: Send complete ms only. Responds in 2 months. Accepts simultaneous and previously published work. Sample copy for 6 × 9 SAE and 2 first-class stamps. Guidelines free with sample copy only.

Payment/Terms: Pays up to 5¢/word for stories and 2 contributor's copies. Pays on acceptance for one-time rights.

Advice: Many stories are "situational—how to respond to dilemmas. Write crisp, action moving, personal style, focused upon an individual, a group of people, or an organization. The story form is an excellent literary device to use in exploring discipleship issues. There are many issues to explore. Each writer brings a unique solution. The first two paragraphs are crucial in establishing the mood/issue to be resolved in the story. Work hard on developing these."

$☐ ☑ ELLERY QUEEN'S MYSTERY MAGAZINE, Dell Magazines, 475 Park Ave. S., New York NY 10016. (212)686-7188. (212)686-7414. Website: www.mysterypages.com (includes writer's guidelines, short fiction, book reviews and magazine's history and awards). **Contact:** Janet Hutchings, editor. Magazine: 5⅜ × 8½; 144 pages with special 240-page combined September/October issue. Magazine for lovers of mystery fiction. Published 11 times/year. Estab. 1941. Circ. 500,000 readers.

● This publication ranked #7 on the *Writer's Digest* Fiction 50 list of top markets for fiction writers. *EQMM* has won numerous awards and sponsors its own award for best stories of the year, nominated by its readership.

Needs: "We accept only mystery, crime, suspense and detective fiction." No explicit sex or violence. Wants more classical who-dun-its. Receives approximately 400 unsolicited fiction mss each month. Accepts 10-15 mss/issue. Publishes ms 6-12 months after acceptance. Agented fiction 50%. **Publishes 11 new writers/year.** Recently published work by Laurence Block, Joyce Carol Oats, John Mortimer and Minette Walters. Length: 7,000 words maximum. Publishes 1-2 short novels of up to 17,000 words/year by established authors; minute mysteries of 250 words; short, humorous mystery verse. Critiques rejected mss "only when a story might be a possibility for us if revised." Sometimes recommends other markets.

How to Contact: Send complete ms with SASE. Cover letter should include publishing credits and brief biographical sketch. Accepts simultaneous submissions. Responds in 3 months to mss. Guidelines with SASE. Sample copy for $5.

Payment/Terms: Pays 3¢/word and up. Pays on acceptance for first North American serial rights. Occasionally buys reprints.

Advice: "We have a Department of First Stories and usually publish at least one first story an issue—i.e., the author's first published fiction. We select stories that are fresh and of the kind our readers have expressed a liking for. In writing a detective story, you must play fair with the reader, providing clues and necessary information. Otherwise you have a better chance of publishing if you avoid writing to formula."

$☐ RADIANCE, The Magazine for Large Women, Box 30246, Oakland CA 94604. (510)482-0680. Website: www.radiancemagazine.com. Editor: Alice Ansfield. **Contact:** Alice Ansfield and Catherine Taylor, fiction editors. Magazine: 8½ × 11; 64 pages; glossy/coated paper; 70 lb. cover stock; illustrations; photos. "Theme is to encourage women to live fully now, whatever their body size. To stop waiting to live or feel good about themselves until they lose weight." Quarterly. Estab. 1984. Circ. 17,000. Readership: 80,000.

Needs: Adventure, contemporary, erotica, ethnic, fantasy, feminist, historical, humor/satire, mainstream, mystery/suspense, prose poem, science fiction, spiritual, sports, young adult/teen. "Want fiction to have a larger-bodied character; living in a positive, upbeat way. Our goal is to empower women." Receives 150 mss/month. Accepts 40 mss/year. Publishes ms within 1-2 years of acceptance. Published work by Marla Zarrow, Sallie Tisdale and Mary Kay Blakely. Publishes 15 new writers/year. Length: 1,000-5,000 words; average length: 2,000 words. Publishes short shorts. Sometimes comments on rejected mss.

How to Contact: Query with clips of published work and send complete ms with cover letter. Responds in 4 months. SASE. Accepts reprint submissions. Sample copy for $5. Guidelines for #10 SASE. Reviews novels and short story collections "with at least one large-size heroine."

Payment/Terms: Pays $35-100 and contributor's copies on publication for one-time rights. Sends galleys to the author if requested.

Advice: "Read our magazine before sending anything to us. Know what our philosophy and points of view are before sending a manuscript. Look around your community for inspiring, successful and unique large women doing things worth writing about. At this time, prefer fiction having to do with a larger woman (man, child). *Radiance* is one of the leading resources in the size-acceptance movement. Each issue profiles dynamic large women from all walks of life, along with articles on health, media, fashion and politics. Our audience is the 30 million American women who wear a size 16 or over. Feminist, emotionally-supportive, quarterly magazine."

N **$** **⬛** **⬛** **RANGER RICK MAGAZINE, (II)**, National Wildlife Federation, 8925 Leesburg Pike, Vienna VA 22184. (703)790-4000. Editor: Gerald Bishop. **Contact:** Deborah Churchman, fiction editor. Magazine: 8×10; 40 pages; glossy paper; 60 lb. cover stock; illustrations; photos. "*Ranger Rick* emphasizes conservation and the enjoyment of nature through full-color photos and art, fiction and nonfiction articles, games and puzzles, and special columns. Our audience ranges in ages from 7-12, with the greatest number in the 7 and up. We aim for a fourth grade reading level. They read for fun and information." Monthly. Estab. 1967. Circ. 650,000.

• *Ranger Rick* has won several Ed Press awards. The editors say the magazine has had a backlog of stories recently, yet they would like to see more *good* mystery and science fiction stories (with nature themes).

Needs: Adventure, fantasy, humor, mystery (amateur sleuth), science fiction and sports. "Interesting stories for kids focusing directly on nature or related subjects. Fiction that carries a conservation message is always needed, as are adventure stories involving kids with nature or the outdoors. Moralistic 'lessons' taught children by parents or teachers are not accepted. Human qualities are attributed to animals only in our regular feature, 'Adventures of Ranger Rick.'" Receives about 150-200 unsolicited fiction mss each month. Accepts about 6 mss/year. Published fiction by Leslie Dendy. Length: 900 words maximum. Comments on rejected mss "when there is time."

How to Contact: Query with sample lead and any clips of published work with SASE. May consider simultaneous submissions. Very rarely buys reprints. Responds in 3 months to queries and mss. Publishes ms 8 months to 1 year after acceptance, but sometimes longer. Sample copy for $2. Guidelines for legal-sized SASE.

Payment/Terms: Pays $600 maximum/full-length ms. Pays on acceptance for all rights. Sends galleys to author.

Advice: "For our magazine, the writer needs to understand kids and that aspect of nature he or she is writing about—a difficult combination! Manuscripts are rejected because they are contrived and/or condescending—often overwritten. Some manuscripts are anthropomorphic, others are above our readers' level. We find that fiction stories help children understand the natural world and the environmental problems it faces. Beginning writers have a chance equal to that of established authors *provided* the quality is there. Would love to see more science fiction and fantasy, as well as mysteries."

✓ **⬛** **REDBOOK**, The Hearst Corporation, 224 W. 57th St., New York NY 10019. (212)649-2000. **Contact:** Julia Dahl, fiction editor. Magazine: 8×10¾; 150-250 pages; 34 lb. paper; 70 lb. cover; illustrations; photos. "*Redbook's* readership consists of American women, ages 25-44. Most are well-educated, married, have children and also work outside the home." Monthly. Estab. 1903. Circ. 3,200,000.

Needs: Query. *Redbook* was not accepting unsolicited mss at the time of publication.

✓ **$** **⬛** **⬛** **⬛** **REFORM JUDAISM**, Union of American Hebrew Congregations, 633 3rd Ave., 6th Floor, New York NY 10017-6778. Website: www.uahc.org/rjmag/ (includes writer's guidelines, general information, past issues, and more). Editor: Aron Hirt-Manheimer. **Contact:** Joy Weinberg, managing editor. Magazine: 8×10¾; 80-112 pages; illustrations; photos. "We cover subjects of Jewish interest in general and Reform Jewish in particular, for members of Reform Jewish congregations in the United States and Canada." Quarterly. Estab. 1972. Circ. 310,000.

• Recipient of The Simon Rockower Award for Excellence in Jewish Journalism for feature writing, graphic design and photography. The editor says they would publish more stories if they could find excellent, sophisticated, contemporary Jewish fiction.

Needs: Humor/satire, religious/inspirational. Receives 75 unsolicited mss/month. Buys 3 mss/year. Publishes ms 6 months after acceptance. Published work by Frederick Fastow and Bob Sloan. Length: 600-3,500 words; average length: 1,500 words.

How to Contact: Send complete ms with cover letter. Responds in 6 weeks. SASE for ms. "For quickest response send self-addressed stamped postcard with choices: "Yes, we're interested in publishing; Maybe, we'd like to hold for future consideration; No, we've decided to pass on publication." Accepts simultaneous submissions. Sample copy for $3.50.

Payment/Terms: Pays 30¢/word. Pays on publication for first North American serial rights.

✓ **$** **⬛** **⬛** **ST. ANTHONY MESSENGER**, 1615 Republic St., Cincinnati OH 45210-1298. (513)241-5615. Fax: (513)241-0399. E-mail: stanthony@americancatholic.org. Website: www.AmericanCatholic.org (includes Saint of the day, selected articles, product information). **Contact:** Father Jack Wintz, O.F.M., editor. Magazine: 8×10¾; 60 pages; illustrations; photos. "*St. Anthony Messenger* is a Catholic family magazine which aims to help its readers lead more fully human and Christian lives. We publish articles which report on a changing church and world, opinion pieces written from the perspective of Christian faith and values, personality profiles, and fiction which entertains and informs." Monthly. Estab. 1893. Circ. 340,000.

● This is a leading Catholic magazine, but has won awards for both religious and secular journalism and writing from the Catholic Press Association, the International Association of Business Communicators, the Society of Professional Journalists and the Cincinnati Editors Association.

Needs: Contemporary, religious/inspirational, romance, senior citizen/retirement and spiritual. "We do not want mawkishly sentimental or preachy fiction. Stories are most often rejected for poor plotting and characterization; bad dialogue—listen to how people talk; inadequate motivation. Many stories say nothing, are 'happenings' rather than stories." No fetal journals, no rewritten Bible stories. Receives 70-80 unsolicited fiction mss/month. Accepts 1 ms/issue; 12 mss/year. Publishes ms up to 1 year after acceptance. **Publishes 3 new writers/year.** Recently published work by Geraldine Marshall Gutfreund, John Salustri, Beth Dotson, Miriam Pollikatsikis and Joseph Pici. Length: 2,000-3,000 words. Comments on rejected mss "when there is time." Sometimes recommends other markets.

How to Contact: Send complete ms with SASE. Queries should usually come by regular mail, but will also accept them by e-mail and fax. Responds in 2 months. Sample copy and guidelines available. Reviews novels and short story collections. Send books to Barbara Beckwith, book review editor.

Payment/Terms: Pays 16¢/word maximum and 2 contributor's copies; $1 charge for extras. Pays on acceptance for first serial rights.

Advice: "We publish one story a month and we get up to 1,000 a year. Too many offer simplistic 'solutions' or answers. Pay attention to endings. Easy, simplistic, deus ex machina endings don't work. People have to feel characters in the stories are real and have a reason to care about them and what happens to them. Fiction entertains but can also convey a point and sound values."

$◨ SEEK, Standard Publishing, 8121 Hamilton Ave., Cincinnati OH 45231-2396. (513)931-4050. Fax: (513)931-0950. Website: www.standardpub.com. **Contact:** Eileen H. Wilmoth, editor. Magazine: 5½×8½; 8 pages; newsprint paper; art and photos in each issue. "Inspirational stories of faith-in-action for Christian young adults; a Sunday School take-home paper." Weekly. Estab. 1970. Circ. 40,000.

Needs: Religious/inspirational. Accepts 150 mss/year. Publishes ms an average of 1 year after acceptance. **Publishes 20-30 new writers/year.** Length: 500-1,200 words.

How to Contact: Send complete ms with SASE. No queries by fax or e-mail. Buys reprints. Responds in 3 months. Free sample copy and guidelines.

Payment/Terms: Pays 5¢/word on acceptance.

Advice: "Write a credible story with Christian slant—no preachments; avoid overworked themes such as joy in suffering, generation gaps, etc. Most manuscripts are rejected by us because of irrelevant topic or message, unrealistic story, or poor character and/or plot development. We use fiction stories that are believable."

☑ $◨ SEVENTEEN, Primedia Consumer Magazines, 850 Third Ave., New York NY 10022-6258. **Contact:** Darcy Jacobs, fiction editor. Magazine: 8½×11; 125-400 pages; 40 lb. coated paper; 80 lb. coated cover stock; illustrations; photos. A general interest magazine with fashion; beauty care; pertinent topics such as current issues, attitudes, experiences and concerns of teenagers. Monthly. Estab. 1944. Circ. 2.5 million.

● *Seventeen* sponsors an annual fiction contest for writers age 13-21. *Seventeen* ranked #14 on *Writer's Digest*'s Fiction 50 list of top fiction markets. See the interview with *Seventeen* editors Darcy Jacobs and Patrice Adcroft on page 379.

Needs: High-quality literary fiction. No science fiction, action/adventure or pornography. Receives 200 unsolicited fiction mss/month. Accepts 6-9 mss/year. Agented fiction 50%. Published work by Margaret Atwood, Edna O'Brien, Blake Nelson, Joyce Carol Oates, Ellen Gilchrist and Pagan Kennedy. Publishes 4-5 new writers/year. Length: approximately 750-3,000 words.

How to Contact: Send complete ms with SASE and cover letter with relevant credits. Responds in 3 months to mss. Guidelines for submissions with SASE.

Payment/Terms: Pays $700-2,500 on acceptance for one-time rights.

Advice: "Respect the intelligence and sophistication of teenagers. *Seventeen* remains open to the surprise of new voices. Our commitment to publishing the work of new writers remains strong; we continue to read every submission we receive. We believe that good fiction can move the reader toward thoughtful examination of her own life as well as the lives of others—providing her ultimately with a fuller appreciation of what it means to be human. While stories that focus on female teenage experience continue to be of interest, the less obvious possibilities are equally welcome. We encourage writers to submit literary short stories concerning subjects that may not be immediately identifiable as 'teenage,' with narrative styles that are experimental and challenging. Too often, unsolicited submissions possess voices and themes condescending and unsophisticated. Also, writers hesitate to send stories to *Seventeen* which they think too violent or risqué. Good writing holds the imaginable and then some, and if it doesn't find its home here, we're always grateful for the introduction to a writer's work. We're more inclined to publish cutting edge fiction than simple, young adult fiction."

insider report

Seventeen magazine: looking for fiction to inspire

Darcy Jacobs

Patrice Adcroft

Seventeen is a magazine with a mission. At a time when many consumer magazines are abandoning their fiction departments, *Seventeen* magazine is renewing its commitment to publishing short fiction for its audience of young adult women. Seventeen already has a long and respected history of fiction publishing: Joyce Carol Oates, Margaret Atwood, Amy Tan, Chaim Potok and Pagan Kennedy have appeared in its pages. The magazine has also demonstrated a long-term commitment to encouraging new voices. Previously unpublished authors regularly find a place in its pages, and *Seventeen* sponsors an annual fiction contest for young writers. Fiction editor Darcy Jacobs and editor-in-chief Patrice Adcroft aren't looking to fill the fiction pages of *Seventeen* with mind candy for the lip gloss set. They publish fiction with a purpose: to inspire.

Both Adcroft and Jacobs believe that fiction is especially important to today's fast-paced, gadget-based teen culture. The Internet, television and electronic gaming provide plenty of high-tech distraction. According to Jacobs, today's visual culture makes the written word even more important. "Reading fiction is a chance to be exposed to how beautiful words are," she explains. One reason *Seventeen* believes that publishing fiction is so important is because fewer consumer magazines are doing it. "Thirty years ago, a chance encounter with fiction was much more likely," Adcroft says. "Today's teens are pulled in countless directions, and I think fiction needs to be reintroduced to them, or vice versa."

Adcroft and Jacobs warn against stereotyping today's young adult audience. According to Jacobs, *Seventeen*'s primarily female audience of twelve- to twenty-four-year-olds is becoming increasingly sophisticated. "Teens are very smart, sometimes smarter than we are," says Adcroft. Although Jacobs and Adcroft select fiction with themes that relate to *Seventeen*'s young adult readership, they want to avoid patronizing their audience with exclusively "young adult" fiction. "The line is blurring between 'young adult,' 'twenty-something' and 'adult,'" Jacobs explains. "*Seventeen* wants to publish great fiction, not just great young adult fiction. A piece by Margaret Atwood belongs in *Seventeen* as much as a piece by Francesca Lia Block." Jacobs and Adcroft see fiction as more than a form of entertainment—they see it as a vehicle for contemplation and growth. *Seventeen*'s writer's guidelines request fiction that deals "with issues that are familiar and important to our readers . . . but they should also challenge them and make them think." Adcroft perceives fiction readers as seekers of truth. "Oftentimes you get closer to the truth with fiction than with nonfiction," she explains. "As compelling as nonfiction can be, fiction can transport you, transform you." She adds, "What's great about fiction is that everybody can take what they individually need or want from it. If you are reading fiction, you may remember a struggle during your adolescence, you may remember a romance, you may be inspired to make a change in your life." With this in mind, *Seventeen*'s editors don't shy away from what many might consider adult or controversial themes. However, they are careful not to use fiction for didactic purposes—for teaching morals or standards of behavior. Nor do they seek out specific themes for the purpose of raising social consciousness. "We don't use fiction to advise our readers," states Jacobs. "The point of fiction isn't to give advice." At the same time, Jacobs stays away from fiction that glorifies criminal or self-destructive behavior. "I won't send a message that doesn't belong on our pages, but I don't look for fiction to send a message. It's dangerous to use fiction as a vehicle to teach a lesson to our readers."

"Teens can see through that anyway," adds Adcroft. Presenting or portraying controversial points of view "shouldn't be gratuitous, but illuminating."

But Jacobs and Adcroft want to do more than inspire *Seventeen*'s audience to read. They want to inspire them to write. "We don't want just to expose our audience to fiction, we want to give them an opportunity to show their work," explains Jacobs. "Our readers love to write short stories, poetry, journals. . . . it's part of who *Seventeen* is." *Seventeen* sponsors an annual short fiction contest open to young writers between the ages of thirteen and twenty-one. The winning submission is published in the magazine, and the top five submissions receive publicity and other prizes. Sylvia Plath was one such contest winner.

Writers should note that *Seventeen* always accepts manuscript submissions from previously unpublished authors. Although *Seventeen*'s writer's guidelines request that the cover letter include previous publishing credits, Jacobs says "it's the work you'll be judged on, not your accomplishments. Everyone is happy to be the one to discover a bright new talent." Jacobs doesn't consider age, gender, or even necessarily the genre of a piece when reviewing it for publication. "Everything is evaluated on its own merit," states Adcroft.

As a long-standing member of the *Writer's Digest* "Fiction 50" list, *Seventeen* has a reputation for being an author-friendly publication. Jacobs and her fiction assistant look at every fiction submission they receive—five or six a day. Jacobs also solicits the opinions of other editors within the magazine. "It's not about personal taste, but what is right for our readers, what would appeal to our readers," explains Jacobs, who plans on publishing between six and nine pieces of fiction annually. She advises writers who are considering submitting to *Seventeen*—or to any periodical, for that matter—to do their homework. "Look at recent issues and familiarize yourself with the type of work we're publishing. Try to read a year's worth, if possible. And make sure you send your work to the correct person. Call and check—positions can change." Jacobs *doesn't* recommend that an author call to chat with an editor about a piece. "Most of all, read and follow the writer's guidelines carefully." Adcroft adds that it is important for all writers, especially young ones, to write what they know. Otherwise, "the same rules apply at *Seventeen* that would apply to good writing for any publication. There is no unique *Seventeen* formula."

Seventeen may not be a literary magazine, but that doesn't prevent its editors from publishing high-quality fiction. "We put a lot of pride in the quality of our writing throughout the entire magazine," Jacobs notes. "It's not just what we say, but how it is said that is important."

—*Nicole R. Klungle*

☐ ◎ **SOJOURNER, The Women's Forum**, 42 Seaverns Ave., Jamaica Plain MA 02130. (617)524-0415. E-mail: info@sojourner.org. Website: www.sojourner.org. **Contact:** Amy Pett, editor. Magazine: 11×17; 48 pages; newsprint; illustrations; photos. "Feminist journal publishing interviews, nonfiction features, news, viewpoints, poetry, reviews (music, cinema, books) and fiction for women." Published monthly. Estab. 1975. Circ. 45,000.

Needs: "Writing on race, sex, class and queerness." Experimental, fantasy, feminist, lesbian, humor/satire, literary, prose poem and women's. Query for upcoming themes. Receives 20 unsolicited fiction mss/month. Accepts 10 mss/year. Agented fiction 10%. Published work by Ruth Ann Lonardelli and Janie Adams. Published new writers within the last year. Length: 1,000-4,000 words; average length: 2,500 words.

How to Contact: Send complete ms with SASE and cover letter with description of previous publications; current works. Accepts simultaneous submissions. Responds in 8 months. Publishes ms an average of 6 months after acceptance. Sample copy for $3 with 10×13 SASE. Guidelines for SASE.

Payment/Terms: Pays subscription to magazine and 2 contributor's copies, $15 for first rights. No extra charge up to 5 contributor's copies; $1 charge each thereafter.

Advice: "Pay attention to appearance of manuscript! Very difficult to wade through sloppily presented fiction, however good. Do write a cover letter. If not cute, it can't hurt and may help. Mention previous publication(s)."

$ ◨ **SPIDER, The Magazine for Children,** Carus Publishing Co./Cricket Magazine Group, P.O. Box 300, Peru IL 61354. 1-800-588-8585. **Contact:** Marianne Carus, editor-in-chief. Senior Editor: Tracy Schoenle. Magazine: 8×10; 33 pages; illustrations; photos. "*Spider* publishes high-quality literature for beginning readers, mostly children ages 6 to 9." Monthly. Estab. 1994. Circ. 81,000.

● Carus Publishing also publishes *Cricket* magazine, *Ladybug, the Magazine for Young Children*, *Babybug* and *Cicada*.

Needs: Children's/juvenile (6-9 years), fantasy (children's fantasy). "No religious, didactic, or violent stories, or anything that talks down to children." Accepts 4 mss/issue. Publishes ms 2-3 years after acceptance. Agented fiction 2%. Published work by Lissa Rovetch, Ursula K. LeGuin and Eric Kimmel. Length: 300-1,000 words; average length: 775 words. Also publishes poetry. Often comments on rejected ms.

How to Contact: Send complete ms with a cover letter. Include exact word count. Responds in 3 months. Send SASE for return of ms. Accepts simultaneous and reprint submissions. Sample copy for $5. Guidelines for #10 SASE.

Payment/Terms: Pays 25¢/word and 2 contributor's copies; additional copies $2. Pays on publication for first rights or one-time rights.

Advice: "Read back issues of *Spider*." Looks for "quality writing, good characterization, lively style, humor."

☑ **$** ☐ **SPIRIT,**, Good Ground Press, 1884 Randolph Ave., St. Paul MN 55105. (651)690-7010. Fax: (651)690-7039. Website: www.goodgroundpress.com. **Contact:** Joan Mitchell, editor. Magazine: 8 ½×11; 4 pages; 50 lb. paper. Religious education magazine for Roman Catholic teens. "Stories must be realistic, not moralistic or pietistic. They are used as catalysts to promote teens' discussion of their conflicts." Biweekly (28 issues). Estab. 1988. Circ. 25,000.

Needs: Feminist, religious/inspirational, young adult/teen. Upcoming themes: Christmas and Easter. List of upcoming themes available for SASE. Receives 20 unsolicited mss/month. Accepts 1 mss/issue; 12 mss/year. Publishes ms 6-12 months after acceptance. Published work by Margaret McCarthy, Kathleen Y Choi, Heather Klassen, Kathleen Cleberg, Bob Bartlett and Ron LaGro. Length: 1,000-1,200 words. Sometimes comments on rejected mss.

How to Contact: Send complete ms with a cover letter. Include estimated word count. Responds in 6 months to mss. SASE for return of ms or send a disposable copy of ms. Accepts simultaneous submissions and reprints. Sample copy and guidelines free.

Payment/Terms: Pays $200 minimum and 5 contributor's copies. Pays on publication for first North American serial rights.

Advice: Looks for "believable conflicts for teens. Just because we're religious, don't send pious, moralistic work."

☑ **$** ◨ ◎ **STANDARD,** Nazarene International Headquarters, 6401 The Paseo, Kansas City MO 64131. (816)333-7000. Fax: (816)333-4439. E-mail: ssm@nazarene.org. Website: www.nazarene.org. **Contact:** Everett Leadingham, editor. Magazine: 8½×11; 8 pages; illustrations; photos. Inspirational reading for adults. Weekly. Estab. 1936. Circ. 165,000.

● *Standard* ranked #40 on the *Writer's Digest* Fiction 50 list of top markets for fiction writers.

Needs: "Looking for stories that show Christianity in action." Publishes ms 14-18 months after acceptance. **Published new writers within the last year.** Length: 500-1,200 words; average length: 1,200 words.

How to Contact: Send complete ms with name, address and phone number. Responds in 3 months to mss. SASE. Accepts simultaneous submissions but will pay only reprint rates. Sample copy and guidelines for SAE and 2 first-class stamps.

Payment/Terms: Pays 3½¢/word; 2¢/word (reprint). Pays on acceptance. Pays contributor's copies on publication.

$ ✪ STORY FRIENDS, Mennonite Publishing House, 616 Walnut Ave., Scottdale PA 15683-1999. (724)887-8500. Fax: (724)887-3111. E-mail: rstutz@mph.org. **Contact:** Rose Mary Stutzman, editor. A magazine which portrays Jesus as a friend and helper. Nonfiction and fiction for children 4-9 years of age. Monthly.
   ● The Mennonite Publishing House also published *On the Line*, *Purpose* and *With* magazines.
Needs: Juvenile. Stories of everyday experiences at home, in church, in school or at play, which provide models of Christian values. "Wants to see more fiction set in African-American, Latino or Hispanic settings. No stories about children and their grandparents or children and their elderly neighbors. I have more than enough." **Publishes 10-12 new writers/year.** Published work by Virginia Kroll and Lisa Harkrader. Length: 300-800 words.
How to Contact: Send complete ms with SASE. Seasonal or holiday material should be submitted 6 months in advance. Buys reprints. Free sample copy with SASE.
Payment/Terms: Pays 3-5¢/word. Pays on acceptance for one-time rights. Not copyrighted.
Advice: "I am buying more 500-word stories since we switched to a new format. It is important to include relationships, patterns of forgiveness, respect, honesty, trust and caring. Prefer exciting yet plausible short stories which offer varied settings, introduce children to wide ranges of friends and demonstrate joys, fears, temptations and successes of the readers. Read good children's literature, the classics, the Newberry winner and the Caldecott winners. Respect children you know and allow their resourcefulness and character to have a voice in your writing."

☑ $ ✪ THE SUN, The Sun Publishing Company, Inc., 107 N. Roberson St., Chapel Hill NC 27516. (919)942-5282. Fax: (919)932-3101. Website: www.thesunmagazine.org (includes guidelines, staff list and order forms). **Contact:** Sy Safransky, editor. Magazine: 8½×11; 48 pages; offset paper; glossy cover stock; photos. "While we tend to favor personal writing, we're open to just about anything—even experimental writing, if it doesn't make us feel stupid. Surprise us; we often don't know what we'll like until we read it." Monthly. Estab. 1974. Circ. 50,000.
   ● *The Sun* ranked #37 on the *Writer's Digest* Fiction 50 list of top markets for fiction writers.
Needs: Open to all fiction. Receives approximately 500 unsolicited fiction mss each month. Accepts 2 ms/issue. **Publishes 4-6 new writers/year.** Published work by Poe Ballantine, Sybil Smith and Gillian Kendall. Length: 7,000 words maximum. Also publishes poetry.
How to Contact: Send complete ms with SASE. Responds in 3 months. Publishes ms an average of 6-12 months after acceptance. Sample copy for $5
Payment/Terms: Pays up to $500, 2 contributor's copies, and a complimentary one-year subscription. Pays on publication for one-time rights. Publishes reprints.
Tips: "We favor honest, personal writing with an intimate point of view."

[N] $ ✪ 'TEEN MAGAZINE, Petersen Publishing Co., 6420 Wilshire Blvd., Los Angeles CA 90048-5515. (213)782-2955. Fax: (213)782-2660. Website: www.teenmag.com. **Contact:** Tommi Lewis, editor. Magazine: 100-150 pages; 34 lb. paper; 60 lb. cover; illustrations; photos. "The magazine contains fashion, beauty and features for the young teenage girl. The median age of our readers is 16. Our success stems from our dealing with relevant issues teens face." Monthly. Estab. 1957. Circ. 1.1 million.
Needs: Adventure, humor, mystery, romance and young adult. Every story, whether romance, mystery, humor, etc., must be aimed at teenage girls. The protagonist should be a teenage girl. Subject matter should be appropriate for the average 15-year-old reader. No experimental, science fiction, fantasy or horror. Buys 1 ms/issue; 12 mss/year. Generally publishes ms 3-5 months after acceptance. Length: 2,500-4,000 words. Publishes short shorts.
How to Contact: Send complete ms and short cover letter with SASE. Responds in 10 weeks to mss. Sample copy for $2.50. Guidelines for SASE.
Payment/Terms: Pays $500. Pays on acceptance for all rights.
Advice: "Try to find themes that suit the modern teen. We need innovative ways of looking at the age-old problems of young love, parental pressures, making friends, being left out, etc. Subject matter and vocabulary should be appropriate for an average 16-year-old reader. *'TEEN* would prefer to have romance balanced with a plot, re: a girl's inner development and search for self. Handwritten mss will not be read."

☑ $ ✪ ▼ TOUCH, GEMS (Girls Everywhere Meeting the Savior) Girls' Clubs, Box 7259, Grand Rapids MI 49510. (616)241-5616. Fax: (616)241-5558. E-mail: sara@gemsgc.org. Editor: Jan Boone. **Contact:** Sara Lynne Hilton, managing editor. Magazine: 8½×11; 24 pages; 50 lb. paper; 50 lb. cover stock; illustrations; photos. "Our purpose is to lead girls into a living relationship with Jesus Christ and to help them see how God is at work in their lives and the world around them. Puzzles, poetry, crafts, stories, articles, and club input for girls ages 9-14." Monthly. Circ. 16,000.
   ● *Touch* has received awards for fiction and illustration from the Evangelical Press Association.

Needs: Adventure, ethnic, juvenile and religious/inspirational. Write for upcoming themes. Each year has an overall theme and each month has a theme to fit with yearly themes. Receives 50 unsolicited fiction mss/month. Buys 3 mss/issue; 30 mss/year. **Published new writers within the last year.** Published work by A.J. Schut. Length: 400-1,000 words; average length: 800 words.

How to Contact: Send complete ms with 8 × 10 SASE. Cover letter with short description of the manuscript. Responds in 2 months. Accepts simultaneous, multiple and previously published submissions. Sample copy for 8 × 10 SASE. Free guidelines.

Payment/Terms: Pays 3-5¢/word. Pays on publication for simultaneous, first or second serial rights.

Advice: "Try new and refreshing approaches. No fluffy fiction with Polyanna endings. We want stories dealing with real issues facing girls today. The one-parent, new girl at school is a bit overdone in our market. We have been dealing with issues like AIDS, abuse, drugs, and family relationships in our stories—more awareness-type articles."

☑ $◐ TROIKA MAGAZINE, Wit, Wisdom, and Wherewithal, Lone Tout Publications, Inc., P.O. Box 1006, Weston CT 06883. (203)319-0873. Fax: (203)319-0874. E-mail: etroika@aol.com. Website: www.troik amagazine.com. **Contact:** Celia Meadow, editor. Magazine: 8⅛ × 10⅝; 100 pages; 45 lb. Expression paper; 100 lb. Warren cover; illustrations; photos. "Our general interest magazine is geared toward an audience aged 30-50 looking to balance a lifestyle of family, community and personal success." Quarterly. Estab. 1994. Circ. 100,000.

Needs: Humor/satire, literary, mainstream/contemporary. No genre, experimental or children's. List of upcoming themes available for SASE. Receives 200 unsolicited mss/month. Accepts 2-5 mss/issue; 8-20 mss/year. Publishes ms 3-6 months after acceptance. **Publishes 40-50 new writers/year.** Recently published work by Daniel Etessani, J.P. Maney and Olivia Goldsmith. Length: 2,000-3,000 words. Also publishes literary essays and literary criticism. Sometimes comments on rejected ms.

How to Contact: Send complete ms with a cover letter giving address, phone/fax number and e-mail address. Accepts queries/mss by e-mail. Include estimated word count, brief bio, SASE and list of publications with submission. Responds in 3 months. Send SASE for reply to query. Send a disposable copy of ms. Accepts simultaneous and electronic submissions. Sample copy for $5. Guidelines for #10 SASE.

Payment/Terms: Pays $250 maximum. Pays on publication for first North American serial rights.

Tips: "What makes a manuscript stand out? An authentic voice, an original story, a strong narrative, a delight in language, a sharp eye for detail, a keen intelligence. But proper grammar and spelling don't hurt either."

◐ ⛊ TURTLE MAGAZINE FOR PRESCHOOL KIDS, Children's Better Health Institute, Benjamin Franklin Literary & Medical Society, Inc., Box 567, 1100 Waterway Blvd., Indianapolis IN 46206. (317)636-8881. **Editor:** Terry Harshman. Magazine of picture stories and articles for preschool children 2-5 years old.
  ● The Children's Better Health Institute also publishes *Children's Digest, Children's Playmate, Jack and Jill* and *Humpty Dumpty*, also listed in this section.

Needs: Juvenile (preschool). Special emphasis on health, nutrition, exercise and safety. Also has need for "action rhymes to foster creative movement, very simple science experiments, and simple food activities." Receives approximately 100 unsolicited fiction mss/month. Published new writers within the last year. Length: 100-300 words.

How to Contact: Send complete ms with SASE. No queries. Responds in 10 weeks. Send SASE for Editorial Guidelines. Sample copy for $1.75.

Payment/Terms: Pays up to 22¢/word (approximate); varies for poetry and activities; includes 10 complimentary copies of issue in which work appears. Pays on publication for all rights.

Advice: "Become familiar with recent issues of the magazine and have a thorough understanding of the preschool child. You'll find we are catering more to our youngest readers, so think simply. Also, avoid being too heavy-handed with health-related material. First and foremost, health features should be fun! Because we have developed our own turtle character ('PokeyToes'), we are not interested in fiction stories featuring other turtles."

Ⓝ $◐ TWA AMBASSADOR, Pohly & Partners, 27 Melchor St., Floor 2, Boston MA 02210. (617)451-1700. Fax: (617)338-7767. **Contact:** Michael Buller, editor. Magazine: 8½ × 11; 82 pages; illustrations; photos. Monthly. Circ. 180,000. Member: MPA.

Needs: Humor/satire. List of upcoming themes available for SASE. Receives 10 unsolicited mss/month. Accepts 2 mss/issue. Publishes ms 4-6 months after acceptance. Length: 2,000-3,500 words; average length: 1,500 words. Sometimes comments on rejected mss.

How to Contact: Include brief bio and list of publications. Responds in 3 weeks to queries; 2 months to mss. Send a disposable copy of ms and #10 SASE for reply only. Accepts simultaneous submissions. Sample copy free for SASE. Guidelines for SASE.

Payment/Terms: Pays $750-2,000 and 5 contributor's copies. Pays on acceptance for first rights. Sends galleys to author.

$◐ ◎ WITH: The Magazine for Radical Christian Youth, Faith & Life Press, Box 347, Newton KS 67114-0347. (316)283-5100. **Contact:** Carol Duerksen, editor. Editorial Assistant: Delia Graber. Magazine:

8½×11; 32 pages; 60 lb. coated paper and cover; illustrations; photos. "Our purpose is to help teenagers understand the issues that impact them and to help them make choices that reflect Mennonite-Anabaptist understandings of living by the Spirit of Christ. We publish all types of material—fiction, nonfiction, teen personal experience, etc." Published 6 times/year. Estab. 1968. Circ. 6,100.

• *With* ranked #34 on the *Writer's Digest* Fiction 50 list of top markets for fiction writers.

Needs: Contemporary, ethnic, humor/satire, mainstream, religious, young adult/teen (15-18 years). "We accept issue-oriented pieces as well as religious pieces. No religious fiction that gives 'pat' answers to serious situations." Would like to see more humor. Receives about 50 unsolicited mss/month. Accepts 1-2 mss/issue; 10-12 mss/year. Publishes ms up to 1 year after acceptance. Published work by Shirley Byers Lalonde. Publishes 1-3 new writers/year. Length: 400-2,000 words; 1,500 words preferred.

How to Contact: Send complete ms with cover letter, include short summary of author's credits and what rights they are selling. Responds in 2 months to mss. SASE. Accepts simultaneous and reprint submissions. Sample copy for 9×12 SAE and $1.21 postage. Guidelines for #10 SASE.

Payment/Terms: Pays 4¢/word for reprints; 6¢/word for simultaneous rights (one-time rights to an unpublished story); 6-10¢/word for assigned stories (first rights). Supplies contributor's copies; charge for extras.

Advice: "Each story should make a single point that our readers will find helpful through applying it in their own lives. Request our theme list and detailed guidelines (enclose SASE). All our stories are theme-related, so writing to our themes greatly improves your odds."

☑ ★ $□ **WOMAN'S WORLD MAGAZINE, The Woman's Weekly**, 270 Sylvan Ave., Englewood Cliffs NJ 07632. E-mail: dearww@aol.com. **Fiction Editor:** Johnene Granger. Magazine; 9½×11; 54 pages. We publish short romances and mini-mysteries for all women, ages 18-68." Weekly. Estab. 1980. Circ. 1.5 million.

Needs: Romance (contemporary), mystery. "We buy contemporary romances of 1,500 words. Stories must revolve around a compelling, true-to-life relationship dilemma; may feature a male or female protagonist, and may be written in either the first or third person. We are *not* interested in stories of life-or-death, or fluffy, fly-away style romances. When we say romance, what we really mean is relationship, whether it's just beginning or is about to celebrate its 50th anniversary." Receives 2,500 unsolicited mss/month. Accepts 2 mss/issue; 104 mss/year. Publishes mss 2-3 months after acceptance. Recently published work by Linda S. Reilly, Linda Yellin and Tim Myers. Length: romances—1,500 words; mysteries—1,000 words.

How to Contact: Send complete ms, "double spaced and typed in number 12 font." Cover letter not necessary. Include name, address, phone number and fax on first page of mss. *No queries.* Responds in 8 months. SASE. Guidelines free.

Payment/Terms: Romances—$1,000, mysteries—$500. Pays on acceptance for first North American serial rights only.

Advice: "Familiarize yourself totally with our format and style. Read at least a year's worth of *Woman's World* fiction. Analyze and dissect it. Regarding romances, scrutinize them not only for content but tone, mood and sensibility."

🌐 ▼ **THE WORLD OF ENGLISH**, P.O. Box 1504, Beijing China. **Contact:** Yu-Lun Chen, chief editor. Monthly. Circ. 300,000.

• *The World of English* was named among the 100 Key National Social Periodicals for 2000-2001.

Needs: "We welcome contributions of short and pithy articles that would cater to the interest of our reading public, new and knowledgeable writings on technological finds, especially interesting stories and novels, etc."

How to Contact: Accepts mss by e-mail or fax.

Payment/Terms: "As our currency is regrettably inconvertible, we send copies of our magazines as the compensation for contributions."

Advice: "Aside from literary works, we put our emphasis on the provision of articles that cover various fields in order to help readers expand their vocabulary rapidly and enhance their reading level effectively, and concurrently to raise their level in writing. Another motive is to render assistance to those who, while learning English, are able also to enrich their knowledge and enlarge their field of vision."

◯ **WY'EAST HISTORICAL JOURNAL**, Crumb Elbow Publishing, P.O. Box 294, Rhododendron OR 97049. (503)622-4798. **Contact:** Michael P. Jones, editor. Journal: 5½×8½; 60 pages; top-notch paper; hardcover and softbound; illustrations; photos. "The journal is published for Cascade Geographic Society, a nonprofit educational organization. Publishes historical or contemporary articles on subjects like the history of Oregon's Mt. Hood, the Columbia River, the Pacific NW, the Old Oregon Country, Indian myths and legends, westward trails, the Pony Express and mining. For young adults to elderly." Quarterly. Estab. 1992. Circ. 2,500.

Needs: Open. Special interests include wildlife and fisheries, history of fur trade in Pacific Northwest, the Oregon Trail and Indians. "All materials should relate—somehow—to the region the publication is interested in." Publishes annual special fiction issue in winter. Receives 10 unsolicited mss/month. Accepts 1-2 mss/issue;

22-24 mss/year. Publishes ms up to one year after acceptance. Published work by Joel Palmer. Publishes 5-10 new writers/year. Publishes short shorts. Recommends other markets. "We have several other publications through Crumb Elbow Publishing where we can redirect the material."

How to Contact: Query with clips of published work or send complete ms with cover letter. Responds in 2 months "depending upon work load." SASE (required or material will *not* be returned). Accepts simultaneous and reprint submissions. Guidelines for #10 SASE.

Payment/Terms: Pays contributor's copies on publication. Acquires one-time rights.

Advice: "A ms has to have a historical or contemporary tie to the Old Oregon Country, which was the lands that lay west of the Rocky Mountains to the Pacific Ocean, south to and including Northern California, and north to and including Alaska. It has to be about such things as nature, fish and wildlife, the Oregon Trail, pioneer settlement and homesteading, the Indian wars, gold mining, wild horses, Native American way of life and culture—which are only a few ideas. It has to be written in a non-offensive style, meaning please remove all four-letter words or passages dealing with loose sex and racist comments. Do not be afraid to try something a little different. If you write for the marketplace you might get published, but you loose something in the creative presentation. Write to please yourself and others will recognize your refreshing approach. We have a special need for ghost stories of the Old and New West."

YANKEE MAGAZINE, Yankee Publishing Inc., P.O. Box 520, Dublin NH 03444. (603)563-8111. Fax: (603)563-8252. E-mail: queries@yankeepub.com. Editor: Jim Collins. **Contact:** Editorial Assistant. Magazine: 6×9; 176 pages; glossy paper; 4-color glossy cover stock; illustrations; color photos. "Entertaining and informative New England regional on current issues, people, history, antiques and crafts for general reading audience." Published 10 times/year. Estab. 1935. Circ. 500,000.

• *Yankee* ranked #9 in the *Writer's Digest* Fiction 50 list of top markets for fiction writers.

Needs: Literary. Fiction is to be set in New England or compatible with the area. No religious/inspirational, formula fiction or stereotypical dialect, novels or novellas. Accepts 3-4 mss/year. Published work by Andre Dubus, H. L. Mountzoures and Fred Bonnie. Published new writers within the last year. Length: 2,500 words. Publishes short shorts.

How to Contact: Send complete ms with SASE and previous publications. "Cover letters are important if they provide relevant information: previous publications or awards; special courses taken; special references (e.g. 'William Shakespeare suggested I send this to you . . . .')" Accepts simultaneous submissions, "within reason." Responds in 2 months.

Payment/Terms: Pays $1,000. Pays on acceptance; rights negotiable. Makes "no changes without author consent." Supplies contributor copies; sends galleys to authors.

Advice: "Read previous ten stories in *Yankee* for style and content. Fiction must be realistic and reflect life as it is—complexities and ambiguities inherent. Our fiction adds to the 'complete menu'—the magazine includes many categories—humor, profiles, straight journalism, essays, etc. Listen to the advice of any editor who takes the time to write a personal letter. Go to workshops; get advice and other readings before sending story out cold."

$ **YOUNG SALVATIONIST**, The Salvation Army, P.O. Box 269, 615 Slaters Lane, Alexandria VA 22313. (703)684-5500. Fax: (703)684-5539. E-mail: ys@usn.salvationarmy.org. Website: publications.salvationa rmyusa.org (includes selected articles, writer's guidelines and discussion forums). **Contact:** Tim Clark, managing editor. Magazine: 8×11; 24 pages; illustrations; photos. Christian emphasis articles for youth members of The Salvation Army. 10 issues/year. Estab. 1984. Circ. 50,000.

Needs: Religious/inspirational, young adult/teen. No historical. Would like to see "contemporary, real-life stories that don't preach or talk down to readers." Receives 60 unsolicited mss/month. Buys 9-10 ms/issue; 90-100 mss/year. Publishes ms 3-4 months after acceptance. **Publishes 5 new writers/year.** Published work by Teresa Cleary and Betty Steele Everett. Length: 600-1,200 words; 1,000 words preferred. Publishes short shorts. Sometimes comments on rejected mss and recommends other markets.

How to Contact: Send complete ms. Accepts queries/mss by fax and e-mail. Responds in 2 weeks to queries; 1 month to mss. SASE. Accepts simultaneous and reprint submissions. Sample copy for 9×12 SAE and 3 first-class stamps. Guidelines and theme list for #10 SASE.

Payment/Terms: Pays 15¢/word for all rights, first rights, first North American serial rights and one-time rights; 10¢/word for reprint rights. Pays on acceptance.

Advice: "Don't write about your high school experience. Write about teens now. Know the magazine, its readers and its mission."

Book Publishers

In this section, you will find many of the "big-name" book publishers. Many of these publishers remain tough markets for new writers or for those whose work might be considered literary or experimental. Indeed, some only accept work from established authors, and then often only through an author's agent. However, although having your novel published by one of the big commercial publishers listed in this section is difficult, it is not impossible. The trade magazine *Publishers Weekly* regularly features interviews with writers whose first novels are being released by top publishers. Many editors at large publishing houses find great satisfaction in publishing a writer's first novel.

Also listed here are "small presses" publishing four or more titles annually. Included among them are small and mid-size independent presses, university presses and other nonprofit publishers. Introducing new writers to the reading public has become an increasingly more important role of these smaller presses at a time when the large conglomerates are taking less chances on unknown writers. Many of the successful small presses listed in this section have built their reputations and their businesses in this way and have become known for publishing prize-winning fiction.

These smaller presses also tend to keep books in print longer than larger houses. And, since small presses publish a smaller number of books, each title is equally important to the publisher, and each is promoted in much the same way and with the same commitment. Editors also stay at small presses longer because they have more of a stake in the business—often they own the business. Many smaller book publishers are writers themselves and know first-hand the importance of a close editor-author or publisher-author relationship.

At the end of this section, we've included information on a number of "micropresses," small presses publishing three or fewer books per year.

TYPES OF BOOK PUBLISHERS

Large or small, the publishers in this section publish books "for the trade." That is, unlike textbook, technical or scholarly publishers, trade publishers publish books to be sold to the general consumer through bookstores, chain stores or other retail outlets. Within the trade book field, however, there are a number of different types of books.

The easiest way to categorize books is by their physical appearance and the way they are marketed. Hardcover books are the more expensive editions of a book, sold through bookstores and carrying a price tag of around $20 and up. Trade paperbacks are soft-bound books, also sold mostly in bookstores, but they carry a more modest price tag of usually around $10 to $20. Today a lot of fiction is published in this form because it means a lower financial risk than hardcover.

Mass market paperbacks are another animal altogether. These are the smaller "pocket-size" books available at bookstores, grocery stores, drug stores, chain retail outlets, etc. Much genre or category fiction is published in this format. This area of the publishing industry is very open to the work of talented new writers who write in specific genres such as science fiction, romance and mystery.

At one time publishers could be easily identified and grouped by the type of books they do. Today, however, the lines between hardcover and paperback books are blurred. Many publishers known for publishing hardcover books also publish trade paperbacks and have paperback imprints. This enables them to offer established authors (and a very few lucky newcomers) hard-soft deals in which their book comes out in both versions. Thanks to the mergers of the past decade, too, the same company may own several hardcover and paperback subsidiaries and imprints, even though their editorial focuses may remain separate.

CHOOSING A BOOK PUBLISHER

In addition to checking the bookstores and libraries for books by publishers that interest you, you may want to refer to the Category Index at the back of this book to find publishers divided by specific subject categories. If you write genre fiction, check our new genre sections for lists of book publishers: (mystery, page 57; romance, page 68; science fiction/fantasy & horror, page 78). The subjects listed in the Indexes are general. Read individual listings to find which subcategories interest a publisher. For example, you will find several romance publishers listed in the For Romance Writers Section, but read the listings to find which type of romance is considered—gothic, contemporary, Regency or futuristic. See How to Use This Book to Publish Your Fiction for more on how to refine your list of potential markets.

The icons appearing before the names of the publishers will also help you in selecting a publisher. These codes are especially important in this section, because many of the publishing houses listed here require writers to submit through an agent. A ◙ icon identifies those that mostly publish established and agented authors, while a ◲ points to publishers most open to new writers. See the inside front and back covers of this book for a complete list and explanations of symbols used in this book.

IN THE LISTINGS

As with other sections in this book, we identify new listings with a ◪ symbol. In this section, most with this symbol are not new publishers, but instead are established publishers who decided to list this year in the hope of finding promising new writers.

In addition to the ◪ symbol indicating new listings, we include other symbols to help you in narrowing your search. English-speaking foreign markets are denoted by a ⊕ . The maple leaf symbol ◪ identifies Canadian presses. If you are not a Canadian writer, but are interested in a Canadian press, check the listing carefully. Many small presses in Canada receive grants and other funds from their provincial or national government and are, therefore, restricted to publishing Canadian authors.

We continue to include editorial comments set off by a bullet (●) within listings. This is where we include information about any special requirements or circumstances that will help you know even more about the publisher's needs and policies. The ◪ symbol identifies publishers who have recently received honors or awards for their books. And the ◪ symbol indicates that a publisher accepts agented submissions only.

Each listing includes a summary of the editorial mission of the house, an overarching principle that ties together what they publish. Under the heading **Contact**: we list one or more editors, often with their specific area of expertise. An imprint listed in boldface type means there is an independent listing arranged alphabetically within this section.

Book editors asked us again this year to emphasize the importance of paying close attention to the Needs and How to Contact subheads of listings for book publishers. Unlike magazine editors who want to see complete manuscripts of short stories, most of the book publishers listed here ask that writers send a query letter with an outline and/or synopsis and several chapters of their novel. The Business of Fiction Writing, beginning on page 105 of this book, outlines how to prepare work to submit directly to a publisher.

There are no subsidy book publishers listed in *Novel & Short Story Writer's Market*. By subsidy, we mean any arrangement in which the writer is expected to pay all or part of the cost of producing, distributing and marketing his book. We feel a writer should not be asked to share in any cost of turning his manuscript into a book. All the book publishers listed here told us that they *do not charge writers* for publishing their work. *If any of the publishers listed here ask you to pay any part of publishing or marketing your manuscript, please let us know.*

A NOTE ABOUT AGENTS

Many publishers are willing to look at unsolicited submissions, but most feel having an agent is to the writer's best advantage. In this section more than any other, you'll find a number of publishers who prefer submissions from agents. That's why we've included a section of agents open to submissions from fiction writers (page 115).

For listings of more agents and additional information on how to approach and deal with them, see the 2001 *Guide to Literary Agents*, published by Writer's Digest Books. The book separates nonfee- and fee-charging agents. While many agents do not charge any fees up front, a few charge writers to cover the costs of using outside readers. Be wary of those who charge large sums of money for reading a manuscript. Reading fees do not guarantee representation. Think of an agent as a potential business partner and feel free to ask tough questions about his or her credentials, experience and business practices.

For More Information

Some of the mystery, romance and science fiction publishers included in this section are also included in *Mystery Writer's Sourcebook*, *Romance Writer's Sourcebook* or *Science Fiction and Fantasy Writer's Sourcebook* (all published by Writer's Digest Books). These books include in-depth interviews with editors and publishers. Also check issues of *Publishers Weekly* for publishing industry trade news in the U.S. and around the world or *Quill & Quire* for book publishing news in the Canadian book industry.

For more small presses see the *International Directory of Little Magazines and Small Presses* published by Dustbooks (P.O. Box 100, Paradise CA 95967). To keep up with changes in the industry throughout the year, check issues of two small press trade publications: *Small Press Review* (also published by Dustbooks) and *Independent Publisher* (Jenkins Group, Inc., 121 E. Front St., 4th Floor, Traverse City MI 49684).

✓ ◎ **ABSEY & CO., INC.,** 23011 Northcrest Dr., Spring TX 77389. (888)41ABSEY (412-2739). Fax: (281)251-4676. E-mail: abseyandco@aol.com. Website: www.absey.com (includes authors, titles and descriptions, contact information). **Contact:** Trey Hall, editor-in-chief. "We are interested in book-length fiction of literary merit with a firm intended audience." Publishes hardcover and paperback originals. Averages 6-10 titles/ year. **Published 3-10 new writers within the last year.**
Needs: Juvenile, mainstream/contemporary, short story collections. Also publishes poetry. Published *The Legacy of Roxaboxen*, by Alice McLerran; *Where I'm From*, by George Ella Lyon; *Brothers of the Bat*, by James LeBuffe; *Phonics Friendly Books*, by Joyce Armstrong Carroll; and *Phonics Friendly Families*, by Kelley R. Smith.
How to Contact: Accepts unsolicited mss. Send query letter. Send SASE or IRC for return of ms. Responds in 3 months to queries; 9 months to mss.
Terms: Pays royalties of 8-15% on wholesale price. Publishes ms 1 year after acceptance. Writer's guidelines for #10 SASE.
Advice: "Since we are a small, new press looking for good manuscripts with a firm intended audience, we tend to work closely and attentively with our authors. Many established authors who have been with the large New York houses have come to us to publish their work because we work closely with them."

◎ **ACADEMY CHICAGO PUBLISHERS,** 363 W. Erie St., Chicago IL 60610. (312)751-7300. **Contact:** Anita Miller, senior editor. Estab. 1975. Midsize independent publisher. Publishes hardcover and paperback originals and paperback reprints.
Needs: Biography, history, academic and anthologies. Only the most unusual mysteries, no private-eyes or thrillers. No explicit sex or violence. Serious fiction, no romance/adventure. "We will consider historical fiction that is well researched. No science fiction/fantasy, no religious/inspirational, no how-to, no cookbooks. In general,

we are very conscious of women's roles. We publish very few children's books." Published *The Man Who Once Played Catch with Nellie Fox*, by John Mandarino; *Glass Hearts*, by Terri Paul; and *Murder at Heartbreak Hospital*, by Henry Slesar.

How to Contact: Does not accept unsolicited mss. Query with first three consecutive chapters, triple spaced. Include cover letter briefly describing the content of your work. Send SASE or IRC for return of ms. "Manuscripts without envelopes will be discarded. *Mailers* are a *must*."

Terms: Pays royalties of 5-10% on net; no advance. Publishes ms 18 months after acceptance. Sends galleys to author.

Advice: "At the moment we are swamped with manuscripts and anything under consideration can be under consideration for months."

ACE SCIENCE FICTION, Berkley Publishing Group, Imprint of Penguin Putnam Inc., 375 Hudson St., New York NY 10014. (212)366-2000. **Contact:** Susan Allison, editor-in-chief; Anne Sowards, assistant editor. Estab. 1948. Publishes paperback originals and reprints and 6-10 hardcovers per year. Number of titles: 6/month. Buys 85-95% agented fiction.

Needs: Science fiction and fantasy. No other genre accepted. No short stories. Published *Forever Peace*, by Joe Haldeman; *Neuromancer*, by William Gibson; *King Kelson's Bride*, by Katherine Kurtz.

How to Contact: Accepts unsolicited mss. Query with outline/synopsis and 3 sample chapters. Send SASE. No simultaneous submissions. Responds in 2 months minimum to mss. "Queries answered immediately if SASE enclosed." Publishes ms an average of 18 months after acceptance.

Terms: Standard for the field. Sends galleys to author.

Advice: "Good science fiction and fantasy are almost always written by people who have read and loved a lot of it. We are looking for knowledgeable science or magic, as well as sympathetic characters with recognizable motivation. We are looking for solid, well-plotted science fiction: good action adventure, well-researched hard science with good characterization and books that emphasize characterization without sacrificing plot. In fantasy we are looking for all types of work, from high fantasy to sword and sorcery." Submit fantasy and science fiction to Anne Sowards.

ADVENTURE BOOK PUBLISHERS, Durksen Enterprises Ltd., 3545-32 Ave. NE, #712, Calgary, Alberta T1Y 6M6 Canada. Phone/fax: (403)285-6844. E-mail: adventure@puzzlesbyshar.com. Website: www.puzzlesbyshar.com/adventurebooks/ (includes e-book sales with secure ordering, basic instructions for queries, FAQs, who and where we are, how we publish and all about e-books, including browsing samples). **Contact:** S. Durksen, editor. Estab. 1998. "Small, independent. e-books and some print versions (trade edition style). We are unique in that we are beginning to supply 'physical' e-books to bookstores." Publishes e-books (download and disk versions). **Published 20 new writers within the last year.** Plans 40 first novels in 2001. Averages 50 total titles, 45 fiction titles/year.

Needs: Adventure, children's/juvenile, fantasy (space fantasy, sword and sorcery), historical (general), humor/satire, military/war, mystery/suspense (amateur sleuth, cozy, police procedural, private eye/hardboiled), romance (contemporary, historical, romantic suspense), science fiction (hard science/technological, soft/sociological), thriller/espionage, western (frontier saga, traditional), young adult/teen (adventure, fantasy/science fiction, mystery/suspense, problem novels, romance, series, sports, western). Recently published *Wolfe's Pack*, by Robert M. Blacketer (adventure/military); *The Triumph Mine*, by AJ Lee (fiction); and *Blood Drops Through Time*, by Christine Westendorp (historical fiction/fantasy).

How to Contact: Does not accept unsolicited mss; returns mss "if adequate international postage and envelopes are provided." Query via e-mail with 1-2 page synopsis. Include estimated word count and brief bio. Responds in 3 weeks to queries; up to 6 months to mss. Accepts ms submissions "only by invitation and in accordance with guidelines given to those invited." Always comments on rejected mss.

Terms: Pays royalties of 20%. Does not send galleys to author. Publishes ms 7-10 months after acceptance. Writer's guidelines on website.

Advice: "Good stories can be told without excessive sex and violence graphically detailed for shock value only. We do not consider works of a pornographic, illegal or harmful nature. Preference is given to mainstream manuscripts as opposed to topics with time or issue limitations. Please take the time to proofread with a critical eye before submitting."

ADVOCACY PRESS, Box 236, Santa Barbara CA 93102-0236. (805)962-2728. Fax: (805)963-3508. E-mail: advpress@impulse.net. Website: www.advocacypress.com (includes book catalog, order form, mission statement). **Contact:** Curriculum Specialist. Estab. 1983. "We promote gender equity and positive self-esteem through our programs and publications." Small publisher. Publishes hardcover and paperback originals. Books: perfect or Smyth-sewn binding; illustrations. Average print order: 5,000-10,000. First novel print order: 5,000-10,000. Averages 3-5 total titles, 2 children's fiction titles/year. Promotes titles through catalogs, distributors, tradeshows, individuals, schools and bookstores.

● Advocacy Press books have won the Ben Franklin Award and the Friends of American Writers Award. The press also received the Eleanor Roosevelt Research and Development Award from the American Association of University Women for its significant contribution to equitable education.

Needs: Juvenile. Wants only gender equity/positive esteem messages to boys and girls—picture books; self-esteem issues. Published *Minou*, by Mindy Bingham (picture book); *Kylie's Song*, by Patty Sheehan (picture book); *Nature's Wonderful World in Rhyme*, by William Sheehan.

How to Contact: Accepts unsolicited mss. Submit complete manuscript with SASE for return. Accepts queries by e-mail and fax. Responds in 3 months to queries. Accepts simultaneous submissions.

Terms: Pays royalties of 5-10%. Book catalog for SASE.

Advice: Wants "stories for children that give messages of self-sufficiency/self esteem. Please review some of our publications *before* you submit to us. For layout and writing guidelines, we recommend that you read *The Children's Book: How to Write It, How to Sell It* by Ellen Roberts, Writers Digest Books. *Because of our limited focus, most of our titles have been written inhouse.*"

⊘ ◎ ALASKA NATIVE LANGUAGE CENTER, University of Alaska, P.O. Box 757680, Fairbanks AK 99775-7680. (907)474-7874. **Contact:** Tom Alton, editor. Estab. 1972. Small education publisher limited to books in and about Alaska native languages. Generally nonfiction. Publishes hardcover and paperback originals. Books: 60 lb. book paper; offset printing; perfect binding; photos, line art illustrations. Average print order: 500-1,000 copies. Averages 6-8 total titles/year.

Needs: Ethnic. Publishes original fiction only in native language and English by Alaska native writers. Published *A Practical Grammar of the Central Alaskan Yup'ik Eskimo Language*, by Steven A. Jacobson; *One Must Arrive With a Story to Tell*, by the Elders of Tununak, Alaska.

How to Contact: Does not accept unsolicited mss. Accepts electronic submissions via ASCII for modem transmissions or Macintosh compatible files on 3.5 disk.

Terms: Does not pay. Sends galleys to author.

[N] [◒] [Ψ] [▣] ALEXANDRIA DIGITAL LITERATURE, 701 Fifth Ave., Suite 4380, Seattle WA 98104. (206)464-2841. E-mail: info@alexlit.com. Website: www.alexlit.com (includes catalog, all titles; authors can access a password-protected service to view up-to-the-minute sales data on their works). **Contact:** Kathy Ice (science fiction, fantasy) and Rhias K. Hall (dark fantasy, horror, all poetry), fiction editors. Estab. 1996. "Alexandria Digital Literature publishes previously-published science fiction, fantasy and horror on the Internet. We accept all lengths—poetry through novels—but specialize in shorter works and works that are out of print." Averages 300 total titles, 300 fiction titles/year.

● ADL has been recognized by the Page One Literary Award (1998), *Net Magazine*'s Top 100 (1998-99) and Netscape Cool Site of the Day (1999).

Needs: Fantasy, horror, science fiction. Recently published *Tower of Glass*, by Robert Silverberg; *Izzy and the Father of Terror*, by Eliot Fintushel; and *The Adventure of the Field Theorems*, by Vonda N. McIntyre.

How to Contact: Accepts unsolicited mss. Submit complete ms with cover letter. Accepts queries by e-mail. Include estimated word count and preferred contract terms. Send SASE or disposable copy of ms. Agented fiction 10%. Responds in 1 month to queries; 3 months to mss. Accepts electronic submissions. Sometimes comments on rejected mss.

Terms: Pays royalties of 10-30% or advance. Sends galleys to author. Publishes ms 6-12 months after acceptance. Writer's guidelines free for SASE; book catalogs available online.

Advice: "We're coming to a point where all writers need to be aware of e-publishing—who the players are, what the issues are, how it works, etc. Educate yourself. Find out what's happening in your genre and identify some electronic resources."

⊘ ALGONQUIN BOOKS OF CHAPEL HILL, Subsidiary of Workman Publishing, P.O. Box 2225, Chapel Hill NC 27515-2225.

Imprint(s): Front Porch Paperbacks.

● Algonquin Books is not accepting unsolicited mss or queries at this time.

✓ ⊘ ALYSON PUBLICATIONS, INC., 6922 Hollywood Blvd., Suite 1000, Los Angeles CA 90028. (323)860-6065. Fax: (323)467-6805. Website: www.alyson.com (includes guidelines, calls for submissions, synopses of books and mission statement). **Contact:** Scott Brassart and Angela Brown, fiction editors. Estab. 1979. Medium-sized publisher specializing in lesbian- and gay-related material. Publishes paperback originals, reprints and some hardcover. Books: paper and printing varies; trade paper, perfect-bound. Average print order: 8,000. First novel print order: 6,000. **Published new writers within the last year.** Plans 50 total titles, 25 fiction titles/year.

Imprint(s): Alyson Wonderland, Advocate Books.

● In addition to adult titles, Alyson Publications has been known for its line of young adult and children's books.

Needs: "We are interested in all categories; *all* materials must be geared toward lesbian and/or gay readers. No poetry." Recently published *Silk Road*, by Jane Summer; *Trailblazing*, by Eric Anderson; and *The New York Years*, by Felice Picano. Publishes anthologies. Authors may submit to them directly.
How to Contact: Query first with SASE. Responds in up to 3 months.

ARCADE PUBLISHING, 141 Fifth Ave., New York NY 10010. (212)475-2633. Fax: (212)353-8148. President, Editor-in-Chief: Richard Seaver. **Contact:** Jeannette Seaver, Cal Barksdale and Webster Younce. Estab. 1988. Independent publisher. Publishes hardcover originals and paperback reprints. Books: 50-55 lb. paper; notch, perfect-bound; illustrations. Average print order: 10,000. First novel print order: 3,500-7,500. **Published new writers within the last year.** Averages 40 total titles, 12-15 fiction titles/year. Distributes titles through Time Warner Trade Publishing.
Needs: Literary, mainstream/contemporary, mystery/suspense, translations. No romance, science fiction, young adult. Published *Trying to Save Piggy Sneed*, by John Irving; *Europa*, by Tim Parks; *Dreams of My Russian Summers*, by Andrei Makine; *The Brush-Off*, by Shane Maloney; and *The Queen's Bastard*, by Robin Maxwell.
How to Contact: Does not accept unsolicited mss. Submit through an agent only. Agented fiction 100%. Responds in 2 weeks to queries; 4 months to mss.
Terms: Pays negotiable advances and royalties and 10 author's copies. Writer's guidelines and book catalog for SASE.

ARCHWAY PAPERBACKS, Imprint of Pocket Books for Young Readers, 1230 Avenue of the Americas, New York NY 10020. (212)698-7669. Website: www.simonsayskids.com. **Contact:** Patricia MacDonald, vice president/editorial director. Published by Pocket Books. Publishes paperback originals and reprints. **Published new writers within the last year.**
Imprint(s): Minstrel Books (ages 7-12); and **Archway** (ages 12 and up).
Needs: Young adult: horror, mystery, suspense/adventure, thrillers. Young readers (80 pages and up): adventure, animals, humor, family, fantasy, friends, mystery, school, etc. No picture books. Published *Fear Street: The New Boy*, by R.L. Stine; and *Aliens Ate My Homework*, by Bruce Coville.
How to Contact: Not accepting unsolicited mss.
Payment/Terms: Pays royalties of 6-8%. Publishes ms 2 years after acceptance.

ARSENAL PULP PRESS, 103-1014 Homer St., Vancouver, British Columbia V6B 2W9 Canada. (604)687-4233. Fax: (604)669-8250. E-mail: contact@arsenalpulp.com. Website: www.arsenalpulp.com (includes guidelines, ordering information, book catalog and publicity information). **Contact:** Linda Field, editor. Literary press. Publishes paperback originals. Average print order: 1,500-3,500. First novel print order: 1,500. **Published new writers within the last year.** Averages 12-15 total writers, 2 fiction writers/year. Distributes titles through Whitecap Books (Canada) and LPC Group/In Book (U.S.). Promotes titles through reviews, excerpts and print advertising.
● Arsenal Pulp Press has received 3 Alcuin Society Awards for Excellence in Book Design.
Needs: Ethnic/multicultural (general), feminist, gay, lesbian, literary, short story collections. No genre fiction, i.e. westerns, romance, horror, mystery, etc. Recently published *Quickies 2*, by James E. Johnstone, editor (anthology, gay erotic fiction); and *Hot & Bothered 2*, by Karen X. Tulchinsky, editor (anthology, lesbian erotic fiction).
How to Contact: Accepts unsolicited mss. Query with cover letter, outline/synopsis and 2 sample chapters. Include list of publishing credits. Send SASE for return of ms or send disposable copy of ms and SASE for reply only. Agented fiction 10%. Responds in 1 month to queries; 4 months to mss. Accepts simultaneous submissions. Sometimes comments on rejected mss.
Terms: Pays royalties of 10%. Negotiable advance. Sends galleys to author. Publishes ms 1 year after acceptance. Writer's guidelines and book catalog free for 9×11 SASE.
Advice: "We very rarely publish American writers."

ARTE PUBLICO PRESS, University of Houston, 4800 Calhoun, Houston TX 77204-2174. (713)743-2841. Fax: (713)743-2847. **Contact:** Dr. Nicolás Kanellos, publisher. Estab. 1979. "Small press devoted to the publication of contemporary U.S.-Hispanic literature. Mostly trade paper; publishes 4-6 clothbound books/year. Publishes fiction and belles lettres." Publishes 36 paperback originals and occasionally reprints. Average print order 2,000-5,000. First novel print order 2,500-5,000.
Imprint(s): Piñata Books featuring children's and young adult literature by U.S.-Hispanic authors.
● Arte Publico Press is the oldest and largest publisher of Hispanic literature for children and adults in the United States.
Needs: Childrens/juvenile, contemporary, ethnic, feminist, literary, short story collections, young adult written by US-Hispanic authors. Published *A Perfect Silence*, by Alba Ambert; *Song of the Hummingbird*, by Graciela Limón; and *Little Havana Blues: A Cuban-American Literature Anthology*.
How to Contact: Accepts unsolicited mss. Query with outline/synopsis and sample chapters or complete ms with cover letter. Send SASE or IRC for return of ms. Agented fiction 1%. Responds in 1 month to queries; 4 months to mss. Sometimes comments on rejected mss.

Terms: Pays royalties of 10% on wholesale price. Average advance: $1,000-3,000. Provides 20 author's copies; 40% discount on subsequent copies. Sends galleys to author. Publishes ms minimum 2 years after acceptance. Guidelines for SASE; book catalog free on request.

Advice: "Include cover letter in which you 'sell' your book—why should we publish the book, who will want to read it, why does it matter, etc."

ATHENEUM BOOKS FOR YOUNG READERS, Imprint of the Simon & Schuster Children's Publishing Division, 1230 Avenue of the Americas, New York NY 10022. (212)698-2721. Vice President/Editorial Director: Jonathan J. Lanman. Editorial Coordinator: Howard Kaplan. **Contact:** Marcia Marshall, executive director; Caitlyn Dlouhy, senior editor; Anne Schwartz, editorial director, Anne Schwartz Books. Second largest imprint of large publisher/corporation. Publishes hardcover originals. Books: illustrations for picture books, some illustrated short novels. Average print order: 6,000-7,500. First novel print order: 5,000. Averages 50 total titles, 25 middle grade and YA fiction titles/year.

• Books published by Atheneum Books for Children have received the Newbery Medal (*The View From Saturday*, by E.L. Konigsburg) and the Christopher Award (*The Gold Coin*, by Alma Flor Ada, illustrated by Neal Waldman).

Needs: Juvenile (adventure, animal, contemporary, fantasy, historical, sports, preschool/picture book), young adult/teen (fantasy/science fiction, historical, mystery, problem novels, sports, spy/adventure). No "paperback romance type" fiction. Published *Lottie's New Beach Towel*, by Petra Matthers (3-8, picture book); *Achingly Alice*, by Phyllis Reynolds Naylor (10-14, middle grade novel); *Rearranging*, by David Gifaldi (12 & up young adult fiction).

How to Contact: Does not accept unsolicited mss. Send query letter. Send SASE or IRC for return of the ms. Agented fiction 40%. Responds in 6 weeks to queries. Accepts simultaneous submissions "if we are so informed and author is unpublished."

Terms: Pays royalties of 10%. Average advance: $3,000. "Along with advance and royalties, authors receive ten free copies of their book and can purchase more at a special discount." Sends galleys to author. Writer's guidelines for #10 SASE.

Advice: "We publish all hardcover originals, occasionally an American edition of a British publication. Our fiction needs have not varied in terms of quantity—of the 50-60 titles we do each year, 25 are fiction in different age levels. We are less interested in specific topics or subject matter than in overall quality of craftsmanship. First, know your market thoroughly. We publish only children's books, so caring for and *respecting* children is of utmost importance. Also, fad topics are dangerous, as are works you haven't polished to the best of your ability. (Why should we choose a 'jewel in the rough' when we can get a manuscript a professional has polished to be ready for publication?) The juvenile market is not one in which a writer can 'practice' to become an adult writer. In general, be professional. We appreciate the writers who take the time to find out what type of books we publish by visiting the libraries and reading the books. Neatness is a pleasure, too."

AUNT LUTE BOOKS, P.O. Box 410687, San Francisco CA 94141. (415)826-1300. Fax: (415)826-8300. E-mail: books@auntlute.com. Website: www.auntlute.com (includes writer's guidelines, book catalog, author interviews). **Contact:** Shahara Godfrey, first reader. Small feminist and women-of-color press. Publishes hardcover and paperback originals. Averages 4 total titles/year.

Needs: Ethnic/multicultural, feminist, lesbian.

How to Contact: Accepts unsolicited mss. Query with outline/synopsis and sample chapters. Send SASE for return of ms. Responds in 4 months.

Terms: Pays in royalties. Guidelines and catalog for free.

Advice: "We seek manuscripts, both fiction and nonfiction, by women from a variety of cultures, ethnic backgrounds and subcultures; women who are self-aware and who, in the face of all contradictory evidence, are still hopeful that the world can reserve a place of respect for each woman in it. We seek work that explores the specificities of the worlds from which we come, and which examines the intersections between the borders which we all inhabit."

AUTHORS ONLINE LTD, Adams Yard, Maidenhead St., Herford SG14 1DR England. Phone: (+44)1992-503151. Fax: (+44)207-6812847. E-mail: theeditor@authorsonline.co.uk. Website: www.authorsonline.co.uk (includes books for sale, all genre, in e-format only). **Contact:** Editor. Estab. 1998. "Four-man company allowing self-publishing of previously unpublished titles, reverted rights and works from publishers." Publishes e-books only. First novel print order: 2,000. **Published 71 new writers within the last year.** Averages as many as possible total titles and fiction titles/year.

Needs: Adventure, children's/juvenile, comics/graphic novels, erotica, ethnic/multicultural, experimental, family saga, fantasy, feminist, gay, glitz, historical, horror, humor/satire, lesbian, literary, mainstream, military/war, mystery/suspense, new age/mystic, psychic/supernatural, regional, religious, romance, science fiction, short story collections, thriller/espionage, translations, western, and young adult.

How to Contact: Accepts unsolicited mss. Submit complete ms with cover letter in e-format only. No paper. Include estimated word count and biography. Responds in days to queries and mss. Only accepts electronic submissions or on diskette.
Payment/Terms: Pays royalties of up to 60%. Publishes ms couple of days after acceptance.
Tips: "Send your work in now."

✔ ◐ **AVALON BOOKS,** Imprint of Thomas Bouregy Company, Inc., 160 Madison Ave., New York NY 10016. (212)598-0222. **Contact:** Erin Cartwright, senior editor; Mira Son, assistant editor. Publishes hardcover originals. **Published new writers within the last year.** Averages 60 titles/year. Distributes titles through libraries, Barnes&Noble.com and Amazon.com. Promotes titles through *Library Journal*, Booklist and local papers.
Needs: "Avalon Books publishes wholesome romances, mysteries, westerns. Intended for family reading, our books are read by adults as well as teenagers and their characters are all adults. There is no graphic sex in any of our novels. Currently, we publish 10 books bimonthly: four romances, two career romances, two mysteries and two westerns. All the romances are contemporary; all the westerns are historical." Published *Ten and Me*, by Johnny Boggs (western); *The Marriage Scheme*, by Patricia Azeltine (romance); *Death Spiral*, by Clyde Linsley (mystery); *The Key*, by Eric C. Evans (mystery); and *Bachelor Father*, by Jean Gordon (career romance).
How to Contact: Does not accept unsolicited mss. Query with the first 3 chapters and a brief synopsis (2-3 pages). "We'll contact you if we're interested." Send SASE (ms size) or IRC for return of ms. Responds in about 4 months. "Send SASE for a copy of our writer's guidelines or visit our website www.avalonbooks.com."
Terms: The first half of the advance is paid upon signing of the contract; the second within 30 days after publication. Usually publishes ms within 6-8 months.

✔ ◐ **AVON BOOKS,** Imprint of HarperCollins Children's Books Group, HarperCollins Publishers, 10 E. 53 St., New York NY 10022. (212)207-7000. Website: www.harpercollins.com. **Contact:** Michael Morrison, publisher. Estab. 1941. Large hardcover and paperback publisher. Publishes hardcover and paperback originals and reprints. Averages more than 400 titles a year.
Imprint(s): Avon, Avon EOS.
Needs: Literary fiction and nonfiction, health, history, mystery, science fiction, romance, young adult, pop culture.
How to Contact: Does not accept unsolicited mss. Send query letters only. SASE to insure response.
Terms: Vary.

◐ **BAEN BOOKS,** P.O. Box 1403, Riverdale NY 10471. (718)548-3100. Website: www.baen.com (includes writer's guidelines, chat line, annotated catalog, author bios, tour information). Publisher and Editor: Jim Baen. **Contact:** Toni Weisskopf, executive editor. Estab. 1983. "We publish books at the heart of science fiction and fantasy." Independent publisher. Publishes hardcover and paperback originals and paperback reprints. **Published new writers within the last year.** Plans 2-3 first novels in 2001. Averages 60 fiction titles/year. Distributes titles through Simon & Schuster.
Imprint(s): Baen Science Fiction and Baen Fantasy.
Needs: Fantasy and science fiction. Interested in science fiction novels (based on real science) and fantasy novels "that at least strive for originality." Published *A Civil Campaign*, by Lois McMaster Bujold; *Ashes of Victory*, by David Weber; *Sentry Peak*, by Harry Turtledove.
How to Contact: Accepts unsolicited mss. Submit ms or outline/synopsis and 3 consecutive sample chapters with SASE (or IRC). Responds in 9 months. Accepts simultaneous submissions, "but grudgingly and not as seriously as exclusives." Occasionally comments on rejected mss.
Terms: Pays in royalties; offers advance. Sends galleys to author. Writer's guidelines for SASE.
Advice: "Keep an eye and a firm hand on the overall story you are telling. Style is important but less important than plot. Good style, like good breeding, never calls attention to itself. Read *Writing to the Point*, by Algis Budrys. We like to maintain long-term relationships with authors."

✔ ◐ Ⓐ **BALLANTINE BOOKS,** The Ballantine Publishing Group, A Division of Random House, Inc., 1540 Broadway, New York NY 10036. Fax: (212)792-8442. Website: www.randomhouse.com/BB (includes a complete catalog, author interviews, author chat opportunities, reading guides and topical newsletters). **Contact:** Leona Nevler, editor (all fiction); Peter Borland, executive editor (commercial fiction); Elisa Wares, senior editor (romance, mystery); Joe Blades, associate publisher (mystery). Publishes originals (general fiction, mass-market, trade paperback and hardcover). **Published new writers within the last year.** Averages over 120 total titles/ year.
Needs: Major historical fiction, women's mainstream and general fiction. Recently published *While I Was Gone*, by Sue Miller (fiction); *Hanna's Daughters*, by Marianne Fredriksson (fiction); and *Gone for Soldiers*, by Jeff Shaara.
How to Contact: Does not accept unsolicited proposals or mss. Agented proposals and mss only. Responds in 2 months to queries; 5 months to mss.
Terms: Pays in royalties and advance.

Advice: "Writers should obtain representation by a literary agent."

✓ ◎ **BANKS CHANNEL BOOKS,** P.O. Box 80058, Simpsonville SC 29680. (910)762-4677. Fax: (864)243-9589. E-mail: bankschan@aol.com. **Contact:** E.R. Olefsky, managing editor. Estab. 1993. "We are a regional press doing books *by Carolina authors only*. We look at fiction through our novel contest only." Publishes hardcover and paperback originals and paperback reprints. Books: 50-60 lb. paper; perfect or hardcase bound; illustrations sometimes. Average print order: 3,000. First novel print order: 3,000-5,000. **Published new writers within the last year.** Plans 2 novels in 2001.
Needs: Literary. Published *Styles by Maggie Sweet*, by Judith Minthorn Stacy; *Takedown*, by E.M.J. Benjamin; *Festival in Fire Season* (reprint), by Ellyn Bache.
How to Contact: Does not accept unsolicited mss. Send query letter. Include 1-paragraph bio and list of publishing credits. Send SASE or IRC for return of ms. Responds in 1 week to queries; 2 months to mss. No simultaneous submissions. Charges entry fee for contest.
Payment/Terms: Pays royalties of 6-10%. Sends galleys to author. Publishes ms 1 year after acceptance. Contest guidelines for #10 SASE.
Advice: "We are seeing work that ten years ago would have been snapped up by the big New York presses— and we are delighted to have it. Send a beautifully crafted piece of literary fiction to our contest. It doesn't need to have a Carolina setting, but it helps."

✓ ◎ **BANTAM BOOKS,** The Bantam Dell Publishing Group, A Division of Random House, Inc., 1540 Broadway, New York NY 10036. Website: www.bantamdell.com.
 • See The Bantam Dell Publishing Group listing below.

✓ Ⓐ **THE BANTAM DELL PUBLISHING GROUP,** A Division of Random House, Inc., 1540 Broadway, New York NY 10036. Website: www.bantamdell.com. **Contact:** Jackie Cantor, fiction editor (literary, women's fiction and historical romance); Kara Cesare, fiction editor (romance and women's fiction); Beth DeGuzman, fiction editor (romance, women's fiction, suspense); Tracy Devine, fiction editor (literary, women's fiction, general commercial fiction, suspense, romance); Anne Groell, fiction editor (fantasy and science fiction); Jackie Farber, fiction editor (women's fiction and general commercial fiction); Katie Hall, fiction editor (military, historical); Susan Kamil, fiction editor (The Dial Press—literary, historical); Kathleen Jayes, fiction editor (literary); Kate Miciak, fiction editor (mystery, suspense and historical fiction); Wendy McCurdy, fiction editor (romance and women's fiction); Tom Spain, fiction editor (Americana, historical); Mike Shohl, fiction editor (fantasy and science fiction). The Bantam Dell Publishing Group is composed of seven imprints (Bantam, Delacorte Press, Dell, Delta, DTP, Island and The Dial Press) which collectively publish hardcover, trade paperback, mass market paperback originals and mass market paperback reprints for adult commercial and literary fiction and nonfiction markets.
Imprint(s): Fiction categories are printed under Bantam, Delacorte, Dell, Island and The Dial Press.
Needs: Adventure, fantasy, feminist, historical, literary, mainstream/contemporary, mystery, romance, science fiction and suspense. Recently published *Irresistible Forces*, by Danielle Steel (Delacorte); *The Testament*, by John Grisham (Dell); *Tara Road*, by Maeve Binchy (Delacorte); *The Loop*, by Nicholas Evans (Delacorte); *The Killing Game*, by Iris Johansen (Bantam); *Ashes to Ashes*, by Tami Hoag (Bantam); *Cloud Nine*, by Luanne Rice (Bantam); *War of the Rats*, by David L. Robbins (Bantam); *Losing Julia*, by Jonathan Hull (Delacorte); and *Dating Big Bird*, by Laura Zigman (The Dial Press).
How to Contact: Does not accept unsolicited mss. Accepts agent submissions and single-page query letters with SASE. Include description of work (category and subject matter) and author biography. Query letters or unsolicited mss submitted without SASE will not be returned.

✓ Ⓐ Ⓨ **BANTAM, DOUBLEDAY, DELL/DELACORTE, KNOPF AND CROWN BOOKS FOR YOUNG READERS,** Random House Children's Books, A Division of Random House, Inc., 1540 Broadway, New York NY 10036. (212)782-9000 or (800)200-3552. Website: www.randomhouse.com/kids. Vice President/ Publisher: Beverly Horowitz, Vice President/Editorial Director, Paperbacks: Michelle Poploff. *Bantam, Doubleday, Dell/Delacorte:* Executive Editors: Francoise Bui, Wendy Lamb, Joan Slattery, Karen Wojtyla. Managing Editor: Fiona Simpson. **Contact:** Wendy Loggia, senior editor; Diana Capriotti, editor.
 • *Bud, Not Buddy*, by Christopher Paul Curtis won the Newbery Medal and the Coretta Scott King Award.
Imprint(s): Delacorte Books for Young Readers, Doubleday Books for Young Readers; Laurel Leaf; Skylark; Starfire; Yearling Books.
Needs: Fiction, nonfiction, humor, mystery, adventure, historical, picture books, chapter books, middle-grade, young adult. Recently published *Bud, Not Buddy*, by Christopher Paul Curtis; *White Fox*, by Gary Paulsen; and *Beetle Boy*, by Lawrence David.
How to Contact: Agented fiction only. Can submit to Delacorte Contest for a First Young Adult Novel or Marguerite de Angeli Contest for contemporary or historical fiction set in North America for readers age 7-10. Send SASE for contest guidelines. Responds in up to 4 months. Accepts simultaneous submissions but must be indicated as such.

☑ Ⓐ ☒ **BANTAM, DOUBLEDAY, DELL/DELACORTE, KNOPF AND CROWN BOOKS FOR YOUNG READERS**, Random House Children's Books, A Division of Random House, Inc., 1540 Broadway, New York NY 10036. (212)782-9000 or (800)200-3552. Website: www.randomhouse.com/kids. Vice President/Publisher: Beverly Horowitz, Vice President/Editorial Director, Paperbacks: Michelle Poploff. *Alfred A. Knopf and Crown Books for Young Readers:* Vice President/Publishing Director: Simon Boughton. Vice President/Editor-at-Large: Janet Schulman. **Contact:** Tracy Gates, Nancy Siscoe, senior editors.
Imprint(s): Alfred A. Knopf Books for Young Readers; Crown Books for Young Readers.
Needs: Fiction, nonfiction, mystery, adventure, historical, picture books, chapter books, middle-grade, young adult. Recently published *Stargirl*, by Jerry Spinelli; *The Golden Compass, The Subtle Knife* and *The Amber Spyglass*, by Philip Pullman; *Spirit of Endurance*, by Jennifer Armstrong; and *And to Think that We Thought that We'd Never be Friends*, by Mary Ann Hoberman, illustrated by Kevin Hawkes.
How to Contact: Accepts unsolicited mss. Send SASE for return of ms. Responds in up to 4 months. Accepts simultaneous submissions but must be indicated as such.

☙ ☑ ◑ ◎ **BEACH HOLME PUBLISHERS LTD.**, 226-2040 W. 12th Ave., Vancouver, British Columbia V6J 2G2 Canada. (604)733-4868. Fax: (604)733-4860. E-mail: bhp@beachholme.bc.ca. Website: www.beach holme.bc.ca (includes guidelines, authors, excerpts, titles, ordering information). **Contact:** Michael Carroll, managing editor; Phil Di Tomaso, marketing manager. Estab. 1971. Publishes trade paperback originals. Averages 14 titles/year. "Accepting only Canadian submissions." **Published 6 new writers within the last year.**
Needs: Adult literary fiction from authors published in Canadian literary magazines. Young adult (Canada historical/regional). "Interested in excellent quality, imaginative writing." Recently published *Let the Day Perish*, by Christian Petersen (short fiction); *The Allegra Series*, by Barbara Lambert.
How to Contact: Query with outline and two chapters. Responds in 2 months. Accepts simultaneous submissions, if so noted.
Terms: Pays royalties of 10% on retail price. Average advance: $500. Publishes ms 1 year after acceptance. Writer's guidelines free.
Advice: "Make sure the manuscript is well written. We see so many that only the unique and excellent can't be put down. Prior publication is a must. This doesn't necessarily mean book length manuscripts, but a writer should try to publish his or her short fiction."

◑ **FREDERIC C. BEIL, PUBLISHER, INC.**, 609 Whitaker St., Savannah GA 31401. E-mail: beilbook@beil .com. Website: www.beil.com. **Contact:** Frederic C. Beil III, president; Mary Ann Bowman, editor. Estab. 1983. "Our objectives are (1) to offer to the reading public carefully selected texts of lasting value; (2) to adhere to high standards in the choice of materials and in bookmarking craftsmanship; (3) to produce books that exemplify good taste in format and design; and (4) to maintain the lowest cost consistent with quality." General trade publisher. Publishes hardcover originals and reprints. Books: acid-free paper; letterpress and offset printing; Smyth-sewn, hardcover binding; illustrations. Average print order: 3,000. First novel print order: 3,000. Plans 2 first novels in 2001. Averages 14 total titles, 4 fiction titles/year.
Imprint(s): The Sandstone Press, Hypermedia, Inc.
Needs: Historical, biography, literary, regional, short story collections, translations. Published *A Woman of Means*, by Peter Taylor; *An Exile*, by Madison Jones; and *Delirium of the Brave*, by William C. Harris, Jr.
How to Contact: Does not accept unsolicited mss. Send query letter. Responds in 1 week to queries.
Terms: Payment "all negotiable." Sends galleys to author. Book catalog free on request.

◑ Ⓐ **THE BERKLEY PUBLISHING GROUP**, Imprint of Penguin Putnam Inc., 375 Hudson St., New York NY 10014. (212)366-2000. Publisher/Editor-in-Chief: Leslie Gelbman. Associate Director, Editorial: Susan Allison. **Contact:** Natalee Rosenstein, Judith Palais, Tom Colgan, Gail Fortune, Ginjer Buchanan, Lisa Considine, Denise Silvestro and Christine Zika, fiction editors. Large commercial category line. Publishes paperback originals, trade paperbacks and hardcover and paperback reprints. Books: paperbound printing; perfect binding. Average print order: "depends on position in list." Plans approximately 10 first novels in 2001. Averages 1,180 total titles, 1,000 fiction titles/year.
Imprint(s): Berkley, Jove, Boulevard, **Ace Science Fiction.**
Needs: Fantasy, mainstream, mystery/suspense, romance (contemporary, historical), science fiction. Published works by Tom Clancy and Patricia Cornwell.
How to Contact: *Strongly* recommends agented material. Queries answered if SASE enclosed. Accepts simultaneous submissions. Responds in 3 months minimum to mss.
Terms: Pays royalties of 4-10%. Provides 10 author's copies. Publishes ms 2 years after acceptance. Writer's guidelines and book catalog not available.
Advice: "Aspiring novelists should keep abreast of the current trends in publishing by reading *The New York Times* Bestseller Lists, trade magazines for their desired genre and *Publishers Weekly*."

☑ ◑ ◎ **BETHANY HOUSE PUBLISHERS**, 11400 Hampshire Ave. S., Minneapolis MN 55438. (952)829-2500. Fax: (952)829-2768. Website: www.bethanyhouse.com. Publisher: Gary Johnson. **Contact:**

Sharon Madison, ms review editor; David Horton, senior editor (adult fiction); Barbara Lilland, senior editor (adult fiction); Rochelle Gloege, senior editor (children and youth). Estab. 1956. "The purpose of Bethany House Publisher's publishing program is to relate biblical truth to all areas of life—whether in the framework of a well-told story, of a challenging book for spiritual growth, or of a Bible reference work." Publishes hardcover and trade paperback originals and mass market paperback reprints. Averages 120-150 total titles/year.

Needs: Adult historical fiction, teen/young adult, children's fiction series (age 8-12) and Bethany Backyard (age 6-12). New interest in contemporary fiction. Recently published *The Crossroad*, by Beverly Lewis (fiction).

How to Contact: Does not accept unsolicited fiction. First send SASE or visit website for guidelines. Responds in 3 months. Accepts simultaneous submissions.

Terms: Pays negotiable royalty on net price. Offers negotiable advance. Publishes ms 1 year after acceptance. Writer's guidelines free or on website. Book catalog for 9×12 SAE with 5 first-class stamps.

☑ ◎ **BIRCH BROOK PRESS,** P.O. Box 81, Delhi NY 13753. (212)353-3326. Fax: (607)746-7453. E-mail: birchbrkpr@prodigy.net. Website: www.birchbrookpress.com. **Contact:** Tom Tolnay, publisher. Estab. 1982. Small publisher of popular culture and literary titles in handcrafted letterpress editions. Specializes in fiction anthologies with specific theme. Books: 80 lb. vellum paper; letterpress printing; wood engraving illustrations. Average print order: 500-1,000. Averages 4-6 total titles, 2-3 fiction titles/year. Distributes titles through Ingram, Baker and Taylor, Barnes&Noble.com Amazon.com. Promotes titles through catalogs, direct mail and group ads.

Imprint(s): Birch Brook Press, Persephone Press and Birch Brook Impressions.

Needs: Literary. "We make specific calls for fiction when we are doing an anthology." Plans to publish literary-quality anthology of mysterious short stories on loneliness and another containing short fiction relating to fly fishing. Published *Magic & Madness in the Library*, edited by Eric Graeber (fiction collection); *Kilimanjaro Burning*, by John Robinson (novella); *Autobiography of Maria Callas: A Novel*, by Alma Bond; *The Derelict Genius of Martin M*, by Frank Fagan; and *In Foreign Parts*, by Elisabeth Stevens (stories).

How to Contact: Prefers samples with query letter. Must include SASE. Responds in up to 6 weeks to queries; 3 months to mss. Accepts simultaneous submissions. Sometimes comments on rejected mss.

Terms: Pays modest flat fee on anthologies. Writers guidelines and catalog for SASE.

Advice: "Write well on subjects of interest to BBP such as outdoors, fly fishing, baseball, music and literate mysteries."

☑ ◑ **BJU PRESS,** (formerly Journey Books), 1700 Wade Hampton Blvd., Greenville SC 29614-0001. (864)242-5100, ext. 4316. E-mail: jb@bjup.com. Website: www.bjup.com. **Contact:** Nancy Lohr, editor (juvenile fiction). Estab. 1974. "Small independent publisher of excellent, trustworthy novels, information books, audio tapes and ancillary materials for readers pre-school through high school." Publishes paperback originals and reprints. Books: 50 lb. white paper; Webb lithography printing; perfect-bound binding. Average print order: 5,000. First novel print order: 5,000. **Published new writers within the last year.** Plans 3 first novels in 2001. Averages 12 total titles, 10 fiction titles/year. Distributes titles through Spring Arbor and Appalachian. Promotes titles through CBA Marketplace.

Needs: Children's/juvenile (adventure, animal, easy-to-read, historical, mystery, series, sports), young adults (adventure, historical, mystery/suspense, series, sports, western). Recently published *Songbird*, by Nancy Lohr (adventure ages 6-10); *The Theft*, by Betty Gaard (young adult fiction); *Out of Hiding*, by Catherine Farnes (young adult fiction); and *Little Bear's Secret*, by Kathleen Allan-Meyer (picture book).

How to Contact: Accepts unsolicited mss. Query with outline and 5 sample chapters or submit complete ms with cover letter. Include estimated word count, short bio, Social Security number and list of publishing credits. Send SASE or IRC for return of ms or send disposable copy of ms and SASE for reply only. Responds in 3 weeks to queries; 6 weeks to mss. Accepts simultaneous and disk submissions (IBM compatible preferred).

Terms: "Pay flat fee for first-time authors; royalties for established authors." Sends final ms to author. Publishes ms 12-18 months after acceptance. Writer's guidelines and book catalog free. "Check our webpage for guidelines."

Advice: Needs "more upper-elementary adventure/mystery or a good series. No picture books. No didactic stories. Read guidelines carefully. Send SASE if you wish to have ms returned. Give us original, well-developed characters in a suspenseful plot with good moral tone."

◑ **BLACK HERON PRESS,** P.O. Box 95676, Seattle WA 98145. **Contact:** Jerry Gold, publisher. Estab. 1984. One-person operation; no immediate plans to expand. "We're known for literary fiction. We've done several Vietnam War titles and several surrealistic fictions." Publishes paperback and hardback originals. Average print order: 2,000; first novel print order: 1,500. Averages 4 fiction titles/year. Distributes titles nationally.

● Four books published by Black Heron Press have won awards from King County Arts Commission. This press received Bumbershoot Most Significant Contribution to Literature in 1996.

Needs: Adventure, contemporary, experimental, humor/satire, literary, science fiction. Vietnam war novel—literary. "We don't want to see fiction written for the mass market. If it sells to the mass market, fine, but we don't see ourselves as a commercial press." Published *Charlie & The Children*, by Joanna C. Scott; *The Fruit 'N Food*, by Leonard Chang; and *In A Cold Open Field*, by Sheila Solomon Klass.

How to Contact: Query with first 50 pages only. Responds in 3 months to queries. Accepts simultaneous submissions.

Terms: Pays standard royalty rates. No advance.

Advice: "A query letter should tell me: 1) number of words; 2) number of pages; 3) if ms is available on floppy disk; 4) if parts of novel have been published; 5) if so, where?"

[N] [icons] BLACK LACE BOOKS, Virgin Publishing, Thames Wharf Studios, Rainville Rd., London W6 9IIA United Kingdom. Phone: +44(0207)386 3300. Fax: +44(0207)386 3360. E-mail: ksharp@virgin-pub.co.uk. Website: www.blacklace-books.co.uk (includes book catalog, mission statements). **Contact:** Kerri Sharp, senior commissioning editor. Estab. 1993. Publishes paperback originals. Plans 15 first novels in 2001. Averages 24 fiction titles/year.

Imprint(s): Nexus Fetish Erotic Fiction for Men; Paul Copperwaite, editor; Black Lace Erotic Fiction for Women; Kerri Sharp, editor. "Nexus and Black Lace are the leading imprints of erotic fiction in the UK."

Needs: Erotica. "Female writers only." Especially needs erotic fiction in contemporary settings. Publishes erotic short story anthology by women. Recently published *Asking for Trouble*, by Kristina Lloyd (women's erotic fiction); *Shameless*, by Stella Black (women's erotic fiction); and *Tongue in Cheek*, by Tabitha Flyte (women's erotic fiction). Publishes the women's erotic fiction series Black Lace.

How to Contact: Accepts unsolicited mss. Query with synopsis and 2 sample chapters. Include estimated word count. Send SASE or IRC for return of ms. Agented fiction 25%. Responds in 1 month to queries; 6 months to mss. Accepts simultaneous submissions. Always comments on rejected mss.

Terms: Pays royalties of 7½%. Average advance: $1,000. Sends galleys to author. Publishes ms 7 months after acceptance. Writer's guidelines for SASE; book catalogs free.

Advice: "Contemporary settings are strongly preferred. Open to female authors only. Read the guidelines first."

[icons] JOHN F. BLAIR, PUBLISHER, 1406 Plaza Dr., Winston-Salem NC 27103. (336)768-1374. Fax: (336)768-9194. **Contact:** Carolyn Sakowski, president. Estab. 1954. Small independent publisher. Publishes hardcover and paperback originals. Books: Acid-free paper; offset printing; illustrations. Average print order: 5,000. "Among our 17-20 books, we do one novel a year."

Needs: Prefers regional material dealing with southeastern U.S. No confessions or erotica. "Our editorial focus concentrates mostly on nonfiction." Published *Freedom's Altar*, by Charles Price; *Caveat*, by Laura Kalpakian; and *Something Blue*, by Jean Spaugh.

How to Contact: Accepts unsolicited mss. Send query letter or submit complete ms with cover letter (prefers query). Send SASE or IRC for return of ms. Accepts simultaneous submissions. Responds in 1 month.

Terms: Negotiable. Publishes ms 1-2 years after acceptance. Book catalog for free.

Advice: "We are primarily interested in nonfiction titles. Most of our titles have a tie-in with North Carolina or the southeastern United States. Please enclose a cover letter and outline with the manuscript. We prefer to review queries before we are sent complete manuscripts. Queries should include an approximate word count."

[icon] THE BLUE SKY PRESS, Imprint of Scholastic Inc., 555 Broadway, New York NY 10012. (212)343-6100. Website: www.scholastic.com. **Contact:** The editors. Blue Sky Press publishes primarily juvenile picture books. Publishes hardcover originals. Averages 15 titles/year.

• Because of a long backlog of books, the Blue Sky Press is not accepting unsolicited submissions.

Needs: Juvenile: adventure, fantasy, historical, humor, mainstream/contemporary, picture books, multicultural, folktales. Published *Bluish*, by Virginia Hamilton (novel); *No, David!*, by David Shannon (picture book); and *To Every Thing There is a Season*, by Leo and Diane Dillon (multicultural/historical).

How to Contact: Agented fiction 25%. Responds in 6 months to queries from previously published authors.

Terms: Pays 10% royalty on wholesale price, between authors and illustrators. Publishes ms 2½ years after acceptance.

[icons] BOREALIS PRESS, 110 Bloomingdale St., Ottawa, Ontario K2C 4A4 Canada. Fax: (613)829-7783. E-mail: borealis@istar.ca. Website: www.borealispress.com (includes names of editors, authors, all Borealis Press and Tecumseh Press books in print in 2000). **Contact:** Frank Tierney, editor; Glenn Clever, editor. Estab. 1970. "Publishes Canadiana, especially early works that have gone out of print, but also novels of today and shorter fiction for young readers." Publishes hardcover and paperback originals and reprints. Books: standard book-quality paper; offset printing; perfect and cloth binding. Average print order: 1,000. Buys juvenile mss with b&w illustrations. **Published new writers within in the last year.** Averages 10 total titles/year. Promotes titles through website, catalogue distribution, fliers for titles, ads in media.

Imprint(s): *Journal of Canadian Poetry*, Tecumseh Press Ltd., Canadian Critical Editions Series.

• Borealis Press has a "New Canadian Drama," with 7 books in print. The series won Ontario Arts Council and Canada Council grants.

Needs: Contemporary, literary, juvenile, young adult. "Must have a Canadian content or author; query first." Recently published *Blue: Little Cat Come Home to Stay*, by Donna Richards (young adult); *An Answer for Pierre*, by Gretel Fisher (novel); *The Lore of Women*, Jennifer McVaugh (comic novel).

How to Contact: Send query letter. Send SASE (Canadian postage) or IRC. Accepts queries by e-mail, fax. No simultaneous submissions. Responds in 2 weeks to queries; 4 months to mss. Publishes ms 1-2 years after acceptance.

Terms: Pays royalties of 10% and 3 free author's copies. No advance. Sends galleys to author. Publishes ms 18 months after acceptance. Free book catalog with SASE.

Advice: "Have your work professionally edited. Our greatest challenge is finding good authors, i.e., those who submit innovative and original material."

✓ ◎ BOYDS MILLS PRESS, Subsidiary of Highlights for Children, 815 Church St., Honesdale PA 18431. (800)490-5111. Website: www.boydsmillspress.com (includes names of editors, author information, book information and reviews). **Contact:** Larry Rosler, editorial director; Beth Troop, manuscript coordinator. Estab. 1990. "Independent publisher of quality books for children of all ages." Publishes hardcover. Books: Coated paper; offset printing; case binding; 4-color illustrations. Average print order: varies. **Published 2 new writers within the last year.** Plans 4 fiction titles in 2001. Distributes titles through independent sales reps and via order line directly from Boyds Mills Press. Promotes titles through sales and professional conferences, sales reps, reviews.

Needs: Juvenile, young adult (adventure, animal, contemporary, ethnic, historical, sports). Recently published *Mr. Beans*, by Dayton O. Hyde (YA novel); *Waiting for Dolphins*, by Carole Crowe (middle grade novel); and *Cat on Wheels*, by Larry Dane Brimner (picture book).

How to Contact: Accepts unsolicited mss. Query with first 3 chapters and synopsis. Responds in 1 month. Accepts simultaneous submissions.

Terms: Pays standard rates. Sends pre-publication galleys to author. Time between acceptance and publication depends on "what season it is scheduled for." Writer's guidelines for #10 SASE.

Advice: "Read through our recently-published titles and review our catalogue. If your book is too different from what we publish, then it may not fit our list. Feel free to query us if you're not sure."

✓ ◎ BRANDEN BOOKS, Subsidiary of Branden Press, P.O. Box 812 094, Wellesley MA 02482. (781)235-3634. Fax: (781)790-1056. E-mail: branden@branden.com. Website: www.branden.com. **Contact:** Adolph Caso, editor. Estab. 1967. Publishes hardcover and paperback originals and reprints. Books: 55-60 lb. acid-free paper; case- or perfect-bound; illustrations. Average print order: 5,000. Plans 5 first novels in 2001. Averages 15 total titles, 5 fiction titles/year.

Imprint(s): I.P.L.

Needs: Ethnic, historical, literary, military/war, short story collections and translations. Looking for "contemporary, fast pace, modern society." No porno, experimental or horror. Published *I, Morgain*, by Harry Robin; *The Bell Keeper*, by Marilyn Seguin; and *The Straw Obelisk*, by Adolph Caso.

How to Contact: Does not accept unsolicited mss. Query *only* with SASE. Responds in 1 week to queries, with either "we cannot use" or "send entire manuscript."

Terms: Pays royalties of 5-10% minimum. Advance negotiable. Provides 10 author's copies. Sends galleys to author. Publishes ms "several months" after acceptance.

Advice: "Publishing more fiction because of demand. *Do not make phone, fax or e-mail inquiries.* Do not oversubmit; single submissions only; do not procrastinate if contract is offered. Our audience is a well-read general public, professionals, college students, and some high school students. We like books by or about women."

✓ ◎ Ⓐ BROADWAY BOOKS, The Doubleday Broadway Publishing Group, A Division of Random House, Inc. 1540 Broadway, New York NY 10036. (212)354-6500. Website: www.broadwaybooks.com. **Contact:** Gerald Howard, publisher/editor-in-chief. Broadway publishes general interest nonfiction and fiction for adults. Publishes hardcover and trade paperback originals and reprints.

Needs: Commercial literary fiction. Published *Freedomland*, by Richard Price.

How to Contact: Accepts agented fiction only.

Ⓝ ◯ ◎ BROKEN BOULDER PRESS, P.O. Box 172, Lawrence KS 66044. (785)331-0270. E-mail: apowell10@hotmail.com. Website: www.brokenboulder.com (includes guidelines, catalog, press info, editorial info). **Contact:** Adam Powell, fiction editor. Estab. 1996. "We are a two-person not-for-profit and tax-exempt literary press. We have quickly gained a reputation for publishing highly progressive and avant garde fiction; nothing is too experimental for us." Publishes paperback originals. Books: plain paper; photocopy printing; saddle-stapled; several illustrations. Average print order: 100. First novel print order: 100. **Published 3 new writers within the last year.** Averages 8 total titles, 3 fiction titles/year. Promotes titles through the Internet and "extensive word-of-mouth."

Needs: Experimental, literary, short story collections, translations. "We always need progressive fiction and visual art." Recently published *Eating Kafka*, by Bayard (experimental novella); *Reptile Appliance*, by Mark Kipniss (experimental short fiction); and *Neotrope #1*, by Adam Powell, editor (experimental literary journal).

How to Contact: Accepts unsolicited mss. Send query letter. Accepts queries by e-mail. Include estimated word count and brief bio. Send disposable copy of ms and SASE for reply only. Responds in 1 month to queries; 2 months to mss. Accepts simultaneous and electronic submissions. Always comments on rejected mss.

Terms: Pays in author's copies, 10-20% of press run. Sends galleys to author. Publishes ms 2-6 months after acceptance. Writer's guidelines for SASE or on website; book catalogs for #10 SASE and 33¢ postage.

Advice: "We're publishing more fiction, especially small novellas or collections of short fiction. Avoid conventions and traditions—let the literary id run amok."

BROKEN JAW PRESS, Box 596, Stn. A, Fredericton, New Brunswick E3B 5A6 Canada. Phone/fax: (506)454-5127. E-mail: jblades@nbnet.nb.ca. Website: www.brokenjaw.com. **Contact**: Joe Blades, publisher. "We are a small, mostly literary, Canadian publishing house. We accept only Canadian authors." Publishes Canadian-authored trade paperback originals and reprints. **Published 1 new writer within the last year.** Averages 10-15 titles/year, plus *New Muse of Contempt* magazine. Distributes titles through General Distribution Services Ltd. (Toronto, Vancouver and Buffalo).

● *What Was Always Hers*, by Uma Parameswaran won the 2000 Canadian Authors Association Jubilee Award for Short Stories.

Imprint(s): Book Rat, SpareTime Editions, Dead Sea Physh Products, Maritimes Arts Projects Productions.

Needs: Literary. Published *Rum River*, by Raymond Fraser; *Herbarium of Souls*, by Vladimir Tasic; and *Reader Be Thou Also Ready*, by Robert James (novel).

How to Contact: Not currently accepting unsolicited book mss or queries. Only accepting mss or queries pertaining to the contest for first book for unpublished fiction writers (New Muse Award). For details visit website.

Terms: Pays royalties of 10% on retail price. Average advance: $0-100. Publishes ms 1 year after acceptance. Writer's guidelines for #10 SASE (Canadian postage or IRC or visit website). Book catalog for 9 × 12 SAE with 2 first-class Canadian stamps or IRC or visit website.

CAITLIN PRESS, INC., P.O. Box 2387 Station B, Prince George, British Columbia V2N 2S6 Canada. (250)964-4953. Fax: (250)964-4970. E-mail: caitlin_press@telus.net. Website: www.caitlin-press.com (includes writer's guidelines, catalogue, what's new, author tours, interviews, author bios, about US order info). **Contact**: Cynthia Wilson. Estab. 1977. "We publish books about the British Columbia interior or by people from the interior." Publishes trade paperback and soft cover originals. Averages 6-7 titles/year. Distributes titles directly from publisher and through general distribution and Harbour Publishing. Promotes titles through *BC Book World*, *Candian Books in Print* and website.

Needs: Adventure, historical, humor, mainstream/contemporary, short story collections, young adult.

How to Contact: Accepts unsolicited mss. Send query letter with SASE. Responds in 3 months to queries. Accepts simultaneous submissions.

Terms: Pays royalties of 15% on wholesale price. Publishes ms 18 months after acceptance.

Advice: "Our area of interest is British Columbia and Northern Canada. Submitted manuscripts should reflect our interest area."

CANDLEWICK PRESS, Subsidiary of Walker Books Ltd. (London), 2067 Massachusetts Ave., Cambridge MA 02140. (617)661-3330. Fax: (617)661-0565. **Contact:**Liz Bicknell, editorial director/associate publisher; Mary Lee Donovan, executive editor (nonfiction/fiction); Gale Pryor, editor (nonfiction/fiction); Amy Ehrlich, editor at large (picture books); Kara LaReau, associate editor (fiction/poetry); Cynthia Platt, associate editor (fiction/nonfiction). Candlewick Press publishes high-quality illustrated children's books for ages infant through young adult. "We are a truly child-centered publisher." Estab. 1991. Publishes hardcover originals, trade paperback originals and reprints. Publishes 200 titles/year.

Needs: Juvenile. Recently published *Because of Winn-Dixie*, by Kate DiCamillo; and *Grandad's Prayers of the Earth*, by Douglas Wood.

How to Contact: For novels: Query first with synopsis and 2 sample chapters to the attention of Manuscripts Editor. Send SASE or IRC for reply. For picture books: Submit complete ms to the attention of Manuscripts Editor. Send SASE or IRC for return of ms. Responds in 3 months. Accepts simultaneous submissions, if so noted.

Terms: Pays royalties of 10% on retail price. Advance varies. Publishes ms 3 years after acceptance for illustrated books, 1 year for others.

CAROLRHODA BOOKS, INC., Division of the Lerner Publishing Group, 241 First Ave. N., Minneapolis MN 55401. (612)332-3344. Fax: (612)332-7615. Website: www.lernerbooks.com. **Contact:** Rebecca

Poole, submissions editor. Estab. 1969. Carolrhoda Books seeks creative K-6 children's nonfiction and historical fiction with unique and well-developed ideas and angles. Publishes hardcover originals. Averages 50-60 titles/year.

Needs: Juvenile, historical, picture books, multicultural, fiction for beginning readers. "We continue to add fiction for middle grades and 1-2 picture books per year. Not looking for folktales or anthropomorphic animal stories." Published *Come Morning*, by Leslie Davis Guccione (historical); *Fire in the Sky*, by Candice Ransom (historical); and *Fire at the Triangle Factory*, by Holly Littlefield (easy reader historical).

How to Contact: "Submissions are accepted in the months of March and October only. Submissions received in any other month will be returned unopened." Query with SASE or send complete ms for picture books. Send SASE or IRC for return of ms. Responds in 6 months. Accepts simultaneous submissions.

Terms: Pays royalty on wholesale price, makes outright purchase or negotiates payments of advance against royalty. Advance varies. Publishes ms 18 months after acceptance. Writer's guidelines and book catalog for 9×12 SASE with $3 in postage. No phone calls.

Advice: "Our audience consists of children ages four to eleven. We publish very few picture books. We prefer manuscripts that can fit into one of our series. Spend time developing your idea in a unique way or from a unique angle; avoid trite, hackneyed plots and ideas."

● **CARROLL & GRAF PUBLISHERS, INC.**, Avalon Publishing Group, 19 W. 21st St., Suite 601, New York NY 10010. (212)627-8590. Fax: (212)627-8490. **Contact:** Kent Carroll, publisher/executive editor. Estab. 1983. "Carroll and Graf is one of the few remaining independent trade publishers and is therefore able to publish successfully and work with first-time authors and novelists." Publishes hardcover and paperback originals and paperback reprints. First novel print order: 7,500. Plans 5 first novels in 2001. Averages 120 total titles, 50 fiction titles/year.

Needs: Contemporary, science fiction, literary, mainstream and mystery/suspense. No romance.

How to Contact: Does not accept unsolicited mss. Query first or submit outline/synopsis and sample chapters. Send SASE or IRC for reply. Responds in 2 weeks. Occasionally comments on rejected mss.

Terms: Pays royalties of 6-15%. Advance negotiable. Sends galleys to author. Publishes ms 9 months after acceptance. Free book catalog on request.

● Ⓐ **CARTWHEEL BOOKS**, Imprint of Scholastic, Inc., 555 Broadway, New York NY 10012. (212)343-6100. Fax: (212)343-4444. Website: www.scholastic.com. Vice President/Editorial Director: Bernette Ford. **Contact:** Grace Maccarone, executive editor; Sonia Black, editor; Jane Gerver, executive editor; Liza Baker, acquisitions editor. Estab. 1991. "Cartwheel Books publishes innovative books for children, ages 3-9. We are looking for 'novelties' that are books first, play objects second. Even without its gimmick, a Cartwheel Book should stand alone as a valid piece of children's literature." Publishes hardcover originals. Averages 85-100 titles/year.

Needs: Children's/juvenile (fantasy, humor, juvenile, mystery, picture books, science fiction). "The subject should have mass market appeal for very young children. Humor can be helpful, but not necessary. Mistakes writers make are a reading level that is too difficult, a topic of no interest or too narrow, or manuscripts that are too long." Published *Little Bill (series)*, by Bill Cosby (picture book); *Dinofours* (series), by Steve Metzger (picture book); and *The Haunted House*, by Fiona Conboy (3-D puzzle storybook).

How to Contact: *Agented submissions or previously published authors only.* Responds in 2 months to queries; 6 months to mss. Accepts simultaneous submissions.

Terms: Pays royalty on retail price. Offers advance. Publishes ms 2 years after acceptance. Book catalog for 9×12 SAE. Writer's guidelines free.

Advice: Audience is young children, ages 3-9. "Know what types of books the publisher does. Some manuscripts that don't work for one house may be perfect for another. Check out bookstores or catalogs to see where your writing would 'fit' best."

✓ ● **CATBIRD PRESS**, 16 Windsor Rd., North Haven CT 06473-3015. (800)360-2391. E-mail: catbird@pipeline.com. Website: www.catbirdpress.com (includes writer's guidelines, author and book information, excerpts). **Contact:** Robert Wechsler, publisher. Estab. 1987. Small independent trade publisher. "Catbird Press specializes in sophisticated, imaginative prose humor as well as fiction and Central European literature in translation." Publishes cloth and paperback originals. Books: acid-free paper; offset printing; paper binding; illustrations (where relevant). Average print order: 3,000. First novel print order: 2,500. **Published no new English language writers within the last year.** Averages 4 total titles, 2-3 fiction titles/year. Promotes titles through Independent Publishers Group, all wholesalers, etc. Promotes titles through reviews, publicity, advertising, readings and signings.

Needs: Humor (specialty); literary, translations (specialty Czech, French and German read in-house). No thriller, historical, science fiction, or other genre writing; only writing with a fresh style and approach. Recently published *Labor Day*, by Floyd Kemske (literary); *A Double Life*, by Frederic Raphael (literary); *The 1898 Base-Ball Fe-As-Ko*, by Randall Beth Platt (humor).

How to Contact: Accepts unsolicited mss but no queries. Submit outline/synopsis with sample chapter. Accepts queries (but no mss) by e-mail. Send SASE. Responds in 1 month to mss. Accepts simultaneous submissions, "but let us know if simultaneous."

Terms: Pays royalties of 7½-10%. Average advance: $2,000; offers negotiable advance. Sends galleys to author. Publishes ms approximately 1 year after acceptance. Terms depend on particular book. Writer's guidelines for #10 SASE or available at website.

Advice: "Book publishing is a business. If you're not willing to learn the business and research the publishers, as well as learn the craft, you should not expect much from publishers. It's a waste of time to send genre or other derivative writing to a literary press. We are interested in novelists who combine a sense of humor with a true knowledge of and love for language, a lack of ideology, care for craft and self-criticism."

CENTENNIAL PUBLICATIONS, 256 Nashua Ct., Grand Junction CO 81503. (970)243-8780. **Contact:** Dick Spurr, publisher. Publishes hardcover and trade paperback originals and reprints. Averages 4-5 titles/year.

Needs: Humor, mystery. "We are very selective in this market." Published *In Over My Waders*, by Jack Sayer (humor).

How to Contact: Does not accept unsolicited mss. Query with synopsis and SASE or IRC for return. Responds in 1 week to queries; 1 month to mss.

Terms: Pays royalties of 8-10% on retail price. Average advance: $1,000. Publishes ms 8 months after acceptance. Book catalog free.

CHARLESBRIDGE PUBLISHING, 85 Main St., Watertown MA 02472-2535. (617)926-0329, ext. 140. Fax: (617)926-5720. E-mail: ewright@charlesbridge.com. Website: www.charlesbridge.com (includes writer's guidelines, names of editors, authors, titles, chat lines). **Contact:** Elena Dworkin Wright, editorial director. Estab. 1980. "We are looking for picture book stories with levels of meaning and humor." **Published 1 new writer within the last year.** Publishes school programs and hardcover and trade paperback originals. Averages 40 titles/year. Distributes titles through schools, bookstores, book clubs, sales reps, catalogs, direct mail offers, distributors and international conventions. Promotes titles through catalogs, sales reps, trade shows, conventions and author presentations.

Needs: Math concepts in nonrhyming story. Recently published *Sir Cumference and the First Round Table*, by Cindy Neuschwander (a math adventure/picture book); *Cut Down to Size at HIGH NOON*, by Scott Sundby (historical fictional mathematical humorous picture book); and *Sold*, by Nathan Zimelman (a contemporary mathematical humorous picture book).

How to Contact: Responds in 2 months.

Terms: Publishes ms 1 year after acceptance.

Advice: "We look for stories with enough science, problem solving, or historical context to interest parents and teachers as well as the humor to interest kids."

CHINA BOOKS & PERIODICALS, INC., 2929 24th St., San Francisco CA 94110-4126. (415)282-2994. Fax: (415)282-0994. Website: www.chinabooks.com. **Contact:** Greg Jones, editor. Estab. 1960. "China Books is the main importer and distributor of books and magazines from China, providing an ever-changing variety of useful tools for travelers, scholars and others interested in China and Chinese culture." Publishes hardcover and trade paperback originals. Averages 5 titles/year.

Needs: Ethnic, experimental, historical, literary. "*Must* have Chinese, Chinese-American or East Asian theme. We are looking for high-quality fiction with a Chinese or East Asian theme or translated from Chinese that makes a genuine literary breakthrough and seriously treats life in contemporary China or Chinese-America. No fiction that is too conventional in style or treats hackneyed subjects. No fiction without Chinese or Chinese-American or East Asian themes, please." Recently published *Ward Four*, by Ba Jin (1999).

How to Contact: Query with outline/synopsis and sample chapters. Query for electronic submissions. Responds in 3 months to queries. Accepts simultaneous submissions.

Terms: Pays royalties of 6-8% on net receipts. Average advance: $1,000. Publishes ms 1 year after acceptance. Book catalog free. Writer's guidelines for #10 SASE.

Advice: "We are looking for original ideas, especially in language study, children's education, adoption of Chinese babies, or health issues relating to Traditional Chinese medicine. No adventure novels or thrillers with Chinese settings. See our website for author guidelines."

CIRCLET PRESS, 1770 Massachusetts Ave., #278, Cambridge MA 02140. (617)864-0492 (noon-4p.m. EST). Fax: (617)864-0663, call before faxing. E-mail: circlet-info@circlet.com. Website: www.circlet.com/ (includes previews of upcoming books, catalog of complete books in print, links to authors' web pages and other publishers). **Contact:** Cecilia Tan, publisher. Estab. 1992. Small, independent specialty book publisher. "We are the only book publisher specializing in science fiction and fantasy of an erotic nature." Publishes paperback originals. Books: perfect binding; illustrations sometimes. Average print order: 2,500. **Published 50 new writers**

within the last year. Averages 6-8 anthologies/year. Distributes titles through the LPC Group in the US/Canada, Turnaround UK in the UK and Bulldog Books in Australia. Promotes titles through reviews in book trade and general media, mentions in *Publishers Weekly, Bookselling This Week* and regional radio/TV.

Imprints: The Ultra Violet Library (non-erotic lesbian/gay fantasy and science fiction).

Needs: "We publish only short stories of erotic science fiction/fantasy, of all persuasions (gay, straight, bi, feminist, lesbian, etc.). No horror! No exploitative sex, murder or rape. No degradation." No novels. All books are anthologies of short stories. Recently published *Through a Brazen Minor*, by Delia Sherman (fantasy); *Nymph*, by Francesca Lia Block; *Fetish Fantastic*, edited by Cecilia Tan (science fiction erotica).

How to Contact: Accepts unsolicited mss between April 15 and August 31. Accepts queries (no mss) by e-mail. "Any manuscript sent other than this time period will be returned unread or discarded." Submit complete short story with cover letter. Include estimated word count, 50-100 word bio, list of publishing credits. Send SASE for reply, return of ms or send a disposable copy of ms. Agented fiction 5%. Responds in up to 18 months. Accepts simultaneous submissions. Always comments on rejected mss.

Terms: Pays ½¢/word minimum for 1-time anthology rights only, plus 2 copies; author is free to sell other rights. Sends galleys to author. Publishes ms 1-24 months after acceptance. Writer's guidelines for #10 SASE; book catalog for #10 SAE and 2 first-class stamps.

Advice: "Read what we publish, learn to use lyrical but concise language to portray sex positively. Make sex and erotic interaction integral to your plot. Stay away from genre stereotypes. Use depth of character, internal monologue and psychological introspection to draw me in."

CLARION BOOKS, Imprint of Houghton Mifflin Company, 215 Park Ave. S., New York NY 10003. Website: www.houghtonmifflinbook.com. **Contact:** Dinah Stevenson, editorial director; Michele Coppola, editor; Jennifer B. Greene, associate editor; Julie Strauss-Gabel, associate editor. Estab. 1965. "Clarion is a strong presence in the fiction market for young readers. We are highly selective in the areas of historical and contemporary fiction. We publish chapter books for children ages 7-10 and middle grade novels for ages 9-14, as well as picture books and nonfiction." Publishes hardcover originals. Averages 50 titles/year.

How to Contact: Does not accept unsolicited mss at this time. "Clarion is swamped with submissions."

CLEIS PRESS, P.O. Box 14684, San Francisco CA 94114. (415)575-4700. E-mail: cleis@aol.com. **Contact:** Frederique Delacoste, editor. Estab. 1980. Midsize independent publisher. Publishes paperback originals. **Published new writers within the last year.** Plans 1 first novel every other year. Averages 15 total titles, 5 (3 are anthologies) fiction titles/year.

● Cleis Press has received the Best Fiction Firecracker for *The Leather Daddy and the Femme*, by Carol Queen, the Fab Award, and the Firecracker for Outstanding Press for 1999.

Needs: Comics/graphic novels, erotica, ethnic/multicultural (gay/lesbian), feminist, gay, historical (gay/lesbian), human rights, humor/satire, lesbian, novels, thriller/espionage, translations. Published *Sexually Speaking: Collected Sex Writings*, by Gore Vidal (essays); and *A Fragile Union*, by Joan Nestle (essays), which won a Lambda Literary Award.

How to Contact: Accepts unsolicited mss. Accepts queries by e-mail. Send complete ms with cover letter. Include 1- or 2-page bio, list of publishing credits. Send SASE or IRC for return of ms or send disposable copy of ms and SASE for reply only. Agented fiction 25%. Responds in 6 weeks.

Payment/Terms: Pays royalty of 7%. Advance is negotiable. Sends galleys to author. Publishes ms 12-18 months after acceptance. Catalogue for SASE and 2 first-class stamps.

COFFEE HOUSE PRESS, 27 N. Fourth St., Minneapolis MN 55401. (612)338-0125. **Contact:** Allan Kornblum and Chris Fischbach, editors. Estab. 1984. "Nonprofit publisher with a small staff. We publish literary titles: fiction and poetry." Publishes hardcover and paperback originals. Books: acid-free paper; cover illustrations. Average print order: 3,000. First novel print order: 3,000-4,000. **Published new writers within the last year.** Plans 2 first novels in 2001. Averages 12 total titles, 6 fiction titles/year.

● This successful nonprofit small press has received numerous grants from various organizations including the NEA, the Mellon Foundation and Lila Wallace/Readers Digest.

Needs: Contemporary, ethnic, experimental, literary. Looking for "non-genre, contemporary, high quality, unique material." No westerns, romance, erotica, mainstream, science fiction or mystery. Publishes anthologies, but they are closed to unsolicited submissions. Published *Ex Utero*, by Laurie Foos (first novel); *Gunga Din Highway*, by Frank Chin (novel); and *A .38 Special & a Broken Heart*, by Jonis Agee (short stories).

How to Contact: Accepts unsolicited mss. Query with samples and SASE. Agented fiction 10%. Responds in 2 months to queries; 6 months to mss.

Terms: Pays royalties of 8%. Average advance: $3,000. Provides 15 author's copies. Writer's guidelines for #10 SASE with 55¢ postage.

COMPASS POINT MYSTERIES™/TORY CORNER EDITIONS™, The Quincannon Publishing Group, P.O. Box 8100, Glen Ridge NJ 07028. Phone/fax: (973)669-8367. E-mail: editors@Quincannon.bizland.com. Website: www.Quincannon.bizland.com (includes everything necessary—contacts, writers' etiquette and guidelines, catalogue, sales channels). **Contact:** Holly Benedict, editor (mystery fiction); Alan Quincannon, editor (miscellaneous fiction). Estab. 1990. "Compass Point Mysteries™ specializes in regional mystery novels made unique by involving some element of a region's history (the setting and time-frame or the mystery's origin). If at all possible, we like to tie each of these novels to a regional museum where they can be sold with some degree of exclusivity. From time to time Tory Corner Editions™ considers fiction which is set at a particular historic site but whose subject matter may fall outside the parameters of the mystery genre." Publishes paperback originals and reprints (on very rare occasions if they meet the specified criteria). Books: trade paperbacks; perfect binding. Average print order: 500; first novel print order: 500. Averages 3 total titles, 1-2 fiction titles/year. "We seek to place our novels almost exclusively in the gift shops of the regional museums they feature and schedule periodic booksignings at those locales. Our novels are also offered through Internet booksellers and local independent bookstores."

Needs: Mystery/suspense (amateur sleuth, cozy, psychic/supernatural), regional (mysteries). Recently published *Wind of Time* (romantic mystery) and *Wicked is the Wind* (cozy mystery), both by John Dandola; and *Echoes from the Castle Walls*, by John Hays Hammond, Jr. (collection of mystery/horror stories).

How to Contact: Does not accept unsolicited mss. Send query letter; no agented submissions. Include estimated word count and brief bio; also "a letter of intent from the museum director and/or museum board of directors of the featured historic site stating that the manuscript has been read and approved and that, if published, the title will be stocked by the museum gift shop." Responds in 6 weeks to queries; up to 9 months to mss. Always comments on rejected mss.

Terms: "Books are published in runs of 500 and reprinted as supplies necessitate. Authors are paid a flat fee per run. Fees vary as to the cover price of each book." Sends galleys to author. Publishes ms 1 year after acceptance. Writer's guidelines and book catalog on website.

Advice: "Unfortunately, we are finding that many would-be authors consider that once they have created a plot and a premise and their computers have made their submissions look pretty, editors can be relied upon to anonymously rewrite their manuscripts. Editors are only a part of the guiding process and storytelling requires an awareness of succinctness and pacing, a mastery of language and grammar, and a willingness to polish and restructure. Our mystery novels should first tell a good interesting story which just happens to be a mystery, and they should usually not run more than 224 typeset pages. Besides using an historic site as a locale, our fiction must be well-written; it will be judged first and foremost on that merit. Please also bear in mind that an affiliation with a specific museum does not guarantee acceptance of any manuscript."

✔ ◯ **CONCORDIA PUBLISHING HOUSE,** 3558 S. Jefferson Ave., St. Louis MO 63118-3968. (314)268-1187. Fax: (314)268-1329. E-mail: boverton@cphnet.org. Website: www.cph.org (includes guidelines, editorial contacts, products, question/answer). **Contact:** Dawn Weinstock, managing editor (youth fiction); Jane Wilke, acquisitions editor (children's product, teaching resources). Estab. 1869. "We publish Protestant, inspirational, theological, family and juvenile books. All manuscripts should conform to the doctrinal tenets of The Lutheran Church—Missouri Synod." Publishes hardcover and trade paperback originals. Averages 150 titles/year.

Needs: Juvenile novels. "We will consider preteen and children's fiction and picture books. All books must contain Christian content. No adult Christian fiction." Published *Ask Willie*, by Paul Buchanan (juvenile); and *Desert Dictives*, by Mona Gainsburg Hodgson.

How to Contact: No phone queries, please. Query with SASE first. Responds in 3 months to queries. Simultaneous submissions discouraged.

Terms: Pays royalty or makes outright purchase. Publishes ms 15 months after acceptance. Writer's guidelines for #10 SASE.

Advice: "Our needs have broadened to include writers of books for lay adult Christians."

🍁 ◎ 🔽 **COTEAU BOOKS,** Thunder Creek Publishing Co-operative Ltd., 401-2206 Dewdney Ave., Regina, Saskatchewan S4R 1H3 Canada. (306)777-0170. Fax: (306)522-5152. E-mail: coteau@coteau.unibase.com. Website: coteau.unibase.com. **Contact:** Barbara Sapergia, acquisitions editor. Estab. 1975. "Coteau Books publishes the finest Canadian fiction, poetry, drama and children's literature, with an emphasis on western writers." Independent publisher. Publishes paperback originals. Books: #2 offset or 60 lb. hi-bulk paper; offset printing; perfect bound; 4-color illustrations. Average print order: 1,500-3,000; first novel print order: approx. 1,500. **Published new writers within the last year.** Averages 14 total titles, 6-8 fiction titles/year. Distributes titles through General Distribution Services.

● Books published by Coteau Books have received awards including the City of Edmonton Book Prize for *Banjo Lessons*, Jubilee Fiction Award for *In the Misleading Absence of Light*, and the Danuta Gleed Literary Award for *The Progress of an Object in Motion*.

Needs: Novels, short fiction, middle years and young adult fiction. No science fiction. No children's picture books. Publishes Canadian authors only.

How to Contact: *Canadian writers only.* Accepts unsolicited mss. Submit complete ms with cover letter and résumé to Acquisitions Editor. Accepts queries by e-mail. Send SASE or IRC for return of ms. Responds in 3 months to queries and mss. Sometimes comments on rejected mss.

Terms: "We're a co-operative and receive subsidies from the Canadian, provincial and local governments. We do not accept payments from authors to publish their works." Sends galleys to author. Publishes ms 1-2 years after acceptance. Book catalog for 8½×11 SASE.

Advice: "We publish short-story collections, novels, drama, nonfiction and poetry collections, as well as literary interviews and children's books. This is part of our mandate. The work speaks for itself! Be bold. Be creative. Be persistent!"

CROSSWAY BOOKS, Division of Good News Publishers, 1300 Crescent, Wheaton IL 60187-5800. Fax: (630)682-4785. **Contact:** Jill Carter. Estab. 1938. " 'Making a difference in people's lives for Christ' as its maxim, Crossway Books lists titles written from an evangelical Christian perspective." Midsize independent evangelical religious publisher. Publishes paperback originals. Average print order 5,000-10,000 copies. Averages 85 total titles, 10-15 fiction titles/year. Distributes titles through Christian bookstores and catalogs. Promotes titles through magazine ads, catalogues.

- *King of the Stable*, by Melody Carlson received the "Gold Medallion" award from the Evangelical Christian Publishers Association.

Needs: Contemporary, adventure, historical, literary, religious/inspirational, young adult. "All fiction published by Crossway Books must be written from the perspective of evangelical Christianity. It must understand and view the world through a Christian worldview." No sentimental, didactic, "inspirational" religious fiction, heavy-handed allegorical or derivative fantasy. Recently published *Fool's Gold*, by Stephen Bly (historical fiction); *To Dream Again*, by Sally John (inspirational/romance); *Cry Freedom*, by Mark Schalesky (historical fiction).

How to Contact: Does not accept unsolicited mss. Query with synopsis and sample chapters only. Accepts queries by fax. Responds in 2 months to queries. Publishes ms 1-2 years after acceptance.

Terms: Pays royalties. Negotiates advance. Writer's guidelines for SASE; book catalog for 9×12 SAE and 6 first-class stamps.

Advice: "We feel called to publish fiction in the following categories: Christian realism, historical fiction, intrigue, western fiction and children's fiction. All fiction should include explicit Christian content, artfully woven into the plot, and must be consistent with our statements of vision, purpose and commitment. Crossway can successfully publish and market *quality* Christian novelists. Also read John Gardner's *On Moral Fiction*. We require a minimum word count of 25,000 words."

CROWN BOOKS FOR YOUNG READERS, Bantam, Doubleday, Dell/Delacorte, Knopf and Crown Books for Young Readers, Random House Children's Books, A Division of Random House, Inc., 1540 Broadway, New York NY 10036. (212)782-9000 or (800)200-3552. Website: www.randomhouse.com/kids.

- See listing for Bantam, Doubleday, Dell/Delacorte, Knopf and Crown Books for Young Readers, page 395.

CUMBERLAND HOUSE PUBLISHING, 431 Harding Industrial Dr., Nashville TN 37211. (615)832-1171. Fax: (615)832-0633. E-mail: info@cumberlandhouse.com. **Contact:** Ron Pitkin, president. "We look for unique titles with clearly defined audiences." Publishes hardcover and trade paperback originals and reprints. Averages 35 titles/year. Imprint averages 5 titles/year.

Imprint(s): Cumberland House Hearthside; Julia M. Pitkin, editor-in-chief.

Needs: Mystery, historical. Published *Skeleton Crew*, by Beverly Connor (mystery); and *Manassas*, by James Reasoner.

How to Contact: Does not accept unsolicited mss. Send query letter. Writers should know "the odds are really stacked against them." Agented fiction 20%. Responds in 2 months to queries; 4 months to mss. Accepts simultaneous submissions.

Terms: Pays royalties of 10-20% on wholesale price. Average advance: $1,000-10,000. Publishes ms an average of 8 months after acceptance. Book catalog for 8×10 SAE and 4 first-class stamps. Writer's guidelines free.

Advice: Audience is "adventuresome people who like a fresh approach to things. Writers should tell what their idea is, why it's unique and why somebody would want to buy it—but don't pester us."

DAN RIVER PRESS, Conservatory of American Letters, P.O. Box 298, Thomaston ME 04861-0298. Phone/fax: (207)354-0998. E-mail: cal@americanletters.org. Website: www.americanletters.org (includes guidelines, editors, book catalog). **Contact:** Richard S. Danbury, fiction editor. Estab. 1977. "Small press publisher of fiction and biographies owned by a non-profit foundation." Publishes hardcover and paperback originals. Books: paperback; offset printing; perfect and cloth binding; illustrations. Average print order: 500; first novel print order: 500-1,000. Averages 2-3 total titles, 2-3 fiction titles/year. Promotes titles through the author's sphere of influence. Distributes titles by mail order to libraries and bookstores.

Needs: Family saga, fantasy (space fantasy, sword and sorcery), historical (general), horror (dark fantasy, futuristic, psychological, supernatural), humor/satire, literary, mainstream, mystery/suspense (amateur sleuth, police procedural, private eye/hardboiled), New Age/mystic, psychic/supernatural, regional, religious (general religious, inspirational, religious mystery/suspense, religious thriller, religious romance), romance (contemporary, futuristic/time travel, gothic, historical, romantic suspense), science fiction (hard science/technological, soft/sociological), short story collections, thriller/espionage, western (frontier saga, traditional), outdoors/fishing. Publishes poetry and fiction anthology (submission guidelines to *Dan River Anthology* on the Web). Recently published *Dan River Anthology 2001*, by R.S. Danbury III, editor (poetry and short stories); and *Wytopitloc: Tales of a Deer Hunter*, by Ed Rau Jr. (hunting stories).

How to Contact: Accepts unsolicited mss. Submit complete ms with cover letter. Include estimated word count, brief bio, Social Security number and list of publishing credits. Send SASE or IRC for return of ms or send disposable copy of ms and SASE for reply only. Responds in 1 month to queries; 2 months to mss. Accepts simultaneous submissions.

Terms: Pays royalties of 10-15%. Average advance: $250. Pays 1 author's copy. Sends galleys to author. Publishes ms 8-12 months after acceptance. Writer's guidelines on website; book catalog for 6×9 SAE and 55¢ postage or on website.

Advice: "Spend some time developing a following."

N. JOHN DANIEL AND COMPANY, PUBLISHERS, P.O. Box 21922, Santa Barbara CA 93121. (805)962-1780. Fax: (805)962-8835. E-mail: dand@danielpublishing.com. **Contact:** John Daniel, publisher. Estab. 1980. Publishes hardbound and paperback originals. Publishes poetry, fiction, nonfiction. Average print order: 2,000. Averages 4 total titles/year.

Needs: Publishes poetry, fiction and nonfiction; specializes in belles lettres, literary memoir. Recently published *A Night at the Y*, by Robert Garner McBrearty (short stories).

How to Contact: Accepts unsolicited mss. Responds in 2 months. Accepts simultaneous submissions.

Terms: Pays royalties of 10% of net receipts. No advance.

✔ ◐ ◎ MAY DAVENPORT, PUBLISHERS, 26313 Purissima Rd., Los Altos Hills CA 94022. (650)947-1275. Fax: (650)947-1373. E-mail: cvz28@aol.com. Website: www.maydavenportpublishers.com (includes catalog, author information). **Contact:** May Davenport, editor/publisher. Estab. 1976. "We prefer books which can be *used* in high schools as supplementary readings in English or creative writing courses. Reading skills have to be taught, and novels by humorous authors can be more pleasant to read than Hawthorne's or Melville's novels, war novels, or novels about past generations. Humor has a place in literature." Publishes hardcover and trade paperback originals. Averages 4 titles/year. Distributes titles through direct mail order.

Imprint(s): md Books (nonfiction and fiction).

Needs: Humor, literary. "We want to focus on novels junior and senior high school teachers can share with their reluctant readers in their classrooms." Recently published *To Touch the Sun*, by Andrea Ross (novel); *Dirty Mary No More*, by Marion Page (novel); and *A Taste of the Elephant—A Gold Rush Mystery*, by Robert Nathan Farley (novel).

How to Contact: Query with SASE. Responds in 1 month.

Terms: Pays royalties of 15% on retail price. No advance. Publishes ms 1 year after acceptance. Book catalog and writer's guidelines for #10 SASE.

Advice: "Just write humorous fictional novels about today's generation with youthful, admirable, believable characters to make young readers laugh. TV-oriented youth need role models in literature, and how a writer uses descriptive adjectives and similes enlightens youngsters who are so used to music, animation, special effects with stories."

✔ ◯ DAW BOOKS, INC., Distributed by Penguin Putnam Inc., 375 Hudson St., 3rd Floor, New York NY 10014-3658. (212)366-2096. Fax: (212)366-2090. E-mail: daw@penguinputnam.com. Website: www.dawbooks.com. Publishers: Elizabeth Wollheim and Sheila Gilbert. **Contact:** Peter Stampfel, submissions editor. Estab. 1971. Publishes hardcover and paperback originals and reprints. Averages 60-80 titles/year.

Needs: "We are interested in science fiction and fantasy novels. We need science fiction more than fantasy right now, but we're still looking for both. We like character-driven books with attractive characters. We're not looking for horror novels, but we are looking for mainstream suspense thrillers. We accept both agented and unagented manuscripts. Long books are absolutely not a problem. We are not seeking collections of short stories or ideas for anthologies." Recently published *Mountains of Black Glass*, by Tad Williams (science fiction).

How to Contact: First send query letter with SASE or IRC for reply. Simultaneous submissions "returned unread at once unless prior arrangements are made by agent." Responds in 6 weeks "or longer if a second reading is required."

Terms: Pays in royalties with an advance negotiable on a book-by-book basis. Sends galleys to author. Book catalog free.

Advice: "We strongly encourage new writers. Research your publishers and submit only appropriate work."

✔ ◐ ◎ DEL REY BOOKS, The Ballantine Publishing Group, A Division of Random House, Inc., 1540 Broadway, New York NY 10036. (212)782-8393. E-mail: Delray@randomhouse.com. Website: www.randomhouse.com/delrey/ (includes writers guidelines, names of editors, a writers workshop where you can get your work critiqued, an online newsletter with updates, author interviews and contests). **Contact:** Shelly Shapiro, senior

insider report

Robert McBrearty: Succeeding in the short story form

Robert McBrearty

"I try to write stories that are funny, touching, and offer some insight into life and what it means to be human." In talking with short story writer Robert McBrearty, one gets the distinct impression that to McBrearty realizing this personal goal, more than anything else, means success.

McBrearty's recent collection of short fiction, *A Night at the Y* (John Daniel & Co., 1999), is filled with characters whose creation stands as evidence of the author's goal: the stories revolve around their characters' search for meaning. "I think the lack of a sense of purpose actually is one of the themes that runs through the collection—however, not in a negative sort of way. Usually there's a search going on, a search for that purpose, and the characters make some progress along the way with that search," says McBrearty.

McBrearty freely admits that the searches his characters are involved in are not merely the fruit of his imagination, but are often based on his own human experiences. "Probably my own search is reflected in the stories. A lot of times, the viewpoint character—the 'I' character—is somewhat like myself, or maybe I'll draw on different aspects of myself."

For a first collection, *A Night at the Y* has drawn some encouraging cricital attention. "Every now and then one encounters a book whose every sentence is so finely crafted as to approach perfection. (This) is such a book," wrote a critic for the *Denver Rocky Mountain News*. And a critic from *The Chicago Tribune* wrote, "What threads through McBrearty's warm and engaging collection is a humaneness toward his characters, and a gentle, sad irony that pervades their world views."

Translating life into art

The short stories in *A Night at the Y* are all written from the point of view of ordinary men making their way through a complex world. "I guess I feel more comfortable writing from a male point of view," McBrearty says. "I feel it's what I know, so it's the place I usually come from." It is often the ordinariness of these characters that makes their respective plights so accessible to readers: the night clerk who re-evaluates his definition of a hero, the husband and new father for whom house shopping becomes a flight for freedom, the dishwasher whose job parallels his relationship woes. For McBrearty, the characters represent a payoff of sorts for years of "frustrating, demoralizing experiences," he says. "A lot of the stories came out of various drudge kinds of jobs I worked—dishwashing, night clerk, construction. There was a period of one job after another, mostly fairly unrewarding stuff. To some extent, writing was the thing that kept me going. Those kinds of jobs, while painful, provide some great experiences to write about." McBrearty also points to his life as a family man, with a marriage and children, as a source of inspiration for his writing. "Ordinary life has much richness in it if one is alert and perceptive," he says.

McBrearty's writing roots

The inception of McBrearty's writing career can be traced back to a high school experience which he remembers as a defining moment. "In my freshman year of high school, our English teacher asked us to write a short story at the end of the year, and I worked on it for a couple of weeks and just discovered it was something that I really liked doing," he says. "I guess it was one of the first things in school that I got really excited about, and I sort of knew right then what I wanted to do with my life."

After high school, McBrearty attended the University of Texas, then went to study creative writing at the University of Guanajuato in San Miguel de Allende, Mexico (the town where he set the collection's title story), and stayed on for a few years to teach English. He is a graduate of the Iowa Writers' Workshop and has received numerous awards for his fiction, such as a Pushcart Prize for his first published piece, "The Dishwasher," and fellowships to the MacDowell Colony and the Fine Arts Work Center in Provincetown, Massachusetts. He has taught writing part-time at the University of Colorado for the past ten years.

However, before the awards and well-received collection, McBrearty discovered the invaluable resource provided by small press publications to beginning writers, especially writers of short stories, a form often singled out as dying due to dwindling venues for publication. "I think the short story form is still going quite strong. Maybe not too much in a commercial sense—that is, it's difficult to make money at it—but I think it's going very strong, primarily in the small presses. You can use those small press publications in a lot of ways—help to get jobs, fellowships—so even though they are not that rewarding financially right up front, there are a lot of kind of spin-offs to them."

McBrearty also points to the networking opportunities that small press publications provide for writers. "I think establishing contacts, a network of writers and editors that you know, is very important. That starts slowly, but as you go on with your writing career, it expands so you know other writers and the editors of various magazines, if not personally, then at least through letters and phone calls." He mentions *The Missouri Review* and *The Green Hills Literary Lantern* as two magazines in which he has had the fortune of having repeat stories appear. Making use of small press publications requires one to have persistence, however, and McBrearty is quick to warn against expecting overnight success.

On discipline and finding your voice

McBrearty stresses that being able to develop a writing routine has been key to the success of his career. "I think especially when writers are getting going, it's really important to develop some good work habits, try to get into a routine. I wouldn't be inflexible about it—that is, I think writers can really drive themselves crazy if they have this inflexible schedule that they can never vary from. You should have some days when you let yourself rest, but in general I think you need some real good work habits, especially when you're starting out. If beginning writers never really get a good work habit going, then it's very hard to accomplish anything." His personal routine involves writing in the morning, sometimes getting up as early as five and working until seven, "partly because I have children and the rest of the household doesn't get up until about seven, so I can get quiet time," and sometimes allowing himself to shift to writing for two to three hours later in the morning. "I set up various routines, and I'll go along with one routine for a while until it seems to need some change. I'm always experimenting."

Another lesson McBrearty learned early is that writers should be willing to experiment with their work in order to find where their strengths lie. "In my own case, when I was in college, I was writing kind of somber, serious stories—the situations all seemed bleak, the characters seemed bleak. One of my creative writing teachers said, 'Why don't you try writing some comedy?' And I did. My next story had some comedy in it, and I figured out that was one of my real strengths. So I think sometimes finding your strengths and what kind of writer you are can make a huge difference."

With reviewers quick to praise his mastery of wit and compassionate rendering of characters, one may feel that McBrearty has, indeed, realized his personal goal with the stories in *A Night at the Y*. And with a novel and second short story collection forthcoming, as well as numerous teaching opportunities and readings being offered him, McBrearty has found that his determination has garnered success well beyond his expectations.

—*Rodney A. Wilson*

editor; Steve Saffel, senior editor. Estab. 1977. "In terms of mass market, we basically created the field of fantasy bestsellers. Not that it didn't exist before, but we put the mass into mass market." Publishes hardcover originals and paperback originals and reprints. Plans 6-7 first novels in 2001. Averages 70 fiction titles/year.

Needs: Fantasy ("should have the practice of magic as an essential element of the plot"), alternate history ("novels that take major historical events, such as the Civil War, and bend history in a new direction sometimes through science fiction and fantasy devices"), science fiction ("well-plotted novels with good characterization, exotic locales, and detailed alien cultures"). Recently published *Darwin's Radio*, by Greg Bear; *The Great War: Walk in Hell*, by Harry Turtledove; *The Master Harper of Pern*, by Anne McCaffrey.

How to Contact: Does not accept unsolicited mss. Query first with detailed outline and synopsis of story from beginning to end. Accepts queries by e-mail. Responds in 6 months, occasionally longer. Sometimes comments on rejected mss.

Terms: Pays royalty on retail price. "Advance is competitive." Publishes ms 1 year after acceptance. Sends galleys to author. Writer's guidelines for #10 SASE.

Advice: Has been publishing "more fiction and hardcovers, because the market is there for them. Read a lot of science fiction and fantasy, such as works by Anne McCaffrey, David Eddings, Larry Niven, Arthur C. Clarke, Terry Brooks, Frederik Pohl, Barbara Hambly. When writing, pay particular attention to plotting (and a satisfactory conclusion) and characters (sympathetic and well-rounded) because those are what readers look for."

☑ ◎ **DELACORTE PRESS**, The Bantam Dell Publishing Group, A Division of Random House, Inc., 1540 Broadway, New York NY 10036. Website: www.bantamdell.com.
• See The Bantam Dell Publishing Group listing, page 394.

Ⓝ ◍ **DELACORTE BOOKS FOR YOUNG READERS**, Bantam, Doubleday, Dell/Delacorte, Knopf and Crown Books for Young Readers, Random House Children's Books, 1540 Broadway, New York NY 10036. (212)782-9000 or (800)200-3552. Website: www.randomhouse.com/kids.
• See listing for Bantam, Doubleday, Dell/Delacorte, Knopf and Crown Books for Young Readers, page 394.

Ⓝ **DELL**, The Bantam Dell Publishing Group, A Division of Random House, Inc., 1540 Broadway, New York NY 10036. Website: www.bantamdell.com.
• See The Bantam Dell Publishing Group listing, page 394.

☑ ◎ **DIAL BOOKS FOR YOUNG READERS**, Children's Division of Penguin Putnam Inc., 345 Hudson St., 14th Floor, New York NY 10014-3657. (212)414-3416. Website: www.penguinputnam.com. President/Publisher: Nancy Paulsen. Editorial Director: Lauri Hornik. **Contact:** Submissions Editor. Estab. 1961. Trade children's book publisher, "looking for picture book mss and novels." Publishes hardcover originals. Plans 2 first novels in 2001. Averages 50 titles/year, mainly fiction.

Imprint(s): Easy-to-Read Books.

Needs: Juvenile (1-9 yrs.), especially animal and contemporary; young adult/teen (9-16 years), especially literary fiction. Recently published *A Long Way from Chicago*, by Richard Peck; *What! Cried Granny*, by Kate Lum and Adrian Johnson; and *My Man Blue*, by Nikki Grimes and Jerome Lagarrigue.

How to Contact: Does not accept unsolicited mss. Send query letter with SASE. Occasionally comments on rejected ms.

Terms: Pays advance against royalties. "We will send a catalog to anyone who sends 4 first-class stamps with a self-addressed, 9 × 12 envelope."

Advice: "To agents. We are publishing more fiction books than in the past, and we publish only hardcover originals, most of which are fiction. At this time we are particularly interested in both fiction and nonfiction for the middle grades, and innovative picture book manuscripts. We also are looking for easy-to-reads for first and second graders. Plays, collections of games and riddles, and counting and alphabet books are generally discouraged. Before submitting a manuscript to a publisher, it is a good idea to request a catalog to see what the publisher is currently publishing."

✓ ⊘ 🅰 **THE DIAL PRESS**, The Bantam Dell Publishing Group, A Division of Random House, Inc., 1540 Broadway, New York NY 10036. Website: www.bantamdell.com.
- See The Bantam Dell Publishing Group listing, page 394.

🅽 ◯ **DISKUS PUBLISHING**, P.O. Box 43, Albany IN 47320. E-mail: books@diskuspublishing.com. Website: www.diskuspublishing.com (includes writer's guidelines, names of editors, book catalog, interviews with authors, About Us, submission status log, About Our Authors). **Contact:** Marilyn Nesbitt, editor-in-chief; Joyce McLaughlin, inspirational and children's editor; Holly Janey, submissions editor. Estab. 1997. Publishes paperback originals and e-books. **Published 10 new writers within the last year.** Averages 60 total titles, 50 fiction titles/year. Member: AEP, PMA.
- *The Best Laid Plans*, by Leta Nolan Childers was the #1 bestselling e-book of 1999. *Paper Roses* was a winner of The Rising Star Contest for Historical Fiction. *Eye of the Beholder* was a finalist (inspirational genre) in the Eppie Awards.

Needs: Adventure, children's/juvenile, ethnic/multicultural (general), family saga, fantasy (space fantasy), historical, horror, humor/satire, literary, mainstream, military/war, mystery/suspense, psychic/supernatural, religious, romance, science fiction, short story collections, thriller/espionage, western, young adult/teen. Recently published *The Best Laid Plans*, by Leta Nolan Childers (romance); *Brazen*, by Lori Foster (adventure/romance); and *A Change of Destiny*, by Marilynn Mansfield (science fiction/futuristic).

How to Contact: Accepts unsolicited mss. No queries; complete ms only. Include estimated word count, brief bio, list of publishing credits and genre. Send SASE or IRC for return of ms or send disposable copy of ms and SASE for reply only. Agented fiction 5%. Accepts simultaneous submissions and submissions on disk plus printout of synopsis and first chapter. Sometimes comments on rejected mss.

Terms: Pays royalties of 40%. Sends galleys to author. Publishes ms 6-8 months after acceptance. Writer's guidelines free for #10 SASE. Book catalog available for #10 SASE or online.

✓ ☺ 🅰 **DOUBLEDAY ADULT TRADE**, The Doubleday Broadway Publishing Group, A Division of Random House, Inc., 1540 Broadway., New York NY 10036. (212)782-9000. Fax: (212)782-9700. Website: www.doubleday.com. **Contact:** William Thomas, vice president/editor-in-chief. Estab. 1897. Publishes hardcover and paperback originals and paperback reprints.

Imprint(s): Currency (contact Roger Scholl); **Nan A. Talese** (contact Nan A. Talese); Religious Division (contact Eric Major); Image (contact Trace Murphy).

Needs: "Doubleday is not able to consider unsolicited queries, proposals or manuscripts unless submitted through a bona fide literary agent."

Terms: Pays in royalties; offers advance. Publishes ms 1 year after acceptance.

🅽 **DOUBLEDAY BOOKS FOR YOUNG READERS**, Bantam, Doubleday, Dell/Delacorte, Knopf and Crown Books for Young Readers, Random House Children's Books, A Division of Random House, Inc., 1540 Broadway, New York NY 10036. (212)782-9000 or (800)200-3552. Website: www.randomhouse.com/kids.
- See listing for Bantam, Doubleday, Dell/Delacorte, Knopf and Crown Books for Young Readers, page 394.

🅽 ☘ ⊘ 🅰 **DOUBLEDAY CANADA**, Random House Canada, A Division of Random House, Inc., 1 Toronto St., Suite 300, Toronto, Ontario M5C 2V6 Canada. Website: www.randomhouse.ca. Publishes hardcover and paperback originals. Averages 50 total titles/year.

Imprint(s): Seal Books (mass market publisher).

How to Contact: Does not accept unsolicited mss. Agented fiction only.

■ ◎ **DOWN EAST BOOKS**, Division of Down East Enterprise, Inc., P.O. Box 679, Camden ME 04843-0679. Fax: (207)594-7215. E-mail: adevine@downeast.com. Senior Editor: Karin Womer. **Contact:** Acquisitions Editor. Estab. 1954. "We are primarily a regional publisher concentrating on Maine or New England." Publishes hardcover and trade paperback originals and trade paperback reprints. Averages 20-24 titles/year. First novel print order: 3,000.

- Down East Books has published Elisabeth Ogilvie, Michael McIntosh, Louise Dickinson Roch and John N. Cole.

Imprint(s): Silver Quill (outdoor sportsmen market).
Needs: Juvenile, regional. "We publish 1-2 juvenile titles/year (fiction and non-fiction), and 1-2 adult fiction titles/year." Published *Tides of the Heart*, by Thomas M. Sheehan (novel); *Day Before Winter*, by Elisabeth Ogilvie (novel); and *My Brothers' Keeper*, by Nancy Johnson (young adult novel).
How to Contact: Query first with small sample of text, outline and SASE. Responds in 2 months. Accepts simultaneous submissions.
Terms: Pays royalties of 10-15% on receipts. Average advance: $200. Publishes ms 1 year after acceptance. Writer's guidelines for 9×12 SAE with 3 first-class stamps.

N ✓ ○ ◎ **DUCKWORTH PRESS**, 3005 66th St., Lubbock TX 79413-5707. Phone/fax: (806)799-3706. E-mail: msuniver@swbell.net. **Contact:** Ann Thompson, fiction editor (romance); L.K. Thompson, fiction editor (action, mainstream). Estab. 1991. "We prefer writers who live in Texas and New Mexico who write about those areas, who are well established, and who are known in the areas where they live since we apply a regional approach to marketing. We do small editions and intense marketing in an author's region. We don't do very much business in major metropolitan areas." Publishes some hardcover originals, mostly paperback originals. Books: 20 lb. paper; electronic press; perfect binding; a few illustrations. Average print order: 250. First novel print order: 100-500. **Published 2 new writers within the last year.** Plans 2 first novels in 2001. Averages 4 total titles, 2 fiction titles/year.
Needs: Adventure, children's/juvenile (adventure, easy-to- read, fantasy, historical, mystery), family saga, historical, humor/satire, mainstream/contemporary, mystery/suspense (amateur sleuth, police procedural), regional (Texas, New Mexico), romance (contemporary, historical, romantic suspense), western (traditional). Recently published *The Bonners*, by John W. Curry (historical fiction); *Thorns on the Laurel*, by Katherine Gonzales (historical romance); *Never Say Crash*, by Bill Nile (historical fiction).
How to Contact: Query letter only first. Accepts unsolicited queries/correspondence by e-mail. Include estimated word count and bio (3 pages or less). Send SASE for reply, return of ms or send a disposable copy of ms. Responds in 1 month to queries; 2 months to mss. Accepts simultaneous and electronic submissions (disk). Often comments on rejected mss.
Terms: Pays royalties of 10-25% on gross sales. Average advance: small. Also pays 5 author's copies. "If the author helps with legwork, we pay a higher royalty." Sends galleys to author. Publishes ms up to 2 months after acceptance. Writer's guidelines for #10 SASE.
Advice: "Pick a topic based on your region's history, make it something that a broad spectrum of locals would be interested in, and then write it."

■ ◎ **DUFOUR EDITIONS**, P.O. Box 7, Chester Springs PA 19425. (610)458-5005. Fax: (610)458-7103. E-mail: dufour8023@aol.com. **Contact:** Thomas Lavoie, associate publisher. Estab. 1940s. Small independent publisher, tending toward literary fiction. Publishes hardcover and paperback originals and reprints. Averages 6-7 total titles, 1-2 fiction titles/year. Promotes titles through catalogs, reviews, direct mail, sales reps, Book Expo and wholesalers.
Needs: Literary, short story collections, translations. Published *Tideland*, by Mitch Cullin; *The Case of the Pederast's Wife*, by Clare Elfman.
How to Contact: Send query letter only. Include estimated word count, bio and list of publishing credits. Include SASE for reply. Responds in 3 weeks to queries; 3 months to mss.

THOMAS DUNNE BOOKS, Imprint of St. Martin's Press, 175 Fifth Ave., New York NY 10010. (212)674-5151. **Contact:** Tom Dunne. Publishes wide range of fiction and nonfiction. Publishes hardcover originals, trade paperback originals and reprints. Averages 90 titles/year.
Needs: Mainstream/contemporary, mystery/suspense, "women's" thriller. Recently published *Winter Solstice*, by Rosamunde Pilcher; and *Marines of Autumn*, by James Brady.
How to Contact: Query or submit synopsis and 100 sample pages with SASE. Responds in 2 months to queries. Accepts simultaneous submissions.
Terms: Pays royalties of 10-15% on retail price for hardcover, 7½% for paperback. Advance varies with project. Publishes ms 1 year after acceptance. Book catalog and writer's guidelines free.

✓ ◐ Ⓐ **DUTTON**, Imprint of Penguin Putnam Inc., 375 Hudson St., New York NY 10014. (212)366-2000. Website: www.penguinputnam.com. **Contact:** Brian Tart, editor-in-chief (mainstream and commercial fiction, narrative nonfiction); Laurie Chittenden, senior editor (commercial and mainstream fiction). Estab. 1948. Publishes hardcover originals. **Published new writers within the last year.**

Needs: "All kinds of commercial and literary fiction, including mainstream, historical, New Age, thriller and gay. Full length novels and collections." Recently published *Code to Zero*, by Ken Follett; *Life on the Other Side*, by Sylvia Browne; and *Scarlet Feather*, by Maeve Binchy.

How to Contact: Agented mss only. Accepts simultaneous submissions. Responds in 3 months.

Terms: Pays royalties and author's copies; offers advance. Sends galleys to author. Publishes ms 12-18 months after acceptance. Book catalog for SASE.

Advice: "Write the complete manuscript and submit it to an agent or agents."

✓ ◐ **DUTTON CHILDREN'S BOOKS**, Imprint of Children's Division, Penguin Putnam Inc., 345 Hudson St., New York NY 10014. (212)414-3700. Website: www.penguinputnam.com. **Contact:** Lucia Monfried, associate publisher and editor-in-chief. Estab. 1852. Dutton Children's Books publishes fiction and nonfiction for readers ranging from preschoolers to young adults on a variety of subjects. Publishes hardcover originals. Averages 80 titles/year.

Needs: Dutton Children's Books has a complete publishing program that includes picture books; easy-to-read books; and fiction for all ages, from "first-chapter" books to young adult readers. Published *The Iron Ring*, by Lloyd Alexander; *How Yussel Caught the Gefilte Fish*, by Charlotte Herman, illustrated by Katya Krenina.

How to Contact: Does not accept unsolicited mss. Send query with SASE.

Terms: Pays royalty on retail price.

✓ ◯ ◎ **E.M. PRESS, INC.,** P.O. Box 336, Warrenton VA 20188. Phone/fax: (540)349-9958 (call first for fax). E-mail: empress2@erols.com. Website: www.empressinc.com. President: Beth A. Miller. **Contact:** Montana Umbel, assistant publisher. Estab. 1991. "Expanding small press." Publishes paperback and hardcover originals. Books: 50 lb. text paper; offset printing; perfect binding; illustrations. Average print order: 1,200-5,000. Averages 8 total titles, fiction, poetry and nonfiction, each year. Distributes titles through wholesalers and direct sales. Promotes titles through radio and TV, Interview Report, direct mailings and Ingram's catalogs.

Needs: "We are focusing more on Virginia/Maryland/DC authors and subject matter. We're emphasizing nonfiction and a children's line, though we still consider 'marketable' fiction." Recently published *The Relationship*, by John Hyman (young adult); *Sassparilla's New Shoes*, by Ming and Wah Chen (children's); and *Can You Come Here Where I Am? The Poetry and Prose of Seven Breast Cancer Survivors*.

How to Contact: Accepts unsolicited mss. Submit outline/synopsis and sample chapters or complete ms with cover letter. Include estimated word count. Send SASE or IRC for return of ms or send disposable copy of the ms and SASE for reply only. Agented fiction 10%. Responds in 3 months to queries; 3 months to mss. Accepts simultaneous submissions.

Terms: Amount of royalties and advances varies. Sends galleys to author. Publishes ms 18 months after acceptance. Writer's guidelines for SASE.

Advice: Publishing "less fiction, more regional work, though we look for fiction that will do well in secondary rights sales."

◐ ▼ **THE ECCO PRESS**, Imprint of HarperCollins General Books Group, HarperCollins Publishers, 10 E. 53rd St., New York NY 10022. (212)207-7000. Website: www.harpercollins.com. **Contact:** Daniel Halpern, editor-in-chief. Estab. 1970. Publishes hardcover and paperback originals and reprints. Books: acid-free paper; offset printing; Smythe-sewn binding; occasional illustrations. First novel print order: 3,000 copies. Averages 60 total titles, 20 fiction titles/year.

● *Vita Nova*, by Louise Glück won last year's *The New Yorker* Award.

Needs: "We can publish possibly one or two original novels a year." Literary, short story collections. No science fiction, romantic novels, western (cowboy) or historical novels. Recently published *Blonde*, by Joyce Carol Oates; *Pitching Around Fidel*, by S.L. Price.

How to Contact: Does not accept unsolicited mss.

Terms: Pays royalties. Advance is negotiable. Publishes ms 1 year after acceptance. Writer's guidelines for SASE; book catalog free on request.

Advice: "We are always interested in first novels and feel it's important they be brought to the attention of the reading public."

Ⓝ ❖ ▼ **LES ÉDITIONS DU VERMILLON**, 305 St. Patrick St., Ottawa, Ontario K1N 5K4 Canada. (613)241-4032. Fax: (613)241-3109. E-mail: editver@magi.com. Website: www.francoculture.ca/edition/vermillon (includes book catalog). **Contact:** Jacques Flamand, editorial director. Publishes trade paperback originals. **Published new writers within the last year.** Averages 15 books/year. Distributes titles through Prologue in Canada. Promotes titles through advertising, book fairs and media.

● *Lithochronos*, by Andrée Christensen and Jacques Flamand was awarded the Prix Trillium.

Needs: Juvenile, literary, religious, short story collections, young adult. Recently published *Le chien de Shibuya*, by J.-Fr. Samadu (adventure, youth); *Ottawa, P.R.*, by Jean Taillefer (novel); and *A coeur d'ombre*, by Jacqueline L'Heureux-Hart (poetry).
How to Contact: Query with SASE or IRC for reply. Responds in 1 year to mss.
Terms: Pays royalties of 10%. Offers no advance. Publishes ms 18 months after acceptance. Book catalog free.

ÉDITIONS LA LIBERTÉ INC., 3020 Chemin Ste-Foy, Ste-Foy, Quebec G1X 3V6 Canada. Phone/fax: (418)658-3763. **Contact:** Nathalie Roy, director of operations. Publishes trade paperback originals. **Published 1 new writer within the last year.** Averages 4-5 titles/year.
Needs: Historical, juvenile, literary, mainstream/contemporary, short story collections, young adult. Published *L'espace Montauban/Le Dernier Roman Scout*, by Jean Désy.
How to Contact: Accepts only mss written in French. Query with synopsis. Accepts simultaneous submissions.
Terms: Pays royalties of 10% on retail price. Publishes ms 4 months after acceptance. Book catalog free.

WM. B. EERDMANS PUBLISHING CO., 255 Jefferson Ave. SE, Grand Rapids MI 49503-4570. (800)253-7521. Fax: (616)459-6540. Website: www.eerdmans.com. **Contact:** Jon Pott, editor-in-chief, fiction editor (adult fiction); Judy Zylstra, fiction editor (children); Gwen Penning, assistant to the editor-in-chief. Estab. 1911. "Although Eerdmans publishes some regional books and other nonreligious titles, it is essentially a religious publisher whose titles range from the academic to the semi-popular. Our children's fiction is meant to help a child explore life in God's world and to foster a child's exploration of her or his faith. We are a midsize independent publisher. We publish the occasional adult novel, and these tend to engage deep spiritual issues from a Christian perspective." Publishes hardcover and paperback originals and reprints. **Published 1 new writer within the last year.** Averages 140 total titles, 6-8 fiction titles (mostly for children)/year.
Imprint(s): Eerdmans Books for Young Readers.
• Wm. B. Eerdmans Publishing Co.'s titles have won awards from the American Library Association and The American Bookseller's Association.
Needs: Religious (children's, general, fantasy). Published *At Break of Day*, by Nikki Grimes (children's); *The Goodbye Boat*, by Mary Joslin (children's); and *A Traitor Among Us*, by Elizabeth Van Steenwyk (middle reader).
How to Contact: Accepts unsolicited mss. Query with outline/synopsis and 2 sample chapters. Accepts queries by fax. Include 150- to 200-word bio and list of publishing credits. Send either SASE or IRC for return of ms or send disposable copy of ms and SASE for reply only. Agented fiction 25%. Responds in 1 month to queries; 3 months to mss. Accepts simultaneous submissions, "if notified." Accepts electronic submissions (fax). Sometimes comments on rejected ms.
Terms: Pays royalties of 7% minimum. Average advance: negotiable. Sends galleys to author. Publishes ms 12-18 months after acceptance. Writer's guidelines and book catalog free.
Advice: "Our readers are educated and fairly sophisticated, and we are looking for novels with literary merit."

ENIGMATIC PRESS, 117 Birchanger Lane, Birchanger, Bishop's Stortford, Hertfordshire CM23 5QF United Kingdom. Phone: 01279 817708. E-mail: michael@micksims.force9.co.uk. Website: www.epr ess.force9.co.uk (includes guidelines, *Enigmatic Electronic* e-zine, author pages, art gallery, links, current and forthcoming titles, news, fiction). **Contact:** Mick Sims, editor; Len Maynard, editor. Estab. 1998. "Small two-man operation in UK. Independent. Professional standards on amateur budget. Funded partly by arts board. Publishes new, established authors as well as rare fiction from the past. Any length fiction." Publishes paperback originals. Books: 100 gsm ordinary paper; Docutech; perfect bound; b&w full page illustrations. Average print order: 300. **Published 32 new writers within the last year.** Averages 10 fiction titles/year. Distributes titles through subscription, single sales, bookshops, distributors.
• Nominated in 2000 for International Horror Awards and British Fantasy Awards.
Imprint(s): Enigmatic Tales; Enigmatic Variations; Enigmatic Electronic; Mick Sims, Len Maynard, editors (supernatural fiction).
Needs: Horror (dark fantasy, psychological, supernatural, ghosts). Publishes anthology of supernatural fiction (closed to submissions). Recently published *Enigmatic Tales 8* (anthology supernatural fiction); *Millennium Macabre*, by William Meikle (supernatural fiction); and *The Shadows Beneath*, by Paul Finch (supernatural fiction). Publishes the Enigmatic Tales series.
How to Contact: Accepts unsolicited mss. Submit complete ms with cover letter. Accepts queries by e-mail. Include estimated word count, brief bio and list of publishing credits. Send disposable copy of ms and SASE for reply only. Responds in 1 week to queries; 3 weeks to mss. Accepts electronic submissions and disk. Often comments on rejected mss.
Terms: Pays 1 author's copy. Does not send galleys to author. Publishes ms 5-15 months maximum after acceptance. Writer's guidelines free for SASE. Book catalogs free.
Advice: "We were first published ourselves 26 years ago. We thought we knew it all. Be humble but persistent. Be polite but assertive. Be good—we only publish quality."

PAUL S. ERIKSSON, PUBLISHER P.O. Box 125, Forest Dale VT 05745. (802)247-4210 Fax: (802)247-4256. **Contact:** Paul S. Eriksson, editor; Peggy Eriksson, associate publisher/co-editor. Estab. 1960. "We look for intelligence, excitement and saleability." Publishes hardcover and paperback originals. First novel print order: 3,000-5,000.
Needs: Mainstream. Published *The Headmaster's Papers*, by Richard A. Hawley; *The Year that Trembled*, by Scott Lax; and *Hand in Hand*, by Tauno Yliruusi.
How to Contact: Query first. Publishes ms an average of 6 months after acceptance.
Terms: Pays royalties of 10-15%; advance offered if necessary. Free book catalog.
Advice: "Our taste runs to serious fiction."

M. EVANS & CO., INC., 216 E. 49th St., New York NY 10017. (212)688-2810. Fax: (212)486-4544. E-mail: editorial@mevans.com. Website: www.mevans.com (includes book catalog). **Contact:** Editor. Estab. 1960. Publishes hardcover and trade paper nonfiction and a small fiction list. Averages 30-40 titles/year.
Needs: "Small general trade publisher specializing in nonfiction titles on health, nutrition, diet, cookbooks, parenting, popular psychology."
How to Contact: Does not accept unsolicited mss. Agented fiction: 100%. Accepts simultaneous submissions.
Terms: Pays in royalties and offers advance; amounts vary. Sends galleys to author. Publishes ms 6-12 months after acceptance.

FARRAR, STRAUS & GIROUX, 19 Union Square W., New York NY 10003.
• Farrar, Straus & Giroux is not accepting any mss/queries at this time.
Imprint(s): Hill & Wang, Farrar, Straus & Giroux Paperbacks, North Point Press, **Farrar, Straus & Giroux/Children's Books** and Sunburst Books.

FARRAR, STRAUS & GIROUX/CHILDREN'S BOOKS, 19 Union Square W., New York NY 10003. (212)741-6900. **Contact:** Margaret Ferguson, editor-in-chief. Estab. 1946. "We publish original and well-written material for all ages." **Published new writers within the last year.** Averages 70 total titles/year.
Needs: Children's picture books, juvenile novels, nonfiction. Published *Holes*, by Louis Sacher; *The Trolls*, by Polly Horvath; and *Tribute to Another Dead Rock Star*, by Randy Powell.
How to Contact: Query with outline/synopsis and 3 sample chapters. Include brief bio, list of publishing credits with submission. Agented fiction 25%. No electronic submissions. Responds in 3 months to queries; 3 months to mss.
Terms: Pays royalties; offers advance. Publishes ms 18-24 months after acceptance. Book catalog with 9 × 12 SASE and $1.87 postage.
Advice: "Study our list to avoid sending something inappropriate. Send query letters for long manuscripts; don't ask for editorial advice (just not possible, unfortunately); and send SASEs!"

FAWCETT, The Ballantine Publishing Group, A Division of Random House, Inc., 1540 Broadway, New York NY 10036. Estab. 1955. Major publisher of mass market and trade paperbacks. Publishes paperback originals and reprints. Averages 160 titles/year. Encourages new writers. "Always looking for *great* first novels."
Needs: Mysteries. Published *Noelle*, by Diana Palmer; *Writing for the Moon*, by Kristin Hannah.
How to Contact: Agented material only. Unsolicited mss will be promptly returned unopened.
Advice: "Gold Medal list consists of four paperbacks per month—usually three are originals."

FC2, Dept. of English, FSU, Tallahassee FL 32306-1580. (850)644-2260. E-mail: fc2@english.fsu.edu. Publishers: R.M. Berry, Jeffrey DeShell. Estab. 1974. Publisher of innovative fiction. Publishes hardcover and paperback originals. Books: perfect/Smyth binding; illustrations. Average print order: 2,200. First novel print order: 2,200. **Published new writers within the last year.** Plans 2 first novels, 4 novels total; 1 first story collection in 2001. Averages 6 total titles, 6 fiction titles each year. Often comments on rejected mss.
Needs: Formally innovative, experimental, modernist/postmodern, avant-garde. anarchist, feminist, gay, minority, cyberpunk. Published *Book of Lazarus*, by Richard Grossman; *Is It Sexual Harassment Yet?*, by Cris Mazza; *Nature Studies*, by John Henry Ryskamp; and *Latino Heretics Anthology*, edited by Tony Diaz.
How to Contact: Accepts unsolicited mss. Query first with outline/synopsis. Include 1-page bio, list of publishing credits. SASE with ms. Agented fiction 5%. Responds in 3 weeks to queries; 4 months to mss. Accepts simultaneous submissions. Send queries to: FC2, Unit for Contemporary Literature, Illinois State University, 109 Fairchild Hall, Normal IL 61790-4241.
Terms: Pays royalties of 7½%. Sends galleys to author. Publishes ms 1 year after acceptance.
Advice: "Be familiar with our list."

THE FEMINIST PRESS AT THE CITY UNIVERSITY OF NEW YORK, 365 Fifth Ave., New York NY 10016. Website: www.feministpress.org (includes writer's guidelines, online catalog, teacher's resources). **Contact:** Florence Howe, publisher; Jean Casella, senior editor; Sara Cahill, editor; Amanda Hanlin, assistant editor. Estab. 1970. "Nonprofit, tax-exempt, education and publishing organization interested in changing the curriculum, the classroom and consciousness." Publishes hardcover and paperback reprints. "We use an acid-free paper, perfect-bind our books, four color covers; and some cloth for library sales if the book has been out of print for some time; we shoot from the original text when possible. We always include a scholarly and literary afterword, since we are introducing a text to a new audience. Average print run: 4,000." Publishes no original fiction; exceptions are anthologies and international works. Averages 10-15 total titles, 4-8 fiction titles/year (reprints of feminist classics only). Distributes titles through Consortium Book Sales and Distribution. Promotes titles through author tours, advertising, exhibits and conferences.

Needs: Contemporary, ethnic, feminist, gay, lesbian, literary, regional, science fiction, translations, women's. Published *Apples From the Desert*, by Savyon Liebrecht (short stories, translation); *Confessions of Madame Psyche*, by Dorothy Bryant (novel); and *Mulberry and Peach*, by Hualing Nen (novel, translation).

How to Contact: Accepts unsolicited mss. Query with outline/synopsis and 1 sample chapter. Accepts queries by fax. Send SASE. Responds in 1 month to queries; 3 months to mss. Accepts simultaneous submissions.

Terms: Pays royalties of 10% on net sales. Average advance: $100. Pays 10 author's copies. Sends galleys to author. Book catalog free.

FENN PUBLISHING COMPANY LTD., H.B. Fenn and Company Ltd., 34 Nixon Rd., Bolton, Ontario L7E 1W2 Canada. (905)951-6600. Fax: (905)951-6601. Website: www.hbfenn.com. **Contact:** C. Jordan Fenn, publisher. Estab. 1982. Member: CPC.

How to Contact: Accepts unsolicited mss. Submit complete ms with cover letter. Include brief bio and list of publishing credits. Send SASE or IRC for return of ms or send disposable copy of ms and SASE for reply only. Responds in 2 months to queries; 3 months to mss. Accepts simultaneous submissions.

Terms: Pays in royalties. Publishes ms 1 year after acceptance.

FIREBRAND BOOKS, 141 The Commons, Ithaca NY 14850. (607)272-0000. Website: www.firebrandbooks.com. **Contact:** Nancy K. Bereano, publisher. Estab. 1985. "Our audience includes feminists, lesbians, ethnic audiences, and other progressive people." Independent feminist and lesbian press. Publishes quality trade paperback originals. Averages 6-8 total titles/year.

● Firebrand has won the Lambda Literary Award Organization's Publisher's Service Award.

Needs: Feminist, lesbian. Published *The Gilda Stories*, by Jewelle Gomez (novel); and *Stone Butch Blues*, by Leslie Feinberg (novel).

How to Contact: Accepts unsolicited mss. Query with outline/synopsis and sample chapters or send complete ms with cover letter. Send SASE or IRC for return of ms. Responds in 2 weeks to queries; 2 months to mss. Accepts simultaneous submissions with notification.

Terms: Pays royalties. Publishes ms 1 year after acceptance.

FORGE BOOKS, Tom Doherty Associates, LLC, 175 5th Ave., New York NY 10010. (212)388-0100. Fax: (212)388-0191. Website: www.tor.com (includes FAQ, writer's guidelines, info on authors and upcoming books, first chapter of selected books, list of award winners). **Contact:** Melissa Ann Singer, senior editor (general fiction, mysteries, thriller, horror); Natalia Aponte, senior editor (general fiction, thrillers); Patrick Nielsen Hayden, senior editor (science fiction, fantasy). Estab. 1980. "Forge imprint specializes in thrillers, historicals, and mysteries; Tor imprint in science fiction and fantasy." Publishes hardcover and paperback originals. **Published new writers within the last year.** Plans 2-3 first novels in 2001. Averages 130 total titles, 129 fiction titles/year.

Imprint(s): Forge, Tor, Orb.

● Recently won the Locus Award and the Western Writers of America Award for best publisher.

Needs: Erotica, historical, horror, mainstream/contemporary, mystery/suspense (amateur sleuth, cozy, police procedural, private eye/hardboiled), thriller/espionage, western (frontier saga, traditional), science fiction, fantasy.

How to Contact: Accepts unsolicited mss. Query with outline/synopsis and first 3 sample chapters. Include estimated word count, bio and list of publishing credits. SASE for reply. Agented fiction 95%. Responds in 4 months to proposals. Sometimes comments on rejected mss.

Terms: Pays royalties. Sends galleys to author. Publishes ms 12-18 months after acceptance.

Advice: "The writing mechanics must be outstanding for a new author to break into today's market."

FORT ROSS INC., 26 Arthur Place, Yonkers NY 10701-1703. (914)375-6448. Fax: (914)375-6439. E-mail: ftross@ix.netcom.com. Website: www.fortross.net (includes description of Fort Ross Inc., including examples of published books, available rights and catalog of the authors and artists). **Contact:** Dr. Vladimir P. Kartsev. Estab. 1992. "We publish only well-established American/Canadian fantasy, science fiction and romance writers who would like to have their novels translated in Russia and Easter Europe by our publishing house in cooperation with the local publishers." Publishes hardcover and paperback translations. **Published 3 new writers within the last year.** Averages 10 total titles/year.

Needs: Adventure, fantasy (space fantasy, sword and sorcery), mystery/suspense (amateur sleuth, police procedural, private eye/hardboiled), romance (contemporary, futuristic/time travel), science fiction (hard science/technological, soft/sociological), thriller/espionage. Recently published *The Harem*, by Liza Dulby; *Lolita's Diary*, by Pia Pera (novel); and *Killers Are Storming . . .*, by Aleshkin (mystery).
How to Contact: Does not accept unsolicited mss. Send query letter. Include estimated word count, brief bio and list of publishing credits. Send SASE or IRC for reply. Responds in 1 month. Accepts simultaneous submissions.
Terms: Pays royalties of 4-9%. Average advance: $500-1,000; negotiable. Does not send galleys of translated novels to author. Publishes ms 1 year after acceptance.

N **FOUNTAINHEAD PRODUCTIONS, INC.**, 755 Highway 34, Matawan NJ 07747. (732)583-2138. Fax: (732)566-7336. E-mail: exec@fountainheadpub.com. Website: www.fountainheadpub.com. **Contact:** J.G. Fennessy, editor; Kathleen M. Leo, associate editor; Michael McMahon, associate editor. Estab. 1999. "Small independent publisher. We publish a wide range of titles and are not 'niche' publishers. We also sponsor the national writing contest and publish the contest winners." Publishes hardcover and paperback originals and hardcover and paperback reprints. Books: type of paper, method of printing, binding and illustrations vary. Average print order: varies; first novel print order: varies. **Published 1 new writer within the last year.** Plans 5-10 first novels in 2001. Averages 10 total titles, 7 fiction titles/year. Distributes titles through Ingram Books. Promotes titles through pre-press reviews.
Needs: Adventure, ethnic/multicultural, fantasy, historical, horror, humor/satire, literary, mainstream, military/war, mystery/suspense, psychic/supernatural, regional, religious, romance, science fiction, thriller/espionage, western; special interests (Irish/Celtic science fiction). Recently published *Domestics*, by J.G. Fennessy (Irish). Publishes *In the Parishes of Ireland* trilogy.
How to Contact: Does not accept or return unsolicited mss. Query with 2-3-page outline/synopsis. Accepts queries by e-mail and fax. Include estimated word count, brief bio and list of publishing credits. Responds in 2 months to queries; 3 months to mss. Accepts simultaneous submissions, electronic submissions (proposals only) and disk. Often comments on rejected mss.
Terms: Pays royalties of 5-15%. Sends galleys to author. Publishes ms 8-12 months after acceptance. Writer's guidelines available on Internet.
Advice: "The availability of electronic media and publishing are making fiction more desirable than ever. Follow our guidelines and send your best writing when requested."

N **FOUR WALLS EIGHT WINDOWS**, 39 W. 14th St., #503, New York NY 10011. (212)206-8965. E-mail: edit@fourwallseightwindows.com. Website: www.4w8w.com (includes complete catalog, featured books and ordering information). **Contact:** John Oakes, publisher. Estab. 1987. "We are a small independent publisher." Publishes hardcover and paperback originals and paperback reprints. Books: quality paper; paper or cloth binding; illustrations sometimes. Average print order: 3,000-7,000. First novel print order: 3,000-5,000. **Published new writers within the last year.** Averages 28 total titles; approximately 9 fiction titles/year. Distributes titles through Publishers Group West, the largest independent distributor in the country. Promotes titles through author tours, bound galleys, select advertising, postcard mailing. etc.
• Four Walls Eight Windows' books have received mention from the *New York Times* as "Notable Books of the Year" and have been nominated for *L.A. Times* fiction and nonfiction prizes. Won Special Citation, Philip K. Dick Award for Paul DiFilippo's *Lost Pages*.
Needs: Literary, nonfiction. Published *The Angle Quickest for Flight*, by Steven Kotler (novel); *Extremities*, by Kathe Koja (stories); *Beast of the Heartland*, by Lucius Shepard (stories).
How to Contact: Does not accept unsolicited submissions. "Query letter accompanied by sample chapter, outline and SASE is best. Useful to know if writer has published elsewhere, and if so, where." Accepts electronic queries. Agented fiction 70%. Responds in 2 months. Accepts simultaneous submissions. No electronic submissions.
Terms: Pays standard royalties. Average advance: varies. Sends galleys to author. Publishes ms 1-2 years after acceptance. Book catalog free on request.
Advice: "Please read our catalog and/or our website to be sure your work would be compatible with our list."

FRONT STREET BOOKS, 20 Battery Park Ave., #403, Asheville NC 28801. (828)236-3097. Fax: (828)236-3098. E-mail: nhz@frontstreetbooks.com. Website: www.frontstreetbooks.com (includes writer's guidelines, names of editors, book catalog, interviews with authors, first chapters of some books). **Contact:** Stephen Roxburgh, president and publisher; Joy Neaves, assistant editor. Estab. 1994. "Small independent publisher of high-quality picture books and literature for children and young adults." Publishes hardcover originals.
• *Asphalt Angels*, by Ineke Holtwijk won the 2000 Mildred L. Batchelder Award.
Needs: Children's/juvenile (adventure, animal, easy-to-read, fantasy, historical, mystery, preschool/picture book, sports), young adult/teen (adventure, fantasy/science fiction, historical, horror, mystery/suspense, problem novels,

romance, sports, western). Recently published *Myrtle of Willendorf*, by Rebecca O'Connell (young adult fiction); *Paper Trail*, by Barbara Snow Gilbert (young adult fiction); *Letters from Vinnie*, by Maureen Sappéy (fiction); *A Day, A Dog*, by Gabrielle Vincent (picture book).

How to Contact: Accepts unsolicited mss. Query with outline/synopsis and a few sample chapters or submit complete ms with cover letter. Accepts queries by e-mail. Include short bio and list of publishing credits. Send SASE for reply, return of ms or send disposable copy of ms. Agented fiction 10%. Responds in 2 weeks to queries; 3 months to mss. Accepts simultaneous submissions. No electronic submissions.

Terms: Pays royalties. Offers negotiable advance.

✅ ◯ **LAURA GERINGER BOOKS**, Imprint of HarperCollins Children's Books Group, HarperCollins Publishers, 1350 Avenue of the Americas, New York NY 10019. (212)261-6500. Website: www.harpercollins.com. **Contact:** Laura Geringer, senior vice president/publisher. "We look for books that are out of the ordinary, authors who have their own definite take, and artists that add a sense of humor to the text." Publishes hardcover originals. **Published new writers within the last year.** Averages 15-20 titles/year.

Needs: Adventure, fantasy, historical, humor, literary, young adult. Recently published *Regular Guy*, by Sarah Weeks; and *Throwing Smoke*, by Bruce Brooks.

How to Contact: Accepts unsolicited mss. Submit complete ms with cover letter. Send SASE or IRC for return of ms. Agented fiction 75%. Responds in 4 months to queries.

Terms: Pays royalties of 10-12½% on retail price. Advance varies. Publishes ms 6-12 months after acceptance for novels. Writer's guidelines for #10 SASE. Book catalog for 8 × 10 SAE with 3 first-class stamps.

Advice: "A mistake writers often make is failing to research the type of books an imprint publishes, therefore sending inappropriate material."

N **A** **DAVID R. GODINE, PUBLISHER, INC.**, P.O. Box 9103, 9 Lewis St., Lincoln MA 01773. Fax: (617)259-9198. E-mail: godine@godine.com. Website: www.godine.com. President: David R. Godine. **Contact:** Mark Polizzotti, editorial director. Estab. 1970. Small independent publisher (5-person staff). Publishes hardcover and paperback originals and reprints. Average print order: 2,500-5,000; first novel print order: 2,500. **Published new writers within the last 3-5 years.**

Imprint(s): Nonpareil Books (trade paperbacks), Verba Mundi (translations), Imago Mundi (photography).

Needs: Literary, historical, children's. Published *Last Trolley from Beethovenstraat*, by Grete Weil (novel in translation); and *The Last Worthless Evening*, by Andre Dulous (short stories).

How to Contact: Does not accept unsolicited mss.

Terms: Pays standard royalties; offers advance. Publishes ms 3 years after acceptance.

Advice: "Have your agent contact us."

🔆 ◯ ◎ **☖** **GOOSE LANE EDITIONS**, 469 King St., Fredericton, New Brunswick E3B 1E5 Canada. (506)450-4251. Fax: (506)459-4991. **Contact:** Laurel Boone, editorial director. Estab. 1957. Publishes hardcover and paperback originals and occasional reprints. Books: some illustrations. Average print order: 3,000. First novel print order: 1,500. Averages 14 total titles, 4-5 fiction titles/year. Distributes titles through General Distribution Services. Promotes titles through Literary Press Group (Canada).

● Goose Lane author Lynn Coady was a finalist for the Governor General's Award for fiction for *Strange Heaven*. Luther Corhern's *Salmon Camp Chronicles* was a finalist for the Stephen Leacock Medal for Humuor.

Needs: Contemporary, historical, literary, short story collections. "Not suitable for mainstream or mass-market submissions. No genres i.e.: modern and historical adventure, crime, modern and historical romance, science fiction, fantasy, westerns, confessional works (fictional and autobiographical), and thrillers and other mystery books." Recently published *Overnight Sensation*, by Colleen Curran; *Sisters of Grass*, by Theresa Kishkan; *The Time of Her Life*, by David Helwig.

How to Contact: Considers unsolicited mss. Submit outline/synopsis and 30-50 page sample. Send SASE "with Canadian stamps, International Reply Coupons, cash, check or money order. No U.S. stamps please." Responds in 6 months.

Terms: Pays royalties of 8-12%. Average advance: $100-200, negotiable. Sends galleys to author. Writers guidelines for SAE and IRC or Canadian stamps.

Advice: "We do not consider submissions from outside Canada."

◐ **☖** **GRAYWOLF PRESS**, 2402 University Ave., Suite 203, St. Paul MN 55114. (651)641-0077. Fax: (651)641-0036. E-mail: wolves@graywolfpress.org. Website: www.graywolfpress.org (includes writers' guidelines, catalog, author bios, news). Director: Fiona McCrae. **Contact:** Anne Czarniecki, executive editor; Katie Dublinski, assitant editor. Estab. 1974. "Graywolf Press is an independent, nonprofit publisher dedicated to the creation and promotion of thoughtful and imaginative contemporary literature essential to a vital and diverse culture." Growing small literary press, nonprofit corporation. Publishes hardcover and paperback originals. Books: acid-free quality paper; offset printing; hardcover and soft binding; illustrations occasionally. Average print order: 3,000-10,000. First novel print order: 2,000-6,000. Averages 14-16 total titles, 4-6 fiction titles/year. Distributes titles nationally through Consortium Book Sales and Distribution. "We have an in house marketing staff and an advertising budget for all books we publish."

• *The Wedding Jester*, by Steve Stern won the National Jewish Book award.

Needs: Literary, and short story collections. Literary fiction; no genre books (romance, western, science fiction, suspense). Recently published *Ana Imagined*, by Perrin Ireland (novel); *Graveyard of the Atlantic*, by Alyson Hagy (short stories); *Glyph*, by Percival Everett (novel).

How to Contact: Query with SASE. "Please do not fax or e-mail queries or submissions." Responds in 3 months. Accepts simultaneous submissions.

Terms: Pays in royalties of 7½-10%; negotiates advance and number of author's copies. Sends galleys to author. Publishes ms 18 months after acceptance. Guidelines for #10 SASE; book catalog free.

Advice: "Please review the catalog and submission guidelines before submitting your work. We rarely publish collections or novels by authors who have not published work previously in literary journals or magazines."

✓ ◐ **GREENE BARK PRESS,** P.O. Box 1108, Bridgeport CT 06601. (203)372-4861. E-mail: greenebark@ aol.com. Website: www.greenebarkpress.com. **Contact:** Michele Hofbauer, associate publisher. "We only publish children's fiction—all subjects, but in reading picture book format appealing to ages 3-9 or all ages." Publishes hardcover originals. **Published new writers within the last year.** Averages 5 titles/year. Distributes titles through Baker & Taylor, Partners Book Distributing and Quality Books. Promotes titles through ads, trade shows (national and regional), direct mail campaigns.

Needs: Juvenile. Recently published *A Pumpkin Story*, by Mariko Shinju.

How to Contact: Submit complete ms with SASE. Does not accept queries or ms by e-mail. Responds in 3 months to mss. Accepts simultaneous submissions.

Terms: Pays royalties of 10-15% on wholesale price. Publishes ms 1 year after acceptance. Writer's guidelines for SASE; book catalog for $2.

Advice: Audience is "children who read to themselves and others. Mothers, fathers, grandparents, godparents who read to their respective children, grandchildren. Include SASE, be prepared to wait, do NOT inquire by telephone, fax or e-mail."

✓ ◉ **GREENWILLOW BOOKS,** Imprint of HarperCollins Children's Books Group, HarperCollins Publishers, 1350 Avenue of the Americas, New York NY 10019. (212)261-6500. Website: www.harperchildrens.com. **Contact:** Fiction Editor. Estab. 1974. "Greenwillow Books publishes quality hardcover books for children." Publishes hardcover originals and reprints. **Published new writers within the last year.** Averages 70-80 titles/ year.

Needs: Juvenile, picture books: fantasy, historical, humor, literary, mystery. Recently published *The Queen of Attolia*, by Megan Whalen Turner; *All Alone in the Universe*, by Lynne Rae Perkins; *One Lighthouse, One Moon*, by Anita Lobel; *Cold Little Duck, Duck, Duck*, by Lisa Westburg Peters, illustrated by Sam Williams.

How to Contact: Agented fiction 70%. Responds in 3 months to mss. Accepts simultaneous submissions.

Terms: Pays royalties of 10% on wholesale price for first-time authors. Average advance varies. Publishes ms 2 years after acceptance. Writer's guidelines for #10 SASE; book catalog available for $1.50 and 9×12 SASE.

◐ **GROLIER PUBLISHING,** Grolier Inc., Sherman Turnpike, Danbury CT 06816. (203)797-3500. Fax: (203)797-3197. Estab. 1895. "Grolier Publishing is a leading publisher of reference, educational and children's books. We provide parents, teachers and librarians with the tools they need to enlighten children to the pleasure of learning and prepare them for the road ahead." Publishes hardcover and trade paperback originals.

Imprint(s): Children's Press, Franklin Watts, **Orchard Books**.

• Grolier was recently purchased by Scholastic Inc.

N A **GROVE/ATLANTIC, INC.,** 841 Broadway, New York NY 10003. (212)614-7850, 7860. Fax: (212)614-7886, 7915. "Grove/Atlantic publishes serious nonfiction and literary fiction." Publishes hardcover originals, trade paperback originals and reprints. Averages 60-70 titles/year.

Imprint(s): Grove Press (Estab. 1952), Atlantic Monthly Press (Estab. 1917).

Needs: Experimental, literary. Recently published *Four Blondes*, by Candace Bushnell (Atlantic Monthly); and *How the Dead Live*, by Will Self (Grove Press).

How to Contact: Does not accept unsolicited mss. Agented submissions only. Accepts simultaneous submissions.

Terms: Pays royalties of 7½-15% on retail price. Advance varies considerably. Publishes ms 1 year after acceptance. Book catalog free.

✓ ◐ **GRYPHON BOOKS,** P.O. Box 209, Brooklyn NY 11228. (718)646-6126 (after 6 pm EST). Website: www.gryphonbooks.com. **Contact:** Gary Lovisi, owner/editor. Estab. 1983. Publishes paperback originals and trade paperback reprints. Books: bond paper; offset printing; perfect binding. Average print order: 500-1,000. **Published new writers within the last year.** Plans 2 first novels in 2001. Averages 10-15 total titles, 12 fiction titles/year.

Imprint(s): Gryphon Books, Gryphon Doubles, Gryphon SF Rediscovery Series.

Needs: Mystery/suspense (private eye/hardboiled, crime), science fiction (hard science/technological, soft/socio-logical). No supernatural, horror, romance or westerns. Published *The Dreaming Detective*, by Ralph Vaughn (mystery-fantasy-horror); *The Woman in the Dugout*, by Gary Lovisi and T. Arnone (baseball novel); and *A Mate for Murder*, by Bruno Fischer (hardboiled pulp). Publishes Gryphon Double novel series.

How to Contact: "I am not looking for novels now but will see a *1-page synopsis* with SASE." Include estimated word count, 50-word bio, short list of publishing credits, "how you heard about us." Do not send ms. Agented fiction 5-10%. Responds in 1 month to queries; 2 months to mss. Accepts simultaneous and electronic submissions (with hard copy—disk in ASCII). Often comments on rejected mss.

Terms: For magazines, $5-45 on publication plus 2 contributor's copies; for novels/collections payment varies and is much more. Sends galleys to author. Publishes ms 1-3 years after acceptance. Writers guidelines and book catalog for SASE.

Advice: "I am looking for better and better writing, more cutting-edge material with *impact*! Keep it lean and focused."

GUERNICA EDITIONS, Box 117, Station P, Toronto, Ontario M5S 2S6 Canada. (416)658-9888. Fax: (416)657-8885. E-mail: guernicaeditions@cs.com. Website: www.guernicaeditions.com. **Contact:** Antonio D'Alfonso, fiction editor (novel and short story). "Guernica Editions is a small press that produces works of fiction and nonfiction on the viability of pluriculturalism." Publishes paperback originals and reprints. Books: various paper; offset printing; perfect binding. Average print order: 1,500; first novel print order: 1,500. **Published 6 new writers within the last year.** Plans 4 first novels in 2001. Averages 25 total titles, 18-20 fiction titles/year. Distributes titles through professional distributors.

• Two titles by Guernica Editions have won American Book Awards.

Imprint(s): Prose Series, Antonio D'Alfonso, editor, all; Picas Series, Antonio D'Alfonso, editor, reprints.

Needs: Erotica, literary, translations. "We are open to all styles, but especially shorter pieces." Publishes anthology of Arab women writers/Italian women writers. Recently published *The Embrace*, by Irene Guilford (novel); *Stay With Me, Lella*, by Marisa Labozzetta (novel); and *Lydia Thrippe!*, by Daniel Sloate (literary fiction).

How to Contact: Accepts unsolicited mss. Send query letter. Include estimated word count, brief bio and list of publishing credits. Send IRC for return of ms. Responds in weeks to queries; months to mss.

Terms: Pays royalties of 10%. Average advance: $500-1,000. Sends galleys to author. Publishes ms 12 months after acceptance. Book catalogs for $5 and on website.

Advice: "Know what publishers do, and send your works only to publisher whose writers you've read and enjoyed."

ROBERT HALE LIMITED, Clerkenwell House, 45/47 Clerkenwell Green, London EC1R 0HT England. Fax: 020-7490-4958. **Contact:** Fiction Editor. Publishes hardcover and trade paperback originals and hardcover reprints. **Published approximately 50 new writers within the last year.**

Imprint(s): J.A. Allen; Caroline Burt, editor (horse books nonfiction).

Needs: Historical (not U.S. history), mainstream and western. Length: 40,000-150,000 words. Recently published *Midnight Clear*, by Kathy Hogan Trocheck (crime); *Light of the Moon*, by Barbara Cartland (historical romance); and *Honour Thy Wife*, by Norman Bogner (general ficiton).

How to Contact: Query with synopsis and 2 sample chapters. Acceptes queries by fax.

Advice: "Write well and have a strong plot!"

HAMPTON ROADS PUBLISHING COMPANY, INC., 134 Burgess Ln., Charlottesville VA 22902. (804)296-2772. Fax: (804)296-5096. E-mail: editorial@hrpub.com. Website: www.hrpub.com (includes writer's guidelines, authors, titles, synopsis of books, message board, guest book). **Contact:** Rebecca Williamson, managing editor. Estab. 1989. Publishes and distributes hardcover and paperback originals on subjects including metaphysics, health, complementary medicine, visionary fiction and other related topics. "We work as a team to produce the best books we are capable of producing which will impact, uplift and contribute to positive change in the world. We publish what defies or doesn't quite fit the usual genres. We are noted for visionary fiction." Average print order: 3,000-5,000. **Published 6 new writers within the last year.** Averages 60 total titles/year, 5-6 fiction titles/year. Distributes titles through distributors. Promotes titles through advertising, representatives, author signings and radio-TV interviews with authors.

Needs: Literary, New Age/mystic/spiritual, psychic/supernatural/occult. Looking for "visionary fiction, past-life fiction, based on actual memories." Recently published *Rogue Messiahs*, by Colin Wilson; *Spirit Matters*, by Michael Lerner; and *The Authenticator*, by William M. Valtos.

How to Contact: Does not accept unsolicited mss. Query with synopsis, chapter-by-chapter outline and 2 sample chapters. Accepts queries by e-mail and fax. Send SASE or IRC for return of ms or send disposable copy of ms and SASE for reply only (preferred). Agented fiction 5%. Responds in 1 month to queries; up to 5 months to mss. Accepts simultaneous submissions.

Terms: Pays in royalties; advance is negotiable. Sends galleys to author.

Advice: "Send us something new and different. Be patient. We take the time to give each submission the attention it deserves."

HARCOURT INC., 525 B St., Suite 1900, San Diego CA 92101. (619)231-6616. Fax: (619)699-6777. Publisher: Louise Pelan. **Contact:** Jeannette Larson, senior editor (general fiction); Allyn Johnston, editorial director of Harcourt Brace Children's Books; Elizabeth Van Doren, editorial director of Gulliver Books; Paula Wiseman, editorial director of Silver Whistle. Publishes hardcover originals and paperback reprints. **Published "very few" new writers within the last year.** Averages 150 titles/year.

Imprint(s): Harcourt Trade Children's Books, Gulliver Books, Red Wagon Books and Silver Whistle.

- Books published by Harcourt Trade Publishers have received numerous awards including the Caldecott and Newbery medals and selections as the American Library Association's "Best Books for Young Adults." Note that the publisher only accepts manuscripts through an agent. Unagented writers may query only.

Needs: Nonfiction for all ages, picture books for very young children, historical, mystery. Published *To Market, To Market*, by Ann Miranda; *Antarctic Antics*, by Judy Sierra; *Armageddon Summer*, by Bruce Coville and Jane Yolen; *Count On Me*, by Alice Provensen.

How to Contact: Does not accept unsolicited mss. Submit through agent only.

Terms: Terms vary according to individual books; pays on royalty basis. Book catalog for 9 × 12 SASE.

Advice: "Read as much current fiction as you can; familiarize yourself with the type of fiction published by a particular house; interact with young people to obtain a realistic picture of their concerns, interests and speech patterns."

HARLEQUIN ENTERPRISES, LTD., 225 Duncan Mill Rd., Don Mills, Ontario M3B 3K9 Canada. (416)445-5860. Website: www.eHarlequin.com (includes product listings, guidelines, author information, a full range of related information). Chairman and CEO: Brian E. Hickey. Vice President Editorial: Isabel Swift. **Contact:** Randall Toye, editorial director (Harlequin, Gold Eagle, Worldwide Library); Tara Gavin, editorial director (Silhouette, Steeple Hill); Diane Moggy, editorial director (MIRA). Estab. 1949. Publishes paperback originals and reprints. Books: Newsprint paper; web printing; perfect-bound. **Published new writers within the last year.** Averages 700 total titles/year. Distributes titles through retail market, direct mail market and overseas through operating companies. Promotes titles through trade and consumer advertising: print, radio, TV.

Imprint(s): Harlequin, **Silhouette**, MIRA, Gold Eagle, Worldwide Mysteries, **Steeple Hill.**

Needs: Romance, heroic adventure, mystery/suspense (romantic suspense *only*). Will accept nothing that is not related to the desired categories.

How to Contact: Send query letter or query with outline and first 50 pages (2 or 3 chapters) or submit through agent with SASE (Canadian). Does not accept simultaneous or electronic submissions. Responds in 6 weeks to queries; 6 months to mss.

Terms: Offers royalties, advance. Must return advance if book is not completed or is unacceptable. Sends galleys to author. Publishes ms 1 year after acceptance. Guidelines available.

Advice: "The quickest route to success is to follow directions for submissions: Query first. We encourage first novelists. Before sending a manuscript, read as many current Harlequin titles as you can. It's very important to know the genre and the series most appropriate for your submission." Submissions for Harlequin Romance and Harlequin Presents should go to: Mills & Boon Limited Eton House, 18-24 Paradise Road, Richmond, Surrey TW9 1SR United Kingdom, Attn: Karin Stoecker; Superromances: Paula Eykelhof, senior editor, (Don Mills address); Temptation: Birgit Davis-Todd, senior editor (Don Mills address). Intrigue: Denise O'Sullivan, associate senior editor, Harlequin Books, 6th Floor, 300 E. 42 Street, New York, NY 10017. Silhouette and Steeple Hill submissions should also be sent to the New York office, attention Tara Gavin. MIRA submissions to Dianne Moggy, editorial director (Don Mills address); Gold Eagle and Worldwide Mysteries submissions to Feroze Mohammed, senior editor (Don Mills address). "The relationship between the novelist and editor is regarded highly and treated with professionalism."

HARPERCOLLINS CHILDREN'S BOOKS, HarperCollins Publishers, 1350 Avenue of the Americas, New York NY 10019. (212)261-6500. Website: www.harperchildrens.com. Editor-in-Chief: Kate Morgan Jackson. **Contact:** Alix Reid, editorial director Robert Warren, editorial director; Phoebe Yeh, editorial director. Publishes hardcover originals. Averages 350 total titles/year.

Imprint(s): Avon; Joana Cotler Books (Joana Cotler, editorial director); **Laura Geringer Books** (Laura Geringer, editorial director); **Greenwillow**; HarperFestival (Suzanne Daghlian, editorial director); HarperTempest (Elise Howard, vice president/publisher); HarperTrophy (Ginee Seo, editorial director).

Needs: Adventure, fantasy, historical, humor, juvenile, literary, picture books, young adult. Recently published *Today I Feel Silly*, by Jamie Lee Curtis (picture book); *Ella Enchanted*, by Gail Carson Levine (novel).
How to Contact: Does not accept unsolicited mss. Send query letter only with SASE or IRC for reply. Responds in 1 month to queries and proposals; 4 months to mss. Accepts simultaneous submissions.
Terms: Pays royalties of 10-12½% on retail price. Advance varies. Publishes novel 1 year, picture books 2 years after acceptance. Writer's guidelines for #10 SASE. Book catalog for 8 × 10 SAE with 3 first-class stamps.
Advice: "We have no rules for subject matter, length or vocabulary, but look instead for ideas that are fresh and imaginative. Good writing that involves the reader is essential."

⊕ ✓ ◎ HARPERCOLLINS PUBLISHERS (NEW ZEALAND) LIMITED, P.O. Box 1, Auckland, New Zealand. Website: www.harpercollins.co.nz. **Contact:** Ian Watt, publisher. Averages 4-6 fiction titles/year (20-25 nonfiction).
Imprint(s): Flamingo, HarperCollins.
Needs: Adult fiction: Flamingo and HarperCollins imprints (40,000+ words); Junior fiction: 8-11 years (15-17,000 words).
How to Contact: Full ms preferred.
Terms: Pays royalties. "Write and ask for guidelines."
Advice: "It helps if the author and story have New Zealand connections/content."

✓ ⊘ HARPERTORCH, (formerly HarperPaperbacks), Division of HarperCollins Publishers, 10 E. 53rd St., New York NY 10022. (212)207-7000. Fax: (212)207-7901. Publisher: Michael Morrison. **Contact:** Jennifer Hershey, editorial director. Publishes paperback originals and reprints. **Published new writers within the last year.**
Needs: Mainstream/contemporary, mystery/suspense, romance (contemporary, historical, romantic suspense), thriller/espionage.
How to Contact: Does not accept unsolicited mss. Query by letter or through agent. Send SASE or IRC for reply.
Terms: Pays advance and royalties.

⊘ HARVEST HOUSE PUBLISHERS, 1075 Arrowsmith, Eugene OR 97402-9197. (541)343-0123. Editorial Managing Director: LaRae Weikert. Vice President of Editorial: Carolyn McCready. **Contact:** Acquisitions. Estab. 1974. "The foundation of our publishing program is to publish books that 'help the hurts of people' and nurture spiritual growth." Midsize independent publisher. Publishes hardcover and paperback originals and reprints. Books: 40 lb. ground wood paper; offset printing; perfect binding. Average print order: 10,000. First novel print order: 10,000-15,000. Average 120 total titles, 6 fiction titles/year.
How to Contact: Does not accept unsolicited mss. Recommends using Evangelical Christian Publishers Association website (www.ecpa.org) or the Writer's Edge.

Ⓝ ⊘ HAWK PUBLISHING GROUP, 6420 S. Richmond Ave., Tulsa OK 74136-1619. (918)492-3677. Fax: (918)492-2120. E-mail: wb@hawkpub.com. Website: www.hawkpub.com (includes writer's guidelines, book catalog, forthcoming titles, author information). **Contact:** Kirsten Bernhardt, editor-in-chief. Estab. 1999. Independent publisher of general trade/commercial books, fiction and nonfiction. Publishes hardcover and paperback originals and paperback reprints. **Published 3 new writers within the last year.** Plans 3 first novels in 2001. Averages 15 total titles, 12 fiction titles/year. Member: PMA, SPAN. Distributes titles through all major wholesalers.
Needs: Adventure, fantasy, historical, horror, humor/satire, literary, mainstream, mystery/suspense, science fiction, thriller/espionage. Recently published *Remnants of Glory*, by Teresa Miller (literary); and *Old Fears*, by John Wooley and Ron Wolfe (horror).
How to Contact: Accepts unsolicited mss. Query with outline/synopsis and sample chapters. Accepts queries by e-mail and fax. Include brief bio and list of publishing credits. Send disposable copy of ms and SASE for reply only. Agented fiction 60%. Responds in 2 weeks to queries; 2 months to mss. Accepts simultaneous submissions. Often comments on rejected mss.
Terms: Pays royalty plus advance; terms vary. Sends galleys to author. Writer's guidelines free.
Advice: "We're publishing more fiction, more hardcovers. Send us something different and really, really good."

✓ ⊘ Ⓥ HELICON NINE EDITIONS, Subsidiary of Midwest Center for the Literary Arts, Inc., P.O. Box 22412, Kansas City MO 64111-2820. (816)753-1016. E-mail: helicon9@aol.com. Website: www.heliconnine. com (includes general information about title, book and author, ording information for books). **Contact:** Gloria Vando Hickok, publisher; Patty Seyburn, editor; Pat Breed, editor (general fiction); Ann Slegman, editor (general fiction); Steve Shapiro, editor (general fiction). Estab. 1990. Small press publishing poetry, fiction, creative nonfiction and anthologies. Publishes paperback originals. Books: 60 lb. paper; offset printing; perfect-bound; 4-color cover. Average print order: 1,000-5,000. **Published one new writer within the last year.** Averages 4 total titles, 2-4 fiction titles/year. Also publishes one-story chapbooks called *feuillets*, which come with envelope,

250 print run. Distributes titles through Baker & Taylor, The Booksource, Brodart, Ingrams, Follett (library acquisitions), Midwest Library Service, all major distributors and booksellers. Promotes titles through reviews, readings, radio and television interviews.

• Helicon Nine Editions has received the Society of Midland Authors Prize as well as grants from the Kansas Arts Commission, the Missouri Arts Council and the National Endowment for the Arts. *Diasporadic*, by Patty Seyburn received the Notable Book Award, and Amy Tan selected "Africans" from Sheila Kohler's *One Girl* for *Best American Short Stories*.

Needs: Contemporary, ethnic, experimental, literary, short story collections, translations. "We're only interested in fine literature." Nothing "commercial." Recently published *Climbing the God Tree*, by Jamie Wriston Colbert (short story collection); *Galaxy Girls: Wonder Women*, by Anne Whitney Pierce (short story collection); and *Eternal City*, by Molly Shapiro (short story collection).

How to Contact: Does not accept unsolicited mss. Send query first with SASE. Responds in 1 week to queries.

Terms: Pays royalties, advance and author's copies. "Individual arrangement with author." Sends galleys to author. Publishes ms 6-12 months after acceptance.

Advice: "We accept short story collections. We welcome new writers and first books. Submit a clean, readable copy in a folder or box—paginated with title and name on each page. Also, do not pre-design book, i.e., no illustrations. We'd like to see books that will be read 50-100 years from now." Helicon Nine Editions sponsors the annual Willa Cather Fiction Prize—a $1,000 prize plus publication. Send a SASE for guidelines.

N ⊕ ◑ **HODDER & STOUGHTON/HEADLINE**, Hodder Headline, 338 Euston Rd., London NW1 3BH England. Phone: (020)7873 6000. Fax: (020)7873 6024. **Contact:** Mrs. Betty Schwartz, submissions editor, Hodder & Stoughton (adult fiction, nonfiction); Caroline Stofer, submissions editor, Headline (adult fiction). "Big commercial, general book publishers of general fiction/nonfiction, thrillers, romance, sagas, contemporary original, literary, crime." Publishes hardcover and paperback originals and paperback reprints. **Published 5 new writers within the last year.**

Imprint(s): Coronet, Sceptre, Flame, Hodder & Stoughton, NEL, LIR (Headline, Review, Feature).

Needs: Family saga, historical (general), literary, mainstream, mystery/suspense (amateur sleuth, cozy, police procedural, private eye/hardboiled), romance (contemporary, romantic suspense), thriller/espionage.

How to Contact: Accepts unsolicited mss. Query with outline/synopsis and first sample chapter. Accepts queries by e-mail. Include estimated word count and brief bio. Send disposable copy of ms and SASE for reply only. Responds in 2 weeks minimum to queries; 1 month to mss. Accepts simultaneous submissions.

Terms: Writer's guidelines for SASE. Book catalogs for flat A4 SASE.

Advice: "Minimum 80,000 words. Send covering letter, short synopsis (1-2 pages) and first sample chapter, typewritten, double-spaced. Writing should be of good quality, and commercial. No single short stories."

◑ ⓥ **HOLIDAY HOUSE, INC.,** 425 Madison, New York NY 10017. (212)688-0085. Fax: (212)421-6134. Editor-in-Chief: Regina Griffin. **Contact:** Michelle Frey, associate editor. Estab. 1935. "Holiday House has a commitment to publishing first-time authors and illustrators." Independent publisher of children's books, picture books, nonfiction and novels for young readers. Publishes hardcover originals and paperback reprints. **Published new writers within the last year.** Averages approximately 50 hardcovers and 15 paperbacks/year.

• *The Wright Brothers: How They Invented the Airplane* by Russell Freedman and published by Holiday House was a Newbery Honor Book.

Needs: Children's books only: literary, contemporary, Judaica and holiday, adventure, humor and animal stories for young readers. Recently published *Give Me Liberty: The Story of the Declaration of Independence*, by Russell Freedman; *The Jar of Fools*, by Eric A. Kimmel, illustrated by Mordicai Gerstern; *The Blues of Flats Brown*, by Walter Dean Myers, illustrated by Nina Laden. "We're not in a position to be too encouraging, as our list is tight, but we're always open to good writing."

How to Contact: "We ask for query letters only with SASE. We do not accept simultaneous submissions. No phone calls, please."

Terms: Royalties, advance are flexible, depending upon whether the book is illustrated. Publishes ms 1-2 years after acceptance.

Advice: "Please submit only one project at a time."

✓ ◐ Ⓐ **HENRY HOLT & COMPANY**, 115 W. 18th St., 6th Floor, New York NY 10011. (212)886-9200. **Contact**: Sara Bershtel, associate publisher (Metropolitan Books, literary fiction); Jennifer Barth, executive editor (adult literary fiction). Publishes hardcover and paperback originals and reprints.

Imprint(s): Owl Books; John Macrae Books; Metropolitan Books; **Henry Holt & Company Books for Young Readers**.

How to Contact: Accepts queries; no unsolicited mss. Agented fiction 95%.

✓ ◑ **HENRY HOLT & COMPANY BOOKS FOR YOUNG READERS**, Imprint of Henry Holt & Co., Inc., 115 W. 18th St., New York NY 10011. (212)886-9200. Fax: (212)645-5832. Website: www.henryholt.com/byr/. **Contact:** Laura Godwin, vice president and associate publisher; Nina Ignatowicz, executive editor; Marc

Aronson, senior editor-at-large (young adult nonfiction and fiction); Christy Ottaviano, executive editor (picture books, middle grade fiction); Reka Simonsen, editor (fiction and nonfiction). Estab. 1866 (Holt). Henry Holt Books for Young Readers publishes excellent books of all kinds (fiction, nonfiction, illustrated) for all ages, from the very young to the young adult. Publishes hardcover and trade paperback originals. Averages 50-60 titles/year.

Imprint(s): Edge Books (Marc Aronson, senior editor, "a high caliber young adult fiction imprint"); Red Feather Books ("covers a range between early chapter and younger middle grade readers"); Owlet Paperbacks.

Needs: Juvenile: adventure, animal, contemporary, fantasy, history, humor, multicultural, religion, sports, suspense/mystery. Picture books: animal, concept, history, humor, multicultural, religion, sports. Young adult: contemporary, fantasy, history, multicultural, nature/environment, problem novels, sports. Recently published *The Road to Home*, by Mary Jane Auch (middle grade fiction); *Where Once There Was a Wood*, by Denise Fleming (picture book paperbacks); and *Ola's Wake*, by B.J. Stone (middle grade fiction).

How to Contact: Accepts unsolicited mss. Query with outline/synopsis or submit complete ms with cover letter. Include estimated word count, brief bio and list of publishing credits. Send SASE or IRC for return of ms. Responds in 4 months to queries and mss. No longer accepts multiple or simultaneous submissions.

Terms: Pays royalty and advance. Publishes ms 18 months after acceptance. Book catalog and writer's guidelines upon request with SASE or visit website.

✔ ◐ ♈ HOUGHTON MIFFLIN BOOKS FOR CHILDREN, Imprint of Houghton Mifflin Company, 222 Berkeley St., Boston MA 02116-3764. (617)351-5000. Fax: (617)351-1111. E-mail: hmco.com. Website: www.children's_books@hmco.com (includes titles, job postings, etc.) **Contact:** Hannah Rodgers, submissions coordinator; Margaret Raymo, senior editor; Amy Flynn, editor; Dinah Stevenson (New York City); W. Lorraine (Walter Lorraine Books). "Houghton Mifflin gives shape to ideas that educate, inform, and above all, delight." Publishes hardcover and trade paperback originals and reprints. **Published 12 new writers within the last year.** Averages approximately 60 titles/year. Promotes titles through author visits, advertising, reviews.

Imprint(s): Clarion Books, New York City, Walter Lorraine Books.

● Houghton Mifflin Books for Children received the Caldecott Award in 1999 for *Snowflake Bentley*.

Needs: Adventure, ethnic, historical, humor, juvenile (early readers), literary, mystery, picture books, suspense, young adult, board books. Recently published *Night Hoops*, by Carl Deuker; *Gathering Blue*, by Lois Lowery; *The Circuit*, by Francisco Jimenez.

How to Contact: Submit complete ms with appropriate-sized SASE. Responds in 3 months. Accepts simultaneous submissions. No mss or proposals by e-mail, fax or disk.

Terms: Pays royalties of 5-10% on retail price. Average advance: dependent on many factors. Publishes ms 18 months after acceptance. Writer's guidelines for #10 SASE; book catalog for 9×12 SASE with 3 first-class stamps.

✔ ◐ HOUGHTON MIFFLIN COMPANY, 222 Berkeley St., Boston MA 02116. (617)351-5000. Fax: (617)351-1202. Website: www.houghtonmifflinbooks.com. **Contact:** Submissions Editor. Estab. 1832. Publishes hardcover and paperback originals and paperback reprints. **Published new writers within the last year.** Averages 100 total titles, 50 fiction titles/year.

Needs: Ethnic, feminist, gay, historical, lesbian, literary, mainstream/contemporary.

How to Contact: Does not accept unsolicited mss. Agented fiction 80%.

Terms: Pays royalties of 10-15%. Average advance: varies. Publishes ms 1-2 years after acceptance.

Ⓝ ❦ ◐ ◎ ♈ HOUSE OF ANANSI PRESS, Stoddart Publishing, 34 Lesmill Rd., Toronto, Ontario M3B 2T6 Canada. (416)445-3333. Fax: (416)445-5967. E-mail: info@anansi.ca. Website: www.anansi.ca (includes submission guidelines, book catalog, names of editors, news, awards info, order form). **Contact:** Martha Sharpe, publisher, editor; Adrienne Leahey, assistant editor. Estab. 1967. "House of Anansi Press finds and publishes innovative literary works of fiction, nonfiction and poetry by Canadian writers. Anansi acquired a reputation early on for its editors' ability to spot talented writers who push the boundaries and challenge the expectations of the literary community." Publishes hardcover and paperback originals and paperback reprints. Books: perfect binding. **Published 2 new writers within the last year.** Plans 2 first novels in 2001. Averages 10-15 total titles, 2-5 fiction titles/year. Member: ACP, LPG, OBPO. Distributes titles through General Distribution Services.

● Anansi Press received the Giller Prize (shortlist) for 1999.

Needs: Ethnic/multicultural (general), experimental, feminist, gay, literary, short story collections, translations. "All books must be by Canadians or Canadian landed immigrants." Recently published *19 Knives*, by Mark Anthony Jarman (short stories); *This All Happened*, by Michael Winter (literary novel); and *Am I Disturbing You?*, by Anne Hébert (novel in translation). Publishes the CBC Massey Lectures Series.

How to Contact: Accepts unsolicited mss. Query with outline/synopsis and 2 sample chapters. Accepts queries by regular mail only. Include brief bio and list of publishing credits. Send SASE or IRC for return of ms OR send disposable copy of ms and SASE for reply only. Agented fiction 60%. Responds in 6 months to queries and mss. Accepts simultaneous submissions. Sometimes comments on rejected mss.

Terms: Pays royalties of 8-12%. Average advance. Sends first proofs only to author. Publishes ms 6-12 months after acceptance. Writer's guidelines on website. Book catalogs free or on website.
Advice: "Read and submit your work to literary journals and magazines. Attend or participate in literary events—readings, festivals, book clubs. Visit our website, see the kinds of books we publish, think about whether we're the right publisher for your work."

HUNTINGTON HOUSE PUBLISHERS, P.O. Box 53788, Lafayette LA 70505. (318)237-7049. Fax: (318)237-7060. E-mail: ladawn@eatel.net. Website: www.huntingtonhousebooks.com. **Contact:** Editorial Department. Estab. 1983. **Published 9 new writers within the last year.** Plans 4 first novels in 2001. Averages 30 total titles, 10 fiction titles/year.
Needs: Young adult/teen (adventure, easy-to-read, fantasy/science fiction, historical, mystery/suspense, series). Recently published *High On Adventure III*, by Steve Arrington; *Patriots*, by James Wesley Rawles (first novel); *Slash Brokers*, by Jeff Barganier (first novel).
How to Contact: Accepts unsolicited mss. Query with outline/synopsis and sample chapters. Include estimated word count and brief bio. Send a disposable copy of the ms. Agented fiction 5%. Responds in 3 weeks to mss. Accepts simultaneous submissions.
Terms: Pays royalties of 10-15%. Sends prepublication galleys to author. Writer's guidelines for SASE.
Advice: "Submit an outline (two to four pages) and chapter by chapter synopsis of your idea. Even if the breakdown is still only tentative, this provides us with the information we need to determine which of our series your piece could join. Note any previously published material and include excerpts (no more than two pages each). Enclose any peer reviews, recommendations, and references in the proposal package."

HYPERION BOOKS FOR CHILDREN, Imprint of Hyperion, 114 Fifth Ave., New York NY 10011. (212)633-4400. Fax: (212)633-4833. **Contact:** Editorial Director. "The aim of Hyperion Books for Children is to create a dynamic children's program informed by Disney's creative vision, direct connection to children, and unparalleled marketing and distribution." Publishes hardcover and trade paperback originals. Averages 210 titles/year.
Needs: Juvenile, picture books, young adult. Published *McDuff*, by Rosemary Wells and Susan Jeffers (picture book); *Split Just Right*, by Adele Griffin (middle grade).
How to Contact: Submit through agent only. Accepts simultaneous submissions.
Terms: Pays royalty, "varies too widely to generalize." Average advance: varies. Publishes ms 1 year after acceptance. Writer's guidelines and book catalog free.
Advice: "Hyperion Books for Children are meant to appeal to an upscale children's audience. Study your audience. Look at and research current children's books. Who publishes what you like? Approach them."

IMAJINN BOOKS, ImaJinn, P.O. Box 162, Hickory Corners MI 49060-0162. (616)671-4633. Fax: (616)671-4535. E-mail: imajinn@worldnet.att.net. Website: www.imajinnbooks.com (includes book list, writer's guidelines, author pictures and bios, contests, ImaJinn book news, tips for writers, author questions/answers from readers, etc.). **Contact:** Linda J. Kichline, editor. Estab. 1998. "ImaJinn Books is a small independent publishing house that specializes in romances with story lines involving ghosts, psychics or psychic phenomena, witches, vampires, werewolves, angels, reincarnation, time travel, space travel, the future, and any other form of 'other worldly' or 'new-age' type story line. Occasionally, ImaJinn Books will publish a straight fantasy or general fiction novel that falls into the above categories and has romantic elements in it, but is not a traditional romance. We also intend to publish a science fiction young adult series beginning in 2001." Publishes paperback originals and reprints. Books: 60 lb. text stock paper; camera ready and disk to film printing; perfect binding; illustrations occasionally but rare. Average print order: 2,500. First novel print order: 1,000. **Published 2 new writers within the last year.** Plans 3 first novels in 2001. Averages 12-24 total titles, 12-24 fiction titles/year. Member: SPAN and PMA. Distributes titles through Baker & Taylor, Ingram Books, Amazon.com, BN.com and imajinnbooks.com. Promotes titles through advertising review magazines.
  • ImaJinn Books has won the Reviewers International Organization (RIO) 1999 Dorothy Parker Award for Best Fantasy. Two titles were nominated for the PEARL (Paranormal Excellence in Romantic Literature) Award and one book cover was nominated for best paranormal cover of the year.
Needs: Children's/juvenile (fantasy), fantasy (romance), horror (romance), New Age/mystic, psychic/supernatural, romance (futuristic/time travel), science fiction (romance), young adult/teen (fantasy/science fiction). "We look for specific story lines based on what the readers are asking for and what story lines in which we're short. We post our current needs on our website." Recently published *Dreamsinger*, by J.A. Ferguson (fantasy romance); *Midnight Enchantment*, by Nancy Gideon (vampire romance); and *Time of the Wolf*, by Julie D'Arcy (fantasy).
How to Contact: Does not accept or return unsolicited mss. Send query letter. Accepts queries by e-mail. Include estimated word count, brief bio and list of publishing credits. Send disposable copy of ms and SASE for reply only. Agented fiction 20%. Responds in 3 months to queries; 6 months to mss. Accepts simultaneous submissions, electronic submissions and disk. Often comments on rejected mss.
Terms: Pays royalties of 10%. Sends galleys to author. Publishes ms up to 2 years after acceptance. Writer's guidelines free for #10 SASE and 33¢ postage. Book catalogs free.

Advice: "Carefully read the author guidelines, and read books published by ImaJinn Books."

INSOMNIAC PRESS, 192 Spadina Ave., Suite 403, Toronto, Ontario M5T 2C2 Canada. (416)504-6270. Fax: (416)504-9313. E-mail: mike@insomniacpress.com. Website: www.insomniacpress.com (includes writer's guidelines, author tour info, book descriptions). **Contact:** Fiction Editor. Estab. 1992. "Midsize independent publisher with a mandate to produce edgy experimental fiction." Publishes paperback originals. First novel print order: 3,000. **Published 4 new writers within the last year.** Plans 2 first novels in 2001. Averages 10 total titles, 5 fiction titles/year. Member: Literary Press Group of Canada. Distributes titles through PGW Canada (trade) and Seven Hills Distribution (US, trade).

Needs: Experimental, gay, lesbian, literary, mainstream, mystery/suspense. Recently published *Pray For Us Sinners*, by Patrick Taylor (novel); *Just for Comfort*, by Ralph Osborne (novel); and *Happy Pilgrims*, by Stephen Finucan (short story).

How to Contact: Accepts unsolicited mss. Send query by e-mail. Include estimated word count, brief bio and list of publishing credits. Send SASE or IRC for return of ms or send disposable copy of ms and SASE for reply only. Agented fiction 5%. Responds in 2 weeks to queries; 3 weeks to mss. Accepts simultaneous submissions. Sometimes comments on rejected ms.

Terms: Pays royalties of 10% maximum. Advance is negotiable. Sends galleys to author. Publishes ms 8 months after acceptance. Writer's guidelines free on website.

Advice: "Visit our website, read our writer's guidelines."

INTERLINK PUBLISHING GROUP, INC., 46 Crosby St., Northampton MA 01060-1804. Fax: (413)582-7057. E-mail: interpg@aol.com. **Contact:** Michel Moushabeck, publisher; Pam Thompson, fiction editor. Contemporary fiction in translation published under Emerging Voices: New International Fiction. Estab. 1987. "Midsize independent publisher specializing in world travel, world literature, world history and politics." Publishes hardcover and paperback originals. Books: 55 lb. Warren Sebago Cream white paper; web offset printing; perfect binding. Average print order: 5,000. First novel print order: 5,000. **Published new writers within the last year.** Plans 2 first novels in 2001. Averages 30 total titles, 2-6 fiction titles/year. Distributes titles through distributors such as Baker & Taylor. Promotes titles through book mailings to extensive, specialized lists of editors and reviewers, authors read at bookstores and special events across the country.

Imprint(s): Interlink Books, Olive Branch Press and Crocodile Books USA.

Needs: "Adult translated fiction from around the world." Published *House of the Winds*, by Mia Yun (first novel); *The Gardens of Light*, by Amin Maalouf (novel translated from French); and *War in the Land of Egypt*, by Yusef Al-Qaid (novel translated from Arabic). Publishes the International Folk Tales series.

How to Contact: Does not accept unsolicited mss. Submit query letter and brief sample only. No queries by e-mail or fax. Send SASE. Responds within 6 weeks to queries.

Terms: Pays royalties of 6-7%. Sends galleys to author. Publishes ms 1-1½ years after acceptance.

Advice: "Our Emerging Voices Series is designed to bring to North American readers the once-unheard voices of writers who have achieved wide acclaim at home, but were not recognized beyond the borders of their native lands. We are also looking for folktale collections (for adults) from around the world that fit in our International Folk Tale Series."

ISLAND, (formerly Dell Publishing Island), The Bantam Dell Publishing Group, A Division of Random House, Inc., 1540 Broadway, New York NY 10036. Website: www.bantamdell.com.

• See The Bantam Dell Publishing Group listing, page 394.

JAMESON BOOKS, 722 Columbus St., P.O. Box 738, Ottawa IL 61350. (815)434-7905. Fax: (815)434-7907. E-mail: 72557.3635@compuserve.com. **Contact:** Jameson G. Campaigne, Jr., publisher/editor Estab. 1986. "Jameson Books publishes conservative/libertarian politics and economics, history, biography, Chicago-area themes and pre-cowboy frontier novels (1750-1840)." Publishes hardcover and paperback originals and reprints. Books: free sheet paper; offset printing. Average print order: 10,000. First novel print order: 5,000. Plans 6-8 novels this year. Averages 12-16 total titles, 4-8 fiction titles each year. Distributes titles through LPC Group/Chicago (book trade).

Needs: Very well-researched western (frontier pre-1850). No cowboys, no science fiction, mystery, poetry, et al. Published *Yellowstone Kelly*, by Peter Bowen; *Wister Trace*, by Loren Estelman; and *One-Eyed Dream*, by Terry Johnston.

How to Contact: Does not accepted unsolicited mss. Submit outline/synopsis and 3 consecutive sample chapters. Send SASE. Agented fiction 50%. Responds in 2 weeks to queries; up to 5 months to mss. Accepts simultaneous submissions. Occasionally comments on rejected mss.

Terms: Pays royalties of 5%-15%. Average advance: $1,500. Sends galleys to author. Publishes ms 1-12 months after acceptance.

KAEDEN BOOKS, 19915 Lake Rd., Box 16190, Rocky River OH 44116. (440)356-0030. Fax: (440)356-5081. E-mail: kaeden01@aol.com. Website: www.kaeden.com (includes samples of books, reviews and titles).

Acquisitions: Kathleen Urmston, fiction editor (children's K-3); Karen Tabak, fiction editor (children's grades 3-6). Estab. 1990. "Children's book publisher for education K-6 market: reading stories, science, math and social studies materials, also poetry." Publishes paperback originals. Books: offset printing; saddle binding; illustrations. Average print order: 5,000. First novel print order: 5,000. **Published 5 new writers within the last year.** Plans 8 first novels in 2001. Averages 8-16 total titles/year.

Needs: Adventure, children's/juvenile (adventure, animal, easy-to-read, fantasy, historical, mystery, preschool/picture book, series, sports), ethnic/multicultural, fantasy (space fantasy), historical (general), humor/satire, mystery/suspense (amateur sleuth), romance (romantic suspense), science fiction (soft/sociological), short story collections, thriller/espionage. Plans a poetry anthology/associated stories. Submit stories and poetry to editor.

How to Contact: Accepts unsolicited mss. Query with outline/synopsis. Include 1-page bio and list of publishing credits. Send a disposable copy of ms and SASE for reply only. Responds "if interested."

Terms: Negotiable, either royalties or flat fee by individual arrangement with author depending on book. No advance. Publishes ms 6-24 months after acceptance.

Advice: "Our line is expanding with particular interest in poetry and fiction/nonfiction for grades three to six. Material must be suitable for use in the public school classroom, be multicultural and be high interest with appropriate word usage and a positive tone for the respective grade."

○ Ⓐ KENSINGTON PUBLISHING CORP., 850 Third Ave., 16th Floor, New York NY 10022. (212)407-1500. Fax: (212)935-0699. Editor-in-Chief: Paul Dinas. **Contact:** Tracy Bernstein, editorial director; Kate Duffy, editorial director; John Scognamiglio, editorial director; Ann LaFarge, executive editor; Karen Thomas, executive editor (Dafina Books); Claire Gerus, senior editor (Twins Streams health books); Diane Stockwell, senior editor (Encanto Books); Tomasita Ortiz, editor; Amy Garvey, consulting editor (romance); Hilary Sares, consulting editor (romance). Full service trade commercial publisher, all formats. Averages over 500 total titles/year.

Imprint(s): Kensington Books; Zebra Books; Pinnacle Books; Dafina Books; Twin Streams Books; Citadel Books; Brava Books; Encanto Books; Precious Gems; BET Books.

Needs: "Romance (contemporary, historical, Regency, erotica), mysteries, true crime, westerns, multicultural women's fiction, mainstream women's commercial fiction, gay and lesbian fiction and nonfiction, thrillers, romantic suspense, biographies, humor, paranormal, self-help, alternative health, pop culture nonfiction. No science fiction/fantasy, experimental fiction, business texts or children's titles."

How to Contact: Does not accept unsolicited mss. Agented submissions only.

Terms: Pays industry standard royalties and advances.

✔ ○ ALLEN A. KNOLL, PUBLISHERS, 200A W. Victoria St., Suite 3, Santa Barbara CA 93101-3627. Fax: (805)966-6657. E-mail: bookinfo@knollpublishers.com. Website: www.knollpublishers.com (includes book catalog, interviews with authors, special news items). **Contact:** Fiction Editor. Estab. 1990. Small independent publisher. "We publish books for intelligent people who read for fun." Publishes hardcover originals. Books: offset printing; sewn binding. Member: PMA, SPAN, ABA. Distributes titles through Ingram, Baker & Taylor, Brodart, Sunbelt. Promotes titles through advertising in specialty publications, direct mail, prepublication reviews and advertising.

Needs: Published *Flip Side*, by Theodore Roosevelt Gardner II (suspense); *The Unlucky Seven*, by Alistair Boyle (mystery); *Phantom Virus*, by David Champion (courtroom drama). Publishes A Bomber Hanson Mystery (courtroom drama series) and A Gil Yates Private Investigator Novel (P.I. series).

How to Contact: Does not accept unsolicited mss. Book catalog free.

✔ ○ Ⓐ ALFRED A. KNOPF, The Knopf Publishing Group, A Division of Random House, Inc., 299 Park Ave., New York NY 10171. (212)751-2600. Website: www.aaknopf.com. **Contact:** Senior Editor. Estab. 1915. Book-length fiction of literary merit by known and unknown writers. Publishes hardcover originals. Averages 200 titles/year. **Published new writers in the last year.** Also publishes nonfiction.

Needs: Contemporary, literary and spy. No western, gothic, romance, erotica, religious or science fiction.

How to Contact: Does not accept unsolicited mss. Query with outline or synopsis. Send SASE or IRC for reply. Agented fiction 90%. Responds within 3 months to mss.

Terms: Pays royalties of 10-15%; offers advance. Must return advance if book is not completed or is unacceptable. Publishes ms 1 year after acceptance.

✔ ○ ALFRED A. KNOPF BOOKS FOR YOUNG READERS, Bantam, Doubleday, Dell/Delacorte, Knopf and Crown Books for Young Readers, Random House Children's Books, A Division of Random House, Inc., 1540 Broadway, New York NY 10036. (212)782-9000 or (800)200-3552. Website: www.randomhouse.com/kids.

● See listing for Bantam, Doubleday, Dell/Delacorte, Knopf and Crown Books for Young Readers, page 395.

insider report

Published author goes it alone for second novel

As a longtime publisher of small, independently-produced magazines—or "zines"—Toronto-based writer Jim Munroe has been distributing his own work into the public domain for many years, and he believes the traditional model of publishing success is overrated. As a former editor for the politically-conscious, anti-corporate zine *Adbusters*, Munroe has long been critical of mainstream media's trend toward monopolization, but his perspective is not completely that of the outsider. He has had an inside view of how a major publishing company works. And after publishing his first novel with HarperCollins Canada, Munroe chose to go it alone for his second novel, further positioning himself not just as a maverick in the field but a staunch champion of self-publishing.

Jim Munroe

"This isn't for everyone, obviously," Munroe says. "Lots of people would be happy to hand over a manuscript and hang out at the café until it's time to sign books. Lots of people like to have editors and publicists and agents, for practical and prestige reasons. I've made my own zines and books for ten years, and I've developed skills and relationships that allow me to produce the same quality product without the overhead. As interesting as it was to have things done for me, it only confirmed my suspicions that there was basically no difference between professionals and talented amateurs. Basically, a corporate publisher offered me services I didn't need."

With his first novel, *Flyboy Action Figure Comes with Gasmask*—the farcical love story of a college student with the power to turn into a fly—Munroe initially hoped he could avoid the big publishing houses and sign a contract with an independent publisher. Negotiations with several independent publishers fell through, while other independents subsequently failed to follow up on their initial interest. Meanwhile, at the Canadian branch of HarperCollins, a young editor pulled *Flyboy* out of the slush pile and lobbied for its publication. As a staunch critic of media consolidation, Munroe viewed HarperCollins' interest with suspicion because of the company's ties to Rupert Murdoch's publishing empire. But the editor's personal enthusiasm for his book surprised Munroe enough to explore further his ideas about large media corporations and the people who work there. "So, I met with the young editor and the publisher, both of whom I found charming and enthusiastic. They told me about HarperCollins, and I listened, curious to see how they'd spin it—and ended up pleased by their candor. At the end of it, I was given a contract. I said I'd need a month to think it over."

Munroe sought advice from the Writer's Union and also from friends. His networking led him to a literary agent who offered to represent him in negotiations, but Munroe ultimately passed on the offer. "I had already secured the contract and the language of the contract was plain enough that I felt I could deal with it myself. I also was hesitant to sacrifice any control of my business to someone else—DIY [Do It Yourself] unless there's a good reason not to—so when I met the agent, and we didn't click, I declined the offer of representation."

In subsequent negotiations, HarperCollins pleased Munroe with their willingness to make concessions, and let him consider the contract without pressure. Munroe secured what he felt was a reasonable advance, along with control over important aspects of the book, such as the cover art and back jacket blurb. However, his hands-on style did not mesh well with the corporate way of doing things, and the remainder of the publication process proved difficult. "I was focused on trying to make each detail of the process interesting and creative, and it was draining to try to fight against the way things are usually done," he says. "Corporate specialization fragments a project into several pieces and creates lots of cracks for things to disappear into."

HarperCollins negotiated a U.S. publishing deal with Avon books in New York, but the American publisher didn't grant Munroe the level of editorial involvement he had hoped for. In addition, the subsequent acquisition of Avon by Rupert Murdoch had further soured Munroe's hopes of dealing with a company outside Murdoch's media domain. Further disillusioned by the firing of the editor who had initially championed *Flyboy* at HarperCollins, Munroe decided it was time to go it alone. HarperCollins graciously absolved Munroe of any further contractual obligations, and he was once again a free agent.

After finishing his second novel, the science fiction satire *Angry Young Spaceman*, Munroe founded his own independent imprint, No Media Kings. He also built a matching website (www.nomediakings.org) where he has anthologized numerous articles and essays regarding the writing process, the cultural politics of publishing and what Munroe perceives are the less-than-glamorous financial realities hidden behind the major publishing deal. True to his philosophy as a politically aware zinester—and contrary to the widespread image of self-publishing as nothing more than a form of vanity publishing—Munroe believes the decision to self-publish can be an important political statement, and he aims to educate others about the possibilities. "I get a lot of great feedback from people who say they find the site inspiring, which is what it's for," he says. "Whether people choose to self-publish or have someone else do it, they should know they have the option. Of course they should consider it, but it's always going to be an individual decision. They just should always remember self-publishing can be a shameless and politically powerful act."

Although he built an ordering page into the website for *Angry Young Spaceman* and made sure it was widely publicized and linked to other high-traffic sites, Munroe still concluded distribution through mainstream channels would be essential. While proceeds from Internet sales are advantageous compared to bookstore sales, Munroe's sales figures have since proven the worth of standard bookstore sales. "Distribution and retail through the normal channels account for 60% of the cover price, so bypassing them means a self-published author would only have to make a fraction of the sales an author with a corporate house has to make to earn enough to live off of," Munroe says. "I've made 20 online sales after three months, while projected sales of the book through bookstores are currently at about 1,400 in Canada: a whopping 1.4 percent. My readers are young and net savvy, but until people get more comfortable with ordering online, online sales are no replacement for getting your book into the bookstores."

After checking around and asking advice from distributors and independent publishers,

Munroe established a distribution deal with Insomniac Press, an independent publishing house. In this case, he admits his previous track record with HarperCollins and *Flyboy* was helpful in landing a distribution deal, but asserts that previously unpublished writers should not consider it a major obstacle. "When I approached the distributor's sales rep team, she knew of me from my first book. So, she suggested I could get around the official requirement of having two books in my backlist by making a deal with an established indie publisher who also knew of me. The publisher, however, has told me he would consider anyone's proposal for a similar deal."

When it comes to marketing a self-published book to the public, Munroe believes the credibility question is more a matter of perception. "Credibility isn't a big deal when it comes to marketing—if you can produce an engaging enough campaign and an appealing product, the general public doesn't care as much when it comes to the brand name. It helped when it came to reporters, however, since they're afraid to look stupid by endorsing something that isn't 'real.' It was my intention from the beginning to confront people's notions of a 'real' book by going against the publishing norm, and it was satisfying to see the snowballing of media attention."

However, he's also quick to point out a self-publisher must wear many hats and that a successful editorial process for a self-published book will still require the input of others. "One thing I'd like to stress is that it's not enough to be a good writer and designer. You have to have marketing and planning skills to pull it off properly. A network of people to give feedback on the editing and production process is also essential. You can do it without a company and without professionals, but not entirely alone."

Despite the inherent obligations and responsibilities involved in successfully self-publishing a book, Munroe concludes business and creativity each have their complementary challenges and pleasures. "Actually, I've relished the opportunity to do the marketing and the production of the book. I have that kind of split personality that allows me to enjoy the inner and outer worlds. Because I was involved in every element of the process with HarperCollins anyway, it wasn't a change—except I got to make the final decisions."

—Ian Bessler

LAUREL LEAF, Bantam, Doubleday, Dell/Delacorte, Knopf and Crown Books for Young Readers, Random House Children's Books, A Division of Random House, Inc., 1540 Broadway, New York NY 10036. (212)782-9000 or (800)200-3552. Website: www.randomhouse.com/kids.
   • See listing for Bantam, Doubleday, Dell/Delacorte, Knopf and Crown Books for Young Readers, page 394.

LEE & LOW BOOKS, 95 Madison Ave., New York NY 10016. (212)779-4400. Fax: (212)683-1894. Website: www.leeandlow.com. **Contact:** Philip Lee, publisher; Louise May, senior editor. Estab. 1991. "Our goals are to meet a growing need for books that address children of color, and to present literature that all children can identify with. We only consider multicultural children's picture books. Of special interest are stories set in contemporary America." Publishes hardcover originals—picture books only. Averages 12-15 total titles/year.
Needs: Children's/juvenile (historical, multicultural, preschool/picture book for children ages 2-10). "We do not consider folktales, fairy tales or animal stories." Published *Dear Ms. Parks: A Dialogue With Today's Youth*, by Rosa Parks (collection of correspondence); *Giving Thanks: A Native American Good Morning Message*, by Chief Jake Swamp (picture book); and *Sam and the Lucky Money*, by Karen Chinn (picture book).
How to Contact: Accepts unsolicited mss. Send complete ms with cover letter or through an agent. Send SASE for return of ms or send a disposable ms and SASE for reply only. Agented fiction 30%. Responds in 4 months. Accepts simultaneous submissions. Sometimes comments on rejected mss.
Terms: Pays royalties. Offers advance. Sends galleys to author. Writer's guidelines for #10 SASE or on website. Book catalog for SASE with $1.43 postage.

Advice: "Writers should familiarize themselves with the styles and formats of recently published children's books. Lee & Low Books is a multicultural children's book publisher. We would like to see more contemporary stories set in the U.S. Animal stories and folktales are not considered at this time."

☑ ◎ **LEISURE BOOKS,** Division of Dorchester Publishing Co., Inc., 276 Fifth Ave., Suite 1008, New York NY 10001. (212)725-8811. Fax: (212)532-1054. E-mail: dorchedit@aol.com. Website: www.dorchesterpub.com (includes writer's guidelines, names of editors, authors, titles, etc.). **Contact:** Joanna Rulf or Leah Hultenschmidt, editorial assistants. Mass-market paperback publisher—originals and reprints. Publishes romances, westerns, horrors and technothrillers only. Books: Newsprint paper; offset printing; perfect-bound. Average print order: variable. First novel print order: variable. Plans 25 first novels in 2001. Averages 150 total titles, 145 fiction titles/year. Promotes titles through ads in *Romantic Times*, author readings, promotional items.
Imprint(s): Leisure Books (contact: Alicia Condon), **Love Spell Books** (contact: Christopher Keeslar).
Needs: Historical romance, horror, technothriller, western. Looking for "historical romance (90,000-115,000 words)." Published *Pure Temptation*, by Connie Mason (historical romance); and *Frankly My Dear*, by Sandra Hill (time-travel romance).
How to Contact: Accepts unsolicited mss. Send query letter. Accepts queries by e-mail. Include SASE. Agented fiction 70%. Responds in 1 month to queries; 4 months to mss. "All mss must be typed, double-spaced on one side and left unbound." No electronic submissions. Comments on rejected ms "only if requested ms requires it."
Terms: Offers negotiable advance. Payment depends "on category and track record of author." Sends galleys to author. Publishes ms within 2 years after acceptance. Romance guidelines for #10 SASE.
Advice: Encourages first novelists "if they are talented and willing to take direction, *and* write the kind of genre fiction we publish. Please include a brief synopsis if sample chapters are requested."

☑ ◎ **LERNER PUBLICATIONS COMPANY,** 241 First Ave. N., Minneapolis MN 55401. (612)332-3344. Fax: (612)332-7615. Website: www.lernerbooks.com. **Contact:** Jennifer Zimian, submissions editor. Estab. 1959. "Midsize independent *children's* publisher." Publishes hardcover originals and paperback reprints. Books: Offset printing; reinforced library binding; perfect binding. Average print order: 5,000. First novel print order: 5,000. Averages 75 total titles, 1-2 fiction titles/year.
Needs: Young adult: general, problem novels, sports, adventure, mystery (young adult). Looking for "well-written middle grade and young adult. No *adult fiction* or single short stories." Recently published *Dressed for the Occasion*, by Brandon Marie Miller; and *Ida B. Wells-Barnett*, by Catherine A. Welch.
How to Contact: "Submissions are accepted in the months of March and October only. Work received in any other month will be returned unopened." Accepts unsolicited mss. Query first or submit outline/synopsis and 2 sample chapters. Responds in up to 6 months. Accepts simultaneous submissions.
Terms: Pays royalties. Offers advance. Provides author's copies. Sends galleys to author. Publishes ms 12-18 months after acceptance. Writer's guidelines for #10 SASE. Book catalog for 9×12 SAE with $3.20 postage.
Advice: Would like to see "less gender and racial stereotyping; protagonists from many cultures."

N ◎ **ARTHUR LEVINE BOOKS,** Imprint of Scholastic Inc., 555 Broadway, New York NY 10012. (212)343-6100. **Contact:** Arthur Levine, publisher. "Arthur Levine Books is looking for distinctive literature, for whatever's extraordinary." Averages 14 titles/year.
Needs: Juvenile, picture books. Published *When She Was Good*, by Norma Fox Mazer.
How to Contact: Query only. Send SASE. "We are willing to work with first-time authors, with or without agent."
Terms: Pays variable royalty on retail price. Advance varies. Book catalog available for 9×12 SASE.

◎ **LINTEL,** 24 Blake Lane, Middletown NY 10940. (212)674-4901. **Contact:** Walter James Miller, editorial director. Estab. 1977. Two-person organization on part-time basis. Publishes hardcover and paperback originals. Books: 90% opaque paper; photo offset printing; perfect binding; illustrations. Average print order: 1,000. First novel print order: 1,200.
Needs: Experimental, feminist, gay, lesbian, regional short fiction. Recently published *June*, by Mary Sanders Smith; and *Notes from a Dark Street*, by Edward Adler.
How to Contact: Accepts unsolicited mss in January and July only. Query with SASE. Accepts simultaneous and photocopied submissions. Responds in 2 months to queries; 3 months to mss. Occasionally comments on rejected mss.
Terms: Negotiated. No advance except 100 copies. Sends galleys to author. Publishes ms 6-8 months after acceptance. Book catalog free.
Advice: "Lintel is devoted to the kinds of literary art that will never make The Literary Guild or even the Book-of-the-Month Club; that is, literature concerned with the advancement of literary art. We still look for the innovative work ignored by the commercial presses. We consider any ms on its merits alone. We encourage first

novelists. Be innovative, advance the *art* of fiction, but still keep in mind the need to reach reader's aspirations as well as your own. Originality is the greatest suspense-building factor. Consistent spelling errors, errors in grammar and syntax can mean only rejection."

LIONHEARTED PUBLISHING, INC., P.O. Box 618, Zephyr Cove NV 89448-0618. (775)588-1388. Fax: (775)588-1386. E-mail: admin@LionHearted.com. Website: www.LionHearted.com (includes writer's guidelines, authors, titles, articles and writing tips for authors). **Contact:** Historical or Contemporary Acquisitions Editor. Estab. 1994. Independent. "We publish entertaining, fun, romantic genre fiction—single title releases." Publishes paperback originals. Books: mass market paperback; perfect binding. Also expanded romance into e-book formats. **Published new writers within the last year.** Plans 12 first novels in 2001. Averages 12-72 fiction titles/year. Distributes titles through Ingram, Barnes & Noble, Baker & Taylor, Amazon and Internet website. Promotes titles through trade romance reader magazines, website and Internet.

• *P.S. I've Taken a Lover*, by Patricia Lucas White won the National Reviewer's Choice Award for Best Book of the Year. *The Alliance*, by Patricia Waddell was a nominee for Best Electronic Book of the Year by *Romantic Times*. *My Captain Jack*, by Diane Drew was an EPPIE Award finalist.

Needs: Romance (contemporary, futuristic/time travel, historical, Regency period, romantic suspense; over 65,000 words only). Recently published *Knight's Desire*, by Elizabeth Taylor George (historical romance); *P.S. I've Taken a Lover*, by Patricia Lucas White (romance); and *The Alliance*, by Patricia Waddell (futuristic romance).

How to Contact: Accepts unsolicited mss. Query with outline/synopsis and 3 sample chapters. Accepts queries by e-mail. Include estimated word count, list of publishing credits, cover letter and 1 paragraph story summary in cover or query letter. Send SASE or IRC for return of ms or send disposable copy of ms and SASE for reply only. Agented fiction less than 10%. Responds in 1 month to queries; 3 months to mss. No simultaneous submissions. Always comments on rejected mss.

Terms: Pays royalties of 10% maximum on paperbacks; 30% on electronic books. Average advance: $1,000. Sends galleys to author. Publishes ms 18-24 months after acceptance. Writer's guidelines free for #10 SASE; book catalog for SASE.

Advice: "If you are not an avid reader of romance, don't attempt to write romance, and don't waste your time or an editor's by submitting to a publisher of romance. Read a few of our single title releases (they are a bit different) before submitting your romance novel."

LITTLE, BROWN AND COMPANY, 1271 Avenue of the Americas, New York NY 10020 and 3 Center Plaza, Boston MA 02108. (212)522-8700 and (617)227-0730. Fax: (212)522-2067. Website: www.twbookmark.com. **Contact:** Editorial Department. Estab. 1837. "The general editorial philosophy for all divisions continues to be broad and flexible, with high quality and the promise of commercial success always the first considerations." Medium-size house. Publishes adult and juvenile hardcover and paperback originals. **Published new writers within the last year.** Averages 125 total adult titles/year. Number of fiction titles varies.

Imprint(s): Little, Brown; Back Bay; Bulfinch Press.

• Children's submissions: Submissions Editor, Children's Books, at Boston address. Bulfinch submissions: Submissions Editor, Bulfinch Press, at Boston address. Include SASE.

Needs: Open. No science fiction. Published *When the Wind Blows*, by James Patterson; *Angels Flight*, by Michael Connelly; and *The Pilot's Wife*, by Anita Shreve.

How to Contact: Unable to consider unsolicited materials by mail, but encourages submissions to iPublish.com (online publishing company).

Terms: "We publish on a royalty basis, with advance."

LITTLE, BROWN AND COMPANY CHILDREN'S BOOKS, Trade Division; Children's Books, 3 Center Plaza, Boston MA 02108. (617)227-0730. Website: www.littlebrown.com. **Contact:** Maria Modugno, editorial director and associate publisher. Estab. 1837. Books: 70 lb. paper; sheet-fed printing; illustrations. Sometimes buys juvenile mss with illustrations "if by professional artist." **Published "a few" new writers within the last year.** Distributes titles through sales representatives. Promotes titles through author tours, book signings, posters, press kits, magazine and newspapers and Beacon Hill Bookbay.

• *Maniac Magee*, by Jerry Spinelli and published by Little, Brown and Company Children's Books, received a Newbery Award. *Toot and Puddle*, by Holly Hobbie was named an ABBY Honor Book.

Imprint(s): Megan Tingley Books; Megan S. Tingley, editorial director.

Needs: Middle grade fiction and young adult. Recently published *The Tale I Told Sasha*, by Nancy Willard, illustrated by David Christiana; *Look-Alikes*, by Joan Steiner (picture book); and *Define Normal*, by Julie Anne Peters (middle grade novel).

How to Contact: Submit through agent only.

Terms: Pays on royalty basis. Sends galleys to author. Publishes ms 1-2 years after acceptance.

Advice: "We are looking for trade books with bookstore appeal. We are especially looking for young children's (ages 3-5) picture books. New authors should be aware of what is currently being published. We recommend they spend time at the local library and bookstore familiarizing themselves with new publications." Known for "humorous middle grade fiction with lots of kid appeal. Literary, multi-layered young adult fiction with distinctive characters and complex plots."

LITTLE SIMON, Imprint of Simon & Schuster Children's Publishing Division, 1230 Avenue of the Americas, New York NY 10022. (212)698-7200. Website: www.simonsays.com. **Contact**: Submissions Editor. "Our goal is to provide fresh material in an innovative format for pre-school age. Our books are often, if not exclusively, illustrator driven." Averages 65 total titles/year. This imprint publishes novelty books only (pop-ups, lift-the-flaps board books, etc.).
How to Contact: Does not accept unsolicited mss. Query for more information. Responds in 8 months. Accepts simultaneous submissions.
Terms: Negotiable.

LIVINGSTON PRESS, Station 22, University of Alabama, Livingston AL 35470. Fax: (205)652-3717. E-mail: jwt@uwamail.westal.edu. Website: www.livingstonpress@westal.edu/ (includes catalog). **Contact**: Joe Taylor, editor. Estab. 1982. "Literary press. We publish offbeat and/or southern literature. Emphasis on offbeat." Publishes hardcover and paperback originals. Books: acid-free paper; offset printing; perfect binding. Average print order: 1,500. First novel print order: 1,500. **Published new writers within the last year.** Plans 2 first novels in 2001. Averages 4-6 total titles, 5 fiction titles/year. Distributes titles through Yankee Book, Baker & Taylor, Blackwell North America. Promotes titles through catalogs, readings, postcards, 75-100 review copies.
Imprint(s): Swallows Tale Press.
Needs: Literary, short story collections. No genre. Published *Detecting Metal*, by Fred Bonnie (novel).
How to Contact: Does not accept unsolicited mss. Query first. Include bio, list of publishing credits. Send SASE for reply, return of ms or send a disposable copy of ms. Responds in 3 weeks to queries; 6 months to mss. Accepts simultaneous submissions. Sometimes comments on rejected mss.
Terms: Pays 12% of press run in contributor's copies. Sends galleys to author. Publishes ms 1-2 years after acceptance. Book catalog free.
Advice: "Our readers are interested in literature, often quirky literature."

JAMES LORIMER & CO., PUBLISHERS, 35 Britain St., 3rd Floor, Toronto, Ontario M5A 1R7 Canada. (416)362-4762. Fax: (416)362-3939. E-mail: jlc@sympatico.ca. **Contact**: Diane Young, editor-in-chief. "James Lorimer & Co. publishes Canadian authors only, on Canadian issues/topics. For juvenile list, realistic themes only, especially mysteries and sports." Publishes trade paperback originals. **Published new writers within the last year.** Averages 30 titles/year.
Needs: Juvenile, young adult. "No fantasy, science fiction, talking animals; realistic themes only. Currently seeking sports novels for ages 9-13 (Canadian writers only)."
How to Contact: Does not accept unsolicited mss. Query with synopsis and 2 sample chapters. Responds in 4 months.
Terms: Pays royalties of 5-10% on retail price. Offers negotiable advance. Publishes ms about 1 year after acceptance. Book catalog for #10 SASE.

LOST HORSE PRESS, 9327 S. Cedar Rim Lane, Spokane WA 99224 or No. 105 Lost Horse Rd., Sandpoint ID 83864. (509)448-4047. Fax: (509)448-3986. E-mail: losthorse@ior.com. **Contact:** Christine Holbert, editor of novels, novellas. Estab. 1998. Publishes hardcover and paperback originals and reprints. Books: 60-70 lb. Natural paper; offset printing; Smyth-sewn cloth or trade paperback; b&w illustration. Average print order: 1,000-2,500. First novel print order: 1,000. **Published 2 new writers within the last year.** Plans 2 first novels in 2001. Averages 4 total titles, 2 fiction titles/year. Member: PNBA, PMA, Women Writing the West. Distributes titles through SPD, IPG, Amazon.com and Baker & Taylor.
Needs: Erotica, ethnic/multicultural, experimental, feminist, gay, historical, humor/satire, lesbian, literary, regional (Pacific NW), short story collections, translations. Recently published *Tales of a Dalai Lama*, by Pierre Delattre (literary fiction); *Love*, by Valerie Martin (short stories); *Sailing Away*, by Richard Morgan (short stories).
How to Contact: Accepts unsolicited mss. Submit complete ms with cover letter. Accepts queries by e-mail. Include brief bio and list of publishing credits. Send SASE or IRC for return of ms or send disposable copy of ms and SASE for reply only. Responds in 3 months to queries and mss. Accepts submissions on disk. Sometimes comments on rejected mss.
Terms: Pays royalties of 10% and 20 author's copies. Sends galleys to author. Publishes ms 1-2 years after acceptance. Writer's guidelines for SASE; book catalog free.

LOVE SPELL, Leisure Books, Division of Dorchester Publishing Co., Inc., 276 Fifth Ave., Suite 1008, New York NY 10001-0112. (212)725-8811. Website: www.dorchesterpub.com (includes submission guidelines, author bios and upcoming release info). Editor: Christopher Keeslar. **Contact**: Joanna Rulf and Leah Hultenschmidt, editorial assistants. "Love Spell publishes quirky sub-genres of romance: time-travel, paranormal, futuristic, lighthearted contemporaries and historicals. Despite the exotic settings, we are still interested in character-driven plots." Mass market paperback publisher—originals and reprints. Books: newsprint paper; offset printing; perfect-bound. Average print order: varies. First novel print order: varies. Plans 15 first novels in 2001. Averages 10-12 original titles/month.

Needs: Romance (futuristic, time travel, paranormal, historical). Looking for romances of 90,000-115,000 words. Recently published *High Intensity*, by Dara Joy.

How to Contact: Accepts unsolicited mss. Query first. "All mss must be typed, double-spaced on one side and left unbound." Send SASE or IRC for return of ms. Agented fiction 70%. Responds in up to 6 months. Comments "only if requested ms requires it."

Terms: Offers negotiable advance. "Payment depends on category and track record of author." Sends galleys to author. Publishes ms within 2 years after acceptance. Writer's guidelines for #10 SASE.

Advice: "The best way to learn to write a Love Spell Romance is by reading several of our recent releases. The best written stories are usually ones writers feel passionate about—so write from your heart! Also, the market is very tight these days so more than ever we are looking for refreshing, standout original fiction."

LTD BOOKS, 200 N. Service Rd. West, Unit 1, Suite 301, Oakville, Ontario L6M 2Y1 Canada. Phone/fax: (905)825-8420. E-mail: publisher@ltdbooks.com. Website: www.ltdbooks.com. **Contact:** Dee Lloyd, Terry Sheils, editors. Estab. 1999. "LTD Books, an energetic new presence in the rapidly expanding e-book market, is a multi-genre, royalty-paying fiction publisher specializing in high quality stories with strong characters and great ideas." Publishes electronic books on disk or by download. Books: 3½" floppy disk with cover and jewel case, or as a download. **Published 3 new writers within the last year.** Averages 36 total titles, 36 fiction titles/year. Member: Association of Electronic Publishers. Distributes titles through the Internet, Barnes&Noble.com and Powells.

● *Knights Tiger*, by Terry Sheils (Horror category) and *Ties That Blind*, by Dee Lloyd (Contemporary Romance category) were finalists for the EPPIE 2000 Awards, presented by Electronically Published Internet Connection (EPIC).

Needs: Adventure, fantasy (space fantasy, sword and sorcery), historical (general), horror (dark fantasy, futuristic, psychological, supernatural), literary, mainstream, mystery/suspense (amateur sleuth, cozy, police procedural, private eye/hardboiled), romance (contemporary, futuristic/time travel, gothic, historical, regency period, romantic suspense), science fiction (hard science/technological, soft/sociological), thriller/espionage, western, young adult/teen (adventure, fantasy/science fiction, historical, horror, mystery/suspense, problem novels, romance, series, sports, western). Recently published *Prince of Shadows*, by C. Anne Williams (historical); and *Rendezvous At Boomer Greer*, by Robert Russell (science fiction).

How to Contact: Accepts unsolicited mss. Query with synopsis and 3 sample chapters. Accepts queries by e-mail. Include estimated word count, brief bio and list of publishing credits. Send disposable copy of ms and SASE for reply only. Responds in 2 weeks to queries; 6 weeks to mss. Accepts simultaneous submissions, electronic submissions and disk. Always comments on rejected mss.

Terms: Pays royalties of 30%. Sends galleys to author. Publishes ms 3-5 months after acceptance. Writer's guidelines on website.

Advice: "We publish only fiction. All of our books are electronic (as download or on disk) at this time. We are researching the viability of print-on-demand and the new technologies."

MACADAM/CAGE PUBLISHING, 155 Sansome St., Suite 520, San Francisco CA 94104. (415)986-7502. Fax: (415)986-7414. E-mail: pat@macadamcage.com. Website: www.macadamcage.com (includes catalog, authors, book excerpts, submission guidelines, purchasing details). **Contact:** Pat Walsh (all genres). Estab. 1999. Midsize independent publisher. Publishes hardcover and paperback originals. Books: web offset printing; case binding. Average first novel print order: 5,000-15,000. **Published 3 new writers within the last year.** Averages 10 total titles, 8 fiction titles/year. Member: PMA, ABA, NCIBA. Distributes titles through Baker & Taylor, Ingram, Brodart and Bookpeople. Promotes titles through public relations firm.

Needs: Experimental, historical, literary, mainstream. Recently published *Confessions of Brother Eli*, by Joseph DiPrisco (literary); *Peter Squared*, by Ken Oldberg (contemporary); and *The Family Man*, by Michael S. Patterson (thriller).

How to Contact: Accepts unsolicited mss. Submit complete ms with cover letter. Include estimated word count and brief bio. Send SASE or IRC for return of ms. Agented fiction 50%. Responds in 3 months to queries and mss. Accepts simultaneous submissions. Often comments on rejected mss.

Terms: Pays royalties of 8-10%. Offers negotiable advance. Sends galleys to author. Publishes ms 6-12 months after acceptance. Writer's guidelines free for SASE.

Advice: "We publish almost all fiction. Large publishers are releasing fewer novels and taking fewer risks. We believe there is a market for literary fiction that is being ignored. Strong writing is mandatory, as is a command of the language."

◎ **MAGE PUBLISHERS,** 1032 29th St. NW, Washington DC 20007. (202)342-1642. Fax: (202)342-9269. E-mail: info@mage.com. Website: www.mage.com. **Contact:** Amin Sepehri, assistant to publisher. Estab. 1985. "Small independent publisher." Publishes hardcover originals. Averages 4 total titles, 1 fiction title/year.
Needs: "We publish only books on Iran and Persia and translations of Iranian fiction writers." Ethnic (Iran) fiction. Published *My Uncle Napoleon*, by Iraj Pezeshkzad; *King of the Benighted*, by M. Irani; and *Sutra and Other Stories*, by Simin Daneshvar.
How to Contact: Does not accept unsolicited mss. Send query letter with SASE or IRC. Responds in 3 months to queries. Accepts simultaneous and electronic submissions.
Terms: Pays royalties. Publishes ms 1 year after acceptance. Writer's guidelines on web.
Advice: "If it isn't related to Persia/Iran, don't waste our time or yours."

N ◻ **MAJESTIC BOOKS,** P.O. Box 19097, Johnston RI 02919. E-mail: majesticbk@aol.com. **Contact:** Cindy MacDonald, publisher. Estab. 1992. "Majestic Books is a small press. We publish young writers under the age of 18 in an anthology filled with poems and short stories." Publishes paperback originals. Books: 60 lb. white paper; offset printing; perfect binding. Average print order: 300. **Published new writers within the last year.** Averages 3 total titles, 3 fiction titles/year. Distributes titles through mail order. Promotes titles through mailings.
Needs: Adventure, family saga, fantasy, mainstream, mystery/suspense, psychic/supernatural, romance, science fiction (soft/sociological), thriller/espionage, western, young adult/teen. Recently published *Tribute to Talent*; *Mysteries, Monsters, Memories and More VIII*; *Dawn of Distinction*, all by various authors (anthologies).
How to Contact: Accepts unsolicited mss. Submit complete ms with cover letter. Include estimated word count and age (for under-18 authors only). Send SASE or IRC for return of ms or send disposable copy of ms and SASE for reply only. Responds in 2 weeks to mss. Accepts simultaneous and electronic submissions.
Terms: Pays royalties of 10% on sales relating directly to author's inclusion. Publishes ms 1 year after acceptance. Writer's guidelines for SASE.
Advice: "Our press only publishes talented young writers under the age of 18. Please include age with all submissions and keep stories under 2,000 words. Originality is a must."

◑ **MARCH STREET PRESS,** 3413 Wilshire, Greensboro NC 27408-2923. Phone/fax: (336)282-9754. E-mail: rbixby@aol.com. Website: http://users.aol.com/marchst (includes writer's guidelines; names of editors, authors, titles; free websites, business directory, library of books and past issues). **Contact:** Robert Bixby, editor/publisher. Estab. 1988. Publishes paperback originals. Books: vellum paper; photocopy; saddle-stitch binding. Averages 4-6 total titles, 1 or fewer fiction titles/year.
Needs: Literary. Short story collections. Published *Jailer's Inn*, by Deborah Bayer (very short fiction).
How to Contact: *"Accepts unsolicited mss if $10 reading fee enclosed."* Submit complete ms with a cover letter and reading fee. Send SASE for return of ms or send a disposable copy of ms and SASE for reply only. Responds in 1 week to queries; 6 months to mss. Accepts simultaneous submissions. Sometimes comments on a rejected ms.
Terms: Pays royalty of 15%. Provides 10 author's copies. Sends galleys to author. Publishes ms 6-12 months after acceptance. Writer's guidelines for #10 SASE or on website.

N ◖ ◎ **McBOOKS PRESS,** 120 W. State St., Ithaca NY 14850. (607)272-2114. Fax: (607)273-6068. E-mail: mcbooks@mcbooks.com. Website: www.McBooks.com (includes some guidelines, staff names, book catalog). **Contact:** S.K. List, editorial director. Estab. 1980. "Small independent publisher; specializes in historical nautical fiction, American publisher of Alexander Kent's Richard Bolitho series, Dudley Pope's Ramage novels." Publishes paperback reprints "mostly." Averages 19 total titles, 17 fiction titles/year. Distributes titles through LPC Group.
Needs: Historical (nautical). Recently published *Ramage*, by Dudley Pope (nautical fiction); *The Privateersman*, by Capt. Frederick Marryat (nautical fiction); and *The Only Victor*, by Alexander Kent (Douglas Reeman) (nautical fiction). Publishes the continuing Bolitho and Ramage series.
How to Contact: Accepts unsolicited mss. Query with outline/synopsis and 1-2 sample chapters. Accepts queries by e-mail. Include list of publishing credits. Send SASE or IRC for return of ms. Mostly agented fiction. Responds in 3 months to queries. Accepts simultaneous submissions.

◑ **MARGARET K. McELDERRY BOOKS,** Imprint of the Simon & Schuster Children's Publishing Division, 1230 Sixth Ave., New York NY 10020. (212)698-2761. **Contact:** Emma D. Dryden, executive editor. Estab. 1971. Publishes hardcover originals. Books: high quality paper; offset printing; three-piece and POB bindings; illustrations. Average print order: 10,000. First novel print order: 6,000. **Published new writers within the last year.** Averages 25 total titles/year.
● Books published by Margaret K. McElderry Books have received numerous awards including the Newbery and the Caldecott Awards.
Needs: All categories (fiction and nonfiction) for juvenile and young adult: adventure, contemporary, early chapter books, fantasy, poetry, literary and picture books. "We will consider any category. Results depend on the

quality of the imagination, the artwork and the writing." Recently published *Ebb and Flo and the Greedy Gulls*, by Jane Simmons (picture book); *King of Shadows*, by Susan Cooper (middle grade fiction); *River Boy*, written by Janet S. Wong and illustrated by Julie Paschkis (poetry/picture book).

How to Contact: Send query letter.

Terms: Pays in royalties; offers advance. Publishes ms 18 months after acceptance.

Advice: "Imaginative writing of high quality is always in demand; also picture books that are original and unusual. Keep in mind that McElderry Books is a very small imprint, so we are very selective about the books we will undertake for publication. The YA market is tough right now, so we're being very picky. We try not to publish any 'trend' books. Be familiar with our list and with what is being published this year by all publishing houses."

N ⬛ ◎ **MERIWETHER PUBLISHING LTD.**, 885 Elkton Dr., Colorado Springs CO 80907. (719)594-4422. Website: www.contemporarydrama.com (includes products sold and catalog information). **Contact:** Rhonda Wray, associate editor/religious topics; Ted Zapel, plays & books editor. Estab. 1970. "Midsize, independent publisher. We publish plays for teens, mostly one-act comedies, holiday plays for churches and musical comedies. Our books are on the theatrical arts." Publishes paperback originals. Books: quality paper; Printing House Specialist; paperback binding. Average print order: 5,000-10,000. **Published new writers within the last year.** Averages 10 total titles/year. Distributes titles through catalog, website and distributors.

Needs: No fiction books; plays only. Religious (children's religious plays and religious fantasy plays).

How to Contact: Accepts unsolicited mss with SASE. Send query letter. Accepts queries by e-mail. Include list of publishing credits. Send SASE or IRC for return of ms or send disposable copy of ms and SASE for reply only. Responds in 3 weeks to queries; 2 months to mss. Accepts simultaneous submissions. Sometimes comments on rejected mss.

Terms: Pays in royalties; percentage varies to buy-out. Sends galleys to author. Publishes ms 6-12 months after acceptance. Writer's guidelines for SASE. Book catalog for $1.50.

N ⬛ **MICAH PUBLICATIONS, INC.**, 255 Humphrey St., Marblehead MA 01945. (781)631-7601. Fax: (781)639-0772. E-mail: micah@micahbooks.com. Website: www.micahbooks.com (includes lists of our publications; "writers can survey the website to see what we are interested in"). **Contact:** Roberta Kalechofsky, editor. Estab. 1975. "One-person operation on part-time basis. We only publish about 3 titles a year." Publishes paperback originals and reprints. Books: 60 lb. paper; perfect bound; some illustrations. Average print order: 800. First novel print order: 800. Averages 3 total titles, 1 fiction title/year. Promotes titles through exhibits and direct mailings.

Needs: Children's/juvenile (animal), family saga, literary, short story collections, translation, animal stories.

How to Contact: Does not accept unsolicited mss; advisable to query with outline/synopsis and 2 sample chapters. Include estimated word count, brief bio and list of publishing credits. Send SASE or IRC for return of ms or send disposable copy of ms and SASE for reply only. Responds in 3 months to queries and mss. Accepts simultaneous submissions. Sometimes comments on rejected mss.

Terms: Pays in 12 author's copies. Additional copies at 50% discount. Will divide spin-off benefits if there are any. "We have to insist that the author take responsibility for promoting his/her work." Sends galleys to author. Publishes ms 6-8 months after acceptance. Writer's guidelines for SASE. Book catalogs free upon request.

Advice: "Be honest. Make sure your work is of high literary quality. We don't have time and money to waste on anything but writing excellence."

N ⬛ **THE MIDKNIGHT CLUB**, P.O. Box 25, Browns Mills NJ 08015. (609)735-9043. E-mail: info@midknightclub.net. Website: www.midknightclub.net (includes book catalog, product info, chats and booksignings page). **Contact:** Faith Ann Hotchkin, editor-in-chief. Estab. 1999. "The Midknight Club is a midsized publishing house that publishes both fiction and nonfiction books in the religion, philosophy, metaphysics, occult category." Publishes hardcover and paperback originals. Books: offset web paper; lithography (some digital) printing; perfect binding. Average print order: 2,000-5,000; first novel print order: 2,000. **Published 1 new writer within the last year.** Plans 1 first novel in 2001. Averages 4-5 total titles, 1-2 fiction titles/year. Member: NAPRA. Distributes titles through New Leaf, Baker & Taylor and website.

Needs: Comics/graphic novels, horror (dark fantasy, psychological, supernatural), New Age/mystic, religious (general religious, religious fantasy, religious mystery/suspense, religious thriller), science fiction, short story collections. Planning anthology of horror fiction and poetry. Editors will select from submissions. Recently published *Shangri-La*, by Michael Szul (religious/horror fiction).

How to Contact: Does not accept unsolicited mss. Query with outline/synopsis and 3 sample chapters. Accepts only query letters by e-mail. Include brief bio and list of publishing credits. Send SASE or IRC for return of ms OR send disposable copy of ms and SASE for reply only. Responds in 2 weeks to queries; 1 month to mss. Accepts simultaneous submissions, electronic submissions and disk. Always comments on rejected mss.

Terms: Pays royalties of 10-12%. Sends galleys to author. Publishes ms 6-12 months after acceptance. Writer's guidelines on website.

Advice: "We're not trend followers and we pay no attention to them. We do our own thing. Don't be afraid to try new things with your work. We comment on all submissions and we prefer them by e-mail."

N ○ MIGHTYBOOK, Guardian Press, 10924 Grant Rd., #225, Houston TX 77070. (281)955-9855. Fax: (281)469-6466. E-mail: reaves@houston.rr.com. Website: www.mightybook.com. **Contact:** Richard Eaves, acquisitions director. Estab. 1991. "Small independent publisher of electronic, read-aloud picture books, books on audio cassette/CD, and print-on-demand books. Much of our marketing and sales are done on the Internet." Publishes hardcover and paperback originals. Books: matte paper; offset/litho printing; perfect binding; 4-color illustrations. **Published 5 new writers within the last year.** Averages 6 total titles, 4 fiction titles/year. Distributes/ promotes titles through the Internet, trade shows and toys and merchandising.
Needs: Children's/juvenile, young adult/teen. Very short children's picture books (100-200 words). Recently published *Furello*, by Harriett Fabrick (juvenile adventure); *Sabboth Queen*, by Myra Lichtman-Fields (children's); and *Cloud That Covered My Head*, by Ilana Levinski (children's).
How to Contact: Accepts unsolicited mss. Submit complete ms with cover letter. Accepts queries by e-mail and phone. Include estimated word count and brief bio. Send disposable ms and SASE for reply only. Agented fiction 5%. Responds in 6 weeks to queries and mss. Accepts simultaneous submissions, electronic submissions and submissions by disk.
Terms: Pays royalties of 20% of gross. No advance. Publishes ms 3-6 months after acceptance. Writer's guidelines and book catalog on website.
Advice: "Write really good, very short stories for children."

✓ ○ ♥ MILKWEED EDITIONS, 1011 Washington Ave. S., Suite 300, Minneapolis MN 55415. (612)332-3192. Fax: (612)332-6248. E-mail: books@milkweed.org. Website: www.milkweed.org (includes writer's guidelines, mission statement, catalog, poem of day, excerpts from titles). **Contact:** Emilie Buchwald, publisher; Elisabeth Fitz, manuscript coordinator. Estab. 1980. Nonprofit publisher. Publishes hardcover and paperback originals and paperback reprints. Books: book text quality—acid-free paper; offset printing; perfect or hardcover binding. Average print order: 4,000. First novel print order depends on book. **Published new writers within the last year.** Averages 20 total titles/year. Number of fiction titles "depends on manuscripts."
- Milkweed Editions books have received numerous awards, including Finalist, *LMP* Individual Achievement Award for Editor Emilie Buchwald, awards from the American Library Association, a *New York Times* Notable and several Pushcarts.
Needs: For adult readers: literary fiction, nonfiction, poetry, essays; for children (ages 8-12): fiction and biographies. Translations welcome for both audiences. No legends or folktales for children. No romance, mysteries, science fiction. Recently published *Falling Dark*, by Tim Tharp (fiction).
How to Contact: Send for guidelines first, then submit complete ms. Responds in 6 months. Accepts simultaneous submissions.
Terms: Pays royalties of 7½% on list price. Advance varies. Sends galleys to author. Publishes ms 1-2 years after acceptance. Book catalog for $1.50 postage. "Send for guidelines. Must enclose SASE."
Advice: "Read good contemporary literary fiction, find your own voice, and persist. Familiarize yourself with our list before submitting."

✓ ○ Ⓐ MINSTREL BOOKS, Imprint of Pocket Books for Young Readers, Imprint of Simon & Schuster, 1230 Avenue of the Americas, New York NY 10020. (212)698-7000. Website: www.simonandschuster.com. Editorial director: Patricia MacDonald. **Contact** Attn: Manuscript proposals. Estab. 1986. "Minstrel publishes fun, kid-oriented books, the kinds kids pick for themselves, for middle grade readers, ages 8-12." Publishes hardcover originals and reprints, trade paperback originals. Averages 125 titles/year.
Needs: Middle grade fiction for ages 8-12: animal stories, fantasy, humor, school stories, mystery, suspense. No picture books. Published *Upchuck and the Rotten Willy*, by Bill Wallace; *The Flood Disaster*, by Peg Kehret; and *I Was A Sixth Grade Alien*, by Bruce Coville.
How to Contact: Does not accept unsolicited mss unless they are agented or from a writer who has been previously published.
Terms: Pays royalty on retail price. Advance varies. Publishes ms 2 years after acceptance. Writer's guidelines and book catalog free.
Advice: "Hang out with kids to make sure your dialogue and subject matter are accurate."

✓ ○ MOREHOUSE PUBLISHING CO., 4475 Linglestown Rd., Harrisburg PA 17112. Fax: (717)541-8136. Website: www.morehousegroup.com. **Contact:** Mark J.H. Fretz, editorial director. Estab. 1884. Morehouse publishes a wide variety of religious nonfiction and children's fiction with an emphasis on the Anglican faith. Publishes hardcover and paperback originals. Averages 35 titles/year.
Needs: Christian picture books for ages 3-8. Artwork essential. Published *Bless All Creatures Here Below*, by Judith Gwyn Brown; and *Angel and Me*, by Sara Maitland.

How to Contact: Submit entire ms (1,500 words maximum), résumé and SASE. Note: Manuscripts from outside the US will not be returned. Please send copies only. Responds in 2 months. Accepts simultaneous submissions.

Terms: Pays royalties of 7-10%. Average advance: $500-1,000. Publishes ms 18 months after acceptance. Book catalog for 9×12 SAE with $1.01 in postage stamps.

✓ A **WILLIAM MORROW**, Imprint of HarperCollins General Books Group, HarperCollins Publishers, 10 E. 53rd St., New York NY 10022. (212)207-7000. Fax: (212)207-7921. **Contact**: Acquisitions Editor. Estab. 1926. Approximately one fourth of books published are fiction.

Needs: "Morrow accepts only the highest quality submissions" in contemporary, literary, experimental, adventure, mystery/suspense, spy, historical, war, feminist, gay/lesbian, science fiction, horror, humor/satire and translations. Juvenile and young adult divisions are separate.

How to Contact: Does not accept unsolicited mss or queries. *Submit through agent.*

Terms: Pays royalties; offers advance. Sends galleys to author. Publishes ms 2 years after acceptance. Free book catalog.

✓ ◐ ▼ **MULTNOMAH PUBLISHERS, INC.**, P.O. Box 1720, Sisters OR 97759. (541)549-1144. Fax: (541)549-0260. Website: www.multnomahbooks.com. **Contact**: Editorial Dept. Estab. 1987. Midsize independent publisher of evangelical fiction and nonfiction. Publishes paperback originals. Books: perfect binding. Average print order: 12,000. Averages 120 total titles, 20-25 fiction titles/year.

● Multnomah Books has received several Gold Medallion Book Awards from the Evangelical Christian Publishers Association.

Needs: Literary, mystery/suspense, religious/inspirational issue or thesis fiction. Published *Home to Harmony*, by Philip Gulley (short stories/inspirational); *Margaret's Peace*, by Linda Hall (suspense); and *A Gathering of Finches*, by Jane Kirkpatrick (historical novel).

How to Contact: Does not accept simultaneous submissions. Query with outline/synopsis and 3 sample chapters. "Include a cover letter with any additional information that might help us in our review." Send SASE or IRC for return of ms or send a disposable copy of ms with SASE for reply only. Responds in 10 weeks. Accepts simultaneous submissions.

Terms: Pays royalties. Provides 100 author's copies. Sends galleys to author. Publishes ms 1-2 years after acceptance. Writer's guidelines for SASE or on website.

Advice: "Looking for clean, moral, uplifting fiction. We're particularly interested in contemporary women's fiction, historical fiction, superior romance, mystery/suspense and thesis fiction."

🌐 ◉ **MY WEEKLY STORY COLLECTION,** D.C. Thomson and Co., Ltd., 22 Meadowside, Dundee DD19QJ, Scotland. **Contact:** Mrs. D. Hunter, fiction editor. "Cheap paperback story library with full-colour cover. Material should not be violent, controversial or sexually explicit." Averages 48 romantic novels/year. Distributes titles through national retail outlets. Promotes titles through dispaly cards in retail outlets and in-house magazine adverts.

Needs: Contemporary and historical novels. Length: approximately 30,000 words.

How to Contact: Query with outline/synopsis and 3 opening chapters.

Terms: Writers are paid on acceptance. Writers guidelines available on request.

Advice: Avoid too many colloquialisms/Americanisms. Stories can be set anywhere but local colour not too 'local' as to be alien."

◐ A ▼ **THE MYSTERIOUS PRESS**, Crime and mystery fiction imprint for Warner Books, 1271 Avenue of the Americas, New York NY 10120. (212)522-7200. Website: www.warnerbooks.com. (includes authors, titles, guidelines, bulletin board, tour info, contests). **Contact**: Sara Ann Freed, editor-in-chief; William Malloy, executive editor. Estab. 1976. Publishes hardcover and paperback originals, trade and paperback reprints. Books: hardcover (some Smythe-sewn) and paperback binding; illustrations rarely. First novel print order: 10,000 copies. **Published new writers within the last year.**

Needs: Mystery/suspense. Recently published *Storm Track*, by Margaret Moran; *Listen to the Silence*, by Marcia Muller; *The Hook* by Donald E. Westlake; *The Hours of the Virgin*, by Loren D. Estleman.

How to Contact: Submit through an agent only.

Terms: Pays royalties of 10% minimum. Average advance: negotiable. Sends galleys to author. Buys hard and softcover rights. Publishes ms 1 year after acceptance.

Advice: "Write a strong and memorable novel, and with the help of a good literary agent, you'll find the right publishing house. Don't despair if your manuscript is rejected by several houses. All publishing houses are looking for new and exciting crime novels, but it may not be at the time your novel is submitted. Hang in there, keep the faith—and good luck."

Ⓝ ○ ◉ **THE NAIAD PRESS, INC.**, P.O. Box 10543, Tallahassee FL 32302. (850)539-5965. Fax: (850)539-9731. E-mail: naiadpress@aol.com. Website: www.naiadpress.com (includes complete and detailed

insider report

Philip Gulley: Finding his niche in the Christian fiction market

The first time a publisher contacted Quaker minister Philip Gulley requesting that he write a book, Gulley hung up on him. Gulley thought it was a friend playing a joke, but the publisher was truly interested in acquiring a collection of the essays Gulley had written for his Quaker church in Indianapolis. The essays, written for the front page of his church newsletter, were brought to the publisher's attention by Paul Harvey Jr., who showed them to him after attending Gulley's church. Harvey was impressed by the beauty of Gulley's essays, which embrace down-home values and promote fulfillment in simplicity, in a message that transcends religious denominations yet still upholds Christian traditions. This collection of essays became Gulley's first book, *Front Porch Tales: Warm-Hearted Stories of Family, Faith, Laughter and Love* (Multnomah).

Philip Gulley

Gulley went on to publish two more collections of inspirational essays—*Hometown Tales* and *For Everything a Season*—and has recently finished *Home to Harmony* (Multnomah), his first short story collection. *Home to Harmony*, set in the fictional town of Harmony, Indiana, relates the experiences of Sam Gardner, pastor of the Harmony Friends Meeting.

Gulley faced some challenges switching to fiction after his first three books of short nonfiction essays. "Moving from a story format to a chapter format was a trick. With essays, at the end of every story I had this little reflection where I could interject my own opinion, but with fiction you can't do that. You can't have this remote third party just intoning down from above some moral, objective, or lesson," he says. "You have to have the characters convey that, and you have to do it in a creative way that doesn't look and feel manipulative."

Gulley's entry into the Christian fiction market was timed perfectly—industry watchers are reporting a sharp increase in the market, which *Publishers Weekly* says "has grown from an ugly duckling into a swan." With Americans as a culture seeking a return to spirituality and faith, authors such as Frank Peretti, Tim LaHaye and Jerry Jenkins are finding growing audiences, leading another *Publishers Weekly* writer to observe that Christian fiction is changing "to tell a good story and tell it well—and to illuminate the values of faith along the way."

With reviewers comparing his writing to that of Garrison Keillor, it seems Gulley knows how to tell a story. And he's found a rich mine of inspiration in his hometown. Gulley acknowledges some advantages and disadvantages of using your hometown as a source of inspiration for writing. He finds it awkward to write nonfiction about his own community while living in it because of all of the suggestions for story topics friends and family give him. But he also cites some advantages, such as the chance to use the wealth of stories from the past. "You grow up in a place, and you think you know the people. But when you sit and talk with them, you realize your knowledge and understanding of them is not complete," he says. "The people you thought were just kind of boring are actually fascinating people and have done really interesting things."

He advises writers who want to draw inspiration from their past to have the people they write about read the material before publication. "I have heard horror stories from people who have written stories from their memories about people they knew but they never bothered to have the people read them first, and it was just catastrophic," he says. "Always have people read what you write if it involves them."

One of Gulley's current projects is the sequel to *Home to Harmony*, titled *Searching for Harmony* (available from Multnomah in June 2001). It will feature three scenarios of people searching for meaning and harmony in life in different ways: through religious fulfillment, love or money. Gulley finds parallels between the spiritual search his characters struggle with and society's similar struggles. "I think people are seeking a relationship with God to help them order their lives and find perspective and balance," he says. "They want some sense of the divine in their lives, some perspective that helps them negotiate life."

The other project Gulley is currently working on is a theology title, *A Grace is True* (Multnomah, 2001), about the idea of ultimate reconciliation—the belief that God ultimately will redeem everyone. "The theological premise is rooted in early Christianity, and has kind of faded over the years as we became more interested in heaven and hell and the saved and the damned. These are concepts I've never really bought into, so this is a theological book based on the nature of God," he says.

Gulley balances his time among his duties as a Quaker minister, a father and a writer with discipline, writing fiction three days a week and nonfiction every Thursday. "It takes a long time to write a well-crafted essay or story. It usually takes me one week—and that is when I am writing three solid days," he says. "That is always my goal, to write one well-crafted essay, story or chapter a week."

He advises first-time authors interested in writing for a Christian audience to "hone your subject matter to the truth. There is a lot of bad Christian writing out there, and what makes it bad is the author's unwillingness to really search for the truth," he says. "They settle for cliché and for the worst images of God instead of for truth and grace. I would encourage writers to have a well-thought out theology which speaks the truth about God."

Gulley believes that society has a spiritual hunger for practical Christianity. "I know that what I hunger for is intimacy with God, and I suspect that there are a lot of people with the same need. I think people are looking for authenticity."

—*Karen Roberts*

catalog, order capacity). **Contact**: Barbara Grier, editorial director. Estab. 1973. "Oldest and largest lesbian publishing company. We are scrupulously honest and we keep our books in print for the most part." Books: 50 lb. offset paper; sheet-fed offset; perfect-bound. Average print order: 12,000. First novel print order: 12,000. Averages 34 total titles/year. Distributes titles through distributors, direct sales to stores and individuals and over the Web. Promotes titles through a first class mailing to over 26,000 lesbians monthly; 2,300 bookstores on mailing list.

● The Naiad Press is one of the most successful and well-known lesbian publishers. They have also produced eight of their books on audio cassette.

Needs: Lesbian fiction, all genres. Published *Love in the Balance*, by Marianne K. Martin; *Bad Moon Rising*, by Barbara Johnson; and *Endless Love*, by Lisa Shapiro.

How to Contact: Does not accept unsolicited mss. Query with outline/synopsis. Include estimated word count and 2-sentence bio. Send SASE or IRC for reply. Responds in 3 weeks to queries; 3 months to mss.

Terms: Pays royalties of 15% using a standard recovery contract. Occasionally pays royalties of 7½% against cover price. "Seldom gives advances and has never seen a first novel worthy of one. Believes authors are investments in their own and the company's future—that the best author is the author who produces a book every 12-18 months forever and knows that there is a *home* for that book." Publishes ms 1-2 years after acceptance. Book catalog for legal-sized SASE and $1.50 postage and handling.

Advice: "We publish lesbian fiction primarily and prefer honest work (i.e., positive, upbeat lesbian characters). Lesbian content must be accurate . . . a lot of earlier lesbian novels were less than honest. No breast beating or complaining. Our fiction titles are becoming increasingly *genre* fiction, which we encourage. Original fiction in paperback is our main field, and its popularity increases. We publish books BY, FOR AND ABOUT lesbians. We are not interested in books that are unrealistic. You know and we know what the real world of lesbian interest is like. Don't even try to fool us. Short, well-written books do best. Authors who want to succeed and will work to do so have the best shot."

THE NAUTICAL & AVIATION PUBLISHING CO. OF AMERICA INC., 1250 Fairmont Ave., Mt. Pleasant SC 29464. (843)856-0561. Fax: (843)856-3164. President: Jan Snouck-Hurgronje. **Contact:** Heather Parker, editor. Estab. 1979. Small publisher interested in quality military and naval history and literature. Publishes hardcover originals and reprints. Averages 10 total titles, 1-4 fiction titles/year.

Needs: Revolutionary War, War of 1812, Civil War, WWI and II, Persian Gulf and Marine Corps. history. Looks for "novels with a strong military history orientation." Recently published *The Black Flower*, by Howard Bahn; *Lieutenant Christopher and Normandy*, by VADM William P. Mack; and *The General*, by C.S. Forester (all military fiction).

How to Contact: Accepts unsolicited mss. Send query letter or query with cover letter and 2 chapters or brief synopsis. SASE necessary for return of mss. Agented fiction "miniscule." Responds in 3 weeks to queries and mss. Accepts simultaneous submissions. Sometimes comments on rejected mss.

Terms: Pays royalties of 10-12% on selling price. After acceptance publishes ms "as quickly as possible—next season." Book catalog free on request.

Advice: Publishing more fiction. Encourages first novelists. "We're interested in good writing—first novel or last novel. Keep it historical, put characters in a historical context. Professionalism counts. Know your subject. *Convince us.*"

NAVAL INSTITUTE PRESS Imprint of U.S. Naval Institute, 291 Wood Rd., Annapolis MD 21402-5034. Fax: (410)295-1084. E-mail: esecunda@usni.org. Website: www.nip.org. Press Director: Ronald Chambers. **Contact:** Paul Wilderson, executive editor; Tom Cutler, senior acquisitions editor; Eric Mills, acquisitions editor. Estab. 1873. The Naval Institute Press publishes general and scholarly books of professional, scientific, historical and literary interest to the naval and maritime communities. First novel print order: 2,500. Averages 80 titles/year.

Imprint(s): Bluejacket Books (paperback reprints).

Needs: Limited fiction on military and naval themes. Recently published *Dog Company Six*, by Edwin P. Simmons (Age of Sail historical novel).

How to Contact: Send query letter only.

Terms: Pays royalties of 5-10% on net sales. Publishes ms 1 year after acceptance. Writer's guidelines for #10 SASE; book catalog free for 9×12 SASE.

THOMAS NELSON PUBLISHERS, NelsonWorld Publishing Group, Box 141000, Nashville TN 37214-1000. Estab. 1798. **Contact:** Acquisitions Editor. "Largest Christian book publishers." Publishes hardcover and paperback originals. Averages 150-200 total titles/year.

Imprint(s): Janet Thoma Books; Oliver Nelson Books.

Needs: Seeking successfully published commercial fiction authors who write for adults from a Christian perspective. Published *A Skeleton in God's Closet*, by Paul Maier (suspense/mystery); *The Twilight of Courage*, by Brock and Bodie Thoene (historical suspense); and *The Secrets of the Roses*, by Lila Peiffer (romance).

How to Contact: Corporate office does not accept unsolicited mss. "No phone queries." Send brief prosaic résumé, 1-page synopsis and one sample chapter. Send SASE or IRC for reply. Responds in 3 months.

Terms: Pays royalty on net sales with rates negotiated for each project. Publishes ms 1-2 years after acceptance. Writer's guidelines for #10 SASE. Accepts simultaneous submissions if so noted.

Advice: "We are a conservative publishing house and want material which is conservative in morals and in nature."

TOMMY NELSON, Thomas Nelson, Inc., 404 BNA Dr., Bldg. 200, Suite 508, Nashville TN 37217. Fax: (615)902-2415. Website: www.tommynelson.com. Publisher of children's Christian fiction and nonfiction for boys and girls up to age 14. "We honor God and serve people through books, videos, software and Bibles for children that improve the lives of our customers." Publishes hardcover and trade paperback originals. Averages 50-75 total titles/year.

Imprint(s): Word Kids.

Needs: Adventure, juvenile, mystery, picture books, religious. "No stereotypical characters without depth."
How to Contact: Does not accept unsolicited mss or simultaneous submissions.
Terms: Pays royalty on wholesale price or makes outright purchase. Average advance: $1,000 minimum. Publishes ms 18 months after acceptance.
Advice: "Know the CBA market. Check out the Christian bookstores to see what sells and what is needed."

N ☺ A NEW AMERICAN LIBRARY (NAL), Division of Penguin Putnam Inc., 375 Hudson St., New York NY 10014. (212)366-2000. Fax: (212)366-2889. **Contact:** Carolyn Nichols, executive director, NAL Editorial (fiction, nonfiction); Ellen Edwards, executive editor (commercial women's fiction); Laura Anne Gilman, executive editor (science fiction/fantasy/horror); Audrey LeFehr, executive editor (contemporary and historical romance, multicultural fiction); Hilary Ross, associate executive editor (Regency, romance); Doug Grad, senior editor (thrillers, historical and military fiction/nonfiction); Dan Slater, senior editor (westerns, thrillers, commercial fiction, media tie-ins); Marie Timell, senior editor (New Age, inspirational); Genny Ostertag, editor (mystery, women's fiction); Cecilia Oh, associate editor (Regency, romance, inspirational). Estab. 1948. Publishes hardcover and paperback originals and paperback reprints. **Published new writers within the last year.**
Imprint(s): Signet, Onyx, Signet Classic, **ROC,** NAL Accent.
Needs: "All kinds of commercial and literary fiction, including mainstream, historical, Regency, New Age, western, thriller, science fiction, fantasy. Full length novels and collections." Recently published *On Secret Service*, by John Jakes; *False Pretenses*, by Catherine Coulter; *Suspicion of Betrayal*, by Barbara Parker; and *The Quiet Game*, by Greg Iles.
How to Contact: Agented mss only. Queries accepted with SASE. "State type of book and past publishing projects." Simultaneous submissions OK. Responds in 3 months.
Terms: Pays in royalties and author's copies; offers advance. Sends galleys to authors. Publishes ms 18 months after acceptance. Book catalog for SASE.
Advice: "Write the complete manuscript and submit it to an agent or agents. We publish The Trailsman, Battletech and other western and science fiction series—all by ongoing authors. Would be receptive to ideas for new series in commercial fiction."

N ◑ A NEW HOPE BOOKS, INC., P.O. Box 38, New Hope PA 18938. (888)741-BOOK. Fax: (215)244-0935. E-mail: NewHopeBks@aol.com. Website: www.NewHopeBooks.net (includes book catalogue, featured authors, submission guidelines, contact information). **Contact:** Barbara Taylor, publisher; Tamara Hayes, assistant editor. Estab. 1999. "We are a small but quickly growing press that savors zippy, mainstream page turners, which readily adapt to feature film." Publishes hardcover and paperback originals and reprints. **Published 1 new writer within the last year.** Plans 3 first novels in 2001. Averages 6 total titles, 6 fiction titles/year.
Needs: Adventure, literary, mainstream, mystery/suspense, thriller/espionage. "Plot-driven fiction only that tugs on the heartstrings." Recently published *The Boardwalkers* (murder mystery); and *A Run to Hell* (crime/espionage), both by Frederick Schofield.
How to Contact: Does not accept unsolicited mss. Query with outline/synopsis and 1 sample chapter. Include estimated word count. Send SASE or IRC for return of ms or send disposable copy of ms and SASE for reply only. "Almost all of our fiction is agented." Responds in 1 month to queries; 6 weeks to mss. Accepts simultaneous submissions.
Terms: Pays royalty. Offers negotiable advance. Sends galleys to author. Publishes ms 1 year after acceptance. Writer's guidelines free for #10 SASE; book catalog on website.
Advice: "Current industry trends heavily favor our approach. Submissions must pluperfectly fit our guidelines for consideration."

◑ ◎ NEW VICTORIA PUBLISHERS, P.O. Box 27, Norwich VT 05055-0027. Phone/fax: (802)649-5297. E-mail: newvic@aol.com. Website: www.NewVictoria.com (includes list of titles). **Contact:** Claudia Lamperti, editor; ReBecca Béguin, editor. Estab. 1976. "Publish mostly lesbian fiction—strong female protagonists. Most well known for Stoner McTavish mystery series." Small, three-person operation. Publishes trade paperback originals. Plans 2-5 first novels in 2001. **Published 3 new writers within the last year.** Averages 8-10 titles/year. Distributes titles through LPC Group (Chicago), Airlift (London) and Bulldog Books (Sydney, Australia). Promotes titles "mostly through lesbian feminist media."
   • *Shaman's Moon*, by Sarah Dreher won the Lambda Literary Award for Mystery.
Needs: Lesbian/feminist: adventure, fantasy, historical, humor, mystery (amateur sleuth), romance. Looking for "strong feminist characters, also strong plot and action. We will consider most anything if it is well written and appeals to a lesbian/feminist audience; mostly mysteries." Publishes anthologies or special editions. Published *Killing at the Cat*, by Carlene Miller (mystery); *Queer Japan*, by Barbara Summerhawk (anthology); *Skin to Skin*, by Martha Miller (erotic short fiction); *Talk Show*, by Melissa Hartman (novel); *Flight From Chador*, by Sigrid Brunel (adventure); and *Do Drums Beat There*, by Doe Tabor (novel),
How to Contact: Does not accept unsolicited mss. Query with outline/synopsis and sample chapters. Accepts queries by e-mail, fax. Send SASE or IRC for reply. Responds in 2 weeks to queries; 1 month to mss.

Terms: Pays royalties of 10%. Publishes ms 1 year after acceptance. Writer's guidelines for SASE; book catalog free.

Advice: "We are especially interested in lesbian or feminist mysteries, ideally with a character or characters who can evolve through a series of books. Mysteries should involve a complex plot, accurate legal and police procedural detail, and protagonists with full emotional lives. Pay attention to plot and character development. Read guidelines carefully."

NEWEST PUBLISHERS LTD., 201, 8540-109 St., Edmonton, Alberta T6G 1E6 Canada. (780)432-9427. Fax: (780)433-3179. E-mail: info@newestpress.com. **Contact:** Ruth Linka, general manager. Estab. 1977. Publishes trade paperback originals. **Published new writers within the last year.** Averages 12 total titles/year, fiction and nonfiction. Distributes titles through General Distribution Services. Promotes titles through book launches, media interviews, review copy mailings and touring.

Needs: Literary. "Our press is interested in western Canadian writing." Published *The Widows*, by Suzette Mayr (novel); *The Blood Girls*, by Meira Cook (novel); and *Baser Elements*, by Murray Malcolm (crime fiction). Publishes the Nunatak New Fiction Series.

How to Contact: Accepts unsolicited mss. Accepts queries by e-mail. SASE necessary for return of ms. Responds in 2 months to queries; 6 months to mss.

Terms: Pays royalties of 10% minimum. Sends galleys to author. Publishes ms at least 1 year after acceptance. Book catalog for 9 × 12 SASE.

Advice: *"We publish western Canadian writers only or books about western Canada.* We are looking for excellent quality and originality."

NEXUS, Virgin Publishing, Thames Wharf Studios, Rainville Rd., London W6 9HA England. Phone: 0207-386-3312. Fax: 0207-386-3360. E-mail: jmarriott@virgin-pub.co.uk. Website: www.virginbooks. com (includes book catalog, guidelines; guidelines can also be found on the Erotic Readers Association website: www.erotica-readers.com). **Contact:** James Marriott, commissioning editor. Estab. 1988. "We are an imprint of Virgin Publishing. We publish only fetish-oriented erotic fiction." Publishes paperback originals and reprints. Books: perfect bound. **Published 1 new writer within the last year.** Averages 36 fiction titles/year.

Imprints: Sapphire Books

Needs: Erotica. Recently published *Plaything*, by Penny Birch; *The Young Wife*, by Stephanie Calvin; *Candy in Captivity*, by Arabella Knight.

How to Contact: Accepts unsolicited mss with SASE. Query with outline/synopsis and 3 sample chapters. Accepts queries by e-mail, fax and phone. Include estimated word count. Send SASE or IRC for return of ms. Agented fiction 10%. Responds in 2 weeks to queries; 6 months to mss. Accepts simultaneous submissions. Always comments on rejected mss.

Terms: Pays royalties of 7½%. Advance is negotiable. Sends galleys to authors. Publishes ms 1 year after acceptance. Writer's guidelines for SASE. Book catalogs free upon request or on website.

Advice: "Think original."

NORTH-SOUTH BOOKS, affiliate of Nord-Sud Verlag AG, 1123 Broadway, Suite 800, New York NY 10010. (212)463-9736. Website: www.northsouth.com. **Contact:** Julie Amper. Estab. 1985. "The aim of North-South is to build bridges—bridges between authors and artists from different countries and between readers of all ages. We believe children should be exposed to as wide a range of artistic styles as possible with universal themes." **Published new writers within the last year.** Averages 100 titles/year.

● North-South Books is the publisher of the international bestseller, *The Rainbow Fish*.

Needs: Picture books, easy-to-read. "We are currently accepting only picture books; all other books are selected by our German office." Published *The Rainbow Fish & the Big Blue Whale*, by Marcus Pfister (picture); *The Other Side of the Bridge*, Wolfram Hänel (easy-to-read); and *A Mouse in the House*, by G. Wagener.

How to Contact: Agented fiction only. Query. Does not respond unless interested. All unsolicited mss returned unopened. Returns submissions accompanied by SASE.

Terms: Pays royalty on retail price. Publishes ms 2 years after acceptance.

W.W. NORTON & COMPANY, INC., 500 Fifth Ave., New York NY 10110. (212)354-5500. Fax: (212)869-0856. Website: www.wwnorton.com. **Contact:** Editorial Department. Estab. 1924. Midsize independent publisher of trade books and college textbooks. Publishes literary fiction. Publishes hardcover originals.

● *Ship Fever*, by Andrea Barrett, published by W.W. Norton & Company, Inc., won the National Book Award.

Needs: High-quality literary fiction. No occult, science fiction, religious, gothic, romances, experimental, confession, erotica, psychic/supernatural, fantasy, horror, juvenile or young adult. Published *Ship Fever*, by Andrea Barrett; *Oyster*, by Jannette Turner Hospital; and *Power*, by Linda Hogan.

How to Contact: Does not accept unsolicited mss. Send query letter to "Editorial Department" listing credentials and briefly describing ms. Send SASE or IRC for reply. Accepts simultaneous submissions. Responds in 10 weeks. Packaging and postage must be enclosed to ensure safe return of materials. Occasionally comments on rejected mss.

Advice: "We will occasionally encourage writers of promise whom we do not immediately publish. We are principally interested in the literary quality of fiction manuscripts. A familiarity with our current list of titles will give you an idea of what we're looking for. If your book is good and you have no agent you may eventually succeed; but the road to success will be easier and shorter if you have an agent backing the book."

☑ ⦸ **ORCHARD BOOKS**, An imprint of Scholastic Inc., 95 Madison Ave., New York NY 10016. (212)951-2600. Fax: (212)213-6435. Website: www.scholastic.com. **Contact:** Ana Cerro, editor. Orchard specializes in children's illustrated and picture books. Publishes hardcover originals. **Published new writers within the last year.**

Needs: Picture books, young adult, middle reader, board book, novelty and some nonfiction. Recently published *Mouse in Love*, by Robert Kraus, illustrated by Jose Aruego and Ariane Dewey; and *Pete and Polo's Big School Adventure*, by Adrian Reynolds.

How to Contact: Currently not accepting queries or unsolicited mss.

Terms: Pays royalties of 7½-10% on retail price. Advance varies. Publishes ms 1 year after acceptance.

Advice: "Go to a bookstore and read several Orchard Books to get an idea of what we publish. Write what you feel. It's worth finding the right publishing match."

⊕ ⦸ **ORIENT PAPERBACKS**, A Division of Vision Books Pvt Ltd., Madarsa Rd., Kashmere Gate, Delhi 110 006 India. **Contact:** Sudhir Malhotra, editor. Averages 10-15 novels or story collections/year. "We are one of the largest paperback publishers in S.E. Asia and publish English fiction by authors from this part of the world."

Needs: Length: 40,000 words minimum.

How to Contact: Send cover letter, brief summary, 1 sample chapter and author's bio data. "We send writers' guidelines on accepting a proposal."

Terms: Pays royalty on copies sold.

⊕ ☑ **PETER OWEN PUBLISHERS**, 73 Kenway Rd., London SW5 ORE England. Phone: 44+ 020 7373 6760. E-mail: admin@peterowen.com. Website: www.peterowen.com (includes complete backlists, book catalog plus ordering information). **Contact:** Antonia Owen, editorial director/fiction editor. "Independent publishing house now 50 years old. Publish fiction from around the world, from Russia to Japan. Publishers of Shusaku Endo, Paul and Jane Bowles, Hermann Hesse, Octavio Paz, Colette, etc." Averages 15 fiction titles/year.

Needs: Does not accept short stories, only excerpts from novels of normal length. Recently published *Hermes in Paris*, by Peter Vansittost (literary fiction); *Doubting Thomsas*, by Atle Naesr (translated literary fiction); *Lying*, by Wendy Perriam (fiction).

How to Contact: Query with synopsis and/or sample chapter or submit through agent (preferred). Send SASE (or IRC).

Terms: Pays standard royalty. Average advance. Book catalog for SASE, SAE with IRC or on website.

Advice: "Be concise. It would help greatly if author was familiar with the list. U.K. bookselling, especially since end of net book agreement, is making new fiction very hard to sell; it is also hard to get fiction reviewed. At the moment we are publishing less fiction than nonfiction."

☑ ⦸ **RICHARD C. OWEN PUBLISHERS INC.**, P.O. Box 585, Katonah NY 10536. Fax: (914)232-3977. Website: www.rcowen.com (includes guidelines, book-of-the-month sample book, teacher development). **Contact:** Janice Boland, director of children's books. "We believe children become enthusiastic, independent, life-long readers when supported and guided by skillful teachers who choose books with real and lasting value. The professional development work we do and the books we publish support these beliefs." Publishes hardcover and paperback originals. **Published 15 new writers within the last year.** Distributes titles to schools via mail order. Promotes titles through website, database mailing, reputation, catalog, brochures and appropriate publications—magazines, etc.

Needs: Picture books. "Brief, strong story line, real characters, natural language, exciting—child-appealing stories with a twist. No lists, alphabet or counting books." Also seeking mss for new anthologies of short, snappy stories for 7-8-year-old children (2nd grade). Subjects include humor, careers, mysteries, science fiction, folktales, women, fashion trends, sports, music, myths, journalism, history, inventions, planets, architecture, plays, adventure, technology, vehicles. Recently published *Armadillo*, by Marjorie Jackson (factual nonfiction story); *Wolf Song*, by Margo Lemieux (factual nonfiction story); and *Super Duper Sandwich*, by Bernice Meyers (humor).

How to Contact: Send for ms guidelines, then submit full ms with SASE. Responds in 1 month to queries; 2 months to mss. Accepts simultaneous submissions, if so noted.

Terms: Pays royalties of 5% on wholesale price; Books for Young Learners Anthologies and picture storybooks: flat fee for all rights. Publishes ms 3 years after acceptance. Writer's guidelines for SASE with 52¢ postage.

Advice: "We don't respond to queries. Send entire ms. Write clear strong stories with memorable characters and end with a big wind-up finish. Write for today's children—about real things that interest them. Read books that your public library features in their children's room to acquaint yourself with the best modern children's literature."

✓ ◑ Ⓐ **OWL BOOKS**, Imprint of Henry Holt & Co., Inc., 115 W. 18th St., New York NY 10011. (212)886-9200. Fax: (212)633-0748. **Contact:** Jennifer Barth, senior editor; Tom Bissell, associate editor. Estab. 1996.
Needs: Literary mainstream/contemporary. Published *White Boy Shuffle*, by Paul Beatty; and *The Debt to Pleasure*, by John Lanchester.
How to Contact: Holt does not accept unagented submissions.
Terms: Pays royalties of 6-7½% on retail price. Advance varies. Publishes ms 1 year after acceptance.

✓ ◔ **PANTHEON BOOKS**, The Knopf Publishing Group, A Division of Random House, Inc., 299 Park Ave., New York NY 10171. (212)751-2600. Fax: (212)572-6030. Website: www.pantheonbooks.com or www.ran domhouse.com/knopf/pantheon. Editorial Director: Dan Frank. Senior Editor: Shelley Wagner. Executive Editor: Erroll McDonald. **Conatct**: Editorial Department. Estab. 1942. "Small but well-established imprint of well-known large house." Publishes hardcover and trade paperback originals and trade paperback reprints. Averages 75 total titles, about 25 fiction titles/year.
Needs: Quality fiction and nonfiction. Published *Crooked Little Heart*, by Anne Lamott.
How to Contact: Does not accept unsolicited mss. Query with cover letter and sample material. Send SASE or IRC for return.
Payment/Terms: Pays royalties; offers advance.

✓ ◑ ◔ ❥ **PAPIER-MACHE PRESS**, 40 Commerce Park, Milford CT 06460. (203)877-8573. Estab. 1984. "Small women's press." Publishes anthologies, novels. Books: 60-70 lb. offset paper; perfect-bound or case-bound. Average print order: 25,000.
Needs: Not publishing new titles at this time. Published *At Our Core: Women Writing About Power*, by Sandra Martz (anthology); and *Generation to Generation*, by Sandra Martz and Shirley Coe (anthology).

✓ ◎ **PEACHTREE PUBLISHERS, LTD.,** 1700 Chattahoochee Ave., Atlanta GA 30318. (404)876-8761. Fax: (404)875-2578. Website: www.peachtree-online.com (includes writer's guidelines, current catalog of titles, upcoming promotional events, behind-the-scenes look at creating a book). President: Margaret Quinlin. **Contact**: Helen Harriss, fiction editors. Estab. 1977. Small, independent publisher specializing in general interest publications, particularly of Southern origin. Publishes hardcover and paperback originals and hardcover reprints. First novel print run 3,000. **Published 2 new writers within the last year.** Averages 18-20 total titles, 1-2 fiction titles/year. Promotes titles through review copies to appropriate publications, press kits and book signings at local bookstores.
Imprint(s): Freestone and Peachtree Jr.
Needs: Young adult and juvenile fiction. Contemporary, literary, mainstream, regional. No adult science fiction/fantasy, horror, religious, romance, historical or mystery/suspense. "We are seeking YA and juvenile works including mystery and historical fiction, however."
How to Contact: Accepts unsolicited mss. Query, submit outline/synopsis and 50 pages, or submit complete ms with SASE. Responds in 1 month to queries; 3 months to mss. Accepts simultaneous submissions. Do not fax or e-mail queries, manuscripts or submissions
Terms: Pays in royalties. Sends galleys to author. Free writer's guidelines. Publishes ms 2 years after acceptance. Book catalog for 2 first-class stamps.
Advice: "We encourage original efforts in first novels."

◎ ❥ **PELICAN PUBLISHING COMPANY**, Box 3110, Gretna LA 70054-3110. (504)368-1175. Website: www.pelicanpub.com (includes writer's guidelines, featured book, index of Pelican books). **Contact**: Nina Kooij, editor-in-chief. Estab. 1926. "We seek writers on the cutting edge of ideas. We believe ideas have consequences. One of the consequences is that they lead to a bestselling book." Publishes hardcover and paperback originals and reprints. Books: hardcover and paperback binding; illustrations sometimes. Buys juvenile mss with illustrations. Distributes titles internationally through distributors, bookstores, libraries. Promotes titles at reading and book conventions, in trade magazines, in radio interviews, print reviews and TV interviews.
  • *The Warlord's Puzzle*, by Virginia Walton Pilegard was #2 on *Independent Bookseller*'s Book Sense 76 list. *Dictionary of Literary Biography* lists *Unforgotten*, by D.J. Meador as "one of the best of 1999."
Needs: Juvenile fiction, especially with a regional and/or historical focus. No young adult fiction, contemporary fiction or fiction containing graphic language, violence or sex. Also no "psychological" novels. Recently published *The Loki Project*, by Benjamin King (adult historical fiction); and *The Warlord's Puzzle*, by Virginia Walton Pilegard (children's fairytale).

How to Contact: Does not accept unsolicited mss. Send query letter. May submit outline/synopsis and 2 sample chapters with SASE. "Not responsible if writer's only copy is sent." Responds in 1 month to queries; 3 months to mss. Comments on rejected mss "infrequently."

Terms: Pays royalties of 10% and 10 contributor's copies; advance considered. Sends galleys to author. Publishes ms 9-18 months after acceptance. Catalog of titles and writer's guidelines for SASE.

Advice: "Research the market carefully. Request our catalog to see if your work is consistent with our list. For ages 8 and up, story must be planned in chapters that will fill at least 90 double-spaced manuscript pages. Topic for ages 8-12 must be Louisiana related and historical. We look for stories that illuminate a particular place and time in history and that are clean entertainment. The only original adult work we might consider is historical fiction, preferably Civil War (not romance). Please don't send three or more chapters unless solicited. Follow our guidelines listed under 'How to Contact.' "

☑ **PENGUIN PUTNAM INC.**, 375 Hudson St., New York NY 10014. Website: www.penguinputnam.com. See the listings for Ace Science Fiction, Berkley Publishing Group, Dutton, New American Library (NAL), Plume, G.P. Putnam's Sons and Viking.

☑ ◑ ◎ **PERFECTION LEARNING CORP.**, 10520 New York Ave., Des Moines IA 50322-3775. (515)278-0133. Fax: (515)278-2980. E-mail: sthies@plconline.com. Website: www.perfectionlearning.com (includes writer's guidelines, names of editors, book catalog). **Contact:** Sue Thies, editorial director. "We are an educational publisher of hi/lo fiction and nonfiction with teacher support material." **Published 10 new writers within the last year.** Publishes 50-75 total titles/year, fiction and nonfiction. Distributes titles through sales reps, direct mail and online catalog. Promotes titles through educational conferences, journals and catalogs.

Imprint(s): Cover-to-Cover; Sue Thies, editorial director (all genres).

Needs: Hi/lo mss in all genres. Readability of ms should be at least two grade levels below interest level. "Please do not submit mss with fewer than 4,000 words or more than 20,000 words." Published *Tall Shadow*, by Bonnie Highsmith Taylor (Native American); *The Rattlesnake Necklace*, by Linda Baxter (historical fiction); and *Tales of Mark Twain*, by Peg Hall (retold short stories)."

How to Contact: Accepts unsolicited mss. Query with outline/synopsis and 3-4 sample chapters or submit complete ms with a cover letter. Accepts queries by e-mail and fax. Include 1-page bio, estimated word count and list of publishing credits. Send SASE or IRC for return of ms or send a disposable copy of ms and SASE for reply only. Responds in 5 months. Accepts simultaneous submissions.

Terms: Publishes ms 6-8 months after acceptance. Writer's guidelines on website; book catalog for 9×12 SAE with $2.31 postage.

Advice: "We are an educational publisher. Check with educators to find out their needs, their students' needs and what's popular."

◑ **PHILOMEL BOOKS**, Imprint of the Children's Division of Penguin Putnam Inc., 345 Hudson St., New York NY 10014. (212)414-3610. **Contact**: Patricia Lee Gauch, editorial director; Michael Green, senior editor. Estab. 1980. "A high quality-oriented imprint focused on stimulating picture books, middle-grade novels, and young adult novels." Publishes hardcover originals and paperback reprints. Averages 25 total titles, 5-7 novels/ year.

Needs: Adventure, ethnic, family saga, fantasy, historical, juvenile (5-9 years), literary, preschool/picture book, regional, short story collections, translations, western (young adult), young adult/teen (10-18 years). Looking for "story-driven novels with a strong cultural voice but which speak universally." No "generic, mass-market oriented fiction." Published *The Long Patrol*, by Brian Jacques; *I Am Mordred*, by Nancy Springer; and *Choosing Up Sides*, by John H. Ritter.

How to Contact: Accepts unsolicited mss. Query first or submit outline/synopsis and first 3 chapters. Send SASE or IRC for return of ms. Agented fiction 40%. Responds in 10 weeks to queries; up to 4 months to mss. Accepts simultaneous submissions. Sometimes comments on rejected ms.

Terms: Pays royalties, negotiable advance and author's copies. Sends galleys to author. Publishes ms anywhere from 1-3 years after acceptance. Writer's guidelines for #10 SASE. Book catalog for 9×12 SASE.

Advice: "We are not a mass-market publisher and do not publish short stories independently. In addition, we do just a few novels a year."

◑ Ⓐ **PICADOR USA**, St. Martin's Press, 175 Fifth Ave., New York NY 10010. **Contact:** Publisher. Estab. 1994. "We publish high-quality literary fiction and nonfiction. We are open to a broad range of subjects, well written by authoritative authors." Publishes hardcover originals and trade paperback originals and reprints.

Needs: Literary. Recently published *Grange House*, by Sarah Blake.

How to Contact: Does not accept unsolicited mss. Query only with SASE. Publishes few unagented writers. Responds in 2 months to queries. Accepts simultaneous submissions.

Terms: Pays royalties of 7½-12½% on retail price. Advance varies. Publishes ms 18 months after acceptance. Writer's guidelines for #10 SASE. Book catalog for 9×12 SASE and $2.60 postage.

☑ ◙ **PIÑATA BOOKS,** Imprint of Arte Publico Press, University of Houston, Houston TX 77204-2174. (713)743-2841. Fax: (713)743-3080. Website: www.arte.uh.edu. **Contact:** Nicolas Kanellos, president. Estab. 1994. "We are dedicated to the publication of children's and young adult literature focusing on U.S. Hispanic culture." Publishes hardcover and trade paperback originals. **Published new writers within the last year.** Averages 10-15 titles/year.
Needs: Adventure, juvenile, picture books, young adult. Published *Trino's Choice*, by Diane Gonzales Bertrand (ages 11-up); *Delicious Hullabaloo/Pachanga Deliciosa*, by Pat Mora (picture book); and *The Year of Our Revolution*, by Judith Ortiz Cofer (young adult).
How to Contact: Does not accept unsolicited mss. Query with synopsis, 2 sample chapters and SASE or IRC for reply. Responds in 1 month to queries, 6 months to mss. Accepts simultaneous submissions.
Terms: Pays royalties of 10% on wholesale price. Average advance: $1,000-3,000. Publishes ms 2 years after acceptance. Writer's guidelines and book catalog free via website or with #10 SASE.
Advice: "Include cover letter with submission explaining why your manuscript is unique and important, why we should publish it, who will buy it, relevance to the U.S. Hispanic culture, etc."

☑ ◙ ◎ **PINEAPPLE PRESS,** P.O. Box 3899, Sarasota FL 34230-3899. (800)746-3275. Fax: (941)351-9988. E-mail: info@pineapplepress.com. Website: www.pineapplepress.com (includes searchable database of titles, news events, featured books, company profile, and option to request a hard copy of catalog). **Contact:** June Cussen, executive editor. Estab. 1982. Small independent trade publisher. Publishes hardcover and paperback originals. Books: quality paper; offset printing; Smyth-sewn or perfect-bound; illustrations occasionally. **Published new writers within the last year.** Plans 1-2 first novels in 2001. Averages 20 total titles/year. Distributes titles through Pineapple, Ingram and Baker & Taylor. Promotes titles through reviews, advertising in print media, direct mail, author signings and the World Wide Web.
Needs: Historical, literary, mainstream, regional (most fiction is set in Florida). Recently published *The Return*, by Mark Mustian (novel).
How to Contact: No unsolicited mss. Query with outline, brief synopsis and sample chapters. Send SASE or IRC for reply. Responds in 3 months. Accepts simultaneous submissions.
Terms: Pays royalties of 6½-15% on net price. Advance is not usually offered. "Basically, it is an individual agreement with each author depending on the book." Sends galleys to author. Publishes ms 18 months after acceptance. Book catalog for 9 × 12 SAE with $1.24 postage.
Advice: "Quality first novels will be published, though we usually only do one or two novels per year. We regard the author/editor relationship as a trusting relationship with communication open both ways. Learn all you can about the publishing process and about how to promote your book once it is published. A query on a novel without a brief sample seems useless."

◙ **PIPPIN PRESS,** 229 E. 85th Street, Gracie Station Box 1347, New York NY 10028. (212)288-4920. Fax: (732)225-1562. **Contact:** Barbara Francis, publisher; Joyce Segal, senior editor. Estab. 1987. "Small, independent children's book company, formed by the former editor-in-chief of Prentice Hall's juvenile book division." Publishes hardcover originals. Books: 135-150 GSM offset-semi-matte paper (for picture books); offset, sheet-fed printing; Smythe-sewn binding; full color, black and white line illustrations and half tone, b&w and full color illustrations. Averages 5-6 titles/year.
Needs: Juvenile only for ages 4-12. "I am interested in humorous novels for children of about 7-12. Also interested in autobiographical novels for 8-12 year olds and selected historical fiction and idiosyncratic nonfiction for the same age group. Less interested in picture books at this time."
How to Contact: Does not accept unsolicited mss. Send query letter with SASE or IRC for reply. Responds in 3 weeks to queries. Accepts simultaneous submissions. Sometimes comments on rejected mss.
Terms: Pays royalties. Sends galleys to author. Publication time after ms is accepted "depends on the amount of revision required, type of illustration, etc." Writer's guidelines for #10 SASE.

☑ ◙ **PLEASANT COMPANY PUBLICATIONS,** Subsidiary of Pleasant Company, 8400 Fairway Place, Middleton WI 53528. (608)836-4848. Fax: (608)836-1999. Website: www.americangirl.com (includes writer's guidelines, names of editors, press releases, e-store including book list). **Contact:** Erin Falligant, submissions editor; Andrea Weiss, senior editor (contemporary fiction); Peg Ross, editor (history mysteries). Estab. 1986. Midsize independent publisher. "Moving in new directions, and committed to high quality in all we do. Pleasant Company has specialized in historical fiction and contemporary nonfiction for girls 7-12 and is now actively seeking strong authors for middle-grade contemporary fiction, historical fiction and fantasy for all ages." Publishes hardcover and paperback originals. Averages 30-40 total titles, 3 fiction titles/year.
● *The Night Flyers*, by Elizabeth McDavid Jones won the 2000 Edgar Allan Poe Award for Best Children's Mystery.
Imprints: The American Girls Collection and American Girls Library.
Needs: Children's/juvenile (historical, mystery, contemporary for girls 8-12). Pleasant Company Publications also seeks mss for its contemporary fiction imprint. "Novels should capture the spirit of contemporary American girls and also illuminate the ways in which their lives are personally touched by issues and concerns affecting

America today. We are looking for thoughtfully developed characters and plots, and a discernible sense of place." Stories must feature an American girl, aged 11-12; reading level 4th-6th grade. No science fiction or first-romance stories. Recently published *The Night Flyer*, by Elizabeth McDavid Jones (historical fiction); *A Song for Jeffrey*, by Constance M. Foland (contemporary fiction); and *Going for Great*, by Carolee Brockman (contemporary fiction).

How to Contact: Accepts unsolicited mss. Query with outline/synopsis and 3 sample chapters for series submissions. Submit complete ms with cover letter for stand-alone fiction and picture books. Include list of publishing credits. "Tell us why the story is right for us." Send SASE or IRC for return of ms or send disposable copy of ms and SASE for reply only. Agented fiction 5%. Responds in 10 weeks to queries; 4 months to mss. Accepts simultaneous submissions.

Payment/Terms: Advance against royalties. Publishes ms 3-12 months after acceptance. Writer's guidelines for SASE.

Advice: For historical fiction "your story *must* have a girl protagonist age 8-12. No early reader. Our readers are girls 10-12, along with parents and educators. We want to see character development and strong plotting."

☑ ☺ Ⓐ **PLUME**, (formerly Dutton Plume), Division of Penguin Putnam Inc., 375 Hudson St., New York NY 10014. (212)366-2000. Website: www.penguinputnam.com. **Contact:** Rosemary Ahern, editor-in-chief (literary fiction). Estab. 1948. Publishes paperback originals and reprints. **Published new writers within the last year.**

Needs: "All kinds of commercial and literary fiction, including mainstream, historical, New Age, western, thriller, gay. Full length novels and collections." Recently published *Girl with a Pearl Earring*, by Tracy Chevalier; *Liar's Moon*, by Philip Kimball; and *The True History of Paradise*, by Margaret Cezair-Thompson.

How to Contact: Agented mss only. Send query with SASE. "State type of book and past publishing projects." Accepts simultaneous submissions. Responds in 3 months.

Terms: Pays in royalties and author's copies; offers advance. Sends galleys to author. Publishes ms 12-18 months after acceptance. Book catalog for SASE.

Advice: "Write the complete manuscript and submit it to an agent or agents."

◖ **POCKET BOOKS**, Imprint of Simon & Schuster, 1230 Avenue of the Americas, New York NY 10020. (212)698-7000. Website: www.simonandschuster.com. **Contact:** Tracy Behar, vice president/editorial director. "Pocket Books publishes general interest nonfiction and adult fiction." Publishes paperback originals and reprints, mass market and trade paperbacks and hardcovers. **Published new writers within the last year.** Averages 250 titles/year.

Needs: Mysteries, romance, Star Trek® novels, thriller/psychological suspense, westerns. Recently published *Star Trek Avenger*, by William Shatner (fiction).

How to Contact: Does not accept unsolicited mss. Send query letter with SASE or IRC for reply. Responds in 1 month.

Terms: Pays royalties of 6-8% on retail price. Publishes ms 2 years after acceptance. Writer's guidelines for #10 SASE; book catalog free.

🇳 ⊕ ◖ **POWER OF LOVE PUBLISHING**, P.O. Box 145, O'Connor, Canberra ACT 2602 Australia. Phone/fax: 61 2 62556264. E-mail: info@poweroflove.com.au. Website: www.poweroflove.com.au (includes writer's guidelines, articles on fiction writing, discussion list, about us, info on writers/books). **Contact:** Jenny Millea, fiction editor (romance). Estab. 1997. "We're a category romance start-up aiming to publish innovative, interesting, intelligent romance fiction that provides readers with an enjoyable, entertaining reading experience." Publishes paperback originals. Books: web press printing; paperback binding; front cover illustrations. Average print order: 5,000; first novel print order: 5,000. Plans 4 first novels in 2001. Averages 12 fiction titles/year. Member: Publishers ACT. Distributes titles through website. Promotes titles through writer's networks, paid radio advertising and general media.

Imprint(s): Mature Delight, Inner City, Crossings, Dare to Dream.

Needs: Romance (contemporary). Especially needs "romances that are innovative, fresh with a new spin, style and appeal." Recently published *Strictly Business*, by Annie West (Dare to Dream Romance); and *High Flying Love*, by Ramona Crawford (Crossings Romance).

How to Contact: Accepts unsolicited mss. Query with outline/synopsis and first 3 chapters. Accepts queries by e-mail and fax (only for writers outside Australia). Include estimated word count, brief bio and list of publishing credits. Send SASE or IRC for return of ms. Agented fiction 10%. Responds in 14 weeks to queries and mss. Accepts simultaneous submissions. Always comments on rejected mss.

Terms: Pays royalties. Publishes ms 6-12 months after acceptance.

Advice: "Make the effort and do one more draft before you send it to a publisher."

🇳 ✂ ◯ ◎ 🅨 **PRAIRIE JOURNAL PRESS**, Prairie Journal Trust, P.O. Box 61203, Brentwood Postal Services, Calgary, Alberta T2L 2K6 Canada. E-mail: prairiejournal@iname.com. Website: www.geocities.com/Athens/Ithaca/4336 (includes guidelines, subscription information and home page). **Contact:** Anne Burke, literary editor. Estab. 1983. Small-press, noncommercial literary publisher. Publishes paperback originals. Books: bond paper; offset printing; stapled binding; b&w line drawings. **Published new writers within the last year.** Averages 2 total titles or anthologies/year. Distributes titles by mail and in bookstores and libraries (public and university). Promotes titles through direct mail and in journals.

- Prairie Journal Press authors have been nominated for The Journey Prize in fiction.

Needs: Literary, short stories. No romance, horror, pulp, erotica, magazine type, children's, adventure, formula, western. Published *Prairie Journal Fiction, Prairie Journal Fiction II* (anthologies of short stories); *Solstice* (short fiction on the theme of aging); and *Prairie Journal Prose.* "Our new series *Prairie Annals* is 8½×11, stapled, soft cover, full color art."

How to Contact: Accepts unsolicited mss. Query first and send Canadian postage or IRCs and $8 for sample copy, then submit 1-2 stories with SAE and IRCs (sorry, no US stamps). Responds in 6 months or sooner. Occasionally comments on rejected mss if requested.

Terms: Pays 1 author's copy; honorarium depends on grant/award provided by the government or private/corporate donations. Sends galleys to author. Book catalog free on request to institutions; SAE with IRC for individuals. "No U.S. stamps!"

Advice: "We wish we had the means to promote more new writers. We look for something different each time and try not to repeat types of stories if possible. We receive fiction of very high quality. Short fiction is preferable although excerpts from novels are considered if they stand alone on their own merit."

PRESIDIO PRESS, 505B San Marin Dr., Suite 300, Novato CA 94945. (415)898-1081, ext. 125. Fax: (415)898-0383. **Contact:** E.J. McCarthy, editor-in-chief. Estab. 1976. Small independent general trade—specialist in military. Publishes hardcover originals. Publishes an average of 2 works of fiction per list. **Published new writers within the past year.** Averages 24 new titles/year.

Needs: Historical with military background, war, thriller/espionage. Published *Synbat*, by Bob Mayer; *Proud Legions*, by John Antal; and *A Murder of Crows*, by Steve Shepard.

How to Contact: Accepts unsolicited mss. Send query letter with SASE or IRC for reply. Responds in 2 weeks to queries; 3 months to mss. Accepts simultaneous submissions. Comments on rejected ms.

Terms: Pays royalties of 15% of net minimum. Average advance: $1,000. Sends edited manuscripts and page proofs to author. Publishes ms 12-18 months after acceptance. Book catalog and guidelines for 9×12 SASE with $1.30 postage.

Advice: "Think twice before entering any highly competitive genre; don't imitate; do your best. Have faith in your writing and don't let the market disappoint or discourage you."

PRIDE & IMPRINTS, 7419 Ebbert Drive SE, Port Orchard WA 98367. **Contact:** Cris Newport, senior editor. Estab. 1989. Publishes paperback originals and reprints. **Published new writers within the last year.** Averages 50 total titles/year.

- Chosen as the "Best Example of an Independent Publisher" by BookWatch (Midwest Book Review).

Needs: Contemporary, fantasy, gay/lesbian/bisexual, historical, science fiction, young adult. No children's books, horror, "bestseller" fiction, spy or espionage novels, "thrillers," any work which describes childhood sexual abuse or in which this theme figures prominently. Recently published *Bones Become Flowers*, by Jess Mowry (contemporary fiction); *Annabel and I*, by Chris Anne Wolfe (lesbian fiction); *Journey of a Thousand Miles*, by Peter Kasting (gay fiction).

How to Contact: Does not accept unsolicited mss. Query with cover letter and 1-page synopsis which details the major plot developments. "Visit website for detailed submission instructions." Responds in 6 months to mss.

Terms: Pays royalties of 10-15% on wholesale price. Publishes ms 1-2 years after acceptance. Guidelines online only.

Advice: "Read our books before you even query us."

PUFFIN BOOKS, Imprint of Penguin Putnam Inc., 345 Hudson St., New York NY 10014-3657. (212)414-2000. Website: www.penguinputnam.com. **Contact:** Sharyn November, senior editor; Kristin Gilson, executive editor; Joy Peskin, assistant editor. "Puffin Books publishes high-end trade paperbacks and paperback reprints for preschool children, beginning and middle readers, and young adults." Publishes trade paperback originals and reprints. Averages 175-200 titles/year.

Imprint(s): PaperStar.

Needs: Picture books, young adult novels, middle grade and easy-to-read grades 1-3. "We publish mostly paperback reprints. We do few original titles." Published *A Gift for Mama*, by Esther Hautzig (Puffin chapter book).

How to Contact: Does not accept unsolicited mss. Send query letter with SASE or IRC for reply. Responds in 3 months to mss. Accepts simultaneous submissions, if so noted.

Terms: Royalty and advance vary. Publishes ms 1 year after acceptance. Book catalog for 9×12 SASE with 7 first-class stamps; send request to Marketing Department.

Advice: "Our audience ranges from little children 'first books' to young adult (ages 14-16). An original idea has the best luck."

☑ ⊘ 🄰 **G.P. PUTNAM'S SONS**, Imprint of Penguin Putnam Inc., 375 Hudson St., New York NY 10014. (212)366-2000. Fax: (212)366-2666. Website: www.penguinputnam.com. **Contact**: Acquisitions Editor. Publishes hardcover originals. **Published new writers within the last year.**
Imprint(s): Putnam, Riverhead, Jeremy P. Tarcher.
Needs: Adventure, literary, mainstream/contemporary, mystery/suspense, women's. Recently published *The Bear and the Dragon*, by Tom Clancy (adventure); *Perish Twice*, by Robert B. Parker (mystery/thriller); and *Vector*, by Robin Cook (medical thriller).
How to Contact: Does not accept unsolicited mss. Prefers agented submissions. Responds in 6 months to queries. Accepts simultaneous submissions.
Payment/Terms: Pays variable royalties on retail price. Advance varies.

🄽 🌐 **QUARTET BOOKS LIMITED**, 27 Goodge Street, London W1P 1FD England. Fax: 0171 637 1866. E-mail: quartetbooks@easynet.co.uk. **Contact:** Stella Kane, publishing director. Publishes "cutting-edge, avant-garde literary fiction." **Published new writers within the last year.** Averages 30 novels/year. Distributes titles through Plymbridge Distribution Services. Promotes titles through trade advertising mostly.
Needs: "Contemporary literary fiction including translations, popular culture, biographies, music, history and politics. *No* romantic fiction, science fiction or poetry."Recently published *Resentment*, by Gary Indiana (literary-black comic); *As Good As It Gets*, by Simon Nolan (edgy, Brit-lit); and *The Romance Reader*, by Pearl Abraham (rites of passage-literary).
How to Contact: Query with brief synopsis and sample chapters. Accepts queries by e-mail and fax.
Terms: Pays advance—half on signature, half on delivery or publication.

☑ ◎ **QUIXOTE PRESS**, 1854 345th Ave., Wever IA 52658. (800)571-2665 or (319)372-7480. Fax: (319)372-7485. E-mail: maddmack@interl.net. **Contact:** Bruce Carlson, president. Quixote Press specializes in humorous regional folklore and special interest cookbooks. Publishes trade paperback originals and reprints. **Published mostly new writers within the last year.**
Needs: Adventure, ethnic, experimental, humor, short story collections, children's. Published *Eating Ohio*, by Rus Pishnery (short stories about Ohio); *Lil' Red Book of Fishing Tips*, by Tom Whitecloud (fishing tales); and *How to Talk Hoosier*, by Netha Bell (humor).
How to Contact: Query with synopsis and SASE. Responds in 2 months. Accepts simultaneous submissions.
Terms: Pays royalties of 10% on wholesale price. No advance. Publishes ms 1 year after acceptance. Writer's guidelines and book catalog for #10 SASE.
Advice: "Carefully consider marketing considerations. Audience is women in gift shops, on farm site direct retail outlets. Contact us at *idea* stage, not complete manuscript stage. Be receptive to design input by us."

🍁 ☑ ◯ ◎ **RAGWEED PRESS INC./gynergy books**, P.O. Box 2023, Charlottetown, Prince Edward Island C1A 7N7 Canada. (902)566-5750. Fax: (902)566-4473. E-mail: editor@ragweed.com. Website: www.ragweed.com or www.gynergy.com. **Contact**: Managing Editor. Estab. 1980. "Independent Canadian-owned feminist press." Publishes paperback originals. Books: 60 lb. paper; perfect binding. Average print order: 2,000. Averages 8 total titles, 3 fiction titles/year. **Published new writers within the last year.**
Needs: *Canadian-authors only.* "We do accept submissions to anthologies from U.S. writers." Children's/juvenile (adventure, picture book, girl-positive), feminist, lesbian, regional, young adult. Published *The Dog Wizard*, by Anne Louise MacDonald (children's picture book); and *Fragment by Fragment*, by Margo Rivera.
How to Contact: Accepts unsolicited mss. Include cover letter, brief bio, list of publishing credits. Send SASE or IRC for return of ms. Responds in 6 months. Accepts simultaneous submissions.
Terms: Pays royalties of 10%; offers negotiable advance. Provides 10 author's copies. Sends galleys to author. Publishes ms 1-2 years after acceptance. Writer's guidelines for #10 SASE. Book catalog for large SAE and 2 first-class stamps or IRC.
Advice: "Send us your full manuscript, and be patient. Please remember SASE—no phone calls or e-mail."

☑ ◎ **RAINBOW BOOKS, INC.**, P.O. Box 430, Highland City FL 33846. (863)648-4420. Fax: (863)647-5951. E-mail: rbibooks@aol.com. **Contact:** Besty A. Lampe, editorial director. Estab. 1979. Publishes hardcover and trade paperback originals. Averages 12-15 titles/year.
Needs: "Mainly, we're looking for well-written mystery books that deserve to be published." Recently published *Biotechnology is Murder*, by Dirk Wyle (fiction).
How to Contact: Does not accept unsolicited mss. Query with synopsis and first chapter. Send SASE or IRC for reply. Responds in 1 month to queries and proposals; 2 months to mss. Accepts simultaneous submissions.
Terms: Pays royalties of 6-12% on retail price. Offers advance. Publishes ms 1 year after acceptance. Writer's guidelines for #10 SASE.
Advice: "Be professional in presentation of queries and manuscripts, and always provide a return mailer with proper postage attached in the event the materials do not fit our list. In mystery fiction, we don't want to see books with violence for violence's sake."

☑ Ⓐ **RANDOM HOUSE BOOKS FOR YOUNG READERS**, Random House Children's Books, A Division of Random House, Inc., 1540 Broadway, New York NY 10036. (212)782-9000 or (800)200-3552. Website: www.randomhouse.com/kids. Vice President/Publisher: Kate Klimo. Editor-in-Chief: Mallory Loehr. Executive Editor: Heidi Kilgras. **Contact:** Alice Jonaitis, senior editor; Jim Thomas, editor; Alice Alfonsi, editorial director (Star Wars); Courtney Devon Silk, editorial director (mass market); Kerry Milliron, editor/licensing manager; Naomi Kleinberg, editorial director (Sesame Workshop); Apple Jane Jordan, associate editor (Sesame Workshop). *Disney Books:* Editorial Director: Chris Angellili. Executive Editor: Andrea Posner-Sanchez. **Contact:** Dennis Shealy, senior editor; Mark McVeigh, editor.
Needs: Humor, juvenile, mystery, early picture/board books, picture books, chapter books, middle-grade, young adult. Recently published the works of Dr. Seuss, P.D. Eastman and the Berenstain Bears; *The Story of Babar*; the Step into Reading beginning readers series; the Junie B. Jones series; the Magic Tree House series; *The Protector of the Small Quartet*, by Tamora Pierce; and *The Phantom Tollbooth*, by Norman Juster.
How to Contact: Agented fiction only. Responds in up to 4 months. Accepts simultaneous submissions but must be indicated as such.

✦ ☑ ☺ Ⓐ **RANDOM HOUSE CANADA**, A Division of Random House, Inc., 1 Toronto St., Suite 300, Toronto, Ontario M5C 2V6 Canada. Website: www.randomhouse.ca. Publishes hardcover and paperback originals. Averages 56 titles/year.
Imprint(s): Vintage Canada.
How to Contact: Does not accept unsolicited mss. Agented fiction only. All unsolicited mss returned unopened. "We are *not* a mass market publisher."

☑ **RANDOM HOUSE CHILDREN'S BOOKS**, 1540 Broadway, New York NY 10036. (212)782-9000 or (800)200-3552. Website: www.randomhouse.com/kids. President/Publisher: Craig W. Virden. Vice President/Associate Publisher: Kevin Jones.
• See listings for **Bantam, Doubleday, Dell/Delacorte, Knopf and Crown Books for Young Readers** and **Random House Books for Young Readers**.
Advice: (for all imprints) "We look for original, unique stories. Do something that hasn't been done before."

☑ ☺ Ⓐ **RANDOM HOUSE, INC.**, 299 Park Ave., New York NY 10171. (212)751-2600. Website: www.randomhouse.com. Estab. 1925. Publishes hardcover and paperback originals.
Imprint(s): The following Random House publishing groups and their imprints consider fiction; those printed in boldface type have individual listings in this book. *Ballantine Publishing Group* (**Ballantine Books, Del Rey, Fawcett**); *The Bantam Dell Publishing Group* (Bantam, Delacorte Press, Dell, The Dial Press, Island); *The Doubleday Broadway Publishing Group* (**Broadway Books,** Currency, **Doubleday,** Doubleday Religious Publishing, Doubleday/Image, **Nan A. Talese**); *The Knopf Publishing Group* (**Alfred A. Knopf, Pantheon Books, Vintage**); *Random House Children's Books* (**Bantam, Doubleday, Dell/Delacorte, Knopf and Crown Books for Young Readers** [including Delacorte Books for Young Readers, Doubleday Books for Young Readers, Laurel Leaf, Skylark, Starfire, Yearling Books] and **Random House Books for Young Readers** [including Disney]).

✦ ☑ ☺ ◎ ▼ **RED DEER PRESS**, MacKimmie Library Tower, Room 13, 2500 University Dr., NW, Calgary, Alberta T2N 1N4 Canada. (403)220-4334. Fax: (403)210-8191. E-mail: cdearden@rdc.ab.ca. Website: www.bookpublishers.ab.ca/redeerco.reddeerc.html. **Contact**: Dennis Johnson, managing editor; Aritha van Herk, fiction editor. Estab. 1975. Publishes adult and young adult hardcover and paperback originals "focusing on books by, about, or of interest to Western Canadians." Books: offset paper; offset printing; hardcover/perfect-bound. Average print order: 5,000. First novel print order: 2,500. Averages 14-16 total titles, 2 fiction titles/year. Distributes titles in Canada, the US, the UK, Australia and New Zealand.
Imprint(s): Roundup Books (edited by Ted Stone), Inprints (fiction reprint series, edited by Aritha van Herk).
• Red Deer Press has received numerous honors and awards from the Book Publishers Association of Alberta, Canadian Children's Book Centre, the Governor General of Canada and the Writers Guild of Alberta. *A Fine Daughter*, by Catherine Simmons Niven received the Georges Bugnet Award for Best Novel.
Needs: Contemporary, experimental, literary, young adult. No romance, science fiction or horror. Published anthologies under Roundup Books imprint focusing on stories/poetry of the Canadian and American West. Published *Great Stories of the Sea*, edited by Norma Ravvin (anthology); *A Fine Daughter*, by Catherine Simmons Niven (novel); and *Great Stories from the Prairies* (anthology).
How to Contact: *Canadian authors only.* Does not accept unsolicited mss in children's and young adult genres. Query first or submit outline/synopsis and 2 sample chapters. Send SASE or IRC. Responds in 6 months to queries and mss. Accepts simultaneous submissions. Final mss must be submitted on Mac disk in MS Word.
Terms: Pays royalties of 8-10%. Advance is negotiable. Sends galleys to author. Publishes ms 1 year after acceptance. Book catalog for 9×12 SASE.

Advice: "We're very interested in literary and experimental fiction from Canadian writers with a proven track record (either published books or widely published in established magazines or journals) and for manuscripts with regional themes and/or a distinctive voice. We publish Canadian authors exclusively."

Ⓝ Ⓞ Ⓞ REGENCY PRESS, Crack of Noon Enterprises, P.O. Box 18908, Cleveland Heights OH 44118-0908. (216)932-5319. Website: www.regency-press.com (includes sales, contest, helpful info, writer's guidelines, book catalog). **Contact:** Kelly Ferjutz, editor. Estab. 1998. Publisher of Regency fiction—new and reprints in paperback and hardcover, eventually large print. Publishes hardcover and paperback originals and paperback reprints. **Published 2 new writers within the last year.** Plans 4 first novels in 2001. Averages 6-8 fiction titles/year.

Needs: Fantasy, historical, mystery/suspense, romance and nonfiction about Regency period. Plans contest for Regency short-story anthology. Recently published *The Marplot Marriage*, by Beth Andrews (Regency); and *The Reluctant Guardian*, by Jo Manning (Regency).

How to Contact: Accepts unsolicited mss. Query with 1 page outline/synopsis. Include estimated word count, brief bio and list of publishing credits. Send SASE or IRC for return of ms OR send disposable copy of ms and SASE for reply only. Responds in 3 months to queries; 6 months to mss. Accepts simultaneous submissions. Always comments on rejected mss.

Terms: Pays royalties of 7%. Sends galleys to author. Publishes ms 12-18 months after acceptance. Writer's guidelines free for #10 SASE. Book catalogs for $1.

Ⓞ REVELL PUBLISHING, Subsidiary of Baker Book House, P.O. Box 6287, Grand Rapids MI 49516-6287. (616)676-9185. Fax: (616)676-9573. E-mail: lholland@bakerbooks.com or petersen@bakerbooks.com. Website: www.bakerbooks.com. **Contact:** Sheila Ingram, assistant to the editorial director; Jane Campbell, editorial director (Chosen Books). Estab. 1870. Midsize publisher. "Revell publishes to the heart (rather than to the head). For 125 years, Revell has been publishing evangelical books for personal enrichment and spiritual growth of general Christian readers." Publishes hardcover, trade paperback and mass market originals and reprints. Average print order: 7,500. **Published new writers within the last year.** Plans 1 first novel in 2001. Averages 60 total titles, 8 fiction titles/year.

Imprint(s): Spire Books.

Needs: Religious/inspirational (general). Published *Triumph of the Soul*, by Michael R. Joens (contemporary); *Daughter of Joy*, by Kathleen Morgan (historical); and *Blue Mist on the Danube*, by Doris Eliane Fell (contemporary).

How to Contact: Query with outline/synopsis. Include estimated word count, bio and list of publishing credits. Send SASE or IRC for return of ms or send disposable copy of ms and SASE for reply only. Agented fiction 20%. Responds in 3 weeks to queries; 2 weeks to mss. Accepts simultaneous submissions. Sometimes comments on rejected mss.

Terms: Pays royalties. Sends galleys to author. Publishes ms 1 year after acceptance. Writer's guidelines for SASE.

☑ Ⓞ RISING TIDE PRESS, 3831 N. Oracle Rd., Tucson AZ 85705. (520)888-1140. Fax: (520)888-1123. E-mail: rmilestonepress@gateway.net. Website: www.risingtidepress.com (includes book catalog, writer's guidelines, about our authors). **Contact:** Debra S. Tobin and Brenda J. Kazen. Estab. 1988. "Independent women's press, publishing lesbian and feminist nonfiction and fiction." Publishes paperback trade originals. Books: 60 lb. vellum paper; sheet fed and/or web printing; perfect-bound. Average print order: 2,000. First novel print order: 2,000. **Published 4-5 new writers within the last year.** Plans 10-12 first novels in 2001. Averages 12 total titles/year. Distributes titles through Bookpeople, Baker & Taylor, Alamo Square, Marginal (Canada), Turnaround (UK) and Banyon Tree (Pacific Basin). Promotes titles through magazines, journals, newspapers, *PW*, Lambda Book Report, distributor's catalogs, special publications and Internet.

Needs: Lesbian adventure, contemporary, erotica, fantasy, feminist, romance, science fiction, suspense/mystery, western. Looking for romance and mystery. Recently published *Storm Rising*, by Linda Kay Silva (adventure); *Called to Kill*, by Joan Albarella (mystery); and *Side Dish*, by Kim Taylor (romance). Seeking "coming out stories" and stories about growing up in a gay household for anthologies.

How to Contact: Accepts unsolicited mss. Query with 1-page outline/synopsis and SASE. Responds in 3 months to mss.

Terms: Pays 10% royalties. Publishes ms 6-18 months after acceptance. Writer's guidelines for #10 SASE.

Advice: "Outline your story to give it boundaries and structure. Find creative ways to introduce your characters and begin the story in the middle of some action and dialogue. Our greatest challenge is finding quality manuscripts that are well plotted and not predictable, with well-developed, memorable characters."

Ⓞ ROC, Imprint of New American Library, A Division of Penguin Putnam, Inc., 375 Hudson St., New York NY 10014. (212)366-2000. Website: www.penguinputnam.com. **Contact:** Laura Anne Gilman, executive editor;

Jennifer Heddle, assistant editor. "Roc tries to strike a balance between fantasy and science fiction. We're looking for books that are a good read, that people will want to pick up time and time again." Publishes mass market, trade and hardcover originals. Averages 36 total titles/year.

Needs: Fantasy, horror, science fiction. Recently published *Queen of the Darkness*, by Anne Bishop; and *On the Oceans of Eternity*, by S.M. Stirling.

How to Contact: Does not accept unsolicited mss. Query with synopsis and 1-2 sample chapters. Send SASE or IRC for reply. Responds in 3 month to queries. Accepts simultaneous submissions.

Terms: Pays royalty. Advance negotiable.

ROUSSAN PUBLISHERS INC., Roussan Editeur Inc., 4710 St.-Ambroise, Suite 154, Montreal, Quebec H4C 2C7 Canada. (514)481-2895. Fax; (514)487-2899. Website: www.magnet.ca/roussan. **Contact:** Kathryn Rhoades; Jane Frydenlund, editor-in-chief. Roussan Publishers Inc., specializes in reality-based fiction for young adults and pre-teens. Canadian authors only. Publishes trade paperback originals. **Published 5 new writers within the last year.** Averages 12 titles/year; each division publishes 6 titles/year.

● Roussan Publishers Inc. has published such authors as George Bowering, Dayle Gaetz and Beth Goobie.

Needs: *Roussan is not currently accepting non-Canadian mss.* Young adult and junior readers only—adventure, fantasy, feminist, historical, juvenile, mystery, science fiction. No picture books. Published *Home Child*, by Barbara Haworth-Attard (historical); *The Vampire's Visit*, by David Poulsen; and *Gone to Maui*, by Cherylyn Stacey (young adult).

How to Contact: Query with synopsis and 3 sample chapters. Responds in 3 months. Accepts simultaneous submissions.

Terms: Pays royalties of 8-10% on retail price. Publishes ms 1 year after acceptance.

ST. MARTIN'S PRESS, 175 Fifth Ave., New York NY 10010. Estab. 1952. General interest publisher of both fiction and nonfiction. Publishes hardcover and paperback trade and mass market originals. Averages 1,500 total titles/year.

Imprint(s): Bedford Books; Buzz Books; **Thomas Dunne Books; Forge;** Minotaur; **Picador USA; Stonewall Inn Editions; TOR Books.**

Needs: General fiction: fantasy, historical, horror, literary, mainstream, mystery, science fiction, suspense, thriller, western (contemporary).

Terms: Pays royalty. Offers advance.

SALVO PRESS, P.O. Box 9095, Bend OR 97708. Phone/fax: (541)330-8746. E-mail: salvopress@hotmail.com. Website: www.salvopress.com (includes book catalog, writer's guidelines, author pages, sample chapters, author tours and links). **Contact:** Scott Schmidt, publisher (mystery, suspense, thriller & espionage). Estab. 1998. "We are a small press specializing in mystery, suspense, espionage and thriller fiction. We plan on expanding into science fiction and literary fiction. Our press publishes in trade paperback and e-book format simultaneously." Publishes paperback originals and e-books. Books: 5½×8½ or 6×9 paper; offset printing; perfect binding. Average print order: 2,000; first novel print order: 1,500. **Published 3 new writers within the last year.** Plans 3 first novels in 2001. Averages 6 fiction titles/year. Distributes titles through Seven Hills Book Distributors.

Needs: Adventure, literary, mystery/suspense (amateur sleuth, police procedural, private eye/hardboiled), science fiction (hard science/technological), thriller/espionage. Recently published *The Dolomite Solution*, by Trevor Scott (mystery/thriller); and *Snake Song*, by Gerald Duff (mystery).

How to Contact: Does not accept unsolicited mss. Send query letter. Accepts queries by e-mail; no queries by fax. Include estimated word count, brief bio, list of publishing credits "and something to intrigue me so I ask for more." Send SASE or IRC for return of ms or send disposable copy of ms and SASE for reply only. Agented fiction 15%. Responds in 3 weeks to queries; 1 month to mss. Accepts simultaneous and electronic submissions. Sometimes comments on rejected mss.

Terms: Pays royalties of 10-15%. No advance. Sends galleys to author. Publishes ms 9 months after acceptance. Writer's guidelines and book catalogs can be found on website.

SANS SOLEIL, Expanded Media Ed., P.O. Box 190136, Bonn 53037 Germany. Phone: 228-22-9583. Fax: 228-21-9507. E-mail: pociao@t-online.de. Website: www.sanssoleil.de (includes presentation of books and CD's, reviews). **Contact:** Dociao, director. Estab. 1997. "Independent publisher. We publish only female writing or texts about outstanding women. Biography, letters. Second part of our business is music. Also audio poetry, spoken word, etc. Again, reserved to women." Publishes paperback originals. Average print order: 1,000. First novel print order: 1,000. Averages 2 total titles, 1 fiction title/year.

Needs: Lesbian, literary. Spoken word audio material is welcome. Recently published *Jane Bowles*, by goNza magilla (letters); and *Ana Miranda*, by Clarice Lispector (literary portrait).

How to Contact: Accepts unsolicited mss. Query with outline/synopsis and 2 sample chapters. Include estimated word count and brief bio. Send disposable copy of ms and SASE for reply only. Agented fiction 50%. Responds in weeks to queries; in months to mss. Accepts simultaneous submissions.

Terms: Pays royalties of 10%. Advance is negotiable. Sends galleys to author upon request. Book catalog available on website.

N **◉** **◐** **◎** **☟** **SAPPHIRE BOOKS**, Virgin Publishing, Thames Wharf Studios, Rainville Rd., London W6 9HA England. Phone: 0207-386-3312. Fax: 0207-386-3360. E-mail: kbryson@virgin-pub.co.uk. Website: www.sapphire-books.co.uk. **Contact:** Kathleen Bryson, commissioning editor. Estab. 1999. Publishes paperback originals. **Published new writers within the last year.** Plans 4 first novels in 2001. Averages 6 total titles; 6 fiction titles/year.
* *Big Deal*, by Helen Sandler was named Erotic Book of the Year by Libertas Bookshop.
Imprint(s): Nexus.
Needs: Erotica, lesbian. Recently published *Getaway*, by Suzanne Blaylock (lesbian erotica).
How to Contact: Accepts unsolicited mss. Query with outline/synopsis and 2 sample chapters. Include estimated word count. Send SASE or IRC for return of ms. Agented fiction 25%. Responds in 1 month to queries; 5 months to mss. Accepts simultaneous submissions. Always comments on rejected mss.
Terms: Pays royalties of 5½%. Average advance: $1,000. Sends galleys to author. Publishes ms 7 months after acceptance. Writer's guidelines for SASE. Book catalog free.
Advice: "Open to lesbian/bisexual women only. Read guidelines first."

◐ **☟** **SARABANDE BOOKS, INC.**, 2234 Dundee Rd., Suite 200, Louisville KY 40205-1845. Fax: (502)458-4065. E-mail: sarabandek@aol.com. Website: www.SarabandeBooks.org (includes authors, forthcoming titles, backlist, writer's guidelines, names of editors, author interviews and excerpts from their work and ordering and contest information). **Contact:** Sarah Gorham, editor-in-chief; Kirby Gann, fiction editor. Estab. 1994. "Small literary press publishing poetry and short fiction." Publishes hardcover and paperback originals. **Published new writers within the last year.** Averages 8 total titles, 4-5 fiction titles/year. Distributes titles through Consortium Book Sales & Distribution. Promotes titles through advertising in national magazines, sales reps, brochures, newsletters, postcards, catalogs, press release mailings, sales conferences, book fairs, author tours and reviews.
* Books published by Sarabande Books have received the following awards: 1997/98 Society of Midland Authors Award and 1997 Carl Sandburg Award—Sharon Solwitz, *Blood & Milk*; 1997 Poetry Center Book Award and First Annual Levis Reading Prize—Belle Waring, *Dark Blonde*; GLEA New Writers Award—Becky Hagenston, *A Gram of Mars*.
Needs: Short story collections, 300 pages maximum (or collections of novellas, or single novellas of 150 pages). "Short fiction *only*. We do not publish full-length novels." Published *Mr. Dalloway*, by Robin Lippincott (novella); *A Gram of Mars*, by Becky Hagenston (short stories); and *The Baby Can Sing and Other Stories*, by Judith Slater.
How to Contact: Submit in September only. Query with outline/synopsis and 1 sample story or 10-page sample. Include 1 page bio, listing of publishing credits. Send SASE or IRC for reply. Responds in 3 months to queries; 6 months to mss. Accepts simultaneous submissions.
Terms: Pays in royalties, author's copies. Sends galleys to author. Writer's guidelines available (for contest only) for #10 SASE. Book catalog available.
Advice: "Make sure you're not writing in a vacuum, that you've read and are conscious of your competition in contemporary literature. Have someone read your manuscript, checking it for ordering, coherence. Better a lean, consistently strong manuscript than one that is long and uneven. Old fashioned as it sounds, we like a story to have good narrative, or at least we like to be engaged, to find ourselves turning the pages with real interest."

N **☟** **SCHOLASTIC CANADA LTD.**, 175 Hillmount Rd., Markham, Ontario L6C 1Z7 Canada. (905)887-7323. Fax: (905)887-3643. Website: www.scholastic.ca. **Contact:** Editors. Publishes hardcover and trade paperback originals. Averages 30 titles/year.
Imprint(s): North Winds Press; Les Éditions Scholastic (contact Sylvie Andrews, French editor).
Needs: Children's/juvenile, young adult. Published *After the War*, by Carol Matas (juvenile novel).
How to Contact: *Scholastic Canada is not accepting unsolicited mss in 2001.* Query with synopsis, 3 sample chapters and SASE. Responds in 3 months to queries.
Terms: Pays royalties of 5-10% on retail price. Average advance: $1,000-5,000 (Canadian). Publishes ms 1 year after acceptance. Book catalog for 8½×11 SAE with 2 first-class stamps (IRC or Canadian stamps only).

◐ **☟** **Ⓐ** **SCHOLASTIC INC.**, 555 Broadway, New York NY 10012-3999. (212)343-6100. Website: www. scholastic.com (includes general information about Scholastic). **Contact:** Jean Feiwel, senior vice president/ publisher, Book Group Scholastic Inc. Estab. 1920. Publishes books for children ages 4-young adult. "We are proud of the many fine, innovative materials we have created—such as classroom magazines, book clubs, book fairs, and our new literacy and technology programs. But we are most proud of our reputation as 'The Most Trusted Name in Learning.' " Publishes juvenile hardcover picture books, novels and nonfiction. Distributes titles through Scholastic Book Clubs, Scholastic Book Fairs, bookstores and other retailers.
Imprint(s): Blue Sky Press (contact: Bonnie Verberg, editorial director); **Cartwheel Books** (contact: Bernette Ford, editorial director); **Arthur Levine Books** (contact: Arthur Levine, editorial director); Mariposa (Spanish

language contact: Susana Pasternac, editorial director); **Scholastic Press** (contact: Elizabeth Szabla); Scholastic Trade Paperbacks (contact: Craig Walker, editorial director; Maria Weisbin, assistant to Craig Walker); Scholastic Reference (contact: Wendy Barish, editorial director).

● Scholastic published *Out of the Dust*, by Karen Hesse, winner of the Newbery Medal.

Needs: Hardcover—open to all subjects suitable for children. Paperback—family stories, mysteries, school, friendships for ages 8-12, 35,000 words. Young adult fiction, romance, family and mystery for ages 12-15, 40,000-45,000 words for average-to-good readers. Published *Her Stories: African American Folktales, Fairy Tales and True Tales*, by Virginia Hamilton, illustrated by Leo and Diane Dillon; and *Pigs in the Middle of the Road*, by Lynn Plourde.

How to Contact: Does not accept unsolicited manuscripts. Submissions (agented) may be made to the Editorial Director. Responds in 6 months.

Terms: Pays advance and royalty on retail price. Writer's guidelines for #10 SASE.

Advice: "Be current, topical and get an agent for your work."

SCHOLASTIC PRESS, Imprint of Scholastic Inc., 555 Broadway, New York NY 10012. (212)343-6100. Fax: (212)343-4713. Website: www.scholastic.com (includes information for teachers, parents and children, games/contests and information for children as well as book and author information—no guidelines online). **Contact:** Elizabeth Szabla, editorial director; Dianne Hess, executive editor (picture books, middle grade, young adult); Tracy Mack, senior editor (picture books, middle grade, young adult); Lauren Thompson, senior editor (picture books); Jennifer Braunstein, editorial assistant (picture books, middle grade, young adult). Scholastic Press publishes a range of picture books, middle grade and young adult novels. Publishes hardcover originals. **Published new writers within the last year.** Promotes titles through trade and library channels.

Needs: Juvenile, picture books. Recently published *Amelia and Eleanor Go for a Ride*, by Pam Muñoz Ryan, illustrated by Brian Selznick; and *Snail Mail No More*, by Paula Danziger and Ann M. Martin (middle grade fiction/YA).

How to Contact: Does not accept unsolicited mss. Agented submissions only. Responds in 6 months to submissions from SCBWI members and previously-published authors.

Terms: Pays royalty on retail price. Royalty and advance vary. Publishes ms 18 months after acceptance.

Advice: "Be a BIG reader of juvenile literature before you write and submit!"

SCRIBNER, An imprint of Simon & Schuster, 1230 Avenue of the Americas, New York NY 10020. (212)698-7000. Publishes hardcover originals. Averages 70-75 total titles/year.

Imprint(s): Rawson Associates; Lisa Drew Books.

Needs: Literary, mystery/suspense. Published *Accordion Crimes*, by E. Annie Proulx (novel, Pulitzer Prize-winning author); *Underworld*, by Don Delillo; and *Go Now*, by Richard Hell (novel).

How to Contact: *Agented fiction only.* Responds in 3 months to queries. Accepts simultaneous submissions.

Terms: Pays royalties of 7½-12½% on wholesale price. Advance varies. Publishes ms 9 months after acceptance.

SCRIVENERY PRESS, P.O. Box 740969-1003, Houston TX 77274-0969. (713)665-6760. Fax: (713)665-8838. E-mail: books@scrivenery.com. Website: www.scrivenery.com (includes writer's guidelines, catalog of books, sample chapters, interactive message boards, unique database of bookstores and more). **Contact:** Leila B. Joiner, editor (literary fiction); Chris Coleman, editor (mainstream and historical fiction). Estab. 1999. "As a newer publisher, we are actively seeking new mainstream/literary novels and collections for publication as trade paperback originals. As our backlist grows, we anticipate our requirements will become more stringent regarding unpublished wrtiers." Publishes hardcover and paperback originals and paperback reprints. Books: 60 lb. acid free paper; direct CTP printing; perfect bound; line art and gray scale illustrations. Average print order: 2,000. First novel print order: 1,000. **Published 3 new writers within the last year.** Plans 3 first novels in 2001. Averages 20 total titles, 10 fiction titles/year. Member: Publishers Marketing Association. Distributes all titles through Ingram Book Group, Ingram International and Baker & Taylor.

Needs: Experimental, historical (general, pre-WWII), literary, mainstream, mystery/suspense, short story collections, thriller/espionage, translations. "We need polished, literate work that could be construed as a crossover between genre and literary fiction." Short story anthology in planning for 2001/2002. Recently published *Good King Sauerkraut*, by Barbara Paul (mystery); *A Journey to the Interior*, by E.A. Blair (historical); and *Cleaning Up the Mess*, by Paul F. Ferguson (collection/literary).

How to Contact: Does not accept unsolicited mss. Query with outline/synopsis and 3 sample chapters. Include estimated word count, brief bio, list of publishing credits and genre/target market. Send SASE or IRC for return of ms or send disposable copy of ms and SASE for reply only. Agented fiction 50%. Responds in 2 months to queries; 3 months to mss. Accepts simultaneous submissions.

Terms: Pays royalties of 8½-15%. Average advance: seldom offered. Sends galleys to author. Publishes ms 6-12 months after acceptance. Writer's guidelines free for #10 SASE. Book catalogs for $2.

Advice: "Scrivenery Press is open to unpublished talent, but not writers new to the craft. Polish your manuscript as best you can; expect to be judged against seasoned pros. Submit material in industry-standard format, but be aware we will need electronic word processor files for the final manuscript. If you send us a simultaneous submission, please note that in your cover letter."

☑ ◯ ◎ ⚥ **SEAL PRESS**, 3131 Western Ave., Suite 410, Seattle WA 98121. Fax: (206)285-9410. E-mail: sealpress@sealpress.com. Website: www.sealpress.com. **Contact:** Faith Conlon, editor/publisher; Jennie Goode, managing editor. Estab. 1976. "Midsize independent feminist book publisher interested in original, lively, radical, empowering and culturally diverse books by women." Publishes hardcover and trade paperback originals. Books: 55 lb. natural paper; Cameron Belt, Web or offset printing; perfect binding; illustrations occasionally. Averages 6 total titles/year.
   • Seal has received numerous awards including Lambda Literary Awards for mysteries, humor and translation.
Needs: Ethnic, feminist, gay/lesbian, literary. Recently published *Bruised Hibiscus*, by Elizabeth Nunez (fiction).
How to Contact: Does not accept unsolicited mss. Query with outline/synopsis and 2 sample chapters. Send SASE or IRC for reply. Responds in 2 months to queries.
Terms: Pays royalties of 7-10% on retail price. Average advance: $500-2,000. Publishes ms 18 months after acceptance. Writer's guidelines and book catalog are free.

[N] ⊕ ☑ [A] **SECKER & WARBURG**, Random House, 20 Vauchall Bridge Rd., London SW1V 2SA England. Phone: 0207-8408400. Fax: 0207-2336117. Website: www.randomhouse.co.uk. **Contact:** Geoff Mulligan, editorial director; David Milner, editor. Estab. 1936. Publishes hardcover and paperback originals and reprints. First novel print order: 3,000. **Published 2 new writers within the last year.** Plans 1 first novel in 2001. Averages 20 total titles, 10 fiction titles/year. Member: PA. Distributes titles through Random House.
   • Secker & Warburg's illustrious publishing history includes 10 Nobel Prize winners and 6 Booker Prize winners among many other honors and achievements.
Needs: Literary, short story collections (rarely publishes). Recently published *Disgrace*, by J.M. Coetzee (literary); *Inishowen*, by J. O'Connor (literary); and *The Lightning Cage*, by Alan Wall (literary).
How to Contact: Does not accept unsolicited mss. *Submit through agent only.* Include estimated word count, brief bio and list of publishing credits. Agented fiction 99%. Responds in 1 month to queries; 2 months to mss. Accepts simultaneous submissions.
Terms: Pays in royalties and advance. Sends galleys to author. Publishes ms 10-12 months after acceptance. Book catalog free upon request or on website.

☑ ◑ ⚥ **SECOND CHANCE PRESS AND THE PERMANENT PRESS**, 4170 Noyac Rd., Sag Harbor NY 11963. (631)725-1101. Fax: (631)725-8215. E-mail: shepard@thepermanentpress.com. Website: www.thepermanentpress.com (includes titles, authors, descriptions of backlist and frontlist titles and an order form). **Contact:** Judith and Martin Shepard, publishers. Estab. 1977. Mid-size, independent publisher of literary fiction. Publishes hardcover originals and trade paperbacks. Average print order: 1,500-2,000. First novel print order: 1,500-2,000. **Published new writers within the last year.** Averages 12 fiction titles/year. Distributes titles through Ingram, Baker & Taylor and Brodart. Promotes titles through reviews.
   • Received a Literary Marketplace Award for Editorial Excellence and a Small Press Book Award for Best Gay/Lesbian Title for Elise O'Haene's *Licking Our Wounds*.
Needs: Contemporary, erotica, ethnic/multicultural, experimental, family saga, literary, mainstream. "We like novels with a unique point of view and a high quality of writing." No genre novels. Recently published *Whompy-jawed*, by Mitch Cullen (literary fiction); *Manifesto for the Dead*, by Domenic Stansberry (mystery); and *Bloodlines*, by Bruce Ducker (literary fiction).
How to Contact: Does not accept unsolicited mss. Query with outline and no more than 2 chapters. No queries by e-mail or fax. Send SASE or IRC for reply. Agented fiction 35%. Responds in 6 weeks to queries; 6 months to mss. Accepts simultaneous submissions.
Terms: Pays royalties of 10-20%. Average advance: $1,000. Sends galleys to author. Book catalog for $3.
Advice: "We are looking for good books, be they tenth novels or first ones, it makes little difference. The fiction is more important than the track record. Send us the beginning of the story, it's impossible to judge something that begins on page 302. Also, no outlines and very short synopsis—let the writing present itself."

◐ ◎ ▣ **SERENDIPITY SYSTEMS**, P.O. Box 140, San Simeon CA 93452. (805)927-5259. E-mail: bookware@thegrid.net. Website: www.s-e-r-e-n-d-i-p-i-t-y.com (includes guidelines, sample books, writer's manuscript help, catalog). **Contact:** John Galuszka, publisher. Estab. 1985. "Electronic publishing for IBM-PC compatible systems." Publishes "electronic editions originals and reprints." Books on disk. **Published new writers within the last year.** Averages 36 total titles, 15 fiction titles/year (either publish or distribute).
Imprint(s): Books-on-Disks™, Bookware™ and RocketEditions™.

Needs: "Works of fiction which use, or have the potential to use, hypertext, multimedia or other computer-enhanced features. We cannot use on-paper manuscripts." No romance, religion, New Age, children's, young adult, occult. Recently published *The Blue-Eyed Muse*, by John Peter (novel).

How to Contact: Query by e-mail. Submit complete ms with cover letter and SASE. *IBM-PC compatible disk required.* ASCII files required unless the work is hypertext or multimedia. Send SASE or IRC for return of ms or send disposable copy of ms and SASE for reply only. Responds in 2 weeks to queries; 1 month to mss. Often comments on rejected mss.

Terms: Pays royalties of 25%. Publishes ms 2 months after acceptance. Writer's guidelines on website.

Advice: "We are interested in seeing multimedia works suitable for Internet distribution. Would like to see: more works of serious literature—novels, short stories, plays, etc. Would like to not see: right wing adventure fantasies from 'Tom Clancy' wanna-be's."

✔ ⊘ ▼ **SEVEN STORIES PRESS,** 140 Watts St., New York NY 10013. (212)226-8760. Fax: (212)226-1411. E-mail: info@sevenstories.com. Website: www.sevenstories.com. **Contact:** Daniel Simon, Michael Manckin, Violaine Huysman, fiction editors. Estab. 1995. "Publishers of a distinguished list of authors in fine literature, journalism, contemporary culture and alternative health." Publishes hardcover and paperback originals and paperback reprints. Average print order: 5,000. **Published new writers within the last year.** Averages 20 total titles, 10 fiction titles/year.

- *Borrowed Hearts*, by Rick DeMarinis won the 2000 Independent Publisher Book Award for Short Story Fiction. *Parable of the Talents*, by Octavia E. Butler won the 2000 Nebula Award. *The Undiscovered Chekhov*, translated by Peter Constantine won the 1999 National Translation Award of the American Literary Translators Association (ALTA).

Needs: Literary. Plans anthologies. Ongoing series of short story collections from other cultures (e.g., *Contemporary Fiction from Central America*; from Vietnam, etc. Recently published *The Free Thinkers*, by Layle Silbert (novel); *So Vast the Prison*, by Assia Djebar; and *Borrowed Hearts*, by Rick DeMarinis (short stories).

How to Contact: Query with outline/synopsis and 1 sample chapter. Include list of publishing credits. Send SASE or IRC for reply. Agented fiction 60%. Responds in 1 month to queries; 4 months to mss. Accepts simultaneous submissions. Sometimes comments on rejected mss.

Payment/Terms: Pays standard royalty; offers advance. Sends galleys to author. Publishes ms 1-2 years after acceptance. Free book catalog.

Advice: "Writers should only send us their work after they have read some of the books we publish and find our editorial vision in sync with theirs."

✔ ○ ⊚ ▼ **SILHOUETTE BOOKS,** Harlequin Enterprises, 300 E. 42nd St., 6th Floor, New York NY 10017. (212)682-6080. Fax: (212)682-4539. Website: www.eHarlequin.com (includes guidelines, features regarding romance, book catalog, author interviews and features of interest to women). **Contact:** Mary-Theresa Hussey, senior editor (Silhouette Romance); Joan Marlow Golan, senior editor (Silhouette Desire); Karen Taylor Richman, senior editor (Silhouette Special Edition); Leslie Wainger, executive senior editor (Silhouette Intimate Moments); Tracy Farrell, senior editor/editorial coordinator (Harlequin Historicals). Estab. 1980. International publisher of category romance. Publishes paperback originals. **Published 10-20 new writers within the last year.** Averages 350-400 fiction titles/year.

Imprint(s): Silhouette Romance, Silhouette Special Edition, Silhouette Desire, Silhouette Intimate Moments, Harlequin Historicals.

- Titles by Silhouette Books have received numerous awards from *Romantic Times*, the Rita Award from Romance Writers of America and best selling awards from national bookstores.

Needs: Romance (contemporary, futuristic/time travel, historical, romantic suspense). Published *Callaghan's Bride*, by Diana Palmer (SR); *Rio: Man of Destiny*, by Cait London (SD); and *The Perfect Neighbor*, by Nora Roberts (SSE).

How to Contact: Does not accept unsolicited mss. Query with brief synopsis. Accepts queries by fax. Include estimated word count, brief bio and list of published credits. Send SASE or IRC for return of ms. Responds in 3 months to queries and mss. Sometimes comments on rejected mss.

Terms: Pays in royalties; offers advance (negotiated on an individual basis). Must return advance if book is not completed or is unacceptable. Sends galleys to author. Publishes ms 3 years after acceptance. Writer's guidelines for SASE.

Advice: "Study the market. Category Romance is a dynamic, ever-changing market with a readership who expect quality, imagination and a love of the genre from their writers."

Ⓝ ⊘ ⊚ **SILVER DAGGER MYSTERIES,** The Overmountain Press, P.O. Box 1261, Johnson City TN 37605. (423)926-2691. Fax: (423)929-2464. E-mail: bethw@overmtn.com. Website: www.silverdaggerstore.com (includes submission guidelines, book catalog, author bios, newsletter). **Contact:** Alex Foster, acquisitions editor (mystery). Estab. 1999. "Small imprint of a larger company. We publish Southern mysteries. Our house is unique in that we are a consortium of authors who communicate and work together to promote each other." Publishes hardcover and paperback originals and reprints. Books: 60 lb. offset paper; perfect/case binding. Average print order: 2,000-5,000; first novel print order: 2,000. **Published 3 new writers within the last year.** Plans 6 first novels in 2001. Averages 15 fiction titles/year. Member: PAS. Distributes titles through direct mail, Ingram, Partners, trade shows.

Needs: Mystery/suspense (amateur sleuth, cozy, police procedural, private eye/hardboiled), young adult/teen (mystery/suspense). Publishes *Magnolias & Mayhem,* an anthology of Southern short mysteries. Submissions "closed—editor solicits prior to contract signing." Recently published *Midnight Hour,* by Mary Saums (mystery); *In the Spirit of Murder,* by Laura Belgrave (mystery); and *A Whiff of Garlic,* by David Hunter (mystery).

How to Contact: Does not accept or return unsolicited mss. Query with outline/synopsis and first 3 chapters. Accepts queries by e-mail. Include estimated word count, brief bio and list of publishing credits. Send SASE or IRC for return of ms. Agented fiction 30%. Responds in 1 month to queries; 3 months to mss.

Terms: Pays royalties of 15%. Sends galleys to author. Publishes ms 1 year after acceptance. Writer's guidelines and book catalogs on website.

Advice: "We tend to be very author friendly from editing to promotion. Make sure your book is 'Southern' or set in the South before taking the time to submit."

SIMON & SCHUSTER, 1230 Avenue of the Americas, New York NY 10020. Website: www.simonsays.com. *Adult Trade:* Simon & Schuster Trade (Fireside, The Free Press, Kaplan, **Scribner** [Lisa Drew, Rawson Associates, Scribner], Simon & Schuster, Touchstone, Scribner Paperback Fiction); *Simon & Schuster Children's Publishing* (Aladdin Paperbacks, **Atheneum Books for Young Readers, Margaret K. McElderry Books**), Nickelodeon, Simon Spotlight [**Little Simon**], **Simon & Schuster Books for Young Readers,** Simon & Schuster New Media; *Mass Market:* **Pocket Books** (Pocket Books for Young Adults [**Archway Paperbacks, Minstrel Books,** Pocket Books for Young Adults Pocket Pulse], MTV Books, Nickelodeon, *Star Trek,* Washington Square Press, Pocket Pulse).

✓ ⊘ ♈ SIMON & SCHUSTER BOOKS FOR YOUNG READERS, Subsidiary of Simon & Schuster Children's Publishing Division, 1230 Avenue of the Americas, New York NY 10020. (212)698-2851. Fax: (212)698-2796. Website: www.simonsayskids.com. **Contact:** Stephen Geck, vice president/associate publisher; David Gale, editorial director; Kevin Lewis, senior editor; Jessica Schulte, editor; Amy Hampton-Knight, associate editor. "We're looking for complex, challenging YA novels and middle-grade fiction with a fresh, unique slant." Publishes hardcover originals. **Published 3 new writers within the last year.** Plans 4 first novels in 2001. Averages 80 total titles, 20 fiction titles/year. Promotes titles through trade magazines, conventions and catalog.

● Books from Simon & Schuster Books for Young Readers have received the following awards: 2000 Michael L. Printz Honor Award for *Hard Love*; 1999 Coretta Scott King Author Award and ALA Best Book for Young Adults for *Heaven*, by Angela Johnson.

Needs: Children's/juvenile, young adult/teen (adventure, historical, mystery, contemporary fiction). No problem novels. No anthropomorphic characters. Publishes anthologies; editor solicits from established writers. Recently published *The Janitor's Boy,* by Andrew Clements (middle-grade fiction); *The Raging Quiet,* by Sheryl Jordan (young adult fiction); and *Hard Love,* by Ellen Wittlinger (young adult fiction).

How to Contact: *Does not accept unsolicited mss.* Send query letter and SASE. Agented fiction 90%. Responds in 2 months to queries. Accepts simultaneous submissions.

Terms: Pays royalties. Offers negotiable advance. Sends galleys to author. Publishes ms within 2 years of acceptance. Writer's guidelines for #10 SASE. Book catalog available in libraries.

Advice: "Study our catalog and read books we have published to get an idea of our list. The fiction market is crowded and writers need a strong, fresh, original voice to stand out."

⊞ SKYLARK, Bantam, Doubleday, Dell/Delacorte, Knopf and Crown Books for Young Readers, Random House Children's Books, A Division of Random House, Inc., 1540 Broadway, New York NY 10036. (212)782-9000 or (800)200-3552. Website: www.randomhouse.com/kids.

● See listing for Bantam, Doubleday, Dell/Delacorte, Knopf and Crown Books for Young Readers, page 394.

✓ ⊘ ◎ ♈ GIBBS SMITH, PUBLISHER/PEREGRINE SMITH, P.O. Box 667, Layton UT 84041. (801)544-9800. Fax: (801)544-5582. Website: www.gibbs~smith.com/. **Contact:** Gail Yngve, editor (poetry); Suzanne Taylor, senior editor; Madge Baird, editorial director (humor). Estab. 1969. Small independent press. "We publish books that make a difference." Publishes hardcover and paperback originals and reprints. Averages 40-60 total titles, 1-2 fiction titles/year.

● Gibbs Smith is the recipient of a Western Writers Association Fiction Award. Publishes the winner of the Peregrine Smith Poetry Contest (accepts entries only in April).

Needs: Only short works oriented to gift market. Publishes *The Peregrine Reader,* a series of anthologies based upon a variety of themes. Recently published *The Lesson,* by Carol Lynn Pearson.

How to Contact: Send query letter or short gift book ms directly to the editor. Send SASE or IRC for return of the ms. Responds in 1 month to queries; 4 months to mss. Accepts simultaneous submissions. Sometimes comments on rejected mss.

Terms: Pays royalty depending on the book. Provides 10 author's copies. Sends galleys to author. Publishes ms 1-2 years after acceptance. Writer's guidelines and book catalog for #10 SASE.

N̄: ◯ ◎ SOFT SKULL PRESS INC., 100 Suffolk St., Basement, New York NY 10002. (212)673-2502. Fax: (212)673-0787. E-mail: nick@softskull.com. Website: www.softskull.com. **Contact:** Sander Hicks, publisher; Nick Mamatas, senior editor. Estab. 1992. "A small press combining the ferocity of the zine scene, the power of punk and the speed of the modern copy shop. Especially interested in authors under 35." Publishes hardcover and paperback originals. Books; 55 lb. paper; offset printing, cloth/paperback binding; illustrations. Average print order: 3,000; first novel print order: 3,000. **Published 8 new writers within the last year.** Plans 2 first novels in 2001. Averages 12 total titles, 6 fiction titles/year. Member: SPAN, PMA, Small Press Center and Union of Progressive Presses. Distributes titles through PGW.

Needs: Experimental, gay, humor/satire, lesbian, literary, science fiction (experimental). "We are inundated with 'drug and rock & roll' novels. We love left-of-center political material." Publishes *What the Fuck: The Avant Porn Anthology*. Recently published *Outline Of My Lover*, by Douglas A. Martin (gay/experimental); *Ripe Tomatoes*, by Nora Ruth Roberts (political satire); and *Document Zippo*, by L.A. Ruocco (experimental).

How to Contact: Accepts unsolicited mss. Query with 3-page outline only. "Nick Mamatas accepts e-mail queries—Sander Hicks does *not*. Firm. See submission guidelines on our website." Include estimated word count. Send SASE or IRC for return of ms or send disposable copy of ms and SASE for reply only. Agented fiction 30%. Responds in 1 month to queries; 3 months to mss. Accepts simultaneous submissions.

Terms: Pays royalties of 7-9%. Average advance: $100-15,000. Sends galleys to author. Publishes ms 1 year after acceptance. Writer's guidelines free for SASE. Book catalogs free or on website.

Advice: "Make the commonplace extraordinary. Don't be afraid to be political, even radical. Know our list before submitting. We are interested in challenging and aggressive literature. No mainstream genre material, but cutting edge books that thwart genre expectations can be cool. We are moving away from 'drug and rock' novels. We may start looking at experimental or New Wave science fiction, urban fantasy, absurdist stuff."

◖ SOHO PRESS, 853 Broadway, New York NY 10003. (212)260-1900. Website: www.sohopress.com. **Contact:** Juris Jurjevics, Laura M.C. Hruska and Melanie Fleishman, editors. Publishes hardcover originals and trade paperback reprints. **Published 7-10 new writers within the last year.** Averages 40 titles/year. Distributes titles through Farrar, Straus & Giroux. Promotes titles through readings, tours, print ads, reviews, interviews, advance reading copies, postcards and brochures.

Imprint(s): Soho Crime, edited by Laura Hruska, Juris Jurjevics and Melanie Fleishman (mystery).

Needs: Ethnic, literary, mystery (procedural), suspense. "We do novels that are the very best of their kind." Recently published *The Farming of Bones*, by Edwidge Danticat; *The Gravity of Sunlight*, by Rosa Shand; and *Murder in the Marais*, by Cara Black.

How to Contact: Query with SASE or IRC. Responds in 1 month to queries; 6 weeks to mss. Accepts simultaneous submissions.

Terms: Pays royalties of 10-15% on retail price. For trade paperbacks pays 7½%. Offers advance. Publishes ms 10 months after acceptance. Book catalog for SASE plus $1.

Advice: Greatest challenge is "introducing brand new, untested writers. We do not care if they are agented or not. Half the books we publish come directly from authors. We look for a distinctive writing style, strong writing skills and compelling plots. We are not interested in trite expression of mass market formulae."

☑ ◖ SOUNDPRINTS, Division of Trudy Corporation, 353 Main Ave., Norwalk CT 06851-1552. Fax: (203)846-1776. E-mail: sndprnts@ix.netcom.com. Website: www.soundprints.com. **Contact:** Chelsea Shriver, editorial assistant. Publishes hardcover originals. **Published 4 new writers within the last year.** Averages 20 titles/year.

Needs: Juvenile.

How to Contact: Send query letter. Responds in 3 months to queries. Accepts simultaneous submissions.

Terms: Makes outright purchase. No advance. Publishes ms 2 years after acceptance. Writer's guidelines for #10 SASE; book catalog for 9 × 12 SAE with $1.33 postage.

Advice: "Our books are written for children from ages 4-8. Our most successful authors can craft a wonderful story which is derived from authentic wildlife facts. First inquiry to us should ask about our interest in publishing a book about a specific animal or habitat. When we publish juvenile fiction, it will be about wildlife and all information in the book *must* be accurate."

☑ ◖ SOUTHERN METHODIST UNIVERSITY PRESS, P.O. Box 750415, Dallas TX 75275-0415. (214)768-1433 (acquisitions). Fax: (214)768-1428. **Contact:** Kathryn M. Lang, senior editor. Estab. 1936. "Small university press publishing in areas of film/theater, Southwest life and letters, religion/medical ethics and contemporary fiction." Publishes hardcover and paperback originals and reprints. Books: acid-free paper; perfect-bound;

some illustrations. Average print order: 2,000. **Published 2 new writers within the last year.** Averages 10-12 total titles, 3-4 fiction titles/year. Distributes titles through Texas A&M University Press Consortium. Promotes titles through writers' publications.

Needs: Literary novels and story collections. "We are always willing to look at 'serious' or 'literary' fiction." No "mass market, science fiction, formula, thriller, romance." Published *One Day's Perfect Weather*, by Dan Stern (short stories); *Champeen*, by Heather Ross Miller (novel); and *The Rules of the Lake*, by Irene Ziegler (short stories).

How to Contact: Accepts unsolicited mss. Query with outline/synopsis and 3 sample chapters. Send SASE or IRC for return of ms. Responds in 3 weeks to queries; up to 1 year to mss. Sometimes comments on rejected mss.

Terms: Pays royalties of 10% net, negotiable small advance, 10 author's copies. Publishes ms 1 year after acceptance. Book catalog free.

Advice: "We view encouraging first-time authors as part of the mission of a university press. Send query describing the project and your own background. Research the press before you submit—don't send us the kinds of things we don't publish." Looks for "quality fiction from new or established writers."

✔ ◑ ◎ ▼ SPECTRA BOOKS, Subsidiary of Random House, Inc., 1540 Broadway, New York NY 10036. (212)782-8771. Fax: (212)782-9523. Website: www.bantamdell.com. **Contact:** Anne Lesley Groell, senior editor; Michael Shohl, editor. Estab. 1985. Large science fiction, fantasy and speculative fiction line. Publishes hardcover originals, paperback originals and trade paperbacks. Averages 60 fiction titles/year.

● Many Bantam Spectra Books have received Hugos and Nebulas.

Needs: Fantasy, literary, science fiction. Needs include novels that attempt to broaden the traditional range of science fiction and fantasy. Strong emphasis on characterization. Especially well written traditional science fiction and fantasy will be considered. No fiction that doesn't have at least some element of speculation or the fantastic. Published *A Clash of Kings*, by George R. Martin (medieval fantasy); *Ship of Magic*, by Robin Hobb (coming of age fantasy); and *Antarctica*, by Stanley Robinson (science fiction).

How to Contact: Query with 3 chapters and a short (no more than 3 pages double-spaced) synopsis. Send SASE or IRC for return of ms. Agented fiction 90%. Responds in 6 months. Accepts simultaneous submissions if noted.

Terms: Pays in royalties; negotiable advance. Sends galleys to author. Writer's guidelines for #10 SASE.

Advice: "Please follow our guidelines carefully and type neatly."

✔ ◑ ◎ ▼ SPINSTERS INK, 32 E. First St., #330, Duluth MN 55802-2002. (218)727-3222. Fax: (218)727-3119. E-mail: spinsters@aol.com. Website: www.lesbian.org/spinsters-ink (includes online catalog, writer's guidelines, staff list, chat rooms, excerpts from books, discussion forums). **Contact:** Nancy Walker. Estab. 1978. Moderate-size women's publishing company growing steadily. "We are committed to publishing works by women writing from the periphery: fat women, Jewish women, lesbians, poor women, rural women, women of color, etc." Publishes paperback originals and reprints. Books: 55 lb. acid-free natural paper; photo offset printing; perfect-bound; illustrations when appropriate. Average print order: 5,000. **Published new writers within the last year.** Plans 2 first novels in 2001. Averages 6 total titles, 3-5 fiction titles/year. Distributes titles through Words Distributing and all wholesalers. Promotes titles through Women's Review of Books, Feminist Bookstore News, regional advertising, author interviews and reviews.

● Spinsters Ink won the 2000 PMA Benjamin Franklin Award for *Maid Order Catalog*.

Needs: Feminist, lesbian. Wants "full-length quality fiction—thoroughly revised novels which display deep characterization, theme and style. We *only* consider books by women. No books by men, or books with sexist, racist or ageist content." Published *Silent Words*, by Joan Drury (feminist mystery); *The Activist's Daughter*, by Ellyn Bache (feminist); and *Living at Night*, by Mariana Romo-Carmona (lesbian). Publishes anthologies. Writers may submit directly.

How to Contact: Send query letter or submit outline/synopsis and 2-5 sample chapters (not to exceed 50 pages) with SASE. Responds in 1 month to queries; 3 months to mss. Accepts simultaneous submissions. Prefers hard copy submission. Occasionally comments on rejected mss.

Terms: Pays royalties of 7-10%, plus 10 author's copies; unlimited extra copies at 40% discount. Publishes ms 18 months after acceptance. Free book catalog.

Advice: "In the past, lesbian fiction has been largely 'escape fiction' with sex and romance as the only required ingredients; however, we encourage more complex work that treats the lesbian lifestyle with the honesty it deserves. Look at our catalog and mission statement. Does your book fit our criteria?"

◪ STARBURST PUBLISHERS, P.O. Box 4123, Lancaster PA 17604. (717)293-0939. Fax: (717)293-1945. E-mail: starburst@starburstpublishers.com. Website: www.starburstpublishers.com (includes writer's guidelines, authors, titles, editorial information, catalog, rights, distribution, etc.). **Contact:** David A. Robie, editorial director. Estab. 1982. Midsize independent press specializing in inspirational and self-help books. Publishes trade paperback and hardcover originals and trade paperback reprints. **Published new writers within the last year.** Averages 10-15 total titles/year. Distributes titles through all major distributors and sales reps. Promotes titles through print, radio, and major distributors.

Needs: Religious/inspirational: Adventure, contemporary, fantasy, historical, horror, military/war, psychic/supernatural/occult, romance (contemporary, historical), spiritual, suspense/mystery, western. Wants "inspirational material." Published *The Fragile Thread*, by Aliske Webb; and *The Miracle of the Sacred Scroll*, by Johan Christian.

How to Contact: Does not accept unsolicited mss. Query with outline/synopsis and 3 sample chapters. Accepts queries by e-mail. Include bio. Send SASE or IRC for return of ms. Agented fiction less than 25%. Responds in 1 month to queries; 2 months to manuscripts. Accepts electronic submissions via disk and modem, "but also wants clean double-spaced typewritten or computer printout manuscript."

Terms: Pays royalties of 6-16%. "Individual arrangement with writer depending on the manuscript as well as writer's experience as a published author." Publishes ms up to one year after acceptance. Writer's guidelines for #10 SASE. Book catalog for 9 × 12 SAE and 4 first-class stamps.

Advice: "50% of our line goes into the inspirational marketplace; 50% into the general marketplace. We are one of the few publishers that has direct sales representation into both the inspirational and general marketplace."

STARFIRE, Bantam, Doubleday, Dell/Delacorte, Knopf and Crown Books for Young Readers, Random House Children's Books, A Division of Random House, Inc., 1540 Broadway, New York NY 10036. (212)782-9000 or (800)200-3552. Website: www.randomhouse.com/kids.
● See listing for Bantam, Doubleday, Dell/Delacorte, Knopf and Crown Books for Young Readers, page 394.

STEEPLE HILL, Harlequin Enterprises, 300 E. 42nd Street, 6th Floor, New York NY 10017. Website: www.harlequin.com. Editorial Director: Tara Gavin. Senior Editor: Tracy Farrell. **Contact:** Ann Leslie Tuttle, Patience Smith, Karen Kosztolnyik, acquisitions editors; and all Silhouette/Harlequin Historicals editors. Estab. 1997. Publishes mass market paperback originals.

Imprint(s): Love Inspired.

Needs: Christian romance. Recently published *A Mother at Heart*, by Carolyne Aarsen.

How to Contact: Does not accept unsolicited mss. Send query letter or submit synopsis and 3 sample chapters. Send SASE or IRC for reply.

Terms: Pays royalty. Writer's guidelines for #10 SASE.

Advice: "Drama, humor and even a touch of mystery all have a place in this series. Subplots are welcome and should further the story's main focus or intertwine in a meaningful way. Secondary characters (children, family, friends, neighbors, fellow church members, etc.) may all contribute to a substantial and satisfying story. These wholesome tales of romance include strong family values and high moral standards. While there is no premarital sex between characters, a vivid, exciting romance that is presented with a mature perspective, is essential. Although the element of faith must clearly be present, it should be well integrated into the characterizations and plot. The conflict between the main characters should be an emotional one, arising naturally from the well-developed personalities you've created. Suitable stories should also impart an important lesson about the powers of trust and faith."

STONE BRIDGE PRESS, P.O. Box 8208, Berkeley CA 94707. (510)524-8732. Fax: (510)524-8711. E-mail: sbp@stonebridge.com. Website: www.stonebridge.com (includes complete catalog, contact information, related features, submission guidelines and excerpts). **Contact:** Peter Goodman, publisher. Estab. 1989. "Independent press focusing on books about Japan in English (business, language, culture, literature, animation)." Publishes paperback originals and reprints. Books: 60-70 lb. offset paper; web and sheet paper; perfect-bound; some illustrations. Averages 6 total titles, 2 fiction titles/year. Distributes titles through Consortium. Promotes titles through Internet announcements, special-interest magazines and niche tie-ins to associations.

Imprint(s): Rock Spring Collection of Japanese Literature, edited by Peter Goodman.
● Stone Bridge Press received a Japan-U.S. Friendship Prize for *Ravine and Other Stories*, by Yoshikichi Furni.

Needs: Japan-themed. No poetry. "Primarily looking at material relating to Japan. Mostly translations, but we'd like to see samples of work dealing with the expatriate experience." Also Asian- and Japanese-American.

How to Contact: Accepts unsolicited mss. Query with 1-page cover letter, outline/synopsis and 3 sample chapters. Accepts queries by e-mail and fax. Send SASE or IRC for return of the ms. Agented fiction 25%. Responds in 1 month to queries; up to 8 months to mss. Accepts simultaneous submissions. Sometimes comments on rejected ms.

Terms: Pays royalties, offers negotiable advance. Publishes ms 18-24 months after acceptance. Catalog for 1 first-class stamp.

Advice: "As we focus on Japan-related material there is no point in approaching us unless you are very familiar with Japan. We'd especially like to see submissions dealing with the expatriate experience. Please, absolutely no commercial fiction."

◖ **STONEWALL INN**, Imprint of St. Martin's Press, 175 Fifth Ave., New York NY 10010. (212)674-5151. Website: www.stonewallinn.com. **Contact:** Keith Kahla, general editor. "Stonewall Inn is the only gay and lesbian focused imprint at a major house . . . and is more inclusive of gay men than most small presses." Publishes trade paperback originals and reprints. Averages 20-23 titles/year. **Published new writers within the last year.**
Needs: Gay, lesbian, literary, mystery. Recently published *The Coming Storm*, by Paul Russell; and *Out of the Ordinary*, by Noelle Howey and Ellen Samuels.
How to Contact: Query with SASE. Responds in 6 months to queries. Accepts simultaneous submissions.
Terms: Pays standard royalty on retail price. Average advance: $5,000 (for first-time authors). Publishes ms 1 year after acceptance. Book catalog free.
Advice: "Anybody who has any question about what a gay novel is should go out and read half a dozen. For example, there are hundreds of 'coming out' novels in print."

◎ ☑ **SUNSTONE PRESS**, P.O. Box 2321, Santa Fe NM 87504-2321. (505)988-4418. **Contact:** James C. Smith, Jr. Estab. 1971. Midsize publisher. Publishes hardcover and paperback originals. First novel print order: 2,000. **Published new writers within the last year.** Plans 2 first novels in 2001. Averages 16 total titles, 2-3 fiction titles/year.
  ● Sunstone Press published *Ninez*, by Virginia Nylander Ebinger which received the Southwest Book Award from the Border Regional Library Association.
Needs: Western. "We have a Southwestern theme emphasis. Sometimes buy juvenile mss with illustrations." No science fiction, romance or occult. Published *Apache: The Long Ride Home*, by Grant Gall (Indian/Western); *Sorrel*, by Rita Cleary; and *To Die in Dinetah*, by John Truitt.
How to Contact: Accepts unsolicited mss. Query first or submit outline/synopsis and 2 sample chapters with SASE. Responds in 2 weeks. Accepts simultaneous submissions.
Terms: Pays royalties of 10% maximum and 10 author's copies. Publishes ms 9-12 months after acceptance.

◙ ◙ **TAB BOOK CLUB, (TEEN AGE BOOK CLUB)**, Scholastic Inc., 555 Broadway, New York NY 10012. **Contact:** Greg Holch, senior editor.
Needs: "TAB Book Club publishes novels for young teenagers in seventh through ninth grades. At the present time these novels are all reprints from Scholastic's trade division or from other publishers. The Tab Book Club is not currently publishing original novels."
How to Contact: "We are not looking at new manuscripts this year."
Advice: "The books we are publishing now are literary works that we hope will become the classics of the future. They are novels that reveal the hearts and souls of their authors."

☑ ◙ Ⓐ **NAN A. TALESE**, The Doubleday Broadway Publishing Group, A Division of Random House, Inc., 1540 Broadway, New York NY 10036. (212)782-8918. Fax: (212)782-9261. Website: www.nanatalese.com. **Contact:** Nan A. Talese, editorial director. "Nan A. Talese publishes nonfiction with a powerful guiding narrative and relevance to larger cultural trends and interests, and literary fiction of the highest quality." Publishes hardcover originals. Averages 15 titles/year.
Needs: Literary. Published *Alias Grace*, by Margaret Atwood (novel); *Desire of Everlasting Hills*, by Thomas Cahill; *Amsterdam*, by Ian McEwan; and *Great Shame*, by Thomas Keneally.
How to Contact: Agented fiction only. Responds in 1 week to queries; 1 month to mss. Accepts simultaneous submissions.
Terms: Pays royalty on retail price, varies. Advance varies. Publishes ms 8 months after acceptance.
Advice: "We're interested in literary narrative, fiction and nonfiction—we do not publish genre fiction. Our readers are highly literate people interested in good story-telling, intellectual and psychologically significant. We want well-written material."

☑ ◙ ☑ **TEXAS CHRISTIAN UNIVERSITY PRESS**, P.O. Box 298300, TCU, Fort Worth TX 76129. (817)257-7822. Fax: (817)257-5075. E-mail: tcupress@tcu.edu. Website: www.prs.tcu.edu/prs/ (includes staff, awards, authors' guidelines, catalog, ordering general info and newsletter). Director: Judy Alter. **Contact:** James Ward Lee, acquisitions consultant. Estab. 1966. Texas Christian publishes "scholarly monographs, other serious scholarly work and regional titles of significance focusing on the history and literature of the American West." Publishes hardcover originals, some reprints. **Published new writers within the last year.** Averages 15 titles/ year. Distributes titles through consortium headquarted at Texas A&M. Promotes titles through catalog, reviews and some paid advertising.
  ● Texas Christian University Press won the Texas Institute of Letters design award.
Needs: Regional fiction. Recently published *Auslander*, by Mary Powell (regional); *Memorial Day and Other Stories*, by Paul Scott Malone; and *Snake Mountain*, by Jerry Craven (regional).
How to Contact: Considers mss by invitation only. Please do not query. Responds in 3 months.
Terms: Pays royalties of 10% on net price. Publishes ms 16 months after acceptance.
Advice: "Regional and/or Texana nonfiction or fiction have best chance of breaking into our firm."

Jennifer Egan: Painstaking revisions, attention to detail pay off

Jennifer Egan didn't plan on becoming a writer. "I actually wanted to be a doctor, and I was convinced I would be," Egan says. "But at a certain point I got very squeamish, and suddenly the whole doctor thing just didn't quite appeal to me in the way it had." Egan's next plan was to become an archaeologist, but when she was eighteen, she changed her mind a final time. "I took a year off between high school and college and sort of rambled around and went to Europe. I think it was then I realized how crucial writing was to my relationship to the world. I wrote frenetically in this journal I had, and somehow it became clear to me that writing was the thing that gave the world order and meaning for me, and I would have to pursue it completely in my life."

Egan considers her first writing attempts as less than successful. "I began with short stories, and I had an idea for a novel at the end of college, and I tried to write it. I just didn't really understand the basic craft of writing. It was an 800-page book, lacking drama or characters. When I moved to New York and started sending this around, I quickly discovered it was not the masterpiece I had hoped."

Unsure what to do with her novel, Egan set it aside, joined a writing group and went back to writing short stories. "In a way, the stories became smaller canvases on which to work out technical problems, and I began to improve in my story writing. After a year of that, I re-read the novel, and then I knew myself what was wrong. I thought I would let the whole thing go and try something totally different, but I found the idea—of the two sisters and the journey and the 60s and 70s—still really haunted me. So I decided to start from scratch and take another attempt."

The result of that attempt was Egan's first novel, *The Invisible Circus* (Nan A. Talese/Doubleday, 1995), which prompted critics to hail her as "a writer of tremendous elegance and grace" (*The Philadelphia Enquirer*) and "a generous, gifted and spellbinding writer" (*Booklist*). Before that novel was published, Egan had her first short story publication in *The New Yorker*, and has followed up with stories appearing in *GQ*, *Ploughshares* and *The New York Times Magazine*. The film version of *The Invisible Circus*, starring Cameron Diaz, is scheduled for release in January 2001. And Egan's most recent publication, a collection of short stories titled *Emerald City: Stories* (Picador USA, 1997), did not disappoint critics' high expectations.

Egan credits writing groups for giving her valuable feedback on her stories, but makes special mention of the first group she worked with. "The real emphasis in that group was getting at raw emotional material. I think that was helpful for me, because there was *no* raw emotional material in the novel or stories I had written." She describes the process as "scraping away so you would get to the deeper feelings, with particular emphasis on emotional truth. Without that, you don't have much, even with all the technique in the world. Something that is written beautifully and leaves you cold is not much fun to read. That was the first lesson I learned: What is the story, why does it matter, and to whom?" Knowing the importance of feedback, Egan has since taken other workshops and still has informal groups of peers read her work.

Another lesson Egan learned and now teaches to her students at Columbia University is the importance of creating complex characters. "You can afford to work against the things you've established in a character when you're writing," Egan says. "There's a tendency to think, 'This person wouldn't do that!' Well, what if they *would* do that? What if that's the amazing thing? If they do it and it makes no sense at all, and yet somehow, that feels right?" She describes such a character named Wolf in *The Invisible Circus* whose complexities took her a long time to work out. "He has to do a lot of things," Egan explains. "He gets involved with this young girl, he's hiding important information, and yet I've always really liked him in my mind, although on the page he was often a very unlikable character!"

Unlike many writers, Egan never bases a character on people she knows. "I absolutely invent them out of thin air," she says. "And if they remind me of someone I know, that is usually a detriment—I will have to overcome that in trying to make the character work."

While noting the importance of her characters to the story, Egan is quick to add they arrive only after she has chosen a setting. "I tend to begin with a place and a time, some kind of atmosphere, and the characters grow out of that. It's like I make the appointment and the guests show up." Once Egan has intuitively found her characters, she maintains it still takes time to straighten out the wrinkles. "I spend hours and hours agonizing over how to make people work better as characters, so there's plenty of sweat and agony," she says.

Once she has an idea of a time and place, Egan begins the writing process with only a vague outline. "In a way, writing is not unlike reading for me," Egan says. "As I'm doing it the first time, I actually don't know what will happen or who will appear or anything. If I see all the way to the end and it's very clear to me, I don't want to write it. It seems boring because I don't feel I will discover anything in the process. Now, obviously this has many pitfalls, because you take a lot of wrong turns," Egan says, explaining how a wrong turn can take a hundred pages before she realizes she's off course.

After completing the original draft in longhand, Egan types it into the computer and then begins her meticulous revision process, beginning with detailed outlines. "The first one I had for the second draft of this book was about seventy-five pages, single-spaced," Egan says. "I have these long lists of things I need to do, like checklists, and also lots of cogitation about the overall goal of the chapter in the context of the book."

After a year of revisions, she reads the entire manuscript through. "It's usually a horrific experience," Egan says. "I see all the things that are still wrong and need change, and I try to understand the book a little better than I did before."

Currently working on the sixth draft of her new book, Egan says, "I have as many as thirty drafts of some chapters. I number them to keep track. Sometimes I'll feel I've drifted some-where I didn't want to be, and it's helpful to have the drafts numbered so I can go back and find earlier drafts and see if there really is something there I need."

Egan says she wrote the first draft by hand in three or four months, but has continued to revise it for five years. "I write very quickly, which you would never know from my output," she says of her painstakingly thorough revision process. Yet inevitably, with each draft, Egan's checklists get shorter. "I'm doing one more little re-write of it now, and this outline is ten pages," Egan says with obvious relief. "So it has this feeling of tracing smaller and smaller circles around something until finally I've really got it in my sights. But it's a mysterious and disorderly process for me."

Nevertheless, Egan's tenacity sees her through to the completed project. "Some days I'm at my desk all day, but at a minimum, three or four hours in the morning. I think it's very hard to perpetuate a writing career if you aren't pretty self-disciplined. If you really look at which careers are thriving and moving forward, it's the people who just keep doing it again and again."

Once Egan feels the manuscript is finished, she says she's ready to let go of it and move on to the next project. In fact, Egan didn't even want to be a part of the adaptation process when *The Invisible Circus* was optioned for a screenplay. "Creatively, I had nothing to do with it at all," Egan says, grateful she had an agent to handle the negotiations.

Egan thinks of her book and the movie as two separate visions. "I don't feel proprietary about the characters," Egan explains, unconcerned by any identity makeovers they could undergo in the movie's version of them. "I think if you're going to sell an option on your book, and you don't have control over the movie, you better get used to the idea that it has nothing to do with you—or potentially, with your book. You just can't control everything, much as I might like to."

Dealing with publishers directly is another thing Egan prefers not to handle. Instead, she opts to use an agent to sell her books. "Your agent is really acting as your lawyer in that situation, and you have a contract you will need to sign with the publisher," notes Egan. "In my case, I didn't know a thing about any of that, so I really did need an agent."

Egan acknowledges choosing an agent can be a tricky ordeal. "Because I had published some stories, I talked to a few agents, and I just picked one. It was kind of like picking a college," Egan admits with a laugh. "You want someone who has enough of a reputation and respect to get their phone calls returned, and then you try to find someone who responds to your work. But in the end, the decision feels a tiny bit arbitrary. There are a large number of agents in New York respected enough to get their clients' work out there, and that's all the client can ask of an agent. They can't make the work better than it is. That's up to the writer."

Short stories are another matter. "If you've published one or two, you can probably get the stories read even if you just send them out yourself," Egan says. "Getting the first one or two published is hard, but people do it." While novels are the projects Egan has the most passion for, she continues to write stories. "There aren't many places to sell them and it is hard to publish them, but I really like doing it," she says.

As for the current book she's working on, Egan keeps a tight lip on the details but lets slip a few clues. "It's extremely different in every respect from anything I've done before, and I'm proud of that. It's ambitious and complicated, and it's definitely longer—which may not be so good!" Egan jokes. "It's more than one story intertwined; that automatically creates a certain textured quality that wasn't the case in a more straight-forward story like *The Invisible Circus*. Will I pull it off? I don't know. I'm keeping my fingers crossed."

—*Rachel Vater*

✓ ◯ ◎ **TIDEWATER PUBLISHERS,** Imprint of Cornell Maritime Press, Inc., P.O. Box 456, Centreville MD 21617-0456. (410)758-1075. Fax: (410)758-6849. E-mail: cornell@crosslink.net. **Contact:** Charlotte Kurst, managing editor. Estab. 1938. "Tidewater Publishers issues adult nonfiction works related to the Chesapeake Bay area, Delmarva or Maryland in general. The only fiction we handle is juvenile and must have a regional focus." Publishes hardcover and paperback originals. **Published new writers within the last year.** Averages 7-9 titles/year.
Needs: Regional juvenile fiction only. Published *Toulouse: The Story of a Canada Goose*, by Priscilla Cummings (picture book); and *Oyster Moon*, by Margaret Meacham (adventure).

How to Contact: Query or submit outline/synopsis and sample chapters. Responds in 2 months.
Terms: Pays royalties of 7½-15% on retail price. Publishes ms 1 year after acceptance. Book catalog for 10×13 SAE with 5 first-class stamps.
Advice: "Our audience is made up of readers interested in works that are specific to the Chesapeake Bay and Delmarva Peninsula area."

✓ Ø Ⓐ **TOR BOOKS**, Tom Doherty Associates, 175 Fifth Ave., New York NY 10010. (212)388-0100. Website: www.tor.com. **Contact:** Patrick Nielsen Hayden, manager of science fiction; Melissa Singer (Forge Books). Estab. 1980. Publishes hardcover and paperback originals, plus some paperback reprints. Books: 5 point Dombook paper; offset printing; Bursel and perfect binding; few illustrations. Averages 200 total titles/year, mostly fiction. Some nonfiction titles.
Imprint(s): Forge Books.
Needs: Fantasy, mainstream, science fiction and horror. Published *The Path of Daggers*, by Robert Jordan; *1916*, by Morgan Llywelyn; *The Predators*, by Harold Robbins; and *Ender's Shadow*, by Orson Scott Card.
How to Contact: Agented mss preferred. Agented fiction 90%. No simultaneous submissions. Address manuscripts to "Editorial," *not* to the Managing Editor's office.
Terms: Pays in royalties and advance. Writer must return advance if book is not completed or is unacceptable. Sends galleys to author. Publishes ms 1-2 years after acceptance. Free book catalog on request.

✓ **TSR, INC.**, Wizards of the Coast, P.O. Box 707, Renton WA 98057-0707. (425)226-6500. Website: www.wizards.com. Executive Editor: Mary Kirchoff. **Contact:** Novel Submissions Editor. Estab. 1974. "We publish original paperback and hardcover novels and 'shared world' books." TSR publishes games as well, including the Dungeons & Dragons® role-playing game. Books: standard paperbacks; offset printing; perfect binding; b&w (usually) illustrations. Average first novel print order: 75,000. Averages 50-60 fiction titles/year.
Imprint(s): Dragonlance® Books; Forgotten Realms® Books; Greyhawk Novels; Magic: The Gathering® Books; Legend of the Five Rings Novels; Star*Drive Books.
Needs: Fantasy, science fiction, short story collections. "We currently publish only work-for-hire novels set in our trademarked worlds. No violent or gory fantasy or science fiction."
How to Contact: Request guidelines first, then query with outline/synopsis and 3 sample chapters. Agented fiction 65%. Responds in 4 months 2 queries. Accepts simultaneous submissions.
Terms: Pays royalties of 4-8% on retail price. Average advance: $4,000-6,000. Publishes ms 1 year after acceptance. Writer's guidelines for #10 SASE.

✓ Ø Ø ◎ ♈ **TYNDALE HOUSE PUBLISHERS, INC.**, 351 Executive Dr., Carol Stream IL 60188. (608)668-8300. Website: www.tyndale.com. **Contact:** Linda Washington, fiction acquisitions assistant. Estab. 1962. Privately-owned religious press. Publishes hardcover and paperback originals. Books: industry-standard paper; hardcover and softcover bindings. First novel print order: 7,500. **Published 1-2 new writers within the last year.** Plans 1-2 first novels in 2001. Averages 150 total titles, 25-30 fiction titles/year. Member: ECPA. Distributes titles through catalog houses, rackers and distributors. Promotes titles through print ads in trade publications, radio, point of sale materials and catalogs.
Imprint(s): Heart Quest; Anne Goldsmith, fiction editor (inspirational romance), Jan Strob, fiction editor (genre and mainstream inspirational fiction), and Virginia Williams, editor (inspirational children's fiction).
  • Three books published by Tyndale House have received the Gold Medallion Book Award. They include *The Last Sin Eater*, by Francine Rivers; *The Sword of Truth*, by Gilbert Morris; and *A Rose Remembered*, by Michael Phillips.
Needs: Religious (children's, general, inspirational, mystery/suspense, thriller, romance). "We primarily publish Christian historical romances, with occasional contemporary, suspense or standalones." Recently published *Left Behind*, by Tim Lattaye and Jerry Jenkins (general/inspirational); *Hope*, by Lori Copeland (inspirational romance); and the *Left Behind—Kids* series, by Tim Lattaye and Jerry Jenkins (children's religious).
How to Contact: Does not accept unsolicited mss. Queries with outline/synopsis and 3 sample chapters. Include estimated word count, brief bio and list of publishing credits. Send SASE or IRC for return of ms or send disposable copy of ms and SASE for reply only. Agented fiction 20%. Responds in 3 months to queries and mss. Accepts simultaneous submissions.
Terms: Advance negotiable. Sends galleys to authors. Publishes ms 9 months after acceptance. Writer's guidelines for 9×12 SAE and $2.40 for postage or visit website.
Advice: "We are a religious publishing house with a primarily evangelical Christian market. We are looking for spiritual themes and content within established genres."

Ⓝ ♜ ♈ **TYRO PUBLISHING**, 194 Carlbert St., Sault Ste. Marie, Ontario P6A 5E1 Canada. (705)253-6402. E-mail: tyro@sympatico.ca. **Contact:** Lorelee Gordon, editor. Estab. 1984. "We are a small press. Currently we publish only talking books on CD-ROM." Average print order: 200. First novel print order: 200. **Published 4 new writers within the last year.** Plans 2 first novels in 2001. Averages 8 total titles, 2 fiction titles/year. Distributes titles directly to booksellers, libraries and distributors.

Needs: Recently published *A Saga of Sable Island*, by Helen Hodgson (historical).
How to Contact: Accepts unsolicited mss by e-mail only. Query with outline/synopsis and 3 sample chapters only by e-mail. Accepts queries by e-mail. Include estimated word count and brief bio. Agented fiction 2%. Responds in 2 weeks to queries; 1 month to mss. Accepts electronic submissions. Often comments on rejected mss.
Terms: Pays royalties of 15%. "Normally checks are sent every three months as books are sold." Sends galleys to author. Publishes ms 6 months after acceptance. Writer's guidelines and book catalog available by e-mail only.

✓ ◐ **UNITY HOUSE**, (formerly Unity Books), Unity School of Christianity, 1901 NW Blue Parkway, Unity Village MO 64065-0001. (816)524-3550 ext. 3190. Fax: (816)251-3552. E-mail: ~books@unityworldhq.org. Website: www.unityworldhq.org. **Contact**; Michael Maday, editor; Raymond Teague, associate editor. "We are a bridge between traditional Christianity and New Age spirituality. Unity School of Christianity is based on metaphysical Christian principles, spiritual values and the healing power of prayer as a resource for daily living." Publishes hardcover and trade paperback originals and reprints. **Published 9 new writers within the last year.** Averages 18 titles/year.
Needs: Spiritual, inspirational, metaphysical.
How to Contact: Query with synopsis and sample chapter. Responds in 1 month to queries; 2 months to mss.
Terms: Pays royalties of 10-15% on net receipts. Publishes ms 13 months after acceptance of final ms. Writer's guidelines and book catalog free.

✓ ◎ **UNIVERSITY OF NEBRASKA PRESS**, 233 N. Eighth St., P.O. Box 880255, Lincoln NE 68588-0255. (402)472-3581. Fax: (402)472-0308. E-mail: pressmail@unl.edu. Website: http://nebraskapress.unl.edu. **Contact**: Daniel Ross, director. Estab. 1941. "The University of Nebraska Press seeks to encourage, develop, publish and disseminate research, literature and the publishing arts. The Press maintains scholarly standards and fosters innovations guided by referred evaluations." Publishes hardcover and paperback originals and reprints. **Published new writers within the last year.**
Imprint(s): Bison Books (paperback reprints).
Needs: Accepts fiction translations but no original fiction. Also welcomes creative nonfiction.
How to Contact: Query first with outline/synopsis, 1 sample chapter and introduction. Responds in 4 months.
Terms: Pays graduated royalty on original books. Occasional advance. Writer's guidelines and book catalog for 9×12 SAE with 5 first-class stamps.

◐ ♉ **UNIVERSITY PRESS OF NEW ENGLAND**, 23 S. Main St., Hanover NH 03755-2048. (603)643-7100. Fax: (603)643-1540. E-mail: university.press@dartmouth.edu. Website: www.dartmouth.edu/acad-inst/up ne/ (includes writer's guidelines, names of editors, authors, titles, etc.). Director: Richard M. Abel. **Contact:** Phil Pochoda, editorial director (literary, New England); Phyllis Deutsch, editor. Estab. 1970. "University Press of New England is a consortium of six university presses. Some books—those published for one of the consortium members—carry the joint imprint of New England and the member: Wesleyan, Dartmouth, Brandeis, Tufts, University of New Hampshire and Middlebury College." New England settings only. Publishes hardcover originals. Averages 85 total titles, 6 fiction titles/year. Promotes titles through catalog, magazine advertisements, trade journal ads, mailings.
Imprint(s): HardScrabble.
 ● University Press of New England received the Commonwealth Club of California Silver Medal (Best First Fiction) for *Leaving Pico*, by Frank X. Gaspar.
Needs: Literary, regional (New England) novels and reprints. Recently published *Rain Line*, by Anne Whitney Pierce; *The Day Laid on the Altar*, by Adria Bernardi; and *Pipers at the Gates of Dawn*, by Lynn Stegner.
How to Contact: Does not accept unsolicited mss. Query with outline and 1-2 sample chapters. Accepts queries by e-mail and fax. Include list of publishing credits. Send SASE or IRC for return. Agented fiction 50%. Responds in 2 months. Accepts simultaneous submissions. Sometimes comments on rejected mss.
Terms: Pays standard royalty. Offers advance occasionally. Writer's guidelines and book catalog for 9×12 SAE with 5 first-class stamps.

✓ ◎ Ⓐ **VIKING**, Imprint of Penguin Putnam Inc., 375 Hudson St., New York NY 10014. (212)366-2000. Website: www.penguinputnam.com. **Contact:** Acquisitions Editor. Publishes a mix of academic and popular fiction and nonfiction. Publishes hardcover and trade paperback originals.
Needs: Literary, mainstream/contemporary, mystery, suspense. Published *Out to Canaan*, by John Karon (novel).
How to Contact: Agented fiction only. Responds in up to 6 months to queries. Accepts simultaneous submissions.
Terms: Pays royalties of 10-15% on retail price. Advance negotiable. Publishes ms 1 year after acceptance.
Advice: "Looking for writers who can deliver a book a year (or faster) of consistent quality."

✓ ◐ **VIKING CHILDREN'S BOOKS,** Imprint of the Children's Division of Penguin Putnam Inc., 345 Hudson St., New York NY 10014-3657. (212)366-2000. Fax: (212)414-3399. Website: www.penguinputnam.com

(includes online catalog of all imprints, feature articles and interviews, young readers site, order information, education and teacher's resources). "Viking Children's Books publishes the highest quality trade books for children including fiction, nonfiction, and novelty books for pre-schoolers through young adults." Publishes hardcover originals. **Published new writers within the last year.** Averages 80 titles/year. Promotes titles through press kits, institutional ads.

Needs: Juvenile, young adult. Recently published *Keeping the Moon*, by Sarah Dessen (novel); *Joseph Had a Little Overcoat*, by Simms Taback (picture book); *See You Later, Gladiator*, by Jon Scieszka (chapter book).

How to Contact: Accepts unsolicited mss. For picture books and novels submit entire ms. Responds in 4 months to queries. SASE mandatory for return of materials.

Terms: Pays royalties of 5-10% on retail price. Advance negotiable. Publishes ms 12-18 months after acceptance.

Advice: No "cartoony" or mass-market submissions for picture books.

N: VINTAGE, The Knopf Publishing Group, A Division of Random House, Inc., 299 Park Ave., New York NY 10171. Website: www.vintagebooks.com. **Contact:** Submissions Editor. Publishes trade paperback originals and reprints. **Published new writers within the last year.**

Needs: Literary, mainstream/contemporary, short story collections. Published *Snow Falling on Cedars*, by Guterson (contemporary); and *Martin Dressler*, by Millhauser (literary).

How to Contact: Does not accept unsolicited mss. Query with synopsis and 2-3 sample chapters. Responds in 6 months. Accepts simultaneous submissions. No submissions by fax or e-mail.

Terms: Pays 4-8% on retail price. Offers $2,500 and up advance. Publishes ms 1 year after acceptance.

VISION BOOKS PVT LTD., Madarsa Rd., Kashmere Gate, Delhi 110006 India. Phone: (+91)11 2962267 or (+91)11 2962201. Fax: (+91)11 2962935. E-mail: orientpbk@vsnl.com. **Contact:** Sudhir Malhotra, fiction editor. Publishes 25 titles/year.

Needs: "We are a large multilingual publishing house publishing fiction and other trade books."

How to Contact: "A brief synopsis should be submitted initially. Subsequently, upon hearing from the editor, a typescript may be sent."

Terms: Pays royalties.

VISTA PUBLISHING, INC., 422 Morris Ave., Suite One, Long Branch NJ 07740-5901. (732)229-6500. Fax: (732)229-9647. E-mail: czagury@vistapubl.com. Website: www.vistapubl.com (includes titles, authors, editors, pricing and ordering information). **Contact:** Carolyn Zagury, president. Estab. 1991. "Small, independent press, owned by women and specializing in fiction by nurses and allied health professional authors." Publishes paperback originals. **Published 3 new writers within the last year.** Plans 3 first novels in 2001. Averages 12 total titles, 6 fiction titles/year. Distributes titles through catalogs, wholesalers, distributors, exhibits, website, trade shows, book clubs and bookstores. Promotes titles through author signings, press releases, author speakings, author interviews, exhibits, website, direct mail and book reviews.

Needs: Adventure, humor/satire, mystery/suspense, romance, short story collections. Published *Eucarion*, by Curt Samlaska (action thriller); *Deathtone*, by John Riva (mystery thriller); and *Memories of the Dance*, by Keith Neely (action).

How to Contact: Accepts unsolicited mss. Query with complete ms. Accepts queries by e-mail and fax. Include bio. Send SASE or IRC for return of ms or send disposable copy of ms and SASE for reply only. Responds in 2 months to mss. Accepts simultaneous submissions. Comments on rejected mss.

Terms: Pays royalties. Sends galleys to author. Publishes ms 2 years after acceptance. Writer's guidelines and book catalog for SASE.

Advice: "We prefer to read full mss. Authors should be nurses or allied health professionals."

WALKER AND COMPANY, Walker Publishing Co., 435 Hudson St., New York NY 10014. Fax: (212)727-0984. **Contact:** Michael Seidman, Emily Easton, Jacqueline Johnson, Tim Travaglini, editors. Estab. 1959. Publishes hardcover and trade paperback originals. **Published new writers within the last year.** Averages 70 total titles/year.

Needs: Adult mystery, juvenile fiction and picture books. Recently published *Captain's Command*, by Anna Myers (juvenile).

How to Contact: *Does not accept unsolicited mss.* Submit outline and chapters as preliminary. Query letter should include "a concise description of the story line, including its outcome, word length of story (we prefer 70,000 words), writing experience, publishing credits, particular expertise on this subject and in this genre. Common mistakes: Sounding unprofessional (i.e. too chatty, too braggardly). Forgetting SASE." Agented fiction 50%. Notify if multiple or simultaneous submissions. Responds in 3 months.

Terms: Pays royalty on retail price, 7½-12% on paperback, 10-15% on hardcover. Offers competitive advance.

Advice: "As for mysteries, we are open to all types, including suspense novels and offbeat books that maintain a 'play fair' puzzle. We are always looking for well-written western novels that are offbeat and strong on characterization. Character development is most important in all Walker fiction. We expect the author to be expert in the categories, to know the background and foundations of the genre. To realize that just because some subgenre is hot it doesn't mean that that is the area to mine—after all, if everyone is doing female p.i.s, doesn't it make more sense to do something that isn't crowded, something that might serve to balance a list, rather than make it top heavy? Finally, don't tell us why your book is going to be a success; instead, show me that you can write and write well. It is your writing, and not your hype that interests us."

✔ ⊘ Ⓐ ♛ **WARNER ASPECT,** Imprint of Warner Books, 1271 Avenue of the Americas, New York NY 10020. Fax: (212)522-7990. Website: www.twbookmark.com (includes each month's new titles, advice from writers, previous titles and interviews with authors, "hot news," contests). **Contact:** Betsy Mitchell, editor-in-chief. "We're looking for 'epic' stories in both fantasy and science fiction." Publishes hardcover, trade paperback, mass market paperback originals and mass market paperback reprints. **Published 2 new writers within the last year.** Distributes titles through nationwide sales force.
  ● Warner Aspect published *Parable of the Talents*, by Octavia E. Butler, winner of the Nebula Award for best novel.
Needs: Fantasy, science fiction. Published *The Naked God*, by Peter F. Hamilton (science fiction); and *A Cavern of Black Ice*, by J.V. Jones (fantasy).
How to Contact: Agented fiction only. Responds in 10 weeks to mss.
Terms: Pays royalty on retail price. Average advance: $5,000 and up. Publishes ms 14 months after acceptance.
Advice: "Think epic! Our favorite stories are big-screen science fiction and fantasy, with plenty of characters and subplots. Sample our existing titles—we're a fairly new list and pretty strongly focused." Mistake writers often make is "hoping against hope that being unagented won't make a difference. We simply don't have the staff to look at unagented projects."

✔ ⊘ Ⓐ **WARNER BOOKS,** Time & Life Building, 1271 Avenue of the Americas, New York NY 10020. (212)522-7200. Website: www.twbookmark.com. Publishes hardcover, trade paperback and mass market paperback originals and reprints. Warner publishes general interest fiction. Averages 350 total titles/year.
Imprint(s): Mysterious Press, Warner Aspect, Walk Worthy.
Needs: Fantasy, mainstream, mystery/suspense, romance, science fiction, thriller. Recently published *Wish You Well*, by David Baldacci; *Standoff*, by Sandra Brown; and *The Rescue*, by Nicholas Sparks.
How to Contact: Accepts agented submissions *only*.

◓ **WESLEYAN UNIVERSITY PRESS,** 110 Mount Vernon St., Middletown CT 06459. (860)685-2420. **Contact:** Suzanna Tamminen, editor-in-chief. "We are a scholarly press with a focus on cultural studies." Publishes hardcover originals. **Published new writers within the last year.** Averages 20-25 titles/year.
Needs: Science fiction. "We publish very little fiction." Published *Dhalgren*, by Samuel R. Delany.
How to Contact: Query with outline. Responds in 1 month to queries; 3 months to mss. Accepts simultaneous submissions.
Terms: Pays royalties of 6%. Publishes ms 1 year after acceptance. Writer's guidelines for #10 SASE. Book catalog free.
Advice: Audience ranges from the informed general reader to specialized academic reader.

Ⓝ ◓ **WHITE PINE PRESS,** P.O. Box 236, Buffalo NY 14201. Phone/fax: (716)627-4665. E-mail: wpine@ whitepine.org. Website: www.whitepine.org (includes book catalog). **Contact:** Elaine LaMattina, editor (all fiction). Estab. 1973. Small, not-for-profit literary publisher. Publishes paperback originals. Books: text paper; offset printing; perfect binding. Average print order: 1,500. First novel print order: 1,500. Plans 1 first novel in 2001. Averages 8 total titles, 4 fiction titles/year. Distributes titles through Consortium Book Sales.
Needs: Ethnic/multicultural, feminist, literary, short story collections, translations. Recently published *A Sketch of the Fading Sun*, by Won-Suh Park (Korean fiction); *Afterwards*, by A. Zawacki, editor (Slovenian literature); and *In Lithuanian Wood*, by Wendell Mayo (American fiction). Publishes the New American Fiction series.
How to Contact: Accepts unsolicited mss. Send query letter. "We do not accept queries via e-mail or fax." Include estimated word count and list of publishing credits. Send SASE or IRC for return of ms or send disposable copy of ms and SASE for reply only. Agented fiction 1%. Responds in 1 month to queries; 6 months to mss. Accepts simultaneous submissions. Sometimes comments on rejected mss.
Terms: Pays 100 author's copies. Sends galleys to author. Publishes ms 1-2 years after acceptance. Writer's guidelines free for SASE.
Advice: "Send query letter first detailing project. Stick to our guidelines. Don't telephone to see if we received it. We're interested in what's good, not what's trendy."

◓ ◎ **WILSHIRE BOOK CO.,** 12015 Sherman Rd., North Hollywood CA 91605-3781. (818)765-8579. Fax: (818)765-2922. E-mail: mpowers@mpowers.com. Website: www.mpowers.com (includes types of books published). **Contact:** Melvin Powers, publisher; Marcia Powers, senior editor (adult fables). Estab. 1947. "You are not only what you are today, but also what you choose to become tomorrow." Looking for adult fables that teach principles of psychological growth. Publishes trade paperback originals and reprints. **Published 7 new writers within the last year.** Averages 15 titles/year. Distributes titles through wholesalers, bookstores and mail order. Promotes titles through author interviews on radio and television.

Needs: Allegories that teach principles of psychological/spiritual growth or offer guidance in living. Min. 30,000 words. Published *The Princess Who Believed in Fairy Tales*, by Marcia Grad; *The Knight in Rusty Armor*, by Robert Fisher. Allegories only. No standard novels or short stories.

How to Contact: Accepts unsolicited mss. Query with synopsis, 3 sample chapters and SASE or submit complete ms with cover letter. Accepts queries by e-mail. Responds in 2 months.

Terms: Pays standard royalty. Publishes ms 6 months after acceptance.

Advice: "We are vitally interested in all new material we receive. Just as you hopefully submit your manuscript for publication, we hopefully read every one submitted, searching for those that we believe will be successful in the marketplace. Writing and publishing must be a team effort. We need you to write what we can sell. We suggest that you read the successful books mentioned above or others that are similar: *Greatest Salesman in the World*, *Illusions*, *Way of the Peaceful Warrior*, *Celestine Prophecy*. Analyze them to discover what elements make them winners. Duplicate those elements in your own style, using a creative new approach and fresh material, and you will have written a book we can successfully market."

THE WONDERLAND PRESS, INC., 160 Fifth Avenue, Suite 723, New York NY 10010. (212)989-2550. E-mail: litraryagt@aol.com. **Contact:** John Campbell. Estab. 1985. Member: American Book Producers Association. Represents 24 clients. Specializes in high-quality nonfiction, illustrated, reference, how-to and entertainment books. "We welcome submissions from new authors, but proposals must be unique, of high commercial interest and well written." Currently handles: 90% nonfiction books; 10% novels.

● The Wonderland Press is also a book packager and "in a very strong position to nurture strong proposals all the way from concept through bound books."

Represents: Interested in reviewing nonfiction books, novels. Considers these nonfiction areas: art/architecture/design; biography/autobiography; enthnic/cultural interests; gay/lesbian issues; health/medicine; history; how-to; humor; interior design/decorating; language/literature/criticism; photography; popular culture; psychology; self-help/personal improvement. Considers these fiction areas: action/adventure; literary; picture book; thriller.

How to Contact: Send outline/proposal with SASE. Responds in 3-5 days to queries; 2 weeks to mss.

Needs: Does not want to receive poetry, memoir, children's or category fiction. Recently published *Body Knots*, by Howard Schaty (Rizzoli); and *Nude Body Nude*, by Howard Schaty (HarperCollins).

Terms: Agent receives 15% commission on domestic sales. Offers written contract. 30-90 days notice must be given to terminate contract. Offers criticism service, included in 15% commission. Charges for photocopying, long-distance telephone, overnight express-mail, messengering.

Tips: "Follow your talent. Write with passion. Know your market. Submit work in final form; if you feel a need to apologize for its mistakes, typos, or incompleteness, then it is not ready to be seen. We want to see your best work."

WORLDWIDE LIBRARY, Division of Harlequin Books, 225 Duncan Mill Rd., Don Mills, Ontario M3B 3K9 Canada. (416)445-5860. **Contact**: Feroze Mohammed, senior editor/editorial coordinator. Estab. 1979. Large commercial category line. Publishes paperback originals and reprints. Averages 72 fiction titles/year. "Mystery program is reprint; no originals please."

Imprint(s): Worldwide Mystery; Gold Eagle Books.

Needs: "Action-adventure series and future fiction."

How to Contact: Query with outline/synopsis/series concept or overview and sample chapters. Send SAE with International Reply Coupons or money order. Responds in 10 weeks to queries. Accepts simultaneous submissions.

Terms: Advance and sometimes royalties; copyright buyout. Publishes ms 1-2 years after acceptance.

Advice: "Publishing fiction in very selective areas."

WRITE WAY PUBLISHING, P.O. Box 441278, Aurora CO 80044. (800)680-1493. Fax: (303)617-1440. E-mail: writewy@aol.com. Website: www.writewaypub.com (includes first chapter, reviews and sales information on every title). **Contact:** Dorrie O'Brien, owner/editor. Estab. 1993. "Write Way is a book-only, fiction-only independent press concentrating on genre publications such as mysteries, soft science fiction, fairy tale/fantasy and horror/thrillers." Publishes hardcover originals. Average print order: 2,500. First novel print order: 2,000. **Published new writers within the last year.** Averages 10-12 fiction titles/year. Distributes titles through Midpoint Trade Books. Promotes titles through newspapers, magazines and trade shows.

Needs: Fantasy/fairy tale, horror (soft), mystery/suspense (amateur sleuth, cozy, police procedural, private eye/hardboiled), psychic/supernatural, science fiction (soft/sociological, space trilogy/series). Recently published *The Music Box Murders*, by Larry Karp; *Killing Thyme*, by Peter Abresch; and *Plot Twist*, by Jane Rubins.

How to Contact: Query with short outline/synopsis and 1-2 sample chapters. Include estimated word count, bio (reasonably short) and list of publishing credits. Send SASE or IRC for return of ms or send disposable copy of ms and SASE for reply only. Agented fiction 10%. Responds in 1 month to queries; up to 8 months to mss. Accepts simultaneous submissions. Often comments on rejected mss.

Terms: Pays royalties of 8-10%. Does not pay advances. Sends galleys to author. Publishes ms within 3 years after acceptance. Writer's guidelines for SASE.

Advice: "Always have the query letter, synopsis and the first chapters edited by an unbiased party prior to submitting them to us. Remember: first impressions are just as important to a publisher as they might be to a prospective employer."

☑ ◐ **WRITERS PRESS, INC.,** 2309 Mountainview Dr., Suite 185, Boise ID 83706. (208)327-0566. Fax: (208)327-3477. E-mail: publish@writerspress.com. Website: www.writerspress.com. **Contact:** John Ybarra, editor. "By publishing high-quality children's literature that is both fun and educational, we are striving to make a difference in today's educational world." Publishes hardcover and trade paperback originals. **Published new writers within the last year.** Averages 3-4 titles/year.

Imprints: Premier Books®, digital printing on demand.

Needs: Adventure, historical, juvenile, picture books, young adult, inclusion, special education.

How to Contact: Does not accept unsolicited mss. Send query letter. Accepts queries by e-mail and fax. Responds in 1 month to queries; 4 months to mss.

Terms: Pays royalties of 4-12% or makes outright purchase of up to $1,500. Publishes ms 6 months after acceptance. Writer's and catalog guidelines free.

N: YEARLING, Bantam, Doubleday, Dell/Delacorte, Knopf and Crown Books for Young Readers, Random House Children's Books, A Division of Random House, Inc., 1540 Broadway, New York NY 10036. (212)782-9000 or (800)200-3552. Website: www.randomhouse.com/kids.

• See listing for Bantam, Doubleday, Dell/Delacorte, Knopf and Crown Books for Young Readers, page 394.

♣ ◐ **YORK PRESS LTD.,** 152 Boardwalk Dr., Toronto, Ontario M4L 3X4 Canada. (416)690-3788. Fax: (416)690-3797. E-mail: yorkpress@sympatico.ca. Website: www3.sympatico.ca/yorkpress. **Contact:** Dr. S. Elkhadem, general manager/editor. Estab. 1975. "We publish scholarly books and creative writing of an experimental nature." Publishes trade paperback originals. **Published new writers within the last year.** Averages 10 titles/year.

Needs: "Fiction of an experimental nature by well-established writers." Published *The Moonhare*, by Kirk Hampton (experimental novel).

How to Contact: Query first. Responds in 2 months.

Terms: Pays royalties of 10-20% on wholesale price. Publishes ms 6 months after acceptance.

◉ ♟ **ZOLAND BOOKS, INC.,** 384 Huron Ave., Cambridge MA 02138. (617)864-6252. Fax: (617)661-4998. E-mail: info@zolandbooks.com. Website: www.zolandbooks.com. **Contact:** Roland Pease, publisher/editor; Stephen Hull, marketing director. Estab. 1987. "We are a literary press, publishing poetry, fiction, nonfiction, photography, and other titles of literary interest." Publishes hardcover and paperback originals and reprints. Books: acid-free paper; sewn binding; some with illustrations. Average print order: 2,000-5,000. **Published 1-2 new writers within the last year.** Averages 14 total titles/year. Distributes titles through Consortium Book Sales and Distribution. Promotes titles through catalog, publicity, advertisements, direct mail.

• Awards include: Hemingway/PEN Award, Kafka Prize for Women's Fiction, National Book Award finalist, *New York Times* Notable Book, *Publishers Weekly* Best Book of the Year.

Needs: Contemporary, feminist, literary, African-American interest. Published *Courting Disaster*, by Julie Edelson (literary novel); *A Citizen of the World*, by Maclin Bocock (short stories); and *The Long Run of Myles Mayberry*, by Alfred Acorn (literary novel).

How to Contact: Accepts unsolicited mss. Query first, then send complete ms with cover letter and SASE. Responds in 6 weeks to queries; 6 months to mss.

Terms: Pays royalties of 5-8%. Average advance: $1,500; negotiable (also pays author's copies). Sends galleys to author. Publishes ms 1-2 years after acceptance. Book catalog for 6×9 SAE and 2 first-class stamps.

Advice: "Be original."

☑ ◉ ◎ **ZONDERVAN,** Imprint of HarperCollins Publishers, 5300 Patterson SE, Grand Rapids MI 49530. (616)698-6900. E-mail: zondervan@zph.com. Website: www.zondervan.com. **Contact:** Manuscript Review Editor. Estab. 1931. "Our mission is to be the leading Christian communication company meeting the needs of people with resources that glorify Jesus Christ and promote biblical principles." Large evangelical Christian publishing house. Publishes hardcover and paperback originals and reprints, though fiction is generally in paper only. First novel print order: 5,000. **Published new writers in the last year.** Averages 150 total titles, 15-20 fiction titles/year.

Needs: Adult fiction, (mainstream, biblical, historical, suspense, mystery), "Inklings-style" fiction of high literary quality. Christian relevance necessary in all cases. Will *not* consider collections of short stories. Published *Glimpses of Truth*, by Jack Ceranaugh (historical); *Seasons Under Heaven*, by Terri Blackstock and Bev Lattaye (mainstream); and *Tonopah*, by Christopher Lane (suspense).

How to Contact: Accepts unsolicited mss but prefers queries with outline and 2 sample chapters. *Write for writer's guidelines first.* Include #10 SASE. Responds in 2 months to queries; 4 months to mss.

Terms: "Standard contract provides for a percentage of the net price received by publisher for each copy sold, usually 14-17% of net."

Advice: "Almost no unsolicited fiction is published. Send plot outline and one or two sample chapters. Editors will *not* read entire manuscripts. Your sample chapters will make or break you."

MICROPRESSES

The very small presses listed here are owned or operated by one to three people, often friends or family members. Some are cooperatives of writers and most of these presses started out publishing their staff members' books or books by their friends. Even the most successful of these presses are unable to afford the six-figure advances, lavish promotional budgets and huge press runs possible in the large, commercial houses. These presses can easily be swamped with submissions, but writers published by them are usually treated as "one of the family."

ACME PRESS, P.O. Box 1702, Westminster MD 21158. (410)848-7577. **Contact**: Ms. E.G. Johnston, managing editor. Estab. 1991. "We operate on a part-time basis and publish 1-2 novels/year." Publishes hardcover and paperback originals. **Published new writers within the last year.** Averages 1-2 fiction titles/year.

Needs: Humor/satire. "We publish only humor novels, so we don't want to see anything that's not funny." Published *She-Crab Soup*, by Dawn Langley Simmons (fictional memoir/humor); *Biting the Wall*, by J. M. Johnston (humor/mystery); and *Hearts of Gold*, by James Magorian (humor/mystery).

How to Contact: Accepts unsolicited mss. Query with outline/synopsis and first 50 pages or submit complete ms with cover letter. Include estimated word count. Send SASE for reply, return of ms or send a disposable copy of ms. Agented fiction 25%. Responds in 2 weeks to queries; 6 weeks to mss. Accepts simultaneous submissions. Always comments on rejected mss.

Terms: Pays 25 author's copies and 50% of profits. Sends galleys to author. Publishes ms 1 year after acceptance. Writer's guidelines and book catalog for #10 SASE.

AFFABLE NEIGHBOR, P.O. Box 3635, Ann Arbor MI 48104. E-mail: affableneighbor@yahoo.com. Editor-in-Chief: Joe Henry Fisher. **Contact:** Marshall Stanley, assistant editor (fiction); Leigh Chalmers, editor (poetry). Estab. 1994. "*Affable Neighbor* is currently a part-time operation. Noted for outrageous and boundary-pushing material, often pushing the limits of good taste/censorship. (But not exclusively, by any means.)" Publishes paperback originals. Books: white paper; photostatic printed; varied binding; illustrations. Average print order: small. **Published 1 new writer within the last year.** Averages 6 total titles/year. Distributes titles through mail order. Promotes titles through reviews.

Needs: Comics/graphic novels, erotica, experimental, fantasy, gay, horror, humor/satire, lesbian, literary, psychic/supernatural, science fiction. Need short stories for possible publication in a small magazine.

How to Contact: Accepts unsolicited mss. Submit complete ms with cover letter. Include brief bio and photograph. Send SASE or IRC for return of ms or send a disposable copy of ms and SASE for reply only. Responds in weeks to queries; in months to mss. Accepts simultaneous submissions. Often comments on rejected mss.

Terms: Pays by individual arrangement with author.

Advice: "Your work should make me feel that I *have* to publish it. Photographs/drawings are often a plus."

AGELESS PRESS, P.O. Box 5915, Sarasota FL 34277-5915. Phone/fax: (941)952-0576. E-mail: irishope@home.com. Website: http://members.home.net/irishope/ageless.htm (includes contest winners, articles, book excerpts). **Contact**: Iris Forrest, editor. Estab. 1992. Independent publisher. Publishes paperback originals. Books: acid-free paper; notched perfect binding; no illustrations. Average print order: 5,000. First novel print order: 5,000. **Published new writers within the last year.** Averages 1 title/year.

Needs: Experimental, fantasy, humor/satire, literary, mainstream/contemporary, mystery/suspense, New Age/mystic/spiritual, science fiction, short story collections, thriller/espionage. Looking for material "based on personal computer experiences." Stories selected by editor. Published *Computer Legends, Lies & Lore*, by various (anthology); and *Computer Tales of Fact & Fantasy*, by various (anthology).

How to Contact: Does not accept unsolicited mss. Send query letter. Accepts queries by e-mail and fax. Send SASE or IRC for return of ms or send a disposable copy of ms and SASE for reply only. Responds in 1 week. Accepts simultaneous submissions, electronic (disk, 5¼ or 3.5 IBM) submissions in ASCII format. Sometimes comments on rejected mss.
Terms: Average advance: negotiable. Publishes ms 6-12 months after acceptance.

ANVIL PRESS, Bentall Centre, P.O. Box 1575, Vancouver, British Columbia V6C 2P7 Canada; or Lee Building, #204-A, 175 E. Broadway, Vancouver, British Columbia V5T 1W2 Canada. (604)876-8710. Fax: (604)879-2667. E-mail: subter@portal.ca. Website: www.anvilpress.com (includes writer's guidelines, names of editors, book catalog, sample of magazine, contest info). **Contact:** Brian Kaufman, managing editor; Grant Buday, fiction editor. Estab. 1988. "1½-person operation with volunteer editorial board. Anvil Press publishes contemporary fiction, poetry and drama, giving voice to up-and-coming Canadian writers, exploring all literary genres, discovering, nurturing and promoting new Canadian literary talent." Publishes paperback originals. Books: offset or web printing; perfect-bound. Average print order: 1,000-1,500. First novel print order: 1,000. **Published new writers within the last year.** Plans 2 first novels in 2001. Averages 2-3 fiction titles/year.
• Anvil Press titles have been nominated for the Journey Prize, the BC Book Prize and the City of Vancouver Prize.
Needs: Experimental, contemporary modern, literary, short story collections. Recently published *White Lung*, by Grant Buday (novel); *Airborne Photo*, by Clint Burnham (contemporary); *Touched*, by Jodi Lundgren; and *Skin*, by Bonnie Bowan. Publishes the Anvil Pamphlet series: shorter works (essays, political tracts, polemics, treatises and works of fiction that are shorter than novel or novella form).
How to Contact: *Canadian writers only.* Accepts unsolicited mss. Send query letter or query with outline/synopsis and 1-2 sample chapters. Include estimated word count and bio. Send SASE or IRC for return of ms or send a disposable copy of ms and SASE for reply only. Responds in 1 month to queries; up to 4 months to mss. Accepts simultaneous submissions (please note in query letter that manuscript is a simultaneous submission). Often comments on rejected mss.
Terms: Pays royalties of 15% (of final sales). Average advance: $400. Sends galleys to author. Publishes ms within contract year. Book catalog for 9×12 SASE and 2 first-class stamps.
Advice: "We are only interested in writing that is progressive in some way—form, content. We want contemporary fiction from serious writers who intend to be around for awhile and be a name people will know in years to come. Read back titles, look through our catalog before submitting."

ARTEMIS PRESS, DeeMar Communications, PMB 320, 6325-9 Falls of Neuse Rd., Raleigh NC 27615-6809. (919)870-6423. E-mail: artemispress@aol.com. Website: www.angelfire.com/nc2/artemispress (includes guidelines, titles list, order page). **Contact:** Diane Tait, owner. Estab. 2000. "Woman-owned independent press which publishes women writers of short stories and novellas. We are unique in that we are approachable and give personalized services. We work with you on all phases of publication." Publishes paperback originals. Books: 60 lb. paper; perfect binding. Average print order: 100. First novel print order: 100. Plans 1 first novel in 2001. Averages 1 total title, 1 fiction title/year. Distributes titles through Amazon.com, writer's lists, book fairs and contests.
Needs: Erotica, fantasy, New Age/mystic, romance, short story collections (all women themed).
How to Contact: Accepts unsolicited mss. Submit complete ms with cover letter. Include brief bio, list of publishing credits and potential market base. Send disposable copy of ms and SASE for reply only. Responds in 2 weeks to queries and mss. Often comments on rejected mss.
Terms: Pays royalties of 10-15% and 10 author's copies. Sends galleys to author. Publishes ms up to 1 year after acceptance. Writer's guidelines on website.
Advice: "In addition to submitting required material, we like to know why you think we should publish your work. We work collaboratively with all writers in all phases of publication. We are looking for 'team' players."

ATTIC PRESS, Crawford Business Park, Crosses Green, Cork, Ireland. E-mail: e.ocarrol@ucc.ie. Website: www.iol.ie/~atticirl/. **Contact:** Managing Editor. "Attic Press is an independent, export-oriented, Irish-owned publishing house with a strong international profile. The press specializes in the publication of women's fiction, politics, sociology, narratives and current affairs." Averages 2-3 fiction titles/year.
How to Contact: Does not accept unsolicited mss. Send query letter. "Unsolicited proposals will be returned without acknowledgement." Publishes an award-winning series of teenage fiction, Bright Sparks.
Terms: Pays royalties; advance on signing contract. Catalog available.

AVID PRESS, LLC, 5470 Red Fox Dr., Brighton MI 48114-9079. Website: www.avidpress.com. **Contact:** Colleen Gleason Shulte or Kate Gleason, publishers. "Avid Press is a royalty-paying publisher of fiction and non-fiction, electronic and print books. Avid Press is dedicated to building and maintaining a reputation as an author-friendly publisher. It is important that our authors are pleased and proud to be associated with Avid Press." Publishes e-books and paperback originals and reprints.
Imprints: VIM (young adult titles)

Needs: Romance (historical, contemporary, humorous, paranormal, gothic, suspense/mystery), thriller suspense, mystery, young adult. No science fiction, children's, general nonfiction, short stories, poetry. Recently published *Hunter's Song*, by Natalie Damschroder (romance); *When the Lilacs Bloom*, by Linda Colwell (romance); and *Electronic Publishing: The Definitive Guide*, by Karen Weisner (nonfiction instructional).

How to Contact: Query with synopsis and one sample chapter (send as e-mail attachment). Accepts queries by e-mail at subs@avidpress.com. Include brief author bio.

Terms: Pays royalty. Guidelines on website or for SASE.

Advice: "There are no 'rules' for being published by Avid Press; instead, we are looking for manuscripts that are written from the heart-books the author would want to read-not books that follow a specific guideline or formula. We are looking for entertaining stories and compelling characters."

BANCROFT PRESS, P.O. Box 65360, Baltimore MD 21209. (410)358-0658. Fax: (410)764-1967. E-mail: bruceb@bancroftpress.com. Website: www.bancroftpress.com (includes booklist, guidelines and mission statement). **Contact:** Bruce Bortz, editor. Estab. 1991. "Small independent press publishing literary and commercial fiction, often by journalists." Publishes hardcover and paperback originals. First novel print order: 5,000-7,500. **Published 2 new writers within the last year.** Plans 2 first novels in 2001. Averages 4-6 total titles, 2-4 fiction titles/year.

● *The Re-Appearance of Sam Webber*, by Scott Fuqua is an ALEX Award winner.

Needs: Ethnic/multicultural (general), family saga, feminist, gay, glitz, historical, horror (dark fantasy, futuristic, psychological, supernatural), humor/satire, lesbian, literary, mainstream, military/war, mystery/suspense (amateur sleuth, cozy, police procedural, private eye/hardboiled), New Age/mystic, psychic/supernatural, regional, science fiction (hard science/technological, soft/sociological), thriller/espionage, translations, western (frontier saga, traditional), young adult/teen (historical, problem novels, series). Published *Those Who Trespass*, by Bill O'Reilly (thriller); *The Re-Appearance of Sam Webber*, by Scott Fuqua (literary); and *Malicious Intent*, by Mike Walker (Hollywood).

How to Contact: Accepts unsolicited mss. Query with outline/synopsis and 3 sample chapters. Accepts queries by e-mail and fax. Include bio and list of publishing credits. Send SASE for reply, return of ms or send a disposable copy of ms. Agented fiction 100%. Responds in 6 months. Accepts simultaneous submissions. Sometimes comments on rejected mss.

Terms: Pays royalties of 6-12½%. Average advance: $1,500. Sends galleys to author. Publishes ms 18 months after acceptance.

Advice: "Be patient, send a sample, know your book's audience."

BEGGAR'S PRESS, 8110 N. 38th St., Omaha NE 68112-2018. (402)455-2615. **Contact:** Richard R. Carey, publisher. Estab. 1952. Small independent publisher. "We are noted for publishing books and periodicals in the styles of the great masters of the past. We publish three periodicals (literary) and novels, poetry chapbooks, and collections of short stories." Publishes paperback originals. Books: 20 lb. paper; offset; perfect binding; some illustrations. Average print order: 500-700. First novel print order: 500. **Published new writers within the last year.** Plans 2 first novels in 2001. Averages 3-5 total titles, 4 fiction titles/year. Member: International Association of Independent Publishers and Federation of Literary Publishers.

Imprint(s): *Lamplight; Raskolnikov's Cellar; Beggar's Review.*

Needs: Adventure, historical (general, 1800's), horror (psychological), humor/satire, literary, mystery/suspense, short story collection. Published *An Evening Studying the Anatomy of Jena Kruger*, by Richard Carey; *My Doorknob Is Female*, by Diane Jensen; and *Seduction of An Olive*, by Debra Knight. Plans series.

How to Contact: Does not accept unsolicited mss. "We are not accepting queries or manuscripts at the present time. We are completely scheduled for the next two years."

Terms: Pays royalties of 10-15%; provides 2 author's copies

BENEATH THE UNDERGROUND, 132 Woodycrest Dr., East Hartford CT 06118. (860)569-3101. E-mail: vfrazer@home.com. **Contact:** Vernon Frazer, editor. Estab. 1998. One-person operation specializing in cutting-edge poetry and fiction. Publishes paperback originals. Books: 60 lb. paper; offset printing; perfect binding. Average print order: 300. First novel print order: 500. Averages 2 total titles, 1 fiction title/year. Distributes titles through Ingram Book Company.

Needs: Experimental, literary, short story collections, avant-pop, magic realism. Recently published *Stay Tuned to This Channel*, by Vernon Frazer (avant-pop).

How to Contact: Does not accept unsolicited mss. Self-publisher.

Advice: "Start your own press. Preserve your independence."

BILINGUAL PRESS/EDITORIAL BILINGÜE, Hispanic Research Center, Arizona State University, Tempe AZ 85287-2702. (480)965-3867. **Contact:** Gary Keller, editor. Estab. 1973. "University affiliated." Publishes hardcover and paperback originals and reprints. Books: 60 lb. acid-free paper; single sheet or web press printing; case-bound and perfect-bound; illustrations sometimes. Average print order: 4,000 copies (1,000 case-bound, 3,000 soft cover). **Published new writers within the last year.** Plans 2 first novels in 2001. Averages 12 total titles, 6 fiction titles/year.

Needs: Ethnic, literary, short story collections, translations. "We are always on the lookout for Chicano, Puerto Rican, Cuban-American or other U.S.-Hispanic themes with strong and serious literary qualities and distinctive and intellectually important themes. We have been receiving a lot of fiction set in Latin America (usually Mexico or Central America) where the main character is either an ingenue to the culture or a spy, adventurer or mercenary. We don't publish this sort of 'Look, I'm in an exotic land' type of thing. Also, novels about the Aztecs or other pre-Columbians are very iffy." Published *MotherTongue*, by Demetria Martinez (novel); *Rita and Los Angeles*, by Leo Romero (short stories); and *Sanctuary Stories*, by Michael Smith (stories and essays).

How to Contact: Does not accept unsolicited mss. Send query letter with SASE or IRC for reply. Responds in 3 weeks to queries; 2 months to mss. Accepts simultaneous submissions. Sometimes comments on rejected mss.

Terms: Pays royalties of 10%. Average advance: $500. Provides 10 author's copies. Sends galleys to author. Publishes ms 1 year after acceptance. Writer's guidelines available. Book catalog free.

Advice: "Writers should take the utmost care in assuring that their manuscripts are clean, grammatically impeccable, and have perfect spelling. This is true not only of the English but the Spanish as well. All accent marks need to be in place as well as other diacritical marks. When these are missing it's an immediate first indication that the author does not really know Hispanic culture and is not equipped to write about it. We are interested in publishing creative literature that treats the U.S.-Hispanic experience in a distinctive, creative, revealing way. The kinds of books that we publish we keep in print for a very long time irrespective of sales. We are busy establishing and preserving a U.S.-Hispanic canon of creative literature."

BOOKS FOR ALL TIMES, INC., Box 2, Alexandria VA 22313. Website: www.bfat.com. **Contact:** Joe David, publisher/editor. Estab. 1981. One-man operation. Publishes paperback originals. Will be testing print-on-demand. Has published 2 fiction titles to date. Plans 3 books for 2001.

Needs: Contemporary, literary, short story collections. "No novels at the moment; hopeful, though, of publishing a collection of quality short stories. No popular fiction or material easily published by the major or minor houses specializing in mindless entertainment. Only interested in stories of the Victor Hugo or Sinclair Lewis quality."

How to Contact: Send query letter with SASE. Responds in 1 month to queries. Accepts simultaneous submissions. Occasionally comments on rejected mss.

Terms: Pays negotiable advance. "Publishing/payment arrangement will depend on plans for the book." Book catalog free with SASE.

Advice: Interested in "controversial, honest stories which satisfy the reader's curiosity to know. Read Victor Hugo, Fyodor Dostoyevsky and Sinclair Lewis for an example."

BOSON BOOKS, C&M Online Media, Inc., 3905 Meadow Field Lane, Raleigh NC 27606. (919)233-8164. Fax: (919)233-8578. E-mail: cm@cmonline.com. Website: www.cmonline.com. (All books may be downloaded from the website. It is a sales site). **Contact:** Acquisitions Editor. Estab. 1994. "We are an online book company with distribution at our website and through ten separate distributors such as softlock.com and barnesandnoble.com." Publishes online originals and reprints. **Published 6 new writers within the last year.** Plans 6 first novels in 2001. Averages 12 total titles, 9 fiction titles/year. Member: Association of Online Publishers.

Needs: "The quality of the writing is our only consideration." Publishes ongoing series of Holocaust narratives by eyewitnesses.

How to Contact: Does not accept or return unsolicited mss. Query with synopsis and 2 sample chapters. Accepts queries by e-mail and fax. Send SASE or IRC for return of ms or send disposable copy of ms and SASE for reply only. Accepts simultaneous and electronic submissions.

Terms: Pays royalties of 20%. Sends galleys to author. Writer's guidelines and book catalog on website.

Advice: "We want to see only excellence in writing."

CADMUS EDITIONS, Box 126, Tiburon CA 94920. (707)762-1050. **Contact:** Jeffrey Miller, editor. Estab. 1979. Emphasis on quality literature. Publishes hardcover and paperback originals. Books: approximately 25% letterpress; 75% offset printing; perfect and case binding. Average print order: 2,000. First novel print order: 2,000. Averages 1-3 total titles/year.

Needs: Literary. Published *The Wandering Fool*, by Yunus Emre, translated by Edouard Roditi and Guzin Dino; *The Hungry Girls*, by Patricia Eakins; and *Zig-Zag*, by Richard Thornley.

How to Contact: No unsolicited mss. Agented material only.

Terms: Pays negotiated royalty.

CALYX BOOKS, P.O. Box B, Corvallis OR 97339-0539. (503)753-9384. Fax: (541)753-0515. E-mail: calyx@proaxis.com. **Contact:** M. Donnelly, director; Micki Reaman, managing editor. Estab. 1986. "Calyx exists to publish women's literary and artistic work and is committed to publishing the works of all women, including women of color, older women, lesbians, working-class women, and other voices that need to be heard." Publishes hardcover and paperback originals. Books: offset printing; paper and cloth binding. Average print order: 4,000-10,000 copies. First novel print order: 4,000-5,000. **Published 1 new writer within the last year.** Averages 3 total titles/year. Distributes titles through Consortium Book Sales and Distribution. Promotes titles through author reading tours, print advertising (trade and individuals), galley and review copy mailings, presence at trade shows, etc.

- Past anthologies include *Forbidden Stitch: An Asian American Women's Anthology*; *Women and Aging*; *Present Tense: Writing and Art by Young Women*; and *A Line of Cutting Women*.

Needs: Contemporary, ethnic, experimental, feminist, lesbian, literary, short story collections, translations. Published *Into the Forest*, by Jean Hegland (women's literature); *Switch*, by Carol Guess (lesbian literature); and *The End of the Class Wars*, by Catherine Brady (short stories).

How to Contact: Send SASE for submission guidelines. Accepts requests by e-mail.

Terms: Pays royalties of 10% minimum, author's copies (depends on grant/award money). Average advance: $200-500. Sends galleys to author. Publishes ms 2 years after acceptance. Writer's guidelines for #10 SASE. Book catalog free on request.

Advice: "We are closed for book submissions until further notice."

CAROLINA WREN PRESS, INC., 120 Morris St., Durham NC 27701. (919)560-2738. Fax: (919)560-2759. E-mail: carolinawrenpress@compuserve.com. **Contact:** Cherryl Floyd-Miller and Sonja Stone, editors (Carolina Wren Press, contest specific). Estab. 1976. "Small, one person, part-time, nonprofit. We depend on grants to operate. We cater to new writers who have been historically under-represented, especially women, people of color, minorities, etc." Publishes paperback originals. Books: 6×9 paper; typeset; various bindings; illustrations. Average print order: 1,500. First novel print order: 1,500. **Published 1 new writer within the last year.** Averages 2 total titles, 1 fiction title/year. Member: SPD. Distributes titles through Amazon.com, Barnes & Noble, Borders, Ingram and Baker & Taylor.

Imprint(s): Lollipop Power Books; Jacqueline Ogburn, editor (nonstereotypical children's literature).

Needs: Children's/juvenile (non-stereotypical), ethnic/multicultural, experimental (poetry), feminist, gay, lesbian, literary, short story collections. Recently published *Letters Lost & Found*, by Elaine Goolsly; *Succory*, by Andrea Selch; and *Gold Indigoes*, by George Elliott Clarke.

How to Contact: Does not accept unsolicited mss; will return if supplied with postage. Send query letter. Accepts queries by e-mail, fax and phone. Include brief bio. Send SASE or IRC for return of ms. Agented fiction "only one of 40" submissions. Responds in 3 months to queries; 6 months to mss.

Terms: Pays in author's copies (10% of print run) and 50% off list price for additional copies. Sends galleys to author. Publishes ms 6 months after acceptance.

Advice: "Please do not submit unless in response to advertised call on specific topic. Workshop your manuscript before submitting."

CAVE BOOKS, 756 Harvard Ave., St. Louis MO 63130. (314)862-7646. E-mail: rawatson@artsci.wustl.edu. **Contact:** Richard Watson, editor. Estab. 1985. Small press devoted to books on caves, karst and speleology. Publishes hardcover and paperback originals and reprints. Books: acid free paper; offset printing. Average print order: 1,500. **Published 2 new writers within the last year.** Averages 4 total titles, 1 or no fiction titles/year.

Needs: Fiction: novels about cave exploration only. Adventure, caves, karst, speleology. Recently published *Emergence*, by Marian McConnell (novel).

How to Contact: Accepts unsolicited mss. Send query letter. Accepts queries by e-mail. Send SASE or IRC for return of ms or send disposable copy of ms and SASE for reply only. Responds in 2 weeks to queries; 2 months to mss. Accepts simultaneous submissions. Sometimes comments on rejected mss.

Terms: Pays royalties of 10%. Sends galleys to author. Publishes ms 18 months after acceptance. Writer's guidelines on website.

Advice: "In the last three years we have received only three novels about caves, and we have published one of them. We get dozens of inappropriate submissions."

CHRISTCHURCH PUBLISHERS LTD., 2 Caversham St., London SW3 4AH United Kingdom. Fax: 0044 171 351 4995. **Contact:** James Hughes, fiction editor. Averages 25 fiction titles/year. Length: 30,000 words minimum.

Needs: "Miscellaneous fiction, also poetry. More 'literary' style of fiction, but also thrillers, crime fiction, etc."

How to Contact: Query with synopsis ("brief synopsis favored").

Terms: Pays royalties and advance. "We have contacts and agents worldwide."

CREATIVITY UNLIMITED PRESS, 30819 Casilina, Rancho Palos Verdes CA 90274. (310)377-7908. **Contact:** Rochelle Stockwell. Estab. 1980. One-person operation with plans to expand. Publishes paperback originals and self-hypnosis cassette tapes. Books: perfect binding; illustrations. Average print order: 2,500. First novel print order 1,000. Averages 2 total titles/year.

Needs: Published *Insides Out*, by Shelley Stockwell (plain talk poetry); *Sex and Other Touchy Subjects* (poetry and short stories); *Time Travel: Do-It-Yourself Past Life Regression Handbook*; *Denial is Not a River in Egypt*; and *Hypnosis: How to Put a Smile on Your Face and Money in Your Wallet*.
How to Contact: Write for more information.

CROSS-CULTURAL COMMUNICATIONS, 239 Wynsum Ave., Merrick NY 11566-4725. (516)868-5635. Fax: (516)379-1901. E-mail: cccmia@juno.com. **Contact:** Stanley H. Barkan, editorial director. Estab. 1971. "Small/alternative literary arts publisher focusing on the traditionally neglected languages and cultures in bilingual and multimedia format." Publishes chapbooks, magazines, anthologies, novels, audio cassettes (talking books) and video cassettes (video books, video mags); hardcover and paperback originals. Publishes new women writers series, Holocaust series, Israeli writers series, Dutch writers series, Asian-, African- and Italian-American heritage writers series, Polish writers series, Armenian writers series, Native American writers series, Latin American writers series.
- Authors published by this press have received international awards including Nat Scammacca, who won the National Poetry Prize of Italy and Gabriel Preil, who won the Bialik Prize of Israel.
Needs: Contemporary, literary, experimental, ethnic, humor/satire, juvenile and young adult folktales, and translations. "Main interests: bilingual short stories and children's folktales, parts of novels of authors of other cultures, translations; some American fiction. No fiction that is not directed toward other cultures. For an annual anthology of authors writing in other languages (primarily), we will be seeking very short stories with original-language copy (other than Latin, script should be print quality 10/12) on good paper. Title: *Cross-Cultural Review Anthology: International Fiction 1*. We expect to extend our *CCR* series to include 10 fiction issues: *Five Contemporary* (Dutch, Swedish, Yiddish, Norwegian, Danish, Sicilian, Greek, Israeli, etc.) *Fiction Writers*." Published *Sicilian Origin of the Odyssey*, by L.G. Pocock (bilingual English-Italian translation by Nat Scammacca); *Sikano L'Americano!* and *Bye Bye America*, by Nat Scammacca; and *Milkrun*, by Robert J. Gress.
How to Contact: Accepts unsolicited mss. Query with SAE with $1 postage to include book catalog. "Note: Original language ms should accompany translations." Accepts simultaneous submissions. Responds in 1 month.
Terms: Pays "sometimes" 10-25% in royalties and "occasionally" by outright purchase, in author's copies— "10% of run for chapbook series" and "by arrangement for other publications." No advance.
Advice: "Write because you want to or you must; satisfy yourself. If you've done the best you can, then you've succeeded. You will find a publisher and an audience eventually. Generally, we have a greater interest in nonfiction, novels and translations. Short stories and excerpts from novels written in one of the traditional neglected languages are preferred—with the original version (i.e., bilingual). Our kinderbook series will soon be in production with a similar bilingual emphasis, especially for folktales, fairy tales, and fables."

DARKTALES PUBLICATIONS, P.O. Box 675, Grandview MO 64030. Phone/fax: (718)889-3405. E-mail: dave@darktales.com. Website: www.darktales.com (includes an entire Web community for horror writers and fans—horror discussion listserve, webring, chatroom, fiction bulletin boards, book catalog, interviews and commentary in e-zine, *Sinister Element*, and more). **Contact**: Butch Miller, editor-in-chief (noir, speculative fiction, horror); David Nordhaus, CFO/editor (dark fantasy, horror); Keith Herber, editor (horror, "Lovecraftian"). Estab. 1998. Small independent publisher. "Our publishing focus is on horror, from extreme to esoteric. We hope to add some truly wonderful new titles to the body of horror. What makes us unique is that so many of the authors we are working with are new names to the horror scene. We hope to make them succeed, or at least help them on their way." Publishes paperback originals. Books: trade paper; print-on-demand technology; Perma-bound. Average print order: 750. **Published 8 new writers within the last year.** Plans 8 first novels in 2001. Plans 15 total titles, all fiction, this year. Member: Horror Writers Association. Distributes titles through online sales and self-distribution. Promotes titles through print, radio and Internet ads.
Needs: Comics/graphic novels, erotica (must be dark), horror (dark fantasy, futuristic, psychological, supernatural, extreme). "We are looking to expand our line of chapbooks with long fiction pieces around 1,500 words. We are also considering concepts for dark fantasy/horror role-playing game companions or originals. Publishes *The Asylum* horror anthology series; writers may submit to Victor Heck, editor (see website for details). Recently published *Scary Rednecks and Other Inbred Horrors*, by David Whitman and Weston Ochse (horror anthology); *Demonesque*, by Steven L. Climer (horror novel); and *Tribulations*, by J. Michael Straczynski (dark fantasy). Publishes the *Sinister Element* series.
How to Contact: Does not accept unsolicited mss. Query with outline/synopsis and 2-3 sample chapters. Accepts queries by e-mail. Include estimated word count, brief bio and list of publishing credits. Send a disposable copy of ms and SASE for reply only. Agented fiction 20%. Responds in 1 month to queries; 4 months to mss. Accepts simultaneous and electronic submissions and disk. Often comments on rejected mss.
Terms: Pays royalties of 6-8%. Average advance: $100. Sends galleys to author as an electronic typeset version in PDF format. Publishes ms within 2 years of acceptance. Writer's guidelines and book catalog on website.
Advice: "We are the first horror independent press to effectively integrate print-on-demand technology, thus enabling us to publish more books with lower risk than traditional offset publishers. Plus our book quality is second to none. Please follow our submission guidelines. Always query first. We publish only horror and dark erotica. Anything else and we won't be interested."

○ ⚤ **THE DESIGN IMAGE GROUP INC.**, 231 S. Frontage Rd., Suite 17, Burr Ridge IL 60521. (630)789-8991. Fax: (630)789-9013. E-mail: dig1956@aol.com. Website: www.designimagegroup.com (includes book catalog and links). **Contact**: Editorial Committee. Estab. 1998. "Horror/genre fiction micropublisher distributing exclusively through normal trade channels." Publishes paperback originals. Books: offset paper; offset printing; perfect binding. Average print order: 3,000. First novel print order: 3,000. **Published 1 new writer within the last year.** Plans 4 first novels in 2001. Averages 3 total titles, 3 fiction titles/year. Member: AMA, SPMA. Distributes titles through Ingram, Baker & Taylor and Diamond.
  ● The Design Image Group Inc. has been an International Horror Guild Award Nominee for First Novel and HWA Stoker Award Nominee for first novel. They are members of the Publishers Marketing Association and Horror Writers Association.
Needs: Horror, supernatural. Looking for "traditional supernatural horror fiction." Publishes horror anthology. Guidelines announced in writers' and genre publications in advance. Recently published *Gothique*, by Kyle Marffin (vampire); *A Face Without a Heart*, by Rick R. Reed (horror); and *Whispered From the Grave* (anthology).
How to Contact: Accepts unsolicited mss. Send query letter or query with synopsis and 3 sample chapters. Send SASE or IRC for return of ms or send a disposable copy of the ms and SASE for reply only. Agented fiction 25%. Responds in 4 months to queries and mss. Accepts simultaneous submissions. Often comments on rejected mss.
Terms: Pays royalties of 10-20% on wholesale price, not cover. Average advance: $3,000. Sends galleys to author. Publishes ms 3 months after acceptance. Writer's guidelines for SASE. Book catalog for 6×9 SASE or see website.
Advice: "We publish traditional supernatural horror ONLY—vampires, ghosts, werewolves, witches, etc. No thrillers, serial killers, etc. Please send for writers guidelines, they're quite specific and helpful."

◑ ◎ **DOWN THERE PRESS**, Subsidiary of Open Enterprises Cooperative, Inc., 938 Howard St., #205, San Francisco CA 94103. (415)974-8985 ext 205. Fax: (415)974-8989. E-mail: goodvibe@well.com. Website: www.goodvibes/dtp/dtp.html (includes titles, author bios, excerpts, guidelines, calls for submissions). **Contact:** Leigh Davidson, managing editor. Estab. 1975. Small independent press with part-time staff; part of a large worker-owned cooperative. Publishes paperback originals. Books: Web offset printing; perfect binding; some illustrations. Average print order: 5,000. First novel print order: 3,000-5,000. **Published new writers within the last year.** Averages 1-2 total titles, 1 fiction title each year. Member: Publishers Marketing Association and Northern California Book Publicity and Marketing Association.
Imprint(s): Yes Press and Red Alder Books.
Needs: Erotica, feminist, lesbian. Published *Herotica 6*, edited by Marcy Sheiner (anthology); *Sex Spoken Here: Erotic Reading Circle Stories*, edited by Carol Queen and Jack Davis (anthology); and *Sex Toy Tales*, edited by A. Semans and Cathy Winks.
How to Contact: Accepts unsolicited mss. Submit partial ms with cover letter, synopsis and table of contents (short stories for anthologies only). Accepts queries and correspondence by fax. Include estimated word count. Send SASE or IRC for return of ms or send disposable copy of ms and SASE for reply only. Responds in up to 9 months to mss. Accepts simultaneous submissions. Sometimes comments on rejected mss.
Terms: Pays royalties and author's copies. Sends galleys to author. Publishes ms 18 months after acceptance. Writer's guidelines and book catalog for #10 SASE.

🅽 ◑ **FIRST AMENDMENT PRESS INTERNATIONAL COMPANY**, 38 E. Ridgewood Ave., PMB 217, Ridgewood NJ 07450-3808. (888)277-1251. Fax: (810)314-6739. E-mail: fapic@msn.com. Website: www.fapic.com. ("Our website is a showcase and point-of-purchase for all of our newly released titles. The website also has a message board and an archive of past essays and articles.") **Contact:** John Rimpington, fiction editor. Estab. 1997. "First Amendment Press International Company (FAPIC) proudly publishes books true to the voices of its authors and their intent by delivering completely unedited, uncut, quality literature to the reading public. Founded in 1997, FAPIC has since become a leader among small to midsized presses by preserving the distinct talents of its authors." Publishes hardcover originals. Books: 60 lb. Joy white offset paper; press printing; cloth binding. Average print order: 2,000. First novel print order: 2,000. **Published 3 new writers within the last year.** Plans 2 first novels in 2001. Averages 5 total titles, 3 fiction titles/year. Member: Publishers Marketing Association, Small Press Association. Distributes titles through the Internet, PMA programs, Baker & Taylor, Ingram Book Company and ARC mailings.
Needs: Erotica, fantasy (space fantasy, sword and sorcery), feminist, gay, horror (dark fantasy, futuristic, psychological, supernatural), humor/satire, lesbian, literary, mainstream, mystery/suspense, New Age/mystic, psychic/supernatural, regional, religious (general religious, religious fantasy, religious mystery/suspense, religious thriller, religious romance), romance (contemporary, futuristic/time travel, gothic, romantic suspense), science fiction (soft/sociological), short story collections, thriller/espionage, translations, western (frontier saga, traditional). Recently published *Noble McCloud—A Novel* (fiction); and *The Imam—A Novel*, both by Harvey Havel (fiction).

How to Contact: Does not accept unsolicited mss. Send query letter. Accepts queries by e-mail and fax. Include estimated word count, brief bio and list of publishing credits. Send disposable copy of ms and SASE for reply only. Agented fiction 33%. Responds in 1 month to queries; 2 months to mss. Accepts electronic submissions. Always comments on rejected mss.

Terms: Pays royalties of 20-50%. Offers negotiable advance (individual arrangement with author depending on the book.) Sends galleys to author. Publishes ms 5-12 months after acceptance. Book catalog on website.

Advice: "As an independent small press our strength has always been fiction, but we have also seen opportunity in nonfiction titles as well. Overall, however, we aim to publish as many quality fiction titles as possible, given our budget."

FP HENDRIKS PUBLISHING LTD., 4806-53 St., Stettler, Alberta T0C 2L2 Canada. Phone/fax: (403)742-6483. E-mail: editor@fphendriks.com. Website: www.fphendriks.com. **Contact:** Faye Boer, managing editor. Estab. 1994. "Small independent publisher. Noted for personal contact with authors." Publishes paperback originals. **Published 2 new writers within the last year.** Plans 1 first novel in 2001. Averages 2-4 total titles, 1-2 fiction titles/year. Member: Book Publishers Association of Alberta. Distributes titles through Fitzhenry & Whiteside. Distributes titles through catalogs, sales reps and distributor catalog.

• *From Your Child's Teacher* won the 1999 *Parent's Guide* Honor Award.

Needs: Young adult/teen (adventure, easy-to-read, fantasy/science fiction, historical, horror, mystery/suspense, romance, sports, western). Needs "young adult fiction in most genres."

How to Contact: Accepts unsolicited mss. Query with outline/synopsis and 2-3 sample chapters. Accepts queries by e-mail. Include estimated word count, brief bio and list of publishing credits. Send SASE or IRC for return of ms or send disposable copy of ms and SASE for reply only. Responds in 4 months to queries; up to 6 months to mss. Accepts simultaneous submissions, electronic submissions and disk (depending on format).

Terms: Pays royalties of 10%. Sends galleys to author. Publishes ms 1 year after acceptance. Writer's guidelines free for 3×8 SAE and 46¢ postage (Canadian) or IRC or visit website. Book catalog for 9×12 SAE and $1.50 postage (Canadian).

Advice: "Attend always to audience."

GASLIGHT PUBLICATIONS, Empire Publishing Services, P.O. Box 1344, Studio City CA 91614-0344. (818)784-8918. **Contact:** Simon Waters, fiction editor (Sherlock Holmes only). Estab. 1960. Publishes hardcover and paperback originals and reprints. Books: paper varies; offset printing; binding varies; illustrations. Average print order: 5,000. First novel print order: 5,000. **Published 1 new writer within the last year.** Plans 1 first novel in 2001. Averages 4-12 total titles, 2-4 fiction titles/year. Promotes titles through sales reps, trade, library, etc.

Needs: Sherlock Holmes only. Recently published *On the Scent with Sherlock Holmes*, by Walter Shepherd; *Sherlock Holmes, The Complete Bagel Street Saga*, by Robert L. Fish; and *Subcutaneously, My Dear Watson*, by Jack Tracy (all Sherlock Holmes). Publishes the Sherlock Holmes Mysteries series.

How to Contact: Accepts unsolicited mss. Send query letter. Include estimated word count, brief bio and list of publishing credits. Send SASE or IRC for return of ms or send disposable copy of the ms and SASE for reply only. Agented fiction 12%. Responds in 2 weeks to queries; up to 1 year to mss.

Terms: Pays royalties of 8-10%. (Royalty and advances dependant on the material.) Sends prepublication galleys to author. Publishes ms 1-6 months after acceptance. Writer's guidelines for SASE. Book catalog for 9×12 SAE and $2 postage.

Advice: "Please send only Sherlock Holmes material. Other stuff just wastes time and money."

THE GLENCANNON PRESS, P.O. Box 633, Benicia CA 94510. (707)745-3933. Fax: (707)747-0311. E-mail: captjoff@pacbell.net. Website: www.glencannon.com (includes book catalog). **Contact:** Bill Harris (maritime, maritime children's). Estab. 1993. "We publish quality books about ships and the sea." Publishes hardcover and paperback originals and hardcover reprints. Books: Smyth-sewn or perfect binding; illustrations. Average print order: 1,000. First novel print order: 750. **Published 1 new writer within the last year.** Averages 4-5 total titles, 1 fiction title/year. Member: PMA. Distributes titles through Ingram and Baker & Taylor. Promotes titles through direct mail, magazine advertising and word of mouth.

Imprint(s): Palo Alto Books (any maritime); Glencannon Press (merchant marine); Bill Harris, editor.

Needs: Adventure, children's/juvenile (adventure, fantasy, historical, mystery, preschool/picture book), ethnic/multicultural (general), historical (maritime), humor/satire, mainstream, military/war, mystery/suspense, thriller/espionage, western (frontier saga, traditional maritime), young adult/teen (adventure, historical, mystery/suspense, western). Currently emphasizing children's maritime, any age. Recently published *White Hats*, by Floyd Beaver (navy short stories); and *Holy Glencannon*, by Guy Gilpatric (merchant marine short story).

How to Contact: Accepts unsolicited mss. Submit complete ms with cover letter. Include brief bio and list of publishing credits. Send SASE or IRC for return of ms OR send disposable copy of ms and SASE for reply only. Responds in 1 month to queries; 2 months to mss. Accepts simultaneous submissions. Often comments on rejected mss.

Terms: Pays royalties of 10-20%. "Usually author receives $1-2 per copy for each book sold." Sends galleys to author. Publishes ms 6-24 months after acceptance. Book catalog free and on website.
Advice: "Write a good story in a compelling style."

○ GOLDENISLE PUBLISHERS, INC., 2395 Hawkinsville Hwy., Eastman GA 31023. (912)374-9455. Fax: (912)374-9720. **Contact**: Tena Ryals. Estab. 1998. "Small independent publisher." Publishes hardcover and paperback originals and hardcover reprints. Average print order: 2,000. First novel print order: 1,000. **Published 1 new writer within the last year.** Plans 1 first novel in 2001. Averages 3-5 total titles, 3 fiction titles/year. Member: PMA. Distributes titles through Baker & Taylor, Ingram, Brodart and Barnes & Noble. Promotes titles through PMA programs, Booklist and *Publishers Weekly*.
Needs: Historical (general), humor satire, mainstream, religious (inspirational), romance (historical), western (frontier saga). Recently published *The Third Season*, by Jack P. Jones (mainstream, contemporary); *Unforgettable*, by Fern Smith-Brown (historical romance); and *Cast Down the Waters: A Bosnia in Flames*, by Clifford J. Moody.
How to Contact: Does not accept unsolicited mss. Send query letter. Include estimated word count, 1 page bio and list of publishing credits. Send SASE or IRC for reply. Responds in 6 weeks to queries; 4 months to mss. Sometimes comments on rejected mss.
Terms: Pays royalties. Sends galleys to author. Publishes ms 1-2 years after acceptance.
Advice: "We do not publish material containing the 'f-word,' hard profanity, explicit sex or 'thrown-in violence.' Write what you enjoy writing and revise until it touches your heart."

Ⓝ GOTHIC CHAPBOOK SERIES, Gothic Press, 4998 Perkins Rd., Baton Rouge LA 70808-3043. (225)925-2917. E-mail: gwriter602@aol.com. Website: www.gothicpress.com (includes information and catalog request e-mail). **Contact:** Gary W. Crawford, editor. Estab. 1979. "One person operation on a part-time basis. Publishes horror fiction, poetry, and scholarship and criticism." Publishes paperback originals. Books: printing or photocopying; saddle stitched. Average print order: 150-200. Averages 1-2 total titles and fiction titles/year. Member: Horror Writers Association, Science Fiction Poetry Association. Distributes titles through the Internet, direct mail and Amazon.com.
Needs: Horror (dark fantasy, psychological, supernatural). Need novellas and short stories. Gothic Press is not always an open market. Query first before submitting anything.
How to Contact: Accepts unsolicited mss. Send query letter. Accepts queries by e-mail or phone. Include estimated word count, brief bio and list of publishing credits. Send SASE or IRC for return of ms or send disposable copy of ms and SASE for reply only. Responds in 2 weeks to queries; 4 weeks to mss. Sometimes comments on rejected ms. Pays royalties of 10%. Sends galleys to author. Writer's guidelines send SASE.
Advice: "Know gothic and horror literature well."

Ⓝ ○ GREYCORE PRESS, 2646 New Prospect Rd., Pine Bush NY 12566. (914)744-5081. Fax: (914)744-8081. Website: www.greycore.com. **Contact:** Polly Lindenbaum, editor. Estab. 1999. Small independent publisher of quality fiction and nonfiction titles. Publishes hardcover originals. Books: cloth binding. Average print order: 2,000. First novel print order: 2,000. **Published 3 new writers within the last year.** Plans 2 first novels in 2001. Averages 3 total titles, 2 fiction titles/year. Member: Dustbooks. Distributes titles through Alliance House.
Needs: Literary, mainstream, short story collections. Recently published *The Secret Keepers*, by Julie Mars; and *The Queen of Hearts: Tales of Middle Age Passion*, by Millie Crace-Brown.
How to Contact: Does not accept unsolicited mss. Send query letter. Accepts queries by e-mail and fax. Include estimated word count and list of publishing credits. Send SASE or IRC for return of ms. Responds in weeks to queries; in months to mss. Accepts simultaneous submissions. Sometimes comments on rejected mss.
Terms: Pays royalties of 50% after production costs. Sends galleys to author. Publishes ms 18 months after acceptance.
Advice: "We prefer to get cover letters that include author credentials and the ways in which they are willing to help publicize their work."

⊕ ✓ ◎ HANDSHAKE EDITIONS, Atelier A2, 83 rue de la Tombe Issoire, 75014 Paris France. Fax: 33-1-4320-4195. E-mail: jim_haynes@wanadoo.fr. **Contact:** Jim Haynes, editor. Averages 4 story collections or novels/year. "Only face-to-face submissions accepted. More interested in 'faction' and autobiographical writing." Pays in copies. Writers interested in submitting a manuscript should "have lunch or dinner with me in Paris."

⊕ ✓ HEMKUNT PRESS, Hemkunt Publishers (P) Ltd., A-78 Naraina Industrial Area Phase-I, New Delhi India 110028. Phone: +91-11-579-5079. Fax: +91-11-611-3705. E-mail: hemkunt1@vsnl.com. Website: www.hemkuntpress.com (includes company profile, book jackets, prices, ISBN, brief summary). **Contact**: Arvinder Singh, director. "We specialize in children's fiction and storybooks as well as novels and short stories." Distributes titles through direct sales, direct mailings and distributors.

Needs: "We would be interested in novels, preferably by authors with a published work. Unpublished work can also be considered. Would like to have distribution rights for US, Canada and UK besides India." Charges fee depending on author profile, ms and marketability. Recently published *More Tales of Birbal & Akbar*, by Sanjana Singh.

How to Contact: Send a cover letter, brief summary, 3 sample chapters (first, last and one other chapter). Accepts queries by e-mail and fax.

Terms: Catalog on request.

Advice: "Send interesting short stories and novels pertaining to the global point of view."

N ◑ ◎ HILL STREET PRESS, Hill Street Press LLC, 191 E. Broad St., #209, Athens GA 30601-2848. (706)613-7200. Fax: (706)613-7204 E-mail: info@hillstreetpress.com. Website: www.hillstreetpress.com (includes writer's guideline, mission statement, book catalog and interviews). **Contact:** Patrick Allen and Judy Long, editors. Estab. 1998. "Small independent press specializing in Southern belles lettres." Publishes hardcover and paperback originals and paperback reprints. Books: acid-free paper; conventional printing; photos/drawings. Average print order: 7,500. First novel print order: 7,500. **Published 5 new writers within the last year.** Plans 2 first novels in 2001. Averages 26 total titles; 5 fiction titles/year. Member: PAS. Distributes and promotes titles electronically, through the gift trade and national distribution group.

Needs: Gay, historical (southern U.S.), lesbian, literary, regional (southern U.S.). Recently published *Total View of Taftly*, by Scott Morris (literary); *Strange Birds in the Tree of Heaven*, by Karen S. McElmurray (literary); and *The Bearded Lady*, by Sharlee Dieugez (commercial).

How to Contact: Accepts unsolicited mss. Query with outline/synopsis and 3 sample chapters. Include estimated word count, brief bio, list of publishing credits and résumé. Send SASE or IRC for return of ms or send disposable copy of ms and SASE for reply only. Agented fiction 5%. Responds in 3 months to queries; 6 months to mss. Accepts simultaneous submissions.

Payment/Terms: Pays royalties. Sends galleys to author. Publishes ms up to 2 years after acceptance. Writer's guidelines free for SASE. Book catalog available for 11 × 8 SAE with $1.24 postage.

Advice: "Give a good synopsis; tell us what other published books it might resemble and your educational/professional background."

☑ ◑ HOLLOW EARTH PUBLISHING, P.O. Box 1355, Boston MA 02205-1355. (617)249-0161. E-mail: hep2@hotmail.com. **Contact:** Helian Grimes, editor/publisher. Estab. 1983. "Small independent publisher." Publishes hardcover and paperback originals and reprints. Books: acid-free paper; offset printing; Smythe binding.

Needs: Comics/graphic novels, fantasy (sword and sorcery), feminist, gay, lesbian, literary, New Age/mystic/spiritual, translations. Looking for "computers, Internet, Norse mythology, magic." Publishes various computer application series.

How to Contact: Does not accept unsolicited mss. Contact by e-mail only. Include estimated word count, 1-2 page bio and list of publishing credits. Agented fiction 90%. Responds in 2 months. Accepts submissions on disk.

Terms: Pays in royalties. Sends galleys to author. Publishes ms 6 months after acceptance.

Advice: Looking for "less fiction, more computer information."

N ◯ HUNTINGTON PRESS, 3687 S. Procyon Ave., Las Vegas NV 89103. (702)252-0655. Fax: (702)252-0675. E-mail: books@huntingtonpress.com. Website: www.huntingtonpress.com. **Contact:** Deke Castleman, senior editor. Publishes hardcover and paperback originals. Books: offset printing. First novel print order: 3,000-5,000. **Published 2 new writers within the last year.** Plans 2 first novels in 2001. Averages 12 total titles, 2 fiction titles/year. Member: PMA/SPAN.

Needs: Adventure, historical (general), mainstream, mystery/suspense. Recently published *Keeps*, by A.D. "Pete" Fowler (gambling); and *Spider Snatch*, by Bill Branon (action adventure).

How to Contact: Accepts unsolicited mss. Send query letter. Accepts queries by e-mail. Responds in 3 months to queries; 6 weeks to mss. Accepts simultaneous and electronic submissions. Often comments on rejected mss.

Terms: Pays royalties. Sends galleys to author. Publishes ms 1 year after acceptance. Writer's guidelines for SASE. Book catalogs free.

◑ ◎ ⛉ ILLUMINATION PUBLISHING CO., P.O. Box 1865, Bellevue WA 98009. (425)644-7185. Fax: (425)644-9274. E-mail: liteinfo@illumin.com. Website: www.illumin.com. **Contact:** Ruth Thompson, editorial director. Estab. 1987. "Illumination Arts is a small publishing company publishing high quality, uplifting and inspirational children's picture books that create transformation." Publishes hardcover originals. Averages 6-8 children's picture books/year. Distributes titles through New Leaf, De Vorss, Book People, Quality, Ingram, Baker & Taylor, Koen Pacific and bookstores. Promotes titles through direct mailings, website, book shows, flyers and posters, catalogs. Publisher arranges author and illustrator signings but expects authors/illustrators to actively promote. Enters many book award events. Member: Book Publishers of the Northwest.

● Illumination Publishing's *Dragon* was selected Best Children's Book 2000 by The Coalition of Visionary Retailers. *The Right Touch* was a winner of the 1999 Ben Franklin Award (parenting).

Needs: Children's/juvenile (adventure, inspirational, preschool/picture books). Recently published *To Sleep with the Angels, The Doll Lady* and *Wings of Change* (children's picture books).
How to Contact: Accepts unsolicited mss. Query first or submit complete ms with cover letter. Include estimated word count and list of publishing credits. Send SASE or IRC for return of ms. Responds in 3 weeks to queries; 2 months to mss. Accepts simultaneous submissions. Often comments on rejected mss.
Terms: Pays royalties. Sends galleys to author. Publishes ms 18 months-2 years after acceptance. Writer's guidelines for SASE and on website.
Advice: "Submit full manuscripts, neatly typed without grammatical or spelling errors. Expect to be edited many times. Be patient. We are very *painstaking*. Read and follow the guidelines posted on our website."

IVY LEAGUE PRESS, INC., P.O. Box 3326, San Ramon CA 94583-8326. (925)736-0601 or 800-IVY-PRESS. Fax: (925)736-0602 or (888)IVY-PRESS. E-mail: ivyleaguepress@worldnet.att.net. **Contact**: Maria Thomas, editor. Publishes hardcover and paperback originals. Specializes in medical thrillers. Books: perfect binding. First novel print order: 5,000. Plans 1 novel in 2001. Averages 2 total titles, 1-2 fiction titles/year. Distributes titles through Baker & Taylor and Ingram. Promotes titles through TV, radio and print.
Needs: Mystery/suspense(medical). Published *Allergy Shots*, by Litman.
How to Contact: Accepts unsolicited mss. Query with outline/synopsis. Include estimated word count, bio and list of publishing credits. Send SASE or IRC for return of the ms or send disposable copy of ms and SASE for reply only. Responds in 2 months to queries. Accepts electronic submissions. Always comments on rejected mss.
Terms: Royalties vary. Sends galleys to author.
Advice: "If you tell a terrific story of medical suspense, one which is hard to put down, we may publish it."

JESPERSON PRESS LTD., 39 James Lane, St. John's, Newfoundland A1E 3H3 Canada. (709)753-0633. **Contact:** John Simmonds, publisher. Midsize independent publisher. Publishes hardcover and paperback originals. Averages 3-4 total titles, 1-2 fiction titles/year.
Needs: Solid contemporary fiction by Newfoundland authors about Newfoundland, preferably novel-length or short story collection. Not interested in young adult, childrens' or poetry of any kind.
How to Contact: Does not accept unsolicited mss. Query with synopsis and SASE (Canadian postage or IRCs, please) only. Responds in 6 months or less. Sometimes comments on rejected mss.
Terms: Pays negotiable royalties. Sends galleys to author. Book catalog free.

KARNAK HOUSE, 300 Westbourne Park Road, London W11 1EH England. Fax: 0171-221-6490. **Contact**: Amon Saba Saakana, managing editor. Averages 3-4 fiction titles annually.
Needs: "An Afro-Caribbean publishing company concerned with global literary concerns of the African community, whether in North and South America, the Caribbean, Africa or Europe. We look for innovative work in the areas outlined above and work which attempts to express the culture, language, mythology—ethos—of the people. No fantasy, science fiction. We are literary publishers. We look for work which tries to break away from standard English as the dominant narrative voice."
Terms: "We rarely pay advances, and if so, very small, but pay a royalty rate of 8-10% on the published price of the book."

KAWABATA PRESS, Knill Cross House, Knill Cross, Millbrook, Torpoint, Cornwall PL10 1DX England. **Contact:** Colin Webb, fiction editor.
 ● "No longer publishing separate books/booklets—but still publish short stories in *Sepia* magazine."
Needs: "Mostly poetry—but prose should be realistic, free of genre writing and clichés and above all original in ideas and content."
How to Contact: "Don't forget return postage (or IRC)."
Advice: "Avoid clichés; avoid obnoxious plots; avoid the big themes (life, death, etc.); be original; find a new angle or perspective; try to be natural rather than clever; be honest."

LEAPFROG PRESS, P.O. Box 1495, 95 Commercial St., Wellfleet MA 02667-1495. (508)349-1925. Fax: (508)349-1180. E-mail: leapfrog@capecod.net. Website: www.leapfrogpress.com (includes description of press, mission statement, writer's guidelines, e-mail link, description of books, sample poems, link to distributor, cover designs). **Contact:** David Witkowsky, acquisitions editor. Estab. 1996. "We publish book-length literary fiction and literate nonfiction that reflects a strong personal story. We publish books that are referred to by the large publishers as midlist but which we believe to be the heart and soul of literature. We're a small shop, so the small number of books we choose receive a lot of attention." Publishes hardcover and paperback originals and paperback reprints. Books: acid-free paper; sewn binding. Average print order: 5,000. First novel print order: 4,000 (average). Averages 4 total titles, 3-4 fiction titles/year. Distributes titles through Consortium Book Sales and Distribution, St. Paul, MN. Promotes titles through all national review media, bookstore readings, author tours, website, radio shows, chain store promotions, advertisements. Member: Publishers Marketing Association, Bookbuilders of Boston and PEN.

● Leapfrog Press titles have been nominated for the American Library Association—Best of the Year Award and the National Book Critics Circle Award and have been finalists for the Firecracker Alternative Press Book of the Year Award, New York Public Library Best of the Teenage List 2000 Award and the Benjamin Franklin Award.

Needs: "Genres often blur; we're interested in good writing. We'd love to see memoirs as well as fiction that comments on the world through the lens of personal, political or family experience." Recently published *Rookie Cop*, by Richard Rosenthal; *The Dangerous Age*, by Anette Williams Jaffee; *Leo@Fergusrules.com*, by Anne Taugherlini; and *Look at Me*, by Lauren Mitchell.

How to Contact: Does not accept unsolicited mss. Query with brief description of book and 2-4 sample chapters (50 pages). Accepts queries by e-mail. Send SASE or IRC for return of ms or send disposable copy of ms and SASE for reply only. Responds in 3 months to queries; 6 months to mss. No simultaneous submissions. "Please see website for information. Do not call the office." Sometimes comments on rejected mss.

Terms: Pays royalties of 4-8%. Offers negotiable advance. Provides negotiable number of author's copies. Sends galleys to author. Publishes ms 1-2 years after acceptance.

Advice: "Send us a manuscript that educates us somewhat about our world and does not dwell on personal problems only. And, it must be well written. We strongly push sales of secondary rights (translations, foreign sales, theatrical, etc.) and expect the author and publisher to participate equally in the proceeds. Writers must be willing to accept and incorporate editorial advice and cannot shirk their responsibility to publicize their own work by giving readings, contacting book stores, drumming up local media attention, etc. We believe in strong marketing with an author who can publicize him/herself."

LIVINGSTON PRESS, Station 22, University of West Alabama, Livingston AL 35470. **Contact:** Joe Taylor, editor. Estab. 1984. "Small university press specializing in offbeat and/or Southern literature." Publishes hardcover and paperback originals. Books: acid-free paper; offset; perfect bindings; illustrations sometimes. Average print order: 2,500. First novel print order: 2,500. **Published 3 first novels within the last year.** Averages 6 total titles, 1 fiction title/year. Member: Publishers Association of the South. Distributes titles through Ingram, Baker & Taylor, Amazon, Blackwell N.A., Brodart and Yankee Book.

Imprints: Swallow's Tale Press.

Needs: Literary, short story collections, off-beat or Southern. Recently published *Widening the Road*, by Fred Bonnie (stories); *The High Traverse*, by Richard Blanchard (novel); *The Drinking of Spirits*, by Tom Abrams (stories).

How to Contact: Accepts unsolicited mss. Query with outline/synopsis and 3 sample chapters. Accepts queries by e-mail only. Include estimated word count, brief bio and list of publishing credits. Send SASE or IRC for return of ms or send a disposable copy of ms and SASE for reply only. Responds in 2 months to queries; 8 months to mss. Accepts simultaneous submissions.

Terms: Pays in author's copies (12%) and royalties after 1,500 copies. Sends galleys to author. Publishes ms up to 2 years after acceptance. Book catalog available for SASE.

LOLLIPOP POWER BOOKS, 120 Morris St., Durham NC 27701. (919)560-2738. **Contact:** Jackie Ogburn, editor. Estab. 1970. "Children's imprint of the Carolina Wren Press, a small, nonprofit press which publishes non-sexist, multi-racial picture books." Publishes paperback originals. First novel print order: 3,000. Averages 1 fiction title every other year.

Needs: Not currently reviewing mss. Recently published *Puzzles*, by Dana Walker.

Terms: Pays royalties of 10%.

Advice: "Lollipop Power Books must be well-written stories that will appeal to children. We are not interested in preachy tales where message overpowers plot and character. We look for good stories told from a child's point of view. Our books present a child's perspective and feelings honestly and without condescension."

MID-LIST PRESS, Jackson, Hart & Leslie, Inc., 4324-12th Ave. S., Minneapolis MN 55407-3218. (612)822-3733. Fax: (612)823-8387. E-mail: guide@midlist.org. Website: www.midlist.org (includes writer's guidelines, history and mission, book catalog, ordering information and news). Associate Publisher: Marianne Nora. **Contact:** Lane Stiles, senior editor. Estab. 1989. "We are a nonprofit literary press dedicated to the survival of the mid-list, those quality titles that are being neglected by the larger commercial houses. Our focus is on first-time writers, and we are probably best known for the Mid-List Press First Series Awards." Publishes hardcover and paperback originals and reprints. Books: acid-free paper; offset printing; perfect or Smyth-sewn binding. Average print order: 2,000. **Published 2 new writers within the last year.** Plans 1 first novel in 2001. Averages 3 fiction titles/year. Distributes titles through Small Press Distribution, Ingram, Baker & Taylor, Midwest Library Service, Brodart, Follett, Bookmen and Emery Pratt. Promotes titles through publicity, direct mail, catalogs, author's events and reviews and awards.

Needs: General fiction. No children's/juvenile, romance, young adult, religious. Recently published *Quick Bright Things*, by Ron Wallace (short fiction); *The Hand Before the Eye*, by Donald Friedman (novel); and *Leaving the Neighborhood*, by Lucy Ferriss (short fiction). Publishes First Series Award for the Novel and First Series Award for Short Fiction. *There is a $20 reading fee for a First Series Award but no charge for publication.*

How to Contact: Accepts unsolicited mss. Send query letter first. Send disposable copy of the ms and SASE for reply only. Agented fiction less than 10%. Responds in 3 weeks to queries; 3 months to mss. Accepts simultaneous submissions.
Terms: Pays royalty of 40-50% of profits. Average advance: $1,000. Sends galleys to author. Publishes ms 6-12 months after acceptance. Writer's guidelines for #10 SASE or visit website.
Advice: "Write first for guidelines or visit our website before submitting a query, proposal or manuscript. And take the time to read some of the titles we've published."

☑ ☷ **MILKWEEDS FOR YOUNG READERS**, Imprint of Milkweed Editions, 1011 Washington Ave. S., Suite 300, Minneapolis MN 55415-1246. (612)332-3192. Fax: (612)215-2550. **Contact:** Elisabeth Fitz, first reader. Estab. 1984. "Milkweeds for Young Readers are works that embody humane values and contribute to cultural understanding." Publishes hardcover and trade paperback originals. **Published new writers within the last year.** Averages 3 total titles/year. Distributes titles through Publishers Group West. Promotes titles individually through print advertising, website and author tours.
   • *PU-239 & Other Russian Fantasies*, by Ken Kalfus won the Pushcart Prize.
Needs: For ages 8-12: adventure, animal, fantasy, historical, juvenile and mainstream/contemporary. Recently published *The Ocean Within*, by V.M. Caldwell; *The #66 Summen*, by John Armistead; *My Lord Bag of Rice*, by Carol Bly (short stories); and *Falling Dark*, by Tim Tharp (novel).
How to Contact: Submit complete ms with cover letter. Agented fiction 30%. Responds in up to 6 months to mss. Accepts simultaneous submissions.
Terms: Pays royalty of 7½% on retail price. Advance varies. Publishes ms 1 year after acceptance. Writer's guidelines for #10 SASE. Book catalog for $1.50.

Ⓝ ◪ **MOON MOUNTAIN PUBLISHING**, 80 Peachtree Rd., N. Kingstown RI 02852-1933. (401)884-6703. Fax: (401)884-7076. E-mail: hello@moonmountainpub.com. Website: www.moonmountainpub.com (includes catalog, guidelines, contact info, news, children's activities, business-to-business custom publishing).
Contact: Cathy Monroe, president (juvenile); Robert Holtzman, vice president (juvenile). Estab. 1999. "Small publisher of beautifully illustrated children's picture books that delight, occasionally inspire." Publishes hardcover originals. Books: non-acid paper; offset, 4-color printing. Average print order: 4,000. First novel print order: 4,000. **Published 1 new writer within the last year.** Averages 5 total titles, 5 fiction titles/year. Member: PMA, IPNE.
Needs: Children's/juvenile (adventure, animal, easy-to-read, fantasy, historical, preschool/picture book). Recently published *Hello Willow*, by Kimberly Poulton; and *Petronella*, by Jay Williams.
How to Contact: Accepts unsolicited mss. Submit complete ms with cover letter. Accepts queries by e-mail. Include estimated word count. Send SASE or IRC for return of ms or send disposable copy of ms and SASE for reply only. Responds in 1 month to queries; 3 months to mss. Accepts simultaneous submissions.
Terms: Pays royalty and advance. Sends galleys to author. Publishes ms 1-2 years after acceptance. Writer's guidelines for SASE or on website. Book catalog on website.
Advice: "Let us see positive, not preachy, stories with an element of whimsy or fantasy and definitely some fun."

◎ **MOUNTAIN STATE PRESS**, 2300 MacCorkle Ave. SE, Charleston WV 25304-1099. (304)357-4767. Fax: (304)357-4715. E-mail: msp1@newwave.net. **Contact:** Lisa Contreras, fiction editor. Estab. 1978. "A small nonprofit press run by a board of 13 members who volunteer their time. We specialize in books about West Virginia or by authors from West Virginia. We strive to give a voice to Appalachia" Publishes paperback originals and reprints. **Published new writers within the last year.** Plans 2-3 first novels in 2001. Averages 3 total titles, 1-2 fiction titles/year. Distributes titles through bookstores, distributors, gift shops and individual sales (Amazon.com and Barnes & Noble online carry our titles). Promotes titles through newspapers, radio, TV (local author series), mailings and book signings.
Needs: Family saga, historical (West Virginia), military/war, New Age/mystic/spiritual, religious. Currently compiling an anthology. Recently published *Homesick for the Hills*, by Alyce Faye Bragg (memoirs, humor); and *Under the Shade of the Trees: Thomas (Stonewall) Jackson's Life at Jackson's Mill*, by Dennis Norman (historical).
How to Contact: Accepts unsolicited mss. Query with outline/synopsis and 3 sample chapters or submit complete ms with cover letter. Accepts queries by e-mail and fax. Include estimated word count and bio. Send SASE or IRC for return of ms or send disposable copy of ms with SASE for reply only. Responds in 6 months to mss. Accepts electronic submissions. Often comments on rejected mss.
Terms: Pays royalties.
Advice: "Topic of West Virginia is the best choice for our press. Send your manuscript in and it will be read and reviewed by the members of the Board of Mountain State Press."

☑ ◎ ☷ **NEW RIVERS PRESS**, 420 N. Fifth St., Suite 1180, Minneapolis MN 55401-1384. Fax: (612)339-9047. E-mail: contact@newriverspress.org. Website: www.newriverspress.org (includes guidelines, authors, all books—current and backlist, history, mission, ordering information, excerpts and events calendar). **Contact:** Eric Braun, editor. Estab. 1968. "Our mission is to publish the best writing by *new* writers—those at the beginnings of their careers. We publish mostly short fiction but are interested in novels as well. Many houses work with authors of note—New Rivers Press discovers those authors." Distributes titles through Consortium Book Sales and Distribution. "All books get at least 2 ads in prominent journals. We go to several conventions and book shows, do thorough direct mail campaigns and work with Consortium to promote in the most efficient ways we can."

• Honors for New Rivers Press titles include Book-of-the-Month Club Alternate Selection and finalists for Minnesota Book Awards and Foreword Book of the Year.

Needs: Contemporary, experimental, literary, translations. "No popular fantasy/romance. Nothing pious, polemical (unless other very good redeeming qualities). We are interested in only quality literature and always have been (though our concentration in the past has been poetry)." Recently published *Tilting the Continent: Southeast Asian American Writing*, edited by Shirley Geok-Lin Lim and Cheng Lok Chua; *Alone with the Owl*, by Alan Davis (short fiction); *The Record Player*, by Winifred Moranville (short fiction); *The Pact*, by Walter J. Roers (novel); and *Woman Lake*, by Richard Broderick.

How to Contact: "At this time we cannot accept unsolicited submissions. You must submit through the Minnesota Voices Project, open to residents of Minnesota, or the Headwaters Literary Contest, open to residents of the United States." (See Contests & Awards).

Terms: Minnesota Voices Project Series pays authors $1,000. Publishes ms 2 years after acceptance. Guidelines for SASE. Book catalog free.

Advice: "We read for quality, which experience has taught can be very eclectic and can come sometimes from out of nowhere. We are interested in publishing short fiction (as well as poetry and translations) because it is and has been a great indigenous American form and is almost completely ignored by the commercial houses. Find a *real* subject, something that belongs to you and not what you think or surmise that you should be doing by current standards and fads."

OUR CHILD PRESS, P.O. Box 74, Wayne PA 19087-0074. (610)964-0606. Fax: (610)964-0938. E-mail: ocp98@aol.com. Website: www.ourchildpress.com. **Contact:** Carol Hallenbeck, CEO. Estab. 1984. Publishes hardcover and paperback originals and reprints. Plans 2 first novels in 2001.

• Received the Ben Franklin Award for *Don't Call Me Marda*, by Sheila Welch.

Needs: Especially interested in books on adoption or learning disabilities. Recently published *Things Little Kids Need to Know*, by Susan Uhlig.

How to Contact: Does not accept unsolicited mss. Send query letter. Responds in 2 weeks to queries; 2 months to mss. Accepts simultaneous submissions. Sometimes comments on rejected mss.

Terms: Pays royalties of 5% minimum. Publishes ms up to 6 months after acceptance. Book catalog free.

PALARI PUBLISHING, P.O. Box 9288, Richmond VA 23227-0288. (804)537-5394. Fax: (804)537-5164. E-mail: palaripub@aol.com. Website: www.palari.net (includes writer's guidelines). **Contact:** David Smitherman, fiction editor. Estab. 1998. Small publisher specializing in Southern mysteries and nonfiction. Publishes hardcover and paperback originals. **Published 2 new writers within the last year.** Plans 2 first novels in 2001. Averages 4 total titles, 2 fiction titles/year. Distributes titles through Baker & Taylor, Ingram, mail order and website. Promotes titles through book signings, direct mail and the Internet. Member: Publishers Marketing Association.

Needs: Adventure, erotica, gay, historical, horror, lesbian, literary, mainstream, mystery/suspense, thriller/espionage. Recently published *The Guessing Game*, by Ted Randler (mystery).

How to Contact: Accepts unsolicited mss. Query with outline/synopsis and 3 sample chapters. Accepts queries by e-mail and fax. Include estimated word count, 1 page bio, Social Security number and list of publishing credits. Send SASE or IRC for return of ms or send disposable copy of ms and SASE for reply only. Responds in 1 month to queries; 2 months to mss. Accepts simultaneous and electronic submissions. Often comments on rejected mss.

Terms: Pays royalties. Publishes ms within 1 year after acceptance. Writer's guidelines available on website.

Advice: "Send a good bio. I'm interested in a writer's experience and unique outlook on life."

PAPYRUS PUBLISHERS & LETTERBOX SERVICE, P.O. Box 27383, Las Vegas NV 89126-1383. (702)256-3838. Managing Editor: Anthony Wade. Public Relations and Publicity: Erica Neubauer. **Contact:** Geoffrey Hutchison-Cleaves, editor-in-chief; Jessie Rosé, fiction editor. Estab. London 1946; USA 1982. Mid-size independent press. Publishes hardcover originals. Books: audio. Average print order 2,500. Averages 3 total titles/year. Promotes titles through mail, individual author fliers, author tours.

Imprint(s): Letterbox Service; Difficult Subjects Made Easy.

How to Contact: "Not accepting right now. Fully stocked."

Advice: "Don't send it, unless you have polished and polished and polished. Absolutely no established author sends off a piece that has just been 'written' once. That is the first draft of many!"

N⊘◎❤ PIANO PRESS, P.O. Box 85, Del Mar CA 92014-0085. (858)481-5650. Fax: (858)755-1104. E-mail: pianopress@aol.com. Website: http://pianopress.iuma.com (includes company description, product line, ordering information and writer's guidelines). **Contact:** Elizabeth C. Axford, M.A., editor (short stories/picture books). Estab. 1999. "Piano Press is an independent publisher. We publish books, songbooks and CDs on music-related topics, as well as some poetry." Books: medium weight paper; mimeo/offset printing; comb, saddle stitched or perfect bound; music manuscripts as illustrations. Average print order: 1,000-5,000. Averages 1-7 total titles, 1 fiction title/year. Member: PMA, ASCAP, NARAS. Distributes titles through wholesale distribution, Baker & Taylor, The Orchard (NYC distributor).

● Honored by San Diego Local Authors in 1999 and 2000.

Needs: Children's/juvenile (preschool/picture book, music related), ethnic/multicultural (music), short story collections. "Looking for short stories on music-related topics only. Also short stories and/or essays for our annual anthology, *The Art of Music—A Collection of Writings.*" Writers may submit and/or enter annual contest. See Contests & Awards. Recently published *Merry Christmas, Happy Hanukkah—A Multilingual Songbook & CD.*

How to Contact: Accepts unsolicited mss. Send query letter. Accepts queries by e-mail. Include estimated word count, brief bio, list of publishing credits and music background. Send SASE or IRC for return of ms or send disposable copy of ms and SASE for reply only. Responds in 6 weeks to queries; 3 months to mss. Accepts simultaneous and electronic submissions. Sometimes comments on rejected mss.

Terms: Pays 5 author's copies. Pay depends on grants/awards. Sends galleys to author. Publishes ms 6-18 months after acceptance. Writer's guidelines and book catalog free for #10 SAE and 33¢ postage.

Advice: "We feel there is a need for more original writings on music-related topics. Work should be complete, original, fresh and legible. Typewritten manuscripts only, please."

N⊘ PICK POCKET BOOKS, Phony Lid Publications, P.O. Box 2153, Rosemead CA 91770. E-mail: lou@fyuocuk.com. Website: www.fyuocuk.com (includes writer's guidelines, book catalog, sample fiction, cover art, author profiles). **Contact:** Louis Baudrey, editor. Estab. 1998. "The Pick Pocket Books are handmade, quarter-sized books featuring fiction, poetry, comics and art. Printed on selected papers with the quasi-knopf, 'not-so-perfect' binding and designed with a passion for the craft of book making on a budget so tight, it's criminal . . . disposable verse, adventures from the edge, frenzies of vice and other tales of degradation: Read Cheap." Publishes paperback originals. Books: 32 lb. text, 100 lb cover paper; docutech printing; hand binding; illustrations throughout. Average print order: 300. **Published 8 new writers within the last year.** Plans 1 first novel in 2001. Averages 20 total titles, 10 fiction titles/year. Distributes and promotes titles through the Internet, mail marketing, advertisements and reviews in trade magazines.

Needs: Comics/graphic novels, erotica, humor/satire, literary. Short fiction 2,000-3,000 words with strong story lines that are able to stand alone as an individual work. "We're particularly interested in urban tales, drug/counterculture, aggressive fiction that can be complimented by illustrations and presented in a concise format." Recently published *Fizz,* by Paul A. Toth; and *Pork Bellies & the Saki Bottle,* by Arin Greenwood.

How to Contact: Accepts unsolicited mss. Query with up to 3 short stories. Include estimated word count and brief bio. Send SASE or IRC for return of ms. Responds in 3 weeks to queries; 3 months to mss. Accepts electronic submissions (only per editor's request) and disk. Sometimes comments on rejected mss.

Terms: Pays in author's copies (25% of print order). Sends galleys to author. Publishes ms 3-12 months after acceptance. Writer's guidelines and book catalog free for #10 SASE.

Advice: "Read Pick Pocket Books. We are concentrating more on fiction, using illustrations to enhance the story so that they are appealing to the potential reader."

⊘◎ PIG IRON PRESS, 26 N. Phelps, Box 237, Youngstown OH 44501-0237. (330)747-6932. Fax: (330)747-0599. **Acquisitons:** Jim Villani, editor/publisher. Small independent publisher. Publishes hardcover originals, paperback originals and reprints. Books: 60 lb. offset paper; offset lithography; paper/casebound; illustration on cover only. Average print order: 1,000. First novel print order: 800. Averages 2 total titles, 1 fiction title/year.

Needs: Adventure, experimental, science fiction, short story collections. Published *The Harvest,* by Judith Hemschemeyer (social realism).

How to Contact: Not accepting unsolicited mss at this time.

Terms: Sends galleys to author. Writer's guidelines for #10 SASE. Book catalog for SASE.

N⊕○ PIPERS' ASH LTD., Church Rd., Christian Malford, Chippenham, Wiltshire SN15 4BW United Kingdom. Phone: 01249 720563. Fax: +44 870 0568916. E-mail: pipersash@supamasu.com. Website: www.supamasu.com. **Contact:** Acquisitions Editor. Estab. 1976. "Small press publisher. Considers all submitted manuscripts fairly—without bias or favor. This company is run by book-lovers, not by accountants." Publishes hardcover and paperback originals and reprints. Books: 80 gsm paper; digital printing; illustrations on covers only. **Published 12 new writers within the last year.** Plans 6 first novels in 2001. Averages 18 total titles, 12 fiction titles/year. Distributes and promotes titles through direct mail and the Internet.

Needs: Adventure, children's/juvenile (adventure), literary, romance (contemporary, romantic suspense), science fiction (hard science/technological, soft/sociological), short story collections, translations, western (frontier saga, traditional), young adult/teen (adventure, fantasy/science fiction). Currently emphasizing stage plays. Planning anthologies: short stories, science fiction, poetry. "Authors are invited to submit collections of short stories and poetry for consideration for our ongoing programs." Recently published *Russian Girl's Story*, by Jeanne Feasey (mystery); *Frank Riddle: Frontiersman*, by Mark Bannerman (western); and *Kaleidoscope*, by Bill Smurthwaite (short stories). Publishes children's adventure stories.

How to Contact: Accepts unsolicited mss. Query with synopsis and first chapter. Accepts queries by e-mail, fax and phone. Include estimated word count. Send SASE or IRC for return of ms or send disposable copy of ms and SASE for reply only. Responds in 1 week to queries; up to 3 months to mss. Accepts electronic submissions and disk. Always comments on rejected mss.

Terms: Pays royalties of 10-15% and 5 author's copies. No advance. Sends galleys to author. Publishes ms 2 months after acceptance. Writer's guidelines on website. Book catalog for A5 SASE and on website.

Advice: "Study the market! Check your selected publisher's catalogue."

N ⊘ PLEASURE BOAT STUDIO, 8630 NE Wardwell Rd., Bainbridge Island WA 98110. (206)842-9772. Fax: (206)842-9773. E-mail: pleasboat@aol.com. Website: www.pbstudio.com (includes sample works, writer's guidelines, company philosophy, authors and titles). **Contact:** Jack Estes, fiction editors. Estab. 1996. "We publish high-quality literary (not mainstream) fiction in original or in translation." Publishes paperback originals. Books: 55 lb. paper; perfect binding. Average print order: 1,500. First novel print order: 1,000. **Published 2 new writers within the last year.** Averages 4-5 total titles; 3 fiction titles/year.

Needs: Ethnic/multicultural, feminist, gay, historical, humor/satire, literary, regional, short story collections, translations. Recently published *Another Life and Other Stories*, by Edwin Weihe (short story collection); *The Eighth Day of the Week*, by Alfred Kessler (novel); and *If You Were with Me, Everything Would Be All Right*, by Ken Harvey (short story collection).

How to Contact: Accepts unsolicited mss. Query with outline/synopsis and 1-2 sample chapters. Accepts queries by e-mail. Include estimated word count, 1-page bio and list of publishing credits. Send SASE or IRC for return of ms. Responds in 1 month to queries. Accepts simultaneous submissions.

Terms: Pays royalty of 10%. Provides 25 author's copies. "Payment by individual arrangement." Sends galleys to author. Publishes ms 1-2 years after acceptance.

Advice: "Send query only, not complete manuscript, and don't get discouraged."

N ✚ ⊘ PONDER PUBLISHING INC., P.O. Box 23037, RPO McGillivray, Winnipeg, Manitoba R3T 5S3 Canada. (204)269-2985. Fax: (204)888-7159. E-mail: service@ponderpublishing.com. Website: www.ponder publishing.com (includes title information, distribution information, book excerpts, reader survey, website survey, romance/relationship column, writing contest information, editorial staff, contact information). **Contact:** Mary Barton, senior editor (romance); Pamela Walford, assistant editor (romance). Estab. 1996. "Small, independent publisher. Our submissions team is always on the lookout for diamonds in the rough, writers with a unique voice. We feel we've taken the best of formula romance and mainstream romance and combined them into a short, fast-paced, entertaining read." Publishes paperback originals. Books: groundwood paper; mass market format printing; perfect binding. Average print order: 5,000-15,000. First novel print order: 3,000-5,000. **Published 1 new writer within the last year.** Plans 2 first novels in 2001. Averages 2 total titles, 2 fiction titles/year. Member: Small Publishers Association of North America. Distributes titles through four major American and one Canadian distributor. Promotes titles through advertising, the Internet, trade shows and newsletter.

Needs: Romance (contemporary, futuristic/time travel, romantic suspense). "We are looking for a variety of voices and styles, anything unique, for our Ponder Romance line. We like light, highly entertaining story lines that are as enjoyable as the romance." Recently published *Oh Susannah*, by Selena Mindous; *Autumn's Eve*, by Jordanna Boston; and *Sand Pirates*, by Ellis Hoff (all romance).

How to Contact: Accepts unsolicited mss. Query with outline/synopsis and 3 sample chapters. Include estimated word count, brief bio and list of publishing credits. Send IRC for return of ms or send disposable copy of ms and IRC for reply only. Responds in 3 months to queries; 5 months to mss. Accepts simultaneous submissions. Often comments on rejected mss.

Terms: "Contracts are confidential and negotiable. We pay signing bonuses (as opposed to advances) in addition to royalties." Does not send galleys to author. Publishes ms 1-3 years after acceptance. Writer's guidelines and book catalog for SASE and $1 postage (Canadian).

Advice: "Read our books. They are unique to the genre in a way that the writer's guidelines cannot fully convey. Ponder romances go right down the middle between category and mainstream romance."

⊘ THE POST-APOLLO PRESS, 35 Marie St., Sausalito CA 94965. (415)332-1458. Fax: (415)332-8045. E-mail: tpapress@dnai.com. Website: www.dnai.com/~tpapress/ (includes excerpts, catalog, reviews and ordering links). **Contact:** Simone Fattal, publisher. Estab. 1982. Specializes in "women writers published in Europe or the Middle East who have been translated into English for the first time." Publishes paperback originals. Book: acid-free paper; lithography printing; perfect-bound. Average print order: 1,000. First novel print order: 1,000.

Published new writers within the last year. Averages 2 total titles/year. Distributes titles through Small Press Distribution, Berkeley, California. Promotes titles through advertising in selected literary quarterlies, SPD catalog, Feminist Bookstore News & Catalog, ALA and ABA and SF Bay Area Book Festival participation.

Needs: Feminist, lesbian, literary, spiritual, translations. No juvenile, horror, sports or romance. "Many of our books are first translations into English." Recently published *Some Life*, by Joanne Kyger; and *Happily*, by Lyn Hejinian.

How to Contact: "The Post-Apollo Press is not accepting manuscripts or queries currently due to a full publishing schedule."

Terms: Pays royalties of 6½% minimum or by individual arrangement. Sends galleys to author. Publishes ms 1½ years after acceptance. Book catalog free.

Advice: "We want to see serious, literary quality, informed by an experimental aesthetic."

THE PRAIRIE PUBLISHING COMPANY, Box 2997, Winnipeg, Manitoba R3C 4B5 Canada. (204)837-7499. **Contact:** Ralph Watkins, publisher. Estab. 1969. Buys juvenile mss with illustrations. Books: 60 lb. high-bulk paper; offset printing; perfect-bound; line-drawings. Average print order: 2,000. First novel print order: 2,000. **Published new writers within the last year.**

Needs: Open. Published *The Homeplace* (historical novel); *My Name is Marie Anne Gaboury* (first French-Canadian woman in the Northwest); and *The Tale of Jonathan Thimblemouse*.

How to Contact: Does not accept unsolicited mss. Send query letter with SASE or IRC. Responds in 1 month to queries; 6 weeks to mss. Publishes ms 4-6 months after acceptance.

Terms: Pays royalties of 10%. No advance. Book catalog free.

Advice: "We work on a manuscript with the intensity of a Max Perkins. A clean, well-prepared manuscript can go a long way toward making an editor's job easier. On the other hand, the author should not attempt to anticipate the format of the book, which is a decision for the publisher to make. In order to succeed in today's market, the story must be tight, well written and to the point. Do not be discouraged by rejections."

PUBLISHERS SYNDICATION, INTERNATIONAL, P.O. Box 6218, Charlottesville VA 22906-6218. (804)964-1194. Fax: (804)964- 0096. **Contact:** A. Samuels. Estab. 1979.

Needs: Adventure, mystery/suspense (amateur sleuth, police procedural), thriller/espionage, western (frontier saga).

How to Contact: Accepts unsolicited mss. Submit complete ms with cover letter. Include estimated word count. Send SASE or IRC for return of ms. Responds in 1 month.

Terms: Pays royalties of .05-2%. Advance is negotiable. Writer's guidelines for SASE.

Advice: "The type of manuscript we are looking for is devoid of references which might offend. Remember you are writing for a general audience."

PUDDING HOUSE PUBLICATIONS, 60 N. Main St., Johnstown OH 43031. (614)967-6060. E-mail: pudding@johnstown.net. Website: www.puddinghouse.com (includes staff, departments, photos, guidelines, books for direct and wholesale purchase, publications list, writing games, poem of the month, Unitarian Universalist poets page, calls, etc.). **Contact:** Jennifer Bosveld, editor (short short stories only). Estab. 1979. "Small independent publisher seeking outrageously fresh short short stories." Publishes paperback originals. Books, chapbooks, broadsides: paper varies; side stapled; b&w illustrations. **Published new writers within the last year.** Promotes titles through direct mail, conference exhibits, readings, workshops.

Needs: Experimental, literary, the writing experience, liberal/alternative politics or spirituality, new approaches. Recently published *In the City of Mystery*, by Alan Ziegler (short short stories); and *Karmic 4-Star Buckaroo*, by John Bennett (short short stories).

How to Contact: Accepts unsolicited mss. Submit complete ms with cover letter and ample SASE. Include short bio and list of publishing credits. Send SASE for return of ms. Responds immediately unless traveling. No simultaneous submissions. Sometimes comments on rejected mss for various fee, if close.

Terms: Pays in author's copies. Sends galleys to author for chapbooks. Publishes ms 2-24 months after acceptance. Writer's guidelines free for SASE. Publication list available.

Advice: "Be new!"

RAVENHAUS PUBLISHING, 227 Willow Grove Rd., Stewartsville NJ 08886. (908)859-4331. Fax: (908)859-3088. E-mail: ravenhaus@publicist.com. Website: www.ravenhauspublishing.com (includes general book information, previews and sample book chapters). **Contact:** Dolores Dowd, publisher. Estab. 1997. Small independent press. Publishes hardcover and paperback originals. Average print order: 5,000. First novel print order: 3,000-5,000. **Published 2 new writers within the last year.** Plans 2 first novels in 2001. Averages 3 total titles, 2 fiction titles/year. Member: Publisher Marketing Association. Distributes titles through national distributor.

Needs: Adventure, fantasy, horror (dark fantasy, futuristic, psychological, supernatural), mystery/suspense (amateur sleuth, cozy, police procedural, private eye/hardboiled), New Age/mystic, psychic/supernatural, romance (contemporary, futuristic/time travel, gothic, historical, Regency period, romantic suspense), science fiction (hard science/technological, soft/sociological), short story collections, thrillers/espionage. "We are currently very interested in horror and science fiction." Recently published *The Nova Affair* (espionage); and *The Plains of Heaven* (science fiction), both by Bloom.

How to Contact: Accepts unsolicited mss. Query with outline/synopsis and 2 sample chapters. Accepts queries by fax. Include brief bio and list of publishing credits. Send disposable copy of ms and SASE for reply only. Agented fiction 20%. Responds in 3 months to queries; 6 months to mss. Accepts simultaneous submissions.

Terms: Pays royalties of 10-20%. Average advance: $1,500. Sends galleys to author. Publishes ms 1 year after acceptance. Writer's guidelines free for #10 SASE.

Advice: "We are currently expanding our number of titles but still require exceptional writing skills. Edit your queries carefully if you want us to seriously consider your work."

N **⊘** **RECONCILIATION PRESS**, P.O. Box 3709, Fairfax VA 22038. (703)691-8416. Fax: (703)691-8466. E-mail: publisher@reconciliation.com. Website: www.reconciliation.com (includes historical fiction series, study guides and online stories). **Contact:** John Jenkins, publisher. Estab. 1997. "Small publisher to home school and Christian school market. Online serial historical novels." Publishes paperback originals and online stories. **Published 2 new writers within the last year.** Plans 2 new first novels in 2001. Averages 4 total titles, 4 fiction titles/year. Distributes titles through Amazon.com and the Internet.

Needs: Historical (Christian American 19th and 20th century), young adult/teen (historical). Recently published *Cry of the Blood*, by J.L. Jenkins (historical fiction); *The Gift*, by K. O'Hara (historical fiction); and *Fool's Gold*, by E. Stobbe (historical fiction).

How to Contact: Does not accept unsolicited mss. Query with outline/synopsis and 2 sample chapters. Accepts queries by e-mail. Include estimated word count, brief bio and list of publishing credits. Send disposable copy of ms and SASE for reply only. Responds in 2 weeks to queries; 2 months to mss. Accepts electronic submissions. Often comments on rejected mss.

Terms: Pays royalties of 7-30%. Publishes ms 3-6 months after acceptance. Writer's guidelines on website.

Advice: "Follow our guidelines."

✓ **⊘** **⚐** **RED SAGE PUBLISHING, INC.**, P.O. Box 4844, Seminole FL 33775-4844. Phone/fax: (727)391-3847. E-mail: alekendall@aol.com. Website: www.RedSagePub.com (includes authors and guidelines). **Contact:** Alexandria Kendall, editor (romance erotica). Estab. 1995. Publishes "romance erotica or ultra-sensual romance novellas written by romance writers." Publishes paperback originals. Books: perfect binding. **Published 4 new writers within the last year.** Averages 1 total title, 1 fiction title/year. Distributes titles through Amazon, Barnes & Noble, Borders and independent bookstores as well as mail order. Promotes titles through national trade publication advertising, author interviews and book signings.

● Red Sage Publishing received the Fallot Literary Award for Fiction.

Imprint(s): The *Secrets* Collections (romance, ultra-sensual), edited by Alexandria Kendall.

Needs: Romance (ultra-sensual) novellas for *The Secrets Collections: The Best in Women's Sensual Fiction* anthology. Length: 20,000-30,000 words. Writers may submit to anthology editor. Recently published *Insatiable*, by Chevon Gael; and *Strictly Business*, by Shannon Hollis.

How to Contact: Accepts unsolicited mss. Query with outline/synopsis and 10 sample pages. Include estimated word count and list of publishing credits if applicable. Send SASE or IRC for return of ms. Responds in 3 months. Sometimes comments on rejected ms.

Terms: Pays advance and royalty. Sends galleys to author. Publishes ms 1-2 years after acceptance. Writer's guidelines for SASE.

Advice: "Know your reader."

⊕ **✓** **◎** **RENDITIONS**, Research Centre for Translation, Institute of Chinese Studies, Chinese University of Hong Kong, Shatin, New Territories, Hong Kong. Phone: 852-26097399. Fax: 852-26035110. E-mail: renditions@cuhk.edu.hk. Website: www.renditions.org (includes sections about Research Centre for Translation, the Chinese University of Hong Kong, *Renditions* magazines, Renditions Paperbacks, Renditions Books, forthcoming, ordering information and related sites). **Contact:** Dr. Eva Hung, editor. Academic specialist publisher. Averages 2 fiction titles/year. Distributes titles through local and overseas distributors and electronically via homepage and Amazon.com. Promotes titles through homepage, exchange ads with *China Now* and *China Review International* and paid ads in *Feminist Bookstore News* and *Journal of Asian Studies* of AAS.

Needs: Will only consider English translations of Chinese fiction, prose, drama and poetry. Fiction published either in semiannual journal (*Renditions*) or in the Renditions Paperback series. Recently published *Marvels of a Floating City*, by Xi Xi (Hong Kong stories); *Hong Kong Stories: Old Themes New Voices*, by Eva Hung, editor; and *Traces of Love and Other Stories*, by Eileen Chang.

How to Contact: For fiction over 5,000 words in translation, sample is required. Sample length: 1,000-2,000 words. Send sample chapter. "Submit only works in our specialized area. Two copies of translation accompanied by two copies of original Chinese text." Accepts fax and e-mail requests for information and guidelines.

Terms: Pays royalties for paperback series; honorarium for publication in *Renditions*.

RONSDALE PRESS, 3350 W. 21 Ave., Vancouver, British Columbia V6S 1G7 Canada. (604)738-4688. Fax: (604)731-4548. E-mail: ronhatch@pinc.com. Website: www.ronsdalepress.com (includes guidelines, catalog, events). **Contact**: Ronald B. Hatch, president/editor; Veronica Hatch, editor (YA historical). Estab. 1988. Ronsdale Press is "dedicated to publishing books that give Canadians new insights into themselves and their country." Publishes paperback originals. Books: 60 lb. paper; photo offset printing; perfect binding. Average print order: 1,000. First novel print order: 1,500. **Publishes new writers within the last year.** Plans 1 first novel in 2001. Averages 3 fiction titles/year. Distributes titles through General Distribution and Partners West. Promotes titles through ads in BC Bookworld and Globe & Mail, and interviews on radio.

● Ronsdale author, Janice MacDonald won the Alberta Import Award for *The Ghoul's Night Out*. *Eyewitness*, by Margaret Thompson was chosen as a B.C. Millennium Book.

Needs: Literary. Published *The City in the Egg*, by Michel Trembly (novel); *Tangled in Time*, by Lynne Fairbridge (children's); and *Daruma Days*, by Terry Watada (short stories).

How to Contact: *Canadian authors only.* Accepts unsolicited mss. Submit outline/synopsis and at least first 100 pages. Accepts queries/correspondence by e-mail. Send SASE or IRC for return of ms. Short story collections must have some magazine publication. Responds in 2 weeks to queries; 2 months to mss. Sometimes comments on rejected mss.

Terms: Pays royalties of 10%. Provides author's copies. Sends galleys to author. Publishes ms 6 months after acceptance.

Advice: "We publish both fiction and poetry. Authors *must* be Canadian. We look for writing that shows the author has read widely in contemporary and earlier literature. Ronsdale, like other literary presses, is not interested in mass-market or pulp materials."

JAMES RUSSELL PUBLISHING, 780 Diogenes Dr., Reno NV 89512-1336. E-mail: scrnplay@powernet.net. Website: www.powernet.net/~scrnplay (includes sample query letter, guidelines, advice for writers, catalog). **Contact**: James Russell, publisher. Estab. 2000. "We are a new small publisher in the novel market. We will publish novels with an educational angle. We want readers to learn as they are entertained." Publishes paperback originals and e-books. Books: white 50 lb. paper; web and sheet printing; perfect binding. Plans 1 first novel in 2001. Averages 7 total titles/year. Member: PMA. Distributes titles through Ingram and Baker & Taylor. Promotes titles through websites, distributors' catalogs, PMA, marketing and print ads.

Needs: Adventure, historical (1800s western), humor/satire, literary, regional (Nevada, California), religious (general religious, inspirational), romance (western), western (frontier saga), young adult/teen (adventure, western).

How to Contact: Does not accept or return unsolicited mss. Send query letter. Accepts queries by e-mail. Include estimated word count. Send disposable copy of ms and SASE for reply only. Responds in 3 weeks to queries; 1 month to mss. Accepts simultaneous submissions. Often comments on rejected mss.

Terms: Pays royalties of 10-15%. Sends galleys to author. Publishes ms 3 months after acceptance. Writer's guidelines for #10 SASE. Book catalog for SASE and 33¢ postage.

Advice: "Employ a proofreader/editor prior to submission. We need manuscripts ready for publishing. Visit our website for advice, guidelines and a free query letter sample. Tell us why your book is better than others on the market. Who do you feel will buy your book? Send query letter only. Keep query to one page. Include SASE. Do not call, use e-mail or postal letter to follow up."

SCHERF BOOKS, Subsidiary of Scherf, Inc., P.O. Box 80180, Las Vegas NV 89180-0180. (702)243-4895. Fax: (702)243-7460. E-mail: ds@scherf.com. Website: www.scherf.com (includes book catalog). **Contact**: Dietmar Scherf (all fiction); Gail Kirby, editor (all fiction). Estab. 1990. "Small publisher concentrating on selective titles. We want to discover the next John Grisham, Danielle Steel, Nora Roberts, Tom Clancy, Michael Crichton, Ernest Hemingway, Anne Rice, Stephen King, etc. Based on our parent company we have vast resources and are known to get behind our books and authors just like a major publishing house would." Publishes hardcover and paperback originals. Average print order: 2,500-50,000. First novel print order: 2,500-20,000. Plans 10 first novels in 2000. Averages 2-4 total titles, 2 fiction titles/year. Distributes titles through Ingram Book Company, Baker & Taylor, Amazon.com and through most Internet bookstores. Promotes titles through advertisements, Internet, direct mail and PR.

Needs: Adventure, ethnic/multicultural (general), family saga, horror (dark fantasy, futuristic, psychological, supernatural), literary, mainstream, mystery/suspense, religious (inspirational, religious mystery/suspense, religious thriller), thriller/espionage, young adult/teen (adventure, easy-to-read, mystery/suspense, series). "We consistently look for thrillers and mystery/suspense novels that appeal to a broad audience. But also quality literary fiction is very interesting. We're searching for great unpublished writers and new ideas."

How to Contact: Does not accept or return unsolicited mss. Send query letter. Include estimated word count and 1-paragraph bio. Send SASE for return of ms or send disposable copy of ms and SASE for reply only. Responds in 1 month to queries; up to 4 months to mss. Accepts simultaneous submissions. Sometimes comments on rejected mss.

Terms: Pays royalties of 5-10%. Offers negotiable advance. Sends galleys to author. Publishes ms 12-18 months after acceptance.

Advice: "We're concentrating on novels, now. There are many manuscripts out there, but it is difficult to find an excellent piece of work. But once we find that certain exceptional novel, we're getting behind it full throttle. Write the greatest book possible about a story that you love and are truly excited about. Learn some writing skills, especially grammar, characterization, dialogue or strong narrative qualities, plot, etc. A great story is a beginning, but the writer has to have excellent writing skills. Read books from authors that you like, but develop your own unique voice."

[N] [globe] [disk] SERPENT'S TAIL, 4 Blackstock Mews, London N4 2BT United Kingdom. Phone: (020)7354 1949. E-mail: info@serpentstail.com. Website: www.serpentstail.com. **Contact:** Laurence O'Toole, fiction editor. "We are an up-market literary house whose tastes are well out of the mainstream. We see our audience as young and urban-based." Publishes hardcover and paperback originals and reprints. Averages 40 total titles, 30 fiction titles/year.
Needs: Short stories. "Translations, literary fiction and cultural studies are our forte."
How to Contact: Accepts unsolicited mss. "Send query letter first, and only after you have looked at the books we publish." Accepts queries by e-mail, fax and phone. Include estimated word count and brief bio. Send IRC or return postage. Responds to queries in 3 weeks; 3 months to ms. Accepts simultaneous submissions.
Terms: Pays advance plus royalties. Write for catalog.
Tips: "For us, writers need not give extra background to their work, its context, etc. regarding the fact that they are not British. We are a pretty cosmopolitan bunch."

[N] [disk] SIGNAL CREST, Tiptoe Literary Service, 434 Sixth St., #206, Raymond WA 98577-1804. (360)942-4596. E-mail: anne@willapabay.org. Website: www.willapabay.org/~anne (includes publishing, product and general information and links). **Contact:** Anne Grimm-richardson, editor. Estab. 1985. "One-person operation, in-house publishing and syndication." Publishes paperback originals and reprints. Books: 20 lb. paper; photocopy printing; coil bound; pen and ink illustrations. Averages 6 total titles, 3 fiction titles/year.
Needs: Children's/juvenile (adventure, fantasy, read-aloud), feminist, science fiction (hard science/technological, soft/sociological), young adult/teen (amateur radio). Currently emphasizing feminist/family, fantasy/science fiction/amateur radio short stories. Planning domestic violence anthology. Editor will select stories.
How to Contact: Does not accept or return unsolicited mss. Send query letter by e-mail. Include 100-word summary. Send disposable copy of ms and SASE for reply only. Responds in 1 month to queries; 3 months to mss. Sometimes comments on rejected mss.
Terms: No payment (or by negotiation). Self-publisher. Book catalog on website.
Advice: "Look into publishing your own work—keep the profits from your own work."

[maple leaf] [check] [disk] SNOWAPPLE PRESS, P.O. Box 66024, Heritage Postal Outlet, Edmonton, Alberta T6J 6T4 Canada. (780)437-0191. **Contact:** Vanna Tessier, editor. Estab. 1991. "We focus on topics that are interesting, unusual and controversial." Small independent literary press. Publishes hardcover and paperback originals. Books: non-acid paper; offset printing; perfect binding; illustrations. Average print order: 500. First novel print order: 500. Plans 1 first novel in 2001. Averages 3-4 total titles, 1-2 fiction titles/year. Distributes titles through bookseller and library wholesalers. Promotes titles through press releases and reviews.
Needs: Adventure, children's/juvenile (adventure, fantasy, mystery), experimental, historical, literary, mainstream/contemporary, short story collections, translations, young adult/teen (adventure, mystery/suspense). Published *A Crop Of Stones: Graphic Means*, by Vanna Tessier (short stories); *The Last Waltz Of Chopin*, translated by Gilberto Finzi (novel).
How to Contact: Does not accept unsolicited mss. Query with 1-page cover letter. Include estimated word count, 300-word bio and list of publishing credits. Send SASE with sufficient IRCs. Responds in 1 month to queries; 3 months to mss. Accepts simultaneous submissions.
Terms: Pays honorarium; provides 10-25 author's copies. Sends galleys to author. Publishes ms 12-18 months after acceptance.
Advice: "Query first with proper SASE and IRCs to obtain guidelines."

[N] [disk] [A] [Y] STONES POINT PRESS, P.O. Box 384, Belfast ME 04915. (207)338-1921. Fax: (207)338-8379. E-mail: books@stonespointpress.com. Website: www.stonespointpress.com (includes book catalog, author bios). **Contact:** Chris Redfern, manager. Estab. 1992. "One-person operation on a part-time basis. Publishes an eclectic assortment of titles." Publishes paperback originals. Books: 50 lb. white paper; offset printing; perfect binding. Average print order: 2,000. First novel print order: 1,000. Plans 1 first novel in 2001. Averages 2 total titles, 1 fiction title/year. Member: MWPA. Promotes titles over the Internet and through magazine ads.
  • A Stones Point Press title, *The Bud Wilson Dream Book*, by Barbara Kramer won a 1997 Maine Arts Commission Individual Fellowship Award.
Needs: Children's/juvenile (verse), family saga, literary, mainstream, military/war, romance (contemporary), short story collections.

How to Contact: Does not accept or return unsolicited mss. Submit through agent only. Accepts queries by e-mail and fax. Include estimated word count, brief bio and list of publishing credits. Send SASE or IRC for return of ms. Responds in 2 months to queries; 4 months to mss. Accepts electronic submissions and disk.

Terms: Pays royalty of 15%. Offers negotiable advance, pays honorarium or does not pay. Sends galleys to author. Publishes ms 1 year after acceptance. Book catalog for SASE.

STORMLINE PRESS, P.O. Box 593, Urbana IL 61801. **Contact:** Raymond Bial, publisher. Estab. 1985. "Small independent literary press operated by one person on a part-time basis, publishing one or two books annually." Publishes hardcover and paperback originals. Books: acid-free paper; paper and cloth binding; b&w illustrations. Average print order: 1,000-2,000. First novel print order: 1,000-2,000. Averages 1-2 total titles/year.

• Stormline's title, *First Frost*, was selected for a Best of the Small Presses Award.

Needs: *Publishes by invitation only.* Literary. Looks for "serious literary works, especially those which accurately and sensitively reflect rural and small town life." Published *Silent Friends: A Quaker Quilt*, by Margaret Lacey (short story collection).

How to Contact: Does not accept unsolicited submissions.

Terms: Pays royalties of 10% maximum. Provides author's copies. Sends galleys to author. Publishes ms 6-12 months after acceptance. Writer's guidelines for SASE. Book catalog free.

Advice: "We look for a distinctive voice and writing style. We are always interested in looking at manuscripts of exceptional literary merit. We are not interested in popular fiction or experimental writing. Please review other titles published by the press, notably *Silent Friends: A Quaker Quilt*, to get an idea of the type of books published by our press."

SWEET LADY MOON PRESS, P.O. Box 1076, Georgetown KY 40324. (502)868-6573. Fax: (502)868-6566. E-mail: troyteegarden@worldradio.org. **Contact:** Troy Teegarden, editor. Estab. 1995. "Small press: fiction under 3,500 words in literary magazine *Stovepipe*; chapbooks maximum 60 pages, 8½×5½." Publishes paperback originals. Books: offset printing; stapled binding; illustrations. Average print order: 250. **Published 30 new writers within the last year.** Averages 4 total titles, 2 fiction titles/year. Distributes titles through the Internet, catalog, stores and mail order.

Needs: Comics/graphic novels, experimental, humor/satire, literary, short story collections. Recently published *Why I Hate Reading Books*, by Mike Francis; and *Twenty Shots*, by J. Todd Dockery.

How to Contact: Accepts unsolicited mss. Accepts queries by e-mail. Include estimated word count and brief bio. Send SASE or IRC for return of ms or send disposable copy of ms and SASE for reply only. Responds in 1 month to queries and mss. Accepts simultaneous submissions. Sometimes comments on rejected mss.

Terms: Pays author's copies. Sends galleys to author. Publishes ms 3-6 months after acceptance. Writer's guidelines and book catalog for SASE.

Advice: "We publish who we like. Read our current authors."

THISTLEDOWN PRESS, 633 Main St., Saskatoon, Saskatchewan S7H 0J8 Canada. (306)244-1722. Fax: (306)244-1762. E-mail: thistle@sk.sympatico.ca. Website: www.thistledown.sk.ca (includes guidelines, catalog, teaching materials). Editor-in-Chief: Patrick O'Rourke. **Contact:** Jesse Stothers, editor. Estab. 1975. Publishes paperback originals—literary fiction, young adult fiction, poetry. Books: quality stock paper; offset printing; perfect-bound; occasional illustrations. Average print order 1,500-2,000. First novel print order: 1,000-1,500. **Published new writers within the last year.** Averages 12 total titles, 6-7 fiction titles/year. Distributes titles through General Distribution Services. Promotes titles through intensive school promotions, online, advertising, special offers.

• Thistledown's *Prisoner in a Red-Rose Chain*, by Jeffrey Moore won the Commonwealth Writers Prize for Best New Book.

Needs: Literary, experimental, short story collections, novels.

How to Contact: Does not accept unsolicited mss. Query first with SASE or IRC for reply. Accepts queries by e-mail and fax. "We *only* want to see Canadian-authored submissions. We will *not* consider multiple submissions." Accepts photocopied submissions. Responds in 2 months to queries. Publishes anthologies. "Stories are nominated." Published *Prisoner in a Red-Rose Chain*, by Jeffrey Moore (literary/novel); *Aphid & the Shadow Drinkers*, by Steven Lattey (short fiction); and *The Lady at Batoche*, by David Richards (young adult historical novel). Also publishes The Mayer Mystery Series (mystery novels for young adults) and The New Leaf Series (first books for poetry and fiction—Saskatchewan residents only).

Terms: Pays standard royalty on retail price. Publishes ms 1-2 years after acceptance. Writer's guidelines and book catalog for #10 SASE.

Advice: "We are primarily looking for quality writing that is original and innovative in its perspective and/or use of language. Thistledown would like to receive queries first before submission—perhaps with novel outline, some indication of previous publications, periodicals your work has appeared in. *We publish Canadian authors only.* We are continuing to publish more fiction and are looking for new fiction writers to add to our list. New Leaf Editions line is first books of poetry or fiction by emerging Saskatchewan authors. Familiarize yourself with some of our books before submitting a query or manuscript to the press."

◑ **TROPICAL PRESS, INC.**, P.O. Box 161174, Miami FL 33116-1174. Fax: (305)378-1595. E-mail: tropicb ook@aol.com. Website: www.tropicalpress.com. **Contact**: Susan Diez and Gordon Witherspoon, fiction editors. Estab. 1997. Independent publisher. Publishes paperback originals. **Published 2 new writers within the last year.** Plans 1 first novel in 2001. Averages 4 total titles, 2 fiction titles/year.
Needs: Adventure, historical (general), mystery/suspense.
How to Contact: Accepts unsolicited mss. Query with outline/synopsis and 1 sample chapter. Send SASE or IRC for return of ms. Agented fiction 50%. Responds in 1 month to queries. Accepts simultaneous submissions. Sometimes comments on rejected mss.
Terms: Pays royalties of 5% minimum. Pay depends on grants/awards. Sends galleys to author. Publishes ms 1 year after acceptance. Writer's guidelines for #10 SASE.
Advice: "We see a niche for all good writing that doesn't require the sale of 25,000 copies to break even. Present a clean, well-conceived presentation. Give us your credits, if any, and let the writing speak for itself."

🏂 ✅ ▣ ◎ ▼ **TURNSTONE PRESS**, 607-100 Arthur St., Winnipeg, Manitoba R3B 1H3 Canada. (204)947-1555. Fax: (204)942-1555. E-mail: editor@turnstonepress.mb.ca. Website: www.TurnstonePress.com (includes submission guidelines, new titles, selected backlist, excerpts and author tour information). **Contact**: Manuela Dias, editor. Estab. 1976. "Turnstone Press is a literary press that publishes Canadian writers with an emphasis on writers from, and writing on, the Canadian West." Focuses on eclectic new writing, prairie writers, travel writing and regional mysteries. Books: offset paper; perfect-bound. First novel print order: 1,500. **Published 5 new writers within the last year.** Averages 12-15 total titles/year. Distributes titles through General Distribution Services (Canada and US). Promotes titles through Canadian national and local print media and select US print advertising.
  • *Summer of My Amazing Luck*, by Miriam Toews was nominated for the Stephen Leacock Award for Humor. Melissa Steele, author of *Donut Shop Lovers*, won the John Hirsch Award for Most Promising Manitoba Writer. *Bread, Wine and Angels*, by Anna P. Zurzolo was runner-up for the Commonwealth Writer's Prize for Best First Book. *Hoot to Kill*, by Karen Dudley was shortlisted for the Arthur Ellis Award.
Imprints: Ravenstone.
Needs: Literary, regional (Western Canada), mystery, gothic, noir. "We will be doing only 4-5 fiction titles a year. Interested in new work exploring new narrative/fiction forms, travel/adventure/nature writing of a literary nature and writing that pushes the boundaries of genre." Recently published *This Place Called Absence*, by Lydia Kwa (novel); and *Choke Hold*, by Todd Babiak (comic novel).
How to Contact: *Canadian authors only.* Accepts unsolicited mss. Query with 20-40 sample pages. Include list of publishing credits. Send SASE or IRC for return of ms. Responds in 2 months to queries; up to 4 months to mss. Accepts simultaneous submissions if notified.
Terms: Pays royalties of 10% and 10 author's copies. Average advance: $500. Publishes ms 1 year after acceptance. Sends galleys to author. Book catalog free with SASE.
Advice: "As a Canadian literary press, we have a mandate to publish Canadian writers only. Do some homework before submitting work to make sure your subject matter/genre/writing style fall within the publisher's area of interest."

▣ Ⓐ **ULTRAMARINE PUBLISHING CO., INC.**, Box 303, Hastings-on-the-Hudson NY 10706. (914)478-1339. Fax: (914)478-1365. **Contact:** Christopher P. Stephens, publisher. Estab. 1973. Small publisher. "We have 200 titles in print. We also distribute for authors where a major publisher has dropped a title." Averages 15 total titles, 12 fiction titles/year.
Needs: Experimental, fantasy, mainstream, science fiction, short story collections. No romance, westerns, mysteries.
How to Contact: Does not accept unsolicited mss. Agented fiction 90%. Occasionally comments on rejected mss.
Terms: Pays royalties of 10% minimum; advance is negotiable. Publishes ms an average of 8 months after acceptance. Free book catalog.

▣ ▣ ◎ **UNIVERSITY OF NEVADA PRESS**, MS 166, Reno NV 89557-0076. (775)784-6573. Fax: (775)784-6200. E-mail: dalrympl@scs.unr.edu. Director: Ronald E. Latimer. **Contact:** Margaret Dalrymple, editor-in-chief. Estab. 1961. "Small university press. Publishes fiction that focuses primarily on the American West." Publishes hardcover and paperback originals and paperback reprints. Books: acid-free paper. Averages 25 total titles, 2 fiction titles/year. Member: AAUP.
  • *The Blossom Festival*, by Lawrence Coates won the WESTAF Award for Fiction.
Needs: Ethnic/multicultural (general), family saga, historical (American West), humor/satire, mystery/suspense (U.S. West), regional (U.S. West). Published *Wild Indians & Other Creatures*, by Adrian Louis (short stories); *Gunning for Ho*, by H. Lee Barnes (short stories); and *The Blossom Festival*, by Lawrence Coates (novel). "We have series in Basque Studies, Gambling Studies, history and humanities, ethnonationalism, Western literature."

How to Contact: Accepts unsolicited mss. Query with outline/synopsis and 2-4 sample chapters. Accepts queries by e-mail and fax. Include estimated word count, 1-2 page bio and list of publishing credits. Send SASE or IRC for return of ms or send disposable copy of ms and SASE for reply only. Agented fiction 20%. Responds in 3 weeks to queries; 4 months to mss. Sometimes comments on rejected mss.

Terms: Pays royalties; negotiated on a book-by-book basis. Sends galleys to author. Publishes ms up to 2 years after acceptance. Writer's guidelines for #10 SASE.

Advice: "We are not interested in genre fiction."

VAN NESTE BOOKS, 12836 Ashtree Rd., Midlothian VA 23113-3095. Phone/fax: (804)897-3568. E-mail: kvno@aol.com. Website: members.aol.com/kvno/vbooks/van_neste_books.htm (current and backlist books, author information and contact information). **Contact:** Karen Van Neste Owen, publisher. Estab. 1996. "We are a small independent publisher interested in publishing serious fiction." Publishes hardcover originals. Books: 55 lb. acid-free paper; cloth binding; illustrations (cover only). Average print order: 1,000. **Published 2 new writers within the last year.** Plans 2-4 first novels in 2001. Averages 2-4 total titles, 2-4 fiction titles/year. Distributes titles through Van Neste Books. Promotes titles through bound galleys mailed to book reviewers throughout the U.S. and representation by foreign and Hollywood agents.

Needs: Feminist, historical, humor/satire, literary, mainstream/contemporary, mystery/suspense, regional (southern), thriller/espionage. Recently published *Lumen*, by Ben Pastor (historical mystery); *A Better Man*, by Enid Harlow (mainstream contemporary); and *Survivors*, by Valerie Nieman (mainstream contemporary).

How to Contact: Accepts unsolicited mss. Query with "brief" synopsis and 3 sample chapters. Accepts queries by e-mail; no mss. Include estimated word count, 2-paragraph bio, Social Security number and list of publishing credits. Send SASE for return of ms or send disposable copy of ms and SASE for reply only. Responds in 2 months to queries; 6 months to mss. Sometimes comments on rejected mss.

Terms: Pays royalties of 10-15% on print runs of more than 2,500 copies; half that on print runs under 2,500 copies. Average advance: $500 for finished disk. Sends galleys to author. Publishes ms 12-18 months after acceptance.

Advice: "I am looking for serious, mainstream contemporary fiction and will consider first-time novelists. However, because the business is so small, I need the copy to be as clean (free of mistakes) as possible. No collections of short stories, poetry or juvenile fiction, please. Because of the difficulty for first-time and midlist authors to find a publisher, we like to think that we offer a chance for quality fiction to see the light—to publish an author's novel that might not be published otherwise."

VANESSAPRESS, P.O. Box 82761, Fairbanks AK 99708. (907)452-5070. Website: www.mosquitonet.com/~inkworks/vanessapress.html (includes names of editors, authors, titles, general contact information and prices). **Contact:** Sue Mitchell. Estab. 1984. "Vanessapress is Alaska's only women's publishing company. Our focus is on work by Alaskan women authors. We publish fiction, nonfiction and poetry." Publishes paperback originals and reprints. Average print order: 1,000. **Published 1 new writer within the last year.** Averages 1 title/year.

Needs: "We accept manuscripts of all genres." Recently published *O Rugged Land of Gold*, by Martha Martin; and *Tides of Morning* (anthology, poems and stories).

How to Contact: Accepts unsolicited mss. Query with outline/synopsis and 3 sample chapters. Include list of publishing credits and marketing plan. Send SASE or IRC for return of ms. Responds in 2 months to queries; 3 months to mss.

Terms: Publishes ms 1-2 years after acceptance. Sometimes comments on rejected ms.

Advice: "We only accept submissions from Alaskan women authors."

VÉHICULE PRESS, Box 125, Place du Parc Station, Montreal, Quebec H2W 2M9 Canada. **Contact:** Simon Dardick, publisher/editor. Estab. 1973. Small publisher of scholarly, literary and cultural books. Publishes hardcover and paperback originals. Books: good quality paper; offset printing; perfect and cloth binding; illustrations. Average print order: 1,000-3,000. Averages 15 total titles/year.

Imprint(s): Signal Editions (poetry).

Needs: Feminist, literary, regional, short story collections, translations—"*by Canadian residents only.*" No romance or formula writing. Published *Rembrandt's Model*, by Yeshim Ternar; and *Ice in Dark Water*, by David Manicom.

How to Contact: Send query letter or query with sample chapters. Send SASE or IRC for reply ("no U.S. stamps, please"). Responds in 3 months to mss.

Terms: Pays in royalties of 10-12%. "Depends on press run and sales. Translators of fiction can receive Canada Council funding, which publisher applies for." Sends galleys to author. Book catalog for 9×12 SASE.

Advice: "Quality in almost any style is acceptable. We believe in the editing process."

VOICES FROM MY RETREAT, P.O. Box 1077, S, Fallsburg NY 12779. (914)436-7455. Fax: (718)885-0066. E-mail: myretreat2@aol.com. Website: www.myretreat.net. **Contact:** Cora Schwartz, editor. Estab. 1999. "Small independent publisher focusing on novels and short story collections with an international

slant, i.e. characters, setting, themes." Publishes paperback originals. Plans 1 first novel this year. Averages 2 total titles, 2 fiction titles/year. Distributes titles through Amazon.com or direct. Promotes titles through Amazon.com, I.W.W.G. conferences and Small Press (NYC).
- Voices From My Retreat is a member of Small Press (NYC) and the International Womens Writing Guild.

Needs: Ethnic/multicultural (general), experimental, feminist, historical (general), humor satire, literary, mainstream, short story collections, all must have an international slant. Recently published *Beneath the Hill*, by Pat Carr (literary); and *All There Is*, by Maria Butler (mainstream).
How to Contact: Does not accept unsolicited mss. Submit complete ms with cover letter. Include estimated word count, and 1-page bio. Send SASE or IRC for return of ms or send disposable copy of ms and SASE for reply only. Responds in 2 months to mss. Accepts simultaneous and electronic submissions. Sometimes comments on rejected mss.
Terms: Pays royalties of 10% minimum. Publishes ms 6 months after acceptance.
Advice: "Be gut level honest. We are not interested in fiction in which the author uses a point of view of the opposite sex or of a race, class, or nationality which he/she is not. We are looking for both experience and authenticity."

W.W. PUBLICATIONS, 4108 Menton, Flint MI 48507. **Contact**: Philip Helms, editor. Estab. 1967. One-man operation on part-time basis. Publishes paperback originals and reprints. Books: typing paper; offset printing; staple-bound; black ink illustrations. Average print order: 500. First novel print order: 500. Averages 1 fiction title/year.
Imprint(s): *Minas Tirith Evening Star.*
Needs: Fantasy, science fiction. "Specializes in Tolkien-related or middle-earth." Published *The Adventures of Fungo Hafwirse*, by Philip W. Helms and David L. Dettman.
How to Contact: Accepts unsolicited mss. Submit complete ms with SASE. Responds in 1 month. "Submit hardy copy by mail only. No phone inquiries, no fax and no e-mail. No exceptions." Occasionally comments on rejected mss.
Terms: Individual arrangement with author depending on book, etc.; provides 5 author's copies.
Advice: "We are publishing more fiction and more paperbacks. The author/editor relationship: a friend and helper."

WAVERLY HOUSE PUBLISHING, P.O. Box 1053, Glenside PA 19038. (215)884-5873. E-mail: info@natsel.com. Website: www.natsel.com (includes book catalog and interviews with authors). **Contact**: Nora Wright, publisher. Estab. 1997. 'Small independent publisher publishing works of high entertainment value which also convey a message of social significance to the African-American community." Publishes hardcover and paperback originals. Books: offset printing; casebound with perfect binding. Average print order: 2,000. First novel print order: 2,000. **Published 1 new writer within the last year.** Plans 1 first novel in 2001. Averages 2-3 total titles, 2-3 fiction titles/year. Distributes titles through Cultured Plus, Ingram and Baker & Taylor. Promotes titles through advertisement in African-American literary journals and the use of publicity consultant. Member: PMA and SPAN.
Needs: Ethnic/multicultural (specific culture, African-American). Recently published *Damaged!*, by Bernadette Y. Connor (novel); and *The Rest of Our Lives*, by Dawn Connelly-Craig.
How to Contact: Does not accept unsolicited mss. Send query letter. Accepts queries by e-mail. Include estimated word count and 50-word bio. Send SASE or IRC for return of ms or send disposable copy of ms and SASE for reply only. Responds in 1 month to queries; 2 months to mss. Accepts simultaneous submissions.
Terms: Pays royalties of 6% minimum. Sends galleys to author. Publishes ms 9-12 months after acceptance.

WOODLEY MEMORIAL PRESS, English Dept., Washburn University, Topeka KS 66621. (785)234-1032. E-mail: zzlaws@washburn.edu.Website: www.wuacc.edu/reference/woodley-press/index.html (includes writer's guidelines, editors, authors, titles). **Contact**: Robert N. Lawson, editor. Estab. 1980. "Woodley Memorial Press is a small, nonprofit press which publishes book-length poetry and fiction collections by Kansas writers only; by 'Kansas writers' we mean writers who reside in Kansas or have a Kansas connection." Publishes paperback originals. Averages 2 titles/year.
Needs: Contemporary, experimental, literary, mainstream, short story collection. "We do not want to see genre fiction, juvenile, or young adult." Published *Gathering Reunion*, by David Tangeman (stories and poetry); *The Monday, Wednesday, Friday Girl*, by Stuart Levine (short stories); and *Rudolph, Encouraged by His Therapist*, by Eugene Bales (satiric).
How to Contact: *Charges $5 reading fee.* Accepts unsolicited mss. Submit complete ms with cover letter. Accepts queries by e-mail. Send SASE or IRC for return of ms. Responds in 2 weeks to queries; 2 months to mss. Sometimes comments on rejected ms.
Terms: "Terms are individually arranged with author after acceptance of manuscript." Publishes ms one year after acceptance. Writer's guidelines on website.

Advice: "We only publish one work of fiction a year, on average, and definitely want it to be by a Kansas author. We are more likely to do a collection of short stories by a single author."

■ **WRITERS DIRECT**, Imprint of Titlewaves Publishing, Book Division of H&S Publishing, 1351 Kuhio Highway, Kapaa HI 96746. (808)822-7449. Fax: (808)822-2312. E-mail: rs@hshawaii.com. Website: www.bestpl acesonearth.com (includes book catalog). **Contact:** Rob Sanford, editor. Estab. 1985. "Small independent publishing house founded and run by published authors." Publishes hardcover and paperback originals and reprints. Books: recycled paper; digital printing; perfect binding; illustrations. **Published 4 new writers within the last year.** Plans 1 first novel in 2001. Averages more than 6 total titles, 2 fiction titles/year.

Needs: Adventure, children's/juvenile, humor satire, literary, mainstream, New Age/mystic, psychic/supernatural, regional (Hawaii), religious (children's religious, inspirational, religious mystery/suspense, religious thriller), science fiction, thriller/espionage.

How to Contact: Accepts unsolicited mss. Query with outline/synopsis and 3 sample chapters. Include estimated word count, 1-page bio, list of publishing credits, why author wrote book, marketing plan. Send SASE for return of ms or send disposable copy of ms and SASE for reply only. Responds in 1 month to queries; 3 months to mss. Accepts simultaneous submissions. Sometimes comments on rejected mss.

Terms: Pays royalties of 15-35%. Sometimes sends galleys to author. Book catalog for legal-size SASE.

Advice: "Do what you do best and enjoy most. Your writing is an outcome of the above."

Contests & Awards

In addition to honors and, quite often, cash awards, contests and awards programs offer writers the opportunity to be judged on the basis of quality alone without the outside factors that sometimes influence publishing decisions. New writers who win contests may be published for the first time, while more experienced writers may gain public recognition of an entire body of work.

Listed here are contests for almost every type of fiction writing. Some focus on form, such as short stories, novels or novellas, while others feature writing on particular themes or topics. Still others are prestigious prizes or awards for work that must be nominated, such as the Pulitzer Prize in Fiction. Chances are no matter what type of fiction you write, there is a contest or award program that may interest you.

SELECTING AND SUBMITTING TO A CONTEST

Use the same care in submitting to contests as you would sending your manuscript to a publication or book publisher. Deadlines are very important, and where possible, we've included this information. At times contest deadlines were only approximate at our press deadline, so be sure to write or call for complete information.

Follow the rules to the letter. If, for instance, contest rules require your name on a cover sheet only, you will be disqualified if you ignore this and put your name on every page. Find out how many copies to send. If you don't send the correct amount, by the time you are contacted to send more, it may be past the submission deadline. An increasing number of contests invite writers to query by e-mail, and many post contest information on their websites. Check listings for e-mail and website addresses.

One note of caution: Beware of contests that charge entry fees that are disproportionate to the amount of the prize. Contests offering a $10 prize, but charging $7 in entry fees, are a waste of your time and money.

If you are interested in a contest or award that requires your publisher to nominate your work, it's acceptable to make your interest known. Be sure to leave the publisher plenty of time, however, to make the nomination deadline.

THE EDWARD ABBEY FICTION AWARD, The Bear Deluxe Magazine, P.O. Box 10342, Portland OR 97296. (503)242-1047. Fax: (503)243-2645. E-mail: bear@teleport.com. Website: www.orlo.org. **Contact:** Steven Babcock, senior editor. Award to "recognize short fiction in the spirit of Edward Abbey, noted environmental author and activist." Annual award for short stories. Award: $500. Competition receives 80-150 submissions per category. Judged by magazine creative review group. $5 entry fee. Guidelines available June 1. For guidelines, send SASE or e-mail. Accepts inquiries by e-mail. Entries must be postmarked by first Monday after Labor Day. Entries should be previously unpublished. Contest open to all writers. Length: 4,000 words. Winners announced in December following deadline. Winners notified by phone. For list of winners send SASE.

ELEANOR ABRAM PRIZE FOR FICTION, The Harpweaver, Breck University, St. Catharines, Ontario L2S 3A1 Canada. (905)688-5550, ext. 3472. Fax: (905)688-5550, ext. 4492. **Contact:** Angus Somorville or Lynn Peppus, co-editors. Annual award for short stories. Award: $150. Guidelines available July 2000. For guidelines, e-mail, visit website or call. Accepts inquiries by fax, phone. Deadline September 2001. Entries should be unpublished. Contest open to all writers. Length: 5,000 words. Winners announced November 2001. Winners notified by mail or phone.

ADVENTURES IN STORYTELLING MAGAZINE'S NATIONAL STORIES INTO PRINT WRITING CONTEST, *Adventures in Storytelling Magazine*, 1702 Eastbrook Dr., Columbus OH 43223. (614)274-8234. E-mail: Alamarr@aol.com. **Contact:** Chris Irvin, associate editor. Annual competition with theme for stories 500 words or less. Prizes: 1st, 2nd and 3rd place winner and 3 honorable mentions. Cash awards are given based on total entry fees. First place will receive 25% of total entry fees; 2nd place, 15%; and 3rd place, 10%. Competition receives approximately 50 submissions. $3 fee per entry. Guidelines available February 2001 for SASE or e-mail. Accepts inquiries by e-mail. Deadline: November 30. Winners announced and notified by January 1. For a list of winners, send SASE or e-mail. "Follow guidelines carefully. Be sure your story does not exceed word limit and conforms to contest themes."

N **AIM MAGAZINE'S SHORT STORY CONTEST**, AIM Magazine, P.O. Box 1174, Maywood IL 60153. (708)344-4414. Website: www.aimmagazine.org. **Contact:** Ruth Apilado, associate editor. This annual award is for short stories that embody our goals of furthering the brotherhood of man by way of the written word. Award: $100 and publications. Competition receives 20 submissions per category. Judge: Staff members. No entry fee. Guidelines available anytime. Accepts inquiries by e-mail and phone. Entries should be unpublished. Contest open to everyone. Length: 4,000 word or less. Winners are announced in the autumn issue. Winners notified by mail on Sept 1. For list of winners send SASE.

☑ ○ **AKRON MANUSCRIPT CLUB ANNUAL FICTION CONTEST**, Akron Manuscript Club and A.U., Falls Writer's Workshop, P.O. Box 1101, Cuyahoga Falls OH 44223-0101. (330)923-2094. E-mail: mmlop @aol.com. Website: www.aol.hometown. **Contact:** M.M. LoPiccolo, contest director. Award to "encourage writers with cash prizes and certificates and to provide in-depth critique that most writers have never had the benefit of seeing." Annual competition for short stories. Award: certificates to $50 (1st Prize in three fiction categories dependent on funding); certificates for 2nd and 3rd Prizes. Competition receives 50-75 submissions per category. Judge: M.M. LoPiccolo. $25 fee for each entry in one category. Guidelines will be sent *only* with SASE. Deadline: January 1-March 15. Unpublished submissions. Length: 2,500 words (12-13 pages). Send all mail to: Fiction Contest, P.O. Box 1101, Cuyahoga Falls OH 44223-0101, Attn: M.M. LoPiccolo. "Send *no* manuscript without obtaining current guidelines. *Nothing* will be returned without SASE." Winners announced in May. Winners notified by mail. List of winners available after May for SASE.

N ◎ **ALABAMA STATE COUNCIL ON THE ARTS INDIVIDUAL ARTIST FELLOWSHIP**, 201 Monroe St., Montgomery AL 36130-1800. (205)242-4076, ext. 224. Fax: (334)240-3269. E-mail: randy@arts.stat e.al.us. Website: www.arts.state.al.us. **Contact:** Randy Shoults, Literature program manager. "To recognize the achievements and potential of Alabama writers." Annual. Competition receives 25 submissions annually. Judge: independent peer panel. No entry fee. Guidelines available January 2001. For guidelines, fax, e-mail, visit website. Accepts inquiries by fax, e-mail, phone. Deadline March 1, 2001. "Two copies of the following should be submitted: a resume and a list of published works with reviews, if available. A minimum of ten pages of poetry or prose, but no more than twenty pages. Please label each page with title, artist's name and date. If published, indicate where and the date of publication." Winners announced in June. Winners notified by mail and e-mail. For list of winners, send SASE, fax, e-mail, or visit website.

N ◎ **ALASKA STATE COUNCIL ON THE ARTS CAREER OPPORTUNITY GRANT AWARD**, Alaska State Council on the Arts, 411 West 4th Ave., Suite 1E, Anchorage AK 99501-2343. (907)269-6610 and 1-888-ARTSGCI. Fax: (907)269-6601. E-mail: info@aksca.org. **Contact:** Director. Grants help artists take advantage of impending, concrete opportunities that will significantly advance their work or careers. Professional artists working in the literary arts who are requesting support for unique, short-term opportunities are eligible. Awards up to $1,000. Deadline: applications must be received in the office 30 days prior to dates of career opportunity. Alaskan residents only.

○ ◎ **ALLIGATOR JUNIPER NATIONAL WRITING CONTEST**, Prescott College, 301 Grove Ave., Prescott AZ 86301. (520)778-2090, ext. 2012. Fax: (520)776-5137. Annual competition for fiction, creative nonfiction, poetry. "We aim to publish work that is original, graceful, skillful, authentic, moving, and memorable." Award: $500 plus publication for 1st place in each category. Non-winners chosen for publication paid in copies. Competition receives 250 submissions. Fiction is judged by editors and staff of *Alligator Juniper*. Entry fee $10 for each story up to 30 pages. Additional entries require additional fee. All entrants receive the next issue, a $7.50 value. Guidelines available for SASE. Postmark deadline: October 1. Winners announced January. Winners notified by phone. List of winners mailed to all entrants.

○ **AMELIA MAGAZINE AWARDS**, 329 "E" St., Bakersfield CA 93304. (805)323-4064. **Contact:** Frederick A. Raborg, Jr., editor. The Reed Smith Fiction Prize; The Willie Lee Martin Short Story Award; The Cassie Wade Short Fiction Award; The Patrick T. T. Bradshaw Fiction Award; and four annual genre awards in science fiction, romance, western and fantasy/horror. Estab. 1984. Annual. "To publish the finest fiction possible and reward the writer; to allow good writers to earn some money in small press publication. *Amelia* strives to fill that gap between major circulation magazines and quality university journals." Unpublished submissions. Length: The Reed Smith—3,000 words maximum; The Willie Lee Martin—3,500-5,000 words; The Cassie Wade—4,500 words maximum; The Patrick T. T. Bradshaw—25,000 words; the genre awards—science fiction, 5,000 words; romance, 3,000 words; western, 5,000 words; fantasy/horror, 5,000 words. Award: "Each prize consists of $200 plus publication and two copies of issue containing winner's work." The Reed Smith Fiction Prize offers two additional awards when quality merits of $100 and $50, and publication; Bradshaw Fiction Award: $250, 2 copies. Deadlines: The Reed Smith Prize—September 1; The Willie Lee Martin—March 1; The Cassie Wade—June 1; The Patrick T. T. Bradshaw—February 15; *Amelia* fantasy/horror—February 1; *Amelia* western—April 1; *Amelia* romance—October 1; *Amelia* science fiction—December 15. Entry fee: $7.50. Sample copies: $10.95. Bradshaw Award fee: $15. Contest rules for SASE. Looking for "high quality work equal to finest fiction being published today."

▥ AMERICAN LITERARY SHORT FICTION AWARD, American Literary Review, Dept. of English, Univ. of North Texas, P.O. Box 311307, Denton TX 76203-1307. (940)565-2755. Fax: (940)565-4355. Website: www.engl.unt.edu/alr. **Contact:** Lee Martin, editor. "This biannual award for short stories is meant to award excellence in short fiction." Award: $500 and publication. Competition receives 300 submissions per category. Judge: screened internally. Finalists sent to outside judge. Past judges have included Marly Swick, Antonya Nelson and Janis Agee. Entry fee $10/story. Guidelines are currently available. For guidelines, send SASE or visit website. Accepts inquiries by fax and phone. Deadline October 1, 2001. Entries should be unpublished. Contest open to anyone not affiliated with the University of North Texas. "Only solidly crafted, character-driven stories will have the best chance for success." Winners are announced February 1, 2002. Winners notified by mail and phone on February 1, 2002. For list of winners send SASE.

▥ AMERICAN MARKETS NEWSLETTER SHORT STORY COMPETITION, American Markets Newsletter, 2531 39th Ave., San Francisco CA 94116. Fax: (415)753-6057. E-mail: sheila.oconnor@juno.com. **Contact:** Sheila O'Connor, publisher/editor. Award is to "give short story writers more exposure—all entries are considered for worldwide syndication whether they win or not." Biannual competition for short stories. Award: 1st place, $250; 2nd place, $100; 3rd place: $50, and worldwide syndication for all eligible entries whether they win or not. Judge: editor of American Markets Newsletter. $5 per entry; $9 for 2; $12 for 3; and $4 each entry thereafter. For guidelines, send SASE, fax, or e-mail. Accepts inquiries by fax and e-mail. Deadline June 30 and December 31. Published or previously unpublished entries are actively encouraged. Add a note of where and when previously published. Contest open to all. Length: 2,000 words or fewer. "All kinds of fiction are considered—we especially want women's pieces—romance, twist in the tale, but all will be considered." Winners announced "within 3 months of deadlines." Winners notified by mail if they include SASE.

◐ SHERWOOD ANDERSON SHORT FICTION AWARD, *Mid-American Review*, Dept. of English, Bowling Green State University, Bowling Green OH 43403. (419)372-2725. **Contact:** Michael Czyzniejewski, fiction editor. Annual. "Contest is open to all writers. It is judged by a well-known writer, e.g., June Spence or Melanie Rae Thon. Editors choose the top five entries, then the winner is selected by judge and guaranteed publication in the spring issue of *Mid-American Review*, plus $300. All entrants receive a copy of the issue where the winners are printed." Competition receives 100-200 submissions. $10 fee per story. Guidelines available for SASE. Deadline: October 1. Unpublished material. Winners announced in Spring issue. Winners notified before end of year by phone or mail. For list of winners, send SASE.

▥ SHERWOOD ANDERSON WRITER'S GRANT, Sherwood Anderson Foundation, 216 College Rd., Richmond VA 23229. (804)282-8008. Fax: (804)287-6052. E-mail: mspear@richmond.edu. Website: www.richmond.edu/~journalm/comp.html. **Contact:** Michael M. Spear, foundation co-president. Award to "encourage and support developing writers." Annual award for short stories and chapters of novels. Award: range $5,000 to $10,000. Entries are judged by a committee established by the foundation. No entry fee. Guidelines available on website. Accepts inquiries by e-mail. Deadline April 1, 2001. Published or previously unpublished entries. "The contest is open to all struggling writers in the United States." No word length specifications. "Send in your best, most vivid prose that clearly shows talent." Winners announced in mid-summer each year. Winners notified by phone. For list of winners visit website.

⊕ ▢ ◎ ANDREAS-GRYPHIUS-PREIS (LITERATURPREIS DER KÜNSTLERGILDE), Die Kunstlergilde e.V., Hafenmarkt 2, D-73728 Esslingen a.N., Germany. Phone: 0049/711/3969010. Fax: 0049/711/39690123. **Contact:** Ramona Rauscher-Steinebrunner, chief secretary. "The prize is awarded for the best piece of writing or for complete literary works." Annual competition for short stories, novels, story collections, translations. Award: 1 prize of DM 25,000; 1 prize of DM 7,000. Competition receives 50 entries. Accepts inquiries by fax. Judges: Jury members (7 persons). Guidelines available. Fiction should be published in German in the last 5 years. Deadline: October. "The prize is awarded to writers who are dealing with the particular problems of the German culture in eastern Europe." Winners announced beginning of year following deadline. Winners notified by mail.

ANNUAL FICTION CONTEST, Women In The Arts, P.O. Box 2907, Decatur IL 62524. (217)872-0811. **Contact:** Vice President. Award to "encourage new writers, whether published or not." Annual competition for short stories. Award: At least $30. Competition receives 25-30 submissions. Judges: professional writers. Entry fee $2 for each story submitted. Guidelines available for SASE. Deadline: November 1 annually. Published or previously unpublished submissions. Open to anyone. Word length: 1,500 words maximum. "Entrants must send for our contest rules and follow the specific format requirements."

ANNUAL JUVENILE-FICTION CONTEST, Women In The Arts, P.O. Box 2907, Decatur IL 62524. (217)872-0811. **Contact:** Vice President. Award to "encourage writers of children's literature, whether published or not." Annual competition for short stories. Award: At least $30. Competition receives 30-40 submissions. Judges: professional writers. Entry fee $2 for each story submitted. Guidelines available for SASE. Deadline: November 1 annually. Published or previously unpublished submissions. Open to anyone. Word length: 1,500 words maximum. "Entrants must send for our contest rules and follow the specific format requirements."

N ANNUAL POETRY/FICTION CONTEST, Rambunctious Press, Inc.1221 W. Pratt Blvd., Chicago IL 60626. (773)338-2439. **Contact:** E. Hausler, editor. Annual competition for short stories. Award: $100 (1st prize), $75 (2nd prize), $50 (3rd prize). Competition receives 200+ submissions. Entry fee $3 per story or $12 subscription. For guidelines send SASE. Deadline: December 31, 2001. Entries should be previously unpublished. Contest open to everyone. Length: 10 pages. "Follow theme with creativity. Each contest has theme. Examples: 'Senses,' 'Luck,' 'Colors.'" Winners announced three months after contest deadline. "All contestants will receive list of winners."

THE ANNUAL/ATLANTIC WRITING COMPETITIONS, Writers' Federation of Nova Scotia, 1113 Marginal Rd., Halifax, Nova Scotia B3H 4P7 Canada. (902)423-8116. E-mail: talk@writers.ns.ca. Website: www.writers.ns.ca. **Contact:** Jane Buss, executive director. "To recognize and encourage unpublished writers in the region of Atlantic Canada. (Competition only open to residents of Nova Scotia, Newfoundland, Prince Edward Island and New Brunswick, the four Atlantic Provinces.)" Annual competition for short stories, novels, poetry, children's writing and drama. Award: Various cash awards. Competition receives approximately 10-12 submissions for novels; 75 for poetry; 75 for children's; 75 for short stories; 10 for nonfiction. Judges: Professional writers, librarians, booksellers. $15 fee/entry. Guidelines available after May for SASE. Accepts inquiries by e-mail. Deadline: July 31. Unpublished submissions. Winners announced in March. Winners notified by mail. List of winners available on website.

ANTIETAM REVIEW LITERARY AWARD, *Antietam Review*, 41 S. Potomac St., Hagerstown MD 21740. Phone/fax: (301)791-3132. **Contact:** Ethan Fischer, executive editor. Annual award to encourage and give recognition to excellence in short fiction. Open only to writers from Maryland, Pennsylvania, Virginia, West Virginia, Washington DC and Delaware. "We consider only previously unpublished work. We read manuscripts between June 1 and September 1." Award: $100 for the story; the story is printed in the magazine with citation as winner of Literary Contest. Competition receives 100 submissions. "We consider all fiction mss sent to *Antietam Review* Literary Contest as entries for inclusion in each issue. We look for well-crafted, serious literary prose fiction under 5,000 words." $10 fee for each story submitted. Guidelines available for #10 SASE. Accepts inquiries by phone. Deadline: September 1. Winners announced in October. Winners notified by phone and mail in October.

ANVIL PRESS INTERNATIONAL 3-DAY NOVEL WRITING CONTEST, Anvil Press, 204-A 175 E. Broadway, Vancouver, British Columbia V5T 1W2 Canada. (604)876-8710. Fax: (604)879-2667. E-mail: subter@portal.ca. **Contact:** Brian Kaufman, managing editor. Annual prize for best novel written in 3 days, held every Labor Day weekend. Award: Offer of publication with percentage of royalties (grand prize); $500 Canadian (1st runner up); $250 Canadian (2nd runner up). Competition receives 400-500 submissions. Judges: Anvil Press Editorial Board. $25 entry fee. Guidelines available June 1 for SASE fax, e-mail, or visit website. Accepts inquiries by fax and e-mail. Deadline: September 3. "Runner up categories may not be offered every year. Please query." Winners announced November 30. Winners notified by phone and mail. List of winners available November 30 for SASE or on website. "This is a short novel and should contain all the ingredients found in any good novel: character development, a strong story plot line and dramatic action. Don't think of a movie treatment or TV-style scenario, and read past winners!"

ARIZONA COMMISSION ON THE ARTS CREATIVE WRITING FELLOWSHIPS, 417 W. Roosevelt St., Phoenix AZ 85003. (602)255-5882. E-mail: general@arizonaarts.org. Website: http://az.arts.asu .edu/artscomm/. **Contact:** Jill Bernstein, literature director. Fellowships awarded in alternate years to fiction writers and poets. Award: $5,000-7,500. Competition receives 120-150 submissions. Judges: Out-of-state writers/

editors. Guidelines available for SASE. Accepts inquiries by fax and e-mail. Deadline: September 13. Arizona resident poets and writers over 18 years of age only. Winners announced by March 2001. Winners notified in writing. List of winners available for SASE.

N ◎ ARROWHEAD REGIONAL ARTS COUNCIL INDIVIDUAL ARTIST CAREER DEVELOP-MENT GRANT, Arrowhead Regional Arts Council, 101 W. Second St. Suite 204, Duluth MN 55802-2086. (218)722-0952. Fax: (218)722-4459. E-mail: aracouncil@aol.com. Website: www.members.aol.com/aracouncil. **Contact:** Robert DeArmond, executive director. Award to "provide financial support to regional artists wishing to take advantage of impending, concrete opportunities that will advance their work or careers. Applicants must live in the seven-county region of Northeastern Minnesota." Award is granted 3 times a year Competition open to short stories, novels, story collections and translations. Award: up to $1,000. Competition receives 15-20 submissions per category. Judge: ARAC Board. No entry fee. Guidelines now available. For guidelines, e-mail or phone, Accepts inquiries by fax, e-mail and phone. Deadline April, July and November 2001. Entries should be unpublished. Winners announced approximately 6 weeks after deadline date. Winners notified by mail or phone. For list of winners send e-mail.

N ◎ THE ART OF MUSIC ANNUAL WRITING CONTEST, Piano Press, P.O. Box 85, Del Mar CA 92014-0085. (858)481-5650. Fax: (858)755-1104. E-mail: eaxford@aol.com. Website: http://pianopress.iuma.c om. **Contact:** Elizabeth C. Axford, owner. Contest to promote the art of music through writing; to encourage more writing on music-related topics. Award: First, second, and third prizes in each of 3 age groups. Prizes include a medal and publication in the annual anthology *The Art of Music—A Collection of Writings.* Judge: Panel of published writers. Entry fee $20/story, essay or poem. Guidelines available after September. Guidelines for SASE or e-mail. Deadline: June 30. Entries should be previously unpublished. Contest open to all writers. "Make sure all work is fresh and original. Music-related topics only." Winners announced on September 1. Winners notified by mail in September. For list of winners send SASE.

✓ ◯ ◎ ASF TRANSLATION PRIZE, American-Scandinavian Foundation, 58 Park Ave., New York NY 10016. (212)879-9779. Fax: (212)249-3444. E-mail: agyongy@amscan.org. Website: www.amscan.org. **Contact:** Publishing office. Estab. 1980. "To encourage the translation and publication of the best of contemporary Scandinavian poetry and fiction and to make it available to a wider American audience." Annual competition for poetry, drama, literary prose and fiction translations. Award: $2,000, a bronze medallion and publication in *Scandinavian Review.* Competition receives 20-30 submissions. Competition rules and entry forms available with SASE. Accepts inquiries by fax and e-mail. Deadline: June 1, 2001. Submissions must have been previously published in the original Scandinavian language. No previously-published translated material. Original authors should have been born within past 200 years. Winners announced in September. Winners notified by mail. List of winners available for SASE. "Select a choice literary work by an important Scandinavian author whose work has not yet been translated into English."

◯ ◎ THE ISAAC ASIMOV AWARD, International Association for the Fantastic in the Arts and *Asimov's* magazine, School of Mass Communications, U. of South Florida, 4202 E. Fowler, Tampa FL 33620. (813)974-6792. Fax: (813)974-2591. E-mail: rwilber@chuma.cas.usf.edu. **Contact:** Rick Wilber, administrator. "The award honors the legacy of one of science fiction's most distinguished authors through an award aimed at undergraduate writers." Annual award for short stories. Award: $500 and consideration for publication in *Asimov's.* Winner receives all-expenses paid trip to Ft. Lauderdale, Florida, to attend Conference on the Fantastic in mid-March where award is given. Competition receives 100-200 submissions. Judges: *Asimov's* editors. Entry fee: $10 for up to 3 submissions. Guidelines available for SASE. Accepts inquiries by fax and e-mail. Deadline: December 15. Unpublished submissions. Full-time college undergraduates only. Winners announced in February. Winners notified by telephone. List of winners available in March for SASE.

⬧ ◐ ◎ ASTED/GRAND PRIX DE LITTERATURE JEUNESSE DU QUEBEC-ALVINE-BE-LISLE, Association pour l'avancement des sciences et des techniques de la documentation, 3414 Avenue du Parc, Bureau 202, Montreal, Quebec H2X 2H5 Canada. (514)281-5012. Fax: (514)281-8219. E-mail: info@asted.org. Website: www.asted.org. **Contact:** Micheline Patton, president. "Prize granted for the best work in youth literature edited in French in the Quebec Province. Authors and editors can participate in the contest." Annual competition for fiction and nonfiction for children and young adults. Award: $500. Deadline: June 1. Contest entry limited to editors of books published during the preceding year. French translations of other languages are not accepted.

◐ ◎ THE ATHENAEUM LITERARY AWARD, The Athenaeum of Philadelphia, 219 S. Sixth St., Philadelphia PA 19106. (215)925-2688. Fax: (215)925-3755. Website: www.libertynet.org/athena. **Contact:** Literary Award Committee. Annual award to recognize and encourage outstanding literary achievement in Philadelphia and its vicinity. Award: A bronze medal bearing the name of the award, the seal of the Athenaeum, the title of the book, the name of the author and the year. Competition receives 10-20 submissions. Judged by committee appointed by Board of Directors. Deadline: December. Submissions must have been published during the preceding year. Nominations shall be made in writing to the Literary Award Committee by the author, the publisher or a member of the Athenaeum, accompanied by a copy of the book. The Athenaeum Literary Award is granted for a work of general literature, not exclusively for fiction. Juvenile fiction is not included. Winners announced spring 2002. Winners notified by mail. List of winners available on website.

N **AUTUMN 2001 SHORT STORY COMPETITION**, Write Spot Publishers International, P.O. Box 221, The Gap, Brisbane, Queensland 4061 Australia. (07)33001948. Fax: (07)33005677. E-mail: frontdesk@write rsspot.com. Website: www.writersspot.com. **Contact:** D. Murray, submissions editor. The annual award for short stories "offers writers the opportunity to win cash prizes and the possibility of being published in an anthology of short stories. Stories selected for inclusion will be offered royalties on the sales of the publication." Awards: $750 for first prize, $250 for second prize, $100 for third prize, $50 for editor's choice, plus up to 10 prizes of publication in anthology. Judge: a panel of 4-6 judges from our publications committee. Entry fee: $8/entry; $12/2 entries; $5 each/3 or more entries. For guidelines, send SASE, fax, e-mail, visit website or call. Accepts inquiries by fax, e-mail and phone. Deadline May 31, 2001. Entries should be unpublished. Entries must be typed, should not have been previously published and should not have previously won a prize. Contest open to writers of all ages, nationalities, locations, and genres. Length: fewer than 5,000 words. "Originality counts! The works enjoyment/entertainment factor is deemed more relevant than its literary brilliance." Winners are announced two weeks after closing date. Winners are notified by mail, phone and e-mail. For list of winners send SASE, fax, e-mail or visit website.

AWP AWARD SERIES IN POETRY, CREATIVE NONFICTION AND SHORT FICTION, AWP/Thomas Dunne Books Novel Award, The Associated Writing Programs, Tallwood House, Mail Stop 1E3, George Mason University, Fairfax VA 22030. (703)993-4301. Fax: (703)993-4302. E-mail: awp@gmu.edu. Website: http://awpwriter.org. **Contact:** David Sherwin. Annual award. The AWP Award Series was established in cooperation with several university presses in order to publish and make fine fiction, nonfiction, and poetry available to a wide audience. The competition is open to all authors writing in English. Awards: $2,000 plus publication for short story collection; $10,000 advance plus publication by Thomas Dunne Books for Novel, an imprint of St. Martin's Press. In addition, AWP tries to place mss of finalists with participating presses. Competition receives 700 novel and 400 short fiction submissions. Novels are judged by editors at Thomas Dunne Books. Short fiction is judged by a leading author in the field (2000—Jill McCorkle). Entry fee $20 nonmembers, $10 AWP members. Contest/award rules and guidelines for business-size SASE or visit our website. No phone calls please. Mss must be postmarked between January 1-February 28. Only book-length mss in the novel and short story collections are eligible (60,000 word minimum for novels; 150-300 pages for story collections). Open to all authors writing in English regardless of nationality or residence. Manuscripts previously published in their entirety, including self-publishing, are not eligible. No mss returned. Winners announced in August. Winners notified by phone. Send SASE for list of winners.

AWP INTRO JOURNALS PROJECT, Tallwood House, Mail Stop 1E3, George Mason University, Fairfax VA 22030. **Contact:** David Sherwin. "This is a prize for students in AWP member university creative writing programs only. Authors are nominated by the head of the creative writing department. Each school may send 2 nominated short stories." Annual competition for short stories and poetry. Award: $50 plus publication in participating journal. 1999 journals included *Puerto del Sol*, *Quarterly West*, *Mid-American Review*, *Cimmaron Review*, *Willow Springs*, *Fourth Genre* and *Hayden's Ferry Review*. Judges: AWP. Deadline: December. Unpublished submissions only.

N **AWP PRAGUE SUMMER SEMINARS FELLOWSHIP**, Associated Writing Programs, Tallwood House, MS 1E3, George Mason University, Fairfax VA 22030. E-mail: awp@gmu.edu. Website: http://awpwriter.org. **Contact:** David Sherwin, editor. Award to "grant fellowships to promising writers so they can attend the Prague Summer Seminars." Annual award for short stories or novel excerpts. Award: tuition to summer seminars (but not transportation). Competition receives 150-200 submissions per category. Judge: published writers in each field. $5 entry fee. For guidelines, send SASE or visit website. Entries should be previously unpublished. Contest open to "any writer writing in English who has yet to publish a first book. Length: 20 pages maximum. Winners announced Spring 2001. Winners notified by phone. For list of winners send SASE.

N **BAKELESS LITERARY PUBLICATION PRIZES**, Bread Loaf Writers' Conference, Middlebury College, Middlebury VT 05753. (802)443-2018. Fax: (802)443-2087. Annual award to recognize and publish an author's first novel or short story collection. Award: tuition, room and board at the conference and publication by Middlebury College/University Press of New England. Judge for 2001 is Howard Norman. Entry fee: $10. Guidelines available April 1 for SASE. Unpublished submissions. Length: 150-450 pages. List of winners available for SASE.

BEACON STREET REVIEW EDITOR'S CHOICE AWARD, Beacon Street Review, Emerson College, 100 Beacon St., Boston MA 02116. (617)824-8750. E-mail: beaconstreetreveiw@hotmail.com. **Contact:** Prose or Poetry Editor. Award to "recognize highest degree of creative talent and a true seriousness of effort." Annual award for short stories, nonfiction or poetry. Award: $75. Judge: an established local author. No entry fee. For guidelines send SASE. Deadline October 4, 2001. Entries should be previously unpublished. Contest open to all writers. Length: 4,000 words maximum for prose entries or 5 poems.

THE BEACON, First Coast Romance Writers, P.O. Box 8604, Jacksonville FL 32239-8604. E-mail: dianah2o@aol.com. Website: www.angelfire.com/fl/RomanceWriting. **Contact:** Heather Waters, contest coordinator. Award to "provide published authors with a chance at greater success." Annual competition for novels. Award: a lighthouse pennant. Judge: finalists are read by book retailers. $25 entry fee. Guidelines available June 2000. For guidelines, send SASE or e-mail. Accepts inquiries by e-mail. Deadline February 1, 2001. Entries should be published (romance genre; 3 autographed copies of book; not returned; must be copyrighted 2000). Contest open to writers of all romance categories. Winners announced May 2001. Winners notified by mail. For list of winners send SASE or visit website.

GEORGE BENNETT FELLOWSHIP, Phillips Exeter Academy, 20 Main St., Exeter NH 03833-2460. Website: www.exeter.edu. **Contact:** Charles Pratt, coordinator, selection committee. "To provide time and freedom from monetary concerns to a person contemplating or pursuing a career as a professional writer." The committee favors applicants who have not yet published a book-length work with a major publisher." Annual award of writing residency. Award: A stipend ($6,000 at present), plus room and board for academic year. Competition receives approximately 150 submissions. Judges are a committee of the English department. Entry fee $5. Application form and guidelines for SASE, or obtain from the Academy website: www.exeter.edu. Deadline: December 1. Winners announced in March. Winners notified by letter or phone. List of winners available in March. All applicants will receive an announcement of the winner.

BERTELSMANN'S WORLD OF EXPRESSIONS SCHOLARSHIP PROGRAM, Bertelsmann USA, 1540 Broadway, New York NY 10036. (212)930-4520. Fax: (212)930-4783. E-mail: bwoesp@bmge.com. Website: www.worldofexpression.org. **Contact:** Melanie Fallon-Houska, director. Annual competition for short stories and poems. Award: $500-10,000, 68 awards total. Competition receives 2,000 submissions per category. Judges: various city officials, executives, authors, editors. Guidelines available October 1 for SASE, fax or e-mail. Deadline: February 1. Winners announced mid-May. Winners notified by mail and phone. For list of winners, send SASE, fax, e-mail or visit website. All the entrants must be public New York City high school seniors. Word length: 2,500 words or less.

BEST LESBIAN EROTICA, Cleis Press, P.O. Box 4108, Grand Central Station, New York NY 10163. Fax: (718)499-0338. E-mail: tristan@puckerup.com. Website: www.puckerup.com. **Contact:** Tristan Taormino, series editor. Submit short stories, novel excerpts, other prose; poetry will be considered, but poetry is not encouraged. Unpublished and previously published material will be considered, provided it was published between September 1999 and December 31, 2000. Include cover page with author's name, title of submission(s), address, phone/fax, and e-mail. All submissions must be typed and double-spaced. Also number the pages. Length: 5,000. You may submit a maximum of 3 different pieces of work. Submit 2 hard copies of each submission. No e-mail submissions will be accepted; accepts inquiries by e-mail. All submissions must include a SASE or an e-mail address for response. No mss will be return.

"BEST OF OHIO WRITERS" CONTEST, *Ohio Writer Magazine*, P.O. Box 91801, Cleveland OH 44101. (216)932-8444. E-mail: poetsleague@yahoo.com. **Contact:** Ron Antonucci, editor. Award "to encourage and promote the work of writers in Ohio." Annual competition for short stories. Awards: $150 (1st

FOR EXPLANATIONS OF THESE SYMBOLS,
SEE THE INSIDE FRONT AND BACK COVERS OF THIS BOOK.

Prize), $50 (2nd Prize). Competition receives 100 submissions. Judges: "a selected panel of prominent Ohio writers." $10 entry fee; includes subscription to *Ohio Writer*. Guidelines available after January 1 for SASE or e-mail. Accepts inquiries by e-mail and phone. Deadline: July 31. Unpublished submissions. Ohio writers only. Length: 2,500 words. "No cliché plots; we're looking for fresh, unpublished voices." Winners announced November 1. Winners are notified by mail. List of winners available November 1 for SASE or e-mail.

☑ ◎ **DORIS BETTS FICTION PRIZE**, North Carolina Writers' Network, 3501 Hwy. 54 W., Studio C, Chapel Hill NC 27516. (919)967-9540. Fax: (919)929-0535. E-mail: mail@ncwriters.org. Website: www.ncwriters.org. **Contact:** Jenn Habel, program coordinator. Award to "encourage and recognize the work of emerging and established North Carolina writers." Annual competition for short stories. Awards: $150 1st Place, $100 2nd Place, $50 3rd Place. Competition receives 100-150 submissions. Judges change annually. Entry fee $8 for NCWN members; $12 for nonmembers. Guidelines available in July for SASE or on website. Deadline: February 28. Unpublished submissions. "The award is available only to legal residents of North Carolina or out-of-state NCWN members." Word length: 6 double-spaced pages (1,500 words maximum). Winners announced in May. Winners notified by phone and letter. List of winners available for SASE.

☑ ◐ **IRMA S. AND JAMES H. BLACK CHILDREN'S BOOK AWARD**, Bank Street College, 610 W. 112th St., New York NY 10025-1898. (212)875-4450. Fax: (212)875-4558. E-mail: lindag@bnkst.edu. Website: http://streetcat.bnkst.edu/html/isb.html. **Contact:** Linda Greengrass, award director. Annual award "to honor the young children's book published in the preceding year judged the most outstanding in text as well as in art. Book must be published the year preceding the May award." Award: Press function at Harvard Club, a scroll and seals by Maurice Sendak for attaching to award book's run. Judges: adult children's literature experts and children 6-10 years old. No entry fee. Guidelines available by SASE, fax, e-mail, or on website. Accepts inquiries by phone, fax and e-mail. Deadline: December 15. "Write to address above. Usually publishers submit books they want considered, but individuals can too. No entries are returned." Winners announced in May. Winners notified by phone. For list of winners, visit website.

⊕ ☑ ◑ ◎ **JAMES TAIT BLACK MEMORIAL PRIZES**, Department of English Literature, University of Edinburgh, David Hume Tower, George Square, Edinburgh EH8 9JX Scotland. Phone: 44 0131 650 2252. Fax: 44 0131 650 6898. E-mail: communications.office@ed.ac.uk/englit. Website: www.ed.ac.uk/englit. **Contact:** Anne McKelvie, deputy director of communications and public affairs. "Two prizes are awarded: one for the best work of fiction, one for the best biography or work of that nature, published during the calendar year: October 1st to September 30th." Annual competition. Award: £3,000 each. Competition receives approximately 300 submissions. Judge: Professor R.D.S. Jack, Dept. of English Literature. Guidelines for SASE or SAE and IRC. Guildlines available Sept. 30. Deadline: September 30. Previously published submissions. "Eligible works are those written in English, originating with a British publisher, and first published in Britain in the year of the award. Works should be submitted by publishers." Winners announced in January. Winners notified by phone, via publisher. Contact Department of English Literature for list of winners or check website.

☑ ◑ **THE BLACK WARRIOR REVIEW LITERARY AWARD**, P.O. Box 862936, Tuscaloosa AL 35486-0277. (205)348-4518. Website: www.sa.ua.edu/osm/bwr. **Contact:** T.J. Beitelman. "Award is to recognize the best fiction published in *BWR* in a volume year. Only fiction accepted for publication is considered for the award." Competition is for short stories and novel chapters. Award: $500. Competition receives approximately 3,000 submissions. Prize awarded by an outside judge. Guidelines available for SASE. Winners announced in the Fall. Winners notified by phone or mail. List of winners available for purchase in Fall issue.

⊕ ◑ ◎ **BOARDMAN TASKER PRIZE**, 14 Pine Lodge, Dairyground Rd., Bramhall, Stockport, Cheshire SK7 2HS United Kingdom. Phone/fax: 0161 439 4624. **Contact:** Mrs. Dorothy Boardman. "To reward a book which has made an outstanding contribution to mountain literature. A memorial to Peter Boardman and Joe Tasker, who disappeared on Everest in 1982." Award: £2,000. Competition receives 20 submissions. Judges: A panel of 3 judges elected by trustees. Guidelines for SASE. Deadline: August. Limited to works published or distributed in the UK for the first time between November 1 and October 31. Publisher's entry only. "May be fiction, nonfiction, poetry or drama. Not an anthology. Subject must be concerned with a mountain environment. Previous winners have been books on expeditions, climbing experiences; a biography of a mountaineer; novels." Winners announced October or November. Winners notified by mail. Short list, available in September, will be sent to all publishers who have entered books.

⊕ ☑ ◎ **BOOKER PRIZE FOR FICTION**, Book Trust, Book House, 45 E. Hill, London SW18 2QZ England. Phone: 020 8516 2973. Fax: 020 8516 2978. E-mail: sandra@booktrust.org.uk. **Contact:** Sandra Vince, prizes manager. Award to the best novel of the year. Annual competition for novels. Award: £20,000. Each of the short listed authors receive £1,000. Competition receives 100 submissions. Judges: five judges appointed by the Booker Management Committee. Deadline: July 1. Published submissions. A full-length novel written in English by a citizen of the Commonwealth or Republic of Ireland.

BOSTON GLOBE-HORN BOOK AWARDS, *Horn Book Magazine, Inc.*, 56 Roland St., Suite 200, Boston MA 02129. (617)628-0225. Fax: (617)628-0882. E-mail: info@hbook.com. Website: www.hbook.com. **Contact:** Karen Walsh, marketing and advertising director. Annual award. "To honor excellence in children's fiction or poetry, picture and nonfiction books published within the US." Award: $500 and engraved silver bowl first prize in each category; engraved silver plate for the 2 honor books in each category. Competition receives 2,000 submissions. No entry fee. Guidelines available after January 15 for SASE, fax, e-mail, or on website. Accepts inquiries by fax and e-mail. Entry forms or rules for SASE. Deadline: May 15. Previously-published material between June 1, 2000-May 31, 2001. Books are submitted by publishers. Winners announced in August. Winners notified by phone. List of winners available in September on website.

THE BRIAR CLIFF REVIEW POETRY & FICTION COMPETITION, *The Briar Cliff Review*, Briar Cliff College, 3303 Rebecca St., Sioux City IA 51104-0100. (712)279-5321. Fax: (712)279-5410. E-mail: currans@briar-cliff.edu. Website: www.briar-cliff.edu/bcreview. **Contact:** Tricia Currans-Sheehan, editor. Award "to reward good writers and showcase quality writing." Annual award for short stories and poetry. Award: $200 and publication in spring issue. Competition receives 100-125 submissions. Judges: editors. "All entries are read by at least 3 editors." $10 entry fee. Guidelines for SASE. Deadline: submissions between August 1 and November 1. Previously unpublished submissions. Word length: 5,000 words maximum. "Send us your best work. We want stories with a plot." Winners announced December or January. Winners notified by letter. List of winners available for SASE sent with submission.

THE BRIDPORT PRIZE, Bridport Arts Centre, South Street, Bridport, Dorset DT6 3NR United Kingdom. (01308)424183. Fax: (01308)454166. E-mail: arts@bridport.co.uk. Website: www.wdi.co.uk/arts. **Contact:** Francesca Pashby, marketing officer. Awarded to "promote literary excellence, discover new talent." Annual competition for short stories. Award: £2,500 sterling (1st prize), £1,000 sterling (2nd prize), £500 sterling (3rd prize) plus various runners-up prizes and publication of approximately 10 best stories in anthology. Judge: One judge. £5 sterling entry fee. Guidelines available January 2001; send SASE or visit website. Accepts inquiries by fax, e-mail and phone. Deadline June 30, 2001. Entries should be unpublished. Contest open to anyone. Length: 5,000 words maximum. Winners announced in October of year of contest. Winners notified by mail or phone in September. For list of winners send SASE.

BRONX RECOGNIZES ITS OWN (B.R.I.O.), Bronx Council on the Arts, 1738 Hone Ave., Bronx NY 10461-1486. (718)931-9500. Fax: (718)409-6445. E-mail: artserv@mail.binc.org. Website: www.bronxarts.org. **Contact:** Ed Friedman, director, community arts services. Award to "recognize artistic talent in Bronx County." Annual competition for novels. Award: $2,500 (awards 20/year in visual, media, performing and literary arts). Competition receives approximately 50 literary submissions. Judges: peer panel of non-Bronx artists. Guidelines available mid-December by a phone call, fax, written request or on website. Deadline: March. Only Bronx artists may apply. Proof of Bronx residency required. Word length: 20 typed pages of ms. Winners announced in May. Winners notified by mail in May. For a list of winners, send SASE.

ARCH & BRUCE BROWN FOUNDATION, The Arch & Bruce Brown Foundation, PMB 503, 31855 Date Palm Drive #3, Cathedral City CA 92234. (760)202-1125. E-mail: archwrite@aol.com. Website: www.aabbfoundation.org. **Contact:** Arch Brown, president. Contest for "gay-positive works based on history." Annual contest; type of contest changes each year: short story (2001); playwrighting (2002); novel (2003). Award: $1,000 (not limited to a single winner). No entry fee. For guidelines, send SASE or visit website. Deadline November 30, 2001. Entries should be unpublished. Contest open to all writers. Winners announced Spring 2002. Winners notified by mail April 1, 2002. For list of winners send SASE or visit website.

BURNABY WRITERS' SOCIETY ANNUAL COMPETITION, 6584 Deer Lake Ave., British Columbia V5G 3T7 Canada. (604)444-1228. E-mail: lonewolf@portal.ca. Website: www.bws.bc.ca. Annual competition to encourage creative writing in British Columbia. "Category varies from year to year." Award: $200, $100 and $50 (Canadian) prizes. Receives 400-600 entries for each award. Judge: "independent recognized professional in the field." Entry fee $5. Guidelines available for SASE or on website. Contest requirements after March for SASE. Deadline: May 31. Open to British Columbia authors only. Winners announced in September. Winners notified by phone, mail or e-mail. List of winners available for SASE.

BUSH ARTIST FELLOWS PROGRAM, Bush Foundation, E-900 First Nat'l Bank Building, 332 Minnesota St., St. Paul MN 55101-1387. (651)227-5222. Fax: (651)297-6485. E-mail: kpolley@bushfound.org.

Contact: Kathi Polley, program assistant. Award to "provide artists with significant financial support that enables them to further their work and their contribution to their communities. Fellows may decide to take time for solitary work or reflection, engage in collaborative or community projects, or embark on travel or research." Annual grant. Award: $40,000 for 12-18 months. Competition receives 200-300 submissions. Literature (fiction, creative nonfiction, poetry) offered every other year. Next offered 2002 BAF. Applications available August. Accepts inquiries by fax and e-mail. Deadline: October. Must meet certain publication requirements. Judges: a panel of artists and arts professionals who reside outside of Minnesota, South Dakota, North Dakota or Wisconsin. Applicants must be at least 25 years old, and Minnesota, South Dakota, North Dakota or Western Wisconsin residents. Students not eligible. Winners announced in Spring. Winners notified by letter. List of winners available in May; will be sent to all applicants.

□ ◎ *BYLINE* SHORT FICTION & POETRY AWARDS, P.O. Box 130596, Edmond OK 73013-0001. Phone/fax: (405)348-5591. E-mail: bylinemp@aol.com. Website: www.bylinemag.com. **Contact:** Marcia Preston, executive editor/publisher. "To encourage our subscribers in striving for high quality writing." Annual awards for short stories and poetry. Award: $250 in each category. Competition receives approximately 200 submissions in each category. Judges are published writers not on the *ByLine* staff. Entry fee $5 for stories; $3 for poems. Guidelines available for SASE. Accepts inquiries by e-mail and phone. Postmark deadline: November 1. "Judges look for quality writing, well-drawn characters, significant themes. Entries should be unpublished and not have won money in any previous contest. Winners announced in February issue and published in February or March issue with photo and short bio. Winners notified by mail and phone in January. For list of winners, send SASE, read magazine or visit website. Open to subscribers only."

□ CALIFORNIA WRITERS' CLUB CONTEST, California Writers' Club, P.O. Box 1281, Berkeley CA 94701. **Contact:** Contest Coordinator. Cash awards "to encourage writing." Competition is held annually. Competition receives varying number of submissions. Judges: Professional writers, members of California Writers' Club. Entry fee to be determined. Guidelines available January 1 through March 30 by mail or on website. Accepts inquiries by fax, phone and e-mail. Deadline: May 1. Unpublished submissions. "Open to all." Winners announced at annual conference. Winners notified by mail, fax, phone or phone. List of winners available July 1.

☑ ◎ JOHN W. CAMPBELL MEMORIAL AWARD FOR THE BEST SCIENCE FICTION NOVEL OF THE YEAR; THEODORE STURGEON MEMORIAL AWARD FOR THE BEST SCIENCE FIC-TION SHORT FICTION, Center for the Study of Science Fiction, English Dept., University of Kansas, Lawrence KS 66045. (785)864-3380. Fax: (785)864-4298. E-mail: jgunn@falcon.cc.ukans.edu. Website: www.falcon.cc.ukans.edu/~sfcenter/. **Contact:** James Gunn, professor and director. "To honor the best novel and short science fiction of the year." Annual competition for short stories and novels. Award: Certificate. "Winners' names are engraved on a trophy." Campbell Award receives approximately 200 submissions. Judges: 2 separate juries. Accepts inquiries by e-mail and fax. Deadline: December 31. For previously published submissions. "Ordinarily publishers should submit work, but authors have done so when publishers would not. Send for list of jurors." Entrants for the Sturgeon Award are selected by nomination only. Winners announced in July. List of winners available for SASE.

Ⓝ THE CAPRICORN AWARD, The Writer's Voice, 5 W. 63rd St., New York NY 10023. (212)875-4124. Fax: (212)875-4184. E-mail: wswritersvoice@ymcanyc.org. Website: www.ymcanyc.org. **Contact:** David Andrews, literary manager. Annual competition for novels or story collections. Award: $1,000, plus featured reading. Entry fee $15. Deadline: December 31. Applicants may submit excerpts of work that have been previously published, however complete work cannot have been previously published elsewhere. Submit first 150 pgs. of novel/story collection. Guidelines/entry form for SASE by e-mail or at website. Accepts inquiries by e-mail. Winners announced mid-summer 2002. Winners notified by mail, phone.

□ CAPTIVATING BEGINNINGS CONTEST, *Lynx Eye*, 1880 Hill Dr., Los Angeles CA 90041-1244. (323)550-8522. E-mail: pamccully@aol.com. **Contact:** Pam McCully, co-editor. Annual award for stories "with engrossing beginnings, stories that will enthrall and absorb readers." Award: $100 plus publication, 1st Prize; $10 each for 4 honorable mentions plus publication. Competition receives 600-700 submissions. Judges: *Lynx Eye* editors. Entry fee $5/story. Guidelines available for SASE or by e-mail. Accepts inquiries by e-mail, phone. Unpublished submissions. Length: 7,500 words or less. "The stories will be judged on the first 500 words." Deadline: January 31. Winners announced March 15. Winners notified by phone, mail or e-mail. List of winners available March 31 for SASE.

☑ □ WILLA CATHER FICTION PRIZE, Helicon Nine Editions, 3607 Pennsylvania, Kansas City MO 64111-2820. (816)753-1095. Fax: (816)753-1016. E-mail: helicon9@aol.com. Website: www.heliconnine.com.

Contact: Gloria Vando Hickok, publisher. Annual competition for novels, story collections and novellas. Award: $1,000. Competition receives 200-250 submissions. Winners chosen by nationally-recognized writers. Entry fee $20. Guidelines for SASE, by e-mail or on website. Accepts inquiries by e-mail and phone. Deadline: May 1. Unpublished submissions. Open to all writers residing in the US and its territories and Canada. Manuscripts will not be returned. Judge: Rosellen Brown of Chicago. Past judges include William Gass, Robley Wilson, Daniel Stern, Leonard Michaels, Carolyn Doty. Winners announced in the fall. Winners notified by phone. Finalists notified by mail with critique of ms. List of winners available in November for SASE. "Helicon Nine is interested only in fine literature. Do not send trendy or commercial manuscripts."

THE *CHELSEA* AWARDS, P.O. Box 773, Cooper Station, New York NY 10276-0773. E-mail: rafoerster@aol.com. *Mail entries to*: Chelsea Awards, %Richard Foerster, Editor, P.O. Box 1040, York Beach ME 03910-1040. Annual competition for short stories. Award: $1,000 and publication in *Chelsea* (all entries are considered for publication). Competition receives 300 submissions. Judges: the editors. Entry fee $10 (for which entrants also receive a subscription). Guidelines available for SASE. Deadline: June 15. Unpublished submissions. Manuscripts may not exceed 30 typed pages or about 7,500 words. The stories must not be under consideration elsewhere or scheduled for book publication within 8 months of the competition deadline. Include separate cover sheet; no name on ms. Mss will not be returned; include SASE for notification of results. Winners announced August 15. Winners notified by telephone. List of winners available August 20 for SASE.

THE CHILDREN'S BOOK AWARD, Federation of Children's Book Groups, The Old Malt House, Aldbourne, Marlborough, Wilts SN8 2DW England. Award to "promote good quality books for children." Annual award for short stories, novels, story collections and translations. Award: "Portfolio of children's writing and drawings and a magnificent trophy of silver and oak." Judges: Thousands of children from all over the United Kingdom. Guidelines for SASE or SAE and IRC. Deadline: December 31. Published and previously unpublished submissions (first publication in UK). "The book should be suitable for children."

CHILDREN'S WRITERS FICTION CONTEST, Stepping Stones, P.O. Box 8863, Springfield MO 65801-8863. (417)863-7670. Fax: (417)864-4745. E-mail: wilyams4@vista_business.zzn.com. **Contact:** V.R. Williams, coordinator. Award to "promote writing for children by encouraging children's writers and giving them an opportunity to submit their work in competition." Annual competition for short stories and translations. Award: $150 and/or publication in *Hodge Podge*. Competition receives 150 submissions. "Judged by Goodin, Williams, Goodwin and/or associates. Entries are judged for clarity, grammar, punctuation, imagery, content and suitability for children." Entry fee $5. Guidelines available for SASE, fax or e-mail. Accepts inquiries by fax, phone and e-mail. Deadline: July 31. Previously unpublished submissions. Word length: 1,000 words. "Work submitted on colored paper, book format or illustrated is not acceptable. Stories should have believable characters." Winners announced in September. Winners notified by mail. List of winners for SASE or fax.

THE CHRISTOPHER AWARDS, The Christophers, 12 E. 48th St., New York NY 10017-1091. (212)759-4050. Fax: (212)838-5073. E-mail: awards_coordinator@christophers.org. Website: www.christophers.org. **Contact:** Judith Trojan, program manager. Annual award "to encourage creative people to continue to produce works which affirm the highest values of the human spirit in adult and children's books." Published submissions only. Award: Bronze medallion. "Award judged by a grassroots panel and a final panel of experts. Juvenile works are 'children tested.' " No entry forms or submission fees. "Potential winners are nominated and reviewed throughout the year by panels of media professionals, members of the Christopher staff and by specially supervised children's reading groups. Friends of The Christophers are also encouraged to nominate titles." For guidelines send 6x9 SASE or fax. Accepts inquiries by fax, e-mail and phone. Two deadlines: June 1 and November 1 every year. Books may be submitted any time in between as well. Winners announced in January. Winners notified by mail and phone late January. List of winners available for SASE, by fax or visit website. Example of book award: *I Love You, Blue Kangaroo!*, by Emma Chichester Clark (children's book category 2000).

CINESTORY SCREENWRITING AWARDS, CineStory, PMB 272, Dearborn Station, 47 W. Polk St., Chicago IL 60605-2000. (312)322-9060. Fax: (312)322-0962. E-mail: cinestory@aol.com. Website: www.cinestory.com. "CineStory, a national non-profit screenwriter's center, is committed to the development of the authentic voice of the cinematic storyteller. We nurture non-formulaic scripts that trigger moving pictures inspired directly by the writer's words. And we encourage writers to grow as producers of their own work." Annual award for screenplays. Award: $2,000 (1st prize). Three winners, 8 finalists and 16 semi-finalists will be selected. Judge: industry experts. $40 entry fee. For guidelines, send SASE or visit website. Deadline September 15, 2001. Entries should be previously unpublished. Contest open to any writer without produced feature film credits. Length: 90-130 pages. "CineStory supports the unique power of the screenwriter's vision and the writer's significance as a primary film creator." For list of winners visit website.

○ **CNW/FFWA FLORIDA STATE WRITING COMPETITION,** Florida Freelance Writers Association, P.O. Box A, North Stratford NH 03590. (603)922-8338. Fax: (603)922-8339. E-mail: danakcnw@ncia.net. Website: www.writers-editors.com. **Contact:** Dana K. Cassell, executive director. Award "to recognize publishable writing." Annual competition for short stories and novels. Awards: $100 (first place), $75 (second place), $50 (third place). Competition receives 50-100 submissions in short story/novel division. Total 400-500 in all divisions. Judges: published authors, teachers, editors. Entry fee ($5-20) varies with membership status. Guidelines available for SASE or on website. Deadline: March 15. Previously unpublished submissions. Winners will be notified by mail by May 31. For list of winners, send SASE or visit website.

N ⊕ ◎ **COMMONWEALTH WRITERS PRIZE,** The Commonwealth Foundation, %Book Trust, Book House, 45 East Hill, London SW18 2QZ England. (020)8516-2973/2. Fax: (020)8516-2978. E-mail: sandra@boo ktrust.org.uk or tarryn@booktrust.org.uk. Website: www.oneworld.org/com_fnd/contents.html. **Contact:** Sandra Vince, prizes manager or Tarryn McKay, prizes assistant. "This award was set up to recognise and reward the diverse talent within the Commonwealth. It awards well established as well as first-time novelists, and is unique in the fact that the overall Best Book winner has an audience with the Queen." Annual prize for short stories (published as a collection) and novels. Award: Regional winners £1,000, Overall Best First Book £3,000 and Overall Best Book £10,000. Number of submissions varies. Judge: Regional judges for 2001 include Mr. Kevin Baldeosingh, Mr. Valentine Cunningham and others. The judging criterion is confidential. No entry fee. For 2001 guidelines either request direct from Book Trust, or "ask publisher to contact us." Accepts inquiries by fax, e-mail, phone and post. "The deadline for entry is November 15; any books we are advised of that are not published by this date must be in by December 31." Entries should be published during the preceding year. Contest open to all fiction writers from Commonwealth countries. Length: Open. Writers may submit their own fiction only if it is published. Regional winners announced in February and the overall winners in April. "Publishers will be notified of regional win, and winners are invited to a gala dinner for the announcement of the overall winners." List of winners "should be in the papers, or contact us for a press release."

N ⊕ **COMPLETE NOVEL COMPETITION,** The David Thomas Charitable Trust, P.O. Box 6055, Nairn 1V124YB Scotland. (0044)1667453351. Fax: (0044)1667452365. **Contact:** Lorna Edwardson, competition director. Award: Winner will be announced in *Writers' News* or *Writing Magazine*. Also an extract from the novel may be published in one or other. Winning entry to be read by a publisher, plus £250. Competition receives 100 submissions per category. £10 per entry. Guidelines available January 2001. For guidelines send SASE. Accepts inquiries by fax and phone. Deadline May 31, 2001. Entries should be unpublished. Contest open to anyone not connected with Writers' News Ltd. Length: No restrictions. Winners are announced autumn 2001. Winners notified by mail, phone by approximately the end of June 2001.

✓ ◎ **CONNECTICUT COMMISSION ON THE ARTS ARTIST FELLOWSHIPS,** One Financial Plaza, Hartford CT 06103-2601. (860)566-4770. Fax: (860)566-6462. E-mail: kdemeo@csunet.ctstateu.edu. Website: www.ctarts.org/artfellow.htm (to download application from website). **Contact:** Linda Dente, program manager. "To support the creation of new work by creative artists *living in Connecticut*." Biennial competition for the creation or completion of new works in literature, i.e., short stories, novels, story collections, poetry and playwriting. Awards: $5,000 and $2,500. Competition receives 50-75 submissions. Judges: Peer professionals (writers, editors). Guidelines available in June by e-mail or on website. Accepts inquiries by phone and e-mail. Deadline: September 18. Writers may send either previously published or unpublished submissions—up to 25 pages of material. Connecticut residents only. "Write to please yourself. If you win, that's a bonus." Winners announced in January. Winners notified by mail. For list of winners, send SASE.

❧ ✓ ◗ ◎ **CONSEIL DE LA VIE FRANCAISE EN AMÉRIQUE/PRIX CHAMPLAIN,** Conseil de la vie Française en Amérique, Maison de la Francophonie 39, rue Dalhousie, Quebec G1K 8R8 Canada. (418)646-9117. Fax: (418)644-7670. E-mail: cvfa@cvfa.ca. Website: www.cvfa.ca. Prix Champlain estab. 1957. Annual award to encourage literary work in novel or short story in French by Francophiles living outside Quebec, in the US or Canada. "There is no restriction as to the subject matter. If the author lives in Quebec, the subject matter must be related to French-speaking people living outside of Quebec." Award: $1,500 in Canadian currency. The prize will be given alternately; one year for fiction, the next for nonfiction. Next fiction award in 2001. 3 different judges each year. Guidelines for SASE or IRC. Deadline: December 31. For previously published or contracted submissions, published no more than 3 years prior to award. Author must furnish 4 examples of work, curriculum vitae, address and phone number.

○ **THE *CRUCIBLE* POETRY AND FICTION COMPETITION,** *Crucible*, Barton College, College Station, Wilson NC 27893. Annual competition for short stories. Award: $150 (1st Prize); $100 (2nd Prize) and publication in *Crucible*. Judges: The editors. Guidelines for SASE. Deadline: April. "The best time to submit is December through April." Unpublished submissions only. Fiction should be 8,000 words or less.

☑ ◎ **DANA AWARD IN SHORT FICTION**, 7207 Townsend Forest Court, Browns Summit NC 27214-9634. (336)656-7009. E-mail: danaawards@pipeline.com. Website: http://danaawards.home.pipeline.com. **Contact:** Mary Elizabeth Parker, chair, Dana wards. Award "to reward work that has been previously unrecognized in the area of fiction. All genres, including literary/mainsream, and speculative fiction—science fiction, fantasy, horror, surrealism—previously was a separate award category discontinued due to lack of response. No work for or by children/young adults. Let authors be aware work must meet standards of literary complexity and excellence. That is, character development, excellence of style are as important as the plot line." Annual competition. Award: $1,000. Competition receives 100-200 submissions. Entry fee $10/short story. Make checks payable to Dana Awards. Guidelines for SASE, by e-mail or on website. Accepts inquiries by e-mail. Unpublished submissions and not under contract to any publisher. Word length: no minimum, but no longer than 10,000 words. 3,000 word average preferred. Postmark deadline. October 31. Winners announced early Spring. Winners notified by phone; then by letter. Send SASE with submissions to receive competition results letter.

DANA AWARD IN THE NOVEL, 7207 Townsend Forest Court, Browns Summit NC 27214-9634. (336)656-7009. E-mail: danaawards@pipeline.com. Website: http://danaawards.home.pipeline.com. **Contact:** Mary Elizabeth Parker, chair, Dana Awards. Award to "reward work that has not yet been recognized, since we know from firsthand experience how tough the literary market is." Annual competition for novels. Award: $1,000. Competition receives 300 submissions. Judges: nationally-published novelists. $20 fee for each submission. Guidelines for SASE, e-mail or on website. Accepts inquiries by e-mail. Postmark deadline October 31. Unpublished submissions and not under contract to be published. Novelists should submit first 50 pages only of a novel either completed or in progress. No novels for or by children/young adults. In-progress submissions should be as polished as possible. Multiple submissions accepted, but each must include a separate $20 entry fee. Make checks payable to Dana Awards. Winners announced March-April. Winners notified by phone, mail, or e-mail. List of winners available early spring for SASE, e-mail, or on website. Send SASE for results letter along with submissions.

☑ **THE DOROTHY DANIELS ANNUAL HONORARY WRITING AWARD**, National League of American Pen Women, Simi Valley Branch, P.O. Box 1485, Simi Valley CA 93062. **Contact:** Carol Doering, contest chair. Award "to honor excellent writing." Annual competition for short stories. Award: $100 (1st Place). Judges: Pen Women members. Competition receives approximately 150 entries. $5 fee/short story. Guidelines for SASE. Deadline: July 30. Unpublished submissions: not currently submitted elsewhere; entries must have received no prior awards. No limit on number of entries. Any person except Simi Valley Pen Women, interns, and their immediate families are eligible. Any genre. Word length: 2,000 words maximum. "Entries must follow rules exactly." Winners announced November 1. Winners notified by mail. List of winners available for SASE.

☑ ○ ◎ **MARGUERITE DE ANGELI PRIZE**, Delacorte Press Books for Young Readers, 1540 Broadway, New York NY 10036. (212)782-8633. Fax: (212)782-9452. **Contact:** Pearl N. Young, editorial assistant. "To encourage the writing of fiction for middle grade readers (either contemporary or historical) in the same spirit as the works of Marguerite de Angeli." Open to US and Canadian writers. Annual competition for first novels for middle-grade readers (ages 7-10). Award: One BDD hardcover and paperback book contract, with $1,500 cash prize and $3,500 advance against royalties. Competition receives 350 submissions. Judges: Editors of Delacorte Press Books for Young Readers. Send SASE for guidelines. Deadline: Submissions must be postmarked by June 30. Previously unpublished (middle-grade) fiction. Length: 40-144 pages. Winners announced by October 31. Winners notified by phone. List of winners available by SASE or fax.

☑ **DEAD METAPHOR PRESS CHAPBOOK CONTEST**, Dead Metaphor Press, P.O. Box 2076, Boulder CO 80306-2076. (303)417-9398. E-mail: dmetaphorp@earthlink.net. **Contact:** Richard Wilmarth. Award to "promote quality writing." Annual competition for short stories. Award: 10% of the press run plus discounted copies. Books distributed by Small Press Distribution. Competition receives 250-300 submissions. Judge: Richard Wilmarth. Entry fee $10. Guidelines available for SASE. Deadline: October 31. Maximum length: 24 pages. Winners announced at end of summer. Winners notified by mail. For list of winners, send SASE.

🄽 ⊕ ◎ **DEBUT DAGGER**, Crime Writers' Association, P.O. Box 6939, Birmingham B14-7LT, United Kingdom. Phone: 0121-446-2536. Fax: 0121-666-2536. E-mail: judith.cutler@virgin.net. Website: www.twbooks.co.uk/cwa/cwa.html. **Contact:** Judith Cutler, secretary. Competition to stimulate new crime writing. Annual competition for first 3,000 words of novel and 500 word outline. Award: £250 cash and free tickets for Dead on Deansgate crime writing convention. Entry fee: £10. Guidelines available April/May 2001. For guidelines visit website. Deadline: Mid-August. Entries should be unpublished. Contest open to anyone who has not had a novel published in any genre. Deadline: First 3,000 words (maximum) of novel and outline of 500 words (maximum). Winners announced October 2001. Winners notified by phone.

☑ ◯ ◎ **DELAWARE DIVISION OF THE ARTS,** 820 N. French St., Wilmington DE 19801. (302)577-8284. Fax: (302)577-6561. E-mail: kpleasanton@state.de.us. Website: www.artsdel.org **Contact:** Kristin Pleasanton, coordinator. "To help further careers of emerging and established professional artists." Annual awards for Delaware residents only. Awards: $10,000 for masters, $5,000 for established professionals; $2,000 for emerging professionals. Competition receives 100 submissions. Judges are out-of-state professionals in each division. Entry forms or rules available after January 1 for SASE. Accepts inquiries by fax and e-mail . Deadline: August 1. Winners announced in December. Winners notified by mail.

[N] **THE DREADED SYNOPSIS,** First Coast Romance Writers, P.O. Box 8604, Jacksonville FL 32239-8604. E-mail: lbarone21@aol.com. Website: www.angelfire.com/fl/RomanceWriting. **Contact:** Laura Barone, president. Competition to provide "the opportunity to have your synopsis critiqued by trained and experienced judges to see if you have the elements required to catch an editor's attention." Annual competition for synopses. Award: 1st prize, $50; 2nd prize, $25; and 3rd prize $15. Judge: Elizabeth Sinclair, author of "The Dreaded Synopsis" is the final judge. Judged on content and efficiency. $15 entry fee. Guidelines available June 2000. Accepts inquiries by e-mail. Deadline October 1, 2001. Entries should be unpublished. Contest open to all writers. Length: 10 pages maximum. "Use hooks. Limit using names other than the main characters." Winners announced January 2, 2002. Winners notified by mail and e-mail. For list of winners send SASE or visit website.

[N] ⊕ **DUNCTON COTTAGE SHORT STORY AND POETRY COMPETITION,** Duncton Cottage Bird and Animal Sanctuary, 12 Hylton Terrace, Rookhope, County Durham DL13 2BB United Kingdom. (+44)01388-517005. Fax: (+44)01388-517044. E-mail: farplace@hotmail.com. **Contact:** Mr. N. Robson, or Mrs. V. Robson, manager. Award to "raise funds to support a small U.K. animal sanctuary." Annual award for short stories and poetry. Award: cash prize of ⅓ entry fees, divided amongst a winner receiving ¾ of this prize fund in each category and a runner-up receiving the remaining quarter (UK sterling cheque only at present). Judge: Mr. N. Robson, after short-listing by others. £5 UK sterling for up to 2 entries. Additional entries £2.50 UK sterling each. Guidelines available July 2000. For guidelines, send SASE, fax, e-mail or call. Accepts inquiries by fax, e-mail and phone. Deadline July 31, 2001. Entries should be unpublished. Contest open to anyone worldwide, but at present we can only accept fees in UK sterling. (Prize fund also UK sterling). Length: 4,000 words. Winners are announced in early September 2001. Winners are notified by mail (if SAE), phone and e-mail in August 2001. For list of winners send SASE, fax, e-mail.

[N] ⊕ ◎ **DUNDEE BOOK PRIZE,** City of Discovery Campaign, University of Dundee, Poltgor, City of Discovery Press Office, Prospect RR3 Business Covers, Dundee Technology Park, Dundee DD2 1SN Scotland. (01382)434275. Fax: (01382)434096. E-mail: annerendall@dundeecity.gov.uk. Website: http://www.cityofdiscovery.com. **Contact:** Petra Kydd, account director. Award to "raise the profile of the City of Dundee through press coverage of the book prize and to encourage writers to set novels in and around Dundee." Biannual competition for novels. Award: £6,000. Competition receives 100 submissions per category. Judge: a panel of 3 judges. No entry fee. For guidelines, send SASE, fax, e-mail, visit website or call. Accepts inquiries by fax, e-mail or phone. Deadline August 2001. Entries should be unpublished. Contest open to anyone. Length: 65,000 words average. Winners are announced in spring 2002. Winners notified by phone. For list of winners send SASE, fax, e-mail, or visit website.

☑ ◯ **JACK DYER FICTION PRIZE,** *Crab Orchard Review,* English Dept., Southern Illinois University, Carbondale IL 62901-4503. (618)453-6833. Fax: (618)453-8224. Website: www.siu.edu/~crborchd. **Contact:** Jon Tribble, managing editor. Award to "reward and publish exceptional fiction." Annual competition for short stories. Award: $1,000 and publication. Competition receives approximately 200 submissions. Judges: prescreened by *Crab Orchard* staff; winner chosen by outside judge. Entry fee $10; year's subscription included. Guidelines available after January for SASE. Deadline March 15. Previously unpublished submissions. Word length: 6,000. "Please note that no stories will be returned." Winners announced by August 15. Winners notified by phone in July. List of winners available for SASE or on website.

◯ **EATON LITERARY ASSOCIATES' LITERARY AWARDS PROGRAM,** Eaton Literary Associates, P.O. Box 49795, Sarasota FL 34230-6795. (941)366-6589. Fax: (941)365-4679. E-mail: eatonlit@aol.com. Website: www.eatonliterary.com. **Contact:** Richard Lawrence, vice president. Biannual award for short stories and novels. Award: $2,500 for best book-length ms, $500 for best short story. Competition receives approx. 2,000 submissions annually. Judges are 2 staff members in conjunction with an independent agency. Guidelines for SASE, fax, e-mail or on website. Accepts inquiries by fax, phone and e-mail. Deadline: March 31 for short stories; August 31 for book-length mss. Winners announced in April and September. Winners notified by mail. For list of winners, send SASE, fax, e-mail or on website.

☑ ◨ ◎ **EMERGING LESBIAN WRITERS FUND AWARDS**, Astraea National Lesbian Action Foundation, 116 E. 16th St., 7th Floor, New York NY 10003. (212)529-8021. Fax: (212)982-3321. E-mail: info@astraea.org. Website: www.astraea.org. **Contact:** Christine Lipat, program officer. Award to "recognize and encourage new/emerging lesbian writers and poets." Annual competition for fiction and poetry. Award: $10,000 (one-time only grantees). Competition receives 200 submissions. Judges: Established writers/poets (2 each category). $5 entry fee. Guidelines for SASE or e-mail (application form required). Deadline: March 8. Previously published submissions. U.S. residents only. Write for guidelines. "Must have at least one published work. No submissions accepted without application form." Winners announced in July. Winners notified by mail and phone. For list of winners, visit website.

⬛**N** ◎ **THE EMILY CONTEST**, West Houston Chapter Romance Writers of America, 5603 Chantilly Lane, Houston TX 77092. (713)804-0734. E-mail: ellen_watkins@juno.com. Website: http://www.poboxes.com/whrwa. **Contact:** Ellen Watkins, Emily contest chair. Purpose is "to help people writing romance novels learn to write better books and to help them make contacts in the publishing world." Annual competition for novels. First-place entry in each category receives the Emily brooch; all finalists receive certificates. Competition receives 40-60 submissions per category. First round judges are published authors and experienced critiquers. Final round judges (for finalists) are editors at a major romance publishing house. $15 entry fee for WHRWA members, $25 for non-members. Guidelines available September 2000. For guidelines, send SASE, e-mail or visit website. Accepts inquiries by e-mail. Contest open to all unpublished romance writers. Length: first 35 pages of novel. "We look for dynamic, interesting romantic stories with a hero and heroine readers can relate to and love. Hook us from the beginning and keep the excitement level high." Winners announced May 2001. Winners notified by mail or phone. For list of winners send SASE or visit website.

◨ ◎ **VIRGINIA FAULKNER AWARD FOR EXCELLENCE IN WRITING**, *Prairie Schooner*, 201 Andrews Hall, University of Nebraska, Lincoln NE 68588-0334. (402)472-0911. Fax: (402)472-9771. E-mail: eflanaga@unlnotes. Website: www.unl.edu/schooner/psmain.htm. **Contact:** Hilda Raz, editor. "An award for writing published in *Prairie Schooner* in the previous year." Annual competition for short stories, novel excerpts and translations. Award: $1,000. Judges: Editorial Board. Guidelines for SASE or at website. Accepts inquiries by fax and e-mail. "We only read mss from September through May." Work must have been published in *Prairie Schooner* in the previous year. Winners will be notified by mail. List of winners will be published in spring *Prairie Schooner.*

☑ ◯ **WILLIAM FAULKNER COMPETITION IN FICTION**, The Pirate's Alley Faulkner Society Inc., 632 Pirate's Alley, New Orleans LA 70116-3254. (504)586-1612. Fax: (504)522-9725. E-mail: faulkhouse@aol.com. Website: www.wordsandmusic.org. **Contact:** R. James, contest director. "To encourage publisher interest in writers with potential." Annual competition for short stories, novels, novellas, personal essays and poetry. Award: $7,500 for novel, $2,500 for novella, $1,500 for short story, $1,000 personal essay, $750 poetry and gold medals, plus trip to New Orleans for presentation. Competition receives 1,500-1,800 submissions. Judges: professional writers, academics. $25 fee for each poem, essay, short story; $30 for novella; $35 for novel. Guidelines for SASE or on website. Accepts inquiries by e-mail. Deadline: April 1. Unpublished submissions. Word length: for novels, over 50,000; for novellas, under 50,000; for short stories, under 20,000. All entries must be accompanied by official entry form which is provided with guidelines. Winners announced September 1. Winners notified by mail. List of winners available for SASE or on website.

☑ ◎ **FAUX FAULKNER CONTEST**, *Hemispheres* Magazine, *Faulkner Newsletter* of Yoknapatawpha Press and University of Mississippi, P.O. Box 248, Oxford MS 38655. (601)234-0909. E-mail: boozernhb@aol.com. Website: www.watervalley.net/yoknapatawphapress/index.htm. Award "to honor William Faulkner by imitating his style, themes and subject matter in a short parody." Annual competition for a 500-word (2-pages) parody. Award: 2 round-trip tickets to Memphis, plus complimentary registration and lodging for the annual Faulkner and Yoknapatawpha Conference at the University of Mississippi. Competition receives approximately 200-300 submissions. Past judges have included George Plimpton, Tom Wicker, John Berendt and Arthur Schlesinger, Jr. (judges rotate every year or so—well-known authors). Guidelines for SASE. Deadline: April 1. Previously unpublished submissions. Winner announced July 1. Winner notified May 1. Contestants grant publication rights and the right to release entries to other media and to the sponsors.

⬛**N** **FAW AWARDS**, Friends of American Writers, 400 E. Randolph, Apt. 2123, Chicago IL 60601. (312)856-1147. **Contact:** Jane Larson, chairman. Contest is to support emerging author. Award: $900. Competition receives 100 submissions per category. Judge: Juvenile award committee. No entry fee. Guidelines available now. For guidelines send SASE. Accepts inquiries by phone. Entries should be previously published. Contest open to anyone. Winners will be announced in April. For list of winners send SASE.

FEMINIST WRITER'S CONTEST, NW Suburban Chicago NOW Chapter, % Kate Hutchinson, Buffalo Grove H.S., 1100 W. Dundee, Buffalo Grove IL 60089. (847)718-4075. E-mail: khutchin@dist214.k12.il.us. Website: www.northwestsub@ad.con. **Contact:** Kate Hutchinson, contest director. "To encourage, to reward feminist writers, and to be published in our chapter newsletter." Annual competition for short stories and essays. Award: $100 (1st place), $50 (2nd place). Competition receives approximately 50-60 submissions. Judges are feminist teachers, writers, political activists, social workers and entrepeneurs. Entry fee $10. Guidelines available after January for SASE. Accepts inquiries by e-mail, fax and phone. Deadline: October 31 of each year. May be either published or unpublished. "We accept both foreign or domestic entries. Stories/essays may be on any subject, but should reflect feminist awareness." Word length: 3,000 words or less. Winners announced January. Winners notified by letter. List of winners available for SASE or visit website.

FISH SHORT STORY PRIZE, Fish Publishing, Durrus, Bantry, Co. Cork, Ireland. Phone: (00)353-27-61246. E-mail: fishpublishing@eircom.net. Website: www.fishpublishing.com. **Contact:** Clem Cairns, editor. Award to "discover, encourage, and publish new literary talent." Annual competition for short stories. Award: First prize $1,200 and publication; second prizes (two) one week residence at Anam Cara Writers Retreat, Ireland, and a residential writing course at Dingle Writing Courses, Ireland, and publication. Competition receives 1,200 submissions per category. Judge: Entries are shortlisted to approximately 100. These are sent to independent judges, who are well-known writers. $12 entry fee. Guidelines available April 2001. For guidelines, send SASE, e-mail or visit website. Deadline November 30, 2001. Entries should be previously published. Entries may have been published in local magazines. Contest open to everybody. Length: 5,000 words or fewer. "Send your most finished, polished work. Don't be afraid of originality." Winners announced March 17. Winners notified by mail in February. For list of winners send SASE, e-mail, or visit website.

DOROTHY CANFIELD FISHER AWARD, Vermont Dept. of Libraries, 109 State St., Montpelier VT 05609-0601. (802)828-3261. Fax: (802)828-2199. E-mail: ggreene@dol.state.vt.us. Website: www.dol.state.vt.us. **Contact:** Grace Greene, Children's Services Consultant. Estab. 1957. Annual award. "To encourage Vermont schoolchildren to become enthusiastic and discriminating readers and to honor the memory of one of Vermont's most distinguished and beloved literary figures." Award: Illuminated scroll. Publishers send the committee review copies of books to consider. Only books of the current publishing year can be considered for next year's master list. Master list of titles is drawn up in March each year. Children vote each year in the spring and the award is given before the school year ends. Submissions must be "written by living American authors, be suitable for children in grades 4-8, and have literary merit. Can be nonfiction also." Accepts inquiries by e-mail. Deadline: December 1. Winners announced in April. Winners notified by mail and phone. Call, write or e-mail for list of winners.

FLORIDA FIRST COAST WRITERS' FESTIVAL NOVEL, SHORT FICTION & POETRY AWARDS, Writers' Festival & Florida Community College at Jacksonville, FCCJ North Campus, 4501 Capper Rd., Jacksonville FL 32218-4499. (904)766-6559. Fax: (904)766-6654. E-mail: hdenson@fccj.org. Website: www.fccj.org/wf/. **Contact:** Howard Denson and Brian Hale, festival contest directors. Conference and contest "to create a healthy writing environment, honor writers of merit, select some stories for *The State Street Review* (a literary magazine) and find a novel manuscript to recommend to St. Martin's Press for 'serious consideration.'" Annual competition for short stories and novels. Competition receives 65 novel, 150-250 short fiction and 300-600 poetry submissions. Judges: university faculty and freelance and professional writers. Entry fees $30 (novels), $10 (short fiction), $5 (poetry). Guidelines available in the fall for SASE. Accepts inquiries by fax and e-mail. Deadlines: Decenber 1 for novels; January 1 for poetry and short fiction. Unpublished submissions. Word length: none for novel; short fiction, 6,000 words; poetry, 30 lines. Winners announced at the Florida First Coast Writers' Festival held in May.

FLORIDA STATE WRITING COMPETITION, Florida Freelance Writers Association, P.O. Box A, North Stratford NH 03590-0167. (603)922-8338. Fax: (603)922-8339. E-mail: danakcnw@ncia.net. Website: www.writers-editors.com. **Contact:** Dana K. Cassell, executive director. "To offer additional opportunities for writers to earn income and recognition from their writing efforts." Annual competition for short stories and novels. Award: varies from $50-100. Competition receives approximately 100 short stories; 50 novels; total 400-500 entries in all categories. Judges: authors, editors and teachers. Entry fee from $5-20. Guidelines for SASE. Deadline: March 15. Unpublished submissions. Categories include short story and novel chapter. "Guidelines are revised each year and subject to change. New guidelines are available in summer of each year." Accepts inquiries by fax and e-mail. Winners announced May 31. Winners notified by mail. List of winners available for SASE marked "winners" and on website.

FOOD, RECIPES, WINES & SUCH CONTEST, Creative With Words Publications, P.O. Box 223226, Carmel CA 93922. (831)655-8627. E-mail: cwwpub@usa.net. Website: members.tripod.com/CreativeWithWor ds. **Contact:** Brigitta Geltrich. editor and publisher. 25th Anniversary award. Competition for short stories, poetry and recipes. Award: $25 (1st Prize); $10 (2nd Prize); $5 (3rd Prize); $1 (4rd-13th Prizes); small gift (3 honorable mentions). "We will close the competition when 300 manuscripts from 300 individual writers have been received." Judges: CWW editors and readers. Guidelines for SASE. Inquiries by e-mail OK with e-mail return address. Previously unpublished submissions. Word length: 800 words or less. "Recipes must be tried and approved; stories/poetry must be original (the old told in a new exciting way); guidelines must be followed." Winners announced one month after contest closes. Winners notified by mail and e-mail. List of winners available on website.

✓ ◯ ◎ **FOOL FOR LOVE FIRST CHAPTER CONTEST**, Virginia Romance Writers, P.O. Box 35, Midlothian VA 23113. E-mail: vrwfoolforlove@hotmail.com. Website: www.geocities.com/SoHo/Museum/2164. **Contact:** Contest Coordinator. Award to "recognize unpublished writers in romance fiction." Annual competition for novels. Award: $25; certificate. Competition receives 100 submissions per category. Judges: experienced critiquers and/or published romance authors. Final judges are acquiring editors. $25 entry fee. Guidelines available January 2001. Guidelines for SASE, e-mail or on website. Accepts inquiries by e-mail. Deadline: April 1, 2001. Previously unpublished submissions. Award is for romance only. Categories include historical/Regency; long contemporary; short contemporary. Word length: prologue/ first chapter up to 20 pages. "Know your market and genre." Winners announced August 2001. Winners notified by e-mail and phone. For list of winners, check website, e-mail, send SASE.

✓ ◯ **H.E. FRANCIS SHORT STORY AWARD,** Ruth Hindman Foundation, University of Alabama, English Department, Patricia Sammon, Huntsville AL 35899. E-mail: maryh71997@aol.com. **Contact:** Patricia Sammon, chairperson. Annual short story competition to honor H.E. Francis, retired professor of English at the University of Alabama in Huntsville. Award: $1,000. Competition receives approximately 500 submissions. Judges: distinguished writers. $15 fee per entry. Guidelines for SASE. Deadline: December 31. Unpublished submissions. Winners announced March. Winners notified by mail. List of winners available for SASE.

✓ 🌐 ◐ ◎ **MILES FRANKLIN LITERARY AWARD,** Arts Management Pty. Ltd., Station House, Rawson Place, 790 George St., Sydney NSW 2000 Australia. Fax: 61-2-9211 7762. E-mail: claudia@artsmanagement.com.au. **Contact:** Claudia Crosariol, associate director, projects & artists. Award "for the advancement, improvement and betterment of Australian literature." Annual award for novels. Award: AUS $28,000 (in 2000), to the author "who presents the novel which is of the highest literary merit and which must present Australian life in any of its phases." Competition receives 50 submissions. Judges: Peter Rose, Dagmar Schmidmaier, Professor Elizabeth Webby, Hilary McPhee and Father Ed Campion (in 2000). Guidelines available in October. For guidelines send SASE, fax or e-mail. Accepts inquiries by fax, phone and e-mail. Deadline: December 15. Previously published submissions. "The novel must have been published in the year prior to competition entry and must present Australian life in any of its phases." Winners announced May/June. Winners notified by phone. List of winners for SASE.

✓ **FRENCH BREAD AWARDS,** *Pacific Coast Journal*, P.O. Box 23868, San Jose CA 95153-3868. E-mail: paccoastj@bjt.net. Website: http://frenchbread.freeservers.com. **Contact:** Stillson Graham, editor. Award with the goal of "finding the best fiction and poetry out there." Annual competition for short stories and poetry. Award: $50 (1st Prize), $25 (2nd Prize). Competition receives approximately 50 submissions. Judges: Editorial staff of *Pacific Coast Journal*. $6 fee per entry. Guidelines for SASE, e-mail or on website. Accepts inquiries by e-mail. Deadline: September 1. Unpublished submissions. Length: 4,000 words. "Manuscripts will not be returned. Send SASE for winners' list. All entrants will receive issue in which first place winners are published." Winners announced in December. Winners notified by mail and/or e-mail. List of winners available for SASE, e-mail or on website.

🆕 **JEROME FUHDED RETREAT,** New York Mills Arts Retreat, 24 N. Main Ave. P.O. Box 246, New York Mills MN 56567. (218)385-3339. Fax: (218)385-3366. E-mail: nymills@uslink.net. Website: http://www.kulcher.org. **Contact:** Kent Scheer, coordinator. "The purpose is to reward writers and other artists of merit with a financial stipend and a one-month getaway." Biannual competition for short stories, novels, or story collections. Award: "one-month of retreat at our small-town facility including a $1,500 stipend." Competition receives 35-50 submissions per category. Judge: "All entries are juried together at the same time by a panel of five professionals in diverse art forms." No entry fee. Guidelines available year round. For guidelines, send SASE, fax, e-mail or visit website. Accepts inquiries by fax, e-mail, phone. Deadlines: April 1, 2001 and October 1, 2001. Contest open to US citizens. Length: 12 pages of fewer. "Our stipend retreat awards require a community outreach proposal. It is very important that entries have strong educational value." Winners announced 2 months following each deadline. Winners notified by phone.

N 🎯 **THE FUNNY PAPER COMPETITION**, F/J Writers Service, P.O. Box 22557, Kansas City MO 64113-0557. E-mail: felix22557@aol.com. Website: http://www.angelfire.com/biz/funnypaper. **Contact:** F.H. Fellhauer, editor. Award to "provide readership, help, and the opportunity to write for money to budding authors of all ages." Competition for short stories, fillers, jokes, poems, cartoons held 4 times/year. Award: $5-100. Competition receives 50-300 submissions per category. Judge: editors and selected assistants. No entry fee. Guidelines in every issue. For guidelines, send SASE, e-mail or visit website. Accepts inquiries by e-mail. No deadline (unused entries are held for next contest). Entries should be unpublished, or published only if we are advised where and when. Contest open to all writers. Length: 1,000 words maximum. Winners announced in each issue. Winners notified by mail on publication.

N 🎯 **THE JANE GESKE AWARD**, *Prairie Schooner*, 201 Andrews Hall, P.O. Box 880034, Lincoln NE 68588-0334. (402)472-0911. Fax: (402)472-9771. E-mail: eflanga@unlnotes.ul.edu. Website: www.unl.edu/scho oner/psmain.htm. **Contact:** Hilda Raz, editor-in-chief or Erin Flanagan, managing editor. Annual award "to honor work published the previous year in *Prairie Schooner* including fiction, essays, and poetry. Award: $200. Competition is judged by the editorial staff of *Prairie Schooner*." No entry fee. For guidelines send SASE or visit website. "We prefer inquiries by mail. Writers published in the past year in *Prairie Schooner* are automatically entered." Work is nominated by the editorial staff. Winners announced in the spring issue. Winners notified by February or March.

☐ **GLIMMER TRAIN'S FALL SHORT STORY AWARD FOR NEW WRITERS**, Glimmer Train Press, Inc., 710 SW Madison St., Suite 504, Portland OR 97205-2900. (503)221-0836. Fax: (503)221-0837. Website: www.glimmertrain.com (includes writers' guidelines and a Q&A section for writers). **Contact:** Linda Burmeister Davies, contest director. Contest offered for any writer whose fiction hasn't appeared in a nationally-distributed publication with a circulation over 5,000. "Send original, unpublished short (1,200-8,000 words) story with $12 reading fee for each story entered. Guidelines available for SASE. Must be postmarked between August 1 and September 30. Title page to include name, address, phone, and Short Story Award for New Writers must be written on outside of envelope. No need for SASE as materials will not be returned. Notification on January 2. Winner receives $1,200, publication in *Glimmer Train Stories* and 20 copies of that issue. First/second runners-up receive $500/$300, respectively, and consideration for publication. All applicants receive a copy of the issue in which winning entry is published and runners-up announced."

☐ **GLIMMER TRAIN'S FICTION OPEN**, Glimmer Train Press, Inc., 710 SW Madison St., Suite 504, Portland OR 97205-2900. (503)221-0836. Fax: (503)221-0837. Website: www.glimmertrain.com (includes writers' guidelines and a Q&A section for writers). **Contact:** Linda Burmeister Davies, contest director. Contest for short story, open to all writers. Award: First place $2,000, publication in *Glimmer Train Stories* (circ. 13,000) and 20 copies of that issue. First/second runners-up receive $1,000/$600 respectively and consideration for publication. Reading fee $15 for each story submitted. Guidelines for SASE. Must be postmarked between May 1 and June 30 and please write "FICTION OPEN" on the outside of the envelope. Unpublished submissions. No theme or word-count limitations. Winners will be called by October 15. List of winners available for SASE with story.

☐ **GLIMMER TRAIN'S SPRING SHORT STORY AWARD FOR NEW WRITERS**, Glimmer Train Press, Inc., 710 SW Madison St., Suite 504, Portland OR 97205-2900. (503)221-0836. Fax: (503)221-0837. Website: www.glimmertrain.com (includes writers' guidelines and a Q&A section for writers). **Contact:** Linda Burmeister Davies, contest director. Contest offered for any writer whose fiction hasn't appeared in a nationally-distributed publication with a circulation over 5,000. "Send original, unpublished short (1,200-8,000 words) story with $12 reading fee for each story entered. Guidelines available for SASE. Must be postmarked between February 1 and March 31. Title page to include name, address, phone, and Short Story Award for New Writers must be written on outside of envelope. No need for SASE as materials will not be returned. Notification on July 1. Winner receives $1,200, publication in *Glimmer Train Stories* and 20 copies of that issue. First/second runners-up receive $500/$300, respectively, and consideration for publication. All applicants receive a copy of the issue in which winning entry is published and runners-up announced."

GLIMMER TRAIN'S VERY SHORT FICTION SUMMER AWARD, *Glimmer Train Stories*, 710 SW Madison St., Suite 504, Portland OR 97205. (503)221-0836. Fax: (503)221-0837. Website: www.glimmertrain.com (includes writers' guidelines and Q&A section for writers). **Contact:** Linda Burmeister Davies, editor. Annual award offered to encourage the art of the very short story. Contest opens May 1 and ends July 31; entry must be postmarked between these dates. Awards: $1,200 and publication in *Glimmer Train Stories* (1st Place); $500 (2nd Place); $300 (3rd Place). Competition receives 1,500 submissions. $10 fee per story. Guidelines available for SASE or check website. Length: 2,000 words maximum. First page of story should include name, address, phone number and word count. "VSF AWARD" must be written on outside of envelope. Materials will not be returned. Include SASE for list of winning entries. Notification on November 1.

GLIMMER TRAIN'S VERY SHORT FICTION WINTER AWARD, *Glimmer Train Stories*, 710 SW Madison St., Suite 504, Portland OR 97205. (503)221-0836. Fax: (503)221-0837. Website: www.glimmertrain.com (includes writer's guidelines and a Q&A section for writers). **Contact:** Linda Burmeister Davies, editor. Award offered to encourage the art of the very short story. Contest opens November 1 and ends January 31; entry must be postmarked between these dates. Awards: $1,200 and publication in *Glimmer Train Stories* (1st Place); $500 (2nd Place); $300 (3rd Place). $10 fee per story. Guidelines available for SASE or check website. Length: 2,000 words maximum. First page of story should include name, address, phone number and word count. "VSF AWARD" must be written on outside of envelope. Materials will not be returned. Include SASE for list of winners. Notification on May 1.

GOVERNMENT OF NEWFOUNDLAND AND LABRADOR ARTS AND LETTERS COMPETITION Government of Newfoundland and Labrador Dept. of Tourism and Culture, P.O. Box 1854, St. John's, Newfoundland A1C 5P9 Canada. (709)729-5253. Fax: (709)729-5952. **Contact:** Regina Best, coordinator. Award "to encourage the creative talent of people of the Province of Newfoundland and Labrador." Annual competition for arts and letters. Award: Senior division: $600 (1st Prize), $300 (2nd Prize), $150 (3rd Prize); Junior division: $300 (1st Prize), $200 (2nd Prize), $100 (3rd Prize). Competition receives approximately 1,000 submissions and 60-70 fiction entries. Judges: Blind judging by outside people who are professionals in their field. Guidelines for SASE. Deadline: February. Unpublished submissions. Competition is only open to residents of this province. "There are two divisions in this competition: Junior (12-18 years) and Senior (19-on). Each entry receives a written adjudication. There are prizes in several categories; fiction; nonfiction; poetry; dramatic script; painting; 3-D art; drawing and print-making; photography; musical composition. Categories in the Junior division are poetry, prose and visual arts. Applications and rules and regulations for entering are available at the above address." Winners announced in May. Winners notified by press release. List of winners available.

GREAT AMERICAN BOOK CONTEST, Book Deals, Inc., 417 N. Sangamon St., Chicago IL 60622. (312)491-0300. Fax: (312) 491-8091. E-mail: greatamericanbk@aol.com. Website: www.BookDealsInc. com. **Contact:** Caroline Francis Carney, director. Award to "discover American authors of exceptional talent whose work equals or surpasses the finest of American's past and future." Annual competition for book-length prose. Award: Grand Prize $3,000 and a meeting with a book editor and a film scout; $750 honorable mention for an author 30 years or younger whose "strong voice exhibits the next generation's literary promise." Competition receives 600+ submissions. Judges: jury of authors, literary experts, academics. Entry fee $30. Guidelines available January 2001 for SASE. Accepts inquiries by fax and e-mail. Deadline: December 31. Previously unpublished submissions. "Story must have an American setting, authors must have an exceptional narrative voice and the recommended length is between 45,000-300,000 words." Winners announced on or by April 1, 2002. Winners notified by phone. For list of winners send SASE or visit website.

GREAT BEGINNINGS, Utah Romance Writers of America, 1570 N. 4150 W., Plain City UT 84404. (801)731-5225. E-mail: pwv@uswest. Website: www.xmission.com/~utahrwa. **Contact:** Teresa Versey, chapter president. Annual competition for novels. Award: First place receives a plaque and 2nd through 4th place receive certificates. Competition receives 100 submissions per category. Judges: experienced, published and unpublished authors and editors in the final round. $10 entry fee. Guidelines available January 1, 2001. For guidelines, send SASE, e-mail or visit website. Accepts inquiries by e-mail. Deadline March 17, 2001. Entries should be unpublished. Contest is open to both unpublished authors, and to published authors submitting unpublished, uncontracted works. Length: 3 ms pages. Winners are announced on May 12, 2001. Winners notified by mail, phone, e-mail on May 12, 2001. For list of winners send SASE, e-mail or visit website.

THE GREAT BLUE BEACON SHORT-SHORT STORY CONTEST, *The Great Blue Beacon: The Newsletter for Writers of All Genres and Skill Levels*, 1425 Patriot Dr., Melbourne FL 32940. (321)253-5869. E-mail: ajircc@juno.com. **Contact:** A.J. Byers, editor/publisher. Award to "recognize outstanding short-short story." Annual award for short-short stories. Award: $50 (1st prize); $25 (2nd prize); $10 (3rd prize), plus publication of winning entry in *The Great Blue Beacon*. Judges: outside panel of judges. Entry fee $5 ($4 for subscribers). Guidelines available December. For guidelines send SASE or e-mail. Accepts inquiries by e-mail. Deadline: March 15. Entries should be previously unpublished. Open to all writers. Length: 750 words or fewer. Winners announced in May. Winners notified by phone. List of winners available for SASE or by e-mail.

GREAT LAKES BOOK AWARDS, Great Lakes Booksellers Awards, 208 Franklin St., Grand Haven MI 49417. (616)847-2460. Fax: (616)842-0051. E-mail: glba@books-glba.org. Website: www.books-glba.org. Award to "recognize and reward excellence in the writing and publishing of books that capture the spirit and enhance awareness of the region." Annual competition for fiction, children's and nonfiction. Award: $500 plus bookstore promotion. Competition receives approximately 90 submissions. Five judges each category. No entry fee. Guidelines available. Deadline: May 31, 2001. Writer must be nominated by members of the GLBA. Winners announced September 2001.

GREAT LAKES COLLEGES ASSOCIATION NEW WRITERS AWARD, Great Lakes Colleges Association Inc., 535 W. William, Suite 301, Ann Arbor MI 48103. (734)761-4833. Fax: (734)761-3939. E-mail: krumhol z@cc.denison.cc. Annual award. Winners are invited to tour the GLCA colleges. An honorarium of at least $300 will be guaranteed the author by each of the GLCA colleges they visit. Receives 30-40 entries in each category annually. Judges: Professors from member colleges. No entry fee. Guidelines available after August 1. Accepts inquiries by fax and e-mail. Deadline: February 21. Unpublished submissions. First publication in fiction or poetry. Writer must be nominated by publisher. Four copies of the book should be sent to: Director, New Writers Award. Winners announced in May. Letters go to publishers who have submitted.

■ **GREAT PLAINS STORYTELLING & POETRY READING CONTEST**, P.O. Box 492, Anita IA 50020. Phone/fax: (712)762-4363. **Contact:** Robert Everhart, director. Estab. 1976. Annual award "to provide an outlet for writers to present not only their works but also to provide a large audience for their presentation *live* by the writer. Attendance at the event, which takes place annually in Avoca, Iowa, is *required.*" Awards: $50 (1st Prize); $25 (2nd Prize); $15 (3rd Prize); $10 (4th Prize); $5 (5th Prize). $5 entry fee. Entry forms available at contest only. Deadline is day of contest, which takes place over Labor Day Weekend. Previously published or unpublished submissions.

Ⓝ ◎ **THE JUDY & A.C. GREENE LITERARY FESTIVAL CONTEST**, The Living Room Theatre of Salado, P.O. Box 1023, Salado TX 76571-1023. (254)913-1432. E-mail: lrts@vvm.com. Website: www.vvm.com/ ~lrts. **Contact:** Dr. Raymond Carver, contest/festival manager. "The purpose of the festival is development of unpublished works by Texas writers. The Festival seeks unpublished literary works which may be adapted by staff of the Living Room Theatre for dramatic performance with two to five actors using scripts and lecture stands but no other theatrical elements." Annual competition for short stories, novels, story collections. Award: 1st prize $1,500; 3 finalists $250 each. Competition receives about 50 submissions per category. Judge: contest/ festival staff. $20 entry fee. Guidelines available now. For guidelines, send e-mail or visit website. Accepts inquiries by e-mail or phone. Deadline March 31. Entries should be unpublished. Contest open to Texas residents or former residents. Length: 60-90 minutes reading aloud time. "No poems or discursive writing." Winners announced in June. Winners notified by phone. For list of winners send e-mail.

◯ **THE GREENSBORO REVIEW LITERARY AWARDS**, English Dept., 134 McIver Bldg, UNC-Greensboro, P.O. Box 26170, Greensboro NC 27402-6170. (336)334-5459. E-mail: jlclark@uncg.edu. Website: www.un cg.edu/eng/mfa. **Contact:** Jim Clark, editor. Annual award. Award: $250. Competition receives 1,000 submissions. Guidelines for SASE. Accepts inquiries by e-mail. Deadline: September 15. Unpublished submissions. "All manuscripts meeting literary award guidelines will be considered for cash award as well as for publication in *The Greensboro Review.*" Winners notified in December. List of winners published in the Spring issue of *The Greensboro Review.*

◯ ✔ **HEADWATERS LITERARY COMPETITION**, New Rivers Press, 420 N. 5th St. #1180, Minneapolis MN 55401. (612)339-7114. Fax: (612)339-9047. E-mail: contact@newriverspress.org. Website: www.newriver spress.org. **Contact:** Eric Braun, editor. Award to "find and publish the best creative prose book-length manuscripts written by emerging writers living in the U.S." Annual competition for novels or story collections. Award: $1,000 and publication of book. Competition receives 100 prose and 100 poetry submissions. Judges: "We hire outside judges who work together with our editorial staff." Entry fee $20. Guidelines available February 2001 for SASE. Deadline: September 30. Previously unpublished submissions. "Individual stories may have been published, but not as a book length collection. Open to all U.S. writers. Short fiction, novellas, memoirs, personal essays and other forms of creative prose." Word length: 100-200 pages for prose; 40-60 pages for poetry. "Look at recent NRP books, particularly contest winners." Winners announced May/June 2002. "All entrants will receive letter notifying them of the panelists' decisions." List of winners available for SASE.

Ⓝ ◎ **HEART OF THE WEST WRITERS CONTEST**, Utah Romance Writers of America, 1570 N. 4150 W., Plain City UT 84404. (801)731-5225. E-mail: pwv@uswest. Website: www.xmission.com/~utahrwa. **Contact:** Teresa Versey, chapter president. Annual competition for novels. Award: First place winners will receive a golden locket, second through fourth place winners receive certificates. Competition receives 80 submissions per category. Judge: published and experienced, unpublished authors in the first round; editors in the second round. $25 entry fee. Guidelines available April 1, 2001. For guidelines, send SASE, e-mail or visit website.

Accepts inquiries by e-mail. Deadline July 15, 2001. Entries should be unpublished. Contest open to unpublished authors, and to published authors submitting unpublished, uncontracted work. Length: 20 ms pages. Winners are announced in November 2001. Winners notified by mail, phone and e-mail. For list of winners send SASE, e-mail or visit website.

● DRUE HEINZ LITERATURE PRIZE, University of Pittsburgh Press, 3347 Forbes Ave., Pittsburgh PA 15261. (412)383-2456. Fax: (412)383-2466. E-mail: press@pitt.edu. Website: www.pitt.edu/~press. Annual award "to support the writer of short fiction at a time when the economics of commercial publishing make it more and more difficult for the serious literary artist working in the short story and novella to find publication." Award: $10,000 and publication by the University of Pittsburgh Press. "It is imperative that entrants request complete rules of the competition by sending an SASE before submitting a manuscript." Submissions will be received only during the months of May and June. Postmark deadline: June 30. Manuscripts must be unpublished in book form. The award is open to writers who have published a book-length collection of fiction or a minimum of three short stories or novellas in commercial magazines or literary journals of national distribution. Winners announced in February. Winners notified by phone or mail. List of winners available for SASE sent with manu-script.

☑ ● ERNEST HEMINGWAY FOUNDATION/PEN AWARD FOR FIRST FICTION, PEN New England, P.O. Box 725, North Cambridge MA 02140. Fax: (617)353-7134. E-mail: awards@pen-ne.org. **Contact:** Mary Louise Sullivan, awards coordinator. Annual award "to give beginning writers recognition and encourage-ment and to stimulate interest in first books of fiction among publishers and readers." Award: $7,500. Novels or short story collections must have been published during calendar year under consideration. Entry form or rules for SASE. Deadline: December 15. "The Ernest Hemingway Foundation/PEN Award For First Fiction is given to an American author of the best first-published book-length work of fiction published by an established publish-ing house in the US each calendar year." Winners will be announced mid-March. Winners will be notified through publisher or PEN NE Executive Board member.

☑ ○ LORIAN HEMINGWAY SHORT STORY COMPETITION, P.O. Box 993, Key West FL 33041-0993. (305)294-0320. Fax: (305)292-3653. E-mail: calico2419@aol.com. Website: www.shortstorycompetition.com. **Contact:** Carol Shaughnessy, co-director. Award to "encourage literary excellence and the efforts of writers who have not yet had major-market success." Annual competition for short stories. Awards: $1,000 (1st Prize); $500 (2nd Prize); $500 (3rd Prize); honorable mentions. Competition receives approximately 850 submissions. Judges: A panel of writers, editors and literary scholars selected by novelist Lorian Hemingway. Entry fee $10 for each story postmarked by June 1, 2001; $15 for each story postmarked between June 1 and June 15, 2001. Guidelines for SASE after February 1. Accepts inquiries by SASE, fax, e-mail or visit website. Deadline: June 1, 2001 and June 15, 2001. Unpublished submissions. "Open to all writers whose fiction has not appeared in a nationally distributed publication with a circulation of 5,000 or more." Word length: 3,000 words maximum. "We look for excellence, pure and simple—no genre restrictions, no theme restrictions—we seek a writer's voice that cannot be ignored." Winners announced before August 1. Winners notified by phone or e-mail. For list of winners, e-mail, visit website. "All entrants will receive a letter from Lorian Hemingway and a list of winners by October 1."

☑ ○ ◎ HIGHLIGHTS FOR CHILDREN, 803 Church St., Honesdale PA 18431. (570)253-1080. **Contact:** Marileta Robinson, senior editor. Award "to honor quality stories (previously unpublished) for young readers." Three $1,000 awards. Competition receives 1,500 submissions. Judges: *Highlights* editors. Guidelines available July 2000 for SASE. Deadline February 28, 2001. Length: 500 words maximum for beginning readers (to age 8) and 900 words for more advanced readers (ages 9 to 12). No minimum word length. No entry form necessary. To be submitted between January 1 and February 28 to "Fiction Contest" at address above. "No violence, crime or derogatory humor. Obtain a copy of the guidelines, since the theme changes each year." Nonwinning entries returned in June if SASE is included with ms. Winners announced in June. Winners notified by phone or letter. List of winners will be sent with returned mss.

☑ ● THE ALFRED HODDER FELLOWSHIP, The Council of the Humanities, Princeton University, 122 E. Pyne, Princeton NJ 08544. **Contact:** Cass Garner, program manager. "This fellowship is awarded for the pursuit of independent work in the humanities. The recipient is usually a writer or scholar in the early stages of his or her career, a person 'with more than ordinary learning' and with 'much more than ordinary intellectual and literary gifts.' " Traditionally, the Hodder Fellow has been a humanist outside of academia. Candidates for the Ph.D. are not eligible. Award: $46,500. The Hodder Fellow spends an academic year in residence at Princeton working independently. Competition receives 300 submissions. Judges: Princeton Committee on Humanistic Studies. Deadline: November 1. Applicants must submit a résumé, a sample of previous work (10 page maximum, not returnable), and a project proposal of 2 to 3 pages. Letters of recommendation are not required.

[N] [◎] PEARL HOGREFE FELLOWSHIP, The Pearl Hogrefe Fund and Department of English, 203 Ross Hall, Iowa State University, Ames IA 50011. (515)294-2477. Fax: (515)294-6814. E-mail: englgrad@iastate.edu. Website: www.engl.iastate.edu. **Contact:** Kathleen Hickok, graduate studies coordinator. "To provide new M.A. students with writing time." Annual competition for manuscript sample of 25 pages, any genre. Award: $1,000/month for 9 months and full payment of tuition and fees. Competition receives 60-75 submissions. Judges: the creative writing staff at Iowa State University. Guidelines available by e-mail. Accepts inquiries by fax, e-mail, phone. Deadline: January 31. Either published or unpublished submissions. "No restrictions, except the applicant cannot hold or expect to receive a masters in English or creative writing during the current year." Winners announced and notified by phone on April 1.

[N] [⊕] [◎] THE WINIFRED HOLTBY MEMORIAL PRIZE, The Royal Society of Literature, 3J Somerset House, Strand, London WC2R 0RN United Kingdom. E-mail: rslit@aol.com. Website: http://www.rslit.org. **Contact:** Julia Abel Smith. Award for "regional fiction, i.e., fiction with a strong sense of a particular place." Annual competition for novels. Award: £1,000. Competition receives 60 submissions per category. Judge: 3 judges, who are as yet unchosen. No entry fee. Guidelines available in 2001. For guidelines, send fax, e-mail or call. Accepts inquiries by fax, e-mail, phone. Deadline December 15, 2001. Entries should be previously published. Contest open to citizens of the Commonwealth who may enter and only publishers can submit books. Publishers must nominate work. Winners are announced June 2002. Winners notified by mail April 2002.

[ ] [◎] HONOLULU MAGAZINE/BORDERS BOOKS & MUSIC FICTION CONTEST, *Honolulu* Magazine, 36 Merchant St., Honolulu HI 96813. (808)524-7400. **Contact:** A. Kam Napier, associate editor. "We do not accept fiction except during our annual contest, at which time we welcome it." Annual award for short stories. Award: $1,000 and publication in the April issue of *Honolulu* Magazine. Competition receives approximately 400 submissions. Judges: Panel of well-known Hawaii-based writers. Rules for SASE. Deadline: early December. "Stories must have a Hawaii theme, setting and/or characters. Author should enclose name and address in separate small envelope. Do not put name on story."

[✓] [ ] [◎] L. RON HUBBARD'S WRITERS OF THE FUTURE CONTEST, Author Services, Inc., P.O. Box 1630N, Los Angeles CA 90078. (323)466-3310. Website: www.authorservicesinc.com/wof_home.htm. **Contact:** Nathalie Cordebard, contest administrator. Estab. 1984. Quarterly. "Foremost contest for new writers of science fiction, fantasy and horror, short stories and novelettes." Awards $1,000, $750, $500 in quarterly prizes, annual $4,000 Grand Prize, five-day Writer's Workshop with major authors, publication in leading international anthology. Judge: professional panel. No entry fee. Entrants retain all rights. Guidelines available for SASE or check website. Accepts inquiries by phone. Deadlines March 31, June 30, September 30, and December 31. Length: 17,000 words maximum." Winners announced quarterly. Winners notified by mail. For list of winners visit website.

[✓] [ ] [◎] ZORA NEALE HURSTON/RICHARD WRIGHT AWARD, Zora Neale Hurston/Richard Wright Foundation, English Dept., Virginia Commonwealth University, P.O. Box 842005, Richmond VA 23284-2005. (804)225-4729. Fax: (804)828-8684. E-mail: information@hurston-wright.org. Website: www.hurston-wright.org. President/Founder: Marita Golden. **Contact:** Donna Champ Banks, executive director. "Awards excellence in fiction for writing by students of African descent enrolled full time as an undergraduate or graduate student in any college or university in the U.S." Annual award for previously unpublished short stories and novel excerpts. Awards: $1,000; $500. Competition receives 50-75 submissions. Judges: published writers. Guidelines available in September for SASE. Unpublished submissions. Word length: 25 pages maximum. Winners announced in March. Winners notified by mail. List of winners available in April, visit website.

[✓] [ ] INDIANA REVIEW FICTION PRIZE, *Indiana Review*, Ballantine Hall 465, 1020 E. Kirkwood Ave., Bloomington IN 47405-7103. (812)855-3439. Website: www.indiana.edu/~inreview/ir.html. **Contact:** Shannon Gibney, associate editor. Contest for fiction in any style and on any subject. Alternates each year with poetry contest. Award: $1,000, publication in the *Indiana Review* and contributor's copies (1st place). Each entrant will receive the prize issue. Competition receives 500 submissions. Judges: *Indiana Review* staff and outside judges. Guidelines for SASE or on website after May. Accepts inquiries by phone. Deadline: November 12, 2001. All entries considered for publication. Cover letter must include name, address, phone number, and title of story. Entrant's name should appear only in the cover letter, as all entries will be considered anonymously. Manuscripts will not be returned. No previously published works, or works forthcoming elsewhere, are eligible. Simultaneous submissions acceptable, but in event of entrant withdraw, contest fee will not be refunded. Length: 40 pages maximum, double spaced. Winners announced on December 10. Winners notified by mail, e-mail, or phone. For list of winners, send SASE.

☑ ◎ **INDIVIDUAL ARTIST FELLOWSHIP**, Nebraska Arts Council, 3838 Davenport, Omaha NE 68131-2329. (402)421-3627. Fax: (402)595-2334. E-mail: swise@nebraskaartscouncil.org. Website: www.nebraskaartsc ouncil.org. **Contact:** Suzanne Wise, program manager. Award to "recognize outstanding achievement by Nebraska writers." Competition every third year for short stories and novels. Award: $5,000 Distinguished Achievement; $1,000-2,000 Merit Awards. Competition receives 70-80 submissions per category. Judges: panel of 3. Next deadline for literature: November 15, 2002. Published or previously unpublished submissions. Nebraska residents only. Length: 50 pages.

◎ **INTERNATIONAL IMITATION HEMINGWAY COMPETITION**, PEN Center USA West, 672 S. Lafayette Park Pl. #44, Los Angeles CA 90057. (213)365-8500. Fax: (213)365-9616. E-mail: pen@pen-usa west.org. Website: www.pen-usa-west.org. **Contact:** Eric Chow, administrative coordinator. Write one page of Imitation Hemingway. Must sound like Hemingway, read like Hemingway, and must be funny. Annual competition. Competition receives 1,000 submissions. Guidelines available on website. Accepts inquiries by fax, e-mail. Deadline: mid-April. Previously unpublished submissions. Word length: one page. Winners announced and notified by phone in mid-June. List of winners for SASE. "Call PEN for further details or visit our website."

Ⓝ ◎ **INTERNATIONAL READING ASSOCIATION CHILDREN'S BOOK AWARDS**, Sponsored by IRA, P.O. Box 8139, 800 Barksdale Rd., Newark DE 19714-8139. (302)731-1600. E-mail: exec@reading.org. Annual awards given for a first or second book. Four IRA Children's Book Awards at US$500 each will be offered for an author's first or second published book. Awards will be given for fiction and nonfiction in two age categories: younger readers (ages 4-10) and older readers (ages 10-17). This award is intended for newly-published authors who show unusual promise in the children's book field. Books from any country and in any language copyrighted during the 2000 calendar year will be considered. Entries in a language other than English must include a one-page abstract in English and a translation into English of one chapter or similar selection that in the submitter's estimation is representative of the book. Entries must be received by November 1. For guidelines with specific information write to Executive Office, International Reading Association, PO Box 8139, Newark, DE 19714-8139, USA.

◯ **IOWA SCHOOL OF LETTERS AWARD FOR SHORT FICTION, THE JOHN SIMMONS SHORT FICTION AWARD**, Iowa Writers' Workshop, 102 Dey House, 507 N. Clinton St., Iowa City IA 52242-1000. Annual awards for short story collections. To encourage writers of short fiction. Award: publication of winning collections by University of Iowa Press the following fall. Entries must be at least 150 pages, typewritten, and submitted between August 1 and September 30. Stamped, self-addressed return packaging must accompany manuscript. Rules for SASE. Iowa Writer's Workshop does initial screening of entries; finalists (about 6) sent to outside judge for final selection. "A different well-known writer is chosen each year as judge. Any writer who has not previously published a volume of prose fiction is eligible to enter the competition for these prizes. Revised manuscripts which have been previously entered may be resubmitted."

Ⓝ **THE IOWA SHORT FICTION AWARD**, University of Iowa Press, 100 Kuhl House, Iowa City IA 52242-1000. (319)335-2000. Fax: (319)335-2055. Website: http://www.uiowa.edu/~uipress. **Contact:** Holly Carver, director. Award to "give exposure to promising writers who have not yet published a book of prose." Annual competition for story collections. Award: Publication only under Press's standard contract. Competition receives 300-400 mss. Judge: "Senior Iowa Writers' Workshop members screen manuscripts; published fiction author of note makes final two selections." No entry fee. For guidelines, send SASE or visit website. Accepts inquiries by fax, phone. Deadline: Entries accepted during August and September. "Individual stories can have been previously published (as in journals) but never in *book* form." Stories in English. Length: "at least 150 word-processed, double-spaced pages; 8-10 stories on average for manuscript." Winners announced January following competition. Winners notified by phone in January.

☑ ◯ ◎ **JOSEPH HENRY JACKSON AWARD**, Intersection for the Arts/The San Francisco Foundation, 446 Valencia St., San Francisco CA 94103-3415. (415)626-2787. Fax: (415)626-1636. E-mail: info@theintersecti on.org. Website: www.theintersection.org. **Contact:** Kevin Chen, program director. Award "to encourage young, unpublished writers." Annual award for short stories, novels and story collections. Award: $2,000. Competition receives 150-200 submissions. Entry form and rules available in mid-October for SASE. Deadline: January 31. Unpublished submissions only. Applicant must be resident of northern California or Nevada for 3 consecutive years immediately prior to the deadline date. Age of applicant must be 20 through 35. Work cannot exceed 100 double-spaced, typed pages. "Submit a serious, ambitious portion of a book-length manuscript." Winners announced June 15. Winners notified by mail. "Winners will be announced in letter mailed to all applicants."

☑ ◎ **JAPAN FOUNDATION ARTIST FELLOWSHIP PROGRAM**, 152 W. 57th St., 39th Floor, New York NY 10019. (212)489-0299. Fax: (212)489-0409. E-mail: info@jfny.org. Website: www.jfny.org/jfny. **Con-**

tact: Yuika Goto, program assistant: . "This program provides artists and specialists in the arts with the opportunity to pursue creative projects in Japan and to meet and consult with their Japanese counterparts." Annual competition. Several artists fellowships from two to six months' duration during the Japanese fiscal year (April 1-March 31) are available to artists, such as writers, musicians, painters, sculptors, stage artists, movie directors, etc.; and specialists in the arts, such as scenario writers, curators, etc. Benefits include transportation to and from Japan; settling-in, research, activities and other allowances and a monthly stipend. See brochure for more details. Competition receives approximately 30-40 submissions. Judges: Foundation staff in Japan. Guidelines available after August by fax or e-mail. Accepts inquiries by fax, phone and e-mail. Deadline: December 1. Work should be related to Japan. Applicants must be accredited artists or specialists. Affiliation with a Japanese artist or institution is required. Three letters of reference, including one from the Japanese affiliate must accompany all applications. Winners announced in April. Winners notified by mail. List of winners available by phone.

✅ ◐ ◎ JAPANOPHILE SHORT STORY CONTEST, *Japanophile*, P.O. Box 7977, Ann Arbor MI 48107-7977. (734)930-1553. Fax: (734)930-9968. E-mail: japanophile@aol.com. Website: www.japanophile.c om. **Contact:** Susan Aitken Lapp, editor. Estab. 1974. Annual award "to encourage quality writing on Japan-America understanding." Award: $100 plus possible publication. Competition receives 200 submissions. Entry fee: $5. Send $4 for sample copy of magazine. Guidelines available by August for SASE, e-mail or on website. Accepts inquiries by fax and e-mail. Deadline: December 31. Prefers unpublished submissions. Stories should involve Japanese and non-Japanese characters, maximum 5,000 words. Winners notified in March. Winners notified by mail. List of winners available in March for SASE.

◐ JAMES JONES FIRST NOVEL FELLOWSHIP, James Jones Society, Wilkes University, Wilkes-Barre PA 18766. (570)408-4530. Fax: (570)408-7829. E-mail: english@wilkesl.wilkes.edu. Website: wilkes.edu/acade mics/casps/eng-jjs.html. **Contact:** J. Michael Lennon, English department professor. Award to "honor the spirit of unblinking honesty, determination, and insight into modern culture exemplified by the late James Jones by encouraging the work of an American writer who has not published a book-length work of fiction." Annual award for unpublished novel, novella, or collection of related short stories in progress. Award: $5,000. Receives approximately 600 applications. Application fee: $15. Guidelines for SASE. Accepts inquiries by e-mail and fax. Deadline: Postmark March 1. Unpublished submissions. "Award is open to American writers." Word length: 50 opening pages and a two-page thematic outline. "Name, address, telephone number on title page only." Winners announced early September. Winners notified by phone. List of winners available October 1 for SASE. "For more information, visit us on the Web."

✅ KATHA: INDIAN AMERICAN FICTION CONTEST, *India Currents* Magazine, P.O. Box 21285, San Jose CA 95148. (408)274-6966. Fax: (408)274-2733. E-mail: editor@indiacurrents.com. Website: www.indiacurr ents.com. **Contact:** Vandana Kumar, managing editor. Award "to encourage creative writing which has as its focus India, Indian culture, Indian-Americans and America's views of India." Annual competition for short stories. Awards: $300 (1st Prize), $200 (2nd Prize), $100 (3rd Prize), 2 honorable mentions. Competition received 50 submissions last year. Judges: "A distinguished panel of Indian-American authors. Guidelines for SASE, e-mail, or on website. Accepts inquiries by e-mail and phone. Deadline: December 31. Unpublished submissions. Length: 3,000 words maximum. Winners announced on April 1. Winners notified by mail. For list of winners, send SASE. "Write about something you have experienced personally or do extensive research, so that you can write knowledgebly."

Ⓝ ◎ KILLER FROG CONTEST, *Scavenger's Newsletter*, 833 Main, Osage City KS 66523-1214. (785)528-3538. E-mail: foxscav1@jc.net. Website: http://www.jlgiftsshop.com/scav/index.html. **Contact:** Janet Fox, editor/publisher. Competition "to see who can write the funniest/most overdone horror story, or poem, or produce the most outrageous artwork on a horror theme." Annual award for short stories, poems and art. Award: $50 for each of 4 categories and "coveted froggie statuette. Four runners-up in each category will receive a year's free *Scavenger* subscription." Winners will be published electronically on website. Competition receives 50 submissions per category. Judge: Editor/Publisher of *Scavenger*, Janet Fox. Guidelines available January 1 for SASE, e-mail or on website. Guidelines will also run in February or March issue of *Scavenger's Newsletter*. Accepts inquiries by e-mail, phone. Submissions must be postmarked between April 1 and July 1. Published or previously unpublished submissions. Limited to horror/humor. Length: up to 4,000 words. "Write badly, throw good taste out the window, have fun!" Winners will be announced in the September issue of *Scavenger*. Winners notified by mail and e-mail in August. List of winners available for SASE, e-mail, or visit website.

Ⓝ THE *KRATER* PROSODY AWARDS FOR SHORT FICTION AND POETRY, 2001, *Krater Quarterly*, P.O. Box 1371, Lincoln Park MI 48146. E-mail: kraterquarterly@aol.com. Website: www.KraterQuarterly.c om. **Contact:** Leonard Fritz, editor. Award "to honor writers for their creativity." Annual competition for short stories and poetry. Award: $500 and publication in the Winter 2002 issue for short fiction and poetry. Competition receives 350-400 submissions. Judge: the magazine's staff. $10 fee 1st entry; $7 fee each additional. Guidelines available February 2001. For guidelines, send SASE, e-mail or visit website. Deadline February 2001 to August 1, 2001. Entries should be previously unpublished. Contest open to all writers. Length: 5,000 words maximum. Winners announced mid-September. Winners notified by mail and e-mail. For list of winners send SASE or visit website.

N ◯ ◎ LAURIE, Smoky Mountain Romance Writers, P.O. Box 70268, Knoxville TN 37938. Phone/fax (call first): (865)922-7700. E-mail: skunkoml@aol.com. Website: www.smrw.org. **Contact:** Deborah Ledgerwood, contest coordinator. Award to "honor excellence in romance fiction." Annual competition for novels. Award: First place in each category wins a Laurie pendant, and finalist and winner receive certificates. "We accept 50 entries maximum for each category." Judge: Finalists are judged by an acquisitions editor. $25 entry fee. Guidelines available November 2000. For guidelines, send SASE, e-mail or visit website. Accepts inquiries by e-mail. Deadline March 1, 2001. Entries should be unpublished. Contest open to Romance Writers of America members. Length: 5-page synopsis, prologue, and first chapter (not to exceed 30 pages). Winners announced May 19, 2001. Winners notified by phone and e-mail May 20, 2001. For list of winners send e-mail or visit website.

◢ ◎ THE LAWRENCE FOUNDATION AWARD, *Prairie Schooner*, 201 Andrews Hall, P.O. Box 880334, Lincoln NE 68588-0334. (402)472-0911. Fax: (402)472-9771. E-mail: eflanaga@unlnotes.unl.edu. Website: www.unl.edu/schooner/psmain.htm. **Contact:** Hilda Raz, editor-in-chief or Erin Flanagan, managing editor. Award "to honor and recognize the best short story published in *Prairie Schooner* in the past year." Annual competition for short stories. Award: $1,000. Judge: The editorial staff of *Prairie Schooner*. No entry fee. For guidelines send SASE or visit website. "We prefer inquiries by mail. Writers published in the past year in *Prairie Schooner* are automatically entered." Work is nominated by editorial staff. Winners announced in the Spring issue. Winners notified by mail in February or March.

N ◎ URSULA K. LE GUIN PRIZE FOR IMAGINATIVE FICTION, *Rosebud*, P.O. Box 459, Cambridge WI 53523. (608)423-9609. Website: www.rsbd.net. **Contact:** John Smelcer, publisher or John Lehman, associate publisher. This annual competition is to select the very best imaginative short story entered. Award: $1,000 and publication in *Rosebud*. Competition receives 200-250 entries per category. Judge: a panel of 2-3 pre-judges and Ursula K. Le Guin is final judge. Entry fee is $10. Guidelines available in the fall. For guidelines visit website. Deadline: December 31st annually unless specified. Entries should be previously unpublished. Contest open to anyone. Winners announced in mid-spring of each year. Winners notified by mail, phone, or e-mail. For list of winners send SASE.

LITERAL LATTÉ FICTION AWARD, *Literal Latté*, 61 E. 8th St., Suite 240, New York NY 10003. (212)260-5532. E-mail: litlatte@aol.com. Website: www.literal-latte.com. **Contact:** Jenine Gordon Bockman, editor/publisher. Award to "provide talented writers with three essential tools for continued success: money, publication and recognition." Annual competition for short stories. Award: $1,000 (1st Prize); $200 (2nd Prize); $100 (3rd Prize); up to 7 honorable mentions. Competition receives 400-600 submissions. Judges: the editors. Entry fee $10 ($15 includes subscription) for each story submitted. Guidelines available for SASE. Accepts inquiries by e-mail. Deadline: mid-January. Previously unpublished submissions. Open to new and established writers worldwide. Word length: 6,000 words maximum. "The First Prize Story in the First Annual *Literal Latté* Fiction Awards has been honored with a Pushcart Prize." Winners notified by phone. List of winners available in late April for SASE.

N ◎ LITERALLY HORSES POETRY/SHORT STORY CONTEST, *Literally Horses*, P.O. Box 51554, Kalamazoo MI 49005. (616)345-5915. **Contact:** Laurie A. Cerny, publisher. Award to "promote/recognize horse/Western lifestyle-related poetry and short stories." Annual competition for short stories and poetry. Award: $100 first place short story; $75 first place poetry; honorable mention prizes in each category. "Anticipate at least 100 entries." Judge: a panel of judges—including *Literally Horses* publisher. $9.95 per entry (includes a 1-year subscription). Guidelines available fall 2000. For guidelines, send SASE. Deadline May 15, 2001. Entries should be previously unpublished. Contest open to anyone. Length: 2,500 words. "Make sure the topic has something to do with horses: racing, driving, riding, showing, backyard horse, etc. Also, cowboy/Western lifestyle theme oriented is OK. Something different. Inspirational." Winners announced Fall 2001. Winners notified by mail July 15, 2001. For list of winners send SASE.

◯ LONG FICTION CONTEST INTERNATIONAL, White Eagle Coffee Store Press, P.O. Box 383, Fox River Grove IL 60021-0383. (847)639-9200. E-mail: wecspress@aol.com. Website: http://members.aol.com/wecspress. **Contact:** Publisher. To promote and support the long fiction form. Annual award for short stories. "Entries accepted from anywhere in the world; story must be written in English." Winning story receives A.E.

Coppard Award—publication as chapbook plus $500, 25 contributor's copies; 40 additional copies sent to book publishers/agents and 10 press kits. Entry fee $15 US, ($5 for second story in same envelope). Must be in US funds. Competition receives 200 entries. Guidelines available in April. Accepts inquiries by e-mail. Deadline: December 15. Accepts previously unpublished submissions, but previous publication of small parts with acknowledgements is OK. Accepts simultaneous submissions. No limits on style or subject matter. Length: 8,000-14,000 words (30-50 pages double spaced) single story; may have multiparts or be a self-contained novel segment. Send cover with title, name, address, phone; second title page with title only. Submissions are not returned; they are recycled. "Previous winners include Adria Bernardi, Doug Hornig, Christy Sheffield Sanford, Eleanor Swanson, Gregory J. Wolos and Joe Hill. SASE for most current information." Winners announced March 30, 2001. Winners notified by phone. List of winners available March 30 for SASE. "Write with richness and depth."

☑ ♥ ◎ **LOS ANGELES TIMES BOOK PRIZES**, *L.A. Times*, % Public Affairs Dept. 202 W. First St., Los Angeles CA 90012. (213)237-5775. Fax: (213)237-4609. E-mail: tom.crouch@latimes.com. Website: www.la times.com. **Contact:** Tom Crouch, administrative coordinator. Annual award. For books published between January 1 and December 31. Award: $1,000 cash prize in each of the following categories: fiction, first fiction (the Art Seidenbaum Award) and young adult fiction. In addition, the Robert Kirsch Award recognizes the body of work by a writer living in and/or writing on the American West. Entry is by nomination of juries—no external nominations or submissions are accepted. Juries appointed by the *L.A. Times*. No entry fee. "Works must have their first U.S. publication during the calendar year." Writers must be nominated by committee members. "The *Times* provides air fare and lodging in Los Angeles for the winning authors to attend the awards ceremony held in April as part of the *Los Angeles Times Festival of Books*."

N **A LOVE AFFAIR LITERARY CONTEST**, Arts Station/Abraham Baldwin College, ABAC 45, 2802 Moore Hwy., Tifton GA 31794. Website: http://www.tiftononline.com/loveaffair. **Contact:** Liz Carson, contest director. Award to "nurture the writer while celebrating the South." Annual competition for short stories. Award: $500 (total prizes). Competition receives 50 submissions. Judge: "All judged by contest director." $7 per entry. Guidelines available Fall 2000. For guidelines, send SASE or visit website. Deadline February 14, 2001. Entries should be previously unpublished. Contest open to all writers. Length: 2,500 words. "Send literary quality ficiton; a Southern theme is helpful but not required." Winners announced at May Love Affair Festival. Winners notified by mail, phone by April 1. For list of winners send SASE or visit website.

N ◎ **THE HUGH J. LUKE AWARD**, *Prairie Schooner*, 201 Andrews Hall, P.O. Box 880334, Lincoln NE 68588-0334. (402)472-0911. Fax: (402)472-9771. E-mail: eflanaga@unlnotes.unl.edu. Website: www.unl.edu/ schooner/psmain.htm. **Contact:** Hilda Raz, editor-in-chief or Erin Flanagan, managing editor. Award "an annual cash prize to honor work published in the previous year in *Prairie Schooner*, including essays, fiction and poetry." Award: $250. Judge: Competition is judged by the editorial staff of *Prairie Schooner*. No entry fee. For guidelines, send SASE or visit website. "We prefer inquiries by mail. Writers published in the past year in *Prairie Schooner* are automatically entered." Work is nominated by the editorial staff. Winners announced in the Spring issue. Winners notified by mail in February or March.

N ⊕ ◎ **MAIL ON SUNDAY/JOHN LLEWELLYN RHYS PRIZE**, *The Mail On Sunday*, % Book Trust, Book House, 45 E. Hill, London, SW18 2QZ England. Phone: 020-856-2973/2. Fax: 020-8516-2978. E-mail: sandra@booktrust.org.uk or tarryn@booktrust.org.uk. Website: www.booktrust.org.uk. **Contact:** Sandra Vince, prizes manager or Tarryn McKay, prizes assistant. "The prize was set up by Jane Oliver, the widow of John Lewellyn Rhys, a young writer killed in action in World War II. It is awarded to a writer under the age of 35 and brings to light new and exciting talent." Annual award for short stories, novels, nonfiction and poetry. £500 to shortlist authors and £5,000 to winner. Number of submissions. No entry fee. "For 2001 guidelines either request direct from Book Trust, or ask publisher to contact us." Accepts inquiries by fax, e-mail, phone and post. Entries should be published during year preceding award. Open to any author who is British or Commonwealth citizen. Writers may submit their own fiction only if it is published. Publishers will be notified of winners. List of winners should be in the papers, or contact us for a press release.

☑ ⊕ ○ ◎ **THE MARTEN BEQUEST TRAVELLING SCHOLARSHIP**, Arts Management Pty. Ltd., Station House Rawson Place, 790 George St., Sydney NSW 2000 Australia. Phone: +61-2-9212-5066. Fax: +61-2-9211-7762. E-mail: claudia@artsmanagement.com.au. **Contact:** Claudia Crosariol, associate director, artists and projects. "The Marten Bequest is intended to augment a scholar's own resources towards affording him or her a cultural education by means of a travelling scholarship, to be awarded to one or more applicants who fulfill the required conditions and who are of outstanding ability and promise in one or more categories of the arts. The scholarships shall be used for study, maintenance and travel either in Australia or overseas. One scholarship is granted in each of nine categories which rotate in two groups on an annual basis: Instrumental Music, Painting, Singing, Prose, Poetry, Acting, Architecture, Sculpture and Ballet." 6 scholarships of $18,000.

Award: AUS $18,000 payable in two installments of $9,000 per annum. Applicants must be Australian-born, age 21-35 years at time of applying (except Ballet, 17-35 years). Competition receives 50 submissions in each category. Panel of 6 judges. Guidelines for SASE. Accepts inquiries by fax, e-mail, phone. Deadline: last Friday in October. Winners announced in March. Winners notified by phone and mail. List of winners available by SASE, fax in late March.

WALTER RUMSEY MARVIN GRANT, Ohioana Library Association, 65 S. Front St., Room 1105, Columbus OH 43215-4163. (614)466-3831. Fax: (614)728-6974. E-mail: ohioana@winslo.state.oh.us. **Contact:** Linda Hengst. "To encourage young unpublished (meaning not having a book published) writers (30 years of age or under)." Annual competition for short stories. Award: $1,000. Guidelines for SASE. Deadline: January 31. Open to unpublished authors born in Ohio or who have lived in Ohio for a minimum of five years. Must be 30 years of age or under. Up to six pieces of prose may be submitted; maximum 60 pages, minimum 10 pages.

MASSACHUSETTS CULTURAL COUNCIL ARTIST GRANTS PROGRAM, Massachusetts Cultural Council, 120 Boylston St., Boston MA 02116-4600. (617)727-3668. Fax: (617)727-0044. E-mail: mcc@art.state.ma.us. Website: www.massculturalcouncil.org. **Contact:** Michael Brady, program officer for artists. Award: "The Artist Grants Program provides direct support to artists in recognition of exceptional work." Biannual competition for short stories and novels. Award: artist grant $12,500; finalist $1,000. Competition receives 395 fiction submissions. Judge: "The MCC convenes independent peer panels to review applications. The panels are composed of artists and arts professionals representing diverse stylistic perspectives. The review process is anonymous." No entry fee. Guidelines available fall 2001 (for 2002 competition). For guidelines, fax, e-mail or visit website. Accepts inquiries by fax, e-mail, phone. Deadline December 2001 (for 2002 competition). Contest open to Massachusetts residents only, 18 years or older; must be legal resident for the last two years at the time of application. Recipients and finalist must be resident of Massachusetts at the time grants are awarded (June 2002). Length: 30 pages or fewer. "The Artist Grants Program is highly competitive. Submit your strongest work—you do not need to submit a work-in-progress." Winners announced June 2002. Winners notified by mail, phone. For list of winners visit website.

MASTERS LITERARY AWARD, Center Press, P.O. Box 17897, Encino CA 91416-7897. Website: members.xoom.com/centerpress. "One yearly Grand Prize of $1,000, and four quarterly awards of 'Honorable Mention' each in 1) fiction; 2) poetry and song lyrics; and 3) nonfiction." Judges: Gabriella Stone, Scott A. Sonders and Sandra Gilbert. $15 entry fee. Awards are given on March 15, June 15, September 15 and December 15. Any submission received prior to an award date is eligible for the subsequent award. Submissions accepted throughout the year. Fiction and nonfiction must be no more than 20 pages (5,000 words); poetry no more than 150 lines. All entries must be in the English language. #10 SASE required for guidelines. "Be persistant, be consistent, be professional."

THE JOHN H. McGINNIS MEMORIAL AWARD, *Southwest Review*, P.O. Box 750374, 307 Fondren Library West, Southern Methodist University, Dallas TX 75275-0374. (214)768-1037. **Contact:** Elizabeth Mills, senior editor. Annual awards (fiction and nonfiction). Stories or essays must have been published in the *Southwest Review* prior to the announcement of the award. Awards: $1,000. Pieces are not submitted directly for the award but for publication in the magazine.

JENNY McKEAN MOORE WRITER IN WASHINGTON, Jenny McKean Moore Fund & The George Washington University, Dept. of English, George Washington University, Washington DC 20052. (202)994-6180. Fax: (202)994-7915. **Contact:** D. McAleavey, professor of English. Annual award "of a teaching residency for a different genre each year." Award: $46,000 and an "attractive benefits package." Receives 200 submissions. Judges: George Washington University English faculty and members of the J.M. Moore Fund. Guidelines for SASE. Deadline: November 15. Previously published submissions. Winners announced in February. Winners notified by phone.

MID-LIST PRESS FIRST SERIES AWARD FOR SHORT FICTION, Mid-List Press, 4324-12th Ave. South, Minneapolis MN 55407-3218. (612)822-3733. Fax: (612)823-8387. E-mail: guide@midlist.org. Website: www.midlist.org. **Contact:** Lane Stiles, senior editor. To encourage and nurture short fiction writers who have never published a collection of fiction. Annual competition for fiction collections. Award: $1,000 advance and publication. Competition receives 300 submissions. Judges: manuscript readers and the editors of Mid-List Press. $20 entry fee. Guidelines available in September for SASE or on website. Deadline: July 1. Previously published or unpublished submissions. Word length: 50,000 words minimum. "Application forms and guidelines are available for a #10 SASE or visit our website." Winners announced in January. Winners notified by phone and mail in January. For a list of winners, send SASE or visit website.

○ **MID-LIST PRESS FIRST SERIES AWARD FOR THE NOVEL**, Mid-List Press, 4324-12th Ave. South, Minneapolis MN 55407-3218. (612)822-3733. Fax: (612)823-8387. E-mail: guide@midlist.org. Website: www.m idlist.org. **Contact:** Lane Stiles, senior editor. To encourage and nurture first-time novelists. Annual competition for novels. Award: $1,000 advance and publication. Competition receives approximately 500 submissions. Judges: manuscript readers and the editors of Mid-List Press. $20 entry fee. Guidelines available for SASE or on website. Deadline: February 1. Unpublished submissions. Word length: minimum 50,000 words. "Application forms and guidelines are available for a #10 SASE, or visit our website." Winners announced in July. Winners notified by phone and mail. Winners' list published in *Poets & Writers* and *AWP Chronicle*; also available by SASE, e-mail or on website.

☑ ○ **MILKWEED EDITIONS NATIONAL FICTION PRIZE**, Milkweed Editions, 1011 Washington Ave. S., Suite 300, Minneapolis MN 55415-1246. (612)332-3192. Fax: (612)215-2550. E-mail: editor@milkweed .org. Website: www.milkweed.org. **Contact:** Emilie Buchwald, publisher. Annual award for a novel, a short story collection, one or more novellas, or a combination of short stories and novellas. Award: $7,500 cash advance as part of any royalties agreed upon at the time of acceptance. Contest receives 3-5000 submissions per category. Judged by Milkweed Editions. Guidelines available for SASE or check website. Accepts inquiries by e-mail and phone. "Please look at previous winners: *The Empress of One*, by Faith Sullivan; *Falling Dark*, by Tim Tharp; *Montana 1948*, by Larry Watson; and *Aquaboogie*, by Susan Straight—this is the caliber of fiction we are searching for. Catalog available for $1.50 postage, if people need a sense of our list."

○ ◎ **MILKWEED EDITIONS PRIZE FOR CHILDREN'S LITERATURE**, Milkweed Editions, 430 First Ave. N., Suite 400, Minneapolis MN 55401. (612)332-3192. Fax: (612)215-2350. Website: www.milkweed.o rg. **Contact:** Emilie Buchwald, publisher. "Our goal is to encourage writers to create books for the important age range of middle readers." Annual award for novels for children ages 8 to 12. The Milkweed prize will be awarded to the best work for children ages 8 to 12 that Milkweed accepts for publication during each calendar year by a writer not previously published by Milkweed. The winner will receive $10,000 cash advance as a part of any royalties agreed upon at the time of acceptance. There is no deadline. Judges: Milkweed Editions. Guidelines for SASE. Unpublished in book form. Page length: 150-300 pages. "Send for guidelines for children's literature and check our website to review previous winners. Winners notified upon acceptance for publication."

☑ ⊕ ○ ◎ **MIND BOOK OF THE YEAR**, Granta House, 15-19 Broadway, London E15 4BQ England. **Contact:** Ms. A. Brackx. "To award a prize to the work of fiction or nonfiction which outstandingly furthers public understanding of the causes, experience or treatment of mental health problems." Annual competition for novels and works of nonfiction. Award: £1,000. Competition receives approximately 50-100 submissions. Judges: A panel drawn from MIND's Council of Management. Deadline: December. Author's nomination is accepted. All books must be published in English in the UK.

Ⓝ ◎ **MINNESOTA STATE ARTS BOARD/ARTIST ASSISTANCE FELLOWSHIP**, Park Square Court, 400 Sibley St., Suite 200, St. Paul MN 55101-1928. (612)215-1600. Fax: (612)215-1602. **Contact:** Amy Frimpong, artist assistance program associate. "To provide support and recognition to Minnesota's outstanding literary artists." Annual award for fiction writers, creative nonfiction writers and poets. Award: up to $8,000. Competition receives approximately 150 submissions/year. Deadline: October. Previously published or unpublished submissions. Send request or call the above number for application guidelines. *Minnesota residents only.*

☑ ◎ **MINNESOTA VOICES PROJECT**, New Rivers Press, 420 N. Fifth St., #1180, Minneapolis MN 55401. (612)339-7114. E-mail: contact@newriverspress.org. Website: www.newriverspress.org. **Contact:** Eric Braun, editor. Annual award "to foster and encourage new and emerging regional writers of short fiction, novellas, personal essays and poetry." Requires entry form. Awards: $1,000 to each author published in the series plus "a generous royalty agreement if book goes into second printing." Competition receives 80-100 submissions. No entry fee. Guidelines available in January for SASE, e-mail, or visit website. Accepts queries by e-mail. Deadline: April 1. Restricted to new and emerging writers residing in Minnesota. Winners announced October. Winners notified by mail. List of winners available for SASE or e-mail.

☑ ***THE MISSOURI REVIEW* EDITORS' PRIZE CONTEST**, 1507 Hillcrest Hall, Columbia MO 65211. (573)882-4474. Fax: (573)884-4671. Website: www.missourireview.org. **Contact:** Hoa Ngo, managing editor. Annual competition for short stories, poetry and essays. Award: $1,500 for fiction and poetry, $1,000 for essay and publication in *The Missouri Review*. Competition receives more than 1,000 submissions. Judges: *The Missouri Review* editors. $15 entry fee (checks payable to *The Missouri Review*). Each fee entitles entrant to a one-year subscription to *The Missouri Review*, an extension of a current subscription, or a gift subscription. Guidelines available June for SASE. Deadline: October 15. Outside of envelope should be marked "Fiction," "Essay," or "Poetry." Enclose an index card with author's name, address, and telephone number in the left corner and, for fiction and essay entries only, the work's title in the center. Entries must be previously unpublished and will not be returned. Page length restrictions: 25 typed, double-spaced, for fiction and essays, 10 for poetry. Winners announced in January. Winners notified by phone and mail. List of winners available for SASE. "Send fully realized stories with a distinctive voice, style and subject."

◻ MODEST CONTEST, *New Stone Circle,* 1185 E. 1900 North Rd., White Heath IL 61884. (217)762-5801. **Contact:** Mary Lucille Hays, fiction editor. Award "to encourage good writing." Annual competition for short stories. Awards: $100 (1st Prize). All contestants receive a copy of the contest issue. Competition receives approximately 100 submissions. Judge: Mary Hays. Entry fee $10. Guidelines for SASE. Deadline: June 1. Unpublished submissions. Winners announced in September. Winners notified by mail.

◎ MONEY FOR WOMEN, Money for Women/Barbara Deming Memorial Fund, Inc., Box 630125, Bronx NY 10463. **Contact:** Susan Pliner, administrator. "Small grants to individual feminists in the arts." Biannual competition. Award: $500-1,000. Competition receives approximately 150 submissions. Judges: Board of Directors. Guidelines for SASE. Deadline: December 31, June 30. Limited to US and Canadian citizens. Word length: 25 pages. May submit own fiction. "Only for feminists in the arts." Winners announced five months after deadline. Winners notified by mail.

[N] MOONLIGHT & MAGNOLIA FICTION WRITING CONTEST: SF, F, H, Genre Writing Program, P.O. Box 180489, Richland MS 39218-0489. (601)932-6670. E-mail: hoover59@aol.com. **Contact:** K. Mark Hoover, contest administrator. This annual award for short stories recognizes and encourages new and unpublished writers throughout the South while rewarding excellence in genre writing. Award: $250 (1st prize); $100 (2nd prize); $50 (3rd prize); top ten finalists receive certificates suitable for framing. Entries must be in competition format. Judges: This year James Van Pett; changes annually. Entry fees $7.50/story; $2.50/additional entry. Guidelines presently available through October 31. Guidelines for SASE or by e-mail. Accepts inquiries by e-mail. Deadline: October 31, 2001. Open to unpublished writers and those who have not published more than 2 stories in a nationally-distributed publication with a circulation over 5,000. Length: 10,000 words. "We are open to multiple submissions, but please send only your best work. Southern writers are encouraged to participate, but the contest is world-wide. Regional contestants will not be given preference during judging." Winners will be announced January 31, 2002. Winners will be notified by mail, phone, or e-mail. For list of winners, send SASE.

[N] ⊕ BRIAN MOORE SHORT STORY AWARDS, Creative Writers' Network, 15 Church St., Belfast, BT1 1PG Northern Ireland. Phone: (44) 028-90312361. Fax: (44) 028-90434669. E-mail: mmooney.cwn@virgin. net. **Contact:** Martin Mooney, development officer. This annual award is to promote short story form. Award: £500 (first prize). Judge: Established Irish fiction writer. Entry fee £5/1st story, £4/2nd story. Guidelines available May 2001. For guidelines send SASE or e-mail. Accepts inquiries by fax, e-mail, and phone. Deadline: Mid-September 2001. Entries should be unpublished. Contest open to any writer in English. Length: 3,500 words. Winners are announced in November 2001. For list of winners, send fax or e-mail.

◻ ◎ MYSTERY MAYHEM CONTEST, *Mystery Time*/Hutton Publications, P.O. Box 2907, Decatur IL 62524. **Contact:** Linda Hutton, editor. Award "to encourage writers to have fun writing a mystery spoof." Annual competition for short stories. Award: $10 cash and publication in *Mystery Time.* Competition receives approximately 100 submissions. Judge: Linda Hutton, editor of *Mystery Time.* No entry fee. Guidelines for SASE. Deadline: September 15 annually. Unpublished submissions. Word length: Must be one sentence of any length. "One entry per person, of one sentence which can be any length, which is the opening of a mystery spoof. Must include SASE. Entry form not required. All material must be typed. Flyer of previous years' winners available for $1 plus #10 SASE." Winners announced in October in *Mystery Time Anthology* Autumn issue.

✔ ⤵ ◻ ◎ THE NATIONAL CHAPTER OF CANADA IODE VIOLET DOWNEY BOOK AWARD, The National Chapter of Canada IODE, 254-40 Orchard View Blvd., Toronto, Ontario M4R 1B9 Canada. (416)487-4416. Fax: (416)487-4417. **Contact:** Sandra Connery, chairman, book award committee. "The award is given to a Canadian author for an English-language book suitable for children 13 years of age and under, published in Canada during the previous calendar year. Fairy tales, anthologies and books adapted from another source are not eligible." Annual competition for novels, children's literature. Award: $3,000. Competition receives 100-120 submissions. Judges: A six-member panel of judges including four National IODE officers and two non-members who are recognized specialists in the field of children's literature. Guidelines for SASE. Deadline: December 31. Previously published January 1, 2000 and December 31, 2000. "The book must have been written by a Canadian citizen and must have been published in Canada during the calendar year." Word length: Must have at least 500 words of text preferably with Canadian content.

N NATIONAL LITERISTIC CIRCLE PRIZE FOR SHORT FICTION; NLC PRIZE FOR POETRY, National Literistic Circle, 2655 Springwells, Detroit MI 48209. **Contact:** Mary Anne Lovell, submissions supervisor. Award to recognize the best in short fiction and poetry. Annual. Award: $500 short fiction; $500 poetry. Competition receives about 300 submissions per category. Judge: NLC directors. $12 each entry (for each story or for set of 3 poems). Guidelines available February 2001. For guidelines, send SASE or e-mail. Deadline July 31, 2001. Entries should be previously unpublished. Contest open to all writers. Length: no more than 5,000 words fiction; no more than 100 lines each poem. Winners announced September. Winners notified by mail. For list of winners, send SASE.

N ◎ NATIONAL OUTDOOR BOOK AWARDS, Association of Outdoor Recreation and Education and Idaho State University, P.O. Box 8128, Pocatello ID 83209. (208)282-3912. Fax: (208)282-4600. E-mail: wattron@isu.edu. Website: www.isu.edu/outdoor/bookpol.htm. **Contact:** Ron Watters, chairman. Award "honors outstanding writing and publishing in the outdoor field." Annual competition includes awards for novels and story collections. Award: Extensive national publicity, including display of all submitted titles at the International Conference on Outdoor Recreation and Education; announcement of winning titles to the media; reviews, cover scans and publisher links of winning titles on Association website; use of award medallion and logo on book covers and promotions. Competition receives from 20 to 40 submissions in "Literature" category. Judge: nationwide panel includes book reviewers, columnists, authors, academics and trade representatives. A $45 application fee should accompany each nominated title. Guidelines available April 2001. For guidelines, send fax, e-mail, visit website or call. Accepts inquiries by fax, e-mail, phone. Award nominations open in April and are due September 1st of the award year. Entries should be previously published. "Must be bound—galleys not acceptable. Must have been released after June 1 of the previous year. Contest open to authors of any nationality, but books must be in English." Length: open. Fictional works should be entered in the "Literature" category. Winners announced "early November at the International Conference on Outdoor Recreation and Education." Winners notified by mail in early November. For list of winners visit website.

○ NATIONAL WRITERS ASSOCIATION ANNUAL NOVEL WRITING CONTEST, National Writers Association, 3140 Peoria St., PMB 295, Aurora CO 80014. (303)841-0246. **Contact:** Sandy Whelchel, executive director. Annual award to "recognize and reward outstanding ability and to increase the opportunity for publication." Award: $500 (1st Prize); $300 (2nd Prize); $100 (3rd Prize). Award judged by editors and agents. $35 entry fee. Judges' evaluation sheets sent to each entry with SASE. Contest rules and entry forms available with SASE. Opens December 1. Deadline: April 1. Unpublished submissions, any genre or category. Length: 20,000-100,000 words.

○ NATIONAL WRITERS ASSOCIATION ANNUAL SHORT STORY CONTEST, National Writers Association, 3140 S. Peoria #295, Aurora CO 80014-3155. (303)841-0246. Fax: (303)751-8593. E-mail: sandywrter@aol.com. Website: www.nationalwriters.com. **Contact:** Sandy Whelchel, executive director. Annual award to encourage and recognize writing by freelancers in the short story field. Award: $200 (1st Prize); $100 (2nd Prize); $50 (3rd Prize). Competition receives 200 submissions for short story category. Opens April 1. Entry fee $15. Guidelines available in January for SASE, fax, e-mail, or on website. All entries must be postmarked by July 1. Accepts inquiries by fax, phone and e-mail. Evaluation sheets sent to each entrant if SASE provided. Unpublished submissions. Length: No more than 5,000 words. Winners announced at the NWA Summer Conference in June. Winners notified by phone or e-mail. List of winners published in *Authorship* or on website.

✓ THE NEBRASKA REVIEW AWARD IN FICTION, *The Nebraska Review*, University of Nebraska at Omaha, Omaha NE 68182-0324. (402)554-3159. E-mail: jreed@unomaha.edu. **Contact:** James Reed, managing editor. Award to "recognize short fiction of the highest possible quality." Annual competition for short stories. Award: publication plus $500. Competition receives 400-500 submissions. Judges: staff. $10 entry fee for each story submitted. Guidelines for SASE. Accepts inquiries by e-mail, phone. Deadline: November 30. Previously unpublished submissions. Length: 5,000 words. Winners announced March 15. Winners notified by phone, e-mail and/or mail in February. List of winners for SASE.

○ ◎ NESFA SCIENCE FICTION SHORT STORY CONTEST, New England Science Fiction Association, P.O. Box 809, Framingham MA 01701-0203. (617)625-2311. Fax: (617)776-3243. E-mail: info@nesfa.org. Website: www.nesfa.org. **Contact:** Suford Lewis, short story contest chair. Contest to encourage people to write science fiction and fantasy short stories. Annual competition for short stories. Award: plaque and $50 of NESFA merchandise. Competition receives 20-50 submissions. Judges: well-known, professional science fiction and fantasy writers. Contest guidelines available for SASE. Accepts inquiries by fax and e-mail. Deadline November 15. Unpublished submissions. Limited to writers who have had no fiction published. Length: 7,500 words or fewer. "Read a lot of science fiction and fantasy. Write using good grammar. Have a plot, a beginning, middle and end." Winners announced at banquet in February. Winners notified by mail. List of winners will be sent to all entrants at the end of February.

☑ ◖ ◎ **NEUSTADT INTERNATIONAL PRIZE FOR LITERATURE**, *World Literature Today*, 110 Monnet Hall, University of Oklahoma, Norman OK 73019-4033. **Contact:** Robert Con Davis-Undiano, director. Biennial award to recognize distinguished and continuing achievement in fiction, poetry or drama. Awards: $40,000, an eagle feather cast in silver, an award certificate, and a special issue of *WLT* devoted to the laureate. "We are looking for outstanding accomplishment in world literature. The Neustadt Prize is not open to application. Nominations are made only by members of the international jury, which changes for each award. Jury meetings are held in February or March of even-numbered years. Unsolicited manuscripts, whether published or unpublished, cannot be considered."

NEW MILLENNIUM WRITING AWARDS, Room S, P.O. Box 2463, Knoxville TN 37901-2463. (423)428-0389. E-mail: donwill@aol.com. Website: www.mach2.com/books. **Contact:** Don Williams, editor. Award "to promote literary excellence in contemporary fiction." Semiannual competition for short stories. Award: $1,000 plus publication in *New Millennium Writings*. Competition receives approximately 1,000 submissions. Judges: Novelists and short story writers. Entry fee: $15. Guidelines for SASE available year round and on website. Accepts inquiries by e-mail. Deadlines: June 15 and November 15. Unpublished submissions. No required word length. "Provide a bold, yet organic opening line, sustain the voice and mood throughout, tell an entertaining and vital story with a strong ending." Winners announced August and February. Winners notified by mail and phone. All entrants will receive a list of winners, plus a copy of the journal. Send letter-sized SASE with entry for list.

Ⓝ ◖ ◎ **NEW YORK STATE EDITH WHARTON CITATION OF MERIT, (State Author)**, NYS Writers Institute, Humanities 355, University at Albany, Albany NY 12222. (518)442-5620. **Contact:** Donald Faulkner, associate director. Awarded biennially to honor a New York State fiction writer for a lifetime of works of distinction. Fiction writers living in New York State are nominated by an advisory panel. Recipients receive an honorarium of $10,000 and must give two public readings a year.

☑ ◖ ◎ **JOHN NEWBERY AWARD**, American Library Association (ALA) Awards and Citations Program, Association for Library Service to Children, 50 E. Huron St., Chicago IL 60611. (312)280-2168. Fax: (312)944-7671. E-mail: alsc@ala.org. Website: www.ala.org/alsc. **Contact:** Executive Director. Annual award. Only books for children published in the US during the preceding year are eligible. Award: Medal. Entry restricted to US citizens-residents. Guidelines available February 1. Accepts inquiries by fax and e-mail. Deadline: December. Winners announced in January. Winners notified by phone. List of winners available in February on website.

◖ ◎ **96 INC'S BRUCE P. ROSSLEY LITERARY AWARDS**, 96 Inc., P.O. Box 15559, Boston MA 02215-0010. (617)267-0543. Fax: (617)262-3568. E-mail: to90inc@ici.net. **Contact:** Vera Gold, director. Award "to increase the attention for writers of merit who have received little recognition." Biennial award for short stories, novels and story collections. Award: $1,000 for the literary award and $100 for Bruce P. Rossley New Voice Award. Competition receives 400-500 submissions. Judges: Professionals in the fields of writing, journalism and publishing. Entry fee $10. Guidelines available after July 2001 for SASE. Deadline: September 30. Published or unpublished submissions. "In addition to writing, the writer's accomplishments in the fields of teaching and community service will also be considered." Open to writers from New England. Work must be nominated by "someone familiar with the writer's work." Winners announced November. Winners notified by mail early November. Winners are honored at a reception near the end of the year. List of winners available in November for #10 SASE.

☑ **NTPWA ANNUAL POETRY & FICTION CONTEST**, North Texas Professional Writers' Association, P.O. Box 563, Bedford TX 76095-0563. (817)428-2822. Fax: (817)428-2181. E-mail: through website. Website: www.startext.net/homes/prowritr. **Contact:** Elaine Lanmon. Award "to recognize and encourage previously unpublished writers." Annual competition for short stories, novels and poetry. Fiction awards: $50 (1st Prize), $25 (2nd Prize). Poetry awards: $25 (1st Prize), $10 (2nd Prize). Judges: Published writers. Entry fee: $7 fiction, $5/2 poems. Guidelines for SASE. Inquiries by fax and e-mail OK. Deadline: May 31, 2001. Unpublished submissions. Length: 20 pages (fiction); 30 lines (each poem). Winners announced July 31, 2001. List of winners available for SASE.

☑ ◖ **O! GEORGIA!, O! GEORGIA TOO! WRITING COMPETITIONS**, (formerly Southeastern Regional Writing Competitions), Humpus Bumpus, P.O. Box 1303, Roswell GA 30077-1303. (770)781-9705. Fax: (770)781-4676. E-mail: paulcossman@mindspring.com. Website: www.humpusbumpus.com. **Contact:** Paul A.

Cossman. Mission: to "identify and publish new writers in order to help them launch their writing careers." Annual competitions for adults and students (K-12th grade). Award: publication in trade paperback book sold at Humpus Bumpus Books and stores throughout Georgia. Contest receives 350-400 submissions. Entry fee: $10. Guidelines available on website or phone. Deadline: March 15. Winners announced June 30. Winners notified by mail. List of winners available. "Be original, creative and fresh. Have good character development, good imagery, (good grammar and spelling)."

☐ **THE FLANNERY O'CONNOR AWARD FOR SHORT FICTION**, The University of Georgia Press, 330 Research Dr., Athens GA 30602-4901. (706)369-6135. Fax: (706)369-6131. E-mail: mnunnell@ugapress.uga .edu. Website: www.uga.edu/ugapress. **Contact:** Margaret Nunnelley, award coordinator. Annual award "to recognize outstanding collections of short fiction. Published and unpublished authors are welcome." Award: $1,000 and publication by the University of Georgia Press. Competition receives 330 submissions. Guidelines for SASE, fax, e-mail or on website. Accepts inquiries by fax, e-mail, phone. Deadline: April 1-May 31. "Manuscripts cannot be accepted at any other time." $15 entry fee. Ms will not be returned. Winners announced in November. Winners notified by mail. List of winners for SASE, fax, e-mail or on website.

☐ **FRANK O'CONNOR FICTION AWARD**, *descant*, Dept. of English, Texas Christian University, Box 297270, Fort Worth TX 76129. (817)921-7240. **Contact:** Claudia Knott, business manager. Estab. 1979 with *descant*; earlier awarded through *Quartet*. Annual award to honor the best published fiction in *descant* for its current volume. Award: $500 prize. Competition receives 500-6,000 submissions. Judge: *descant* editor. No entry fee. Guidelines available for SASE. Deadline April 30, 2001. Winners announced August 2001. Winners notified by phone. "About 12 to 15 stories are published annually in *descant*. Winning story is selected from this group."

◪ **OHIO STATE UNIVERSITY PRESS**, 1070 Carmack Rd., Columbus OH 43210-1002. (614)292-6930. Fax: (614)292-2065. E-mail: ohiostatepress@osu.edu. Website: www.ohiostatepress.org. **Contact:** Jeanette Rivard. Estab. 1957. "Small-sized university press." Publishes "scholarly and trade books." Member of Association of American University Presses (AAUP), International Association of Scholarly Publishers (IASP) and Association of American Publishers (AAP). Publishes one annual winner of poetry contest and of short fiction prize. Guidelines available on website. Inquiries by e-mail and fax OK. Competition receives 400-500 submissions.

◎ **OHIOANA AWARD FOR CHILDREN'S LITERATURE, ALICE WOOD MEMORIAL**, Ohioana Library Association, 65 S. Front St., Room 1105, Columbus OH 43215-4163. (614)466-3831. Fax: (614)728-6974. E-mail: ohioana@winslo.state.oh.us. **Contact:** Linda Hengst, director. Competition "to honor an individual whose body of work has made, and continues to make, a significant contribution to literature for children or young adults." Annual award of $1,000. Guidelines for SASE. Inquiries by fax and e-mail OK. Deadline: December 31 prior to year award is given. "Open to authors born in Ohio or who have lived in Ohio for a minimum of five years." Winners announced in August or September. Winners notified by letter in May. Entrants can call or e-mail for winner.

◪ ◎ **OHIOANA BOOK AWARDS**, Ohioana Library Association, 65 S. Front St., Room 1105, Columbus OH 43215-4163. (614)466-3831. Fax: (614)728-6974. E-mail: ohioana@winslo.state.oh.us. **Contact:** Linda R. Hengst, director. Annual awards granted (only if the judges believe a book of sufficiently high quality has been submitted) to bring recognition to outstanding books by Ohioans or about Ohio. Five categories: Fiction, Nonfiction, Juvenile, Poetry and About Ohio or an Ohioan. Criteria: Books written or edited by a native Ohioan or resident of the state for at least 5 years; two copies of the book MUST be received by the Ohioana Library by December 31 prior to the year the award is given; literary quality of the book must be outstanding. Awards: Certificate and glass sculpture (up to 6 awards given annually). Each spring a jury considers all books received since the previous jury. Award judged by a jury selected from librarians, book reviewers, writers and other knowledgeable people. No entry forms are needed, but they are available July 1, 2000. "We will be glad to answer letters asking specific questions." Winners announced in August or September. Winners notified by mail in May.

✓ ☐ **OPEN VOICE AWARDS**, Westside YMCA—Writer's Voice, 5 W. 63rd St., New York NY 10023. (212)875-4124. Fax: (212)875-4184. E-mail: wswritersvoice@ymcanyc.org. Website: www.ymcanyc.org. **Con-**

TO RECEIVE REGULAR TIPS AND UPDATES about writing and Writer's Digest publications via e-mail, send an e-mail with "SUBSCRIBE NEWSLETTER" in the body of the message to newsletter-request@writersdigest.com

tact: David Andrews, literary manager. Competition for fiction or poetry. Award: $1,000 honorarium and featured reading. Entry fee $15. Deadline: December 31. Unpublished submissions. "Submit a maximum of 10 pages of poetry or 15 double-spaced pages of fiction." Guidelines for SASE, on website, or request via e-mail. Accepts inquiries by e-mail. All entrants notified of winners by mid-summer.

◯ **OPUS MAGNUM DISCOVERY AWARDS,** C.C.S. Entertainment Group, 433 N. Camden Dr., #600, Beverly Hills CA 90210. (310)288-1881. Fax: (310)475-0193. E-mail: awards@screenwriters.com. **Contact:** Carlos Abreu, president. Award "to discover new unpublished manuscripts." Annual competition for novels. Award: Film rights options up to $10,000. Judges: Industry professionals. Entry fee $75. Deadline: August 1 of each year. Unpublished submissions.

◯ **ORANGE BLOSSOM FICTION CONTEST,** *The Oak*, 1530 Seventh St., Rock Island IL 61201. (309)788-3980. **Contact:** Betty Mowery, editor. "To build up circulation of publication and give new authors a chance for competition and publication along with seasoned writers." Award: Subscription to *The Oak*. Competition receives approximately 75 submissions. Judges: Various editors from other publications, some published authors and previous contest winners. Entry fee six 33¢ stamps. Guidelines available after January for SASE. Word length: 500 words maximum. "May be on any subject, but avoid gore and killing of humans or animals." Deadline: April 1. Winners announced mid-July. Winners notified by mail.

[N] ⊕ ◎ **ORANGE PRIZE IN FICTION,** Orange pcs, %Book Trust, Book House, 45 East Hill, London SW18 2QZ England. (020)8516-2973/2. Fax: (020)8516-2978. E-mail: sandra@booktrust.org.uk or tarryn@book trust.org.uk. Website: www.orangeprize.com. **Contact:** Sandra Vince, prizes manager or Tarryn McKay, prizes assistant. "This award was set up to find and reward the very best in women's fiction writing." Annual competition for novels only. Award: £30,000 and a "Bessie" statue to the winner. Number of entries varies. Judges have not been confirmed for 2001. No entry fee. Guidelines available. Authors should "either request direct from Book Trust, or ask their publisher to contact us. We accept inquiries by fax, e-mail, phone and post. Entries should be previously published novels by women, all nationalities." Length: open. Publishers will be notified of winning entry. Winner should be announced in the papers "or contact us for press release."

☑ ◯ ◎ **OREGON INDIVIDUAL ARTIST FELLOWSHIP,** Oregon Arts Commission, 775 Summer St. N.E., Suite 350, Salem OR 97301-1284. (503)986-0082. Fax: (503)986-0260. E-mail: oregon.artscomm@state .or.us. Website: art.econ.state.or.us. **Contact:** Michael Faison, assistant director. "Award, in recognition of artistic excellence, enables professional artists to undertake projects to assist their professional development." Biennial competition for short stories, novels, poetry and story collections. Award: $3,000. (Please note: ten $3,000 awards are spread over 5 disciplines—literature, music/opera, media arts, dance and theatre awarded in even-numbered years.) Competition receives 150 submissions. Guidelines available after March. Judges: Peer panel from outside the state. Deadline: September 1. Competition limited to Oregon residents. Winners announced in late December. Winners notified by mail. List of winners can be requested from Oregon Arts Commission or check the website.

◎ **DOBIE PAISANO FELLOWSHIPS,** Dobie House, 702 E. Dean Keeton St., Austin TX 78705. (512)471-8542. Fax: (512)471-9997. E-mail: aslate@mail.utexas.edu. **Contact:** Audrey N. Slate, director. Annual fellowships for creative writing (includes short stories, novels and story collections). Award: 6 months residence at ranch; $1,200 monthly living stipend. Competition receives approximately 100 submissions. Judges: faculty of University of Texas and members of Texas Institute of Letters. $10 entry fee. Application and guidelines available in October on request by letter, fax or e-mail. "Open to writers with a Texas connection—native Texans, people who have lived in Texas at least two years, or writers with published work on Texas and Southwest." Deadline: January 26. Winners announced in May. Winners notified by telephone followed by mail.

☑ **THE PATERSON FICTION PRIZE,** The Poetry Center at Passaic County Community College, One College Boulevard, Paterson NJ 07505-1179. (973)684-6555. Fax: (973)684-5843. E-mail: m.gillan@pccc.cc.nj. us. Website: www.pccc.cc.nj.us/poetry. **Contact:** Maria Mazziotti Gillan, director. Award to "encourage recognition of high-quality writing." Annual competition for books of short stories and novels. Award: $1,000. Competition receives 1,000 submissions. Judge: A different one every year. Guidelines available for SASE or on website. Deadline: April 1, 2001. Winners announced in July. Winners notified by mail. For list of winners, send SASE or visit website.

☑ ◯ *PEARL* **SHORT STORY CONTEST,** *Pearl* Magazine, 3030 E. Second St., Long Beach CA 90803-5163. Phone/fax: (562)434-4523. E-mail: mjohn5150@aol.com. Website: www.pearlmag.com. **Contact:** Marilyn Johnson, fiction editor. Award to "provide a larger forum and help widen publishing opportunities for fiction writers in the small press; and to help support the continuing publication of *Pearl*." Annual competition for short stories. Award: $100, publication in *Pearl* and 10 copies. Competition receives approximately 100 submissions.

Judges: Editors of *Pearl* (Marilyn Johnson, Joan Jobe Smith, Barbara Hauk). $10 entry fee per story. Includes copy of magazine featuring winning story. Guidelines for SASE or visit website. Accepts inquiries by e-mail. Deadline: March 15. Unpublished submissions. Length: 4,000 words maximum. Include a brief biographical note and SASE for reply or return of manuscript. Accepts simultaneous submissions, but asks to be notified if story is accepted elsewhere. All submissions are considered for publication in *Pearl*. "Although we are open to all types of fiction, we look most favorably upon coherent, well-crafted narratives, containing interesting, believable characters and meaningful situations." Winners announced and notified by mail and phone in June. List of winners available for SASE, fax, e-mail or on website.

☑ ○ ◎ WILLIAM PEDEN PRIZE IN FICTION, *The Missouri Review*, 1507 Hillcrest Hall, University of Missouri, Columbia MO 65211. (573)882-4474. Website: www.missourireview.org. **Contact:** Speer Morgan, Evelyn Somers, Hoa Ngo, editors. Annual award "to honor the best short story published in *The Missouri Review* each year." Submissions are to be previously published in the volume year for which the prize is awarded. Award: $1,000. No application process; all fiction published in *MR* is automatically entered.

☑ ◢ ◎ PEN CENTER USA WEST LITERARY AWARD IN FICTION, PEN Center USA West, 672 S. LaFayette Park Place, #41, Los Angeles CA 90057. (213)365-8500. Fax: (213)365-9616. E-mail: pen@pen-usa-west.org. Website: www.pen-usa-west.org. **Contact:** Eric Chow, awards coordinator. To recognize fiction writers who live in the western United States. Annual competition for published novels and story collections. Award: $1,000, plaque, and honored at a ceremony in Los Angeles. Competition receives 125 submissions. Judges: panel of writers, booksellers, editors. $20 fee for each book submitted. Guidelines available in August for SASE, fax, e-mail or on website. Accepts inquiries by fax, phone and e-mail. Deadline: December 31. Books published between January 1 and December 31. Open only to writers living west of the Mississippi. All entries must include 4 non-returnable copies of each submission and a completed entry form. Winners announced in May. Winners notified by phone and mail. List of winners available for SASE or on website.

☑ ◎ PEN NEW ENGLAND/L.L. WINSHIP AWARD, P.O. Box 725, N. Cambridge MA 02140. (617)499-9550. Fax: (617)353-7134. E-mail: awards@pen-ne.org. Website: www.pen-ne.org. **Contact:** Mary L. Sullivan, coordinator. Award to "acknowledge and praise a work of (published 2000) fiction, nonfiction or poetry with a New England topic and setting and/or by an author whose main residence is New England." Annual competition for novels and poetry. Award: $2,500. Competition receives 150 submissions. Five judges. Guidelines available in October for SASE. Accepts inquiries by fax and e-mail. Deadline: December 15. Previously published submissions that appeared between January 1 and December 31 of the preceeding year. Winners announced mid-March. Winners will be notified through publisher or PEN-NE Executive Board member. List of winners available in April by fax or phone.

◢ ◎ PEN/BOOK-OF-THE-MONTH CLUB TRANSLATION PRIZE, PEN American Center, 568 Broadway, New York NY 10012. (212)334-1660. E-mail: jm@pen.org. **Contact:** John Morrone, awards coordinator. Award "to recognize the art of the literary translator." Annual competition for translations. Award: $3,000. Deadline: December 15. Previously published submissions within the calendar year. "Translators may be of any nationality, but book must have been published in the US and must be a book-length literary translation." Books may be submitted by publishers, agents or translators. No application form. Send three copies. "Early submissions are strongly recommended."

Ｎ ○ PENMANSHIP: A Creative Arts Calendar Contest, P.O. Box 2475, Staunton VA 24402. E-mail: penmanship@hotmail.com. **Contact:** Tameka Norris, director (submissions, awards); Sheredia Norris, assistant director (guidelines, comments, questions). Ongoing competition for poetry, short stories and photography/artwork. Award: $100 poetry, $150 short story, $250 photography/artwork (one winner in each category); winner also receives contributor copy and certificate of notability. $10 fee per entry. For guidelines, send SASE. Deadline: September 1, 2001. Entries may be unpublished or previously published. *Penmanship* accepts first, one-time and second serial (reprint) rights. Contest open to all artists. Winners list for SASE and published in calendar and online.

◖ ◎ PEN/NORMA KLEIN AWARD, PEN American Center, 568 Broadway, New York NY 10012. (212)334-1660. E-mail: jm@pen.org. **Contact:** John Morrone, award director. "Established in 1990 in memory of the late PEN member and distinguished children's book author, the biennial prize recognizes an emerging voice of literary merit among American writers of children's fiction. Candidates for the award are new authors whose books (for elementary school to young adult readers) demonstrate the adventuresome and innovative spirit that characterizes the best children's literature and Norma Klein's own work (but need not resemble her novels stylistically)." Award: $3,000. Judges: a panel of three distinguished children's authors. Guidelines for SASE. Previously published submissions. Writer must be nominated by other authors or editors of children's books. Next award: 2001.

◎ **PEW FELLOWSHIP IN THE ARTS, The University of the Arts**, 230 S. Broad St., Suite 1003, Philadelphia PA 19102. (215)875-2285. Fax: (215)875-2276. E-mail: pewarts@mindspring.com. Website: www.p ewarts.org. **Contact:** Melissa Franklin, director. Program Assistant: Christine Miller. "The Pew Fellowships in the Arts provides financial support directly to artists so that they may have the opportunity to dedicate themselves wholly to the development of their artwork for up to two years. A goal of the Pew Fellowships in the Arts is to provide such support at a critical juncture in an artist's career, when a concentration on artistic development and exploration is most likely to contribute to personal and professional growth." Annual fellowship is awarded in three of 12 fields. The 2001 awards will be in fiction and creative nonfiction, media arts, and photography and works on paper. Award: up to 12 $50,000 fellowships/year. Competition receives 100-200 submisions per category. Judges: a panel of artists and arts professionals. Application and guidelines available in late August for SASE. Accepts inquiries by SASE, fax, e-mail, phone, website. Limited to 2 year or longer residents of Bucks, Chester, Delaware, Montgomery or Philadelphia counties who are 25 years of age or older. Winners announced June 2001. Winners notified by mail. List of winners will be mailed to entrants.

N: MARY ANN PFENNINGER LITERARY AWARD, GEM Literary, 4717 Poe Rd., Medina OH 44256-9745. (330)725-8807. Fax: (330)725-8763. E-mail: gemlit@earthlink.net. Website: www.gembooks.com. **Contact:** Larua Weber, acquisitions. Award to "honor unpublished authors in memory of the founder of the company and an author." Annual award for novels or story collections. Award: literary representation and cash awards for top three winners, as well as certificates for top ten. Competition receives 50 submissions per category. Judge: local and company readers give point values. Readers are assigned by genre; synopsis required. $20 entry fee plus return postage. Guidelines available July 2000. For guidelines, send SASE, e-mail or visit website. Accepts inquiries by e-mail. Deadline June 30, 2001. Entries should be unpublished but will accept self-published, or e-books. Contest open to anyone over the age of 18. Winners announced in August 2001. Winners notified by mail or webpage. For list of winners send SASE, e-mail, or visit website.

☑ ◯ ◎ **JAMES D. PHELAN AWARD**, Intersection for the Arts/The San Francisco Foundation, 446 Valencia St., San Francisco CA 94103-3415. (415)626-2787. Fax: (415)626-1636. E-mail: info@theintersection.o rg. Website: www.theintersection.org. **Contact:** Kevin B. Chen, program director. Annual award "to author of an unpublished work-in-progress of fiction (novel or short story), nonfiction prose, poetry or drama." Award: $2,000 and certificate. Competition receives more than 160 submissions. All submissions are read by three initial readers (change from year to year) who forward ten submissions each on to three judges (change from year to year). Judges are established Bay Area writers with extensive publishing and teaching histories. Rules and entry forms available after October 15 for SASE. Deadline: January 31. Unpublished submissions. Applicant must have been born in the state of California, but need not be a current resident; must be 20-35 years old. Winners announced June 15. Winners notified by letter.

☑ ◯ *POCKETS FICTION WRITING CONTEST*, *Pockets Magazine*, Upper Room Publications, P.O. Box 340004, Nashville TN 37203-0004. (615)340-7333. Fax: (615)340-7267. (Do not send submissions via fax.) E-mail: pockets@upperroom.org. Website: www.upperroom.org/pockets. **Contact:** Patricia McIntyre, editorial assistant. The purpose of the contest is to "find new freelance writers for the magazine." Annual competition for short stories. Award: $1,000 and publication. Competition receives 600 submissions. Judged by *Pockets* editors and editors of other Upper Room publications. Guidelines available upon request and SASE or on website. Accepts inquiries by e-mail and fax. Submissions must be postmarked between March 1 and August 15. Deadline August 15, 2001. Former winners may not enter. Unpublished submissions. Word length: 1,000-1,600 words. "No historical fiction or fantasy." Winner announced November 1. Winner notified by mail.

◯ ☑ **KATHERINE ANNE PORTER PRIZE FOR FICTION**, *Nimrod International Journal of Prose and Poetry*, University of Tulsa, 600 S. College, Tulsa OK 74104. (918)631-3080. E-mail: nimrod@utulsa.edu. Website: www.utulsa.edu/nimrod. **Contact:** Michelle McRuiz, associate editor. "To award promising writers and to increase the quality of manuscripts submitted to *Nimrod*." Annual award for short stories. Award: $2,000 (1st Prize), $1,000 (2nd Prize) plus publication and two contributors copies. Competition receives approximately 500 entries/year. Judge varies each year. Past judges: Ron Carlson, Anita Shreve, Mark Doty, Gordon Lish, George Garrett, Toby Olson, John Leonard and Gladys Swan. $20 entry fee. Guidelines available after January for #10 SASE. Deadline: April 20. Previously unpublished manuscripts. Length: 7,500 words maximum. "Must be typed, double-spaced. Our contest is judged anonymously, so we ask that writers take their names off of their manuscripts. Include a cover sheet containing your name, full address, phone and the title of your work. Include a SASE for notification of the results. We encourage writers to read *Nimrod* before submission to discern whether or not their work is compatible with the style of our journal. Single issues are $10 (book rate postage included)." Winners announced in June. Winners notified by phone. List of winners available for SASE with entry.

N **◎** *PRAIRIE SCHOONER* **READERS' CHOICE AWARDS**, *Prairie Schooner*, 201 Andrews Hall, P.O. Box 880334, Lincoln NE 68588-0334. (402)472-0911. Fax: (402)472-9771. E-mail: eflanaga@unlnotes.unl.edu. Website: www.unl.edu/schooner/psmain.htm. **Contact:** Hilda Raz, editor-in-chief or Erin Flanagan, managing editor. Awards to "honor work published the previous year in *Prairie Schooner*, including poetry, essays and fiction." Award: $250 each. "We usually award 6-12 of these." Judge: the editorial staff of *Prairie Schooner*. No entry fee. For guidelines, send SASE or visit website. "We prefer inquiries by mail. Writers published in the past year in *Prairie Schooner* are automatically entered." Work is nominated by the editorial staff. Winners announced in the Spring issue. Winners notified by mail in February or March.

◎ **PREMIO AZTLAN**, University of New Mexico, Department of English Language and Literature, Albuquerque NM 87131. **Contact:** Rudolfo Anaya. Submit entries to: Maria Teresa Márquez, Center for Southwest Research, Zimmerman Library, University of New Mexico, Albuquerque NM 87131. "National literary prize established for the purpose of encouraging and rewarding new Chicano and Chicana writers." Annual competition. Award: $2,000. Guidelines for SASE. Deadline: December 1. "New writers are those who have published no more than two books of fiction. Any writer or publisher may submit five copies of a work of fiction published in 2000. The 2000 publication may serve as the second book. The writer's current vita must accompany the materials, which will not be returned." Award will be made in the spring of 2001, and the winner will be invited to read his or her work at the University of New Mexico.

N **🌐** **MATHEW PRICHARD AWARD FOR SHORT STORY WRITING**, SAMWAW (South and Mid Wales Association of Writers), 6 Lias Cottages Porthcawl, Bridgend CF36 3RD South Wales. 01656-786531 **Contact:** Jean Barraclough, organiser. Award to "encourage writers." Annual award for short stories. Award: £2,000. Competition receives 350-400 submissions per category. Judges: two writers who are secondary adjudicators and a famous writer who is the final adjudicator, not named yet. £4 entry fee (£3 for SAMWAW members). Guidelines available August 2000. For guidelines, send SASE. Accepts inquiries by phone. Deadline: February 28, 2001. Entries should be unpublished. Contest open to all. Length: 2,500 words or fewer. Winners are announced in mid-May 2001. Winners notified by mail, phone before mid-May. For list of winners send SASE.

🍁 **✔** **◯** *PRISM INTERNATIONAL* **SHORT FICTION CONTEST**, *Prism International*, Dept. of Creative Writing, University of British Columbia, Buchanan E462-1866 Main Mall, Vancouver, British Columbia V6T 1Z1 Canada. (604)822-2514. Fax: (604)822-3616. E-mail: prism@interchange.ubc.ca. Website: www.arts.ubc.ca/prism. **Contact:** Director. Award: $2,000; five $200 runner-up prizes. Competition receives 650 submissions. Deadline: December 31 of each year. Entry fee $22 plus $5 reading fee for each story; 1 year subscription included. Guidelines available May 2000 for SASE, fax, e-mail, or visit website. Accepts inquiries by fax, phone and e-mail. Winners announced in June. Winners notified in May by phone or e-mail. List of winners available in June for SASE, e-mail or on website. "Read a fiction contest issue of *PRISM International* to see what editors are looking for. The fiction contest issue comes out each summer in July or August."

✔ **♥** **◎** **PULITZER PRIZE IN FICTION**, Columbia University, 709 Journalism Bldg., Mail Code 3865, New York NY 10027-6902. (212)854-3841. Fax: (212)854-3342. E-mail: pulitzer@www.pulitzer.org. Website: www.pulitzer.org. **Contact:** Professor Seymour Topping, administrator. Annual award for distinguished short stories, novels and story collections *first* published in U.S. in book form during the year by an American author, preferably dealing with American life. Award: $7,500 and certificate. Competition receives 200 submissions. Guidelines and entry forms available for SASE or request by phone, e-mail or on website. Accepts inquiries by fax, phone and e-mail. Deadline: Books published between January 1 and June 30 must be submitted by July 1. Books published between July 1 and October 31 must be submitted by November 1; books published between November 1 and December 31 must be submitted in galleys or page proofs by November 1. Submit 4 copies of the book, entry form, biography and photo of author and $50 handling fee. Open to American authors. Winners announced April 16. Winners notified by telegram. For list of winners, visit website.

N **◎** *PULP ETERNITY* **BEST OF THE 90s SMALL PRESS**, Anthology Series, P.O. Box 930068, Norcross GA 30003. (770)934-6598. E-mail: pulpeternity@hotmail.com. Website: www.pulpeternity.com. **Contact:** Steve Algieri, publisher. Held to "reward and feature the best in short fiction from the small press published during the 90s." One-time award for short stories. "All stories selected for this electronic anthology will receive $5 and publication. The top story, as selected by readers, will receive $500 cash." Receives 1,500 entries per category. "A panel of editors will select the 100 best stories. The readers themselves select the grand prize winners." No entry fee. Guidelines available for SASE. Accepts inquiries by e-mail. Deadline: February 15, 2001. Entries should be previously published only. "Stories must have been published online or in print from January 1, 1990 to December 31, 1999. 'Small Press' is defined as any publications paying less than .03/word for fiction and/or having less than 5,000 circulation. We will choose stories for the following genres: 1) science fiction, 2) fantasy

& magic realism, and 3) horror & crime fiction." Length: under 40,000/words. "Please visit the guidelines online for full list of qualifications, helpful tips, and submission requirements." Winners notified by mail and e-mail. For list of winners for SASE.

PUSHCART PRIZE, Pushcart Press, P.O. Box 380, Wainscott NY 11975. (516)324-9300. **Contact:** Bill Henderson, president. Annual award "to publish and recognize the best of small press literary work." Previously published submissions, short stories, poetry or essays on any subject. Must have been published during the current calendar year. Award: Publication in *Pushcart Prize: Best of the Small Presses.* Deadline: December 1. Nomination by small press publishers/editors only.

◖ QUARTERLY WEST NOVELLA COMPETITION, University of Utah, 200 S. Central Campus Dr., Room 317, Salt Lake City UT 84112-9109. (801)581-3938. Website: www.chronicle.utah.edu/QW/QW.html. **Contact:** Margot Schilpp or Lynn Kilpatrick, editors. Biennial award for novellas. Award: 2 prizes of $500 and publication in *Quarterly West.* Competition receives 300 submissions. Guidelines for SASE. Accepts inquiries by phone. Deadline: Postmarked between October 1 and December 31. Winners announced in late May. Winners notified by phone. List of winners available for SASE.

✓◖ QUINCY WRITERS GUILD ANNUAL CREATIVE WRITING CONTEST, P.O. Box 433, Quincy IL 62306-0433. (217)885-3327. E-mail: chillebr@adams.net. Website: www.quincylibrary.org/guild.htm. **Contact:** Carol Hillebrenner, treasurer. "A contest to promote new writing." Annual competition for short stories, nonfiction, poetry. Awards: Cash for 1st, 2nd, 3rd Place entries; certificates for honorable mention. Competition receives approximately 35 submissions. Judges: Writing professionals not affiliated with Quincy Writers Guild. Entry fee $4 (fiction and nonfiction, each entry); $2 (poetry each entry). "Guidelines are very important." For guidelines, send SASE, e-mail or visit website. Accepts inquiries by e-mail (preferred) or phone. Deadline: April 1, 2001. Unpublished submissions. Word length: fiction and nonfiction, 2,000 words; poetry, 3 pages maximum, any style. No entry form is required. Entries accepted after January 1. Winners announced June 2001 and at July annual meeting. Winners notified by mail in late June. List of winners available after July 2001 for SASE or by e-mail.

▣ QUOTH THE RAVEN'S SHORT STORY AND FLASH FICTION COMPETITIONS, *Quoth the Raven Literary Review,* 29 Spring St., Bristol VT 05443. (802)453-4773. E-mail: linda@quoththeraven.com. Website: www.quoththeraven.com. **Contact:** Linda Wiggin or Michael Torre, directors. "Our goal is to provide both the emerging and experienced writers of poetry and fiction an opportunity for recognition and wide exposure. The online format of the magazine has the advantage over the small literary publications in that it reaches a worldwide audience." Annual competition for short stories. Award: First prize, $400 plus publication; second prize, $125; third prize, $50. Competition receives 50-200 submissions per category. Judge: Michael Torre and Linda Wiggin. There may be a guest judge for one of the contests. $12 entry fee. Guidelines available Fall 2000. For guidelines, visit website. Accepts inquiries by e-mail, phone. Entries should be unpublished. Contest open to writers over 18. Length: short story (less than 6,000 words); flash fiction (less than 1,000 words). "What is most important is good, sound writing. Any genre is acceptable. However we are looking for work that appeals to a wide range of readers. Poetry that shows an appreciation of the innovative use of language and traditional styles has the advantage. A touch of humor helps. Also read some of our previous winners." Winners announced 6 weeks after deadline. Winners notified by mail, phone 3-4 weeks after deadline. For list of winners send SASE.

▣ DAVID RAFFELOCK AWARD FOR PUBLISHING EXCELLENCE, National Writers Assn., 3140 S. Peoria #295, Aurora CO 80014. (303)841-0246. Fax: (303)841-2607. E-mail: sandywrter@aol.com. Website: www.nationalwriters.com. **Contact:** Sandy Whelchel, executive director. Award to "assist published authors in marketing their works and promoting them." Annual award for novels, story collections. Award: $5,000 value promotional tour and services of a publicist. Judges: publishers and agents. $100 entry fee. Guidelines available. For guidelines, send SASE, e-mail or visit website. Accepts inquiries by fax, e-mail, phone. Deadline May 1, 2001. Entries should be previously published. Contest open to anyone with a published book in the English language. Winners are announced in June 2001 at the June NWAF Conference. Winners notified by mail or phone. For list of winners send SASE or visit website.

✓◖◎ SIR WALTER RALEIGH AWARD, North Carolina Literary and Historical Association, 4611 Mail Service Center., Raleigh NC 27699-4610. (919)733-9375. **Contact:** Jerry C. Cashion, awards coordinator. "To promote among the people of North Carolina an interest in their own literature." Annual award for novels. Award: Statue of Sir Walter Raleigh. Competition receives 8-12 submissions. Judges: University English and history professors. Guidelines available in August for SASE. Accepts inquiries by fax. Deadline: July 15, 2001. Book must be an original work published during the 12 months ending June 30 of the year for which the award is given. Writer must be a legal or physical resident of North Carolina for the three years preceding the close of the contest period. Authors or publishers may submit 3 copies of their book to the above address. Winners announced November. Winners notified by mail. List of winners available for SASE.

◎ **THE REA AWARD FOR THE SHORT STORY**, Dungannon Foundation, 53 W. Church Hill Rd., Washington CT 06794. (860)868-9455. **Contact:** Elizabeth Rea, president. Annual award for "a writer who has made a significant contribution to the short story form." Award: $30,000. Judges: 3 jurors. Work must be nominated by the jury. Award announced in spring annually. "This award cannot be applied for."

N ⊕ **REAL WRITERS SHORT STORY COMPETITION**, Real Writers Support and Appraisal Services for Aspiring Writers, P.O. Box 170, Chesterfield, Derbyshire, S40 1FE United Kingdom. Phone: (+44)01246-238492. Fax: (+44)01246-238492. E-mail: realwrtrs@aol.com. Website: www.turtledesign.com/RealWriters/. **Contact:** Lynne Patrick, coordinator. Award to "provide a regular outlet for short fiction." Annual competition for short stories. Award: One prize of £1,000 ($1,500), other cash prizes decided on merit; sponsored prizes of weekend breaks, writers' workshop places and magazine subscriptions—these change annually. "We publish a winners' anthology, and runners-up are considered for publication in a leading magazine for writers." Competition receives 1,100 submissions per category. Judge: Winners selected for a shortlist by a well-known writer or personality with a writing connection. Lesley Claister, Anjéle Lambert and Colin Baker are past judges. Shortlist chosen by an experienced panel. £5 or $10 plus critique fee/entry. Guidelines available May 2001. For guidelines, send SASE, fax, e-mail, visit website or call. Accepts inquiries by fax, e-mail, phone. Deadline September 2, 2001. Entries should be unpublished. Contest open to anyone as long as the work entered is unpublished. Length: 5,000 words. Winners are announced January 2002. Winners notified by mail. For list of winners send SASE.

◖ ◎ **RHODE ISLAND STATE COUNCIL ON THE ARTS**, Individual Artist's Fellowship in Literature, 95 Cedar St., Suite 103, Providence RI 02903-1062. (401)222-3880. Fax: (401)521-1351. Website: www.RISCA.state.ri.us. **Contact:** Randall Rosenbaum, executive director. Award: $5,000; runner-up $1,000. Competition receives approximately 50 submissions. In-state panel makes recommendations to an out-of-state judge, who recommends finalist to the council. Entry forms and guidelines for SASE. Accepts inquiries by e-mail and fax. Deadline: April 1. Artists must be Rhode Island residents and not undergraduate or graduate students. "Program guidelines may change. Prospective applicants should contact RISCA prior to deadline." Winners announced in July. Winners notified by mail.

◐ ◎ **HAROLD U. RIBALOW PRIZE**, *Hadassah Magazine*, 50 W. 58th St., New York NY 10019. (212)688-0227. Fax: (212)446-9521. E-mail: hadamag@aol.com. **Contact:** Alan M. Tigay, executive editor. Estab. 1983. Annual award "for a book of fiction on a Jewish theme. Harold U. Ribalow was a noted writer and editor who devoted his time to the discovery and encouragement of young Jewish writers." Book should have been published the year preceding the award. Award: $1,000 and excerpt of book in *Hadassah Magazine*. Deadline is April of the year following publication.

✅ ◉ **THE MARY ROBERTS RINEHART FUND**, Mail Stop Number 3E4, English Dept., George Mason University Creative Writing Program, 4400 University Dr., Fairfax VA 22030-4444. (703)993-1185. E-mail: wmiller@gmu.edu. **Contact:** William Miller, director. Annual award in fiction, nonfiction, and poetry by unpublished writers (that is, no book publications, and no previously published work may be submitted to this competition). Award: Three awards, one in each category each year (about $2,000 each). Competition receives approximately 125 submissions. Guidelines for SASE or e-mail. Accepts inquiries by e-mail and phone. Deadline: November 30. Writers must be nominated by a sponsoring writer, writing teacher, editor, or agent. Winners announced in Spring. Winners notified by mail. List of winners available for SASE.

N ◎ **ROMANCE AND BEYOND CONTEST**, *Romance and Beyond Magazine*, 3527 Ambassador Caffery Parkway; PMB9, Lafayette LA 70503-5130. (318)991-9095. E-mail: RBeyond@aol.com. Website: www.RomanceandBeyond.com. **Contact:** Mary Tarver, editor. Award to "encourage excellence in speculative romantic fiction." Annual competition for short stories. Award: publication plus cash awards; $50 grand prize; $20, first in each category; $15, second; $10, third. Competition receives 30 submissions per category. Judge: "We use a detailed numerical system of judging by three judges, including editors and published authors." $10 entry fee. Guidelines available October. For guidelines, send SASE, or visit website. Accepts inquiries by e-mail. Deadline February. Entries should be previously unpublished. Contest open to all writers. Length: 10,000 words maximum. "Read our magazine." Winners announced April. Winners notified by phone and e-mail. For list of winners send SASE or visit website. All entrants will receive their scoresheets with comments.

◎ **ROTTEN ROMANCE**, Hutton Publications, P.O. Box 2907, Decatur IL 62524. **Contact:** Linda Hutton, editor. Award to "have fun writing a spoof of genre fiction." Annual competition for short stories. Award: $10 and publication. Competition receives 100 submissions. Judge: Linda Hutton, editor. Guidelines available for SASE. Deadline: Valentine's Day annually. Previously unpublished submissions. Open to anyone. Word length: no more than 1 sentence, any length. "An entry form is available, but not required. Handwritten envelopes and/or entries will be discarded; all material must be typed. SASE required with entry. Tickle your sense of humor and ally it with your best writing. Study paperback romances to get a feel for the genre." Winners announced March 1. Winners notified by mail.

SALIVAN SHORT STORY CONTEST, Salivan Enterprises, 41 Sunnydale, D.D.O., Quebec H9B 1E3 Canada. (514)683-6767. Fax: (450)668-1679. E-mail: salivan@ctrl-fz.org. Website: www.salivan.com. **Contact:** Tammy Mackenzie, contest coordinator. Award "to promote excellence in short stories and to see them published." Biannual award for short stories. Three categories include science fiction/fantasy, horror and romance. Award: 1st Place: $50 U.S. and 90-day publication on the website; 2nd and 3rd Place: 90-day publication on the website. Top 20-30 per category eligible for publication in the contest anthology. All entrants receive a judge's critique. Competition receives 150-500 entries. Judges: editors and publishers in the given genre. No entry fee. Guidelines for SASE, e-mail or on website. Accepts inquiries by fax and e-mail. Deadlines: February 28 and October 31. Submissions should be the exclusive property of the author, published or unpublished. "Only stories in science fiction/fantasy, horror or romance." Word length: 6,000 words maximum. "Know your genre and submit stories that stretch that genre." Winners announced within 3 months of deadline. Winners notified by mail, phone May 1 and January 1. List of winners available three months after deadline for SASE, e-mail, fax or on website.

THE SCARS/CC&D EDITOR'S CHOICE AWARDS, Scars Publications and Design/*Children, Churches & Daddies Magazine*. E-mail: ccandd96@pa.freei.net or ccandd96@aol.com. Website: www.yotko.com/scars. **Contact:** Janet Kuypers, editor/publisher. Award to "showcase good writing in an annual book." Annual competition for short stories. Award: publication of story/essay and one copy of book. $11 entry fee. For guidelines, e-mail or visit website. Accepts inquiries by e-mail. Deadline November. Entries may be unpublished or previously published. Contest open to anyone. Length: "We appreciate shorter works. Shorter stories, more vivid and more real storylines in writing have a good chance." Winners announced at book publication, online. Winners notified by mail when book is printed. For list of winners send SASE or e-mail.

SCIENCE FICTION WRITERS OF EARTH (SFWoE) SHORT STORY CONTEST, Science Fiction Writers of Earth, P.O. Box 121293, Fort Worth TX 76121-1293. (817)451-8674. E-mail: sfwoe@flash.net. Website: www.flash.net/~sfwoe. **Contact:** Gilbert Gordon Reis, SFWoE administrator. Purpose "to promote the art of science fiction/fantasy short story writing." Annual award for short stories. Award: $200 (1st Prize); $100 (2nd Prize); $50 (3rd Prize). First place story is published by *Altair—Magazine of Speculative Fiction*. *Altair* also pays 1¢/word to the author of the winning story on publication. Competition receives approximately 250 submissions/year. Judge: Author Edward Bryant. Entry fee $5 for first entry; $2 for additional entries. Guidelines available after November for SASE, e-mail, or print from website. Accepts inquiries by e-mail. Deadline: October 30. Submissions must be unpublished. Stories should be science fiction or fantasy, 2,000-7,500 words. "Visit our website and read in our online newsletter what the judge looks for in a good story. Contestants enjoy international competition." Winners announced January 31. Winners notified by phone, e-mail, mail. "Each contestant is mailed the contest results, judge's report, and a listing of the top ten contestants." Send separate SASE for complete list of the contest stories and contestants (or print from website).

SCRIPTAPALOOZA, Final Draft Inc., 7775 Sunset Blvd. PMB #200, Hollywood CA 90046. (323)654-5809. E-mail: info@scriptapalooza.com. Website: www.scriptapalooza.com. **Contact:** Mark Andrushko, president. Award to "discover genuine talent, regardless of writer's location, or lack of relatives in the business. We help push individuals through the 'Hollywood Door.'" Annual competition for screenwriting. Award: first prize, $2,500; 2nd prize, $1,500; third place, $500. All three winners will be considered by major production companies. All three receive software. Ten runners-up have loglines submitted to same production companies. Competition receives 1,000-2,000 submissions. Judge: Three founders of the company—Mark Andrushko, Genevieve Cibor and Kelli Bennett. $35-45 entry fee. Guidelines available now. For guidelines, send SASE, e-mail or visit website. Accepts inquiries by e-mail, phone. Deadline January 2 (earlybird deadline $35); March 1 (first deadline $40); April 15 (final deadline $45). Entries should be unpublished. Contest open to anyone 18 or older; entered screenplays may not have been previously optioned, sold or produced. No pornography accepted. Length: 80-130 pages (proper screenwriting format). Winners announced August 15. Winners notified by mail, phone. For list of winners visit website.

SCRIPTAPALOOZA TV, 7775 Sunset Blvd. PMB #200, Hollywood CA 90046. (323)654-5809. E-mail: info@scriptapalooza.com. Website: www.scriptapaloozatv.com. **Contact:** Mark Andrushko, president. Award to "discover talented writers who have an interest in American television writing." Biannual competition for TV spec scripts and pilots. Award: $500 to top three winners in each category (total $1,500), plus software, production company consideration and possible pitch meetings. Competition receives 100-300 submissions in each category. Judge: Three founders of the company—Mark Andrushko, Genevieve Cibor and Kelli Bennett. $35 entry fee. Guidelines available now. For guidelines, send SASE, visit website. Accepts inquiries by e-mail, phone. Deadline May 15, 2001 and November 15, 2001. Entries should be unpublished. Contest open to any writer 18 years or older. Length: standard television format whether one hour, one-half hour or pilot. "Pilots should be fresh and new and easy to visualize. Spec scripts should be current with the shows, up-to-date storylines, characters, etc." Winners announced February 15 and August 15. Winners notified by mail, phone as soon as possible. For list of winners visit website.

7 HILLS SHORT FICTION CONTEST, Tallahassee Writers Association, P.O. Box 6996, Tallahassee FL 32314. (850)222-8731. E-mail: verna@talstar.com. Website: www.twaonline.org. **Contact:** Verna Safran, fiction chair. Competition to "stimulate good writing, to use proceeds for book donations to library and to produce a literary magazine." Annual competition for short stories. Awards: $100 (1st Prize); $75 (2nd Prize); $50 (3rd Prize); plus honorable mentions and publication. Competition receives 100-150 submissions. Judges: different each year. $10 entry fee. Guidelines available in March for SASE. Accepts inquiries by e-mail. Deadline: August 15. Unpublished submissions and not submitted elsewhere. "We want literary fiction, not genre fiction." Length: 1,500-2,000 words. Winners announced in October. Winners notified at Fall Writer's Conference and by mail. List of winners available in October for SASE.

SEVENTEEN MAGAZINE FICTION CONTEST, *Seventeen Magazine,* 850 Third Ave., New York NY 10022-6258. (212)407-9700. Fax: (212)407-9899. Website: www.seventeen.com. **Contact:** Attn: Writer's Guidelines. To honor best short fiction by a young writer. Competition receives 5,000 submissions. Guidelines for SASE. Rules published in the November issue. Contest for 13-21 year olds. Deadline: April 30. Submissions judged by a panel of outside readers, former winners and *Seventeen*'s editors. Cash awarded to winners. First-place story published in the December or January issue. Winners announced in late 2001. Winners notified by phone or mail. List of winners available in an early issue in year 2002.

FRANCES SHAW FELLOWSHIP FOR OLDER WOMEN WRITERS, The Ragdale Foundation, 1260 N. Green Bay Rd., Lake Forest IL 60045-1106. (847)234-1063. Fax: (847)234-1075. E-mail: ragdale1@aol.com. Website: www.ragdale.org. **Contact:** Sylvia Brown, director of programming and marketing. Award to "nurture and support older women writers who are just beginning to write seriously." Annual competition for short stories, novels and poetry. Award: 2 months free residency at Ragdale, plus domestic travel. Competition receives 150 submissions. Judges: a panel of four anonymous women writers. Guidelines for SASE. Accepts inquiries by fax and e-mail. Deadline: February 1. Previously unpublished submissions. Females over 55. Length: 20 pages/12 short poems. "Make your letter of application interesting, covering your desire to write and the reasons you have been thwarted to this point." Winners announced in April. Winners notified by phone.

SHORT GRAIN CONTEST, Box 1154, Regina, Saskatchewan S4P 3B4 Canada. (306)244-2828. Fax: (306)244-0255. E-mail: grain.mag@sk.sympatico.ca. Website: www.skwriter.com. ("E-mail entries not accepted.") **Contact:** Elizabeth Philips. Annual competition for postcard stories, prose poems, dramatic monologues and creative non-fiction. Awards: 3 prizes of $500 in each category. "All winners and Honourable Mentions will also receive regular payment for publication in *Grain.*" Competition receives approximately 900 submissions. Judges: Canadian writers with national and international reputations. Query first. Entry fee $22 for 2 entries in one category (includes one-year subscription); each additional entry in the same category $5. U.S. and International entries in U.S. dollars. U.S. writers add $4 U.S. postage. International writers add $6 U.S. postage. Guidelines for SASE or SAE and IRC. Deadline: January 31. Unpublished submissions. Contest entries must be either an original postcard story (a work of narrative fiction written in 500 words or less) or a prose poem (a lyric poem written as a prose paragraph or paragraphs in 500 words or less), or a dramatic monologue (a self-contained speech given by a single character in 500 words or less). Winners announced in April. Winners notified by phone, e-mail and mail. List of winners available for SASE.

SHORT, SHORT FICTION CONTEST, New England Writers, P.O. Box 483, Windsor VT 05089-0483. (802)674-2315. Fax: (802)674-5503. E-mail: newvtpoet@aol.com. Website: http://hometown.aol.com/newvtpoet/myhomepage/index.html. **Contact:** Frank Anthony, director. Competition for publication in annual *Anthology of New England Writers.* Annual competition for short stories. Award: $300. Competition receives 125 submissions. Judge: TBA. $6 entry fee. Guidelines available for SASE, e-mail or on website. Accepts inquiries by e-mail and phone. Deadline: June 15. Unpublished submissions. Length: 1,000 words maximum. "We want well-crafted stories written for an audience with high standards." Winners announced at annual N.E.W. conference in July. Winners notified by mail right after conference. List of winners available for SASE.

☑ ◑ *SIDE SHOW* **8TH SHORT STORY CONTEST**, Somersault Press, P.O. Box 1428, El Cerrito CA 94530-1428. (510)965-1250. E-mail: jisom@atdial.net. **Contact:** Shelley Anderson, editor. Award "to attract quality writers for our 300-odd page paperback fiction anthology." Awards: $200 (1st Prize); $100 (2nd Prize); $75 (3rd Prize); $5/printed page paid to all accepted writers (on publication). Competition receives 1,000 submissions. Judges: The editors of *Side Show*. $10 entry fee; year's subscription included. Leaflet available but no guidelines or restrictions on length, subject or style. For leaflet, send SASE or e-mail. Accepts inquiries by e-mail. Sample copy for $10 plus $2 postage. Multiple submissions (in same mailing envelope) encouraged (only one entry fee required for each writer). Will critique if requested. "No deadline. Book published when we accept 20-25 stories." Winners announced when book published. Winners notified before book is printed. "A story from *Side Show* was selected for inclusion in *Pushcart Prize XVIII· Best of the Small Presses.*"

N: THE JOHN SIMMONS SHORT FICTION AWARD, University of Iowa Press, 100 Kuhl House, Iowa City IA 52242-1000. (319)335-2000. Fax: (319)335-2055. Website: www.uiowa.edu/~uipress. **Contact:** Holly Carver, director. Award to "give exposure to promising writers who have not yet published a book of prose." Annual competition for story collections. Award: Publication only under Press's standard contract. Competition receives 300-400 mss. Judge: Senior Iowa Writers' Workshop members screen manuscripts; published fiction author of note makes final two selections. No entry fee. For guidelines, send SASE or visit website. Accepts inquiries by fax, phone. Deadline: Entries accepted during August and September. "Individual stories can have been previously published (as in journals) but never in *book* form." Stories must be in English language. Length: "at least 150 word-processed, double-spaced pages; 8-10 stories on average for manuscript." Winners announced January following competition. Winners notified by phone.

☑ ◎ *SKIPPING STONES* **HONOR AWARDS**, P.O. Box 3939, Eugene OR 97403-0939. (541)342-4956. Fax: (541)342-4956. E-mail: skipping@efn.org. Website: www.efn.org/~skipping. **Contact:** Arun N. Toké, executive editor. Award to "promote multicultural and/or nature awareness through creative writings for children and teens." Annual competition for short stories, novels, story collection and nonfiction. Award: honor certificates; seals; reviews; press release/publicity. Competition receives 125 submissions. Judges: "A multicultural committee of readers, reviewers and editors." $50 entry fee ($25 for small/low income publishers/self-publishers). Guidelines for SASE or e-mail. Accepts inquiries by e-mail, fax and phone. Deadline: January. Previously published submissions that appeared in print during calendar year preceding award. Writer may submit own work or can be nominated by publisher, authors or illustrators. "We seek authentic, exceptional, child/youth-friendly books that promote intercultural/international/intergenerational harmony and understanding through creative ways. Writings that come out of your own experiences/cultural understanding seem to have an edge." Winners announced in April. Winners notified through press release, personal notifications and by publishing reviews of winning titles. List of winners available for SASE, e-mail or on website.

☑ ◎ **THE BERNICE SLOTE AWARD**, *Prairie Schooner*, 201 Andrews Hall, P.O. Box 880334, Lincoln NE 68588-0334. (402)472-0911. Fax: (402)472-9771. E-mail: eflanaga@unlnotes.unl.edu. Website: www.unl.edu/schooner/psmain.htm. **Contact:** Hilda Raz, editor-in-chief or Erin Flanagan, managing editor. Award to "recognize the best work by a beginning writer published in *Prairie Schooner* in the previous year, including stories, essays and poetry." Award: $500. Judge: Competition is judged by the editorial staff of *Prairie Schooner*. No entry fee. For guidelines, send SASE, or visit website. "We prefer inquiries by mail. Writers published in the past year in *Prairie Schooner* are automatically entered." Work is nominated by the editorial staff. Winners announced in the Spring issue. Winners notified by mail in February or March.

N: ◎ SMOKY MOUNTAIN VALENTINE CONTEST, Smoky Mountain Romance Writers, 521 Woodland Dr., Clinton TN 37716-3422. (865)457-4571. Fax: (865)457-8189. E-mail: LKL77@aol.com. Website: www.smrw.org. **Contact:** Katie Lorette, contest coordinator. Award to "encourage all authors, published or unpublished, by rewarding their creativity in the romance genre." Annual competition for novels. Award: Heart pendant and certificate. Competition receives 30 submissions. Judge: First round judges are experienced critiquers and published authors; final round judges are multi-published authors. $10 entry fee. Guidelines available June. For guidelines, send SASE, e-mail or visit website. Accepts inquiries by e-mail, phone. Deadline first Saturday in December. Entries should be unpublished. Contest open to writers unpublished in book-length in past five years. Length: submit one scene (5 pages maximum). Follow guidelines closely. Know the romance market. Winners announced February 14. Winners notified by phone and e-mail. For list of winners send SASE or visit website.

☑ ◯ ◎ **KAY SNOW CONTEST**, Willamette Writers, 9045 SW Barbur Blvd., Suite 5-A, Portland OR 97219-4027. (503)452-1592. Fax: (503)452-0372. E-mail: wilwrite@teleport.com. Website: www.willamettewriters.com. **Contact:** Bill Johnson, office manager. Award "to create a showcase for writers of all fields of literature." Annual competition for short stories; also poetry (structured and nonstructured), nonfiction, juvenile and student writers and screenwriters. Award: $300 (1st Prize) in each category, second and third prizes, honorable mentions. Competition receives approximately 500 submissions. Judges: nationally-recognized writers and teachers. $15 entry fee, nonmembers; $10, members; students free. Guidelines for #10 SASE. Accepts inquiries by fax and e-mail. Deadline: May 15 postmark. Unpublished submissions. 1 poem with maximum 5 double-spaced pages per entry fee. Winners announced August. Winners notified by mail and phone. List of winners available for SASE. Prize winners will be honored at the two-day August Willamette Writers Conference. Press releases will be sent to local and national media announcing the winners, and excerpts from winning entries may appear in our newsletter.

☑ ◎ **SOUTH DAKOTA ARTS COUNCIL**, 800 Governors Dr., Pierre SD 57501-2294. (605)773-3131. **Contact:** Dennis Holub, executive director. "Individual Artist Grants are planned for the fiscal year 2002 through 2003—Artist Mentorship Grant (up to $3,000) and Artists Collaboration Grant (up to $6,000)." Guidelines available. Deadline: March 1. Grants are open only to residents of South Dakota.

[N] ◖ ◎ **SOUTHERN HEAT CONTEST**, Romance Writers of America—East Texas Chapter, P.O. Box 131322, Tyler TX 75713-1322. E-mail: j.justiss@juno.com. Website: www.home.earthlink.net/~ralsobrook/rwaet c.htm. **Contact:** Janet Justiss, contest coordinator. Competition "to bring talented unpublished writers to the attention of editors who buy the type of fiction they write—historical, contemporary, paranormal/time travel/futuristic or mainstream romance fiction." Annual award for romance novels. Award: $15 (1st Prize); $10 (2nd Prize); certificates to all finalists. Winner in each category has complete ms read by judge/editor. Competition receives 5-30 submissions per category. First round judged by published authors who provide extensive critiques. Final round judged by editors of major publishing houses (Avon, NAL, etc.). $15 entry fee. Guidelines available late fall 2000. For guidelines, send SASE, e-mail or visit website. Accepts inquiries by e-mail, phone. Deadline March 15. Entries should be unpublished. Published authors may submit entry in category in which they are not previously published. Entrants must be over 18 years of age. The contest is for romance fiction of novel length; fiction in other genres will not be judged. Length: Submit first 10 ms pages plus 5-page synopsis. "Editors like an intriguing 'hook' that is appropriate to category (historical, contemporary, single title, paranormal) and strong brief summary (synopsis). Entrant should be familiar with current published romance fiction to know what editors are looking for." Winners announced June 15. Winners notified by phone after June 15. For list of winners send SASE, e-mail, visit website.

◖ **THE SOUTHERN REVIEW/LOUISIANA STATE UNIVERSITY SHORT FICTION AWARD**, *The Southern Review*, 43 Allen Hall, Louisiana State University, Baton Rouge LA 70803-5005. (225)388-5108. Fax: (225)388-5098. E-mail: bmacon@unix1.sncc.lsu.edu. Website: www.lsu.edu/guests/wwwtsm. **Contact:** Michael Griffith, associate editor. Annual award "to recognize the best first collection of short stories by an American writer published in the United States during the past year." Award: $500. Possible campus reading. Competition receives 40-60 submissions. Judges: A committee of editors and faculty members. Guidelines available for SASE. Accepts inquiries by fax and e-mail. Deadline: January 31. Two copies to be submitted by publisher or author. Looking for "style, sense of craft, plot, in-depth characters." Winners announced summer. Winners notified by mail or phone.

[N] ⊕ **SPRING 2001 SHORT STORY COMPETITION**, Writespot Publishers International, P.O. Box 221, The Gap, Brisbane, Queensland 4061 Australia. (07)33001948. Fax: (07)33005677. E-mail: frontdesk@write rsspot.com. Website: www.writersspot.com. **Contact:** D. Murray, submission editor. Award to offer writers the opportunity to win cash prizes and the possibility of being published in an anthology of short stories. Stories selected for inclusion will be offered royalties on the sales of the publication. Awards: First Place $750, Second Place $250, Third Place $100, Editor's Choice $50. Plus up to 10 prizes of publication in anthology. Judge: a panel of 4-6 judges from our Publications Committee. $8/entry, $12/2 stories, $5 each/3 or more entries. Guidelines available July 2001. For guidelines, send SASE, fax, e-mail, visit website, or call. Accepts inquiries by fax, e-mail, phone. Deadline November 30, 2001. Entries should be unpublished. Entries must be typed, previously unpublished, and should not have previously won a prize. Length: 5,000 words or fewer. Winners are announced mid-December 2001. Winners notified by mail, phone, e-mail in mid-December 2001. For list of winners send SASE, fax, e-mail or visit website.

☑ ⊕ ◖ **STAND MAGAZINE SHORT STORY COMPETITION**, *Stand Magazine*, Haltwhistle House, George St., Newcastle upon Tyne NE4 7JL England. Annual award for short stories. Award: total £1,500 (or US $ equivalent). Entry fee $8. Guidelines and entry form on receipt of UK SAE or 2 IRCs. Deadline: May 31, 2001.

◖ ◎ **WALLACE E. STEGNER FELLOWSHIP**, Creative Writing Program, Stanford University, Stanford CA 94305-2087. (650)723-2637. Fax: (650)723-3679. E-mail: gay-pierce@forsythe.stanford.edu. Website: www. stanford.edu/dept/english/cw. **Contact:** Gay Pierce, program administrator. Annual award for short stories, novels, poetry and story collections. Five fellowships in fiction ($15,000 stipend plus required tuition of approximately $6,000). Competition receives 600 submissions. $40 entry fee. Guidelines available in June for SASE. Accepts inquiries by fax and e-mail. Deadline: December 1. For unpublished or previously published fiction writers. Residency required. Word length: 9,000 words or 40 pages. Winners announced April. Winners notified by telephone. All applicants receive notification of winners.

SUB-*TERRAIN* ANNUAL SHORT STORY CONTEST, *sub-TERRAIN Magazine*, P.O. Box 1575, Bentall Center, Vancouver, British Columbia V6C 2P7 Canada. (604)876-8710. Fax: (604)879-2667. E-mail: subter@pinc.com. Website: www.anvilpress.com. **Contact:** Brian Kaufman, managing editor. Award "to inspire writers to get down to it and struggle with a form that is condensed and difficult. To encourage clean, powerful writing." Annual award for short stories. Award: $500 and publication. Runners-up also receive publication. Competition receives 150-200 submissions. Judges: An editorial collective. Entry fee $15 for one story, $5 extra for each additional story (includes 3-issue subscription). Guidelines available in November for SASE. "Contest kicks off in November." Deadline: May 15. Unpublished submissions. Length: 2,000 words maximum. Winners announced in July issue. Winners notified by phone call and press release. "We are looking for fiction that has MOTION, that goes the distance in fewer words. Also, originality and a strong sense of voice are two main elements we look for."

TALL GRASS WRITERS GUILD LITERARY ANTHOLOGY/CONTEST, Outrider Press, 937 Patricia, Crete IL 60417-1375. (708)672-6630 or (800)933-4680 (code 03). Fax: (708)672-5820. E-mail: outriderpr@aol.com. Website: www.OutriderPress.com. **Contact:** Whitney Scott, senior editor. 2001 competition to collect diverse writings by authors of all ages, genders and orientations on the theme of romantic love: "A kiss is still a kiss." Open to poetry, short stories and creative nonfiction. Award: publication in anthology; free copy to all published contributors. $1,000 in cash prizes. Competition receives 400-600 submissions. Judges: Mark Richard Zubro (prose), Pamela Miller (poetry). Entry fee $16; $12 for members. Guidelines and entry form available for SASE. Accepts inquiries by e-mail. Deadline: February 28, 2001. Unpublished and published submissions. Word length: 2,500 words or less. Maximum 2 entries per person. Include SASE. Winners announced in July. List of winners available for SASE.

THE PETER TAYLOR PRIZE FOR THE NOVEL, Knoxville Writers Guild and University of Tennessee Press, P.O. Box 10326, Knoxville TN 37939. Website: www.knoxvillewritersguild.com. **Contact:** Brian Griffin, contest manager. Competition to identify and publish novels of high literary quality. Annual competition for novels. Award: $1,000, publication by the University of Tennessee Press, standard royalty contract. Runners-up will be considered for publication. Competition receives 600 (estimate) submissions. Entries are read and judged anonymously. The judge for 2000 was the novelist George Garrett. Doris Betts will judge in 2001. $20 entry fee. Guidelines available October. For guidelines, send SASE or visit website. Deadline April 30. Entries should be unpublished. Contest open to both published and unpublished novelists. Any US resident writing in English may enter. Length: 40,000 words minimum. "Write fiction that matters, that will always matter." Winners announced in November. Winners notified by mail and phone in September. For list of winners send SASE or visit website.

TENNESSEE ARTS COMMISSION LITERARY FELLOWSHIP, 401 Charlotte Ave., Nashville TN 37243-0780. (615)741-1701. Fax: (615)741-8559. E-mail: dadkins@mail.state.tn.us. **Contact:** Dennis Adkins, communications coordinator. Award to "honor promising writers." Annual award for fiction or poetry. Award: $5,000. Competition receives approximately 30 submissions. Judges are out-of-state jurors. Previously published and unpublished submissions. Writers must be previously published writers and residents of Tennessee. Length: 15 ms pages. Write for guidelines. Accepts inquiries by fax and e-mail. This year's award is for prose.

TEXAS INSTITUTE OF LETTERS ANNUAL AWARD, Texas Institute of Letters, Center for the Study of the Southwest, Southwest Texas State University, San Marcos TX 78666. (512)245-2232. Fax: (512)245-7462. E-mail: mb13@swt.edu. Website: www.English.swt.edu/css/TIL/rules.htm. **Contact:** Dr. Mark Busby, secretary. Award to recognize writers of Texas literature. Annual competition for short stories and novels. Award: The Book Publishers of Texas Award for the best book published for children or young people ($250), The Stanley Marcus Award for the best book design ($750) and the Fred Whitehead Award for the best design of a trade book ($750), The Brazos Bookstore Short Story Award for best short story given in memory of Bill Shearer ($750), and the Natalie Ornish Poetry Award for the best book of poetry ($1,000). Judge: committees to be set up. No entry fee. Guidelines available by August on website. Accepts inquiries by fax, e-mail and phone. Deadline in January. Entries should be previously published. Each entry should be accompanied by a statement of the entrant's eligibility: birth in Texas or 2 years consecutive residence in the state at some time. A work whose subject matter substantially concerns Texas is also eligible. For list of winners, send e-mail.

✓ *TEXAS REVIEW* **PRESS BOOK COMPETITIONS**, Texas Review Press, English Department, Box 2146, Sam Houston State University, Huntsville TX 77341-2146. (409)294-1992. Fax: (409)294-1408. E-mail: eng_be m@shsu.edu. Website: shsu.edu/~eng_www/trp2.html. **Contact:** Barbara Miles, senior administrative assistant. The *Texas Review* has two annual competitions for fiction: the George Garrett Fiction Prize for a book of stories or short novel and the *Texas Review* Novella Prize for novellas. Competitions receive approximately 125 submissions. Judges: final judges are George Garrett and X. J. Kennedy. Entry fee $20. Guidelines available for SASE. Accepts inquiries by fax and e-mail. Deadline: George Garret Fiction Prize, September 15; *Texas Review* Novella Prize, October 15. Previously unpublished submissions. Word length: George Garret Fiction Prize, up to 250 pages; *Texas Review* Novella Prize, up to 150 pages. "Get your hands on previous winners and read them, but notice their diversity—we are not looking for the same thing twice." Winners announced by mail, time varies. Winners notified by phone.

✓ ◐ **THURBER HOUSE RESIDENCIES**, The Thurber House, 77 Jefferson Ave., Columbus OH 43215-3840. (614)464-1032. Fax: (614)228-7445. E-mail: thhouse@thurberhouse.org. Website: www.thurberhouse.org. **Contact:** Michael J. Rosen, literary director. "Four writers/year are chosen as writers-in-residence, one for each quarter." Award for writers of novels and story collections. Award: $6,000 stipend and housing for a quarter in the furnished third-floor apartment of James Thurber's boyhood home. Competition receives 50 submissions. Judges: Advisory panel. Guidelines available in August for SASE. To apply, send letter of interest and curriculum vitae. Deadline: December 15. "The James Thurber Writer-in-Residence will teach a class in the Creative Writing Program at The Ohio State University in either fiction, nonfiction or poetry and will offer one public reading and a short workshop for writers in the community. Significant time outside of teaching is reserved for the writer's own work-in-progress. Candidates should have published at least one book with a major publisher, in any area of fiction, nonfiction, or poetry and should possess some experience in teaching." Winners announced in March. Winners notified by mail. List of winners available in April for SASE.

✓ ◔ ◎ **THE THURBER PRIZE FOR AMERICAN HUMOR**, The Thurber House, 77 Jefferson Ave., Columbus OH 43215-3840. (614)464-1032. Fax: (614)228-7445. E-mail: thhouse@thurberhouse.org. Website: www.thurberhouse.org. **Contact:** Michael J. Rosen, literary director. Award "to give the nation's highest recognition of the art of humor writing." Biannual competition for novels and story collections. Award: $5,000; Thurber statuette. Up to 3 Honor Awards may also be conferred. Judges: Well-known members of the national arts community. Entry fee $25/title. Guidelines for SASE. Published submissions or accepted for publication in US for first time. No reprints or paperback editions of previously published books. Word length: no requirement. Primarily pictorial works such as cartoon collections are not considered. Work must be nominated by publisher.

✓ *TICKLED BY THUNDER* **ANNUAL FICTION CONTEST**, *Tickled By Thunder*, 14076-86A Ave., Surrey, British Columbia V3W 0V9 Canada. (604)591-6095. E-mail: thunder@istar.ca. Website: home.istar.ca/~thunder. **Contact:** Larry Lindner, editor. "To encourage new writers." Annual competition for short stories. Award: 50% of all fees, $150 minimum (Canadian), 1 year's (4-issue) subscription plus publication. Competition receives approximately 30 submissions. Judges: The editor and other writers. Entry fee $10 (Canadian) per entry (free for subscribers but more than one story requires $5 per entry). Guidelines available for SASE, e-mail, website. Accepts inquiries by e-mail. Deadline: February 15. Unpublished submissions. Word length: 2,000 words or less. Winners announced in May. Winners notified by mail. List of winners available for SASE.

Ⓝ **JOHN TIGGES WRITING CONTEST**, Loras College, 1450 Alta Vista, Dubuque IA 52004-0178. (319)588-7138. Fax: (319)588-7964. E-mail: lcrosset@loras.edu. Website: www.loras.edu/conted. **Contact:** Linda Crossett, director of continuing education. This annual award encourages and recognizes writers. Prizes given for fiction, nonfiction, and poetry. Awards: $100 and publication in *Julien's Journal*, Dubuque area magazine (1st prize, fiction prize); $50 (2nd prize); and $25 (3rd prize). Poetry and nonfiction receive same monetary awards. First place in both are published in Dubuque *Telegraph Herald*. Receives 25-30 fiction entries, 20-25 nonfiction entries, and 50-60 poetry entries. Judges are either faculty or graduates of Loras College English Department. Entry fee: $5/entry. Guidelines available February 1, 2001 for SASE, fax, e-mail, or phone. Accepts

**FOR EXPLANATIONS OF THESE SYMBOLS,
SEE THE INSIDE FRONT AND BACK COVERS OF THIS BOOK.**

inquiries by fax, e-mail, or phone. Deadline: April 9, 2001. Entries should be unpublished. Length: 1,500 words. Winners announced at the Sinipee Writer's Workshop, April 29, 2001. Winners notified by mail, first week in May. For list of winners send SASE.

◎ ROBERT TRAVER FLY-FISHING FICTION AWARD, *Fly Rod & Reel Magazine*, P.O. Box 370, Camden ME 04843-0370. (207)594-9544. Fax: (207)594-5144. E-mail: pguernsey@flyrodreel.com. Website: www.flyrodreel.com. **Contact:** Paul Guernsey, senior editor. "The Traver Award is given annually for a work of short fiction that embodies an implicit love of fly-fishing, respect for the sport and the natural world in which it takes place and high literary values." Award: $2,500 and publication. Competition receives approximately 200 submissions. Judges: Members of John D. Voelker Foundation and *Fly Rod & Reel* editorial staff. Accepts inquiries by fax, e-mail, phone. Deadline: March 30. Include SASE. Winners announced in late summer/early fall publication. Winners notified by mail upon publication.

✔ ◯ TROUBADOUR'S SHORT STORY CONTEST, Troubadour's Writers Group, P.O. Box 138, Woodstock IL 60098-0138. E-mail: ghstwn46@aol.com. Website: www.owc.net/~mason/troubadours.html. **Contact:** Carla Fortier, contest coordinator. Contest "for those who enjoy writing competitions and/or appreciate feedback from judges." Annual competition for short stories. Award: $75 (1st prize); $50 (2nd prize); $25 (3rd prize); each entry is given a written critique, which is returned to the author with SASE; winner are offered the opportunity to have the their stories published in *The Lantern*. Competition receives 100 submissions. Judges: published authors. $5 entry fee per story; accepts multiple entries if each is accompanied by $5 fee. Guidelines available for SASE, by e-mail or on website. Accepts inquiries by e-mail. Deadline March 1. Unpublished submissions. Length: 1,500 words maximum. "Follow the format guidelines and enter a complete story with a beginning, middle and end. No poetry, vignettes or essays." Judges look for "a well-conceived storyline that revolves around characters in conflict with themselves or others. Writing should grab reader's attention and display a vitality of language and style through a balanced use of dialogue and narrative." Winners announced before July. Winners notified by mail. For list of winners, visit website.

✔ ♡ ◎ MARK TWAIN AWARD, Missouri Association of School Librarians, 1552 Rue Riviera, Bonne Terre MO 63628-9349. Phone/fax: (573)358-1053. E-mail: masl@i1.net. Website: www.coe.missouri.edu/~mas1/. **Contact:** Frederica Coleman. Estab. 1970. Annual award to introduce children to the best of current literature for children and to stimulate reading. Award: A bronze bust of Mark Twain, created by Barbara Shanklin, a Missouri sculptor. A committee selects pre-list of the books nominated for the award; statewide reader/selectors review and rate the books, and then children throughout the state vote to choose a winner from the final list. Books must be published two years prior to nomination for the award list. Publishers may send books they wish to nominate for the list to the committee members. 1) Books should be of interest to children in grades 4 through 8; 2) written by an author living in the US; 3) of literary value which may enrich children's personal lives. Accepts inquiries by fax and e-mail. Winners announced in May. Winners notified in April by phone. List of winners available.

N UNDERGRADUATE SHORT FICTION CONTEST, Sulisa Publishing, 818 SW Third Ave., #1388, Portland OR 97204. (541)996-8033. Fax: (541)994-8024. E-mail: sulisa2@yahoo.com. **Contact:** Amy Buringrud, publisher. Competition "to assist undergraduate writers in their budding careers." Annual competition for short stories. Award: Publication in an annual anthology. Competition receives 150-300 submissions per category. Entries are judged by a panel of 10 graduate writing students. $10 entry fee. Guidelines available now. For guidelines, send SASE or e-mail. Accepts inquiries by e-mail. Deadline November 15. Entries should be previously unpublished. Contest open to any writer currently enrolled in a college or university. Length: 20 pages maximum. "Let someone you admire read your work and consider his or her opinion before submitting. Proofread well. Be confident and take a chance." Winners announced in February. Winners notified by mail. For list of winners send SASE.

N ◎ THE UNDISCOVERED WRITER, Love Designers Writers' Club, Inc., 1507 Burnham Ave., Calumet City IL 60409. (708)862-9797. E-mail: exchbook@aol.com. **Contact:** Nancy McCann, president. Award "to give unpublished writers a chance at having their stories looked at." Annual competition for novels. Two prizes are awarded. Each winner will have her ms read by an editor. "Each member of our club (reviewers of *Rendezvous*, a monthly review magazine) reads and judges. Each manuscript has at least three readers." $20 entry fee. Guidelines available Autumn 2000. For guidelines send SASE or e-mail. Accepts inquiries by e-mail, phone. Entries must be previously unpublished. Contest open to any genre as long as it has romance in it. Length: 3-page synopsis or 10 pages of beginning novel. Winners announced 2 months after close of contest. Winners notified by mail.

✔ 🌐 ◯ ◎ UPC SCIENCE FICTION AWARD, Universitat Politècnica de Catalunya Board of Trustees, gran capità 2-4, Edifici NEXUS, 08034 Barcelona Spain. Phone: 34 93 4016343. Fax: 34 93 4017766. E-mail: consell.social@upc.es. Website: www.upc.es/op/english/sciencefiction/sciencefiction.htm. **Contact:** Anna Serra, secretary. "The award is based on the desire for integral education at UPC. The literary genre of science fiction is undoubtedly the most suitable for a university such as UPC, since it unifies the concepts of science and literature." Annual award for short stories: 1,000,000 pesetas (about $10,000 US). Competition receives 140 submissions. Judges: Professors of the university and science fiction writers. Guidelines available January 2001 by mail, e-mail, fax, phone, or website. Deadline: September 14, 2001. Previously unpublished entries. Length: 70-115 pages, double-spaced, 30 lines/page, 70 characters/line. Submissions may be made in Spanish, English, Catalan or French. The author must sign his work with a pseudonym and enclose a sealed envelope with full name, a personal ID number, address and phone. The pseudonym and title of work must appear on the envelope. Winners announced December 2001. Winners notified by phone November 2001. List of winners sent to all entrants; also available by mail and on website.

VOGELSTEIN FOUNDATION GRANTS, The Ludwig Vogelstein Foundation, Inc., P.O. Box 510, Shelter Island NY 11964-0510. **Contact:** Willi Kirkham, executive director. "A small foundation awarding grants to individuals in the arts and humanities. Criteria are merit and need. No student aid given." Award $1,000-3,500 grants. Contest receives 50-100 submissions. Guidelines available between September 1 and February 1 for SASE. Deadline: Last initial A-M, April 5-16; last initial N-Z, April 17-30. Winners announced in November. Winners notified November-December by mail.

WALDEN FELLOWSHIP, Coordinated by: Extended Campus Programs, Southern Oregon University, 1250 Siskiyou Blvd., Ashland OR 97520-5038. (503)552-6901. Fax: (541)552-6047. E-mail: friendly@sou.edu. **Contact:** Brooke Friendly, arts coordinator. Award "to give Oregon writers the opportunity to pursue their work at a quiet, beautiful farm in southern Oregon." Annual competition for all types of writing. Award: 3-6 week residencies. Competition receives approximately 30 submissions. Judges: Committee judges selected by the sponsor. Guidelines for SASE. Accepts inquiries by fax and e-mail. Deadline: end of November. Oregon writers only. Word length: maximum 30 pages prose, 8-10 poems. Winners announced in January. Winners notified by mail. List of winners available for SASE.

EDWARD LEWIS WALLANT MEMORIAL BOOK AWARD, 3 Brighton Rd., West Hartford CT 06117. Sponsored by Dr. and Mrs. Irving Waltman. **Contact:** Mrs. Irving Waltman. Annual award. Memorial to Edward Lewis Wallant offering incentive and encouragement to beginning writers, for books published the year before the award is conferred in the spring. Award: $500 plus award certificate. Books may be submitted for consideration to Dr. Sanford Pinsker, Department of English, Franklin & Marshall College, P.O. Box 3003, Lancaster PA 17604-3003. Deadline: December 31. "Looking for creative work of fiction by an American which has significance for the American Jew. The novel (or collection of short stories) should preferably bear a kinship to the writing of Wallant. The award will seek out the writer who has not yet achieved literary prominence." Winners announced January-February. Winners notified by phone.

WE DARE YOU CONTEST, Saskatchewan Romance Writers, 817 Cathcart St., Winnipeg Manitoba R3R 3C1 Canada. E-mail: sask.romance.writers@home.com or judwar@hotmail.com. Website: www.members.home.net/sask.romance.writers/srw.htm. **Contact:** Judy Reynolds, contest coordinator. Award to "provide romance writers with an opportunity to be critiqued by experienced judges, with the five top entries read and ranked by Silhouette Books editor Mary-Theresa Hussey." Annual competition for novels. Award: every entry receives 3 critiques of first 25 pages; top five will be read and ranked by a Silhouette editor; first place receives $50 (Canadian), a critique of the entire manuscript and a certificate; second to 5th receive a certificate. Competition accepts a maximum of 40 submissions. Judges: three members of Saskatchewan Romance Writers. Judged on "hook, dialogue, characterization, conflict, and other essential writing elements." $15 US or $20 Canadian entry fee. Guidelines available in January for SASE. Accepts inquiries by e-mail or check website. Deadline: July 1. Previously unpublished submissions. "The contest and awards are available to romance writers. Judging is based on standards and accepted practices used in the romance genre. Writers from any geographical area are welcome." Length: submit the first 25 double-spaced pages. "Since the premise of the 'We Dare You' contest is to hook us on your story, the best tip I can offer is to give us an interesting opening that grabs us and makes us want to continue reading. Also, please read and follow the competition guidelines carefully." Winners announced in September. Winners notified by phone or e-mail. List of winners available in September for SASE or by e-mail.

WESTERN HERITAGE AWARDS, National Cowboy Hall of Fame, 1700 NE 63rd St., Oklahoma City OK 73111. (405)478-2250. Fax: (405)478-4714. **Contact:** M.J. Van Deuenter, director of publications. Annual award "to honor outstanding quality in fiction, nonfiction and art literature." Submissions are to have been published during the previous calendar year. Award: The Wrangler, a replica of a C.M. Russell Bronze.

Competition receives 350 submissions. Entry fee $35. Entry forms and rules available October 1 for SASE. Accepts inquiries by fax. Deadline: November 30. Looking for "stories that best capture the spirit of the West. Submit five actual copies of the work." Winners announced April. Winners notified by letter.

N ⊕ ◎ WHITBREAD BOOK AWARDS, Whitbread-Karen Earl Limited, 2-3 Ledbury Mews West, London W11-2AE England. Phone: (020)7243-0064. Fax: (020)7792-1220. Website: www.whitbread-bookaward s.co.uk. **Contact:** Bud McLintock, director. This annual award is for first novels, novel, biography, poetry, Whitbread children's book of the year. "Celebrating the best contemporary British writing." Awards: £3,500 per category (First novel, novel, biography, poetry, and Whitbread Children's Book of the Year); £22,500 (Whitbread Book of the Year). Receives 65 first novel entries; 110 novel entries, 90 biography entries; 70 poetry entries; and 86 Whitbread Children's Book of the Year entries. Each category has 3 judges. No entry fee. Guidelines available June 2001 for SASE. Accepts inquiries by fax and phone. Deadline: July 2001. Entries must be published in the United Kingdom and must be nominated by publishers. "Writers who have been living in the UK for the last 3 year." Winners announced January 2002. Winners notified by phone. For list of winners for SASE.

N ◎ LAURA INGALLS WILDER AWARD, American Library Association/Association for Library Service to Children, 50 E. Huron St., Chicago IL 60611. **Contact:** Executive Director. Award offered every 2 years; next award year is 2001. "To honor a significant body of work for children, for illustration, fiction or nonfiction." Award: Bronze medal. Authors must be nominated by ALSC members.

◑ ◎ WISCONSIN INSTITUTE FOR CREATIVE WRITING FELLOWSHIP, University of Wisconsin—Creative Writing, English Department, 600 N. Park St., Madison WI 53706. Website: polyglot.lss.wisc.edu/ english. **Contact:** Jesse Lee Kercheval, director. Competition "to provide time, space and an intellectual community for writers working on first books." Six annual awards for short stories, novels and story collections. Awards: $23,000/9-month appointment. Competition receives 500 submissions. Judges: English Department faculty. Guidelines available for SASE; write to Ron Kuka or check website. Deadline: February. Published or unpublished submissions. Applicants must have received an M.F.A. or comparable graduate degree in creative writing and not yet published a book. Limit 1 story up to 30 pages in length. No name on writing sample. Two letters of recommendation and vita or resume required.

◑ ◎ PAUL A. WITTY SHORT STORY AWARD, International Reading Association, P.O. Box 8139, 800 Barksdale Rd., Newark DE 19714-8139. (302)731-1600, ext. 293. Fax: (302)731-1057. E-mail: jbutler@readi ng.org. Website: www.reading.org. **Contact:** Janet Butler, public information coordinator. Annual award given to the author of an original short story published for the first time in 2000 in a periodical for children. Award: $1,000. "The short story should serve as a literary standard that encourages young readers to read periodicals." For guidelines write to: Executive Office. Deadline: December 1. Published submissions.

◑ TOBIAS WOLFF AWARD FOR FICTION, Mail Stop 9053, Western Washington University, Bellingham WA 98225. Annual competition for novel excerpts and short stories. Award: $1,000 (1st Prize); $250 (2nd Prize); $100 (3rd Prize). Judge: To be announced. Entry fee $10 for the first entry, $5/story or chapter thereafter. Guidelines for SASE. Deadline: January 4 to March 1. Unpublished submissions. Length: 10,000 words or less per story or chapter. Winner announced July. List of winners available for SASE.

N ⊕ ◎ DAVID T.K. WONG FELLOWSHIP, University of East Anglia, School of English & American Studies, Norwich, Norfolk NR4 7TJ United Kingdom. Phone: (00)44 1603 592810. Fax: (00)44 1603 507728. E-mail: v.striker@uea.ac.uk. Website: www.uea.ac.uk/eas/intro/prizes/wong/intro.htm. **Contact:** Val Striker, fellowship administrator. Annual award for short stories, novels and story collections. Award £25,000 (pounds sterling). Competition receives 120 submissions per category. Judge: by international panel nominated by various institutions including UEA's Professor of Creative Writing, biographer and Poet Laureate, Andrew Motion. £5 sterling/entry. Guidelines are currently available. For guidelines, fax, e-mail, visit website or call. Accepts inquiries by fax, e-mail, phone. Deadline October 31. Entries should be unpublished. "The Fellow will be someone of exceptional talent who plans to write in English about life in the Far East." Length: 5,000 words or fewer. Winners are announced in late March/early April 2001. Winners notified by mail or e-mail.

◎ WORLD FANTASY AWARDS, World Fantasy Awards Association, P.O. Box 43, Mukilteo WA 98275-0043. E-mail: sfexessec@aol.com. **Contact:** Peter Dennis Pautz, president. Award to "recognize excellence in fantasy literature worldwide." Annual competition for short stories, novels, story collections, anthologies, novellas and life achievement. Award: Bust of HP Lovecraft. Judge: Panel. Guidelines available for SASE. Deadline: June 30. Published submissions from previous calendar year. Word length: 10,000-40,000 novella; 10,000 short story. "All fantasy is eligible, from supernatural horror to Tolkienesque to sword and sorcery to the occult, and beyond." Winners announced November 1. List of winners available November 1.

N ⊕ **WORLD WIDE WRITERS AWARD**, Writers International Ltd., P.O. Box 3229, Bournemouth BH1 12S United Kingdom. Phone: (44)1202 716043. Fax: (44)1202 740995. E-mail: writintl@globalnet.co.uk. Website: www.worldwidewriters.com. **Contact:** John Jenkins, publisher. Award "to encourage the art of short story writing." Awards annual and bimonthly prizes (six times a year) for short stories. Annual Prizes: (Best Short Story of the Year): £3,000 ($5,000) (1st Prize); £625 ($1,000) (2nd and 3rd Prize). Prizes per issue: £625 ($1,000) (1st Prize); £315 ($500) (2nd Prize); £200 ($200) (3rd Prize). Competition receives approximately 200 submissions per month. Judge: Panel provides a short list to the editor. £6 ($10) entry fee. Guidelines available. For guidelines, send SASE, e-mail or visit website. Accepts inquiries by e-mail. Entries should be unpublished. Contest open to anyone. Length: 2,000-5,000 words. "Read *World Wide Writers*." Winners announced in every issue of *World Wide Writers*. Winners notified by mail within 3 months. For list of winners, visit website.

☑ **WORLD'S BEST SHORT-SHORT STORY CONTEST**, English Department Writing Program, Florida State University, Tallahassee FL 32306-1036. (850)644-4230. **Contact:** Mark Winegardner, director, Writing Program. Annual award for short-short stories, unpublished, maximum 300 words. Prizewinning story gets $300 and a crate of Florida oranges; winner and finalists are published in *SunDog: The Southeast Review*. Competition receives approx. 5,000 submissions. Entry fee $1. SASE for rules. Deadline: April 15. Open to all. Length: 300 words maximum. Winners are announced on May 15. Winners are notified by mail between May 15 and June 15.

N ✿ **☑** ⊚ **WRITE YOUR HEART OUT**, Ponder Publishing Inc., P.O. Box 23037, RPO McGillivray, Winnipeg, Manitoba R3T 5S3 Canada. (204)269-2985. Fax: (204)888-7159. E-mail: service@ponderpublishing.com. Website: www.ponderpublishing.com. **Contact:** Mary Barton, senior editor. "We are looking for potential Ponder Romances, and we felt the contest would be incentive for writers to pen something specifically for us since the mss do not have to be in a complete state." Awards: $500 CDN (grand prize); $100 CDN (2nd prize); and 10 consolation prizes (detailed critiques). Receives 100 entries per category. "Judged by our entire submissions team: Assistant Submissions Editors, Senior Submission Editor, and Assistant & Senior Editors." Entry fee: $10 U.S. & international; $15 Canadian. Guidelines now available for SASE, fax, e-mail or visit website. Accepts inquiries by fax and e-mail. Deadline: April 30, 2001 (midnight). Entries should be unpublished. Open to anyone with romance mss. Length: First 3 chapters and 2 page synopsis. "Read our Ponder Romances. They are unique to the romance market." Winners announced September 1, 2001. Winner notified by mail before September 1, 2001. For list of winners send SASE, e-mail or visit website.

N ⊕ **THE WRITERS BUREAU POETRY AND SHORT STORY COMPETITION**, The Writers Bureau, Sevendale House, 7 Dale St., Manchester M1 1JB England. Phone: (+44)161 228 2362. Fax: (+44)161 228 3533. E-mail: comp@writersbureau.com. Website: www.writersbureau.com/comp.html. **Contact:** Angela Cox, competition secretary. Annual competition for short stories. Award: £1,000 (1st Prize), £400 (2nd Prize), £200 (3rd Prize), £100 (4th Prize), 6 awards of £50 (5th Prize). Judge: Iain Pattison, competition adjudicator. £4 fee per entry. Guidelines available April 2001. For guidelines, send SASE, fax, e-mail, visit website or call. Accepts inquiries by fax, e-mail, phone. Deadline July 31, 2001. Entries should be unpublished. Contest open to anyone. Length: 2,000 words. Winners announced September 30, 2001. Winners notified by mail. For list of winners send SASE or visit website.

◯ **WRITER'S DIGEST ANNUAL WRITING COMPETITION, (Short Story Division)**, *Writer's Digest*, 1507 Dana Ave., Cincinnati OH 45207. (513)531-2690, ext. 328. E-mail: competitions@fwpubs.com. Website: www.writersdigest.com. **Contact:** Contest Director. Grand Prize $1,500 cash and your choice of a trip to New York City to meet with editors and agents or a trip to the 2002 Maui Writer's Conference. Other awards include cash, reference books and certificates of recognition. Names of grand prize winner and top 100 winners are announced in the November issue of *Writer's Digest*. Top entries published in booklet ($6). Send SASE to *WD* Annual Writing Competition for rules and entry form, or see January through May issues of *Writer's Digest*. Deadline: May 31. Entry fee $10 per manuscript. All entries must be original, unpublished and not previously submitted to a *Writer's Digest* contest. Length: 4,000 words maximum. No acknowledgment will be made of receipt of mss nor will mss be returned. Three of the ten writing categories target short fiction: mainstream/literary, genre and children's fiction.

WRITER'S DIGEST NATIONAL SELF-PUBLISHED BOOK AWARDS, *Writer's Digest*, 1507 Dana Ave., Cincinnati OH 45207. (513)531-2690, ext. 328. E-mail: competitions@fwpubs.com. Website: www.writersdigest.com. **Contact:** Contest Director. Award to "recognize and promote excellence in self-published books." Annual competition with 9 categories: mainstream/literary fiction; genre fiction; nonfiction; inspirational (spiritual, New Age); life stories; children's and young adult books; reference books; poetry; and cookbooks. Grand prize: $1,500 plus an ad in *Publishers Weekly* and promotion in *Writer's Digest*. Category winners receive $500 and promotion in *Writer's Digest*. Judges: Final judges are successful self-published authors and book editors. Entry fee $100 for first entry; $50 for each additional entry. Guidelines available for SASE. Deadline: December 15. Published submissions. Author must pay full cost and book must have been published in year of contest or two years prior.

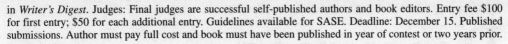 **WRITERS' JOURNAL ANNUAL FICTION CONTEST**, Val-Tech Media, P.O. Box 394, Perham MN 56573-0394. (218)346-7921. Fax: (218)346-7924. E-mail: writersjournal@wadena.net. Website: www.writer sjournal.com. **Contact:** Leon Ogroske, publisher/managing editor. Award: $50 (1st Place); $25 (2nd Place); $15 (3rd Place). Publishes prize winners and selected honorable mentions. Competition receives approximately 250 submissions/year. Entry fee $5 each. Unpublished submissions. Entry forms or rules available for SASE. Deadline: December 31 annually. Maximum length is 2,000 words. Two copies of each entry are required—one *without* name or address of writer. Winners notified by mail and list published in *Writer's Journal*.

WRITERS' JOURNAL ROMANCE CONTEST, Val-Tech Media, P.O. Box 394, Perham MN 56573-0394. (218)346-7921. Fax: (218)346-7924. E-mail: writersjournal@wadena.net. Website: www.writersjournal.c om. **Contact:** Leon Ogroske, editor. Annual competition for short stories. Award: $50 (1st Prize); $25 (2nd Prize); $15 (3rd Prize); publishes prize winers plus honorable mentions. Competition receives 350 submissions. Entry fee $5/entry. Guidelines available for SASE (4 entries/person). Deadline: July 31. Unpublished submissions. Word length: 2,000 words maximum. Winners announced in December. Winners notified by mail and winners list published in *Writers' Journal*. "Enclose #10 SASE for winner's list."

THE WRITERS' WORKSHOP INTERNATIONAL FICTION CONTEST, The Writers' Workshop, 387 Beaucatcher Rd., Asheville NC 28805. Phone/fax: (828)254-8111. **Contact:** Karen Ackerson, executive director. Annual awards for fiction. Awards: $350 (1st Prize); $250 (2nd Prize); $100 (3rd Prize). Competition receives approximately 350 submissions. Past judges have been Peter Matthiessen, Kurt Vonnegut, E.L. Doctorow. Entry fee $18/$15 members. Guidelines for SASE. Unpublished submissions. Length: 10,000 words typed, double-spaced pages per story. Multiple submissions are accepted.

Resources

Conferences & Workshops 545

Organizations 591

Publications of Interest 599

Websites of Interest 603

Canadian Writers Take Note 607

Printing & Production Terms Defined 608

Glossary 610

Category Index 613

General Index 655

Conferences & Workshops

Why are conferences so popular? Writers and conference directors alike tell us it's because writing can be such a lonely business otherwise—that at conferences writers have the opportunity to meet (and commiserate) with fellow writers, as well as meet and network with publishers, editors and agents. Conferences and workshops provide some of the best opportunities for writers to make publishing contacts and pick up valuable information on the business, as well as the craft, of writing.

The bulk of the listings in this section are for conferences. Most conferences last from one day to one week and offer a combination of workshop-type writing sessions, panel discussions, and a variety of guest speakers. Topics may include all aspects of writing from fiction to poetry to scriptwriting, or they may focus on a specific area such as those sponsored by the Romance Writers of America for writers specializing in romance or the SCBWI conferences on writing for children's books.

Workshops, however, tend to run longer—usually one to two weeks. Designed to operate like writing classes, most require writers to be prepared to work on and discuss their work-in-progress while attending. An important benefit of workshops is the opportunity they provide writers for an intensive critique of their work, often by professional writing teachers and established writers.

Each of the listings here includes information on the specific focus of an event as well as planned panels, guest speakers and workshop topics. It is important to note, however, some conference directors were still in the planning stages for 2000 when we contacted them. If it was not possible to include 2000 dates, fees or topics, we have provided information from 1999 so you can get an idea of what to expect. For the most current information, it's best to send a self-addressed, stamped envelope to the director in question about three months before the date(s) listed.

FINDING A CONFERENCE

Many writers try to make it to at least one conference a year, but cost and location count as much as subject matter or other considerations when determining which conference to attend. There are conferences in almost every state and province and even some in Europe open to North Americans.

To make it easier for you to find a conference close to home—or to find one in an exotic locale to fit into your vacation plans—we've divided this section into geographic regions. The conferences appear in alphabetical order under the appropriate regional heading.

Note that conferences appear under the regional heading according to where they will be held, which is sometimes different than the address given as the place to register or send for information. The regions are as follows:

Northeast (pages 547-555): Connecticut, Maine, Massachusetts, New Hampshire, New York, Rhode Island, Vermont

Midatlantic (pages 555-558): Washington DC, Delaware, Maryland, New Jersey, Pennsylvania

Midsouth (pages 558-560): North Carolina, South Carolina, Tennessee, Virginia, West Virginia

Southeast (pages 560-564): Alabama, Arkansas, Florida, Georgia, Louisiana, Mississippi, Puerto Rico
Midwest (pages 564-570): Illinois, Indiana, Kentucky, Michigan, Ohio
North Central (pages 570-574): Iowa, Minnesota, Nebraska, North Dakota, South Dakota, Wisconsin
South Central (pages 574-579): Colorado, Kansas, Missouri, New Mexico, Oklahoma, Texas
West (pages 579-585): Arizona, California, Hawaii, Nevada, Utah
Northwest (pages 585-587): Alaska, Idaho, Montana, Oregon, Washington, Wyoming
Canada (pages 587-589)
International (pages 589-590)

LEARNING AND NETWORKING

Besides learning from workshop leaders and panelists in formal sessions, writers at conferences also benefit from conversations with other attendees. Writers on all levels enjoy sharing insights. Often, a conversation over lunch can reveal a new market for your work or let you know which editors are most receptive to the work of new writers. You can find out about recent editor changes and about specific agents. A casual chat could lead to a new contact or resource in your area.

Many editors and agents make visiting conferences a part of their regular search for new writers. A cover letter or query that starts with "I met you at the National Writers Association Conference," or "I found your talk on your company's new romance line at the Moonlight and Magnolias Writer's Conference most interesting . . ." may give you a small leg up on the competition.

While a few writers have been successful in selling their manuscripts at a conference, the availability of editors and agents does not usually mean these folks will have the time there to read your novel or six best short stories (unless, of course, you've scheduled an individual meeting with them ahead of time). While editors and agents are glad to meet writers and discuss work in general terms, usually they don't have the time (or energy) to give an extensive critique during a conference. In other words, use the conference as a way to make a first, brief contact.

SELECTING A CONFERENCE

Besides the obvious considerations of time, place and cost, choose your conference based on your writing goals. If, for example, your goal is to improve the quality of your writing, it will be more helpful to you to choose a hands-on craft workshop rather than a conference offering a series of panels on marketing and promotion. If, on the other hand, you are a science fiction novelist who would like to meet your fans, try one of the many science fiction conferences or "cons" held throughout the country and the world.

Look for panelists and workshop instructors whose work you admire and who seem to be writing in your general area. Check for specific panels or discussions of topics relevant to what you are writing now. Think about the size—would you feel more comfortable with a small workshop of eight people or a large group of 100 or more attendees?

If your funds are limited, start by looking for conferences close to home, but you may want to explore those that offer contests with cash prizes—and a chance to recoup your expenses. A few conferences and workshops also offer scholarships, but the competition is stiff and writers interested in these should find out the requirements early. Finally, students may want to look for conferences and workshops that offer college credit. You will find these options included in the listings here. Again, send a self-addressed, stamped envelope for the most current details.

> ## For More Information
>
> For more information on conferences and even more conferences from which to choose, check the May issue of *Writer's Digest*. *The Guide to Writers Conferences* (ShawGuides, 10 W. 66th St., Suite 30H, New York NY 10023) is another helpful resource now available on the *Writer's Digest* website at www.writersdigest.com.

Northeast (CT, MA, ME, NH, NY, RI, VT)

☑ **BECOME A MORE PRODUCTIVE WRITER**, P.O. Box 1310, Boston MA 02117-1310. (617)266-1613. E-mail: marcia@yudkin.com. Website: www.yudkin.com/publish.htm. **Contact:** Marcia Yudkin, director. Estab. 1991. Workshop held approximately 3 times/year. Workshop held on one Saturday in May, October, February. Average attendance 15. "Creativity workshop for fiction writers and others. Based on latest discoveries about the creative process, participants learn to access their unconscious wisdom, find their own voice, utilize kinesthetic, visual and auditory methods of writing, and bypass longstanding blocks and obstacles. Held at a hotel in central Boston."
Costs: $149.
Accommodations: List of area hotels and bed & breakfasts provided.
Additional Information: Conference information available after August. Accepts inquiries by mail, phone, e-mail. "Audiotapes of seminar information also available."

Ⓝ THE BLUE MOUNTAIN CENTER, Blue Mountain Lake, New York NY 12812-0109. (518)352-7391.
Contact: Harriet Barlow, director. Residencies for established writers. "Provides a peaceful environment where residents may work free from distractions and demands of normal daily life." Residencies awarded for 1 month between June 19 and November 1 (approx.). For more information, send SASE for brochure.
To Apply: Send for brochure. Application deadline: February 1.

BREAD LOAF WRITERS' CONFERENCE, Middlebury College, Middlebury VT 05753. (802)443-5286. Fax: (802)443-2087. E-mail: blwc@mail.middlebury.edu. **Contact:** Carol Knauss, administrative coordinator. Estab. 1926. Annual. Conference held in late August. Conference duration: 11 days. Average attendance: 230. For fiction, nonfiction and poetry. Held at the summer campus in Ripton, Vermont (belongs to Middlebury College).
Costs: $1,780 (includes room/board) (2000).
Accommodations: Accommodations are at Ripton. Onsite accommodations $620 (2000).
Additional Information: Conference information available January 2001. Accepts inquiries by fax and e-mail.

Ⓝ CHENANGO VALLEY WRITERS' CONFERENCE, Office of Summer Programs, Colgate University, Hamilton NY 13346. (315)228-7770. Fax: (315)228-7975. Website: http://clark.colgate.edu/cvwritersconference/. **Contact:** Matt Leone, director. Estab. 1996. Annual. Conference held June 2001. Conference duration: 1 week. Average attendance: 50-60. Conference focuses on fiction, poetry and publishing. Site: Colgate University is located in Hamilton, New York. "The campus is a nationally-known jewel of intellectual achievement and physical beauty." In 2000, Kelly Cherry, Tom Sleigh, Lee Abbott, Pam Durban, Sheila Kohler and Christopher Tilghman particiapted as faculty members; and Fred Busch, Peter Balakian, Caroline Preston, Gioia Timpanelli and William Clark participated as guest speakers.
Costs: 2000: Tuition, room and board—$975; before March 1, $895. Tuition for day students—$650; before March 1 $595.
Accommodations: "We will pick up participants from local airports, train and bus stations for a $25 fee." Offers overnight accommodations. "We reside in the air-conditioned Drake Hall, one of our newest dorms."
Additional Information: "Please send in mss you wish to have workshopped before May 1. Please submit: fiction—no more than 25 pages, both story and novel; poetry—a sheaf of 4-5 poems." Conference information available mid-January 2001. For brochure send e-mail, visit website, call or fax. Accepts inquiries by e-mail, phone, fax. Agents and editors participate in conference.

insider report

Michael Collier: "Word has gotten out, Bread Loaf has a new vitality"

© Lorin Klaris Photography

Michael Collier

Over the past 75 years, the Bread Loaf Writers' Conference has included its share of literary heavyweights: Tim O'Brien, Joan Didion, Richard Ford, Eudora Welty, Walter Mosely, Carson Mc-Cullers, Rita Dove. A pretty impressive faculty list, right?

Guess again. These writers were *students* at Bread Loaf. Like many budding authors, they participated in the conference's workshops early in their careers, though some did return as teachers—not unusual, as Bread Loaf alumni tend to form lifelong bonds with the program.

"On our application form, we ask how the applicant heard about Bread Loaf," says Michael Collier, director of the conference. "Most respond by saying they don't know, because somehow they've always known about the conference. This is because Bread Loaf, unlike any other writers' conference, has the status of being an American literary institution.

"References to Bread Loaf are found in most of the biographies of major American writers," he says. "When participants attend readings in the Little Theatre, they know they are sitting in the place where W.H. Auden, Robert Frost, Willa Cather, Anne Sexton, May Sarton, Toni Morrison, Ralph Ellison, William Carlos Williams, John Irving, Joyce Carol Oates, Richard Wright, and many other great American writers once addressed similar audiences."

The oldest writers' conference in the United States, Bread Loaf was founded in 1926 at Middlebury College, also home to *The New England Review*. Since its inception, the conference has attracted hundreds of writers each August for its eleven-day program, held at the edge of the Green Mountain Forest in Ripton, Vermont on the college's auxiliary campus—a rolling expanse of fields dotted with late 19th-Century New England clapboard cottages and the conference's trademark Adirondack chairs.

Today, Bread Loaf continues to be a mecca for promising writers, thanks in large part to an extensive financial aid program that includes fellowships, scholarships, and a work-study program where writers pay their way by serving meals in the dining hall at the Bread Loaf Inn.

The conference's chief drawing card, however, is its reputation in the world of American letters. Bread Loaf boasts enough history to fill a book—and it has. *Whose Woods These Are: A History of the Bread Loaf Writers' Conference, 1926-1992*, by David Haward Bain (Ecco Press), was published in 1993 and chronicles the conference's first sixty-six years.

With more than 250 participants each year, Bread Loaf isn't only the country's most storied conference, it's also one of the largest. The program includes workshops in fiction, poetry, and nonfiction—19 in all, each made up of ten participants, a faculty member, and a fellow. Though some special guests (such as agents and editors) usually aren't able to stay the whole

12 days, at any given time the conference hosts 135 contributors (paying customers), 10 auditors, 25 waiters, 15 scholars, 15 administrative staff, 19 fellows, 19 faculty, and 20 editors, agents, publishers, and special guests.

In an effort to maintain continuity while still keeping the conference fresh, Collier seeks a balance between returning faculty members and new faces. Last year, for example, the faculty included nonfiction writers Patricia Hampl and Garret Hongo; poets Toi Derricotte, Edward Hirsch and Yusef Komunyakaa; and fiction writers Charles Baxter, Lynn Freed, David Huddle, Beverly Lowry, Antonya Nelson, Jay Parini and Helen Schulman, all of whom have previously taught at Bread Loaf. These regulars were complemented by first-timers David St. John, Randall Kenan, Michael Palmer, Barry Lopez, Susan Shreve, and Linda Gregerson.

"We hire writers who are not only distinguished, but who are also tremendously effective teachers of literary writing," says Collier. "We have also found that introducing new faculty to the conference each year helps attract applicants as well as encourages past participants to reapply."

The approach seems to be working. In the past two years, applications are up more than 50 percent, from 650 in 1998 to almost 1,000 in 2000. The bad news is, it's getting harder to get into Bread Loaf.

Admissions are handled on a competitive basis, with the writing sample being the most important component of the application. Bread Loaf has an admissions board of two poets and four prose writers. Each application is read closely and ranked, usually by two board members.

"In the past two years," Collier says, "the conference has been in the enviable position of admitting only applicants who have mostly received rankings of 'excellent' and 'very good.' "

The scholarship applications go through a slightly different process: the admissions committee creates a generous finalist list from the initial applicant pool. These finalists are then considered in round-table fashion until a consensus is reached concerning awards. Do the committee members draw blood at these meetings? "I wouldn't say that," Collier says, "but passions can run high, certainly."

The committee considers many factors when reading the writing sample, but in general, freshness and verbal mastery are highly prized. (Work the applicant wishes to present in the workshop can be substituted for the writing sample after the applicant is accepted.)

"An applicant can best serve him- or herself by sending a strong, polished piece for the writing sample and by keeping to the page limitation," says Collier. "It's also important to be persistent, especially if applying for scholarships. The admissions committee takes note of persistence and often rewards it."

Collier describes the admission board's job as "almost impossible." The conference's 25 work-study scholarships (waiterships) are selected from an applicant pool of more than 300. Similarly, 19 fellows are chosen from a pool of more than 150.

"What's been most interesting to watch about the growing volume of applications is how the sophistication of the writing has grown as well," says Collier. "We're not just logging in more applications, but we are attending to more highly-qualified writers at the same time. In part, the rise in applications can be attributed to the prosperity of the times, but I also think it's a response to the changes we have made to the conference program over the past five years. Word has gotten out that Bread Loaf has a new vitality."

Before Collier became director in 1995, the workshops met only twice to discuss participants' work. This made it impossible for the faculty to cover many of the stories or poems they were given. Collier, an award-winning poet and professor at the University of Maryland, recognized the need for more individualized attention. Now the workshops meet five times, and they've been trimmed from a maximum of 20 members to ten, allowing teachers to spend more time on each student's work.

"I believed that making the workshop the most important aspect of the conference would create a strong sense of community and a clearer idea of what Bread Loaf was about," Collier says. "We did other simple things, too, such as sending the faculty copies of the workshop manuscripts in advance of the conference."

Before Collier, there had also been criticism that Bread Loaf was too hierarchical, limiting participant interaction with faculty members. Other critics suggested there was too much interaction, dubbing the conference "Bed Loaf."

Those critics have been silenced, thanks in large part to Collier, whose laid-back hospitality and genial sense of integrity set the tone for the conference. He gives the impression he's ever mindful of being the custodian of a national literary treasure, and it's not a responsibility he takes lightly.

"I do think the conference is less hierarchical now, more friendly and inclusive," he says. "We try to hire faculty who have a real interest in teaching. They're also more accessible." Back in the old days, for instance, faculty members customarily met for pre-lunch Bloody Marys. Collier discontinued the tradition. "Now, instead of gathering in the faculty lounge for drinks after a workshop, the faculty members have the opportunity to eat lunch with students."

Bread Loaf is still famous for its social life, but these days, there is a general consensus among attendees that the conference has struck an ideal balance between work and play. "There is a seriousness of purpose about Bread Loaf," Collier says. "Everyone feels, while they are on the mountain, that writing is the most important and most necessary thing they could do."

(For information on applications, fees, and deadlines, see the Bread Loaf Writers' Conference listing on page 547. Also, see the Insider Report with novelist and Bread Loaf alumnus Elizabeth Graver on page 571.)
—*Will Allison*

N CREATIVITY WORKSHOP, 444 E. 82nd St., #16H, New York NY 10028. (212)249-1602. E-mail: admin@creativityworkshop.com. Website: www.creativityworkshop.com. **Contact:** Karen Bell, administrative assistant. Estab. 1995. Workshop held March 4-18 (Egypt); last weekend in March (NYC). Also summer workshops in Italy, Greece, Spain and France (dates TBA). Average attendance: 10. "This is a workshop for writers of all genres in which we do exercises aimed at process not product. It is a workshop geared to learning one's own creative process and experimenting with many tools to spark inspiration." Site: "Sites differ as to the locations the workshop is held." In 2000, faculty members included Shelley Berc and Alejandro Fogel.
Costs: NYC 2-day conference: $280 (food and lodging not included); Egypt Tour: $2,000 (includes workshop, lodging, some meals).
Additional Information: For brochure send e-mail or visit website. Accepts inquiries by e-mail, phone.

DOWNEAST MAINE WRITER'S WORKSHOPS, P.O. Box 446, Stockton Springs ME 04981. (207)567-4317. Fax: (207)567-3023. E-mail: redbaron@ime.net. Website: www.maineweb.com/writers/. **Contact:** Janet J. Barron, director. Estab. 1994. Annual. Tentative dates 2000, last week in July and second week in August. Writing workshops geared towards aspiring writers. "We hold small, 3-day workshops during the summer each year. In intense, experimental hands-on workshops, we address, in-depth, the subject of 'How to Get Your Writing Published' and 'Writing for the Children's Market' via expert, individual, personalized, practical guidance and inside-the-industry info from a 30-year professional writer and acquisition editor of several well-known publishing houses. Upon registration, students receive a questionnaire requesting responses re: their writing level, writing interests, and expectations from the conference. From this information, we build the workshop which is entirely geared around participants' information and needs. Each workshop is limited to 12 students."

Costs: Tuition (includes lunch): 3-day, $295, $19.95 for 300-page textbook and $4 shipping and handling ("we accept Visa and MC"). Reasonable local accommodations and meals additional (except lunch during conference).
Accommodations: Upon registration, participants receive a list of local B&Bs and Inns, most of which include large, full breakfasts in their reasonable rates. They also receive a list of area activities and events.
Additional Information: Upon registration, students receive a comprehensive, confidential questionnaire. DEMWW workshops are completely constructed around participant's answers to questionnaires. Also offers a writer's clinic for writing feedback if participants seek this type of assistance. No requirements prior to registration. For more details and free brochures, contact DEMWW at any of the numbers listed. Conference information available April 2000.

☑ **FEMINIST WOMEN'S WRITING WORKSHOPS, INC.**, P.O. Box 6583, Ithaca NY 14851. **Contact:** Margo Gumosky, director. Estab. 1975. Workshop held every summer. Workshop duration: 8 days. Average attendance: 30-40 women writers. "Workshops provide a women-centered community for writers of all levels and genres. Workshops are held on the campuses of Hobart/William Smith Colleges in Geneva, NY. Geneva is approximately mid-way between Rochester and Syracuse. Each writer has a private room and 3 meals daily. College facilities such as pool, tennis courts and weight room are available. FWWW invites all interests. Past speakers include Dorothy Allison, National Book Award Finalist for *Bastard Out of Carolina*, and Ruth Stone, author of *Second-Hand Coat, Who Is The Widow's Muse?* and *Simplicity*.
Costs: $545 for tuition, room, board.
Accommodations: Shuttle service from airports available for a fee.
Additional Information: "Writers may submit manuscripts 4-10 pages with application." For brochures/guidelines send SASE.

[N] **GOTHAM WRITERS' WORKSHOP**, WritingClasses.com (online division), 1841 Broadway, Suite 809, New York NY 10023-7603. (212)974-8377. Fax: (212)307-6325. E-mail: office@write.org. Website: www.WritingClasses.com. **Contact:** Dana Miller, director of student affairs. Estab. 1993. "Classes are held throughout the year. There are four terms, beginning in January, April, June/July, September/October in 2001." Workshop duration: 10-week, 1-day, and online courses offered. Average attendance: approximately 1,000 students per term, 4,000 students per year. Offers craft-oriented creative writing courses in fiction writing, screenwriting, nonfiction writing, memoir writing, novel writing, children's book writing, playwriting, poetry, sketch comedy and business writing. Also, Gotham Writers' Workshop offers a teen program and private instruction. Site: Classes are held at various schools in New York City as well as online at www.WritingClasses.com. View a sample online class on the website.
Costs: Ten-week and online courses—$415 (includes $20 registration fee); one-day courses—$165 (includes $20 registration fee). These fees are before any discounts. For information regarding our discounts, please contact us for a catalog. Meals and lodging not included.
Additional Information: "Participants do not need to submit workshop material prior to their first class." Sponsors a contest for a free 10-week online creative writing course (value = $415) offered each term. Students should fill out a form online at www.WritingClasses.com to participate in the contest. The winner is randomly selected. For brochure send e-mail, visit website, call or fax. Accepts inquiries by SASE, e-mail, phone, fax. Agents and editors participate in some workshops.

[N] **GREEN MOUNTAIN WRITERS CONFERENCE**, 47 Hazel Street, Rutland VT 05701. (802)775-5326. E-mail: ommar@stanford.edu. Website: www.vermontwriters.com. **Contact:** Yvonne Daley, director. Estab. 1999. Annual. Conference to be held July 30-Aug. 3, 2001. Average attendance: 40. "Focus is to teach and celebrate writing across the genres. We have workshops in fiction, creative non-fiction, memoir, poetry, magazine writing, opinion writing, and travel writing. Conference held at an old dance pavillion on a 5-acre site on a remote pond in Tinmouth, VT." Features: Place in Story—The Importance of Environment; Creative Character through Description, Dialogue, Action, Reaction, and Thought; The Collision of Real Events and Imagination. Panelists, lecturers have included Grace Paley, Chris Bohjalian, David Budbill, and many more.
Costs: In 2000 cost was $500 (including lunch, snacks, beverages).
Accommodations: Transportation can be made at cost from area airports. Offers list of area hotels and lodging.
Additional Information: Participants' mss can be read and commented on at a cost. Sponsors contests. Requirements: Free tuition, no lodging ($500); reading cost fee: $15. Essays plus 3 poems or 10 pages of fiction/nonfiction. Essays should say why the writer wants to attend our conference. Length: 1,000 words. Brochures available February, 2001 or on website. Brochures for SASE, e-mail, website or call. Accepts inquiries by SASE, e-mail, phone. Editors participate in conferences. "We aim to create a community of writers who support one another and serve as audience/mentors for one another. Participants often continue to correspond and share work after conferences."

☑ **HOFSTRA UNIVERSITY SUMMER WRITERS' CONFERENCE**, 250 Hofstra University, UCCE, Hempstead NY 11549. (516)463-5016. Fax: (516)463-4833. E-mail: uccelibarts@hofstra.edu. Website: Continuing Learners at www.hofstra.edu. **Contact:** Kenneth Henwood, director, Liberal Arts Studies. Estab. 1972. Annual (every summer, starting week after July 4). Conference to be held July 9-20, 2001. Average attendance: 65. Conference offers workshops in fiction, nonfiction, poetry, juvenile fiction, stage/screenwriting, and on occasion, one other genre such as detective fiction or science fiction. Workshops in prose and poetry for high school student writers are also offered. Site is the university campus, a suburban setting, 25 miles from NYC. Guest speakers are not yet known. "We have had the likes of Oscar Hijuelos, Robert Olen Butler, Hilma and Meg Wolitzer, Budd Schulberg and Cynthia Ozick."

Costs: Non-credit (no meals, no room): approximately $400 per workshop or $625 for two workshops. Credit: Approximately $1,100/workshop (2 credits) undergraduate and graduate; $2,100 (4 credits) undergraduate and graduate.

Accommodations: Free bus operates between Hempstead Train Station and campus for those commuting from NYC. Dormitory rooms are available for approximately $350 for the 2 week conference. Those who request area hotels will receive a list. Hotels are approximately $75 and above/night.

Additional Information: "All workshops include critiquing. Each participant is given one-on-one time of ½ hour with workshop leader. We submit work to the Shaw Guides Contest and other Writer's Conferences and Retreats contests when appropriate." Conference information available March 2000. Accepts inquiries by fax, e-mail.

IWWG MEET THE AGENTS AND EDITORS: THE BIG APPLE WORKSHOPS, ℅ International Women's Writing Guild, P.O. Box 810, Gracie Station, New York NY 10028-0082. (212)737-7536. Fax: (212)737-9469. E-mail: iwwg@iwwg.com. Website: www.iwwg.com. **Contact:** Hannelore Hahn, executive director. Estab. 1980. Biannual. Workshops held April 21-22, 2001, and in October 2001. Average attendance: 200. Workshops to promote creative writing and professional success. Site: Private meeting space of the City Athletic Club, mid-town New York City. Saturday: One day workshop. Sunday morning: open house/meet the authors and panel discussion with eight recently-published authors. Sunday afternoon: open house/meet the authors, independent presses and editors.

Costs: $110 for the weekend.

Accommodations: Information on transportation arrangements and overnight accommodations made available.

Additional Information: For workshop information send SASE. Accepts inquires by fax, e-mail.

THE MACDOWELL COLONY, 100 High St., Peterborough NH 03458. (603)924-3886. Fax: (603)924-9142. Website: www.macdowellcolony.org. **Contact:** Pat Dodge, admissions coordinator. Estab. 1907. Open to writers, composers, visual artists, film/video artists, interdisciplinary artists and architects. Includes main building, library, 3 residence halls and 32 individual studios on over 450 mostly wooded acres, 1 mile from center of small town in southern New Hampshire. Available up to 8 weeks year-round. Provisions for the writer include meals, private sleeping room, individual secluded studio. Accommodates variable number of writers, 10 to 20 at a time.

Costs: Artists are asked to contribute toward the cost of their residency according to their financial resources.

To Apply: Application forms available. Application deadline: January 15 for summer, April 15 for fall/winter, September 15 for winter/spring. Writing sample required. For novel, send a chapter or section. For short stories, send 2-3. Send 6 copies. Brochure/guidelines available; SASE appreciated.

✓ MANHATTANVILLE COLLEGE SUMMER WRITERS' WEEK, School of Graduate and Professional Studies, 2900 Purchase St., Purchase NY 10577-2103. (914)694-3425. Fax: (914)694-3488. E-mail: rdowd@mville.edu. Website: www.mville.edu. **Contact:** Ruth Dowd, R.S.C.J., dean, School of Graduate and Professional Studies. Estab. 1982. Annual. Conference held June 25-29, 2001. Average attendance: 90. Workshops include children's literature, journal writing, creative nonfiction, personal essay, poetry, screenwriting, fiction, travel writing and short fiction. There is also a workshop in the writer's craft for beginners. The Conference is designed not only for writers but for teachers of writing. Students do intensive work in the genre of their choice. Manhattanville is a suburban campus 30 miles from New York City. The campus centers around Reid Castle, the administration building, the former home of Whitelaw Reid. Workshops are conducted in Reid Castle. We feature a major author as guest lecturer during the Conference. Past speakers have included such authors as Toni Morrison, Andy Bienen, Gail Godwin, Richard Peck and poet Mark Doty.

Costs: Conference cost was $560 in 1999 plus $30 fee.

Accommodations: Students may rent rooms in the college residence halls. More luxurious accommodations are available at neighboring hotels. In the summer of 1999 the cost of renting a room in the residence halls was $25 per night.

Additional Information: Conference information available March 15, 2001. For brochure send e-mail, visit website, call or fax. Accepts inquiries by SASE, e-mail, fax, phone.

N NEW ENGLAND WRITERS, P.O. Box 483, 151 Main St., Windsor VT 05089. (802)674-2315. Fax: (802)674-3503. E-mail: newvtpoet@aol.com. Website: http://hometown.aol.com/newvtpoet/myhomepage/profile.html. **Contact:** Dr. Frank Anthony, president. Estab. 1988. Annual. Conference held July 21, 2001. Conference duration: 1 day. Average attendance: 150. The purpose is "to bring an affordable literary conference to any

writers who can get there, and to expose them to emerging excellence in the craft." Site: The Grace Outreach Building, 1 mile south of the Dartmouth campus, Hanover NH. In 2000, panels included On Becoming A Writer, Methods Of Line Breaking, Where's The Story? and How To Get An Agent. In 2000 Dana Gioia, Wesley McNair, Tim Parrish, Don Pease, PhD and John Talbot participated as faculty members or speakers.
Costs: $10 (includes lunch). No pre-registration required.
Accommodations: Provides a list of area hotels or lodging options.
Additional Information: Sponsors poetry and fiction contests as part of conference (award announced at conference). Conference information available now. For brochure send SASE or visit website. Accepts inquiries by SASE, e-mail, phone. Agents and editors participate in conference. (University Press of New England and Dartmouth Bookstore of Hanover sit in on panels and offer books for sale.) Open readings and door prizes.

■ ODYSSEY, 20 Levesque Lane, Mont Vernon NH 03057. Phone/fax: (603)673-6234. E-mail: jcavelos@sff.net. Website: www.sff.net/odyssey. **Contact:** Jeanne Cavelos, director. Estab. 1995. Annual. Workshop to be held June 11 to July 20, 2001. Attendance limited to 20. "A workshop for fantasy, science fiction and horror writers that combines an intensive learning and writing experience with in-depth feedback on students' manuscripts. The only workshop to combine the overall guidance and in-depth feedback of a single instructor with the varied perspectives of guest lecturers and the only such workshop run by an editor." Conference held at New Hampshire College in Manchester, New Hampshire. Previous guest lecturers included: Harlan Ellison, Ben Bova, Dan Simmons, Jane Yolen, Elizabeth Hand, Craig Shaw Gardner, Melissa Scott, Patricia McKillip and John Crowley.
Costs: In 2000: $1,160 tuition, $337 housing (double room), $20 application fee, $525 food (approximate), $55 processing fee to receive college credit.
Accommodations: "Workshop students stay at New Hampshire College townhouses and eat at college."
Additional Information: Students must apply and include a writing sample. Students' works are critiqued throughout the 6 weeks. Workshop information available in September. For brochure/guidelines send SAE, e-mail, visit website, call or fax. Accepts inquiries by SASE, e-mail, fax, phone.

THE OLDERS' TRAVEL WRITING WORKSHOP, 84 New St., Albany VT 05820. (802)755-6774. E-mail: julvt@together.net. **Contact:** Jules Older. Estab. 1988. Annual. Workshop held in the summer and fall. Workshop duration: 1 full Saturday. Average attendance: 12-16. Workshop on travel writing. Workshop held at mountain resorts in Vermont, New Hampshire and Cooperstown, NY. Themes include "Bringing Your Passions Into Travel Writing" and "Travel Writing in Fiction, for Adults and Kids." Workshop speakers are Jules and Effin Older.
Costs: $225.
Accommodations: Information on discounted overnight accommodations is available.
Additional Information: Workshop brochures available year round. Inquiries by e-mail encouraged.

ROBERT QUACKENBUSH'S CHILDREN'S BOOK WRITING & ILLUSTRATING WORKSHOPS, 460 E. 79th St., New York NY 10021-1443. (212)744-3822. Fax: (212)861-2761. E-mail: rqstudios@aol.com. Website: www.rquackenbush.com. **Contact:** Robert Quackenbush, director. Estab. 1982. Annual. Workshop held July 9-13, 2001. Average attendance: limited to 10. Workshops to promote writing and illustrating books for children. Held at the Manhattan studio of Robert Quackenbush, author and illustrator of over 170 books for young readers. "Focus is generally on picture books, easy-to-read and early chapter books. All classes led by Robert Quackenbush."
Costs: $650 tuition covers all costs of the workshop, but does not include housing and meals. A $100 nonrefundable deposit is required with the $550 balance due two weeks prior to attendance.
Accommodations: A list of recommended hotels and restaurants is sent upon receipt of deposit.
Additional Information: Class is for beginners and professionals. Critiques during workshop. Private consultations also available at an hourly rate. "Programs suited to your needs; individualized schedules can be designed. Write or phone to discuss your goals and you will receive a prompt reply." Conference information available July 2000. For brochure send SAE, e-mail, visit website, call or fax. Accepts inquiries by fax, e-mail, phone, SASE.

Ⓝ SEACOAST WRITER'S ASSOCIATION SPRING AND FALL CONFERENCES, 59 River Rd., Stratham NH 03885-2358. E-mail: riverrd@tiac.net. Website: www.whitepinescollege.edu. **Contact:** Pat Parnell, conference director. Annual. Conferences held in May and October. Conference duration: 1 day. Average attendance: 50. "Our conferences offer workshops covering various aspects of fiction, nonfiction and poetry."
Costs: $50.
Additional Information: "We sometimes include critiques. It is up to the speaker." Spring meeting includes a contest. Categories are fiction, nonfiction (essays) and poetry. Judges vary from year to year. Conference information available for SASE April 1 and September 1. Accepts inquiries by SASE, e-mail, fax, phone.

STATE OF MAINE WRITERS' CONFERENCE, 18 Hill Rd., Belmont MA 02478. (617)489-1548. **Contact:** June Knowles and Mary Pitts, co-chairs. Estab. 1941. Annual. Conference held in August. Conference duration:

4 days. Average attendance: 40. "We try to present a balanced as well as eclectic conference. There is quite a bit of time and attention given to poetry but we also have children's literature, travel, novels/fiction and other issues of interest to writers. Our speakers are publishers, editors, illustrators and other professionals. Our concentration is, by intention, a general view of writing to publish. We are located in Ocean Park, a small seashore village 14 miles south of Portland. Ours is a summer assembly center with many buildings from the Victorian Age. The conference meets in Porter Hall, one of the assembly buildings which is listed on the National Register of Historic Places. Within recent years our guest list has included Lewis Turco, Amy MacDonald, Jeffrey Aronson, Wesley McNair, John N. Cole, Betsy Sholl, John Tagliabue, Roy Fairfield, Oscar Greene and many others. We usually have about 10 guest presenters a year."

Costs: $90-100 includes the conference banquet. There is a reduced fee, $45, for students ages 21 and under. The fee does not include housing or meals which must be arranged separately by the conferees.

Accommodations: An accommodations list is available. "We are in a summer resort area and motels, guest houses and restaurants abound."

Additional Information: "We have a list of about nine contests on various genres. The prizes, all modest, are awarded at the end of the conference and only to those who are registered." Send SASE for program guide and contest announcements.

STONECOAST WRITERS' CONFERENCE, University of Southern Maine, 37 College Ave., Gorham ME 04038. (207)780-5617. **Contact:** Barbara Hope, conference director. Estab. 1979. Annual. Conference held in mid-July. Conference duration: 10 days. Average attendance: 90-100. "Conference concentrates on fiction, poetry, popular fiction and creative nonfiction. Freeport, Maine, is the site of the conference. Workshops are at the University of Southern Maine Stone House Conference Center." Past speakers include Joyce Johnson, Manette Ansay, Jonathan Lethem, David Huddle, Colin Harrison and David Bradley.

Costs: $510 includes tuition.

Accommodations: Accommodations provided in university housing.

Additional Information: Scholarships available for various groups.

N **⊕** **THE TUSCANY WORKSHOPS,** 817 West End Ave., #11D, New York NY 10025. (212)666-6505. Fax: (212)666-7103. E-mail: jmworks@angel.net. Website: www.tuscanyworkshops.com. **Contact:** Maggie Barrett, co-director. Estab. 1995. Two annual conferences. June 3-16, 2001 (in Tuscany); September 15-22, 2001 (on Cape Cod). Average attendance: 8. Conference focuses on fiction writing. Site: A 2,000-acre estate in Tuscany, with swimming and horseback riding; a day's drive from Florence, Assisi and Pisa. Novelist Susan Schwartz Senstad is scheduled to participate as a faculty member.

Costs: Tuscany, $2,950; Cape Cod, $1,500. Accommodation, 3 meals/day, tuition, ground transportation, the estate's own wine, housekeeping, classes, critiques, lectures and readings, use of projectors and lightboxes, delivery and pickup of processing, use of printers, paper, duplicating service, and guided field trips.

Accommodations: Cost for both Tuscany and Cape Cod is inclusive for shared or individual accommodations (five 18th-century farmhouses, all with double bedrooms and shared bathrooms. Main building for workshops, readings, lectures and slide shows.)

Additional Information: Submit fiction sample (max. 15 pages) with registration. Conference information available January 2001. For brochure send e-mail, visit website, call or fax. Accepts inquiries by e-mail, phone, fax. Agents and editors participate in conference.

WESLEYAN WRITERS CONFERENCE, Wesleyan University, Middletown CT 06459. (860)685-3604. Fax: (860)685-2441. E-mail: agreene@wesleyan.edu. Website: www.wesleyan.edu/writing/conferen.html. **Contact:** Anne Greene, director. Estab. 1956. Annual. Conference held the last week in June. Average attendance: 100. For fiction techniques, novel, short story, poetry, screenwriting, nonfiction, literary journalism, memoir. The conference is held on the campus of Wesleyan University, in the hills overlooking the Connecticut River. Meals and lodging are provided on campus. Features readings of new fiction, guest lectures on a range of topics including publishing and daily seminars. "Both new and experienced writers are welcome."

Costs: In 2000, day rate $690 (including meals); boarding students' rate $805 (including meals and room for 5 nights).

Accommodations: "Participants can fly to Hartford or take Amtrak to Meriden, CT. We are happy to help participants make travel arrangements." Overnight participants stay on campus.

Additional Information: Manuscript critiques are available as part of the program but are not required. Participants may attend seminars in several different genres. Scholarships and teaching fellowships are available, including the Jakobson awards for new writers and the Jon Davidoff Scholarships for journalists. Accepts inquiries by e-mail, fax.

✓ **THE WRITER'S VOICE OF THE WEST SIDE YMCA,** 5 West 63rd St., New York NY 10023. (212)875-4124. (212) 875-4184. E-mail: wswritersvoice@ymcanyc.org. Website: http://ymcanyc.org/wvoice/. **Contact:** David Andrews, assistant. Estab. 1981. Workshop held four times/year (summer, spring, winter and

fall). Workshop duration: 6-10 weeks, two hours one night/week. Average attendance: 15. Workshop on "fiction, poetry, writing for performance, non-fiction, multi-genre, playwriting and writing for children." Workshop held at the West Side YMCA.
Costs: $325/workshop.
Additional Information: Sponsors several contests including awards for poetry, fiction and nonfiction and a literary magazine. For workshop brochures/guidelines send SASE, e-mail, visit website, call or fax. Accepts inquiries by SASE, e-mail, fax, phone. "The Writer's Voice of the West Side Y is the largest non-academic literary arts center in the U.S."

☑ **WRITING, CREATIVITY AND RITUAL: A WOMAN'S RETREAT**, 995 Chapman Rd., Yorktown Heights NY 10598. E-mail: emily@emilyhanlon.com. Website: www.emilyhanlon.com. **Contact:** Emily Hanlon. Estab. 1998. Annual. Retreat held July 2001. Average attendance: 20 is the limit. Retreat for "fiction, memoir, creative nonfiction and the creative process." Location varies. "I try to find places conducive to creativity and the imagination. July 2001, Glastonbury, England." The theme of the retreat is "the passion and risk of the creative journey. Writing emphasis on the writer's voice through opening to characters that come from the writer's unconscious."
Costs: 2000 fees: $1,700-2,000 depending on choice of room. Includes workshop, room and all meals.
Additional Information: Conference information free and available spring 2001. Accepts inquiries by e-mail, phone. "This retreat is open only to women. Enrollment is limited to 20. More than just a writing workshop or conference, the retreat is an exploration of the creative process through writing—3-hour writing workshops daily, time to write and explore Glastonbury. Three days of traveling/touring the English countryside are planned."

YADDO, Box 395, Saratoga Springs NY 12866-0395. (518)587-4886. Fax: (518)584-1312. E-mail: chwait@aol.com. **Contact:** Admissions Committee. Estab. 1926. "Those qualified for invitations to Yaddo are highly-qualified writers, visual artists, composers, choreographers, performance artists and film and video artists who are working at the professional level in their fields. Artists who wish to work collaboratively are encouraged to apply. An abiding principle at Yaddo is that applications for residencies are judged on the quality of the artists' work and professional promise." Provisions include room, board and studio space. No stipends are offered. Site includes four small lakes, a rose garden, woodland. Two seasons: large season is mid-May-Labor Day; small season is October-May (stays from 2 weeks to 2 months; average stay is 5 weeks). Accommodates approximately 16 writers in large season.
Costs: No fee is charged; residency includes room, board and studio space. Limited international travel expenses are available to artists accepted for residencies at Yaddo.
To Apply: Filing fee is $20 (checks to Corporation of Yaddo). Two letters of recommendation are requested. Applications are considerd by the Admissions Committee and invitations are issued by April (deadline: January 15) and September (deadline: August 1). Conference information available for SASE. Accepts inquiries by e-mail, fax.

ZEN MOUNTAIN MONASTERY, Mt. Tremper NY 12457. (914)688-2228. Fax: (914)688-2415. E-mail: zmmtrain@zen-mtn.org. Website: www.sen-mtn.org/zmm. **Contact:** Training office. On-going writer retreats. Duration: 1 weekend. Average attendance: 15-20. Workshop on "Zen and its relation to the creative process. The retreat takes place within the context of Zen training. Participants will be introduced to Zazen (the formal seated meditation). We offer retreats in Haiku, poetry and journal writing." Workshops held at an American Zen Buddhist Monastery located in the Catskill Mountains retreat cabin. Speakers include Anne Waldman, Christian McEwen, Gail Sher (*One Continuous Mistake*) and Hannah Hinchman.
Costs: $195 includes meals, lodging and Zen training.
Accommodations: Direct bus line for NY Port Authority Adirondack Trailways provided. "Participants are expected to stay here for the entirety of the retreat. Dormitory style lodging for men and women."
Additional Information: Workshop brochures/guidelines for SASE. Accepts inquiries by fax and e-mail.

Midatlantic (DC, DE, MD, NJ, PA)

N **BOUCHERCON: THE WORLD MYSTERY CONVENTION**, P.O. Box 11700, Washington DC 20008. E-mail: info@bouchercon2001.com. Website: www.bouchercon2001.com. **Contact:** William L. Starvck, registrar. Estab. 1970. Annual. Conference held November 1-4, 2001. Average attendance: 1,000-2,000. Boucher-

CAN'T FIND A CONFERENCE? Conferences are listed by region. Check the introduction to this section for a list of regional categories.

con, in its 32nd year, focuses on mystery. Site: Hyatt Regency Crystal City, Washington, D.C. Plans 6-8 tracks of mystery-related themes for conference. Sue Grafton, Peter Lovesey, Lew and Nancy Buckingham and Michael Connelly are scheduled to participate.

Costs: $150 (doesn't include meal event tickets).

Accommodations: Free shuttle from airport to hotel for Hyatt Regency Crystal City guests. Offers overnight accommodations.

Additional Information: For conference brochure send SASE, e-mail or visit website. Accepts inquiries by SASE, e-mail. Agents and editors participate in conference.

THE COLLEGE OF NEW JERSEY WRITERS' CONFERENCE, English Dept., The College of New Jersey, P.O. Box 7718, Ewing NJ 08628-0718. (609)771-3254. Fax: (609)637-5112. E-mail: write@tcnj.edu. **Contact:** Jean Hollander, director. Estab. 1980. Annual. Conference held April 2001. Conference duration: 9 a.m. to 10:30 p.m. Average attendance: 600-1,000. "Conference concentrates on fiction (the largest number of participants), poetry, children's literature, play and screenwriting, magazine and newspaper journalism, overcoming writer's block, nonfiction books. Conference is held at the student center at the college in two auditoriums and workshop rooms; also Kendall Theatre on campus." The focus is on various genres: romance, detective, mystery, TV writing, etc. Topics have included "How to Get Happily Published," "How to Get an Agent" and "Earning a Living as a Writer." The conference usually presents twenty or so authors, plus two featured speakers, who have included Arthur Miller, Saul Bellow, Toni Morrison, Joyce Carol Oates, Erica Jong, Alice Walker, Joseph Heller, John Updike, Anna Quindlen, etc.

Costs: General registration $45, plus $10 for each workshop. Lower rates for students.

Additional Information: Conference information available for SASE. Accepts inquiries by SASE, e-mail, fax, phone.

N **DEADLY INK MYSTERY CONFERENCES**, 15 Mohawk Ave., Rockawam NJ 07866. (973)627-2806. E-mail: pab@nac.net. Website: www.deadlyink.com. **Contact:** Patti Biringer, conference manager. Estab. 2000. Annual. Conference held June 22-23, 2001. Conference duration: from 6 p.m. Friday to 5 p.m. Saturday. Average attendance: 125. Focuses on mystery writing for mystery fans and authors. Conference held at Four Points Sheraton in Mt. Arlington, New Jersey. Features humor in mystery, historical mysteries, what do emotions look like, growing series characters, computer crime. Faculty includes Parnell Hall (guest of honor), Jonathan Harrington, Irene Marcuse, Nancy Tesler, Jane Rubino, and many more.

Costs: $85 includes 1 workshop, 1 critique group Friday night, breakfast, banquet lunch with guest speaker, 8 workshops, book signings, book sellers.

Accommodations: Offers overnight accommodations. Special conference rate at on-site hotel.

Additional Information: Sponsors contests. Short story contest: 3,000 words, 2 winners will receive $50 cash and publication in program book setting in New Jersey. Judged by multi-published short story authors. For brochures e-mail or phone. "Small, friendly conference where fans meet writers, and writers have the opportunity to get new readers."

N **MID ATLANTIC LITERARY SMALL PRESS CONFERENCE AND BOOK FAIR**, 4508 Walsh St., Bethesda MD 20815. (301)654-8664. Fax: (301)654-8667. E-mail: postmaster@writer.org. Website: www.writer.org/bookfair. **Contact:** Jo Ann Billings, coordinator. Estab. 1994. Annual. Conference held April 28, 2001. Average attendance: 750. Conference focuses on poetry, fiction and literary nonfiction. Purpose is to bring together independent publishers for a conference and afternoon fair. The Writer's Center has a large, theater-line space in which the morning conference is held. The afternoon fair takes place outside, under tents. Walsh St. in Bethesda is closed of for the fair. "Our 2000 theme was Electronic and Print-on-Demand Publishing. We had a panel and discussion on the topic." In 2000 faculty, guests speakers and panelists included Barbara Bole (cash cares.org), Terence Mulligan (Minimus), Dorothy Phaire, Carol Harrison (Xlibris).

Costs: Free to the public. $30 fee for presses and literary organizations includes conference and table for the fair.

Additional Information: Conference information available January 1, 2001. For brochure send e-mail, visit website or call. Accepts inquiries by e-mail, phone. Editors participate in conference. "We also offer workshops year-round in all genres.'

MID-ATLANTIC MYSTERY BOOK FAIR & CONVENTION, Detecto Mysterioso Books at Society Hill Playhouse, 507 S. Eighth St., Philadelphia PA 19147. (215)923-0211. Fax: (923)923-1789. E-mail: shp@erols.com. Website: www.erols.com/SHP. **Contact:** Deen Kogan, chairperson. Estab. 1991. Annual. Convention held October 13-15, 2000. Average attendance: 450-500. Focus is on mystery, suspense, thriller, true crime novels. "An examination of the genre from many points of view." The convention is held at the Wyndham Franklin Plaza, located in the historic area of Philadelphia. Previous speakers included Lawrence Block, Jeremiah Healy, Neil Albert, Michael Connelly, Paul Levine, Eileen Dreyer, Earl Emerson, Wendy Hornsby.

Costs: $125 registration fee.

Accommodations: Attendees must make their own transportation arrangements. Special room rate available at convention hotel.

Additional Information: "The Bookroom is a focal point of the convention. Twenty-five specialty dealers are expected to exhibit and collectables range from hot-off-the-press bestsellers to 1930's pulp; from fine editions to reading copies. Conference information available by mail or telephone after June 15. Accepts inquiries by e-mail, fax; provide address."

☑ **MONTROSE CHRISTIAN WRITER'S CONFERENCE**, 5 Locust St., Montrose Bible Conference, Montrose PA 18801-1112. (570)278-1001 or (800)598-5030. Fax: (570)278-3061. E-mail: mbc@montrosebible.org. Website: www.montrosebible.org. **Contact:** Donna Kosik, MBC Secretary/Registrar. Estab. 1990. Annual. Conference held July 22-27, 2001. Average attendance: 75. "We try to meet a cross-section of writing needs, for beginners and advanced, covering fiction, poetry and writing for children. It is small enough to allow personal interaction between conferees and faculty. We meet in the beautiful village of Montrose, Pennsylvania, situated in the mountains. The Bible Conference provides hotel/motel-like accommodations and good food. The main sessions are held in the chapel with rooms available for other classes. Fiction writing has been taught each year." **Costs:** In 2000 registration was $110.

Accommodations: Will meet planes in Binghamton NY and Scranton PA; will meet bus in Great Bend PA. Information on overnight accommodations is available. On-site accommodations: room and board $170-255/conference; $38-$57/day including food.

Additional Information: "Writers can send work ahead and have it critiqued for $25. The attendees are usually church related. The writing has a Christian emphasis." Conference information available March 2001. For brochure send SASE, visit website, e-mail, call or fax. Accepts inquiries by SASE, e-mail, fax, phone.

JENNY McKEAN MOORE COMMUNITY WORKSHOPS, English Dept., George Washington University, Washington DC 20052. (202)994-8223. Fax: (202)363-8628. **Contact:** D. McAleavey, professor. Estab. 1976. Workshop held each semester. Length: semester. Average attendance: 15. Workshop concentration varies depending on professor—usually fiction or poetry. Workshop held at university.

Costs: Free.

Additional Information: Admission is competitive and by ms.

☑ **OUTDOOR WRITERS ASSOCIATION OF AMERICA ANNUAL CONFERENCE**, 158 Lower Georges Valley Rd., Spring Mills PA 16875. (814)364-9557. Fax: (814)364-9558. E-mail: eking4owaa@cs.com. Website: www.owaa.org. **Contact:** Eileen King, meeting planner. Estab. 1927. Annual. Conference held June 2-6, 2000, in St. George, UT. Average attendance: 800-950. Conference concentrates on outdoor communications (all forms of media). Featured speakers have included Don Ranley, University of Missouri, Columbia; US Forest Service Chief Michael Dombeck; Nina Leopold Bradley (daughter of Aldo Leopold); Secretary of the Interior, Bruce Babbitt.

Costs: $140 for nonmembers; "applicants must have prior approval from Executive Director." Registration fee includes cost of most meals.

Accommodations: List of accommodations available after April. Special room rate for attendees.

Additional Information: Sponsors contests, "but all is done prior to the conference and you must be a member to enter them." Conference information available March 2001. For brochure visit website, send e-mail, call or fax. Accepts inquiries by e-mail, fax.

PENNWRITERS CONFERENCE, RR #2, Box 241, Middlebury Center PA 16935. (717)871-0599. (717)871-6104. E-mail: elizwrite8@aol.com. Website: www.pennwriters.org. **Contact:** Elizabeth Darrach. Estab. 1987. Annual. Conference held May 18-20, 2001. Average attendance: 120. "We encompass all genres and will be aiming for workshops to cover many areas, including fiction (long and short), nonfiction, etc." Workshop held at the Holiday Inn Grantville. Theme for 2001 is "A Way with Words." Speakers include Leonard Bishop, *Writer's Digest* columnist Amanda Lynch, Valerie Maimont and motivational speaker Bill Foster.

Costs: 2000 fees: $125 for members.

Accommodations: Special rate of $82/night if reservation is made by April 20.

Additional Information: Sponsors contest: published authors judge fiction in 2 categories, short stories and Great Beginnings (novels). For conference information send SASE. Accepts inquiries by fax and e-mail. "Agent/editor appointments are available on a first-come, first serve basis."

☑ **SUSPENSE, MYSTERY & INTRIGUE II**, % Novel Explorations, 10705 Charter Dr., Suite 350, Columbia MD 21044. (800)432-6659. Fax: (410)964-0878. E-mail: novelexp@home.com. Website: http://users.erols.com/novelexp/. **Contact:** Patty Suchy, coordinator. Estab. 1998. Conference held every 2 years. Next conference: March 2002. Conference duration: one week. Average attendance: 60. Conference concentrates on fiction, mystery, suspense, romantic suspense, short stories and horror. Conference held aboard cruise ship. Workshops include

"Murder With Only One Witness"; "Mind of a Serial Killer"; "PI's Real & Fictional"; "Balancing Plot and Characters"; "How to Get Happily Published"; "Can You Really Do That?"; and "From Book to Movie." Conference speakers are well-known authors and crime specialists.

Costs: $700-1500. Includes one week's stay aboard cruise ship plus all meals.

Accommodations: Airline discounts available.

Additional Information: Conference information available early 2001. For brochure/guidelines e-mail, phone, fax or visit website. Accepts inquiries by fax, e-mail, phone. "Books for sale on ship; shipboard autographing; dinner with authors; relaxed, personal atmosphere."

WASHINGTON INDEPENDENT WRITERS (WIW) SPRING WRITERS CONFERENCE, #220, 733 15th St. NW, Suite 220, Washington DC 20005-2112. (202)347-4973. Fax: (202)628-0298. E-mail: washwrite r@aol.com. Website: www.washwriter.org. Executive Director: Isolde Chapin. Estab. 1975. Annual. Conference held May 14-15. Conference duration: Friday evening and Saturday. Average attendance: 250. "Gives participants a chance to hear from and talk with dozens of experts on book and magazine publishing as well as on the craft, tools and business of writing." National Press Club as conference site. Past keynote speakers include Erica Jong, Haynes Johnson, Diane Rehm and Kitty Kelley.

Costs: $125 members; $150 nonmembers; $185 membership and conference.

Additional Information: Conference information available for SASE in February. Accepts inquiries by fax, e-mail.

WINTER POETRY & PROSE GETAWAY IN CAPE MAY, 18 North Richards Ave., Ventnor NJ 08406-2136. (609)823-5076. E-mail: wintergetaway@hotmail.com. Website: www.wintergetaway.com. **Contact:** Peter E. Murphy, founder/director. Estab. 1994. Annual. Workshop held January 12-15, 2001. Average attendance: 150. "Open to all writers, beginners and experienced over the age of 18. Prose workshops meet all day Saturday and Sunday and on Monday morning. Participants choose one workshop from among the following choices: short story (beginning and advanced), memoir, novel, drama, poetry, photography, story telling and pottery. Classes are small so each person receives individual attention for the new writing or work-in-progress that they are focusing on. The workshops are held at the Grand Hotel on the oceanfront in historic Cape May, New Jersey. Individual tutorials are available for fiction writers at an additional cost." 2001 speakers include Renee Ashley, Robert Carnevale, Cat Doty, Penny Dugan, Donna Perry, Mimi Schwartz, Robbie Clipper Jethi, and Richard Weems.

Costs: Cost for 2001 is $380 which includes breakfast and lunch for three days, all workshop session and evening activities, and a double room. Dinners are not included. Participants may choose a single room at an additional cost. Some workshops require additional material fees. Commuters who make their own arrangements are welcome. A $25 early bird discount is available if full payment is made by November 15.

Accommodations: "Participants stay in comfortable rooms, most with an ocean view, perfect for thawing out the muse. Hotel facilities include a pool, sauna and a whirlpool, as well as a lounge and disco for late evening dancing."

Additional Information: "Individual critiques are available to prose writers at an additional cost. Work-in-progress should be sent ahead of time." For conference information (after September 15) send e-mail, visit website or call. Accepts inquiries by SASE, e-mail, phone. "The Winter Getaway is known for its challenging and supportive workshops that encourage imaginative risk-taking and promote freedom and transformation in the participants' writing."

Midsouth (NC, SC, TN, VA, WV)

☑ **CHATTANOOGA CONFERENCE ON SOUTHERN LITERATURE**, c/o Arts & Education Council, P.O. Box 4203, Chattanooga TN 37405-0203. (423)267-1218 or (800)267-4232. Fax: (423)267-1018. E-mail: srobinson@artsedcouncil.org. Website: www.artsedcouncil.org. **Contact:** Susan Robinson, executive director. Estab. 1981. Biennial. Conference held April 19-21, 2001. Average attendance: 1,200. Conference on fiction, nonfiction, drama and poetry. Conference held in downtown Chattanooga on the campus of the University of Tennessee and in the historic Tivoli Theatre. 2001 speakers include Pearl Cleage, George Garrett, E.L. Konigsburg and Robert Morgan. 2001 panels feature members of the Fellowship of Southern Writers.

Costs: $50 (covers conference registration only).

Accommodations: "Radisson Read House Hotel offers a rate of $82/night for conference attendees." Shuttle service provided from the Radisson Read House Hotel to the University of Tennessee at Chattanooga.

Additional Information: Conference brochures with schedule available in January 2001. For brochure send SASE e-mail, visit website, call. Accepts inquiries by phone, SASE, e-mail.

[N] **DUEL ON THE DELTA WRITERS' CONFERENCE**, P.O. Box 241149, Memphis TN 38117-1149. (901)726-9683. E-mail: DuelontheDelta@aol.com. Website: www.rivercityrw.com. **Contact:** Kathleen Hodges, conference coordinator. Estab. 1992. Annual. Conference held March 2-3, 2001. Average attendance: 200. Conference sponsored by River City Romance Writers. Areas of focus include romance, romantic suspense, suspense, mystery, mainstream, multicultural. Site: Full-service hotel with banquet and meeting facilities. Conference includes tracks specially designed for the beginning, advanced and published writer; industry track featuring editors and agents from major publishers, small presses and electronic publishers; special track for mystery/suspense genre; round table discussions on genre specific topics; Meet the Experts. 2000 guests included Heather Graham, Debra Dixon, Joan Johnston, Deborah Smith, Elizabeth Daniels Squire, David Hunter, Felicia Mason, Lynn Emery, Sabrina Jeffries, Patricia Potter; editors from Berkley, Silhouette, Avon/HarperCollins, ImaJinn Books, Silver Dagger Mysteries and Starlight Writers.

Costs: Last year $135 (included Friday reception, Friday workshops; Saturday workshops, breakfast, lunch, dinner). Hotel/travel responsibility of individuals.

Accommodations: Hotel provides free shuttle and lower room rate on a selected/reserved block of rooms. 2000 room rate was $99.

Additional Information: First-chapter critique service available. Submit up to 25 pages prior to conference for review and personal interview during conference. Deadline February 15. $25 fee. Sponsors a contest. First 25 pages judged in 2 rounds: first round (experienced critiquers/published authors); final round (editor/agent). 1st place: plaque and pendant. Finalists: plaque. $20 fee. Deadline: November 1. See website for more details. Conference information is available December 2000. For brochure send SASE, e-mail, visit website, call. Accepts inquiries by SASE, e-mail and phone. Agents and editors participate in conference. "Editor/agent appointments available. Round table discussions. Night Owl Sessions on Friday. Chartered casino bus to Tunica on Friday. Literacy fundraiser. Two book fairs. Professional audiotaping. Book signing. All published authors attending are invited to participate in booksigning."

✅ **NORTH CAROLINA WRITERS' NETWORK FALL CONFERENCE**, P.O. Box 954, Carrboro NC 27510-0954. (919)967-9540. Fax: (919)929-0535. E-mail: mail@ncwriters.org. Website: www.ncwriters.org. **Contact:** Linda W. Hobson, executive director. Estab. 1985. Annual. Conference held in November 2001. Average attendance: 450. "The conference is a weekend full of workshops, panels, readings and discussion groups. It endeavors to serve writers of all levels of skill from beginning, to emerging, to established. We try to have *all* genres represented. In the past we have had novelists, poets, journalists, editors, children's writers, young adult writers, storytellers, playwrights, screenwriters, etc. We take the conference to a different location in North Carolina each year in order to best serve our entire state. We hold the conference at a conference center with hotel rooms available."

Costs: "Conference cost is approximately $175 and includes two meals."

Accommodations: "Special conference hotel rates are obtained, but the individual makes his/her own reservations."

Additional Information: Conference information available in late August 2001. For brochure send SASE with 2 first-class stamps, e-mail, visit website, fax or phone. Accepts inquiries by SASE, phone, fax, e-mail.

SEWANEE WRITERS' CONFERENCE, 310 St. Luke's Hall, Sewanee TN 37383-1000. (931)598-1141. Fax: (931)598-1145. E-mail: cpeters@sewanee.edu. Website: www.sewanee.edu/writers_conference/home.html. **Contact:** Cheri B. Peters, creative writing programs manager. Estab. 1990. Annual. Conference held July 17-29, 2001. Average attendance: 110. "We offer genre-based workshops in fiction, poetry, and playwriting. The Sewanee Writers' Conference uses the facilities of the University of the South. Physically, the University is a collection of ivy-covered Gothic-style buildings, located on the Cumberland Plateau in mid-Tennessee. We allow invited editors, publishers, and agents to structure their own presentations, but there is always opportunity for questions from the audience." The 2000 faculty included Laura Maria Censabella, Tony Earley, Barry Hannah, Andrew Hudgins, Diane Johnson, Romulus Linney, Alice McDermott, Erin McGraw, Claire Messud, Padgett Powell, Francine Prose, Mary Jo Salter, Dave Smith and Mark Strand.

Costs: Full conference fee (tuition, board, and basic room) is $1,205; a single room costs an additional $50.

Accommodations: Complimentary chartered bus service is available, on a limited basis, on the first and last days of the conference. Participants are housed in University dormitory rooms. Motel or B&B housing is available but not abundantly so. Dormitory housing costs are included in the full conference fee.

Additional Information: "We offer each participant (excluding auditors) the opportunity for a private manuscript conference with a member of the faculty. These manuscripts are due one month before the conference begins." Conference information available after February. For brochure send address and phone number, e-mail, visit website or call. "The conference has available a limited number of fellowships and scholarships; these are awarded on a competitive basis." Accepts inquiries by website, e-mail, phone, regular mail (send address and phone number).

🅽 **VIRGINIA FESTIVAL OF THE BOOK**, 145 Ednam Dr., Charlottesville VA 22903. (804)924-6890. Fax: (804)296-4714. E-mail: vabook@virginia.edu. Website: www.vabook.org. **Contact:** Nancy Damon. Estab. 1995. Annual. Festival held March 21-25, 2001. Average attendance: 13,500. Festival held to celebrate books and promote reading and literacy. Held throughout the Charlottesville/Albemarle area.

Costs: $35 fee for luncheon and reception.
Accommodations: Overnight accommodations can be found on the web.
Additional Information: "Authors must 'apply' to the festival to be included on a panel. Others can observe but not participate on panel." Conference information is available in November. For brochure visit website. Accepts inquiries by e-mail, fax. Agents and editors participate in conference. "The festival is a five-day event featuring authors, illustrators and publishing professionals. The featured authors are invited or write and inquire to participate. All attendees welcome."

N VIRGINIA ROMANCE WRITER'S CONFERENCE: Step Back in Time; Romance, History, and Crime, 13 Woodlawn Terrace, Fredericksburg VA 22405. E-mail: spggreenman@aol.com. Website: www.geociti es.com/SoHo/museum/2164. **Contact:** Sandra Greenman. Estab. 1993. Biannual. Conference held March 23-25, 2001. Average attendance: 250-300 (limited to first 300 who register). Focus fiction. Workshops include basic and advanced writing, history, and criminology. VRW is a non-profit organization. Our goal is to stimulate interest in the art of writing by inspiring, encouraging, educating, and bringing together authors, editors, agents, and other related professionals for the mutual benefit of all. Conference at the Williamsburg Marriott. Features basic & advanced writing, plotting, screenwriting, how to create sexual tension, brainstorming (interactive), writing historical fiction, private programs by Mariners' Museum, personality types and deviant behavior, criminology. Some faculty includes Leanne Banks (author); Carolyn Green (author); Felicia Hall (author); Tracey Neikirk (special history speaker from Mariners' Museum); Dr. C. Thomas Somma (criminology, Auxilary Police Officer with the VBPD Forensic Pathologist); Newton DeShazo (Ed.D. LMFT LPC, psychologist); and more.
Costs: $150 (VRW members); $165 (non-members). Friday reception $17. Includes all workshops, handouts, continental breakfast & lunch on Saturday, and Sunday breakfast. After February 14 there will be a $15 late fee. Saturday only $125 (only includes lunch). Extra lunch tickets $45; extra banquet tickets $55.
Accommodations: List of area hotels on request. Rooms available at Marriott. Rates are $89/night. Must identify themselves as VRW Conference attendees and make own reservations. Hotel fills up by Feb. 1.
Additional Information: "Editor or agent appointments are scheduled in advance on a first-come, first-served basis." Forms are include in confirmation packages and must be returned ASAP. Brochures available October 2000 for SASE and e-mail. Accepts inquiries by SASE, e-mail. Agents and editors participate in conference.

THE WRITERS' WORKSHOP, 387 Beaucatcher Rd., Asheville NC 28805. (828)254-8111. **Contact:** Karen Ackerson, executive director. Estab. 1984. Held throughout the year. Conference duration: 1-3 days. Sites are throughout the South, especially North Carolina. Past guest speakers include John Le Carré, Peter Matthiessen and Eudora Welty.
Costs: Vary. Financial assistance available to low-income writers. Information on overnight accommodations is made available.

Southeast (AL, AR, FL, GA, LA, MS, PR [Puerto Rico])

ALABAMA WRITERS' CONCLAVE, P.O. Box 230787, Montgomery AL 36123-0787. (334)244-8920. Fax: (334)387-9123. E-mail: poettennis@aol.com. Editor: D.J. Tennis. **Contact:** Kay Blankenship, president. Estab. 1923. Annual. Conference held for three days, the first week in August. Average attendance: 75-100. Conference to promote "all phases" of writing. Held at the Ramsay Conference Center (University of Montevallo). "We attempt to contain all workshops under this roof."
Costs: Fees for 3 days are $45 for members; $55 for nonmembers (which includes membership). Lower rates for 1- or 2-day attendance. Meals and awards banquet additional cost.
Accommodations: Accommodations available on campus. $18 for single, $36 for double.
Additional Information: "We have 'name' speakers and workshops with members helping members. We offer open mike readings every evening. We sponsor a contest each year with a published book of winners." Conference brochures/guidelines available for SASE after June. Accepts inquiries by fax, e-mail. Membership dues are $15 and include a quarterly newsletter. Membership information from Donna Jean Tennis at above address.

■ ARKANSAS WRITERS' CONFERENCE, 6817 Gingerbread, Little Rock AR 72204. (501)565-7220. Fax: (501)565-8889. E-mail: pvining@aristotle.net. **Contact:** Clouita Rice, registrar/treasurer. Estab. 1944. Annual. Conference held June 1-2, 2001. Average attendance: 225. "We have a variety of subjects related to writing—we have some general sessions, some more specific, but try to vary each year's subjects."
Costs: Registration: $10; luncheon: $15; banquet: $17.50, contest entry $5.
Accommodations: "We meet at a Holiday Inn Select—rooms available at reasonable rate." Holiday Inn has a bus to bring anyone from airport. Rooms average $67.
Additional Information: "We have 36 contest categories. Some are open only to Arkansans, most are open to all writers. Our judges are not announced before conference but are qualified, many from out of state."

Conference information available February 15, 2001. For brochure send SASE, call or fax. Accepts inquiries by SASE, fax, phone. "We have had 226 attending from 12 states—over 2,000 contest entries from 40 states and New Zealand, Mexico and Canada."

FLORIDA CHRISTIAN WRITERS CONFERENCE, 2600 Park Ave., Titusville FL 32780. (407)269-6702, ext. 202. Fax: (407)383-1741. E-mail: writer@digital.net. Website: www.kipertek.com/writer. **Contact:** Billie Wilson, conference director. Estab. 1988. Annual. Conference is held in late January. Conference duration: 5 days. Average attendance: 200. To promote "all areas of writing." Conference held at Park Avenue Retreat Center, a conference complex at a large church near Kennedy Space Center. Editors will represent over 30 publications and publishing houses.
Costs: Tuition $360, included tuition, room and board (double occupancy).
Accommodations: "We provide shuttle from the airport and from the hotel to retreat center. We make reservations at major hotel chain."
Additional Information: Critiques available. "Each writer may submit three works for critique. We have specialists in every area of writing to critique." Conference brochures/guidelines are available for SASE.

FLORIDA FIRST COAST WRITERS' FESTIVAL, 101 W. State St., FCCJ Downtown Campus, Jacksonville FL 32202-3056. (904)633-8327. Fax: (904)633-8435. E-mail: kclower@fccj.org. Website: www.fccj.org/wf/. **Contact:** Kathleen Clower, media production manager. Estab. 1985. Annual. Festival held May 17-19, 2001. Average attendance: 300-350. All areas: mainstream plus genre. Held at Sea Turtle Inn on Atlantic Beach.
Costs: "Early bird special $175 for 2 days (including lunch and banquet) or $150 for 2 days (including lunch) or $75 for each day; pre-conference workshops extra."
Accommodations: Sea Turtle Inn, (904)249-7402 or (800)874-6000, has a special festival rate.
Additional Information: Sponsors contests for short fiction, poetry and novels. Novel judges are David Poyer and Lenore Hart. Entry fees: $30, novels; $10, short fiction; $5, poetry. Deadline: November 1 for novels, short fiction, poems. Conference information available March 2001. For brochures/guidelines visit website, e-mail, fax, call. Accepts inquiries by e-mail, SASE, phone, fax. E-mail contest inquiries to hdenson@fccj.org.

HEMINGWAY DAYS WRITER'S WORKSHOP AND CONFERENCE, P.O. Box 4045, Key West FL 33041-4045. (305)294-4440. Fax: (305)292-3653. E-mail: calico2419@aol.com. Director of Workshop: Dr. James Plath. Festival Director: Carol Shaughnessy. Estab. 1989. Annual. Conference held July. Conference duration: 3½ days. Average attendance: 60-100. "We deliberately keep it small so that there is a greater opportunity for participants to interact with presenting writers. The Hemingway Days Writer's Workshop and Conference focuses on fiction, poetry and Ernest Hemingway and his work. The workshop and conference is but one event in a week-long festival which honors Ernest Hemingway. The first evening features a reception and presentation of the Conch Republic Prize for Literature to a writer whose life's work epitomizes the creative spirit of Key West. Then, one day focuses on the writing of fiction, one day on the writing of poetry, and one day on Ernest Hemingway's life and work. We are offering more hands-on directed writing sessions than ever before, and combine them with our traditionally-offered presentations and after-sunset readings by critically-acclaimed writers. Most years, we also offer the opportunity for participants to have their own work critiqued. Traditionally, the Workshop & Conference is held at a resort in Key West's historic Old Town section. Directed writing exercises take place at a variety of locations in the Old Town area such as gardens and historic sites, while after-sunset readings will take place at an open-air atrium or restaurant."
Costs: $120 (1998); included all panels, directed writing exercises, attendance at all literary receptions and after-sunset readings.
Accommodations: Material available upon request.
Additional Information: Brochures/guidelines are available for SASE. "The conference/workshop is unique in that it combines studies in craft with studies in literature, and serious literary-minded events to celebrate Hemingway the writer with a week-long festival celebrating 'Papa' the myth."

HOW TO BE PUBLISHED WORKSHOPS, P.O. Box 100031, Birmingham AL 35210. (205)907-0140. E-mail: mgteach@earthlink.net. Website: home.earthlink.net/~mgteach. **Contact:** Michael Garrett. Estab. 1986. Workshops held January 21 (9 am-4 pm), 22nd (9 am-4 pm and 6-9 pm), and 23rd (9 am-4 pm). Workshop duration: 1 day. Average attendance: 10-15. Workshop to "move writers of category fiction closer to publication." Workshop held at college campuses and universities. Themes include "Marketing," "Idea Development" and a manuscript critique.
Costs: $49-79.
Additional Information: "Special critique is offered, but advance submission is not required." Accepts inquiries by e-mail.

N KEY WEST LITERARY SEMINAR, 4 Portside Lane, Searsport ME 04974. (888)293-9291. E-mail: keywest@mint.net. Website: http://KeyWestLiterarySeminar.org. **Contact:** Miles Frieden. Estab. 1981. Annual. Spirit of Place: American Literary Landscapes January 7-13, 2002. Workshop duration: 7 days. Average attendance: 400.
Costs: $400 plus tax.
Accommodations: Provides list of area hotels or lodging options.
Additional Information: For brochure send e-mail, visit website or call. Accepts inquiries by e-mail, phone. Agents and editors participate in conference.

N KEY WEST WRITERS' WORKSHOP, 5901 College Rd., Key West FL 33040. (305)296-9087, ext. 302. Fax: (305)292-2392. E-mail: weinman_i@firn.edu. Website: www.firn.edu/fkcc/kwww.htm. **Contact:** Irving Weinman, director. Estab. 1996. Held 5 weekends/season (January-March). Workshop duration: 5 weekends. Average attendance: 10-12 participants in each workshop. Workshop focuses on fiction and poetry. John Ashbery (poetry), Sharon Olds (poetry), Joy Williams (fiction), Carolyn Forché (poetry) and Robert Stone (fiction) are scheduled to participate in the 2001 conference.
Costs: $275 for tuition only.
Accommodations: Provides a list of area hotels or lodging options.
Additional Information: "It's very competitive; many more applicants than places. Early application is essential." Workshop information is available now. For brochure send SASE, e-mail, visit website, call, fax. Accepts inquiries by SASE, e-mail, phone, fax. High standards. "Informal, intimate, intense."

☑ MOONLIGHT AND MAGNOLIAS WRITER'S CONFERENCE. E-mail: info@georgiaromancewrite rs.org. Website: www.georgiaromancewriters.org/maggies.html. Estab. 1982. Annual. Conference held 3rd weekend in September. Average attendance: 300. "Conference focuses on writing of women's fiction with emphasis on romance. Includes agents and editors from major publishing houses. Workshops have included: beginning writer track, general interest topics, and professional issues for the published author, plus sessions for writing for children, young adult, inspirational, multicultural and Regency. Speakers have included experts in law enforcement, screenwriting and research. Literacy raffle and advertised speaker and GRW member autographing open to the public." Published authors make up 25-30% of attendees. Brochure available for SASE in June or check website. Accepts inquiries by e-mail.
Costs: Hotel $74/day, single, double, triple, quad (1997). Conference: non-GRW members $145 (early registration). See website for full information.
Additional Information: Maggie Awards for excellence are presented to unpublished writers. The Maggie Award for published writers is limited to Region 3 members of Romance Writers of America. Proposals per guidelines must be submitted in early June. Published authors judge first round, category editors judge finals. Guidelines available for SASE in spring or on website.

N OZARK CREATIVE WRITERS, INC., 6817 Gingerbread Lane, Little Rock AR 72204. (501)565-8889. Fax: (501)565-7220. E-mail: puining@gristotts.net. President: Dusty Richards. **Contact:** Peggy Vining, OCWI board. Estab. 1973. Annual. Conference always held 2nd weekend in October. Conference duration: 2½ days. Average attendance: 250. "All types of writing. Main speaker for workshop in morning sessions—usually a novelist. Satellite speakers—afternoon—various types, including a Poetry Seminar. Conference site is the convention center. Very nice for a small group setting. Reserve early, prior to September 1, to insure place."
Costs: $50 plus approximately $30 for 2 banquets. Rooms are approximately $65/night; meals extra. Registration fee allows you to enter the writing contests.
Accommodations: Chamber of Commerce will send list; 60 rooms are blocked off for OCW prior to August 15th. Accommodations vary at hotels. Many campsites also available. "Eureka Springs is a resort town near Branson, Missouri, the foothills of the beautiful Ozark Mountains."
Additional Information: "We have approximately 20 various categories of writing contests. Selling writers are our judges. Entry fee required to enter. Brochures are available for SASE after May 1." Accepts inquiries by SASE, e-mail, fax, phone.

MARJORIE KINNAN RAWLINGS: WRITING THE REGION, P.O. Box 12246, Gainesville FL 32604. (888)917-7001. Fax: (352)373-8854. E-mail: shakes@ufl.edu. Website: www.afn.org/~gaca/writers/writers.html. **Contact:** Norma M. Homan, executive director. Estab. 1997. Annual conference held in July/August 2001. Conference duration: 5 days. Average attendance: 100. Conference concentrates on fiction, writing for children, poetry, nonfiction, drama, screenwriting, writing with humor, setting, character, etc. Conference held at historic building, formerly the Thomas Hotel. 2000 speakers included Patrick Smith, June and David Cussen and Mark Ryan.
Costs: $355 for 5 days including meals; $335 "early bird" registration; $125 single day; $75 half day.
Accommodations: Special conference rates at area hotels available.

Additional Information: Manuscript consultation on an individual basis by application only and $100 additional fee. Sponsors essay contest for registrants on a topic dealing with Marjorie Kinnan Rawlings. For brochures/guidelines send SASE. Accepts inquiries by fax, e-mail.

N SCBWI SOUTHERN BREEZE FALL CONFERENCE, "Writing and Illustrating for Kids," P.O. Box 26282, Birmingham AL 35260. E-mail: joanbroerman@home.com. Website: http://members.home.net/south ernbreeze/. **Contact:** Joan Broerman, regional advisor. Estab. 1992. Annual. Conference held in October. One-day Saturday conference. Average attendance: 125. "All Southern Breeze SCBWI conferences are geared to the production and support of quality children's literature."
Costs: About $60 for SCBWI members, $75 for non-members, plus lunch (about $6). Individual critiques are available for additional fees.
Accommodations: "We have a room block with a conference rate. The conference is held at a nearby school If we can get an airline discount, we publish this in our newsletter and on our webpage."
Additional Information: "The fall conference offers 30 workshops on craft and the business of writing, including a basic workshop for those new to the children's field." Manuscript critiques are offered; manuscripts must be sent by deadline. Conference information is included in the SCBWI newsletter, mailed in September. Brochure is available for SASE, by e-mail or visit website for details. Accepts inquiries by SASE, e-mail. Agents and editors attend/participate in conference.

N SCBWI SOUTHERN BREEZE SPRING CONFERENCE, "Springmingle '01," P.O. Box 26282, Birmingham AL 35260. E-mail: joanbroerman@home.com. Website: http://members.home.net/southernbreeze/. **Contact:** Joan Broerman, regional advisor. Estab. 1992. Annual. Conference held in February. Conference duration is 3 days. Average attendance: 60. "All Southern Breeze SCBWI conferences are geared to the production and support of quality children's literature." Event is held "in a hotel in one of the 3 states which compose our region: Alabama, Georgia or Mississippi." Springmingle '01 will include Richard Peck, National Book Award finalist; Patricia Lee Gauch, vice president and editorial director of Philomel Books, Penguin Putnam Books for Young Readers; and an illustrator to be announced.
Costs: "About $100; SCBWI non-members pay $10-15 more. Sometimes 1 or 2 meals are included."
Accommodations: "We have a room block with a conference rate in the hotel conference site. Individuals make their own reservations. If we can get an airline discount, we publish this in our newsletter and on our webpage."
Additional Information: Sometimes individual manuscript consultations are offered; manuscripts must be sent ahead of time. Conference information is included in the SCBWI newsletter, mailed in January. Brochure is available for SASE, by e-mail or visit website for details. Accepts inquiries by SASE, e-mail. Agents and editors participate in conference.

SCBWI/FLORIDA ANNUAL FALL CONFERENCE, 2158 Portland Ave., Wellington FL 33414. E-mail: barcafer@aol.com. **Contact:** Barbara Casey, Florida regional advisor. Estab. 1985. Annual. Conference duration: one-half day. Average attendance: 70. Conference to promote "all aspects of writing and illustrating for children. Time and location to be announced."
Costs: $50 for SCBWI members, $55 for non-SCBWI members. Ms and art evaluations, $30.
Accommodations: Special conference rates at Airport Hilton, West Palm Beach, Florida.
Additional Information: Accepts inquiries by e-mail.

N SOUTHERN LIGHTS, P.O. Box 8604, Jacksonville FL 32239-8604. (352)687-3902. E-mail: LBarone21 @aol.com. Website: www.angelfire.com/fl/Romancewriting. **Contact:** Laura Barone, president. Estab. 1995. Annual. Conference held May 2001. Conference duration: 2 days. Average attendance: 100. The focus of the conference is fiction writing. Site: Holiday Inn Baymeadows, which is "close to beaches, local attractions and shopping." Panels for the 2000 conference included plotting, character development, sexual tension, avoiding contrivances, and editor/agent appointments. Cheryl Anne Porter (St. Martins, Harlequin), Vicki Heinze (St. Martins, Silhouette, Kensington), Katherine Garbera (Silhouette Desire), Lorna Tedder (Silhouette, Kensington), Jennifer Weis (editor, St. Martins Press), and Marge Smith (Harlequin, Silhouette, Kensington) participated in 2000.
Costs: $65 fee includes lunch; $55/night hotel.
Accommodations: "If request is made early we can arrange pickup at airport." Offers overnight accommodations at a special room rate at the conference site.
Additional Information: Conference information is available March 2001. For brochure send SASE, e-mail, visit website, or call. Accepts queries by SASE, e-mail, phone. Agents and editors participate in conference.

✓ ⊕ WRITE IT OUT, P.O. Box 704, Sarasota FL 34230-0704. (941)359-3824. Fax: (941)359-3931. E-mail: rmillerwio@aol.com. Website: www.writeitout.com. **Contact:** Ronni Miller, director. Estab. 1997. Workshops held 2-3 times/year in March, June and August, 2001. Duration: 5-10 days. Average attendance: 4-10.

Workshops on "fiction, travel writing, poetry, memoirs." Workshops held across the United States as well as in Italy in a Tuscan villa, in Bermuda at a hotel or in Cape Cod at an inn. Theme: "Landscape—Horizon." Past speakers included Arturo Vivante, novelist.

Costs: 2000 fees: Italy $2,150; Bermuda $895; Cape Cod $795. Price includes tuition, room and board. Airfare not included.

Additional Information: "Critiques on work are given at the workshops." Conference information available November 2000. For brochures/guidelines e-mail, fax, phone or visit website. Accepts inquiries by fax, phone, e-mail. Workshops have "small groups, option to spend time writing and not attend classes, with personal appointments made with instructors for feedback."

✔ **WRITING STRATEGIES FOR THE CHRISTIAN MARKET**, 2712 S. Peninsula Dr., Daytona Beach FL 32118-5706. (904)322-1111. Fax: (904)322-1111*9. E-mail: romy14@juno.com. Website: www.amyfound. org. **Contact:** Rosemary Upton, instructor. Estab. 1991. Independent studies with manual. Includes Basics I, Marketing II, Business III, Building the Novel. Critique by mail with SASE. Question and answer session via e-mail or U.S. mail. Critique shop included once a month, except summer (July and August). Instructors include Rosemary Upton, novelist; Kistler London, editor.

Costs: $30 for manual and ongoing support.

Additional Information: "Designed for correspondence students as well as the classroom experience, the courses are economical and include all materials, as well as the evaluation of assignments." Those who have taken Writing Strategies instruction are able to attend an on-going monthly critiqueshop where their peers critique their work. Manual provided. For brochures/guidelines/newsletter send SASE, e-mail, fax or call. Accepts inquiries by fax, e-mail. Independent study by mail only offered at this time.

WRITING TODAY—BIRMINGHAM-SOUTHERN COLLEGE, Box 549003, Birmingham AL 35254. (205)226-4921. Fax: (205)226-3072. E-mail: dcwilson@bsc.edu. Website: www.bsc.edu. **Contact:** Martha Ross, director. Estab. 1978. Annual. Conference held March 16-17, 2001. Average attendance: 400-500. "This is a two-day conference with approximately 18 workshops, lectures and readings. We try to offer workshops in short fiction, novels, poetry, children's literature, magazine writing, and general information of concern to aspiring writers such as publishing, agents, markets and research. The conference is sponsored by Birmingham-Southern College and is held on the campus in classrooms and lecture halls." The 2000 conference featured Ernest Gaines, Sena Jeter Naslund, Ishmael Reed and Claudia Johnson.

Costs: $120 for both days. This includes lunches, reception and morning coffee and rolls.

Accommodations: Attendees must arrange own transportation. Local hotels and motels offer special rates, but participants must make their own reservations.

Additional Information: "We usually offer a critique for interested writers. We have had poetry and short story critiques. There is an additional charge for these critiques." Sponsors the Hackney Literary Competition Awards for poetry, short story and novels. Guidelines available for SASE.

Midwest (IL, IN, KY, MI, OH)

ANTIOCH WRITERS' WORKSHOP, P.O. Box 494, Yellow Springs OH 45387. E-mail: info@antiochwriter sworkshop.com. Website: www.antiochwritersworkshop.com. Estab. 1984. Annual. Conference held August. Average attendance: 80. Workshop concentration: poetry, nonfiction and fiction. Workshop located on Antioch College campus in the Village of Yellow Springs. Speakers have included Sue Grafton, Imogene Bolls, George Ella Lyon, Herbert Martin, John Jakes, Virginia Hamilton and Natalie Goldberg.

Costs: Tuition is $485—lower for local and repeat—plus meals.

Accommodations: "We pick up attendees free at the airport." Accommodations made at dorms and area hotels. Cost is $16-26/night (for dorms).

Additional Information: Offers mss critique sessions. Conference information is available after March 2000.

THE COLUMBUS WRITERS CONFERENCE, P.O. Box 20548, Columbus OH 43220. (614)451-3075. Fax: (614)451-0174. E-mail: AngelaPL28@aol.com. **Contact:** Angela Palazzolo, director. Estab. 1993. Annual. Conference held in September. Average attendance: more than 200. "The conference covers a variety of fiction and nonfiction topics presented by writers, editors and literary agents. Writing topics have included novel, short story, children's, young adult, poetry, historical fiction, science fiction, fantasy, humor, mystery, playwriting,

SENDING TO A COUNTRY other than your own? Be sure to send International Reply Coupons (IRC) instead of stamps for replies or return of your manuscript.

screenwriting, travel, humor, cookbook, technical, queries, book proposals and freelance writing. Other topics have included finding and working with an agent, targeting markets, time management, obtaining grants, sparking creativity and networking." Speakers have included Lee K. Abbott, Lore Segal, Jack Matthews, David Baker, Mike Harden, Oscar Collier, Maureen F. McHugh, Ralph Keyes, Stephanie S. Tolan, J. Patrick Lewis, Tracey E. Dils, Dennis L. McKiernan, Karen Harper, Melvin Helitzer, Susan Porter, Les Roberts, Tracey E. Dils, J. Patrick Lewis and many other professionals in the writing field.

Costs: Early registration fee is $149 for the full conference (Friday afternoon sessions, dinner, after-dinner program and Saturday program); otherwise fee is $169. Early registration for the Saturday program (includes continental breakfast, lunch, and afternoon refreshments) is $119; otherwise fee is $139.

Additional Information: Call, write, e-mail or send fax to obtain a conference brochure, available mid-summer.

N GREEN RIVER WRITERS NOVELS-IN-PROGRESS WORKSHOP, 11906 Locust Rd., Middletown KY 40243-1413. (502)245-4902. E-mail: mary_odell@ntr.net. **Contact:** Mary E. O'Dell, director. Estab. 1991. Annual. Conference held in March. Conference duration: 1 week. Average attendance: 50. Open to persons, college age and above, who have approximately 3 chapters (60 pages) or more of a novel. Mainstream and genre novels handled by individual instructors. Short fiction collections welcome. "Each novelist instructor works with a small group (5-7 people) for five days; then agents/editors are there for panels and appointments on the weekend." Site: The University of Louisville's Shelby Campus, suburban setting, graduate dorm housing (private rooms available with shared bath for each 2 rooms). "Meetings and classes held in nearby classroom building. Grounds available for walking, etc. Lovely setting, restaurants and shopping available nearby. Participants carpool to restaurants, etc." Past workshops have covered mystery, fantasy, mainstream/literary, suspense, historical.

Costs: Tuition—$375, housing $22 per night private, $18 shared. Does not include meals.

Accommodations: "We do meet participants' planes and see that participants without cars have transportation to meals, etc. If participants would rather stay in hotel, we will make that information available."

Additional Information: Participants send 60 pages/3 chapters with synopsis and $25 reading fee which applies to tuition. Deadline will be in late January. Conference information available after January 1. For brochures/guidelines send SASE. Accepts inquiries by e-mail.

IMAGINATION, Cleveland State University, Division of Continuing Education, 2344 Euclid Ave., Cleveland OH 44115. (216)687-4522. **Contact:** Dan Chaon, director. Estab. 1990. Annual. Conference lasts 5 days and is held late June/early July. Average attendance: 60. "Conference concentrates on fiction, poetry and nonfiction. Held at Mather Mansion, a restored 19th century mansion on the campus of Cleveland State University." Past themes have included Writing Beyond Realism and Business of Writing. E-mail, fax or mail for brochure after January 2001.

✔ INDIANA UNIVERSITY WRITERS' CONFERENCE, 464 Ballantine Hall, Bloomington IN 47405-7103. (812)855-1877. Fax: (812)855-9535. E-mail: rrubinas@indiana.edu. Website: http://php.indiana.edu/~iuwc/. **Contact:** Romayne Rubinas, director. Estab. 1940. Annual. Conference/workshops held from June 24-29, 2001. Average attendance: 100. "Conference to promote poetry, fiction and nonfiction." Located on the campus of Indiana University, Bloomington. "We do not have themes, although we do have panels that discuss issues such as how to publish. We also have classes that tackle just about every subject of writing." Michael Martone, Kate Daniels, Timothy Liu, Jonis Agee and Beckian Fritz Goldberg spoke and taught workshops at the 2000 conference.

Costs: Approximately $300; does not include food or housing. This price does *not* reflect the cost of taking the conference for credit. "We supply conferees with options for overnight accommodations. We offer special conference rates for both the hotel and dorm facilities on site."

Additional Information: "In order to be accepted in a workshop, the writer must submit the work they would like critiqued. Work is evaluated before accepting applicant. Scholarships are available determined by an outside reader/writer, based on the quality of the manuscript." Conference information available in January 2001. For brochures/guidelines send SASE, visit website, e-mail, or call. Accepts inquiries by SASE, e-mail, phone. Application deadline is in early May. Apply early as workshops fill up quickly. "We are the second oldest writer's conference in the country. We are in our 60th year."

N KENTUCKY WOMEN WRITERS CONFERENCE, % The Carnegie Center, 251 W. Second St., Lexington KY 40507-1135. (859)254-4175. Fax: (859)281-1151. E-mail: kywwc@hotmail.com or CCLL1@carn egieliteracy.org. Website: www.carnegieliteracy.org. **Contact:** Jan Isenhour, director. Estab. 1979. Fall event/annual spring conference. Conference held March 24-26, 2001. Average attendance: 100-150. "Conference is a gathering to foster feminist creativity highlighting readings, panel discussions, workshops, performances and films. Features all genres including memoir, poetry, fiction, nonfiction, and feminist theory." Site: "Located in historic Gratz Park in downtown Lexington, The Carnegie Center for Literacy and Learning is in walking distance of all facilities. This center for community literacy was dedicated by Barbara Bush on September 11, 1992 and hailed as unique with programs for all ages and abilities; reading, writing, and literacy-related workshops;

presentations; after-school tutoring; visiting poets, writers, storytellers and artists." 2001 conference theme is Claiming Identities/Writing Identities. 2000 conference featured Judith Ortiz Cofer, Sena Jeter Naslund, Karen Sayler McElmurray, Patricia Johnson, Gloria Velasquez and Margarita Donnelly.
Costs: $100-150 (TBA) for entire conference (meals and lodging not included).
Accommodations: Provides a list of area hotels or lodging options (there are hotels within walking distance of conference site).
Additional Information: Sponsors a contest as part of conference. Conference information is available January 2001. For brochure send SASE, e-mail, visit website, call, fax. Accepts inquiries by SASE, e-mail, phone, fax. Agents and editors participate in conference.

N: KENYON REVIEW WRITERS WORKSHOP, *The Kenyon Review*, Kenyon College, Gambier OH 43022. (740)427-5207. Fax: (740)427-5417. E-mail: kenyonreview@kenyon.edu. Website: www.kenyonreview.org. **Contact:** David Lynn, director. Estab. 1990. Annual. Workshop held late June through early July. Workshop duration: 10 days. Average attendance: 35-40. Participants apply in poetry, fiction or creative nonfiction, and then participate in intensive daily workshops which focus on the generation and revision of significant new work. The conference takes place on the campus of Kenyon College in the rural village of Gambier, Ohio. Students have access to college computing and recreational facilities, and are housed in campus housing. 2000 faculty: Fiction, Keith Banner and Sharon Dilworth; Poetry, Erin Belieu and David Bergman; Nonfiction, Rebecca McClanahan.
Costs: $1,450 including room and board.
Accommodations: The workshop operates a shuttle from Gambier to the airport in Columbus, Ohio. Offers overnight accommodations. Students are housed in Kenyon College student housing. The cost is covered in the tuition.
Additional Information: Application includes a writing sample. Admission decisions are made on a rolling basis beginning Februrary 1. Workshop information is available in November. For brochure send e-mail, visit website, call, fax. Accepts inquiries by SASE, e-mail, phone, fax.

N: MAUMEE VALLEY FREELANCE WRITERS' FIFTH ANNUAL CONFERENCE, Lourdes College, 6832 Convent Blvd., Sylvania OH 43560. (419)824-3707. Fax: (419)824-3514. E-mail: gburke@lourdes.edu. Website: www.lourdes.edu. **Contact:** Gloria Burke, conference coordinator. Estab. 1997. Annual. Conference held April 21, 2001. Average attendance: 50. "The purpose is to provide a venue for freelance writers in a variety of genres. For example, in 2000 we offered sessions on e-publishing, writing for the confession market, writing for alumni magazines, how to write for the *Chicken Soup* books, the art and business of children's writing, travel writing, how to write query letters and writing for local and area publications. This is a small Franciscan facility located in Sylvania OH, 10 miles from Toledo OH. Buildings are of Spanish-style architecture, many adorned with large, exquisite tile murals. Many inside hallways are decorated with statues, paintings, tiles, and unusual designs imported from Italy and Spain. The conference itself begins in the beautiful Planetarium Lobby; classes are held in Mother Adelaide Hall." Keynote speaker for the 2001 conference will be Barbara Kuroff, Editorial Director of Writer's Digest Market Books.
Costs: $69/person including lunch.
Additional Information: Conference information is available January, 2001. For brochure send SASE, e-mail, visit website, call, fax. Accepts inquiries by SASE, e-mail, phone, fax. Agents and editors participate in conference. "Evaluations show that this is a well-planned, well-organized conference. Every effort has been made to reach freelance writers in the Maumee Valley and Southeastern Michigan areas. We have had anywhere from 38-65 people in attendance; as the conference coordinator, it is my goal to reach for the 100+ mark—hopefully, in 2001."

THE MID AMERICA MYSTERY CONFERENCE, Magna cum Murder, The E.B. Ball Center, Ball State University, Muncie IN 47306. (765)285-8975. Fax: (765)747-9566. E-mail: kkenniso@wp.bsu.edu. Estab. 1994. Annual. Conference held in October. Average attendance: 400. Conference for crime and detective fiction held in the Horizon Convention Center and Historic Radisson Hotel Roberts. Past speakers included Mickey Spillane, Anne Perry, Jeremiah Healy, John Gilstrap and Tess Gerritsen.
Costs: $165, which includes continental breakfasts, boxed lunches, a reception and a banquet (1997).
Additional Information: Brochures or guidelines available for SASE. Accepts inquiries by fax, e-mail.

MIDLAND WRITERS CONFERENCE, Grace A. Dow Memorial Library, 1710 W. St. Andrews, Midland MI 48640-2698. (517)835-7151. Fax: (517)835-9791. E-mail: kred@vlc.lib.mi.us. Website: www.gracedowlibrary.org. **Contact:** Katherine Redwine, conference chair. Estab. 1980. Annual. Conference held in June. Average attendance: 100. "The Conference is composed of a well-known keynote speaker and workshops on a variety of subjects including poetry, children's writing, freelancing, agents, etc. The attendees are both published and

unpublished authors. The Conference is held at the Grace A. Dow Memorial Library in the auditorium and conference rooms. Keynoters in the past have included Dave Barry, Pat Conroy, Kurt Vonnegut, Peggy Noonan, Roger Ebert."
Costs: Adult—$50 before May 26, $60 after May 27; students, senior citizens and handicapped—$40 before May 26, $50 after May 26. A box lunch is available. Costs are approximate until plans for upcoming conference are finalized.
Accommodations: A list of area hotels is available.
Additional Information: Conference brochures/guidelines are mailed mid-April. Call or write to be put on mailing list. Accepts inquiries by e-mail, fax.

MIDWEST WRITERS' CONFERENCE, 6000 Frank Ave. NW, Canton OH 44720-7599. (216)499-9600. Fax: (330)494-6121. E-mail: Druhe@Stark.Kent.Edu. **Contact:** Debbie Ruhe, conference director. Estab. 1968. Annual. Conference held in early October. Conference duration: 2 days. Average attendance: 350. "The conference provides an atmosphere in which aspiring writers can meet with and learn from experienced and established writers through lectures, workshops, competitive contest, personal interviews and informal group discussions. The areas of concentration include fiction, nonfiction, juvenile literature and poetry. The Midwest Writers' Conference is held on Kent State University Stark Campus in Canton, Ohio. This two-day conference is held in Main Hall, a four-story building and wheel chair accessible."
Costs: $125 includes Friday workshops, keynote address, Saturday workshops, box luncheon and manuscript entry fee (limited to two submissions); $70 for contest only (includes two manuscripts).
Accommodations: Arrangements are made with a local hotel which is near Kent State and offers a special reduced rate for conference attendees. Conferees must make their own reservations 3 weeks before the conference to be guaranteed this special conference rate.
Additional Information: Each manuscript entered in the contest will receive a critique. If the manuscript is selected for final judging, it will receive an additional critique from the final judge. Conference attendees are not required to submit manuscripts to the writing contest. Manuscript deadline is early August. For contest: A maximum of 1 entry for each category is permitted. Entries must be typed on 8½×11 paper, double-spaced. A separate page must accompany each entry bearing the author's name, address, phone, category and title of the work. Entries are not to exceed 3,000 words in length. Work must be original, unpublished and not a winner in any contest at the time of entry. Conference brochures and guidelines are available after June for SASE. Accepts inquiries by e-mail, fax.

THE MINISTRY OF WRITING: AN ANNUAL COLLOQUIUM, Earlham School of Religion, 228 College, Richmond IN 47374. (800)432-1377. Fax: (765)983-1668. E-mail: billbr@earlham.edu. Website: www.earlh am.edu/~esr/napoli.html. **Contact:** J. Brent Bill, director. Estab. 1992. Annual conference held October 19-20, 2001. Conference duration: 1½ days. Average attendance: 175. Conference "to encourage writers to see writing as ministry." Workshops are held on fiction, nonfiction, editing, marketing, etc. Held on the campus of Earlham School of Religion in Richmond, IN—using classrooms, worship spaces, etc. Novelist Elizabeth Cox is the 2001 keynote speaker. 2000 conference featured Donna Jo Napoli (keynoter, young adult); Kathleen Bolduc (personal narrative); Joyce & Josh Brown (self-publishing), Barbara Bennett Mays (editing), C. Michael Curtis of the *Atlantic Monthly* (fiction), James Yerkes (anthology) and David Yount (nonfiction).
Costs: $55 for entire conference (including meals); $45 for Saturday only; $25 student fee (graduate/undergrad).
Accommodations: Hotel lists available.
Additional Information: Conference information available after August 1 every year. For brochures/guidelines send SASE, visit website, e-mail, fax or call. Accepts inquiries by SASE, e-mail, fax, phone.

☑ **OAKLAND UNIVERSITY WRITERS' CONFERENCE**, 221 Varner Hall, Rochester MI 48309-4401. (248)370-3125. Fax: (248)370-4280. E-mail: gjboddy@oakland.edu. Website: www.oakland.edu/contin-ed/writer sconf/. **Contact:** Gloria J. Boddy, program director. Estab. 1961. Annual. Conference held in October 2001. Average attendance: 400. Held at Oakland University: Oakland Center: Vandenburg Hall and O'Dowd Hall. Each annual conference covers all aspects and types of writing in 36 concurrent workshops on Saturday. Major writers from various genres are speakers for the Saturday conference and luncheon program. Individual critiques and hands-on writing workshops are conducted Friday. Areas: poetry, articles, fiction, short stories, playwriting, nonfiction, young adult, children's literature. Keynote speaker in 2000: Patricia Polacco.
Costs: 2000: Conference registration: $85; lunch, $15; individual ms, $58; writing workshop, $48.
Accommodations: List is available.
Additional Information: Conference information available after August 2001. For brochures/guidelines send SASE, visit website, e-mail, fax, call. Accepts inquiries by e-mail, fax, phone, SASE.

OF DARK & STORMY NIGHTS, Mystery Writers of America—Midwest Chapter, P.O. Box 1944, Muncie IN 47308-1944. (765)288-7402. E-mail: spurgeonmwa@juno.com. **Contact:** W.W. Spurgeon, director. Estab. 1982. Annual. Workshop held June 9, 2001. Average attendance: 200. Dedicated to "writing *mystery* fiction and crime-related nonfiction. Workshops and panels presented on techniques of mystery writing from ideas to revision, marketing, investigative techniques and more, by published writers, law enforcement experts and publishing professionals." Site is Holiday Inn, Rolling Meadows IL (suburban Chicago).

Costs: $125 for MWA members; $150 for non-members; $50 extra for ms critique.

Accommodations: Easily accessible by car or train (from Chicago) Holiday Inn, Rolling Meadows $89 per night plus tax; free airport bus (Chicago O'Hare) and previously-arranged rides from train.

Additional Information: "We accept manuscripts for critique (first 30 pages maximum); $50 cost. Writers meet with critics during workshop for one-on-one discussions." Conference information available January 1, 2001. For brochures/guidelines send SASE, e-mail, call. Accepts inquiries by SASE, phone, e-mail.

N OPEN WRITING WORKSHOPS, Creative Writing Program, Dept. of English, Bowling Green State University, Bowling Green OH 43403-0215. (419)372-8370. Fax: (419)372-6805. E-mail: mmcgowa@bgnet.bgs u.edu. Website: http://personal.bgsu.edu/~wmayo/wshop.html. **Contact:** Mary McGowan, creative writing secretary. Estab. Spring 1999. Twice per academic year (fall and spring). Workshop held Spring, 2001: Date to be determined. Workshop duration: 1 day. Average attendance: 15-20/workshop. Intensive manuscript-based workshops in fiction and poetry. The open workshops are open to writers of all levels of achievement. Workshops are lead by creative writing program faculty who read, comment on and distribute mss ahead of time. Beginning or advanced—each ms is addressed on its particular merits. Wendell Mayo (fiction; Director of Creative Writing Program), John Wylam (Poetry; Advisor to BFA Writing Program), Karen Craigo (poetry; Poetry Editor, *Mid American Review*) aer scheduled to participate.

Costs: $50/person per ms. Does not include meals, lodging.

Accommodations: No. "We provide parking on campus."

Additional Information: Participants need to submit workshop material prior to conference. Fiction: 1 story, 15 pages double-spaced maximum; send 2 copies. Poetry: 3 poems, a total of 100 lines for all 3, send 2 copies. "Deadlines are set about 3 weeks before the workshops. This gives us time to copy all the mss and mail to all participants with detailed instructions." For brochure send SASE, e-mail, visit website, call, fax. Accepts inquiries by SASE, e-mail, phone, fax. Editors participate in conference. "This is a no-nonsense workshop whose purpose is to 'open' doors for writers who are writing in comparative isolation. We provide guidance on preparation of mss for publication as well."

GARY PROVOST'S WRITERS RETREAT WORKSHOP, % Write It/Sell It, 2507 South Boston Place, Tulsa OK 74114. Phone/fax: (918)583-1471. E-mail: wrwwisi@aol.com. Website: www.channel1.com/wisi. **Contact:** Gail Provost Stockwell, director. Assistant Director: Lance Stockwell; Workshop Leader: Carol Dougherty. Estab. 1987. Workshop held May 25-June 3, 2001. Average attendance: 30. Focus on fiction and narrative nonfiction books in progress. All genres. Site: Marydale Retreat Center in Erlanger, KY (just south of Cincinnati, OH). "The Writers Retreat Workshop is an intensive learning experience for small groups of serious-minded writers. Founded by the late Gary Provost, one of the country's leading writing instructors and his wife Gail, an award-winning author, the WRW is a challenging and enriching adventure. The goal of the WRW core staff and visiting agents/editors/authors is for students to leave with a solid understanding of the marketplace as well as the craft of writing a novel. In the heart of a supportive and spirited community of fellow writers, students learn Gary Provost's course and make remarkable leaps in their writing, editing and marketing skills."

Costs: $1,635 for 10 days which includes all food and lodging (discount for past participants). The Marydale Retreat Center is 5 miles from the Cincinnati airport and offers shuttle services.

Additional Information: Participants are selected based upon the appropriateness of this program for the applicant's specific writing project. Participants are asked to submit a brief overview and synopsis before the workshop and are given assignments and feedback during the 10-day workshop. Workshop information available October 2000. For brochures/guidelines call 1-800-642-2494, e-mail, fax or visit website. Accepts inquiries by fax, e-mail, phone, SASE.

N RETREAT FROM HARSH REALITY, Mid-Michigan RWA Chapter, P.O. Box 278, Climax MI 49034-0278. (616)746-4789. Fax: (616)746-5184. E-mail: soulem@aol.com. Website: www.net-link.net/MMRWA. **Contact:** Maris Soule, retreat chair. Estab. 1985. Annual. Conference held May 4-6, 2001. Average attendance: limited to 50. Conference focuses on romance and fiction writing. Site: The W.K. Kellogg Biological Station Conference Center, on Gull Lake (Michigan) is the former summer home of cereal manufacturer and philanthropist W.K. Kellogg and one of the most picturesque estates in southwestern Michigan. This quiet country atmosphere lends itself to a productive and relaxing weekend. "We do not have panels. Emphasis is on one speaker and her or his expertise." Betina Krahn, award-winning author of romantic fiction, is the scheduled speaker for 2001.

Costs: Fees range from $30 (Saturday only, lunch only) to $145 (weekend package, all meals, single room).

Accommodations: On-site rooms offer view of lake, kitchenette, twin beds. Handicapped rooms available.

Additional Information: Two types of critiques are offered: 1. Published author critique, 50 pages maximum, $15. Open to MMRWA members or retreat attendees. 2. Saturday night group critique (no charge). Bring 5 copies of 5-10 pages each for group critique. Conference information is available now. For brochure send SASE, e-mail, visit website, phone, fax. Accepts inquiries by SASE, e-mail, phone, fax. "Dress is casual—sweatshirts and jeans. One-on-one conversation with speaker and attendees is emphasized. A chance to relax, talk writing, learn and share ideas. We have a book sale and author signing. Waldenbooks has put this on for the past three years."

ROPEWALK WRITERS' RETREAT, 8600 University Blvd., Evansville IN 47712. (812)464-1863. E-mail: lcleek@usi.edu. **Contact:** Linda Cleek, conference coordinator. Estab. 1989. Annual. Conference held in June. Average attendance: 42. "The week-long RopeWalk Writers' Retreat gives participants an opportunity to attend workshops and to confer privately with one of four or five prominent writers. Historic New Harmony, Indiana, site of two 19th century utopian experiments, provides an ideal setting for this event with its retreat-like atmosphere and its history of creative and intellectual achievement. At RopeWalk you will be encouraged to write—not simply listen to others talk about writing. Each workshop will be limited to twelve participants. The New Harmony Inn and Conference Center will be headquarters for the RopeWalk Writers' Retreat. Please note that reservations at the Inn should be confirmed by May 1." 2000 faculty included Kim Barnes, Stephen Dobyns, Heather McHugh, Victoria Redel and Robert Wrigley.
Costs: $435 (2000), includes breakfasts and lunches.
Accommodations: Information on overnight accommodations is made available. "Room-sharing assistance; some low-cost accommodations."
Additional Information: For critiques submit mss approx. 6 weeks ahead. Brochures are available after January 15.

SKYLINE WRITERS' CONFERENCE, P.O. Box 33343, N. Royalton OH 44133. **Contact:** Eleanor Behman, conference director. Estab. 1983. Annual. Conference held August 2001. Average attendance: 50-60. Features fiction, nonfiction, poetry, children's, science fiction, and inspirational. Conference held in N. Royalton High School.
Costs: $50 (non-members); $55 (members). Includes continental breakfast, full buffet lunch, snacks and 6 workshops.
Additional Information: Includes literary contest, 2 mss in two of the following categories: fiction, nonfiction, children's and poetry. "We are totally non-profit, supported only by members and attendees of conference." Brochures available for SASE.

WALLOON WRITERS' RETREAT, Michigania on Walloon Lake, Boyne City MI. (248)589-3913. Fax: (248)589-3913. E-mail: info@springfed.org. Website: www.springfed.org. **Contact:** John D. Lamb, director. Estab. 1999. Annual. Conference held September 27-30, 2001. Average attendance: 50. Focus includes fiction, poetry, creative nonfiction. Michigania is owned and operated by the University of Michigan Alumni Association. Located on Walloon Lake. Attendees stay in spruce-paneled cabins and seminars are held in a large conference lodge with fieldstone fireplaces and dining area. Features and faculty includes Joyce Maynard (The Terror of the Blank Page); Jacquelyn Mitchard (When Fiction Outs the Truth); Keith Taylor (short stories); and Michael Moore & Ben Hamper (panel discussions).
Costs: Single occupancy is $495, $425 (3 nights, 2 nights). $245 no lodging.
Accommodations: Shuttle rides from Traverse City Airport. Offers overnight accommodations. Provides list of area lodging options.
Additional Information: Optional: Attendees may submit 3 poems or 5 pages of prose for conferences with a staff member. Brochures available mid-June. For brochure e-mail, visit website or call. Accepts inquiries by SASE, e-mail, phone. Editors participate in conference. "Walloon Lake in Northern Michigan is the same lake where Ernest Hemingway spent the first 19 years of his life at his family's Windemere Cottage. The area plays a role in some of his early short stories. Notably in a couple of his Nick Adams stories."

WRITE-TO-PUBLISH CONFERENCE, Wheaton College, 501 College Ave., Wheaton IL 60187. (847)299-4755. Fax: (847)296-0754. E-mail: linjohnson@compuserve.com. **Contact:** Lin Johnson, director. Estab. 1971. Annual. Conference held from June 6-9, 2001. Average attendance: 175. Conference on "writing all types of manuscripts for the Christian market."
Costs: $325.
Accommodations: Shuttle service provided. Accommodations in campus residence halls or discounted hotel rates. Costs $180-$320.
Additional Information: Optional critiquing available. Conference information available in February 2001. For brochures/guidelines visit website, e-mail, fax or call. Accepts inquiries by e-mail, fax, phone.

North Central (IA, MN, NE, ND, SD, WI)

PETER DAVIDSON'S WRITER'S SEMINAR, 982 S. Emerald Hills Dr., P.O. Box 497, Arnolds Park IA 51331-0497. (712)332-9329. Fax: (712)362-8363. **Contact:** Peter Davidson, seminar presenter. Estab. 1985. Seminars held about 30 times annually, in various sites. Offered year round. Seminars last 1 day, usually 9 a.m.- 4 p.m. Average attendance: 35. "All writing areas including books of fiction and nonfiction, children's works, short stories, magazine articles, poetry, songs, scripts, religious works, personal experiences and romance fiction. All seminars are sponsored by community colleges or colleges across the U.S. Covers many topics including developing your idea, writing the manuscript, copyrighting, and marketing your work. The information is very practical—participants will be able to put into practice the principles discussed. The seminar is fast-paced and should be a lot of fun for participants."
Costs: Each sponsoring college sets own fees, ranging from $42-59, depending on location, etc.
Accommodations: "Participants make their own arrangements. Usually, no special arrangements are available."
Additional Information: "Participants are encouraged to bring their ideas and/or manuscripts for a short, informal evaluation by seminar presenter, Peter Davidson." Conference brochures/guidelines are available for SASE. No inquiries by fax or e-mail. "In even-numbered years, usually present seminars in Colorado, Wyoming, Nebraska, Kansas, Iowa, Minnesota and South Dakota. In odd-numbered years, usually present seminars in Illinois, Iowa, Minnesota, Arkansas, Missouri, South Dakota, Nebraska and Tennessee."

GREAT LAKES WRITER'S WORKSHOP, Alverno College, 3400 S. 43 St., P.O. Box 343922, Milwaukee WI 53234-3922. (414)382-6176. Fax: (414)382-6332. **Contact:** Cindy Jackson, assistant director, Professional and Community Education. Estab. 1985. Annual. Workshop held the third Friday and Saturday in June. Average attendance: 150. "Workshops focus on a variety of subjects including fiction, writing for magazines, freelance writing, writing for children, poetry, marketing, etc. Participants may select a portion of the workshop or attend the full 2 days. Classes are held during the evening and weekend. The workshop is held in Milwaukee, WI at Alverno College."
Costs: In 1999, cost was $80 for entire workshop.
Accommodations: Attendees must make their own travel arrangments. Accommodations are available on campus; rooms are in residence halls and are not air-conditioned. Cost in 1997 was $25 for single, $20 per person for double. There are also hotels in the surrounding area. Call (414)382-6040 for information regarding overnight accommodations.
Additional Information: "Some workshop instructors may provide critiques, but this changes depending upon the workshop and speaker. This would be indicated in the workshop brochure." Brochures are available for SASE after March. Accepts inquiries by fax.

IOWA SUMMER WRITING FESTIVAL, 116 International Center, University of Iowa, Iowa City IA 52242-1802. (319)335-2534. E-mail: peggy-houston@uiowa.edu; amy-margolis@uiowa.edu. Website: www.edu/~iswfe st. **Contact:** Peggy Houston, Amy Margolis, directors. Estab. 1987. Annual. Festival held in June and July. Workshops are one week or a weekend. Average attendance: limited to 12/class—over 1,500 participants throughout the summer. "We offer courses in most areas of writing: novel, short story, essay, poetry, playwriting, screenwriting, humor, travel, writing for children, memoir, women's writing, romance and mystery." Site is the University of Iowa campus. Guest speakers are undetermined at this time. Readers and instructors have included Lee K. Abbott, Susan Power, Joy Harjo, Gish Jen, Abraham Verghese, Robert Olen Butler, Ethan Canin, Clark Blaise, Gerald Stern, Donald Justice, Michael Dennis Browne, Marvin Bell, Hope Edelman.
Costs: $400/week; $175, weekend workshop (1999 rates). Discounts available for early registration. Housing and meals are separate.
Accommodations: "We offer participants a choice of accommodations: dormitory, $27/night; Iowa House, $65/night; Holiday Inn, $70/night (rates subject to changes)."
Additional Information: Conference information available in February. Accepts inquiries by fax, e-mail.

Ñ SINIPEE WRITERS' WORKSHOP, Continuing Education Loras College, Dubuque IA 52001-0708. (319)588-7139. Fax: (319)588-7964. E-mail: lcrosset@loras.edu/~corted. Website: www.loras.edu. **Contact:** Linda Crossett, director, continuing education. Estab. 1985. Annual. Workshop held April 28, 2001. Average attendance: 40-50. The conference provides general information for writers on how to get published. There are several speakers at each workshop, usually someone for fiction, poetry, nonfiction and either a publisher, editor or agent. The conference is held in the Alumni Campus Center on the Loras College campus. The Campus Center is handicapped accessible. For 2000 fiction themes included a romance writer talking about how she got started and the romance market today. Also a short story author spoke on how she got her first book of short stories published. Speakers for 2000 were Linda H. Wallerich (Jessica Douglas/Linda Benjamin) romance writing;

insider report

Elizabeth Graver on building community among writers

Does writing leave you feeling lonesome? Are you weary of that isolated one-on-one with a blank sheet of paper (or computer screen)? Have you begun to regard your work sessions as bouts of solitary confinement?

Maybe what you need is connection—the sense of community that comes from joining a writer's group, taking part in a conference or retreat, or simply making contact with another writer.

Elizabeth Graver knows from experience that the creative process requires more than seclusion. The acclaimed author of *Have You Seen Me* (University of Pittsburgh Press), *Unravelling* and *The Honey Thief* (both from Hyperion) has belonged to her Boston writers' group for more than 12 years. In addition, atten-

Elizabeth Graver

dance at the Bread Loaf Writers' Conference, and residencies at the MacDowell Colony and Blue Mountain Center, have revealed to her the power of combining literary production with social interaction.

On one hand, the "long, long stretches of time to really dive deep" into her writing were a great gift, she says. "I have a full-time teaching job, so it's very hard during the school year." She adds with a laugh, "Even during the summer when I'm home, the phone rings, I decide to go look at my garden or wipe the kitchen counter. There are just so many ways to distract yourself."

The MacDowell Colony (Peterborough, New Hampshire) provides private studios to the 20-30 artists who are in residence at any given time. Uninvited visits to fellow "colonists" during the day are prohibited, and lunch is delivered to artists so their creativity remains uninterrupted. However, breakfast and dinner are taken in the dining room, and evening hours may include readings, informal performances and slide shows.

"For me, that mix of intense solitude and really scintillating conversation and community is hard to come by in the outside world," says Graver. "It was incredibly nourishing to my work. I also loved the fact that both McDowell and Blue Mountain Center are interdisciplinary. They had composers and visual artists there as well as writers, and it was really great to see people working in other mediums. I also made some friends who have become really good readers of my work and whose work has inspired me."

Compared to her stints at these colonies, Graver's experience at the Bread Loaf Writers' Conference in the mountains near Ripton, Vermont was less productive but no less stimulating. She was fresh out of college, attending the venerable conference on a working scholarship.

"I didn't write while I was there, I was much too busy," Graver recalls. "My scholarship involved being a waitress, so it was really intense. But I liked it." Fortunately she did have time for the generous schedule of readings that Bread Loaf is known for. "As someone who was just starting out, what was exciting was going to all the readings and being saturated by other people's work. I've always found going to readings sends me home wanting to write.

"I had some good instructors, so it was much more like being a student," Graver continues. "At a colony you're off doing your own thing. It's not like there's anyone there to teach you, although there was a kind of teaching going on through the work we shared with each other."

Whether at a colony or conference, Graver stresses, connecting with fellow writers is especially rewarding. "I had a friend at Bread Loaf named Audrey," Graver says. "When I left I didn't get her address, but when I moved to Boston I remembered that she lived there." With the assistance of the Bread Loaf administrator, Graver was able to reconnect with Audrey. "Now she's one of my close friends. We started my Boston writers' group and have been in it together for years. So one of the biggest things I got out of Bread Loaf was that relationship."

Graver notes that over the years the group has had "many permutations. It started out with four women. We were all about the same age, totally unpublished. Now all of us have published something like three books. We had a lot of perseverance, a kind of will power, and we were all very supportive of each other."

That support was something Graver depended on as she grew and developed as a writer. "Even when I was away at graduate school or wherever, I would send them work. It was really one of the main reasons I wanted to move back to Boston. We became friends as well as writing colleagues."

Those writing colleagues provide her with thorough feedback and something Graver especially prizes—an opportunity to present unpolished writing. "I can go with ideas half-formed and then use the others as a sounding board," she explains. "They'll look at things very much bit-by-bit, but I can also give them a whole draft of a novel and say, 'Okay, take this, read the entire thing. Does it work?' It's a real ongoing process where I can show very raw work and not feel as if it needs to be complete."

Of course, not every writer flourishes in a group situation or feels comfortable submitting work to others for criticism. Graver concedes it's all very personal—what works for one writer may not for another. She believes even the ideal size of a writers' group is a matter of individual preference. For Graver, a tighter, more intimate circle is the way to go.

"In a smaller group I can get and give more attention. If I was in a group with 12 people, I don't think we'd all be able to read each other's work in a consistent, weekly way." Graver points out that a larger group could also make it difficult "to figure out who's a really good reader for me. They wouldn't all be in a larger group, and I wouldn't be for them."

Regardless of its size, "community" is important to a writer, a point Graver emphasizes to her students. "Sometimes they'll say, 'I'm graduating, what am I going to do? I bet I'll never write again.' I tell them, 'There are ways to create a structure without being inside an academy.' And in some ways it's a better structure because it's less hierarchical. I always encourage them to try literally to create community in some way."

To Graver, it helps to know that others are writing, too. What's more, making a commitment to show work to someone at a specific time is motivating. "It both forces you to produce a little more and puts you more in dialogue with other people." She adds, "I'll always have some sort of group."

(For more information on the Bread Loaf Writers' Conference, see the Insider Report with Director Michael Collier on page 548.)

—*Nancy Breen*

Sharon Helgens, short story writer; David Rusk, publisher; Nancy Clark Scobie, poet; and Jan Ford, nonfiction/ short stories. Speakers for 2001 (not a complete list) include Carrie Rodabaugh, editor; and Paul Polansky, nonfiction.

Costs: $60 ($65 at the door); $30 ($32.50 at door) for senior citizens and students.

Accommodations: Provides a list of area hotels or lodging options.

Additional Information: No prior submissions required. Sponsors a contest as part of workshop. Requirements: $5 entry fee/$15 additional fee for written critique. Poetry must not exceed 40 lines and short fiction and nonfiction entries must be 1,500 words or less. Style and subject are open and work by aspiring writers as well as seasoned professionals is welcome. Contest judges are faculty in the Loras College English Department who teach creative writing, or graduates of the creative writing program. Workshop information is available February 1, 2001. For brochure send e-mail, call, fax. Accepts inquiries by SASE, e-mail, phone, fax. Agents and editors participate in conference.

🄽 UNIVERSITY OF NORTH DAKOTA WRITERS CONFERENCE, Box 7209 UND, Grand Forks ND 58202-7209. (701)777-2768. Fax: (701)777-2373. E-mail: James_McKenzie@UND.nodak.edu. Website: www.UND.edu/culture/WC. **Contact:** James McKenzie, director. Estab. 1969. Annual. Conference held March 19-23, 2001. Average attendance: 800/day. Covers all genres, focused around a specific theme (war in 2000, work for 2001). The conference is a regional cultural and intellectual festival that puts nationally-known writers in intimate and large audience contact with other writers and the student, academic and general public. Almost all events take place in the campus memorial union which has a variety of small rooms and a 1,500 seat main hall. Tessa Bridal was a fiction writer in residence in 2000. Other fiction writers at the 2000 conference were Ha Jin and Robert Olen Butler, and memoirists Helen Fremont, John Balaban and Eavan Boland.

Costs: Free, open to the public.

Accommodations: Offers overnight accommodations. "Campus residence halls are available at very good prices." Also provides a list of area hotels or lodging options.

Additional Information: Conference information is available January 31, 2001. For brochure send SASE, e-mail, visit website, call, fax. Accepts inquiries by SASE, e-mail, phone, fax.

🄽 WISCONSIN REGIONAL WRITER'S ASSOCIATION SPRING AND FALL CONFERENCES, 510 W. Sunset Ave., Appleton WI 54911-1139. (920)734-3724. E-mail: wrwa@lakefield.net. Website: www.wkw ells.net/wrwa. **Contact:** Donna Potrykus, vice president. Estab. 1948. Annual. Conferences held in May and September. Average attendance: 100-150. Conferences are dedicated to self-improvement through speakers, workshops and presentations. We honor all genres of writing. Fall conference is a one-day event that features speakers and awards for membership only. The Jade Ring contest has six genre categories—winner receives a cash prize and jade ring. Site: Ramada Conference Center—Wausau WI. 2000 topics included plotting short stories, escaping the slush pile and children's fiction. Past presenters have included Marcia Preston, Pamela Kuck and John Kaminski.

Costs: $75-100.

Accommodations: Provides a list of area hotels or lodging options. "We negotiate for special rates at each facility. A block of rooms is set aside for a specific time period."

Additional Information: Awards are presented for The Jade Ring Contest at the Fall conference. Must be a member to enter. Awards presented on Saturday night at the Jade Ring Banquet. For brochure send e-mail, visit website, call. Accepts inquiries by e-mail, phone. Agents and editors participate in conference.

🄽 WRITERS INSTITUTE, 610 Langdon St., Room 621, Madison WI 53703. (608)262-3447. Fax: (608)265-2475. Website: www.dcs.wisc.edu/lsa/writing. **Contact:** Christine DeSmet. Estab. 1989. Annual. Held July 12-13, 2001. Average attendance: 200. Covers fiction and nonfiction. Site: University of Wisconsin Madison, Memorial Union. Panels planned for the 2001 conference include the craft of writing and business/marketing for writers. Marshall J. Cook, Laurel Yorke and Christine DeSmet are scheduled to participate.

Costs: $195 includes materials, breaks.

Accommodations: Provides a list of area hotels or lodging options.

Additional Information: Sponsors contest. Submit 1-page writing sample and $5 entry fee. Conference speakers are judges. Conference information is available in April. For brochure send e-mail, visit website, call, fax. Accepts inquiries by SASE, e-mail, phone, fax. Agents and editors participate in conference.

INTERESTED IN A PARTICULAR GENRE? Check our sections for: **Mystery**, page 57; **Romance**, page 68; **Science Fiction/Fantasy & Horror**, page 78.

South Central (CO, KS, MO, NM, OK, TX)

[N] ART AND SOUL, P.O. Box 97404, Baylor University, Waco TX 76798-7404. (254)710-6879 or 4805. Fax: (254)710-3894. E-mail: Rel_Lit@baylor.edu. Website: www.baylor.edu/~Rel_lit. **Contact:** Greg Garrett, director. Estab. 2000. Annual. Conference held in February. Average attendance: 200-400. Areas of focus include fiction, poetry, spiritual autobiography, humor, creative nonfiction, religion and creativity. Sessions take place in auditoriums, conference rooms, and classrooms on the historic campus of Baylor University in Waco, Texas. 2000 panels, workshops, and master classes included humor, fiction and autobiography, creativity and spirituality, agent representation and submission and publication. Lee Smith, Anne Lamott, Bruce Hornsby and Hal Crowther are scheduled to participate in the 2001 conference.
Costs: Tuition costs range from $30 for advance student registration to $75 for regular registration. One meal is included.
Accommodations: Offers shuttle service to hotels from campus, plus discounts on airfare and car rental. No overnight accommodations. List of area hotels/lodging options provided.
Additional Information: Registrants requesting an individual ms consultation should contact the conference to check on availability. Conference information is available fall 2000. For brochure send SASE, e-mail, visit website, phone, fax. Accepts inquiries by SASE, e-mail, phone, fax. Agents and editors participate in conference.

[N] THE BAY AREA WRITERS GUIDE 13TH ANNUAL CONFERENCE, P.O. Box 728, Seabrook TX 77586. (281)268-7500. E-mail: bawlconference@aol.com. Website: www.angelfire.com/tx2/bawl/. **Contact:** Committee Member. Estab. 1988. Annual. Conference held May 13-14, 2001. Average attendance: 100. Conference focuses on all genres: fiction, non-fiction, poetry, screenwriting, journalism and children. The conference is held on the campus of the University of Houston Clear Lake, a typical college satellite campus. Features writing for children, marketing mass-market paperbacks, e-publishing, legal aspects of crime in fiction, romance markets, mythic character patterns, erotica and writing for screen and television. Faculty includes Julie Duffy (X-libris Press); Marianne Dyson (author); Michelle Brummer (literary agent); Cheryl Bolen (author); Kim Rangel (author); Howard Bushart (author); Angela Adair Hoy (e-books.com); Chris Rogers (author); and Kasey Kelly (screenwriter).
Costs: $100 for both days, includes lunch, Friday reception and 1 year membership. $65/day; $35/students.
Accommodations: Offers a list of overnight accommodations.
Additional Information: Sponsors several contests, including long fiction (first chapter, 20 pp. max. plus synopsis); short fiction (5,000 words); long nonfiction (first chapter, 20 pp max. plus synopsis); short nonfiction (5,000 words); poetry (100 lines). This contest is limited to writers who have not been published in the category they submit. Judges are editors, agents, and published authors. Brochures available March 2001 for SASE, e-mail, website, or call. Accepts inquiries by SASE, e-mail, phone. Agents and editors participate in conferences. "Has two or three editors and agents who conduct private interviews with participants."

[N] CAT WRITERS ASSOCIATION WRITERS CONFERENCE, P.O. Box 1904, Sherman TX 75091-1904. (903)868-1022. Fax: (903)893-1731. E-mail: amy@shojai.com. Website: www.catwriters.org. **Contact:** Amy D. Shojai, president. Estab. 1994. Annual. Conference held November 16-18, 2001. Average attendance: 100-120. The conference provides basic-to-advanced information on how to get published, research sources, market work (nonfiction and fiction); offers networking opportunities between writers, editors, publishers, broadcasters, illustrators; and celebrates good writing that has a focus on cats. The conference is held in a new city each year, typically in conjunction with the Cat Fanciers Association International Cat Show. 16 seminars are held in a hotel conference facility. A major book-signing event is held in the cat show hall, typically a large convention center. 2000 conference included writing for children panel; understanding 'net rights; book editors' panel; working with a publicist; magazine editors' panel; media training; and a fiction authors' panel. 2000 included authors Peter Mandel, Shirley Rousseau Murphy, Ann Whitehead Nagola and Suzzanne Liurance; and agents Meredith Bernstein and Lucy Lourien.
Costs: Cost for 2000 conference was $65 for CWA members; $88 for nonmembers. (Included all seminars; reception; book-signing event; night cocktail reception/awards banquet; Sunday morning breakfast and members meeting; press pass into the cat show hall.)
Accommodations: Hosting hotel offers reduced rate for conference attendees. Will also provide a list of area hotels or lodging options. Hotels run about $90/night.
Additional Information: Sponsors a contest. "Work must have been published in contest year July-June; cost is $10/entry for members, $15/entry for nonmembers; more than 30 categories; contest judged by professional CWA members. Conference information available June/July 2001. For brochure send SASE, visit website. Accepts inquiries by SASE, e-mail. Agents and editors participate in conference. "We make available one-on-one appointments with editors/agents for writers to 'pitch' their projects. Also, the Dog Writers Association is a sponsor of the seminars, so those who attend have an interest in both cat and dog topics. All seminars are applicable to all writing disciplines and not restricted to cat writing."

N FALL INSPIRATION RETREAT 2000, P.O. Box 272, Tinnie NM 88351. Phone/fax: (505)653-4437. E-mail: mysticsprings@magicplace.com. Website: www.guardians.nativeland.com. **Contact:** Deborah Vanderlee-lie, director. Estab. 1999. Annual. Workshop held October 20-22, 2001 (tentative). Average attendance: 30. "Conference sessions cover poetry, fiction, nonfiction and journaling. Workshops are geared towards achieving deeper levels of creativity for all writers." Site: A guest ranch featuring large casitas (homes) fully equipped. Catering is also available. All homes and cabins have decks and grills. The ranch is surrounded by national forest and is nestled in the pines of The Capitan Mountains. An adobe pavillion is on site for workshops. 2000 sessions covered meditation writing, journaling and creative expression. Also included "Circle of Souls" discussion forum where all attendees shared on-site writing.
Costs: $295-395; also offers couples packages for $495 (2000 rates). Fee covered 2 nights' lodging and all workshops.
Accommodations: Offers overnight accommodations, included in price of conference. If staying more nights than are included in conference package, room rental is $59-89/night.
Additional Information: Conference information is available on website only. Accepts inquiries by e-mail, phone. Editors participate in conference.

FLATIRONS BLUNT INSTRUMENT MYSTERY WORKSHOP, c/o Thora Chinnery, 415 Erie Dr., Boulder CO 80303. (303)499-0203. (303)494-5995. E-mail: chinnery@chisp.net. Website: http://bcn.boulder.co.us/arts/blunt. **Contact:** Thora Chinnery, workshop coordinator. Estab. 1996. Annual. Conference held June 23, 2001. Average attendance: 70. Conference for "mystery writers and readers." Conference held in "two very large auditorium size rooms at the local Elks club." 2000 speakers included Michael Siedman (Walker Press), Christine Jorgensen and James Doss.
Costs: 2000 fees: $50 (included continental breakfast and buffet with lunch). "Out-of-town guests were given free bed and breakfast with local members."
Additional Information: "Limited critiquing is available from published authors on a first-come basis." Conference information available January 2001. For brochure/guidelines send SASE, visit website, e-mail, and call. Accepts inquiries by phone, SASE, e-mail. "It is the only genre-specific mystery workshop in the Rocky Mountain area. The scenery is fabulous. The conference is sponsored by the Rocky Mountain Chapter of Sisters in Crime."

N GEMINI INK 2001 SUMMER FESTIVAL: "SOUTHERN STATES OF MIND", 121 W. Woodlawn, San Antonio TX 78212-3457. Toll free (877)734-9673 or (210)734-9673. Fax: (210)737-0688. E-mail: info@geminiink.org. Website: www.geminiink.org. **Contact:** Dave Rutschman, director, university. Estab. 1998. Annual. Conference to be held June 9-30, 2001. Average attendance: 270. "Gemini Ink's mission is to celebrate art in literature. Since 1992, we have sought to expose as wide a segment of the San Antonio area population as possible to the best current and classical literature in a way that is entertaining, educational, and enlightening. Conference focus areas: fiction, memoir, poetry, nonfiction. Most of the Writing Workshops and the Receptions are held in a two-story house in the historic Monte Vista neighborhood, giving visiting writers a first-hand flavor of the Alamo City. Its cozy atmosphere corresponds to San Antonio's grace and charm, and its homelike surroundings encourage informal bonding, causing casual friendships to develop, enabling students the freedom to work and, ultimately, stimulating them to return. Other classes will be held at two visual arts centers, the Southwest School of Art and Craft (also the location for two faculty readings) and the McNay Art Museum (also the location for a dramatic reader's theater production). The opening event will hopefully be our first faculty reading at the Institute of Texan Cultures during the Texas Folklife Festival." Focuses on "Writing for the Long Haul: Novel Writing"; "Creating & Recreating Your Life: Fiction"; "Fast Readers, Slow Stories: Fiction." Faculty includes Charles M. Baxter, Patricia Spears, Elizabeth Forsythe Hailey, Babsi Sidwa, and many more.
Costs: There is no overall conference cost. Rather, students pay for the classes they want to take. Summer Festival 2000 rates were $40-120, with free receptions for students and members. Faculty readings and a readers theater production are also free and open to the public.
Accommodations: Participants can save 5% off lowest published fare at the time of ticket purchase when they arrange their travel through The Adventure Group, (888) 434-4241. Some restrictions may apply. Provides list for lodging.
Additional Information: Submit workshop material prior to arrival. Most classes require mss of varying length/topic (depending on course) to be submitted by the registration deadline (a few weeks before each course begins). Brochures available April, 2001 by e-mail, website, fax, or call. Accepts inquiries by SASE, e-mail, phone, fax. Agents and editors participate in conferences.

GOLDEN TRIANGLE WRITERS GUILD, 4245 Calder, Beaumont TX 77706. (409)898-4894. **Contact:** D.J. Resnick, advisor. E-mail: gtwg@juno.com. Estab. 1983. Annual. Conference held during third weekend in October. Attendance limited to 350. Held at the Hilton Hotel on IH10 at Washington in Beaumont, Texas.
Costs: $210-235 before October 2nd; $235-260 after October 2nd. Cost includes meals and 1 year membership.
Accommodations: Special conference rates available at Holiday Inn (Beaumont).

Additional Information: Sponsors a contest. Attendance required. Preliminary judging done by published authors and/or specialists in each specific genre. Final judging done by editors and/or agents specializing in each specific area.

HOUSTON WRITERS CONFERENCE 2000, P.O. Box 742683, Houston TX 77274-2683. (281)342-5924. E-mail: houwrites@aol.com. Website: www.houstonwrites.com. **Contact:** Ted Simmons. Estab. 1997. Conference held annually in March. Average attendance: 250. Conference includes all genres, fiction and nonfiction. Conference is held at the Houston Marriott Westside Hotel. Previous dinner and luncheon speakers were Anita Richmond Bunkley, Melanie Lawson and Susan Wiggs. Every year there is also a agent/editor Q&A panel.
Costs: $225 before November 1; $240 November 2-February 1; $255 after February 2.
Accommodations: Special rate for participants of $65 at Houston Marriott Westside. Check website for additional information.
Additional Information: E-mail or check website for contest information. Conference brochures/guidelines available for SASE after September. Accepts inquiries by e-mail. Conference includes "approximately 50 multi-track workshops over 2½ days, multi-genre, all experience levels, bookstore and author signings."

N MISSOURI WRITERS GUILD 2001 ANNUAL CONVENTION, 5433 Rockhill Rd., Kansas City MO 64110-2451. (816)361-1281. E-mail: eblivingsfun@hotmail.com. **Contact:** Jane Simmons, chair. Annual. Conference to be held April 27-29, 2001. Average attendance: 100+. Annual convention where members come together to visit, network, meet agents, learn, and receive any awards from the annual contests. "Our members have work published as novels, poetry, magazine articles, children's books, etc . . . Features important tips for submitting fiction to a publisher, ins and outs of self-publishing, honoring KC area authors at Friday night reception, banquet, and art to show-off the words."
Accommodations: Offers overnight accommodations.
Additional Information: Submit workshop materials prior to arrival. Sponsors contest. To enter, one must be a MWG member. Brochures available by Thanksgiving 2000 by e-mail. Accepts inquiries by e-mail. Agents and editors participate in conference. "Come to KC in April 2001 for two days of professional networking and just plain ole' fun."

☑ NATIONAL WRITERS ASSOCIATION CONFERENCE, 3140 S. Peoria, Suite 295, Aurora CO 80014. (303)841-0246. Fax: (303)841-2607. E-mail: sandywriter@aol.com. Website: www.nationalwriters.com. **Contact:** Sandy Whelchel, executive director. Estab. 1926. Annual. Conference held June 8-10, 2001, in Denver, CO. Average attendance: 200-300. Conference focuses on general writing and marketing.
Costs: $300 (approx.).
Additional Information: Awards for previous contests will be presented at the conference. Conference information available in December 2000. For brochures/guidelines send SASE, visit website, e-mail, fax, or call. Accepts inquiries by SASE, e-mail, fax, phone.

☑ NIMROD ANNUAL WRITERS' WORKSHOP, (formerly Oklahoma Writers' Workshop), *Nimrod*, University of Tulsa, 600 S. College, Tulsa OK 74104. (918)631-3080. Fax: (918)631-3033. E-mail: nimrod@utulsa.edu. Website: www.utulsa.edu/nimrod. **Contact:** Francine Ringold, PhD, editor-in-chief. Estab. 1978. Workshop held annually in October. Workshop duration: 1 day. Average attendance: 100-150. Workshop in fiction and poetry. "Prize winners (*Nimrod*/Hardman Prizes) conduct workshops as do contest judges. Past judges: Rosellen Brown, Stanley Kunitz, Toby Olson, Lucille Clifton, W.S. Merwin, Ron Carlson, Mark Doty, Anita Shreve and Francine Prose."
Costs: Approximately $30-40. Lunch provided.
Additional Information: *Nimrod International Journal* sponsors *Nimrod*/Hardman Literary Awards: The Katherine Anne Porter Prize for fiction and The Pablo Neruda Prize for poetry. Poetry and fiction prizes: $2,000 each and publication (1st prize); $1,000 each and publication (2nd prize). Deadline: must be postmarked no later than April 20. Guidelines for SASE.

☑ NORTHWEST OKLAHOMA WRITER'S WORKSHOP, 1118 Lookout Dr., Enid OK 73701. Phone/fax: (580)237-2744. E-mail: enidwriters@yahoo.com. Website: www.scribequill.com/enidwriters. **Contact:** Tracye White, workshop coordinator. Estab. 1991. Annual. Conference held in March or April (date set in January). Conference duration: 6 hours. Average attendance: 20-30. "Usually fiction is the concentration area. The purpose is to help writers learn more about the craft of writing and encourage writers 'to step out in faith' and submit." Held in Cherokee Strip Conference Center. Past speakers have been Norma Jean Lutz, inspirational and magazine writing; Deborah Bouziden, fiction and magazine writing; Anna Meyers, children's writing; Sondra Soli, poetry; Marcia Preston, magazines, Mary Lynn, manuscript preparation and submission protocol; Jean Hager, writing mysteries; Annie Jones, romance; Carolyn D. Wall, *ByLine* fiction editor.
Costs: $40; includes catered lunch.

Additional Information: Conference guidelines are available for SASE. Accepts inquiries by SASE, e-mail, phone.

N OKLAHOMA WRITERS FEDERATION CONFERENCE, 8416 Huckleberry, Edmond OK 73034. (405)348-0276. Fax: (405)282-7230. E-mail: DBouziden@worldnet.att.net. Website: http://members.tripod.com/OWFI. **Contact:** Deborah Bouziden, president, or Lou Mansfield, treasurer. Estab. 1968. Annual. Conference held May 4-5, 2001. Average attendance: 250-300. Conference covers all genres, fiction, poetry, nonfiction. Site: "Our conference is held at the Embassy Suites Hotel. It has 6 floors. Everything, all meetings are contained within the hotel." 2000 presenters included Robert Tabian, agent; Leslie Wainger, editor, Silhouette; and Craig Nelsen, publisher, Rodgers & Nelsen Publishing. Merline Lovelace, Christine Rimmer, and many other authors spoke.
Costs: Full conference, $100; one day only, $50; authors' banquet, $30; awards banquet, $30 (2000 fees).
Accommodations: The hotel provides a shuttle to and from airport. Embassy Suites room rates have been $79. Guests of the hotel get free buffet breakfast.
Additional Information: "The annual OWFI contest is open only to paid-up members. It features competitions for cash prizes in 28 unpublished ms categories and awards 4 trophies for the best books published during the previous calendar year. A $20 entry fee entitles participants to enter as many categories as they want, but they may enter no single category more than once. Since the contest's purpose is to encourage writers to produce professionally-acceptable mss, the contest rules are very explicit, and contestants must follow them closely. Categories include mainstream novel; contemporary romance novel; historical romance novel; mystery/suspense novel; Western novel; science fiction/fantasy/horror novel; nonfiction book; picture book; middle reader book; and young adult book." For brochures/guidelines send SASE, e-mail, visit website, call. Accepts inquiries by SASE, e-mail, phone. Agents and editors participate in conference.

✓ ROCKY MOUNTAIN BOOK FESTIVAL, 2123 Downing St., Denver CO 80205. (303)839-8320. Fax: (303)839-8319. E-mail: ccftb@compuserve.com. Website: www.coloradobook.org. **Contact:** Christiane Citron, executive director. Estab. 1991. Annual. Festival held in March. Average attendance: 10,000. Festival promotes published work from all genres. Held at Denver Merchandise Mart. Offers a wide variety of panels. Approximately 200 authors are scheduled to speak at the next festival.
Costs: $4 (adult); $2 (child).
Additional Information: Brochures/guidelines available. Accepts inquiries by e-mail, fax.

✓ ROCKY MOUNTAIN CHILDREN'S BOOK FESTIVAL, 2123 Downing St., Denver CO 80205-5210. (303)839-8320. Fax: (303)839-8319. E-mail: ccftb@compuserve.com. Website: www.coloradobook.org. **Contact:** Christiane Citron, executive director. Estab. 1996. Annual festival held in March. Festival duration: 2 days. Average attendance: 10,000. Festival promotes published work for and about children/families. It is solely for children's authors and illustrators—open to the public. Held at Denver Merchandise Mart. Approximately 100 authors speak annually. Past authors include Ann M. Martin, Sharon Creech, Nikki Grimes, T.A. Barron, Laura Numeroff, Jean Craighead George and Robert Munsch.
Costs: $2 children, $4 adults.
Accommodations: "Information on accommodations available."
Additional Information: Send SASE for brochure/guidelines. Accepts inquiries by fax, e-mail.

✓ ROMANCE WRITERS OF AMERICA NATIONAL CONFERENCE, 3707 FM 1960 West, Suite 555, Houston TX 77068. (281)440-6885, ext. 27. Fax: (281)440-7510. E-mail: info@rwanational.com. Website: www.rwanational.com. Executive Director: Allison Kelley. **Contact:** Jane Detloff, office manager. Estab. 1981. Annual. Conference held July 18-22, 2001. Average attendance: 1,500. Over 100 workshops on writing, researching and the business side of being a working writer. Publishing professionals attend and accept appointments. Keynote speaker is renowned romance writer. Conference will be held in Washington, D.C. in 2000.
Costs: $300.
Additional Information: Annual RITA awards are presented for romance authors. Annual Golden Heart awards are presented for unpublished writers. Conference brochures/guidelines are available for SASE in May 2001. Accepts inquiries by SASE, e-mail, fax, phone.

N SCBWI INSIDE THE CHILDREN'S BOOK BIZ CONFERENCE, Wyndham Garden Hotel, 8051 LBJ Freeway, Dallas TX 75251-8051. Website: http://star-telegram.com/homes/SCBWI. **Contact:** Vickie Perez, conference public relations. Estab. 1983. Annual. One-day conference held in September, usually the 4th Saturday. Average attendance: 200. Conference focusing on children's fiction and nonfiction, from picture books to young adult, with illustrator interests as well. Sponsored by the NC/NE Texas Chapter of the Society of Children's Book Writers and Illustrators (SCBWI). The 2000 faculty included Connie Epstein, Publisher's Corner/*SCBWI Bulletin*; Stephen Geck, vice president and associate publisher, Simon & Schuster Books for Young Readers; Wendy

Loggia, senior editor, Random House Children's Books; George Nicholson, senior agent, Sterling Lord Literistic; David Saylor, vice president and creative director, Scholastic; Phoebe Yeh, editorial director, HarperCollins Children's Books. Speakers give inside information on the current trends.

Costs: In 2000 Early Bird registration fee was $75 for national SCBWI members, $80 for non-members. Late registration fee was $85 for national SCBWI members, $90 for non-members. Cost includes lunch.

Accommodations: Wyndham Garden Hotel, easily accessible off LBJ Freeway in Dallas, TX. Offers food, lodging and spacious conference room. 2000 room rates were $69 double/single, $79 triple, $89 quad (price includes breakfast buffet for two).

Additional Information: "We always have 'Pitch to the Pros' 15-minute consultations with speakers on a first-registered, first-scheduled basis." There is also an illustrator's table for displays and an author autographs table for published SCBWI members. Conference brochure is available in July by e-mail, phone or visit website. Accepts inquiries by SASE, e-mail, phone. Agents and editors attend/participate in this conference.

✔ **SOUTHWEST WRITERS WORKSHOP CONFERENCE**, 8200 Mountain Rd. NE, Suite 106, Albuquerque NM 87110-7835. (505)265-9485. Fax: (505)265-9483. E-mail: swriters@aol.com. Website: www.southwestwriters.org. **Contact:** Stephanie Dooley, conference chair. Estab. 1983. Annual. Conference held in September. Average attendance: about 400. "Conference concentrates on all areas of writing and includes preconference sessions, appointments and networking." Workshops and speakers include writers and editors of all genres for all levels from beginners to advanced. 2000 keynote speaker was Lorna Luft, actress, singer and author of *Me and My Shadow.*

Costs: $265 (members) and $320 (nonmembers); includes conference sessions and 2 luncheons.

Accommodations: Usually have official airline and discount rates. Special conference rates are available at hotel. A list of other area hotels and motels is available.

Additional Information: Sponsors a contest judged by authors, editors and agents from New York, Los Angeles, etc., and from major publishing houses. Eighteen categories. Deadline: May 1. Entry fee is $29 (members) or $39 (nonmembers). Conference information available in April 2001. For brochures/guidelines send SASE, visit website, e-mail, fax, call. Accepts inquiries by SASE, e-mail, fax, phone. "An appointment (10 minutes, one-on-one) may be set up at the conference with editor or agent of your choice on a first-registered/first-served basis."

STEAMBOAT SPRINGS WRITERS GROUP, P.O. Box 774284, Steamboat Springs CO 80477. (970)879-8079. E-mail: freiberger@compuserve.com. **Contact:** Harriet Freiberger, director. Estab. 1982. Annual. Conference held July 2001. Conference duration: 1 day. Average attendance: 30. "Our conference emphasizes instruction within the seminar format. Novices and polished professionals benefit from the individual attention and the camaraderie which can be established within small groups. A pleasurable and memorable learning experience is guaranteed by the relaxed and friendly atmosphere of the old train depot. Registration is limited." Steamboat Arts Council sponsors the group at the restored train depot.

Costs: $35 before June 1, $45 after. Fee covers all conference activities, including lunch. Lodging available at Steamboat Resorts; 10% discount for participants. Optional dinner and activities during evening preceding conference.

Additional Information: Available April 2001. Accepts inquiries by e-mail, phone, mail.

ℕ TAOS INSTITUTE OF ARTS, 108 Civic Plaza Dr., Taos NM 87571. Phone/fax: (505)758-2793. E-mail: tia@taosnet.com. Website: www.tiataos.com. Estab. 1988. Annual. Workshops held June-October 2001. Workshop duration: 1 week. Average attendance: 12 students maximum/workshop. Covers general fiction, travel writing, mystery writing, the business of publishing, children's book writing, free-association writing. Workshops take place in a variety of locations in Taos. 2000 topics included a general fiction workshop and a mystery novel workshop. Melanie Sumner, Robert Westbrook, Margaret Klee Lichtenberg and Donna Guthrie were among the presenters in 2000.

Costs: $380 ($40 registration fee and $340 tuition). Meals, lodging, etc., are separate.

Accommodations: Provides a list of area hotels or lodging options.

Additional Information: In mystery writing workshops, participants may send 1 chapter (30-page limit). Deadline at least 2 weeks prior to workshop. Conference information available March 2001. For brochure send e-mail, call. Accepts inquiries by SASE, e-mail, phone, fax.

ℕ UNIVERSITY OF NEW MEXICO'S TAOS SUMMER WRITERS CONFERENCE, Dept. of English, Humanities 255, University of New Mexico, Albuquerque NM 87131-1106. (505)277-6248. Fax: (505)277-2950. E-mail: taosconf@unm.edu. Website: www.unm.edu/~taosconf. **Contact:** Sharon Oard Warner, director. Estab. 1999. Annual. Conference held July 14-21, 2001 (weekend workshops July 14-15, week-long workshop July 15-20). Average attendance: 100. Conference offers both weekend and week-long workshops for beginning and experienced writers. Workshop size is a maximum of 12, which allows for both group support and individual attention. "We offer workshops in novel writing, short story writing, screenwriting, poetry, creative nonfiction, travel writing, and in special topics, such as historical fiction and revision. Workshops and readings are all held at the Sugarbrush Inn Conference Center, part of the Sugarbrush Inn, an historic hotel and Taos landmark since 1929."

Costs: Week-long workshop tuition is $475, includes a Sunday evening Mexican buffet dinner, a Friday evening barbecue, and evening museum tour. A Wednesday weekend workshop tuition is $200.

Accommodations: "We offer a discounted car rental rate through the Sugarbrush Inn." Offers overnight accommodations. Participants may choose to stay at either the Sugarbrush Inn or the adjacent Comfort Suites. Conference participants receive special discounted rates $59-99 per night. Room rates at both hotels include a full hot breakfast.

Additional Information: Participants do not submit mss in advance. Instead, they bring copies to distribute at the first meeting of the workshop. Sponsors contest. "We offer two merit-based scholarships to participants and one D. H. Lawrence Fellowship. Scholarship awards are based on submissions of poetry and fiction. They provide tuition remission for 2 week-long workshops, transportation and lodging not provided." To apply, participants simply check the "Scholarship" box on the application and include 10 pages of poetry or fiction along with deposit. Applicants should be registered for the conference. The Fellowship is for emerging writers with one book in print or press, provides tuition remission and the cost of lodging. Brochures available late January-early February 2001. For brochures send e-mail, visit website, call or fax. Accepts inquiries by SASE, e-mail, phone, fax. "The conference offers a balance of special events and free time. If they take a morning workshop, they'll have afternoons free, and vice versa. We've also included several outings, including an evening tour of the Harwood Arts Center and a visit to historic D. H. Lawrence Ranch outside Taos."

N ROBERT VAUGHAN'S "WRITE ON THE BEACH", ATAP Financial Corp., P.O. Box 1092, Addison TX 75001-1092. (972)381-7250. Fax: (206)493-2702. E-mail: writeonthebeach@aol.com. Website: www.robertv aughan.com. **Contact:** Robert Vaughan, director. Estab. 1998. Annual. Conference held February and March. Average attendance: 10. Focus is on fiction, nonfiction and screenwriting. The retreat is held in a very large beach house. Each attendee has private room & bath, most with a view of the Gulf. It is held at Gulf Shores, Alabama. Ratio of writers to staff is never higher than 2:1 thus affording maximum consultation time. Faculty includes Greg Tobin (editor-in-chief & sr. vp at Ballentine); Pat LoBruto, (sr. editor Bantam); Bob Robison (agent with Robison & Assoc.); Jim Harris (film producer, Paragon Pictures); and Robert Vaughan (author, screenwriter).

Costs: $1,250 for 6 days. Includes all meals and lodging.

Accommodations: Shuttle service is provided by retreat staff from Pensacola or mobile airports.

Additional Information: Brochures available in April. For brochure e-mail, visit website, phone or fax. Accepts inquiries by e-mail, phone, and fax. Agents and editors participate in conference. "This is a very unique conference, more of a retreat. As attendees have a need for consultation with an editor, they just walk up them, call them by their first name and begin talking."

✓ WRITERS WORKSHOP IN SCIENCE FICTION, English Department/University of Kansas, Lawrence KS 66045-2115. (785)864-3380. Fax: (785)864-4298. E-mail: jgunn@ukans.edu. Website: http://falcon.cc. ukans.edu/~sfcenter/. **Contact:** James Gunn, professor. Estab. 1985. Annual. Conference held June 25-July 8, 2001. Average attendance: 15. Conference for writing and marketing science fiction. "Housing is provided and classes meet in university housing on the University of Kansas campus. Workshop sessions operate informally in a lounge." The workshop is "small, informal and aimed at writers on the edge of publication or regular publication." Past guests include: Frederik Pohl, SF writer and former editor and agent; John Ordover, writer and editor; and Kij Johnson and Christopher McKittrick, writers.

Costs: Tuition: $400. Housing and meals are additional.

Accommodations: Several airport shuttle services offer reasonable transportation from the Kansas City International Airport to Lawrence. During past conferences, students were housed in a student dormitory at $12/day double, $22/day single.

Additional Information: "Admission to the workshop is by submission of an acceptable story. Two additional stories should be submitted by the end of June. These three stories are copied and distributed to other participants for critiquing and are the basis for the first week of the workshop; one story is rewritten for the second week." Conference information available in December. For brochures/guidelines send SASE, visit website, e-mail, fax, call. Accepts inquiries by SASE, phone, fax, e-mail. "The Writers Workshop in Science Fiction is intended for writers who have just started to sell their work or need that extra bit of understanding or skill to become a published writer."

West (AZ, CA, HI, NV, UT)

BE THE WRITER YOU WANT TO BE MANUSCRIPT CLINIC, 23350 Sereno Court, Villa 30, Cupertino CA 95014. (415)691-0300. **Contact:** Louise Purwin Zobel. Estab. 1969. Workshop held irregularly—usually semiannually at several locations. Workshop duration: 1-2 days. Average attendance: 20-30. "This manuscript clinic enables writers of any type of material to turn in their work-in-progress—at any stage of development—to receive help with structure and style, as well as marketing advice." It is held on about 40 campuses at different times, including University of California and other university and college campuses throughout the west.

Costs: Usually $45-65/day, "depending on campus."

Additional Information: Brochures/guidelines available for SASE.

✓ **CALIFORNIA WRITER'S CLUB CONFERENCE AT ASILOMAR**, P.O. Box 1281, Berkeley CA 94701. Website: www.calwriters.com. Estab. 1941. Annual. Check website for dates or send SASE for information. Conference duration: Friday afternoon through Sunday lunch. Average attendance: 350. Conference offers opportunity to learn from and network with successful writers, agents and editors in Asilomar's beautiful and historic beachside setting on the shores of Monterey Bay. Presentations, panels, hands-on workshops and agent/editor appointments focus on writing and marketing short stories, novels, articles, books, poetry and screenplays for children and adults.

Costs: Registration includes all conference privileges, shared lodging and 6 meals. There is a surcharge for a single room.

Accommodations: Part of the California State Park system, Asilomar is rustic and beautiful. Julia Morgan-designed redwood and stone buildings share 105 acres of dunes and pine forests with modern AIA and National Academy of Design-winning lodges. Monterey airport is a 15-minute taxi drive away.

Additional Information: First prize winners in all 7 categories of the *California Writers' Club* writing competitions receive free registration to conference. Cash prizes awarded to first three places in all categories. $10 entry fee. Visit the website for categories, rules and deadlines.

N **COLORADO MOUNTAIN WRITERS' WORKSHOP**, P.O. Box 85394, Tucson AZ 85754. (520)206-9479. E-mail: megfiles@compuserve.com. Website: www.sheilabender.com. **Contact:** Meg Files, director. Estab. 1999. Annual. Conference to be held in July 2001. Average attendance: 30. Focuses on fiction, poetry, and personal essay. Conference is held in an isolated mountaintop campus of Colorado Mountain College, near Glenwood Springs, Colorado. Features writing in voice and point of view. Faculty includes Meg Files, Sheila Bender, and Jack Heffron.

Costs: $300.

Accommodations: Offers overnight lodging in on-site dormitory $342 (6 nights, also meals).

Additional Information: Brochures available January, 2001 for SASE, e-mail, on website or call. Accepts inquiries by SASE, e-mail, phone. Editors participate in conferences. The conference is designed to lift writers, novice or experienced, to the next level. It offers writers isolation, intimacy, and inspiration. Daily activities include craft talks, small group workshops, readings, and ms consultations, as well as writing time.

N **FALLBROOK WRITER'S COLONY**, P.O. Box 976, Fallbrook CA 92088-0976. Phone/fax: (760)451-1669. E-mail: carolroper@writersconsortium.com. Website: www.writersconsortium.com. **Contact:** Jay Orkin. Estab. 1995. Ongoing seminars twice monthly. Seminar duration: 2-7 days. Average attendance: 4-6. "*The Fallbrook Writer's Colony* is a branch of the Writer's Consortium. Writers live and write in Carol Roper's rustic and spacious home. Writers may enjoy the kinship of other talented and dedicated individuals. Writers stay and work in a peaceful, creative environment unrestrained by the demands of everyday obligations and are free to set their own schedules, or attend a workshop seminar conducted by a professional guest faculty of writers and visitors." Site: "Fallbrook, California is a small, friendly town, famous for its avocados and citrus groves, 50 miles north of San Diego's Lindbergh Field and 90 miles south of Los Angeles. The town boasts respected art galleries, several excellent restaurants, and four championship golf courses nearby. There are nature preserves to enjoy. Local horseback riding is available for an additional fee, as are a massage or yoga class." Panels planned for upcoming workshops include How to Write a Novel on Weekends; Find Your Writer's Voice; Overcome Fear of Rejection; Write for Life; and Writing Books That Sell. Carol Roper, Drusilla Campbell and Dale Fetherling are scheduled to participate as speakers.

Costs: $525/week; includes room, meals, orientation and feedback. $400/week without meals. Individual feedback and/or instruction available at $50/hour. Weekend Rates: Private room with bath $175 (includes meals). Special weekend programs are priced differently. If you are here for a week, you may participate in weekend programs at no extra charge.

Accommodations: Up to 4 writers at a time in residence. Private or shared rooms. Writers may stay from 1 week to a month. Each room is comfortably decorated and contains a desk, bed and books or scripts. Writers are advised to bring their laptops or favorite writing tools. FWC is a nonsmoking, vegetarian community (chicken and fish served).

Additional Information: Unpublished or unproduced writers must submit a 10-page writing sample with registration. For brochure send e-mail, visit website, call. Accepts inquiries by SASE, e-mail, phone.

N **FOOTHILL WRITERS' CONFERENCE**, 12345 El Monte Rd., Los Altos Hills CA 94022-4599. (650)949-7316. Fax: (650)949-7375 (include cover sheet; attn: Wolterbeek). E-mail: ksw4102@mercury.fhda.e

du. **Contact:** Kim Wolterbeek. Annual. Conference held in June. Conference duration: 6 days. Average attendance: 150-200. Conference includes fiction, nonfiction, poetry, memoir, screenwriting. Held at Foothill College. Previous topics include "Let's Write: In-Class Exercises for Jumpstarting the Muse"; "Writing the Erotic"; and "Nature Poems: The Power of Place." Past faculty members include Chitia Divakaruni, Lawson Inada and Mary Jane Moffat.
Costs: Approximately $100.
Accommodations: Bus service provided. Offers list of area hotels.
Additional Information: Manuscript to be critiqued may be submitted the first day of workshop. Conference information is available in May. For brochure send SASE or e-mail.

✅ **INTERNATIONAL READERS THEATRE WORKSHOPS**, P.O. Box 17193, San Diego CA 92177-7193. (619)276-1948. Fax: (858)576-7369. E-mail: RTInst@aol.com. Website: www.readerstheatre.net. **Contact:** Bill Adams, director. Estab. 1974. Workshop held July 15-27, 2001. Average attendance: 70. Workshop on "all aspects of Readers Theatre with emphasis on scriptmaking." Workshop held at Wellington Hall on King's College Campus in London.
Costs: "$1,395 includes housing for two weeks (twin accommodations), traditional English breakfast, complimentary mid-morning coffee break and all institute fees."
Additional Information: "One-on-one critiques available between writer and faculty (if members)." Conference information available in December. For brochures/guidelines send SASE, visit website, e-mail, fax, call. Accepts inquiries by SASE, fax, phone, e-mail. Conference offers "up to 12 credits in Theatre (Speech) and/or Education from the University of Southern Maine at $127/unit."

I'VE ALWAYS WANTED TO WRITE BUT . . . , 23350 Sereno Court, Villa 30, Cupertino CA 95014. (415)691-0300. **Contact:** Louise Purwin Zobel. Estab. 1969. Workshop held irregularly, several times a year at different locations. Workshop duration: 1-2 days. Average attendance: 30-50. Workshop "encourages real beginners to get started on a lifelong dream. Focuses on the basics of writing." Workshops held at about 40 college and university campuses in the West, including University of California.
Costs: Usually $45-65/day "depending on college or university."
Additional Information: Brochures/guidelines are available for SASE after August.

IWWG EARLY SPRING IN CALIFORNIA CONFERENCE, International Women's Writing Guild, P.O. Box 810, Gracie Station, New York NY 10028-0082. (212)737-7536. Fax: (212)737-9469. E-mail: iwwg@iwwg.com. Website: www.IWWG.com. **Contact:** Hannelore Hahn, executive director. Estab. 1982. Annual. Conference held March 16-18, 2001. Average attendance: 80. Conference to promote "creative writing, personal growth and empowerment." Site: Busch Bahái School, a redwood forest mountain retreat in Santa Cruz, California. Lisa Dale Norton, Marguerite Rigoglioso, Lynne M. Ruegger and Judith Searle are scheduled to lead workshops.
Costs: $345 for weekend program with room and board ($325 for members); $90 per day for commuters ($80 for members), $170 for weekend program without room and board ($150 for members).
Accommodations: Accommodations are all at conference site.
Additional Information: Conference information is available after August. For brochures/guidelines send SASE. Accepts inquiries by e-mail, fax.

✅ **LEAGUE OF UTAH WRITERS ROUND-UP**, 4621 W. Harman Dr., W.V.C. UT 84120-3752. Phone/fax: (801)964-0861. E-mail: crofts@numucom.com. Website: http://luwrite.tripod.com/. **Contact:** Dorothy Crofts. Estab. 1935. Annual. Conference held in September. Conference duration: 2 days, Friday and Saturday. Average attendance: 200. "The purpose of the conference is to award the winners of our annual contest as well as instruction in all areas of writing. Speakers cover subjects from generating ideas to writing a novel and working with a publisher. We have something for everyone." Conference held at hotel conference rooms and ballroom facilities with view of lakeside for awards banquet. Dinner at poolside. Past themes included "Generating Ideas"; "25 Ideas on How to Work Well with a Publisher"; "Script to Screen"; "On Writing a Novel"; "What an Editorial Consultant Can Do For You." Past speakers included Jim Cypher, literary agent; Gerald Lund, historical novelist; Dick Siddoway, author; Dave Wolverton, author; Jennie Hansen, romance writer and Duane Crowther, publisher.
Costs: 1999 costs: $100 for LUW members ($80 if registered before August 31); $150 for nonmembers (fee includes 4 meals).
Accommodations: Shuttle service is available from Salt Lake International Airport to Salt Lake Airport Hilton. List of hotel/motel accommodations available. Special hotel rate for conference attendees $79.
Additional Information: Opportunity for writers to meet one-on-one with literary agent from New York, 10 pages of their novel will be read and reviewed with writer. Sponsors contests for eight fiction categories, three open to nonmembers of League. Word limits vary from 1,500 to 75,000. Conference brochures/guidelines available for SASE after January 2000. Accepts inquiries by fax, e-mail.

LOS ANGELES WRITERS CONFERENCE, Universal City Walk, Universal City CA 91608. (310)825-9415. Fax: (310)206-7382. E-mail: writers@unex.ucla.edu. Website: www.unex.edu/writers. **Contact:** Madeleine Laird. Estab. 1997. Annual. Conference held in February. Average attendance: 150-200. Conference on "creative writing—memoir, novel, short story writing." Located in UCLA extension classrooms on Universal City Walk. Panels include "sources of motivation and inspiration for writers." Speakers include Ray Bradbury, Carolyn See and L.A. Theatresports.

Costs: $545 before December 1; $645 after December 1 (includes parking, one event with food each day and guest speakers).

Accommodations: "The workshops and special events are all held on City Walk, which is the equivalent of one city block." Information on overnight accommodations is available.

Additional Information: Conference brochures available late September for SASE. Accepts inquiries by fax, e-mail. "Our conference focuses on the writing process, sources of motivation and inspiration."

N MORMON WRITERS' CONFERENCE, Association for Mormon Letters, 1925 Terrace Dr., Orem UT 84097-8060. (801)226-5585. E-mail: aml@mail.xmission.com. or bronsonjscott@juno.com. **Contact:** Scott Bronson, conference chair. Estab. 1999. Annual. Conference held November 2001. Conference duration: one day. Average attendance: 150. The conference will cover anything to do with writing by, for, or about Mormons, including fiction, poetry, drama, personal essay, nonfiction magazine, and children's literature. Site: Utah Valley State Collete, Orem UT (large conference room, smaller classrooms). Panels for the 2000 conference included contemporary Mormon theater, science fiction in the Mormon market, finding a personal voice, and three novelist identities: author, narrator, characters. Josh Brady, Gideon Burton, Carolyn Campbell, Ann Cannon and Chris Crowe participated as faculty in 2000.

Costs: $35 (2000 cost).

Additional Information: Conference information is available in August. For brochures/guidelines send SASE, e-mail, visit website. Accepts inquiries by SASE, e-mail. Editors participate in conference. "You don't have to be Mormon to enjoy and benefit from this conference, but Mormonism as a culture is a primary focus."

MOUNT HERMON CHRISTIAN WRITERS CONFERENCE, P.O. Box 413, Mount Hermon CA 95041-0413. (831)430-1238. Fax: (831)335-9218. E-mail: slist@mhcamps.org. Website: www.mounthermon.org. **Contact:** David R. Talbott, director of specialized programs. Estab. 1970. Annual. Conference held Friday-Tuesday over Palm Sunday weekend. Average attendance: 350. "We are a broad-ranging conference for all areas of Christian writing, including fiction, children's, poetry, nonfiction, magazines, books, educational curriculum and radio and TV scriptwriting. This is a working, how-to conference, with many workshops within the conference involving on-site writing assignments. The conference is sponsored by and held at the 440-acre Mount Hermon Christian Conference Center near San Jose, California, in the heart of the coastal redwoods. Registrants stay in hotel-style accommodations, and full board is provided as part of conference fees. Meals are taken family style, with faculty joining registrants. The faculty/student ratio is about 1:6 or 7. The bulk of our faculty are editors and publisher representatives from major Christian publishing houses nationwide."

Costs: Registration fees include tuition, conference sessions, resource notebook, refreshment breaks, room and board and vary from $545 (economy) to $770 (deluxe), double occupancy (2000 fees).

Accommodations: Airport shuttles are available from the San Jose International Airport. Housing is not required of registrants, but about 95% of our registrants use Mount Hermon's own housing facilities (hotel-style double-occupancy rooms). Meals with the conference are required and are included in all fees.

Additional Information: Registrants may submit 1 work for critique in advance of the conference, then have personal interviews with critiquers during the conference. No advance work is required, however. Conference brochures/guidelines are available in December for SASE or by calling (888)MH-CAMPS. Accepts inquiries by e-mail, fax. "The residential nature of our conference makes this a unique setting for one-on-one interaction with faculty/staff. There is also a decided inspirational flavor to the conference, and general sessions with well-known speakers are a highlight."

NO CRIME UNPUBLISHED™ MYSTERY WRITERS' CONFERENCE, Sisters in Crime/Los Angeles, P.O. Box 251646, Los Angeles CA 90025. (213)694-2972. E-mail: sincla@email.com. Website: www.sistersincrimela.com. Estab. 1995. Annual. Conference duration: 1 day. Average attendance: 200. Conference on mystery and crime writing. Usually held in hotel near Los Angeles airport. Two-track program: Craft and forensic sessions; keynote speaker, luncheon speaker, agent panel, book signings. In 1999: Earlene Fowler, keynote speaker; authors, agents, forensic experts, public defender.

Costs: $80, included continental breakfast, snacks, lunch, souvenir items and all sessions (1999).
Accommodations: Airport shuttle to hotel. Optional overnight stay available. Hotel conference rate available. Arrangements made directly with hotel.
Additional Information: Conference brochure available for SASE.

PALM SPRINGS WRITERS CONFERENCE, 2700 N. Cahuenga Blvd., Suite 4204, Los Angeles CA 90068. (213)874-5158. Fax: (213)874-5767. E-mail: valtrain@aol.com. Website: http://home.earthlink.net/~pswriterc onf/. **Contact:** Mary Valentine. Estab. 1992. Annual. Conference held in April. Average attendance: 230. Conference concentration is on the teaching and marketing of publishable fiction and nonfiction. "Conference is held at Marquis Hotel Resort, a first-class resort in the heart of Palm Springs. Classes on all aspects of fiction, short and long; stresses commercial, saleable fiction." Featured speakers/panelists include Catherine Coulter, Ray Bradbury, Tami Hoag, Harlan Ellison, Gerald Petievich, V.C. Andrews (Andrew Neiderman), Dianne Pugh, Arthur Lyons.
Costs: $345-395.
Accommodations: Complimentary hotel shuttle service from Palm Springs Regional Airport. Special hotel rates for Marquis Hotel.
Additional Information: "We offer critiques (half hour) for manuscripts by qualified professional writers (there is a charge), as well as free ten-minute one-on-one with agents and editors."Guidelines available for SASE. Accepts inquiries by fax, e-mail.

PASADENA WRITERS' FORUM, P.C.C. Extended Learning Dept., 1570 E. Colorado Blvd., Pasadena CA 91106-2003. (626)585-7608. **Contact:** Meredith Brucker, coordinator. Estab. 1954. Annual. Conference held in March. Average attendance: 200. "For the novice as well as the professional writer in any field of interest: fiction or nonfiction, including scripts, children's, humor and poetry." Conference held on the campus of Pasadena City College. A panel discussion by agents, editors or authors is often featured at the end of the day.
Costs: $100, including box lunch and coffee hour.
Additional Information: Brochure upon request, no SASE necessary. "Pasadena City College also periodically offers an eight-week class 'Writing for Publication'."

✓ SAN DIEGO STATE UNIVERSITY WRITERS' CONFERENCE, SDSU College of Extended Studies, 5250 Campanile Drive, San Diego State University, San Diego CA 92182-1920. (619)594-2517. E-mail: xtension @mail.sdsu.edu. Website: www.ces.sdsu.edu. **Contact:** Paula Pierce, assistant director. Estab. 1984. Annual. Conference held on 3rd weekend in January. Conference duration: 2 days. Average attendance: approximately 350. "This conference is held in San Diego, California, at the Town & Country Hotel, Mission Valley. Each year the SDSU Writers Conference offers a variety of workshops for the beginner and the advanced writer. This conference allows the individual writer to choose which workshop best suits his/her needs. In addition to the workshops, editor/agent appointments and office hours are provided so attendees may meet with speakers, editors and agents in small, personal groups to discuss specific questions. A reception is offered Saturday immediately following the workshops where attendees may socialize with the faculty in a relaxed atmosphere. Keynote speaker is to be determined."
Costs: Approximately $230. This includes all conference workshops and office hours, coffee and pastries in the morning, lunch and reception Saturday evening. Editor/agent appointments extra fee.
Accommodations: Town & Country Hotel, Mission Valley, (800)772-8527. Conference rate available for SDSU Writers Conference attendees. Attendees must make their own travel arrangements.
Additional Information: Editor/agent sessions are private, one-on-one opportunities to meet with editors and agents to discuss your submission. To receive a brochure, e-mail, fax, call or send a postcard to above address. No SASE required.

✓ THE WILLIAM SAROYAN WRITER'S CONFERENCE, P.O. Box 5331, Fresno CA 93755-5331. Phone/fax: (559)224-2516. E-mail: law@pacbell.net. **Contact:** Nannette Potter, conference chairperson. Estab. 1991. Annual. Conference held March 30-April 1, 2001. Conference duration: "Friday noon to Sunday noon."

**FOR EXPLANATIONS OF THESE SYMBOLS,
SEE THE INSIDE FRONT AND BACK COVERS OF THIS BOOK.**

Average attendance: 250. Conference on "how to write and how to get published." The conference is held at Piccadilly Inn which is "close to the airport, other hotels and all workshops in one section of the hotel." 2000 speakers included John Baker, John Kremer, Linda Mead, James Frey, Barbara Kuroff and Andrea Brown.

Costs: 2000 fees: $225 for all workshops (choice of 39), most meals, critique sessions, one-on-ones with agents, editors, etc. Overnight accommodations listed in brochure. On-site accommodations approximately $80/night.

Additional Information: Conference information available February 2001. For brochures/guidelines visit website, e-mail, fax or call. Accepts inquiries by fax, SASE, phone, e-mail. The conference is "small, intimate—easy to talk with agents, editors, etc."

SCBWI/NATIONAL CONFERENCE ON WRITING & ILLUSTRATING FOR CHILDREN, 8271 Beverly Blvd., Los Angeles CA 90048. (323)782-1010. Fax: (323)782-1892. E-mail: scbwi@scbwi.org. Website: www.scbwi.org. **Contact:** Lin Oliver, executive director. Estab. 1972. Annual. Conference held in August. Conference duration: 4 days. Average attendance: 350. Writer and illustrator workshops geared toward all levels. Covers all aspects of children's magazine and book publishing.

Costs: Approximately $350; includes all 4 days and one banquet meal. Does not include hotel room.

Accommodations: Information on overnight accommodations made available.

Additional Information: Manuscript and illustration critiques are available. Brochure/guidelines available for SASE or visit website.

SQUAW VALLEY COMMUNITY OF WRITERS FICTION WORKSHOP, P.O. Box 2352, Olympic Valley CA 96146-2352. (530)274-8551. Fax: (530)274-0986. E-mail: svcw@oro.net. Website: www.squawvalley writers.org. **Contact:** Brett Hall Jones, executive director. Estab. 1969. Annual. Conference held in August. Conference duration is 7 days. Average attendance: 120. "The Fiction Workshop assists talented writers by exploring the art and craft as well as the business of writing." Offerings include daily morning workshops lead by writer-teachers, editors, or agents of the staff, limited to 12-13 participants; seminars; panel discussions of editing and publishing; craft colloquies; lectures; and staff readings. Themes and panels in 2000 included "Personal History in Fiction," "Narrative Structure," "Roots" and "Anatomy of a Short Story." Faculty and speakers included Will Allison, Max Byrd, Mark Childress, Carolyn Doty, Jennifer Egan, Molly Giles and Bharati Mukherjee.

Costs: 2000 tuition was $590, which included six dinners. See "Accommodations" below for housing costs.

Accommodations: The Community of Writers rents houses and condominiums in the Valley for participants to live in during the week of the conference. Single room (one participant): $385/week. Double room (twin beds, room shared by conference participant of the same sex): $275/week. Multiple room (bunk beds, room shared with two or more participants of the same sex): $175/week. All rooms subject to availability; early requests are recommended. Can arrange airport shuttle pick-ups for a fee.

Additional Information: Admissions are based on submitted manuscript (unpublished fiction, a couple of stories or novel chapters); requires $20 reading fee. Brochure/guidelines available February, 2001 by phone, e-mail or visit website. Accepts inquiries by SASE, e-mail, phone. Agents and editors attend/participate in conference.

UCLA EXTENSION WRITERS' PROGRAM, 10995 Le Conte Ave., #440, Los Angeles CA 90024-2883. (310)825-9415 or (800)388-UCLA. Fax: (310)206-7382. E-mail: writers@uclaextension.org. Website: www.uclaextension.org/writers. **Contact:** Cindy Lieberman, conference coordinator. Estab. 1981. Courses held year-round with one-day or intensive weekend workshops to 12-week courses. Conference held in February. A year-long Master Sequence is also offered every fall. "The diverse offerings span introductory seminars to professional novel and script completion workshops. The annual Los Angeles Writers Conference and a number of 1, 2 and 4-day intensive workshops are popular with out-of-town students due to their specific focus and the chance to work with industry professionals. The most comprehensive and diverse continuing education writing program in the country, offering over 400 courses a year including: screenwriting, fiction, writing for young people, poetry, nonfiction, playwriting, publishing and writing for interactive multimedia. Courses are offered in Los Angeles on the UCLA campus, Santa Monica and Universal City as well as online over the Internet. Adult learners in the UCLA Extension Writers' Program study with professional screenwriters, fiction writers, playwrights, poets, nonfiction writers, and interactive multimedia writers, who bring practical experience, theoretical knowledge, and a wide variety of teaching styles and philosophies to their classes."

Costs: Vary from $75-695.

Accommodations: Students make own arrangements. The program can provide assistance in locating local accommodations.

Additional Information: Conference information available in October. For brochures/guidelines visit website, e-mail, fax or call. Accepts inquiries by e-mail, fax, phone. "Some advanced-level classes have manuscript submittal requirements; instructions are always detailed in the quarterly UCLA Extension course catalog. An annual fiction prize, The James Kirkwood Prize in Creative Writing, has been established and is given annually to one fiction writer who has produced outstanding work in a Writers' Program course."

☑ **VOLCANO WRITERS' RETREAT**, P.O. Box 163, Volcano CA 95689-0163. (209)296-7945. E-mail: khexberg@volcano.net. Website: www.volcano.net/~khexberg. **Contact:** Karin Hexberg. Estab. 1998. Biannual. Retreat held in April and October. Duration: 3 days. Average attendance: 20-30 (limited). Retreat for writing "fiction, poetry, essay, memoir." Held at the St. George Hotel. Hotel is 150 years old and located in the most picturesque of all the Gold Country towns, Volcano.
Costs: 1999 fees: $200-250 (including lodging and some meals).
Accommodations: Most attendees stay at the site although individuals may make other arrangements.
Additional Information: "Absolutely no critiquing. The purpose of this retreat is to create a non-competitive, non-judgmental, safe atmosphere where we are all free to write the worst stuff in the world." Brochures/guidelines for SASE. Accepts inquiries by e-mail.

WRANGLING WITH WRITING, Society of Southwestern Authors, P.O. Box 30355, Tucson AZ 85751. (520)296-5299. E-mail: wporter202@aol.com. **Contact:** Penny Porter, director. Estab. 1971. Annual. Conference held 3 days in January. Attendance: limited to 350. Conference "to assist writers in whatever ways we can. We cover all areas." Held at the Holiday Inn with hotel rooms available. Keynote speaker for 2001 conference will be Ray Bradbury. Plus 36 workshops for all genres of writing.
Costs: $200; includes meals.
Accommodations: Holiday Inn Pala Verde in Tucson. Information included in brochure available for SASE.
Additional Information: Critiques given if ms sent ahead. Sponsors short story contest (2,500 words or less) separate from the conference. Deadline May 31. Awards given September 21. Brochures/guidelines available after October 15 for SASE. Accepts inquiries by e-mail.

Ⓝ **WRITE NOW! WORKSHOP**, P.O. Box 50993, Phoenix AZ 85076-0993. (408)783-9863. Fax: (408)783-9863. E-mail: infor@creativecopyink.com. Website: www.creativecopyink.com. **Contact:** Kitty Bucholtz, director. Estab. 1997. Annual. Conference held in February. Average attendance: 100. The purpose is to provide a hands-on workshop where attendees immediately put into practice what they are learning. Fiction and screenwriting are always included. Other areas vary each year but may include nonfiction books, magazines, children's books, self-publishing, queries and book proposals. Conference to be held in the Phoenix metro area. In 2000, workshops included characterization, dialogue, story structure, and crime scene fiction. Faculty include Kitty Bucholtz, Helen Gaither, Pamela Kaye Tracy, and more.
Costs: For 2000: $69/person, $59 if registered by 12/31/00. Includes lunch, snacks, handouts and door prizes.
Accommodations: Provides list of area hotel or lodging options.
Additional Information: Brochures available in September for SASE, e-mail, visit website, call or fax. Accepts inquiries by SASE, e-mail, phone, fax. Editors participate in conference. "This workshop is always held the first Saturday in February."

☑ **WRITE YOUR LIFE STORY FOR PAY**, 23350 Sereno Court, Villa 30, Cupertino CA 95014-6507. (650)691-0300. E-mail: lzobelwriter@cs.com. **Contact:** Louise Purwin Zobel. Estab. 1969. Workshop held irregularly, usually semiannually at several locations. Workshop duration: 1-2 days. Average attendance: 30-50. "Because every adult has a story worth telling, this conference helps participants to write fiction and nonfiction in books and short forms, using their own life stories as a base." This workshop is held on about 40 campuses at different times, inluding University of California and other university and college campuses in the West.
Costs: Usually $45-65/day, "depending on campus."
Additional Information: Brochures/guidelines available for SASE. Accepts inquiries by SASE, e-mail, fax, phone.

Northwest (AK, ID, MT, OR, WA, WY)

CLARION WEST WRITERS' WORKSHOP, 340 15th Ave. E., Suite 350, Seattle WA 98112-5156. (206)322-9083. E-mail: KFISHLER@fishler.com. Website: www.sff.net/clarionwest. **Contact:** Leslie Howle, administrator. Estab. 1983. Annual. Workshop held June 17-July 28, 2001. Average attendance: 20. "Conference to prepare students for professional careers in science fiction and fantasy writing. Held at Seattle Central Community College on Seattle's Capitol Hill, an urban site close to restaurants and cafes, not too far from downtown." Deadline for applications: April 1.
Costs: Workshop: $1,400 ($100 discount if application received by March 1). Dormitory housing: $800, meals not included.
Accommodations: Students are strongly encouraged to stay on-site, in dormitory housing at Seattle University. Cost: $800, meals not included, for 6-week stay.
Additional Information: "This is a critique-based workshop. Students are encouraged to write a story a week; the critique of student material produced at the workshop forms the principal activity of the workshop. Students and instructors critique manuscripts as a group." Conference information available in fall 2000. For brochures/

guidelines send SASE, visit website, e-mail or call. Accepts inquiries by e-mail, phone, SASE. Limited scholarships are available, based on financial need. Students must submit 20-30 pages of ms with $25 application fee to qualify for admission. Dormitory and classrooms are handicapped accessible.

N FISHTRAP, P.O. Box 38, Enterprise OR 97828. (503)426-3623. E-mail: rich@fishtrap.org.. Website: www. fishtrap.org. **Contact:** Rich Wardschneider, director. Estab. 1988. Conferences held in July (2 days, plus 4 days of workshops) and February (2 days). Average attendance: 100-120. Focus of the conference is "Writing and the West" (including fiction, nonfiction, poetry, songwriting). Site: old Methodist Church Camp. 2000 faculty members included Ursula Le Guin, Molly Gloss, Luis Alberto Urrea, Jarold Ramsey, Kim Stafford and Beth Hadas (University of New Mexico Press).
Costs: Workshop (4 days, 12 classroom hours) $225; Conference (2 days) $180; Food and Lodging $34/day; food only $20/day.
Accommodations: Offers overnight accommodations (see above). Also provides list of area hotels. (Nearby motels $60-100/night).
Additional Information: Five fellowships given annually. Submit 8 pages of poetry or 2,500 words of prose (no name on ms) by February 7. Entries judged by a workshop instructor. Awards announced March 15. Conference information available November 2000. For brochures/guidelines send SASE, e-mail, visit website or call. Accepts inquiries by SASE, e-mail, phone. Agents and editors occasionally participate in conference. "Fishtrap Gatherings are about writing and the West. They are about ideas more than mechanics and logistics of writing/publishing. Workshops are not manuscript reviews, but writing sessions."

N SEDUCTION, DEDUCTION, AND CHOCOLATE, % Robin Lee Hatcher, P.O. Box 4722, Boise ID 83711-4722. (541)262-3684. E-mail: cmulvany@ruralnetwork.net. Website: www.robinleehatcher.com/cbc. **Contact:** Catherine Mulvany, conference chair. Estab. 1998. Conference held every 2 years (next conference in 2002). Conference duration: 1 day. Average attendance: 50-75. "Romance fiction is our main focus since we are a chapter of Romance Writers of America (Coeur du Bois Chapter)." Site: Owyhee Plaza Hotel in downtown Boise, Idaho. Jennifer Crusie, Evan Fogelman, Robin Lee Hatcher, Ann Elizabeth Cree and Catherine Mulvany participated as faculty members at the 2000 conference.
Costs: 2000 fees were $55 (included lunch plus the afternoon's Dastardly Dessert Bar).
Accommodations: The hotel operates a free airport shuttle. Overnight accommodations available. Special conference rate offered at the Owyhee Plaza Hotel.
Additional Information: Sponsors contest for book-length romantic fiction published the year preceeding the conference—"The Heart of Romance Readers' Choice Award"—which is judged by readers who do not belong to RWA. Conference information is available January 2002. For brochure send SASE, e-mail, visit website or call. Accepts inquiries by SASE, e-mail, phone. Agents and editors participate in conference.

N SITKA CENTER FOR ART AND ECOLOGY, P.O. Box 65, Otis OR 97368. (541)994-5485. Fax: (541)994-8024. E-mail: info@sitkacenter.org. Website: www.sitkacenter.org. **Contact:** Amy Buringrud, associate director. Estab. 1970. Annual workshop program. "We don't have conferences. Our workshop program is open to all levels and is held annually from late May until late March. We also have a residency program from September through May." Average attendance: 10-16/workshop. A variety of workshops in creative processes, including book arts and other media. The Center borders a Nature Conservancy Preserve, the Siuslaw National Experiemental Forest and the Salmon River Estuary, located just north of Lincoln City, Oregon.
Costs: "Workshops are generally $50-300; they do not include meals or lodging."
Accommodations: Does not offer overnight accommodations. Provides a list of area hotels or lodging options.
Additional Information: Brochure available in February of each year by phone, e-mail, fax or visit website. Accepts inquiries by SASE, e-mail, phone, fax.

☑ WHIDBEY ISLAND WRITERS' CONFERENCE, 5456 Pleasant View Lane, Freeland WA 98249. (360)331-6714. E-mail: writers@whidbey.com. Website: www.whidbey.com/writer. **Contact:** Celeste Mergens, director. Annual. Conference held March 2-4, 2001. Conference held in "a state-of-the-art high school and at local homes by the sea on Whidbey Island. A variety of informative classes and hands-on interactive writing workshops are offered. Expert panel discussions are held where agents and editors share inside details, devulge what they are looking for and offer important how-to's in skill-building sessions." Speakers include Marian Blue, Elizabeth Engstrom, Eric Larson, Jennifer Crusie Smith, Bruce Holland Rogers, Gary Ferguson, Susan Wiggs, Gabrielle Daniels, Bob Mayer and more.
Costs: $258 for the weekend not including meals and lodging.
Accommodations: Shuttle from Sea-tac Airport to Mukilteo Ferry for Whidbey Island and from the ferry to the conference available. "We have an accommodations hotline available through the Langley Chamber of Commerce. When making lodging reservations please mention the conference to receive a participant discount."

Additional Information: "If registrant desires an agent/editor consultation, they must submit the first five pages for a chapter book or youth novel or entire picture book idea with a written one-page synopsis." Conference information available July 15. For brochures/guidelines send SASE, visit website, e-mail or call. Accepts inquiries by SASE, phone, e-mail.

✓ **WILLAMETTE WRITERS CONFERENCE**, 9045 SW Barbur, Suite 5-A, Portland OR 97219-4027. (503)452-1592. Fax: (503)452-0372. E-mail: wilwrite@teleport.com. Website: www.willamettewriters.com. **Contact:** Bill Johnson, office manager. Estab. 1968. Annual. Conference held in August. Average attendance: 320. "Willamette Writers is open to all writers, and we plan our conference accordingly. We offer workshops on all aspects of fiction, nonfiction, marketing, the creative process, etc. Also we invite top notch inspirational speakers for keynote addresses. Most often the conference is held on a local college campus which offers a scholarly atmosphere and allows us to keep conference prices down. Recent theme was 'The Writers Way.' We always include at least one agent or editor panel and offer a variety of topics of interest to both fiction and nonfiction writers and screenwriters." Recent editors, agents and film producers in attendance have included: Wendy Hubbert, Penguin Putnam; Carrie McGinnis, St. Martin's Press; Leslie Meredith, Ballantine Books; Stanley Brooks, Once Upon a Time Films; Julian Fowles, Asparza-Katz Productions; David Gassman, ICM; Nancy Ellis, Nancy Ellis Literary Agency; and Linda Mead, Linda Mead Literary Agency.
Costs: Cost for full conference including meals is $210 members; $246 nonmembers.
Accomodations: If necessary, these can be made on an individual basis. Some years special rates are available.
Additional Information: Conference brochures/guidelines are available in May for catalog-size SASE. Accepts inquiries by fax, e-mail.

WRITE ON THE SOUND WRITERS' CONFERENCE, 700 Main St., Edmonds WA 98020-3147. (425)771-0228. Fax: (425)771-0253. E-mail: wots@ci.edmonds.wa.us. **Contact:** Frances Chapin, cultural resources coordinator. Sponsored by Edmonds Arts Commission. Estab. 1986. Annual. Conference held October 6-7, 2001. Conference duration: 2 days. Average attendance: 160. "Workshops and lectures are offered for a variety of writing interests and levels of expertise. It is a high-quality, affordable conference with limited registration."
Costs: $85 for 2 days, $50 for 1 day (1999); includes registration, morning refreshments and 1 ticket to keynote lecture.
Additional Information: Brochures available August 1, 2001. Accepts inquiries by e-mail, fax.

N **WRITERS STUDIO**, 42 N.E. Graham St., Portland OR 97212. (503)287-2150. Fax: (503)287-2150. E-mail: Jesswrites@juno.com. Website: http://writingoutthestorm.homepage.com. **Contact:** Jessica Morrell. Estab. 1998. Workshop held in February and October. Session I: Connecting. "This session emphasizes uncovering and strengthening your authentic voice, adding texture, nuance and perfecting description." Session II: Fiction Intensive. "This is a session for writers who are past the starting line, but are daunted by the task of finishing. It will be especially helpful to writers who would like to restart themselves or their project. We'll cover the all-important issues of conflict and motivation and discuss in depth how to handle deadly middles. The session will also refine and define plot elements, including character development, how to insert complications, and maintain tension and a unity of tone." Site: A historic building in a lovely old neighborhood. Shops, restaurants and public transportation are within walking distance. *Writing Out the Storm* author Jessica Morrell and short story writer Marian Pierce are scheduled to participate as faculty.
Costs: $95 (2000 fees).
Accommodations: Provides a list of area hotels or lodging options.
Additional Information: Conference information available August 2000. For brochure send e-mail, call. Accepts inquiries by SASE, e-mail, phone, fax.

Canada

N ☙ **BLOODY WORDS MYSTERY CONFERENCE**, 12 Roundwood Court, Toronto, Ontario M1W 1Z2. Phone/fax: (416)497-5293. E-mail: soles@sff.net. Website: www.bloodywords.com. **Contact:** Caro Soles, chair. Estab. 1999. Annual. Conference held June 8-9, 2001. Average attendance: 200. Focus: Mystery/true crime/forensics, with Canadian slant. Purpose: To bring readers and writers of the mystery genre together in a Canadian setting. Site: Delta Chelsea Inn, Gerrard St., Toronto. Conference includes a workshop and 2 tracks of panels, one on factual information such as forensics, agents, scene of the crime procedures, etc. and one on fiction, such as "Death in a Cold Climate," "Murder on the Menu," "Elementary My Dear Watson," and a First Novelists Panel. 2000 guests included L.R. Wright, Howard Engel and Medora Sale, as well as 4 agents, Dinah Forbes (senior editor at McClelland & Stewart) and Greg Ioannou, an experienced writer/editor.
Costs: 2000 fee: $125 (included the banquet and all panels, readings, dealers room and workshop).

Accommodations: Offers hotel shuttle from the airport. Offers block of rooms in hotel; list of optional lodging available. Call Delta Chelsea Inn for special conference rates (1-800-CHELSEA).

Additional Information: Sponsors short mystery story contest—4,000 word limit; judges are experienced editors of anthologies; fee is $5 (entrants must be registered). Conference information is available now. For brochure visit website. Accepts inquiries by e-mail and phone. Agents and editors participate in conference. "This is a conference for both readers and writers of mysteries, the only one of its kind in Canada. For 2001, we will have a Canadian Guest of Honor as well as an International Guest of Honor."

BOOMING GROUND, Buch E-462, 1866 Main Mall, Creative Writing Program, UBC, Vancouver, British Columbia V6T 121 Canada. (604)822-2469. Fax: (604)822-3616. E-mail: bg@arts.ubc.ca. Website: www.arts. ubc.ca/bg. **Contact:** Andrew Gray, director. Estab. 1998. Annual. Conference held July 7-14, 2001. Average attendance: 70. Conference on "fiction, poetry, nonfiction, screenplays." Conference held at "Green College, a residential college at the University of Columbia, overlooking the ocean." 2000 panels included "The Double Life of Screenwriters," "Between Fiction and Nonfiction," "The First Novel" and "Poetry in the Millennium." 2000 panelists included Bonnie Burnard, Patrick Crean, Lorna Crozier, Paul Durcan and Judith Thompson.

Costs: 2000 fees were $650 (Canadian). Meals and accommodation separate. Some scholarships available.

Accommodations: "Information on overnight accommodations is available and students are encouraged to stay on-site at Green College." On-site accommodations: $360 and $397 (Canadian) for 7 nights.

Additional information: "Workshops are based on works-in-progress. Writers must submit manuscript with application for jury selection." Conference information available January 2001. For brochures/guidelines send SASE, visit website, e-mail, fax or call. Accepts inquiries by SASE, phone, fax, e-mail. "Classes are offered in both standard level and master classes. Standard classes are aimed at early career writers, while master classes are intended for mid-career writers."

THE FESTIVAL OF THE WRITTEN ARTS, Box 2299, Sechelt, British Columbia V0N 3A0 Canada. (800)565-9631 or (604)885-9631. Fax: (604)885-3967. E-mail: written_arts@sunshine.net. Website: www.sunshi ne.net/rockwood. **Contact:** Gail Bull, festival producer. Estab. 1983. Annual. Festival held August 9-12, 2001. Average attendance: 3,500. To promote "all writing genres." Festival held at the Rockwood Centre. "The Centre overlooks the town of Sechelt on the Sunshine Coast. The lodge around which the Centre was organized was built in 1937 as a destination for holidayers arriving on the old Union Steamship Line; it has been preserved very much as it was in its heyday. A new twelve-bedroom annex was added in 1982, and in 1989 the Festival of the Written Arts constructed a Pavilion for outdoor performances next to the annex. The festival does not have a theme. Instead, it showcases 20 or more Canadian writers in a wide variety of genres each year—the only all-Canadian writer's festival."

Costs: $12 per event or $150 for a four-day pass (Canadian funds).

Accommodations: Lists of hotels and bed/breakfast available.

Additional Information: The festival runs contests during the 3½ days of the event. Prizes are books donated by publishers. Festival information available after mid-April 2001. For brochures visit website, e-mail, fax or call. Accepts inquiries by e-mail, fax.

[N] GOD USES INK ANNUAL WRITERS CONFERENCE, M.I.P. Box 3745, Markham, Ontario L3R 0Y4 Canada. (905)479-5885. Fax: (905)479-4742. E-mail: ft@efc-canada.com. Website: www.efc-canada. com. **Contact:** Trish Kimball, help desk. Estab. 1984. Annual. Conference to be held June 14-16, 2001. Average attendance: 100. "The annual G.U.I. conference seeks to encourage writers of all levels and genres, but especially beginners, to integrate their Christian faith and their writing. Much of the event is how-to workshops, plus opportunities to make friends and share expert advice." The conference will be held at a "lush, green retreat centre tucked away in the city of Guelph, Ontario, about 60 miles west of Toronto, 100 miles from Buffalo, and 200 miles from Detroit." In 2000, we features 5 sessions, 1-hour each, on "Creating Suspense in Your Fiction", by Linda Hall (author and fiction instructor at the University of New Brunswick). In 2001, we hope to have as keynote speaker, James Schaap, author of *Romi's Place*, and several other novels. Also features short stories, devotional books and biographies. Schaap is associate professor of English at Dordt College, in Iowa.

Costs: $254 CDN (including meals).

Accommodations: Red car service available for $46 or less from Toronto airport, (519) 824-9344. Offers overnight accommodations. Two nights, from $30-60 per night on-site.

Additional Information: Sponsors contests. Novice contest for unpublished writers. $5. Length: 400 words. Judged by conference organizers. Brochures available each February by e-mail, website, call or fax. Accepts inquiries by SASE, e-mail, phone, fax. Editors participate in conferences. "Non-Christians are welcome."

VISIT THE WRITER'S MARKET WEBSITE at www.writersmarket.com for hot new markets, daily market updates, writers' guidelines and much more.

SUNSHINE COAST FESTIVAL OF THE WRITTEN ARTS, Box 2299, Sechelt, British Columbia V0N 3A0 Canada. (604)885-9631 or (800) 565-9631. Fax: (604)885-3967. E-mail: written_arts@sunshine.net. Website: www.sunshine.net/rockwood. **Contact:** Gail Bull. Estab. 1982. Annual. Festival held August 10-13, 2000. Average attendance: 9,500. Festival "tries to represent all genres." Held in a "500 seat pavilion set in the beautiful Rockwood Gardens in the seaside town of Sechelt, B.C." Past speakers included Maragret Atwood, Arthur Black, Andreas Schroeder, Bill Richardson, Anne Petrie and Margo Button.
Costs: Individual events, $12; Festival pass, $150; student discounts. Meals and lodging are not included.
Accommodations: Information on overnight accommodations is available.
Additional information: Conference brochures/guidelines available in May for SASE. Accepts inquiries by fax, e-mail.

SURREY WRITERS' CONFERENCE, (formerly A Writer's W*O*R*L*D), 12870 72nd Ave., Surrey, British Columbia V4P 1G1 Canada. (604)594-2000. Fax: (604)590-2506. E-mail: phoenixmcf@aol.com. **Contact:** Rollie Koop, principal. Estab. 1992. Annual. Conference held in Fall. Conference duration: 3 days. Average attendance: 350. Conference for fiction (romance/science fiction/fantasy/mystery—changes focus depending upon speakers and publishers scheduled), nonfiction and poetry. "For everyone from beginner to professional." Conference held at Sheraton Guildford. Guest lecturers included authors Diana Gabaldon, Don McQuinn and Daniel Wood; agents and editors.
Accommodations: On request will provide information on hotels and B&Bs. Conference rate, $90. Attendee must make own arrangements for hotel and transportation.
Additional Information: "A drawing takes place and ten people's manuscripts are critiqued by a bestselling author." Writer's contest entries must be submitted about 1 month early. Length: 1,000 words fiction, nonfiction, poetry, young writers (19 or less). 1st Prize $250, 2nd Prize $125, 3rd Prize $75. Contest is judged by a qualified panel of writers and educators. Write, call or e-mail for additional information.

THE VANCOUVER INTERNATIONAL WRITERS FESTIVAL, 1398 Cartwright St., Vancouver, British Columbia V6H 3R8 Canada. (604)681-6330. Fax: (604)681-8400. E-mail: alee@writersfest.bc.ca. Website: www.writersfest.bc.ca. Estab. 1988. Annual. Held in October. Average attendance: 11,000. "This is a festival for readers and writers. The program of events is diverse and includes readings, panel discussions, seminars. Lots of opportunities to interact with the writers who attend." Held on Granville Island—in the heart of Vancouver. Two professional theaters are used as well as Performance Works (an open space). "We try to avoid specific themes. Programming takes place between February and June each year and is by invitation."
Costs: Tickets are $10-15 (Canadian).
Accommodations: Local tourist info can be provided when necessary and requested.
Additional Information: Festival information available on website. Accepts inquiries by e-mail, fax. "A reminder—this is a festival, a celebration, not a conference or workshop."

International

ART WORKSHOPS IN GUATEMALA, 4758 Lyndale Ave. S, Minneapolis MN 55409-2304. (612)825-0747. Fax: (612)825-6637. E-mail: info@artguat.org. Website: www.artguat.org. **Contact:** Liza Fourré, director. Estab. 1995. Annual. Conference held in February. Maximum class size: 10 students per class. Workshop titles include: "Creative Writing—Developing the Novel" with Tessa Bridal.
Costs: $1,695 (includes tuition, air fare to Guatemala from USA, lodging and ground transportation).
Accommodations: All transportation and accommodations included in price of conference.
Additional Information: Conference information available now. For brochure/guidelines visit website, e-mail, fax or call. Accepts inquiries by e-mail, phone, fax.

EDINBURGH UNIVERSITY CENTRE FOR CONTINUING EDUCATION CREATIVE WRITING WORKSHOPS, 11 Buccleuch Place, Edinburgh EH8 9LW Scotland. Phone: 44(0)131 650 4400. Fax: 44(0)131 667 6097. E-mail: ccesummer@ed.ac.uk. Website: www.cce.ed.ac.uk/summer. Administrative Director of International Summer Schools: Bridget M. Stevens. **Contact:** Ursula Michels. Estab. 1990. Short story course July 1-7; playwriting course July 8-21. Average attendance: 15. Courses cover "basic techniques of creative writing, the short story and playwriting. The University of Edinburgh Centre for Continuing Education occupies traditional 18th century premises near the George Square Campus. Located nearby are libraries, banks and recreational facilities. Free use of word-processing facilities."
Costs: In 2000 cost was £215 per one-week course (tuition only).
Accommodations: Information on overnight accommodations is available. Accommodations include student dormitories, self-catering apartment and local homes.
Additional Information: Conference brochures/guidelines available after December for SASE. Accepts inquiries by e-mail and fax.

⊕ ✓ **PARIS WRITERS' WORKSHOP/WICE**, 20, Bd du Montparnasse, Paris, France 75015. Phone: (331)45.66.75.50. Fax: (331)40.65.96.53. E-mail: pww@wice-paris.org. Website: www.wice-paris.org. **Contact:** Rose Burke and Marcia Lebre, directors. Estab. 1987. Annual. Conference held July 1-6, 2001. Average attendance: 40-50. "Conference concentrates on fiction, nonfiction creativity and poetry. Visiting lecturers speak on a variety of issues important to beginning and advanced writers. 2000 lecturers included Speer Morgan, editor of the *Missouri Review*; Steward Lindh, screenplay writer; Stephen Romer, British poet and editor; Kerry Hardie, Irish poet and novelist; and Denis Hirson, South African author. Located in the heart of Paris on the Bd. du Montparnasse, the stomping grounds of such famous American writers as Ernest Hemingway, Henry Miller and F. Scott Fitzgerald. The site consists of 4 classrooms, a resource center/library and private terrace."
Costs: $370—tuition only.
Additional Information: "Students submit 1 copy of complete ms or work-in-progress which is sent in advance to writer in residence. Each student has a one-on-one consultation with writer in residence concerning ms that was submitted." Conference information available late fall 2000. For brochures/guidelines send SASE, visit website, e-mail or fax. Accepts inquiries by SASE, phone, e-mail, fax. "Workshop attracts many expatriate Americans and other English language students from all over Europe and North America. We can assist with finding a range of hotels, from budget to more luxurious accommodations. We are an intimate workshop with an exciting mix of more experienced, published writers and enthusiastic beginners. Past writers include CK Williams, Carolyn Kizer, Grace Paley, Jayne Anne Phillips, Marilyn Hacker, Matthew Sweeney, Carol Shields, Isabelle Huggins, Mary Jo Salter, Brad Leithauser, Cole Swensen and Lee Gutkind."

⊕ ✓ **SUMMER IN FRANCE WRITING WORKSHOPS**, HCOI, Box 102, Plainview TX 79072. Phone/fax: (806)889-3533. E-mail: bettye@parisamericanacademy.edu. Website: www.parisamericanacademy.edu. **Contact:** Bettye Givens, director. Annual. Conference: 27 days in July. Average attendance: 10-15. For fiction, poetry, nonfiction, drama. The classrooms are in the Val de Grace 277 Rue St. Jacques in the heart of the Latin Quarter near Luxeumbourg Park in Paris. Guest speakers include Paris poets, professors and editors (lectures in English and interpreters).
Costs: Costs vary. 2000 cost was $2,850 for shared apartment, no meals except opening and closing dinners. Costs also include literature classes, art history and the writing workshop.
Accommodations: Some accommodations with a French family.
Additional Information: Conference information available. For brochures/guidelines send SASE, e-mail or visit website. Accepts inquiries by SASE, e-mail, fax. "Enroll early. Side trips out of Paris are planned as are poetry readings at the Paris American Academy and at Shakespeare & Co."

⊕ **TŶ NEWYDD WRITER'S CENTRE**, Llanystumdwy, Cricieth Gwynedd LL52 OLW, United Kingdom. Phone: 01766-522811. Fax: 01766 523095. **Contact:** Sally Baker, director. Estab. 1990. Regular courses held throughout the year. Every course held Monday-Saturday. Average attendance: 14. "To give people the opportunity to work side by side with professional writers, in an informal atmosphere." Site is Tŷ Newydd, large manor house, last home of the prime minister, David Lloyd George. Situated in North Wales, Great Britain—between mountains and sea. Past featured tutors include novelists Beryl Bainbridge and Bernice Rubens.
Costs: £300 for Monday-Saturday (includes full board, tuition).
Accommodations: Transportation from railway stations arranged. Accommodation in Tŷ Newydd (onsite).
Additional Information: Conference information available after January by mail, phone, e-mail, fax or visit website. Accepts inquiries by SASE, e-mail, fax, phone. "We have had several people from U.S. on courses here in the past three years. More and more people come to us from the U.S. often combining a writing course with a tour of Wales."

⊕ ✓ **THE WRITERS' SUMMER SCHOOL, SWANWICK**, P.O. Box 5532, Heanor, DE75 7YF England. Phone/fax: 07050-630949. Website: www.wss.org.uk. **Contact:** Brenda Courtie, secretary. Estab. 1949. Annual. Conference held every August. Average attendance: 300 plus. "Conference concentrates on all fields of writing." Speakers in 2000 included Jonathan Gash and Nigel Rees.
Costs: 2000: £200-300 per person inclusive.
Accommodations: Buses from main line station to conference centre provided.
Additional Information: Conference information available after February. Accepts inquiries by mail, e-mail, fax. "The Writers' Summer School is a nonprofit-making organization."

Organizations

When you write, you write alone. It's just you and the typewriter or computer screen. Yet the writing life does not need to be a lonely one. Joining a writing group or organization can be an important step in your writing career. By meeting other writers, discussing your common problems and sharing ideas, you can enrich your writing and increase your understanding of this sometimes difficult, but rewarding life.

The variety of writers' organizations seems endless—encompassing every type of writing and writer—from small, informal groups that gather regularly at a local coffee house for critique sessions to regional groups that hold annual conferences to share technique and marketing tips. National organizations and unions fight for writers' rights and higher payment for freelancers, and international groups monitor the treatment of writers around the world.

In this section you will find state-, province- and regional-based groups. You'll also find national organizations including the National Writers Association. The Mystery Writers of America and the Western Writers of America are examples of groups devoted to a particular type of writing. Whatever your needs or goals, you're likely to find a group listed here to interest you.

SELECTING A WRITERS' ORGANIZATION

To help you make an informed decision, we've provided information on the scope, membership and goals of the organizations listed on these pages. We asked groups to outline the types of memberships available and the benefits members can expect. Most groups will provide additional information for a self-addressed, stamped envelope, and you may be able to get a sample copy of their newsletter for a modest fee.

Keep in mind joining a writers' organization is a two-way street. When you join an organization, you become a part of it and, in addition to membership fees, most groups need and want your help. If you want to get involved, opportunities can include everything from chairing a committee to writing for the newsletter to helping set up an annual conference. The level of your involvement is up to you, and almost all organizations welcome contributions of time and effort.

Selecting a group to join depends on a number of factors. As a first step, you must determine what you want from membership in a writers' organization. Then send away for more information on the groups that seem to fit your needs. Start, however, by asking yourself:

• Would I like to meet writers in my city? Am I more interested in making contacts with other writers across the country or around the world?

• Am I interested in a group that will critique and give me feedback on work-in-progress?

• Do I want marketing information and tips on dealing with editors?

• Would I like to meet other writers who write the same type of work I do or am I interested in meeting writers from a variety of fields?

• How much time can I devote to meetings and are regular meetings important to me? How much can I afford to pay in dues?

• Would I like to get involved in running the group, working on the group's newsletters, planning a conference?

• Am I interested in a group devoted to writers' rights and treatment or would I rather concentrate on the business of writing?

For More Information

Because they do not usually have the resources or inclination to promote themselves widely, finding a local writers' group is usually a word-of-mouth process. If you would like to start a writers' group in your area, ask your local libraries and bookstores if they sponsor writers' groups.

If you have a computer and would like to meet with writers in other areas of the country, you will find many commercial online services, such as Genie and America Online, have writers' sections and "clubs" online. Many free online services available through the Internet also have writers' "boards."

For more information on writers' organizations, check *The Writer's Essential Desk Reference: A Companion to Writer's Market*, 2nd edition (Writer's Digest Books, 1507 Dana Ave., Cincinnati OH 45207). Other directories listing organizations for writers include the *Literary Market Place* or *International Literary Market Place* (R.R. Bowker, 121 Chanlon Rd., New Providence NJ 07974). The National Writers Association also maintains a list of writers' organizations.

ASSOCIATED WRITING PROGRAMS, Tallwood House, Mail Stop 1E3, George Mason University, Fairfax VA 22030-9736. (703)993-4301. Fax: (703)993-4302. E-mail: awp@gmu.edu. Website: www.awpwriter.org (includes FAQ, membership information/ordering, award series guidelines, links to institutional members, AWP news). **Contact:** Membership Services. Estab. 1967. Number of Members: 5,000 individuals and 324 institutions. Types of Membership: Institutional (universities); graduate students; individual writers; and *Chronicle* subscribers. Open to any person interested in writing; most members are students or faculty of university writing programs (worldwide). Benefits include information on creative writing programs; grants, awards and publishing opportunities for writers; job list for academe and writing-related fields; a job placement service for writers in academe and beyond. AWP holds an annual conference in a different US city every spring; also conducts an annual Award Series in poetry, short story collections, novel and creative nonfiction, in which winner receives $2,000 honorarium and publication by a participating press. AWP acts as agent for finalists in Award Series and tries to place their manuscript with publishers throughout the year. Manuscripts accepted January 1-February 28 only. Novel competition: winner receives publication by St. Martin's Press and $10,000 in royalties. Send SASE for new guidelines. Publishes *The Writer's Chronicle* 6 times/year; 3 times/academic semester. Available to members for free. Nonmembers may order a subscription for $20/year; $27/year Canada; call for overseas rates. Also publishes the *AWP Official Guide to Writing Programs* which lists about 330 creative writing programs in universities across the country and in Canada. *Guide* is updated every 2 years; cost is $25.95, which includes shipping and handling. Dues: $57 for individuals; $37 students (must send copy of ID); additional $62 for full placement service. AWP keeps dossiers on file and sends them to school or organization of person's request. Send SASE for information. Inquiries by fax and e-mail OK.

AUSTIN WRITERS' LEAGUE, Austin Writers' League, 1501 W. Fifth, E-2, Austin TX 78703. (512)499-8914. Fax: (512)499-0441. Website: www.writersleague.org. **Contact:** Jim Bob McMillan, executive director. Associate Director: Sally Baker. Estab. 1981. Number of Members: 1,600. Types of Memberships: Regular, student/senior citizen, family. Monthly meetings and use of resource center/library is open to the public. "Membership includes both aspiring and professional writers, all ages and all ethnic groups." Job bank is also open to the public. Public also has access to technical assistance. Partial and full scholarships offered for some programs. Of 1,600 members, 800 reside in Austin. Remaining 800 live all over the US and in other countries. Benefits include monthly newsletter, monthly meetings, study groups, resource center/library-checkout privileges, discounts on workshops, seminars, classes, job bank, discounts on books and tapes, participation in awards programs, technical/marketing assistance, copyright forms and information, Writers Helping Writers (mentoring program). Center has 5 rooms plus 2 offices and storage area. Public space includes reception and job bank area; conference/classroom; library; and copy/mail room. Library includes 1,000 titles. Sponsors fall and spring workshops, weekend seminars, informal classes, sponsorships for special events such as readings, production of original plays, media conferences, creative writing programs for children and youth; Violet Crown Book Awards, newsletter writing awards, Young Texas Writers awards, contests for various anthologies. Publishes *Austin Writer* (monthly newsletter), sponsors with Texas Commission on the Arts Texas Literary Touring Program. Administers literature subgranting program for Texas Commission on the Arts. Membership/subscription: $45, $40-students, senior citizens, $60 family membership. Monthly meetings. Study groups set their own regular meeting schedules. Send SASE for information.

THE AUTHORS GUILD, 330 W. 42nd St., 29th Floor, New York NY 10036-6902. (212)563-5904. E-mail: staff@authorsguild.org. Website: www.authorsguild.org (includes publishing industry news, business, legal and membership information). Executive Director: Paul Aiken. **Contact:** John McCloskey, membership coordinator. Purpose of organization: membership organization of 8,000 members offers services and informational materials intended to help published authors with the business and legal aspects of their work, including contract problems, copyright matters, freedom of expression and taxation. Maintains staff of attorneys and legal interns to assist members. Group health insurance available. Qualifications for membership: book author published by an established American publisher within 7 years or any author who has had 3 works, fiction or nonfiction, published by a magazine or magazines of general circulation in the last 18 months. Associate membership also available. Annual dues: $90. Different levels of membership include: associate membership with all rights except voting available to an author who has a firm contract offer from an American publisher. Workshops/conferences: "The Guild and the Authors Guild Foundation conduct several symposia each year at which experts provide information, offer advice, and answer questions on subjects of concern to authors. Typical subjects have been the rights of privacy and publicity, libel, wills and estates, taxation, copyright, editors and editing, the art of interviewing, standards of criticism and book reviewing. Transcripts of these symposia are published and circulated to members." The *Authors Guild Bulletin*, a quarterly journal, contains articles on matters of interest to published writers, reports of Guild activities, contract surveys, advice on problem clauses in contracts, transcripts of Guild and League symposia, and information on a variety of professional topics. Subscription included in the cost of the annual dues. Inquiries by mail, e-mail and fax OK.

N **BURNABY WRITERS' SOCIETY**, 6584 Deer Lake Ave., Burnaby, British Columbia V5G 3T7 Canada. (604)444-1228. E-mail: lonewolf@portal.ca. Website: www.bws.bc.ba. **Contact:** Heather Hiebert, editor. Estab. 1967. Number of members: 300. "Membership is regional, but open to anyone interested in writing." Benefits include monthly market newsletter; workshops/critiques; guest speakers; information on contests, events, reading venues, etc.; opportunity to participate in public reading series. Sponsors annual competition open to all British Columbia residents; Canada Council sponsored readings; workshops. Publishes *Burnaby Writers Newsletter* monthly (except July/August), available to anyone for $30/year subscription. Dues: $30/year (includes newsletter subscription); $20 seniors, students. Meets second Thursday of each month. Send SASE for information.

CALIFORNIA WRITERS' CLUB, P.O. Box 1281, Berkeley CA 94701. Phone/fax: (760)446-4350. E-mail: writeit@gtc.net. Website: www.calwriters.com. Estab. 1909. Twelve branches. Number of Members: 900. Type of Memberships: Associate and active. Open to all writers. "Includes published authors, those actively pursuing a career in writing and those associated with the field of writing." Benefits include: CWC sponsors annual conference with writing contest. Publishes a monthly newsletter at state level and at branch level. Available to members only. Dues: $35/year. Send SASE for information. Inquiries by e-mail (through website OK).

CANADIAN SOCIETY OF CHILDREN'S AUTHORS, ILLUSTRATORS AND PERFORMERS (CANSCAIP), Northern District Library, 40 Orchard View Blvd., Lower Level, Toronto, Ontario M4R 1B9 Canada. (416)515-1559. Fax: (416)515-7022. E-mail: canscaip@org. Website: www.interlog.com/~canscaip (includes children's authors, seminar information, art collection—samples [traveling]). **Contact:** Nancy Prasad, executive secretary. Estab. 1977. Number of Members: 1,100. Types of membership: Full professional member and friend (associate member). Open to professional active writers, illustrators and performers in the field of children's culture (full members); beginners and all other interested persons and institutions (friends). International scope, but emphasis on Canada. Benefits include quarterly newsletter, minutes of monthly meetings, marketing opportunities, publicity via our website and our "members available" list, jobs (school visits, readings, workshops, residencies, etc.) through our "members available" list, mutual support through monthly meetings. Sponsors annual workshop, "Packaging Your Imagination," held every fall. Publishes *CANSCAIP News*, quarterly, available to all (free with membership, otherwise $25 Canadian). Dues: professional fees: $60 Canadian/year; friend fees: $25/year; institutional $30/year. "Professionals must have written, illustrated or performed work for children commercially, sufficient to satisfy the membership committee (more details on request)." CANSCAIP National has open meetings from September to June, monthly in Toronto. CANSCAIP West holds bimonthly meetings in Vancouver. Also has a London, Ontario branch. Send SASE for information. Inquiries by fax and e-mail OK.

VISIT THE WRITER'S MARKET WEBSITE at www.writersmarket.com for hot new markets, daily market updates, writers' guidelines and much more.

FEDERATION OF BRITISH COLUMBIA WRITERS, MPO Box 2206, Vancouver, British Columbia V6P 6G5 Canada. (604)683-2057. Fax: (604)683-8269. E-mail: fedbcwrt@pinc.com. Website: www.swifty.com/bcwa. **Contact:** Beverly Garry, Brad Cran, co-executive directors. Estab. 1982. Number of Members: 800. Types of Membership: regular. "Open to established and emerging writers in any genre, province-wide." Benefits include newsletter, liaison with funding bodies, publications, workshops, readings, literary contests, various retail and educational discounts. Sponsors readings and workshops. Publishes a newsletter 4 times/year, included in membership. Dues: $60 regular. Send SASE for information. Inquiries by fax and e-mail OK.

HORROR WRITERS ASSOCIATION (HWA), P.O. Box 50577, Palo Alto CA 94303. E-mail: hwa@horror.org. Website: www.horror.org. **Contact:** B.P. Somtow, president. Estab. 1987. Number of Members: 850. Type of Memberships: Active—writers who have one published novel or three professional stories. Associate—nonwriting professionals including editors, artists, agents and booksellers. Affiliate—beginning writers and others interested in the horror genre. Sponsors the "Bram Stoker Awards" for excellence in horror writing. Publishes membership directory, handbook, and monthly newsletter with market reports. Offers comprehensive website available to members only. Dues: $55/year (US); $65/year (overseas); $75/year family membership; $100/year corporate membership. Meets once a year. Send SASE for information or visit website.

MANITOBA WRITERS' GUILD, 206-100 Arthur St., Winnipeg, Manitoba R3B, 1H3 Canada. (204)942-6134. Fax: (204)942-5754. E-mail: mbwriter@escape.ca. Number of members: approximately 550. Type of memberships: Regular, student, senior and fixed income. Open to anyone: writers, emerging and established; readers, particularly those interested in Manitoba literature. "Membership is provincial in general, although we have members from across Canada, USA and the world." Benefits include special discounts on programs, goods and services; regular mailings of program notices; and *WordWrap*, published 6 times/year, featuring articles, regular columns, information on current markets and competitions, announcements, and profiles of Manitoba writers. Programs include Mentor/Apprentice program, small resource center (2-staff, small resource library, nonlending); open workshops once a month in fall and winter; annual conference, usually April; and Cafe Reading series. Dues: $50 regular; $25 seniors, students, fixed-income. Send SASE for information.

MYSTERY WRITERS OF AMERICA (MWA), 17 E. 47th St., 6th Floor, New York NY 10017. (212)888-8171. Fax: (212)888-8107. Website: www.mysterywriters.org (includes information about the newsletter, awards and membership). **Contact:** Lawrence Block, president. Estab. 1945. Number of Members: 2,600. Type of memberships: Active (professional, published writers of fiction or nonfiction crime/mystery/suspense); associate (professionals in allied fields, i.e., editor, publisher, critic, news reporter, publicist, librarian, bookseller, etc.); corresponding (writers qualified for active membership who live outside the US); affiliate (writers unpublished in the mystery field and those interested in the genre). Benefits include promotion and protection of writers' rights and interests, including counsel and advice on contracts, MWA courses and workshops, a national office, an annual conference featuring the Edgar Allan Poe Awards, the *MWA Anthology*, a national newsletter, regional conferences, insurance, marketing tools, meetings and research publications. Newsletter, *The Third Degree*, is published 10 times/year for members. Annual dues: $80 for US members; $60 for corresponding members.

THE NATIONAL LEAGUE OF AMERICAN PEN WOMEN, INC., Headquarters: The Pen Arts Building, 1300 17th St., NW, Washington DC 20036-1973. (202)785-1997. Fax: (202)452-6868. E-mail: nlapw1@juno.com. Website: members.aol.com/penwomen/pen.htm. **Contact:** National President. Estab. 1897. Number of Members: 5,000. Types of Membership: Three classifications: Art, Letters, Music. Open to: Professional women. "Professional to us means our membership is open to women who sell their art, writings, or music compositions. We have over 175 branches in the mainland US plus Hawaii and the Republic of Panama. Some branches have as many as 100 members, some as few as 10 or 12. It is necessary to have 5 members to form a new branch." Benefits include a bimonthly magazine and local and national competitions. Our facility is The Pen Arts Building. It is a 20-room Victorian mansion. One distinguished resident was President Abraham Lincoln's son, Robert Todd Lincoln, the former Secretary of War and Minister of Great Britain. It has rooms available for Pen Women visiting the D.C. area, and for Board members in session 3 times a year. There are Branch and State Association competitions, as well as Biennial Convention competitions. Offers a research library of books by members and histories of the organization. Sponsors awards biennially to Pen Women in each classification: Art, Letters, Music, and $1,000 award biennially in even-numbered year to nonPen Women in each classification for women age 35 and over who wish to pursue special work in art, music or letters field. *The Pen Woman* is the membership magazine, published 6 times a year, free to members, $18 a year for nonmember subscribers. Dues: $40/year for national organization, from $5-10/year for branch membership and from $1-5 for state association dues. Branches hold regular meetings each month, September through May except in northern states which meet usually March through September (for travel convenience). Send SASE for information. Inquiries via e-mail OK, but prefers SASE.

☑ **NATIONAL WRITERS ASSOCIATION**, 3140 S. Peoria, #295, Aurora CO 80014. (303)841-0246. Fax: (303)841-2607. Website: www.nationalwriters.com (includes contests, job listings and all other services). **Contact:** Sandy Whelchel, executive director. Estab. 1937. Number of Members: 4,000. Types of Memberships: Regular membership for those without published credits; professional membership for those with published credits. Open to: "Any interested writer, national/international, plus we have 16 chapters in various states." Benefits include critiques, marketing advice, editing, literary agency, complaint service, chapbook publishing service, research reports on various aspects of writing, 4 contests, National Writers Press—self-publishing operation, regular newsletter with updates on marketing, bimonthly magazine on writing-related subjects, discounts on supplies, magazines and some services. Sponsors periodic conferences and workshops; short story contest opens April, closes July 1; novel contest opens December, closes April 1. Publishes *Flash Market News* (monthly publication for professional members only); *Authorship Magazine* (bimonthly publication available by subscription, $20 to nonmembers). Dues: $65 regular; $85 professional. For professional membership, requirement is equivalent of 3 articles or stories in a national or regional magazine; a book published by a royalty publisher; a play, TV script or movie produced. Chapters hold meetings on a monthly basis. Inquiries by SASE, e-mail and fax OK.

NORTH CAROLINA WRITERS' NETWORK, P.O. Box 954, Carrboro NC 27510-0954. (919)967-9540. Fax: (919)929-0535. E-mail: mail@ncwriters.org. Website: www.ncwriters.org (includes workshop and competition guidelines, links to other organizations, N.C. Literary Hall of Fame bios and more). **Contact:** Linda W. Hobson, executive director. Estab. 1985. Number of Members: 1,800. Open to: All writers, all levels of skill and friends of literature. Membership is approximately 1,600 in North Carolina and 200 in 33 other states and 5 other countries. Benefits include bimonthly newsletter, reduced rates for competition entry fees, fall and spring conferences, workshops, etc., use of critiquing service, use of library and resource center, press release and publicity service, information database(s). Sponsors annual Fall Conference for Writers, Creative Nonfiction Competition, statewide workshops, Doris Betts Fiction Competition, Writers & Readers Series, Randall Jarrell Poetry Prize, Poetry Chapbook Competition, Thomas Wolfe Fiction Prize, Fiction Competition, Paul Green Playwright Prize. Publishes the 28-page bimonthly *Writers' Network News*, and *North Carolina's Literary Resource Guide*. Subscription included in dues. Dues: $55/year individual, $30/year students enrolled in a degree-granting program, and $40/year seniors 65+ and disabled. Events scheduled throughout the year. Send SASE for information.

ROMANCE WRITERS OF AMERICA (RWA), 3707 FM 1960 West, Suite 555, Houston TX 77068. (281)440-6885. Fax: (281)440-7510. E-mail: info@rwanational.com. Website: rwanational.com. **Contact:** Allison Kelley, executive manager. President: Jo Ann Ferguson. Estab. 1981. Number of members: over 8,400. Type of Memberships: General and associate. Open to: "Any person actively pursuing a writing career in the romance field." Membership is international. Benefits include annual conference, contests and awards, magazine, forums with publishing representatives, network for published authors, group insurance, regional newsletters and more. Dues: $75/new members; $65/renewal fee. Send SASE for information.

☑ **SCIENCE FICTION AND FANTASY WORKSHOP**, 1193 S. 1900 East, Salt Lake City UT 84108-1855. (801)582-2090. Fax: (801)650-2168. E-mail: workshop@burgoyne.com. Website: www.sff.net/people/Dalton-Woodbury/sffw.htp (includes description of what's available to members and links to some members' pages). **Contact:** Kathleen D. Woodbury, director/newsletter editor. Estab. 1980. Number of members: 300. Types of memberships: "Active" is listed in the membership roster and so is accessible to all other members; "inactive" is not listed in the roster. Open to "anyone, anywhere. Our scope is international although over 96% of our members are in the US." Benefits include "several different critique groups: short stories, novels, articles, screenplays, poetry, etc. We also offer services such as copyediting, working out the numbers in planet building (give us the kind of planet you want and we'll tell you how far it is from the sun, etc.—or tell us what kind of sun you have and we'll tell you what your planet is like), brainstorming story, fragments or cultures or aliens, etc." Publishes *SF and Fantasy Workshop* (monthly); nonmembers subscribe for $15/year; samples are $1.50 and trial subscription is $8/6 issues. "We have a publication that contains outlines, synopses, proposals that authors submitted or used for novels that sold. The purpose is to show new and aspiring novelists what successful outlines, etc. look like, and to provide authors (with books coming out) advance publicity. Cost is $2.50/issue or $9/4 issues. We also publish a fiction booklet on an irregular basis. It contains one short story and three critiques by professional writers. Cost to anyone is $5/5 issues or $8/10 issues." Dues: Members pay a one-time fee of

$5 (to cover the cost of the roster and the new-member information packet) and the annual $15 subscription fee. To renew membership, members simply renew their subscriptions. "Our organization is strictly by mail though that is now expanding to include e-mail. No SASE necessary for requests for our information sheet."

SCIENCE FICTION WRITERS OF EARTH, P.O. Box 121293, Fort Worth TX 76121-1293. (817)451-8674. E-mail: sfwoe@flash.net. Website: www.flash.net/~sfwoe (includes contest rules, entry form, judge's report, contest results, list of writers who entered contest, interviews with the winners, reviews of the top three stories, short bios of the top 10 contestants, newsletter with articles of interest to contestants and writers in general). **Contact:** Gilbert Gordon Reis, SFWOE administrator. Estab. 1980. Number of Members: 100-150. Open to: Unpublished writers of science fiction and fantasy short stories. "We have writers in Europe, Canada, Australia and several other countries, but the majority are from the US. Writers compete in our annual contest. This allows the writer to find out where he/she stands in writing ability. Winners often receive requests for their story from publishers. Many winners have told us that they believe that placing in the top ten of our contest gives them recognition and has assisted in getting their first story published." Dues: One must submit a science fiction or fantasy short story to our annual contest each year to be a member. Cost is $5 for membership and first story. $2 for each additional ms. The nominating committee meets several times a year to select the top ten stories of the annual contest. Author Edward Bryant selects the winners from the top ten stories. Contest deadline is October 30 and the cash awards and results are mailed out on January 31 of the following year. The first place story is published by *Altair*, magazine of speculative fiction. Inquiries by SASE, e-mail (no contest submissions) or from the Internet OK.

☑ **SCIENCE-FICTION AND FANTASY WRITERS OF AMERICA, INC.**, % SFWA Executive Director, P.O. Box 171, Unity ME 04988-0171. E-mail: execdir@sfwa.org. Website: www.sfwa.org/. **Contact:** Michael Capobianco, president. Executive Director: Sharon Lee. Estab. 1965. Number of Members: 1,400. Type of Memberships: Active, associate, affiliate, institutional, estate and junior. Open to: "Professional writers, editors, anthologists, artists in the science fiction/fantasy genres and allied professional individuals and institutions. Our membership is international; we currently have members throughout Europe, Australia, Central and South America, Canada and some in Asia." We produce a variety of journals for our members, annual membership directory and provide a grievance committee, publicity committee, circulating book plan and access to medical/life/disability insurance. We award the SFWA Nebula Awards each year for outstanding achievement in the genre at novel, novella, novelet and short story lengths." Quarterly *SFWA Bulletin* to members; nonmembers may subscribe at $15/4 issues within US/Canada; $18.50 overseas. Bimonthly *SFWA Forum* for active and associate members only. Annual *SFWA Membership Directory* for members; available to professional organizations for $60. Active membership requires professional sale in the US of at least 3 short stories or 1 full-length book. Affiliate membership is open to professionals affiliated with science fiction writing. Associate membership require at least 1 professional sale in the US or other professional sale in the US or other professional involvement in the field respectively. Dues are pro-rated quarterly; info available upon request. Business meetings are held during Annual Nebula Awards weekend and usually during the annual World SF Convention. Send SASE for information.

☑ **SISTERS IN CRIME**, Box 442124, Lawrence KS 66044-8933. (785)842-1325. E-mail: sistersincrime@juno.com. Website: www.sistersincrime.org. **Contact:** Beth Wasson, executive secretary. Estab. 1986. Number of Members: 3,200. The original purpose of this organization was to combat discrimination against women in the mystery field. Memberships are open to men as well as women, as long as they are committed to the organization and its goals. Offers membership assistance in networking and publicity.

SOCIETY OF SOUTHWESTERN AUTHORS, P.O. Box 30355, Tucson AZ 85751-0355. (520)743-0940. Fax: (520)296-0409. E-mail: 4stern@azstarnet.com. Website: www.azstarnet.com/nonprofit/ssa (includes newsletter, successes, coming events and dates). President/Chairman: Chris Stern. **Contact:** Penny Parker, director and membership. Estab. 1972. Number of Members: 500. Memberships: Professional (published authors of books, articles, poetry, etc.); Associate (aspiring writers not yet published); and Honorary (one whose contribution to the writing profession or to SSA warrants such recognition). Benefits include conference, short story writing contest, critiques, marketing advice. Sponsors annual conference in January and annual short story writing contest. Publishes *The Write Word* which appears 6 times/year. Dues: $45 (includes $25 registration fee and $20 first year's dues). Meets monthly. Inquiries by SASE, e-mail and fax OK.

☑ **WESTERN WRITERS OF AMERICA**, Office of the Secretary Treasurer, 1012 Fair St., Franklin TN 37064-2718. Phone/fax: (615)791-1444. E-mail: tncrutch@aol.com. Website: www.westernwriters.org (includes membership information, authors' profiles and magazine articles). **Contact:** James A. Crutchfield, secretary/treasurer. Estab. 1953. Number of Members: 600. Type of Membership: Active, associate, patron. Open to: Professional, published writers who have multiple publications of fiction or nonfiction (usually at least three) about the West. Associate membership open to those with one book, a lesser number of short stories or publications or participation in the field such as editors, agents, reviewers, librarians, television producers, directors (dealing with the West). Patron memberships open to corporations, organizations and individuals with an interest in the West. Scope is international. Benefits: "By way of publications and conventions, members are kept abreast of developments in the field of Western literature and the publishing field, marketing requirements, income tax problems, copyright law, research facilities and techniques, and new publications. At conventions members have the opportunity for one-on-one conferences with editors, publishers and agents." Sponsors an annual four-day conference during fourth week of June featuring panels, lectures and seminars on publishing, writing and research. Includes the Spur Awards to honor authors of the best Western literature of the previous year. Publishes *Roundup Magazine* (6 times/year) for members. Available to nonmembers for $30. Publishes membership directory. Dues: $75 for active membership or associate membership, $250 for patron. For information on Spur Awards, send SASE. Inquiries by fax and e-mail OK.

WILLAMETTE WRITERS, 9045 SW Barbur Blvd., Suite 5A, Portland OR 97219. (503)452-1592. Fax: (503)452-0372. E-mail: wilwrite@teleport.com. Website: www.teleport.com/~wilwrite/. **Contact:** Bill Johnson, office manager. Estab. 1965. Number of members: 700. "Willamette Writers is a nonprofit, tax exempt corporation staffed by volunteers. Membership is open to both published and aspiring writers. WW provides support, encouragement and interaction for all genres of writers." Open to national membership, but serves primarily the Pacific Northwest. Benefits include a writers' referral service, critique groups, membership discounts, youth programs (4th-12th grades), monthly meetings with guest authors, intern program, annual writing contest, community projects, library and research services, as well as networking with other writing groups, office with writing reference and screenplay library. Sponsors annual conference held the second weekend in August; quarterly workshops; annual Kay Snow Writing Contest; and the Distinguished Northwest Writer Award. Publishes *The Willamette Writer* monthly: a 12-page newsletter for members and complimentary subscriptions. Information consists of features, how-to's, mechanics of writing, profile of featured monthly speaker, markets, workshops, conferences and benefits available to writers. Dues: $36/year; includes subscription to newsletter. Meets first Tuesday of each month; board meeting held last Tuesday of each month. Inquiries by SASE, fax and e-mail OK.

✓ **THE WRITER'S CENTER**, 4508 Walsh St., Bethesda MD 20815-6006. (301)654-8664. Fax: (301)654-8667. E-mail: postmaster@writer.org. Website: www.writer.org. Executive Director: Jane Fox. **Contact:** Sunil Freeman, assistant director. Estab. 1977. Number of Members: 2,200. Open to: Anyone interested in writing. Scope is regional DC, Maryland, Virginia, West Virginia, Pennsylvania. Benefits include newsletter, discounts in bookstore, workshops, public events, subscriptions to *Poet Lore*, use of equipment and annual small press book fair. Center offers workshops, reading series, equipment, newsletter and limited workspace. Sponsors workshops, conferences, award for narrative poem. Publishes *Writer's Carousel*, bimonthly. Nonmembers can pick it up at the Center. Dues: $30/year. Fees vary with service, see publications. Brochures are available for SASE. Inquiries by e-mail and fax OK.

🍁 ✓ **WRITERS' FEDERATION OF NEW BRUNSWICK**, P.O. Box 37, Station A, Fredericton, New Brunswick E3B 4Y2 Canada. Phone/fax: (506)459-7228. E-mail: aa821@fan.com or wfnb@nb.aibn.com. Website: www.sjfn.nb.ca/community_hall/W/Writers_Federation_NB/index.htm. **Contact:** Anna Mae Snider, project coordinator. Estab. 1983. Number of Members: 230. Membership is open to anyone interested in writing. "This is a provincial organization. Benefits include promotion of members' works through newsletter announcements and readings and launchings held at fall festival and annual general meeting. Services provided by WFNB include a Writers-in-Schools Program and manuscript reading. The WFNB sponsors a fall festival and an annual general meeting which feature workshops, readings and book launchings." There is also an annual literary competition, open to residents of New Brunswick only, which has prizes of $150, $75 and $50 in four categories: Fiction, nonfiction, children's literature and poetry; two $400 prizes, one for the best manuscript of poems (48 pgs.) and one for the best short novel or collection of short stories; also a category for young writers (14-18 years of age) which offers $150 (1st prize), $100 (2nd prize), $50 (3rd prize). Publishes a quarterly newsletter. Dues: $30/year; $20/year for students. Board of Directors meets approximately 5 times a year. Annual General Meeting is held in the spring of each year. Inquiries by SASE, e-mail and fax OK.

**FOR EXPLANATIONS OF THESE SYMBOLS,
SEE THE INSIDE FRONT AND BACK COVERS OF THIS BOOK.**

WRITERS' FEDERATION OF NOVA SCOTIA, 1113 Marginal Rd., Halifax, Nova Scotia B3H 4P7 Canada. **Contact:** Jane Buss, executive director. Estab. 1976. Number of Members: 600. Types of Memberships: General membership, student membership, Nova Scotia Writers' Council membership (professional), Honorary Life Membership. Open to anyone who writes. Provincial scope, with a few members living elsewhere in the country or the world. Benefits include advocacy of all kinds for writers, plus such regular programs as workshops and publications, including directories and a newsletter. Sponsors workshops, 2 annual conferences (one for general membership, the other for the professional wing), 4 book awards, one annual competition for unpublished manuscripts in various categories; a writers-in-the-schools program, a manuscript reading service, reduced photocopying rates. Publishes *Eastword*, 6 issues annually, available by subscription for $35 (Canadian) to nonmembers. Dues: $35/year (Canadian). Holds an annual general meeting, an annual meeting of the Nova Scotia Writers' Council, several board meetings annually. Send 5×7 SASE for information.

WRITERS GUILD OF ALBERTA, Percy Page Centre, 11759 Groat Rd., Edmonton, Alberta T5M 3K6 Canada. (780)422-8174. Fax: (780)422-2663. E-mail: wga@oanet.com. Website: www.writersguild.ab.ca. **Contact:** Miki Andrejevic, executive director. Estab. 1980. Number of Members: 750. Membership open to current and past residents of Alberta. Regional (provincial) scope. Benefits include discounts on programs offered; manuscript evaluation service available; bimonthly newsletter; contacts; info on workshops, retreats, readings, etc. Sponsors workshops 2 times/year, retreats 3 times/year, annual conference, annual book awards program (Alberta writers only). Publishes *WestWord* 6 times/year; available for $60/year (Canadian) to nonmembers. Dues: $60/year for regular membership; $20/year senior/students/limited income; $100/year donating membership—charitable receipt issued (Canadian funds). Organized monthly meetings. Send SASE for information.

WRITERS INFORMATION NETWORK, P.O. Box 11337, Bainbridge Island WA 98110. (206)842-9103. Fax: (206)842-0536. E-mail: WritersInfoNetwork@juno.com. Websites: www.bluejaypub.com/win or www.ecpa.org/win. **Contact:** Elaine Wright Colvin, director. Estab. 1980. Number of members: 1,000. Open to: All interested in writing for religious publications/publishers. Scope is national and several foreign countries. Benefits include bimonthly magazine, *The WIN Informer*, market news, advocacy/grievance procedures, professional advice, writers conferences, press cards, author referral, free consultation. Sponsors workshops, conferences throughout the country each year—mailing list and advertised in *The WIN Informer* magazine. Dues: $35 US; $40 foreign/year. Holds quarterly meetings in Seattle, WA. Brochures are available for SASE. Inquiries by fax and e-mail OK.

THE WRITERS ROOM, INC., 10 Astor Place, 6th Floor, New York NY 10003-6935. (212)254-6995. Fax: (212)533-6059. E-mail: writersroom@writersroom.org. Website: www.writersroom.org (includes organization's background information and downloadable application). **Contact:** Donna Brodie, executive director. Estab. 1978. Number of Members: 200 fulltime and 40 part-time. Founded in 1978 to provide a "home away from home" for any writer who needs a place to work. Description: Large room with 35 desks separated by partitions, space for 300 writers each quarter; open 24 hours a day year-round; kitchen, lounge and bathrooms, storage for files and laptops, small reference library; monthly readings. Dues: $110-185 per quarter year, $50 application fee, $60 key deposit. Send SASE for application and background information. Inquiries by SASE, e-mail and fax OK or visit website.

THE WRITERS' WORKSHOP, 387 Beaucatcher Rd., Asheville NC 28805. (828)254-8111. **Contact:** Karen Ackerson, executive director. Estab. 1984. Number of Members: 1,250. Types of Memberships: Student/low income $25; family/organization $65; individual $35. Open to all writers. Scope is national and international. Benefits include discounts on workshops, quarterly newsletter, critiquing services through the mail. Center offers reading room, assistance with editing your work. Publishes a newsletter; also available to nonmembers ($20). Offers workshops year-round in NC and the South; 2 retreats a year, 4 readings with nationally awarded authors. Contests and classes for children and teens as well. Advisory board includes Kurt Vonnegut, E.L. Doctorow, Peter Matthiessen, Reynolds Price, John Le Carre and Eudora Welty. Also sponsors international contests in fiction, memoirs, poetry and creative nonfiction. Brochures are available for SASE.

"WE WANT TO PUBLISH YOUR WORK."

Completely Updated Each Year

Novel & Short Story Writer's Market

2000+ PLACES TO PUBLISH YOUR FICTION

- 400+ new markets
- 60+ new agents
- 500+ book publishers
- 700+ literary markets
- 600+ genre markets
- 450+ contemporary markets
- 300+ electronic markets

From the Publishers of Writer's Market

You would give anything to hear an editor speak those six magic words. So you work hard for weeks, months, even years to make that happen. You create a brilliant piece of work and a knock-out presentation, but there's still one vital step to ensure publication. You still need to submit your work to the right buyers. With rapid changes in the publishing industry it's not always easy to know who those buyers are. That's why each year thousands of writers, just like you, turn to the most current edition of this indispensable market guide.

Keep ahead of the changes by ordering *2002 Novel & Short Story Writer's Market* today! You'll save the frustration of getting manuscripts returned in the mail stamped MOVED: ADDRESS UNKNOWN. And of NOT submitting your work to new listings because you don't know they exist. All you have to do to order the upcoming 2002 edition is complete the attached order card and return it with your payment. Order now and you'll get the 2002 edition at the 2001 price—just $24.99—no matter how much the regular price may increase!

2002 Novel & Short Story Writer's Market will be published and ready for shipment in January 2002.

Turn Over for More Great Books to Help Get Your Fiction Published!

☐ **Yes!** I want the most current edition of *Novel & Short Story Writer's Market*. Please send me the 2002 edition at the 2001 price–$24.99. (NOTE: *2002 Novel & Short Story Writer's Market* will be ready for shipment in January 2002.) #10756

Additional books from the back of this card:

Book	Price
#	$
#	$
#	$
#	$
Subtotal	$

*Add $3.95 postage and handling for one book; $1.95 for each additional book.

Postage & Handling	$

Payment must accompany order. Ohioans add 6% sales tax. Canadians add 7% GST.

Total	$

VISA/MasterCard orders call
TOLL FREE 1-800-289-0963
8:30 to 5:00 Mon.-Fri. Eastern Time
or FAX 1-888-590-4082

☐ Payment enclosed $_____ (or)

Charge my: ☐ Visa ☐ MasterCard   Exp._____

Account #_____

Signature_____

Name_____

Address_____

City_____

State/Prov._____ Zip/PC _____

30-Day Money Back Guarantee on every book you buy!

6635

Mail to: Writer's Digest Books • 1507 Dana Avenue • Cincinnati, OH 45207
www.writersdigest.com

New Writer's Digest Books!

2001 Guide to Literary Agents
edited by Donya Dickerson
Team up with an agent using this invaluable directory (now in its 9th year). Over 500 listings of literary and script agents, plus inside information on the industry will help you choose the right agent to represent you.
#10684/$21.99/335p/pb

Novelist's Essential Guide Series

Creating Plot
Strong plots are the foundation of great fiction. This guide examines every aspect of plot to show you how to write stories filled with depth, complexity and drama.
#10668/$14.99/208p/pb

Crafting Scenes
Packed with illuminating examples and exercises, this guide will show you how to write captivating scenes that develop your characters and propel your plot. A range of scenes are explored, including action scenes, sex scenes, comic scenes and more.
#10693/$14.99/208p/pb

Fiction Writer's Brainstormer
Make your writing richer, livelier and more imaginative with this liberating guide. It supplies clear instruction and provocative brain-teasers that help get your brain going, stimulate the creative flow, and find new and unusual ways of creating professional, salable works.
#10691/#18.99/256p/pb

How Fiction Works
In 1989 Oakley Hall published *The Art and Craft of Novel Writing*, a classic text that Pulitzer Prize winner Robert Stone called "simply the best book in print to examine the strategies and necessities involved in the making of a novel." Now he has expanded and deepened his instruction to include exercises, new examples, and new advice on all forms of fiction.
#48048/$18.99/240p/hc

Howdunit: How Crimes Are Committed & Solved
This hefty resource includes chapters from nine of the best volumes in the Howdunit crime series as well as thirteen new chapters on key topics such as street gangs, drug trade, terrorism, and forensics. It also offers a huge glossary of crime words and phrases, and plenty of photographs.
#10696/$19.99/416p/pb

Books are available at your local bookstore, or directly from the publisher using the order card on the reverse.

Publications of Interest

This section features listings for magazines and newsletters that focus on writing or the publishing industry. While many of these are not markets for fiction, they do offer articles, marketing advice or other information valuable to the fiction writer. Several magazines in this section offer actual market listings while others feature reviews of books in the field and news on the industry.

The timeliness factor is a primary reason most writers read periodicals. Changes in publishing happen very quickly and magazines can help you keep up with the latest news. Some magazines listed here, including *Writer's Digest*, cover the entire field of writing, while others such as *The Mystery Review*, *Locus* (science fiction) and *Romantic Times* focus on a particular type of writing. You'll also find publications which focus on particular segments of the publishing industry.

Information on some publications for writers can be found in the introductions to other sections in this book. In addition, many of the literary and commercial magazines for writers listed in the markets sections are helpful to the fiction writer. Keep an eye on the newsstand and library shelves for others and let us know if you've found a publication particularly useful.

N BOOK, The Magazine for the Reading Life, West Egg Communications LLC, 4645 N. Rockwell St., Chicago IL 60625. (773)267-4300. Fax: (773)267-5496. E-mail: alanger@bookmagazine.com. Website: www.bookmagazine.com. Editor: Jerome Kramer. **Contact:** Adam Langer. Estab. 1998. Bimonthly. Magazine covering books and reading. Includes book excerpts, essays, interview/profile pieces; columns and departments such as Shop Watch (bookstore profiles), Locations (literary travel), Group Dynamics (book-group tips, stories) and Web Catches (related to books online). Sample copy for $4 plus $1 postage.

CANADIAN CHILDREN'S LITERATURE/LITTÉRATURE CANADIENNE POUR LA JEUNESSE, Slapsie, University of Guelph, Guelph, Ontario N1G 2W1 Canada. (519)824-4120, ext. 3189. Editors: Mary Rubio, Daniel Chouinard and Marie Davis. Administrator: Gay Christofides. Quarterly. "In-depth criticism of English and French Canadian literature for young people. Scholarly articles and reviews are supplemented by illustrations, photographs, and interviews with authors of children's books. The main themes and genres of children's literature are covered in special issues." Reviews novels and short story collections. Sample copies available; single copy price is $4 (Canadian) plus $1 postage.

CANADIAN WRITER'S JOURNAL, Box 5180, New Liskeard, Ontario P0J 1P0 Canada. (705)647-5424. Fax: (705)647-8366. E-mail: cwj@ntl.sympatico.ca. Website: www.nt.net/~cwj/index.htm. **Contact:** Carole Manseau, managing editor. Bimonthly. "Mainly short how-to and motivational articles related to all types of writing and of interest to both new and established writers. Fiction is published in limited quantities, and needs are fully supplied through an annual (fall) short fiction contest." SASE with Canadian postage or IRC for contest rules or visit website. Lists markets for fiction. Sample copies available for $5 ($C for Canadian orders, $US for US orders). Subscription price: $22.50 US/year ; $42 US/2 years; $24.08 CDN/year; $44.94 CDN/2 years.

CHILDREN'S BOOK INSIDER, 901 Columbia Rd., Fort Collins CO 80525. (800)807-1916. E-mail: mail@write4kids.com. Website: www.write4kids.com. **Contact:** Laura Backes, editor/publisher. Monthly. "Publication is devoted solely to children's book writers and illustrators. 'At Presstime' section gives current market information each month for fiction, nonfiction and illustration submissions to publishers. Other articles include writing and illustration tips for fiction and nonfiction, interviews with published authors and illustrators, features on alternative publishing methods (self-publishing, co-op publishing, etc.), how to submit work to publishers, industry trends. Also publishes books and writing tools for both beginning and experienced children's book writers." E-mail cbi@sendfree.com for free online catalog. Single copy price: $3.25. Subscription price: $29.95/year (US); $34.95/year (Canadian); $42.95 everywhere else.

FICTION WRITER'S GUIDELINE, P.O. Box 72300, Albuquerque NM 87195. (505)352-9495. E-mail: BCamenson@aol.com. Website: www.fictionwriters.com/. **Contact:** Blythe Camenson, editor. Bimonthly. "Our publication is an eight page newsletter with agent/editor/author interviews, how-to articles on writing fiction and getting it published, fiction markets, conference listings, Q&A column, success stories and more." Sample copies available for $3.50. Subscriptions: $48/year; free to members of Fiction Writer's Connection. "Basic membership in FWC is $74/year; includes a free newsletter, free critiquing, and a toll-free hotline for questions and free advice." Send SASE for information or visit website.

FOLIO: MAGAZINE. Website: www.foliomagazine.com. **Contact:** Teresa Ennis, editor. Estab. 1972. *Folio:* is "the magazine for magazine management," the leading source of ideas for the entire publishing team. Subscriptions: $96/year (US); $116/year (CDN or Mexico); $199/year for all other countries. **For subscriptions only:** P.O. Box 10571, Riverton NJ 08076-0571. Fax: (203)358-5812. Or order online.

GILA QUEEN'S GUIDE TO MARKETS, P.O. Box 97, Newton NJ 07860-0097. (973)579-1537. Fax: (973)579-6441. E-mail: kathryn@gilaqueen.com. Website: www.gilaqueen.com. **Contact:** Kathryn Ptacek, editor. "Includes complete guidelines for fiction (different genres), poetry, nonfiction, greeting cards, etc. Also includes 'theme section' each issue—science fiction/fantasy/horror, mystery/suspense, romance, western, Canadian, regional, women's markets, religious, etc. and 'mini-markets.' Regular departments include new address listings, dead/suspended markets, moving editors, anthologies, markets to be wary of, publishing news, etc. Every issue contains updates (of stuff listed in previous issues), new markets, conferences, contests. Publishes articles on writing topics, self-promotion, reviews of software and books of interest to writers, etc." Sample copy: $6. Subscriptions: $45/year (US); $49/year (Canada); $60/year (overseas).

THE HORN BOOK MAGAZINE, The Horn Book, Inc., 56 Roland St., Suite 200, Boston MA 02129. (617)628-0225. Fax: (617)628-0882. E-mail: magazine@hbook.com. Website: www.hbook.com. **Contact:** Roger Sutton, editor-in-chief. Estab. 1924. Bimonthly. Magazine covering children's literature for librarians, booksellers, professors, teachers and students of children's literature. Includes interview/profile pieces on children's book authors and illustrators as well as topics of interest to the children's book world. Samply copy available on website (includes original content not found in print edition and writer's guidelines).

LAMBDA BOOK REPORT, Lambda Literary Foundation, P.O. Box 73910, Washington DC 20056. (202)462-7924. Fax: (202)462-5264. E-mail: lbreditor@lambdalit.com. **Contact:** Shelley Bindon, senior editor. Monthly. "This review journal of contemporary gay and lesbian literature appeals to both readers and writers. Fiction queries published regularly." Lists fiction markets. Reviews novels, short story collections, poetry and nonfiction. Single copy price is $4.95/US. Subscriptions: $29.95/year (US); international rate: $58.95 (US $); Canada/Mexico: $46.95/year (US $).

LOCUS, The Newspaper of the Science Fiction Field, P.O. Box 13305, Oakland CA 94661. (510)339-9198. Fax: (510)339-8144. E-mail: locus@locusmag.com. Website: www.locusmag.com. **Contact:** Charles N. Brown, editor. Monthly. "Professional newsletter of science fiction, fantasy and horror; has news, interviews with authors, book reviews, column on electronic publishing, forthcoming books listings, monthly books-received listings, etc." Lists markets for fiction. Reviews novels or short story collections. Sample copies available. Single copy price: $4.95. Subscriptions: $46/year (2nd class mail) for US; $50 (US)/year (2nd class) for Canada; $50 (US)/year (sea mail) for overseas.

MYSTERY READERS JOURNAL, P.O. Box 8116, Berkeley CA 94707. E-mail: whodunit@murderonthemenu.com. Website: www.mysteryreaders.org. **Contact:** Editor. Quarterly. Estab. 1984. Includes interviews, essays, mystery news, new bookstores, overseas reports and convention listings. Membership in Mystery Readers International entitles member to 4 yearly issues of *Mystery Readers Journal*. Membership dues: $24/year for US and Canada (US $36 for overseas airmail).

THE MYSTERY REVIEW, A Quarterly Publication for Mystery Readers, P.O. Box 233, Colborne, Ontario K0K 1S0 Canada. (613)475-4440. Fax: (613)475-3400. E-mail: mystrev@reach.net. Website: www.inline-online.com/mystery. **Contact:** Barbara Davey, editor. Quarterly. "Book reviews, information on new releases, interviews with authors and other people involved in mystery, 'real life' mysteries, out-of-print mysteries, mystery/suspense films, word games and puzzles with a mystery theme." Reviews mystery/suspense novels and short story collections. Single copy price is $5.95 CDN in Canada/$5.95 US in the United States. Subscriptions: $21.50/year CDN (includes GST) in Canada; $20/year US in the US and $28/year US elsewhere (US address for subscriptions: P.O. Box 488, Wellesley Island NY 13640-0488).

NEW WRITER'S MAGAZINE, P.O. Box 5976, Sarasota FL 34277. (941)953-7903. E-mail: newwriters@aol.com. Website: www.newwriters.com. **Contact:** George J. Haborak, editor. Bimonthly. "*New Writer's Magazine* is a publication for aspiring writers. It features 'how-to' articles, news and interviews with published and recently-published authors. Will use fiction that has a tie-in with the world of the writer." Lists markets for fiction. Reviews novels and short story collections. Send #10 SASE for guidelines. Sample copies available; single copy price is $3. Subscriptions: $15/year, $25/2 years. Canadian $20 (US funds). International $35/year (US funds).

OHIO WRITER, Poets League of Greater Cleveland, P.O. Box 91801, Cleveland OH 44101. (216)932-8444. **Contact:** Ron Antonucci, editor. Bimonthly. "Interviews with Ohio writers of fiction and nonfiction; current fiction markets in Ohio." Reviews novels and short story collections. Sample copies available for $2.50. Subscriptions: $15/year; $40/3 years; $20/year institutional rate.

☑ **POETS & WRITERS MAGAZINE**, 72 Spring St , New York NY 10012. Fax: (212)226-3963. E-mail: editor@pw.org. Website: www.pw.org. **Contact:** Therese Eiben, editor. Bimonthly. Covers primarily poetry and fiction writing. "Includes profiles of noted authors and publishing professionals, practical how-to articles, a comprehensive listing of grants and awards for writers and special sections on subjects ranging from small presses to writers conferences." Lists markets for fiction. Sample copies available; single copy price is $4.95. Subscriptions: $19.95/year; $38/2 years. Subscriptions ordered through *Poets & Writers Magazine*, P.O. Box 543, Mount Morris IL 61054 or (815)734-1123.

N: PUBLISHERS WEEKLY. Website: www.publishersweekly.com. **Contact:** Nora Rawlinson, editor-in-chief. Weekly. International news magazine of book publishing and bookselling. "Industry professionals depend on *Publishers Weekly* for in-depth interviews with top authors, publishing industry news, bestseller lists, and early reviews of adult and children's books." Subscriptions: $189/year (US); $239/year US (Canada); $319/year US (all other countries). **For subscriptions only:** P.O. Box 16178, North Hollywood CA 91615-6178. (800)278-2991 (within the US), (818)487-4557 (outside the US). Fax: (818)487-4550.

☑ **THE REGENCY PLUME**, 1523 W. Monterey, Denison TX 75020. E-mail: marilynclay@yahoo.com. Website: http://freetown.com/Picadilly/HydePark/1073/RegncyPlume.html. **Contact:** Marilyn Clay, editor. Bimonthly. "The newsletter focus is on providing accurate historical facts relating to the Regency period: customs, clothes, entertainment, the wars, historical figures, etc. I stay in touch with New York editors who acquire Regency romance novels. Current market info appears regularly in newsletter—see Bits & Scraps." Current Regency romances are "Previewed." Sample copy available for $3.35; single copy price is $3, $5 outside US. Subscriptions: $18/year for 6 issues; $22 Canada; $28 foreign. ("Check must be drawn on a US bank. International money order okay.") Back issues available. Send SASE for subscription information, article guidelines or list of research and writing aids, such as audiotapes, historical maps, books on Regency period furniture and Regency romance writing contest.

☑ **ROMANCE WRITERS REPORT**, Romance Writers of America, 3707 F.M. 1960 W., Suite 555, Houston TX 77068. (281)440-6885. Fax: (281)440-7510. E-mail: info@rwanational.com. **Contact:** Charis McEachern, editor. Monthly professional journal of Romance Writers of America, Inc. Subscriptions included as part of RWA membership. Includes articles, essays and tips written by established writers, contest and conference information and articles by romance editors. Membership dues: $75/year plus $25 processing fee for new applicants and $15 postage for journal.

ROMANTIC TIMES MAGAZINE, 55 Bergen St., Brooklyn NY 11201. (718)237-1097. Website: www.romant ictimes.com. Monthly. Features reviews, news and interviews of interest to the romance reader. Each issue also has special features such as photo tours of authors' houses, interviews with male cover models and articles on romantic pursuits (teas, salons, etc.) and mysteries. Subscriptions: $42/year in US; $66/year in Canada.

☑ **SCAVENGER'S NEWSLETTER**, 833 Main, Osage City KS 66523. (913)528-3538. E-mail: foxscav1@jc .net. Website: www.jlgiftshop.com/scav/index.html. **Contact:** Janet Fox, editor. Monthly. "A market newsletter for science fiction/fantasy/horror/mystery writers with an interest in the small press. Articles about writing/marketing." Lists markets for fiction. Sample copies available. Single copy price: $2.50. Subscription price: $17/year. See website for foreign rates.

☑ **SCIENCE FICTION CHRONICLE**, P.O. Box 022730, Brooklyn NY 11202-0056. (718)643-9011. Website: www.dnapublications.com/sfc. **Contact:** Andrew I. Porter, editor. Bimonthly. Publishes nonfiction, nothing about UFOs. "Bimonthly newsmagazine for professional writers, editors, readers of SF, fantasy, horror." Lists markets for fiction "updated every 6 months." Reviews novels, small press publications, audiotapes and short story collections. Sample copies available with 9×12 SAE with $1.43 postage; single copy price is $3.95 (US) or £3.50 (UK). Subscriptions: $45 US; $56 Canada; $80 overseas. **For subscriptions:** DNA Publications, Inc., P.O. Box 2988, Radford VA 24143-2988. *Note: As with other listings in this section, this is not a "market"— Do not send mss or artwork.*

☑ **THE SMALL PRESS BOOK REVIEW**, P.O. Box 176, Southport CT 06490. (203)332-7629. E-mail: henryberry@aol.com. **Contact:** Henry Berry, editor. Quarterly. "Brief reviews of all sorts of books from small presses/independent publishers." Addresses of publishers are given in reviews. Reviews novels and short story collections.

☑ **SMALL PRESS REVIEW/SMALL MAGAZINE REVIEW**, Dustbooks, P.O. Box 100, Paradise CA 95967. (530)877-6110. E-mail: dustbooks@dcsi.net. Website: www.dustbooks.com. **Contact:** Len Fulton, editor. Bimonthly. "Publishes news and reviews about small publishers, books and magazines." Lists markets for fiction and poetry. Reviews novels, short story and poetry collections. Subscription price: $25/year for individuals, $31/year for institutions.

☑ **A VIEW FROM THE LOFT**, Loft Literary Center, Suite 200, Open Book, 1011 Washington Ave. S, Minneapolis MN 55415. (612)215-2575. E-mail: lvilankulu@loft.org. Website: www.loft.org. **Contact:** Lucia Vilankulu, editor. Monthly. "Publishes articles on writing and list of markets for fiction, poetry and creative nonfiction." Sample copies available; single copy price is $4 US. Subscriptions: $45 in Twin Cities metro area; $30 elsewhere in US; $25 low income/student. (Subscription available only as part of Loft membership; rates are membership rates.)

☑ **THE WRITER**, 120 Boylston St., Boston MA 02116-4615. E-mail: writer@user1.channel1.com. Website: www.writermag.com/thewriter.html. **Contact:** Sylvia K. Burack, editor-in-chief/publisher. Monthly. Contains articles on improving writing techniques and getting published. Includes market lists of magazine and book publishers. Subscription price: $29/year, $54/2 years. Canadian: add $10/year. Foreign: add $30/year. **Subscriptions address:** Kalmbach Publishing Co., 21027 Crossroad Circle, P.O. Box 1612, Waukesha WI 53187-1612. Also publishes *The Writer's Handbook*, an annual book on all fields of writing plus market lists of magazine and book publishers.

☑ **WRITER'S CAROUSEL**, The Writer's Center, 4508 Walsh St., Bethesda MD 20815-6006. (301)654-8664. E-mail: jm@writer.org. Website: www.writer.org. **Contact:** Allan Lefcowitz, editor. Bimonthly. "*Writer's Carousel* publishes book reviews and articles about writing and the writing scene." Lists fiction markets. Reviews novels and short story collections. Sample copies available. Subscriptions: $30 Writer's Center Membership; also available online to members.

☑ **THE WRITER'S CHRONICLE**, Associated Writing Programs, George Mason University, Tallwood House, MSN 1E3, Fairfax VA 22030. E-mail: awpchron@masongmu.edu. Website: www.awpwriter.org. 6 times/year. Essays on contemporary literature and articles on the craft of writing. Lists fiction markets. Subscription: $20/year; $29/year Canada; check with office for overseas.

☑ **WRITER'S DIGEST**, 1507 Dana Ave., Cincinnati OH 45207. (513)531-2222. **Contact:** Melanie Rigney, editor. Monthly. "*Writer's Digest* is a magazine of techniques and markets. We *inspire* the writer to write, *instruct* him or her on how to improve that work, and *direct* him or her toward appropriate markets." Lists markets for fiction, nonfiction, poetry. Single copy price: $5. Subscription price: $19.96.

WRITER'S DIGEST BOOKS–MARKET BOOKS, 1507 Dana Ave., Cincinnati OH 45207. (513)531-2690. Annual. In addition to *Novel & Short Story Writer's Market*, Writer's Digest Books also publishes *Writer's Market*, *Poet's Market*, *Children's Writer's and Illustrator's Market* and the *Guide to Literary Agents*. All include articles and listings of interest to writers. All are available at bookstores, libraries or through the publisher. (Request catalog.)

☑ **WRITERS' JOURNAL**, Val-Tech Publishing, Inc., P.O. Box 394, Perham MN 56573-0394. (218)346-7921. E-mail: writersjournal@wadena.net. Website: www.sowashco.com/writersjournal. **Contact:** Leon Ogroske. Bimonthly. "We are an instructional manual giving writers the tools and information necessary to get their work published." Sample copy available for #10 SASE.

☑ **WRITER'S YEARBOOK**, 1507 Dana Ave., Cincinnati OH 45207. (513)531-2690. **Contact:** Dena Eben. Annual. "A collection of the best writing *about* writing, with an exclusive survey of the year's 100 top markets for article-length nonfiction." Single copy price: $6.25.

Websites of Interest

BY MEGAN LANE

More and more these days, I find myself wondering how I ever lived without the Internet and the World Wide Web. I'm sure I got out more in those ancient times, but I never felt as powerful or as confident about being able to find the answer to any question my inquisitive brain might pose. Even if you refuse to use the Internet, it's virtually impossible to ignore it. Web addresses are ubiquitous—on the corners of TV screens, in print ads and even on the packaging of food we eat.

Despite all the naying of the naysayers, there is useful information to be found in the vast network of cyberspace. Even if you don't own a computer, your local library does; and now that you can easily access the Internet through your television, surfing the Web is harder than ever to resist.

So enough with the excuses! It's time to get with the 21st Century. Even though my eyes are bloodshot from surfing for the past several hours (or is it days?), I've managed to compile a tiny (and woefully incomplete) listing of websites that fiction writers shouldn't miss.

GENRE FICTION

Books and Writing Online: www.interzone.com/Books/books.html. This site includes links to helpful resources on writing, literature and publishing for science fiction and fantasy writers in addition to general book-related links useful to any writer regardless of genre.

Children's Literature Web Guide: www.ucalgary.ca/~dkbrown/index.html. This comprehensive site for children's book writers and illustrators includes links to authors, publishers, booksellers, conferences and other sites of interest.

Children's Writing Resource Center: www.write4kids.com. This site just piles up loads of information for the serious children's fiction writer.

The Market List: www.marketlist.com. Web magazine of genre fiction marketing information.

The Mystery Writers' Forum: www.zott.com/mysforum. Discussions are separated into categories including agents, bookstores, contests, critique corner, death details and industry news.

Romance Central: http://romance-central.com. Great place for giving and receiving advice about romance writing.

Roundup Online Magazine: www.westernwriters.org/roundup.html. This site includes contest information, reviews of westerns and essays about the genre.

The Write Page: www.writepage.com. Online newsletter for readers and writers of genre fiction, featuring information on organizations, conferences, public service efforts and writer's rights.

MAGAZINES AND PUBLISHERS

AcqWeb's Directory of Publishers and Vendors: http://acweb.library.vanderbilt.edu/law/acqweb/pubr.html. This site is a gigantic catalog of links to publishers.

Books A to Z: www.booksatoz.com. This website includes links to professional and creative services, production and technical info, bookmaking materials for sale, academic and research tools.

Bookwire: www.bookwire.com. This site is a gateway to finding information about publishers, booksellers, libraries, authors, reviews and awards.

Electronic Newsstand: http://enews.com. This site offers a massive index of commercial magazines, searchable by title, as well as news about the magazine publishing industry.

John Hewitt's Writer's Resource Center: www.poewar.com. Comprehensive writing site that includes links to consumer, trade and literary magazines.

Overbooked Genre Fiction: www.overbooked.org/genre.html. This site is ready to connect genre writers to sites of interest at the click of a mouse.

Publishers' Catalogs: www.lights.com/publisher. This massive site includes a specific geographic index, which lists countries like Albania, Luxembourg, Thailand and Uruguay, as well as the US and UK.

MISCELLANEOUS
Authorlink: www.authorlink.com. This site does more than just connect writers to publishers; it also offers publishing industry news and interviews with editors and agents.

Authors: http://authors.about.com. This site also includes links to genre sites, playwrights and authors of all nationalities and an Authors Chat Room.

Celebration of Women Writers: www.digital.library.upenn.edu/women. This site is an amazing resource of links to the works and biographies of women writers throughout history, as well as other resources for and about women writers.

Delphi Forum: www.delphi.com. This site hosts forums on many topics including writing and publishing.

Exquisite Corpse—A Journal of Letters and Life: www.corpse.org. An interesting little journal for fiction writers, this site features stories and poems, as well as other fun stuff.

RoseDog.com: www.rosedog.com. This site allows writers to post unpublished work to be reviewed by agents and publishers.

ORGANIZATIONS
Canadian Authors Association: www.islandnet.com/~caa/national.html. "The Association was founded to promote recognition of Canadian writers and their works, and to foster and develop a climate favorable to the creative arts."

Horror Writers Association: www.horror.org. "Among other benefits, the organization issues a regular newsletter, presents the Bram Stoker Awards and provides members with the latest news on paying markets."

National Writers Union: www.nwu.org. "We are a modern, innovative union offering grievance-resolution, industry campaigns, contract advice, health and dental plans, member education, job banks, networking, social events and much more."

PEN American Center: www.pen.org. "As a major voice of the literary community, the organization seeks to defend the freedom of expression wherever it may be threatened, and to promote and encourage the recognition and reading of contemporary literature."

Romance Writers of America: www.rwanational.com. "RWA is a non-profit professional/educational association of 8,200 romance writers and other industry professionals. We are 'The Voice of Romance.' "

Society of Children's Book Writers and Illustrators: www.scbwi.org. "Our website has a dual purpose: It exists as a service to our members as well as offering information about the children's publishing industry and our organization to non-members."

The Writers Guild of America: www.wga.org. "Here at our website, we hope to make film, television, interactive and other mass media writing—and writers—more familiar and accessible."

RESEARCH RESOURCES

Arts & Letters Daily: www.cybereditions.com/aldaily. This website is just full of articles and information for fiction writers.

The Crime Writer: www.svn.net/mikekell/crimewriter.html. Includes links to resources that provide information on crime, current crime news and the criminal justice system.

The English Server Fiction Collection: http://eserver.org. "This site offers works of and about fiction collected from our members, contributing authors worldwide and texts in the public domain."

Novel Advice: www.noveladvice.com. Clever puns aside, this site offers some valuable advice in addition to being just a solid site for fiction writers to visit.

Pilot-Search: www.pilot-search.com. This search engine is geared directly to fiction writers who want to be connected to the online writing lifestyle.

Publishing Law Center: www.publaw.com. This website covers all legal issues that may bother fiction writers in the middle of the night or while signing a contract.

ViVa: A Current Bibliography of Women's History in Historical and Women's Studies Journals: www.iisg.nl/~womhist. Great place to find details about the daily lives of women throughout history.

Dr. Jim Weinrich's AIDS and Sexology Page: http://math.ucsd.edu/~weinrich. This site allows fiction writers to safely learn the how's and why's of human sexuality as well as its devastating modern consequences.

Writer Online: www.novalearn.com/wol/. This website is filled with articles on the online business of writng. It is beneficial for writers who want to use the Internet to market their fiction.

Writer's Digest: www.writersdigest.com. This site includes daily markets, articles, interviews and information about writing books and magazines from *Writer's Digest*.

Writer's Internet Resource Guide: www.novalearn.com/wirg. This website is filled with goodies for fiction writers.

WritersMarket.com: www.writersmarket.com. The online version of *Writer's Market*, this website features a market of the day and rotating web resources.

Writer's Toolbox: www.writerstoolbox.com. This website features a plethora of articles on writing fiction.

Zuzu's Petals Literary Resource: www.zuzu.com. Includes links to magazines, readings, conferences, workshops and more.

WRITING RULES

Elements of Style **by William Strunk, Jr.:** www.bartleby.com/141/index.html. The full text of the English language's most used guide to grammar.

Grammar Girl's Guide to the English Language: http://webwitch.dreamhost.com/grammar.girl. This site has compiled a mass of rules and pet peeves to steer any wayward writer back onto the good grammar track.

The Inkspot: www.inkspot.com. This site offers many, many links to writing resources on the Web. Definitely a good place to start looking for answers to any writing-related question.

William Safire's *Rules for Writers:* www.chem.gla.ac.uk/protein/pert/safire.rules.html. File this under great things to tape next to your computer—a tongue-in-cheek look at some important grammar rules.

The best way to find information about specific research topics is through a search engine such as Yahoo (www.yahoo.com), Google (www.google.com), Infoseek (www.infoseek.com) and others. I did an "exact phrase" search on Yahoo for "life in" and came up with 478 matches. The websites covered everything from "life in" concentration camps to "life in" early Wisconsin, from retired "life in" a motor home to "life in" ancient Egypt.

Certainly a vast portion of the Internet is taken up by commercial sites and time wasters, but the rest is filled with invaluable resources that are only a few mouse clicks away. If you lack experience with computers or the Internet, the library may be your best place to start. You'll receive friendly advice and a guiding hand.

Otherwise, hop on board and start surfing! Your fiction will shine with the details you glean from cyberspace, and every little touch can put you that much closer to your ultimate goal—publication.

◪ Canadian Writers Take Note

While much of the information contained in this section applies to all writers, here are some specifics of interest to Canadian writers:

Postage: When sending an SASE from Canada, you will need an International Reply Coupon. Also be aware, a GST tax is required on postage in Canada and for mail with postage under $5 going to destinations outside the country. Since Canadian postage rates are voted on in January of each year (after we go to press), contact a Canada Post Corporation Customer Service Division, located in most cities in Canada, for the most current rates.

Copyright: For information on copyrighting your work and to obtain forms, write Copyright and Industrial Design, Phase One, Place du Portage, 50 Victoria St., Hull, Quebec K1A 0C9 or call (819)997-1936. Website: www.cipo.gc.ca.

The public lending right: The Public Lending Right Commission has established that eligible Canadian authors are entitled to payments when a book is available through a library. Payments are determined by a sampling of the holdings of a representative number of libraries. To find out more about the program and to learn if you are eligible, write to the Public Lending Right Commission at 350 Albert St., P.O. Box 1047, Ottawa, Ontario K1P 5V8 or call (613)566-4378 for information. The Commission, which is part of The Canada Council, produces a helpful pamphlet, *How the PLR System Works,* on the program.

Grants available to Canadian writers: Most province art councils or departments of culture provide grants to resident writers. Some of these, as well as contests for Canadian writers, are listed in our Contests and Awards section. For national programs, contact The Canada Council, Writing and Publishing Section, P.O. Box 1047, Ottawa, Ontario K1P 5V8 or call (613)566-4338 for information. Fax: (613)566-4390. Website: www.canadacouncil.ca.

For more information: More details on much of the information listed above and additional information on writing and publishing in Canada are included in the *Writer's Essential Desk Reference: A Companion to Writer's Market,* 2nd edition, published by Writer's Digest Books. In addition to information on a wide range of topics useful to all writers, the book features a detailed chapter for Canadians, Writing and Selling in Canada, by Fred Kerner.

See the Organizations and Resources section of *Novel & Short Story Writer's Market* for listings of writers' organizations in Canada. Also contact The Writer's Union of Canada, 24 Ryerson Ave., Toronto, Ontario M5T 2P3; call them at (416)703-8982 or fax them at (416)703-0826. E-mail: twuc@the-wire.com. Website: www.swifty.com/twuc. This organization provides a wealth of information (as well as strong support) for Canadian writers, including specialized publications on publishing contracts; contract negotiations; the author/editor relationship; author awards, competitions and grants; agents; taxes for writers, libel issues and access to archives in Canada.

Printing & Production Terms Defined

In most of the magazine listings in this book you will find a brief physical description of each publication. This material usually includes the number of pages, type of paper, type of binding and whether or not the magazine uses photographs or illustrations.

Although it is important to look at a copy of the magazine to which you are submitting, these descriptions can give you a general idea of what the publication looks like. This material can provide you with a feel for the magazine's financial resources and prestige. Do not, however, rule out small, simply produced publications as these may be the most receptive to new writers. Watch for publications that have increased their page count or improved their production from year to year. This is a sign the publication is doing well and may be accepting more fiction.

You will notice a wide variety of printing terms used within these descriptions. We explain here some of the more common terms used in our listing descriptions. We do not include explanations of terms such as Mohawk and Karma which are brand names and refer to the paper manufacturer. *Getting it Printed*, by Mark Beach (Writer's Digest Books), is an excellent publication for those interested in learning more about printing and production.

PAPER
acid-free: Paper that has a low or no acid content. This type of paper resists deterioration from exposure to the elements. More expensive than many other types of paper, publications done on acid-free paper can last a long time.

bond: Bond paper is often used for stationery and is more transparent than text paper. It can be made of either sulphite (wood) or cotton fiber. Some bonds have a mixture of both wood and cotton (such as "25 percent cotton" paper). This is the type of paper most often used in photocopying or as standard typing paper.

coated/uncoated stock: Coated and uncoated are terms usually used when referring to book or text paper. More opaque than bond, it is the paper most used for offset printing. As the name implies, uncoated paper has no coating. Coated paper is coated with a layer of clay, varnish or other chemicals. It comes in various sheens and surfaces depending on the type of coating, but the most common are dull, matte and gloss.

cover stock: Cover stock is heavier book or text paper used to cover a publication. It comes in a variety of colors and textures and can be coated on one or both sides.

CS1/CS2: Most often used when referring to cover stock, CS1 means paper that is coated only on one side; CS2 is paper coated on both sides.

newsprint: Inexpensive absorbent pulp wood paper often used in newspapers and tabloids.

text: Text paper is similar to book paper (a smooth paper used in offset printing), but it has been given some texture by using rollers or other methods to apply a pattern to the paper.

vellum: Vellum is a text paper that is fairly porous and soft.

Some notes about paper weight and thickness: Often you will see paper thickness described in terms of pounds such as 80 lb. or 60 lb. paper. The weight is determined by figuring how many pounds in a ream of a particular paper (a ream is 500 sheets). This can be confusing, however, because this figure is based on a standard sheet size and standard sheet sizes vary depending on the type of paper used. This information is most helpful when comparing papers of the same type. For example, 80 lb. book paper versus 60 lb. book paper. Since the size of the paper is the same it would follow that 80 lb. paper is the thicker, heavier paper.

Some paper, especially cover stock, is described by the actual thickness of the paper. This is expressed in a system of points. Typical paper thicknesses range from 8 points to 14 points thick.

PRINTING

letterpress: Letterpress printing is printing that uses a raised surface such as type. The type is inked and then pressed against the paper. Unlike offset printing, only a limited number of impressions can be made, as the surface of the type can wear down.

offset: Offset is a printing method in which ink is transferred from an image-bearing plate to a "blanket" and from the blanket to the paper.

sheet-fed offset: Offset printing in which the paper is fed one piece at a time.

web offset: Offset printing in which a roll of paper is printed and then cut apart to make individual sheets.

There are many other printing methods but these are the ones most commonly referred to in our listings.

BINDING

case binding: In case binding, signatures (groups of pages) are stitched together with thread rather than glued together. The stitched pages are then trimmed on three sides and glued into a hardcover or board "case" or cover. Most hardcover books and thicker magazines are done this way.

comb binding: A comb is a plastic spine used to hold pages together with bent tabs that are fed through punched holes in the edge of the paper.

perfect binding: Used for paperback books and heavier magazines, perfect binding involves gathering signatures (groups of pages) into a stack, trimming off the folds so the edge is flat and gluing a cover to that edge.

saddle stitched: Publications in which the pages are stitched together using metal staples. This fairly inexpensive type of binding is usually used with books or magazines that are under 80 pages.

Smythe-sewn: Binding in which the pages are sewn together with thread. Smythe is the name of the most common machine used for this purpose.

spiral binding: A wire spiral that is wound through holes punched in pages is a spiral bind. This is the binding used in spiral notebooks.

Glossary

Advance. Payment by a publisher to an author prior to the publication of a book, to be deducted from the author's future royalties.

All rights. The rights contracted to a publisher permitting a manuscript's use anywhere and in any form, including movie and book club sales, without additional payment to the writer.

Anthology. A collection of selected writings by various authors.

Auction. Publishers sometimes bid against each other for the acquisition of a manuscript that has excellent sales prospects.

Backlist. A publisher's books not published during the current season but still in print.

Book producer/packager. An organization that may develop a book for a publisher based upon the publisher's idea or may plan all elements of a book, from its initial concept to writing and marketing strategies, and then sell the package to a book publisher and/or movie producer.

Cliffhanger. Fictional event in which the reader is left in suspense at the end of a chapter or episode, so that interest in the story's outcome will be sustained.

Clip. Sample, usually from a newspaper or magazine, of a writer's published work.

Cloak-and-dagger. A melodramatic, romantic type of fiction dealing with espionage and intrigue.

Commercial. Publishers whose concern is salability, profit and success with a large readership.

Contemporary. Material dealing with popular current trends, themes or topics.

Contributor's copy. Copy of an issue of a magazine or published book sent to an author whose work is included.

Copublishing. An arrangement in which the author and publisher share costs and profits.

Copyediting. Editing a manuscript for writing style, grammar, punctuation and factual accuracy.

Copyright. The legal right to exclusive publication, sale or distribution of a literary work.

Cover letter. A brief letter sent with a complete manuscript submitted to an editor.

"Cozy" (or "teacup") mystery. Mystery usually set in a small British town, in a bygone era, featuring a somewhat genteel, intellectual protagonist.

Cyberpunk. Type of science fiction, usually concerned with computer networks and human-computer combinations, involving young, sophisticated protagonists.

E-mail. Mail that has been sent electronically using a computer and modem.

Electronic submission. A submission of material by modem or on computer disk.

Experimental fiction. Fiction that is innovative in subject matter and style; avant-garde, non-formulaic, usually literary material.

Exposition. The portion of the storyline, usually the beginning, where background information about character and setting is related.

Fair use. A provision in the copyright law that says short passages from copyrighted material may be used without infringing on the owner's rights.

Fanzine. A noncommercial, small-circulation magazine usually dealing with fantasy, horror or science-fiction literature and art.

First North American serial rights. The right to publish material in a periodical before it appears in book form, for the first time, in the United States or Canada.

Galleys. The first typeset version of a manuscript that has not yet been divided into pages.

Genre. A formulaic type of fiction such as romance, western or horror.

Gothic. A genre in which the central character is usually a beautiful young woman and the setting an old mansion or castle, involving a handsome hero and real danger, either natural or supernatural.

Graphic novel. An adaptation of a novel into a long comic strip or heavily illustrated story of 40 pages or more, produced in paperback.

Hard-boiled detective novel. Mystery novel featuring a private eye or police detective as the protagonist; usually involves a murder. The emphasis is on the details of the crime.

Horror. A genre stressing fear, death and other aspects of the macabre.

Imprint. Name applied to a publisher's specific line (e.g. Owl, an imprint of Henry Holt).

Interactive fiction. Fiction in book or computer-software format where the reader determines the path the story will take by choosing from several alternatives at the end of each chapter or episode.

International Reply Coupon (IRC). A form purchased at a post office and enclosed with a letter or manuscript to a international publisher, to cover return postage costs.

Juvenile. Fiction intended for children 2-12.

Libel. Written or printed words that defame, malign or damagingly misrepresent a living person.

Literary. The general category of serious, non-formulaic, intelligent fiction, sometimes experimental, that most frequently appears in little magazines.

Literary agent. A person who acts for an author in finding a publisher or arranging contract terms on a literary project.

Mainstream. Traditionally written fiction on subjects or trends that transcend experimental or genre fiction categories.

Malice domestic novel. A traditional mystery novel that is not hard-boiled; emphasis is on the solution. Suspects and victims know one another.

Manuscript. The author's unpublished copy of a work, usually typewritten, used as the basis for typesetting.

Mass market paperback. Softcover book on a popular subject, usually around 4×7, directed to a general audience and sold in drugstores and groceries as well as in bookstores.

Ms(s). Abbreviation for manuscript(s).

Multiple submission. Submission of more than one short story at a time to the same editor. Do not make a multiple submission unless requested.

Narration. The account of events in a story's plot as related by the speaker or the voice of the author.

Narrator. The person who tells the story, either someone involved in the action or the voice of the writer.

New Age. A term including categories such as astrology, psychic phenomena, spiritual healing, UFOs, mysticism and other aspects of the occult.

Nom de plume. French for "pen name"; a pseudonym.

Novella (also novelette). A short novel or long story, approximately 7,000-15,000 words.

#10 envelope. $4 \times 9\frac{1}{2}$ envelope, used for queries and other business letters.

Offprint. Copy of a story taken from a magazine before it is bound.

One-time rights. Permission to publish a story in periodical or book form one time only.

Outline. A summary of a book's contents, often in the form of chapter headings with a few sentences outlining the action of the story under each one; sometimes part of a book proposal.

Payment on acceptance. Payment from the magazine or publishing house as soon as the decision to print a manuscript is made.

Payment on publication. Payment from the publisher after a manuscript is printed.

Pen name. A pseudonym used to conceal a writer's real name.

Periodical. A magazine or journal published at regular intervals.

Plot. The carefully devised series of events through which the characters progress in a work of fiction.

Proofreading. Close reading and correction of a manuscript's typographical errors.

Proofs. A typeset version of a manuscript used for correcting errors and making changes, often a photocopy of the galleys.

Proposal. An offer to write a specific work, usually consisting of an outline of the work and one or two completed chapters.

Protagonist. The principal or leading character in a literary work.

Public domain. Material that either was never copyrighted or whose copyright term has expired.

Pulp magazine. A periodical printed on inexpensive paper, usually containing lurid, sensational stories or articles.

Query. A letter written to an editor to elicit interest in a story the writer wants to submit.

Reader. A person hired by a publisher to read unsolicited manuscripts.

Reading fee. An arbitrary amount of money charged by some agents and publishers to read a submitted manuscript.

Regency romance. A genre romance, usually set in England between 1811-1820.

Remainders. Leftover copies of an out-of-print book, sold by the publisher at a reduced price.

Reporting time. The number of weeks or months it takes an editor to report back on an author's query or manuscript.

Reprint rights. Permission to print an already published work whose rights have been sold to another magazine or book publisher.

Roman à clef. French "novel with a key." A novel that represents actual living or historical characters and events in fictionalized form.

Romance. The genre relating accounts of passionate love and fictional heroic achievements.

Royalties. A percentage of the retail price paid to an author for each copy of the book that is sold.

SAE. Self-addressed envelope.

SASE. Self-addressed stamped envelope.

Science fiction. Genre in which scientific facts and hypotheses form the basis of actions and events.

Second serial (reprint) rights. Permission for the reprinting of a work in another periodical after its first publication in book or magazine form.

Self-publishing. In this arrangement, the author keeps all income derived from the book, but he pays for its manufacturing, production and marketing.

Sequel. A literary work that continues the narrative of a previous, related story or novel.

Serial rights. The rights given by an author to a publisher to print a piece in one or more periodicals.

Serialized novel. A book-length work of fiction published in sequential issues of a periodical.

Setting. The environment and time period during which the action of a story takes place.

Short short story. A condensed piece of fiction, usually under 700 words.

Simultaneous submission. The practice of sending copies of the same manuscript to several editors or publishers at the same time. Some people refuse to consider such submissions.

Slant. A story's particular approach or style, designed to appeal to the readers of a specific magazine.

Slice of life. A presentation of characters in a seemingly mundane situation which offers the reader a flash of illumination about the characters or their situation.

Slush pile. A stack of unsolicited manuscripts in the editorial offices of a publisher.

Social fiction. Fiction written with the purpose of bringing about positive changes in society.

Speculation (or Spec). An editor's agreement to look at an author's manuscript with no promise to purchase.

Speculative fiction (SpecFic). The all-inclusive term for science fiction, fantasy and horror.

Splatterpunk. Type of horror fiction known for its very violent and graphic content.

Subsidiary. An incorporated branch of a company or conglomerate (e.g. Alfred Knopf, Inc., a subsidiary of Random House, Inc.).

Subsidiary rights. All rights other than book publishing rights included in a book contract, such as paperback, book club and movie rights.

Subsidy publisher. A book publisher who charges the author for the cost of typesetting, printing and promoting a book. Also Vanity publisher.

Subterficial fiction. Innovative, challenging, nonconventional fiction in which what seems to be happening is the result of things not so easily perceived.

Suspense. A genre of fiction where the plot's primary function is to build a feeling of anticipation and fear in the reader over its possible outcome.

Synopsis. A brief summary of a story, novel or play. As part of a book proposal, it is a comprehensive summary condensed in a page or page and a half.

Tabloid. Publication printed on paper about half the size of a regular newspaper page (e.g. *The National Enquirer*).

Tearsheet. Page from a magazine containing a published story.

Theme. The dominant or central idea in a literary work; its message, moral or main thread.

Trade paperback. A softbound volume, usually around 5 × 8, published and designed for the general public, available mainly in bookstores.

Unsolicited manuscript. A story or novel manuscript that an editor did not specifically ask to see.

Vanity publisher. See Subsidy publisher.

Viewpoint. The position or attitude of the first- or third-person narrator or multiple narrators, which determines how a story's action is seen and evaluated.

Western. Genre with a setting in the West, usually between 1860-1890, with a formula plot about cowboys or other aspects of frontier life.

Whodunit. Genre dealing with murder, suspense and the detection of criminals.

Work-for-hire. Work that another party commissions you to do, generally for a flat fee. The creator does not own the copyright and therefore cannot sell any rights.

Young adult. The general classification of books written for readers 12-18.

Zine. Often one- or two-person operations run from the home of the publisher/editor. Themes tend to be specialized, personal, experimental and often controversial.

Category Index

Our Category Index makes it easy for you to identify publishers who are looking for a specific type of fiction. The index is divided into types of fiction, including a section of electronic magazines. Under each fiction category are magazines and book publishers looking for that kind of fiction. Publishers who are not listed under a fiction category either accept all types of fiction or have not indicated specific subject preferences. Also not appearing here are listings that need very specific types of fiction, e.g., "fiction about fly fishing only." To use this index to find a book publisher for your mainstream novel, for instance, go to the Mainstream/Contemporary section and look under Book Publishers. Finally, read individual listings *carefully* to determine the publishers best suited to your work.

For a listing of agents and the types of fiction they represent, see the Literary Agents Category Index beginning on page 133.

ADVENTURE

Magazines
Acorn, The
Advocate, PKA's Publication
Affable Neighbor
Aguilar Expression, The
Amelia
Analecta
Anthology
Armchair Aesthete, The
Art Times
Artemis Magazine
Asian Pacific American Journal
Aura Literary Arts Review
Barbaric Yawp
Bark, The
Beginners
Bibliophilos
Black Jack
Blue Mesa Review
Blue Skunk Companion, The
Blueline
Bowhunter Magazine
Boys' Life
Boy's Quest
Bugle
Capers Aweigh
Cenotaph
Children, Churches and Daddies Magazine
Circle Magazine, The
City Primeval
Climbing Art, The
Clubhouse Magazine
Cochran's Corner
Cosmopolitan Magazine
Cotworld Creative Magazine
CZ's Magazine
Dagger of the Mind
Dialogue
Discovery Trails
Downstate Story
Edge, Tales of Suspense, The
Enigma
Eureka Literary Magazine
Evansville Review
Fugue
Gotta Write Network Litmag
Green Mountains Review
Green's Magazine
Griffin, The
Grit
Hawaii Pacific Review
Home Times
Horsethief's Journal, The
Iconoclast, The
In Posse Review
Indian Life
Indigenous Fiction
Interbang
Irreantum
Japanophile
Journal of African Travel-Writing, The
Karamu
Kids' Highway
Leapings Literary Magazine
Literary Moments
Lynx Eye
MacGuffin, The
Mediphors
Merlyn's Pen
MJ's Walkabout
Monkeyplanet
Musing Place, The
New England Writers' Network
New Writing
Nightfire
Nimrod
Nite-Writer's International Literary Arts Journal
Northwoods Journal
Oak, The

Palo Alto Review
Peninsular
Peralta Press, The
Plot Line Foyer
Portland Review
Post, The
Prisoners of the Night
PSI
Queen's Quarterly
Rabbit Hole Press, The
Ralph's Review
Rosebud™
S.L.U.G. fest, Ltd.
Seeking the Muse
Short Stuff Magazine for Grown-ups
Shyflower's Garden
SPSM&H
State of Unbeing
Storyteller, The
Studentswrite.com
"Teak" Roundup
Thema
3 A.M. Magazine
Threshold, The
Thresholds Quarterly
Tucumcari Literary Review
Urban Spaghetti
Vincent Brothers Review, The
Virginia Adversaria
Virginia Quarterly Review
Weber Studies
Yellow Sticky Notes

Book Publishers
Adventure Book Publishers
Authors Online Ltd.
Bantam Books
Bantam Dell Publishing Group, The
Beggar's Press
Black Heron Press
Caitlin Press, Inc.
Cave Books
Crossway Books
Delacorte Press
Dell
Dial Press, The
DiskUs Publishing
Duckworth Press
Fort Ross Inc.
Fountainhead Productions, Inc.
Geringer Books, Laura
Glencannon Press, The
Harlequin Enterprises, Ltd.
Hawk Publishing Group
Holt & Company, Henry
Houghton Mifflin Books for Children
Huntington Press
Island
LTD Books
Majestic Books
Morrow, William
New American Library

New Hope Books, Inc.
Palari Publishing
Philomel Books
Pig Iron Press
Pipers' Ash Ltd.
Pocket Books
Publishers Syndication, International
Putnam's Sons, G.P.
Quixote Press
Random House, Inc.
RavenHaus Publishing
Russell Publishing, James
Salvo Press
Scherf Books
Snowapple Press
Tropical Press, Inc.
Vista Publishing, Inc.
Worldwide Library
Writers Direct
Writers Press, Inc.

ALL CATEGORIES OF FICTION
Magazines
George & Mertie's Place: Rooms with a View
Half Tones to Jubliee
Parting Gifts
Pembroke Magazine
Peregrine
Pottersfield Portfolio
Sensations Magazine
Sun, The
US1 Worksheets
Voiding the Void™
Wy'East Historical Journal

CHILDRENS/JUVENILE
Magazines
Advocate, PKA's Publication
American Girl
Anthology
Archaeology
Associate Reformed Presbyterian, The
Bark, The
Baseball
Boy's Quest
Bridal Guides
Bugle
Calliope
Chickadee
Children's Digest
Children's Playmate
Clubhouse
Clubhouse Magazine
Cobblestone
Cochran's Corner
Creative Kids
Cricket Magazine
Crusader Magazine
CZ's Magazine
Dance
Discoveries

Discovery Trails
Faces
Friend Magazine, The
Ghost Town
Guideposts for Kids
Highlights for Children
Hopscotch: The Magazine for Girls
Humpty Dumpty's Magazine
Indian Life
Indian Life Magazine
Jack and Jill
Kids' Highway
Kidz Ch@t
Ladybug
Lighthouse Story Collections
Literally Horses
Literary Moments
Majestic Books
MJ's Walkabout
My Friend
Newfangled Fairy Tales and Girls to the Rescue
Odyssey
Pockets
Ranger Rick Magazine
Seeking the Muse
Skipping Stones
Spellbound Magazine
Spider
Stepping Out of the Darkness
Stone Soup
Story Friends
"Teak" Roundup
Touch
Turtle Magazine for Preschool Kids
Yellow Sticky Notes

Book Publishers
Absey & Co., Inc.
Adventure Book Publishers
Advocacy Press
Arte Publico Press
Atheneum Books for Young Readers
Authors Online Ltd.
Bantam, Doubleday, Dell/Delacorte, Knopf and Crown Books for Young Readers
Bethany House Publishers
BJU Press
Blue Sky Press, The
Borealis Press
Boyds Mills Press
Candlewick Press
Carolrhoda Books, Inc.
Cartwheel Books
Concordia Publishing House
Cross-Cultural Communications
Crown Books for Young Readers
Delecorte Books for Young Readers
Dial Books for Young Readers
DiskUs Publishing
Doubleday Books for Young Readers
Down East Books
Duckworth Press

Dutton Children's Books
E.M. Press, Inc.
Éditions du Vermillon, Les
Éditions La Liberté Inc.
Farrar, Straus & Giroux/Children's Books
Front Street Books
Glencannon Press, The
Godine, Publisher, Inc., David R.
Greene Bark Press
Greenwillow Books
Grolier Publishing
Harcourt Inc.
HarperCollins Children's Books
HarperCollins Publishers (New Zealand) Limited
Hemkunt Press
Holiday House, Inc.
Holt & Company Books for Young Readers, Henry
Holt & Company, Henry
Houghton Mifflin Books for Children
Hyperion Books for Children
Illumination Publishing Co.
ImaJinn Books
Kaeden Books
Knopf Books for Young Readers, Alfred A.
Laurel Leaf
Lee & Low Books
Levine Books, Arthur
Little, Brown and Company
Little, Brown and Company Children's Books
Little Simon
Lollipop Power Books
Lorimer & Co., Publishers, James
McElderry Books, Margaret K.
Micah Publications, Inc.
Mightbook
Milkweed Editions
Milkweeds for Young Readers
Minstrel Books
Moon Mountain Publishing
Morehouse Publishing Co.
Nelson, Tommy
North-South Books
Orchard Books
Owen Publishers Inc., Richard C.
Peachtree Publishers, Ltd.
Pelican Publishing Company
Perfection Learning Corp.
Philomel Books
Piano Press
Piñata Books
Pipers' Ash Ltd.
Pippin Press
Pleasant Company Publications
Prairie Publishing Company, The
Puffin Books
Quixote Press
Ragweed Press Inc./gynergy books
Random House Books for Young Readers
Random House Children's Books
Ronsdale Press
Roussan Publishers Inc.

Scholastic Canada Ltd.
Scholastic Inc.
Scholastic Press
Signal Crest
Simon & Schuster Books for Young Readers
Skylark
Snowapple Press
Soundprints
Starfire
Stones Point Press
Tidewater Publishers
Tyndale House Publishers, Inc.
Viking Children's Books
Walker and Company
Writers Direct
Writers Press, Inc.
Yearling

COMICS/GRAPHIC NOVELS

Magazines

Affable Neighbor
Alien Zoo
Bark, The
Carpe Noctem
Corona
Cotworld Creative Magazine
Futures Magazine
Hybolics
Indian Life
Lady Churchill's Rosebud Wristlet
Literally Horses
Long Shot
Nuvein Online
Plot Line Foyer
Stovepipe
3 A.M. Magazine
12-Gauge.com
Urban Graffiti
Weber Studies
WV
Yellow Sticky Notes
Zopilote

Book Publishers

Affable Neighbor
Authors Online Ltd.
Cleis Press
Darktales Publications
Hollow Earth Publishing
Midknight Club, The
Pick Pocket Books
Pride and Imprints
Sweet Lady Moon Press

CONDENSED NOVEL

Magazines

Antietam Review
Ararat Quarterly
Art:Mag
Asian Pacific American Journal
Bathtub Gin

Blue Skunk Companion, The
Bookpress
Brilliant Corners
Cayo
Climbing Art, The
Cozy Detective, The
Crab Orchard Review
Evansville Review
Grit
Journal of African Travel-Writing, The
Kenyon Review, The
Kestrel
Lullwater Review
Lynx Eye
Matriarch's Way: Journal of Female Supremacy
Missouri Review, The
Musing Place, The
New England Writers' Network
New York Stories
Pangolin Papers
Paperplates
Porcupine Literary Arts Magazine
Quarter After Eight
Rosebud™
Samsara
Snake Nation Review
Talking River Review
"Teak" Roundup
Thin Air
Vincent Brothers Review, The
Washington Square
Westcoast Fisherman, The
Yemassee

ELECTRONIC MAGAZINES

Magazines

Absinthe Literary Review, The
adhocity.com
AKP Zine
Anotherealm
Archipelago
Babel
Barcelona Review, The
BEEF
Blue Moon Review, The
Cafe Irreal, The
Cenotaph
Children, Churches and Daddies Magazine
Dargonzine
Dark Matter Chronicles
Deep Outside SFFH
Duct Tape Press
Electric Wine
EWGPresents
Fairfield Review, The
Fullosia Press
Grand Street
Green Tricycle, The
Horsethief's Journal, The
Intertext
Jackhammer E-Zine

Little Magazine, The
Millennium: A Journal for Tomorrowland
Monkeyplanet
moonbomb press
New Writing
News of the Brave New World
Nuvein Online
Orphic Chronicle, The
Oyster Boy Review of Fiction and Poetry
Painted Bride Quarterly
Paperplates
Paumanok Review, The
Pegasus Online
PeopleNet DisAbility DateNet Home Page
Pif
Plaza, The
Plot Line Foyer
Prose Menagerie, The
Pulp Eternity Online
RealPoetik
Recursive Angel
Renaissance Online Magazine
Seed Cake
Shadow Voices
Short Story Writers Showcase
SNReview
State of Unbeing
Story Bytes
Twilight Showcase
Voiding the Void™
Web Del Sol
Weber Studies
Wilmington Blues

New York Stories
News of the Brave New World
Nightfire
Nite-Writer's International Literary Arts Journal
Nugget
Old Crow Review
On Our Backs
Options
Other Voices (Canada)
Peralta Press, The
Poskisnolt Press
Prisoners of the Night
Pulp Eternity Online
Quarter After Eight
QWF (Quality Women's Fiction)
Rabbit Hole Press, The
Rain Crow
Rhino
Rocket Press
Salt Hill
Samsara
Sanskrit
Shattered Wig Review
Shyflower's Garden
Skidrow Penthouse
Slipstream
Snake Nation Review
SPSM&H
State of Unbeing
sub-TERRAIN
Threshold, The
12-Gauge.com
Urban Graffiti
WV
Yellow Silk

EROTICA

Magazines

Adrift
Affable Neighbor
Affair of the Mind
Amelia
Analecta
Art:Mag
Asian Pacific American Journal
babysue
Carpe Noctem
Contact Advertising
Cotworld Creative Magazine
Dream International/Quarterly
Edge, Tales of Suspense, The
Evansville Review
First Class
First Hand
Gargoyle
Gay Chicago Magazine
Happy
Hustler Busty Beauties
In Posse Review
Long Shot
Lynx Eye
Matriarch's Way: Journal of Female Supremacy
Missing Fez, The

Book Publishers

Affable Neighbor
Artemis Press
Authors Online Ltd.
Black Lace Books
Circlet Press
Cleis Press
Darktales Publications
Down There Press
First Amendment Press International Company
Forge Books
Guernica Editions
Leapfrog Press
New American Library
Nexus
Palari Publishing
Pick Pocket Books
Pleasure Boat Studio
Pocket Books
Sapphire Books
Second Chance Press and the Permanent Press

ETHNIC/MULTICULTURAL

Magazines

About Such Things
ACM (Another Chicago Magazine)

Adrift
Advocate, PKA's Publication
Affable Neighbor
Affair of the Mind
African Voices
Aguilar Expression, The
Algonquin Roundtable Review
Amelia
American Writing
Analecta
Antietam Review
Art Times
Art:Mag
Asian Pacific American Journal
Azorean Express, The
Baltimore Review, The
Beneath the Surface
Bibliophilos
Black Jack
Black Lace
BlackFire
Blue Mesa Review
Blue Skunk Companion, The
Boston Review
Briar Cliff Review, The
Brilliant Corners
Brobdingnagian Times, The
Brown Critique, The
Callaloo
Capers Aweigh
Caribbean Writer, The
Cenotaph
Chanteh
Cicada (California)
Climbing Art, The
Collages and Bricolages
Colorado Review
Concho River Review
Cotworld Creative Magazine
Crab Orchard Review
Cream City Review, The
Crucible
Dialogos
Downstate Story
Epoch Magazine
Eureka Literary Magazine
Evansville Review
Feminist Studies
Frontiers
Fugue
Futures Magazine
Gargoyle
Gertrude
Grasslands Review
Green Hills Literary Lantern, The
Griffin, The
Gulf Coast
Happy
Hawaii Pacific Review
Heartlands Today, The
Hemispheres

Hill and Holler
Home Planet News
Horsethief's Journal, The
Hybolics
Iconoclast, The
Illya's Honey
In Posse Review
In the Family
India Currents
Indian Life
Indian Life Magazine
Indiana Review
Indigenous Fiction
Interbang
International Quarterly
Iowa Review, The
Irreantum
Italian Americana
Jabberwock Review, The
Japanophile
Jewish Currents Magazine
Jewish Quarterly
Jive, Black Confessions, Black Romance, Bronze
    Thrills, Black Secrets
Journal of African Travel-Writing, The
Karamu
Karitos Review, The
Kenyon Review, The
Kerem
Leapings Literary Magazine
Left Curve
Lilith Magazine
Live
Long Shot
Long Story, The
Louisiana Review, The
Lullwater Review
Lynx Eye
MacGuffin, The
Many Mountains Moving
Margin
Matriarch's Way: Journal of Female Supremacy
Milkwood Review
Missouri Review, The
MJ's Walkabout
Mobius
Monkeyplanet
Musing Place, The
NA'AMAT Woman
New England Writers' Network
New Letters Magazine
New York Stories
Nimrod
Northeast Arts Magazine
Now & Then
Nuvein Online
Other Voices (Canada)
Oxford Magazine
Pacific Coast Journal
Painted Bride Quarterly
Palo Alto Review

Paperplates
Passages North
Peninsular
Peralta Press, The
Pikeville Review
Pleiades
Plot Line Foyer
Plowman, The
Poetry Forum Short Stories
Porcupine Literary Arts Magazine
Portland Review
Poskisnolt Press
Puerto Del Sol
Pulp Eternity Online
Quarter After Eight
QWF (Quality Women's Fiction)
Rabbit Hole Press, The
Raven Chronicles, The
Reform Judaism
Rhino
River Styx
Rockford Review, The
Rosebud™
S.L.U.G. fest, Ltd.
Salt Hill
Sanskrit
Shattered Wig Review
Shyflower's Garden
Side Show
Skipping Stones
Skylark
Slipstream
Snake Nation Review
So to Speak
South Dakota Review
Southwestern American Literature
Spindrift
SPSM&H
State of Unbeing
Storyboard
Struggle
Studentswrite.com
Sulphur River Literary Review
Talking River Review
Tameme
Tampa Review
"Teak" Roundup
Thin Air
This Magazine
Transition
Tucumcari Literary Review
12-Gauge.com
Urban Spaghetti
Valley Grapevine
Victory Park
Vincent Brothers Review, The
Virginia Adversaria
Virginia Quarterly Review
Washington Square
Weber Studies
West Coast Line

Westview
White Crow, The
Windhover
Witness
Writers' Forum
Writing for Our Lives
Xavier Review
Yarns and Such
Yellow Silk
Yellow Sticky Notes
Yemassee
Zopilote
Zuzu's Petals Quarterly

Book Publishers

Alaska Native Language Center
Arsenal Pulp Press
Arte Publico Press
Aunt Lute Books
Authors Online Ltd.
Bancroft Press
Bilingual Press/Editorial Bilingüe
Branden Books
Calyx Books
Carolina Wren Press, Inc.
China Books & Periodicals, Inc.
Cleis Press
Coffee House Press
Cross-Cultural Communications
DiskUs Publishing
Feminist Press at the City University of New York, The
Fountainhead Productions, Inc.
Glencannon Press, The
Helicon Nine Editions
Houghton Mifflin Books for Children
Houghton Mifflin Company
Interlink Publishing Group, Inc.
Leapfrog Press
Mage Publishers
New American Library
Philomel Books
Piano Press
Pleasure Boat Studio
Pocket Books
Power of Love Publishing
Quixote Press
Scherf Books
Seal Press
Second Chance Press and the Permanent Press
Soho Press
Stone Bridge Press
University of Nevada Press
Voices from My Retreat
Waverly House Publishing
White Pine Press
Zoland Books, Inc.

EXPERIMENTAL

Magazines

Aberrations
Abiko Quarterly with James, The

ACM (Another Chicago Magazine)
Adrift
Advocate, PKA's Publication
Affable Neighbor
Affair of the Mind
Aguilar Expression, The
Alaska Quarterly Review
Algonquin Roundtable Review
Alsop Review, The
Amelia
American Writing
Analecta
Antietam Review
Antioch Review
Artful Dodge
Art:Mag
Asian Pacific American Journal
Aura Literary Arts Review
Azorean Express, The
babysue
Baltimore Review, The
B&A: New Fiction
Barbaric Yawp
Barcelona Review, The
Bathtub Gin
Beneath the Surface
Bitter Oleander, The
Black Petals
Black Warrior Review
Blue Mesa Review
Blue Moon Review, The
Blue Skunk Companion, The
Bogg
Bomb Magazine
Boston Review
Boulevard
Brilliant Corners
Brobdingnagian Times, The
Cafe Irreal, The
Capilano Review, The
Carpe Noctem
Cayo
Century
Chariton Review, The
Chicago Review
Children, Churches and Daddies Magazine
Chiron Review
Chrysalis Reader
Circle Magazine, The
Climbing Art, The
Coe Review, The
Collages and Bricolages
Colorado Review
Compost
Conduit
Corona
Cotworld Creative Magazine
Cream City Review, The
Crucible
CZ's Magazine
Dagger of the Mind

Denver Quarterly
Downstate Story
Dreams & Visions
Duct Tape Press
1812
Enigma
Eureka Literary Magazine
Evansville Review
Explorations
Fiction
Florida Review, The
Free Focus/Ostentatious Mind
Fugue
Futures Magazine
Gargoyle
Georgia Review, The
Gettysburg Review, The
Ginosko
Grain
Grand Street
Grasslands Review
Green Hills Literary Lantern, The
Green Mountains Review
Greensboro Review, The
Gulf Coast
Happy
Hawaii Pacific Review
Hayden's Ferry Review
Heaven Bone
Home Planet News
Hunted News, The
Hurricane Alice
Hybolics
Idaho Review, The
Iksperament
Illya's Honey
In Posse Review
Indigenous Fiction
Interbang
International Quarterly
Iowa Review, The
Iris (VA)
Irreantum
Jabberwock Review, The
Karamu
Karitos Review, The
Kenyon Review, The
Koja
Lady Churchill's Rosebud Wristlet
Leapings Literary Magazine
Left Curve
Licking River Review, The
Liquid Ohio
Lite
Literal Latté
Little Magazine, The
Lost and Found Times
Lullwater Review
Lynx Eye
MacGuffin, The
Madison Review, The

Many Mountains Moving
Margin
Matriarch's Way: Journal of Female Supremacy
Mediphors
Mid-American Review
Milkwood Review
Minnesota Review, The
Missing Fez, The
Mississippi Review
Mobius
Monkeyplanet
Musing Place, The
Neotrope
New Delta Review
New Letters Magazine
New Methods
New Writing
New York Stories
Nightfire
Nimrod
Northwest Review
Northwoods Journal
Notre Dame Review
Nuvein Online
Oak, The
Office Number One
Ohio Review, The
Other Voices (Canada)
Other Voices (Illinois)
Oxford Magazine
Oyster Boy Review of Fiction and Poetry
Pacific Coast Journal
Painted Bride Quarterly
Palo Alto Review
Pangolin Papers
Partisan Review
Paumanok Review, The
Pikeville Review
Pleiades
Poetry Forum Short Stories
Porter Cosmographic, Bern
Portland Review
Poskisnolt Press
Prairie Fire
Puckerbrush Review
Puerto Del Sol
Pulp Eternity Online
QECE
Quarter After Eight
Quarterly West
Queen's Quarterly
QWF (Quality Women's Fiction)
Rabbit Hole Press, The
Rain Crow
Rambunctious Review
Red Rock Review
Rejected Quarterly, The
Rhino
Rio Grande Review
River Styx
Rocket Press

Rockford Review, The
Rosebud™
S.L.U.G. fest, Ltd.
Salt Hill
Samsara
Sanskrit
Santa Monica Review
Seeking the Muse
Shades of December
Shattered Wig Review
Shyflower's Garden
Silver Web, The
Skidrow Penthouse
Skiptracer
Skylark
Slipstream
Snake Nation Review
So to Speak
Spindrift
Spinning Jenny
SPSM&H
State of Unbeing
Storyboard
Stovepipe
Struggle
sub-TERRAIN
Sulphur River Literary Review
Sycamore Review
Talking River Review
Tampa Review
Thema
Thin Air
This Magazine
3 A.M. Magazine
Threshold, The
Tin House
Transcendent Visions
12-Gauge.com
Urban Spaghetti
Urbanite, The
Victory Park
Vincent Brothers Review, The
Washington Square
Weber Studies
Wespennest
West Coast Line
Western Humanities Review
White Crow, The
Wilmington Blues
Windhover
Wisconsin Academy Review
Wisconsin Review
Witness
Writing for Our Lives
WV
Xavier Review
Yellow Silk
Yemassee
Zyzzyva

Book Publishers

Affable Neighbor
Ageless Press
Anvil Press
Authors Online Ltd.
Beneath the Underground
Black Heron Press
Broken Boulder Press
Calyx Books
China Books & Periodicals, Inc.
Coffee House Press
Cross-Cultural Communications
Grove/Atlantic, Inc.
Helicon Nine Editions
Insomniac Press
Lintel
MacAdam/Cage Publishing
Morrow, William
New Rivers Press
Pig Iron Press
Pudding House Publications
Quixote Press
Random House, Inc.
Red Deer Press
Scrivenery Press
Second Chance Press and the Permanent Press
Snowapple Press
Soft Skull Press Inc.
Sweet Lady Moon Press
Thistledown Press
Ultramarine Publishing Co., Inc.
Voices from My Retreat
York Press Ltd.

FAMILY SAGA

Magazines

Affair of the Mind
Analecta
Beginners
Bibliophilos
Cotworld Creative Magazine
In Posse Review
Interbang
Irreantum
Lady, The
Larcom Review, The
Literary Moments
Milkwood Review
Moxie
Nightfire
Other Voices (Canada)
Plot Line Foyer
Seeking the Muse
State of Unbeing
Stepping Out of the Darkness
Storyboard
Victory Park
Virginia Adversaria
Windhover

Book Publishers

Authors Online Ltd.
Bancroft Press
Dan River Press
DiskUs Publishing
Duckworth Press
Hodder & Stoughton/Headline
Leapfrog Press
Majestic Books
Micah Publications, Inc.
Mountain State Press
Philomel Books
Scherf Books
Second Chance Press and the Permanent Press
Stones Point Press
University of Nevada Press

FANTASY

Magazines

Aberrations
About Such Things
Advocate, PKA's Publication
Affable Neighbor
Alembic
Amazing Stories
Amelia
Analecta
Anotherealm
Anthology
Armchair Aesthete, The
Art Times
Art:Mag
Asimov's Science Fiction
Aura Literary Arts Review
Aurealis
Barbaric Yawp
Beneath the Surface
Blue Skunk Companion, The
Cafe Irreal, The
Capers Aweigh
Cenotaph
Century
Climbing Art, The
Companion in Zeor, A
Contact Advertising
Corona
Cotworld Creative Magazine
CZ's Magazine
Dagger of the Mind
Dargonzine
Dark Matter Chronicles
Deep Outside SFFH
Dialogue
Dream International/Quarterly
Dreams & Visions
Eidolon
Electric Wine
Enigma
Eureka Literary Magazine
Evansville Review
Flesh & Blood

Fugue
Gotta Write Network Litmag
Grasslands Review
Green's Magazine
Griffin, The
Happy
Hawaii Pacific Review
Heaven Bone
Ikspcrament
In Posse Review
Indigenous Fiction
Interbang
Irreantum
Jackhammer E-Zine
Karitos Review, The
Lady Churchill's Rosebud Wristlet
Leading Edge, The
Leapings Literary Magazine
Lite
Literal Latté
Literary Moments
Long Shot
Lynx Eye
MacGuffin, The
Magazine of Fantasy & Science Fiction
Margin
Matriarch's Way: Journal of Female Supremacy
Merlyn's Pen
Minas Tirith Evening-Star
Missing Fez, The
Mississippi Review
Mobius
Monkeyplanet
Musing Place, The
Northwoods Journal
Oak, The
Of Unicorns and Space Stations
Office Number One
On Spec
Orphic Chronicle, The
Outer Darkness
Outer Rim—The Zine, The
Palo Alto Review
Pegasus Online
Peninsular
Penny Dreadful
Playboy Magazine
Plot Line Foyer
Poetry Forum Short Stories
Portland Review
Poskisnolt Press
Primavera
Prisoners of the Night
Psychic Radio, The
Pulp Eternity Online
Queen's Quarterly
QWF (Quality Women's Fiction)
Rabbit Hole Press, The
Ralph's Review
Rejected Quarterly, The
Rockford Review, The

Samsara
Scifi.com
Seeking the Muse
Shades of December
Short Story Writers Showcase
Shyflower's Garden
Skylark
Snake Nation Review
Songs of Innocence
Southern Humanities Review
Space and Time
SPSM&H
State of Unbeing
Studentswrite.com
Talebones
Tampa Review
Threshold, The
Thresholds Quarterly
Twilight Showcase
Urban Spaghetti
Urbanite, The
Visions & Voices
Weber Studies
Weird Tales
Windhover
Yellow Silk
Yellow Sticky Notes

Book Publishers

Ace Science Fiction
Adventure Book Publishers
Affable Neighbor
Ageless Press
Alexandria Digital Literature
Artemis Press
Authors Online Ltd.
Baen Books
Bantam Books
Bantam Dell Publishing Group, The
Berkley Publishing Group, The
Circlet Press
Dan River Press
Daw Books, Inc.
Del Rey Books
Delacorte Press
Dell
Dial Press, The
DiskUs Publishing
First Amendment Press International Company
Forge Books
Fort Ross Inc.
Fountainhead Productions, Inc.
Geringer Books, Laura
Hawk Publishing Group
Hollow Earth Publishing
ImaJinn Books
Island
LTD Books
Majestic Books
New American Library
Philomel Books
Pocket Books

Pride and Imprints
Random House, Inc.
RavenHaus Publishing
Regency Press
ROC
St. Martin's Press
Spectra Books
Tor Books
TSR, Inc.
Ultramarine Publishing Co., Inc.
W.W. Publications
Warner Aspect
Warner Books
Write Way Publishing

FEMINIST

Magazines
ACM (Another Chicago Magazine)
Adrift
Advocate, PKA's Publication
Affable Neighbor
Affair of the Mind
Algonquin Roundtable Review
Amelia
American Writing
Analecta
Antietam Review
Art Times
Art:Mag
Asian Pacific American Journal
Aura Literary Arts Review
Bark, The
Beneath the Surface
Blue Mesa Review
Blue Moon Review, The
Bookpress
Briar Cliff Review, The
Callaloo
Calyx
Capers Aweigh
Children, Churches and Daddies Magazine
Collages and Bricolages
Contact Advertising
Corona
Cotworld Creative Magazine
Crucible
CZ's Magazine
Emrys Journal
Eureka Literary Magazine
Evansville Review
Event
Feminist Studies
Firefly, The
Free Focus/Ostentatious Mind
Frontiers
Futures Magazine
Gertrude
Green Hills Literary Lantern, The
Griffin, The
Happy
Home Planet News

Hurricane Alice
Illya's Honey
In Posse Review
In the Family
Indigenous Fiction
Interbang
Iowa Review, The
Iris (VA)
Irreantum
Jabberwock Review, The
Karamu
Kenyon Review, The
Kerem
Kestrel
Lady, The
Lady Churchill's Rosebud Wristlet
Leapings Literary Magazine
Lilith Magazine
Little Magazine, The
Long Shot
Long Story, The
Lullwater Review
Lynx Eye
Many Mountains Moving
Margin
Matriarch's Way: Journal of Female Supremacy
Milkwood Review
Minnesota Review, The
Missing Fez, The
Mobius
Monkeyplanet
Moxie
Musing Place, The
New York Stories
Northwest Review
Notre Dame Review
Other Voices (Canada)
Oxford Magazine
Pacific Coast Journal
Painted Bride Quarterly
Palo Alto Review
Paperplates
Peralta Press, The
Pikeville Review
Pleiades
Poetry Forum Short Stories
Portland Review
Poskisnolt Press
Primavera
Prisoners of the Night
Pulp Eternity Online
Quarter After Eight
QWF (Quality Women's Fiction)
Rabbit Hole Press, The
Radiance
Rambunctious Review
Rhino
Rio Grande Review
River Styx
Room of One's Own
Sanskrit

Seeking the Muse
Shattered Wig Review
Shyflower's Garden
Side Show
Sinister Wisdom
Skipping Stones
Skylark
Snake Nation Review
So to Speak
Sojourner
Southern Humanities Review
Spirit
SPSM&H
State of Unbeing
Struggle
Sulphur River Literary Review
Talking River Review
13th Moon
This Magazine
Transcendent Visions
Urban Spaghetti
Vincent Brothers Review, The
Virginia Quarterly Review
Weber Studies
West Coast Line
Writing for Our Lives
WV
Yellow Silk
Yemassee
Zuzu's Petals Quarterly

Book Publishers
Academy Chicago Publishers
Arsenal Pulp Press
Arte Publico Press
Aunt Lute Books
Authors Online Ltd.
Bancroft Press
Bantam Books
Bantam Dell Publishing Group, The
Calyx Books
Carolina Wren Press, Inc.
Circlet Press
Cleis Press
Delacorte Press
Dell
Dial Press, The
Down There Press
Dufour Editions
FC2
Feminist Press at the City University of New York, The
Firebrand Books
First Amendment Press International Company
Hollow Earth Publishing
Holt & Company, Henry
Houghton Mifflin Company
Island
Kensington Publishing Corp.
Leapfrog Press
Lintel
Morrow, William

New Victoria Publishers
Papier-Mache
Pleasure Boat Studio
Pocket Books
Post-Apollo Press, The
Ragweed Press Inc./gynergy books
Seal Press
Signal Crest
Spinsters Ink
Van Neste Books
Véhicule Press
Voices from My Retreat
White Pine Press
Zoland Books, Inc.

GAY

Magazines
ACM (Another Chicago Magazine)
Adrift
Affable Neighbor
Affair of the Mind
Amelia
American Writing
Analecta
Art Times
Art:Mag
Asian Pacific American Journal
Aura Literary Arts Review
Bark, The
Bathtub Gin
Beneath the Surface
BlackFire
Blue Mesa Review
Blue Moon Review, The
Bookpress
Carpe Noctem
Children, Churches and Daddies Magazine
Contact Advertising
Cotworld Creative Magazine
Edge, Tales of Suspense, The
Enigma
Evansville Review
Feminist Studies
First Hand
Futures Magazine
Gargoyle
Gay Chicago Magazine
Gertrude
Happy
Home Planet News
Hurricane Alice
Illya's Honey
In Posse Review
In Touch for Men
In the Family
Interbang
Iowa Review, The
Jabberwock Review, The
Karamu
Kenyon Review, The
Long Shot

Lullwater Review
Lynx Eye
Many Mountains Moving
Margin
Minnesota Review, The
Missing Fez, The
Mobius
Monkeyplanet
Musing Place, The
New York Stories
Nightfire
96 Inc.
Northeast Arts Magazine
Options
Other Voices (Canada)
Oxford Magazine
Painted Bride Quarterly
Paperplates
Peninsular
Peralta Press, The
Pleiades
Portland Review
Poskisnolt Press
Primavera
Prisoners of the Night
Puckerbrush Review
Pulp Eternity Online
Quarter After Eight
QWF (Quality Women's Fiction)
Rabbit Hole Press, The
Rio Grande Review
River Styx
Salt Hill
Sanskrit
Shattered Wig Review
Shyflower's Garden
Side Show
Snake Nation Review
SPSM&H
State of Unbeing
Talking River Review
This Magazine
Threshold, The
Transcendent Visions
12-Gauge.com
Urban Graffiti
Weber Studies
West Coast Line
WV
Yellow Silk
Yemassee
Zuzu's Petals Quarterly

Book Publishers
Affable Neighbor
Alyson Publications, Inc.
Arsenal Pulp Press
Authors Online Ltd.
Bancroft Press
Carolina Wren Press, Inc.
Circlet Press
Cleis Press

Dutton
FC2
Feminist Press at the City University of New York, The
First Amendment Press International Company
Hill Street Press
Hollow Earth Publishing
Houghton Mifflin Company
Insomniac Press
Kensington Publishing Corp.
Leapfrog Press
Lintel
Morrow, William
Palari Publishing
Pleasure Boat Studio
Plume
Pride and Imprints
Soft Skull Press Inc.
Stonewall Inn

GLITZ
Magazines
Affable Neighbor
Analecta
Aura Literary Arts Review
Cotworld Creative Magazine
Futures Magazine
Interbang
Monkeyplanet
Peralta Press, The
State of Unbeing
12-Gauge.com

Book Publishers
Authors Online Ltd.
Bancroft Press

HISTORICAL
Magazines
About Such Things
Acorn, The
Advocate, PKA's Publication
Affable Neighbor
Affair of the Mind
Amelia
Analecta
Appalachian Heritage
Ararat Quarterly
Archaeology
Armchair Aesthete, The
Art Times
Art:Mag
Asian Pacific American Journal
Aura Literary Arts Review
Barbaric Yawp
Beneath the Surface
Bibliophilos
Blue Mesa Review
Blue Skunk Companion, The
Bookpress
Boy's Quest

Briar Cliff Review, The
Bugle
Callaloo
Calliope
Capers Aweigh
Caribbean Writer, The
Cenotaph
Century
Chantoh
Christian Courier
Chrysalis Reader
Climbing Art, The
Cobblestone
Cochran's Corner
Concho River Review
Cotworld Creative Magazine
Dixie Phoenix
Downstate Story
Dream International/Quarterly
Electric Wine
Enigma
Eureka Literary Magazine
Evansville Review
Fugue
Fullosia Press
Gettysburg Review, The
Ghost Town
Gotta Write Network Litmag
Griffin, The
Home Planet News
Home Times
Horsethief's Journal, The
Hunted News, The
Illya's Honey
In Posse Review
Indian Life
Indian Life Magazine
Inky Trail News
Interbang
Irreantum
Japanophile
Jewish Currents Magazine
Journal of African Travel-Writing, The
Karamu
Karitos Review, The
Kenyon Review, The
Lady, The
Lamplight, The
Left Curve
Lite
Literary Moments
Lonzie's Fried Chicken®
Louisiana Review, The
Lynx Eye
MacGuffin, The
Mail Call Journal
Many Mountains Moving
Margin
Mediphors
Mediphors
Merlyn's Pen

Milkwood Review
Minnesota Review, The
Mobius
Monkeyplanet
Montana Senior News
Musing Place, The
New Methods
96 Inc.
Nite-Writer's International Literary Arts Journal
Northeast Arts Magazine
Notre Dame Review
Other Voices (Canada)
Pacific Coast Journal
Palo Alto Review
Paumanok Review, The
Peninsular
Peralta Press, The
Pipe Smoker's Ephemeris, The
Plot Line Foyer
Poetry Forum Short Stories
Portland Magazine
Portland Review
Pulp Eternity Online
Purpose
Queen's Quarterly
Rabbit Hole Press, The
Raskolnikov's Cellar and The Lamplight
Rejected Quarterly, The
Rosebud™
S.L.U.G. fest, Ltd.
Seeking the Muse
Short Stuff Magazine for Grown-ups
Shyflower's Garden
Songs of Innocence
Spindrift
SPSM&H
State of Unbeing
Stepping Out of the Darkness
Storyteller, The
Struggle
Studentswrite.com
Talking River Review
Tampa Review
"Teak" Roundup
3 A.M. Magazine
Transition
Tucumcari Literary Review
Urban Spaghetti
Victory Park
Vincent Brothers Review, The
Virginia Adversaria
Weber Studies
Westcoast Fisherman, The
Windhover
Wisconsin Academy Review
Xavier Review
Yellow Sticky Notes
Yemassee
Zopilote

Book Publishers
Academy Chicago Publishers
Adventure Book Publishers
Authors Online Ltd.
Avon Books
Ballantine Books
Bancroft Press
Bantam Books
Bantam Dell Publishing Group, The
Beggar's Press
Beil, Publisher, Inc., Frederic C.
Bethany House Publishers
Branden Books
Caitlin Press, Inc.
Carolrhoda Books, Inc.
China Books & Periodicals, Inc.
Cleis Press
Crossway Books
Cumberland House Publishing
Dan River Press
Delacorte Press
Dell
Dial Press, The
DiskUs Publishing
Duckworth Press
Dutton
Éditions La Liberté Inc.
Forge Books
Fountainhead Productions, Inc.
Geringer Books, Laura
Glencannon Press, The
Godine, Publisher, Inc., David R.
GoldenIsle Publishers Inc.
Goose Lane Editions
Hale Limited, Robert
Harcourt Inc
Hawk Publishing Group
Hill Street Press
Hodder & Stoughton/Headline
Holt & Company, Henry
Houghton Mifflin Books for Children
Houghton Mifflin Company
Huntington Press
Island
LTD Books
MacAdam/Cage Publishing
McBooks Press
Morrow, William
Mountain State Press
My Weekly Story Collection
New American Library
Palari Publishing
Philomel Books
Pineapple Press
Pleasure Boat Studio
Plume
Pocket Books
Presidio Press
Pride and Imprints
Random House, Inc.
Reconciliation Press

Regency Press
Russell Publishing, James
St. Martin's Press
Scrivenery Press
Snowapple Press
Tropical Press, Inc.
University of Nevada Press
Van Neste Books
Voices from My Retreat
Writers Press, Inc.
Zondervan

HORROR

Magazines
Aberrations
Affable Neighbor
Affair of the Mind
Aguilar Expression, The
Alembic
Alien Zoo
Amazing Stories
Analecta
Anotherealm
Armchair Aesthete, The
Art:Mag
Aura Literary Arts Review
Aurealis
Barbaric Yawp
Beneath the Surface
Bibliophilos
Black Petals
Blue Skunk Companion, The
Brobdingnagian Times, The
Burning Sky
Carpe Noctem
Century
Children, Churches and Daddies Magazine
Cochran's Corner
Cotworld Creative Magazine
Dagger of the Mind
Dark Matter Chronicles
Deep Outside SFFH
Downstate Story
Dream International/Quarterly
Edge, Tales of Suspense, The
Electric Wine
Enigma
Evansville Review
Eyes
Flesh & Blood
Fugue
Futures Magazine
Grasslands Review
Griffin, The
Grue Magazine
Happy
Hunted News, The
In Posse Review
Indigenous Fiction
Interbang
Irreantum

Jackhammer E-Zine
Lite
Lynx Eye
Margin
Matriarch's Way: Journal of Female Supremacy
Merlyn's Pen
Missing Fez, The
Mobius
Monkeyplanet
Musing Place, The
New Writing
Night Terrors
Office Number One
Orphic Chronicle, The
Outer Darkness
Outer Rim—The Zine, The
Paumanok Review, The
Peninsular
Penny Dreadful
Peralta Press, The
Playboy Magazine
Psychic Radio, The
Pulp Eternity Online
QWF (Quality Women's Fiction)
Ralph's Review
Raskolnikov's Cellar and The Lamplight
Samsara
Seeking the Muse
Shyflower's Garden
Silver Web, The
Snake Nation Review
Space and Time
SPSM&H
State of Unbeing
Strand Magazine, The
3 A.M. Magazine
Threshold, The
Twilight Showcase
Urban Spaghetti
Urbanite, The
Visions & Voices
Weird Tales
Yellow Sticky Notes

Book Publishers

Adventure Book Publishers
Alexandria Digital Literature
Authors Online Ltd.
Bancroft Press
Beggar's Press
Dan River Press
Darktales Publications
Design Image Group Inc., The
DiskUs Publishing
Enigmatic Press
First Amendment Press International Company
Forge Books
Fountainhead Productions, Inc.
Hawk Publishing Group
ImaJinn Books
Leisure Books
LTD Books

Midknight Club, The
Morrow, William
New American Library
Palari Publishing
Pocket Books
Random House, Inc.
RavenHaus Publishing
ROC
St. Martin's Press
Scherf Books
Tor Books
Write Way Publishing

HUMOR/SATIRE

Magazines

About Such Things
Acorn, The
Advocate, PKA's Publication
Affable Neighbor
Affair of the Mind
AKP Zine
Algonquin Roundtable Review
Amelia
Analecta
Anthology
Ararat Quarterly
Armchair Aesthete, The
Art Times
Art:Mag
Asian Pacific American Journal
Aura Literary Arts Review
Azorean Express, The
babysue
Balloon Life
Barbaric Yawp
Bark, The
Bathtub Gin
Bear Essential Deluxe, The
BEEF
Beneath the Surface
Bibliophilos
Black Jack
Blue Mesa Review
Blue Skunk Companion, The
Blueline
Boys' Life
Briar Cliff Review, The
Brobdingnagian Times, The
Callaloo
Capers Aweigh
Caribbean Writer, The
Chanteh
Chiron Review
Circle Magazine, The
Cochran's Corner
Collages and Bricolages
Companion in Zeor, A
Concho River Review
Corona
Cotworld Creative Magazine
Crab Creek Review

Cream City Review, The
CZ's Magazine
Desperate Act
Dialogue
Dixie Phoenix
Downstate Story
Dream International/Quarterly
Dreams & Visions
1812
Enigma
Eureka Literary Magazine
Evansville Review
Event
Explorations
Fiction
Free Focus/Ostentatious Mind
Fugue
Funny Times, The
Futures Magazine
Gertrude
Gettysburg Review, The
Golf Journal
Gotta Write Network Litmag
Grasslands Review
Green Hills Literary Lantern, The
Green Mountains Review
Green's Magazine
Griffin, The
Happy
Harper's Magazine
Hawaii Pacific Review
Heartlands Today, The
Hemispheres
Higginsville Reader, The
High Plains Literary Review
Hill and Holler
Home Times
Hurricane Alice
Hybolics
Iconoclast, The
Idiot, The
Illya's Honey
In Posse Review
In the Family
Indigenous Fiction
Interbang
International Quarterly
Irreantum
Japanophile
Jewish Currents Magazine
Journal of Polymorphous Perversity
Karamu
Karitos Review, The
Kenyon Review, The
Kerem
Krax Magazine
Lamplight, The
Leapings Literary Magazine
Light Quarterly
Liquid Ohio
Lite

Literary Moments
Little Magazine, The
Long Shot
Lonzie's Fried Chicken®
Lullwater Review
Lynx Eye
MacGuffin, The
Many Mountains Moving
Matriarch's Way: Journal of Female Supremacy
Mediphors
Mediphors
Medusa's Hairdo Magazine
Merlyn's Pen
Milkwood Review
Missing Fez, The
Mississippi Review
Missouri Review, The
MJ's Walkabout
Mobius
Monkeyplanet
Musing Place, The
Nebraska Review, The
New Delta Review
New England Writers' Network
New Letters Magazine
New Writing
New York Stories
News of the Brave New World
Nightfire
96 Inc.
Nite-Writer's International Literary Arts Journal
Nuthouse
Oak, The
Office Number One
Other Voices (Canada)
Other Voices (Illinois)
Oxford Magazine
Pacific Coast Journal
Palo Alto Review
Pangolin Papers
Paumanok Review, The
Pearl
Pegasus Review, The
Peninsular
Peralta Press, The
Pikeville Review
Pipe Smoker's Ephemeris, The
Playboy Magazine
Pleiades
Plot Line Foyer
Portland Review
Poskisnolt Press
Primavera
Quarter After Eight
Queen's Quarterly
QWF (Quality Women's Fiction)
Ralph's Review
Rambunctious Review
Raskolnikov's Cellar and The Lamplight
Reform Judaism
Rejected Quarterly, The

Renaissance Online Magazine
Rhino
Rio Grande Review
River Styx
Rocket Press
Rockford Review, The
Rosebud™
S.L.U.G. fest, Ltd.
Salt Hill
Sanskrit
Seeking the Muse
Shades of December
Shattered Wig Review
Short Stuff Magazine for Grown-ups
Shyflower's Garden
Side Show
Skylark
Slipstream
Snake Nation Review
Southern Humanities Review
SPSM&H
State of Unbeing
Stepping Out of the Darkness
Storyteller, The
Stovepipe
Struggle
Studentswrite.com
sub-TERRAIN
Sulphur River Literary Review
Sycamore Review
Talebones
Talking River Review
"Teak" Roundup
Thema
3 A.M. Magazine
Threshold, The
Thresholds Quarterly
Transcendent Visions
Transition
Troika Magazine
Tucumcari Literary Review
TWA Ambassador
12-Gauge.com
Urban Graffiti
Urban Spaghetti
Urbanite, The
Victory Park
Vincent Brothers Review, The
Virginia Adversaria
Virginia Quarterly Review
Wascana Review of Contemporary Poetry and Short
    Fiction
Weber Studies
Westcoast Fisherman, The
Westview
Whetstone
White Crow, The
Wilmington Blues
Windhover
Wisconsin Academy Review
Writer's Guidelines & News

Writing for Our Lives
Yarns and Such
Yellow Silk
Yemassee
Zuzu's Petals Quarterly

Book Publishers

Acme Press
Adventure Book Publishers
Affable Neighbor
Ageless Press
Authors Online Ltd.
Bancroft Press
Beggar's Press
Black Heron Press
Caitlin Press, Inc.
Catbird Press
Centennial Publications
Cleis Press
Cross-Cultural Communications
Dan River Press
Davenport, Publishers, May
DiskUs Publishing
Duckworth Press
First Amendment Press International Company
Fountainhead Productions, Inc.
Geringer Books, Laura
Glencannon Press, The
GoldenIsle Publishers Inc.
Hawk Publishing Group
Holt & Company, Henry
Houghton Mifflin Books for Children
Kensington Publishing Corp.
Leapfrog Press
Morrow, William
Pick Pocket Books
Pleasure Boat Studio
Pocket Books
Quixote Press
Random House, Inc.
Russell Publishing, James
Soft Skull Press Inc.
Sweet Lady Moon Press
University of Nevada Press
Van Neste Books
Vista Publishing, Inc.
Voices from My Retreat
Writers Direct

LESBIAN

Magazines

ACM (Another Chicago Magazine)
Adrift
Affable Neighbor
Affair of the Mind
Amelia
American Writing
Analecta
Art Times
Art:Mag
Asian Pacific American Journal
Aura Literary Arts Review

Bathtub Gin
Beneath the Surface
Black Lace
Blue Mesa Review
Blue Moon Review, The
Bookpress
Carpe Noctem
Children, Churches and Daddies Magazine
Contact Advertising
Cotworld Creative Magazine
Edge, Tales of Suspense, The
Evansville Review
Feminist Studies
Frontiers
Futures Magazine
Gargoyle
Gay Chicago Magazine
Gertrude
Happy
Home Planet News
Hurricane Alice
Iksperament
Illya's Honey
In Posse Review
In the Family
Interbang
Iris (VA)
Jabberwock Review, The
Karamu
Kenyon Review, The
Lilith Magazine
Long Shot
Lullwater Review
Lynx Eye
Many Mountains Moving
Margin
Minnesota Review, The
Mobius
Monkeyplanet
Musing Place, The
New York Stories
On Our Backs
Options
Other Voices (Canada)
Oxford Magazine
Painted Bride Quarterly
Paperplates
Peninsular
Peralta Press, The
Portland Review
Poskisnolt Press
Primavera
Prisoners of the Night
Pulp Eternity Online
Quarter After Eight
QWF (Quality Women's Fiction)
Rio Grande Review
River Styx
Salt Hill
Sanskrit
Shattered Wig Review

Shyflower's Garden
Sinister Wisdom
Snake Nation Review
So to Speak
SPSM&H
State of Unbeing
Talking River Review
This Magazine
Threshold, The
Transcendent Visions
12-Gauge.com
Urban Graffiti
Weber Studies
Writing for Our Lives
WV
Yellow Silk
Yemassee
Zuzu's Petals Quarterly

Book Publishers

Affable Neighbor
Alyson Publications, Inc.
Arsenal Pulp Press
Aunt Lute Books
Authors Online Ltd.
Bancroft Press
Calyx Books
Carolina Wren Press, Inc.
Circlet Press
Cleis Press
DiskUs Publishing
Down There Press
Feminist Press at the City University of New York, The
Firebrand Books
First Amendment Press International Company
Hill Street Press
Hollow Earth Publishing
Houghton Mifflin Company
Insomniac Press
Kensington Publishing Corp.
Leapfrog Press
Lintel
Morrow, William
Naiad Press, Inc., The
New Victoria Publishers
Palari Publishing
Post-Apollo Press, The
Pride and Imprints
Ragweed Press Inc./gynergy books
Rising Tide Press
Sans Soleil
Sapphire Books
Seal Press
Soft Skull Press Inc.
Spinsters Ink
Stonewall Inn

LITERARY

Magazines

Abiko Quarterly with James, The
About Such Things

Absinthe Literary Review, The
ACM (Another Chicago Magazine)
Acorn, The
Adrift
Advocate, PKA's Publication
Aethlon
Affable Neighbor
Affair of the Mind
Aim Magazine
Alaska Quarterly Review
Alembic
Algonquin Roundtable Review
Alsop Review, The
Amelia
American Literary Review
American Writing
Amethyst Review, The
Analecta
Anthology
Antietam Review
Antigonish Review, The
Antioch Review
Apostrophe
Appalachian Heritage
Arachne, Inc.
Ararat Quarterly
Archipelago
Armchair Aesthete, The
Art Times
Artful Dodge
Art:Mag
Asian Pacific American Journal
Atlantic Monthly, The
Aura Literary Arts Review
Aurealis
Azorean Express, The
B&A: New Fiction
Babel
Baltimore Review, The
Barbaric Yawp
Barcelona Review, The
Bark, The
Bathtub Gin
Baybury Review
BBR Magazine
Beacon Street Review
Bear Essential Deluxe, The
BEEF
Bellingham Review, The
Bellowing Ark
Beloit Fiction Journal
Beneath the Surface
Best Magazine
Bibliophilos
Black Jack
Black Warrior Review
Blue Mesa Review
Blue Moon Review, The
Blue Skunk Companion, The
Blueline
Bookpress

Boston Review
Boulevard
Brain, Child
Briar Cliff Review, The
Brilliant Corners
Brobdingnagian Times, The
Brown Critique, The
Button
Byline
Callaloo
Cambrensis
Campus Life Magazine
Capers Aweigh
Capilano Review, The
Caribbean Writer, The
Carolina Quarterly
Carve Magazine
Cayo
Cenotaph
Century
Chanteh
Chapman
Chariton Review, The
Chattahoochee Review, The
Chelsea
Chicago Review
Children, Churches and Daddies Magazine
Chiron Review
Chrysalis Reader
Cimarron Review
Circle Magazine, The
City Primeval
Citycycle Motorcycle News Magazine
Climbing Art, The
Collages and Bricolages
Colorado Review
Columbia: A Journal of Literature & Art
Compost
Concho River Review
Conduit
Confrontation
Corona
Cottonwood
Cotworld Creative Magazine
Country Woman
Crab Creek Review
Crab Orchard Review
Crania
Cream City Review, The
Crescent Review, The
Crucible
CZ's Magazine
Dalhousie Review, The
Dead Mule, The
Denver Quarterly
Descant
Desperate Act
Distillery, The
Dixie Phoenix
Doubletake
Downstate Story

Dream International/Quarterly
Dreams & Visions
Duct Tape Press
1812
Emrys Journal
Epoch Magazine
Esquire
Eureka Literary Magazine
Evansville Review
Event
EWGPresents
Explorations
Feminist Studies
Fiction
Fiddlehead, The
First Class
Florida Review, The
Flyway
Folio: A Literary Journal
Frank
Free Focus/Ostentatious Mind
Fugue
Futures Magazine
Gargoyle
Geist
George & Mertie's Place: Rooms with a View
Georgia Review, The
Gertrude
Gettysburg Review, The
Ginosko
Glimmer Train Stories
Good Housekeeping
Gotta Write Network Litmag
Grain
Grand Street
Granta
Grasslands Review
Green Hills Literary Lantern, The
Green Mountains Review
Green Tricycle, The
Green's Magazine
Greensboro Review, The
Griffin, The
Gulf Coast
Gulf Stream Magazine
Happy
Hard Row to Hoe Division
Hawaii Pacific Review
Hayden's Ferry Review
Heartlands Today, The
Heaven Bone
Hemispheres
Hidden Manna
Higginsville Reader, The
High Plains Literary Review
Hill and Holler
Home Planet News
Home Times
Horsethief's Journal, The
Hudson Review, The
Hunted News, The

Hybolics
Iconoclast, The
Idaho Review, The
Iksperament
Illya's Honey
In Posse Review
Indiana Review
Indigenous Fiction
Interbang
International Quarterly
Iowa Review, The
Ireland's Own
Iris (VA)
Irreantum
Italian Americana
Jabberwock Review, The
Japanophile
Jewish Currents Magazine
Journal, The (Ohio)
Journal of African Travel-Writing, The
Kaleidoscope
Kalliope
Karamu
Karitos Review, The
Kelsey Review
Kenyon Review, The
Kerem
Kestrel
Kiosk
Krater Quarterly
Lady, The
Lady Churchill's Rosebud Wristlet
Lamplight, The
Landfall/University of Otago Press
Larcom Review, The
Leapings Literary Magazine
Left Curve
Licking River Review, The
Light Quarterly
Lilith Magazine
Liquid Ohio
Lite
Literal Latté
Literary Moments
Literary Review, The
Little Magazine, The
Long Shot
Long Story, The
Lonzie's Fried Chicken®
Lost and Found Times
Louisiana Literature
Louisville Review, The
Lullwater Review
Lynx Eye
MacGuffin, The
Madison Review, The
Malahat Review
Manoa
Many Mountains Moving
Margin
Marlboro Review, The

Massachusetts Review, The
Matriarch's Way: Journal of Female Supremacy
McSweeney's
Mediphors
Medusa's Hairdo Magazine
Merlyn's Pen
Michigan Quarterly Review
Mid-American Review
Midday Moon, The
Milkwood Review
Millennium: A Journal for Tomorrowland
Mindprints
Minnesota Review, The
Missing Fez, The
Mississippi Review
Missouri Review, The
Mobius
Monkeyplanet
Ms Magazine
Musing Place, The
NA'AMAT Woman
Nebo
Nebraska Review, The
Nerve Cowboy
New Delta Review
New England Review
New England Writers' Network
New Letters Magazine
New Orleans Review
New Shetlander
New Welsh Review
New Writing
New York Stories
New Yorker, The
Nightfire
96 Inc.
Nite-Writer's International Literary Arts Journal
North American Review, The
Northeast Arts Magazine
Northwest Review
Northwoods Journal
Notre Dame Review
Now & Then
Nuvein Online
Oasis
Office Number One
Ohio Review, The
Old Crow Review
Other Voices (Canada)
Other Voices (Illinois)
Oxford American, The
Oxford Magazine
Oyster Boy Review of Fiction and Poetry
Pacific Coast Journal
Pacific Enterprise
Painted Bride Quarterly
Palo Alto Review
Pangolin Papers
Paperplates
Paris Review, The
Parting Gifts

Partisan Review
Passages North
Paumanok Review, The
Pearl
Pegasus Review, The
Peninsular
Pennsylvania English
People's Friend
Peralta Press, The
Pif
Pig Iron Press
Pikeville Review
Pipe Smoker's Ephemeris, The
PLANET-The Welsh Internationalist
Plaza, The
Pleiades
Ploughshares
Poetry Forum Short Stories
Porcupine Literary Arts Magazine
Porter Cosmographic, Bern
Portland Magazine
Portland Review
Poskisnolt Press
Potomac Review
Prairie Fire
Prairie Journal of Canadian Literature, The
Prairie Schooner
Primavera
Prism International
Prisoners of the Night
Prose Menagerie, The
Provincetown Arts
Puckerbrush Review
Puerto Del Sol
Quarter After Eight
Quarterly West
Queen's Quarterly
QWF (Quality Women's Fiction)
Rain Crow
Ralph's Review
Rambunctious Review
Raskolnikov's Cellar and The Lamplight
Rattapallax
Raven Chronicles, The
RealPoetik
Recursive Angel
Red Cedar Review
Red Rock Review
Red Wheelbarrow
Reflect
Reflections
Rejected Quarterly, The
Rhino
Rio Grande Review
River Styx
Roanoke Review
Rocket Press
Rockford Review, The
Room of One's Own
Rosebud™
S.L.U.G. fest, Ltd.

Salt Hill
Samsara
Sanskrit
Santa Monica Review
Seeking the Muse
Seems
Sepia
Seventeen
Sewanee Review, The
Shades of December
Shadow Voices
Shattered Wig Review
Shenandoah
Short Stories Bimonthly
Shyflower's Garden
Side Show
Skidrow Penthouse
Skiptracer
Skylark
Slipstream
Small Pond Magazine, The
Snake Nation Review
Snowy Egret
SNReview
So to Speak
Soft Door, The
South Carolina Review
South Dakota Review
Southern Review, The
Southwest Review
Southwestern American Literature
Sou'Wester
Spinning Jenny
SPSM&H
Stand Magazine
State of Unbeing
StoryQuarterly
Storyteller, The
Stovepipe
Struggle
Studentswrite.com
sub-TERRAIN
Sulphur River Literary Review
SunDog: The Southeast Review
Sycamore Review
Takahe
Talking River Review
Tameme
Tampa Review
"Teak" Roundup
Tears in the Fence
Texas Review, The
Thema
Thin Air
Third Alternative, The
Third Coast
Third Half Magazine, The
This Magazine
Threepenny Review, The
Threshold, The
Tin House

Transition
Triquarterly
Troika Magazine
Tucumcari Literary Review
12-Gauge.com
Unmuzzled Ox
Up Dare?
Urban Spaghetti
Urbanite, The
Valley Grapevine
Victory Park
Vincent Brothers Review, The
Virginia Adversaria
Virginia Quarterly Review
Wasafiri
Wascana Review of Contemporary Poetry and Short
    Fiction
Washington Square
Web Del Sol
Weber Studies
Wespennest
West Coast Line
Western Humanities Review
Westview
Whetstone
Whiskey Island Magazine
White Crow, The
Willow Springs
Wilmington Blues
Windhover
Wisconsin Academy Review
Wisconsin Review
Witness
Worcester Review, The
World of English, The
Writer to Writer
Writers' Forum
Writer's Guidelines & News
Writing for Our Lives
WV
Xavier Review
Yale Review, The
Yalobusha Review, The
Yankee Magazine
Yellow Silk
Yellow Sticky Notes
Yemassee
Zoetrope
Zopilote
Zuzu's Petals Quarterly
Zyzzyva

Book Publishers
Affable Neighbor
Ageless Press
Anvil Press
Arcade Publishing
Arsenal Pulp Press
Arte Publico Press
Authors Online Ltd.
Avon Books
Bancroft Press

Banks Channel Books
Bantam Books
Bantam Dell Publishing Group, The
Beach Holme Publishers Ltd.
Beggar's Press
Beil, Publisher, Inc., Frederic C.
Beneath the Underground
Bilingual Press/Editorial Bilingüe
Birch Brook Press
Black Heron Press
Books for All Times, Inc.
Borealis Press
Branden Books
Broadway Books
Broken Boulder Press
Broken Jaw Press
Cadmus Editions
Calyx Books
Carolina Wren Press, Inc.
Carroll & Graf Publishers, Inc.
Catbird Press
China Books & Periodicals, Inc.
Christchurch Publishers Ltd.
Coffee House Press
Cross-Cultural Communications
Crossway Books
Dan River Press
Daniel and Company, Publishers, John
Delacorte Press
Dell
Dial Press, The
DiskUs Publishing
Dufour Editions
Dutton
Ecco Press, The
Éditions du Vermillon, Les
Éditions La Liberté Inc.
FC2
Feminist Press at the City University of New York, The
First Amendment Press International Company
Fountainhead Productions, Inc.
Four Walls Eight Windows
Geringer Books, Laura
Godine, Publisher, Inc., David R.
Goose Lane Editions
Graywolf Press
GreyCore Press
Grove/Atlantic, Inc.
Guernica Editions
Hampton Roads Publishing Company, Inc.
Hawk Publishing Group
Helicon Nine Editions
Hill Street Press
Hodder & Stoughton/Headline
Hollow Earth Publishing
Holt & Company, Henry
Houghton Mifflin Books for Children
Houghton Mifflin Company
Insomniac Press
Island

Karnak House
Knopf, Alfred A.
Leapfrog Press
Livingston Press
LTD Books
MacAdam/Cage Publishing
March Street Press
Micah Publications, Inc.
Milkweed Editions
Morrow, William
Multnomah Publishers, Inc.
New American Library
New Hope Books, Inc.
New Rivers Press
Newest Publishers Ltd.
Norton & Company, Inc., W.W.
Owl Books
Palari Publishing
Philomel Books
Picador USA
Pick Pocket Books
Pineapple Press
Pipers' Ash Ltd.
Pleasure Boat Studio
Plume
Pocket Books
Post-Apollo Press, The
Prairie Journal Press
Pudding House Publications
Putnam's Sons, G.P.
Quartet Books Limited
Random House, Inc.
Red Deer Press
Ronsdale Press
Russell Publishing, James
St. Martin's Press
Salvo Press
Sans Soleil
Scherf Books
Scrivenery Press
Seal Press
Secker & Warburg
Second Chance Press and the Permanent Press
Serpent's Tail
Seven Stories Press
Snowapple Press
Soft Skull Press Inc.
Soho Press
Southern Methodist University Press
Spectra Books
Stones Point Press
Stonewall Inn
Stormline Press
Sweet Lady Moon Press
Talese, Nan A.
Thistledown Press
Turnstone Press
University Press of New England
Van Neste Books
Véhicule Press
Viking

Vintage
Voices from My Retreat
White Pine Press
Writers Direct
Zoland Books, Inc.

MAINSTREAM/ CONTEMPORARY

Magazines
ACM (Another Chicago Magazine)
Acorn, The
Adrift
Advocate, PKA's Publication
Aguilar Expression, The
Alaska Quarterly Review
Amelia
American Literary Review
American Writing
Analecta
Antietam Review
Antigonish Review, The
Antioch Review
Ararat Quarterly
Armchair Aesthete, The
Art Times
Art:Mag
Asian Pacific American Journal
Associate Reformed Presbyterian, The
Atlantic Monthly, The
Azorean Express, The
Baltimore Review, The
Barbaric Yawp
Bathtub Gin
Bellowing Ark
Beloit Fiction Journal
Bibliophilos
Black Jack
Black Warrior Review
Blue Mesa Review
Blue Moon Review, The
Blue Skunk Companion, The
Blueline
Bomb Magazine
Boston Review
Boulevard
Brain, Child
Briar Cliff Review, The
Brilliant Corners
Callaloo
Capers Aweigh
Caribbean Writer, The
Cenotaph
Chanteh
Chariton Review, The
Chattahoochee Review, The
Chelsea
Chicago Review
Children, Churches and Daddies Magazine
Chiron Review
Christianity and the Arts
Chrysalis Reader

Cimarron Review
Circle Magazine, The
Clark Street Review
Climbing Art, The
Collages and Bricolages
Colorado Review
Concho River Review
Confrontation
Corona
Cosmopolitan Magazine
Cotworld Creative Magazine
Crab Creek Review
Crucible
CZ's Magazine
Desperate Act
Dialogue
Discovery Trails
Dixie Phoenix
Downstate Story
Dreams & Visions
1812
Emrys Journal
Epoch Magazine
Esquire
Eureka Literary Magazine
Evansville Review
Event
Eyes
Feminist Studies
Fiction
First Class
Florida Review, The
Folio: A Literary Journal
Free Focus/Ostentatious Mind
Fugue
Futures Magazine
Gargoyle
Gertrude
Gettysburg Review, The
Gotta Write Network Litmag
Grain
Grasslands Review
Green Hills Literary Lantern, The
Green Mountains Review
Green's Magazine
Greensboro Review, The
Griffin, The
Grit
Gulf Coast
Gulf Stream Magazine
Harper's Magazine
Hawaii Pacific Review
Hayden's Ferry Review
Heartlands Today, The
Hemispheres
Higginsville Reader, The
High Plains Literary Review
Hill and Holler
Home Planet News
Home Times
Horsethief's Journal, The

CATEGORY INDEX

Hunted News, The
Iconoclast, The
Illya's Honey
Indigenous Fiction
Inky Trail News
Interbang
International Quarterly
Iris (VA)
Irreantum
Jabberwock Review, The
Japanophile
Jewish Currents Magazine
Journal, The (Pennsylvania)
Karamu
Karitos Review, The
Kenyon Review, The
Krater Quarterly
Ladies' Home Journal
Lady, The
Larcom Review, The
Leapings Literary Magazine
Left Curve
Licking River Review, The
Literary Moments
Long Story, The
Lonzie's Fried Chicken®
Lost and Found Times
Louisiana Literature
Lullwater Review
Lynx Eye
MacGuffin, The
Manoa
Many Mountains Moving
Margin
Mediphors
Medusa's Hairdo Magazine
Merlyn's Pen
Midday Moon, The
Missing Fez, The
Mississippi Review
Missouri Review, The
Mobius
Monkeyplanet
Musing Place, The
NA'AMAT Woman
Nebo
Nebraska Review, The
New Delta Review
New England Writers' Network
New Letters Magazine
New Methods
New Orleans Review
New Writing
New York Stories
New Yorker, The
Nightfire
Nite-Writer's International Literary Arts Journal
North Atlantic Review
Northwest Review
Northwoods Journal
Oak, The

Ohio Review, The
Old Crow Review
Other Voices (Illinois)
Painted Bride Quarterly
Palo Alto Review
Paperplates
Partisan Review
Passages North
Paumanok Review, The
Pearl
Pennsylvania English
Peralta Press, The
Pikeville Review
Playboy Magazine
Pleiades
Plot Line Foyer
Poetry Forum Short Stories
Porcupine Literary Arts Magazine
Portland Magazine
Portland Review
Poskisnolt Press
Prairie Fire
Prairie Journal of Canadian Literature, The
Primavera
Prism International
Puerto Del Sol
Pulp Eternity Online
Quarter After Eight
Quarterly West
Queen's Quarterly
Rain Crow
Rambunctious Review
Red Rock Review
Redbook
Rejected Quarterly, The
Rhino
Rio Grande Review
River Styx
Rosebud™
S.L.U.G. fest, Ltd.
St. Anthony Messenger
Samsara
Sanskrit
Seeking the Muse
Sewanee Review, The
Shades of December
Shattered Wig Review
Short Stories Bimonthly
Short Stuff Magazine for Grown-ups
Shyflower's Garden
Side Show
Skidrow Penthouse
Skiptracer
Skylark
Slipstream
Snake Nation Review
SNReview
So to Speak
Soft Door, The
South Carolina Review
South Dakota Review

Southwestern American Literature
Spindrift
SPSM&H
Storyteller, The
Struggle
Studentswrite.com
Sulphur River Literary Review
Sycamore Review
Talking River Review
Tampa Review
"Teak" Roundup
Texas Review, The
Thema
Thin Air
This Magazine
Threshold, The
Triquarterly
Troika Magazine
Tucumcari Literary Review
Unmuzzled Ox
Urban Spaghetti
Valley Grapevine
Victory Park
Vincent Brothers Review, The
Virginia Adversaria
Washington Square
Weber Studies
Westview
Whetstone
Wisconsin Academy Review
Writers' Forum
Writer's Guidelines & News
Xavier Review
Yale Review, The
Yellow Sticky Notes
Zoetrope
Zyzzyva

Book Publishers
Absey & Co., Inc.
Ageless Press
Anvil Press
Arcade Publishing
Arte Publico Press
Authors Online Ltd.
Ballantine Books
Bancroft Press
Bantam Books
Bantam Dell Publishing Group, The
Berkley Publishing Group, The
Black Heron Press
Borealis Press
Branden Books
Caitlin Press, Inc.
Calyx Books
Carroll & Graf Publishers, Inc.
Coffee House Press
Cross-Cultural Communications
Crossway Books
Dan River Press
Delacorte Press
Dell

Dial Press, The
DiskUs Publishing
Duckworth Press
Dunne Books, Thomas
Dutton
Éditions La Liberté Inc.
Eriksson, Publisher, Paul S.
Feminist Press at the City University of New York, The
First Amendment Press International Company
Forge Books
Fountainhead Productions, Inc.
Glencannon Press, The
GoldenIsle Publishers Inc.
Goose Lane Editions
GreyCore Press
Hale Limited, Robert
HarperTorch
Hawk Publishing Group
Helicon Nine Editions
Hodder & Stoughton/Headline
Holt & Company, Henry
Houghton Mifflin Company
Huntington Press
Insomniac Press
Island
Jesperson Press Ltd.
Kensington Publishing Corp.
Knopf, Alfred A.
Leapfrog Press
LTD Books
MacAdam/Cage Publishing
Majestic Books
Morrow, William
New American Library
New Hope Books, Inc.
New Rivers Press
Owl Books
Palari Publishing
Papier-Mache
Pineapple Press
Plume
Pocket Books
Putnam's Sons, G.P.
Random House, Inc.
Red Deer Press
St. Martin's Press
Scherf Books
Scrivenery Press
Second Chance Press and the Permanent Press
Snowapple Press
Stones Point Press
Tor Books
Ultramarine Publishing Co., Inc.
Van Neste Books
Viking
Vintage
Voices from My Retreat
Warner Books
Writers Direct
Zoland Books, Inc.

Zondervan

MILITARY/WAR
Magazines
Affair of the Mind
Analecta
Bibliophilos
Circle Magazine, The
City Primeval
Cotworld Creative Magazine
Fullosia Press
Interbang
Peralta Press, The
Shyflower's Garden
3 A.M. Magazine
Urban Spaghetti
Weber Studies
Yellow Sticky Notes

Book Publishers
Adventure Book Publishers
Authors Online Ltd.
Bancroft Press
Branden Books
DiskUs Publishing
Fountainhead Productions, Inc.
Glencannon Press, The
Insomniac Press
Morrow, William
Mountain State Press
Nautical & Aviation Publishing Co. of America Inc.,
    The
Naval Institute Press
Pocket Books
Presidio Press
Stones Point Press

MYSTERY/SUSPENSE
Magazines
Advocate, PKA's Publication
Aguilar Expression, The
Alembic
Amelia
Analecta
Anthology
Archaeology
Armchair Aesthete, The
Art:Mag
Beginners
Beneath the Surface
Bibliophilos
Blue Murder Magazine
Blue Skunk Companion, The
Boys' Life
Capers Aweigh
Cenotaph
Chat
Children, Churches and Daddies Magazine
Chrysalis Reader
Circle Magazine, The
City Primeval

Climbing Art, The
Cochran's Corner
Cosmopolitan Magazine
Cotworld Creative Magazine
Cozy Detective, The
Crimewave
CZ's Magazine
Dagger of the Mind
Dialogue
Discovery Trails
Downstate Story
Edge, Tales of Suspense, The
Eureka Literary Magazine
Evansville Review
Free Focus/Ostentatious Mind
Fugue
Fullosia Press
Futures Magazine
Green's Magazine
Griffin, The
Grit
Hardboiled
Hemispheres
Hitchcock's Mystery Magazine, Alfred
Horsethief's Journal, The
In Posse Review
Interbang
Irreantum
Japanophile
Kids' Highway
Lady, The
Lamplight, The
Leapings Literary Magazine
Lite
Literary Moments
Lynx Eye
Merlyn's Pen
Missing Fez, The
MJ's Walkabout
Monkeyplanet
Murderous Intent
Musing Place, The
Mystery Time
New England Writers' Network
New Mystery
Nightfire
Northeast Arts Magazine
Northwoods Journal
Outer Darkness
Palo Alto Review
Paumanok Review, The
Peralta Press, The
Plot Line Foyer
Poetry Forum Short Stories
Portland Review
Post, The
Prisoners of the Night
PSI
Pulp Eternity Online
Queen's Mystery Magazine, Ellery
Rejected Quarterly, The

Seeking the Muse
Short Stuff Magazine for Grown-ups
Shyflower's Garden
Skylark
Snake Nation Review
SPSM&H
Storyteller, The
Strand Magazine, The
Studentswrite.com
"Teak" Roundup
Thema
3 A.M. Magazine
Threshold, The
Tucumcari Literary Review
12-Gauge.com
Urban Spaghetti
Vincent Brothers Review, The
Virginia Adversaria
Weber Studies
Woman's World Magazine
Yarns and Such
Yellow Sticky Notes

Book Publishers
Adventure Book Publishers
Ageless Press
Arcade Publishing
Authors Online Ltd.
Avalon Books
Avon Books
Bancroft Press
Bantam Books
Bantam Dell Publishing Group, The
Beggar's Press
Berkley Publishing Group, The
Carroll & Graf Publishers, Inc.
Centennial Publications
Christchurch Publishers Ltd.
Compass Point Mysteries™/Tory Corner Editions™
Cumberland House Publishing
Dan River Press
Delacorte Press
Dell
Dial Press, The
DiskUs Publishing
Duckworth Press
Dunne Books, Thomas
Fawcett
First Amendment Press International Company
Forge Books
Fort Ross Inc.
Fountainhead Productions, Inc.
Gaslight Publications
Glencannon Press, The
Gryphon Books
Harcourt Inc.
Harlequin Enterprises, Ltd.
HarperTorch
Hawk Publishing Group
Hodder & Stoughton/Headline
Holt & Company, Henry
Houghton Mifflin Books for Children

Huntington Press
Insomniac Press
Island
Ivy League Press, Inc.
Kensington Publishing Corp.
LTD Books
Majestic Books
Morrow, William
Multnomah Publishers, Inc.
Mysterious Press, The
New American Library
New Hope Books, Inc.
New Victoria Publishers
Palari Publishing
Philomel Books
Pocket Books
Presidio Press
Publishers Syndication, International
Putnam's Sons, G.P.
Rainbow Books, Inc.
Random House, Inc.
RavenHaus Publishing
Regency Press
St. Martin's Press
Salvo Press
Scherf Books
Scrivenery Press
Silver Dagger Mysteries
Soho Press
Stonewall Inn
Tropical Press, Inc.
Turnstone Press
University of Nevada Press
Van Neste Books
Viking
Vista Publishing, Inc.
Walker and Company
Warner Books
Write Way Publishing
Zondervan

NEW AGE/MYSTIC/SPIRITUAL
Magazines
Affair of the Mind
Analecta
Bitter Oleander, The
Both Sides Now
Chrysalis Reader
Circle Magazine, The
Cotworld Creative Magazine
Foresight
Griffin, The
Interbang
Irreantum
Nightfire
Other Voices (Canada)
Peninsular
Psychic Radio, The
QWF (Quality Women's Fiction)
Shyflower's Garden
Skylark

Songs of Innocence
State of Unbeing
Visions & Voices
Weber Studies

Book Publishers
Ageless Press
Artemis Press
Authors Online Ltd.
Bancroft Press
Dan River Press
Dutton
First Amendment Press International Company
Hampton Roads Publishing Company, Inc.
Hollow Earth Publishing
ImaJinn Books
Midknight Club, The
Mountain State Press
New American Library
Plume
RavenHaus Publishing
Unity House
Writers Direct

PSYCHIC/SUPERNATURAL/ OCCULT
Magazines
Affable Neighbor
Affair of the Mind
Alien Zoo
Analecta
Art:Mag
Barbaric Yawp
Beneath the Surface
Black Petals
Blue Skunk Companion, The
Capers Aweigh
Carpe Noctem
Children, Churches and Daddies Magazine
Circle Magazine, The
Cotworld Creative Magazine
CZ's Magazine
Downstate Story
Dream International/Quarterly
Edge, Tales of Suspense, The
Eidolon
Electric Wine
Eureka Literary Magazine
Evansville Review
Eyes
Foresight
Free Focus/Ostentatious Mind
Futures Magazine
Grue Magazine
Happy
Heaven Bone
Indigenous Fiction
Interbang
Irreantum
Karitos Review, The
Lite

MacGuffin, The
Margin
Matriarch's Way: Journal of Female Supremacy
Missing Fez, The
Murderous Intent
Night Terrors
Nightfire
Northwoods Journal
Office Number One
Old Crow Review
Orphic Chronicle, The
Outer Darkness
Peninsular
Penny Dreadful
Peralta Press, The
Poskisnolt Press
Prisoners of the Night
Psychic Radio, The
Pulp Eternity Online
QWF (Quality Women's Fiction)
Ralph's Review
Rosebud™
Shades of December
Shattered Wig Review
Skidrow Penthouse
Snake Nation Review
Songs of Innocence
State of Unbeing
Thema
3 A.M. Magazine
Threshold, The
Thresholds Quarterly
Urbanite, The
Visions & Voices
Weber Studies
Weird Tales

Book Publishers
Affable Neighbor
Authors Online Ltd.
Bancroft Press
Dan River Press
DiskUs Publishing
First Amendment Press International Company
Fountainhead Productions, Inc.
Hampton Roads Publishing Company, Inc.
ImaJinn Books
Kensington Publishing Corp.
Majestic Books
Pocket Books
RavenHaus Publishing
Wilshire Book Co.
Write Way Publishing
Writers Direct

REGIONAL
Magazines
About Such Things
Acorn, The
Advocate, PKA's Publication
Amelia
Analecta

Antietam Review
Appalachian Heritage
Arachne, Inc.
Arkansas Review
Art:Mag
Asian Pacific American Journal
Azorean Express, The
Barbaric Yawp
Bibliophilos
Blue Mesa Review
Blue Moon Review, The
Blue Skunk Companion, The
Blueline
Bookpress
Boston Review
Briar Cliff Review, The
Callaloo
Capers Aweigh
Cayo
Chattahoochee Review, The
Climbing Art, The
Concho River Review
Confrontation
Corona
Cotworld Creative Magazine
Cream City Review, The
Crucible
Dixie Phoenix
Downstate Story
Emrys Journal
Eureka Literary Magazine
Evansville Review
Event
Fugue
Gettysburg Review, The
Green Hills Literary Lantern, The
Gulf Coast
Hawaii Pacific Review
Hayden's Ferry Review
Heartlands Today, The
Heaven Bone
Hemispheres
High Plains Literary Review
Hill and Holler
Horsethief's Journal, The
Hunted News, The
Illya's Honey
Indiana Review
Interbang
International Quarterly
Irreantum
Jabberwock Review, The
Japanophile
Karamu
Kelsey Review
Lady, The
Left Curve
Lonzie's Fried Chicken®
Louisiana Literature
Louisiana Review, The
Lullwater Review

Manoa
Margin
Monkeyplanet
Musing Place, The
New Methods
New York Stories
Northwoods Journal
Now & Then
Old Crow Review
Oxford American, The
Palo Alto Review
Partisan Review
Passages North
Pikeville Review
Pleiades
Portland Review
Potomac Review
Prairie Journal of Canadian Literature, The
Raven Chronicles, The
Rhino
Rockford Review, The
Rosebud™
S.L.U.G. fest, Ltd.
Sanskrit
Shattered Wig Review
Short Stuff Magazine for Grown-ups
Skylark
Snake Nation Review
So to Speak
South Dakota Review
Southern Humanities Review
Southwestern American Literature
Spindrift
SPSM&H
State of Unbeing
Storyboard
Storyteller, The
Struggle
Sycamore Review
Talking River Review
"Teak" Roundup
Thema
This Magazine
Transition
Tucumcari Literary Review
12-Gauge.com
Valley Grapevine
Victory Park
Vincent Brothers Review, The
Virginia Adversaria
Weber Studies
Westcoast Fisherman, The
Wisconsin Academy Review
Writers' Forum
Wy'East Historical Journal
Xavier Review
Yankee Magazine
Yarns and Such
Yellow Sticky Notes
Yemassee
Zuzu's Petals Quarterly

Zyzzyva

Book Publishers
Authors Online Ltd.
Bancroft Press
Beach Holme Publishers Ltd.
Beil, Publisher, Inc., Frederic C.
Blair, Publisher, John F.
Caitlin Press, Inc.
Compass Point Mysteries™/Tory Corner Editions™
Dan River Press
Down East Books
Duckworth Press
E.M. Press, Inc.
Feminist Press at the City University of New York,
    The
First Amendment Press International Company
Fountainhead Productions, Inc.
Hill Street Press
Jesperson Press Ltd.
Leapfrog Press
Lintel
Mountain State Press
Newest Publishers Ltd.
Philomel Books
Pineapple Press
Pleasure Boat Studio
Quixote Press
Ragweed Press Inc./gynergy books
Red Deer Press
Russell Publishing, James
Silver Dagger Mysteries
Texas Christian University Press
Tidewater Publishers
Turnstone Press
University of Nevada Press
University Press of New England
Van Neste Books
Vanessapress
Véhicule Press
Woodley Memorial Press
Writers Direct

RELIGIOUS/INSPIRATIONAL

Magazines
Abiko Quarterly with James, The
About Such Things
Analecta
Annals of St. Anne De Beaupré, The
Arachne, Inc.
Ararat Quarterly
Associate Reformed Presbyterian, The
Barbaric Yawp
Beloit Fiction Journal
Brown Critique, The
Christian Courier
Christianity and the Arts
Clubhouse
Clubhouse Magazine
Cochran's Corner
Cornerstone Magazine
Cotworld Creative Magazine

Crusader Magazine
CZ's Magazine
Discoveries
Discovery Trails
Dixie Phoenix
Dreams & Visions
Encounter
Evangel
Evansville Review
Friend Magazine, The
Griffin, The
Grit
Hidden Manna
Home Times
Hunted News, The
Indian Life
Indian Life Magazine
Irreantum
Karitos Review, The
Kerem
Kidz Ch@t
Lighthouse Story Collections
Liguorian
Lilith Magazine
Literary Moments
Live
Matriarch's Way: Journal of Female Supremacy
Mature Years
Messenger of the Sacred Heart
Miraculous Medal, The
My Friend
New England Writers' Network
New Era Magazine
Nite-Writer's International Literary Arts Journal
Now & Then
Pegasus Review, The
Plowman, The
Pockets
Poetry Forum Short Stories
Prayerworks
Psychic Radio, The
Purpose
Queen of All Hearts
Rabbit Hole Press, The
Reform Judaism
St. Anthony Messenger
Seek
Shyflower's Garden
Skipping Stones
Spirit
Standard
Stepping Out of the Darkness
Story Friends
Storyteller, The
Studio: A Journal of Christians Writing
"Teak" Roundup
Thresholds Quarterly
Touch
With
Xavier Review
Yellow Sticky Notes

Young Salvationist

Book Publishers
Authors Online Ltd.
Concordia Publishing House
Crossway Books
Dan River Press
DiskUs Publishing
Éditions du Vermillon, Les
Eerdmans Publishing Co., Wm. B.
First Amendment Press International Company
Fountainhead Productions, Inc.
GoldenIsle Publishers Inc.
Hemkunt Press
Leapfrog Press
Midknight Club, The
Morehouse Publishing Co.
Mountain State Press
Multnomah Publishers, Inc.
Post-Apollo Press, The
Revell Publishing
Russell Publishing, James
Scherf Books
Starburst Publishers
Tyndale House Publishers, Inc.
Unity House
Writers Direct
Zondervan

ROMANCE

Magazines
About Such Things
Advocate, PKA's Publication
Affable Neighbor
Aguilar Expression, The
Analecta
Beginners
Bibliophilos
Blue Skunk Companion, The
Bridal Guides
Brilliant Corners
Brobdingnagian Times, The
Carpe Noctem
Chat
Circle Magazine, The
Cochran's Corner
Cosmopolitan Magazine
Cotworld Creative Magazine
CZ's Magazine
Dialogue
Downstate Story
Eidolon
Eureka Literary Magazine
Evansville Review
Fugue
Futures Magazine
Gay Chicago Magazine
Gotta Write Network Litmag
Griffin, The
Grit
Home Times
Irreantum

Jive, Black Confessions, Black Romance, Bronze
   Thrills, Black Secrets
Lamplight, The
Literary Moments
Louisiana Review, The
Lynx Eye
Matriarch's Way: Journal of Female Supremacy
Merlyn's Pen
Moxie
Musing Place, The
New England Writers' Network
New Writing
Nightfire
Nite-Writer's International Literary Arts Journal
Northwoods Journal
Outer Darkness
Palo Alto Review
PeopleNet DisAbility DateNet Home Page
Plot Line Foyer
Poetry Forum Short Stories
Poskisnolt Press
Post, The
PSI
Pulp Eternity Online
Rabbit Hole Press, The
Rejected Quarterly, The
Rosebud™
St. Anthony Messenger
Seeking the Muse
Shades of December
Short Story Writers Showcase
Short Stuff Magazine for Grown-ups
Shyflower's Garden
Skylark
SPSM&H
Storyteller, The
Studentswrite.com
"Teak" Roundup
Threshold, The
Virginia Adversaria
Virginia Quarterly Review
Visions & Voices
Woman's World Magazine
Yellow Sticky Notes

Book Publishers
Adventure Book Publishers
Artemis Press
Authors Online Ltd.
Avalon Books
Avid Press, LLC
Avon Books
Bantam Books
Bantam Dell Publishing Group, The
Berkley Publishing Group, The
Dan River Press
Delacorte Press
Dell
Dial Press, The
DiskUs Publishing
Duckworth Press
First Amendment Press International Company

Are You Ready to Write Better and Get Paid For What You Write?

At **Writer's Digest School,** we want you to have both a "flair for words" *and* the marketing know-how it takes to give your writing the best shot at publication. That's why you'll work with a professional, published writer who has already mastered the rules of the game firsthand. A savvy mentor who can show you, through detailed critiques of the writing assignments you send in, how to effectively target your work and get it into the hands of the right editor.

Whether you write articles or short stories, nonfiction or novels, **Writer's Digest School** has a workshop that's right for you. Each provides a wealth of expertise and one goal: helping you break into the writing market.

So if you're serious about getting published, you owe it to yourself to check out **Writer's Digest School**. To find out more about us, simply fill out and return the card below. There's absolutely no obligation!

Workshop descriptions on the back ➡

Send Me Free Information!

I want to write better and sell more with the help of the professionals at **Writer's Digest School**. Send me free information about the workshop I've checked below:

☐ Novel Writing Workshop   ☐ Writing & Selling Short Stories
☐ Writing & Selling Nonfiction Articles ☐ Writing Life Stories
☐ Writer's Digest Criticism Service   ☐ The Elements of Effective Writing
☐ Getting Started in Writing   ☐ Marketing Your Nonfiction Book
                                         ☐ Screenwriting Workshop

Name _____

Address _____

City _____ State _____ ZIP _____

Phone: (Day) (_____)_____ (Eve.) (_____)_____

Email Address _____

To get your package even sooner, call 1-800-759-0963
Outside the U.S. call 1-513-531-2690 ext. 342

INSXX1X1

Novel Writing Workshop: Iron out your plot, create your main characters, develop a dramatic background, and complete the opening scenes and summary of your novel's complete story. Plus, you'll pinpoint potential publishers for your type of book.

NEW! **Getting Started in Writing:** From short fiction and novels to articles and nonfiction books, we'll help you discover where your natural writing talents lie.

Writing & Selling Short Stories: Learn how to create believable characters, write vivid, true-to-life dialogue, fill your scenes with conflict, and keep your readers on the edge of their seats.

Writing & Selling Nonfiction Articles: Master the components for effective article writing and selling. You'll learn how to choose attention-grabbing topics, conduct stirring interviews, write compelling query letters, and slant a single article for a variety of publications.

Writing Life Stories: Learn how to weave the important events of your personal or family's history into a heartfelt story. You'll plan a writing strategy, complete a dateline of events, and discover how to combine factual events with narrative flow.

Writer's Digest Criticism Service: Have an experienced, published writer review your manuscripts before you submit them for pay. Whether you write books, articles, short stories or poetry, you'll get professional, objective feedback on what's working well, what needs strengthening, and which markets you should pursue.

The Elements of Effective Writing: Discover how to conquer the pesky grammar and usage problems that hold so many writers back. You'll refresh your basic English composition skills through step-by-step lessons and writing exercises designed to help keep your manuscripts out of the rejection pile.

Marketing Your Nonfiction Book: You'll work with your mentor to create a book proposal that you can send directly to a publisher, develop and refine your book idea, write a chapter-by-chapter outline of your subject, line up your sources and information, write sample chapters, and complete your query letter.

Screenwriting Workshop: Learn to write for the silver screen! Work step by step with a professional screenwriter to craft your script, find out how to research the right agent or producer for your work, and get indispensable information about the Hollywood submission process.

Fort Ross Inc.
Fountainhead Productions, Inc.
GoldenIsle Publishers Inc.
Harlequin Enterprises, Ltd.
HarperTorch
Hodder & Stoughton/Headline
ImaJinn Books
Island
Kensington Publishing Corp.
Leisure Books
LionHearted Publishing, Inc.
Love Spell
LTD Books
Majestic Books
New American Library
Pipers' Ash Ltd.
Pocket Books
Ponder Publishing Inc.
Power of Love Publishing
RavenHaus Publishing
Red Sage Publishing, Inc.
Regency Press
Russell Publishing, James
Silhouette Books
Steeple Hill
Stones Point Press
Vista Publishing, Inc.
Warner Books

SCIENCE FICTION

Magazines

Aberrations
About Such Things
Absolute Magnitude
Advocate, PKA's Publication
Affable Neighbor
Alembic
Alien Zoo
Amazing Stories
Amelia
Analecta
Anotherealm
Anthology
Armchair Aesthete, The
Art Times
Artemis Magazine
Art:Mag
Asimov's Science Fiction
Aura Literary Arts Review
Aurealis
Barbaric Yawp
BBR Magazine
Bear Essential Deluxe, The
BEEF
Beginners
Beneath the Surface
Black Petals
Blue Skunk Companion, The
Boys' Life
Brobdingnagian Times, The
Burning Sky

Cafe Irreal, The
Callaloo
Capers Aweigh
Cenotaph
Century
Chat
Chrysalis Reader
Circle Magazine, The
Climbing Art, The
Cochran's Corner
Companion in Zeor, A
Cotworld Creative Magazine
Cozy Detective, The
Dagger of the Mind
Dark Matter Chronicles
Deep Outside SFFH
Dialogue
Downstate Story
Dream International/Quarterly
Dreams & Visions
Eidolon
Electric Wine
Eureka Literary Magazine
Evansville Review
First Class
Fugue
Futures Magazine
Gotta Write Network Litmag
Grasslands Review
Green's Magazine
Griffin, The
Grit
Happy
Hawaii Pacific Review
Home Planet News
Hurricane Alice
Iconoclast, The
In Posse Review
Indigenous Fiction
Interbang
Intertext
Irreantum
Jackhammer E-Zine
Karitos Review, The
Lady Churchill's Rosebud Wristlet
LC-39
Leading Edge, The
Leapings Literary Magazine
Left Curve
Lite
Literal Latté
Literary Moments
Long Shot
Lynx Eye
MacGuffin, The
Magazine of Fantasy & Science Fiction
Margin
Matriarch's Way: Journal of Female Supremacy
Mediphors
Medusa's Hairdo Magazine
Merlyn's Pen

Mindsparks
Missing Fez, The
MJ's Walkabout
Mobius
Monkeyplanet
Murderous Intent
Musing Place, The
Nightfire
Nimrod
Northwoods Journal
Nova Science Fiction Magazine
Of Unicorns and Space Stations
On Spec
Orphic Chronicle, The
Outer Darkness
Outer Rim—The Zine, The
Pacific Coast Journal
Palo Alto Review
Paumanok Review, The
Pegasus Online
Peninsular
Playboy Magazine
Plot Line Foyer
Poetry Forum Short Stories
Portland Review
Primavera
Prisoners of the Night
Psychic Radio, The
Pulp Eternity Online
Queen's Quarterly
QWF (Quality Women's Fiction)
Rabbit Hole Press, The
Rain Crow
Ralph's Review
Rejected Quarterly, The
Rockford Review, The
Rosebud℠
Samsara
Scifi.com
Seeking the Muse
Shades of December
Short Story Writers Showcase
Shyflower's Garden
Silver Web, The
Skidrow Penthouse
Skylark
Snake Nation Review
Space and Time
Spindrift
SPSM&H
State of Unbeing
Struggle
Studentswrite.com
Talebones
Terra Incognita
Thema
3 A.M. Magazine
Threshold, The
Thresholds Quarterly
12-Gauge.com
Urban Spaghetti

Vincent Brothers Review, The
Visions & Voices
Weber Studies
Yellow Silk
Yellow Sticky Notes
Zopilote

Book Publishers

Ace Science Fiction
Adventure Book Publishers
Affable Neighbor
Ageless Press
Alexandria Digital Literature
Authors Online Ltd.
Avon Books
Baen Books
Bancroft Press
Bantam Books
Bantam Dell Publishing Group, The
Berkley Publishing Group, The
Black Heron Press
Carroll & Graf Publishers, Inc.
Circlet Press
Dan River Press
Daw Books, Inc.
Del Rey Books
Delacorte Press
Dell
Dial Press, The
DiskUs Publishing
FC2
Feminist Press at the City University of New York,
   The
First Amendment Press International Company
Forge Books
Fort Ross Inc.
Fountainhead Productions, Inc.
Gryphon Books
Hawk Publishing Group
ImaJinn Books
Island
LTD Books
Majestic Books
Midknight Club, The
Morrow, William
New American Library
Pig Iron Press
Pipers' Ash Ltd.
Pride and Imprints
RavenHaus Publishing
ROC
St. Martin's Press
Salvo Press
Signal Crest
Soft Skull Press Inc.
Spectra Books
Tor Books
TSR, Inc.
Ultramarine Publishing Co., Inc.
Warner Aspect
Warner Books
Wesleyan University Press

Write Way Publishing
Writers Direct
W.W. Publications

SENIOR CITIZEN/ RETIREMENT
Magazines
Acorn, The
Advocate, PKA's Publication
Amelia
Christian Courier
Dialogue
Evansville Review
Liguorian
Mature Years
Montana Senior News
New York Stories
Nite-Writer's International Literary Arts Journal
Poetry Forum Short Stories
Poskisnolt Press
St. Anthony Messenger
Snake Nation Review
SPSM&H
Storyteller, The
Struggle
Tucumcari Literary Review
Vincent Brothers Review, The

SERIALIZED/EXCERPTED NOVEL
Magazines
Agni
American Writing
Art:Mag
Asian Pacific American Journal
Bathtub Gin
Bellowing Ark
Black Jack
Bomb Magazine
Callaloo
Capper's
Cozy Detective, The
Evansville Review
Gettysburg Review, The
Green Mountains Review
Lynx Eye
Madison Review, The
Manoa
Matriarch's Way: Journal of Female Supremacy
Musing Place, The
Now & Then
Nuvein Online
Other Voices (Illinois)
Potomac Review
Prairie Journal of Canadian Literature, The
Prism International
Puerto Del Sol
Quarter After Eight
Raskolnikov's Cellar and The Lamplight
River Styx
Rosebud™

Skylark
South Dakota Review
Southern Review, The
Spindrift
Threshold, The
Vincent Brothers Review, The
Virginia Quarterly Review
Willow Springs
Xavier Review

Book Publishers
Owen Publishers, Peter

SHORT STORY COLLECTIONS
Magazines
Affable Neighbor
Analecta
Ararat Quarterly
Bark, The
Bibliophilos
Brown Critique, The
First Class
Interbang
Lady Churchill's Rosebud Wristlet
News of the Brave New World
Painted Bride Quarterly
Rain Crow
Skiptracer
State of Unbeing
Stovepipe
Weber Studies

Book Publishers
Absey & Co., Inc.
Ageless Press
Anvil Press
Arsenal Pulp Press
Arte Publico Press
Artemis Press
Authors Online Ltd.
Beggar's Press
Beil, Publisher, Inc., Frederic C.
Beneath the Underground
Bilingual Press/Editorial Bilingüe
Books for All Times, Inc.
Branden Books
Broken Boulder Press
Caitlin Press, Inc.
Calyx Books
Carolina Wren Press, Inc.
Dan River Press
DiskUs Publishing
Dufour Editions
Ecco Press, The
Éditions du Vermillon, Les
Éditions La Liberté Inc.
FC2
First Amendment Press International Company
Goose Lane Editions
Graywolf Press
GreyCore Press
Helicon Nine Editions

Livingston Press
March Street Press
Micah Publications, Inc.
Midknight Club, The
New Rivers Press
Philomel Books
Piano Press
Pick Pocket Books
Pig Iron Press
Pipers' Ash Ltd.
Pleasure Boat Studio
Prairie Journal Press
Quixote Press
Random House, Inc.
RavenHaus Publishing
Sarabande Books, Inc.
Scrivenery Press
Secker & Warburg
Serpent's Tail
Signal Crest
Snowapple Press
Southern Methodist University Press
Stones Point Press
Sweet Lady Moon Press
Thistledown Press
TSR, Inc.
Ultramarine Publishing Co., Inc.
Véhicule Press
Vintage
Vista Publishing, Inc.
Voices from My Retreat
White Pine Press

SPORTS
Magazines
Advocate, PKA's Publication
Aethlon
Amelia
Appalachia Journal
Balloon Life
Beloit Fiction Journal
Bowhunter Magazine
Boys' Life
Boy's Quest
Christian Courier
Chrysalis Reader
Climbing Art, The
Clubhouse Magazine
Discovery Trails
Evansville Review
Fugue
Golf Journal
Home Times
Nite-Writer's International Literary Arts Journal
Northwoods Journal
Now & Then
Playboy Magazine
Rejected Quarterly, The
Skylark
Storyteller, The
"Teak" Roundup

Thema
12-Gauge.com

THRILLER/ESPIONAGE
Magazines
Affair of the Mind
Alembic
Analecta
Artemis Magazine
Aura Literary Arts Review
Bibliophilos
Cenotaph
Circle Magazine, The
City Primeval
Cotworld Creative Magazine
Crimewave
Fullosia Press
Futures Magazine
Griffin, The
Horsethief's Journal, The
Interbang
Irreantum
Missing Fez, The
MJ's Walkabout
Monkeyplanet
Plot Line Foyer
Pulp Eternity Online
Rabbit Hole Press, The
Seeking the Muse
Shyflower's Garden
State of Unbeing
Stepping Out of the Darkness
3 A.M. Magazine
Virginia Adversaria
Yellow Sticky Notes

Book Publishers
Ageless Press
Authors Online Ltd.
Avid Press, LLC
Bancroft Press
Bantam Books
Bantam Dell Publishing Group, The
Christchurch Publishers Ltd.
Cleis Press
Dan River Press
Delacorte Press
Dell
Dial Press, The
DiskUs Publishing
Dunne Books, Thomas
Dutton
First Amendment Press International Company
Forge Books
Fort Ross Inc.
Fountainhead Productions, Inc.
Glencannon Press, The
HarperTorch
Hawk Publishing Group
Hodder & Stoughton/Headline
Island
Kensington Publishing Corp.

Knopf, Alfred A.
LTD Books
Majestic Books
Morrow, William
New American Library
New Hope Books, Inc.
Palari Publishing
Plume
Presidio Press
Publishers Syndication, International
RavenHaus Publishing
St. Martin's Press
Salvo Press
Scherf Books
Scrivenery Press
Soho Press
Van Neste Books
Warner Books
Write Way Publishing
Writers Direct
Zondervan

TRANSLATIONS

Magazines
ACM (Another Chicago Magazine)
Adrift
Affable Neighbor
Affair of the Mind
Agni
Alaska Quarterly Review
Algonquin Roundtable Review
Amelia
American Writing
Antigonish Review, The
Antioch Review
Ararat Quarterly
Artful Dodge
Art:Mag
Asian Pacific American Journal
Bibliophilos
Bitter Oleander, The
Blue Moon Review, The
Blue Skunk Companion, The
Boston Review
Brown Critique, The
Cafe Irreal, The
Callaloo
Cenotaph
Chariton Review, The
Chelsea
Climbing Art, The
Colorado Review
Columbia: A Journal of Literature & Art
Compost
Conduit
Confrontation
Cotworld Creative Magazine
Crab Creek Review
Crab Orchard Review
Cream City Review, The
Dialogos

Dixie Phoenix
1812
Eureka Literary Magazine
Evansville Review
Fiction
Folio: A Literary Journal
Gargoyle
Grand Street
Green Mountains Review
Gulf Coast
Hawaii Pacific Review
Higginsville Reader, The
Horsethief's Journal, The
Hunted News, The
Hurricane Alice
Iksperament
India Currents
Indiana Review
Interbang
International Quarterly
Iowa Review, The
Irreantum
Jabberwock Review, The
Jewish Currents Magazine
Journal of African Travel-Writing, The
Karitos Review, The
Kenyon Review, The
Kestrel
Lady Churchill's Rosebud Wristlet
Left Curve
Lilith Magazine
Lynx Eye
MacGuffin, The
Manoa
Many Mountains Moving
Margin
Marlboro Review, The
Mid-American Review
Mississippi Review
New Delta Review
New Letters Magazine
New Orleans Review
New Writing
Nimrod
96 Inc.
Northwest Review
Notre Dame Review
Oasis
Old Crow Review
Oxford Magazine
Painted Bride Quarterly
Palo Alto Review
Pangolin Papers
Paperplates
Partisan Review
Pikeville Review
Pleiades
Porter Cosmographic, Bern
Potomac Review
Prism International
Puerto Del Sol

Quarter After Eight
Quarterly West
QWF (Quality Women's Fiction)
Rain Crow
Raskolnikov's Cellar and The Lamplight
Reflections
River Styx
Rosebud™
Salt Hill
Sanskrit
Skidrow Penthouse
So to Speak
Spindrift
SPSM&H
State of Unbeing
Struggle
Sulphur River Literary Review
Sycamore Review
Tameme
Tampa Review
Transition
Triquarterly
Unmuzzled Ox
Vincent Brothers Review, The
Virginia Quarterly Review
Weber Studies
Weird Tales
Wespennest
White Crow, The
Willow Springs
Writing for Our Lives
Xavier Review
Yellow Silk

Book Publishers
Arcade Publishing
Authors Online Ltd.
Bancroft Press
Beil, Publisher, Inc., Frederic C.
Bilingual Press/Editorial Bilingüe
Branden Books
Broken Boulder Press
Calyx Books
Catbird Press
Cleis Press
Cross-Cultural Communications
Dufour Editions
Feminist Press at the City University of New York, The
First Amendment Press International Company
Guernica Editions
Helicon Nine Editions
Hollow Earth Publishing
Holt & Company, Henry
Interlink Publishing Group, Inc.
Mage Publishers
Micah Publications, Inc.
Milkweed Editions
Morrow, William
New Rivers Press
Philomel Books
Pipers' Ash Ltd.

Pleasure Boat Studio
Post-Apollo Press, The
Quartet Books Limited
Scrivenery Press
Serpent's Tail
Snowapple Press
Stone Bridge Press
University of Nebraska Press
Véhicule Press
White Pine Press

WESTERN
Magazines
Advocate, PKA's Publication
Amelia
Analecta
Armchair Aesthete, The
Azorean Express, The
Bibliophilos
Black Jack
Blue Mesa Review
Boys' Life
Concho River Review
Cotworld Creative Magazine
Downstate Story
Edge, Tales of Suspense, The
Evansville Review
Free Focus/Ostentatious Mind
Fugue
Futures Magazine
Ghost Town
Grasslands Review
Griffin, The
Grit
In Posse Review
Indian Life
Karitos Review, The
Literally Horses
Literary Moments
Lynx Eye
Merlyn's Pen
MJ's Walkabout
Montana Senior News
New Writing
Northwoods Journal
Palo Alto Review
Paumanok Review, The
Playboy Magazine
Plot Line Foyer
Poskisnolt Press
Post, The
PSI
Short Stuff Magazine for Grown-ups
Shyflower's Garden
Skylark
SPSM&H
Storyteller, The
"Teak" Roundup
Thema
Tucumcari Literary Review
Urban Spaghetti

Valley Grapevine
Vincent Brothers Review, The
Weber Studies
Yellow Sticky Notes
Zopilote

Book Publishers
Adventure Book Publishers
Authors Online Ltd.
Avalon Books
Bancroft Press
Dan River Press
DiskUs Publishing
Duckworth Press
Evans & Co., Inc., M.
First Amendment Press International Company
Forge Books
Fountainhead Productions, Inc.
Glencannon Press, The
GoldenIsle Publishers Inc.
Hale Limited, Robert
Kensington Publishing Corp.
Leisure Books
LTD Books
Majestic Books
New American Library
Philomel Books
Pipers' Ash Ltd.
Plume
Pocket Books
Publishers Syndication, International
Russell Publishing, James
St. Martin's Press
Sunstone Press

YOUNG ADULT/TEEN

Magazines

Advocate, PKA's Publication
Alien Zoo
Archaeology
Associate Reformed Presbyterian, The
Baseball
Boys' Life
Bridal Guides
Cicada (Illinois)
Claremont Review, The
Cochran's Corner
Cozy Detective, The
Creative Kids
CZ's Magazine
Dance
Dream International/Quarterly
Eidolon
Encounter
Free Focus/Ostentatious Mind
Futures Magazine
Ghost Town
Indian Life Magazine
Irreantum
Kids' Highway
Lighthouse Story Collections
Lilith Magazine

Literary Moments
Majestic Books
Merlyn's Pen
Mindsparks
MJ's Walkabout
New Era Magazine
Nite-Writer's International Literary Arts Journal
Plot Line Foyer
Poetry Forum Short Stories
Poskisnolt Press
Renaissance Online Magazine
Seeking the Muse
Seventeen
Skipping Stones
Speak Up
Spirit
Stepping Out of the Darkness
Storyteller, The
Struggle
Studentswrite.com
"Teak" Roundup
Teen Magazine
With
Yellow Sticky Notes
Young Salvationist

Book Publishers

Adventure Book Publishers
Archway Paperbacks
Arte Publico Press
Atheneum Books for Young Readers
Authors Online Ltd.
Avid Press, LLC
Avon Books
Bancroft Press
Bantam, Doubleday, Dell/Delacorte, Knopf and Crown Books for Young Readers
Beach Holme Publishers Ltd.
Bethany House Publishers
BJU Press
Borealis Press
Boyds Mills Press
Caitlin Press, Inc.
Coteau Books
Cross-Cultural Communications
Crossway Books
Crown Books for Young Readers
Delecorte Books for Young Readers
DiskUs Publishing
Doubleday Books for Young Readers
Dutton Children's Books
Éditions du Vermillon, Les
Éditions La Liberté Inc.
FP Hendriks Publishing Ltd.
Front Street Books
Geringer Books, Laura
Glencannon Press, The
Godine, Publisher, Inc., David R.
Holt & Company Books for Young Readers, Henry
Holt & Company, Henry
Houghton Mifflin Books for Children
Huntington House Publishers

Hyperion Books for Children
ImaJinn Books
Knopf Books for Young Readers, Alfred A.
Laurel Leaf
Lerner Publications Company
Little, Brown and Company Children's Books
Lorimer & Co., Publishers, James
LTD Books
Majestic Books
McElderry Books, Margaret K.
Mightbook
Morehouse Publishing Co.
Orchard Books
Peachtree Publishers, Ltd.
Perfection Learning Corp.
Philomel Books
Piñata Books
Pipers' Ash Ltd.
Pride and Imprints
Puffin Books
Ragweed Press Inc./gynergy books

Random House Books for Young Readers
Random House Children's Books
Reconciliation Press
Red Deer Press
Ronsdale Press
Russell Publishing, James
Scherf Books
Scholastic Canada Ltd.
Scholastic Inc.
Signal Crest
Silver Dagger Mysteries
Simon & Schuster Books for Young Readers
Skylark
Snowapple Press
Starfire
TAB Book Club
Thistledown Press
Viking Children's Books
Walker and Company
Writers Press, Inc.
Yearling

General Index

Markets that appeared in the 2000 ediion of *Novel & Short Story Writer's Market* but are not included in this edition are identified by a two-letter code explaining why the market was omitted: **(ED)**—Editorial Decision, **(NS)**—Not Accepting Submissions, **(NR)**—No (or late) Response to Listing Request, **(OB)**—Out of Business, **(RR)**—Removed by Market's Request, **(UC)**—Unable to Contact, **(UF)**—Uncertain Future.

A

Abbey Fiction Award, The Edward 495
Aberrations 287
Abiko Quarterly with James, The 287
About Creative Time Spaces (ED)
About Such Things 139
Abram Prize for Fiction, Eleanor 495
Absey & Co., Inc. 388
Absinthe Literary Review, The 140
Absolute Magnitude 321
Academy Chicago Publishers 388
Ace Science Fiction 389
ACM (Another Chicago Magazine) 140
Acme Press 470
Acorn, The 141
Adaex Edutional Publications Limited (NR)
adhocity.com 288
Adrift 141
Adventure Book Publishers 389
Adventures in Storytelling Magazine's National Stories into Print Writing Contest 495
Adventures of Sword & Sorcery (NR)
Advocacy Press 389
Advocate, PKA's Publication 141
Aegean Center for the Fine Arts Workshops, The (NR)
Aethlon 141
Affable Neighbor 321, 470
Affair of the Mind 142
African Voices 345
Ageless Press 470
Agni 142
Aguilar Expression, The 143
Aim Magazine 346
Aim Magazine's Short Story Contest 496
AKC Gazette (NR)
AKP Zine 321
Akron Manuscript Club 496
Alabama State Council on the Arts Individual Artist Fellowship 496
Alabama Writers' Conclave 560
Alaska Native Language Center 390
Alaska Quarterly Review 143

Alaska State Council on the Arts Career Opportunity Grant Award 496
Alembic 288
Alexander Books (NR)
Alexandria Digital Literature 390
Algonquin Books of Chapel Hill 390
Algonquin Roundtable Review 143
Alien Zoo 322
Alive Communications, Inc. 115
Allen, Literary Agent, James 116
Alligator Juniper 144
Alligator Juniper National Writing Contest 496
Alsop Review, The 144
Altair (NR)
Alyson Publications, Inc. 390
Amazing Stories 346
Ambit (NR)
Amelia 144
Amelia Magazine Awards 496
American Christian Writers Conferences (NR)
American Citizen Italian Press, The (NR)
American Diabetes Association (NR)
American Girl 346
American Literary Review 145
American Literary Short Fiction Award 497
American Markets Newsletter Short Story Competition 497
American University in Cairo Press, The (NR)
American Writing 145
Americas Review, The (NR)
Amethyst Review, The 145
Amherst Review (NR)
Amnesia (NR)
Amsterdam Agency, Marcia 116
Analecta 146
Analecta College Fiction Contest (NR)
Anderson Short Fiction Prize, Sherwood 497
Anderson Writer's Grant, Sherwood 497
Andreas-Gryphius-Preis 497
Annals of St. Anne De Beaupré, The 347
Annick Press Ltd. (NR)
Annual Fiction Contest 498
Annual Juvenile-Fiction Contest 498

Annual Poetry/Fiction Contest 498
Annual/Atlantic Writing Competitions, The 498
Anotherealm 322
Anthology 288
Antietam Review Literary Award 498
Antietam Review 146
Antigonish Review, The 146
Antioch Review 147
Antioch Writers' Workshop 564
Anvil Press 471
Anvil Press International 3-Day Novel Writing
    Contest 498
Any Dream Will Do 322
Apostrophe 147
Appalachia Journal 347
Appalachian Heritage 147
Arachne, Inc. 148
Ararat Quarterly 148
Arcade Publishing 391
Archaeology 288
Archipelago 148
Archway Paperbacks 391
Arizona Commission on the Arts Creative Writ-
    ing Fellowships 498
Arkansas Review 148
Arkansas Writers' Conference 560
Armchair Aesthete, The 149
Arrowhead Regional Arts Council Individual
    Artist Career Development Grant 499
Arsenal Pulp Press 391
Art and Soul 574
Art of Music Annual Writing Contest, The 499
Art Times 347
Art Workshops in Guatemala 589
Arte Publico Press 391
Artemis Magazine 289
Artemis Press 471
Artful Dodge 149
Artisan (NR)
Artist Trust Artist Fellowship; Gap Grants (NR)
Art:Mag 322
Arts & Letters 149
Arvon Foundation Ltd. Workshops, The (NR)
ASF Translation Prize 499
Asian Pacific American Journal 150
Asimov Award, The Isaac 499
Asimov's Science Fiction 347
Associate Reformed Presbyterian, The 348
Associated Writing Programs 592
Asted/Grand Prix de Litterature Jeunesse du
    Quebec-Alvine-Belisle 499

Athenaeum Literary Award, The 499
Atheneum Books for Young Readers 392
Atlantic Monthly, The 348
Atom Mind (NR)
Atrocity (NR)
Attic Press 471
Aunt Lute Books 392
Aura Literary Arts Review 150
Aurealis 289
Auricular Immersion Median Online Magazine
    (NR)
Austin Writers' League 592
Austin Writers' League Workshops/Conferences/
    Classes (NR)
Authors Guild, The 593
Authors in the Park/Fine Print Contest (NR)
Authors Online Ltd. 392
Autumn 2001 Short Story Competition 500
Avalon Books 393
Avid Press, LLC 471
Avon Books 393
Avon Books for Young Readers (RR)
Avon Eos (NR)
AWP Award Series 500
AWP Intro Journals Project 500
AWP Prague Summer Seminars Fellowship 500
Axe Factory Review (NR)
Azorean Express, The 150

B

Babel 151
babysue 323
Backspace (NR)
Baen Books 393
Bakeless Literary Publication Prizes 500
Baker Books (NR)
Balch Awards, Emily Clark (NR)
Ballantine Books 393
Balloon Life 348
Baltimore Review, The 151
Bancroft Press 472
B&A: New Fiction 151
Banks Channel Books 394
Bantam Books 394
Bantam Dell Publishing Group, The 394
Bantam, Doubleday, Dell/Delacorte, Knopf and
    Crown Books for Young Readers 394, 395
Barbaric Yawp 151
Barcelona Review, The 152
Bark, The 289

Barrington Area Arts Council/Whetstone Prizes (NR)
Baseball 290
Batchelder Award, Mildred L. (NR)
Bathtub Gin 152
Bay Area Writers Guide 13th Annual Conference, The 574
Baybury Review 152
BBR Magazine 153
BCLT/BCLA Translation Competition (NR)
Be the Writer You Want to Be Manuscript Clinic 579
Beach Holme Publishers Ltd. 395
Beacon Street Review 153
Beacon Street Review Editor's Choice Award 501
Beacon, The 501
Bear Essential Deluxe, The 349
Become a More Productive Writer 547
BEEF 323
Beggar's Press 472
Beginners 290
Beil, Publisher, Inc., Frederic C. 395
Bellingham Review, The 153
Bellowing Ark 154
Beloit Fiction Journal 154
Beneath the Surface 154
Beneath the Underground 472
Bennett Fellowship, George 501
Berkeley Fiction Review (NR)
Berkley Publishing Group, The 395
Bernstein Literary Agency, Meredith 117
Bertelsmann's World of Expression Scholarship Program 501
Best Lesbian Erotica 501
Best Magazine 349
"Best of Ohio Writers" Contest 501
Best of Soft Science Fiction Contest (NR)
Bethany House Publishers 395
Betts Fiction Prize, Doris 502
Bibliophilos 155
Bilingual Press/Editorial Bilingüe 472
Bilson Award for Historical Fiction for Young People, The Geoffrey (NR)
Birch Brook Press 396
Bitter Oleander, The 323
BJU Press 396
BkMk Press (NR)
Black Books Bulletin: Wordswork (NR)
Black Children's Book Award, Irma S. and James H. 502

Black Heron Press 396
Black Jack 155
Black Lace 155
Black Lace Books 397
Black Memorial Prizes, James Tait 502
Black Petals 323
Black Warrior Review 156
Black Warrior Review Literary Award, The 502
BlackFire 290
Blair, Publisher, John F. 397
Bloody Muse (NR)
Bloody Words Mystery Conference 587
Blue Mesa Review 156
Blue Moon Review, The 157
Blue Mountain Center, The 547
Blue Murder Magazine 324
Blue Rose Bouquet, The (NR)
Blue Skunk Companion, The 157
Blue Sky Press, The 397
Blueline 157
Boardman Tasker Prize 502
Bogg 158
Bomb Magazine 349
Book Publishers of Texas Award (NR)
Booker Prize for Fiction 502
Bookpress 158
Books for All Times, Inc. 473
Booming Ground 588
Borealis Press 397
Boson Books 473
Boston Globe-Horn Book Awards 503
Boston Review 349
Boston Review Short Story Contest (NR)
Both Sides Now 324
Bouchercon: The World Mystery Convention 555
Boulevard 158
Bowhunter Magazine 350
Boyds Mills Press 398
Boys' Life 350
Boy's Quest 290
Brain, Child 159
Branden Books 398
Braziller, Inc., George (NR)
Brazo's Bookstore Award (NR)
Bread for God's Children (RR)
Bread Loaf Writers' Conference 547
Breakaway Books (NR)
Breakfast All Day (NR)
Briar Cliff Review, The 159

Briar Cliff Review Poetry & Fiction Competition, The 503
Bridal Guides 291
Bridge, The (NR)
Bridge Works Publishing Co. (NR)
Bridport Prize, The 503
Brilliant Corners 159
British Book Company Inc., The (OB)
British Fantasy Society, The (NR)
Broadway Books 398
Brobdingnagian Times, The 324
Brody Arts Fund (NR)
Broken Boulder Press 398
Broken Jaw Press 399
Bronx Recognizes Its Own (B.R.I.O.) 503
Brown Critique, The 160
Brown Foundation, Arch & Bruce 503
Brownout Laboratories (NR)
Brownstone Review, The (NR)
Brutarian (NR)
Bugle 351
Bugnet Award for the Novel, Georges (NR)
Burn (NR)
Burnaby Writers' Society 593
Burnaby Writers' Society Annual Competition 503
Burning Sky 325
Bush Artist Fellowships 503
Button 160
Byline 160
Byline Short Fiction & Poetry Awards 504

C
Cadmus Editions 473
Cafe Irreal, The 161
Caitlin Press, Inc. 399
California Writers' Club 593
California Writer's Club Conference at Asilomar 580
California Writers' Club Contest 504
Callaloo 161
Calliope 351
Calyx 161
Calyx Books 473
Cambrensis 162
Campbell Memorial Award, John W. 504
Campus Life Magazine 351
Canada Council Governor General's Literary Awards (NR)

Canadian Institute of Ukrainian Studies Press (NR)
Canadian Society of Children's Authors, Illustrators & Performers (CANSCAIP) 593
Candlewick Press 399
Capers Aweigh 162
Capilano Review, The 162
Capper's 352
Capricorn Award, The 504
Captivating Beginnings Contest 504
Caribbean Writer, The 162
Carolina Novel Award, The (NR)
Carolina Quarterly 163
Carolina Wren Press, Inc. 474
Carolrhoda Books, Inc. 399
Carpe Noctem 352
Carroll & Graf Publishers, Inc. 400
Cartwheel Books 400
Carvainis Agency, Inc., Maria 117
Carve Magazine 163
Carver Short Story Contest, Raymond (NR)
Cat Writers Association Writers Conference 574
Catbird Press 400
Cather Fiction Prize, Willa 504
Cave Books 474
Cayo 163
Cenotaph 163
Centennial Publications 401
Center Press (NR)
Centrums Port Townsend Writers' Conference (NR)
Century 164
Ceteris Paribus (NR)
Chanteh 164
Chapman 164
Chariot Victor Publishing (RR)
Chariton Review, The 164
Charlesbridge Publishing 401
Chasm (NR)
Chat 352
Chattahoochee Review, The 165
Chattanooga Conference on Southern Literature 558
Chelsea 165
Chelsea Awards, The 505
Chenango Valley Writers' Conference 547
Chiaroscuro 325
Chicago Review 165
Chicano/Latino Literary Contest (NR)
Chickadee 353

Children, Churches and Daddies Magazine 166, 325
Children's Book Award, The 505
Children's Digest 353
Children's Playmate 353
Children's Writers Fiction Contest 505
China Books & Periodicals, Inc. 401
Chinook Press (NR)
Chinook Quarterly, The (NR)
Chiricú (NR)
Chiron Review 166
Christchurch Publishers Ltd. 474
Christian Century, The (NR)
Christian Courier 291
Christianity and the Arts 166
Christopher Awards, The 505
Chrysalis Reader 167
Cicada (California) 167
Cicada (Illinois) 167
Cimarron Review 168
Cincinnati Writer's Project (NR)
Cinestory Screenwriting Awards 505
Circle Magazine, The 291
Circlet Press 401
City Primeval 168
Citycycle Motorcycle News Magazine 353
Claremont Review, The 168
Clarion Books 402
Clarion West Writers' Workshop 585
Clark Street Review 326
Cleis Press 402
Climbing Art, The 169
Clockwatch Review (NR)
Clubhouse 354
Clubhouse Magazine 292
CNW/FFWA Florida State Writing Competition 506
Cobblestone 354
Cochran's Corner 292
Coe Review, The 169
Coffee House Press 402
Cold-Drill Magazine (NR)
Cole's Comic Desk 326
Collages and Bricolages 169
College of New Jersey Writers' Conference, The 556
Colorado Mountain Writers' Workshop 580
Colorado Review 170
Columbia: A Journal of Literature & Art 170
Columbus Writers Conference, The 564
Commonwealth Club of California (NR)
Commonwealth Writers Prize 506
Companion in Zeor, A 326
Companion Magazine (NR)
Compass Point Mysteries™/Tory Corner Editions™ 402
Compleat Nurse, The (NR)
Complete Novel Competition 506
Compost 170
Concho River Review 170
Concordia Publishing House 403
Conduit 171
Confrontation 171
Congdon Associates, Inc., Don 117
Connecticut Commission on the Arts Artist Fellowships 506
Connor Literary Agency 118
Conseil de la Vie Francaise en Amerique/Prix Champlain 506
Constable and Company (NR)
Contact Advertising 354
Contraband (NR)
Conversely 171
Cornerstone Magazine 355
Corona 172
Cosmopolitan Magazine 355
Coteau Books 403
Cottonwood 172
Cotworld Creative Magazine 355
Country Folk (NR)
Country Woman 355
Cozy Detective, The 292
Crab Creek Review 172
Crab Orchard Review 172
Crania 173
Crawford Literary Agency 118
Cream City Review, The 173
Creative Kids 356
Creativity Unlimited Press 474
Creativity Workshop 550
Crescent Review, The 173
Cricket Magazine 356
Crimewave 174
Cripes! (NR)
Cross-Cultural Communications 475
Crossing Boundaries Writing Awards (NR)
Crossway Books 404
Crown Books for Young Readers 404
Crucible 174
Crucible Poetry and Fiction Competition, The 506
Crusader Magazine 356

Cumberland House Publishing 404
Curio (NR)
Curriculum Vitae (NR)
Curtis Associates, Inc., Richard 118
Cutbank 174
CZ's Magazine 293

D
Dagger of the Mind 293
Dalhousie Review, The 174
Dan River Anthology (NR)
Dan River Press 404
Dana Award in Short Fiction 507
Dana Award in Speculative Fiction (RR)
Dana Award in the Novel 507
Dance 293
Daniel and Company, Publishers, John 405
Daniels Annual Honorary Writing Award, Dorothy 507
Dante University of America Press, Inc. (NR)
Dargonzine 327
Dark Horizons (NR)
Dark Matter (NR)
Dark Matter Chronicles 294
Darktales Publications 475
Davenport, Publishers, May 405
Daves Agency, Joan 119
Davidson's Writer's Seminar, Peter 570
Daw Books, Inc. 405
de Angeli Prize, Marguerite 507
Dead Metaphor Press 507
Dead Mule, The 175
Deadly Ink Mystery Conferences 556
Deadly Nightshade (NR)
Debut Dagger 507
Deep Outside SFFH 294
Del Rey Books 405
Delacorte Books for Young Readers 408
Delacorte Press 408
Delacorte Press Annual Prize for a First Young Adult Novel (NR)
Delaware Division of the Arts 508
Dell 408
Delta Trade Paperbacks (NR)
Denver Quarterly 175
Descant 175
Desert Writers Workshop/Canyonlands Field Institute (NR)
Design Image Group Inc., The 476
Desperate Act 175
Devil Blossoms (NR)

DHS Literary, Inc. 119
Dial Books for Young Readers 408
Dial Press, The 409
Dialogos 294
Dialogue 357
Dirigible (NR)
Discoveries 357
Discovery (NR)
Discovery Trails 357
DiskUs Publishing 409
Distillery, The 176
Dixie Phoenix 327
Dobie/Paisano Fellowships (NR)
Dodobobo (NR)
Doubleday Adult Trade 409
Doubleday Books for Young Readers 409
Doubleday Canada 409
Doubletake 176
Down East Books 410
Down There Press 476
DownEast Maine Writer's Workshops 550
Downstate Story 176
Dreaded Synopsis, The 508
Dream International/Quarterly 295
Dreams & Nightmares (NR)
Dreams & Visions 295
Drinkin' Buddy Magazine, The (NR)
Duckworth Press 410
Duct Tape Press 327
Duel on the Delta Writers' Conference 558
Dufour Editions 410
Duke University Writers' Workshop (NR)
Duncton Cottage Short Story and Poetry Competition 508
Dundee Book Prize 508
Dunne Books, Thomas 410
Dutton 411
Dutton Children's Books 411
Dyer Fiction Prize, Jack 508

E
E.M. Press, Inc. 411
Eakin Press (NR)
Eastern Writers' Conference (NR)
Eaton Literary Associates' Literary Awards Program 508
Ecco Press, The 411
Edge City Review, The (NR)
Edge Science Fiction and Fantasy Publishing (NR)
Edge, Tales of Suspense, The 328

Edinburgh University Centre for Continuing Education Creative Writing Workshops 589
Éditions du Vermillon, Les 411
Éditions La Liberté Inc. 412
Eerdmans Publishing Co., Wm. B. 412
Eidolon 295
1812 176
Electric Wine 176
Ellenberg Literary Agency, Ethan 119
Ellis Awards, Arthur (NR)
Ellison Inc., Nicholas 120
Eloquent Umbrella, The (NR)
Elysian Fields Quarterly 177
Emerging Lesbian Writers Fund Awards 509
Emily Contest, The 509
Emphasis on Faith and Living (NR)
Emploi Plus 177
Empyreal Press (NR)
Emrys Journal 177
Encounter 328
Enigma 296
Enigmatic Press 412
Enterzone (NR)
Epoch Magazine 178
Eriksson, Publisher, Paul S. 413
Esquire 357
Eternal Voice (NR)
Eternity Magazine (NR)
Eureka Literary Magazine 178
Evangel 358
Evans & Co., Inc., M. 413
Evans Inc., Mary 120
Evansville Review 178
Event 179
Evergreen Chronicles (NR)
Evergreen Chronicles Novella Contest (NR)
EWGPresents 179
Explorations 179
Eyes 296

F

Faces 358
Fairfield Review, The 180
Faith Kids (NR)
Fall Inspiration Retreat 2000 575
Fallbrook Writer's Colony 580
Fan Magazine (NR)
Fanfare (OB)
Fantagraphics Books (NR)
Farrar, Straus & Giroux 413

Farrar, Straus & Giroux/Children's Books 413
Farthest Star (RR)
Faulkner Award for Excellence in Writing, Virginia 509
Faulkner Competition in Fiction, William 509
Faultline (NR)
Faux Faulkner Contest, The Jack 509
FAW Awards 509
Fawcett 413
FC2 413
Federation of British Columbia Writers 594
Feminist Press at the City University of New York, The 413
Feminist Studies 180
Feminist Women's Writing Workshops, Inc. 551
Feminist Writer's Contest 510
Fenn Publishing Company, Ltd. 414
Fernandez Agent/Attorney, Justin E. 120
Festival of the Written Arts, The 588
Fiction 180
Fiction Writer (ED)
Fiddlehead, The 180
Firebrand Books 414
Firefly, The 328
First Amendment Press International Company 476
First Class 181
First Hand 358
Fish Drum Magazine (NR)
Fish Memorial Award, Robert L. (NR)
Fish Short Story Prize 510
Fisher Award, Dorothy Canfield 510
Fishtrap 586
Five Points 181
Flaherty, Literary Agent, Joyce A. 121
Flatirons Blunt Instrument Mystery Workshop 575
Flesh & Blood 296
Florida Christian Writers Conference 561
Florida First Coast Writers' Festival 561
Florida First Coast Writers' Festival Novel, Short Fiction & Poetry Awards 510
Florida Review, The 181
Florida Review Editors' Award (NR)
Florida State Writing Competition 510
Florida Suncoast Writers' Conference (NR)
Florida Wildlife (ED)
Flying Horse (NR)
Flying Island, The (NR)
Flyway 181
Focus Publishing, Inc. (NR)

Foliage (OB)
Folio: A Literary Journal 182
Food, Recipes, Wines & Such Contest 510
Fool for Love First Chapter Contest 511
Foothill Writers' Conference 580
Forbidden Donut (NR)
Foresight 296
Forge Books 414
Fort Ross Inc. 414
Foster City International Writers Contest (NR)
Foul Play Press (OB)
Foundations of Creativity Writing Workshop,
    The (NR)
Fountainhead Productions, Inc. 415
Four Walls Eight Windows 415
Fourteen Hills (NR)
FP Hendriks Publishing Ltd. 477
Francis Short Story Award, H.E. 511
Frank 182
Franklin Literary Award, Miles 511
Fraser Award, Souerette Diehl (NR)
Free Focus/Ostentatious Mind 297
French Bread Awards 511
Friend Magazine, The 358
Friends United Press (RR)
Front Street Books 415
Frontiers 182
Frontiers in Writing Conference (NR)
Fugue 182
Fuhded Retreat, Jerome 511
Fullosia Press 328
Funny Paper Competition, The 512
Funny Times, The 329
Futures Magazine 183

G

Gargoyle 183
Gaslight Publications 477
Gathering of the Tribes, A (NR)
Gay Chicago Magazine 297
Gay Sunshine Press and Leyland Publications
    (NR)
Geist 184
Gem, The (NR)
Gemini Ink 2001 Summer Festival 575
Gent (NR)
George & Mertie's Place: Rooms with a View
    184
Georgetown Review (NR)
Georgia Review, The 184

Geringer Books, Laura 416
Gertrude 185
Geske Award, The Jane 512
Gessler Publishing Company (NR)
Gettysburg Review, The 185
Ghost Town 297
Ginosko 185
Glencannon Press, The 477
Glimmer Train Stories 186
Glimmer Train's Fall Short Story Award for New
    Writers 512
Glimmer Train's Fiction Open 512
Glimmer Train's Spring Short Story Award for
    New Writers 512
Glimmer Train's Very Short Fiction Summer
    Award 512
Glimmer Train's Very Short Fiction Winter
    Award 513
Global Tapestry Journal (NR)
God Uses Ink Annual Writers Conference 588
God Uses Ink Christian Writers' Contest (NR)
Godine, Publisher, Inc., David R. 416
Golden Chance (NR)
Golden Triangle Writers Guild 575
GoldenIsle Publishers Inc. 478
Golf Journal 359
Good Housekeeping 359
Goose Lane Editions 416
Gotham Writers' Workshop 551
Gotta Write Network Litmag 329
Government of Newfoundland and Labrador Arts
    and Letters Competition 513
Grade School Press (NR)
Grain 186
Grand Street 186
Granta 186
Grasslands Review 187
Graywolf Press 416
Great American Book Contest 513
Great Beginnings 513
Great Blue Beacon Short-Story Contest, The 513
Great Lakes Book Awards 513
Great Lakes Colleges Association New Writers
    Award 514
Great Lakes Writer's Workshop 570
Great Plains Storytelling & Poetry Reading Con-
    test 514
Green Hills Literary Lantern, The 187
Green Mountain Writers Conference 551
Green Mountains Review 188

Green River Writers Novels-in-Progress Workshop 565
Green Tricycle, The 188
Greene Bark Press 417
Greene Literary Festival Contest, The Judy & A.C. 514
Green's Magazine 188
Greensboro Review, The 189
Greensboro Review Literary Awards, The 514
Greenwillow Books 417
GreyCore Press 478
Griffin, The 189
Griffon House Publications (NR)
Grit 359
Grolier Publishing 417
Grove/Atlantic, Inc. 417
Grue Magazine 297
Gryphon Books 417
Guernica Editions 418
Guideposts for Kids 359
Gulf Coast 189
Gulf Stream Magazine 189

H

Habersham Review (NR)
Hackney Literary Awards (NR)
Hale Limited, Robert 418
Half Tones to Jubliee 190
Halsey North, Reece 121
Hampton Roads Publishing Company, Inc. 418
Handshake Editions 478
Happy 190
Harcourt Inc 419
Hard Row to Hoe Division 298
Hardboiled 298
Harlequin Enterprises, Ltd. 419
Harlequin Mills & Boon Ltd. (NR)
HarperCollins Children's Books 419
HarperCollins Publishers (NR)
HarperCollins Publishers (New Zealand) Limited 420
HarperPerennial (NR)
Harper's Magazine 360
HarperTorch 420
Harpweaver 190
Harris Literary Agency 121
Harris Literary Agency, Inc., The Joy 122
Harvest House Publishers 420
Harwelden Literary Festival (NR)
Hawaii Pacific Review 298

Hawaii Review (NR)
Hawk Publishing Group 420
Hayden's Ferry Review 190
Haystack Writing Program (NR)
Headwaters Literary Competition 514
Heart of the West Writers Contest 514
Heartland Writers Conference (NR)
Heartlands Today, The 191
Heartsong Presents (NR)
Heaven Bone 191
Heights Writer's Conference, The (NR)
Heinz Literature Prize, Drue 515
Heist Magazine (NR)
Helicon Nine Editions 420
Hemingway Days Writer's Workshop and Conference 561
Hemingway Foundation/Pen Award For First Fiction, Ernest 515
Hemingway Short Story Competition, Lorian 515
Hemispheres 360
Hemkunt Press 478
Henshaw Group, Richard 122
Hidden Manna 191
Higginsville Reader, The 192
High Plains Literary Review 192
Highland Summer Conference (NR)
Highlights for Children 364, 515
Hill and Holler 192
Hill Street Press 479
Hitchcock's Mystery Magazine, Alfred 364
Hodder & Stoughton/Headline 421
Hodder Fellowship, The Alfred 515
Hofstra University Summer Writers' Conference 551
Hogrefe Fellowship, Pearl 516
Hohm Press (NR)
Holiday House, Inc. 421
Hollow Earth Publishing 479
Holt & Company, Henry 421
Holt & Company Books for Young Readers, Henry 421
Holtby Memorial Prize, The Winifred 516
Home Planet News 193
Home Times 365
Honolulu Magazine/Borders Books & Music Fiction Contest 516
Hopkins Literary Associates 122
Hopscotch: The Magazine for Girls 298
Horizon (ED)
Horizons (NR)

GENERAL INDEX

Horror Writers of Association 594
Horsethief's Journal, The 193
Houghton Mifflin Books for Children 422
Houghton Mifflin Company 422
Houston Writers Conference 2000 576
How to Be Published Workshops 561
Howells House (NR)
Hubbard's Writers of the Future Contest, L. Ron 516
Hudson Review, The 193
Humpty Dumpty's Magazine 365
Hunted News, The 194
Huntington House Publishers 423
Huntington Press 479
Hurricane Alice 299
Hurston/Richard Wright Award, Zora Neale 516
Hustler Busty Beauties 365
Hybolics 299
Hyperion Books for Children 423

I

Iconoclast, The 194
Idaho Review, The 194
Ideals Children's Books (NR)
Idiot, The 195
Iksperament 329
Illumination Publishing Co. 479
Illuminations (NR)
Illya's Honey 195
Imagination 565
Imagine (NR)
Imago (NR)
ImaJinn Books 423
Implosion (NR)
Imprint (NR)
In Posse Review 330
In the Family 299
In Touch for Men 365
India Currents 368
Indian Life 300
Indian Life Magazine 368
Indiana Review 195
Indiana Review Fiction Prize 516
Indiana University Writers' Conference 565
Indigenous Fiction 196
Individual Artist Fellowship 517
Individual Artist Fellowship Program (Flordia) (NR)
Individual Artist Fellowships (Maine) (NR)
Inky Trail News 300
Inside (NR)

Insomniac Press 424
Instant Classics (NR)
Interbang 196
Interim (NR)
Interlink Publishing Group, Inc. 424
International Imitation Hemingway Competition 517
International Quarterly 196
International Readers Theatre Workshops 581
International Reading Association Children's Book Awards 517
International Writers Contest (NR)
Intertext 330
Interzone (NR)
Iowa Review, The 197
Iowa School of Letters Award for Short Fiction, The John Simmons Short Fiction Award 517
Iowa Short Fiction Award, The 517
Iowa Summer Writing Festival 570
ipsissima Verba (NR)
Ireland's Own 368
Iris 197
Irish Times Literature Prizes, The (NR)
Ironweed Press (NR)
Irreantum 198
Island (NR)
Island 424
Italian Americana 300
Italica Press (NR)
I've Always Wanted to Write But . . . 581
Ivy (NR)
Ivy League Press, Inc. 480
IWWG Early Spring in California Conference 581
IWWG Meet the Agents and Editors 552
IWWG Summer Conference (NR)

J

J de S Associates Inc. 122
Jabberwock Review, The 198
Jabberwocky Literary Agency 123
Jack and Jill 368
Jack Mackerel Magazine (NR)
Jackhammer E-Zine 330
Jackson Award, Joseph Henry 517
Jameson Books 424
Japan Foundation Artist Fellowship Program 517
Japanophile 199
Japanophile Short Story Contest 518
JCA Literary Agency, Inc. 123
Jefferson Cup (NR)

Jeopardy (NR)
Jesperson Press Ltd. 480
Jewish Currents Magazine 301
Jewish Quarterly 301
Jive, Black Confessions, Black Romance, Bronze Thrills, Black Secrets 369
Jones Award for Fiction (Book), Jesse (NR)
Jones First Novel Fellowship, James 518
Journal, The (Ohio) 199
Journal, The (Pennsylvania) 199
Journal of African Travel-Writing, The 200
Journal of Polymorphous Perversity 301
Journey Books (NR)
Jupiter's Freedom (NR)

K

Kaeden Books 424
Kaleidoscope 200
Kalliope 200
Karamu 201
Karawane (NR)
Karitos Review, The 201
Karnak House 480
Kasper Zine (NR)
Katha: Indian American Fiction Contest 518
Kawabata Press 480
Kaya Production (NR)
Kelsey Review 201
Kennedy Book Awards, Robert F. (NR)
Kensington Publishing Corp. 425
Kentucky Arts Council, Kentucky Artists Fellowships (NR)
Kentucky Women Writers Conference 565
Kenyon Review, The 202
Kenyon Review Writers Workshop 566
Kerem 202
Kestrel 202
Key West Literary Seminar 562
Key West Writers' Workshop 562
Kidd Agency, Inc., Virginia 123
Kidde, Hoyt & Picard 124
Kids' Highway 203
Kids' World (NR)
Kidz Ch@t 369
Killer Frog Contest 518
Kimera: A Journal of Fine Writing (NR)
Kiosk 203
Kiriyama Pacific Rim Book Prize (NR)
Knight Agency, The 124
Knoll, Publishers, Allen A. 425

Knopf, Alfred A. 425
Knopf Books for Young Readers, Alfred A. 425
Koja 203
Koster Literary Agency, Elaine, LLC 124
Kraas Agency, Irene 125
Krater Prosody Awards for Short Fiction and Poetry 2001, The 518
Krater Quarterly 204
Krax Magazine 302

L

La Kancerkliniko 204
Ladies' Home Journal 369
Lady, The 369
Lady Churchill's Rosebud Wristlet 331
Ladybug 370
Lagniappe for Literacy (NR)
Lampack Agency, Inc., Peter 125
Lamplight, The 204
Lamp-Post, The (NR)
Landfall/University of Otago Press 204
Larcom Review, The 205
Laurel Books (NR)
Laurel Leaf 428
Laurel Review, The (NR)
Laurie 519
Lawrence Foundation Award, The 519
LC-39 205
Le Forum (NR)
Le Guin Prize for Imaginative Fiction, Ursula K. 519
Leacock Medal for Humour, Stephen (NR)
Leading Edge, The 331
League of Utah Writers Contest (NR)
League of Utah Writers Round-up 581
Leapfrog Press 480
Leapings Literary Magazine 205
Lee & Low Books 428
Left Curve 302
Leisure Books 429
Lemeac Editeur Inc. (NR)
Lerner Publications Company 429
Levine Books, Arthur 429
Libido (OB)
Licking River Review, The 206
Light Quarterly 206
Lighthouse Story Collections 206
Lightwave Publishing Inc. (NR)
Liguorian 370
Lilith Magazine 370

Lilliput Press, The (NR)
Lincoln Literary Agency, Ray 125
Lines in the Sand (NR)
Lines in the Sand Short Fiction Contest (NR)
Lintel 429
LionHearted Publishing, Inc. 430
Liquid Ohio 331
Lite 206
Literal Latté 207
Literal Latté Fiction Award 519
Literally Horses 332
Literally Horses Poetry/Short Story Contest 519
Literary Moments 207
Literary Review, The 207
Literary Witches (NR)
Little, Brown and Company 430
Little, Brown and Company Children's Books 430
Little Magazine, The 208
Little Simon 431
Live 371
Livingston Press 431, 481
Llewellyn Publications (NR)
Lollipop Power Books 481
Long Fiction Contest International 519
Long Shot 302
Long Story, The 208
Lonzie's Fried Chicken® 208
Loonfeather (NR)
Lord Literistic, Inc., Sterling 126
Lorimer & Co., Publishers, James 431
Los Angeles Times Book Prizes 520
Los Angeles Writers Conference 582
Lost and Found Times 209
Lost Horse Press 431
Lost Worlds (NR)
Louisiana Literature 209
Louisiana Review, The 209, 210
Love Affair Literary Contest, A 520
Love Spell 431
LTD Books 432
Lucky Heart Books (NR)
Luke Award, The Hugh J. 520
Lullwater Review 210
Lummox Journal 210
Lutterworth Press, The (NR)
Lynx Eye 210
Lyons Press, The (NR)

M

Maass Literary Agency, Donald 126
MacAdam/Cage Publishing 432
MacDowell Colony, The 552
MacGuffin, The 211
Macmurray & Beck, Inc. (NR)
Macrae Books, John (NR)
Madison Review, The 211
Magazine of Fantasy & Science Fiction 371
Mage Publishers 433
Mail Call Journal 303
Mail on Sunday/John Llewellyn Rhys Prize 520
Main Street Books (NR)
Majestic Books 303, 433
Malahat Review 211
Malice Domestic Grant (NR)
Mangrove (NR)
Manhattanville College Summer Writers' Week 552
Manitoba Writers' Guild 594
Manoa 212
Manushi (NR)
Many Mountains Moving 212
Maple Woods Community College Writer's Conference (NR)
March Street Press 433
Margin 332
Marin Arts Council Individual Artist Grants (NR)
Mariner Books (NR)
Maritime Writers' Workshop (NR)
Markson Literary Agency, Elaine 126
Marlboro Review, The 212
Marten Bequest Travelling Scholarship, The 520
Marvin Grant, Walter Rumsey 521
Massachusetts Cultural Council Artist Grants Program 521
Massachusetts Review, The 213
Masters Literary Award 521
Matriarch's Way: Journal of Female Supremacy 213
Mattoid (NR)
Mature Living (NR)
Mature Years 371
Maumee Valley Freelance Writers' Fifth Annual Conference 566
McBooks Press 433
McCarthy Prize In Short Fiction, Mary (NR)
McElderry Books, Margaret K. 433
McGinnis Memorial Award, The John H. 521
McKean Moore Writer in Washington, Jenny 521
McKee's Story Structure, Robert (NR)

Companies that appeared in the 2000 edition of *Novel & Short Story Writer's Market*, but do not appear this year, are listed in this General Index with the following codes explaining why these markets were omitted: **(ED)**—Editorial Decision, **(NS)**—Not Accepting Submissions, **(NR)**—No (or late) Response to Listing Request, **(OB)**—Out of Business, **(RR)**—Removed by Market's Request, **(UC)**—Unable to Contact, **(UF)**—Uncertain Future.

McKnight Artist Fellowships For Writers (NR)
McSweeney's 213
Meadowbrook Press (NR)
Medicinal Purposes (NR)
Mediphors 214, 303
Medusa's Hairdo Magazine 304
Meridian 214
Mcriwether Publishing Ltd. 434
Merlyn's Pen 214
Mesechabe (NR)
Messages from the Heart (NR)
Messenger of the Sacred Heart 372
Micah Publications, Inc. 434
Michaels Literary Agency, Inc., Doris S. 127
Michigan Author Award (NR)
Michigan Quarterly Review 218
Mid America Mystery Conference, The 566
Mid Atlantic Literary Small Press Conference &
    Book Fair 556
Mid-American Review 218
Mid-Atlantic Mystery Book Fair & Convention
    556
Midday Moon, The 218
Midknight Club, The 434
Mid-List Press 481
Mid-List Press First Series Award for Short Fic-
    tion 521
Mid-List Press First Series Award for the Novel
    522
Midland Writers Conference 566
Midstream (NR)
Midwest Writers' Conference 567
Mightbook 435
Milkweed Editions 435
Milkweed Editions National Fiction Prize 522
Milkweed Editions Prize for Children's Litera-
    ture 522
Milkweeds for Young Readers 482
Milkwood Review 333
Millennium: A Journal for Tomorrowland 333
Minas Tirith Evening-Star 219
Mind Book of the Year 522
Mindprints 219
Mindsparks 304
Ministry of Writing: An Annual Colloquium, The
    567
Minnesota Review, The 219
Minnesota State Arts Board/Artist Assistance
    Fellowship 522
Minnesota Voices Project 522
Minotaur (ED)

Minstrel Books 435
Miraculous Medal, The 304
Missing Fez, The 219
Mississippi Mud (OB)
Mississippi Review 220
Mississippi Review Prize (NR)
Mississippi Valley Writers Conference (NR)
Missouri Review Editors' Prize Contest, The 522
Missouri Review, The 220
Missouri Writers Guild 2001 Annual Convention
    576
Misty Hill Press (NR)
MJ's Walkabout 333
MM Review (NR)
Mobil Pegasus Prize (NR)
Mobius 220
Modest Contest 523
Money for Women 523
Monkeyplanet 221
Montana Arts Council Individual Artist Fellow-
    ship (NR)
Montana Senior News 372
Monthly Independent Tribune Times Journal
    Post Gazette News Chronicle Bulletin (NR)
Montrose Christian Writer's Conference 557
Moon Mountain Publishing 482
moonbomb press 334
Moonlight & Magnolia Fiction Writing Contest
    523
Moonlight and Magnolias Writer's Conference
    562
Moore Community Workshops, Jenny McKean
    557
Moore Short Story Awards, Brian 523
Morehouse Publishing Co. 435
Mormon Writers' Conference 582
Morris Agency, Inc., William 127
Morrison, Inc., Henry 127
Morrow, William 436
Mount Hermon Christian Writers Conference
    582
Mountain Luminary (NR)
Mountain State Press 482
Moxie 304
MSLEXIA 305
Ms Magazine 372
Multnomah Publishers, Inc. 436
Murderous Intent 305
Mushroom Dreams 334
Musing Place, The 221
My Friend 372

My Legacy (NR)
My Weekly (NR)
My Weekly Story Collection 436
Mysterious Press, The 436
Mystery Mayhem Contest 523
Mystery Time 305
Mystery Writers of America 594

N

NA'AMAT Woman 372
Naiad Press, Inc., The 436
National Chapter of Canada IODE Violet Downey Book Award, The 523
National Federation of the Blind Writer's Division Fiction Contest (NR)
National League of American Pen Women, Inc., The 594
National Literistic Circle Prize for Short Fiction; NLC Prize for Poetry 524
National Outdoor Book Awards 524
National Writers Association 595
National Writers Association Annual Novel Writing Contest 524
National Writers Association Annual Short Story Contest 524
National Writers Association Conference 576
National Written & Illustrated By . . . Awards Contest for Students, The (NR)
Nautical & Aviation Publishing Co. of America Inc., The 439
Naval Institute Press 439
NESFA Science Fiction Short Short Story Contest 524
Nebo 221
Nebraska Review, The 221
Nebraska Review Award in Fiction, The 524
Nelson, Tommy 439
Nelson Publishers, Thomas 439
Neotrope 222
Nerve Cowboy 222
Neustadt International Prize for Literature 525
Nevada Arts Council Artists' Fellowships (NR)
Neverworlds (NR)
New American Library 440
New Delta Review 222
New England Review 223
New England Writers 552
New England Writers' Network 306
New England Writers' Workshop at Emerson College (NR)
New Era Magazine 373

New Era Writing, Art, Photography and Music Contest, The (NR)
New Hampshire State Council on the Arts Individual Artist Fellowship (NR)
New Hampshire Writers Project (NR)
New Hope Books, Inc. 440
New Jersey State Council on the Arts Prose Fellowship (NR)
New Laurel Review (NR)
New Letters Literary Award (NR)
New Letters Magazine 223
New Letters Weekend Writers Conference, The (NR)
New Methods 306
New Millennium Writing Awards 525
New Mystery 373
New Orleans Popular Fiction Conference (NR)
New Orleans Review 223
New Rivers Press 482
New Shetlander 224
New Stone Circle 224
New Victoria Publishers 440
New Virginia Review (NR)
New Welsh Review 224
New Writer, The 224
New Writing 225
New Writing Award (NR)
New York State Edith Wharton Citation of Merit 525
New York Stories 225
New Yorker, The 373
Newbery Award, John 525
Newest Publishers Ltd. 441
Newest Review (NR)
Newfangled Fairy Tales and Girls to the Rescue 306
News of the Brave New World 334
Nexus 441
NFB Writers' Fiction Contest (NR)
Night Terrors 307
Nightfire 225
Nightly Gathering (NR)
Nimrod 225
Nimrod Annual Writers Workshop 576
96 Inc. 226
96 Inc's Bruce P. Rossley Literary Awards 525
Nite-Writer's International Literary Arts Journal 226
No Crime Unpublished® Mystery Writers' Conference 582
No Experience Required (NR)

Nocturnal Lyric, The (NR)
Noir Mechanics (NR)
Noma Award for Publishing in Africa, The (NR)
North American Review, The 226
North Atlantic Review 228
North Carolina Arts Council Fellowship (NR)
North Carolina Arts Council Writers' Residencies (NR)
North Carolina Writers' Network 595
North Carolina Writers' Network Fall Conference 559
North Dakota Quarterly (NR)
Northeast Arts Magazine 229
Northeast Corridor (RR)
Northern Michigan Journal, The (NR)
Northland Publishing Co. (RR)
North-South Books 441
Northwest Oklahoma Writer's Workshop 576
Northwest Review 229
Northwoods Journal 229
Norton & Company, Inc., W.W. 441
Norwegian Literature Abroad Grant (NR)
Notre Dame Review 229
Nova Science Fiction Magazine 334
Now & Then 230
NTPWA Annual Poetry & Fiction Contest 525
Nugget 373
Nuthouse 335
Nuvein Online 335

O

O! Georgia!, O! Georgia Too! Writing Competitions 525
Oak, The 307
Oakland University Writers' Conference 567
Oasis 230
Ober Associates, Harold 127
O'Connor Award for Short Fiction, The Flannery 526
O'Connor Fiction Award, Frank 526
Odyssey 374, 553
Of Ages Past: The Online Magazine For Historical Fiction (NR)
Of Dark & Stormy Nights 567
Of Unicorns and Space Stations 335
Office Number One 336
O'Hagan Award For Short Fiction, Howard (NR)
O'Hara Award Chapbook Competition, Frank (NR)
Ohio Review, The 231

Ohio State University Press 526
Ohio Teachers Write (NR)
Ohioana Award for Children's Literature, Alice Wood Memorial 526
Ohioana Book Awards 526
Oklahoma Writers Federation Conference 577
Oklahoma Writers' Workshop (NR)
Old Crow Review 231
Olders' Children's Writing Workshop, The (NR)
Olders' Travel Writing Workshop, The 553
On Our Backs 374
On Spec 307
On the Line (NR)
Once Upon a World (NR)
One World (NR)
Open Spaces Quarterly 231
Open Voice Awards 526
Open Writing Workshops 568
Options 374
Opus Magnum Discovery Awards 527
Oracle Story (NR)
Orange Blossom Fiction Contest 527
Orange Prize in Fiction 527
Orca Book Publishers Ltd. (NR)
Orchard Books 442
Oregon Book Awards (NR)
Oregon Individual Artist Fellowship 527
Orient Paperbacks 442
Orpheus Romance (NR)
Orphic Chronicle, The 336
Other Voices (Canada) 231
Other Voices (Illinois) 232
Our Child Press 483
Outdoor Writers Association of America Annual Conference 557
Outer Darkness 336
Outer Rim—The Zine, The 337
Outerbridge (NR)
Outrider Press (ED)
Owen Publishers, Peter 442
Owen Publishers Inc., Richard C. 442
Owl Books 443
Oxford American, The 232
Oxford Magazine 232
Oyster Boy Review of Fiction and Poetry 233
Ozark Creative Writers, Inc. 562

P

Pablo Lennis (NR)
Pacific Coast Journal 233

Pacific Enterprise 233
Pacific Review (NR)
Painted Bride Quarterly 234
Paisano Fellowships, Dobie 527
Palari Publishing 483
Palm Springs Writers Conference 583
Palo Alto Review 234
Pangolin Papers 234
Pantheon Books 443
Paperplates 235
Papier-Mache 443
Papyrus Journal (NR)
Papyrus Magazine (NR)
Papyrus Publishers & Letterbox Service 483
Paradoxism (NR)
Paris Review, The 235
Paris Writers' Workshop/WICE 590
Parsec (NR)
Parting Gifts 235
Partisan Review 235
Pasadena Writers' Forum 583
Passager (NR)
Passages North 235
Passeggiata Press, Inc. (NR)
Patchen Competition, Kenneth (NR)
Paterson Fiction Prize, The 527
Paterson Literary Review, The (NR)
Paumanok Review, The 236
PBW (NR)
Peachtree Publishers, Ltd. 443
Pearl 236
Pearl Short Story Contest 527
Peden Prize in Fiction, William 528
Peepal Tree Press (NR)
Pegasus Online 337
Pegasus Review, The 236
Pelican Publishing Company 443
Pembroke Magazine 237
Pemmican Publications (NR)
Pen & Sword (NR)
PEN Center USA West Literary Award in Fiction 528
PEN New England/L.L. Winship Award 528
PEN/Book-of-the-Month Club Translation Prize 528
PEN/Faulkner Award for Fiction, The (NR)
Penguin Putnam Inc. 444
Peninsular 237
Penmanship 528
PEN/Norma Klein Award 528
Pennsylvania English 237

Pennwriters Conference 557
Penny Dreadful 338
Penny-a-Liner (NR)
PeopleNet DisAbility DateNet Home Page 338
People's Friend 374
Peralta Press, The 238
Peregrine 238
Perfection Learning Corp. 444
Pew Fellowship in the Arts 529
Pfenninger Literary Award, Mary Ann 529
Phelan Award, James D. 529
Philomel Books 444
Phoebe (New York) (NR)
Piano Press 484
Picador USA 444
Pick Pocket Books 484
Piedmont Literary Review (NR)
Pif 238
Pig Iron Press 239, 484
Pikeville Review 239
Pillow Screams (NR)
Piñata Books 445
Pinder Lane & Garon-Brooke Associates, Ltd. 127
Pineapple Press 445
Pipe Smoker's Ephemeris, The 308
Pipers' Ash Ltd. 484
Pippin Press 445
Pirate Writings (NR)
PLANET-The Welsh Internationalist 239
Play the Odds (OB)
Playboy College Fiction Contest (NR)
Playboy Magazine 375
Plaza, The 239
Pleasant Company Publications 445
Pleasure Boat Studio 485
Pleiades 240
Plot Line Foyer 240
Ploughshares 241
Plowman, The 241
Plume 446
Pocket Books 446
Pockets 375
Pockets Fiction Writing Contest 529
Poe Awards, Edgar Allan (NR)
Poetic Space (NR)
Poetry Forum Short Stories 241
Poet's Fantasy (NR)
Pointed Circle, The (NR)
Ponder Publishing Inc. 485
Porcupine Literary Arts Magazine 242

Porter Cosmographic, Bern 338
Porter Prize for Fiction, Katherine Anne 529
Portland Magazine 375
Portland Review 242
Portland State University Haystack Writing Program (NR)
Poskisnolt Press 308
Post, The 308
Post-Apollo Press, The 485
Postcard (OB)
Potomac Review 242
Potomac Review Fifth Annual Short Story Contest (NR)
Potpourri (NR)
Pottersfield Portfolio 243
Power and Light (NR)
Power of Love Publishing 446
Prague Review, The (NR)
Prairie Fire 243
Prairie Journal of Canadian Literature, The 243
Prairie Journal Press 446
Prairie Publishing Company, The 486
Prairie Schooner 244
Prairie Schooner Readers' Choice Awards 530
Prayerworks 308
Premio Aztlan 530
Presidio La Bahia Award, The (NR)
Presidio Press 447
Press (NR)
Press Gang Publishers (NR)
Prichard Award for Short Story Writing, Mathew 530
Pride and Imprints 447
Priest Literary Agency, Aaron M. 128
Primavera 244
Prism International 245
Prism International Short Fiction Contest 530
Prisoners of the Night 309
Procreation (NR)
Prose Menagerie, The 245
Provincetown Arts 245
Provost's Writers Retreat Workshop, Gary 568
PSI 309
Psychic Radio, The 309
Publishers Syndication, International 486
Puckerbrush Review 246
Pudding House Publications 486
Puerto Del Sol 246
Puffin Books 447
Pulitzer Prize in Fiction 530
Pulp Eternity Best of the 90s Small Press 530

Pulp Eternity Online 309
Purpose 376
Pushcart Prize 531
"Put Your Best Hook Forward" (NR)
Putnam's Sons, G.P. 448

Q

QECE 338
Qspell Awards/Hugh Maclennan Fiction Award (NR)
Quackenbush's Children's Book Writing & Illustrating Workshops, Robert 553
Quadrant (NR)
Quarter After Eight 246
Quarterly West 247
Quarterly West Novella Competition 531
Quartet Books Limited 448
Queen of All Hearts 310
Queen's Mystery Magazine, Ellery 376
Queen's Quarterly 310
Quincy Writers Guild Annual Creative Writing Contest 531
Quixote Press 448
Quoth the Raven's Short Story and Flash Fiction Competitions 531
QWF (Quality Women's Fiction) 247

R

Rabbit Hole Press, The 247
Radiance 376
Raffelock Award for Publishing Excellence, David 531
Rag Mag (OB)
Ragweed Press Inc./gynergy books 448
Rain Crow 248
Rainbow Books, Inc. 448
Raleigh Award, Sir Walter 531
Ralph's Review 339
Rambunctious Review 248
Random House Books for Young Readers 449
Random House Canada 449
Random House Children's Books 449
Random House, Inc. 449
Random House, Inc. Juvenile Books (RR)
Ranger Rick Magazine 377
Raskolnikov's Cellar and The Lamplight 248
Rattapallax 248
Raven Chronicles, The 249
RavenHaus Publishing 486

Raw Seed Review, The (NR)
Rawlings: Writing the Region, Marjorie Kinnan 562
REA Award for the Short Story, The 532
Reader's Break (OB)
Real Writers Short Story Competition 532
RealPoetik 249
Reconciliation Press 487
Recursive Angel 249
Red Cedar Review 250
Red Deer Press 449
Red Rock Review 250
Red Sage Publishing, Inc. 487
Red Wheelbarrow 250
Redbook 377
Reed Magazine (NR)
Reflect 250
Reflections 310
Reform Judaism 377
Regency Press 450
Regina Medal Award,(ED)
Rejected Quarterly, The 251
Renaissance Online Magazine 339
Renditions 487
Retreat from Harsh Reality 568
Revell Publishing 450
Review and Herald Publishing Association (NR)
Review: Latin American Literature and Arts (NR)
Rfd (NR)
Rhino 251
Rhode Island State Council on the Arts 532
Ribalow Prize, Harold U. 532
Rinaldi Literary Agency, Angela 128
Rinehart Fund, The Mary Roberts 532
Rio Grande Press (NR)
Rio Grande Review 251
Rising Tide Press 450
River City (NR)
River City Writing Awards In Fiction (NR)
River Styx 252
Riverwind (NR)
Roanoke Review 252
Robbins Literary Agency, BJ 128
ROC 450
Rocket Press 252
Rockford Review, The 252
Rocky Mountain Book Festival 577
Rocky Mountain Children's Book Festival 577
Romance and Beyond Contest 532
Romance Writers of America 595

Romance Writers of America National Conference 577
Ronsdale Press 488
Room of One's Own 253
RopeWalk Writers' Retreat 569
Rose & Thorn Literary Ezine, The (NR)
Rosebud™ 311
Rotrosen Agency LLC, Jane 129
Rotten Romance 532
Roughneck Review, The (NR)
Round Table, The,(NR)
Roussan Publishers Inc. 451
Rowland Prize for Fiction for Girls, Pleasant T. (ED)
Rubenesque Romances (NR)
Ruby's Pearls (NR)
Russell & Volkening 129
Russell Publishing, James 488

S

S.L.U.G. fest, Ltd. 339
Sage Hill Writing Experience (NR)
Sagive Fiction Prize, Renee (NR)
St. Anthony Messenger 377
St. Augustine Society Press (NR)
St. Davids Christian Writers Conference (NR)
St. James Awards, The Ian (NR)
St. Martin's Press 451
Salivan Short Story Contest 533
Salmagundi (NR)
Salt Hill 253
Salvo Press 451
Samsara 253
San Diego State University Writers' Conference 583
San Diego Writer's Monthly (NR)
Sanders & Associates, Victoria 129
Sans Soleil 451
Sanskrit 254
Santa Barbara Review (NR)
Santa Monica Review 254
Sapphire Books 452
Sarabande Books, Inc. 452
Saroyan Writer's Conference, The William 583
Satire (NR)
Saturday Night (NR)
Savant Garde Workshop, The (NR)
SCBWI Inside the Children's Book Biz Conference 577
SCBWI Midyear Conference, NYC (NR)
SCBWI Southern Breeze Fall Conference 563

SCBWI Southern Breeze Spring Conference 563
SCBWI/Florida, Annual Fall Conference 563
SCBWI/Hofstra Children's Literature Conference (NR)
SCBWI/National Conference on Writing & Illustrating for Children 584
Scars/CC&D Editor's Choice Awards, The 533
Scherf Books 488
Scholastic Canada Ltd. 452
Scholastic Inc. 452
Scholastic Press 453
Science Fiction and Fantasy Workshop 595
Science Fiction Writers of Earth 596
Science Fiction Writers of Earth (SFWoE) Short Story Contest 533
Science-Fiction and Fantasy Writers of America, Inc. 596
Scifi.com 340
Scribner 453
Scriptapalooza 533
Scriptapalooza TV 533
Scrivener Creative Review (NR)
Scrivenery Press 453
Se La Vie Writer's Journal Contest (NR)
Seacoast Writer's Association Spring and Fall Conferences 553
Seal Press 454
Seattle Artists Program (NR)
Seattle Review, The (NR)
Secker & Warburg 454
Second Chance Press and the Permanent Press 454
Seduction, Deduction, and Chocolate 586
Seductive Torture (NR)
Seed Cake (NR)
Seek 378
Seeking the Muse 254
Seems 254
Self Publishing Your Own Book (NR)
Seniors Market, The (ED)
Sensations Magazine 255
Sepia 255
Sepulchre (OB)
Serendipity Systems 454
Serpent's Tail 489
Seven Buffaloes Press (ED)
7 Hills Short Fiction Contest 534
Seven Stories Press 455
Seventeen 378
Seventeen Magazine Fiction Contest 534
17th Street Productions (NR)

Sewanee Review, The 255
Sewanee Writers' Conference 559
Shades of December 255
Shadow Voices 340
Shallowend Ezine, The (NR)
Shattered Wig Review 256
Shaw Fellowship for Older Women Writers, Frances 534
Shaw Publishers, Harold (RR)
Shenandoah 256
Short Course On Professional Writing (NR)
Short Grain Contest 534
Short, Short Fiction Contest 534
Short Stories Bimonthly 256
Short Story Writers Showcase 340
Short Stuff Magazine for Grown-ups 256
Shyflower's Garden 311
Side Show 257
Side Show 8th Short Story Contest 535
Sidewalks (NR)
Siegel, International Literary Agency, Inc., Rosalie 129
Sierra Nevada College Review (NR)
Signal Crest 489
Silhouette Books 455
Silver Dagger Mysteries 455
Silver Web, The 257
Silverfish Review (NR)
Simmons Short Fiction Award, The John 535
Simon & Schuster 456
Simon & Schuster Books for Young Readers 456
Sinipee Writers' Workshop 570
Sinister Wisdom 258
Sisters in Crime 596
Sitka Center for Art and Ecology 586
Skidrow Penthouse 258
Skin Art (NR)
Skipping Stones 311
Skipping Stones Honor Awards 535
Skiptracer 258
Skylark 259
Skylark (A division of Random House, Inc.) 456
Skyline Writers Conference 569
Slate and Style (NR)
Slipstream 259
Slote Award, The Bernice 535
Small Pond Magazine, The 259
Smith, Publisher/Peregrine Smith, Gibbs 456
Smoky Mountain Valentine Contest 535
SNReview 260
Snake Nation Review 260

Snow Contest, Kay 535
Snowapple Press 489
Snowy Egret 260
So to Speak 260
Society of Children's Book Writers and Illustrators Golden Kite Awards (NR)
Society of Children's Book Writers and Illustrators Work-in-Progress Grants (NR)
Society of Midland Authors (NR)
Society of Southwestern Authors 596
Soft Door, The 261
Soft Skull Press Inc. 457
Soho Press 457
Sojourner 381
Songs of Innocence 261
Sonora Review Short Story Contest (NR)
Soundprints 457
South Carolina Arts Commission Literature Fellowships and Literature Grants (NR)
South Carolina Arts Commission/The Post & Courier Newspaper South Carolina Fiction Project (NR)
South Carolina Review 261
South Dakota Arts Council 536
South Dakota Review 262
Southeastern Regional Writing Competitions (NR)
Southern California Anthology (NR)
Southern Heat Contest 536
Southern Humanities Review 262
Southern Lights 563
Southern Methodist University Press 457
Southern Review, The 262
Southern Review/Louisiana State University Short Fiction Award, The 536
Southwest Review 263
Southwest Writers Workshop Conference 578
Southwestern American Literature 263
Sou'Wester 264
Space and Time 312
Sparks (NR)
Speak Up 264
Spectra Books 458
Spectrum Literary Agency 130
Spellbound Magazine 340
Spider 381
Spindrift 264
Spinning Jenny 264
Spinsters Ink 458
Spirit 381
Spirit that Moves Us Press, The (NR)

Spitball (NR)
Split Rock Arts Program (NR)
Spoonfed (NR)
Spout (NR)
Spring 2001 Short Story Competition 536
SPSM&H 265
Spunk (NR)
Squaw Valley Community of Writers Fiction Workshop 584
Stand Magazine 265
Stand Magazine Short Story Competition 536
Standard 381
Staple (RR)
Starburst Publishers 458
Starfire 459
State of Maine Writers' Conference 553
State of Unbeing 341
Steamboat Springs Writers Group 578
Steele-Perkins Literary Agency 130
Steeple Hill 459
Stegner Fellowship, Wallace E. 536
Stepping Out of the Darkness 312
Sternig & Byrne Literary Agency 130
Stone Bridge Press 459
Stone Soup 265
Stonecoast Writers' Conference 554
Stoneflower Literary Journal (NR)
Stones Point Press 489
Stonewall Inn 460
Stony Brook Short Fiction Prize (NR)
Storm Peak Press (NR)
Stormline Press 490
Story Bytes 341
Story Digest 312
Story Friends 382
Story Line Press (NR)
Storyboard 265
StoryQuarterly 266
Storyteller, The 313
Stovepipe 266
Strand Magazine, The 313
Struggle 266
Studentswrite.com 313
Studio: A Journal of Christians Writing 314
sub-TERRAIN 267
sub-TERRAIN Annual Short Story Contest 537
Sullivan Prize in Short Fiction, The Richard (NR)
Sulphur River Literary Review 267
Summer in France Writing Workshops 590
Summer's Reading, A (NR)
Sun, The 382

SunDog: The Southeast Review 267
Sunshine Coast Festival of the Written Arts 589
Sunstone Press 460
Surrey Writers' Conference 589
Suspense, Mystery & Intrigue II 557
Sweet Lady Moon Press 490
Sycamore Review 268
Synaesthesia Press Chapbook Series (RR)

T
Tab Book Club 460
Tailored Tours Publications, Inc. (OB)
Takahe 268
Talbot Agency, The John 130
Tale Spinner, The (NR)
Talebones 314
Talese, Nan A. 460
Talking River Review 268
Tall Grass Writers Guild Literary Anthology/
    Contest 537
Tameme 269
Tampa Review 269
Taos Institute of Arts 578
Taproot Literary Review (NR)
Taste for Flesh, A (NR)
Tattoo Revue (NR)
Taylor Manuscript Competition, Sydney (NR)
Taylor Prize for the Novel, The Peter 537
"Teak" Roundup 269
Teal Literary Agency, Patricia 131
Tears in the Fence 270
Teen Magazine 382
Tennessee Arts Commission Literary Fellowship
    537
Terra Incognita 314
Texas Christian University Press 460
Texas Institute of Letters Annual Award 537
Texas Review, The 270
Texas Review Press Book Competitions 538
Textshop (NR)
Thalia: Studies in Literary Humor (NR)
Thema 270
Thin Air 271
Third Alternative, The 271
Third Coast 271
Third Half Magazine, The 271
Third World Press (NR)
13th Moon 272
This Magazine 272
Thistledown Press 490

Thorndike Press (NR)
Thorngate Road (NR)
3 A.M. Magazine 272
Threepenny Review, The 272
Threshold, The 315
Thresholds Quarterly 315
Thurber House Residencies 538
Thurber Prize for American Humor, The 538
Tickled by Thunder Annual Fiction Contest 538
Tidewater Publishers 463
Tigges Writing Contest, John 538
Timber Creek Review (NR)
Tin House 272
Tinkle Award, Lon (NR)
Toby Press Ltd., The (NR)
Together Time (NR)
Tor Books 464
Touch 382
Touchstone Literary Journal (NR)
Towson University Prize for Literature (NR)
Transcendent Visions 341
Transition 273
Traver Fly-Fishing Fiction Award, Robert 539
Tricycle Press (NR)
Triquarterly 273
Troika Magazine 383
Tropical Press, Inc. 491
Troubadour's Short Story Contest 539
TSR, Inc. 464
Tucumcari Literary Review 273
Turner Award, Steven (NR)
Turnstone Press 491
Turtle Magazine for Preschool Kids 383
Tuscany Workshops, The 554
TWA Ambassador 383
Twain Award for Short Fiction, Mark (NR)
Twain Award, Mark 539
Twilight Showcase 342
Tŷ Newydd Writer's Centre 590
Tyndale House Publishers, Inc. 464
Tyro Publishing 464

U
UCLA Extension Writers' Program 584
Ulitarra (NR)
Ultramarine Publishing Co., Inc. 491
Undergraduate Short Fiction Contest 539
Undiscovered Writer, The 539
Unity House 465
Univeristy of Georgia Press (NR)

University of Iowa Press (NR)
University of Missouri Press (RR)
University of Nebraska Press 465
University of Nevada Press 491
University of New Mexico's Taos Summer Writers Conference 578
University of North Dakota Writers Conference 573
University of Texas Press (NR)
University of Wisconsin at Madison Writers Institute (NR)
University Press of Colorado (NR)
University Press of New England 465
Unlikely Stories (NR)
Unmuzzled Ox 274
Uno Mas Magazine (NR)
UPC Science Fiction Award 539
Up Dare? 316
Urban Graffiti 342
Urban Spaghetti 274
Urbanite, The 274
US1 Worksheets 275

V

Vagabond Press (RR)
Valley Grapevine 275
Van Neste Books 492
Vancouver International Writers Festival, The 589
Vanessapress 492
Vanwell Publishing Limited (NR)
Vassar College Children's Book Institute of Publishing and Writing (NR)
Vaughan's "Write on the Beach," Robert 579
Véhicule Press 492
Victoria School of Writing, The (NR)
Victory Park 275
Viking 465
Viking Children's Books 465
Vincent Brothers Review, The 276
Vines Agency, Inc., The 131
Vintage 466
Vintage Northwest (NR)
Violet Crown Book Award (NR)
Virginia Adversaria 276
Virginia Festival of the Book 559
Virginia Quarterly Review 316
Virginia Romance Writer's Conference 560
Vision Books Pvt Ltd. 466
Visions & Voices 342
Vista Publishing, Inc. 466

Vogelstein Foundation Grants 540
Voices from My Retreat 492
Voiding the Void™ 343
Volcano Writers' Retreat 585
VQ (NR)

W

W.W. Publications 493
Walden Fellowship 540
Walker and Company 466
Wallant Memorial Book Award, Edward Lewis 540
Walloon Writers' Retreat 569
War, Literature & the Arts 277
Warner Aspect 467
Warner Books 467
Wasafiri 277
Wascana Review of Contemporary Poetry and Short Fiction 277
Washington Independent Writers (WIW) Spring Writers Conference 558
Washington Square 277
Watkins Loomis Agency, Inc. 132
Waverly House Publishing 493
We Dare You Contest 540
Weatherford Award (NR)
Web Del Sol 278
Weber Studies 316
Weird Tales 316
Wesleyan University Press 467
Wesleyan Writers Conference 554
Wespennest 278
West Branch (NR)
West Coast Line 278
West Wind Review (NR)
Westcoast Fisherman, The 317
Westerly (NR)
Western Digest (NR)
Western Heritage Awards 540
Western Humanities Review 279
Western Reserve Writers & Freelance Conference (NR)
Western Reserve Writers Mini Conference (NR)
Western Writers of America 596
Westview 279
Whetstone 279
Whidbey Island Writers' Conference 586
Whiskey Island Magazine 279
White Crow, The 317
White Pine Press 467
White Wall Review (NR)

Companies that appeared in the 2000 edition of *Novel & Short Story Writer's Market*, but do not appear this year, are listed in this General Index with the following codes explaining why these markets were omitted: (ED)—Editorial Decision, (NS)—Not Accepting Submissions, (NR)—No (or late) Response to Listing Request, (OB)—Out of Business, (RR)—Removed by Market's Request, (UC)—Unable to Contact, (UF)—Uncertain Future.

GENERAL INDEX

GENERAL INDEX

Whitebread Book Awards 541
Whiting Writers' Awards (NR)
Wicked Mystic (NR)
Wieser & Wieser, Inc. 132
Wilder Award, Laura Ingalls 541
Willamette Writers 597
Willamette Writers Conference 587
William and Mary Review, The (NR)
Willow Springs 280
Wilmington Blues 343
Wilshire Book Co. 467
Wind Magazine (NR)
Wind Magazine Short Story Competition (RR)
Windhover 280
Winter Poetry & Prose Getaway in Cape May 558
Wisconsin Academy Review 317
Wisconsin Arts Board Individual Artist Program (NR)
Wisconsin Institute for Creative Writing Fellowship 541
Wisconsin Regional Writer's Association Spring and Fall Conference 573
Wisconsin Review 280
Wisconsin Writers' Workshop (NR)
With 383
Witness 280
Witty Short Story Award, Paul A. 541
Wolfe Fiction Prize, Thomas (NR)
Wolff Award for Fiction, Tobias 541
Woman's Weekly (NR)
Woman's World Magazine 384
Women's Press, The (NR)
Wonder Time (NR)
Wonderland Press, Inc., The 468
Wong Fellowship, David T.K. 541
Woodley Memorial Press 493
Worcester Review, The 281
Words of Wisdom (NR)
Works & Conversations (NR)
World Fantasy Awards 541
World of English, The 384
World Wide Writers Award 542
World's Best Short-Short Story Contest 542
Worldwide Library 468
WOW (Women on Writing) (ED)
Wrangling with Writing 585
Write It Out 563
Write Now! Workshop 585
Write on the Sound Writers' Conference 587
Write Way Publishing 468

Write Your Heart Out 542
Write Your Life Story for Pay 585
Writer to Writer 281
Writers Bureau Poetry and Short Story Competition, The 542
Writer's Center, The 597
Writers Community Residency Awards, The (NR)
Writers Connection Selling to Hollywood (NR)
Writer's Digest Annual Writing Competition (Short Story Division) 542
Writer's Digest National Self-Published Book Awards 542
Writers Direct 494
Writers' Federation of New Brunswick 597
Writers' Federation of Nova Scotia 598
Writer's Film Project (NR)
Writers' Forum 281
Writer's Guidelines & News 318
Writers Guild of Alberta 598
Writer's Head, The (NR)
Writers House 132
Writers Information Network 598
Writers Institute 573
Writers' International Forum Writing Competition (RR)
Writers' Journal Annual Fiction Contest 543
Writers' Journal Romance Contest 543
Writers News (ED)
Writers Press, Inc. 469
Writers Room, Inc., The 598
Writers Shop, The 132
Writers Studio 587
Writers' Summer School, Swanwick, The 590
Writer's Voice of the West Side YMCA, The 554
Writers' Workshop, The 560, 598
Writers Workshop in Science Fiction 579
Writers' Workshop International Fiction Contest, The 543
Writes of Passage (NR)
Write-To-Publish Conference 569
Writing, Creativity and Ritual 555
Writing for Money Workshop (NR)
Writing for Our Lives 282
Writing for Publication (NR)
Writing Strategies for the Christian Market 564
Writing Today—Birmingham-Southern College 564
Writing Workshop (NR)
WV 282
Wy'East Historical Journal 384

X

Xavier Review 282
Xenith (NR)
Xoddity (NR)

Y

Yaddo 555
Yale Review, The 283
Yalobusha Review, The 283
Yankee Magazine 385
Yarns and Such 318
Yearling 469
Yellow Bay Writers' Workshop (NR)
Yellow Silk 283
Yellow Sticky Notes 318
Yemassee 283
York Press Ltd. 469

Yorkshire Journal (NR)
Young Judaean (NR)
Young Reader'S Choice Award (NR)
Young Salvationist 385
Young Texas Writers Scholarships (NR)

Z

Zaum 284
Zebra Books (RR)
Zen Mountain Monastery 555
Zoetrope 284
Zoland Books, Inc. 469
Zollinger's Taos School of Writing, Norman (NR)
Zondervan 469
Zopilote 319
Zuzu's Petals Quarterly 284
Zyzzyva 285

GENERAL INDEX